Italy

Liguria, Piedmont & the Italian Riviera (p162)

Milan & the Lakes (p238)

Trento & the Dolomites (p300)

Friuli Venezia Giulia (p403)

Venice & the Veneto (p332)

Emilia-Romagna & San Marino (p429)

Florence & Tuscany (p472)

Umbria & Le Marche (p566)

Rome & Lazio (p62)

Abruzzo & Molise (p621)

Naples & Campania (p638)

Sardinia (p831)

Puglia, Basilicata & Calabria (p704)

Sicily (p765)

THIS EDITION WRITTEN AND RESEARCHED BY

Cristian Bonetto

Abigail Blasi, Kerry Christiani, Gregor Clark, Duncan Garwood, Paula
Hardy, Virginia Maxwell, Brendan Sainsbury, Helena Smith,
Donna Wheeler

PLAN YOUR TRIP

CLASSIC ITALIAN DESIGN P284

CAR CULTURE / GETTY IMAGES ©

CINQUE TERRE P183

CHRISTOPHER GROENHOUT / GETTY IMAGES ©

ON THE ROAD

Contents

ON THE ROAD

Contents

UNDERSTAND

SURVIVAL GUIDE

SISTINE CHAPEL, ROME
P66

SPECIAL FEATURES

Welcome to Italy

If you get it right, travelling in the bel paese *(beautiful country) is one of those rare experiences in life that cannot be overrated.*

Cultural Riches

The French may rightfully brag about Paris, but Italy's showstopping cities include Venice, Florence and Rome. Epicentre of the Roman Empire and birthplace of the Renaissance, this sun-kissed over-achiever groans under the weight of its cultural catalogue: it's in Italy that you'll find Michelangelo's *David* and Sistine Chapel frescoes, Botticelli's *Birth of Venus* and *Primavera*, da Vinci's *The Last Supper*, and the classic villas of Andrea Palladio. And we haven't even mentioned the chariot-grooved streets of Pompeii, the Byzantine mosaics of Ravenna, or Giotto's revolutionary frescoes in Padua.

Bella Vita

In few places do art and life intermingle so effortlessly. This may be the land of Dante, Titian and Verdi, but it's also the home of Prada, Gualtiero Marchesi and Renzo Piano. Beauty, style and flair furnish every aspect of daily life, from those immaculately knotted ties and perfect espressos, to the flirtatious smiles of striking strangers. The root of Italian pathology is a dedication to living life well and, effortless as it may seem, driving that dedication is a reverence for the finer things. So slow down, take note, and indulge in a little *bella vita*.

Buon Appetito

It might look like a boot, but food-obsessed Italy feels more like a bountiful table. From delicate *tagliatelle al ragù* to velvety *cannoli,* every bite feels like a revelation. The secret: superlative ingredients and strictly seasonal produce. And while Italy's culinary soul might be earthy and rustic, it's equally ingenious and sophisticated. Expect some of the world's top fine-dining destinations, from San Pellegrino 'World's 50 Best' hot spots to Michelin-starred musts. So whether you're on a degustation odyssey in Modena, truffle hunting in Piedmont, or simply swilling powerhouse reds at Rome's International Wine Academy, prepare to swoon.

Luscious Landscapes

Italy's fortes extend beyond its galleries, plates and wardrobes. The country is one of Mother Nature's darlings, its geography offering rarely rivalled natural diversity. From the north's icy Alps and glacial lakes to the south's volcanic craters and turquoise grottoes, this is a place for doing as well as seeing. One day you're tearing down Courmayeur's powdery slopes, the next you could be riding cowboy-style across the marshes of the Maremma, or diving in coral-studded Campanian waters. Not bad for a country not much bigger than Arizona.

Why I Love Italy

By Cristian Bonetto, Author

Italy's 20 regions feel more like 20 independent states, each with its own dialects, traditions, architecture and glorious food. From nibbling on *knödel* in an Alto Adige chalet, to exploring souk-like market streets in Sicily, the choices are as diverse as they are seductive. Then there's the country's incomparable artistic treasures, which amount to more than the rest of the world put together. It's hard not to feel a little envious sometimes, but it's even harder not to fall madly in love.

For more about our authors, see page 976

Above: Malcesine (p279), Lago di Garda

Italy

ELEVATION

| 2500m |
| 2000m |
| 1500m |
| 1000m |
| 500m |
| 300m |
| 100m |
| 0 |

N

0 — 200 km
0 — 100 miles

Gran Paradiso
Hike across high-altitude passes (p235)

Lago di Como
Cruise Lombardy's VIP Alpine lake (p269)

Dolomites
Scale Italy's most awesome granite peaks (p308)

Venice
Count millions of mosaic tesserae at San Marco (p336)

Emilia-Romagna
Tuck into Italy's culinary epicentre (p431)

Italian Alps
Ski Piedmont's Milky Way (p212)

Italian Riviera
Village-hop along the Cinque Terre (p183)

SWITZERLAND

AUSTRIA

HUNGARY

SLOVENIA

CROATIA

BOSNIA & HERCEGOVINA

SERBIA

MONTENEGRO

LIECHTENSTEIN

BERN ✪
Zürich
Geneva
Courmayeur
Valtournenche
Aosta
Varallo
VADUZ ✪
Innsbruck
Graz
Tarvisio
LJUBLJANA ✪
ZAGREB ✪
Pécs
Osijek
Banja Luka
SARAJEVO ✪
Dubrovnik
PODGORICA ✪

Danube

Geneva
Briançon
Modane
Parco Nazionale del Gran Paradiso
PIEDMONT
Turin
Milky Way
Nice
Tunaro

Parco Nazionale dello Stelvio
Valtellina
Merano
Bolzano
Alpe di Siusi
CARNIA
Tolmezzo
Udine
Gorizia
Trieste
Palmanova
Lignano
Grado

Trento
Rovereto
Dolomites
Pordenone
Lago di Como
Lago di Garda
Bergamo
Brescia
Verona
Vicenza
Padua
Venice
VENETO

LOMBARDY

Milan
Cremona
Mantua
EMILIA-ROMAGNA
Po Delta
Ravenna
Po

Genoa
Gulf of Genoa
LIGURIA
Riviera di Ponente
Riviera di Levante
Parco Nazionale delle Cinque Terre

Bologna
SAN MARINO
Pesaro
Urbino
Ancona

Garfagnana
Lucca
Pisa
Livorno
Massa
Marittima
Volterra
CHIANTI
Florence
Siena
Arezzo
TUSCANY
Arno
Gubbio
Perugia
Assisi
Sarnano
Macerata
Parco Del Conero
Ascoli Piceno
Pescara
Chieti
UMBRIA
Todi
Orvieto
Nocria
Spoleto
Viterbo
LAZIO

Gorgona
Capraia
Elba
Pianosa
Montecristo

Adriatic Sea

Isole Tremiti

43°N

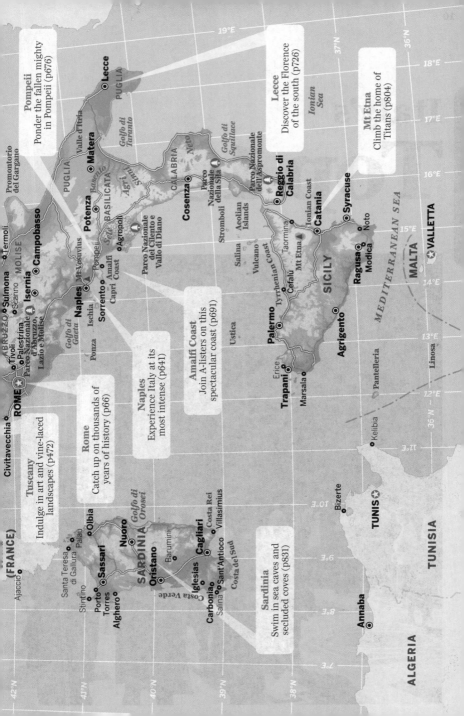

Italy's
Top 18

Eternal Rome

1 Once *caput mundi* (capital of the world), Rome was legendarily spawned by a wolf-suckled wild boy, grew to be Western Europe's first superpower, became the spiritual centrepiece of the Christian world, and is now the repository of over two and a half thousand years of European art and architecture. From the Pantheon (p79) and the Colosseum (p67) to Michelangelo's Sistine Chapel (p112) and countless works by Caravaggio, there's simply too much to see in one visit. So, do as countless others have done before you: toss a coin into the Trevi Fountain (p89) and promise to return. Below left: St Peter's Basilica

Virtuoso Venice

2 Step through the portals of Basilica di San Marco (p337) and try to imagine what it might have been like for a humble medieval labourer glimpsing those glittering gold mosaic domes for the first time. It's not such a stretch – seeing the millions of tiny gilt *tesserae* (hand-cut glazed tiles) fuse into a singular heavenly vision can make every leap of human imagination since the 12th century seem comparatively minor. Below right: Domed roof of Basilica di San Marco

Touring Tuscany

3 Italy's most romanticised region, Tuscany was tailor-made for aesthetes. According to Unesco, Florence (p475) contains 'the greatest concentration of universally renowned works of art in the world', from Brunelleschi's Duomo to Masaccio's Cappella Brancacci frescoes. Beyond its museums and flawless Renaissance streetscapes sprawls an undulating wonderland of regional delights, from the Gothic majesty of Siena, to the Manhattan-esque skyline of medieval San Gimignano, to the vine-laced hills of Italy's most famous wine region, Chianti. Below: Ponte Vecchio, Florence

Amalfi Coast

4 Italy's most celebrated coastline is a bewitching blend of superlative beauty and gripping geology: coastal mountains plunge into milky blue sea in a prime-time vertical scene of precipitous crags, sun-bleached villages and lush forests. While some may argue that the peninsula's most beautiful coast is Liguria's Cinque Terre or Calabria's Costa Viola, it was the Amalfi Coast (p686) that American writer John Steinbeck described as a 'dream place that isn't quite real when you are there and...beckoningly real after you have gone'. Right: Positano, Amalfi Coast

Ghostly Pompeii

5 Nothing piques human curiosity quite like a mass catastrophe and few can beat the ruins of Pompeii (p676), a once-thriving Roman town frozen in time 2000 years ago in its death throes. Wander through Roman streets, snooping around the forum, the erotically frescoed brothel, the 5000-seat theatre and the sumptuous Villa dei Misteri, and ponder Pliny the Younger's terrifying account of the tragedy: 'Darkness came on again, again ashes, thick and heavy. We got up repeatedly to shake these off; otherwise we would have been buried and crushed by the weight'. Left: Statue at the Casa dei Vettii, Pompeii

Mighty Museums

6 Browse through any art-history textbook to highlight seminal movements in Western art, from classical to metaphysical. All were forged in Italy by a roll call of artists including Giotto, da Vinci, Michelangelo, Botticelli, Bernini and Caravaggio. Find the best of them in Rome's Museo e Galleria Borghese (p113) and Vatican Museums (p109), Florence's Uffizi (p477), Venice's Gallerie dell'Accademia (p345), Milan's Museo del Novecento (p243) and Naples' Palazzo Reale di Capodimonte (p653). Below: Uffizi Gallery, Florence

Tackling the Dolomites

7 Scour the globe and you'll find plenty of taller, bigger and more geologically volatile mountains, but few can match the romance of the pink-hued, granite Dolomites (p300). Maybe it's their harsh, jagged summits, the vibrant skirts of spring wildflowers or the rich cache of Ladin legends. Then again, it could just be the magnetic draw of money, style and glamour at Italy's most fabled ski resort, Cortina d'Ampezzo (p401). Whatever the reason, this tiny pocket of northern Italy takes seductiveness to dizzying heights.

TONY C FRENCH / GETTY IMAGES ©

ANDREW PEACOCK / GETTY IMAGES ©

Savouring Emilia-Romagna

8 They don't call Bologna (p431) '*la grassa*' (the fat one) for nothing. Many of Italy's classics call this city home, from mortadella and meat-stuffed tortellini, to its trademark *tagliatelle al ragù*. Shop for produce in the deli-packed Quadrilatero, and side-trip-it to the city of Modena (p443) for world-famous aged balsamic vinegar. Just leave room for a trip to Parma (p448), hometown of *parmigiano reggiano* cheese and the incomparable *prosciutto di Parma*. Wherever you plunge your fork, toast with a glass or three of the region's renowned Lambrusco or sauvignon blanc.

Neapolitan Street Life

9 Nowhere else in Italy are people as conscious of their role in the theatre of everyday life as in Naples (p641). And in no other Italian city does daily life radiate such drama and intensity. Naples' ancient streets are a stage, cast with boisterous matriarchs, bellowing baristas and tongue-knotted lovers. To savour the flavour, dive into the city's rough-and-tumble Porta Nolana market, a loud, lavish opera of hawking fruit vendors, wriggling seafood, and the irresistible aroma of just-baked *sfogliatelle* (sweetened ricotta pastries).

Escaping to Paradiso

10 If you're pining for a soothing retreat, wear down your hiking boots on the 724km of marked trails and mule tracks traversing Gran Paradiso (p235). Part of the Graian Alps and the first of Italy's national parks, Gran Paradiso's pristine spread encompasses 57 glaciers and Alpine pastures awash with wild pansies, gentians and Alpenroses, not to mention a healthy population of Alpine ibexes for whose protection the park was originally established. The eponymous Gran Paradiso mountain (4061m) is the park's only peak, accessed from tranquil Cogne.

Sardinian Shores

11 The English language fails to accurately describe the varied blue, green and, in the deepest shadows, purple hues of Sardinia's seas. While models, ministers and permatanned celebrities wine, dine and sail along the glossy Costa Smeralda, much of Sardinia (p831) remains a wild, raw playground. Slather on that sunscreen and explore the island's rugged coastal beauty, from the tumbledown boulders of Santa Teresa di Gallura and the wind-chiselled cliff face of the Golfo di Orosei, to the windswept beauty of the Costa Verde's dune-backed beaches. Top left: Spiaggia Scivu, Costa Verde

Hiking the Italian Riviera

12 For the sinful inhabitants of Monterosso, Vernazza, Corniglia, Manarola and Riomaggiore – the five villages of the Cinque Terre (p183) – penance involved a lengthy and arduous hike up the vertiginous cliffside to the local village sanctuary to appeal for forgiveness. Scale the same trails today, through terraced vineyards and hillsides smothered in *macchia* (shrubbery) and, as the heavenly views unfurl, it's hard to think of a more benign punishment.

Living Luxe on Lago di Como

13 If it's good enough for George Clooney, it's good enough for mere mortals. Nestled in the shadow of the Rhaetian Alps, dazzling Lago di Como (p269) is the most spectacular of the Lombard lakes, its vain Liberty-style villas home to movie moguls, fashion royalty and Arab sheikhs. Surrounded on all sides by lush greenery, the lake's siren calls include the gardens of Villa Melzi d'Eril, Villa Carlotta and Villa Balbianello, which blush pink with camellias, azaleas and rhododendrons in April and May. Above: Villa Balbianello

Skiing the Alps

14 It might be Italy's smallest and least populous region, but what the Valle d'Aosta (p227) lacks in width it more than makes up for in height. Indeed, this picture-perfect valley is ringed by the icy peaks of some of Europe's highest natural skyscrapers, from Mont Blanc and the Matterhorn, to Monte Rosa and Gran Paradiso. It's equipped with some of the best skiing facilities on the continent, and hitting the slopes here is an international affair, with hair-raising descents into France, Switzerland or Piedmont from the A-list resorts of Courmayeur, Cervinia and Monterosa.

Savoy Palace Envy

15 It wasn't all Florence and the Medici or Rome and the Borghese, darling. In Turin (p197), Savoy princes had a similar penchant for extravagant royal palaces. While Turin's Palazzo Madama and Palazzo Reale are sucker-punching enough, they barely hold a candle to Italy's mini-Versailles, the Reggia di Venaria Reale. In fact, Duke Carlo Emanuele II's oversized hunting lodge is one of the largest royal residences in Europe, its mammoth €200-million restoration involving the preservation of 1022 sq metres of frescoes and 139,400 sq metres of stucco and plasterwork. Above top right: Reggia di Venaria Reale

Murals & Mosaics

16 Often regarded as just plain 'dark', the Italian Middle Ages had an artistic brilliance that's hard to ignore. Perhaps it was the sparkling hand-cut mosaic of Ravenna's Byzantine basilicas (p460) that provided the guiding light, but something inspired Giotto di Bondone to leap out of the shadows with his daring naturalistic frescoes in Padua's Cappella degli Scrovegni (p381) and the Basilica di San Francesco (p583) in Assisi. He gave the world a new artistic language and then it was just a short step to Masaccio's *Trinity* (p485) and the dawning light of the Renaissance. Above right: Basilica di Sant'Apollinare Nuovo, Ravenna

Baroque Lecce

17 There's baroque, and then there's *barocco leccese* (Lecce baroque), the hyperextravagant spin-off defining many Puglian towns. Making it all possible was the local stone, so soft that art historian Cesare Brandi claimed it could be carved with a penknife. Craftspeople crowded facades with swirling designs, gargoyles and strange zoomorphic figures. Queen of the crop is Lecce's Basilica di Santa Croce (p728), so insanely detailed the Marchese Grimaldi said it made him think a lunatic was having a nightmare. Below: Basilica di Santa Croce

Scaling Mount Etna

18 Known to the Greeks as the 'column that holds up the sky', Mt Etna (p804) is not only Europe's largest volcano, it's one of the world's most active. The ancients believed the giant Tifone (Typhoon) lived in its crater and lit the sky with spectacular pyrotechnics. At 3329m it literally towers above Sicily's Ionian coast. Whether you tackle it on foot or on a guided 4WD tour, scaling this time bomb rewards with towering views and the secret thrill of having come cheek-to-cheek with a towering threat.

17

18

Need to Know

For more information, see Survival Guide (p931)

Currency
Euro (€)

Language
Italian

Visas
Generally not required for stays of up to 90 days (or at all for EU nationals); some nationalities need a Schengen visa.

Money
ATMs at every airport, most train stations and widely available in towns and cities. Credit cards accepted in most hotels and restaurants.

Mobile Phones
European and Australian phones work; others should be set to roaming. Use a local SIM card for cheaper rates on local calls.

Time
Central European Time (GMT/UTC plus one hour)

Room Tax
Visitors may be charged an extra €1 to €5 per night 'room occupancy tax' (see p933).

When to Go

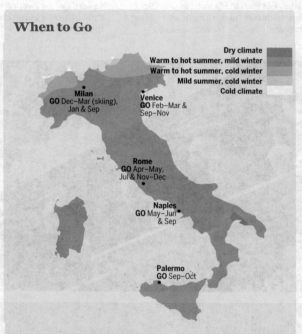

Dry climate
Warm to hot summer, mild winter
Warm to hot summer, cold winter
Mild summer, cold winter
Cold climate

Milan
GO Dec–Mar (skiing), Jan & Sep

Venice
GO Feb–Mar & Sep–Nov

Rome
GO Apr–May, Jul & Nov–Dec

Naples
GO May–Jun & Sep

Palermo
GO Sep–Oct

High Season
(Jul–Aug)

➡ Queues at big sights and on the road, especially in August.

➡ Prices also rocket for Christmas, New Year and Easter.

➡ Late December to March is high season in the Alps and Dolomites.

Shoulder
(Apr–Jun & Sep–Oct)

➡ Good deals on accommodation, especially in the south.

➡ Spring is best for festivals, flowers and local produce.

➡ Autumn provides warm weather and the grape harvest.

Low Season
(Nov–Mar)

➡ Prices up to 30% less than in high season.

➡ Many sights and hotels closed in coastal and mountainous areas.

➡ A good period for cultural events in large cities.

Useful Websites

Lonely Planet (www.lonelyplanet.com/italy) Destination information, hotel bookings, traveller forum and more.

Trenitalia (www.trenitalia.com) Italian railways website.

Agriturismi (www.agriturismi.it) Guide to farm accommodation.

Slow Food (www.slowfood.com) For the best local producers, restaurants and markets.

Enit Italia (www.italiantourism.com) Official Italian-government tourism website.

Important Numbers

To dial listings in the book from outside Italy, dial your international access code, Italy's country code (✆39) then the number (including the '0').

Italy's country code	✆39
International access code	✆00
Ambulance	✆118
Police	✆113
Fire	✆115

Exchange Rates

Australia	A$1	€0.69
Canada	C$1	€0.71
Japan	¥100	€0.75
NZ	NZ$1	€0.61
Switzerland	Sfr1	€0.81
UK	UK£1	€1.19
US	US$1	€0.73

For current exchange rates see www.xe.com.

Daily Costs

**Budget:
Less than €100**

➡ Dorm bed: €15–30

➡ Double room in a budget hotel: €50–110

➡ Pizza or pasta: €6–12

**Midrange:
€100–€250**

➡ Double room in a hotel: €110–200

➡ Lunch and dinner in local restaurants: €25–50

➡ Admission to museum €4–15

**Top End:
More than €250**

➡ Double room in a four- or five-star hotel: €200–450

➡ Top restaurant dinner: €50–150

➡ Opera ticket €40–200

Opening Hours

Opening hours vary throughout the year. We've provided high-season hours; hours decrease in the shoulder and low seasons. In this guide, 'summer' times generally refer to the period from April to September or October, while 'winter' times run from October or November to March.

Banks 8.30am–1.30pm and 3.30–4.30pm Monday to Friday

Restaurants noon–2.30pm and 7.30–11pm or midnight

Cafes 7.30am–8pm

Bars and clubs 10pm–4am

Shops 9am–1pm and 4–8pm Monday to Saturday

Arriving in Italy

Fiumicino airport (Rome; p148)

➡ **Express train:** €14; every 30 minutes, 6.38am to 11.38pm

➡ **Bus:** €4 to €7; 5.35am to 12.30am, plus night services at 1.15am, 2.15am, 3.30am and 5am

➡ **Taxi:** €48 set fare; 45 minutes

Malpensa airport (Milan; p258)

➡ **Express train or shuttle bus:** €10; every 30 minutes, 5am to 10.30pm, plus limited night bus services between 11pm and 5am

➡ **Taxi:** €79 set fare; 50 minutes

Marco Polo airport (Venice; p945)

➡ **Ferry:** €15; every 30 to 60 minutes, 6.10am to 12.15am

➡ **Bus:** €6; every 30 minutes, 7.50am to 12.20am

➡ **Water taxi:** €104; 30 minutes

Capodichino airport (Naples; p659)

➡ **Shuttle bus:** €3; every 20 minutes, 6.30am to 11.40pm

➡ **Taxi:** €19 set fare; 30 minutes

Getting Around

Transport in Italy is affordable, quick and efficient.

Train Reasonably priced, with extensive coverage and frequent departures.

Car Handy for travelling at your own pace, or for visiting regions with minimal public transport. Not a good idea for travelling within major urban areas.

Bus Cheaper and slower than trains. Useful for more remote villages not serviced by trains.

For much more on **getting around**, see p948

First Time Italy

For more information, see Survival Guide (p931)

Checklist

➡ Ensure your passport is valid for at least six months past your arrival date

➡ Check airline baggage restrictions

➡ Organise travel insurance (see p938)

➡ Make bookings (for popular museums, entertainment and accommodation)

➡ Inform your credit-/debit-card company of your travels

➡ Check you can use your mobile (cell) phone

What to Pack

➡ Good walking shoes for those cobblestones

➡ Hat, sunglasses, sunscreen

➡ Electrical adapter

➡ An appetite for Italy's favourite sport: eating!

➡ Smart threads and shoes so you don't look like a heathen in Europe's most stylish nation

➡ Patience: for coping with inefficiency

➡ Phrasebook: for ordering and charming

Top Tips for Your Trip

➡ Visit in spring and autumn – good weather and thinner crowds.

➡ If you're driving, head off the main roads: some of Italy's most stunning scenery is best on secondary or tertiary roads.

➡ Speak at least a few Italian words. A little can go a long way.

➡ Queue-jumping is common in Italy: be polite but assertive.

➡ Avoid restaurants with touts and the mediocre *menu turistico* (tourist menu).

What to Wear

Appearances matter in Italy. Milan, Italy's fashion capital, is rigidly chic. Rome and Florence are marginally less formal, but with big fashion houses in town sloppy attire just won't do. In the cities, suitable wear for men is generally trousers and shirts or polo shirts, and for women skirts, trousers or dresses. Shorts, T-shirts and sandals are fine in summer and at the beach, but long sleeves are required for dining out. For evening wear, smart casual is the norm. A light sweater or waterproof jacket is useful in spring and autumn, and sturdy shoes are good when visiting archaeological sites.

Sleeping

Book ahead for the high season, especially in popular areas, or if visiting cities during major events. See p932 for more accommodation information.

➡ **Hotels** All prices and levels of quality, from cheap-and-charmless to sleek-and-exclusive boutique.

➡ **Farm-stays** Perfect for families and for relaxation, *agriturismi* range from rustic farmhouses to luxe country estates.

➡ **B&Bs** Often great value, can range from rooms in family houses to self-catering studio apartments.

➡ **Pensions** Similar to hotels, though *pensioni* are generally of one- to three-star quality and family-run.

➡ **Hostels** You'll find both official HI-affiliated and privately run *ostelli*, many also offering private rooms with bathroom.

Money

Credit and debit cards can be used almost everywhere with the exception of some rural towns and villages.

Visa and MasterCard are widely recognised. American Express is only accepted by some major chains and big hotels, and few places take Diners Club.

ATMs are everywhere, but be aware of transaction fees. Some ATMs in Italy reject foreign cards. If this happens, try a few before assuming your card is the problem.

For more information, see p940.

Bargaining

Gentle haggling is common in markets. Haggling in stores is generally unacceptable, though goodhumoured bargaining at smaller artisan or craft shops in southern Italy is not unusual if making multiple purchases.

Tipping

Tipping is customary in restaurants, but optional elsewhere.

➡ **Taxis** Optional, but most people round up to the nearest euro.

➡ **Restaurants** Most restaurants have a *coperto* (cover charge), usually €2 to €3. Some also include *servizio* (service charge) of 10% to 15%. If service isn't included a small tip is appropriate.

➡ **Bars** Italians usually leave small change on the bar when ordering coffee. If drinks are brought to your table, tip as you would in a restaurant.

Phrases to Learn Before You Go

English is not widely spoken in Italy. Of course, in the main tourist centres you can get by, but in the countryside and south of Rome you'll need to master a few basic phrases. This will improve your experience no end, especially when ordering in restaurants, some of which have no written menu.

1 **What's the local speciality?**
Qual'è la specialità di questa regione?
kwa·le la spe·cha·lee·ta dee kwes·ta re·jo·ne

A bit like the rivalry between medieval Italian city-states, these days the country's regions compete in speciality foods and wines.

2 **Which combined tickets do you have?**
Quali biglietti cumulativi avete?
kwa·lee bee·lye·tee koo·moo·la·tee·vee a·ve·te

Make the most of your euro by getting combined tickets to various sights; they are available in all major Italian cities.

3 **Where can I buy discount designer items?**
C'è un outlet in zona? che oon owt·let in zo·na

Discount fashion outlets are big business in major cities – get bargain-priced seconds, samples and cast-offs for *la bella figura*.

4 **I'm here with my husband/boyfriend.**
Sono qui con il mio marito/ragazzo.
so·no kwee kon eel mee·o ma·ree·to/ra·ga·tso

Solo women travellers may receive unwanted attention in some parts of Italy; if ignoring fails have a polite rejection ready.

5 **Let's meet at 6pm for pre-dinner drinks.**
Ci vediamo alle sei per un aperitivo.
chee ve·dya·mo a·le say per oon a·pe·ree·tee·vo

At dusk, watch the main piazza get crowded with people sipping colourful cocktails and snacking the evening away: join your new friends for this authentic Italian ritual!

For more information see p953

Etiquette

Italy is a surprisingly formal society; the following tips will help avoid awkward moments.

➡ **Greetings** Shake hands and say *buongiorno* (good day) or *buona sera* (good evening) to strangers; kiss both cheeks and say *come stai* (how are you) to friends. Use *lei* (you) in polite company; use *tu* (you) with friends and children. Only use first names if invited.

➡ **Asking for help** Say *mi scusi* (excuse me) to attract attention; and use *permesso* (permission) when you want to pass someone in a crowded space.

➡ **Religion** Dress modestly (cover shoulders, torsos and thighs) and show respect when visiting religious sites.

What's New

Museums in Bologna

Bologna delivers a trio of new museums under the umbrella of 'Genus Bononiae: Museums in the City'. Top billing goes to the amazing Museo della Storia di Bologna. Set in a medieval *palazzo* (mansion) redesigned by architect Mario Bellini, its high-tech, interactive galleries recount Bologna's action-packed backstory. (p431)

Palazzetto Bru Zane, Venice

Refreshed and restored, the 17th-century Palazzetto Bru Zane is doing what it does best: delighting pleasure seekers with concerts of romantic music by Europe's leading talents. (p376)

Museo Nazionale dell'Automobile, Turin

This museum is back after a major makeover. Drool lasciviously over 200 vehicles, among them an 1892 Peugeot and a 1980 Ferrari 308. (p205)

Museo Casa Enzo Ferrari, Modena

Legendary speed machines and futuristic architecture collide at Modena's latest museum, dedicated to the life and legacy of motor-racing legend and Ferrari company founder, Enzo Ferrari. (p443)

Eataly, Rome

Turin-based food emporium Eataly has opened its biggest outlet yet. The multi-level eating, drinking and food shopping complex reflects Rome's growing trend for all-day dining. (p136)

Museum of Modern and Contemporary Art, Udine

Udine's new museum delivers a fascinating collection of 20th-century Italian artists, a surprise horde of notable Americans, and a boldly reconstructed space by Italian starchitect Gae Aulenti. (p419)

Tunnel Borbonico, Naples

Revisit the Naples of paranoid royals and WWII bombings at the lovingly restored Bourbon Tunnel. Guided tours of this subterranean labyrinth range from standard saunters to speleological adventures. (p654)

Venice Day Trips, Veneto

Dig deeper into Veneto life with this boutique tour outfit. Options include art, food, wine or shopping tours in Venice and Padua, and wonderful wine and food tours of the Veneto countryside. (p361)

Palazzo Margherita, Bernalda

Hollywood meets Italy's deep south at film-maker Francis Ford Coppola's boutique hotel in Basilicata. The luxe, 19th-century villa has been bedding some red-carpet names, including Justin Timberlake. (p745)

Basilica Palladiana, Vicenza

Fresh from a €20 million refit, Vicenza's Basilica Palladiana is once again playing host to world-class temporary exhibitions, some of them utterly extraordinary. (p386)

Villa Romana del Casale

Sparkling from a multiyear renovation, this Roman villa's stunning floor mosaics are back on the A-list of Italy's greatest ancient assets. (p824)

For more recommendations and reviews, see lonelyplanet. com/Italy

If You Like...

Masterpieces

Sistine Chapel More than just Michelangelo's show-stealing ceiling fresco, this world-famous chapel in Rome also features work by Botticelli, Ghirlandaio and Perugino. (p114)

Galleria degli Uffizi Cimabue, Botticelli, da Vinci, Raphael, Titian: Florence's blockbuster art museum delivers a who's who of artistic deities. (p477)

Museo e Galleria Borghese A perfectly sized serve of Renaissance and baroque masterpieces in an elegant villa in Rome. (p113)

Giotto See just how Giotto revolutionised art with his masterly works in the **Cappella degli Scrovegni** (p381) and **Basilica di San Francesco** (p583).

Museo del Novecento Modigliani, de Chirico, Kandinsky, Picasso, Fontana: a first-class 20th-century art museum in modernist Milan. (p243)

Pompeii The Dionysiac frieze in the dining room of the Villa dei Misteri is one of the world's largest ancient frescoes. (p681)

Palazzo Grassi The exceptional contemporary collection of French billionaire François Pinault is showcased against Tadao Ando interior sets in Venice. (p344)

Museion Bolzano's contemporary collection highlights the ongoing dialogue between the Südtirol, Austria and Germany. (p318)

MADRE From site-specific installations by greats like Mimmo Paladino, to the hung statements of Gilbert and George, Naples' modern-art must comes without the crowds. (p647)

Pinturicchio Perugia (p567) and Spello (p590) showcase the work of Umbria's home-grown Renaissance talent, Pinturicchio.

Fabulous Food

Bologna Nicknamed *la grassa* (literally 'the fat'), Bologna straddles Italian food lines between the butter-led north and the tomato-based cuisine of the south. (p438)

Truffles Go to Piedmont (p197), Tuscany (p508) and Umbria (p567) for the world's most coveted fungi.

Osteria Francescana Rave about Massimo Bottura's creative flavour combinations at the world's third-best restaurant. (p446)

Seafood So fresh you can eat it raw in Venice (p332), Sardinia (p831), Sicily (p765) and Puglia (p704). In Campania, order a plate of *spaghetti alle vongole* (spaghetti with clams).

Pizza Italy's most famous export, but who makes the best: Naples or Rome?

Parmesan Parma's cheese is the most famous. Just leave room for Lombardy's Taleggio, Campania's buffalo mozzarella, and Puglia's *burrata* (cheese made from mozzarella and cream).

Eataly Eat, drink and stock larder and cellar at the Rome branch of this giant emporium of top-notch Italian food and drink. (p136)

Il Frantoio The multicourse lunches at this Puglian farmhouse are the very definition of Slow Food. (p722)

Sicily Chickpea fritters in Palermo, fish couscous in San Vito Lo Capo, and chilli-laced chocolate in Modica – Sicily is a cross-cultural feast. (p765)

IF YOU LIKE...SURPRISES

Take a tour of Naples' *sottosuolo* (underground) and explore Greek-era grottoes, Palaeo-Christian burial chambers, royal Bourbon escape routes and WWII air-raid shelters. (p639)

Medieval Hill Towns

Asolo Perched mountainside in the northeast Veneto region, Asolo's nickname is 'the town of 100 vistas'. (p392)

Umbria and Le Marche Medieval hill towns galore: start with Spello and Spoleto, and end with Todi and Urbino. (p566)

Montalcino A Tuscan hill town lined with wine bars pouring the area's celebrated Brunello wines. (p551)

Erice Splendid coastal views from the hilltop Norman castle make this western Sicily's most photogenic village. (p829)

San Gimignano Skyscraping towers make this picture-perfect town look like a medieval Hong Kong or Manhattan. (p544)

Ravello Lording over the Amalfi Coast, this cultured jewel has wowed the best of them, from Wagner to Capote. (p693)

Maratea A 13th-century *borgo* (medieval town) with pint-sized piazzas, winding alleys and startling views across the Gulf of Policastro. (p748)

Puglia From the Valle d'Itria to the sierras of the Salento, Puglia is dotted with biscuit-coloured hilltop villages. (p704)

Wine Tasting

From Etna's elegant whites to Barolo's complex reds, Italian wines are as varied as the country's terrain. Sample them in cellars, over long, lazy lunches or dedicate yourself to a full-blown tour.

Tuscan wine routes Discover why Chianti isn't just a cheap table wine left over from the 1970s. (p538)

(Top) Antiques market, Arezzo (p559)
(Bottom) Ravello (p693), Amalfi Coast

Festa dell'Uva e del Vino In early October the wine town of Bardolino is taken over by wine and food stalls. (p288)

VinItaly Sample exceptional, rarely exported blends at Italy's largest annual wine expo. (p392)

Museo del Vino a Barolo Explore the history of wine through art and film at Barolo's wine museum. (p221)

Colli Orientali and Il Carso These two wine-growing areas in Friuli Venezia Giulia are making international waves for their Friuliano and blended 'super-whites'. Taste test at an *osmize* (rustic pop-up). (p413)

Valpolicella and Soave Wine tastings in these two Veneto regions are free and fabulous. (p395)

Alto Adige's Weinstraße A valley trail where native grapes Lagrein, Vernatsch and Gewürztraminer thrive alongside well-adapted imports pinot blanc, sauvignon, merlot and cabernet. (p324)

Villas & Palaces

Palazzo Reale di Caserta As seen in *Star Wars;* the Italian baroque's spectacular swansong. (p663)

Rome Don't miss Palazzo e Galleria Doria Pamphilj (p90), Palazzo Farnese (p84) and Palazzo Barberini(p89).

Palazzo Reale di Capodimonte Art and blue-blooded ego collide at this hilltop *palazzo* in former royal capital Naples. (p653)

Palazzo Ducale The doge's Venetian palace comes with a golden staircase and interrogation rooms. (p340)

Villa Maser Andrea Palladio and Paolo Veronese conspired

to create the Veneto's finest country mansion. (p392)

Reggia di Venaria Reale Piedmont's sprawling Savoy palace inspired French rival Versailles. (p204)

Palazzi dei Rolli A collection of 42 Unesco-protected lodging palaces in Genoa. (p166)

Villa Romana del Casale See where the home decor obsession began with this Roman villa's 3500-sq-metre mosaic floor. (p824)

Il Vittoriale degli Italiani Gabriele d'Annunzio's estate would put a Roman emperor to shame. (p283)

Markets

Porta Nolana Elbow your way past singsong fishing folk, fragrant bakeries and bootleg CD stalls for a slice of Neapolitan street theatre. (p647)

Pescaria Shop for lagoon specialities in Venice's 600-year-old fish market. (p367)

Mercato di Ballarò Fruit, fish, meat and veg stalls packed under striped awnings down cobbled alleys: Palermo's market is more African bazaar than Italian *mercato*. (p773)

Porta Portese A modern *commedia dell'arte* takes place every Sunday between vendors and bargain hunters at Rome's mile-long flea market. (p146)

Arezzo On the first weekend of every month, Arezzo hosts Italy's oldest and biggest antiques market. (p559)

Luino Straddling the eastern shore of Lago Maggiore, Luino is home to one of northern Italy's largest flea markets, held weekly on Wednesdays. (p267)

Porta Palazzo Turin's outdoor food market is the continent's largest. (p209)

Islands & Beaches

Counting all its offshore islands and squiggly indentations, Italy's coastline stretches 7600km from the sheer cliffs of the Cinque Terre, down through Rimini's brash resorts to the bijou islands in the Bay of Naples and Puglia's sandy shores.

Puglia Italy's best sandy beaches, including the gorgeous Baia dei Turchi and the cliff-backed beaches of the Gargano. (p704)

Aeolian Islands Sicily's seven volcanic islands sport hillsides of silver-grey pumice, black lava beaches and lush green vineyards. (p785)

Borromean Islands Graced with villas, gardens and wandering peacocks, Lago Maggiore's trio of islands are sublimely refined. (p261)

Sardinia Take your pick of our favourite beaches, including the Aga Khan's personal fave, Spiaggia del Principe. (p862)

Procida Pretty, pastel-hued Procida makes cinematographers swoon. (p672)

Rimini Swap high culture for raves on the beach in Rimini. (p464)

Elba This island sits at the heart of the Parco Nazionale Arcipelago Toscano, Europe's largest marine park. (p524)

Gardens

Italy's penchant for the 'outdoor room' has been going strong since Roman

JUAN CARLOS MUÑOZ / GETTY IMAGES ©

Red fox, Parco Nazionale del Gran Paradiso (p235)

emperors landscaped their holiday villas. Renaissance princes refined the practice, but it was 19th-century aristocrats who really went to town.

Reggia di Venaria Reale
Take a botanical, cultural or gastronomic tour to explore the 10 hectares of the Venaria's gardens. (p204)

The Italian Lakes Fringed with fabulous gardens such as those at Isola Madre (p265), Villa Balbianello (p275) and Villa Taranto (p265).

Villa d'Este Tivoli's superlative High Renaissance garden dotted with fantastical fountains and cypress-lined avenues. (p153)

Ravello View the Amalfi Coast from the Belvedere of Infinity and listen to classical-music concerts in romantic 19th-century gardens. (p693)

La Mortella A tropical paradise inspired by the gardens of Granada's Alhambra. (p670)

Giardini Pubblici Venice's first green space and the home of the celebrated Biennale with its avant-garde pavilions. (p357)

Unspoilt Wilderness

Parco Nazionale del Gran Paradiso Spectacular hiking trails, Alpine ibex and a refreshing lack of ski resorts await at Valle d'Aosta's mountain-studded wonderland. (p235)

Parco del Conero Lace up those hiking boots and hit this protected pocket of Le Marche, laced with fragrant forest, gleaming white cliffs and pristine bays. (p609)

Selvaggio Blu Sardinia's toughest hiking trek doesn't short change on rugged beauty – from cliffs and caves to spectacular coastal scenery. (p866)

Parco Nazionale dei Monti Sibillini Head for the border between Umbria and Le Marche for forests and subalpine meadows dotted with peregrine falcons, wolves and wildcats. (p619)

Northern Lagoon, Venice Take a boat tour of Venice's World Heritage–listed lagoon; it's Europe's largest coastal wetland and home to migrating birds from September to January. (p360)

Riserva Naturale dello Zingaro Dip in and out of picturesque coves along the wild coastline of Sicily's oldest nature reserve. (p829)

Month by Month

January

Following hot on the heels of New Year is Epiphany. In the Alps and Dolomites it's ski season, while in the Mediterranean south winters are mild and crowd-free, although many resort towns are firmly shut.

Regata della Befana

Witches in Venice don't ride brooms: they row boats. Venice celebrates Epiphany on 6 January with the Regatta of the Witches, complete with a fleet of brawny men dressed in their finest *befana* (witch) drag.

Ski Italia

Italy's top ski resorts are in the northern Alps and the Dolomites, but you'll also find resorts in Friuli, the Apennines, Le Marche and even Sicily. The best months of the season are January and February.

February

'Short' and 'accursed', is how Italians describe February. In the mountains the ski season hits its peak in line with school holidays. Further south it's chilly, but almond trees blossom and herald the carnival season.

Carnevale

In the period leading up to Ash Wednesday, many Italian towns stage pre-Lenten carnivals, with whimsical costumes, confetti and special festive treats. Venice's Carnevale (p363) is the most famous, while Viareggio's version (www.viareggio.ilcarnevale.com) is well known for its giant papier-mâché floats.

Sa Sartiglia

Masqueraded horse riders and fearless equestrian acrobatics define this historic event (www.sartiglia.info), held in the Sardinian town of Oristano on the last Sunday before Lent and on Shrove Tuesday.

Mostra Mercato del Tartufo Nero

An early-spring taste of truffles from the gastronomic Umbrian town of Norcia. Thousands of visitors sift through booths tasting all things truffle alongside other speciality produce.

March

The weather in March is capricious: sunny, rainy and windy all at once. The official start of spring is 21 March, but the holiday season starts during Easter.

Taste

For three days in March, foodies flock to Florence for Taste (www.pittimmagine.com), a bustling food fair held inside industrial-chic Stazione Leopolda. The program includes culinary-themed talks, cooking demonstrations, and the chance to sample food, coffee and liquor from more than 100 Italian artisan producers.

Settimana Santa

On Good Friday, the Pope leads a candlelit procession

to the Colosseum and on Easter Sunday he gives his blessing in St Peter's Square, while in Florence, a cartful of fireworks explodes in Piazza del Duomo. Other notable processions take place in Procida and Sorrento (Campania), Taranto (Puglia) and Trapani (Sicily).

April

Spring has sprung and April sees the mountains of Sicily and Calabria carpeted with wildflowers, while the gardens of northern Italy show off tulips and early camellias.

◉ Salone Internazionale del Mobile

Held annually in Milan, the world's most prestigious furniture fair (www.cosmit.it) is joined in alternate years by lighting, accessories, office, kitchen and bathroom shows.

◉ Settimana del Tulipano

Tulips erupt in spectacular bloom during the Week of the Tulip, held at Lago Maggiore's Villa Taranto, one of Europe's finest botanical gardens.

🍷 VinItaly

Verona hosts the world's largest wine fair, VinItaly. For four days 4000 international exhibitors will make your head spin with wine tastings, lectures and seminars.

(Top) Il Palio horse race (p536), Siena
(Bottom) Masks for Carnevale, Venice

May

The month of roses and early summer produce makes May a perfect time to travel, especially for walkers. The weather is warm but not too hot and prices throughout Italy are good value. It's also patron-saint season.

✨ Processione dei Serpari

Italy's most peculiar patron-saint day is held on 1 May in Cocullo, Abruzzo. The event sees a statue of St Dominic draped with live snakes and carried in the Snake Charmers' Procession.

✨ Festa di San Gennaro

Naples' Festa di San Gennaro has a lot riding on it: securing the city from volcanic and other disasters. The faithful gather in the cathedral to see their patron-saint's blood liquefy. If it does, the city is safe. Repeat performances take place on 19 September and 16 December.

☆ Ciclo di Rappresentazioni Classiche

Classical intrigue in an evocative setting, the Festival of Greek Theatre, held from mid-May to mid-June, brings Syracuse's 5th-century-BC amphitheatre to life with performances from Italy's acting greats. (p810)

June

The summer season kicks off in June. The temperature cranks up quickly, beach lidos start to open in earnest and some of the big summer festivals commence. Republic Day, on 2 June, is a national holiday.

☆ Napoli Teatro Festival

For three weeks in June, Naples celebrates all things performative with the Napoli Teatro Festival. Using both conventional and unconventional venues, the program ranges from classic works to specially commissioned pieces from both local and international acts. (p655)

✨ La Biennale di Venezia

Held in odd-numbered years, the Venice Biennale (www.labiennale.org) is one of the art world's most prestigious events. Exhibitions are held in venues around the city from June to October.

☆ Ravello Festival

Perched high above the Amalfi Coast, Ravello draws world-renowned artists during its summer-long Ravello Festival (www.ravellofestival.com). Covering everything from music and dance to film and art exhibitions, several events take place in the exquisite Villa Rufolo gardens from June to mid-September. (p694)

☆ Spoleto Festival dei Due Mondi

Held in the Umbrian hill town of Spoleto from late June to mid-July, the Spoleto Festival is an international arts event, featuring music, theatre, dance and art. (p596)

✨ Estate Romana

Between June and September Rome puts on a summer calendar of events that turn the city into an outdoor stage. Dubbed Estate Romana (www.estateromana.comune.roma.it), the program encompasses music, dance, literature and film, with events staged in some of Rome's most evocative venues.

July

School is out and Italians everywhere are heading away from the cities and to mountains or beaches for their summer holidays. Prices and temperatures rise. While the beach is in full swing, many cities host summer art festivals.

✨ Il Palio di Siena

Daredevils in tights thrill the crowds with this chaotic bareback horse race around the piazza in Siena. Preceding the race is a dashing medieval-costume parade. Held on 2 July and 16 August.

☆ Taormina Arte

Ancient ruins and languid summer nights set a seductive scene for Taormina Arte, a major arts festival held through July and August. Events include film screenings, theatre, opera and concerts.

August

August in Italy is hot, expensive and crowded. Everyone is on holiday and, while not everything is shut, many businesses and restaurants do close for part of the month.

✨ Ferragosto

After Christmas and Easter, Ferragosto, on 15 August, is Italy's biggest holiday. It marks the Feast of the Assumption, but even before Christianity the Romans honoured their gods on Feriae Augusti. Naples celebrates with particular fervour.

☆ Mostra Internazionale d'Arte Cinematografica

The Venice International Film Festival (www.labiennale.org/en/cinema) is one of the world's most prestigious silver-screen events. Held at the Lido from late August to early September, it draws the international film glitterati with its red-carpet premieres and paparazzi glamour.

September

This is a glorious month to travel in Italy. Summer wanes into autumn and the start of the harvest season sees local *sagre* (food festivals) spring up. September is also the start of the grape harvest.

✨ Regata Storica

On the first Sunday in September, gondoliers in period dress work those biceps in Venice's Historic Regatta. Period boats are followed by gondola and other boat races along the Grand Canal.

✗ Festival delle Sagre

On the second Sunday in September more than 40 communes in the province of Asti put their wines and local gastronomic products on display at this festival (www.festivaldellesagre.it).

✗ Couscous Fest

The Sicilian town of St Vito celebrates its famous fish couscous at this six-day event in late September (www.couscousfest.it). Highlights include an international couscous cook-off, tastings and world music.

October

October is a fabulous time to visit the south, when the days still radiate with late-summer warmth and the *lidi* (beaches) are emptying. Further north the temperature starts to drop and festival season comes to an end.

☆ Romaeuropa Festival

From late September to November, top international artists take to the stage for Rome's premier festival of theatre, opera and dance (http://romaeuropa.net).

✗ Salone Internazionale del Gusto

Hosted by the Slow Food Movement, this biennial food expo takes place in Turin in even-numbered years. For five days, appetite-piquing events include workshops, presentations and tastings of food, wine and beer from Italy and beyond. (p205)

November

Winter creeps down the peninsula in November, but there's plenty going on. For gastronomes, this is truffle season and the time for the chestnut harvest and mushroom picking.

✨ Ognissanti

Celebrated all over Italy as a national holiday, All Saints' Day on 1 November commemorates the Saint Martyrs, while All Souls' Day, on 2 November, is set aside to honour the deceased.

✗ Truffle Season

From the Piedmontese towns of Alba (www.fieradeltartufo.org) and Asti, to Tuscany's San Miniato, and Le Marche's Acqualagna, November is prime truffle time, with local truffle fairs, events and music.

☆ Opera Season

Italy is home to four of the world's great opera houses: La Scala in Milan, La Fenice in Venice, Teatro San Carlo in Naples and Teatro Massimo in Palermo. The season traditionally runs from mid-October to March, although La Scala opens later on St Ambrose Day, 7 December.

December

December is cold and Alpine resorts start to open for the early ski season, although looming Christmas festivities keep life warm and bright.

✨ Natale

The weeks preceding Christmas are studded with religious events. Many churches set up nativity scenes known as *presepi*. Naples is especially famous for these. On Christmas Eve the Pope serves midnight mass in St Peter's Square.

Itineraries

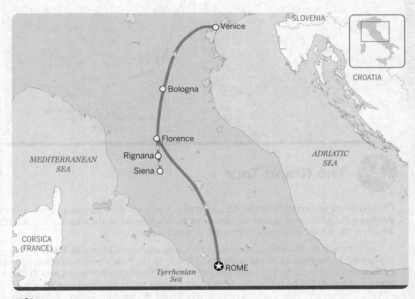

2 WEEKS Rome to Venice

So much to see, so little time. Sample some of Italy's most seductive sights and flavours on this easy route of must-sees. Start with three days in **Rome**, punctuating blockbuster sights with market grazing in the Campo de' Fiori and late-night revelry in Trastevere. On day four, head to Renaissance **Florence**. Drop in on Michelangelo's *David* at the Galleria dell'Accademia and pick your favourite Botticelli at the Uffizi Gallery.

Come day seven, break free to the rolling landscape of Tuscany's Chianti wine region. Recharge with a couple of nights on a farm at **Fattoria di Rignana**, day tripping it to the historic wine cellars at Badia di Passignano and the brooding medieval town of **Siena**.

Gothic beauty also defines **Bologna**, your next stop. Spend a few days soaking up its porticoed streets, museums and superlative regional cooking. Fed and *felice* (happy), continue north for three unforgettable days in **Venice**. Check off musts like the mosaic-encrusted Basilica di San Marco, art-crammed Gallerie dell'Accademia and secret passageways in the Palazzo Ducale, then toast to your trip with a Veneto *prosecco* (sparkling wine).

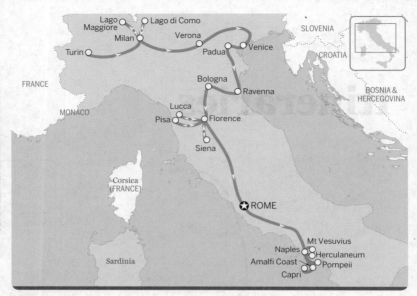

 The Grand Tour

Originally the preserve of aristocratic young men – part scholar's pilgrimage, part rite of passage – the grand tour is now for anyone with enough time on their hands to travel the length of the Italian peninsula from north to south (or vice versa).

The itinerary traditionally started in Turin – and, less often, Milan. In **Turin** you can explore the Savoy palaces, in particular the Venaria Reale, Italy's mini-Versailles, and in **Milan**, admire Leonardo da Vinci's *The Last Supper*. Short excursions to **Lago di Maggiore** or **Lago di Como** might also be in order to enjoy the landscaped lake gardens of Villa Taranto and Villa Carlotta respectively. Board the train for Venice, stopping in **Verona** for a night or two to catch some opera in the Roman Arena. At least four days are needed to enjoy the architectural masterpiece that is **Venice** – the 'locus of decadent Italianate allure'.

During week two start your journey south in **Padua** by taking in Giotto's ground-breaking frescoes in Scrovegni Chapel, dazzling Byzantine mosaics in **Ravenna** and culinary delights in **Bologna** before pausing in **Florence** for a few days. Here you can fill your days with extensive museum visits admiring the monuments and art works of the Renaissance alongside Roman sculptures in the archaeological museum. Day trips to Romanesque **Lucca**, Renaissance **Pisa** or Gothic **Siena** might also feature, time permitting.

By week three you will arrive in **Rome** to study the ruins of the ancient world and the exhaustive art collections at the Vatican, Villa Borghese and Capitoline Hill. Don't try to do it all! Select a few highlights to enjoy and allow plenty of time for coffee in Piazza Navona or dinner in some of Rome's more avant-garde restaurants. Then, head straight to **Naples** for opera at the Teatro San Carlo and archaeological day trips to Herculaneum and Pompeii. Consider also exploring the city's catacombs or scaling Mt Vesuvius. Then end your month-long tour along the romantic **Amalfi Coast** from where you can day trip to offshore **Capri**.

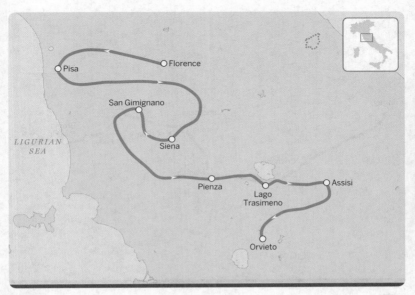

Classic Art Cities

2 WEEKS

The centre of the Renaissance and home to Michelangelo and Dante, Tuscany and Umbria's treasury of architectural styles and artistic expression have made them justifiably world-famous. Start this two-week exploration with three days in **Florence**, where the entire scooter-crammed centre is a World Heritage Site packed with Italy's finest booty of Renaissance art. Climb to the top of Brunelleschi's arresting Duomo, lust after Michelangelo's alpha *David* at the Gallerie dell'Accademia, and meditate on Botticelli's iconic *The Birth of Venus* and *Primavera* at the Uffizi Gallery.

Decamp to **Pisa** to see the architectural ensemble that makes up the Piazza dei Miracoli and then swap Renaissance for Gothic in **Siena**, spending at least two days exploring its brooding streets, frescoed churches and sweeping Piazza del Campo. Tone your thighs and sharpen your orientation by climbing the 400 steps of Torre del Mangia, home to pulse-quickening views of the city. The tower, built on Piazza del Campo in 1344, was at the time a remarkable engineering feat and one of the tallest nonsectarian towers in Italy. From Siena, head on to the fairy-tale medieval towers of **San Gimignano,** a town often dubbed the 'medieval Manhattan' for its dizzying historic skyline. Arrive late in the day so you can enjoy the tiny hill town without the strain of crowds.

On day eight make a slow procession to **Pienza** then skirt the southern shore of **Lago Trasimeno** to reach **Assisi**, where you can admire those Giotto frescoes that caused such a stir in the Middle Ages. Slip into the Romanesque Basilica di Santa Chiara, home to the very cross that reputedly spoke to St Francis. More ethereal energy lingers inside the Santuario di San Damiano, considered the very spot where Assisi's famous saint first heard the voice of God. You'll want at least two days to do them justice before heading southeast to end with the lavish, mosaic-clad cathedral in **Orvieto.**

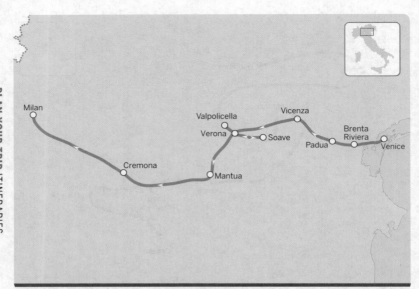

Venice to Milan

2 WEEKS

In the 16th century the Venetian summer began early in June, when every household loaded onto barges for a summer sojourn along the **Brenta Riviera**. You too can make like a Venetian on a boat trip along the Riviera after spending a few days in **Venice**. Marvel at the Tiepolo frescoes of Villa Pisani Nazionale, drop in to the Shoemakers' Museum at Villa Foscarini Rossi and stop in at Palladio's Villa Foscari.

Boat trips along the Brenta Riviera end in **Padua** where you can overnight overlooking the Basilica di Sant'Antonio. Don't miss the small wonders next door: the Oratorio di San Giorgio and the Scoletta del Santo. With advance booking, you can see Padua's crowning glory, Giotto's frescoed Scrovegni Chapel.

On day six hop on the train to **Vicenza**. Spend the afternoon watching sunlight ripple across the soaring facades of Palladio's *palazzi* (mansions) and illuminate the Villa Valmarana 'ai Nani', covered floor-to-ceiling with frescoes by Giambattista and Giandomenico Tiepolo, then head on to **Verona** for three or four days.

Here you can view Mantegnas at Basilica di San Zeno Maggiore, and go window-shopping on Via Mazzini. Then listen to opera in the Roman Arena and wander Verona's balconied backstreets where Romeo wooed Juliet. From Verona, make a day trip northwest to **Valpolicella**, where you can sample the highly prized Amarone (red wine) by appointment at Montecariano Cellars, or back east to **Soave** for a sampling of its namesake Denominazione di origine controllata (DOC) white wine at Azienda Agricola Coffele.

On day 11 dip southwest to regal **Mantua** for an impressive display of dynastic power and patronage at the Gonzagas' fortified family pad, the Palazzo Ducale. Or for something altogether more dramatic, witness the giants trying to storm Mt Olympus in Giulio Romano's fresco in the Camera dei Giganti at Palazzo Te.

Finish up with a two-day stop in **Cremona,** where you can chat with artisans in one of the 100 or so violin-making shops around Piazza del Comune before hearing them in action at the Teatro Amilcare Ponchielli, and then heading on to end your tour in **Milan**.

 1 WEEK ## A Lakes Tour

A short drive northwest of Malpensa airport, **Milan**, and you're on the edge of one of Italy's most serene scenes, Lago Maggiore.

Start with three nights in belle époque **Stresa** and visit the lavish **Borromean Islands**: Isola Madre for its romantic gardens and wisteria-clad Staircase of the Dead; and Isola Bella for its priceless art collection, vast ballrooms and shell-encrusted grotto. Take the funicular up to **Monte Mottarone** and day trip to **Lago d'Orta** and the bijou **Isola San Giulio**.

On day four head north from Stresa to **Verbania**, picnicking amid the tulips of Villa Taranto before gliding east across the lake to **Laveno** and straight on to celebrity haunt **Como**. Amble the flower-laden lakeside to view art exhibits at Villa Olmo before finding a sun lounge at the Lido di Villa Olmo. You could spend days playing in Como, hiring out seaplanes and boats, or hiking the mountainous hinterland of the Triangolo Lariano. If you're ambitious you can walk to chic **Bellagio**. Otherwise take the lake road on day six and lunch on perch in **Lezzeno** before one last romantic night lakeside.

 2 WEEKS ## Northwest Highlights

Often dismissed as little more than the country's economic engine, Italy's north-west packs a surprising cultural and culinary punch. Start with three days in **Milan**, counting masterpieces at the Pinacoteca di Brera, striking a pose in the fashion-obsessed Quadrilatero d'Oro and schmoozing with hip locals in Navigli. Styled up, catch a westbound train to **Turin** for three days of French-influenced architecture, historic cafes, and fabulous museums spanning ancient Egypt to world cinema. Continue south to the foodie town of **Alba**, famed for its prized black truffles. Base yourself here for three days, allowing time to taste-test the winegrowing towns of **Barolo** and **Barbaresco**. Continue south for a day in gritty **Genoa**, sampling its famous *pesto genovese* and taking in the celebrated art and architecture of the Musei di Strada Nuova. The following day, slide on those designer shades and head east for an afternoon of posing in chichi **Portofino** before slumbering in better-value **Santa Margherita**. Spend your final two days hiking the stunning **Cinque Terre** coast, laced with terraced vines, story-book fishing villages and some of Italy's tastiest seafood.

Puglian Promenade
2 WEEKS

Best of Sicily
3 WEEKS

For the majority of visitors to Italy, a trip 'south' means Naples and the Amalfi Coast: what a shame! Puglia, which forms the heel of Lo Stivale (The Boot), is one of the country's most underrated regions. Fly in to **Bari**, where you can find the relics of Father Christmas in the Romanesque cathedral. Strike out south, via **Polignano a Mare**, to the famous **Grotte di Castellana**. From here a two- to three-day drive south will take you through some of the finest Valle d'Itria towns, including **Alberobello**, with its hobbit-like, conical *trulli* houses, wine-producing **Locorotondo**, beautiful baroque **Martina Franca** and chic, whitewashed **Ostuni**. In Martina Franca you get just a small taste of what is awaiting you in **Lecce**, otherwise known as the 'Florence of the south' for its operatic architectural ensembles and scholarly bent. Hire a bike and spend at least three or four days there before striking out to the fortified ports of **Otranto** in the southeast or **Gallipoli** in the southwest, with their sandy blue-flag-accredited beaches. If you don't get caught up gulping raw sea urchins and octopuses, push south to **Santa Maria di Leuca**, the very tip of the Italian stiletto.

Sicily is a sweet, sour, spicy *tajine* of East-West architecture, impossibly ancient ruins, and fiery geology. Fly into **Palermo**, taking three days to savour its raffish palazzi, souklike markets, and the extraordinary mosaics at Cattedrale di Monreale.

On day four, conjure the ancients at the Doric temple in **Segesta**, before continuing to **Trapani** to sample its celebrated Arabesque cuisine. Come morning, hop on the funicular to hilltop **Erice**, but come back down to spend day six sipping sweet local wine in elegant **Marsala** and day seven roaming the Greek ruins of **Selinunte**. The incredible Valle dei Templi in **Agrigento** is your destination on day eight.

On day nine, shoot to the Val di Noto to explore the World Heritage baroque towns of **Ragusa**, **Modica** and **Noto**. Change gear on days 12 and 13 in youthful, worldly **Catania**. Pumped, scale **Mt Etna** on day 14 before two indulgent days of wining, dining and coastal posing in chic **Taormina**. From **Messina**, catch a hydrofoil to the stunning **Aeolian Islands** for five merited days of beach time and volcanic pyrotechnics.

Outdoor vegetable stall, Florence

Plan Your Trip

Eat & Drink
Like a Local

Gastronomy is one of Italy's raisons d'être. The country is like an all-year Christmas stocking, overstuffed with superlative produce and culinary know-how. Locals are fiercely proud of their regions' specialities, and devouring them is an essential part of any Italian sojourn.

The Year in Food

While *sagre* (local food festivals) go into over-drive in autumn, there's never a bad time to raise your fork in Italy. For specific details on food events see p29.

Spring (Mar–May)

Asparagus, artichokes and Easter speciali-ties, plus a handful of festivals like Turin's Cioccolatò and Ascoli Piceno's Fritto Misto all'Italiana.

Summer (Jun–Aug)

Aubergines, peppers and berries. Tuck into tuna at Carloforte's Girotonno tuna catch in June and beat the heat with gelato and Sicilian granita.

Autumn (Sep–Nov)

Food festivals, chestnuts, mushrooms and game. Truffle hunters head to Piedmont, Tuscany and Umbria while wine connoisseurs hit Elba's wine harvest and Merano's wine festival.

Winter (Dec–Feb)

Christmas and Carnevale treats. Fishers serve up sea urchins and mussels on Sar-dinia's Poetto beach, while Umbria celebrates black truffles with the Mostra Mercato del Tartufo Nero.

Food Experiences

So much produce, so many specialities, so little time! Fine-tune your culinary radar with the following edible musts.

Meals of a Lifetime

➡ **Osteria Francescana, Modena** Bold reinterpretations underline the world's third-best restaurant, as voted in the 2013 San Pellegrino World's 50 Best Restaurants. (p446)

➡ **Pizzarium, Rome** Superlative dough and toppings make for unforgettable *pizza al taglio* (pizza by the slice). (p136)

➡ **All'Arco, Venice** Top-of-the-class *cicheti* (Venetian bar snacks) in new- and old-school flavours. (p369)

➡ **Il Santo Bevitore, Florence** Perfectly revamped classics and an infectious buzz make this a Florentine foodie hot spot. (p501)

➡ **Dal Pescatore, Mantua** The first female Italian chef to hold three Michelin stars, Nadia Santini is a self-taught culinary virtuoso. (p297)

➡ **Il Frantoio, Puglia** Legendary eight-course feasts at an olive-grove-fringed *masseria* (working farm). (p722)

Cheap Treats

➡ **Pizza al taglio** 'Pizza by the slice' is the perfect piazza-side nibble.

➡ **Arancini** Deep-fried rice balls stuffed with *ragù* (meat sauce), tomato and vegetables.

➡ **Pecorino** A nutty sheep's-milk cheese perfect with fresh, crunchy *pane* (bread).

➡ **Prosciutto crudo** Sweet-smelling and satisfyingly salty, air-dried ham is another perfect *panino* filler.

➡ **Porchetta rolls** Warm sliced pork (roasted whole with fennel, garlic and pepper) in a crispy roll.

➡ **Pane e panelle** Palermo chickpea fritters on a sesame roll.

➡ **Gelato** The best Italian gelato uses seasonal ingredients and natural colours.

Dare to Try

➡ **Pajata** A creamy Roman pasta dish made with calves' entrails containing the mothers' congealed milk.

➡ **Missoltini** Como's sun-dried fish cured in salt and bay leaves.

➡ **Uove di seppie (cuttlefish eggs)** A Venetian treat, poached in salted water and sometimes spiked with *anice stellato* (star anise).

➡ **Lardo di Colonnata** Tuscany's luscious cured pig lard keeps cardiologists in the black.

➡ **Pani ca meusa** A Palermo sandwich of beef spleen and lungs dipped in boiling lard.

➡ **Zurrette** Sardinian black pudding made of sheep's blood, cooked in a sheep's stomach with herbs and fennel.

Local Specialities

The Italian term for 'pride of place' is *campanilismo*, but a more accurate word would be *formaggismo:* loyalty to the local cheese. Clashes among medieval city-states involving castle sieges and boiling oil have been replaced by competition in producing speciality foods and wines.

Piedmont

Birthplace of the Slow Food Movement. Guzzle Lavazza coffee and vermouth in Turin, also famed for its chocolate and nougat, buzzing *aperitivo* (predinner drinks with snacks) scene and Slow Food emporium Eataly. Alba treats taste buds to white truffles, hazelnuts, and pedigreed Barolo and Barbaresco reds. Hazelnuts and cocoa merge together in Cherasco, known for its chocolates, Baci di Cherasco (Cherasco Kisses), not to mention its lauded *lumache* (snails).

Lombardy

Lombardy is all about *burro* (butter), risotto and gorgonzola cheese. Milan delivers *risotto alla milanese* (saffron and bone-marrow risotto), *panettone* (a yeast-risen sweet bread), uberfashionable restaurants and food emporium Peck. Renaissance

Beef carpaccio

Mantua remains addicted to spiced pumpkin tortelli, wild fowl and *sbrisolona* (a delicious cornmeal cake with almonds, lemon and vanilla). The Valtenesi area is home to some of Italy's finest emerging olive oils, including Comincioli's award-winning Numero Uno.

Venice & the Veneto

Not all bubbly *prosecco* (local sparkling wine) and fiery grappa, Italy's northeast peddles *risotto alle seppie* (cuttlefish-ink risotto), *polenta con le quaglie* (polenta with quails), as well as the odd foreign spice – think *sarde in soar* (grilled sardines in a sweet-and-sour sauce). Sail into Venice for *cicheti* (Venetian bar snacks) at local *bacari* (bars) and to scour Rialto Market produce such as lagoon seafood (look for tags reading *nostrano*, meaning 'ours') and *radicchio di Treviso* (red, bitter chicory). Near Verona, the prime wine region of Valpollicella is celebrated for Amarone, Valpollicella Superiore, Ripasso, Recioto, and inspired renegade Indicazione geografica tipica (IGT) red blends from winemakers like Giuseppe Quintarelli and Romano Dal Forno.

WHAT TO BOOK

Avoid disappointment with the following tips:

➡ Book high-end and popular restaurants, especially for Friday and Saturday evenings and Sunday lunch.

➡ In tourist hot spots, always book restaurants in summer and during Easter and Christmas.

➡ Book cooking courses, such as Bologna's **La Vecchia Scuola Bolognese** (p437), the Cinque Terre's **Arbaspàa** (p185), Lecce's **Awaiting Table** (p729) and Milan's **Teatro 7** (☑02 8907 3719; www.teatro7.com; Via Thaon di Revel 7) and **La Cucina Italiana** (☑02 7064 2242; www. scuolacucinaitaliana.com; Piazza Aspromonte 15).

Pizza

Although Quintarelli passed away in 2012, his family uphold his legacy and continue to produce world-renowned wine in his name.

Emilia-Romagna

Emilia-Romagna claims some of Italy's most iconic edibles, from *tagliatelle alla bolognese* (pasta with white wine, tomato, oregano, beef and pork belly) to *parmigiano reggiano* cheese (Parmesan) and *prosciutto di Parma* (cured ham). Explore the region's flavours with our dedicated regional itinerary on p44.

Tuscany

In Florence, feast on succulent *bistecca alla fiorentina* (T-bone steak), made with world-famous Chianina beef from the Valdichiana valley. The valley is also famous for *ravaggiolo* (sheep's-milk cheese wrapped in fern fronds). Head to Castelnuovo di Garfagnana for autumnal porcini and chestnuts, and to San Miniato for white truffles (from October to December). These prized fungi are celebrated at San Miniato's white-truffle fair (Sagra del Tartufo), held over three weekends in November. Savour *cinta senese* (indigenous Tuscan pig), *pecorino* (sheep's-milk cheese) and prized extra-virgin olive oils in Montalcino, a place also known for its Brunello

Cheese

carbonara, *bucatini all'amatriciana* (with bacon, tomato, chilli and *pecorino* cheese) and *spaghetti cacio e pepe* (with *pecorino* cheese and black pepper). Head to Rome's Testaccio neighbourhood for nose-to-tail staples like *trippa alla romana* (tripe cooked with potatoes, tomato, mint and *pecorino* cheese), and to the Jewish Ghetto for kosher deep-fried *carciofi* (artichokes). Southeast of the city in Frascati, tour the vineyards and swill the area's delicate white vino.

Naples & Campania

Procida lemons get cheeky in *limoncello* (lemon liqueur) while the region's vines create intense red Taurasi and the dry white Fiano di Avellino. Naples is home to superlative pizza and coffee, and on-the-go snacks such as *pizza fritta* (fried pizza dough stuffed with salami, dried lard cubes, smoked *provola* (provolone) cheese, ricotta and tomato). The town of Gragnano produces lauded pasta, perfect for *spaghetti alle vongole* (spaghetti with clam sauce). Leave room for a *sfogliatella* (sweetened ricotta pastry) and *babà* (rum-soaked sponge cake). Both Caserta and the Cilento produce luscious *mozzarella di bufala* (buffalo mozzarella).

Puglia

Head southeast for peppery olive oil, crunchy *pane* and honest *cucina povera* (peasant cooking). Breadcrumbs lace everything from *strascinati con la mollica* (pasta with breadcrumbs and anchovies) to *tiella di verdure* (baked vegetable casserole), while carbolicious snacks include *puccia* (bread with olives) and ring-shaped *taralli* (pretzel-like biscuits). In Salento, linger over lunch at a *masseria* and make a toast with hearty reds like Salice Salentino and Primitivo di Manduria.

Sicily

Pour a devilish Nero d'Avola red to toast your cuisine with kick. Channel ancient Arab influences with fragrant fish couscous and spectacular sweets like *cannoli* (pastry shells filled with sweet ricotta). In Palermo, snack on *sfincione* (spongy, oily pizza topped with onions and *caciocavallo* cheese), and feast on *pasta con le sarde* (pasta with sardines, pine nuts, raisins and wild fennel) and *involtini di pesce spada*

and Rosso di Montalcino reds. Montepulciano is the home of Vino Nobile red, its equally quaffable second-string Rosso di Montepulciano, and Terre di Siena extra-virgin olive oil. Just leave time for Chianti's world-famous vineyards.

Umbria

Uncork a bottle of Sagrantino di Montefalco red and grate a black truffle from Norcia over fresh *tagliatelle* (ribbon pasta). Truffles aside, Norcia is Italy's capital of pork, its famous *norcinerie* (butcher shops) packed with hung hams and stuffed boar's heads. In Lago Trasimeno, freshwater fish flavours dishes like *regina alla porchetta* (roasted carp stuffed with garlic, fennel and herbs) and *tegemacchio* (fish stew made with garlic, onions, tomatoes and a medley of underwater critters). Meanwhile, on the Strada dei Vini del Cantico wine trail, the town of Torgiano celebrates wine and olives with two dedicated museums.

Rome & Lazio

Snack on thin-crust pizza or *supplì* (risotto balls), or carb-up with spaghetti

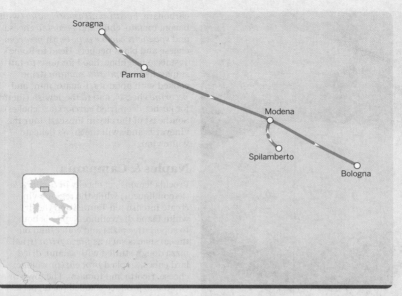

5 DAYS Food Lovers' Tour of Emilia-Romagna

To many gourmands, Emilia-Romagna is Italy's gastronomic queen – no mean feat in a country famed for culinary prowess.

Start your taste test with two days in **Parma**, home to Italy's finest cured ham (*prosciutto di Parma*) and its most revered cheese (*parmigiano reggiano*). Stock up on these, as well as local Lambrusco wines, at Salumeria Garibaldi, and savour classics like *tortelli di zucca* (pumpkin-stuffed pasta) and *cappelletti in brodo* (pasta stuffed with ground meats and *parmigiano* cheese in a beef broth) at foodie favourite Trattoria del Tribunale. If you're a culinary daredevil, look out for *pesto di cavallo* (raw minced horse meat with herbs and parmesan), one of Parma's more unusual specialities. For a cultural take on the world's most grated dairy product, side trip it to the Museo del Parmigiano Reggiano in **Soragna**, 30km northwest of Parma.

Your next stop is culinary hot spot **Modena**. Stock up on the town's world-famous aged *aceto balsamico* (balsamic vinegar) at Enoteca Ducale, or delve deeper on a Modenatur guided visit to local producers. Alternatively, visit the Museo del Balsamico Tradizionale in the town of **Spilamberto**, 17km southeast of Modena. If money permits (and you've booked ahead), dine at boundary-pushing, Michelin-starred darling Osteria Francescana. If it's out of your wallet's reach, graze at Franceschetta 58, its more casual sibling.

From Modena, continue to vibrant **Bologna**, Emilia-Romagna's capital city and your final stop. Spend two days exploring the city's medieval streetscapes and hearty flavours. Stock up on fresh produce at the Mercato delle Erbe and larder essentials in the deli-packed Quadrilatero area, then learn what to do with them with a cooking course at La Vecchia Scuola Bolognese. For cooking books, scour the shelves of Librerie Coop, a multilevel bookshop partnered with Turin's famous food emporium, Eataly. Needless to say, the city has no shortage of nosh spots serving superlative classics like *tagliatelle al ragù*, *mortadella* (pork cold cut) and *stinco di maiale al forno con porcini* (roasted pork shanks with porcini mushrooms) – among the best are Osteria dell'Orsa and Trattoria dal Biassanot. *Buon appetito!*

(thinly sliced swordfish fillets rolled up and filled with breadcrumbs, capers, tomatoes and olives). In Catania, pay tribute to Sicily's Norman invaders with *pasta alla Norma* (pasta with basil, eggplant, ricotta and tomato). Further south, taste-test Modica's spiced chocolate.

How to Eat & Drink

Now that your appetite is piqued, it's time for the technicalities of eating *all'italiana*.

When to Eat

➡ **Colazione (Breakfast)** Often little more than an espresso and a *cornetto* (Italian croissant) or brioche.

➡ **Pranzo (Lunch)** Traditionally the main meal of the day. Standard restaurant times are noon to 2.30pm, though most locals don't lunch before 1pm.

➡ **Aperitivo** Postwork drinks usually take place between 5pm and 8pm, when the price of your drink includes a buffet of tasty morsels.

➡ **Cena (Dinner)** Traditionally lighter than lunch, though still a main meal. Standard restaurant times are 7.30pm to around 11pm.

Where to Eat

➡ **Ristorante (Restaurant)** Formal service and refined dishes.

➡ **Trattoria** Cheaper than a restaurant, with more-relaxed service and regional classics.

➡ **Osteria** Historically a tavern focused on wine, the modern version is often an intimate trattoria or wine bar offering a handful of dishes.

➡ **Enoteca** Wine bars often serve snacks to accompany your tipple.

➡ **Agriturismo** A working farmhouse offering food made with farm-grown produce.

➡ **Pizzeria** Cheap grub, cold beer and a convivial vibe. The best pizzerias are often crowded: be patient.

➡ **Tavola calda** Cafeteria-style spots serving cheap premade food such as pasta and roast meats.

THE CAFFÈ LOW-DOWN

Great *caffè* (coffee) in Italy is not a hipster novelty, it's old-school tradition. Sip *all'italiana* with the following basics, then turn to p422 for more.

➡ Caffè latte and cappuccino are considered morning drinks, with espresso and macchiato the preferred postlunch options.

➡ Baristas may offer a glass of water, either *liscia* (still) or *frizzante* (sparkling), with your espresso. Many (especially southern Italians) drink it before their coffee to cleanse the palate.

➡ Take the edge off with a *caffè corretto*, a shot of espresso spiked with liquer (usually grappa).

➡ Coffee with dessert is fine, but ordering one with your main meal is a travesty.

Menu Decoder

For an explanation of of the dishes you'll find on Italian menus, see p957.

➡ **Menù a la carte** Choose whatever you like from the menu.

➡ **Menù di degustazione** Degustation menu, usually consisting of six to eight 'tasting size' courses.

➡ **Menù turistico** The 'tourist menu' usually signals mediocre fare – steer clear!

➡ **Piatto del giorno** Dish of the day.

➡ **Antipasto** A hot or cold appetiser. For a tasting plate of different appetisers, request an *antipasto misto* (mixed antipasto).

➡ **Primo** First course, usually a substantial pasta, rice or *zuppa* (soup) dish.

➡ **Secondo** Second course, often *carne* (meat) or *pesce* (fish).

➡ **Contorno** Side dish, usually *verdura* (vegetable).

➡ **Dolce** Dessert; including *torta* (cake).

➡ **Frutta** Fruit; usually the epilogue to a meal.

➡ **Nostra produzione** Made in-house.

➡ **Surgelato** Frozen; usually used to denote fish or seafood that's not freshly caught.

Outdoor Experiences

Blessed with mountains, lakes and 7600km of coastline, Italy is like one giant, pulse-racing playground. Whether you're after adrenalin-piquing skiing in the Alps; hard-core hiking in Sardinia; white-water rafting in Calabria, or low-key cycling through Piedmont, Madre Natura (Mother Nature) has you covered.

Best Experiences

Hiking

The Dolomites, Piedmont's Gran Paradiso, Trentino's Stelvio and Calabria's Pollino parks, Umbria's Piano Grande and the coastal tracks of the Cinque Terre, the Amalfi Coast, Sicily and Sardinia.

Cycling

Try the Po Delta and Bolzano, the wine regions of Franciacorta, Barolo, Barbaresco and Chianti. Urban options include Rome's Via Appia Antica, Ferrara, Lucca, Bologna and Lecce.

Skiing

Cross-border skiing into Slovenia at Sella Nevea; skiing and snowboarding in Courmayeur; downhill and cross-country skiing in Cortina d'Ampezzo, the Valle d'Aosta and Sella Ronda.

Diving

The best marine parks are off the Cinque Terre, the Gargano Promontory, Elba, the Sorrento Peninsula, the Aeolian Islands, Ustica and Sardinia.

Best Times to Go

April to June Walk among wildflowers.

July & September Water sports and warm-water diving without the August crowds.

December, February & March The best ski months for atmosphere (Christmas), snow and value respectively.

On Land

From skyscraping Alps to rolling Tuscan hills, Italy's diverse geography provides a plethora of land-locked diversions. The Alps are alive with the sound of skiing, snowboarding and mountain biking, while the vine-laced landscapes of Tuscany and Piedmont put the romance into cycling. Further south, the precipitous peaks of the Amalfi Coast harbour an ancient network of shepherds' paths, making for heavenly hikes.

Hiking & Walking

Italy offers thousands of kilometres of *sentieri* (marked trails). Most local and regional tourist office websites have information about walking in their area. The **Italian Parks** (www.parks.it) organisation lists walking trails through each of the country's 24 national parks, as well as providing updates on Italy's marine parks and other protected areas. Another useful website is that of Italy's major walking club, the **Club Alpino Italiano** (www.cai.it) – follow the *rifugi* (mountain huts) link for information about trail routes and accommodation. For comprehensive coverage of hiking routes across the country, pick up Lonely Planet's *Hiking in Italy*.

The Alps

The Alps stretch from Slovenia in the east, via the southern borders of Austria and Switzerland, to France in the west. For hikers, they offer heady mountain vistas, swooping forested valleys and views over large glacial lakes such as Garda, Como and Maggiore.

To the east in Friuli Venezia Giulia you'll find the Giulie and Carnic Alps, where you can hike in pursuit of lynx, marmots and eagles amid supercute Tyrolean villages. Heading west, the white ridges pass through Trento's Parco Nazionale dello Stelvio, northern Italy's (and the Alps') largest national park, spilling into Lombardy. Lombardy's great lakes – encompassing Garda, Como, Iseo, Maggiore and Orta – are prime hiking territory mixing mountain and lake vistas. Particularly scenic is the crumpled ridge of mountains in Como's Triangolo Lariano, and Garda's Monte Baldo.

Finally, in the far west, dropping into Piedmont and Liguria, are the Graian, Maritime and Ligurian Alps, which take in the Valle d'Aosta, the vast Gran Paradiso park and the lesser-known Parco Naturale delle Alpi Marittime, before making a sharp and dramatic descent to the Cinque Terre and Portofino park on the Ligurian coastline.

Accommodation in the mountains is in *rifugi* (huts) or chalets, which should be booked ahead in high season. For serious hiking you'll need to bring appropriate equipment and get detailed trail maps. Tourist offices and visitor centres provide some information, resources and basic maps for easier tourist routes.

The Dolomites

Soaring across the borders of the Veneto, Trentino and Alto-Adige, the Dolomites are a stunning, Unesco World Heritage–listed mountain range. They offer some of Italy's most scenic (and vertiginous) walking trails, and are equally well known for their skiing and cycling.

Top Trails

➡ **Alpe di Siusi, Alto-Adige** (p327) Europe's largest plateau ends dramatically at the base of the Sciliar Mountains. Average stamina will get you to Rifugio Bolzano, one of the Alps' oldest mountain huts. The more challenging peaks of

GARETH McCORMACK / GETTY IMAGES ©

Valle d'Aosta (p227)

the Catinaccio group and the Sassolungo are nearby.

➡ **Val Pusteria, Alto-Adige** (p330) This narrow Tyrolean valley runs from Bressanone to San Candido. At the far end of the valley are the Sesto Dolomites, criss-crossed with spectacular walking trails, including moderate trails around the iconic Tre Cime di Lavaredo (Three Peaks).

➡ **Val Gardena, Alto-Adige** (p326) One of only five valleys where the Ladin heritage is still preserved. Located amid the peaks of the Gruppo del Sella and Sassolungo there are challenging *alte vie* (high-altitude) trails and easier nature walks such as the Naturonda at Passo di Sella (2244m).

➡ **Brenta Dolomites, Trentino** (p308) The Brenta group is famed for its sheer cliffs and tricky ascents, which are home to some of Italy's most famous *vie ferrate* (trails with permanent steel cables and ladders), including the Via Ferrata delle Bocchette.

➡ **Parco Nazionale delle Dolomiti Bellunesi, Veneto** (p397) A Unesco Heritage park offering trails amid wildflowers. This park also harbours the high-altitude Alte Vie delle Dolomiti trails, accessible between June and September.

ITALY'S BEST PARKS & RESERVES

PARK	FEATURES	ACTIVITIES	BEST TIME TO VISIT	PAGE
Abruzzo, Lazio e Molise	granite peaks, beech woods, bears, wolves	hiking, horse riding	May-Oct	p630
Appennino Tosco-Emiliano	mountains, forests, lakes	skiing, cycling, hiking, horse riding	Feb-Oct	p449
Arcipelago di La Maddalena	rocky islets, beaches, translucent sea	sailing, diving, snorkelling	Jun-Sep	p364
Asinara	albino donkeys, former prison	cycling, boat tours, snorkelling	Jun-Sep	p857
Aspromonte	coniferous forests, high plains, vertiginous villages	hiking	May-Oct	p759
Cilento e Vallo di Diano	Greek temples, dramatic coastline, caves	hiking, swimming, birdwatching	May-Oct	p702
Cinque Terre	Unesco World Heritage Site, colourful fishing villages, ter-raced hillsides	hiking, diving	Apr-Oct	p183
Dolomiti Bellunesi	Unesco World Heritage Site, rock spires, highland mead-ows, chamois	skiing, hiking, mountain biking	Dec-Oct	p397
Dolomiti di Sesto	jagged mountains, Tre Cime di Lavaredo (Three Peaks)	hiking, mountain biking, rock climbing	Jun-Sep	p330
Etna	active volcano, black lava fields, forests	hiking, horse riding	May-Oct	p804
Gargano	ancient forests, limestone cliffs, grottoes	diving, hiking, cycling, snorkelling	Jun-Sep	p714
Golfo di Orosei e del Gennargentu	sheer cliffs, granite peaks, prehistoric ruins	hiking, sailing, rock climb-ing, canyoning	May-Sep	p867
Gran Paradiso	Alpine villages, mountains, meadows, ibex	skiing, snowboarding, hiking, climbing, mountain biking	Dec-Oct	p235
Gran Sasso e Monti della Laga	ragged peaks, birds of prey, wolves	skiing, hiking, climbing	Dec-Mar	p624
Madonie	Sicily's highest peaks, wooded slopes, wolves, wildflowers	hiking, horse riding	May-Jun, Sep-Oct	p783
Majella	mountains, deep gorges, bears	hiking, cycling	Jun-Sep	p627
Maremma	reclaimed marshes, beaches	hiking, horse riding, birdwatching	May-Oct	p557
Monti Sibillini	ancient hamlets, mountains, eagles	hiking, mountain biking, paragliding	May-Oct	p619
Pollino	mountains, canyons, forest, Larico pines, rare orchids	rafting, canyoning, hiking	Jun-Sep	p754
Prigionette	forest paths, albino donkeys, Giara horses, wild boar	hiking, cycling	May-Oct	p857
Sciliar-Catinaccio	pasture lands, valleys, story-book alpine villages	hiking, cycling	Jun-Sep	p327
Sila	wooded hills, lakes, remote villages, mushrooms	skiing, hiking, canyoning, horse riding	Dec-Mar, May-Oct	p753
Stelvio	Alpine peaks, glaciers, forests	year-round skiing, hiking, cycling, mountain biking	Dec-Sep	p325

Central Italy

Abruzzo's national parks are among Italy's least explored. Here, you can climb Corno Grande, the Apennines' highest peak, and explore vast, silent valleys. Likewise, Umbria's Monti Sibillini and Piano Grande are well off the trodden path, and both burst with wildflowers in spring.

Tuscany's only significant park with good walking trails is in the southern Maremma, where you can sign up for walks of medium difficulty. For most people though, an easy amble through picturesque Chianti suits just fine.

The South

For spectacular sea views hit the Amalfi Coast and Sorrento Peninsula, where age-old paths such as the Sentiero degli Dei (Path of the Gods) disappear into wooded mountains and ancient lemon groves. Across the water, Capri subverts its playboy image with a series of bucolic walking trails far from the crowds.

Crossing the border between Calabria and Basilicata is the Parco Nazionale del Pollino, Italy's largest national park. Claiming the richest repository of flora and fauna in the south, its varied landscapes range from deep river canyons to alpine meadows. Calabria's other national parks – the Sila and Aspromonte – offer similarly dramatic hiking, particularly the area around Sersale in the Sila, studded with waterfalls and the possibility of trekking through the Valli Cupe canyon.

Sicily & Sardinia

With their unique topographies, Sicily and Sardinia provide unforgettable walking opportunities. Take your pick of volcano hikes in Sicily: the mother of them all is Mt Etna, but there's a whole host of lesser volcanoes on the Aeolian Islands, from extinct Vulcano, where you can descend to the crater floor, to a three-hour climb to the summit of Stromboli to see it exploding against the night sky. From Etna you can also trek

TOP SKI RESORTS

Friuli Venezia Giulia
➡ **Tarvisio** 60km of cross-country tracks and great freeriding.
➡ **Sella Nevea** 30km of slopes linking to Bovec in Slovenia.
➡ **Forni di Sopra** Family friendly, offering skiing, ice skating and tobogganing.

Valle d'Aosta
➡ **Courmayeur** Dominated by spectacular Mont Blanc, Courmayeur allows access to legendary runs such as the Vallée Blanche.
➡ **Breuil-Cervinia** In the shadow of the Matterhorn and within skiing distance of Zermatt; good for late-season snow and family facilities.
➡ **Monte Rosa** Comprised of three valleys (Val d'Ayas, Val d'Gressoney and Alagna Valsesia) Monte Rosa is characterised by Walser villages and white-knuckle off-piste skiing and heli-skiing.

Piedmont
➡ **Via Lattea** 400km of pistes linking five ski resorts, including one of Europe's most glamorous, Sestriere.
➡ **Limone Piemonte** 80km of runs, including some for Nordic skiing.

Trentino Alto-Adige
➡ **Sella Ronda** This 40km circumnavigation of the Gruppo di Sella range (3151m, at Piz Boé) is one of the Alps' iconic ski routes.
➡ **Alta Badia** 130km of slopes including the legendary Gran Risa.

Veneto
➡ **Cortina d'Ampezzo** Downhill and cross-country skiing with runs ranging from bunny slopes to the legendary Staunies black mogul run.

across into the Madonie park, or, on Sicily's northwest coast, you can track the shoreline in the Riserva Naturale dello Zingaro (p829).

Hiking Sardinia's granite peaks is more challenging. The Golfo di Orosei e del Gennargentu park offers a network of old shepherd tracks on the Supramonte plateau and incorporates the prehistoric site of Tiscali and the Gola Su Gorropu canyon, which requires a guide and a little rock climbing.

Rock Climbing

The huge rock walls of the Dolomites set testing challenges for rock climbers of all levels, with everything from simple, single-pitch routes to long, multipitch ascents, many of which are easily accessible by road. To combine rock climbing with high-level hiking, clip onto the *vie ferrate* in the Brenta Dolomites.

Climbs of all grades are found in the Trentino town of Arco, home to the world-famous **Rock Master Festival** (www.rock-masterfestival.com).

For hard-core mountaineering, alpinists can pit themselves against Europe's highest peaks in the Valle d'Aosta. Courmayeur and Cogne, a renowned ice-climbing centre, make good bases.

To the south, the Gran Sasso massif is a favourite. Of its three peaks, Corno Grande (2912m) is the highest and Corno Piccolo (2655m) the easiest to get to.

Other hot spots include Monte Pellegrino outside Palermo in Sicily, and Domusnovas, Ogliastra and the Supramonte in Sardinia.

The best source of climbing information is the Club Alpino Italiano (p934). Another good information source is the website **Climb Europe** (www.climb-europe.com), which also sells rock-climbing guidebooks covering Italy.

Skiing

Most of Italy's top ski resorts are in the northern Alps, where names like Sestriere, Cortina d'Ampezzo, Madonna di Campiglio and Courmayeur are well known to serious skiers. Travel down the peninsula and you'll find smaller resorts throughout the Apennines, in Lazio, Le Marche and Abruzzo. Even Sicily's Mt Etna is skiable in winter.

Facilities at the bigger centres are generally world-class, with pistes ranging from nursery slopes to tough black runs. As well as *sci alpino* (downhill skiing), resorts might offer *sci di fondo* (cross-country skiing) and *sci alpinismo* (ski mountaineering).

The ski season runs from December to late March, although there is year-round skiing in Trentino Alto-Adige and on Mont Blanc (Monte Bianco) and the Matterhorn in the Valle d'Aosta. Generally, January and February are the best, busiest and priciest months. For better value, consider Friuli's expanding Sella Nevea runs or Tarvisio, one of the coldest spots in the Alps, where the season is often extended into April.

The best bargain of the ski year is the *settimana bianca* (literally 'white week') package covering accommodation, food and ski passes.

Online, **J2Ski** (www.j2ski.com)has detailed information about Italy's ski resorts, including facilities, accommodation and updated snow reports.

Snowboarding

Two snowboarding hot spots are Trentino's Madonna di Campiglio and Valle d'Aosta's Breuil-Cervinia. Madonna's facilities are among the best in the country and include a snowboard park with descents for all levels and a dedicated boarder-cross zone. Breuil-Cervinia, situated at 2050m in the shadow of the Matterhorn, is better suited to intermediate and advanced levels.

SELVAGGIO BLU – THE ULTIMATE TREK

Arguably the toughest trek in Italy, Sardinia's seven-day *Selvaggio Blu* (Savage Blue) is not for the faint-hearted. Stretching 45km along the Golfo di Orosei, the trek traverses wooded ravines, gorges and cliffs and passes many caves. It's not well sign-posted (a deliberate decision to keep it natural) and there's no water en route. Furthermore, it involves rock climbs of up to UIAA grade IV+ (challenging), and abseils of up to 45m.

For information, Italian speakers can consult www.selvaggioblu.it, a website with descriptions of each day's walk, advice on what to take and when to go (namely in spring or autumn).

BIKE TOURS

➡ **I Bike Tuscany** (www.ibiketuscany.com) Year-round one-day tours for riders of every skill level. Transport to Chianti and a support vehicle are provided. Multi-day tours are available through US-based **We Bike Tuscany** (www.webiketuscany.com).

➡ **Iseobike** (www.iseobike.com) Tours around the Franciacorta wine region, with wine tastings.

➡ **Mountainbike Ogliastra** (www.mountainbikeogliastra.it) Organises scenic road cycling itineraries in Sardinia as well as challenging downhill routes on old mule tracks.

➡ **Colpo di Pedale** (www.colpodipedale.it) Trips for all levels on racers, mountain bikes and city bikes around Piedmont's Langhe wine region.

➡ **Ciclovagando** (www.ciclovagando.com) Organises full-day tours of 20km, departing from various Puglian towns including Ostuni and Brindisi.

Cycling

Whether you're after a gentle ride between trattorias, a 100km road race or a teeth-rattling mountain descent, you'll find a route to suit. Tourist offices can usually provide details on trails and guided rides, and bike hire is available in most cities and key activity spots.

Tuscany's rolling countryside is a favourite with cyclists, particularly the wine-producing Chianti area south of Florence. In Umbria, the Valnerina and Piano Grande at Monte Vettore have beautiful trails and quiet country roads to explore. Further north, the flatlands of Emilia-Romagna and the terraced vineyards of Barolo, Barbaresco and Franciacorta are also ideally suited to bike touring. Cycling meets architecture on the Veneto's Brenta Riviera, which offers 150km of bike routes past glorious Venetian villas. In the south, Puglia's flat rolling countryside and coastal paths are also satisfying.

In summer many Alpine ski resorts offer wonderful cycling. Mountain bikers will be spoilt for choice in the peaks around Lago di Garda, Lago Maggiore and the Dolomites in Trentino Alto-Adige. Another challenging area is the granite landscape of the Supramonte in eastern Sardinia.

The best cycling season is spring, when it's not too hot and the countryside looks its best. For detailed information, get hold of Lonely Planet's *Cycling Italy*.

On Water

On the coast, sport goes beyond posing on packed beaches. Sardinia's cobalt waters and Sicily's Aeolian Islands claim some of Italy's best diving. Windsurfers flock to Sardinia, Sicily and the northern lakes, while adrenalin junkies ride rapids from Piedmont to Calabria.

Diving

Diving is one of Italy's most popular summer pursuits, and there are hundreds of schools offering courses, dives for all levels and equipment hire.

Most diving schools open seasonally, typically from about June to October. If possible, avoid August, when the Italian coast is besieged by holidaymakers and peak-season prices.

Information is available from local tourist offices and online in Italian at **Dive-Italy** (www.diveitaly.com).

Top Dive Sites

➡ **Aeolian Islands, Sicily** A volcanic ridge with warm waters encompassing the islands of Vulcano, Lipari, Salina, Panarea, Stromboli, Alicudi and Filicudi. Dive in sea grottoes around the remains of old volcanoes.

➡ **Capri, Ischia & Procida, Campania** These three islands in the Bay of Naples offer exceptional diving amid sun-struck sea caves.

➡ **Cinque Terre marine reserve, Liguria** One of the few places to dive in the north of the country. Dives head out of Riomaggiore and Santa Margherita.

ANDREW BAIN / GETTY IMAGES ©

Above: Sailing on the
Mediterranean Sea

Left: Cyclist in the
Dolomites

➡ **Capo Caccia, Sardinia** The dive site for Sardinia's coral divers, Capo Caccia also features the largest underwater grotto in the Mediterranean.

➡ **Isole Tremiti, Puglia** These wind-eroded islands off Puglia's Gargano Promontory are pock-marked with huge sea caves.

➡ **Pantelleria, Sicily** A spectacular volcanic seabed surrounds the black lava island of Pantelleria.

➡ **Parco Nazionale dell'Arcipelago di La Maddelena** The Maddalena marine park boasts translucent waters and diving around 60 islets.

➡ **Parco Nazionale Arcipelago Toscano, Tuscany** Europe's largest marine park encompasses the Tuscan archipelago and the island of Elba.

➡ **Punta Campanella marine reserve, Campania** Vivid marine life flourishing among underwater grottoes and ancient ruins. Dives head out from Marina del Cantone.

➡ **Ustica, Sicily** Italy's first marine reserve, this volcanic island is rich with underwater flora and fauna and hosts the International Festival of Underwater Activities in late June or July.

Sailing

Italy has a proud maritime tradition and you can hire a paddle boat or sleek sailing yacht almost anywhere in the country. Sailors of all levels are catered for: experienced skippers can island-hop around Sicily and Sardinia, or along the Amalfi, Tuscan, Ligurian or Triestino coasts on chartered yachts; weekend boaters can explore hidden coves in rented dinghies around Puglia, in the Tuscan archipelago and around the Sorrento Peninsula; and speed freaks can take to the Lombard lakes in sexy speedboats.

Down south, on the Amalfi Coast, prime swimming spots are often only accessible by boat. It's a similar story on the islands of Capri, Ischia, Procida and Elba.

In Sicily, the Aeolian Islands' cobalt waters are perfect for idle island-hopping. Across in Sardinia, the Golfo di Orosei, Santa Teresa di Gallura, the Arcipelago di La Maddalena and the Costa Smeralda are all top sailing spots. Sardinia's main sailing portal is www.sailingsardinia.it.

Italy's most prestigious sailing regattas are Lago di Garda's September **Centomiglia** (www.centomiglia.it), which sails just south of Gargnano, and the **Bar-colana** (www.barcolana.it) held in Trieste in October. The latter is the Med's largest regatta.

Reputable yacht charter companies include **Bareboat Sailing Holidays** (www.bareboatsailingholidays.com).

White-Water Sports

A mecca for water rats, the Sesia river in northern Piedmont is Italy's top white-water destination. At its best between April and September, it runs from the slopes of Monte Rosa down through the spectacular scenery of the Valsesia. Operators in Varallo offer various solutions to the rapids: there's canoeing, kayaking, white-water rafting, canyoning, hydrospeed and tubing.

In Alto-Adige, the Val di Sole is another white-water destination, as is Lago di Ledro in Trentino, where you can canyon beneath invigorating waterfalls. Further south, Monti Sibillini in Umbria is another good choice for white-water adventures.

At the southern end of the peninsula, the Lao river rapids in Calabria's Parco Nazionale del Pollino provide exhilarating rafting, as well as canoeing and canyoning. Trips can be arranged in Scalea.

Windsurfing

Considered one of Europe's prime windsurfing spots, Lago di Garda enjoys excellent wind conditions: the northerly *peler* blows in early on sunny mornings, while the southerly *ora* sweeps down in the early afternoon as regular as clockwork. The two main centres are Torbole, home of the World Windsurf Championship, and Malcesine, 15km south.

For windsurfing on the sea, head to Sardinia. In the north, Porto Pollo, also known as Portu Puddu, is good for beginners and experts – the bay provides protected waters for learners, while experts can enjoy the high winds as they funnel through the channel between Sardinia and Corsica. To the northeast, there's good windsurfing on the island of Elba, off the Tuscan coast. Competitions such as the Chia Classic are held off the southwest coast in June

An excellent guidebook to windsurfing and kitesurfing spots across Italy and the rest of Europe is Stoked Publications' *The Kite and Windsurfing Guide: Europe*. Equipment hire is available at all the places mentioned above.

Travel with Children

Italians adore *bambini* (children), but be warned – Italy is a dangerous place for children's cheeks. Indeed, acts of cheek pinching are as prevalent as Gucci shades and heels. On the flipside, the country has few amenities specifically for little ones, which makes a little planning go a long way.

Best Regions for Kids

Milan & the Lakes

Shop Milan, cruise Lago di Como and squeal away at Lago di Garda amusement parks.

Trento & the Dolomites

Ski, snowboard or make a Tyrolean snowman at some of Italy's top family-friendly ski resorts.

Florence & Tuscany

Channel knights in a medieval hilltop town, take a silly photo with a crooked tower in Pisa, then chill at a picture-perfect *agriturismo* (farm stay accommodation).

Campania

Roam subterranean ruins in Naples or play gladiators in Pompeii or Pozzuoli.

Sardinia

An alfresco paradise, packed with spectacular beaches, water sports galore and relaxing hikes and horseback rides.

Italy for Kids

Italy heaves with world-famous archaeological sites, museums and other heritage treasures. But while Pompeian frescoes might thrill mum or dad, they may not excite youngsters. Children's books about the places you visit can help bring these sights to life. Suddenly, those old ruins become the scene of heroic battles, mythical creatures or a blockbuster apocalypse. If visiting Rome with kids aged eight and over, one good choice is Lonely Planet's *Not for Parents: Rome*.

Books aside, keep the pace low key, punctuating museum visits with plenty of gelato stops. Always make a point of asking staff members at tourist offices if they know of any special family activities, and venture into Italy's incredible countryside for some active fun.

Discounted admission for children is available at most Italian tourist attractions, though age limits can vary. Most government-run museums and archaeological sites offer free entry to EU citizens under the age of 18, though some staff may extend this discount to all under 18s, despite the official 'EU-only' policy.

For more information and ideas, see Lonely Planet's *Travel with Children*, the superb website www.italiakids.com or the more general www.travelwithyourkids.com.

Children's Highlights

History Was Here

⇒ **Herculaneum** Smaller than nearby Pompeii, Herculaneum is easier to visit in a shorter time. It's also better preserved, complete with carbonised furniture. (p674)

⇒ **Colosseum** Let your imagination run wild with images of brave gladiators and wild beasts in the Roman Empire's biggest, mightiest stadium. (p67)

⇒ **Medieval Tuscan towns** Climb a brooding tower, catch a medieval horse race or chase imaginary dragons down twisting alleys in story-book towns like Siena and San Gimignano.

⇒ **Castel del Monte** This curious, octagonal 13th-century castle in Puglia is home to Europe's very first flush toilet. (p714)

⇒ **Ostia Antica** (www.ostiaantica.net) Mosaic mermaids and sea monsters, and frescoed advertising conjure up the age of togas at Rome's ancient port.

Rainy Days

⇒ **Museo Nazionale della Scienza e della Tecnologia** Italy's best science and technology museum makes budding inventors go gaga in Milan. (p247)

⇒ **Museo Nazionale del Cinema Multimedia** displays and movie memorabilia make this Turin museum a winner for kids and adults alike. (p202)

⇒ **Explora** Rome's children's museum expands minds with hands-on exhibitions spanning bioscience, society and media. (p120)

⇒ **Casa del Cioccolato Perugina** Live out those Willy Wonka fantasies on a tour of the Baci Perugina chocolate factory in Perugia. (p572)

⇒ **Museo Archeologico dell'Alto Adige** Drop in on Iceman Ötzi, Europe's oldest natural human mummy, in Bolzano. (p317)

Alfresco Fun

⇒ **Sardinia** Go dolphin spotting in the Golfo Aranci, horseback riding along La Giara di Gesturi, or tackle water sports on some of Italy's top beaches. (p831)

⇒ **Aeolian Islands** Seven tiny volcanic islands off Sicily with everything from spewing lava to black-sand beaches. (p785)

⇒ **The Dolomites** Head to Alto Adige's Alpe di Siusi and Kronplatz for abundant blue and red runs, or cycle through orchards and farmland on a Dolomiti di Brenta Bike tour. (p314)

⇒ **Sailing in Venice** Glide across Venetian waters on a customised sailing tour, or learn to row standing up like a verified gondolier. (p361)

Kooky Kicks

⇒ **Catacombe dei Cappuccini** These creepy Palermo catacombs are packed with mummies in their Sunday best. Not for the very young. (p773)

⇒ **Napoli Sotterranea** A secret trap door and war-time hideouts make this guided tour of underground Naples gripping. (p654)

⇒ **Alberobello** Was that Snow White? Imagination runs riot in this World Heritage-listed town in Puglia, famous for its *trulli* (white-washed circular dwellings with cone-shaped roofs). (p721)

LAGO DI GARDA THRILLS & SPILLS

For adrenaline-sparking rides and stunt shows, it's hard to beat northern Italy's Lago di Garda. The lake's eastern bank is home to larger-than-life dinosaurs, pirate ships, roller coasters and a dolphinarium at the kid-oriented Gardaland (p281).

To its north, CanevaWorld (p281) features an aqua park (p281) and **medieval shows** (adult/reduced dinner & show €29/19; ⊘2 shows daily May–mid-Sep) complete with medieval banquet. Within the same sprawling park is CanevaWorld's Movieland Studios (p281), featuring stunt-packed action shows. Opening times vary slightly throughout the year, so check the website for details. Cheaper deals and family tickets are also available online.

Both parks are just off the main lake road. Gardaland is 2km from Peschiera del Garda; CanevaWorld is a similar distance from Lazise. Free buses shuttle visitors to both parks from Peschiera del Garda train station.

MANGIA! MANGIA! EAT! EAT!

Food is a focus of life in Italy and kids are more than welcome at most eateries. High chairs are often available and though kids' menus are rare, it's perfectly acceptable to order a *mezzo piatto* (half-portion).

Pizza al taglio (pizza by the slice) is a great on-the-run snack, as are *panini* from little grocery stores. Markets everywhere, including Rome's Campo de' Fiori, burst with inspiring picnic supplies such as salami, cheese, olives, bread and fruit.

You can buy baby formula in powder or liquid form, as well as sterilising solutions such as Milton, at pharmacies. Fresh cow's milk is sold in cartons in supermarkets and in bars with a 'Latteria' sign. UHT milk is popular and in many out-of-the-way areas the only kind available.

➡ **Leaning Tower** Yes, it's pricey. Yes, it's touristy, but what kid wouldn't want to brag about climbing the legendary Leaning Tower of Pizza...err...Pisa? (p510)

➡ **San Marino** This micro state is packed with kitschy museums, including one dedicated to vampires. (p470)

Planning

When to Go

The best times to visit Italy with young travel companions are April to June and September – temperatures are mild to warm, most hotels and restaurants in coastal holiday areas are open, and tourist numbers are manageable meaning shorter queues and less-irritable little ones.

In July and August prices soar and the country broils. In the Alps, winters are long and severe, but perfect for skiing with many resorts offering family-tailored ac-

tivities. Elsewhere, winters range from dull and rainy (in Milan) to relatively mild (in Rome and further south). Sicily has long summers and short winters , making it a sound choice for coastal family fun.

Where to Stay

Hostels and apartments are sound options for families, offering multibed rooms, guest kitchens, lounge facilities and, in many cases, washing machines. In summer (July and August), camping grounds are buzzing, many offering activities for youngsters. Italy's *agriturismi* are great for fresh air, space and extra perks like animals or a swimming pool.

Book accommodation in advance whenever possible. In hotels, some double rooms can't accommodate an extra bed for kids, so check ahead. If the child is small enough to share your bed, some hoteliers will let you do this for free. The website www.booking.com specifies the 'kid policy' for every hotel listed and any extra charges incurred.

Getting Around

Arrange car rental before leaving home. Car seats for infants and children are available from most car-rental agencies, but should be booked in advance. Driving and parking in the big cities can be highly stressful, so consider using public transport into and within large urban areas. Public-transport discounts are available for children (usually aged under 12).

Intercity trains and buses are safe, convenient and relatively inexpensive. To save money on high-speed Freccia trains (www.trenitalia.com) and Italo trains (www.italotreno.it), book tickets at least a few days in advance, either online, at the self-service ticket machines at train stations, or through a travel agent.

Large car ferries travel between the mainland and Sicily and Sardinia, while smaller ferries and hydrofoils run to other islands. Many large ferries travel overnight, in which case a cabin is worthwhile.

Regions at a Glance

Rome & Lazio

History
Food & Wine
Art

Ancient Icons

Rome's ancient centre is history in 3D. Romulus killed Remus on the Palatino (Palatine Hill), Christians were fed to lions in the Colosseum and emperors soaked at the Terme di Caracalla. Ponder the remains of the great and the good in the catacombs along Via Appia Antica.

Robust Feasting

The Roman palate favours earthy old-school flavours such as pig's cheek, offal, salt cod and *bucatini all'amatriciana* (pasta with tomato, pancetta and chilli-peppers), but that's not to say that dining out is provincial. New-school chefs lend a contemporary twist to stalwart staples.

Museums & Galleries

The breadth of cultural treasures housed in Rome's countless museums and galleries is, quite frankly, embarrassing.

p62

Liguria, Piedmont & the Italian Riviera

Activities
Villages
Food & Wine

Hiking & Skiing

From the slopes of Piedmont's Milky Way and the Valle d'Aosta to coastal hikes along the Cinque Terre, this northwest corner of the country is an outdoor paradise.

Unspoilt Villages

With chic medieval fishing villages along the Cinque Terre, quaint, wine-growing villages on Langhe hilltops and secret villages in the Valle d'Aosta, it's not hard finding your perfect story-book refuge.

Gourmet Paradise

Home to the Slow Food Movement, Piedmont has an embarrassment of culinary riches, from the truffles of Alba and Asti to the renowned wines of the Langhe region.

p162

Milan & the Lakes

Shopping
Gardens
Food & Wine

Fashion Capital

Every fashion addict worth their cashmere cardigan knows that Milan takes fashion and design as seriously as others take biotech or engineering. Top-notch discount outlets mean that everyone can make a *bella figura* (good impression) here.

Villas & Gardens

Framed by gazebos, blushing camellias, artfully tumbling terraces and world-class statuary, Lombardy's lakeside villas knock the socks off the 'luxury getaway' concept.

Culture & Cuisine

Bergamo, Brescia, Cremona and Mantua, the cultured cities of the Po Plain, combine wonderful art and architecture with a slew of sophisticated regional restaurants.

p238

Trento & the Dolomites

Activities
Wellness
Food & Wine

Adrenalin Rush

Ski, hike, ice-climb, sledge-ride or Nordic walk in the Sella Ronda and the remote Parco Nazionale dello Stelvio. Real adrenalin junkies will want to scale the WWI-era *vie ferrate* (trails with permanent cables and ladders).

Thermal Spas

Attend to your wellness in the thermal baths at Terme Merano, then stock up on cosmetics infused with Alpine herbs, grapes, apples and mountain pine, and tisanes.

Austrian Accents

Bolzano beer halls, strudels, Sachertorte, sourdough breads and buckwheat cakes are just some of the region's Austro-Italian specialities. Combine with regional wines such as Gewürztraminer and riesling.

p300

Venice & the Veneto

Art
Architecture
Wine

Moving Pictures

Action-packed paintings by Titian, Veronese and Tintoretto on view at Venice's Biennale illuminate the path to modern art. The Church repeatedly failed to censor these avant-garde artists.

Reflected Glories

Story-book castles, gracious country villas and an entire city of palaces on the water, the Veneto's architectural landmarks admire their own reflections in the snaking canals.

Inspired Wine Pairings

Wine aficionados throng VinItaly to sample Valpolicella's favourite Amarone, Soave and *prosecco* (sparkling wine) – plus innovative blends seldom tasted outside the Veneto.

p332

Friuli Venezia Giulia

History
Wilderness
Food & Wine

Archaeological Sites

Aquileia offers up an entire Roman town for exploration, while Cividale del Friuli and Grado retain some rare, early-Christian churches.

Rural Retreats

The forests of the Carnic and Giulian Alps are wild and verdant, the Laghi di Fusine are still populated by lynx and deer and the Forni di Sopra are spread thick with wild Alpine flowers.

Culinary Crossroad

Friuli's cuisine incorporates smoked trout and DOC prosciutto from San Daniele, spicy brioche, gamey Mittel dishes and traditional sauerkraut. There's also some very exciting wine coming out of the Carso and the Colli Orientali.

p403

Emilia-Romagna & San Marino

Activities
Architecture
Food & Wine

Urban Cycling

Reggio Emilia was voted Italy's best cycling city. Bologna's cobbled streets can look like Oxford, and Parma is largely pedestrianised. Best of all are the 9km of Ferrara's old city walls.

Holy Architecture

Tour the churches for a quick art-history lesson from Ravenna's dazzling Byzantine mosaics, Modena's Romanesque cathedral and Bologna's Gothic-Renaissance Basilica di San Petronio.

Famous Flavours

Come with an empty stomach and try the most famous flavours: Modena's balsamic, Parma's ham and cheese, not to mention Bologna's *bolognese ragù* and *mortadella*.

p428

Florence & Tuscany

Art
Food & Wine
Scenery

Fabulous Frescoes

Read the story of the evolving Renaissance within the vibrant frescoes in Florence, Siena, Arezzo and San Gimignano.

The Tuscan Table

Succulent *bistecche* (steaks), peppery olive oils, pungent autumn truffles – few regions whet the appetite so lasciviously. Then add a glass of Montepulciano's Vino Nobile or Montalcino's world-famous Brunello.

Masterpiece Landscapes

Whether it's cypress-lined gardens in Florence, terraced hills in Chianti, or the Unesco-lauded beauty of the Val d'Orcia and Val di Chiana, Tuscany's landscapes seem sketched by one of the region's artistic greats.

p472

Umbria & Le Marche

Villages
Scenery
Food & Wine

Medieval Towns

Perched snugly on their peaks like storks on chimneys, Umbria's hill towns – Perugia, Assisi, Gubbio, Urbino, Spoleto, Todi – are the postcard-pretty protectors of local traditions.

Spectacular Views

Mountainous and wild, views come at you from all angles. Take the *funivia* (cable car) in Gubbio for views over town and country, or strike out into the snowcapped ranges of Monti Sibillini and the wildflower-flecked Piano Grande.

Forest Fare

Richly forested and deeply rural, the Umbrian larder is stocked with hearty flavours from wild boar and pigeon to Norcia's *cinta senese* (Tuscan pig) salami and black truffles.

p566

Abruzzo & Molise

Scenery
Activities
Wilderness

Road Less Taken

Discover the isolated mountain villages of Pescocostanzo, Scanno, Chieti and Sulmona. En route from Sulmona to Scanno, pass through the dramatically untamed scenery of the Gole di Sagittario gorge.

Mighty Mountains

From Corno Grande to Monte Amaro, Abruzzo's parks offer free-from-the-crowds hiking and skiing. The most popular route is the ascent of Corno Grande.

Back to Nature

It's an area of outstanding beauty and rural, back-country charm. Encompassing three national parks, the ancient forests still harbour bears, chamois and wolves, and are traced with walking trails.

p621

Naples & Campania

Scenery
History
Food & Wine

Cliffs & Coves

From the citrus-fringed panoramas of the Amalfi Coast to Ischia's tropical gardens and Capri's dramatic cliffs, the views from this coastline are as famous as the celebrities who holiday here.

Eerie Ruins

Sitting beneath Mt Vesuvius, the Neapolitans abide by the motto carpe diem. And why not? All around them – at Pompeii, Herculaneum, Cuma and the Campi Flegrei – are reminders that life is short.

Pizza & Pasta

Vying hard for Italy's culinary crown, Campania produces powerhouse coffee, pizzas, tomato pasta, *sfogliatelle* (sweetened ricotta pastries) and an incredible panoply of seafood, eaten every which way you can.

p638

Puglia, Basilicata & Calabria

Beaches
Activities
Food & Wine

Seaside Savvy

Lounge beneath white cliffs in the Gargano, gaze on violet sunsets in Tropea and soak up summer on the golden beaches of Otranto and Gallipoli.

Wild Places

A crush of spiky mountains, Basilicata and Calabria are where the wild things are. Burst through the clouds in mountain-top Pietrapertosa or pick bergamot in the Aspromonte

Culture & Cuisine

Puglia has turned its poverty into a fine art: check out the renovated cave dwellings in Matera and then feast on creamy *burrata* (cheese made from mozzarella and cream) and turnip greens in Ostuni and Lecce.

p704

Sicily

Food & Wine
History
Outdoors

Seafood & Sweets

Sicilian cuisine will dazzle seafood lovers and set sweet teeth on edge. Tuna, sardines, swordfish and shellfish come grilled, fried or seasoned with mint or wild fennel. Desserts are laden with citrus, ricotta, almonds and pistachios.

Cultural Hybrid

A Mediterranean crossroads for centuries, Sicily spoils history buffs with Greek temples, Roman and Byzantine mosaics, Phoenician statues, Norman-Romanesque castles and flouncy art nouveau villas.

Volcanoes & Islands

Outdoor enthusiasts can swim and dive in Ustica's pristine waters, hike the Aeolian Islands' dramatic coastlines or watch the thrilling fireworks of Stromboli and Etna.

p765

Sardinia

Beaches
Activities
History

Sun, Sand & Surf

Famous for its fjord-like coves, crystalline waters and windswept sand dunes, surfers, sailors and divers flock to the Costa Smeralda, Porto Pollo, the Golfo di Orosei and the Archipelago di La Maddalena.

Moving Mountains

Sardinia's awe-inspiring peaks provide a playground for hikers and free climbers. Climbs afford stunning sea views, while Supramonte hikes traverse old shepherd routes.

Prehistoric Rocks

In a landscape of grey granite rocks, Sardinia is littered with strange prehistoric dolmens, menhirs, wells and *nuraghi* (mysterious stone towers built by the island's first inhabitants).

p831

On the Road

**Trento &
the Dolomites**
(p300)

**Friuli
Venezia Giulia**
(p403)

**Liguria,
Piedmont & the
Italian Riviera**
(p162)

**Milan &
the Lakes**
(p238)

**Venice &
the Veneto**
(p332)

**Emilia-Romagna
& San Marino**
(p429)

**Florence &
Tuscany**
(p472)

**Umbria &
Le Marche**
(p566)

**Rome &
Lazio**
(p62)

**Abruzzo &
Molise**
(p621)

**Naples &
Campania**
(p638)

Sardinia
(p831)

**Puglia, Basilicata
& Calabria**
(p704)

Sicily
(p765)

Rome & Lazio

Best Places to Eat

➡ L'Asino d'Oro (p132)

➡ Open Colonna (p133)

➡ Pizzarium (p136)

➡ Enoteca Provincia Romana (p126)

➡ Colline Emiliane (p129)

Best Places to Stay

➡ Palm Gallery Hotel (p125)

➡ Blue Hostel (p123)

➡ Hotel Sant'Anselmo (p124)

➡ Arco del Lauro (p124)

➡ Villa Spalletti Trivelli (p123)

Why Go?

Even in a country of exquisite cities like Italy, Rome is special. An ancient capital that has triumphed through three thousand years of tumultuous history, it's a beautiful, chaotic sprawl of haunting ruins, monumental basilicas and awe-inspiring art. But while history reverberates all around, modern life is lived to the full – priests in designer shades walk through the Vatican talking into smartphones, scooters scream through medieval alleyways, fashionable drinkers sip *aperitivi* on baroque piazzas. A busy cultural calendar and thriving underground scene ensure there's always something going on.

But for all its appeal, Rome can be exhausting and when it all starts to get too much, it's time to change gear and head out of town. The surrounding, often overlooked Lazio region offers natural beauty and cultural riches ranging from sandy beaches and volcanic islands to ancient ruins, Etruscan tombs and remote hilltop monasteries.

When to Go
Rome

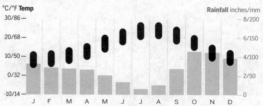

Apr Sunshine, Easter celebrations, Rome's birthday, and azaleas on the Spanish Steps.

May–Jul Rome's festival calendar gets into full swing as summer temperatures soar.

Sep–Oct Still warm but the crowds die down and RomaEuropa theatre festival rolls into town.

Top Roman Sights

With so many world-class monuments, galleries and museums in Rome, it can be difficult to decide which to visit. To help you, here's our selection of must-see sights. The Colosseum is an obvious choice, as are the Vatican Museums – one of the world's great museum complexes and home to the Sistine Chapel. Adjacent to the museums, St Peter's Basilica is the most important church in the Catholic world and a treasure trove of Renaissance and baroque art.

If you like baroque art, you'll love the Museo e Galleria Borghese and Piazza Navona. Not far from the piazza, the Pantheon is the best preserved of Rome's ancient monuments. For the city's finest ancient art check out the Museo Nazionale Romano: Palazzo Massimo alle Terme and the Capitoline Museums on Piazza del Campidoglio. Nearby, ancient ruins lie littered across the atmospheric Palatino (Palatine Hill).

And, of course, to ensure that you return to Rome, be sure to throw a coin into the Trevi Fountain.

DAY TRIPS FROM ROME

The surrounding Lazio region harbours some exceptional sights, most within easy day-trip distance of the capital. Nearest of all are the beautifully preserved ruins of **Ostia Antica**, ancient Rome's main port town. To the east of Rome, and easily accessible by bus or car, **Tivoli** is home to **Villa Adriana**, the vast summer residence of the emperor Hadrian, and **Villa d'Este**, famed for its fabulous fountains. Slightly further afield, Lazio's Etruscan treasures are quite special. The easiest to get to are in **Cerveteri**, but push on up to **Tarquinia** and you'll be rewarded with some truly amazing frescoed tombs. On Rome's southern doorstep, the charming town of **Frascati** is popular with day-tripping Romans who come to take the hilltop air and taste the local *porchetta* (herb-roasted pork) and white wine.

Outstanding Works of Art

➡ Michelangelo's frescoes in the Sistine Chapel are among the world's most famous works of art.

➡ Raphael's great masterpiece *La Scuola di Atene* (The School of Athens) hangs in the Stanze di Raffaello (Raphael Rooms) in the Vatican Museums.

➡ Gian Lorenzo Bernini's sculptures at the Museo e Galleria Borghese show a genius at the top of his game.

➡ Caravaggio's St Matthew cycle in the Chiesa di San Luigi dei Francesi features his signature chiaroscuro (the bold contrast of light and dark) style.

CATACOMBS

Visit the creepy catacombs on Via Appia Antica to see where Rome's pioneering Christians buried their dead. Hundreds of thousands of tombs line the pitch-black tunnels.

ROME & LAZIO

Best Viewpoints

➡ Il Vittoriano (p78)

➡ Dome of St Peter's Basilica (p105)

➡ Priorato dei Cavalieri di Malta (p 98)

➡ Gianicolo (p124)

Lazio's Hidden Gems

➡ Monastero di San Benedetto (p160), Subiaco

➡ Palazzo Farnese (p158), Caprarola

➡ Museo Archeologico Nazionale di Palestrina (p159)

➡ Civita di Bagnoregio (p158)

Resources

➡ **060608** (www.060608.it) Rome's official tourist website.

➡ **Coopculture** (www.coopculture.it) Information and ticket booking for Rome's monuments.

➡ **Vatican Museums** (http://mv.vatican.va) Book tickets and avoid the queues.

➡ **Auditorium** (www.auditorium.com) Check concert listings for the Auditorium Parco della Musica.

Rome & Lazio Highlights

1 Imagine the crowd's roar at the **Colosseum** (p67)

2 Gaze heavenwards in the **Sistine Chapel** (p109)

3 Admire the audacious dome at the **Pantheon** (p79)

4 Gape at the grandeur of **St Peter's Basilica** (p105)

5 Revel in ravishing baroque sculpture at the **Museo e Galleria Borghese** (p113)

6 Check out ancient mosaics at the **Museo Nazionale Romano: Palazzo Massimo alle Terme** (p93)

7 Explore haunting ruins on the **Palatino (Palatine Hill)** (p71)

8 Delve into frescoed Etruscan tombs in **Tarquinia** (p155)

9 Poke around the preserved port town of **Ostia Antica** (p151)

Palestrina (39km)

Via Prenestina

Via Casilina

Frascati (16km)

Furio Camillo Ⓜ

Via Appia Nuova

Colli Albani Ⓜ

Castel Gandolfo (28km)

Marrana della Caffarella

Via Appia Antica (Appian Way)

See Appia Antica Map (p100)

Ponte Lungo Ⓜ

TUSCOLANO

Via La Spezia

Re di Roma Ⓜ

San Giovanni Ⓜ

See Monti, Esquiline & San Lorenzo Map (p94)

Manzoni Ⓜ

See Celian Hill & San Giovanni Map (p97)

APPIO-LATINO

Parco San Sebastiano

EUR (4km)

Circonvallazione Ostiense

Via Cristoforo Colombo

MONTI

Cavour Ⓜ

Campidoglio (Capitoline Hill)

Colosseo Ⓜ

1 Colosseum

7 Palatino (Palatine Hill)

See Ancient Rome Map (p62)

Circo Massimo Ⓜ

Terme di Caracalla

See Centro Storico Map (p80)

Aventine Hill

Viale Aventino

Circo Massimo

Stazione Roma-Ostiense Ⓜ

OSTIENSE

Garbatella Ⓜ

Basilica di San Paolo Fuori le Mura

San Paolo Ⓜ

Via Ostiense

Gianicolo (Janiculum)

TRASTEVERE

Villa Doria Pamphilj

See Trastevere & Gianicolo Map (p102)

See Aventine & Testaccio Map (p134)

Via del Porto Fluviale

Stazione Trastevere Ⓜ

Via Portuense

Viale Guglielmo Marconi

Ostia Antica (25km); Sabaudia (90km)

9 Ostia Antica (p151)

MONTEVERDE

Circonvallazione Gianicolense

GIANCOLENSE

PORTUENSE

ROME

POP 2.61 MILLION

History

According to myth, Rome was founded on the Palatino (Palatine Hill) by Romulus, the twin brother of Remus. Historians proffer a more prosaic version of events, involving Romulus becoming the first king of Rome on 21 April 753 BC and the city comprising Etruscan, Latin and Sabine settlements on the Palatino, Esquiline and Quirinale hills.

Rise and Fall of the Roman Empire

Following the fall of Tarquin the Proud, the last of Rome's seven Etruscan kings, the Roman Republic was founded in 509 BC. From modest beginnings, it spread to become the dominant Western superpower until internal rivalries led to civil war. Julius Caesar, the last of the Republic's consuls, was assassinated in 44 BC, leaving Mark Antony and Octavian to fight for the top job. Octavian prevailed and, with the blessing of the Senate, became Augustus, the first Roman emperor.

Augustus ruled well, and the city enjoyed a period of political stability and unparalleled artistic achievement – a golden age for which the Romans yearned as they endured the depravities of Augustus' successors Tiberius, Caligula and Nero. A huge fire reduced Rome to tatters in AD 64 but the city bounced back and by AD 100 it had a population of 1.5 million and was the undisputed *caput mundi* (capital of the world). It couldn't last, though, and when Constantine moved his power base to Byzantium in 330, Rome's glory days were numbered. In 455 it was routed by the Vandals and in 476 the last emperor of the Western Roman Empire, Romulus Augustulus, was deposed.

The Middle Ages

By the 6th century, Rome was in a bad way and in desperate need of a leader. Into the breach stepped the Church. Christianity had been spreading since the 1st century AD thanks to the underground efforts of apostles Peter and Paul, and under Constantine it received official recognition. In the late 6th century Pope Gregory I did much to strengthen the Church's grip on the city, laying the foundations for its later role as capital of the Catholic world.

The medieval period was a dark age, marked by almost continuous fighting. The city was reduced to a semi-deserted battlefield as the powerful Colonna and Orsini families battled for supremacy and the bedraggled population trembled in the face of plague, famine and flooding (the Tiber regularly broke its banks).

ROME IN...

Two Days

Get to grips with ancient Rome at the **Colosseum** (p67), the **Roman Forum** (p72) and **Palatino** (Palatine Hill) (p71). Spend the afternoon exploring the **Capitoline Museums** (p75) and **Il Vittoriano** (p78) before an evening in the *centro storico* (historic centre). On day two, hit the **Vatican Museums** (p112) and **Sistine Chapel**, and then **St Peter's Basilica** (p105). Afterwards ditch your guidebook and get happily lost in the animated streets around **Piazza Navona** (p83) and the **Pantheon** (p79).

Four Days

On day three, check out the **Trevi Fountain** (p89), the **Spanish Steps** (p85) and the outstanding **Museo e Galleria Borghese** (p113). At night, head to happening **Trastevere**. Next day, visit the **Galleria Doria Pamphilj** (p90) or the **Museo Nazionale Romano: Palazzo Massimo alle Terme** (p93) before exploring the **Jewish Ghetto** and bijou backstreets such as Via del Governo Vecchio and Via dei Coronari. Round the day off in the boho **Monti district**.

A Week

Venture out to **Via Appia Antica** (p99), home of the catacombs, and take a day trip, choosing between **Ostia Antica** (p151) or the Etruscan treasures of **Cerveteri** (p154) or **Tarquinia** (p154).

ⓘ COLOSSEUM TIPS

Some useful tips to beat the Colosseum queues:

➡ Buy your ticket from the Palatino entrance (about 250m away at Via di San Gregorio 30) or at the Roman Forum (Largo della Salara Vecchia).

➡ Get the Roma Pass.

➡ Book your ticket online at www.coopculture.it (plus booking fee of €1.50).

➡ Join an official English-language tour – €5 on top of the regular Colosseum ticket price – and use the dedicated tours queue.

➡ Visit in the late afternoon rather than mid-morning.

Historic Makeovers

But out of the ruins of the Middle Ages grew Renaissance Rome. At the behest of the city's great papal dynasties – the Barberini, Farnese and Pamphilj, among others – the leading artists of the 15th and 16th centuries were summoned to work on projects such as the Sistine Chapel and St Peter's Basilica. But the enemy was never far away, and in 1527 the Spanish forces of Holy Roman Emperor Charles V ransacked Rome.

Another rebuild was in order, and it was to the 17th-century baroque masters Bernini and Borromini that Rome's patrons turned. Exuberant churches, fountains and *palazzi* (palaces) sprouted all over the city, as these two bitter rivals competed to produce ever-more virtuosic masterpieces.

The next makeover followed the unification of Italy and the declaration of Rome as its capital. Mussolini, believing himself a modern-day Augustus, also left an indelible stamp, bulldozing new imperial roads and commissioning ambitious building projects such as the monumental suburb of EUR.

Modern Styling

Post-fascism, the 1950s and '60s saw the glittering era of *la dolce vita* and hasty urban expansion, resulting in Rome's sometimes wretched suburbs. A clean-up in 2000 had the city in its best shape for decades, and in recent years some dramatic modernist building projects have given the Eternal City some edge, such as Richard Meier's Museo dell'Ara Pacis and Massimiliano Fuksas' ongoing Nuvola building in EUR.

⊙ Sights

They say that a lifetime's not enough for Rome *(Roma, non basta una vita!)*. There's simply too much to see. So the best plan is to choose selectively, and leave the rest for next time.

⊙ Ancient Rome

To the southeast of the historic centre, Rome's ancient heart is where you'll find the great icons of the city's golden age: the Colosseum, Palatino (Palatine Hill), the forums and Campidoglio (Capitoline Hill).

★**Colosseum**   AMPHITHEATRE
(Map p68; ☑ 06 3996 7700; www.coopculture. it; Piazza del Colosseo; adult/reduced incl Roman Forum & Palatino €12/7.50; ⊙ 8.30am-1hr before sunset; Ⓜ Colosseo) A monument to raw, merciless power, the Colosseum (Colosseo) is the most thrilling of Rome's ancient sights. It was here that gladiators met in mortal combat and condemned prisoners fought off wild beasts in front of baying, bloodthirsty crowds. Two thousand years on it still exerts a powerful hold, drawing up to five million visitors a year.

Built by Vespasian (r AD 69–79), the Colosseum was inaugurated in AD 80. To mark the occasion, Vespasian's son and successor Titus (r AD 79–81) staged games that lasted 100 days and nights, during which some 5000 animals were slaughtered.

The 50,000-seat arena was originally known as the Flavian Amphitheatre, and although it was Rome's most fearful arena, it wasn't the biggest – the Circo Massimo could hold up to 250,000 people. The name Colosseum, when introduced in medieval times, was not a reference to its size but to the Colosso di Nerone, a giant statue of Nero that stood nearby.

The **outer walls** have three levels of arches, articulated by Ionic, Doric and Corinthian columns. They were originally covered in travertine, and marble statues filled the niches on the 2nd and 3rd storeys. The upper level had supports for 240 masts that held up a canvas awning over the arena, shading the spectators from sun and rain.

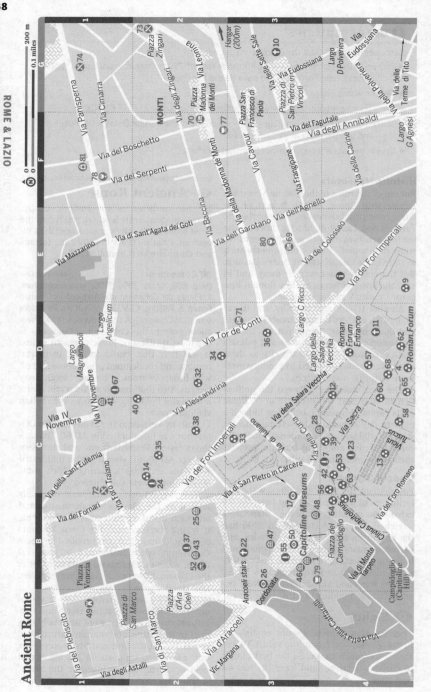

Ancient Rome

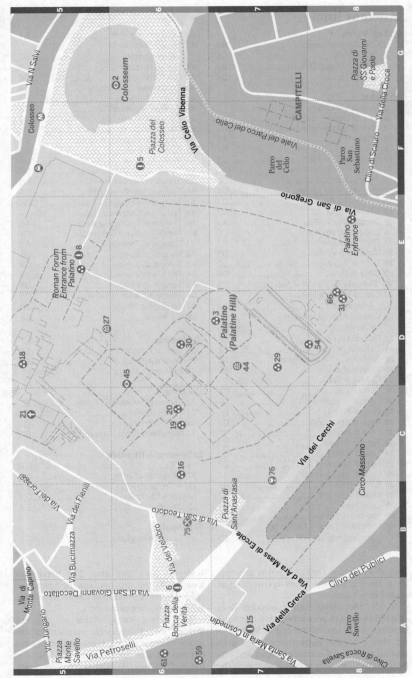

Ancient Rome

The 80 **entrance arches**, known as vomitoria, allowed the spectators to enter and be seated in minutes.

Inside, the **arena** had a wooden floor covered in sand to prevent combatants from slipping and to soak up the blood. Trapdoors led down to the **hypogeum**, an underground complex of corridors, cages and lifts beneath the arena floor, which served as the stadium's backstage area. The hypogeum, along with the top tier, can be visited on guided tours (€8 on top of the normal ticket; advance booking necessary).

The **cavea**, for spectator seating, was divided into three tiers: magistrates and senior officials sat in the lowest tier, wealthy citizens in the middle, and the plebs in the highest tier. Women (except for vestal virgins) were relegated to the cheapest sections at the top. The **podium**, a broad terrace in front of the tiers of seats, was reserved for emperors, senators and VIPs.

With the fall of the Roman Empire in the 5th century, the Colosseum was abandoned. In the Middle Ages it was used as a fortress by two of the city's warrior families, the Frangipani and the Annibaldi. Later, it was used as a quarry for travertine; and marble stripped from it was used in the construction of Palazzo Venezia, Palazzo Barberini and Palazzo Cancelleria, among other buildings. Pollution and vibrations caused by traffic and the metro have also taken a toll. The battle to maintain it is continuous and work is currently underway on a 2½-year €25 million restoration project.

Arco di Costantino   MONUMENT
(Map p68; MColosseo) On the western side of the Colosseum, this triumphal arch was built in 312 to honour the emperor Constantine's victory over rival Maxentius at the battle of Ponte Milvio (Milvian Bridge).

★ Palatino   RUINS
(Palatine Hill; Map p68; ☎06 3996 7700; www.coopculture.it; Via di San Gregorio 30; adult/reduced incl Colosseum & Roman Forum €12/7.50; ☺8.30am-1hr before sunset; MColosseo) Sandwiched between the Roman Forum and the Circo Massimo, the Palatino is a gorgeous, atmospheric area of towering pine trees, majestic ruins and memorable views. According to legend, this is where Romulus and Remus were saved by a wolf and Romulus founded Rome in 753 BC. Archaeological evidence has dated human habitation here to the 8th century BC.

As the most central of Rome's seven hills, and because it was close to the Roman Forum, the Palatino was ancient Rome's most exclusive neighbourhood. The emperor Augustus lived here all his life and successive emperors built increasingly opulent palaces. But after Rome's fall it fell into disrepair and in the Middle Ages churches and castles were built over the ruins. During the Renaissance, wealthy families established gardens on the hill.

Most of the Palatino as it appears today is covered by the ruins of Emperor Domitian's vast complex, which served as the main imperial palace for 300 years. Divided into the **Domus Flavia** (Imperial Palace; Map p68), **Domus Augustana** (Emperor's Residence; Map

p68) and a **stadio** (Stadium; Map p68), it was built in the 1st century AD.

On entering the Palatino from Via di San Gregorio, head uphill until you come to the first recognisable construction, the stadio. This sunken area, which was part of the main imperial palace, was used by the emperor for private games. Adjoining the stadium to the southeast are the impressive remains of a complex built by Septimius Severus, comprising baths, the **Terme di Settimio Severo** (Map p68), and a palace, the **Domus Severiana** (Map p68).

Next to the stadio are the ruins of the Domus Augustana. It was built on two levels, with rooms leading off a *peristilio* (peristyle or garden courtyard) on each floor. You can't get to the lower level, but from above you can see the basin of a fountain and beyond it rooms that were paved with coloured marble. In 2007 a mosaic-covered vaulted cavern was discovered beneath the Domus, which some believed to be the Lupercale, a cave believed by ancient Romans to be where Romulus and Remus were suckled by a wolf.

The grey building near the Domus Augustana houses the **Museo Palatino** (Map p68; admission incl in Palatino ticket; ☺8.30am-1hr before sunset; MColosseo) and its collection of archaeological artefacts, including a beautiful 1st-century bronze, the Ermadi Canefora.

Beyond the museum is the Domus Flavia, the public part of Domitian's palace complex. This was centred on a grand columned peristyle – the grassy area with the base of an octagonal fountain – off which the main halls led.

Among the best-preserved buildings on the Palatino is the **Casa di Livia** (Map p68) (closed to the public), northwest of the Domus Flavia. Home to Augustus' wife Livia, it was built around an atrium leading onto what were once frescoed reception rooms. In front is the **Casa di Augusto** (Map p68;

ROMULUS & REMUS, ROME'S LEGENDARY TWINS

The most famous of Rome's many legends is the story of Romulus and Remus and the city's foundation on 21 April 753 BC.

According to myth, Romulus and Remus were the children of the vestal virgin Rhea Silva and Mars, god of war. While still babies they were set adrift on the Tiber to escape a death penalty imposed by their great-uncle Amulius, who at the time was battling with their grandfather Numitor for control of Alba Longa. However, they were discovered near the Palatino by a she-wolf, who suckled them until a shepherd, Faustulus, found and raised them.

Years later the twins decided to found a city on the site where they'd originally been saved. They didn't know where this was, so they consulted the omens. Remus, on the Aventine, saw six vultures; his brother over on the Palatino saw 12. The meaning was clear and Romulus began building, much to the outrage of his brother. The two subsequently argued and Romulus killed Remus.

Romulus continued building and soon had a city. To populate it he created a refuge on the Capitoline, Aventine, Celian and Quirinale hills, to which a ragtag population of criminals, ex-slaves and outlaws soon decamped. However, the city still needed women. Romulus therefore invited everyone in the surrounding country to celebrate the Festival of Consus (21 August). As the spectators watched the festival games, Romulus and his men pounced and abducted all the women, an act that went down in history as the Rape of the Sabine Women.

⊙ 11am-3.30pm Mon, Wed, Sat & Sun; Ⓜ Colosseo), Augustus' separate residence, which contains superb frescoes in vivid reds, yellows and blues.

Behind the Casa di Augusto are the **Capanne Romulee** (Romulean Huts; Map p68), where it is thought Romulus and Remus were brought up after they were rescued by the shepherd Faustulus.

Northeast of the Casa di Livia lies the **criptoportico** (Map p68), a 128m tunnel where Caligula is thought to have been murdered, and which Nero later used to connect his Domus Aurea with Palatino. Lit by a series of windows, it's now used to stage temporary exhibitions.

In the northwest corner of the Palatino, and covering the Domus Tiberiana (Tiberius' palace), the **Orti Farnesiani** (Map p68) are one of Europe's earliest botanical gardens, dating to the 16th century. Twin pavilions at the garden's northernmost point command breathtaking views over the Roman Forum.

★ **Roman Forum**   RUINS
(Foro Romano; Map p68; ☑ 06 3996 7700; www.coopculture.it; Largo della Salara Vecchia; adult/reduced incl Colosseum & Palatino €12/7.50; ⊙ 8.30am-1hr before sunset; ☐ Via dei Fori Imperiali) Today an impressive, if rather confusing, sprawl of ruins, the Roman Forum was once the beating heart of the ancient world,

a grandiose district of marble-clad temples, basilicas and vibrant public spaces.

Originally an Etruscan burial ground, the area was first developed in the 7th century BC and expanded over subsequent centuries to become the centre of the Roman Republic. In the Middle Ages it was reduced to pasture land – the so-called *Campo Vaccino* (literally 'Cow Field') – and extensively plundered for its marble. The area was systematically excavated in the 18th and 19th centuries and work continues to this day.

Entering from Largo della Salara Vecchia – you can also enter directly from the Palatino – you'll see the **Tempio di Antonino e Faustina** (Map p68) ahead to your left. Erected in AD 141 and dedicated to the empress Faustina and emperor Antoninus Pius, it was transformed into a church in the 8th century, so the soaring columns now frame the **Chiesa di San Lorenzo in Miranda**. To your right the **Basilica Fulvia Aemilia** (Map p68), built in 179 BC, was a 100m-long public hall, with a two-storey porticoed facade.

At the end of the short path, you come to **Via Sacra** (Map p68), the Forum's main thoroughfare, and the **Tempio di Giulio Cesare** (Temple of Julius Caesar; Map p68), built by Augustus in 29 BC on the site of Caesar's cremation.

Head right up Via Sacra and you reach the **Curia** (Map p68), the original seat of the Roman Senate. This was rebuilt on various occasions before being converted into a church in the Middle Ages. What you see today is a 1937 reconstruction of the Curia as it looked during the reign of Diocletian (r 284–305).

In front of the Curia, and hidden by scaffolding, is the **Lapis Niger** (Map p68), a large piece of black marble that covered a sacred area said to be the tomb of Romulus.

At the end of Via Sacra stands the 23m-high **Arco di Settimio Severo** (Arch of Septimius Severus; Map p68), a robust triumphal arch dedicated to the eponymous emperor and his two sons, Caracalla and Geta. Built in AD 203, it commemorates Roman victory over the Parthians. Nearby, at the foot of the Tempio di Saturno, is the **Millarium Aureum** (Map p68), which marked the centre of ancient Rome, from where distances to the city were measured.

On your left are the remains of the **Rostrum** (Map p68), an elaborate podium where Shakespeare had Mark Antony make his famous 'Friends, Romans, countrymen...' speech. In front of this, the **Colonna di Foca** (Column of Phocus; Map p68) marks the centre of the Piazza del Foro, the Forum's main market and meeting place.

The eight granite columns behind the Colonna are all that remain of the **Tempio di Saturno** (Temple of Saturn; Map p68), one of Rome's most important temples that doubled as the state treasury.

Behind it are (from north to south): the ruins of the **Tempio della Concordia** (Temple of Concord; Map p68), the **Tempio di Vespasiano** (Temple of Vespasian and Titus; Map p68) and the **Portico degli Dei Consenti** (Map p68).

> ## ⓘ POSING CENTURIONS
>
> Outside the Roman Forum and Vittoriano, and possibly also the Colosseum, you might find yourself been hailed by costumed Roman soldiers offering to pose for a photo. They are not doing this for love and will expect payment. There's no set rate but coins are sufficient, certainly no more than €5 – and that's €5 in total, not per person.

Passing over to the path parallel to Via Sacra, you'll see the stubby ruins of the **Basilica Giulia** (Map p68), which was begun by Julius Caesar and finished by Augustus. At the end of the basilica are three columns of the **Tempio di Castore e Polluce** (Temple of Castor and Pollux; Map p68), a 5th-century BC temple built to mark the defeat of the Etruscan Tarquins in 489 BC. To the south, the **Chiesa di Santa Maria Antiqua** (Map p68) is the oldest Christian church in the Forum.

Back towards Via Sacra is the **Casa delle Vestali** (House of the Vestal Virgins; Map p68), home of the virgins who tended the sacred flame in the adjoining **Tempio di Vesta** (Map p68).

The six virgin priestesses were selected from patrician families when aged between six and 10 to serve in the temple for 30 years. If the flame in the temple went out, the priestess responsible would be flogged, and if she lost her virginity she would be buried alive, since her blood couldn't be spilled. The offending man would be flogged to death.

Continuing up Via Sacra, past the **Tempio di Romolo** (Temple of Romulus; Map p68),

MUSEUM DISCOUNT CARDS

Several discount cards are available for serious museum-goers. You can buy them at participating museums, or online at www.coopculture.it. The Roma Pass is also available at tourist information points.

Appia Antica Card (www.coopculture.it; adult/reduced €7/4, valid 7 days) For the Terme di Caracalla, Mausoleo di Cecilia Metella and Villa Quintili.

Archaeologia Card (adult/reduced €24.50/14.50, valid 7 days) Covers the Colosseum, Palatino, Roman Forum, Terme di Caracalla, Palazzo Altemps, Palazzo Massimo alle Terme, Terme di Diocleziano, Crypta Balbi, Mausoleo di Cecilia Metella and Villa Quintili.

Roma Pass (www.romapass.it; 3 days €34) Provides admission to two museums or sites (choose from a list of 45), as well as reduced entry to extra sites, unlimited city transport, and reduced entry to other exhibitions and events. If you use this for more-expensive sights such as the Capitoline Museums and the Colosseum you'll save money.

TOP FIVE FILM LOCATIONS

➡ Trevi Fountain (p89) Scene of Anita Ekberg's sensual dip in *La Dolce Vita*.

➡ Bocca della Verità (p79) Gregory Peck goofs around with Audrey Hepburn in *Roman Holiday*.

➡ Piazza Navona (p83) In *Eat Pray Love* Julia Roberts finds ice-cream solace in front of the Chiesa di Sant'Agnese in Agone.

➡ Piazza di Spagna (p85) Drama over drinks at the foot of the Spanish Steps in *The Talented Mr Ripley*.

➡ Pantheon (p79) Tom Hanks checks out Raphael's tomb in *Angels and Demons*.

Other Roman films include: *Three Coins in a Fountain*; *Yesterday, Today and Tomorrow*; *Bicycle Thieves*; *Rome, Open City*; *To Rome with Love*; and *The Great Beauty*.

you come to the **Basilica di Massenzio** (Basilica di Costantino; Map p68), the largest building on the Forum. Started by the Emperor Maxentius and finished by Constantine in 315 – it's also known as the Basilica di Costantino – it originally covered an area of approximately 100m by 65m. A colossal statue of Constantine, pieces of which are on display at the Capitoline Museums, was unearthed here in 1487.

Beyond the basilica is the **Arco di Tito** (Arch of Titus; Map p68), built in AD 81 to celebrate Vespasian and Titus' victories against Jerusalem. In the past, Roman Jews would avoid passing under this arch, the historical symbol of the beginning of the Diaspora.

Basilica di SS Cosma e Damiano   BASILICA
(Map p68; Via dei Fori Imperiali; presepio donation €1; ⊙9am-1pm & 3-7pm, presepio 10am-1pm & 3-6pm Fri-Sun; ☐Via dei Fori Imperiali) Backing onto the Roman Forum, this 6th-century basilica incorporates parts of the **Foro di Vespasiano** and **Tempio di Romolo**, visible at the end of the nave. The real reason to visit, though, are the vibrant 6th-century apse mosaics, depicting Christ's Second Coming. Also worth a look is the 18th-century Neapolitan **presepio** (nativity scene) in a room off the 17th-century cloisters.

Carcere Mamertino   HISTORIC SITE
(Mamertine Prison; Map p68; ☑06 69 89 61; Clivo Argentario 1; adult €6; ⊙9.30am-7pm summer, to 5pm winter, last admission 40min before close; ☐Via dei Fori Imperiali) At the foot of the Campidoglio, the Mamertine Prison was ancient Rome's maximum-security jail. St Peter did time here and while imprisoned supposedly created a miraculous stream of water to baptise his jailers. On the bare stone walls you can make out early Christian frescoes

depicting Jesus and Saints Peter and Paul. Visits are by guided tour only.

Imperial Forums   RUIN
(Map p68; Via dei Fori Imperiali; ☐Via dei Fori Imperiali) The ruins over the road from the Roman Forum are known collectively as the Imperial Forums (Fori Imperiali). Constructed between 42 BC and AD 112 by successive emperors, they were largely buried when Mussolini bulldozed Via dei Fori Imperiali through the area in 1933. Excavations have since unearthed much of them but work continues and visits are limited to the Mercati di Traiano, accessible through the Museo dei Fori Imperiali.

Little that's recognisable remains of the **Foro di Traiano** (Trajan's Forum; Map p68), except for some pillars from the **Basilica Ulpia** (Map p68) and the **Colonna di Traiano** (Trajan's Column; Map p68; Via dei Fori Imperiali; ☐Via dei Fori Imperiali), whose minutely detailed reliefs celebrate Trajan's military victories over the Dacians (from modern-day Romania).

To the southeast, three temple columns arise from the ruins of the **Foro di Augusto** (Augustus' Forum; Map p68), now mostly under Via dei Fori Imperiali. The 30m-high wall behind the forum was built to protect it from the fires that frequently swept the area.

The **Foro di Nerva** (Nerva's Forum; Map p68) was also buried by Mussolini's road-building, although part of a temple dedicated to Minerva still stands. Originally, it would have connected the Foro di Augusto to the 1st-century **Foro di Vespasiano** (Vespasian's Forum; Map p68), also known as the Forum of Peace. On the other side of the road, three columns on a raised platform are the most visible remains of the Foro di Cesare (Caesar's Forum; Map p68).

Mercati di Traiano Museo dei Fori Imperiali
MUSEUM

(Map p68; ✆ 06 06 08; www.mercatiditraiano.it; Via IV Novembre 94; adult/reduced €9.50/7.50; ⏱ 9am-7pm Tue-Sun, last admission 6pm; ⬛ Via IV Novembre) This striking museum brings to life the Mercati di Traiano (Map p68), emperor Trajan's great 2nd-century market complex, while also providing a fascinating introduction to the Imperial Forums with detailed explanatory panels and a smattering of archaeological artefacts.

From the main hallway, a lift whisks you up to the Torre delle Milizie (Militia Tower; Map p68), a 13th-century red-brick tower, and the upper levels of the Mercati. These markets, housed in a three-storey semi-circular construction, hosted hundreds of traders selling everything from oil and vegetables to flowers, silks and spices.

Piazza del Campidoglio
PIAZZA

(Map p68; ⬛ Piazza Venezia) Designed by Michelangelo in 1538, this elegant piazza sits atop the Campidoglio (Capitoline Hill), one of the seven hills on which Rome was founded. In ancient times, it was home to Rome's two most important temples: one dedicated to Jupiter Capitolinus, and one to the goddess Juno Moneta (which housed Rome's mint).

You can reach the piazza from the Roman Forum, but the most dramatic approach is via the Cordonata (Map p68), the graceful staircase that leads up from Piazza d'Ara Coeli. At the top, it is bordered by three palazzi: Palazzo Nuovo (Map p68) to the left, Palazzo Senatorio (Map p68) straight ahead, and Palazzo dei Conservatori (Map p68) on the right. Together, Palazzo Nuovo and Palazzo dei Conservatori house the Capitoline Museums, while Palazzo Senatorio is home to Rome's municipal government.

In the centre, the bronze equestrian statue of Marcus Aurelius (Map p68) is a copy. The original, which dates from the 2nd century AD, is in the Capitoline Museums.

★ Capitoline Museums
MUSEUM

(Musei Capitolini; Map p68; ✆ 06 06 08; www.museicapitolini.org; Piazza del Campidoglio 1; adult/reduced €9.50/7.50; ⏱ 9am-8pm Tue-Sun, last admission 7pm; ⬛ Piazza Venezia) The world's oldest national museums, the Capitoline Museums occupy two palazzi on Piazza del Campidoglio. Their origins date to 1471, when Pope Sixtus IV donated a number of bronze statues to the city, forming the nucleus of what is now one of Italy's finest collections of classical art.

The entrance is in Palazzo dei Conservatori, where you'll find the original core of the sculpture collection on the 1st floor and the museum's picture gallery on the 2nd floor. Before you start on the sculpture collection proper, take a moment to admire the marble body parts littered around the courtyard. The mammoth head, hand and feet all belonged to a 12m-high statue of Constantine that once stood in the Basilica di Massenzio in the Roman Forum.

Of the sculpture on the 1st floor, the Etruscan Lupa Capitolina (Capitoline Wolf) is the most famous piece. Standing in the Sala della Lupa, this 5th-century-BC bronze wolf stands over her suckling wards Romulus and Remus, who were added to the composition in 1471. Other crowd-pleasers include the Spinario, a delicate 1st-century-BC bronze of

ROME & LAZIO SIGHTS

ROME'S LESSER-KNOWN HITS

A tour guide since 2005, Silvia Prosperi knows Rome's great sights inside out. Here she advises on some of the city's lesser-known hits.

Favourite Sights

I love too many sights. The Colonna di Traiano (p74) is a masterpiece that is sometimes neglected. The archaeological museum at Palazzo Massimo alle Terme (p93) is another underrated attraction. I also love the atmosphere of the Etruscan museum at Villa Giulia (p117) and the view from the terrace of Castel Sant'Angelo (p112).

Most Underrated Sights

The Mercati di Traiano (p75) are really interesting, as is Bramante's Tempietto (p104) on the Gianicolo.

Roman Forum

In ancient times, a forum was a market place, civic centre and religious complex all rolled into one, and the greatest of all was the Roman Forum (Foro Romano). Situated between the Palatino (Palatine Hill), ancient Rome's most exclusive neighbourhood, and the Campidoglio (Capitoline Hill), it was the city's busy, bustling centre. On any given day it teemed with activity. Senators debated affairs of state in the **Curia 1** , shoppers thronged the squares and traffic-free streets, crowds gathered under the **Colonna di Foca 2** to listen to politicians holding forth from the **Rostrum 2** . Elsewhere, lawyers worked the courts in basilicas including the **Basilica di Massenzio 3** , while the Vestal Virgins quietly went about their business in the **Casa delle Vestali 4** . Special occasions were also celebrated in the Forum: religious holidays were marked with ceremonies at temples such as the **Tempio di Saturno 5** and the **Tempio di Castore e Polluce 6** , and military victories were honoured with dramatic processions up Via Sacra and the building of monumental arches like the **Arco di Settimio Severo 7** and the **Arco di Tito 8** .

The ruins you see today are impressive but they can be confusing without a clear picture of what the Forum once looked like. This spread shows the Forum in its heyday, complete with temples, civic buildings and towering monuments to heroes of the Roman Empire.

TOP TIPS

» Get grandstand views of the Forum from the Palatino and Campidoglio.

» Visit first thing in the morning or late afternoon; crowds are worst between 11am and 2pm.

» In summer it gets hot in the Forum and there's little shade, so take a hat and plenty of water.

Colonna di Foca & Rostrum

Campidoglio (Capitoline Hill)

The free-standing, 13.5m-high Column of Phocas is the Forum's youngest monument, dating to AD 608. Behind it, the Rostrum provided a suitably grandiose platform for pontificating public speakers.

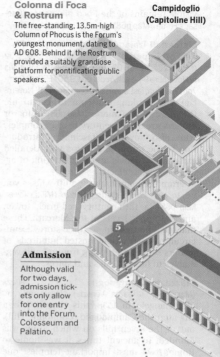

Admission

Although valid for two days, admission tickets only allow for one entry into the Forum, Colosseum and Palatino.

Tempio di Saturno

Ancient Rome's Fort Knox, the Temple of Saturn was the city treasury. In Caesar's day it housed 13 tonnes of gold, 114 tonnes of silver and 30 million sestertii worth of silver coins.

JONATHAN SMITH/GETTY IMAGES©

LONELY PLANET/GETTY IMAGES ©

Tempio di Castore e Polluce

Only three columns of the Temple of Castor and Pollux remain. The temple was dedicated to the Heavenly Twins after they supposedly led the Romans to victory over the Etruscans.

Arco di Settimio Severo

One of the Forum's signature monuments, this imposing triumphal arch commemorates the military victories of Septimius Severus. Relief panels depict his campaigns against the Parthians.

Curia

This big barnlike building was the official seat of the Roman Senate. Most of what you see is a reconstruction, but the interior marble floor dates to the 3rd-century reign of Diocletian.

Basilica di Massenzio

Marvel at the scale of this vast 4th-century basilica. In its original form the central hall was divided into enormous naves; now only part of the northern nave survives.

Julius Caesar RIP

Julius Caesar was cremated on the site where the Tempio di Giulio Cesare now stands.

Via Sacra

Tempio di Giulio Cesare

Casa delle Vestali

White statues line the grassy atrium of what was once the luxurious 50-room home of the Vestal Virgins. The virgins played an important role in Roman religion, serving the goddess Vesta.

Arco di Tito

Said to be the inspiration for the Arc de Triomphe in Paris, the well-preserved Arch of Titus was built by the emperor Domitian to honour his elder brother Titus.

a boy removing a thorn from his foot in the Sala dei Trionfi, and Gian Lorenzo Bernini's *Medusa* bust in the Sala delle Oche.

Also on the 1st floor, in the modern wing known as the **Esedra di Marco Aurelio**, is the original of the equestrian statue that stands in the piazza outside, and foundations of the Temple of Jupiter, the temple that once dominated the Capitoline Hill.

Upstairs, the **Pinacoteca** displays paintings by a long list of major Italian and Flemish artists, including Titian, Tintoretto, Van Dyck, Rubens and Caravaggio. Each room harbours masterpieces but two stand out: the Sala Pietro da Cortona, home to Pietro da Cortona's depiction of the *Ratto delle sabine* (Rape of the Sabine Women), and the Sala di Santa Petronilla, named after Guercino's huge canvas *Seppellimento di Santa Petronilla* (The Burial of St Petronilla). Here you'll also find two Caravaggio canvases: *La Buona Ventura* (The Fortune Teller; 1595), which shows a gypsy pretending to read a young man's hand but actually stealing his ring, and *San Giovanni Battista* (John the Baptist; 1602), a sensual and unusual depiction of the saint.

A tunnel links Palazzo dei Conservatori to Palazzo Nuovo on the other side of the square via the **Tabularium**, ancient Rome's central archive, beneath Palazzo Senatorio.

Palazzo Nuovo displays yet more showstopping classical sculpture. In the Sala del Galata, at the head of the stairs on the 1st floor, is one of the museum's greatest works – the *Galata Morente* (Dying Gaul). A Roman copy of a 3rd-century-BC Greek original, this sublime sculpture movingly captures the quiet, resigned anguish of a dying French warrior. Another superb figurative piece is the sensual yet demure portrayal of the *Venere Capitolina* (Capitoline Venus) in the Gabinetto della Venere, off the main corridor.

Chiesa di Santa Maria in Aracoeli
CHURCH

(Map p68; Piazza Santa Maria in Aracoeli; ⊘ 9am-12.30pm & 2.30-5.30pm; ◻ Piazza Venezia) Atop the 14th-century Aracoeli staircase on the highest point of the Campidoglio, this 6th-century Romanesque church boasts an impressive Cosmatesque floor and an important 15th-century fresco by Pinturicchio. But its main claim to fame is a much-loved wooden baby Jesus believed to have healing powers. In fact, the doll is a copy. The original, which was supposedly made of wood from the garden of Gethsemane, was pinched in 1994 and never recovered.

The church, which sits on the site of the Roman temple to Juno Moneta, has long had an association with the nativity. According to legend, it was here that the Tiburtine Sybil told Augustus of the coming birth of Christ.

Il Vittoriano
MONUMENT

(Map p68; Piazza Venezia; ⊘ 9.30am-5.30pm summer, to 4.30pm winter; ◻ Piazza Venezia) **FREE** Love it or loathe it (as most locals do), you can't ignore the massive mountain of white marble that towers over Piazza Venezia. Known also as the Altare della Patria (Altar of the Fatherland), it was begun in 1885 to commemorate Italian unification and honour Victor Emmanuel II, Italy's first king and the subject of its vast equestrian statue.

The monument also hosts the **Tomb of the Unknown Soldier** and, inside, the **Museo Centrale del Risorgimento** (Map p68; Via di San Pietro in Carcere; ⊘ 9.30am-6.30pm) **FREE**, a free museum documenting Italian unification, and the **Complesso del Vittoriano** (Map p68; ☏ 06 678 06 64; Via di San Pietro in Carcere; ⊘ depends on exhibition), a gallery space that regularly hosts major art exhibitions.

For Rome's best 360-degree views, take the **Roma dal Cielo** (Map p68; adult/reduced €7/3.50; ⊘ 9.30am-6.30pm Mon-Thur, to 7.30pm Fri-Sun) lift up to the top.

Palazzo Venezia
PALACE

(Map p68; Piazza Venezia; ◻ Piazza Venezia) This was the first of Rome's great Renaissance palaces, built between 1455 and 1464. For centuries it served as the embassy of the Venetian Republic, although its best-known resident was Mussolini, who famously made speeches from its balcony. Nowadays, it's home to the **Museo Nazionale del Palazzo Venezia** (Map p80; ☏ 06 678 01 31; Via del Plebiscito 118; adult/reduced €5/2.50; ⊘ 8.30am-7.30pm Tue-Sun; ◻ Piazza Venezia) and its eclectic collection of Byzantine and early Renaissance paintings, tapestries and arms.

Basilica di San Marco
BASILICA

(Map p80; Piazza di San Marco 48; ⊘ 8.30am-noon & 4-6pm Tue-Sat, 9am-1pm & 4-8pm Sun; ◻ Piazza Venezia) The early 4th-century Basilica di San Marco stands over the house where St Mark the Evangelist is said to have stayed while in Rome. Its main attraction is the golden 9th-century apse mosaic.

Bocca della Verità   MONUMENT

(Map p68; Piazza Bocca della Verità 18; donation €0.50; ⊘ 9.30am-4.50pm winter, to 5.50pm summer; 🚇 Piazza Bocca della Verità) A round piece of marble that was once part of an ancient fountain, or possibly an ancient manhole cover, the *Bocca della Verità* (Mouth of Truth) is one of Rome's most popular curiosities. Legend has it that if you put your hand in the carved mouth and tell a lie, it will bite your hand off.

The mouth lives in the portico of the Chiesa di Santa Maria in Cosmedin (Map p68), one of Rome's most beautiful medieval churches. Originally built in the 8th century, the church was given a major revamp in the 12th century, when the seven-storey bell tower and portico were added and the floor was decorated with Cosmati inlaid marble.

Opposite the church are two tiny Roman temples dating to the 2nd century BC: the round Tempio di Ercole Vincitore (Map p68) and the Tempio di Portunus (Map p68), dedicated to the god of rivers and ports, Portunus. Just off the piazza, the Arco di Giano (Map p68) (Arch of Janus) is a four-sided Roman arch that once covered a crossroads.

◉ Centro Storico

The labyrinthine historic centre is the Rome you've come to see – romantic cobbled lanes, operatic piazzas, Renaissance *palazzi*, baroque churches. The Pantheon and Piazza Navona are the stars, but you'll also find a host of monuments, museums and art-rich churches.

★ Pantheon   CHURCH

(Map p80; Piazza della Rotonda; ⊘ 8.30am-7.30pm Mon-Sat, 9am-6pm Sun; 🚇 Largo di Torre Argentina) **FREE** A striking 2000-year-old temple, now church, the Pantheon is the city's best-preserved ancient monument and one of the most influential buildings in the Western world. The greying, pock-marked exterior might look its age, but inside it's a different story, and it's an exhilarating experience to pass through the towering bronze doors and have your vision directed upwards to the largest unreinforced concrete dome ever built.

Its current form dates to AD 120, when Hadrian built over Marcus Agrippa's original 27 BC temple – you can still see Agrippa's name inscribed on the pediment: 'M.AGRIPPA.L.F.COS.TERTIUM.FECIT' or 'Marcus Agrippa, son of Lucius, consul for

the third time, built this'. Hadrian's temple was dedicated to the classical gods – the name Pantheon is a derivation of the Greek words *pan* (all) and *theos* (god) – but in AD 608 it was consecrated as a Christian church and it's now officially known as the Basilica di Santa Maria ad Martyres.

During the Renaissance it was much admired – Brunelleschi used it as inspiration for the Duomo in Florence – and it became an important burial chamber. Inside you'll find the tomb of the artist Raphael, alongside those of kings Vittorio Emanuele II and Umberto I.

However, the real fascination of the Pantheon lies in its massive dimensions and extraordinary dome. Considered the ancient Romans greatest architectural achievement, it was the largest dome in the world until the 15th century and is still the largest unreinforced concrete dome in existence. Its harmonious appearance is due to a precisely calibrated symmetry – its diameter is exactly equal to the Pantheon's interior height of 43.3m. Light enters through the oculus, an 8.7m opening in the dome, which also served as a symbolic connection between the temple and the gods. Rainwater also enters but drains away through 22 almost invisible holes in the sloping marble floor.

The exterior, although somewhat the worse for wear, is still imposing with 16 Corinthian columns supporting a triangular pediment. Little remains of the ancient decor, although rivets and holes in the brickwork indicate where the marble panels were once placed, and the towering 20-tonne bronze doors are 16th-century restorations of the originals.

Chiesa di Santa Maria
Sopra Minerva   CHURCH

(Map p80; Piazza della Minerva; ⊘ 8am-7pm Mon-Fri, 8am-1pm & 3.30-7pm Sat & Sun; 🚇 Largo di Torre Argentina) Bernini's much-loved Elefantino sculpture trumpets the presence of the Dominican Chiesa di Santa Maria Sopra Minerva, Rome's only Gothic church. Built on the site of an ancient temple to Minerva, it has been much altered over the centuries and little remains of its original 13th-century form.

Inside, you'll find two superb 15th-century frescoes by Filippino Lippi and the majestic tomb of Pope Paul IV. Left of the high altar is one of Michelangelo's lesser-known sculptures, *Cristo Risorto* (Christ Bearing the Cross; 1520). An altarpiece of

Centro Storico

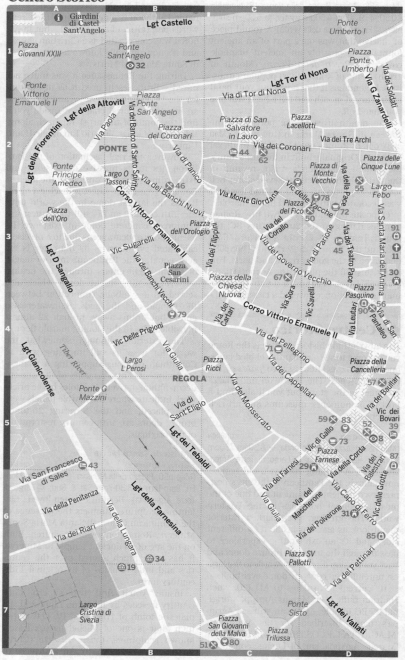

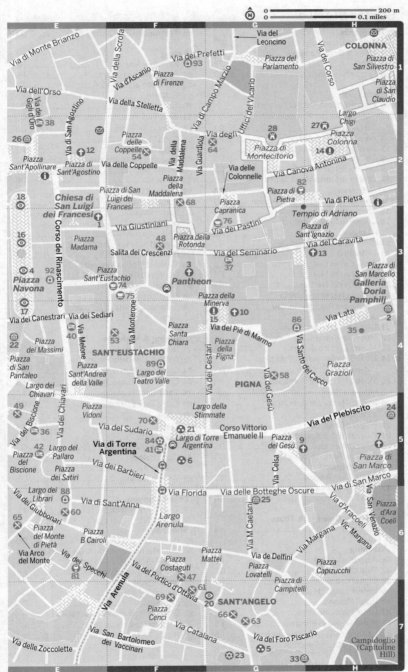

Centro Storico

the *Madonna and Child* in the second chapel in the northern transept is attributed to Fra Angelico, who is buried in the church.

The body of St Catherine of Siena, minus her head (which is in Siena), lies under the high altar, and the tombs of two Medici popes, Leo X and Clement VII, are in the apse.

★ **Chiesa di San Luigi dei Francesi**   CHURCH
(Map p80; Piazza di San Luigi dei Francesi; ⊙ 10am-12.30pm & 3-7pm, closed Thu afternoon; ▣ Corso del Rinascimento) Church to Rome's French community since 1589, this art-rich baroque bonanza boasts no less than three canvases by Caravaggio: *La Vocazione di San Matteo* (The Calling of Saint Matthew), *Il Martirio di San Matteo* (The Martyrdom of Saint Matthew) and *San Matteo e l'Angelo* (Saint Matthew and the Angel), together known as the St Matthew cycle.

These are among Caravaggio's earliest religious works, painted between 1600 and 1602, but they are inescapably his, featuring down-to-earth realism and stunning use of chiaroscuro (the bold contrast of light and dark).

Before you leave the church, take a moment to enjoy Domenichino's colourful 17th-century frescoes of St Cecilia in the second chapel on the right.

Chiesa di Sant'Agostino   CHURCH
(Map p80; Piazza di Sant'Agostino 80; ⊙ 7.30am-12.30pm & 4-6.30pm; ▣ Corso del Rinascimento) This 15th-century early Renaissance church contains two outstanding works of art: Raphael's 1512 *Isaiah* fresco and Caravaggio's *Madonna dei Pellegrini* (Madonna of the Pilgrims), which caused uproar when it was unveiled in 1604, due to its depiction of Mary as barefoot and her two devoted pilgrims as filthy beggars. Also of note is Jacopo Sansovino's 1521 *Madonna del Parto* (Madonna of Childbirth) sculpture, the subject of local devotion by pregnant women.

Museo Nazionale Romano: Palazzo Altemps   MUSEUM
(Map p80; ☑ 06 3996 7700; http://archeo-roma.beniculturali.it/en/museums/national-roman-museum-palazzo-altemps; Piazza Sant'Apollinare 44; adult/reduced €7/3.50; ⊙ 9am-7.45pm Tue-Sun; ▣ Corso del Rinascimento) This gem of a museum houses the best of the Museo Nazionale Romano's formidable collection of classical sculpture. Many pieces come from the celebrated Ludovisi collection, amassed

by Cardinal Ludovico Ludovisi in the 17th century.

Prize exhibits include the beautiful 5th-century *Trono Ludovisi* (Ludovisi Throne), a carved marble block depicting Aphrodite being plucked from the sea. This shares a room with two colossal heads, one of which is the goddess Juno that dates from around 600 BC. The wall frieze (about half of which remains) depicts the 10 plagues of Egypt and the Exodus.

The palazzo's baroque frescoes provide an exquisite decorative backdrop. The walls of the Sala delle Prospettive Dipinte are decorated with landscapes and hunting scenes seen through trompe l'œil windows. These frescoes were painted for Cardinal Altemps, the rich nephew of Pope Pius IV (r 1560–65) who bought the palace in the late 16th century.

The museum also houses the Museo Nazionale Romano's Egyptian collection.

★ **Piazza Navona**   PIAZZA
(Map p80; ▣ Corso del Rinascimento) With its ornate fountains, baroque *palazzi* (mansions), cafes and colourful circus of street performers, hawkers, artists and tourists, Piazza Navona is Rome's most iconic public square. Laid out on the ruins of a 1st-century arena built by the emperor Domitian – the name Navona is a corruption of the Greek word *agon*, meaning public games – it was paved over in the 15th century and for almost 300 years hosted the city's main market.

Of its three fountains, it's Bernini's high-camp **Fontana dei Quattro Fiumi** (Fountain of the Four Rivers; Map p80) that dominates. Depicting personifications of the Nile, Ganges, Danube and Plate, it's festooned with a palm tree, lion and horse, and topped by an obelisk. Legend has it that the figure of the Nile is shielding his eyes from the **Chiesa di Sant'Agnese in Agone** (Map p80; www.santagneseinagone.org; Piazza Navona; concerts €10; ⊙ 9.30am-12.30pm & 4-7pm Tue-Sun; ▣ Corso del Rinascimento), designed by Bernini's hated rival, Francesco Borromini. In truth, it simply indicates that the source of the Nile was unknown at the time.

At the southern end, the **Fontana del Moro** (Map p80) was designed by Giacomo della Porta in 1576. Bernini added the Moor holding a dolphin but the surrounding Tritons are 19th-century copies. The 19th-century **Fontana del Nettuno** (Map p80) at the northern end depicts Neptune fighting with a sea monster, surrounded by sea nymphs.

The piazza's largest building is the 17th-century Palazzo Pamphilj (Map p80), built for Pope Innocent X and now home to the Brazilian Embassy.

Museo di Roma
MUSEUM

(Map p80; ☏ 06 06 08; www.museodiroma.it; entrances Piazza di San Pantaleo 10 & Piazza Navona 2; adult/reduced €8.50/6.50; ⊙10am-8pm Tue-Sun, last admission 7pm; ☐ Corso Vittorio Emanuele II) The baroque Palazzo Braschi houses the Museo di Roma's eclectic collection of paintings, photographs, etchings, clothes and furniture, charting the history of Rome from the Middle Ages to the early 20th century. But as striking as the collection are the palazzo's beautiful frescoed halls, including the extravagant Sala Cinese and the Egyptian-themed Sala Egiziana.

Campo de' Fiori
PIAZZA

(Map p80; ☐ Corso Vittorio Emanuele II) Noisy, colourful 'Il Campo' is a major focus of Roman life: by day it hosts a much-loved market, while at night it morphs into a raucous open-air pub. Towering over the square is a sinister statue of Giordano Bruno, a philosopher monk who was burned at the stake for heresy in 1600.

Palazzo Farnese
PALACE

(Map p80; www.inventerrome.com; Piazza Farnese; admission €5; ⊙ guided tours 3pm, 4pm, 5pm Mon, Wed & Fri; ☐ Corso Vittorio Emanuele II) One of Rome's greatest Renaissance *palazzi*, Palazzo Farnese was started in 1514 by Antonio da Sangallo the Younger, continued by Michelangelo, and finished by Giacomo della Porta. Nowadays, it's home to the French Embassy, and open only to visitors who've booked a guided tour – see the website for details. Visits, for which you'll need to book at least a week in advance, take in the Galleria dei Caracci, home to a cycle of frescoes by Annibale Carracci that are said to rival those of the Sistine Chapel.

Photo ID is required for entry and children under 10 not admitted.

The twin fountains in the square are enormous granite baths taken from the Terme di Caracalla.

Largo di Torre Argentina
RUIN

(Map p80; ☐ Largo di Torre Argentina) A busy public transport hub, Largo di Torre Argentina is set around the sunken Area Sacra (Map p80) and the remains of four Republican-era temples, all built between the 2nd and 4th centuries BC. In the 1st century BC, much of the area was covered by the Teatro di Pompeo, the vast theatre complex where Julius Caesar was stabbed to death on the Ides of March (15 March) 44 BC.

On the piazza's western flank is Rome's premier theatre, Teatro Argentina (Map p80; ☏ 06 684 00 03 11; www.teatrodiroma.net; Largo di Torre Argentina 52; tickets €12-27; ☐ Largo di Torre Argentina).

Chiesa del Gesù
CHURCH

(Map p80; www.chiesadelgesu.org; Piazza del Gesù; rooms admission free; ⊙7am-12.30pm & 4-7.45pm, St Ignatius rooms 4-6pm Mon-Sat, 10am-noon Sun; ☐ Largo di Torre Argentina) An imposing example of late-16th-century Counter-Reformation architecture, this is Rome's most important Jesuit church. The facade by Giacomo della Porta is impressive but it's the awesome gold-and-marble interior that is the real attraction.

The church's great masterpiece is the *Trionfo del Nome di Gesù* (Triumph of the Name of Jesus), the swirling, hypnotic vault fresco by Giovanni Battista Gaulli (aka Il Baciccia), who also painted the cupola frescoes and designed the stucco decoration.

Baroque master Andrea Pozzo designed the Cappella di Sant'Ignazio, where you'll find the opulent tomb of Ignatius Loyola, the Spanish soldier and saint who founded the Jesuits in 1540. The altar-tomb is an opulent marble-and-bronze affair flanked by two sculptures: to the left, *Fede che vince l'Idolatria* (Faith Defeats Idolatry); and on the right, *Religione che flagella l'Eresia* (Religion Lashing Heresy).

The Spanish saint lived in the church from 1544 until his death in 1556. His rooms, which contain a masterful trompe l'œil by Andrea del Pozzo, are to the right of the church entrance.

Museo Nazionale Romano: Crypta Balbi
MUSEUM

(Map p80; ☏ 06 3996 7700; http://archeoroma.beniculturali.it/en/museums/national-roman-museum-crypta-balbi; Via delle Botteghe Oscure 31; adult/reduced €7/3.50; ⊙9am-7.45pm Tue-Sun; ☐ Via delle Botteghe Oscure) The least known of the Museo Nazionale Romano's four museums, the Crypta Balbi is built around the ruins of medieval and Renaissance structures, themselves set atop the ancient Teatro di Balbus (13 BC). Duck down into the underground excavations, then examine artefacts taken from the Crypta, as well as items found in the forums and on the Oppian and Celian Hills.

Jewish Ghetto NEIGHBOURHOOD

(Map p80; 🚊 Lungotevere de' Cenci) Centred on lively Via del Portico d'Ottavia, the Jewish Ghetto is a wonderfully atmospheric area studded with artisans' studios, vintage clothes shops, kosher bakeries and popular trattorias.

Rome's Jewish community dates back to the 2nd century BC, making it one of the oldest in Europe. At one point there were as many as 13 synagogues in the city, but Titus' defeat of Jewish rebels in Jerusalem in AD 70 changed the status of Rome's Jews from citizen to slave. Confinement to the Ghetto came in 1555 when Pope Paul IV ushered in a period of official intolerance that lasted, on and off, until the 20th century.

Museo Ebraico di Roma SYNAGOGUE, MUSEUM

(Jewish Museum of Rome; Map p80; ✆ 06 6840 0661; www.museoebraico.roma.it; Via Catalana; adult/reduced €10/7.50; ⏰ 10am-6.15pm Sun-Thu, 10am-3.15pm Fri mid-Jun–mid-Sep, 10am-4pm Sun-Thu, 9am-1.15pm Fri mid-Sep–mid-Jun; 🚊 Lungotevere de' Cenci) Housed in the city's early-20th-century synagogue, Europe's second largest, this small but engrosssing museum chronicles the historical, cultural and artistic heritage of Rome's Jewish community. Exhibits include copies of Pope Paul IV's papal bull letter confining the Jews to the ghetto and relics from Nazi concentration camps.

Area Archeologica del Teatro di Marcello e del Portico d'Ottavia ARCHAEOLOGICAL SITE

(Map p80; entrances Via del Teatro di Marcello 44 & Via Portico d'Ottavia 29; ⏰ 9am-7pm summer, 9am-6pm winter; 🚊 Via del Teatro di Marcello) FREE Rising like a mini-Colosseum, the Teatro di Marcello (Theatre of Marcellus) is the star of this dusty archaeological area. The 20,000-seat theatre was planned by Julius Caesar and completed in 11 BC by Augustus who named it after a favourite nephew, Marcellus. In the 16th century, a *palazzo*, which now contains several exclusive apartments, was built on top of the original structure.

Beyond the theatre, the Portico d'Ottavia is the oldest *quadriporto* (four-sided porch) in Rome. The dilapidated columns and fragmented pediment once formed part of a vast rectangular portico, supported by 300 columns. From the Middle Ages until the late 19th century, the portico housed Rome's fish market.

Isola Tiberina NEIGHBOURHOOD

(Tiber Island; Map p102) One of the world's smallest inhabited islands, the Isola Tiberina has been associated with healing since the 3rd century BC, when the Romans built a temple to Aesculapius, god of healing, here. These days patients make for the Ospedale Fatebenefratelli whilst church-goers head to the 10th-century Chiesa di San Bartolomeo (Map p102; ⏰ 9am-1pm & 3.30-5.30pm Mon-Sat, 9am-1pm Sun; 🚊 Lungotevere dei Pierleoni) on the site where the temple once stood. Note the church's Romanseque bell tower and, inside, a marble well-head, said to stand over the same spring that supplied healing waters to the temple.

To reach the Isola from the Jewish Ghetto, cross Rome's oldest standing bridge, the 62 BC Ponte Fabricio. Visible to the south are the remains of the Ponte Rotto (Map p102) (Broken Bridge), ancient Rome's first stone bridge, which was all but swept away in a 1598 flood.

⊙ Tridente, Trevi & the Quirinale

Rome's premier shopping district, the Tridente district has long attracted foreigners – Keats, Shelley and Goethe are among the notables to have lived here – and still today visitors flock to the area to browse its boutique-lined streets and hang out on Piazza di Spagna and the Spanish Steps. A short walk away, the Trevi Fountain is another crowd-pleaser.

★ Piazza di Spagna & Spanish Steps PIAZZA

(Map p86; Ⓜ Spagna) A magnet for visitors since the 18th century, the Piazza di Spagna and the Spanish Steps (Scalinata della Trinità dei Monti) provide perfect people-watching perches and you'll almost certainly find yourself taking stock here at some point.

Piazza di Spagna was named after the Spanish Embassy to the Holy See, although the staircase, designed by the Italian Francesco de Sanctis and built in 1725 with a legacy from the French, leads to the French Chiesa della Trinità dei Monti. This landmark church, which was commissioned by King Louis XII of France and consecrated in 1585, commands memorable views and boasts some wonderful frescoes by Daniele da Volterra, including a masterful Deposizione (Deposition).

Tridente & Trevi

ROME & LAZIO ROME

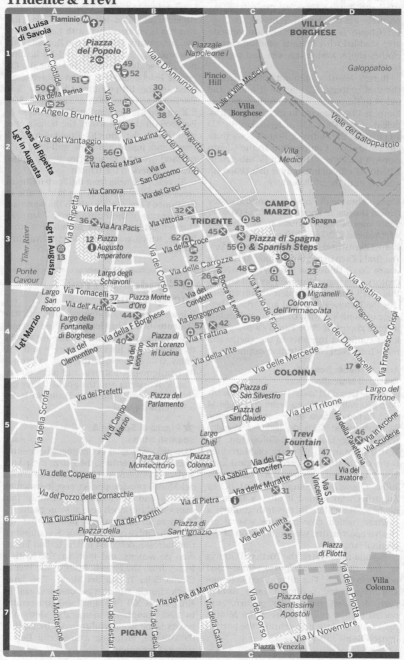

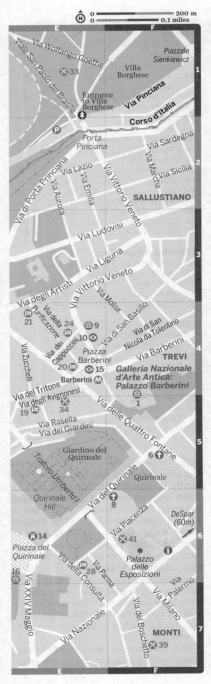

At the foot of the steps, the Barcaccia (the 'sinking boat' fountain) is believed to be by Pietro Bernini, father of the more famous Gian Lorenzo.

To the southeast of the piazza, adjacent Piazza Mignanelli is dominated by the Colonna dell'Immacolata, built in 1857 to celebrate Pope Pius IX's declaration of the Immaculate Conception.

Keats–Shelley House   MUSEUM

(Map p86; ☏06 678 42 35; www.keats-shelley-house.org; Piazza di Spagna 26; adult/reduced €4.50/3.50; ◷10am-1pm & 2-6pm Mon-Fri, 11am-2pm & 3-6pm Sat; Ⓜ Spagna) Overlooking the Spanish Steps, this is where the 25-year-old Romantic poet John Keats died of TB in February 1821. The house is now a small museum crammed with memorabilia relating to the ill-fated poet and his fellow scribes Byron, Mary Shelley and Percy Bysshe Shelley, who drowned off the Tuscan coast in 1822 and is buried with Keats in Rome's non-Catholic cemetery.

★ Piazza del Popolo   PIAZZA

(Map p86; Ⓜ Flaminio) For centuries the site of public executions, this dazzling piazza was originally laid out in 1538 to provide a grandiose entrance to what was then Rome's main northern gateway. It has been remodelled several times since, most recently by Giuseppe Valadier in 1823.

Guarding its southern entry are Carlo Rainaldi's twin 17th-century baroque churches, Chiesa di Santa Maria dei Miracoli and Chiesa di Santa Maria in Montesanto, while over on the northern flank is the Porta del Popolo, created by Bernini in 1655 to celebrate Queen Christina of Sweden's conversion to Catholicism. In the centre, the 36m-high obelisk was brought by Augustus from Heliopolis, in ancient Egypt, and originally stood in the Circo Massimo. To the east are the Pincian (Pincio) Gardens.

Chiesa di Santa Maria del Popolo   CHURCH

(Map p86; Piazza del Popolo; ◷7.30am-noon & 4-7pm; Ⓜ Flaminio) A magnificent repository of art, this is one of Rome's earliest and richest Renaissance churches. The first chapel was built here in 1099 to exorcise the ghost of Nero, who was secretly buried on this spot and whose ghost was thought to haunt the area. Some 400 years later, in 1472, it was given a major overhaul and Pinturicchio added a series of frescoes in the Bramante-designed apse and the Cappella Delle Rovere.

Tridente & Trevi

Raphael's Cappella Chigi – completed by Bernini some 100 years later – features a famous mosaic of a kneeling skeleton, but the church's dazzling highlight is the **Cappella Cerasi** with its two Caravaggio masterpieces: the *Conversione di San Paolo* (Conversion of St Paul) and the *Crocifissione di San Pietro* (Crucifixion of St Peter).

Casa di Goethe   MUSEUM
(Map p86; ☎ 06 3265 0412; www.casadigoethe.it; Via del Corso 18; adult/reduced €5/3; ☺ 10am-6pm Tue-Sun; M Flaminio) The Via del Corso apartment where Goethe enjoyed a happy Italian sojourn (despite complaining of the noisy neighbours) from 1786 to 1788 is now a lovingly maintained museum. Exhibits include documents and some fascinating drawings and etchings.

Museo dell'Ara Pacis   MUSEUM
(Map p86; ☎ 06 06 08; http://en.arapacis.it; Lungotevere in Augusta; adult/reduced €8.50/6.50; ☺ 9am-7pm Tue-Sun, last admission 6pm; M Flaminio) The first modern construction in Rome's historic centre since WWII, Richard Meier's controversial, and widely detested, glass-and-marble pavilion houses the Ara Pacis Augustae (Altar of Peace), Augustus' great monument to peace. One of the most important works of ancient Roman sculpture, the vast marble altar – it measures 11.6m by 10.6m by 3.6m – was completed in 13 BC and positioned near Piazza San Lorenzo in Lucina, slightly to the southeast of its current site.

Over the centuries the altar fell victim to Rome's avid art collectors, and panels ended up in the Medici collection, the Vatican and the Louvre. However, in 1936 Mussolini unearthed the remaining parts and reassembled them in the present location.

Of the reliefs, the most important depicts Augustus at the head of a procession, followed by priests, the general Marcus Agrippa and the entire imperial family.

Mausoleo di Augusto   MONUMENT

(Map p86; Piazza Augusto Imperatore; Piazza Augusto Imperatore) Now an unkempt mound of earth surrounded by unsightly fences, this was once one of ancient Rome's most imposing monuments. The mausoleum was built in 28 BC and is the last resting place of Augustus, who was buried here in AD 14, and his favourite nephew and heir Marcellus. Mussolini had it restored in 1936 with an eye to being buried here himself.

Restoration work is apparently ongoing, though it's proceeding at a slow pace.

★ Trevi Fountain   FOUNTAIN

(Fontana di Trevi; Map p86; Piazza di Trevi; M Barberini) The Fontana di Trevi, scene of Anita Ekberg's dip in *La Dolce Vita*, is Rome's largest and most famous fountain. A flamboyant baroque ensemble of mythical figures, wild horses and cascading rock falls, it takes up the entire side of the 17th-century Palazzo Poli.

The design, the work of Nicola Salvi in 1732, depicts Neptune in a shell-shaped chariot being led by Tritons and two seahorses – one wild, one docile – representing the moods of the sea. In the niche to the left of Neptune, a statue represents Abundance; to the right is Salubrity. The water comes from the aqua virgo, a 1st-century-BC underground aqueduct, and the name Trevi refers to the tre vie (three roads) that converge at the fountain.

The fountain gets very busy during the day as people stop to follow tradition and throw a coin into the water and thus ensure their return to Rome. To avoid the worst of the crowds try to visit in the evening.

In 2012 Karl Lagerfield announced that the Fendi fashion house would be funding a much-needed €2.18m restoration of the fountain.

Piazza Barberini   PIAZZA

(Map p86; M Barberini) More a traffic thoroughfare than a place to linger, this noisy square is named after the Barberini family, one of Rome's great dynastic clans. In the centre, the Bernini-designed **Fontana del Tritone** (Fountain of the Triton) depicts the sea-god Triton blowing a stream of water from a conch while seated in a large scallop shell supported by four dolphins. Bernini also crafted the **Fontana delle Api** (Fountain of the Bees) in the northeastern corner, again for the Barberini family, whose crest features three bees in flight.

★ Galleria Nazionale d'Arte Antica: Palazzo Barberini   GALLERY

(Map p86; 06 3 28 10; www.gebart.it; Via delle Quattro Fontane 13; adult/reduced €7/3.50, incl Palazzo Corsini €9/4.50; 8.30am-7pm Tue-Sun; M Barberini) Commissioned to celebrate the Barberini family's rise to papal power, Palazzo Barberini is a sumptuous baroque palace that impresses even before you go inside and start on the breathtaking art. Many high-profile architects worked on it, including rivals Bernini and Borromini: the former contributed a large squared staircase, the latter a spiral one.

Amid the masterpieces, don't miss Pietro da Cortona's *Il Trionfo della Divina Provvidenza* (Triumph of Divine Providence; 1632–39), the most spectacular of the palazzo's ceiling frescoes in the 1st-floor main salon. Other must-sees include Hans Holbein's famous portrait of a pugnacious Henry VIII (c 1540), Filippo Lippi's luminous *Annunciazione e due devoti* (Annunciation with two Kneeling Donors) and Raphael's

---

THE TREVI COINS

On an average day around €3000 is thrown into the Trevi Fountain. This is collected daily and given to the Catholic charity Caritas, but in 2002, scandal erupted when it emerged that an unemployed man calling himself D'Artagnan had been helping himself for 34 years. He was subsequently banned from the fountain, but eight years later he was caught on film back at his old tricks.

The ensuing controversy highlighted the fact that the only rule D'Artagnan had been breaking was a by-law prohibiting entering Rome's fountains. New legislation was subsequently introduced and as of 2012 it's an offence to remove coins from the water.

ART & POLITICS ON VIA DEL CORSO

On Via del Corso, the arrow-straight road that links Piazza Venezia to Piazza del Popolo, you'll find one of Rome's finest private art galleries. You wouldn't know it from the grimy exterior but the **Galleria Doria Pamphilj** (Map p80; ☑ 06 679 73 23; www.dopart.it; Via del Corso 305; adult/reduced €11/7.50; ⊙ 9am-7pm, last admission 6pm; ☐ Piazza Venezia) houses an extraordinary collection of works by Raphael, Tintoretto, Brueghel, Titian, Caravaggio, Bernini and Velázquez. Masterpieces abound but the undisputed star is Velázquez' portrait of Pope Innocent X, who grumbled that the depiction was 'too real'.

A short walk to the north of the gallery, the 30m-high **Colonna di Marco Aurelio** (Map p80) on Piazza Colonna heralds the presence of **Palazzo Chigi** (Map p80; www.governo.it; Piazza Colonna 370; ⊙ guided visits 9am-1pm Sat Oct-May, booking obligatory) **FREE**, the official residence of the Italian prime minister. Next door, on Piazza di Montecitorio, the Bernini-designed **Palazzo di Montecitorio** (Map p80; ☑ 800 012955; www.camera.it; Piazza di Montecitorio; ⊙ guided visits 10.30am-3.30pm, 1st Sun of month; ☐ Via del Corso) **FREE** is home to Italy's Chamber of Deputies.

La Fornarina (The Baker's Girl), a portrait of his mistress who worked in a bakery in Trastevere. Works by Caravaggio include *San Francesco d'Assisi in meditazione* (St Francis in Meditation), *Narciso* (Narcissus; 1571–1610) and the mesmerisingly horrific *Giuditta e Oloferne* (Judith Beheading Holophernes; c 1597–1600).

Convento dei Cappuccini   MUSEUM
(Map p86; ☑ 06 487 11 85; Via Vittorio Veneto 27; adult/reduced €6/4; ⊙ 9am-7pm daily; Ⓜ Barberini) This church and convent complex has an interesting multimedia museum telling the story of the Capuchin order of monks. The main attraction, however, is the extraordinary **Capuchin cemetery** that lies below, where everything from the picture frames to the light fittings is made of human bones.

Between 1528 and 1870 the resident Capuchin monks used the bones of 4000 of their departed brothers to create this mesmerising, macabre memento mori (reminder of death). There's an arch crafted from hundreds of skulls, vertebrae used as fleurs-de-lis and light fixtures made of femurs.

Palazzo del Quirinale   PALACE
(Map p86; ☑ 06 4 69 91; www.quirinale.it; Piazza del Quirinale; admission €5; ⊙ 8am-noon Sun mid-Sep–Jun; Ⓜ Barberini) Overlooking **Piazza del Quirinale**, this immense palace is the official residence of Italy's head of state, the Presidente della Repubblica. For almost three centuries it was the pope's summer residence but in 1870 Pope Pius IX begrudgingly handed the keys over to Italy's new king. Later, in 1948, it was given to the Italian state.

It's open to the public on Sundays, and at the end of visiting time (at around 12.30pm to 1pm) there's a free concert in the chapel.

On the other side of the piazza, the palace's former stables, the **Scuderie Papali al Quirinale** (Map p86; ☑ 06 3996 7500; www.scuderiequirinale.it; Via XXIV Maggio 16; tickets around €12; ⊙ depends on exhibition), host excellent art exhibitions.

Chiesa di Sant'Andrea
al Quirinale   CHURCH
(Map p86; Via del Quirinale 29; ⊙ 8.30am-noon & 2.30-6pm winter, 9am-noon & 3-6pm summer; ☐ Via Nazionale) It's said that in his old age Bernini liked to enjoy the peace of this late-17th-century church, regarded by many as one of his greatest. Faced with severe space limitations, he managed to produce a sense of grandeur by designing an elliptical floor plan with a series of chapels opening onto the central area.

Chiesa di San Carlo
alle Quattro Fontane   CHURCH
(Map p86; Via del Quirinale 23; ⊙ 10am-1pm & 3-6pm Mon-Fri, 10am-1pm Sat, noon-1pm Sun; ☐ Via Nazionale) A masterpiece of baroque architecture (albeit a grubby one), this was Borromini's first church and bears all the hallmarks of his genius. The elegant curves of the facade, the play of convex and concave surfaces, and the dome illuminated by hidden windows, all combine to transform a minuscule space into a light, airy interior.

The church, completed in 1641, stands at a road intersection known as the Quattro Fontane, after the late-16th-century fountains on its four corners, representing Fidelity, Strength and the rivers Arno and Tiber.

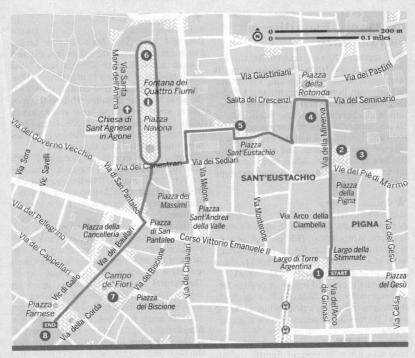

City Walk
Centro Storico

START LARGO DI TORRE ARGENTINA
END PALAZZO FARNESE
LENGTH 1.5KM; THREE HOURS

Follow this tour through Rome's tightly packed historical centre and even without trying you'll come across some of the city's best-known sights.

Start off in ❶ **Largo di Torre Argentina** (p84), a busy square set around the ruins of four Republic-era temples and the site of Julius Caesar's assassination in 44 BC. From here it's a short walk up Via dei Cestari, past Bernini's much-loved ❷ **Elefantino**, to the 13th-century ❸ **Chiesa di Santa Maria Sopra Minerva** (p79), Rome's only Gothic church. Continue past the church to the ❹ **Pantheon** (p79), ancient Rome's best-preserved monument. Built in 27 BC, modified by Hadrian in the 2nd century AD and consecrated as a Christian church in 608, it's an architectural masterpiece capped by the largest unreinforced concrete dome ever built. From the Pantheon, follow signs towards Piazza Navona, stopping off en route for a coffee at ❺ **Caffè Sant'Eustachio** (p139), reckoned by many to serve the capital's best coffee. A short hop away, ❻ **Piazza Navona** (p83) is central Rome's showpiece square, where you can compare the two giants of Roman baroque: Bernini, creator of the Fontana dei Quattro Fiumi, and Borromini, responsible for the Chiesa di Sant'Agnese in Agone. On the other side of Corso Vittorio Emanuel II, the busy road that bisects the *centro storico*, life centres on ❼ **Campo de' Fiori** (p84). By day this noisy square stages a colourful market but at night it transforms into a rowdy open-air pub, beloved of foreign students and lusty Romans. Just beyond, Piazza Farnese is overlooked by the Renaissance ❽ **Palazzo Farnese** (p84), home to some superb frescoes that rival the Sistine Chapel's. To see them, though, you'll need to book well in advance.

⊙ Monti, Esquiline & San Lorenzo

The largest of Rome's seven hills, the Esquiline extends from the Colosseum to Stazione Termini, encompassing Via Cavour (a busy road between Termini and Via dei Fori Imperiali), several impressive museums and churches, and the boho area of Monti, formerly ancient Rome's notorious red-light district. Much of the Esquiline was covered with vineyards and gardens until the late 19th century, when they were dug up to make way for grandiose apartment blocks.

★ Chiesa di Santa Maria della Vittoria
CHURCH

(Map p94; Via XX Settembre 17; ⊙7am-noon & 3.30-7pm; Ⓜ Repubblica) This modest church is an unlikely setting for an extraordinary work of art – Bernini's *Santa Teresa trafitta dall'amore di Dio* (Ecstasy of St Teresa).

This sexually charged sculpture depicts Teresa, engulfed in the folds of a flowing cloak, floating in ecstasy on a cloud while a teasing angel pierces her repeatedly with a golden arrow.

Watching the whole scene from two side balconies are a number of figures, including Cardinal Federico Cornaro, for whom the chapel was built. It's a stunning work, bathed in soft natural light filtering through a concealed window. Go in the afternoon for the best effect.

★ Basilica di Santa Maria Maggiore
BASILICA

(Map p94; Piazza Santa Maria Maggiore; basilica free, museum €3, loggia €2; ⊙7am-7pm, museum & loggia 9.30am-6.30pm; Ⓟ Piazza Santa Maria Maggiore) One of Rome's four patriarchal basilicas, this monumental church stands on the summit of the Esquiline Hill, on the spot where snow is said to have miraculously fallen in the summer of AD 358. In its earliest form it dates to the 5th century but it has been much altered over the centuries.

Outside, the exterior is decorated with glimmering 13th-century mosaics, protected by Ferdinand Fuga's 1741 baroque facade. Rising behind is a 14th-century Romanesque **belfry**, which, at 75m, is the highest in Rome.

The vast interior retains its original 5th-century structure despite the basilica's many overhauls. Particularly spectacular are the 5th-century **mosaics** in the triumphal arch and nave, depicting Old Testament scenes. The central image in the apse, signed by Jacopo Torriti, dates from the 13th century and represents the coronation of the Virgin Mary. Beneath your feet, the nave floor is a fine example of 12th-century Cosmati paving.

The baldachin (ceremonial canopy) over the **high altar** seethes with gilt cherubs; the altar itself is said to contain the relics of St Matthew and other martyrs. A plaque to the right of the altar marks the spot where Gian Lorenzo Bernini and his father Pietro are buried. Steps lead down to the **confessio**, where a statue of Pope Pius IX kneels before a reliquary containing a fragment of Jesus' manger.

ROME'S OPTICAL ILLUSIONS

Aptly for such a theatrical city, Rome contains some magical visual tricks:

Palazzo Spada (Map p80; ☏06 683 24 09; http://galleriaspada.beniculturali.it; Via Capo di Ferro 13; adult/reduced €5/2.50; ⊙8.30am-7.30pm Tue-Sun; Ⓟ Corso Vittorio Emanuele II) This grand mannerist *palazzo* is home to a celebrated illusion known as Borromini's *Prospettiva* (Perspective). What appears to be a 25m-long corridor lined with columns leading to a hedge and life-sized statue is, in fact, only 10m long. The sculpture, which was a later addition, is actually hip-height and the columns diminish in size not because of distance but because they actually get shorter. And look closer at that perfect-looking hedge – Borromini didn't trust the gardeners to clip a real hedge precisely enough so he made one of stone.

Chiesa di Sant'Ignazio di Loyola (Map p80; Piazza di Sant'Ignazio; ⊙7.30am-7pm Mon-Sat, 9am-7pm Sun; Ⓟ Via del Corso) The star at this Jesuit church is Andrea Pozzo's trompe l'œil ceiling fresco depicting St Ignatius Loyola being welcomed into paradise by Christ and the Madonna. For the best views, stand on the small yellow spot and look up at the ceiling, which, despite appearances, is quite flat.

The sumptuously decorated **Cappella Sistina**, last on the right, was built by Domenico Fontana in the 16th century and contains the tombs of Popes Sixtus V and Pius V.

Through the souvenir shop on the right-hand side of the church is a **museum** with a glittering, if slightly dull, collection of religious artifacts. More interesting is the upper **loggia** where you'll get a closer look at the iridescent 13th-century mosaics on the southeast facade.

Basilica di San Pietro in Vincoli   BASILICA

(Map p68; Piazza di San Pietro in Vincoli 4a; ⊙ 8am-12.30pm & 3-7pm Apr-Sep, to 6pm Oct-Mar; M Cavour) Pilgrims and art lovers flock to this 5th-century church for two reasons: to marvel at Michelangelo's macho **Moses** sculpture and to see the **chains** that bound St Peter when he was imprisoned in the Carcere Mamertino.

The church was built specially to house these shackles, which had been sent to Constantinople after the saint's death but were later returned as relics. They arrived in two pieces and legend has it that when they were reunited they miraculously joined together. They are now displayed under the altar.

To the right of the altar, Michelangelo's colossal *Moses* (1505) forms the centrepiece of his unfinished tomb for Pope Julius II. The prophet strikes a muscular pose with well-defined biceps, a magnificent waist-length beard and two small horns sticking out of his head. These were inspired by a mistranslation of a biblical passage: where the original said that rays of light issued from Moses' face, the translator wrote 'horns'. Michelangelo was aware of the mistake, but gave Moses horns anyway. Flanking Moses are statues of Leah and Rachel, probably completed by Michelangelo's students.

The tomb, despite its imposing scale, was never completed – Michelangelo originally envisaged 40 statues but got sidetracked by the Sistine Chapel – and Julius was buried in St Peter's Basilica.

Access to the church is via a flight of steps through a low arch that leads up from Via Cavour.

Domus Aurea   ARCHAEOLOGICAL SITE

(Map p97; ☑ 06 3996 7700; www.coopculture.it; Viale della Domus Aurea; ⊙ closed for restoration; M Colosseo) A monumental exercise in vanity, the Domus Aurea (Golden House) was Nero's great gift to himself. Built after the fire of AD 64 and named after the gold that covered its facade, it was a huge complex covering up to a third of the city, but it's estimated that only around 20% remains of the original complex.

Piazza della Repubblica   PIAZZA

(Map p94; M Repubblica) Flanked by grand neoclassical colonnades, this landmark piazza was laid out as part of Rome's 19th-century post-unification makeover. It follows the lines of the semicircular *exedra* (benched portico) of Diocletian's baths complex and was originally known as Piazza Esedra.

★ Museo Nazionale Romano: Palazzo Massimo alle Terme   MUSEUM

(Map p94; ☑ 06 3996 7700; www.coopculture.it; Largo di Villa Peretti 1; adult/reduced €7/3.50; ⊙ 9am-7.45pm Tue-Sun; M Termini) One of Rome's great unsung heroes, this fabulous museum is a treasure trove of classical art and sculpture. The ground and 1st floors are devoted to sculpture, with some breathtaking pieces. These include the 2nd-century BC Greek bronze, the *Pugile* (Boxer), a crouching Aphrodite from Villa Adriana, the graceful 2nd-century BC *Ermafrodite dormiente* (Sleeping Hermaphrodite), and the idealised *Il discobolo* (Discus Thrower).

However, it's the rich, vivid frescoes on the 2nd floor that are the undoubted highlight. These vibrantly coloured panels illustrate a range of natural, mythological, domestic and erotic themes, as appropriate to the rooms they were originally placed in. There are intimate cubicula (bedroom) frescoes featuring religious, erotic and theatrical subjects, and delicate landscape paintings from the triclinium (dining room). Particularly breathtaking are the frescoes (dating from 30 BC to 20 BC) from Villa Livia, one of the homes of Augustus' wife Livia Drusilla. These cover an entire room and depict a paradisiacal garden full of roses, pomegranates, irises and camomile under a deep-blue sky. They once decorated a summer triclinium, a large living and dining area that had been built half underground to provide protection from the heat.

There are also some exquisitely fine mosaics and rare inlay work on this floor.

In the basement, the unexciting sounding coin collection is far more absorbing than

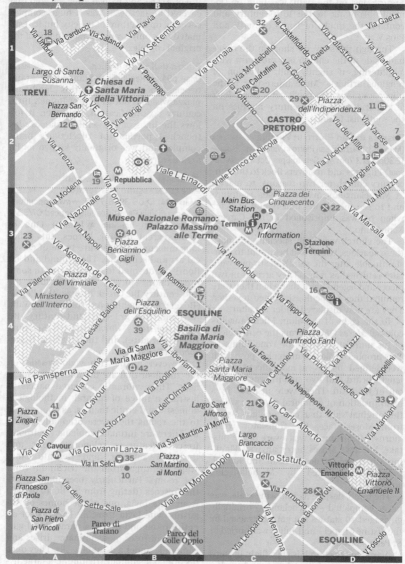

you might expect, tracing the Roman Empire's propaganda offensive through its coins. There's also jewellery dating back several millennia, and the disturbing remains of a mummified eight-year-old girl.

Museo Nazionale Romano: Terme di Diocleziano
MUSEUM

(Map p94; ☏06 3996 7700; www.coopculture.it; Viale Enrico de Nicola 78; adult/reduced €7/3.50; ☺9am-7.30pm Tue-Sun; ⓜTermini) The 3rd-century Terme di Diocleziano was ancient

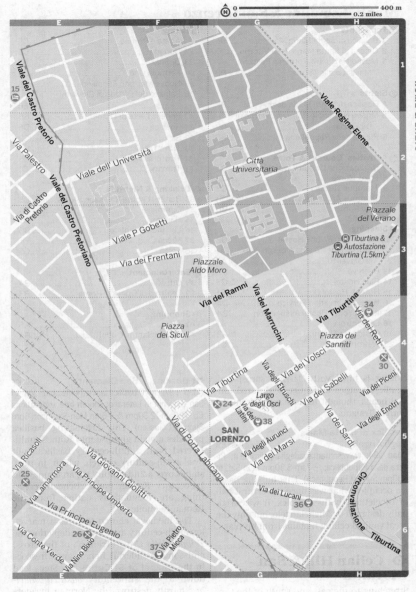

Rome's largest bath complex, covering 13 hectares and accommodating up to 3000 people. Today its ruins house part of the Museo Nazionale Romano. The collection of memorial inscriptions and ancient artefacts provides a fascinating insight into the struc-ture of Roman society, with exhibits relating to cults and the development of Christianity and Judaism.

Upstairs, you can study tomb finds dating from the 11th to 9th centuries BC, whilst outside, the elegant Michelangelo-designed

Monti, Esquiline & San Lorenzo

cloister is lined with classical sarcophagi, headless statues and huge sculptured animal heads, thought to have come from the Foro di Traiano.

Basilica di Santa Maria degli Angeli BASILICA
(Map p94; www.santamariadegliangeliroma.it; Piazza della Repubblica; ⊙ 7am-8.30pm Mon-Sat, to 7.30pm Sun; Ⓜ Repubblica) This hulking basilica occupies what was once the central hall of Diocletian's baths complex. It was originally designed by Michelangelo, but only the great vaulted ceiling remains from his plans.

⊙ Celian Hill & San Giovanni

Stretching to the east and south of the Colosseum, this extensive and oft-overlooked area boasts a couple of Rome's most interesting churches – the landmark Basilica di San Giovanni in Laterano and the Basilica di San Clemente – and some superb ancient ruins.

★**Basilica di San Clemente** BASILICA
(Map p97; www.basilicasanclemente.com; Via di San Giovanni in Laterano; church free, excavations €5; ⊙ 9am-12.30pm & 3-6pm Mon-Sat, noon-6pm Sun; Ⓜ Colosseo) This fascinating basilica provides a vivid glimpse into Rome's multi-layered past: a 12th-century basilica built over a 4th-century church, which, in turn, stands over a 2nd-century pagan temple and 1st-century Roman house. Beneath everything are foundations dating from the Roman Republic.

The medieval church features a marvellous 12th-century apse mosaic depicting the *Trionfo della Croce* (Triumph of the Cross) and some wonderful Renaissance frescoes in the Chapel of St Catherine. Steps lead down to the 4th-century *basilica inferiore*, mostly destroyed by Norman invaders in 1084, but with some faded 11th-century frescoes illustrating the life of San Clemente. Follow the steps down another level and you'll come to a 1st-century Roman house and a dark, 2nd-century temple to Mithras, with an altar showing the god slaying a bull.

Celian Hill & San Giovanni

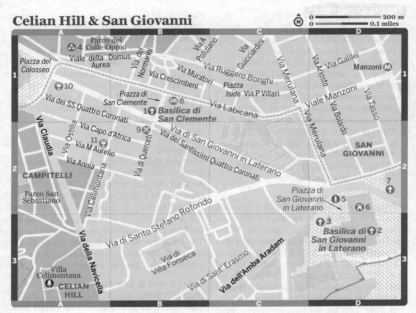

Celian Hill & San Giovanni

Beneath it all, you can hear the eerie sound of a subterranean river, running through a drain dating from the Roman Republic.

★ Basilica di San Giovanni in Laterano

BASILICA

(Map p97; Piazza di San Giovanni in Laterano 4; basilica free, cloister €3; ⊙7am-6.30pm, cloister 9am-6pm; Ⓜ San Giovanni) For a thousand years this monumental cathedral was the most important church in Christendom. Commissioned by the Emperor Constantine and consecrated in AD 324, it was the first Christian basilica built in the city and, until the late 14th century, was the pope's main place of worship. It is still Rome's official cathedral and the pope's seat as the bishop of Rome.

Surmounted by fifteen 7m-high statues – Christ with St John the Baptist, John the Evangelist and the 12 Apostles – Alessandro Galilei's huge white facade is a mid-18th-century example of late-baroque classicism. The central bronze doors were moved here from the Curia in the Roman Forum, while on the far right, the carved Holy Door is only opened in Jubilee years.

The interior has been revamped on numerous occasions, although it owes much of its present look to Francesco Borromini who redecorated it for the 1650 Jubilee. It's a breathtaking sight with a spectacular gilt

THROUGH THE KEYHOLE

Head up to the Aventine Hill for one of Rome's best views. On the ornate cypress-shaded **Piazza dei Cavalieri di Malta** (Map p134; Via di Santa Sabina; ⓘ Lungotevere Aventino) stands the **Priorato dei Cavalieri di Malta**, the Roman headquarters of the *Cavalieri di Malta* (Knights of Malta). The building is closed to the public, but look through its keyhole and you'll see the dome of St Peter's perfectly aligned at the end of a hedge-lined avenue.

ceiling, a beautiful 15th-century **mosaic floor**, and a wide central nave lined with 4.6m-high sculptures of the apostles. At the head of the nave, the Gothic **baldachin** over the papal altar is a dramatic work containing the relics of the heads of saints Peter and Paul. In front of the altar, a double staircase leads down to the **confessio**, which houses the Renaissance tomb of Pope Martin V.

Behind the altar, the massive apse is decorated with sparkling mosaics, parts of which date to the 4th century, but most of which was added in the 19th century.

On the first pilaster in the right-hand nave is an incomplete **Giotto fresco**. While admiring it, cock your ear towards the next pilaster, where a monument to Pope Sylvester II (r 999–1003) is said to sweat and creak when the death of a pope is imminent.

To the left of the altar, the beautiful 13th-century **cloister** is a lovely, peaceful place with graceful Cosmatesque twisted columns set around a central garden.

Palazzo Laterano   PALACE
(Map p97; Piazza di San Giovanni in Laterano; Ⓜ San Giovanni) Flanking Piazza San Giovanni in Laterano, itself dominated by Rome's oldest and tallest **obelisk** (Map p97), is Domenico Fontana's 16th-century Palazzo Laterano. Part of the original 4th-century basilica complex, it was the official papal residence until the papacy moved to the Vatican in 1377, and today houses the diocese of Rome.

Battistero   CHAPEL
(Baptistry; Map p97; Piazza di San Giovanni in Laterano; ⊙ 7am-12.30pm & 4-7pm; Ⓜ San Giovanni) Around the corner from the Basilica di San Giovanni in Laterano is the fascinating octagonal *battistero*. Built by Constantine in the 4th century, it served as the prototype for later Christian churches and bell towers. The chief interest, apart from the architecture, are the decorative mosaics, some of which date to the 5th century.

Scala Santa & Sancta Sanctorum   CHAPEL
(Map p97; Piazza di San Giovanni in Laterano 14; Scala free, Sancta €3.50; ⊙ Scala 6.15am-noon & 3.30-6.30pm summer, 6.15am-noon & 3-6pm winter, Sancta Sanctorum 9.30am-noon & 3-5pm, closed Wed am & Sun year-round; Ⓜ San Giovanni) Brought to Rome by St Helena in the 4th century, the Scala Santa is said to be the staircase that Jesus walked up in Pontius Pilate's palace in Jerusalem. Pilgrims consider it sacred and climb it on their knees, saying a prayer on each of the 28 steps. At the top, the richly frescoed Sancta Sanctorum (Holy of Holies) was formerly the pope's private chapel.

TERME DI CARACALLA

The remnants of emperor Caracalla's vast baths complex **Terme di Caracalla** (📞 06 3996 7700; www.coopculture.it; Viale delle Terme di Caracalla 52; adult/reduced €7/4; ⊙ 9am-1hr before sunset Tue-Sun, 9am-2pm Mon ; ⓘ Viale delle Terme di Caracalla) are among Rome's most awe-inspiring ruins. Inaugurated in 216, the 10-hectare complex comprised baths, gymnasiums, libraries, shops and gardens, and was used by up to 8000 people every day. Underground, slaves sweated in 9.5km of tunnels, tending to the plumbing systems.

Most of what you see today are the remains of the central **bath house**, a huge edifice that measured 218m by 112m. You can also visit the **tunnels** and a recently opened **underground temple** (Mithraeum), dedicated to the Persian god Mithras.

In summer the ruins are used to stage spectacular opera performances.

❶ APPIA ANTICA TIPS

The **Appia Antica Regional Park Information Point** (📞 06 513 53 16; www.par-coappiaantica.it; Via Appia Antica 58-60; ⏱ 9.30am-1pm & 2-5.30pm Mon-Fri, to 5pm winter, 9.30am-6.30pm Sat & Sun, to 5pm winter) sells maps of the park and hires bikes (per hour/day €3/10) and electric bikes (€6/20). It also runs guided tours in English, Spanish and German – book by email at least two weeks before your arrival.

➡ Sunday is a good day to visit as the road is closed to traffic. On other days, the section from Porta San Sebastian for about three miles is not pedestrian-friendly.

➡ The Appia Antica Card (p73) gives admission to the Mausoleo di Cecilia Metella, the Terme di Caracalla and Villa dei Quintili.

➡ To get to Via Appia Antica, catch bus 218 from Piazza di San Giovanni in Laterano, bus 660 from the Colli Albani stop on metro A, or bus 118 from the Piramide stop on metro B.

➡ From Termini, the hop-on, hop-off Archeobus (p118) serves Via Appia Antica, stopping at points of archaeological interest along the way.

◉ Southern Rome

Southern Rome is an extensive and multifaceted neighbourhood that comprises several distinct areas: Via Appia Antica, famous for its catacombs; San Paolo, home of one of the city's great patriarchal basilicas; trendy Via Ostiense, with its cool clubs and post-industrial grit; and EUR, Mussolini's futuristic building development.

Basilica di San Paolo Fuori le Mura BASILICA (www.abbaziasanpaolo.net; Via Ostiense 190; cloisters €4; ⏱ 7am-6.30pm; Ⓜ San Paolo) The largest church in Rome after St Peter's (and therefore the world's third-largest), this magnificent basilica stands on the site where St Paul was buried after being decapitated in AD 67. Built by Constantine in the 4th century, it was largely destroyed by fire in 1823 and much of what you see is a 19th-century reconstruction.

However, many treasures survived, including the 5th-century **triumphal arch**, with its heavily restored mosaics, and the Gothic marble **tabernacle** over the high altar. This was designed around 1285 by Arnolfo di Cambio together with another artist, possibly Pietro Cavallini. To the right of the altar, the elaborate Romanesque Paschal candlestick was fashioned by Nicolò di Angelo and Pietro Vassalletto in the 12th century and features a grim cast of animal-headed creatures. St Paul's tomb is in the nearby **confessio**.

Looking upwards, doom-mongers should check out the papal portraits beneath the nave windows. Every pope since St Peter is represented and legend has it that when there is no room for the next portrait, the world will fall. There are eight places left.

Also well worth a look is the stunning 13th-century Cosmati mosaic work in the **cloisters** of the adjacent Benedictine abbey.

★**Via Appia Antica** HISTORIC SITE (Appian Way; ⬚ Via Appia Antica) Named after consul Appius Claudius Caecus who laid the first 90km section in 312 BC, ancient Rome's *regina viarum* (queen of roads) was extended in 190 BC to reach Brindisi on Italy's southern Adriatic coast. Nowadays, Via Appia Antica (the Appian Way) is one of Rome's most exclusive addresses, a beautiful cobbled thoroughfare flanked by grassy fields, ancient ruins and towering pine trees.

But it has a dark history – it was here that Spartacus and 6000 of his slave rebels were crucified in 71 BC, and it was here that the early Christians buried their dead in 300km of **underground catacombs**. You can't visit all 300km, but three major catacombs (San Callisto, San Sebastiano and Santa Domitilla) are open for guided exploration.

Chiesa del Domine Quo Vadis? CHURCH (Via Appia Antica 51; ⏱ 8am-6.30pm Mon-Fri, 8.15am-6.45pm Sat & Sun winter, to 7.30pm summer; ⬚ Via Appia Antica) This pint-sized church marks the spot where St Peter, fleeing Rome, met a vision of Jesus going the other way. When Peter asked: '*Domine, quo vadis?*' (Lord, where are you going?), Jesus replied, '*Venio Roman iterum crucifigi*' (I am coming to Rome to be crucified again). Reluctantly deciding to join him, Peter tramped

Appia Antica

Chiesa del Domine Quo Vadis? (1km);
Appia Antica Regional Park
Information Point (1.3km)

ROME & LAZIO ROME

Appia Antica

◎ Top Sights
1 Catacombe di San Sebastiano............C1

◎ Sights
Basilica di San Sebastiano..........(see 1)
2 Catacombe di San Callisto.................C1
3 Catacombe di Santa Domitilla............A1
4 Circo di Massenzio...............................D2
5 Mausoleo di Cecilia Metella.................D2
6 Mausoleo di Romolo.............................C2
7 Villa di Massenzio C2

back into town where he was arrested and
executed.

Catacombe di San Callisto CATACOMB
(Map p100; ☑ 06 513 01 51; www.catacombe.roma.
it; Via Appia Antica 110 & 126; adult/reduced €8/5;
⊙9am-noon & 2-5pm, closed Wed mid-Jan–mid-
Feb; ☐Via Appia Antica) These are the largest
and busiest of Rome's catacombs. Founded
at the end of the 2nd century and named after Pope Calixtus I, they became the official
cemetery of the newly established Roman
Church. In the 20km of tunnels explored to
date, archaeologists have found the tombs of
500,000 people and seven popes who were
martyred in the 3rd century.

The patron saint of music, St Cecilia, was
also buried here, though her body was later
removed to the Basilica di Santa Cecilia in
Trastevere. When her body was exhumed
in 1599, more than a thousand years after her death, it was apparently perfectly
preserved.

★**Catacombe di
San Sebastiano** CATACOMB
(Map p100; ☑ 06 785 03 50; www.catacombe.org;
Via Appia Antica 136; adult/reduced €8/5; ⊙10am-
5pm Mon-Sat, closed mid-Nov–mid-Dec; ☐Via Appia Antica) The Catacombe di San Sebastiano
were the first burial chambers to be called
catacombs, the name deriving from the
Greek *kata* (near) and *kymbas* (cavity), because they were located near a cave. During
the persecutory reign of Vespasian, they provided a safe haven for the remains of Saints
Peter and Paul.

The first level is now almost completely
destroyed, but frescoes, stucco work and epigraphs can be seen on the 2nd level. There
are also three perfectly preserved mausole-
ums and a plastered wall with hundreds of
invocations to Peter and Paul, engraved by
worshippers in the 3rd and 4th centuries.

Above the catacombs, the **Basilica di San
Sebastiano** (Via Appia Antica 136; ⊙8am-1pm
& 2-5.30pm daily; ☐Via Appia Antica), a much-
altered 4th-century church, preserves one
of the arrows allegedly used to kill St Sebastian, and the column to which he was tied.

Catacombe di Santa Domitilla CATACOMB
(Map p100; ☑ 06 511 03 42; www.domitilla.info; Via
delle Sette Chiese 283; adult/reduced €8/5; ⊙9am-
noon & 2-5pm Wed-Mon, closed Jan; ☐Via Appia
Antica) Among Rome's largest and oldest,
these wonderful catacombs stretch for about
18km. They were established on the private
burial ground of Flavia Domitilla, niece of
the emperor Domitian and a member of
the wealthy Flavian family. They contain
Christian wall paintings and the haunting

underground **Chiesa di SS Nereus e Achilleus**, a 4th-century church dedicated to two Roman soldiers martyred by Diocletian.

Villa di Massenzio RUIN

(Map p100; ☑06 780 13 24; www.villadimassenzio.it; Via Appia Antica 153; adult/reduced €5/4; ◎9am-4pm Tue-Sat; 🚊Via Appia Antica) The outstanding feature of Maxentius' enormous 4th-century palace complex is the **Circo di Massenzio** (Map p100), Rome's best-preserved ancient racetrack – you can still make out the starting stalls used for chariot races. The 10,000-seat arena was built by Maxentius around 309, but he died before ever seeing a race here.

Above the arena are the ruins of Maxentius' imperial residence, most of which are covered by weeds. Near the racetrack, the **Mausoleo di Romolo** (Tombo di Romolo; Map p100) was built by Maxentius for his son Romulus. The huge mausoleum was originally crowned with a large dome and surrounded by an imposing colonnade, in part still visible.

Mausoleo di Cecilia Metella RUIN

(Map p100; ☑06 3996 7700; www.coopculture.it; Via Appia Antica 161; admission incl Terme di Caracalla & Villa dei Quintili adult/reduced €7/4; ◎9am-1hr before sunset Tue-Sun; 🚊Via Appia Antica) Dating to the 1st century BC, this great drum of a mausoleum encloses a now roofless burial chamber built for the daughter of the consul Quintus Metellus Creticus. The walls are made of travertine and the interior is decorated with a sculpted frieze featuring Gaelic shields, ox skulls and festoons. In the 14th century it was converted into a fort by the Caetani family, who used to frighten passing traffic into paying a toll.

Villa dei Quintili RUIN

(☑06 3996 7700; www.coopculture.it; Via Appia Nuova 1092; adult/reduced incl Terme di Caracalla & Mausoleo di Cecilia Metella €7/4; ◎9am-1hr before sunset Tue-Sun; 🚊Via Appia Nuova) This vast 2nd-century villa was the luxurious abode of two consuls under the emperor Marcus Aurelius. Its highlight is the well-preserved baths complex with a pool, *caldarium* (hot room) and *frigidarium* (cold room).

EUR NEIGHBOURHOOD

(Ⓜ EUR Palasport) This Orwellian quarter of wide boulevards and linear buildings was built for an international exhibition in 1942 and, although war intervened and the exhibition never took place, the name stuck – Esposizione Universale di Roma (Roman Universal Exhibition) or EUR.

The area's main interest lies in its rationalist architecture, which finds perfect form in the **Palazzo della Civiltà del Lavoro** (Palace of the Workers; Quadrato della Concordia; Ⓜ EUR Magliana), aka the Square Colosseum, a 50m-high tower interspersed by rows of orderly arches.

Of EUR's museums, the best is the **Museo della Civiltà Romana** (☑06 06 08; Piazza G Agnelli 10; adult/reduced €7.50/5.50, incl Museo Astronomico & Planetario €9.50/7.50; ◎9am-2pm Tue-Sun; Ⓜ EUR Fermi), a possible kid-pleaser with models of Roman statues and a fascinating room-size re-creation of 4th-century Rome.

⊙ Trastevere & Gianicolo

Over the river from the *centro storico* – hence its name, a derivation of the Latin *trans Tiberim* or across the Tiber – Trastevere is one of Rome's prettiest and most

ROME & LAZIO SIGHTS

THE CATACOMBS

Built as communal burial grounds, the catacombs were the early Christians' solution to the problem of what to do with their dead. Belief in the Resurrection meant that they couldn't cremate their corpses, as was the custom at the time, and Roman law forbade burial within the city walls. Furthermore, as a persecuted minority they didn't have their own cemeteries. So, in the 2nd century they began to dig beneath Via Appia Antica, where a number of converted Christians already had family tombs.

Over time, as Christianity became more popular, competition for burial space became fierce and a cut-throat trade in tomb real estate developed. However, by the late 4th century, Christianity had been legalised and the Christians had begun to bury their dead near the basilicas that were springing up within the city walls. By the Middle Ages the catacombs had been all but abandoned.

More than 30 catacombs have been uncovered in the Rome area since scholars started researching them in the 19th century.

Trastevere & Gianicolo

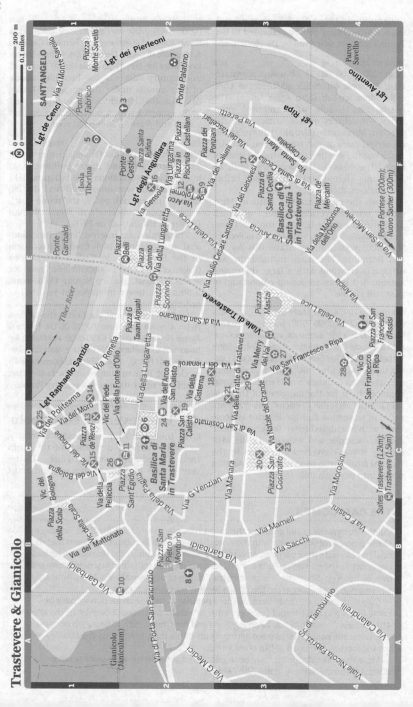

200 m
0.1 miles

Trastevere & Gianicolo

vibrant neighbourhoods, an atmospheric warren of picture-perfect cobbled lanes and colourful *palazzi*. It was originally a bastion of working-class independence and while it retains a strong sense of its roots, it's now a trendy hang-out full of restaurants, cafes, pubs and pizzerias.

Behind it, the Gianicolo (Janiculum) Hill rises serenely above the maelstrom offering incredible bird's-eye views of Rome.

Piazza Santa Maria in Trastevere   PIAZZA
(Map p102; 🚋 Viale di Trastevere, 🚋 Viale di Traste-vere) Trastevere's focal square is a prime people-watching spot. By day it's full of mums with strollers, chatting locals and guidebook-toting tourists; by night it's the domain of foreign students, young Romans and out-of-towners, all in search of a good time. The fountain in the centre is of Roman origin and was restored by Carlo Fontana in 1692.

★ Basilica di Santa Maria
in Trastevere   BASILICA
(Map p102; Piazza Santa Maria in Trastevere; ⊗7.30am-9pm; 🚋 Viale di Trastevere, 🚋 Viale di Trastevere) This glittering basilica is said to be the oldest church in Rome dedicated to the Virgin Mary. Dating to the early 3rd century, it stands on the spot where, according to legend, a fountain of oil miraculously sprang from the ground. Its current form is

the result of a major overhaul in 1138 that saw the addition of a Romanesque bell tower and glittering facade. The portico came later, added by Carlo Fontana in 1702.

Inside, the 12th-century **mosaics** are the headline feature. In the apse, look out for a dazzling gold depiction of Christ and his mother flanked by various saints, and, on the far left, Pope Innocent II holding a model of the church. Beneath this are six mosaics by Pietro Cavallini (c 1291) illustrating the life of the Virgin.

The building itself incorporates 21 ancient Roman columns, some from the Terme di Caracalla, and its wooden ceiling dates from the 17th century.

Villa Farnesina   HISTORIC BUILDING
(Map p80; ☑ 06 6802 7268; Via della Lungara 230; adult/reduced €5/4; ⊗9am-5pm Mon & Sat, 10am-2pm Tue-Fri, 9am-5pm 2nd Sun of month; 🚋 Lgt della Farnesina, 🚋 Viale di Trastevere) This gorgeous 16th-century villa is famous for its stunning frescoes. The most celebrated, in the Loggia of Cupid and Psyche, are attributed to Raphael, who also painted the *Trionfo di Galatea* (Triumph of Galatea) in the room of the same name. On the 1st floor, Peruzzi's dazzling frescoes in the Salone delle Prospettive are a superb illusionary perspective of a colonnade and panorama of 16th-century Rome.

Galleria Nazionale d'Arte Antica di Palazzo Corsini GALLERY

(Map p80; ☎06 6880 2323; galleriacorsini. beniculturali.it/; Via della Lungara 10; adult/reduced €5/2.50, incl Palazzo Barberini €9/4.50; ⏰ 8.30am-7.30pm Tue-Sun; 🚊 Lgt della Farnesina, 🚊 Viale di Trastevere) Once home to Queen Christina of Sweden, whose richly frescoed bedroom witnessed a stready stream of male and female lovers, the 16th-century Palazzo Corsini houses part of Italy's national art collection. Highlights include Caravaggio's mesmerising *San Giovanni Battista* (St John the Baptist) and Rubens' *Testa di Vecchio* (Head of an Old Man).

Tempietto di Bramante & Chiesa di San Pietro in Montorio CHURCH

(Map p102; www.sanpietroinmontorio.it; Piazza San Pietro in Montorio 2; ⏰ Chiesa 8.30am-noon & 3-4pm Mon-Fri, Tempietto 9.30am-12.30pm & 2-4.30pm Tue-Sun; 🚊 Via Garibaldi) Considered the first great building of the High Renaissance, Bramante's sublime Tempietto (Little Temple; 1508) stands in the courtyard of the Chiesa di San Pietro in Montorio, on the spot where St Peter is said to have been crucified. It's a small building with a circular interior surrounded by 16 columns and capped by a proportionally perfect dome. Bernini added a staircase in 1628, as well as a chapel to the adjacent church.

It's quite a climb uphill to get to the church but you can cheat by taking bus 870 from Via Paola just off Corso Vittorio Emanuele II.

★ Basilica di Santa Cecilia in Trastevere BASILICA

(Map p102; Piazza di Santa Cecilia; basilica free, fresco & crypt each €2.50; ⏰ basilica & crypt 9.30am-2.30pm & 4-7.30pm, fresco 10am-2.30pm Mon-Sat; 🚊 Viale di Trastevere, 🚊 Viale di Trastevere) This is the last resting place of St Cecilia, the patron saint of music who was martyred here in AD 230. It features a stunning 13th-century fresco by Pietro Cavallini in the nun's choir, and, in the main body of the basilica, an exquisite sculpture by Stefano Moderno showing exactly how St Cecilia's miraculously preserved body was found in the Catacombe di San Callisto in 1599.

You can also visit the excavations of Roman houses beneath the church, one of which was possibly St Cecilia's.

Chiesa di San Francesco d'Assisi a Ripa CHURCH

(Map p102; Piazza San Francesco d'Assisi 88; ⏰ 7.30am-noon & 2-7.30pm; 🚊 Viale di Trastevere, 🚊 Viale di Trastevere) St Francis is said to have stayed here in the 13th century, and you can still see the rock that he used as a pillow. The church's chief attraction, though, is Bernini's *Beata Ludovica Albertoni* (Blessed Ludovica Albertoni; 1674), a work of highly charged sexual ambiguity that shows Ludovica, a Franciscan nun, in a state of rapture as she reclines, eyes shut, mouth open, one hand touching her breast.

⊙ Vatican City, Borgo & Prati

The Vatican, the world's smallest sovereign state (a mere 0.44 sq km), sits atop the low-lying Vatican hill just a few hundred metres west of the Tiber. Centred on the domed bulk of St Peter's Basilica, it is the capital of the Catholic world and jealous guardian of one of the world's greatest artistic patrimonies.

The state, established under the terms of the 1929 Lateran Treaty, is the modern vestige of the Papal States, the papal fiefdom that ruled Rome and much of central Italy until unification in 1861. As part of the agreement, signed by Mussolini and Pope Pius XI, the Holy See was also given extra-territorial authority over a further 28 sites in and around Rome, including the basilicas of San Giovanni in Laterano, Santa Maria Maggiore and San Paolo Fuori le Mura.

As an independent state, the Vatican has its own postal service, newspaper, radio station and army. The nattily dressed Swiss Guards, all practising Catholics from Switzerland, were first used by Pope Julius II in 1506 and are still responsible for the pope's personal security.

The Vatican's current look is the culmination of more than 1000 years of chipping and chopping. The Leonine walls date from 846 when Leo IV had them put up after a series of Saracen raids, while the Vatican palace, now home to the Vatican Museums, was originally constructed by Eugenius III in the 12th century.

Between the Vatican and the river lies the cobbled, medieval district of the Borgo, while to the north, Prati is a graceful residential area.

★ **St Peter's Basilica** BASILICA

(Map p106; www.vatican.va; St Peter's Square; ⊘7am-7pm Apr-Sep, to 6.30pm Oct-Mar; Ⓜ Ottaviano–San Pietro) **FREE** In this city of outstanding churches, none can hold a candle to St Peter's Basilica (Basilica di San Pietro), Italy's largest, richest and most spectacular church. A monument to centuries of artistic genius, it contains some spectacular works of art, including three of Italy's most celebrated masterpieces: Michelangelo's *Pietà*, his breathtaking dome, and Bernini's baldachin over the papal altar.

It's also one of Rome's busiest tourist attractions, drawing up to 20,000 people on a busy day. So expect queues and remember to dress appropriately – no shorts, miniskirts or bare shoulders.

The original basilica was commissioned by the emperor Constantine and built around 349 on the site where St Peter is said to have been buried between AD 64 and 67. But like many medieval churches, it eventually fell into disrepair and it wasn't until the mid-15th century that efforts were made to restore it, first by Pope Nicholas V and then, rather more successfully, by Julius II.

In 1506 Bramante came up with a design for a basilica based on a Greek-cross plan, with four equal arms and a huge central dome. But on Bramante's death in 1514, construction work ground to a halt as architects, including Raphael and Antonio da Sangallo, tried to modify his original plans. Little progress was made and it wasn't until Michelangelo took over in 1547 at the age of 72 that the situation changed. Michelangelo simplified Bramante's plans and drew up designs for what was to become his greatest architectural achievement, the dome. He never lived to see it built, though, and it was left to Giacomo della Porta and Domenico Fontana to finish it in 1590.

With the dome in place, Carlo Maderno inherited the project in 1605. He designed the monumental facade and lengthened the nave towards the piazza.

Free English-language tours of the basilica are run from the Vatican tourist office, the Centro Servizi Pellegrini e Turisti, at 9.45am on Tuesday and Thursday and at 2.15pm every afternoon between Monday and Friday.

THE FACADE

Built between 1608 and 1612, Carlo Maderno's immense facade is 48m high and 118.6m wide. Eight 27m-high columns support the

ⓘ QUEUE JUMPING AT THE VATICAN MUSEUMS

Here's how to jump the ticket queue – although we can't help with lines for the security checks.

➡ Book **tickets online** (http:// biglietteriamusei.vatican.va/musei/ tickets/do). On payment, you'll receive email confirmation that you should print and present, along with valid ID, at the museum entrance. Note that tickets bought online incur a €4 booking fee. You can also book **guided tours** (adult/reduced €32/24) online.

➡ Time your visit: Tuesday and Thursday are the quietest days. Wednesday morning is also good as everyone is at the pope's weekly audience. Afternoons are better than mornings. Avoid Monday when many other museums are shut.

➡ Book a tour with a reputable guide.

upper attic on which 13 statues stand representing Christ the Redeemer, St John the Baptist and the 11 apostles. The central balcony is known as the **Loggia della Benedizione**, and it's from here that the pope delivers his *Urbi et Orbi* blessing at Christmas and Easter.

INTERIOR

The cavernous 187m-long interior covers more than 15,000 sq metres and contains many spectacular works of art, including Michelangelo's hauntingly beautiful **Pietà** at the head of the right nave. Sculpted when he was only 25, it is the only work he ever signed – his signature is etched into the sash across the Madonna's breast.

Nearby, the **red disc** just inside the main door marks the spot where Charlemagne and later Holy Roman Emperors were crowned by the pope.

Dominating the centre of the basilica is Bernini's 29m-high **baldachin**. Supported by four spiral columns and made with bronze taken from the Pantheon, it stands over the high altar, which itself sits on the site of St Peter's grave. The pope is the only priest permitted to serve at the high altar.

Above, Michelangelo's **dome** soars to a height of 119m. Based on Brunelleschi's design for the Duomo in Florence, the towering cupola is supported by four solid

Vatican City, Borgo & Prati

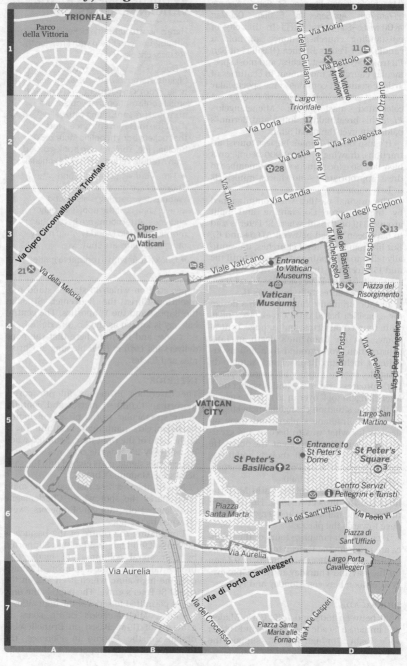

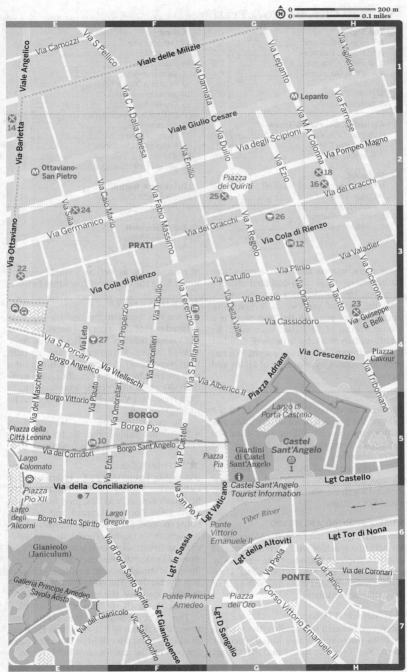

Vatican City, Borgo & Prati

stone piers, named after the saints whose statues adorn the Bernini-designed niches – Longinus, Helena, Veronica and Andrew.

At the base of the Pier of St Longinus, to the right as you face the high altar, is a bronze **statue of St Peter**, believed to be a 13th-century work by Arnolfo di Cambio. It's a much-loved piece and its right foot has been worn down by centuries of kisses and caresses.

DOME
To climb the dome, the entrance is to the right of the basilica. A small lift takes you halfway up, but it's still a long climb to the top (320 steps). Press on, however, and you're rewarded with stunning views. It's well worth the effort, but bear in mind that it's a long and tiring climb and not recommended for those who suffer from claustrophobia or vertigo.

MUSEO STORICO ARTISTICO
Accessed from the left nave, the Museo Storico Artistico sparkles with sacred relics and priceless artefacts, including a tabernacle by Donatello and the 6th-century *Crux Vaticana*, a jewel-studded cross that was a gift of the emperor Justinian II.

VATICAN GROTTOES
Extending beneath the basilica, the Vatican Grottoes were created as a burial place for popes. You'll see the tombs and sarcophagi of many popes, as well as several huge columns from the original 4th-century basilica.

TOMB OF ST PETER
Excavations beneath the basilica have uncovered part of the original church and what the Vatican believes is the Tomb of St Peter. In 1942 the bones of an elderly, strongly built man were found in a box hidden behind a wall covered by pilgrims' graffiti. After more than 30 years of forensic examination, in 1976 Pope Paul VI declared the bones to be those of St Peter.

The excavations can only be visited on a 90-minute guided tour. To book a spot, email the Ufficio Scavi (scavi@fsp.va).

★ **St Peter's Square**   PIAZZA
(Piazza San Pietro; Map p106; ⓂOttaviano–San Pietro) The Vatican's grand central space, St Peter's Square was designed by baroque artist Gian Lorenzo Bernini and laid out between 1656 and 1667. Seen from above, it resembles a giant keyhole with two semicircular colonnades, each consisting of four rows of Doric columns, encircling a giant ellipse that straightens out to funnel believers into the basilica. The effect was deliberate – Bernini described the colonnades as representing 'the motherly arms of the church'.

The 25m obelisk in the centre was brought to Rome by Caligula from Heliopolis in Egypt and later used by Nero as a turning post for the chariot races in his circus.

The scale of the piazza is dazzling: at its largest it measures 340m by 240m. There are 284 columns and, on top of the colonnades, 140 saints. In the midst of all this the pope seems very small as he delivers his weekly address at noon on Sunday.

★ **Vatican Museums**   MUSEUM
(Musei Vaticani; Map p106; ☎ 06 6988 4676; http://mv.vatican.va; Viale Vaticano; adult/reduced €16/8, admission free last Sun of month; ☉ 9am-6pm Mon-Sat, last admission 4pm, 9am-2pm last Sun of month, last admission 12.30pm; Ⓜ Ottaviano–San Pietro) Founded by Pope Julius II in the early 16th century and enlarged by successive pontiffs, the Vatican Museums contain one of the world's greatest art collections, amassed by the popes over the centuries. Exhibits range from Egyptian mummies and Etruscan bronzes to Old Masters and modern paintings, but the main drawcards are the spectacular classical statuary and Michelangelo's frescoes in the Sistine Chapel.

Housing the museums are the lavishly decorated halls and galleries of the Palazzo Apostolico Vaticano. This vast 5.5-hectare complex consists of two palaces – the Vatican palace (nearer to St Peter's) and Belvedere Palace – joined by two long galleries. On the inside are three courtyards: the Cortile della Pigna, the Cortile della Biblioteca and, to the south, the Cortile del Belvedere. You'll never cover it all in one day – there are about 7km of exhibits – so it pays to be selective.

On the whole, exhibits are not well labelled, so consider hiring an audioguide (€7) or buying the *Guide to the Vatican Museums and City* (€14).

The museums are well equipped for visitors with disabilities with suggested itineraries, lifts and specially fitted toilets. Wheelchairs are available free of charge from the Special Permits desk in the entrance hall, and can be reserved by emailing accoglienza.musei@scv.va. Parents with toddlers can take pushchairs (prams) into the museums.

PINACOTECA

Often overlooked by visitors, the papal picture gallery boasts Raphael's last work, *La Trasfigurazione* (Transfiguration; 1517–20), and paintings by Giotto, Bellini, Caravaggio, Fra Angelico, Filippo Lippi, Guido Reni, Van Dyck, Pietro da Cortona and Leonardo da Vinci, whose *San Gerolamo* (St Jerome; c 1480) was never finished.

MUSEO GREGORIANO EGIZIO (EGYPTIAN MUSEUM)

Founded by Gregory XVI in 1839, this museum contains pieces taken from Egypt in Roman times. The collection is small but there are fascinating exhibits including the *Trono di Rameses II*, part of a statue of the seated king, vividly painted sarcophagi dating from around 1000 BC, and some macabre mummies.

MUSEO CHIAROMONTI & BRACCIO NUOVO

The Museo Chiaromonti is effectively the long corridor that runs down the lower east side of the Belvedere Palace. Its walls are lined with thousands of statues representing everything from immortal gods to playful cherubs and ugly Roman patricians. Near the end of the hall, off to the right, is the Braccio Nuovo (New Wing), which contains a famous sculpture of Augustus and a statue depicting the Nile as a reclining god covered by 16 babies.

MUSEO PIO-CLEMENTINO

This stunning museum contains some of the Vatican Museums' finest classical statuary, including the peerless *Apollo Belvedere* and the 1st-century *Laocoön*, both in the Cortile Ottagono (Octagonal Courtyard). Before you go into the courtyard take a moment to admire the 1st-century Apoxyomenos, one of the earliest known sculptures to depict a figure with a raised arm.

To the left as you enter the courtyard, the Apollo Belvedere is a 2nd-century Roman copy of a 4th-century-BC Greek bronze. A beautifully proportioned representation of the sun god Apollo, it's considered one of the great masterpieces of classical sculpture. Nearby, the *Laocoön* depicts a muscular Trojan priest and his two sons in mortal struggle with two sea serpents.

Back inside the museum, the Sala degli Animali is filled with all sorts of sculpted creatures and some magnificent 4th-century mosaics. Continuing through, you come to the Galleria delle Statue, which has several important classical pieces; the Sala delle Buste, which contains hundreds of Roman busts; and the Gabinetto delle Maschere, named after the floor mosaics of theatrical masks. To the east, the Sala delle Muse is centred on the *Torso Belvedere*, another of the museum's must-sees. A fragment of a muscular Greek sculpture from the 1st century BC, it was used by Michelangelo as a model for his *ignudi* in the Sistine Chapel.

The next room, the **Sala Rotonda**, contains a number of colossal statues, including the gilded-bronze figure of an odd-looking *Ercole* (Hercules) and an exquisite floor mosaic. The enormous basin in the centre of the room was found at Nero's Domus Aurea and is made out of a single piece of red porphyry stone.

MUSEO GREGORIANO ETRUSCO

On the upper level of the Belvedere Palace (off the 18th-century Simonetti staircase), the Museo Gregoriano Etrusco contains artefacts unearthed in the Etruscan tombs of northern Lazio, as well as a collection of Greek vases and Roman antiquities. Of particular interest is the *Marte di Todi* (Mars of Todi), a full-length bronze of a warrior dating from the 4th century BC.

GALLERIA DELLE CARTE GEOGRAFICHE (MAP GALLERY)

The last of three galleries – the other two are the **Galleria dei Candelabri** (Gallery of the Candelabra) and the **Galleria degli Arazzi** (Tapestry Gallery) – this 120m-long corridor is hung with 16th-century topographical maps of Italy.

STANZE DI RAFFAELLO (RAPHAEL ROOMS)

These four frescoed chambers were part of Pope Julius II's private apartments. Raphael himself painted the Stanza della Segnatura (1508–11) and the Stanza d'Eliodoro (1512–14), while the Stanza dell'Incendio (1514–17) and Sala di Costantino (1517–24) were decorated by students following his designs.

The first room you come to is the **Sala di Costantino**, which features a huge fresco depicting Constantine's defeat of Maxentius at the battle of Milvian Bridge.

The **Stanza d'Eliodoro**, which was used for private audiences, takes its name from the *Cacciata d'Eliodoro* (Expulsion of Heliodorus from the Temple), an allegorical work reflecting Pope Julius II's policy of forcing foreign powers off Church lands. To its right, the *Messa di Bolsena* (Mass of Bolsena) shows Julius paying homage to the relic of a 13th-century miracle at the lakeside town of Bolsena. Next is the *Incontro di Leone Magno con Attila* (Encounter of Leo the Great with Attila) by Raphael and his school, and, on the fourth wall, the *Liberazione di San Pietro* (Liberation of St Peter), a brilliant

Museum Tour
Vatican Museums

LENGTH THREE HOURS
SEE ALSO VATICAN MUSEUMS (P109)

Follow this three-hour tour to see the museums' greatest hits, culminating in the Sistine Chapel.

Once you've passed through the entrance complex, head up the escalator. At the top, nip out to the terrace for views over St Peter's dome and the Vatican Gardens. Re-enter and go into the **1 Cortile della Pigna**, named after the huge Augustan-era bronze pine cone. Cross the courtyard and enter the long corridor that is the **2 Museo Chiaramonti**. Continue left, up the stairs, to the Museo Pio-Clementino, home of the Vatican's finest classical statuary. Follow the flow of people through to the **3 Cortile Ottagono** (Octagonal Courtyard), where you'll find the celebrated masterpieces, the *Laocoön* and *Apollo Belvedere*.

Continue on through a series of rooms, each more impressive than the last – the **4 Sala degli Animali** (Animal Room), the **5 Sala delle Muse** (Room of the Muses), famous for the *Torso Belvedere*, and the **6 Sala Rotonda** (Round Room) centred on a vast red basin. From the **7 Sala Croce Greca** (Greek Cross Room), stairs lead up to the **8 Galleria dei Candelabri** (Gallery of the Candelabra), the first of three galleries along a lengthy corridor. Then you are funnelled through the **9 Galleria degli Arazzi** (Tapestry Gallery) and onto the **10 Galleria delle Carte Geografiche** (Map Gallery), a 120m-long hall hung with 40 huge maps.

At the end of the corridor, carry on through the **11 Sala Sobieski**, to the **12 Sala di Costantino**, the first of the four Stanze di Raffaello (Raphael Rooms) – the others are the **13 Stanza d'Eliodoro**, the **14 Stanza della Segnatura**, featuring Raphael's superlative *La Scuola di Atene* (The School of Athens), and the **15 Stanza dell'Incendio di Borgo**. Anywhere else these magnificent frescoed chambers would be the star attraction, but here they're the warm-up for the grand finale, the **16 Sistine Chapel**.

VATICAN MUSEUMS

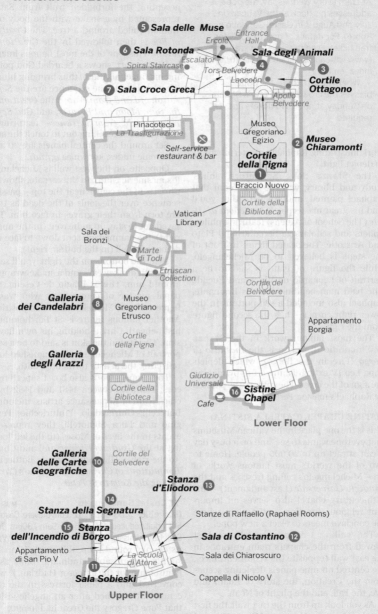

5 Sala delle Muse

Entrance Hall

Ercole

6 Sala Rotonda

Escalator

Spiral Staircase

Sala degli Animali

Tors Belvedere

Laocoon

4

3

Cortile Ottagono

7 Sala Croce Greca

Apollo Belvedere

Pinacoteca
La Trasfigurazione

Museo Gregoriano Egizio

2

Museo Chiaramonti

Self-service restaurant & bar

Cortile della Pigna

1

Braccio Nuovo

Cortile della Biblioteca

Vatican Library

Sala dei Bronzi

Marte di Todi

Etruscan Collection

Cortile del Belvedere

Galleria dei Candelabri

8

Museo Gregoriano Etrusco

Appartamento Borgia

Cortile della Pigna

Galleria degli Arazzi

9

Cortile della Biblioteca

Giudizio Universale

16 **Sistine Chapel**

Cafe

Lower Floor

Galleria delle Carte Geografiche

10

Cortile del Belvedere

Stanza d'Eliodoro **13**

14

Stanza della Segnatura

Stanze di Raffaello (Raphael Rooms)

15 **Stanza dell'Incendio di Borgo**

Sala di Costantino **12**

Appartamento di San Pio V

La Scuola di Atene

Sala dei Chiaroscuro

11

Sala Sobieski

Cappella di Nicolo V

Upper Floor

PAPAL AUDIENCES

At 11am every Wednesday, the pope addresses his flock at the Vatican (in July and August in Castel Gandolfo near Rome). For details of how to apply for free tickets, see the Vatican website (www.vatican.va/various/prefettura/index_en.html).

When he is in Rome, the pope blesses the crowd in St Peter's Square on Sunday at noon. No tickets are required.

work illustrating Raphael's masterful ability to depict light.

The **Stanza della Segnatura**, Julius' study and library, was the first room that Raphael painted, and it's here that you'll find his great masterpiece, *La Scuola di Atene* (The School of Athens) featuring philosophers and scholars gathered around Plato and Aristotle. The seated figure in front of the steps is believed to be Michelangelo, while the figure of Plato is said to be a portrait of Leonardo da Vinci, and Euclide (the bald man bending over) is Bramante. Raphael also included a self-portrait in the lower right corner – he's the second figure from the right.

The most famous work in the **Stanza dell'Incendio di Borgo** is the *Incendio di Borgo* (Fire in the Borgo), which depicts Pope Leo IV extinguishing a fire by making the sign of the cross. The ceiling was painted by Raphael's master, Perugino.

SISTINE CHAPEL (CAPELLA SISTINA)

This is the one place in the Vatican Museums that everone wants to see, and on a busy day it can attract up to 20,000 people. Home to two of the world's most famous works of art – Michelangelo's ceiling frescoes and the *Giudizio Universale* (Last Judgment) – this 15th-century chapel also serves an important religious function as the place where the conclave meets to elect a new pope.

The **ceiling frescoes**, which are best viewed from the chapel's main entrance in the east wall (opposite the visitor entrance), are centred on nine panels depicting scenes from the Creation, the story of Adam and Eve, the Fall, and the plight of Noah.

As you look up from the east wall, the first panel is the *Drunkenness of Noah*, followed by the *Flood*, and *Noah's Sacrifice*. Next, the *Temptation and Expulsion of Adam and Eve from the Garden of Eden* famously depicts Adam and Eve being sent packing after accepting the forbidden fruit from Satan, represented by a snake with the body of a woman coiled around a tree. The *Creation of Eve* is then followed by the *Creation of Adam*. This, one of the most famous images in Western art, shows a bearded God pointing his finger at Adam, thus bringing him to life. Completing the sequence are the *Separation of Land from Water*; the *Creation of the Sun, Moon and Planets*; and *God Separating Light from Darkness*, featuring a fearsome God reaching out to touch the sun.

Set around the central panels are 20 athletic male nudes, known as *ignudi*.

Opposite, on the west wall is Michelangelo's mesmeric **Giudizio Universale**, showing Christ – in the centre near the top – passing sentence over the souls of the dead as they are torn from their graves to face him. The saved get to stay up in heaven (in the upper right), the damned are sent down to face the demons in hell (in the bottom right).

Near the bottom, on the right, you'll see a man with donkey ears and a snake wrapped around him. This is Biagio de Cesena, the papal master of ceremonies, who was a fierce critic of Michelengelo's composition. Another famous figure is St Bartholomew, just beneath Christ, holding his own flayed skin. The face in the skin is said to be a self-portrait of Michelangelo, its anguished look reflecting the artist's tormented faith.

The chapel's **walls** also boast superb frescoes. Painted between 1481 and 1482 by a crack team of Renaissance artists, including Botticelli, Ghirlandaio, Pinturicchio, Perugino and Luca Signorelli, they represent events in the lives of Moses (to the left looking at the *Giudizio Universale*) and Christ (to the right). Highlights include Botticelli's *Temptations of Christ* and Perugino's *Christ Giving the Keys to St Peter*.

⭐ **Castel Sant'Angelo**   MUSEUM
(Map p106; ☎ 06 681 91 11; Lungotevere Castello 50; adult/reduced €8.50/6; ☺ 9am-7.30pm Tue-Sun, last admission 6.30pm ; ▣ Piazza Pia) With its chunky round keep, this castle is an instantly recognisable landmark. Built as a mausoleum for the emperor Hadrian, it was converted into a papal fortress in the 6th century and named after an angelic vision that Pope Gregory the Great had in 590.

Thanks to a secret 13th-century passageway to the Vatican palaces (the Passetto di

Borgo), it provided sanctuary to many popes in times of danger. Most famously, Pope Clemente VI holed up here during the 1527 sack of Rome. Nowadays, it houses an eclectic collection of paintings, sculpture, military memorabilia and medieval firearms.

The upper floors are filled with lavishly decorated Renaissance interiors, including the beautifully frescoed Sala Paolina. Two stories further up, the terrace, immortalised by Puccini in his opera *Tosca*, commands great views over Rome.

Ponte Sant'Angelo   BRIDGE

(Map p80; 🚇Piazza Pia) The emperor Hadrian built Ponte Sant'Angelo in 136 to provide an approach to his mausoleum (now Castel Sant'Angelo), but it was Bernini who brought it to life with his angel sculptures in the 17th century.

👁 Villa Borghese & Northern Rome

This large and attractive area boasts some wonderful art galleries and museums. In the midst of everything, the Villa Borghese park provides a welcome green haven from all the bustle of the city centre.

★ **Museo e Galleria Borghese**   MUSEUM
(Map p113; 📞06 3 28 10; www.galleriaborghese.it; Piazzale del Museo Borghese 5; adult/reduced €9/4.50, plus €2 booking fee and possible exhibition supplement; ⏰9am-7pm Tue-Sun, pre-booking necessary; 🚇Via Pinciana) If you only have time (or inclination) for one art gallery in Rome, make it this one. Housing the 'queen of all private art collections', it provides the perfect introduction to Renaissance and baroque art without ever being overwhelming. To limit numbers, visitors are admitted at two-hourly intervals, so you'll need to pre-book.

The collection, which includes paintings by Caravaggio, Botticelli and Raphael,

Villa Borghese

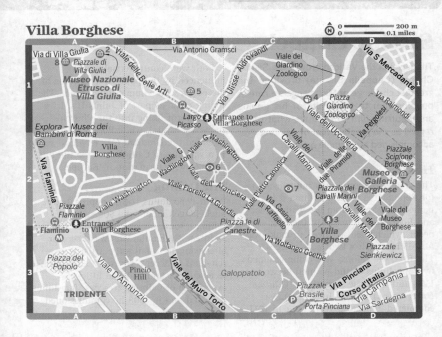

Villa Borghese

Sistine Chapel

The jewel in the Vatican crown, the Sistine Chapel (Cappella Sistina) provided the greatest challenge of Michelangelo's career, pushing him to the limits of his genius and spurring him to produce what many regard as the greatest feat of painting ever accomplished by a single artist.

History

The chapel was originally built in 1483 for Pope Sixtus IV, after whom it is named. But apart from the wall frescoes and floor, little remains of the original decor, which was sacrificed to make way for Michelangelo's two masterpieces. The first, the ceiling, was commissioned by Pope Julius II and painted between 1508 and 1512; the second, the *Giudizio Universale* (The Last Judgment), was completed almost 30 years later in 1541.

Both were controversial works influenced by the political ambitions of the popes who commissioned them. The ceiling came as part of Julius II's drive to transform Rome into the Church's showcase capital, while Pope Paul III intended the *Giudizio Universale* to serve as a warning to Catholics to toe the line during the Reformation in Europe.

The Ceiling

When Pope Julius II first approached Michelangelo about the 800-sq-metre ceiling – some say on the advice of his architect, Bramante, who was keen for Michelangelo to fail – the artist was reluctant to accept. He regarded himself as a sculptor and had had little experience of painting frescoes. But Julius persisted and in 1508 he commissioned

1. Interior of the Sistine Chapel **2.** Detail of Michelangelo's *Giudizio Universale* (The Last Judgment) **3.** Detail from the ceiling of the Sistine Chapel, Michelangelo's *The Creation of Adam*

Michelangelo for a fee of 3000 ducats (approximately €1.5 to €2 million).

Originally, Julius had envisaged a design based on the 12 apostles, but Michelangelo rejected this and came up with a much more complex plan centred on stories from the book of Genesis. And it's this that you see today.

Giudizio Universale (The Last Judgment)

Michelangelo's second stint in the chapel resulted in the *Giudizio Universale*, his highly charged depiction of Christ's second coming on the 200-sq-metre west wall.

The project, commissioned by Pope Clement VII and encouraged by his successor Paul III, was controversial from the start. Critics were outraged when Michelangelo destroyed two Perugino frescoes when preparing the wall, and

when it was unveiled in 1541, its swirling mass of 391 predominantly naked bodies provoked scandal. Pope Pius IV later had Daniele da Volterra cover 41 nudes, earning the artist the nickname *il braghettone* (the breeches maker).

MYTHS DEBUNKED

It's often said that Michelangelo worked alone but throughout the job he employed a stream of assistants to help with the plaster work (producing frescoes involves painting directly onto wet plaster).

Another myth is that Michelangelo painted lying down. In reality, he designed a curved scaffolding system that allowed him to work standing up albeit in an awkward backward-leaning position.

as well as some spectacular sculptures by Bernini, was formed by Cardinal Scipione Borghese (1579–1633), the most knowledgeable and ruthless art collector of his day. It's housed in the Casino Borghese, whose neoclassical look is the result of a 17th-century revamp of Scipione's original villa.

The museum is divided into two parts: the ground-floor gallery, with its superb sculptures, intricate Roman floor mosaics and over-the-top frescoes; and the upstairs picture gallery.

Things get off to a cracking start in the entrance hall, decorated with 4th-century floor mosaics of fighting gladiators and a gravity-defying bas-relief of a horse and rider falling into the void by Pietro Bernini.

Sala I is centred on Antonio Canova's daring depiction of Napoleon's sister, Paolina Bonaparte Borghese, reclining topless as *Venere vincitrice* (Conquering Venus; 1805–08). Yet it's Gian Lorenzo Bernini's spectacular sculptures – flamboyant depictions of pagan myths – that really steal the show. Just look at Daphne's hands morphing into leaves in the swirling *Apollo e Dafne* (Apollo and Daphne; 1622–25) in Sala III, or Pluto's hand pressing into the seemingly soft flesh of Persephone's thigh in the *Ratto di Proserpina* (Rape of Persephone; 1621–22) in Sala IV.

Caravaggio dominates Sala VIII. You'll see a dissipated-looking *Bacchino malato* (Young Sick Bacchus; 1593–94), the strangely beautiful *La Madonna dei Palafenieri*

(Madonna of the Palafrenieri; 1605–06) and *San Giovanni Battista* (St John the Baptist; 1609–10), probably Caravaggio's last work. Then there's the much-loved *Ragazzo col Canestro di Frutta* (Boy with a Basket of Fruit; 1593–95) and the dramatic *Davide con la Testa di Golia* (David with the Head of Goliath; 1609–10) – Goliath's severed head is said to be a self-portrait.

Upstairs, the pinacoteca offers a wonderful snapshot of European Renaissance art. Don't miss Raphael's extraordinary *La Deposizione di Cristo* (The Deposition; 1507) and his *Dama con Liocorno* (Lady with a Unicorn; 1506) in Sala IX. Also in the room is the superb *Adorazione del Bambino* (Adoration of the Christ Child; 1495) by Fra Bartolomeo and Perugino's *Madonna con Bambino* (Madonna and Child; first quarter of the 16th century).

Other highlights include Correggio's erotic *Danae* (1530–31) in Sala X, Bernini's self-portraits in Sala XIV and Titian's early masterpiece, *Amor Sacro e Amor Profano* (Sacred and Profane Love; 1514) in Sala XX.

★ **Villa Borghese**   PARK

(Map p113; Entrances at Piazzale San Paolo del Brasile, Piazzale Flaminio, Via Pinciana, Largo Pablo Picasso; ☉ dawn-dusk; ⊕ Porta Pinciana) Locals, lovers, tourists, joggers – no one can resist the lure of Rome's most celebrated park. Originally the estate of Cardinal Scipione Borghese's 17th-century residence, it covers about 80 hectares and boasts several museums and galleries, as well as the Giardino del Lago (Map p113) and Piazza di Siena (Map p113), an amphitheatre used for Rome's top equestrian event in May.

Bike hire is available at various points, including Largo Pablo Picasso, for about €5/15 per hour/day.

Galleria Nazionale d'Arte Moderna   ART GALLERY

(Map p113; ☎ 06 3229 8221; www.gnam.benicul-turali.it; Viale delle Belle Arti 131, disabled entrance Via Gramsci 71; adult/reduced €8/4; ☉ 8.30am-7.30pm Tue-Sun; ⊕ Piazza Thorvaldsen) Housed in a vast belle époque palace, this impressive but oft-overlooked gallery showcases works by the most important exponents of modern Italian art. There are canvases by the *macchiaioli* (the Italian Impressionists) and futurists Boccioni and Balla, as well as sculptures by Canova and major paintings by Modigliani and De Chirico. International artists are also represented with works by

Degas, Cezanne, Kandinsky, Klimt, Mondrian, Pollock and Henry Moore.

★ **Museo Nazionale Etrusco
di Villa Giulia**   MUSEUM
(Map p113; ☎ 06 322 65 71; www.villagiulia.benicul-
turali.it; Piazzale di Villa Giulia; adult/reduced €8/4;
☺ Villa Giulia 8.30am-7.30pm Tue-Sun, Villa Poniatowski 9am-1.45pm Tue-Sat; ▣ Via delle Belle Arti)
Italy's finest collection of pre-Roman Etruscan treasures is considerately presented in
Villa Giulia, Pope Julius III's 16th-century
pleasure palace, and the nearby **Villa Poniatowski** (Map p113). Exhibits, many of which
came from burial tombs in the surrounding
Lazio region, range from bronze figurines
and black *bucchero* tableware to temple
decorations, terracotta vases and a dazzling
display of sophisticated jewellery.

Must-sees include a polychrome terracotta statue of Apollo, the 6th-century-BC
Sarcofago degli Sposi (Sarcophagus of the
Betrothed) and the Euphronios Krater, a
celebrated Greek vase. The museum ticket
includes admission to Villa Poniatowski.

**Museo Nazionale delle Arti
del XXI Secolo (MAXXI)**   ART GALLERY
(☎ 06 3996 7350; www.fondazionemaxxi.it; Via
Guido Reni 4a; adult/reduced €11/8; ☺ 11am-7pm

GAY & LESBIAN ROME

Rome has a thriving, if low-key, gay scene. By nature the city is conservative and with
the Vatican breathing down the neck of local legislators, it's unlikely to become a Mediterranean San Fran any time soon. That said, the gay community has taken steps out of
the closet and while discretion is still wise – there have been episodes of homophobic
violence in recent years – tolerance is widespread.

The highlights of the city's LGBT calendar are **Gay Pride**, a colourful annual parade
held in mid-June, and **Gay Village**, a temporary complex of bars, clubs, cinema and
fitness areas that hosts a 10-week season of gigs and club nights, usually in EUR.

There are relatively few queer-only venues but many of the city's top clubs host
regular gay and lesbian nights, including Goa (p142) which hosts Venus Rising (www.
venusrising.it) a popular lesbian-only night, and Qube (Via di Portonaccio 212), home of
the Friday-night Muccassassina (www.muccassassina.com) extravaganza. Close to the
Colosseum and dubbed 'gay street', **Via di San Giovanni in Laterano** is a favourite
hang-out with a cluster of popular gay bars. There's also a gay beach, **Settimo Cielo**,
outside town at Capocotta, accessible via bus 61 from Ostia Lido or 70 from EUR.

For local information, pick up the monthly magazine *AUT* published by **Circolo
Mario Mieli** (☎ 800 110611; www.mariomieli.org; Via Efeso 2a), Rome's main cultural and
political gay organisation. AZ Gay (www.azgay.it) also produces an annual gay guide to
Rome, available at tourist kiosks.

Lesbians can find out about the local scene at **Coordinamento Lesbiche Italiano**
(www.clrbp.it; Via San Francesco di Sales 1b), which runs a women-only restaurant, **Luna e
L'Altra** (men are allowed at lunchtime), and hostel La Foresteria Orsa Maggiore (p124).

Other useful sources of information include the international gay guide **Spartacus**
(www.spartacusworld.com), available in app or book form, **Gay Rome** (www.gayrome.
com) and **GayFriendlyItaly** (www.gayfriendlyitaly.com).

Most gay venues (bars, clubs and saunas) require an **Arcigay** (☎ 06 6450 1102; www.
arcigayroma.it; Via Nicola Zabaglia 14) membership card. These cost €15/8 per year/three
months and are available from any venue that requires one.

Popular gay venues include:

Coming Out (Map p97; www.comingout.it; Via di San Giovanni in Laterano 8; ☺ 10.30am-2am;
Ⓜ Colosseo) An easygoing bar in the shadow of the Colosseum recognisable by its rainbow sign and the mixed, convivial crowds that spill out into the street.

Hangar (Map p94; www.hangaronline.it; Via in Selci 69; ☺ 10.30pm-2.30am Wed-Mon, closed 3
weeks Aug; Ⓜ Cavour) Veteran men-only club with a cruisy vibe. Porn-night Mondays and
striptease Thursdays are popular.

L'Alibi (Map p134; www.lalibi.it; Via di Monte Testaccio 44; ☺ 11.30pm-5am Thu-Sun; ▣ Via
Marmorata) Sultry, cavernous gay club playing soulful house. Thursday's Gloss party is
the big one.

Tue-Fri & Sun, to 10pm Sat; ⓔ Viale Tiziano) More than the exhibitions, the highlight of Rome's flagship contemporary art gallery is Zaha Hadid's stunning building. A renovated former barracks, it's impressive inside and out. The multilayered geometric facade faces on to a landscaped courtyard and gives onto a cavernous light-filled interior full of snaking walkways, suspended staircases, glass, cement and steel.

The gallery has a small permanent collection but more interesting are the temporary exhibitions and installations – check the website for details.

Courses

Cooking & Wine Tasting

Roman Kitchen COOKING
(Map p80; ☑ 06 678 57 59; www.italiangourmet.com; per day €200) Cookery writer Diane Seed (*The Top One Hundred Pasta Sauces*) leads one-, two- and three-day courses in her kitchen at Palazzo Doria Pamphilj.

Città di Gusto COOKING
(☑ 06 551 11 21; www.gamberorosso.it; Via Fermi 161) Demonstrations, workshops, lessons and courses are held at this modern complex run by Italian foodie organisation Gambero Rosso.

Vino Roma WINE COURSE
(Map p94; ☑ 328 487 44 97; www.vinoroma.com; Via In Selci 84/G; two-hour tastings per person €50) Vino Roma guides run wine-tasting courses for novices and experts as well as three-hour food tours (€80).

Language

There are hundreds of schools offering individual and group language courses. Costs vary enormously, but bank on €300 to €440 for a two-week group course or €35 to €45 for individual lessons. Some schools also offer accommodation packages.

Arco di Druso LANGUAGE
(Map p106; ☑ 06 3975 0984; www.arcodidruso.com; Via Otranto 12)

Centro Linguistico Italiano Dante Alighieri LANGUAGE
(☑ 06 4423 1490; www.clidante.it; Piazza Bologna 1)

Divulgazione Lingua Italiana Soc LANGUAGE
(DILIT; Map p94; ☑ 06 446 25 93; www.dilit.it; Via Marghera 22)

Italiaidea LANGUAGE
(Map p86; ☑ 06 6994 1314; www.italiaidea.com; 1st fl, Via dei Due Macelli 47)

Torre di Babele Centro di Lingua e Cultura Italiana LANGUAGE
(☑ 06 4425 2578; www.torredibabele.com; Via Cosenza 7)

Arts & Crafts

Art Studio Café ART
(Map p106; ☑ 06 3260 9104; www.artstudiocafe.it; Via dei Gracchi 187a) This cafe, exhibition space and mosaic school offers a range of mosaic and art classes, courses and workshops. Prices vary depending on the course.

☞ Tours

A Friend in Rome WALKING TOUR
(☑ 340 501 92 01; www.afriendinrome.it) Silvia Prosperi organises private tailor-made tours (on foot, by bike or scooter). She covers the Vatican and main historic centre as well as areas outside the capital. Rates are €40 to €50 per hour, with a minimum of three hours for most tours.

Trambus 110open BUS TOUR
(Map p94; ☑ 800 281281; www.trambusopen.com; family/adult/reduced €50/20/18; ⊙ every 15min 8.30am-7pm) A hop-on, hop-off bus tour. It departs from Piazza dei Cinquecento outside Termini and stops at the Colosseum, Bocca della Verità, Piazza Venezia, St Peter's, Ara Pacis and Trevi Fountain. Tickets are valid for 48 hours and are available on board, from authorised dealers, and from kiosks on Piazza dei Cinquecento and at the Colosseum.

Trambus Archeobus BUS TOUR
(Map p94; ☑ 800 281281; www.trambusopen.com; family/adult €40/12; ⊙ half-hourly 9am-12.30pm & 1.30-4.30pm) A stop-and-go bus that runs down Via Appia Antica, stopping at points of archaeological interest along the way. It departs from Piazza dei Cinquecento, and tickets, valid for 48 hours, can be bought online, on board, at the Piazza dei Cinquecento or Colosseum kiosks, and from authorised dealers.

Roma Cristiana WALKING TOUR
(Map p106; ☑ 06 6989 6380; www.operaromana-pellegrinaggi.org) Runs various walking tours, including visits to the Vatican Museums (adult/reduced €26.50/19.50) and St Peter's Basilica (€25).

Bici & Baci
BIKE TOUR

(✆06 482 84 43; www.bicibaci.com; Via del Viminale 5; tours €35; ◷10am, 3pm and 7pm Mar-Oct, on request Nov-Feb) Bici & Baci runs daily bike tours of central Rome, taking in the historical centre, Campidoglio and the Colosseum, as well as tours on vintage Vespas and in classic Fiat 500 cars. For the Vespa and Fiat 500 tours you'll need to book 24 hours ahead. Routes and prices vary according to your requests.

Enjoy Rome
WALKING TOUR

(Map p94; ✆06 445 18 43; www.enjoyrome.com; Via Marghera 8a) Offers three-hour, skip-the-line walking tours of the Vatican (under/over 26yr €27/32) and Ancient & Old Rome (under/over 26yr €25/30) as well as various other tours – see the website for further details. Note that tour prices do not cover admission charges to the Vatican Museums and Colosseum.

🎭 Festivals & Events

Carnevale Romano
CARNIVAL

(www.carnevale.roma.it) Rome goes to town for *carnevale* with horse shows on Piazza del Popolo, costumed parades down Via del Corso and crowds of kids in fancy dress.

Easter
RELIGIOUS

On Good Friday, the pope leads a candlelit procession around the Colosseum. At noon on Easter Sunday he blesses the crowds in St Peter's Square.

Mostra delle Azalee
CULTURE

From mid-April to early May, the Spanish Steps are emblazoned with 600 vases of blooming, brightly coloured azaleas.

Natale di Roma
CULTURE

Rome celebrates its birthday on 21 April with music, historical recreations, fireworks and free entry to many museums. Action is centred on the Campidoglio and Circo Massimo.

Primo Maggio
MUSIC

Rome's May Day rock concert attracts huge crowds and big-name Italian performers to Piazza di San Giovanni in Laterano.

Estate Romana
CULTURE

(www.estateromana.comune.roma.it) From June to October Rome's big summer festival stages hundreds of cultural events and activities across the capital.

Lungo il Tevere
ARTS

(www.lungoiltevereroma.it) Stalls, clubs, bars, restaurants and dance floors line the banks of the Tiber for this summer-long jamboree.

Festa dei Santi Pietro e Paolo
RELIGIOUS

Romans celebrate patron saints Peter and Paul on 29 June. Festivities are centred on St Peter's Basilica and Via Ostiense.

Festa de'Noantri
CULTURE

Trastevere celebrates its roots with a raucous street party in the last two weeks of July. Expect much feasting, drinking, dancing and praying.

Festa della Madonna della Neve
RELIGIOUS

On 5 August, rose petals are showered on celebrants in the Basilica di Santa Maria Maggiore to commemorate a miraculous 4th-century snowfall.

RomaEuropa
PERFORMING ARTS

(http://romaeuropa.net) From late September to November, top international artists take to the stage for Rome's premier festival of theatre, opera and dance.

Festival Internazionale del Film di Roma
FILM

(www.romacinemafest.org) Held at the Auditorium Parco della Musica in early November, Rome's film festival rolls out the red carpet for big-screen big shots.

🛏 Sleeping

While there's plenty of choice, accommodation in Rome is expensive. The nicest place to stay is the *centro storico*, where you'll have everything on your doorstep. Midrange choices abound, but there's only a smattering of good budget options. Near the Vatican, peaceful Prati is a good bet with a decent range of options, excellent restaurants and convenient metro stations (line A). Trastevere is drop-dead gorgeous and a great place to spend summer evenings, but it can be noisy.

The cheapest places are around Stazione Termini. This area, although not as bad as it's sometimes made out to be, is not Rome's most beautiful, and some of the streets to the west of the station, particularly Via Giolitti, can be dodgy at night. Women in particular should be careful. That said, it's convenient and most sights are only a metro ride away.

Rome doesn't really have a low season as such but most hotels drop prices from November to March (excluding Christmas and New Year) and from mid-July through August. Expect to pay top whack in spring (April to June) and autumn (September and October) and over the main holiday periods (Christmas, New Year and Easter).

Always try to book ahead. If you arrive without a reservation, there's a **hotel reservation service** (Map p94; ☎ 06 699 10 00; booking fee €3; ⏰ 7am-10pm) next to the tourist office at Stazione Termini.

You'll find a full list of accommodation options at www.060608.it.

Accommodation Options

The bulk of accommodation in Rome is made up of *alberghi* (traditional hotels) and *pensioni* (cheap family-run hotels often in converted apartments). Most central hotels tend to be three-star and up.

Alongside the hundreds of traditional B&Bs (private homes offering a room or two to paying guests), Rome has a large number of boutique-style B&Bs and guesthouses that offer chic, designer accommodation at mid- to top-end prices. The following agencies all offer online booking services:

Bed & Breakfast Association of Rome (www.b-b.rm.it) Lists B&Bs and short-term apartment rentals.

Bed & Breakfast Italia (www.bbitalia.it) Rome's longest-established B&B network.

Cross Pollinate (www.cross-pollinate.com) Has B&Bs, private apartments and guesthouses.

ROME FOR CHILDREN

Romans love children and even if there are few child-specific sights in town, your little ones will be welcome just about everywhere.

Practicalities

➡ Cobbled streets and badly parked cars make getting around with a pram or pushchair difficult.

➡ Buy baby formula and sterilising solutions at pharmacies. Disposable nappies/diapers (*pannolini* in Italian) are available from supermarkets and pharmacies.

➡ Restaurants are laid-back when it comes to accommodating children and will happily serve a *mezza porzione* (child's portion) and provide a *seggiolone* (highchair). Some hotels can supply a *culla* (cot) on request.

➡ Children under 10 travel free on all public transport.

➡ Check out www.turismoroma.it/piccoli-turisti-curiosi for suggestions on child-friendly things to do.

Sights

Rome's museums and galleries are not ideal for rampaging toddlers, but many of the bigger ones now offer educational services and children's workshops. Some even host kid-friendly events.

Suggested sights for kids include the **Colosseum** (p67), **Villa Borghese** (p116) and Rome's zoo: **Bioparco** (Map p113; ☎ 06 360 82 11; www.bioparco.it; Viale del Giardino Zoologico 1; adult/child over 1m & under 12yr/child under 1m €14/12/free; ⏰ 9.30am-6pm Apr-Oct, to 5pm Nov-Mar; 🚌 Bioparco), Rome's zoo. The catacombs of **Appia Antica** (p99) are best for children over about 12.

Explora (Map p113; ☎ 06 361 37 76; www.mdbr.it; Via Flaminia 82; adult/child 1-3yr €7/3; ⏰ entrance 10am, noon, 3pm, 5pm Tue-Sun; Ⓜ Flaminio) is a hands-on, feet-on museum dedicated to kids under 12. Bookings are advised and essential on weekends. Outside there's a free play park open to all.

Out of town in Tivoli, the gardens at **Villa D'Este** (p153) are fun to explore with their water jets, cascades and grim-faced gargoyles. Nearby, the extensive ruins of **Villa Adriana** (p153) provide ample opportunity for hide and seek.

At **Ostia Antica** (p151), kids can run free amidst the ruins of ancient Rome's main port and give their imagination a work out at the impressively preserved amphitheatre.

Further afield, the haunting Etruscan tombs at **Cerveteri** (p154) and **Tarquinia** (p154) are fascinating for adults and great for little ones.

Rome's hostels cater to everyone from backpackers to budget-minded families. Many hostels offer traditional dorms as well as hotel-style rooms (singles, doubles, even family rooms) with private bathrooms. For information on Rome's official HI hostels, contact the Italian Youth Hostel Association (Associazione Italiana Alberghi per la Gioventù; Map p94; ☑ 06 487 11 52; www.aighostels.com; Via Cavour 44).

Unsurprisingly, Rome is well furnished with religious institutions, many of which offer cheap(-ish) rooms. But bear in mind that many impose curfews and that the accommodation, while spotlessly clean, tends to be basic. For a list of institutions, check out www.santasusanna.org/comingToRome/convents.html.

For longer stays, renting an apartment might well work out cheaper than an extended hotel sojourn. Bank on spending about €900 per month for a studio apartment or a small one-bedroom place. Useful rental resources:

Accommodations Rome (www.accomodationsrome.com)

Flat in Rome (www.flatinrome.it)

Leisure in Rome (www.leisureinrome.com)

Rental in Rome (www.rentalinrome.com)

Sleep in Italy (www.sleepinitaly.com)

⊨ Ancient Rome

Residenza Maritti   GUESTHOUSE €
(Map p68; ☑ 06 678 82 33; www.residenzamaritti.com; Via Tor de'Conti 17; s €50-90, d €80-130, tr €110-150; ✳@🛜; Ⓜ Cavour) Boasting stunning views – from the terrace you can marvel at 360-degrees of ruins and rooftops – this hidden gem is housed in an 18th-century *palazzo* behind the Foro di Augusto. Its rooms, spread over two apartments, are decorated in a simple, cosy style with antiques and family furniture. Each apartment also has a fully equipped kitchen.

Caesar House   HOTEL €€
(Map p68; ☑ 06 679 26 74; www.caesarhouse.com; Via Cavour 310; s €150-200, d €160-260; ✳🛜; Ⓜ Cavour) Quiet and friendly, yet in the thick of it on Via Cavour, this is a small hotel in a renovated apartment. Its public areas are polished and modern, while the six guest rooms feature tiled floors, soothing colours and four-poster beds.

⊨ Centro Storico

Albergo del Sole   PENSION €
(Map p80; ☑ 06 687 94 46; www.solealbiscione.it; Via del Biscione 76; s €70-100, d €100-145, tr €120-180; Ⓟ✳🛜; ☐ Corso Vittorio Emanuele II) One of the few budget options in the historic centre, this is said to be the oldest hotel in Rome, dating to 1462. There's nothing special about the functional rooms but there's a pleasant 2nd-floor roof terrace and the location near Campo de' Fiori is excellent. No credit cards and no breakfast.

Hotel Pensione Barrett   PENSION €€
(Map p80; ☑ 06 686 84 81; www.pensionebarrett.com; Largo di Torre Argentina 47; s €115, d €135, tr €160; ✳🛜; ☐ Largo di Torre Argentina) A charming Aladdin's cave of a pension on Largo di Torre Argentina. The sheer exuberance of the decor is extraordinary, with everything from pot plants and antiques to busts, statues and stucco. Rooms are cosy and come with a range of thoughtful extras including foot spas and fully-stocked fridges.

Dimora degli Dei   BOUTIQUE HOTEL €€
(Map p80; ☑ 06 6819 3267; www.pantheondimoradeglidei.com; Via del Seminario 87; r €120-200; ✳🛜; ☐ Largo di Torre Argentina) Location and discreet style are the selling points of this elegant hideaway near the Pantheon. On the 1st floor of a centuries-old *palazzo*, it has six spacious, high-ceilinged rooms, each named after a Roman god, and each tastefully furnished.

Teatropace 33   HOTEL €€
(Map p80; ☑ 06 687 90 75; www.hotelteatropace.com; Via del Teatro Pace 33; s €80-150, d €130-270; ✳🛜; ☐ Corso del Rinascimento) Near Piazza Navona, this welcoming three-star is a class choice with 23 beautifully appointed rooms decorated with parquet, damask curtains and exposed wood beams. There's no lift, just a monumental 17th-century stone staircase and a porter to carry your bags.

Relais Palazzo Taverna   BOUTIQUE HOTEL €€
(Map p80; ☑ 06 2039 8064; www.relaispalazzotaverna.com; Via dei Gabrielli 92; s €80-150, d €100-210, tr €120-240; ✳🛜; ☐ Corso del Rinascimento) Housed in a 15th-century *palazzo*, this boutique hotel is superbly located off a cobbled pedestrian-only street. Its six rooms cut a stylish dash with white wood-beamed ceilings, funky wallpaper and dark parquet.

Hotel Teatro di Pompeo
HOTEL €€

(Map p80; ☑ 06 6830 0170; www.hotelteatrodi-pompeo.it; Largo del Pallaro 8; s €100-165, d €120-220; ✳ @ ⛾; ☐ Corso Vittorio Emanuele II) Built on top of a 1st-century BC theatre (now the breakfast room), this charming hotel is tucked away behind Campo de' Fiori. Rooms boast a classic old-fashioned feel with polished wood bedsteads and terracotta floor tiles. The best, on the 3rd floor, also have sloping wood-beamed ceilings.

Hotel Navona
HOTEL €€

(Map p80; ☑ 06 6821 1392; www.hotelnavona. com; Via dei Sediari 8; s €60-170, d €60-260; ✳ ⛾; ☐ Corso del Rinascimento) The Navona has a good range of rooms spread over several floors of a 15th-century *palazzo* near Piazza Navona. Those on the reception floor feature gilt-framed decor and antique furniture, while upstairs you'll find modern grey and silvers and mosaic-tiled bathrooms. Breakfast is €10 extra.

★ Hotel Campo de' Fiori
BOUTIQUE HOTEL €€€

(Map p80; ☑ 06 687 48 86; www.hotelcampodefiori. com; Via del Biscione 6; r & apt €90-600; ✳ @ ⛾; ☐ Corso Vittorio Emanuele II) This rakish four-star has got the lot – sexy decor, an enviable location, professional staff and a panoramic roof terrace. Rooms are individually decorated and they all feel delightfully decadent with boldly coloured walls, low wooden ceilings, gilt mirrors and restored bric-a-brac. The hotel also has 13 apartments, ideal for families.

Gigli D'Oro Suite
BOUTIQUE HOTEL €€€

(Map p80; ☑ 06 6839 2055; www.giglidorosuite. com; Via dei Gigli d'Oro 12; r €179-409; ✳ ⛾; ☐ Corso del Risorgimento) A masterclass in interior design, this classy boutique hotel is housed in a 15th-century *palazzo* that once belonged to Pope Sixtus V. Traces of the original building have been left intact so you'll find original stone doorways, antique fireplaces and, in the top-floor executive suite, a low sloping ceiling. Its six suites boast a chic white-leather look and classy designer bathrooms.

🛏 Tridente, Trevi & the Quirinale

La Controra
HOSTEL €

(Map p94; ☑ 06 9893 7366; Via Umbria 7; dm €20-40, d €80-110; ✳ @ ⛾; Ⓜ Barberini, Ⓜ Repubblica) Quality budget accommodation is thin on the ground in the upmarket area north of Piazza Repubblica, but this hidden hostel is a great choice. With its laid-back vibe, cool staff and bright, airy rooms (doubles and dorms for three to four people), it ticks all the right boxes.

Hotel Panda
PENSION €

(Map p86; ☑ 06 678 01 79; www.hotelpanda.it; Via della Croce 35; s €65-80, d €85-108, d €120-140, q €180; ✳ ⛾; Ⓜ Spagna) Only 50m from the Spanish Steps, in an area where a bargain is a Bulgari watch bought in the sales, the friendly, efficient Panda is an anomaly: a budget pension and a splendid one. The clean rooms are smallish but nicely furnished, and there are several triples with a bed on a cosy mezzanine. Air-con costs €6 per night. Book well ahead.

Okapi Rooms
HOTEL €

(Map p86; ☑ 06 3260 9815; www.okapirooms.it; Via della Penna 57; s €65-80, d €85-120, tr €110-140, q €120-180; ✳ ⛾; Ⓜ Flaminio) Twenty-room Okapi occupies a townhouse in a great location near Piazza del Popolo. Rooms are simple and small with cream walls, terracotta floors and double glazing. Some are decorated with ancient-style carvings, and several have small terraces. Bathrooms are tiny but sparkling clean.

★ Town House Fontana di Trevi
B&B €€

(Map p86; ☑ 333 6832012; www.bbfontana-ditrevi.com; Via dei Crociferi 41; r €80-160; ✳ ⛾; Ⓜ Barberini) As the name suggests, this refined bolthole is within a coin's throw of the Trevi Fountain. It's a stylish choice with eight dashing rooms spread over two floors of a typical city centre *palazzo*. Each is individually decorated and the look is contemporary chic with swish trendy furniture, designer bathrooms and handsome parquet floors.

Daphne B&B
B&B €€

(☑ 06 8745 0086; www.daphne-rome.com; Via di San Basilio 55; d €140-235, without bathroom €100-150; ✳ @ ⛾; Ⓜ Barberini) Boutique B&B Daphne is a gem. Run by an American-Italian couple, it has sleek, comfortable rooms, helpful English-speaking staff, top-notch breakfasts and the loan of a mobile phone for your stay. There are rooms in two locations – the one off Via Veneto is the pick, but there's a second at **Via degli Avignonesi 20** (Map p86; Via degli Avignonesi 20). Book months ahead.

La Piccola Maison
B&B €€

(Map p86; ☑ 06 4201 6331; www.lapiccolamaison. com; Via dei Cappuccini 30; s €50-180, d €70-200; ❄ 🛜; Ⓜ Barberini) The excellent Piccola Maison is housed in a 19th-century building in a great location close to Piazza Barberini. It has pleasingly plain, neutrally decorated rooms and thoughtful staff. A great deal.

Hotel Barocco
HOTEL €€

(Map p86; ☑ 06 487 20 01; www.hotelbarocco.com; Piazza Barberini 9; d €170-290; ❄ @ 🛜; Ⓜ Barberini) Very central, this well-run, welcoming hotel overlooking Piazza Barberini (the pricier rooms have views) has a classic feel, with rooms featuring oil paintings, spotless linen, gentle colour schemes and fabric-covered walls. Breakfast is ample and served in a wood-panelled room.

Hotel Modigliani
HOTEL €€

(Map p86; ☑ 06 4281 5226; www.hotelmodigliani. com; Via della Purificazione 42; s €100-180, d €110-200; ❄ 🛜; Ⓜ Barberini) Run by an artistic couple, the Modigliani is all about attention to detail and customer service. The 23 dove-grey rooms are spacious and light, and the best have views and balconies, either outside or over the quiet internal courtyard garden.

Hotel Scalinata di Spagna
HOTEL €€

(Map p86; ☑ 06 6994 0896; www.hotelscalinata. com; Piazza della Trinità dei Monti 17; d €110-190; ❄ @ 🛜; Ⓜ Spagna) Given its location – perched alongside the Spanish Steps – the Scalinata is surprisingly modestly priced. An informal and friendly place, it's something of a warren, with a great roof terrace, and low corridors leading off to smallish, old-fashioned, yet romantic rooms. Book early for a room with a view.

★ Villa Spalletti Trivelli
HOTEL €€€

(Map p86; ☑ 06 4890 7934; www.villaspalletti.it; Via Piacenza 4; r €450-530; Ⓟ ❄ @ 🛜; Ⓜ Spagna) With 12 rooms in a glorious mansion, Villa Spalletti Trivelli has upped the ante for luxurious stays in the capital. Rooms are soberly and elegantly decorated, overlooking the gardens of the Quirinale or the estate's Italian garden. The overall feel is that of staying in the stately home of some aristocratic friends.

★ Babuino 181
BOUTIQUE HOTEL €€€

(Map p86; ☑ 06 3229 5295; www.romeluxurysuites. com/babuino; Via del Babuino 181; r €180-780; ❄ 🛜; Ⓜ Flaminio) A beautifully renovated old *palazzo*, Babuino offers discreet luxury, with great attention to detail, a sleek roof terrace and modern, chic rooms with touches such as a Nespresso machine and fluffy bathrobes. A new annexe across the street has added more suites and rooms that continue the theme of understated elegance.

Portrait Suites
BOUTIQUE HOTEL €€€

(Map p86; ☑ 06 6938 0742; www.portraitsuites. com; Via Bocca di Leone 23; r €450-650; Ⓟ ❄ 🛜; Ⓜ Flaminio) Owned by the Ferragamo family, this is an exclusive residence with 14 exquisite suites and not-huge, but opulent-feeling studios across six floors in an elegant townhouse, plus a dreamy 360-degree roof terrace. There's no restaurant, but you can have meals delivered. Breakfast is served in your room or on the terrace.

🛏 Monti, Esquiline & San Lorenzo

★ Blue Hostel
HOSTEL €

(Map p94; ☑ 340 9258503; www.bluehostel.it; Via Carlo Alberto 13; d €45-100, tr & q €60-120; ❄ 🛜; Ⓜ Vittorio Emanuele) A hostel in name only, this pearl of a place offers hotel-standard rooms sleeping from two to four, each with its own en-suite bathroom and decorated in a tasteful low-key style – think beamed ceilings, wooden floors, French windows, and black-and-white framed photos.

★ Beehive
HOSTEL €

(Map p94; ☑ 06 4470 4553; www.the-beehive.com; Via Marghera 8; dm €25-30, s €50-60, d €90-100, without bathroom s €40-50, d €80-90, tr €95-105; ❄ 🛜; Ⓜ Termini) 🌿 More boutique chic than backpacker crash pad, the Beehive is one of the best hostels in town. Run by a southern-Californian couple, it's an oasis of style with original artworks on the walls, funky modular furniture and a vegetarian cafe (prices don't include breakfast).

Beds are in a spotless, eight-person mixed dorm or in one of six private double rooms, all with fans. Private rooms also have air-con (€10 per night). Book ahead.

Welrome Hotel
HOTEL €

(Map p94; ☑ 06 4782 4343; www.welrome.it; Via Calatafimi 15-19; d/tr/q €110/148/187; ❄ 🛜 ♿; Ⓜ Termini) Not only does owner Mary take huge pride in her small, spotless hotel but she will also enthusiastically point out the cheapest places to eat, tell you where not to waste your time and point you to what's good to do. Families should go for the large room named after Piazza di Spagna; a cot is provided at no extra charge.

Hotel & Hostel Des Artistes
HOTEL €

(Map p94; ☑ 06 445 43 65; www.hoteldesartistes. com; Via Villafranca 20; dm €12-23, s €34-114, d €39-160, tr €80-120, q €100-140; ❄ @; Ⓜ Castro Pretorio) The wide range of rooms here (including triples and family rooms) are decked out in wood and gold with faux-antique furniture and rich reds, gilt lamps and terracotta or tiled floors. Discounts are available for longer stays and/or cash payment.

Alessandro Palace Hostel
HOSTEL €

(Map p94; ☑ 06 446 19 58; www.hostelsalessandro.com; Via Vicenza 42; dm €19-35, d €70-120, tr €95-120; ❄ @ ⓢ; Ⓜ Castro Pretorio) This longstanding favourite offers spick-and-span, terracotta-floored doubles and triples, as well as dorms sleeping from four to eight, all with cheery bedspreads. Every room has its own bathroom plus hairdryer. There's a basement bar and the staff run local tours.

Residenza Cellini
GUESTHOUSE €€

(Map p94; ☑ 06 4782 5204; www.residenzacellini. it; Via Modena 5; d €120-240, tr €150-260; ❄ @ ⓢ; Ⓜ Repubblica) With grown-up furnishings featuring potted palms, polished wood, pale-yellow walls, oil paintings and a hint of chintz, this charming, family run hotel offers spacious, elegant rooms, all with satellite TV and jacuzzi or hydro-massage showers. There's a sunny flower-surrounded terrace for summer breakfasts.

Duca d'Alba
HOTEL €€

(Map p68; ☑ 06 48 44 71; www.hotelducadalba. com; Via Leonina 14; r €70-200; ❄ ⓢ; Ⓜ Cavour) This appealing four-star hotel in the Monti district has small but charming rooms; most have fabric-covered or handpainted walls, wood-beamed ceilings, big flat-screen TVs and sleek button-studded headboards.

🛏 Celian Hill & San Giovanni

Aklesia Suite
B&B €

(Map p97; ☑ 06 6293 1720; www.aklesiasuite.com; Via Labicana 85; d €85-130; ❄ ⓢ; Ⓜ Colosseo) The Aklesia Suite is a lovely B&B five minutes' walk from the Colosseum. On the 3rd floor (no lift) of a handsome Liberty-style apartment block and run by a super-helpful friendly couple, it has three clean, homey rooms and memorable views over the Colosseum.

🛏 Aventine & Testaccio

★ Hotel Sant'Anselmo
HOTEL €€€

(Map p134; ☑ 06 57 00 57; www.aventinohotels. com; Piazza Sant'Anselmo 2; s €130-265, d €150-290; ❄ @; Ⓜ Via Marmorata) A ravishing romantic hideaway set amid the terracotta villas and umbrella pines of the elegant Aventine district. Its rooms are not the biggest but they are stylish, marrying four-poster beds, polished marble and dripping chandeliers with modern touches and contemporary colours. A few also have terraces offering views over southern Rome.

🛏 Trastevere & Gianicolo

La Foresteria Orsa Maggiore
HOSTEL €

(Map p80; ☑ 06 689 37 53; www.casainternazionaledelledonne.org; 2nd fl, Via San Francesco di Sales 1a; dm €26-42, s €55-75, d €110-150, without bathroom s €36-55, d €72-100; @ ⓢ; Ⓜ Piazza Trilussa) This women-only guesthouse (boys aged 12 or younger are welcome) is housed in a lovely 16th-century convent close to the river in Trastevere. The 13 simple rooms sleep two, four, eight or nine, and some have views onto the attractive internal garden. There's a 3am curfew. Wheelchair accessible.

★ Arco del Lauro
B&B €€

(Map p102; ☑ 9am-2pm 06 9784 0350, mobile 346 2443212; www.arcodellauro.it; Via Arco de' Tolomei 27; s €75-125, d €95-145; ❄ @ ⓢ; Ⓜ Viale di Trastevere, Ⓜ Viale di Trastevere) Through a large stone arch and on a narrow cobbled street, this fab six-room B&B in an ancient *palazzo* is a find, offering gleaming white rooms that combine rustic charm with minimalist simplicity. The largest room has a high wood-beamed ceiling. Beds are comfortable, showers are powerful and the owners are eager to please. Book well ahead.

Suites Trastevere
B&B €€

(☑ 347 0744086; www.trastevere.bbsuites.com; Viale di Trastevere 248; s €70-105, d €80-160; ❄ ⓢ; Ⓜ Viale di Trastevere, Ⓜ Viale di Trastevere) On the 4th floor of a honey-hued *palazzo* on Trastevere's wide main drag, this friendly, popular B&B has dramatically frescoed rooms, each themed on local sights such as the Colosseum and Pantheon.

Residenza Arco de' Tolomei
HOTEL €€

(Map p102; ☑ 06 5832 0819; www.bbarcodeitolomei. com; Via Arco de' Tolomei 27; d €140-200; ❄ ⓢ;

ⓠ Viale di Trastevere, ⓠ Viale di Trastevere) This gorgeous place is decorated with polished antiques and rich contrasting chintzes that make the interiors feel like a country cottage. It's a lovely place to stay, and the owners are friendly and helpful.

Hotel Santa Maria
HOTEL €€

(Map p102; ☑06 589 46 26; www.hotelsantamaria. info; Vicolo del Piede 2; s €115-190, d €140-260; P❄@�; ⓠ Viale di Trastevere, ⓠ Viale di Trastevere) Walk along the ivy-lined approach and you'll enter a tranquil haven. Surrounding a spacious modern cloister (a former convent site), shaded by orange trees, rooms are cool and comfortable, with slightly fussy decor and terracotta floors. Staff are helpful and professional, and there's disabled access. There are deals offered for longer stays in summer.

★ Donna Camilla Savelli
HOTEL €€€

(Map p102; ☑06 58 88 61; www.hoteldonnacamillasavelli.com; Via Garibaldi 27; d €180-345; P❄@�; ⓠ Viale di Trastevere, ⓠ Viale di Trastevere) If you have the cash, stay in this converted convent that was designed by baroque genius Borromini. It's been beautifully updated – muted colours complement the serene concave and convex curves of the architecture – and the service is excellent. The pricier of the 78 rooms overlook the lovely cloister garden or have views of Rome.

🛏 Vatican City, Borgo & Prati

Le Stanze di Orazio
B&B €

(Map p106; ☑06 3265 2474; www.lestanzediorazio. com; Via Orazio 3; d €80-130; ❄@�; Ⓜ Lepanto) The inviting Le Stanze di Orazio is a small boutique B&B-style set-up just off Prati's main shopping strip. Three of the five bright, delicately decorated rooms – think soothing whites with lilac and lime-green accents – face onto the street, but effective sound-proofing cuts out most of the noise.

Hotel San Pietrino
HOTEL €

(Map p106; ☑06 370 01 32; www.sanpietrino.it; Via Bettolo 43; s €45-75, d €55-112, without bathroom s €35-55, d €45-85; ❄@�; Ⓜ Ottaviano–San Pietro) Within easy walking distance of St Peter's, San Pietrino is an excellent budget choice. Its cosy rooms are characterful and prettily decorated with terracotta tiled floors and the occasional statue. There's no breakfast but a drinks machine can supply emergency coffee.

Casa di Accoglienza Paolo VI
RELIGIOUS ACCOMMODATION €

(Map p106; ☑06 390 91 41; www.casapaolosesto. it; Viale Vaticano 92; s €35-40, d €65-70, tr €83-88; ❄�; Ⓜ Ottaviano–San Pietro) This tranquil, palm-shaded convent is ideally positioned for the Vatican Museums. The resident nuns keep everything shipshape and the 21 small, sunny rooms are clean as a pin, if slightly institutional in feel. No breakfast.

Colors Hotel
HOTEL €

(Map p106; ☑06 687 40 30; www.colorshotel.com; Via Boezio 31; s €35-90, d €45-125; ❄�; ⓠ Via Cola di Rienzo) Popular with young travellers, this is a bright budget hotel with smart, vibrantly coloured rooms spread over three floors (no lift, though). There are also cheaper rooms with shared bathrooms and, from June to August, dorms (€12 to €35 per person) for guests under 38.

Hotel Bramante
HOTEL €€

(Map p106; ☑06 6880 6426; www.hotelbramante. com; Vicolo delle Palline 24-25; s €100-160, d €140-240, tr €170-250, q €175-260; ❄�; ⓠ Piazza del Risorgimento) Tucked away in an alleyway under the Vatican walls, the Bramante exudes country-house charm with its cosy internal courtyard and quietly elegant rooms – think rugs, wood-beamed ceilings and antiques. It's housed in the 16th-century building where architect Domenico Fontana once lived.

🛏 Villa Borghese & Northern Rome

★ Palm Gallery Hotel
HOTEL €€

(☑06 6478 1859; www.palmgalleryhotel.com; Via delle Alpi 15d; s €100-120, d €90-210; ❄�; ⓠ Via Nomentana, ⓠ Viale Regina Margherita) This gorgeous hotel is housed in an early-20th-century villa in a charming neighbourhood near Villa Torlonia. The individually decorated rooms sport a wonderfully eclectic, ethnic look that effortlessly blends African and Middle Eastern art with original Liberty-syle furniture, patches of exposed brickwork and hand-painted tiles.

✖ Eating

Rome teems with trattorias, *ristoranti*, pizzerias, *enoteche* (wine bars serving food) and gelaterie. Excellent places dot the *centro storico*, Trastevere, Prati, Testaccio and San Lorenzo. Be warned that the area around Termini has quite a few substandard restaurants, as does the Vatican, which is packed with tourist traps.

Many restaurants close for several weeks during the traditional summer holiday month of August.

✕ Ancient Rome

★ Enoteca Provincia
Romana   REGIONAL CUISINE €€
(Map p68; ☑ 06 6994 0273; Via Foro Traiano 82-4; meals €35, aperitifs from €5; ⊙ 11am-11pm Mon-Sat; ⬚ Via dei Fori Imperiali) The best option in the touristy Forum area, this stylish wine bar-cum-restaurant showcases food from the surrounding Lazio region. There's a full daily menu of pastas and mains, as well as finger foods, wine by the glass and evening aperitifs. Lunchtime is busy but it quietens down in the evening.

✕ Centro Storico

★ I Dolci di Nonna
Vincenza   PASTRIES & CAKES €
(Map p80; www.dolcinonnavincenza.it; Via Arco del Monte 98a; pastries from €2.50; ⊙ 9am-9pm; ⬚ Via Arenula) Although a pastry shop – and a delightful one with traditional Sicilian cakes and all manner of tempting gift ideas – it's difficult to resist eating here. Next to the shop is a bar area showcasing a heavenly selection of creamy, flaky, puffy pastries, all just lying there waiting to be gobbled down.

Forno Roscioli   PIZZA BY SLICE, BAKERY €
(Map p80; Via dei Chiavari 34; pizza slices from €2, snacks from €1.50; ⊙ 7.30am-8pm Mon-Fri, 7.30am-2.30pm Sat; ⬚ Via Arenula) Join the lunchtime crowds at this renowned bakery for a slice of pizza (the *pizza bianca* is legendary), fresh-from-the-oven pastries and hunger-sating *supplì* (fried rice croquettes). There's also a counter serving hot pastas and vegetable side dishes.

**Forno di Campo
de' Fiori**   PIZZA BY SLICE, BAKERY €
(Map p80; Campo de' Fiori 22; pizza slices about €3; ⊙ 7.30am-2.30pm & 4.45-8pm Mon-Sat; ⬚ Corso Vittorio Emanuele II) On Campo de' Fiori, this is one of Rome's best takeaways, serving bread, *panini* (sandwiches) and delicious *pizza al taglio* (pizza by the slice). Aficionados swear

by the pizza *bianca* ('white' pizza with olive oil, rosemary and salt), but the *panini* and pizza *rossa* ('red' pizza, with olive oil, tomato and oregano) are just as good.

Antico Forno Urbani   PIZZA BY SLICE, BAKERY €
(Map p80; Piazza Costaguti 31; pizza slices from €2; ⊙ 7.40am-2.30pm & 5-8.45pm Mon-Fri, 9am-1.30pm Sat & Sun; ⬚ Via Arenula) Come mid-morning and you'll find this popular Ghetto bakery packed with locals queueing for their mid-morning snack. Once you get a whiff of the yeasty smells wafting off the freshly baked pizzas, breads, biscuits and focaccias, you'll want to follow suit. Grab a ticket and wait your turn.

Alfredo e Ada   TRATTORIA €
(Map p80; ☑ 06 687 88 42; Via dei Banchi Nuovi 14; meals €20; ⊙ Tue-Sat; ⬚ Corso Vittorio Emanuele II) For a taste of authentic Roman cooking, head to this much-loved trattoria with its wood panelling and spindly, marble-topped tables. It's distinctly no-frills but there's a warm atmosphere and the traditional Roman food is unpretentious and filling.

Enoteca Corsi   OSTERIA €
(Map p80; ☑ 06 679 08 21; www.enotecacorsi.com; Via del Gesù 87; meals €25; ⊙ lunch Mon-Sat; ⬚ Largo di Torre Argentina) Merrily the worse for wear, family-run Corsi is a genuine old-style Roman eatery. The look is rustic – bare wooden tables, paper tablecloths, wine bottles – and the atmosphere one of controlled mayhem. The menu, chalked up on a blackboard, offers no surprises, just honest, homey fare like *melanzane parmigiana* or roast chicken with potatoes.

Pizzeria da Baffetto   PIZZERIA €
(Map p80; ☑ 06 686 16 17; www.pizzeriabaffetto.it; Via del Governo Vecchio 114; pizzas €6-9; ⊙ 6.30pm-1am; ⬚ Corso Vittorio Emanuele II) For the full-on Roman pizza experience, get down to Baffetto. Not everyone likes this historic pizzeria but if you're up for it, meals are raucous, chaotic and fast, and the thin-crust pizzas are spot on. To partake, join the queue and wait to be squeezed in wherever there's room. No credit cards. There's a sister outfit, **Baffetto 2** (Map p80; Piazza del Teatro di Pompeo 18; ⊙ 6.30pm-12.30am Mon & Wed-Fri, 12.30-3.30pm & 6.30pm-12.30am Sat & Sun; ⬚ Corso Vittorio Emanuele II), near Campo de' Fiori.

Bar del Fico   TRADITIONAL ITALIAN €
(Map p80; Via della Pace 34-35; meals €15-20; ⊙ 8am-2am; ⬚ Corso Vittorio Emanuele II)

TOP 10 GELATO

Eating gelato is as much a part of Roman life as traffic jams and dodgy politicians, and the city has some superb *gelaterie artigianale* (artisanal ice-cream shops). To gauge the quality of a place, check out the pistachio flavour: if it's pale olive green it's good; if it's bright green, go elsewhere.

Here's our road-tested guide to Rome's top 10 gelaterie:

★ **Fatamorgana** (Map p106; www.gelateriafatamorgana.it; Via Bettolo 7; cones & tubs from €2; ⊘noon-11pm; Ⓜ Ottaviano–San Pietro) Try the mouthwateringly good *agrumi* (citrus fruit) and *basilico, miele e noci* (basil, honey and hazelnuts). There's another branch at **Piazza Zingari 51** (Map p68; Piazza Zingari), in Monti.

★ **Il Gelato** (Map p86; Piazza Monte d'Oro 91 ; from €2; ☒ Via del Corso) Tuck into creative flavours made by Rome's gelato king, Claudio Torcè.

San Crispino (Map p86; ☑ 06 679 39 24; Via della Panetteria 42; ice cream from €2.30; ⊘noon-12.30am Mon, Wed, Thu & Sun, 11am-1.30am Fri & Sat; Ⓜ Barberini) Delicate, strictly seasonal flavours served only in tubs (cones would detract from the taste). There's a second branch at **Piazza della Maddalena 3** (Map p80; Piazza della Maddalena 3; tubs from €2; ⊘noon-12.30am Mon, Wed, Thu & Sun, noon-1.30am Fri & Sat; ☒ Corso del Rinascimento) in the *centro storico*.

Gelateria del Teatro (Map p80; Via di San Simone 70; cones & tubs from €2; ⊘11am-11.30pm; ☒ Corso del Rinascimento) Does a great turn in Sicilian *pistacchio* (pistachio) and *mandorle* (almonds).

Vice (Map p80; www.viceitalia.it; Corso Vittorio Emanuele II 96; cones & tubs from €2; ⊘11am-1am; ☒ Largo di Torre Argentina) A contemporary outfit serving traditional and modern flavours such as blueberry cheesecake.

Il Caruso (Via Collina 15; ⊘noon-9pm; Ⓜ Repubblica) Top your gelato with *zabaglione* (egg and marsala custard) mixed with *panna* (whipped cream).

Gelarmony (Map p106; Via Marcantonio Colonna 34; ice cream from €1.50; ⊘10am-late; Ⓜ Lepanto) As well as ice cream also does fab Sicilian *cannoli* (pastry tubes filled with creamy ricotta).

Palazzo del Freddo di Giovanni Fassi (Map p94; ☑ 06 446 47 40; www.palazzodelfreddo.it; Via Principe Eugenio 65; from €2; ⊘noon-midnight Tue-Sat, 10am-midnight Sun Mar-Oct, noon-10pm Tue-Thu, noon-midnight Fri & Sat, 10am-10pm Sun Nov-Feb; Ⓜ Vittorio Emanuele) A Roman institution serving classic flavours and great *granite* (crushed-ice drinks).

Giolitti (Map p80; ☑ 06 699 12 43; www.giolitti.it; Via degli Uffici del Vicario 40; ⊘7am-1am; ☒ Via del Corso) Rome's most famous gelateria keeps the hordes happy with succulent sorbets and creamy chocolates.

Old Bridge (Map p106; www.oldbridgelateria.com; Viale dei Bastioni di Michelangelo 5; cones from €1.50; ⊘9am-2am; ☒ Piazza del Risorgimento, ☒ Piazza del Risorgimento) Makes for a refreshing pitstop after visiting the Vatican Museums.

As an alternative to ice cream, Romans like to cool down with a *grattachecca* (crushed ice drowned in fruit syrup) by the river. There are several riverside stands around Rome's central bridges.

Named after the fig tree that shades the chess-playing old boys outside, Bar del Fico is good any time of the day, from breakfast through to dinner. The big bowls of lunchtime pasta hit the spot nicely and the low-key boho decor – rough wooden floors, tin tables and grey, chipped walls – makes for a laid-back ambience.

Chiostro del Bramante Caffè CAFE €
(Map p80; www.chiostrodelbramante.it; Vicolo dell'Arco della Pace 5; dishes €10-14; ⊘10am-8pm; ☏ ; ☒ Corso del Rinascimento) This swish bistro-

cafe is on the 1st floor of Bramante's elegant Renaissance cloisters. It's open throughout the day, so you can drink, snack or lunch on salads, baguettes or light pastas, all the while making use of the free wi-fi. Aperitifs are served in the early evening.

Casa Coppelle
MODERN ITALIAN €€

(Map p80; ☑ 06 6889 1707; www.casacoppelle. it; Piazza delle Coppelle 49; meals €35; ⊙ lunch & dinner; ᵬ Corso del Rinascimento) Exposed brick walls, books, flowers and subdued lighting set the stage for wonderful French-inspired food at this intimate, romantic restaurant. There's a full range of starters and pastas but the real tour de force is the steak served with crunchy, thinly sliced potato crisps. Service is quick and attentive. Book ahead.

Armando al Pantheon
TRATTORIA €€

(Map p80; ☑ 06 6880 3034; www.armandoalpantheon.it; Salita dei Crescenzi 31; meals €40; ⊙ closed Sat dinner, Sun & Aug; ᵬ Largo di Torre Argentina, ᵬ Largo di Torre Argentina) An institution in these parts, wood-panelled Armando is a rare find – a genuine family-run trattoria in the touristy Pantheon area. It's been on the go for more than 50 years and has served its fair share of celebs – philosopher Jean-Paul Sartre and Brazilian footballer Pelé have both eaten here – but the focus remains on traditional Roman food. Reservations recommended.

Cul de Sac
WINE BAR, TRATTORIA €€

(Map p80; ☑ 06 6880 1094; www.enotecaculdesac. com; Piazza Pasquino 73; meals €30; ⊙ noon-4pm & 6pm-12.30am; ᵬ Corso Vittorio Emanuele II) A popular little wine bar, just off Piazza Navona, with an always-busy terrace and narrow, bottle-lined interior. Choose from the encyclopedic wine list and ample menu of Gallic-inspired cold cuts, pâtés, cheeses and main courses. Book for dinner.

Ditirambo
MODERN ITALIAN €€

(Map p80; ☑ 06 687 16 26; www.ristoranteditirambo.it; Piazza della Cancelleria 72; meals €40; ⊙ closed lunch Mon; ᵬ Corso Vittorio Emanuele II) Hugely popular Ditirambo broke culinary ground when it opened in 1996, marrying the informality of an old-school trattoria with forward-looking, creative cooking. Since then it has performed consistently well and it's still a top spot for seasonal, organic cooking and excellent vegetarian dishes. Book ahead.

Sora Margherita
TRATTORIA €€

(Map p80; ☑ 06 687 42 16; Piazza delle Cinque Scole 30; meals €30-35; ⊙ closed dinner Tue & Thu, all day Sun; ᵬ Via Arenula) No-frills Sora Margherita started as a cheap kitchen for hungry locals, but word has spread and it's now a popular lunchtime haunt of everyone from local workers to slumming uptowners. Expect dog-eat-dog queues, a rowdy atmosphere and classic Roman dishes such as *gnocchi al sugo* (gnocchi in tomato sauce) and *fegato* (liver).

Casa Bleve
WINE BAR, GASTRONOMIC €€€

(Map p80; ☑ 06 686 59 70; www.casableve.it; Via del Teatro Valle 48-49; meals €65; ⊙ Tue-Sat, closed Aug; ᵬ Largo di Torre Argentina) Ideal for a romantic assignation, this stately wine bar-cum-restaurant dazzles with its column-lined courtyard and stained-glass roof. Its wine list, one of the best in town, accompanies hard-to-find cheeses and cold cuts, while in the evening there's a full à la carte menu of creative Italian dishes.

✖ Tridente, Trevi & the Quirinale

Al Gran Sasso
TRATTORIA €

(Map p86; ☑ 06 321 48 83; www.trattoriaalgransasso.com; Via di Ripetta 32; meals €25; ⊙ lunch & dinner Sun-Fri; Ⓜ Flaminio) The perfect lunchtime spot, this is a classic, dyed-in-the-wool trattoria serving filling portions of old-school country cooking. It's a relaxed place with a welcoming vibe, garish murals on the walls (strangely, often a good sign) and tasty, value-for-money food. The fried dishes are especially good and there's fresh fish on Tuesdays and Fridays.

Da Michele
PIZZA BY SLICE €

(Map p86; ☑ 349 2525347; Via dell'Umiltà 31; pizza slice from €3; ⊙ 8am-5pm Mon-Fri, to 8pm summer; ᵬ Via del Corso) A handy address near the Trevi Fountain. Buy your fresh, light and crispy *pizza al taglio*, and you'll have a delicious fast lunch. It's all kosher, so meat and cheese is not mixed.

Pompi
DESSERTS €€

(Map p86; Via della Croce 82; tiramisu €3.50; ⊙ 10am-10.30pm; Ⓜ Spagna) Rome's most famous tiramisu vendor sells the deliciously yolky yet light-as-air dessert in three flavours – classic, pistachio and strawberry. You can buy some to eat straight away or get

KOSHER ROME

If you want to eat kosher head to Via del Portico d'Ottavia, the main strip on the Jewish Ghetto. Lined with trattorias and restaurants specialising in kosher food and Roman-Jewish cuisine, it's a lively hang-out, especially on hot summer nights when diners crowd the many sidewalk tables. For a taste of typical Ghetto cooking, try the landmark **Giggetto al Portico d'Ottavia** (Map p80; 06 686 11 05; www.giggettoalportico.it; Via del Portico d'Ottavia 21a; meals €40; Tue-Sun; Via Arenula), or, at No 16, **Nonna Betta** (Map p80; 06 6880 6263; www.nonnabetta.it; Via del Portico d'Ottavia 16; meals €30-35; noon-4pm & 6-11pm, closed Fri dinner & Sat lunch; Via Arenula), a small tunnel of a trattoria serving local staples such as *carciofi alla giudia* (crisp fried artichokes). Further down the road, the unmarked **Gelateria** (Map p80; Via del Portico d'Ottavia 1b; tubs €2-5, cones from €3; 9am-10pm Sun-Fri, to midnight summer; Via Arenula) at No 1b has a small but tasty selection of kosher ice cream.

frozen portions to take away. They also sell ice cream.

Pizzeria al Leoncino
PIZZERIA €

(Map p86; 06 686 77 57; Via del Leoncino 28; pizzas from €6; closed Wed & lunch Sat & Sun; Via del Corso) Some places just never change and this boisterous neighbourhood pizzeria is one of them. A bastion of budget eating in an otherwise expensive area, it has a wood-fired oven, two small rooms and gruff waiters who efficiently serve bruschettas, excellent Roman-style pizza and ice-cold beer. Cash only.

'Gusto
RISTORANTE €

(Map p86; 06 322 62 73; Piazza Augusto Imperatore 9; pizzas €7-10; Via del Corso) This warehouse-style gastronomic complex, all exposed brickwork and industrial chic, is hugely popular with local lunchers who flock here to sit on the sunny terrace and pile into the bountiful midday buffet. It also serves Neapolitan-style pizzas and up-market restaurant fare but these receive mixed reports.

★ Colline Emiliane
EMILIA-ROMAGNA €€

(Map p86; 06 481 75 38; Via degli Avignonesi 22; meals €45; 12.45-2.45pm Tue-Sun & 7.30-10.45pm Tue-Sat, closed Aug; Barberini) This welcoming restaurant just off Piazza Barberini flies the flag for Emilia-Romagna, the well-fed Italian region that has blessed the world with Parmesan, balsamic vinegar, bolognese sauce and Parma ham. It's a consistently excellent place to eat with delicious meats, homemade pasta and rich *ragù*. Try to save room for dessert.

★ Palatium
WINE BAR €€

(Map p86; 06 692 02 132; Via Frattina 94; meals €45; 11am-11pm Mon-Sat, closed Aug; Via del Corso) A rich showcase of regional bounty, run by the Lazio Regional Food Authority, this sleek, ground-breaking wine bar serves excellent local specialities, such as *porchetta* (pork roasted with herbs), artisanal cheese and delicious salami, as well as an impressive array of local wines. *Aperitivo* is a good bet too. One-course meals are priced at a tempting €14.

Matricianella
TRATTORIA €€

(Map p86; 06 683 21 00; www.matricianella.it; Via del Leone 2/4; meals €40; Mon-Sat; Via del Corso) With its gingham tablecloths, chintzy murals and fading prints, this model trattoria is loved for its traditional Roman cuisine. You'll find all the usual menu stalwarts as well as some great Roman-Jewish dishes. Romans go crazy for the fried antipasti, the artichoke *alla giudia* (fried, Jewish style) and the meatballs. Booking is essential.

Il Margutta RistorArte
VEGETARIAN €€

(Map p86; 06 678 60 33; www.ilmargutta.it; Via Margutta 118; meals €45; daily; ; Spagna, Flaminio) Vegetarian restaurants in Rome are rarer than parking spaces, and this airy art gallery-restaurant is an unusually chic way to eat your greens. Dishes are excellent and most produce is organic, with offerings such as artichoke hearts with potato cubes and smoked provolone cheese. Best value is the Saturday and Sunday buffet brunch (€25). It also offers a seven-course vegan menu (€50).

Baccano
BRASSERIE €€

(Map p86; www.baccanoroma.com; Via delle Muratte 23; meals €45; 8.30am-2am; Via del Corso) This is one of a new breed of

Il Tridente

The three streets that radiate south from Piazza del Popolo cut straight to the heart of ancient Rome. Historian and presenter Dan Cruickshank explained the appeal of 'Il Tridente' to *Lonely Planet Traveller* magazine.

Rome is one of the few capital cities whose heart is still girdled by long sections of defensive wall. But what makes Rome different from other great walled cities is its gates. These mighty and majestic works remain portals between different worlds.

For me, most exciting and in many ways perfect, is the Porta del Popolo on the northern tip of the city centre. Perfect not because of its design but because it is the perfect way to enter the magic domain of Rome. Outside the gate all is movement and space: wide modern roads and, to the east, the beautiful gardens of the Villa Borghese.

Pass through the gate, which until the mid-19th century was the main point of entry to the city for travellers, and the heart of Rome opens before you. From the south side of this oval radiate three long, straight streets – the famed Il Tridente – offering heroic and breathtaking vistas through the chaotic fabric of the city.

Via del Babuino

The Via del Babuino is named after an ancient statue that since the 16th century has lolled halfway along its length and is deemed to be so ugly that it's called babuino, the baboon. In the past Romans let off steam by 'talking' through these statues, on which were hung satirical verses that mocked the ruling elite of the city.

1. Piazza del Popolo (p87) at the start of Via del Corso **2.** Via del Corso at sunset **3.** Detail of the Trevi Fountain (p89)

Via del Corso

Running almost due south from Piazza del Popolo is the Via del Corso. It cuts laser-like through the very heart of the city, following the course of the 2200-year-old Via Flaminia, the route along which the legions marched heading north and along which they returned, proclaiming Rome's glory. Go to the east, along Via delle Muratte, and you suddenly find yourself in front of the triumphal façade and fresh waters of the Trevi Fountain, which still manages to rise above the hordes of tourists that engulf it.

Via di Ripetta

The third spoke of the Piazza del Popolo's Il Tridente is the Via di Ripetta, heading southeast, towards the River Tiber and on to the sacred city of the Vatican. The Via di Ripetta also leads to my favourite Rome, the Rome where the past and the present coexist in a most dramatic and intimate manner: narrow rows of artisan shops nestling within the shadow of a rearing palazzo; a mighty church juxtaposed in dramatic contrast with cramped alleys; swirling patterns of eager pedestrians and scooters throbbing and revving as they weave through the city.

restaurant–cafe-bars that are open all day. It serves breakfasts (eggs Benedict etc), then lunch, dinner, burgers, club sandwiches, cocktails, *aperitivi* – you name it, they've got it covered. The look is vintage Parisian glamour combined with 1990s New York City chic.

Vineria Chianti
WINE BAR €€€

(Map p86; ☎ 06 678 75 50; Via del Lavatore 81-82; meals €55; ☺ 12.30-3.30pm & 7-11.30pm; ☐ Via del Tritone) This pretty ivy-clad wine bar is bottle-lined inside, with watch-the-world-go-by streetside seating in summer. Cuisine is Tuscan, so the beef is particularly good, but it also serves imaginative salads and pizza in the evenings.

Babette
ITALIAN €€€

(Map p86; ☎ 06 321 15 59; Via Margutta 1; meals €55; ☺ closed Jan & Aug; ☑; Ⓜ Spagna, Flaminio) Babette is run by two sisters who used to produce a fashion magazine, which accounts for its effortlessly chic *Fried Green Tomatoes*–style interior of exposed brick walls and vintage painted signs. You're in for a feast too, as the cooking is delicious, with a sophisticated, creative French twist (think *tortiglioni* with courgette and pistachio pesto). The daily lunch buffet (€10 Tuesday to Friday, €25 weekends) is a good deal.

✗ Monti, Esquiline & San Lorenzo

Panella l'Arte del Pane
BAKERY, CAFE €

(Map p94; ☎ 06 487 24 35; Via Merulana 54; pizza slices around €3; ☺ noon-midnight Mon-Sat, 10am-4pm Sun Mar-Oct; Ⓜ Vittorio Emanuele) With a sumptuous array of *pizza al taglio*, *supplì*, focaccia and fried croquettes, this is a sublime lunch stop, where you can sip a glass

FAST-FOOD PASTA

For most of the day **Pastificio** (Map p86; Via della Croce 8; pasta dish €4; ☺ lunch 1-3pm Mon-Sat; Ⓜ Spagna) goes about its business as a fresh pasta shop, but at lunchtime it turns itself into the neighbourhood's budget diner. Locals pile in to fill up on the daily pasta dishes (there's a choice of two) eaten out of plastic bowls wherever there's room.

of chilled *prosecco* while eyeing up gastronomic souvenirs from the deli.

Roscioli
PIZZA BY SLICE, BAKERY €

(Map p94; Via Buonarroti 48; pizza slices €3; ☺ 7.30am-8pm Mon-Thu, to 9pm Fri & Sat; Ⓜ Vittorio Emanuele) Off-the-track branch of this splendid deli-bakery-pizzeria, with delish *pizza al taglio*, pasta dishes and other goodies that make it ideal for a swift lunch or picnic stock-up. It's on a road leading off Piazza Vittorio Emanuele II.

Formula Uno
PIZZERIA €

(Map p94; ☎ 06 445 38 66; Via degli Equi 13; pizzas from €6; ☺ 6.30pm-1.30am Mon-Sat; ☐ Via Tiburtina, ☐ Via dei Reti) This basic, historic San Lorenzo pizzeria is as adrenaline-fuelled as its name: waiters zoom around under whirring fans, delivering tomato-loaded bruschetta, fried courgette flowers, *supplì al telefono* (fried rice croquettes with mozzarella) and bubbling thin-crust pizza to eternal crowds of feasting students.

★ L'Asino d'Oro
MODERN ITALIAN €€

(Map p86; ☎ 06 4891 3832; Via del Boschetto 73; meals €45; ☺ Tues-Sat; Ⓜ Cavour) This fabulous restaurant has been transplanted from Orvieto and its Umbrian origins resonate in Lucio Sforza's exceptional cooking. It's unfussy yet innovative, with dishes featuring lots of flavourful contrasts, such as slow-roasted rabbit in a rich berry sauce and desserts that linger long after that last crumb. For such excellent food, this intimate, informal yet classy place is one of Rome's best deals, especially for the set lunch.

Trattoria Monti
RISTORANTE €€

(Map p94; ☎ 06 446 65 73; Via di San Vito 13a; meals €45; ☺ 12.45-2.45pm Tue-Sun, 7.45-11pm Tue-Sat, closed Aug; Ⓜ Vittorio Emanuele) This elegant brick-arched place offers top-notch traditional cooking from the Marches region. There are wonderful *fritti* (fried things), delicate pastas and ingredients such as *pecorino di fossa* (sheep's cheese aged in caves), goose, swordfish and truffles. Try the egg-yolk *tortelli* pasta. Desserts are delectable, including apple pie with *zabaglione*. Book ahead.

La Carbonara
TRATTORIA €€

(Map p68; ☎ 06 482 51 76; Via Panisperna 214; meals €40; ☺ Mon-Sat; Ⓜ Cavour) This busy restaurant was favoured by the Ragazzi di Panisperna (named after the street), a group of young physicists, including Enrico Fermi, whose discoveries led to the first atomic bomb. The waiters are brusque, it crackles with energy and the interior is covered in graffiti – tradition dictates that diners leave their mark on the wall. The speciality is the eponymous carbonara.

Da Danilo TRATTORIA €€
(☑ 06 482 51 76; Via Petrarca 13; meals €45; ☺ Tue-Sat lunch, Mon-Sat dinner; ⓜ Vittorio Emanuele) This upmarket version of the classic neighbourhood trattoria offers icons of Roman cooking in a rustic, eternal-Roman-trattoria atmosphere. It's renowned for its *cacio e pepe* (pasta with pecorino cheese and black pepper) and carbonara. Ideal if you're looking for a fine robust meal.

Tram Tram OSTERIA €€
(Map p94; ☑ 06 49 04 16; www.tramtram.it; Via dei Reti 44; meals around €40; ☺ 12.30-3.30pm & 7.30-11.30pm Tue-Sun; ⓠ Via Tiburtina) This trendy yet old-style lace-curtained trattoria takes its name from the trams that rattle past outside. It's a family run concern whose menu is an unusual mix of Roman and Pugliese (southern Italian) dishes, featuring taste sensations such as *tiella di riso patate e cozze* (baked rice, potatoes and mussels). Book ahead.

Trimani WINE BAR €€
(Map p94; ☑ 06 446 96 30; Via Cernaia 37b; meals €45; ☺ 11.30am-3pm & 5.30-11pm Mon-Sat; ⓜ Termini, ⓠ Termini) Part of the Trimani family's wine empire (their shop just round the corner stocks about 4000 international labels), this is an unpretentious yet highly professional *enoteca*. It stocks a vast selection of Italian regional wines as well as an ever-changing food menu – tuck into local salami and cheese or fresh oysters.

★ Open Colonna MODERN ITALIAN €€€
(Map p86; ☑ 06 4782 2641; www.antonello colonna.it; Via Milano 9a; meals €20-80; ☺ noon-midnight Tue-Sat, lunch Sun; ⓠ Via Nazionale) Spectacularly set at the back of the Palazzo delle Esposizioni, super-chef Antonello Colonna's superb restaurant is tucked onto a mezzanine floor under an extraordinary glass roof. The cuisine is new Roman: innovative takes on traditional dishes, cooked with wit and flair. Best of all, there's a more basic but still delectable fixed two-course lunch for €16, and Saturday and Sunday brunch is €30.

MENU DECODER

The hallmark of an authentic Roman menu is the presence of offal. The Roman love of nose-to-tail eating arose in Testaccio around the city abattoir, and many of the neighbourhood's trattorias still serve traditional offal-based dishes. So whether you want to avoid it or try it, look out for *pajata* (veal's intestines), *trippa* (tripe), *coda alla vaccinara* (oxtail), *coratella* (heart, lung and liver), *animelle* (sweetbreads), *testarella* (head), *lingua* (tongue) and *zampe* (trotters).

Agata e Romeo MODERN ITALIAN €€€
(Map p94; ☑ 06 446 61 15; Via Carlo Alberto 45; meals €120; ☺ Mon-Fri; ⓜ Vittorio Emanuele) This elegant, restrained place was one of Rome's gastronomic pioneers and is still a presence in the city's culinary charts. Its forte is Chef Agata Parisella's light, modern takes on classical Roman staples accompanied by superb wine from the lovingly curated cellar. Bookings essential.

✖ Celian Hill & San Giovanni

Li Rioni PIZZERIA €
(Map p97; ☑ 06 7045 0605; Via dei SS Quattro Coronati 24; pizzas €8; ☺ Thu-Tue, closed Aug; ⓜ Colosseo) Locals swear by Li Rioni, often arriving for the second sitting around 9pm after the tourists have left. A classic neighbourhood pizzeria, it buzzes most nights as diners squeeze into the cosy interior – cheerfully set up as a Roman street scene – and tuck into wood-fired thin-crust pizzas and crispy *supplì*.

✖ Aventine & Testaccio

00100 Pizza PIZZA BY SLICE €
(Map p134; www.00100pizza.com; Via G Branca 88; pizza slices from €3, trapizzini from €3.50; ☺ noon-11pm; ⓠ Via Marmorata) This pocket-sized pizzeria is one of a select group of Roman takeaways with culinary ambitions. As well as pizzas topped with unusual combos such as potato, sausage and beer, you can snack on *supplì* and *trapizzini*, small cones of pizza stuffed with fillers like *polpette al sugo*

Aventine & Testaccio

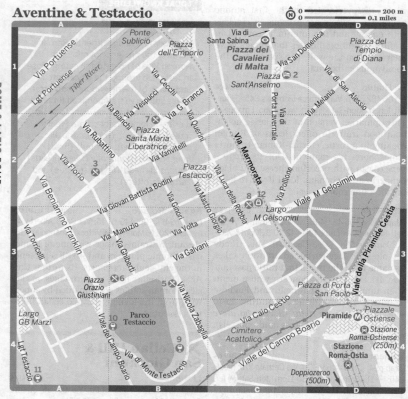

Aventine & Testaccio

◉ Top Sights
1 Piazza dei Cavalieri di Malta.................C1

🛏 Sleeping
2 Hotel Sant'Anselmo.............................C1

🍴 Eating
3 00100 Pizza.. A2
4 Da Felice.. C3
5 Flavio al Velavevodetto B3
6 Nuovo Mercato di Testaccio B3

7 Pizzeria Da Remo B2
8 Volpetti Più...C2

🍷 Drinking & Nightlife
9 ConteStaccio.......................................B4
10 L'Alibi...B4
11 Villaggio Globale................................A4

🛍 Shopping
12 Volpetti C2

(meatballs in tomato sauce) or *seppie con i piselli* (cuttlefish with peas).

Pizzeria Da Remo   PIZZERIA €
(Map p134; ☏ 06 574 62 70; Piazza Santa Maria Liberatrice 44; pizzas from €5.50; ⊙ 7pm-1am Mon-Sat; 🚍 Via Marmorata) Pizzeria Da Remo is one of the city's most popular pizzerias, its spartan interior always crowded with noisy diners. The pizzas are thin Roman classics with toppings loaded onto the crisp, charred base. Place your order by ticking your choiceson a sheet of paper slapped down by an overstretched waiter. Expect to queue.

Volpetti Più   CAFETERIA €
(Map p134; Via Volta 8; mains €8; ⊙ 10.30am-3.30pm & 5.30-9.30pm Mon-Sat; 🚍 Via Marmorata)

One of the few places in town where you can sit down for a full meal for less than €20, Volpetti Più is a sumptuous *tavola calda* (canteen-style buffet) offering an opulent choice of pizza, pasta, soup, meat, vegetables and fried nibbles.

Flavio al Velavevodetto   TRATTORIA €€
(Map p134; ☑ 06 574 41 94; www.flavioalvelavevodetto.it; Via di Monte Testaccio 97-99; meals €30-35; ⊙ closed Sat lunch & Sun summer; ☑ Via Marmorata) This welcoming eatery is the sort of place that gives Roman trattorias a good name. Housed in a rustic Pompeian-red villa, it specialises in earthy, no-nonsense Italian food, prepared with skill and served in mountainous portions. Expect homemade pastas seasoned with veggies and *guanciale* (bacon made from pig's cheek), followed by uncomplicated meaty mains.

Da Felice   REGIONAL CUISINE €€
(Map p134; ☑ 06 574 68 00; www.feliceatestaccio.com; Via Mastro Giorgio 29; meals €35-40; ⊙ lunch & dinner; ☑ Via Marmorata) Foodies swear by this local stalwart, famous for its traditional Roman cuisine. The menu follows a classic weekly timetable with *tonnarelli cacio e pepe* (square-shaped spaghetti with pecorino cheese and black pepper) on Tuesday, *coda alla vaccinara* (oxtail) on Thursday, and pasta *in brodo d'arzilla* (pasta in fish ray broth) on Friday. Reservations essential.

✖ Trastevere & Gianicolo

Sisini   PIZZA BY SLICE €
(Map p102; Via di San Francesco a Ripa 137; pizza & pasta from €2, supplì €1.10; ⊙ 9am-10.30pm Mon-Sat, closed Aug; ☑ Viale di Trastevere, ☑ Viale di Trastevere) Locals love this fast-food takeaway joint (the sign outside says 'Supplì') serving up fresh *pizza al taglio* and various pasta and risotto dishes. It's also worth sampling the *supplì* and roast chicken.

Bir & Fud   PIZZERIA €
(Map p80; Via Benedetta 23; meals €25; ⊙ 7.30pm-midnight, to 2am Fri & Sat; ☑ Piazza Trilussa) This orange-and-terracotta, vaulted pizzeria wins plaudits for its organic take on pizzas, *crostini* and fried things (potato, pumpkin etc). It also has a microbrewery on site, and serves seasonal tipples such as Birrificio Troll Palanfrina (a winter-only beer made from chestnuts).

Brasserie 4:20   RISTORANTE €
(☑ 06 5831 0737; Via Portuense 82; meals around €20; ⊙ 7pm-2am Sun-Wed, to 4am Thu-Sat; ☑ Piazza di Porta Portese) Rome's passion for artisanal beer shows no sign of abating, and this characterful brick-arched place, with kegs outside and a cool neon sign, not only has multiple rare draught beers but takes the concept one step further: many of its dishes are beer based (how about some 'tiramistout'). There are also good burgers, if you're in a burger-and-beer mood.

Da Augusto   TRATTORIA €
(Map p102; ☑ 06 580 37 98; Piazza de' Renzi 15; meals €25; ⊙ lunch & dinner; ☑ Viale di Trastevere, ☑ Viale di Trastevere) For a Trastevere feast, plonk yourself at one of Augusto's rickety tables, either inside or out on the small piazza, and prepare to enjoy some mamma-style cooking. The gruff waiters dish out hearty platefuls of *rigatoni all'amatriciana* (pasta tubes with pancetta, chilli and tomato sauce) and *stracciatella* (clear broth with egg and Parmesan) among a host of Roman classics. Be prepared to queue. Cash only.

Pizzeria Ivo   PIZZERIA €
(Map p102; ☑ 06 581 70 82; Via di San Francesco a Ripa 158; pizzas around €7; ⊙ Wed-Mon; ☑ Viale di Trastevere, ☑ Viale di Trastevere) One of Trastevere's most famous pizzerias, Ivo's has been slinging pizzas for some 40 years, and still the hungry come. With the TV on in the corner and the tables full (including a few outside on the cobbled street), it's a noisy, vibrant place, and the waiters fit the gruff-and-fast stereotype.

Forno la Renella   BAKERY €
(Map p102; ☑ 06 581 72 65; Via del Moro 15-16; pizza slices from €2.50; ⊙ 7am-2am Tue-Sat, to 10pm Sun & Mon; ☑ Piazza Trilussa) The wood-fired ovens at this historical Trastevere bakery have been going for decades, producing a delicious daily batch of pizza, bread and biscuits. Piled-high toppings (and fillings) vary seasonally. It's popular with everyone from skinheads to elderly ladies.

★ La Gensola   SICILIAN €€
(Map p102; ☑ 06 581 63 12; Piazza della Gensola 15; meals €45; ⊙ closed Sun mid-Jun–mid-Sep; ☑ Viale di Trastevere, ☑ Viale di Trastevere) This classy yet unpretentious trattoria thrills gourmets with delicious food that has a Sicilian slant and emphasis on seafood, including an excellent tuna tartare, linguine with fresh

EATALY

Housed in a renovated rail terminal in trendy Ostiense, **Eataly** (✆06 9027 9201; www.roma.eataly.it; Air Terminal Ostiense, Piazzale XII Ottobre 1492; ⊙shop 10am-midnight, restaurants noon-11.30pm; Ⓜ Piramide) is an enormous, mall-like complex devoted to Italian food. As well as shops selling foodstuffs from all over the country, books and kitchenware, it's also home to 19 cafes and restaurants, including a *panini* (sandwich) bar, a gelateria, a *friggitoria* (traditional Roman fried food), a restaurant specialising in Lazio-sourced vegetables, a *rosticceria* (for roasted meats) and a fine-dining restaurant. There's also an excellent pizza and pasta restaurant, and a microbrewery serving craft beers.

The complex is a 10-minute walk from Piramide metro station.

anchovies and divine *zuccherini* (tiny fish) with fresh mint. The set menu costs €41.

Le Mani in Pasta RISTORANTE €€

(Map p102; ✆06 581 60 17; Via dei Genovesi 37; meals €45; ⊙lunch & dinner Tue-Sun; 🚊Viale di Trastevere, 🚊Viale di Trastevere) Popular and lively, this rustic, snug place has arched ceilings and an open kitchen that serves up tasty fresh pasta dishes such as *fettucine con ricotta e pancetta*. The grilled meats are great, too.

Meridionale RISTORANTE €€

(Map p102; www.meridionaletrastevere.com; Via dei Fienaroli; meals €35, Sunday buffet €15; ⊙dinner Tue-Sun, lunch Sat & Sun; 🚊Viale di Trastevere, 🚊Viale di Trastevere) This hidden-away, arch-ceilinged restaurant specialises in southern Italian cooking, with dishes such as spaghetti with squid and cherry tomatoes. The appealing interior has a shabby-chic vibe, with its faded newspaper wallpaper, and glass domes over the desserts. There's a buffet lunch on Sunday.

Glass Hostaria MODERN ITALIAN €€€

(Map p102; ✆06 5833 5903; Vicolo del Cinque 58; meals €80; ⊙from 8pm Tue-Sun; 🚊Piazza Trilussa) Trastevere's foremost foodie address, the Glass is a modernist-styled, sophisticated restaurant with cooking to match. Chef Cristina Bowerman creates inventive, delicate dishes that combine fresh ingredients and

traditional elements to delight and surprise the palate. There are tasting menus at €70 and €90.

Paris RISTORANTE €€€

(Map p102; ✆06 581 53 78; www.ristoranteparis.it; Piazza San Calisto 7a; meals €55; ⊙Tue-Sat, lunch only Sun; 🚊Viale di Trastevere, 🚊Viale di Trastevere) An old-school Roman restaurant set in a 17th-century building, with seating out on the piazza, Paris (named for its founder, not the French capital) is the best place outside the Ghetto to sample Roman-Jewish cuisine, such as delicate *fritto misto con baccalà* (deep-fried vegetables with salt cod) and *carciofi alla giudia* (deep-fried artichokes). There's a sun-shaded terrace.

✖ Vatican City, Borgo & Prati

★ Pizzarium PIZZA BY SLICE €

(Map p106; Via della Meloria 43; pizza slices from €3; ⊙11am-9pm Mon-Sat; Ⓜ Cipro–Musei Vaticani) A gourmet revelation masquerading as an unassuming takeaway, hard-to-find Pizzarium dishes up some of Rome's best sliced pizza. Served on a wooden chopping board, its fluffy dough and perfect crust are topped with original, intensely flavoured ingredients. There's also a daily selection of *supplì*, juices and chilled beers.

Mondo Arancina SICILIAN, FAST FOOD €

(Map p106; Via Marcantonio Colonna 38; arancine from €2.50; ⊙10am-late; Ⓜ Lepanto) All sunny yellow ceramics, cheerful crowds and tantalising deep-fried snacks, this bustling takeaway brings a little corner of Sicily to Rome. Star of the show are the classic fist-sized *arancine*, fried rice balls stuffed with fillers ranging from classic *ragù* to more exotic fare such as truffle risotto and quail eggs.

Dolce Maniera BAKERY €

(Map p106; Via Barletta 27; ⊙24hr; Ⓜ Ottaviano–San Pietro) This 24-hour basement bakery supplies much of the neighbourhood with breakfast. Head here for cheap-as-chips *cornetti* (croissants), slabs of pizza, *panini* and an indulgent array of cakes.

Cacio e Pepe TRATTORIA €

(✆06 321 72 68; Via Avezzana 11; meals €25; ⊙closed Sat dinner & Sun; 🚊Piazza Giuseppe Mazzini) A local institution, this humble trattoria is as authentic as it gets with a menu of traditional Roman dishes, a spartan interior and no-frills service. If you can find a free seat at one of the gingham-clad tables splayed across the pavement, keep it simple with *cacio e pepe* followed by *pollo alla cacciatora* ('hunter's chicken').

Romeo
PIZZERIA, RISTORANTE €€

(Map p106; ☑ 06 3211 0120; www.romeo.roma. it; Via Silla 26a; pizza slices €3.50, meals €35-40; ☺ 9am-midnight Mon-Sat; Ⓜ Ottaviano–San Pietro) One of Rome's new breed of multipurpose gastro outfits, Romeo serves everything from freshly prepared *panini* to fabulous *pizza al taglio* and full restaurant meals. The look is contemporary chic with black walls and sprouting tubular lights; the food is a mix of classic Italian fare and forward-looking international creations.

Velavevodetto
Ai Quiriti
TRADITIONAL ITALIAN €€

(Map p106; ☑ 06 3600 0009; www.ristorantevelavevodetto.it; Piazza dei Quiriti 5; meals €35; ☺ Mon-Sun; Ⓜ Lepanto) Since it opened in spring 2012, this Prati newcomer has won over local diners with its unpretentious earthy food, honest prices and welcoming service. The menu reads like a directory of Roman staples, and while it's all pretty good, standout choices include *polpette di bollito* (fried meat balls) and *carciofi fritti* (fried artichokes).

Osteria dell'Angelo
TRATTORIA €€

(Map p106; ☑ 06 372 94 70; Via Bettolo 24; set menu €25 ; ☺ lunch & dinner Tue-Fri, dinner Mon & Sat; Ⓜ Ottaviano–San Pietro) Laid-back and informal, this hugely popular neighbourhood trattoria (reservations are a must) is a great place to try genuine local cuisine. The set menu features a mixed antipasti, a robust Roman-style pasta and a choice of hearty mains with a side dish. To finish off, you're offered lightly spiced biscuits to dunk in sweet dessert wine.

Hostaria Dino e Tony
TRATTORIA €€

(Map p106; ☑ 06 3973 3284; Via Leone IV 60; meals €30; ☺ Mon-Sat, closed Aug; Ⓜ Ottaviano–San Pietro) Something of a rarity, Dino e Tony is an authentic trattoria in the Vatican area. Kick off with the monumental antipasto, a minor meal in its own right, before plunging into its signature dish, *rigatoni all'amatriciana*. No credit cards.

Dal Toscano
TUSCAN €€

(Map p106; ☑ 06 3972 5717; www.ristorantedaltoscano.it; Via Germanico 58-60; meals €45; ☺ Tue-Sun; Ⓜ Ottaviano–San Pietro) One for the traditionalists, Dal Toscano is an old-fashioned *ristorante* that serves top-notch Tuscan meats. Start with the hand-cut *prosciutto* before attempting the colossal char-grilled *bistecche alla Fiorentina* (Florentine-style steak). You'll need to book.

Pizzeria Amalfi
PIZZERIA €€

(Map p106; ☑ 06 3973 3165; Via dei Gracchi 12; pizzas from €6, mains from €25; ☺ lunch & dinner; Ⓜ Ottaviano–San Pietro) While Roman pizzas are thin and crispy, Neapolitan pizzas are thicker and more doughy. And that's what you get at this brightly coloured pizzeria-cum-restaurant. If pizza doesn't appeal, there's a decent range of grilled meats, pastas, salads and fish dishes. Note that there's a second branch across the road at Via dei Gracchi 5.

Settembrini
CAFE, MODERN ITALIAN €€€

(☑ 06 323 26 17; www.viasettembrini.it; cafe Via Settembrini 21, restaurant Via Settembrini 25; aperitif €8, restaurant meals €60; ☺ cafe 7am-1am daily, restaurant lunch & dinner Mon-Fri, dinner Sat; ☐ Piazza Giuseppe Mazzini) All labels, suits and lipstick, this fashionable watering hole is a hot foodie fixture. Join the sharply dressed darlings for bar snacks, a light lunch or evening *aperitivo* at the cafe, or make an occasion of it and dine on creative Italian cuisine at the smart restaurant next door.

Ristorante L'Arcangelo
GASTRONOMIC €€€

(Map p106; ☑ 06 321 09 92; Via Belli 59-61; meals €60, tasting 'Roman' menu €50; ☺ closed lunch Sat & all day Sun; ☐ Piazza Cavour) Frequented by politicians and local celebs, this smart restaurant enjoys a stellar reputation with local gourmets. The highlights for many are the classic Roman staples such as carbonara and gnocchi, but there's also a tempting choice of innovative modern dishes.

✖ Villa Borghese & Northern Rome

Cinecaffè
CAFE €€

(Map p86; www.cinecaffe.it; Casina delle Rose, Largo Marcello Mastroianni 1; aperitif €6, snacks from €2.50, salads €9; ☺ 9am-7pm; ☐ Porta Pinciana) This slick modern cafe is one of the few places to get a decent bite in Villa Borghese. Stop by for a morning coffee or claim a table on the sunny terrace for an alfresco salad or choice pasta dish. Snacks and *panini*

SELF-CATERING

Rome's fresh-produce markets are a fabulous feature of the city's foodscape, and most neighbourhoods have their own daily market, operating from around 7am to 1.30pm, Monday to Saturday. There are also some excellent farmers markets, mostly taking place on weekends.

Rome's most famous food markets:

Campo de' Fiori (Map p80; 🚇 Corso Vittorio Emanuele II)

Mercato di Circo Massimo (Map p68; www.mercatocircomassimo.it; Via di San Teodoro 74; ⊙ 9am-6pm Sat, to 4pm Sun; 🚇 Via dei Cerchi)

Nuovo Mercato Esquilino (Map p94; Via Lamarmora; Ⓜ Vittorio Emanuele)

Piazza San Cosimato (Map p102; 🚇 Viale di Trastevere, 🚇 Viale di Trastevere)

Nuovo Mercato di Testaccio (Map p134; Via Galvani; ⊙ 6am-3pm Mon-Sat; 🚇 Via Marmorata)

You can also stock up on groceries at the small supermarkets dotted around town:

Conad (Map p94; Stazione Termini)

DeSpar (Map p94; Via Nazionale 212-213)

Carrefour Express (Map p86; Via Vittoria 32)

Sir (Map p94; Piazza dell'Indipendenza 28)

Todis (Map p102; Via Natale del Grande 24)

are also available and brunch is served at weekends.

 ## Drinking & Nightlife

Rome has plenty of drinking venues, ranging from traditional *enoteche* (wine bars) and streetside cafes to dressy lounge bars, pubs (trendy by virtue of their novelty) and counter-culture hang-outs. During the day people usually head to bars for a quick coffee, while early evening sees the city's hipsters turn out for the evening *aperitivo* (aperitif).

Much of the action is in the *centro storico* – Campo de' Fiori fills with young, rowdy drinkers, while the lanes around Piazza Navona host a calmer, dressier scene. Over the river, Trastevere is another popular spot with dozens of bars and pubs, while to the east of Termini, the cheaper, grungier bars of San Lorenzo and Pigneto attract students and an arty alternative crowd.

Rome's clubs cater to most tastes, with DJs spinning everything from lounge and jazz to house, dancehall and hip hop. The scene is centred on Testaccio (mainstream clubs) and Ostiense (industrial, warehouse vibe for serious clubbers), although you'll also find places in Trastevere and the *centro storico*. Out from the centre, San Lorenzo and Pigneto are happening areas.

You'll need to dress the part for the big clubs, which can be tricky to get into, especially for groups of men. Events are often listed for 10pm but don't kick off until around 11pm, while clubs rarely hot up until well after 1am. Drinks are expensive, typically €10 to €16. Note also that many clubs shut between mid-June and mid-September.

 ## Ancient Rome

Cavour 313   WINE BAR
(Map p68; ☎ 06 678 54 96; www.cavour313.it; Via Cavour 313; ⊙ 12.30pm-2.45pm & 7.30pm-12.30am, closed Sun summer; Ⓜ Cavour) Close to the Forum, wood-panelled Cavour 313 attracts everyone from tourists to actors and politicians. Sink into its pub-like cosiness and while away hours over sensational wine (more than 1200 labels) accompanied by cold cuts and cheese (€8 to €12) or a plate of pasta.

Caffè Capitolino   CAFE
(Map p68; Piazzale Caffarelli 4; ⊙ 9am-7.30pm Tue-Sun; 🚇 Piazza Venezia) The charming rooftop cafe of the Capitoline Museums is a good place to relax over a drink or light snack (*panini*, salads and pizza). Although part of the museum complex, you don't need a

ticket to drink here as it's accessible via an independent entrance on Piazzale Caffarelli.

0,75 — BAR

(Map p68; www.075roma.com; Via dei Cerchi 65; ⊘11am-1.30am; 🛜; 🚇Via dei Cerchi) This funky bar on the Circo Massimo is good for a lingering drink, weekend brunch (€15; 11am to 3pm), *aperitivo* (6.30pm onwards) or light lunch (pastas €7 to €8.50, salads €5.50 to €7.50). It's a friendly place with a laid-back vibe, attractive exposed-brick look and cool tunes. Free wi-fi.

🍷 Centro Storico

★ Caffè Tazza d'Oro — CAFE

(Map p80; www.tazzadorocoffeeshop.com; Via degli Orfani 84; ⊘7am-8pm; 🚇Via del Corso) A busy, stand-up bar with polished wood and brass fittings, this is one of Rome's best coffee houses. Its espresso hits the mark perfectly and there's a range of delicious coffee concoctions, including a refreshing *granita di caffè* (a crushed-ice coffee drink served with whipped cream).

Caffè Sant'Eustachio — CAFE

(Map p80; Piazza Sant'Eustachio 82; ⊘8.30am-1am Sun-Thu, to 1.30am Fri, to 2am Sat; 🚇Corso del Rinascimento) This small, unassuming cafe, generally three deep at the bar, is famous for its *gran caffè*, said by many to be the best coffee in town. Created by beating the first drops of espresso and several teaspoons of sugar into a frothy paste, then adding the rest of the coffee, it's superbly smooth and guaranteed to put some zing into your sightseeing.

★ Barnum Cafe — CAFE

(Map p80; www.barnumcafe.com; Via del Pellegrino 87; ⊘9.30am-2am Tue-Sat, to 9pm Mon; 🚇Corso Vittorio Emanuele II) A relaxed, friendly spot to check your email over a freshly squeezed orange juice or spend a pleasant hour reading a newspaper on one of the tatty old armchairs in the white bare-brick interior. If you like tunes with your drinks, stop by on Tuesday evening for the DJ-accompanied Sounds Good *aperitivo* (from 7pm).

Etablì — BAR, RISTORANTE

(Map p80; ☎06 9761 6694; www.etabli.it; Vicolo delle Vacche 9a; ⊘6.30pm-1am Mon-Wed, to 2am Thu-Sat; 🚇Corso del Rinascimento) Housed in a lofty 17th-century *palazzo*, Etablì is a rustic-chic lounge bar and restaurant where Roman beauties drop by to chat over cocktails,

snack on tapas and indulge in *aperitivo*. It's laid-back and good-looking, with occasional jam sessions and original French country decor – think wrought-iron fittings, comfy armchairs and a crackling fireplace.

Open Baladin — BAR

(Map p80; www.openbaladinroma.it; Via degli Specchi 6; ⊘12pm-2am; 🚇Via Arenula) A cool lounge bar near Campo de' Fiori, Open Baladin is a leading light in Rome's thriving beer scene. With more than 40 beers on tap and up to 100 bottled brews, many produced by artisanal microbreweries, it's a great place for buffs of the brown stuff. There's also a decent food menu with *panini*, burgers and daily specials.

Salotto 42 — BAR

(Map p80; www.salotto42.it; Piazza di Pietra 42; ⊘10am-2am Tue-Sat, to midnight Sun & Mon; 🚇Via del Corso) On a picturesque piazza, facing the columns of the Tempio di Adriano, this is a glamorous lounge bar, complete with vintage armchairs, suede sofas and a collection of two-tonne design books. Come for the daily lunch buffet or to hang out with the beautiful people over an *aperitivo*.

Circus — BAR

(Map p80; www.circusroma.it; Via della Vetrina 15; ⊘10am-2am; 🚇Corso del Rinascimento) A great little cafe-bar tucked around the corner from Piazza Navona, popular with American students from the nearby school. It's a funky, informal place where you can drink and catch up on the news from home – wi-fi is free and there are international newspapers to read. Regular events are staged, ranging from retro celebrations of '90s Britpop to themed *aperitivo* nights.

Caffè Farnese — CAFE

(Map p80; Via dei Baullari 106; ⊘7.30am-8pm, to late summer; 🚇Corso Vittorio Emanuele II) On a street between Campo de' Fiori and Piazza Farnese, this unassuming cafe is a top people-watching pad, ideal for whiling away the early afternoon hours. It also does a very fine espresso.

Il Goccetto — WINE BAR

(Map p80; Via dei Banchi Vecchi 14; ⊘11.30am-2pm Tue & Sat, 6.30pm-midnight Mon-Sat, closed Aug; 🚇Corso Vittorio Emanuele II) Should anyone decide to make an Italian version of American TV series *Cheers*, they should set it at this wood-panelled *vino e olio* (wine and oil) shop, where a colourful cast of regulars finish each other's sentences, banter with the owners and work their way through an 800-strong wine list. Eavesdrop over plates of prized north Italian cheese and salami.

Caffè & Bar della Pace
CAFE

(Map p80; www.caffedellapace.it; Via della Pace 5; ⏰9am-3am Tue-Sun, 4pm-3am Mon; 🚌Corso del Rinascimento) Live *la dolce vita* at this perennially fashionable art nouveau cafe. Inside it's all gilt and mismatched wooden tables; outside stylishly dressed drinkers strike poses over their Camparis against a backdrop of cascading ivy.

Vineria Reggio
WINE BAR

(Map p80; www.vineriareggio.com; Campo de' Fiori 15; ⏰8.30am-2am Mon-Sat; 🚌Corso Vittorio Emanuele II) The pick of the bars and cafes on Campo de' Fiori, this has a cosy, bottle-lined interior and outside tables. Busy from lunchtime onwards, it attracts tourists and *fighi* (cool) Romans like bees to a honeypot. Wine by the glass from €3.50 and snacks from €3.

🍸 Tridente, Trevi & the Quirinale

La Scena
BAR

(Map p86; Via della Penna 22; ⏰noon-3am; Ⓜ️Flaminio) Part of the art deco Hotel Locarno, this bar has a lovely, faded Agatha Christie–era feel, and a greenery-shaded outdoor terrace bedecked in wrought-iron furniture. A glass of *prosecco* costs from €5.

Stravinskij Bar – Hotel de Russie
BAR

(Map p86; ☎️06 328 88 70; Via del Babuino 9; ⏰9am-1am; Ⓜ️Flaminio) Can't afford to stay at the celeb-magnet Hotel de Russie? Then splash out on a drink at its swish bar. There are sofas inside, but best is a sunny drink in the courtyard overlooked by terraced

APERITIVO, ANYONE?

Although originally a northern Italian custom, the *aperitivo* has been enthusiastically adopted by Rome's barflies and many bars now serve lavish buffets between 6pm and 9pm. To partake, order a drink – there's usually a standard charge of €8 to €10 – and dig in.

Top spots include Freni e Frizioni (p142), Doppiozeroo (p141) and Etabli (p139).

gardens. Impossibly romantic, it's perfect for a cocktail (€20) and posh snacks.

Rosati
CAFE

(Map p86; ☎️06 322 58 59; Piazza del Popolo 5; ⏰7.30am-11.30pm; Ⓜ️Flaminio) Rosati, overlooking Piazza del Popolo, was once the hang-out of the left-wing chattering classes. Authors Italo Calvino and Alberto Moravia used to drink here while their right-wing counterparts went to Canova (Map p86; ☎️06 361 22 31; Piazza del Popolo 16; ⏰8am-midnight; Ⓜ️Flaminio), across the square. Today tourists are the main clientele, and the views are as good as ever.

Caffè Greco
CAFE

(Map p86; ☎️06 679 17 00; Via dei Condotti 86; ⏰9am-8pm; Ⓜ️Spagna) Casanova, Goethe, Wagner, Keats, Byron, Shelley and Baudelaire are among the luminaries who have sipped at Caffè Greco since it opened in 1760. Now there are fewer artists and lovers and more shoppers and tourists. Prices reflect this, unless you do as the locals do and drink at the bar.

🍸 Monti, Esquiline & San Lorenzo

★ Circolo degli Artisti
CLUB, LIVE MUSIC

(☎️06 7030 5684; www.circoloartisti.it; Via Casilina Vecchia 42; ⏰7pm-2am Tue-Thu, to 4.30am Fri-Sun; 🚌Ponte Casilino) East of the Pigneto district, Circolo offers one of Rome's best nights out with top gigs and DJ sets. Friday night cracks open electronica and house for gay night – Omogenic – and Saturday sees the fun-packed Screamadelica (punk-funk, ska and new wave), usually also featuring a live band. There's a cool garden bar and admission is either free or a snip.

Ai Tre Scalini
WINE BAR

(Map p68; Via Panisperna 251; ⏰12.30pm-1am Mon-Fri, 6pm-1am Sat & Sun; Ⓜ️Cavour) The Three Steps is always packed, with crowds spilling onto the street. As well as a tasty choice of wines, it sells the damn fine Menabrea beer, brewed in northern Italy. You can also tuck into a heart-warming array of cheeses, salami and dishes such as *polpette al sugo* (meatballs with sauce).

2 Periodico Caffè
CAFE

(Map p68; Via Leonina 77; ⏰9am-1am Tue-Thu, to 2am Fri-Sun; Ⓜ️Cavour) This cafe has a funky laid-back vibe, with its mismatched vintage furniture, fairylights in jam jars and personable bar staff. It's the kind of place you might find in Shoreditch in London or the Marais in Paris, but what's uniquely Italian is the coffee and delicious little extras such as lavender-scented More Bianche biscuits.

Solea
BAR

(Map p94; 328 9252925; Via dei Latini 51; 9am-2am; Via Tiburtina, Scalo San Lorenzo) With vintage sofas and chairs, and cushions on the floor, this slightly grungy place has the look of a chill-out room in a gone-to-seed mansion, and is full of lounging San Lorenzo dudes drinking mean mojitos. Fun.

Micca Club
CLUB, LIVE MUSIC

(Map p94; www.miccaclub.com; Via Pietra Micca 7a; 7pm-2am Thu-Sat, Mon & Tue, from 6pm Sun; Vittorio Emanuele) At eclectic Micca, pop art and jelly-bright lighting fill ancient, cathedral-like arched cellars, and there are regular burlesque, drag, swing and rockabilly nights, plus loads of live gigs. There's *aperitivo* nightly until 10pm, and an admission charge if a gig's on and at weekends.

Locanda Atlantide
CLUB, LIVE MUSIC

(Map p94; 06 4470 4540; www.locandatlantide. it; Via dei Lucani 22b; 9pm-2am Oct-Jun; Via Tiburtina, Scalo San Lorenzo) Come tickle Rome's grungy underbelly. Descend through a door in a graffiti-covered wall into this cavernous basement dive, packed to the rafters with studenty, alternative crowds and featuring everything from experimental theatre to DJ-spun electro music.

Dimmidisì
CLUB

(Map p94; 06 446 18 55; dimmidisiclub.org; Via dei Volsci 126b; 6pm-2am Thu-Mon Sep-May; Via dei Reti, Via Tiburtina) The intimate, small-scale 'Tell Me Yes' proffers a wide range of off-beat nights, from reggae to the *taranta* music of southern Italy. There are regular DJs and it's a good place to see live bands.

Bar Zest at the Radisson Blu Es
BAR

(Map p94; Via Filippo Turati 171; 9am-1am; Via Cavour) In need of a cocktail in the Termini district? Pop up to the 7th-floor bar at the Radisson Blu Es. Waiters are cute, chairs are by Jasper Morrison, views are through plate-glass and there's a sexy rooftop pool to look at. A glass of *prosecco* costs €9 and there are light meals and snacks.

Celian Hill & San Giovanni

Il Pentagrappolo
WINE BAR

(Map p97; Via Celimontana 21b; noon-3pm & 6pm-1am Tue-Fri, 6pm-1am Sat & Sun; Colosseo) This relaxed, star-vaulted wine bar is the perfect antidote to sightseeing overload. Join the mellow crowd to sip on wine (choose from about 15 wines by the glass) and chat over piano tunes or live jazz. There's also lunch and a daily *aperitivo* from 6pm.

Aventine & Testaccio

Villaggio Globale
CLUB, LIVE MUSIC

(Map p134; www.ecn.org/villaggioglobale/joomla; Via Monte del Cocci 22; Via Marmorata) For a warehouse-party vibe, head to this historic *centro sociale* (an ex-squat turned cultural centre) occupying the city's graffiti-sprayed former slaughterhouse. Entrance is cheap, the beer flows and there's plenty of music action with live DJ sets and gigs, mostly techno, dancehall, reggae, dubstep and drum 'n' bass.

ConteStaccio
CLUB, LIVE MUSIC

(Map p134; www.contestaccio.com; Via di Monte Testaccio 65b; 7pm-5am Tue-Sun, closed end Jun–mid-Sep; Via Marmorata) With an under-the-stars terrace and cool, arched interior, ConteStaccio is one of the top venues on the Testaccio clubbing strip. Daily gigs by emerging groups set the tone, spanning indie, rock, acoustic, funk and electronic. Admission is usually free with cocktails costing around €8.

Southern Rome

Doppiozeroo
BAR

(06 5730 1961; doppiozeroo.com; Via Ostiense 68; 7am-2am Mon-Sat; Piramide) This easy-going bar was once a bakery, hence the name ('double zero' is a type of flour). But today the sleek, modern interior attracts hungry, trendy Romans, especially for the famously lavish *aperitivo* between 6.30pm and 9pm. There's a buffet lunch on Saturday and Sunday, and DJs every Thursday.

Neo Club
CLUB

(Via degli Argonauti 18; 11pm-4am Fri & Sat; Garbatella) This small, dark two-level club has an underground feel and is one of the funkiest clubs in the zone, featuring a dancetastic mish-mash of breakbeat, techno and old-skool house.

Goa
CLUB

(06 574 82 77; www.goaclub.com; Via Libetta 13; 11.30pm-4.30am Thu-Sat; Garbatella) Goa is Rome's serious super-club, with international-al names, ethnic styling, a fashion-forward crowd, podium dancers and heavies on the door. Look out for the regular lesbian night, Venus Rising (www.venusrising.com).

Rashomon
CLUB

(www.rashomonclub.com; Via degli Argonauti 16; 11pm-4am Fri & Sat Oct-May; Garbatella) Rashomon is sweaty, not posey, and where to head when you want to dance your arse off. Shake it to a music lover's feast of the sound of the underground, especially house, techno and electronica.

🍴 Trastevere & Gianicolo

Ma Che Siete Venuti a Fà
PUB

(Map p80; Via Benedetta 25; 11am-2am; Piazza Trilussa) This pint-sized pub – whose name, a football chant, translates politely as 'What did you come here for?'– is a beer-buff's paradise, packing a huge number of on-tap craft beers and obscure bottled tipples into its tiny interior.

Bar San Calisto
CAFE

(Map p102; 06 589 56 78; Piazza San Calisto 3-5; 6am-2am Mon-Sat; Viale di Trastevere, Viale di Trastevere) Those in the know head to the down-at-heel 'Sanca' for its basic, stuck-in-time atmosphere and cheap prices. It attracts everyone from drug dealers, intellectuals and pseudo-intellectuals to keeping-it-real Romans, alcoholics and American students. It's famous for its chocolate –

SUMMER NIGHTS IN ROME

From mid-June to mid-September, most of the city's clubs and music joints close, with some moving to Fregene or Ostia for a summer of beach-front dancing. However, the Estate Romana (p119) festival supplies ample after-dark entertainment. Concerts, exhibitions, theatrical performances and open-air cinema are staged across town, while the city's nightlife goes alfresco down by the Tiber for the summer-long Lungo il Tevere (p119) festival.

---

drunk hot with cream in winter, eaten as ice cream in summer.

Freni e Frizioni
BAR

(Map p102; 06 5833 4210; www.freniefrizioni. com; Via del Politeama 4-6; 6.30pm-2am; Piazza Trilussa) The hipsters favourite cool Trastevere bar, this was a garage in a former life, hence its name ('brakes and clutches'). The arty crowd flocks here to slurp well-priced drinks (especially mojitos), feast on the good-value *aperitivo* (7pm to 10pm) and spill into the piazza out the front.

Ombre Rosse
BAR

(Map p102; 06 588 41 55; Piazza Sant'Egidio 12; 8am-2am Mon-Sat, 11am-2am Sun; Piazza Trilussa) A seminal Trastevere hang-out; grab a table on the terrace and watch the world go by amid a clientele ranging from elderly Italian wide boys to wide-eyed tourists. Tunes are slinky and there's live music (jazz, blues, world) on Thursday evenings from September to April.

🍴 Vatican City, Borgo & Prati

Passaguai
WINE BAR

(Map p106; www.passaguai.it; Via Leto 1; 10am-2am Mon-Sat; 📶; Piazza del Risorgimento) A small, cavelike basement wine bar, Passaguai has a few outdoor tables on a quiet street and feels pleasingly off-the-radar. It boasts a good wine list and a range of artisanal beers, and the food – think cheese and cured meats – is tasty too. Free wi-fi.

Art Studio Café
CAFE

(Map p106; www.artstudiocafe.it; Via dei Gracchi 187a; Lepanto) A cafe, exhibition space and craft school all in one, this bright and breezy spot serves one of Prati's most popular *aperitivo*. It's also good for a light lunch or restorative mid-afternoon tea.

☆ Entertainment

Entertainment in Rome can be simply parking yourself at a streetside table and watching the world go by. But the city has a thriving cultural scene with a year-round calendar of concerts, performances and festivals. In summer, the Estate Romana (p119) festival sponsors hundreds of cultural events, many staged in atmospheric parks, piazzas and churches. Autumn is another good time, with festivals dedicated to dance, drama and jazz.

A useful listings guide is *Trova Roma*, a free insert with *La Repubblica* newspaper every Thursday. Upcoming events are also listed on www.turismoroma.it, www.060608. it, www.inromenow.com and www.auditorium.com.

For tickets, try **Orbis** (Map p94; ☑ 06 474 47 76; Piazza dell'Esquilino 37), which accepts cash payment only, or the online agency **Hellò Ticket** (☑ 800 907080; www.helloticket.it).

Classical Music
An abundance of spectacular settings makes Rome a superb place to catch a classical music concert. The city's cultural and musical hub is the Auditorium Parco della Musica, but free concerts are often held in churches, especially at Easter, Christmas and New Year. Seats are available on a first-come, first-served basis and the programs are generally excellent. Check newspapers and listings for programs.

Auditorium Parco
della Musica   CONCERT VENUE
(☑ 06 8024 1281; www.auditorium.com; Viale Pietro de Coubertin 30; ☐ shuttle bus M from Stazione Termini, ☐ Viale Tiziano) Rome's main concert venue, this state-of-the-art complex combines architectural innovation with perfect acoustics. Designed by Renzo Piano, its three concert halls and 3000-seat open-air arena host everything from classical music concerts to tango exhibitions, book readings and film screenings.

The auditorium is also home to Rome's top orchestra, the world-class **Orchestra dell' Accademia Nazionale di Santa Cecilia** (www.santacecilia.it).

Teatro Olimpico   THEATRE
(☑ 06 326 59 91; www.teatroolimpico.it; Piazza Gentile da Fabriano 17; ☐ Piazza Mancini, ☐ Piazza Mancini) The Teatro Olimpico is home to the **Accademia Filarmonica Roman** (www.filarmonicaromana.org), one of Rome's major classical music organisations whose past members have included Rossini, Donizetti and Verdi. The theatre offers a varied program that concentrates on classical and chamber music, but also features opera, ballet and contemporary multimedia events.

Opera
Opera is staged in the city's main opera house and, in summer, amidst the spectacular ruins of the Terme di Caracalla.

Teatro dell'Opera di Roma   OPERA
(Map p94; ☑ 06 481 70 03; www.operaroma.it; Piazza Beniamino Gigli; ballet tickets €12-80, opera €17-150; ☒ box office 9am-5pm Mon-Sat, 9am-1.30pm Sun; Ⓜ Repubblica) Built in 1880, the plush and gilt interior of Rome's premier opera house is a stunning surprise after the Fascist-era exterior (which was revamped in the 1920s). This theatre has an impressive history: it premiered Puccini's *Tosca* and Maria Callas once sang here. Contemporary productions don't always match the splendour of the setting, but you may get lucky.

Jazz & Blues
Alexanderplatz   JAZZ
(Map p106; ☑ 06 3974 2171; www.alexanderplatz.it; Via Ostia 9; ☒ concerts 9.45pm Sun-Thu, 10.30pm Fri & Sat ; Ⓜ Ottaviano–San Pietro) Small and intimate, Rome's top jazz joint attracts top Italian and international performers and a respectful, cosmopolitan crowd. Book a table if you want to dine to the tunes.

La Casa del Jazz   JAZZ
(☑ 06 70 47 31; www.casajazz.it; Viale di Porta Ardeatina 55; admission €5-10; ☒ 7pm-midnight; Ⓜ Piramide) In the middle of a park in the southern suburbs, the Casa del Jazz is housed in a villa that once belonged to a Mafia boss. When he was caught, the Comune di Roma (Rome Council) confiscated it and converted it into a jazz-fuelled complex, with a 150-seat auditorium, rehearsal rooms, cafe and restaurant. Some events are free.

Big Mama   BLUES
(Map p102; ☑ 06 581 25 51; www.bigmama.it; Vicolo di San Francesco a Ripa 18; ☒ 9pm-1.30am, shows 10.30pm Thu-Sat, closed Jun-Sep; ☐ Viale di Trastevere, ☐ Viale di Trastevere) To wallow in the Eternal City blues, there's only one place to go – this cramped Trastevere basement, which also hosts jazz, funk, soul and R&B.

Lettere Caffè Gallery   LIVE MUSIC
(Map p102; ☑ 06 9727 0991; www.letterecaffe.org; Vicolo di San Francesco a Ripa 100/101; ☒ 7pm-2am, closed mid-Aug–mid-Sep; ☐ Viale di Trastevere, ☐ Viale di Trastevere) Like books? Poetry? Blues and jazz? Then you'll love this place – a clutter of bar stools and books, where there are regular live gigs, poetry slams, comedy and gay nights, plus DJ sets playing indie and new wave. There's vegetarian nibbles from 7pm to 9pm nightly (€5).

Cinemas

Of Rome's 80-odd cinemas only a handful show films in the original language (marked VO or *versione originale* in listings). Expect to pay around €8, with many cinemas offering discounts on Wednesdays.

In Trastevere, try the **Alcazar Cinema** (Map p102; ✆06 588 00 99; Via Merry del Val 14; Viale di Trastevere, Viale di Trastevere) or **Nuovo Sacher** (✆06 581 81 16; www.sacher-film.eu; Largo Ascianghi 1; Viale di Trastevere, Viale di Trastevere), owned by cult Roman film maker Nanni Moretti.

Sport

Watching a game of football at Rome's **Stadio Olimpico** (✆06 3685 7520; Viale dei Gladiatori 2, Foro Italico) is an unforgettable experience, although you'll have to keep your wits about you as crowd trouble is not unheard of.

Throughout the season (September to May), there's a game most Sundays involving one of the city's two teams: **AS Roma**, known as the *giallorossi* (yellow and reds; www.asroma.it), or **Lazio**, the *biancazzuri* (white and blues; www.sslazio.it, in Italian). Ticket prices start at €16 and can be bought at Lottomatica (lottery centres), the stadium, ticket agencies, www.listicket.it or one of the many Roma or Lazio stores around town.

To get to the stadium take metro line A to Ottaviano and then bus 32.

Shopping

Rome boasts the usual cast of flagship chain stores and glitzy designer outlets but what makes shopping here fun is its legion of small, independent shops – historic, family owned delis, small-label fashion boutiques, artists' studios and neighbourhood markets.

For designer clothes head to Via dei Condotti, Rome's top shopping strip, and the grid of streets around Piazza di Spagna. For something more left field, check out the vintage shops and boutiques on Via del Governo Vecchio, around Campo de' Fiori and in the Monti neighbourhood.

If you're looking for antiques or arty gifts, try Via dei Coronari, Via dei Banchi Vecchi or Via Margutta.

For the best bargains, time your visit to coincide with the *saldi* (sales). Winter sales run from early January to mid-February and summer sales from July to early September.

🅰 Centro Storico

★ Confetteria Moriondo & Gariglio
CHOCOLATE

(Map p80; Via del Piè di Marmo 21-22; ⏰9am-7.30pm Mon-Sat; Via del Corso) Roman poet Trilussa was so smitten with this historic chocolate shop – established by the Torinese confectioners to the royal house of Savoy – that he dedicated several sonnets in its honour. Many of the handmade chocolates and bonbons, laid out in ceremonial splendour in glass cabinets set against dark crimson walls, are still made to 19th-century recipes.

★ Ibiz – Artigianato in Cuoio
ACCESSORIES

(Map p80; Via dei Chiavari 39; ⏰9.30am-7.30pm Mon-Sat; Corso Vittorio Emanuele II) In their diminutive workshop, Elisa Nepi and her father craft exquisite, well-priced leather goods, including wallets, bags, belts and sandals, in simple but classy designs and myriad colours. For €70 you should be able to pick up a purse, while satchels cost around €200.

Le Artigiane
ARTISANAL

(Map p80; www.leartigiane.it; Via di Torre Argentina 72; ⏰10am-7.30pm; Largo di Torre Argentina) A space for local artisans to showcase their wares, this shop is the result of an ongoing project to sustain and promote Italy's artisanal traditions. It's a browser's dream selling an eclectic range of handmade clothes, costume jewellery, design objects and lamps.

daDADA 52
CLOTHING

(Map p80; www.dadada.eu; Via dei Giubbonari 52; ⏰11am-2pm & 2.30-7.30pm Mon, 10am-7.30pm Tue-Sat, 11am-7.30pm Sun; Via Arenula) Every young Roman fashionista makes a stop at daDADA for its funky cocktail dresses, bright print summer frocks, eclectic coats and colourful hats. Prices start at around €100 but many items are north of €200. There's a second **branch** (Map p86; ✆06 6813 9162; www.dadada.eu; Via del Corso 500; Flaminio or Spagna) at Via del Corso 500.

Luna & L'Altra
CLOTHING

(Map p80; Piazza Pasquino 76; ⏰10am-2pm Tue-Sat & 3.30-7.30pm Mon-Sat; Corso Vittorio Emanuele II) This trendy address is one of a number of independent boutiques on and around Via del Governo Vecchio. In its austere, gallery-like interior, clothes and accessories by hip designers Issey Miyake, Marc Le Bihan, Jean Paul Gaultier and Yohji Yamamoto are exhibited in reverential style.

Nardecchia
ART

(Map p80; Piazza Navona 25; ⏱10am-1pm Tue-Sat & 4.30-7.30pm Mon-Sat; 🚌Corso del Rinascimento) You'll be inviting people to see your etchings after a visit to this historic Piazza Navona shop. Famed for its antique prints, Nardecchia sells everything from 18th-century etchings by Giovanni Battista Piranesi to more affordable 19th-century panoramas. Bank on at least €120 for a small framed print.

Officina Profumo Farmaceutica di Santa Maria Novella
COSMETICS

(Map p80; Corso del Rinascimento 47; ⏱10am-7.30pm Mon-Sat; 🚌Corso del Rinascimento) The Roman branch of one of Italy's oldest pharmacies, this bewitching, aromatic shop stocks natural perfumes and cosmetics as well as herbal infusions, teas and pot pourri, all carefully shelved in wooden cabinets under a giant Murano-glass chandelier. The original pharmacy was founded in Florence [in 1]612 by the Dominican monks of Santa [Nov]ia Novella, and many of its cosmetics are [base]d on 17th-century herbal recipes.

SHOES

[...]; Via dei Pettinari 86-87; ⏱9am-1pm Tue-[...]7.30pm Mon-Sat; 🚌Via Arenula) Don't [...] the piles of boxes and the dis-[...]aday look – those in the know [...] seemingly down-at-heel shop, [...]rinis since 1940, for the latest [...] Whatever is 'in' this season, [...] it, at reasonable prices and [...] hue.

Trevi &

ARTISANAL

[...] ⏱9am-1pm & 4-8pm [...] the well-worn stairs [...] from the softest [...]tly be the proud [...]signer-style bag, [...] can even take a [...] produce. Bags [...] around a week [...] overseas, [...] as postage [...] Map p [...] am-7 [...] ART [...] minut [...] m Mon, [...] nd al last- [...] ware [...] er,

... the art of letter writing, plus an ... choice of notebooks, art stuff and ... inspire you to ... di Marmoraro ... ARTISANAL

cards ... bring ... amazi... trinke...

Bottega di Marmoraro
(Map p86; ... Sat; Ⓜ Flamin... wall shop lin... you can get i... any inscription... at lunchtime a... moraro (marble... tripe for his lunch ... ⏱8am-7.30pm Mon... hole-in-the-

Lucia Odescalchi
(Map p86; ☎06 6992 ...; Piazza Santissimi Apostoli ... Fri; Ⓜ Spagna) If you're ... piece of statement jew... place. Housed in the eve... the family *palazzo*, the avant-garde pieces often have an almost medieval beauty, and run from incredible polished steel and chain mail to pieces created out of pearls and fossils. Beautiful. Prices start at around €140.

C.U.C.I.N.A.
HOMEWARES

(Map p86; ☎06 679 12 75; Via Mario de' Fiori 65; ⏱3.30-7.30pm Mon, 10am-7.30pm Tue-Fri, 10.30am-7.30pm Sat; Ⓜ Spagna) If you're into cooking as much for the gear as the food, you'll enjoy this cool kitchenware shop. A branch of the capital's C.U.C.I.N.A chain, it stocks all sorts of sexy pots and pans, designer

---

LOCAL KNOWLEDGE

HELP FIGHT THE MAFIA

To look at it there's nothing special about **Pio La Torre** (Map p80; www.liberaterra.it; Via dei Prefetti 23; ⏱10am-1pm & 3.30-7.30pm Mon-Sat; 🚌Via del Corso), a small, unpretentious food store near Piazza del Parlamento. But shop here and you're making a small but concrete contribution to the fight against the mafia. All the gastro goodies on sale, including organic olive oils, pastas, honeys and wine, are produced on land confiscated from organised crime outfits. The shop is part of a countrywide chain called *I Sapori e I Saperi della Legalità* (The Taste and Awareness of Legality), which distributes food produced on ex-mafia terrain.

cutlery &
range of fash...

and envelope...

CLOTHING
...lino 97;
...m Sun;
...sguises a
...the Tardis-like
...its finger is on the
...selection of designers,
...Gabbana, Fendi, Missoni,
...Sergio Rossi.

SHOES
...; ☏ 06 679 24 67; Via Frattina 85a;
...m-7.45pm Tue-Sat, noon-7.45pm Sun & Mon;
Ⓜ Spagna) If you're female and in need of an Italian shoe fix, this fashionable store sells both classic and on-trend styles – foxy heels, boots and ballet pumps – at extremely reasonable prices. Shoes are soft leather and come in endless colours.

Sermoneta
ACCESSORIES

(Map p86; ☏ 06 679 19 60; www.sermonetagloves.com; Piazza di Spagna 61; ⊙ 9.30am-8pm Mon-Sat, 10am-7pm Sun; Ⓜ Spagna) Buying leather gloves in Rome is a rite of passage for some, and its most famous glove-seller is the place to do it. Choose from a kaleidoscopic range of quality leather and suede gloves lined with silk and cashmere. An expert assistant will size up your hand in a glance. Just don't expect them to smile.

Fausto Santini
SHOES

(Map p86; ☏ 06 678 41 14; Via Frattina 120; ⊙ 11am-7.30pm Mon, 10am-7.30pm Tue-Sat, 11am-2pm & 3-7pm Sun; Ⓜ Spagna) Rome's best-known shoe designer, Fausto Santini is famous for his beguilingly simple, architectural shoe designs, with gorgeous boots and shoes made from butter-soft leather. Colours are beautiful, the quality impeccable. Seek out the end-of-line **discount shop** (Map p94; ☏ 06 488 09 34; Via Cavour 106; Ⓜ Cavour) if this looks out of your price range.

🔒 Monti, Esquiline & San Lorenzo

101
WOMEN'S CLOTH...

(Map p94; Via Urbana; ⊙ 10am-1.30pm & 2...
Ⓜ Cavour) The collection at this indi... boutique might include gossar... jumpers, broad-brimmed hats, ... earrings and silk dresses. It's always ... look to discover a special something.

Tina Sondergaard
CLOTHING

(Map p68; ☏ 06 9799 0565; Via del Boschetto 1d; ⊙ 3-7.30pm Mon, 10.30am-1pm & 1.30-7.30pm Tue-Sat, closed Aug; Ⓜ Cavour) Sublimely cut and whimsically retro-esque, these handmade threads are a hit with female fashion cognoscenti, including Italian rock star Carmen Consoli and the city's theatre and TV crowd. Each piece is a limited edition and new creations hit the racks every week.

🔒 Aventine & Testaccio

Volpetti
FOOD & DRINK

(Map p134; www.volpetti.com; Via Marmorata 47; ⊙ 8am-2pm & 5-8.15pm Mon-Sat; 🚌 Via Marmorata) This superstocked deli, considered by many the best in town, is an Aladdin's cave of gourmet treasures. Helpful staff will guide you through the extensive selection of smelly cheeses, homemade pastas, olive o... vinegars, cured meats, veggie pies, w... and grappas. You can also order online

🔒 Trastevere & Gia...

Porta Portese Flea Market
MARKET

(Piazza Porta Portese; ⊙ 7am-1pm
Trastevere, 🚌 Viale di Trastevere) a mar-
side of Rome, head to this m... every-
ket. With thousands of s... ikes to
thing from rare books... crazily
Peruvian shawls and N... aluables
busy and a lot of fu...
safe and wear your...

ℹ Orienta...

Rome is a spr...
relatively co...
trated in th...
city's ma...
west. H... s great ancient
and P...latino. On the
stor...
Co...
...d walking is often

tre is
are concen-
e Termini, the
Vatican to the
e Pantheon
t of the centro
the south, the

r's Basilica trum-
an.

Main police station (Questura; ☎06 4 68 61; Via San Vitale 11)

INTERNET ACCESS

Free wi-fi is now widely available in hostels, B&Bs and hotels. Some also provide laptops/computers for guest use.

Free public wi-fi is available in hotspots around town, but to use it you have to register with the provider, either the **Provincia di Roma** (www.provincia.roma.it), **Roma Wireless** (www.romawireless.com) or **Digit Roma** (www.digitroma.it), and give an Italian mobile number. Much easier is to head to one of the many cafes or bars offering free wi-fi.

There are a number of internet cafes in the area around Stazione Termini. Costs are usually between €4 and €6 per hour.

MEDIA

The following are available in English:

Osservatore Romano (www.osservatore-romano.va) The online edition of the Vatican's official daily newspaper.

Wanted in Rome (www.wantedinrome.com) A useful expat magazine that comes out every second Wednesday and features classified ads, listings and reviews. The online version is free.

MEDICAL SERVICES

For problems that don't require hospital treatment, call the **Guardia Medica Turistica** (☎06 7730 6650; Via Emilio Morosini 30).

You can also call a private doctor to come to your hotel or apartment; try **Roma Medica** (☎338 6224832; call-out/treatment charge €150; ◷24hr). The call-out/treatment fee will probably be around €150, but it's worth it if you have insurance. For emergency treatment, go to the *pronto soccorso* (casualty) section of an *ospedale* (hospital).

Pharmacists will serve prescriptions and can provide basic medical advice. Night pharmacies are listed in daily newspapers and in pharmacy windows.

Farmacia Vaticana (☎06 6988 9806; Palazzo Belvedere, Via di Porta Angelica; ◷8.30am-6pm Mon-Fri Sep-Jun, 8.30am-3pm Mon-Fri Jul & Aug, plus 8.30am-1pm Sat year-round) In the Vatican. Sells certain drugs that are not available in Italian pharmacies, and will fill foreign prescriptions (something local pharmacies can't do).

Ospedale di Odontoiatria G Eastman (☎06 84 48 31; Viale Regina Elena 287b) For emergency dental treatment.

Ospedale Santo Spirito (☎06 6 83 51; Lungotevere in Sassia 1) Near the Vatican.

Pharmacy (☎06 488 00 19; Piazza Cinquecento 51) Near Stazione Termini. There's also

a pharmacy inside Stazione Termini (next to platform 1), open from 7.30am to 10pm.

Policlinico Umberto I (☎06 4 99 71; www.policlinicoumberto1.it; Viale del Policlinico 155) Near Stazione Termini.

MONEY

ATMs are liberally scattered around the city.

There are money-exchange booths at Stazione Termini and Fiumicino and Ciampino airports. In the centre, there are numerous bureaux de change, including the **American Express** (☎06 6 76 41; Piazza di Spagna 38; ◷9am-5.30pm Mon-Fri, 9am-12.30pm Sat) office.

POST

There are post office branches at Via delle Terme di Diocleziano 30, Via della Scrofa 61-63 and Stazione Termini (next to platform 24).

Main Post Office (Map p80; ☎06 6973 7205; Piazza di San Silvestro 19; ◷8.20am-7.05pm Mon-Fri, 8.20am-12.35pm Sat)

Vatican Post Office (Map p106; ☎06 6988 3406; St Peter's Sq; ◷8.30am-6.30pm Mon-Sat)

TOURIST INFORMATION

For phone enquiries, the Comune di Roma runs a free multilingual **tourist information line** (☎06 06 08; www.060608.it; ◷9am-9pm).

There are tourist information points at Rome's two international airports – **Fiumicino** (Terminal 3, International Arrivals; ◷8am-7.30pm) and **Ciampino** (International Arrivals, baggage reclaim area; ◷9am-6.30pm) – and at the following locations across the city:

Castel Sant'Angelo Tourist Information (Map p80; Piazza Pia; ◷9.30am-7pm)

Piazza delle Cinque Lune Tourist Information (Map p80; Piazza delle Cinque Lune; ◷9.30am-7pm) Near Piazza Navona.

ⓘ **WATCH YOUR VALUABLES**

Rome is a relatively safe city, but petty crime is rife. Pickpockets follow tourists, so watch out around the Colosseum, Piazza di Spagna, St Peter's Square and Stazione Termini. Be particularly vigilant around the bus stops on Via Marsala, where thieves prey on disoriented travellers fresh in from Ciampino Airport. Crowded public transport is another hotspot – the 64 Vatican bus is notorious. If travelling on the metro, try to use the end carriages, which are usually less crowded.

Stazione Termini Tourist Information (Map p94; ⊙8am-8.30pm) In the hall that runs parallel to platform 24.

Fori Imperiali Tourist Information (Map p68; Via dei Fori Imperiali; ⊙9.30am-7pm; 🚃 Via dei Fori Imperiali)

Trevi Fountain Tourist Information (Map p86; Via Marco Minghetti; ⊙9.30am-7pm) Near the Trevi Fountain.

Via Nazionale Tourist Information (Map p86; Via Nazionale; ⊙9.30am-7pm)

For information about the Vatican, contact the **Centro Servizi Pellegrini e Turisti** (Map p106; ✆06 6988 1662; St Peter's Sq; ⊙8.30am-6pm Mon-Sat).

WEBSITES

060608 (www.060608.it) Provides information on sites, accommodation, shows, transport and so on.

Coop Culture (www.coopculture.it) Information and ticketing for Rome's monuments, museums and galleries.

In Rome Now (www.inromenow.com) Savvy internet magazine compiled by two American expats.

Parla Food (www.parlafood.com) Lippy American food blog with excellent links.

Turismo Roma (www.turismoroma.it) Rome's official tourist website. Lists accommodation options, upcoming events and more.

Vatican (www.vatican.va) The Vatican's official website.

ⓘ Getting There & Away

AIR

Rome's main international airport **Leonardo da Vinci** (✆06 6 59 51; www.adr.it/fiumicino), better known as Fiumicino, is on the coast 30km west of the city.

The much smaller **Ciampino Airport** (✆06 6 59 51; www.adr.it/ciampino), 15km southeast of the city centre, is the hub for European low-cost carrier Ryanair.

BOAT

Rome's port is at Civitavecchia, about 80km north of the city. Ferries sail to/from destinations across the Mediterranean, as well as Sicily and Sardinia.

Bookings can be made at the Termini-based **Agenzia 365** (✆06 474 09 23; www.agenzie365.it; ⊙8am-9pm), at travel agents or online at www.traghettiweb.it. You can also buy tickets directly at the port.

Frequent trains depart from Stazione Termini to Civitavecchia (€5 to €15, forty minutes to 1¼ hours). On arrival, it's about 700m to the port (to your right) as you exit the station.

The main ferry companies:

Grimaldi Lines (✆081 49 64 44; www.grimaldi-lines.com) To/from Trapani (Sicily), Porto Torres (Sardinia), Barcelona (Spain) and Tunis (Tunisia).

Tirrenia (✆892123; www.tirrenia.it) To/from Arbatax, Cagliari and Olbia (all Sardinia).

BUS

Long-distance national and international buses use the **Autostazione Tiburtina** (Piazzale Tiburtina) near Stazione Tiburtina, east of the city centre. Take metro line B from Stazione Termini.

You can get tickets at the bus station or at travel agencies.

Interbus (✆091 34 25 25; www.interbus.it) To/from Sicily.

Marozzi (✆080 579 01 11; www.marozzivt.it) To/from Sorrento, Bari, Matera and Lecce.

SENA (✆0861 199 19 00; www.sena.it) To/from Siena, Bologna and Milan.

Sulga (✆800 09 96 61; www.sulga.it) To/from Perugia, Assisi and Ravenna.

For destinations in the Lazio region, **Cotral** (✆800 174471; www.cotralspa.it) buses depart from numerous points across the city. The company is linked with Rome's public transport system, which means that you can buy tickets that cover city buses, trams, metro and train lines, as well as regional buses and trains.

CAR & MOTORCYCLE

Driving into central Rome is a challenge, involving traffic restrictions, one-way systems, a shortage of street parking and aggressive drivers.

Rome is circled by the Grande Raccordo Anulare (GRA) to which all autostradas (motorways) connect, including the main A1 north–south artery (the Autostrada del Sole) and the A12, which connects Rome to Civitavecchia and Fiumicino Airport.

Car Hire

Rental cars are available at the airport and Stazione Termini.

Avis (www.avisautonoleggio.it)

Europcar (www.europcar.com)

Hertz (www.hertz.it)

Maggiore National (www.maggiore.it)

TRAIN

Almost all trains serve **Stazione Termini** (Piazza dei Cinquecento), Rome's main train station and principal transport hub. There are regular connections to other European countries, all major Italian cities and many smaller towns.

Train information is available from the customer service area on the main concourse to the left of the ticket desks. Alternatively, check www.trenitalia.com, or phone ✆892021.

Left luggage (1st 5hr €5, 6-12hr per hr €0.70, 13hr & over per hr €0.30; ⊘ 6am-11pm) is available on the lower-ground floor under platform 24.

Rome's other principal train stations are Stazione Tiburtina, Stazione Roma-Ostiense and Stazione Trastevere.

❶ Getting Around

TO/FROM THE AIRPORT
Fiumicino

The easiest way to get to/from Fiumicino is by train, but there are also buses and private shuttle services.

By taxi, the set fare to/from the city centre is €48, which is valid for up to four passengers with luggage. Note that taxis registered in Fiumicino charge more, so make sure you catch a Comune di Roma taxi – they are white with the words *Roma capitale* on the side along with the driver's ID number.

Leonardo Express (adult/child under 4 €14/ free) Runs to/from Stazione Termini. Departures from the airport every 30 minutes between 6.38am and 11.38pm; from Termini between 5.52am and 10.52pm. Journey time is 30 minutes.

FR1 Train (€8) Connects to Trastevere, Ostiense and Tiburtina stations, but not Stazione Termini. Departures from the airport every 15 minutes (hourly on Sunday and public holidays) between 5.58am and 11.28pm; from Tiburtina every 15 minutes between 5.47am and 7.32pm, then half-hourly to 10.02pm Monday to Saturday, half-hourly between 6.02am and 10.02pm Sunday.

Airport Shuttle (☑ 06 4201 3469; www.airportshuttle.it) Transfers to/from your hotel for €25 for one person, then €6 for each additional passenger up to a maximum of eight.

Cotral (www.cotralspa.it; one way €5, if bought on bus €7) Runs to/from Stazione Tiburtina via Stazione Termini. Eight daily departures including night services from the airport at 1.15am, 2.15am, 3.30am and 5am, and from Tiburtina at 12.30am, 1.15am, 2.30am and 3.45am. Journey time is one hour.

Ciampino

To get into town, the best bet is to take one of the dedicated bus services. You can also take a bus to Ciampino station and pick up a train to Stazione Termini. By taxi, the set fare to/from the airport is €30.

Terravision (www.terravision.eu; one way €4) Twice hourly departures to/from Via Marsala outside Stazione Termini. From the airport services are between 8.15am and 12.15am; from Via Marsala between 4.30am and 9.20pm. Buy tickets at Terracafè in front of the Via Marsala bus stop. Journey time is 40 minutes.

SIT (www.sitbusshuttle.com; from airport €4, to airport €6) Buses run from Ciampino between 7.45am and 11.30am to Via Marsala outside Stazione Termini; from Termini between 4.30am and 9.30pm. Get tickets on board. Journey time is 45 minutes.

Cotral (www.cotralspa.it; one way €3.90) Runs 17 daily services to/from Via Giolitti near Stazione Termini. Also buses to/from Anagnina metro station (€1.20) and Ciampino train station (€1.20), where you can get a train to Termini (€1.30).

CAR & MOTORCYCLE
Access & Parking

Most of the historical centre is closed to normal traffic from 6.30am to 6pm Monday to Friday, from 2pm to 6pm Saturday, and from 11pm to 3am Friday to Sunday. Evening restrictions also apply in Trastevere, San Lorenzo, Monti and

TRAIN SERVICES TO MAJOR CITIES

From Stazione Termini you can catch trains to the following cities and many others. All fares quoted are 2nd class.

TO	SERVICE TYPE	FARE (€)	DURATION (HR)
Florence	fast	43	1½
	slow	20.25	3¾
Milan	fast	76-86	3-3½
	medium	55.50	6¾
Naples	fast	39-43	1¼
	slow	11.20	2½
Palermo	day	73	11½
	night	92.50-99.50	12¼
Venice	fast	80	3¾
	medium	45.50-49.50	6¾-9

TICKETS

Public-transport tickets are valid on all of Rome's bus, tram and metro lines, except for routes to Fiumicino Airport. They come in various forms:

BIT (*biglietto integrato a tempo*, a single ticket valid for 100 minutes and one metro ride) €1.50

BIG (*biglietto integrato giornaliero*, a daily ticket) €6

BTI (*biglietto turistico integrato*, a three-day ticket) €16.50

CIS (*carta integrata settimanale*, a weekly ticket) €24

Abbonamento mensile (a monthly pass) €35

Buy tickets at *tabacchi*, newsstands and from vending machines at main bus stops and metro stations. They must be purchased before you start your journey and validated in the machines on buses, at the entrance gates to the metro or at train stations. Ticketless riders risk an on-the-spot €50 fine. Children under 10 travel free.

The Roma Pass (p73) comes with a three-day travel pass valid within the city boundaries.

Testaccio, typically from 9.30pm or 11pm to 3am on Fridays and Saturdays.

All streets within the 'Limited Traffic Zone' (ZTL) are monitored by electronic-access detection devices. If you're staying in this zone, contact your hotel otherwise you risk a fine. For further information, check www.agenziamobilita.roma.it.

Blue lines denote pay-and-display parking – get tickets from meters (coins only) and *tabacchi*. Expect to pay up to €1.20 per hour between 8am and 8pm (11pm in some places). After 8pm (or 11pm) parking is generally free until 8am the next morning.

Traffic wardens are vigilant and fines are not uncommon. If your car gets towed away, call ☎ 06 6769 2303.

There's a comprehensive list of car parks at www.060608.it – click on the transport tab and car parks link.

Scooter Hire

To hire a scooter, prices range from about €20 for a 50cc scooter to €125 for a 1000cc motorbike. Reliable operators:

Bici e Baci (☎ 06 482 84 43; www.bicibaci.com; Via del Viminale 5)

Eco Move Rent (☎ 06 4470 4518; www.eco-moverent.com; Via Varese 48-50; ⊗8.30am-7.30pm)

PUBLIC TRANSPORT

Rome's public transport system includes buses, trams, metro and a suburban train network.

Metro

Rome has two main metro lines, A (orange) and B (blue), which cross at Stazione Termini, the only point at which you can change from one line

to the other. A third line 'B1' branches off line B and serves the northern suburbs, but you're unlikely to need it.

Trains run between 5.30am and 11.30pm (to 1.30am on Friday and Saturday).

All stations on line B have wheelchair access except Circo Massimo, Colosseo and Cavour; on line A, Cipro–Musei Vaticani is one of the few stations equipped with lifts.

Take line A for the Trevi Fountain (Barberini), Spanish Steps (Spagna) and St Peter's (Ottaviano–San Pietro).

Take line B for the Colosseum (Colosseo).

Bus & Tram

Rome's buses and trams are run by **ATAC** (☎ 06 5 70 03; www.atac.roma.it). The **main bus station** (Map p94; Piazza dei Cinquecento) is in front of Stazione Termini on Piazza dei Cinquecento, where there's an **information booth** (Map p94; ⊗7.30am-8pm). Other important hubs are at Largo di Torre Argentina and Piazza Venezia.

Buses generally run from about 5.30am until midnight, with limited services throughout the night.

Rome's night bus service comprises more than 25 lines, many of which pass Stazione Termini and/or Piazza Venezia. Buses are marked with an 'n' before the number and bus stops have a blue owl symbol. Departures are usually every 15 to 30 minutes between about 1am and 5am, but can be less frequent.

Overground Rail Network

Rome's overground rail network is useful only if you are heading out of town to the Castelli Romani, the beaches at Lido di Ostia or the ruins at Ostia Antica.

Taxi

Official licensed taxis are white with an ID number and *Roma capitale* written on the sides.

Always go with the metered fare, never an arranged price (the set fares to and from the airports are exceptions).

In town (within the ring road) flag fall is €3 between 6am and 10pm on weekdays, €4.50 on Sundays and holidays, and €6.50 between 10pm and 7am. Then it's €1.10 per kilometre. Official rates are posted in taxis and on www. viviromaintaxi.eu.

You can hail a taxi, but it's often easier to wait at a rank or phone for one. There are taxi ranks at the airports, Stazione Termini, the Colosseum, Largo di Torre Argentina, Piazza San Silvestro, Piazza della Repubblica, Piazza Belli in Trastevere and in the Vatican at Piazza del Pio XII and Piazza del Risorgimento.

You can book a taxi by phoning the Comune di Roma's automated taxi line on ☑ 06 06 09, or calling a taxi company direct.

Note that when you call for a cab, the meter is switched on immediately and you pay for the cost of the journey from wherever the driver receives the call.

La Capitale (☑ 06 49 94)
Pronto Taxi (☑ 06 66 45)
Radio Taxi (☑ 06 35 70)
Samarcanda (☑ 06 55 51)
Tevere (☑ 06 41 57)

LAZIO

With a capital like Rome, it's unsurprising that the rest of Lazio gets overlooked. But when Rome starts to feel like the Eternal City for all the wrong reasons, do as the Romans do and leave the city behind. You'll discover a region that's not only beautiful – verdant and hilly in the north, parched and rugged in the south – but also full of historical and cultural interest.

Ostia Antica

An easy and enjoyable day trip from Rome, Ostia Antica is one of Lazio's prize sights. Ostia (referring to the mouth or *ostium* of the Tiber) was ancient Rome's main sea port and its excavated ruins are wonderfully complete, like a smaller version of Pompeii.

Founded in the 4th century BC, the city had a population of around 50,000 at its height and was an important defensive and commercial centre. Decline came in the 5th century AD when barbarian invasions and the outbreak of malaria led to the abandonment of the city, and its slow burial – up to 2nd-floor level – in river silt, hence its survival. Pope Gregory IV re-established the town in the 9th century.

⊙ Sights

★**Scavi Archeologici**
di Ostia Antica RUIN
(☑ 06 5635 2830; www.ostiaantica.net; Viale dei Romagnoli 717; adult/reduced €6.50/3.75; ☉ 8.30am-7.15pm Tue-Sun Apr-Oct, to 6pm Mar, to 5pm Nov-Feb, last admission 1hr before closing) Ostia's ruins are spread out and you'll need a few hours to do them justice. Note also that the site gets busy at weekends but is often empty during the week.

From the **Porta Romana** near the ticket office, the **Decumanus Maximus**, the city's main strip, runs over 1km to **Porta Marina**, a gate which originally led out to the sea.

On the Decumanus, the **Terme di Nettuno** is one of the site's highlights. This baths

BUSES FROM TERMINI

From Piazza dei Cinquecento outside Stazione Termini buses run to all corners of the city.

DESTINATION	BUS NO
Campo de' Fiori	40/64
Colosseum	75
Pantheon	40/64
Piazza Navona	40/64
Piazza Venezia	40/64
St Peter's Square	40/64
Terme di Caracalla	714
Trastevere	H
Villa Borghese	910

Lazio

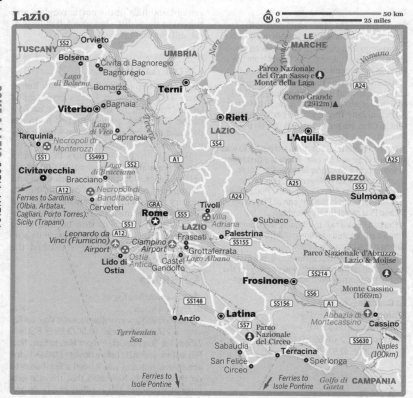

complex, one of 20 that originally stood in town, dates from Hadrian's 2nd-century renovation of the port and boasts some superb mosaics, including a stunning depiction of Neptune driving his sea-horse chariot, surrounded by sea monsters, mermaids and mermen. In the centre of the complex are the remains of a large arcaded courtyard called the **Palaestra**, in which athletes used to train.

Next to the Terme is a good-sized **Teatro** (amphitheatre), built by Agrippa and later enlarged to hold 4000 people. Climb to the top and look out and you'll get a good overview of the site.

Behind the amphitheatre is the **Piazzale delle Corporazioni** (Forum of the Corporations), the offices of Ostia's merchant guilds, which sport mosaics depicting the different interests of each business.

The **Forum**, Ostia's main square, is dominated by the huge **Capitolium**, a temple built by Hadrian and dedicated to the main Roman deities – Jupiter, Juno and Minerva.

Nearby is another must-see: the **Thermopolium**, an ancient cafe. Check out the bar, surmounted by a frescoed menu, the kitchen and small courtyard where customers would have sat next to a fountain and relaxed with a drink. Across the road are some spectacularly well-preserved latrines, set in a sociable crescent, part of the **Terme di Foro** complex.

For more modern facilities, there's a cafeteria/bar complex with toilets, a gift shop and a museum displaying statues and sarcophagi excavated on-site.

Castello di Giulio II
CASTLE

(☑ 06 5635 8044; Piazza della Rocca; ⊙ entry by free guided tours only 11am Thu, 11am & noon Sun) Near the entrance to the excavations is this imposing castle, an impressive example of 15th-century military architecture, which lost its purpose when a freak flood changed the course of the river, making the location less accessible.

Eating

Ristorante Cipriani RISTORANTE €
(✆06 5635 2956; Via del Forno 11; meals €25; ⊙lunch Thu-Tue, dinner Mon, Tue, Thu-Sun) Dine on Roman staples such as *pasta alla gricia* (with lardons and onion) and *cacio e pepe*, while seated in a cobbled street by the castle. They do a bargain menu at €10.

❶ Getting There & Away

From Rome, take the Ostia Lido train from Stazione Porta San Paolo (next to Piramide metro station), getting off at Ostia Antica. Trains leave half-hourly and the trip, which is covered by standard public-transport tickets, takes approximately 25 minutes. On arrival, walk over the pedestrian bridge. Go straight ahead and you'll see the castle to your right and the ruins straight ahead.

By car, take Via del Mare, which runs parallel to Via Ostiense, and follow signs for the *scavi* (ruins).

Tivoli

POP 52,920 / ELEV 225M

A summer retreat for ancient Romans and the Renaissance rich, the hilltop town of Tivoli is home to two Unesco World Heritage Sites: Villa Adriana, the sprawling country estate of Emperor Hadrian, and the 16th-century Villa d'Este, a Renaissance villa famous for its landscaped gardens and lavish fountains.

Information is available from the **tourist information point** (✆0774 31 35 36; Piazzale delle Nazione Unite; ⊙9.30am-5.30pm Tue-Sun) near Piazza Garibaldi, where the bus arrives.

◉ Sights

Villa Adriana ARCHAEOLOGICAL SITE
(✆06 3996 7900; www.villaadriana.beniculturali. it; adult/reduced €8/4, plus possible exhibition supplement, car park €3; ⊙9am-1hr before sunset; 🛜) Some 5km outside Tivoli proper, Emperor Hadrian's sumptuous summer residence set new standards of luxury when it was built between AD 118 and 134 – a remarkable feat given the excesses of the Roman Empire. More like a small town than a villa, it's vast – a model near the entrance gives an idea of the scale of the original complex – and you'll need several hours to explore it. Consider hiring an audioguide (€5), which gives a helpful overview.

Hadrian was a great traveller and enthusiastic architect and he personally designed much of the complex, taking inspiration from buildings he'd seen around the world. The pecile, a large porticoed pool area where the emperor used to stroll after lunch, was a reproduction of a building in Athens. Similarly, the canopo is a copy of the sanctuary of Serapis in the Egyptian town of Canopus, with a long canal of water enclosed by a colonnade. The Serapaeum, which provides a backdrop for the pool, was an outdoor summer dining room, where Hadrian held banquets.

To the east of the pecile is another highlight, the Teatro Marittimo, Hadrian's private retreat. Built on an island in an artificial pool, it was originally a mini-villa accessible only by swing bridges, which the emperor would have raised when he felt like a dip. Nearby, the fish pond is encircled by an underground gallery where Hadrian liked to wander.

There are also several magnificent bath complexes, temples, barracks, and a museum (often closed) with the latest discoveries from ongoing excavations.

Villa d'Este VILLA, GARDEN
(✆0774 331 20 70; www.villadestetivoli.info; Piazza Trento; adult/reduced €8.50/4, plus possible exhibition supplement; ⊙8.30am-1hr before sunset Tue-Sun) In Tivoli's hilltop centre, the steeply terraced gardens of Villa d'Este are a superlative example of the High Renaissance garden, dotted by fantastical fountains all powered by gravity alone. The villa, originally a Benedictine convent, was converted into a pleasure palace by Lucrezia Borgia's son, Cardinal Ippolito d'Este, in 1550. Later, it was home to the composer Franz Liszt who stayed here between 1865 and 1886 and was inspired to write *To the Cypresses of the Villa d'Este* and *To the Fountains of the Villa d'Este*.

---

❶ TIVOLI IN A DAY

Tivoli makes an excellent day trip from Rome but to cover its two main sites – Villa Adriana and Villa d'Este – you'll have to start early. The best way to see both is to visit Villa d'Este first, then take the Rome bus from Piazza Garibaldi, asking the driver to drop you off close to Villa Adriana. After visiting the villa, pick up the bus back to Rome.

Viterbo

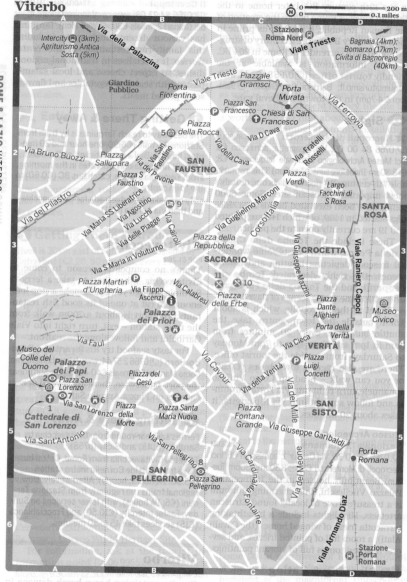

Founded by the Etruscans and eventually taken over by Rome, it was an important medieval centre, and in the 13th century became the residence of the popes. Papal elections were held in the Gothic Palazzo dei Papi where, in 1271, the entire college of cardinals was briefly imprisoned. The story goes that after three years of deliberation the cardinals still hadn't elected a new pope. Mad with frustration, the Viterbesi locked the dithering priests in a turreted hall and starved them into electing Pope Gregory X.

13; meals €50; ⊘ Tue-Sat), with fine food and a graceful terrace. For a more down-to-earth bite, pick up a *panino con porchetta* (sandwich filled with herb-roasted pork) from a stand on **Piazza del Mercato**, or head to a traditional *cantina* (cellar-cum-trattoria) for *porchetta*, cured meats, olives and cheese accompanied by jugs of local white wine.

Grottaferrata

The elegant town of Grottaferrata is worth a quick stop for its fortified abbey, the **Monastero Esarchico di Santa Maria di Grottaferrata** (Abbazia Greca di San Nilo; ✆ 06 945 93 09; www.abbaziagreca.it; Viale San Nilo; ⊘ 7am-12.30pm & 3.30pm-1hr before sunset). Founded in 1004 and subsequently enlarged in the 13th and 15th centuries, this is the last remaining example of the Byzantine-Greek abbeys that once dotted medieval Italy.

Castel Gandolfo

One of the prettiest of the Castelli's towns, Castel Gandolfo is a refined hilltop *borgo* (medieval town). There are no must-see sights but the central **Piazza della Libertà** is a lovely spot for an ice cream, and the views over Lago Albano are gorgeous. Facing onto the piazza is the pope's 17th-century summer residence, the **Palazzo Pontificio** (closed to the public), where he holds his regular weekly audiences in July and August.

Just outside the historic centre, the **Antico Ristorante Pagnanelli** (✆ 06 936 00 04; www.pagnanelli.it; Via Antonio Gramsci 4, Castel Gandolfo; meals €70) is one of the Castelli's top restaurants offering sophisticated food and romantic lakeside views.

Lago Albano

The largest and most developed of the Castelli's two volcanic lakes – the other is Lago di Nemi – Lago Albano is set in a steeply banked wooded crater. It's a popular hangout, particularly in spring and summer, when Romans flock here to top up their tans and eat in the many lakeside eateries.

ⓘ Getting There & Around

The best way to get to Frascati is by train from Stazione Termini (€2.10, 30 minutes, roughly hourly Monday to Saturday, every two hours Sunday). Likewise there are regular trains to Castel Gandolfo from Termini (€2.10, 45 minutes).

To travel between the Castelli towns you'll need to take the bus. To go from Frascati to Grottaferrata (€1.10, 15 minutes, every 30 to 40 minutes) and on to Castel Gandolfo (€1.10, 40 minutes), take the Cotral bus from Piazza Marconi.

If travelling by car, exit Rome on Via Tuscolana (SS215) for Frascati and Grottaferrata or Via Appia (SS7) for Castel Gandolfo and Lago Albano.

Palestrina

POP 20,540 / ELEV 450M

With its hilltop historic centre and fascinating archaeology museum, Palestrina is well worth a visit. In ancient times, the town, then known as Praeneste, was a favourite getaway of wealthy Romans and home to a spectacular mountain-side sanctuary.

The 2nd-century BC **Santuario della Fortuna Primigenia** was a vast temple that extended down the hillside in six terraced levels, covering much of what is now the historic centre. It has long since been built over but there's a model of it in the **Museo Archeologico Nazionale di Palestrina** (✆ 06 953 81 00; Piazza della Cortina; admission incl sanctuary €5; ⊘ 9am-8pm, ticket office closes at 7pm, sanctuary 9am-1hr before sunset), showing what it originally looked like.

The museum, housed in the 17th-century Palazzo Barberini, itself built into the sanctuary's upper terrace, has an interesting collection of ancient sculpture and funerary artefacts, as well as some huge Roman mosaics. Its crowning glory, though, is the breathtaking *Mosaico Nilotico*, an extraordinarily vivid 2nd-century BC mosaic depicting the flooding of the Nile and everyday life in ancient Egypt.

For a bite to eat, the highly regarded **Zi' Rico** (✆ 06 8308 2532; www.zirico.it; Via Enrico Toti 2; meals €35-40; ⊘ Tue-Sat, Sun dinner by reservation only) serves creative Italian fare in an intimate setting near the cathedral. Also in the historic centre, the **Albergo Ristorante Stella** (✆ 06 953 81 72; www.hotelstella.it; Piazza della Liberazione 3; meals €25-30, s/d/tr €50/70/90) offers robust country cooking and modest, no-frills accommodation.

Cotral buses run to Palestrina from Ponte Mammolo metro station in Rome (€2.20, one hour, hourly).

By car it's a straightforward 39km along Via Prenestina (SS155).

South Coast

Lazio's southern coast boasts the region's best beaches and tracts of beautiful, unspoilt countryside around Monte Circeo, a rocky promontory that rises to a height of 541m as it juts into the sea.

Sabaudia

About 90km south of Rome, the modern, rather uninspiring town of Sabaudia makes a convenient base for the Parco Nazionale del Circeo (www.parcocirceo.it), an 800-hectare area of sand dunes, rocky coastline, forest and wetlands.

The park's visitor centre (☑ 07 7351 1385; Via Carlo Alberto 188-190; ☉ visitor centre dawn-dusk, information office 9am-1pm & 2.30-5pm) can provide details on activities available in the area including hiking, fishing, birdwatching, walking and cycling. For further information and accommodation lists, ask at Sabaudia's tourist office (☑ 0773 51 50 46; www.prolocosabaudia.it; Piazza del Comune 18; ☉ 9.15am-12.30pm & 4-7.45pm Mon-Sat, 9.05am-12.45pm Sun).

There's plenty of accommodation in the vicinity, but for a simple beachfront stay, head to Camping Sabaudia (☑ 0773 59 30 20; www.campingsabaudia.it; Via Sant'Andrea 15; camping two people & tent €28-37; ☉ May-Sep), a decent campground immersed in Mediterranean *macchia* (shrubland).

From Rome, Cotral buses leave from Laurentina metro station (line B) for Terracina, stopping off at Sabaudia en route (€5, two to three hours depending on traffic).

Sperlonga

The pick of Lazio's southern coastal towns, Sperlonga is a fashionable summer spot. Its attractive steeply stacked medieval centre buzzes throughout the season, and there are two inviting sandy beaches set either side of a rocky promontory.

Other than the beach – and the great views from the top of the historic centre – the main attraction is the Museo Archeologico di Sperlonga (☑ 0771 54 80 28; Via Flacca, Km1.6; admission/reduced €4/2; ☉ 8.30am-6pm) just south of town. Here you can admire sculptures and masks dating from the 2nd century BC, and poke around the ruins of Villa Tiberio, a sumptuous villa used by the emperor Tiberius.

Near the northern entrance to the historic centre, Hotel Mayor (☑ 0771 54 92 45; www.hotelmayor.it; Via 1 Romita 4; s €60-110, d €75-140; P ❄) offers simple, clean rooms, some with balconies, and its own patch of private beach. Note that minimum stays are required in some summer months.

Of the many eating options, the Pasticceria Gelateria Fiorelli (Via San Rocco 15; cones from €2, aperitivi from €4.50; ☉ Mon-Sun) is a good bet for gelato, whilst up in the medieval quarter, Gli Archi (☑ 07 7154 8300; www.gliarchi.com; Via Ottaviano 17; meals €40-45) specialises in locally caught seafood.

To get to Sperlonga from Rome, take a regional train from Stazione Termini to Fondi-Sperlonga (€6.90, 1¼ hours, hourly) and then a connecting Piazzoli (www.piazzoli.it) bus to Sperlonga (€1, 10 minutes).

WORTH A TRIP

SUBIACO

Set amidst wooded hills in Lazio's remote eastern reaches, Subiaco is one of the region's hidden gems. Nero had a villa here but it was St Benedict who put the town on the map when he spent three years meditating in a local cave. This grotto is now incorporated into the Monastero di San Benedetto (☑ 0774 8 50 39; www.benedettini-subiaco.org; ☉ 9am-12.30pm & 3-6pm), a spectacularly sited hilltop monastery that boasts a series of rich 13th- to 15th-century frescoes.

At the foot of the same hill is a second monastery, the Monastero di Santa Scolastica (☑ 0774 8 55 69; www.benedettini-subiaco.org; ☉ 9.30am-12.15pm & 3.30-6.15pm), which offers accommodation (per person B&B €37) and fixed-price restaurant meals for €19 and €27.

To get to Subiaco from Rome, there's a Cotral bus (1¼ hours, every 15 to 30 minutes Monday to Friday, less frequently at weekends) from Ponte Mammolo metro station. The bus stops a little way from the Monastero di Santa Scolastica, to which it's a scenic, if demanding, 3km uphill walk. Buy a three-zone BIRG ticket (€8) to cover your return journey.

WORTH A TRIP

ABBAZIA DI MONTECASSINO

Dramatically perched on a mountain top near the regional border with Campania, the **Abbazia di Montecassino** (☑0776 31 15 29; www.montecassino.it; ☺9am-12.30pm & 3.30-5pm, to 6pm Apr-Oct) was one of the most important Christian centres in the medieval world. St Benedict founded it in 529 AD, supposedly after three ravens led him to the spot, and lived there until his death in 547.

Throughout its history it has been destroyed and rebuilt several times, most recently after WWII. During the war it was at the centre of heavy fighting as the Germans sought to stop the Allied push north. After almost six months of bloody deadlock, the Allies bombed it to rubble in May 1944 in a desperate bid to break through German defences.

To reach the abbey from Rome, take one of the regular trains from Stazione Termini to Cassino (€7.40, 80 minutes to two hours) and then a local bus up from Piazza San Benedetto.

By car, Sperlonga is 120km from Rome. Take Via Pontina (SS148) and follow signs to Terracina and then Sperlonga.

Isole Pontine

This group of small volcanic islands off the southern Lazio coast serves as an Italian Hamptons. Between mid-June and the end of August, Ponza and Ventotene – the only two inhabited islands – are packed with holidaymakers and Roman weekenders who descend in droves to eat shellfish at little terrace restaurants, swim in emerald coves and take boat trips round the craggy coast. Outside of these months the islands are much quieter, and, although expensive, a joy to explore.

Action centres on Ponza town, a colourful cascade of pastel-coloured houses that rings the hillside above the harbour. Here you'll find the usual array of souvenir shops, cafes and restaurants, as well as a small sandy beach.

Operating out of Ponza, **Cooperativa Barcaioli** (☑0771 80 99 29; www.barcaioliponza.it; Sotto il Tunnel di S Antonio) is one of several outfits offering boat trips around the island (€25 including lunch) and shuttles to the beach at Frontone. Alternatively, the local bus company **Autolinee Ponza** (☑0771 8 04 47) runs hourly panoramic tours of the island (€2.40).

🛏 Sleeping & Eating

Many of the locals rent out individual rooms to tourists; you'll find them touting at the port. Otherwise, the small **tourist office** (☑0771 8 00 31; www.prolocodiponza.it; Via Molo Musco; ☺10am-noon Wed & Sat) can help out.

Villa Ersilia RENTAL ROOMS €
(☑0771 8 00 97; www.villaersilia.it; Via Scotti 2; per person €35-100; ☎) Housed in a mustard-yellow villa a short but steep walk up from the harbour (follow the signs), this friendly place has simple sunny rooms and lovely views out to sea.

★**Tutti Noi** SEAFOOD €€
(☑0771 82 00 44; Via Dante 5; meals €30; ☺Mon-Sun Jun-Aug, closed Sun dinner Sep-May) This welcoming trattoria opposite Ponza's beach is one of many seafood restaurants in town. The fish is as fresh as the morning catch and the pasta seafood dishes are excellent.

ℹ Getting There & Around

Ponza and Ventotene are accessible from Anzio, Terracina, Naples and Formia. Some services run year-round, including daily ferries from Terracina, but most are seasonal, operating from June to September. Timetable information is available from the ferry company websites, travel agents and, in summer, the Rome section of *Il Messaggero* and *Il Tempo* newspapers.

Prices vary according to the point of departure and whether you're on a hydrofoil or car ferry – from Terracina to Ponza the daily ferry costs €20 return plus €1.50 embarkation tax. A hydrofoil on the same route costs €39 return plus tax. Journey time varies from 80 minutes to 2½ hours.

Cars and large motorbikes are forbidden on Ponza in summer, but there's a good local bus service. Otherwise, you can rent a scooter or mini moke.

The major ferry companies are:
Navigazione Libera del Golfo (www.navlib.it)
SNAP (☑0773 79 00 55; www.snapnavigazione.it)
Vetor (☑06 984 50 83; www.vetor.it)

Liguria, Piedmont & the Italian Riviera

Includes ➡

Why Go?

The beauty of northwestern Italy is its diversity. You only have to take a short train ride out of Turin and everything changes: food, culture, scenery – even the language.

The seduction starts in Liguria, a thin, precipitous coastal strip famous for its food (pesto and focaccia), swanky resorts and the once-powerful independent trading empire of Genoa. Piedmont is a flat, fertile medallion of land trapped between the Alps and the Mediterranean – an economic and political powerhouse that provided the nation with its first capital (Turin), a popular car (Fiat) and, more recently, Slow Food and fine wine. Mountainous Aosta, meanwhile, is a semi-autonomous Alpine region with a different history, its own language, and ample skiing and hiking terrain, all guarded by Europe's highest mountains.

If the three regions have anything in common it's their House of Savoy connections and proud sense of history. Italy, in the modern sense, was invented right here.

Best Places to Eat

➡ L'Acino (p208)

➡ Trattoria della Raibetta (p175)

➡ 4 Ciance (p215)

➡ Osteria dei Sognatori (p220)

Best Places to Stay

➡ Hotel Royal Superga (p214)

➡ Hotel Cairoli (p173)

➡ Hotel Langhe (p217)

➡ La Torretta Charme & Relax (p189)

When to Go

Turin

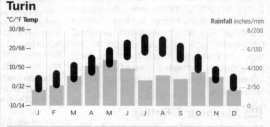

Jan–Mar Most reliable snow cover for skiing in the Alps.

Apr Fewer crowds and better hiking on the Ligurian coast.

Sep & Oct Late-season hiking in the Alps and autumn food festivals in Turin and Alba.

Piedmont Discount Card

Serious sightseers will save a bundle with a **Torino + Piemonte Card** (www.turismotorino.org; 2/3/5 days €25/29/34). It covers admission to 190 of the region's monuments and museums, and offers reductions on various forms of public transport, including Turin's Sassi–Superga tram, GTT boats on the Po river and the Turismo Bus Torino. It also offers discounts on some guided tours and theatres. You can buy the card at Turin's tourist office.

TURIN'S CULINARY CREATIONS

Lavazza The family-run coffee company was founded in Via San Tommaso in 1895 and, along with Trieste-based Illy, dominates Italy's legendary coffee industry with an annual turnover of nearly €1 billion.

Chocolate Though no one city can claim to have invented chocolate, the Torinese have better claims than most: their genius was to blend cocoa with Piedmontese hazelnuts to form the epic *gianduja* (soft hazelnut chocolate), the precursor to Nutella and plenty of other chocolate goodies.

Grissini Breadsticks were allegedly invented by a Torinese baker in the 1670s to help the poor digestion of the future king Vittorio Amedeo II. The crunchy snacks caught on and are ubiquitous in most Italian restaurants and delis.

Cinque Terre – After the Floods

Freakishly wet weather along the Ligurian coast in October 2011 brought devastating flash floods to the two Cinque Terre towns of Vernazza and Monterosso, burying many of their historic streets and houses under several metres of mud. Tragically, half-a-dozen people were killed and Monterosso's mayor emotionally declared that his town no longer existed. However, employing a stoicism shaped by centuries of fighting off tiresome invaders, Cinque Terre has bounced back. As of 2013, most businesses are open again, although you may want to check ahead vis-à-vis the status of the iconic, but increasingly delicate Sentiero Azzurro (blue walking trail).

> **DON'T MISS**
>
> The region's newest sight is an extravagantly refurbished car museum in Turin's up-and-coming Lingotto district, known as the Museo Nazionale dell'Automobile.

Unesco World Heritage Sites

➤ **Cinque Terre** Medieval fishing villages and landscaped cliffsides on the Ligurian coast.

➤ **Residences of the Royal House of Turin** A collection of baroque pleasure palaces in and around Turin, including Palazzo Madama, Palazzo Reale and Venaria Reale.

➤ **Sacri Monti** Nine sacred mountains in Piedmont and Lombardy with chapels and pilgrims' paths dedicated to the Christian faith.

➤ **Palazzi dei Rolli** Forty-two Renaissance and baroque palaces in Genoa.

Resources

➤ **Liguria** www.turismoinliguria.it

➤ **Piedmont** www.piemonteitalia.eu

➤ **Valle d'Aosta** www.lovevda.it

➤ **Turin** www.turismotorino.org

Liguria, Piedmont & the Italian Riviera Highlights

1 Seeing the supersonic spirit that built modern Turin at the freshly refurbished **Museo Nazionale dell'Automobile** (p205).

2 Discovering the art and architecture of a once-great maritime empire in Genoa's amazing **Palazzi dei Rolli** (p167).

3 Discussing terroir, tannins and taste with the wine-quaffers of the **Barolo region** (p221).

4 Hiking the blue trail, the red trail, the sanctuary trails – in fact, any trail on the stunning cliffsides of **Cinque Terre** (p183).

5 Working out who's French, Italian and Swiss-Walser in the multicultural **Valle d'Aosta** (p227).

6 Escaping the clamorous Valle d'Aosta on foot with an excursion into the **Parco Nazionale del Gran Paradiso** (p235).

7 Descending on Alba in October to see white truffles sell for big prices in the annual **Truffle Festival** (p217).

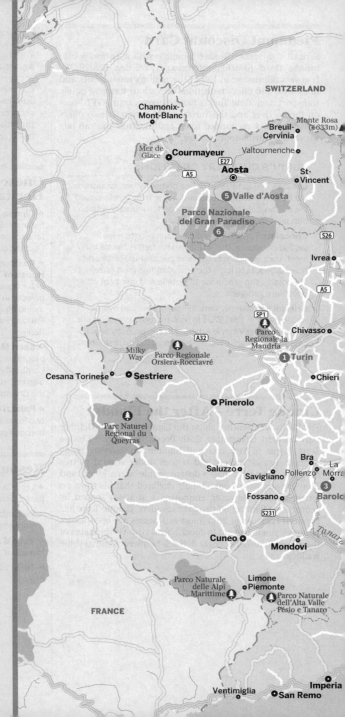

LIGURIA

POP 1.57 MILLION

The first thing to strike you about Liguria is its almost total lack of flatness. Wedged in a sinuous arc between Piedmont and the sea, this is where the Alps and the Apennines cascade precipitously into the Mediterranean. The demanding topography has had an indelible effect on almost every facet of Ligurian life. Farming is carried out on ingeniously terraced cliff faces, and impossibly stacked fishing villages have long plundered the sea both to make their livings and fill their menus.

Anchored beside the region's best natural harbour is noble Genoa. Known as La Superba (the Superb One) to biased locals, it's a city that once ruled over one of the finest maritime empires in medieval Europe. Spread on either side are the swanky resorts of the so-called Italian Riviera, punctuated with pockets of timelessness, most notably the Portofino peninsula and the legendary Cinque Terre. Surprisingly, given its lack of obvious agricultural land, Liguria is renowned for its food: anchovies, lemons, crunchy focaccia bread and an earthy green sauce known to the world as pesto.

Genoa

POP 605,000

Contrasting sharply with the elegance of Turin, Genoa is a big crawling port that's almost Dickensian in places, thanks to its narrow, twisting lanes (caruggi) that are more reminiscent of the clamour of Morocco than the splendour of Venice. A once-important trading centre that bred such historic gamechangers as Columbus and Mazzini, the city breathes a cosmopolitan air, with remnants of empire evident in its weighty art heritage.

Deep in the maze of the gritty old town, beauty and the beast sit side by side in streets that glimmer like a film noir movie set. Old men smoke languidly outside noisy bars and prostitutes stand like sentries in dark doorways, while on the periphery memories of the great years echo through the gold-leaf halls of the Unesco-sponsored Palazzi dei Rolli – a myriad collection of 16th- and 17th-century 'lodging palaces'.

The Most Serene Republic of Genoa ruled the Mediterranean waves during the 12th to the 13th centuries, before deferring to the superior power of Piedmont. Its crusading noblemen once established colonies in the Middle East and North Africa, and its emblematic flag, the red cross of St George, was greedily hijacked by the English.

Since hosting Expo 1992 and being championed as 2004's European City of Culture, Genoa has undergone some radical renovations, with its once-tatty port area now hosting Europe's largest aquarium and one of its best maritime museums.

History

Genoa's name is thought to come from the Latin *ianua,* meaning 'door'. Founded in the 4th century BC, Genoa was an important Roman port and was later occupied by Franks, Saracens and the Milanese. The first ring of Genoa's defensive walls was constructed in the 12th century. (The only remaining section of these walls, Porta Soprana, was built in 1155, although what you see today is a restored version.)

A victory over Venice in 1298 led to a period of growth, but bickering between the Grimaldis, Dorias, Spinolas and other dynasties caused internal chaos. The Grimaldis headed west, establishing the principality of Monaco – hence the similarity of Monaco's language, Monegasque, to the Genoese dialect.

In the 16th century, under the rule of Imperial Admiral Andrea Doria, Genoa benefited from financing Spanish exploration. Its coffers swelled further in the 17th century, which saw an outer ring of walls added as the city expanded, and its newly built palaces filled with art, attracting masters such as Rubens. Celebrated architect Galeazzo Alessi (1512–72) designed many of the city's splendid buildings.

The end of the Age of Exploration came as a blow and, as the Mediterranean's mercantile importance declined, so did Genoa's. The city languished for centuries.

Genoa was the first northern city to rise against Nazi occupation and the Italian Fascists during WWII, liberating itself before Allied troops arrived. After the war the city developed rapidly, although by the 1970s decline had set in as industries folded.

Christopher Columbus is Genoa's most famous son. In 1992 the 500th anniversary of his seminal voyage to America transformed Genoa's ancient harbour from a decaying backwater into a showpiece for the city. Renzo Piano orchestrated the overhaul, adding a number of striking permanent attractions. Two years later, Genoa was named a

European City of Culture, spurring further renovations and additions to the cityscape, including several new museums and a much-needed metro system.

◎ Sights

Aside from its Ligurian cuisine, Genoa's tour de force is its Palazzi dei Rolli. Forty-two of these plush lodging palaces – built between 1576 and 1664 to host visiting European gentry – were placed on the Unesco World Heritage list in 2006. They are mostly on or around Via Garibaldi and Via Balbi.

Musei di Strada Nuova   MUSEUM
(www.museidigenova.it; combined ticket adult/reduced €8/6; ⊘9am-7pm Tue-Fri, 10am-7pm Sat & Sun) Skirting the northern edge of what was once the city limits, pedestrianised Via Garibaldi (formerly called the Strada Nuova) was planned by Galeazzo Alessi in the 16th century. It quickly became the city's most sought-after quarter, lined with the palaces of Genoa's wealthiest citizens. Three of these *palazzi* (mansions) – Rosso, Bianco and Doria-Tursi – comprise the Musei di Strada Nuova. Between them, they hold the city's finest collection of old masters.

Tickets must be purchased at the bookshop inside Palazzo Doria-Tursi (www.museidigenova.it; Via Garibaldi 9). This palace's highlight is the Sala Paganiniana, which showcases a small but absorbing collection of legendary violinist Niccolò Paganini's personal effects. Pride of place goes to his Cannone violin, made in Cremona in 1743. One lucky musician gets to play the maestro's violin during October's Paganiniana festival. Other artefacts on show include letters, musical scores and Paganini's travelling chess set. Elsewhere the collections are centred on ceramics and coins.

Lavishly frescoed rooms in Palazzo Rosso (www.museidigenova.it; Via Garibaldi 18) are the backdrop for several Van Dyck portraits of the local Brignole-Sale family. Other standouts include Guido Reni's *San Sebastiano* and Guercino's *La Morte di Cleopatra* (the Death of Cleopatra), as well as works by Veronese, Dürer and Bernardo Strozzi.

Flemish, Spanish and Italian artists feature at Palazzo Bianco (www.museidigenova.it; Via Garibaldi 11). Rubens' *Venere e Marte* (Venus and Mars) and Van Dyck's *Vertumna e Pomona* are among the highlights, which also include works by Hans Memling, Filippino Lippi and Spanish masters Murillo and Zurbarán.

Palazzo Ducale   MUSEUM
(www.palazzoducale.genova.it; Piazza Giacomo Matteotti 9; admission depends on exhibition; ⊘exhibitions 9am-9pm) Once the seat of an independent republic, this grand palace was built in the mannerist style in the 1590s and largely refurbished after a fire in the 1770s. Today it hosts high-profile temporary art exhibitions (an excellent photography show was running at last visit).

There are several smaller museums inside, including the Stanza del Jazz (Piazza Giacomo Matteotti 9; admission free; ⊘4-7pm Mon-Sat by reservation) **FREE**, with a collection of original recordings. The *palazzo* also has a bookshop and the fine M-Cafe.

Cattedrale di San Lorenzo   CATHEDRAL
(Piazza San Lorenzo; ⊘8am-noon & 3-7pm) Impressive even by Italian standards, Genoa's black-and-white-striped Gothic-Romaesque cathedral owes its continued existence to the poor quality of a British WWII bomb that failed to ignite here in 1941; it still sits on the right side of the nave like an innocuous museum piece.

Fronted by twisting columns and crouching lions, the cathedral was first consecrated in 1118. The two bell towers and cupola were added in the 16th century.

Inside, above the central doorway, there's a great lunette with a painting of the Last Judgment, the work of an anonymous Byzantine painter of the early 14th century. In the sacristy, the Museo del Tesoro (Piazza San Lorenzo; adult/child €5.50/4.50; ⊘tours 9am-noon & 3-6pm Mon-Sat) preserves various dubious holy relics, including the medieval Sacro Catino, a glass vessel once thought to be the Holy Grail. Other artefacts include the polished quartz platter upon which Salome is said to have received John the Baptist's head, and a fragment of the True Cross.

Liguria

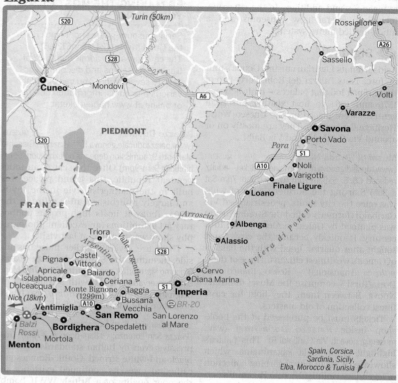

★ **Palazzo Reale**   PALACE, MUSEUM
(www.palazzorealegenova.it; Via Balbi 10; adult/
reduced €4/2; ⊙ 9am-7pm Thu-Sun, to 1.30pm Tue
& Wed) If you only get the chance to visit one
of the Palazzi dei Rolli, make it this one – a
veritable Versailles with terraced gardens,
exquisite furnishings and a fine collection of
Renaissance art. The gilded Hall of Mirrors
is worth the entry fee alone.

Add in frescoes, stuccoes and numerous
other artefacts collected by its two illustrious Genovese owners, the Balbis and the
Durazzos, and you'll be blinking gold for
hours afterwards. Complimentary guided
tours enhance the experience.

Museo del Risorgimento   MUSEUM
(www.istitutomazziniano.it; Via Lomellini 11; adult/
reduced €4/2.80; ⊙ 9am-7pm Tue-Fri, 10am-7pm
Sat) One of numerous Risorgimento (reunification period) museums in Italy, Genoa's
has extra significance: it is housed in the

residence where Italian patriot and activist
Giuseppe Mazzini was born in 1805. Occupying rooms that once sheltered the so-called
'soul of Italy' are flags, personal possessions
and well-laid-out and succinct explanations
(some of them in English) of the complicated process of Italy's unification.

Chiesa del Gesù   CHURCH
(Piazza Giacomo Matteotti; ⊙ 4.30-7pm) Half-
hidden behind the cathedral but emulating it in its ecclesial brilliance, this former
Jesuit church dating from 1597 has an intricate and lavish interior. The wonderfully
frescoed walls and ceiling are anchored by
two works by the great Dutch artist Rubens.
Circoncisione (Circumcision) hangs over
the main altar, and *Miracoli di San Ignazio*
is displayed in a side chapel.

Casa della Famiglia Colombo   MUSEUM
(Piazza Dante; admission €5; ⊙ 9am-noon & 2-6pm
Sat & Sun) Not the only house claiming to

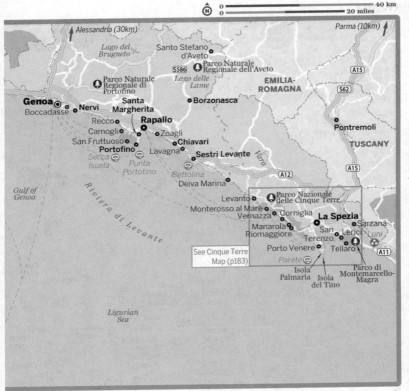

be the birthplace of the navigator Christopher Columbus (Calvi in Corsica is another contender), this one probably has the most merit, as various documents inside testify. Curiously, it stands just outside the old city walls in the shadow of the **Porta Soprana** gate (built in 1155).

Columbus allegedly lived here from 1455 until 1470, when he was between the ages of four and 19. For an extra €2 you can climb the twin-towered Porta Soprana.

Piazza de Ferrari
PIAZZA

After the asphyxiation of the *caruggi* this fountain-embellished main piazza ringed by magnificent buildings feels as if you've just come up for air. Showcase architecture includes the art nouveau **Palazzo della Borsa** (now offices), which was once the country's stock exchange; the hybrid neoclassical-modernist Teatro Carlo Felice (bombed in WW2 and not fully rebuilt until 1991); and the impressive central fountain.

Museo d'Arte Orientale
MUSEUM

(Piazzale Mazzini 1; adult/reduced €4/2.80; ⊙9am-1pm Tue-Fri, 10am-7pm Sat & Sun) Just east of Via Garibaldi, a path from Piazza Corvetto twists through terraced gardens to one of Europe's largest collections of Japanese art, bringing together some 20,000 items, including porcelain, bronzes, costumes and musical instruments.

Old City
NEIGHBOURHOOD

The heart of medieval Genoa – bounded by **Porta dei Vacca**, the streets of Via Cairoli, Via Garibaldi and Via XXV Aprile, and Porta Soprana – is famed for its *caruggi*. As evidenced by the washing pegged on lines strung outside the buildings, these dark, almost cave-like laneways and dank, odoriferous blind alleys are largely residential, with a sprinkling of bars, shops and cafes.

Particularly after dark, parts of the *caruggi* can feel somewhat unnerving. Although it's not overly dangerous (especially

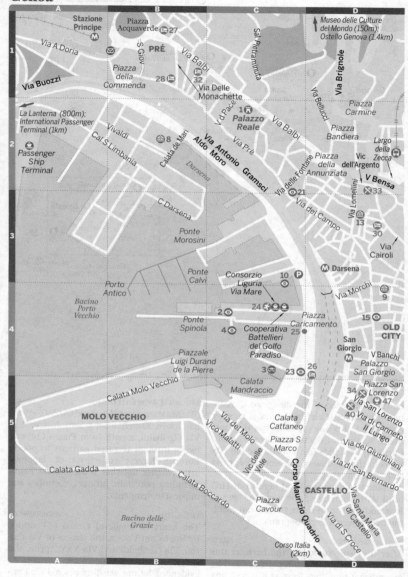

compared with a decade ago), take care in the zone west of Via San Luca and south to Piazza Banchi, where most of the old city's lowlife (prostitution, drugs and so on) concentrates. East of the piazza is Via Orefici, where you'll find market stalls.

Galleria Nazionale
ART GALLERY

(www.palazzospinola.it; Piazza Superiore di Pellicceria 1; adult/reduced €5/3; ⊙9am-8pm Tue-Sat, 2-8pm Sun) This gallery's paintings are wonderfully displayed over four floors of the 16th-century Palazzo Spinola, once owned

worth visiting to gape at the decorative architecture.

Museo delle Culture del Mondo — MUSEUM
(Museum of World Cultures; www.castellodalbertis-genova.it; Corso Dogali 18; adult/reduced €6/4.50; ⊙10am-6pm) Towering over the western end of town, **Castello D'Albertis** houses an eclectic museum showcasing artefacts collected by its globetrotting owner. The neo-Gothic edifice was built in 1892 on the ruins of a much older castle for the Capitano Enrico D'Albertis, who hauled back all manner of 'curiosities' from his extensive sea voyages.

Where else could you find a stuffed platypus, a fragment of the Great Wall of China and a handful of sand from San Salvador (Columbus' first disembarkation point) in the same cabinet? If you don't fancy the climb up to Corso Dogali, there's a lift from Via Balbi (€1) to the castle gates.

Porto Antico — NEIGHBOURHOOD
(www.portoantico.it) The port that once controlled a small empire has reaffirmed itself as one of the best places to enjoy a *passeggiata* (evening stroll) since a decade-long facelift in the late 1990s and early 2000s. Young nightlife searchers and kids are particularly well catered for with an aquarium, the futuristic Bigo (lookout) and a pirate ship (Il Galeone Neptune)..

Acquario — AQUARIUM
(www.acquariodigenova.it; Ponte Spinola; adult/reduced €18/12; ⊙9.30am-7.30pm; ⊞) No glorified fish tank, Genoa's bright-blue aquarium is one of the largest in Europe, with more than 5000 sea creatures, including sharks, swimming in six million litres of water. Moored at the end of a walkway is the ship Nave Blu, refurbished in July 2013 as a unique floating display. It contains 2,700 sq metres of exposition space and specialises in exhibits of coral reefs and a reconstruction of a Madagascan rainforest. The aquarium has disabled access.

Biosfera — BIOSPHERE DOME
(Ponte Spinola; adult/reduced €5/3.50; ⊙10am-7pm mid-Mar–mid-Nov, to 5pm rest of year) A giant glass ball housing a humid mini-ecosystem with tropical plants, butterflies and birds, the Biosphere is an interesting and innovative addition to the port, although its assorted greenery probably won't delay you more than 15 minutes. The ambient temperature inside is controlled by computers.

by the Spinola family, one of the Republic's most formidable dynasties. The main focus is Italian and Flemish Renaissance art of the so-called 'Ligurian School' (look out for Van Dyck, Rubens and Strozzi), but it's also

LIGURIA, PIEDMONT & THE ITALIAN RIVIERA GENOA

Genoa

Bigo　　　　　　　　　　　　　　LOOKOUT

(Calata Cattaneo; adult/reduced €4/3; ⊙10am-11pm Jun-Aug, 2-6pm Mon, 10am-6pm Tue-Sun Mar-May, Sep & Oct) The port's most eye-catching and futuristic structure is this giant spider-like contraption that hoists a cylindrical viewing cabin 200m into the air for mediocre city views that struggle to justify the price tag. The lift has access for visitors with disabilities.

Galata Museo del Mare　　　　　MUSEUM

(www.galatamuseodelmare.it; Calata de Mari 1; admission €12; ⊙10am-7.30pm, closed Mon Nov-Feb) Rivalled only by Barcelona and Venice as a medieval and Renaissance maritime power, Genoa's 'museum of the sea' is, not surprisingly, one of its most relevant and interesting. High-tech exhibits trace the history of seafaring, from Genoa's reign as Europe's greatest dockyard to the ages of sail and steam, and justify the rather steep entry fee.

A section on the ground floor is deservedly dedicated to native son, Christopher Columbus. Alongside is a scale reconstruc-

tion of a 17th-century galley ship, given extra drama by added sound effects and snippets of film. The 2nd floor guards a valuable collection of old maps and globes, while the 3rd floor has a more recent exposé of Italian emigration (using ships). The top-floor mirador has one of Genoa's best cityscape views. Bring a camera.

Il Galeone Neptune　　　　　　PIRATE SHIP

(Mole Ponte Calvi; adult/reduced €5/3; ⊙10am-6pm; ⊕) This full-sized replica pirate ship was built in 1986 as a prop in the Roman Polanski movie *Pirates*. Moored permanently in the port, it is now a favourite playground for kids re-enacting scenes from *Peter Pan* and *Pirates of the Caribbean* with their beleaguered parents.

Genoa-Casella Railway　　　　RAILWAY

Spectacular views of Genoa's forts can be seen from the 1929 narrow-gauge railway, which snakes 25km north from Stazione Genova (www.ferroviagenovacasella.it; Via alla Stazione per Casella 15) to the village of Casella (one way/return €2/3.20, one hour, eight to

12 daily) in the Valle Scrivia. Stazione Genova is 1.3km north of Stazione Brignole: it's 15 minutes by foot or you can catch bus 33.

La Lanterna LIGHTHOUSE

(Via alla Lanterna; admission €6; ☺10am-7pm Sat & Sun) The port may have changed radically since its '90s rebirth, but its omnipresent sentinel hasn't moved an inch since 1543. Genoa's emblematic lighthouse is one of the world's oldest and tallest – and it still works, beaming its light over 50km to warn ships and tankers. Visitors can climb 172 steps and ponder exhibits in an adjacent museum of lamps, lenses and related history.

La Lanterna is best accessed via a special 800m walking trail that starts at the ferry terminal. It's surrounded by a pleasant park.

☞ Tours

Information and tickets for boat trips round the port and destinations further afield are available from the ticket booths (Ponte Spinola; ☺9.30am-6.30pm Sep-Jun, 9am-8pm Jul & Aug) beside the aquarium at the Porto Antico.

Whale Watch Liguria WHALE-WATCHING TOUR
(www.whalewatchliguria.it; tickets €33; ☺1.15pm Sat Apr-Oct) These five-hour spring and summer tours are run in consultation with the WWF and include fascinating background on the world's largest mammals provided by an onboard biologist.

Genova Tours BUS TOUR
(adult/reduced €14/7.50) Runs three or four open-topped bus tours daily, with headphone commentary in five languages. It's best to confirm the departure point for your specific trip; tourist offices can provide departure details. Tickets are sold on the bus.

⚜ Festivals & Events

Slow Fish FOOD
(www.slowfish.it) ✐ Every odd-numbered year in early May, this festival celebrates seafood with a fish market and tastings. Affiliated with the Slow Food Movement, it also runs free workshops focusing on water pollution, good fishing practices and aquaculture.

**Palio delle Quattro Antiche
Repubbliche Marinare** REGATTA
(Regatta of the Four Ancient Maritime Republics) In the Regatta of the Four Ancient Maritime Republics, the four historical maritime rivals – Pisa, Venice, Amalfi and Genoa – meet in June for a procession of boats and a dramatic race; the next will be held in Pisa in 2017.

Premio Paganini MUSIC
In homage to Genoese violinist Niccolò Paganini (1782–1849), this is an international violin competition held in September. The next event is in 2014 and will be held in the Teatro Carlo Felice (p176).

🛏 Sleeping

Dozens of hotels are spread round town. The greatest concentration is near Stazione Principe, on and around Via Balbi.

★**Hotel Cairoli** HOTEL €
(☎010 246 14 54; www.hotelcairoligenova.com; Via Cairoli 14/4; d/tr/qu €85/100/125; ✳@☎) Window-shoppers wouldn't know it, but Mondrian lurks three flights up in this Genoese *palazzo*. Themed on various modern artists, the rooms at the cleverly put-together Cairoli exhibit the personalities and works of various famous artists. Add in a communal library, chill-out area, internet room, fully equipped gym, free newspapers, terrace and informative maps on the wall and you have five stars in a three-star wrapping.

It's multilingual and friendly, too.

B&B Palazzo Morali B&B €
(☎010 246 70 27; www.palazzomorali.com; Piazza della Raibetta; s/d €65/75; P✳☎) Your instant reaction on entering the rarefied world of Palazzo Morali is 'I've stumbled upon a secret Palazzo Rolli that Unesco forgot to list'. When you come to your senses, you'll realise

DON'T MISS

CORSO ITALIA

When you've had your fill of the rats and pungent alleys of the old city, decamp (as locals do) to the oceanside promenade known as Corso Italia, which lies approximately 3km east of the city centre. This broad 2.5km-long pavement is where Genovese Romeos pledge undying love to their Juliets, and joggers justify last night's gelati. The beach here is pebble, but the Corso displays some lovely Liberty facades and ends in unexpectedly cute **Boccadasse**, a once separate fishing village that appears like a sawn-off part of Cinque Terre out of the surrounding urbanity.

LIGURIA, PIEDMONT & THE ITALIAN RIVIERA GENOA

that 'B&B' is a misnomer at this exquisite place on the top two floors of a lofty building overlooking Genoa's port.

Palatial rooms (some with shared bathroom) are embellished with gold-leafed four-poster beds and Genovese art, and breakfast feels more like a banquet than an early-morning snack.

Hotel Meuble Suisse
HOTEL €

(☑ 010 54 11 76; www.meublesuisse.com; 3rd fl, Via XX Settembre 21; s/d €53/71; ☎) Clean rooms, service with a smile and your own personal chandelier. What more could you want? Climb the stairs to the 3rd floor of this strapping Genoa building near Stazione Brignole for a bit of revived fin-de-siècle magic. If the nine spacious rooms are full, climb up another floor to the charming, similarly priced Olympia Hotel Genova (☑ 010 59 25 38; www.olympiahotelgenova.com; 4th fl, Via XX Settembre 21).

Hotel Agnello d'Oro
HOTEL €

(☑ 010 246 20 84; www.hotelagnellodoro.it; Vico delle Monachette 6; s/d €65/85; ☀ @ ☎ ⚑) Economical and close to Stazione Porta Principe the 17-room Agnello has everything a serious traveller needs, such as terrace, reading room, tourist info, buffet breakfasts and family rooms.

Ostello Genova
HOSTEL €

(☑ 010 242 24 57; www.ostellogenova.it; Via Costanzi 120; dm €17, s/d €28/50, shared bathroom s/d €24/44; ☺ reception 24 hrs; P ☎) A steep 2km north of the centre, Genoa's only hostel has rules that won't endear it to free-spirited backpackers: its eight-bed dorms are single-sex, there's a lockout from 9am to 3.30pm, a 1am curfew, and Hostelling International (HI) cards are mandatory. Catch bus 40 from Stazione Brignole to the end of the line. Has access for guests with disabilities.

Hotel Bristol Palace
HOTEL €€

(☑ 010 59 25 41; www.hotelbristolpalace.com; Via XX Settembre 35; s €92/143; P ☀ @ ☎) Under the huge portals of Via XX Settembre lies one of Genoa's fanciest pads, a belle époque masterpiece exhibiting atmospheric, airy rooms with geometric parquet flooring and original antiques (as well as mod cons). Enter the domain via a sweeping staircase with an ornamental glass roof visible at the top.

Grand Hotel Savoia
HOTEL €€

(☑ 010 2 77 21; www.grandhotelsavoiagenova.it; Via Arsenale di Terra 5; s/d €124/169; ☀ @ ☎) Retreat to the land of fluffy bathrobes and the customised shower gel in the aptly named Grand Savoia, a hotel that could still happily accommodate the Italian royal family if they hadn't been abolished in 1946. Decor is elegant but old world and rooms sizes vary (ask for one with a mural behind the bed). It's next to Stazione Porta Principe.

Hotel Cristoforo Colombo
HOTEL €€

(☑ 010 251 36 43; www.hotelcolombo.it; Via di Porta Soprana 27; s €88-160, d €110-170; ☎) A rather charming family-run hotel ideally situated near Cattedrale di San Lorenzo, Cristoforo Colombo has 18 colour-accented rooms with postmodern furnishings. Breakfast is served on an inviting 6th-floor rooftop terrace.

Hotel della Posta Nuova
HOTEL €€

(☑ 010 25 29 29; www.albergopostagenova.com; Via Balbi 24; s €40-115, d €60-130; P ☀) No real surprises at this reliable hotel 150m from Stazione Principe, though it's clean, safe and relatively friendly for such a transient quarter. Rooms are smallish and simple but admit plenty of natural light. The ones on the top floor have a terrace overlooking Via Balbi.

✗ Eating

It's practically impossible to leave town without tasting *pesto genovese* – the famous sauce that appears on menus everywhere. Ubiquitous local specialities focaccia (especially topped with cheese) and *farinata* (flat bread made from chickpea flour) make cheap takeaway snacks. Nail a place with a visible oven and dive in when you see the baker stocking his display cases with a fresh round. *Torta pasqualina* (spinach, ricotta cheese and egg tart), *pansotti* (spinach-filled ravioli with a thick, creamy hazelnut sauce) and freshly caught seafood are also good.

Trattoria Da Maria
TRATTORIA €

(☑ 010 58 10 80; Vico Testadoro 14R; €12; ☺ 11.45am-3pm Mon-Sat, 7-10.30pm Thu & Fri) Pesto is essentially a poor man's cuisine that employs basic ingredients and you'll pay poor man's prices at this no-frills trattoria stuck up a shadowy Genovese alley that opens daily for lunch (and dinner on Thursday and Friday). Tables are shared and the food arrives with the speed and subtlety of an invading Napoleonic army.

The barely legible handwritten menu is essentially whatever's in the pot. Pesto dominates.

M-Cafe
SANDWICH SHOP, CAFE €
(Palazzo Ducale, Piazza Giacomo Mateotti 9; snacks from €4; ☺8am-8pm) It's a testament to Italy's unswerving gastronomic quality that even the museum cafes are top-notch. M-Cafe in the grand lobby of the Palazzo Ducale is regularly frequented by people who have no intention of browsing the exhibits. Abundant servings of apertifs arrive at 6pm-ish. There are additional branches in the Palazzo Rosso and Palazzo Reale.

Pastaway
ITALIAN €
(☑010 247 32 35; Piazza della Meridiana; boxes €4-7) After demolishing your €5 carton of takeaway *trofie* (short, twisted pasta) in pesto sauce, you'll wonder why no one outside of Genoa has yet come up with such an obvious business start-up, ie takeaway (or *portavia* as they say in Italian) handmade pasta that's fast, fresh, ready to eat. Choose your pasta and sauce and...GO!

Trattoria delle Erbe
TRATTORIA, SEAFOOD €
(Piazza delle Erbe 8-10; €20; ☺noon-2.30pm & 7-10.30pm Tue-Sat, noon-2.30pm Sun & Mon) Serving the kind of salt-of-the-sea Genovese food that has been satisfying local bellies since local boy Columbus accidentally bumped into America, this trattoria in the agreeably mildewed Piazza delle Erbe is ideal for *risotto del pescatore* (seafood risotto), gnocchi with rocket and prawns, or a seafood mixed grill.

La Cremeria delle Erbe
GELATO €
(Piazza delle Erbe 15-17; cones from €2; ☺11am-1am Mon-Thu & Sun, to 2am Fri & Sat) There are at least a dozen contenders for the 'best ice cream in Genoa' mantle, but if you like your gelato creamy, look no further than this outlet in agreeably shabby Piazza delle Erbe that snares late-night diners and boozers on their way home from the pubs.

Focaccia e Dintorni
FOCACCERIA €
(Via Canneto Il Curto 7-8; focaccia from €1; ☺7am-8pm) Punt a football anywhere in Genoa and you're bound to hit somewhere that sells focaccia. The bakeries or *focaccerias* are significantly better than the bars, as is this place just off Via San Lorenzo that also sells pizza slices, *farinata* and sweet treats.

★ Trattoria della Raibetta
TRATTORIA €€
(www.trattoriadellaraibetta.it; Vico Caprettari 10-12; mains €14; ☺lunch & dinner Tue-Sun) The most authentic Genoese food can be procured in the family-run joints hidden in the warren of streets near the cathedral. The Raibetta's menu is unfussy and fish-biased. Try the seafood with *riso venere* (a local black rice) or the signature homemade *trofiette al pesto*.

The octopus salad makes a good overture, while the wine is a toss-up between 200 different vintages.

Trattoria Rosmarino
TRATTORIA €€
(☑010 251 04 75; www.trattoriarosmarino.it; Salita del Fondaco 30; meals €30; ☺noon-3pm & 7-11pm Mon-Sat) More chic than shabby, Rosmarino cooks up its local Genovese specialties in a more elegant setting than the other spit and sawdust trattorias of the *caruggi*. Slick service and a modernist presentation make it a romantic nook for lovers and/or lovers of good food. It's popular, so book ahead.

Ombre Rosse
TRADITIONAL ITALIAN €€€
(☑010 27 57 608; Vico Indoratori 20; meals €35-35; ☺12.30-10pm Mon-Fri, 7.45-10.30pm Sat) Encased in one of the oldest medieval houses in the city, dating from the early 13th century, Ombre Rosse offers another dose of urban serendipity. First there's the dark but romantic interior, full of books, posters and interesting nooks. Second is the alfresco seating in a delightful small park (one of the few in Genoa's dense urban grid).

Third and most importantly is the 100% Ligurian food – *trofie al pesto*, pasta with *salsa di noci* (walnut sauce) and fine *verdure torta* (vegetable quiche) with a side salad.

Da Gaia
TRADITIONAL ITALIAN €€€
(Vico dell'Argento 13r; meals €30-50; ☺noon-3pm & 7pm-midnight Mon-Fri, 7pm-midnight Sat) Don't let the dark, Dickensian alley put you off. Gaia is a ray of light in murky surroundings, and is regularly voted the best restaurant in town by those who should know (ie the locals). It's famous for its fish, so try the antipasto vegetable plate before diving into prawns, sea bass or tuna. It also does all the Genovese staples – pesto, *salsa di noci* – and a good stewed rabbit.

 Drinking & Nightlife

The revamped Porto Antico has captured much of the youthful night-time scene, but never underestimate the lure of the *caruggi*. You'll also find sophisticated new drinking spots intermingled with old-time favourites throughout the city, particularly in the streets just northwest of Piazza de Ferrari.

Piazza delle Erbe is clad with cafe terraces where you can linger over a coffee or something stronger.

⭐**La Nouvelle Vague**   WINE BAR
(www.nouvelle-vague.it; Vico de Gradi 4r; ⊗noon-3pm Mon-Fri, 6.30pm-1.30am Mon-Sat) The *caruggi* pull many surprises, but few are as sweet as this enclave of cool underground intellectualism beneath the clammy confusion of Genoa's medieval streets. Nouvelle Vague is a French-themed bookshop and bar where you can sip Italian wine while leafing through the works of Genet and Proust.

Photos of a gamine Jean Seaberg adorn the walls, and the top-drawer aperitif snacks that accompany all drink orders have led to numerous dinner cancellations.

Fratelli Klainguti   CAFE
(Via di Soziglia; ⊗8am-8pm) Pre-dating cappuccinos and Lavazza coffee, Klainguti presumably found other ways to pull in the clientele when it opened in 1828. These days, caffeine and pastries do the trick for most people who are happy to pay over the odds to get served by a waiter in a bow tie under an ostentatious chandelier.

Simple *primi* (first courses) start at a more reasonable €5.

Café degli Specchi   CAFE
(Via Salita Pollaiuoli 43r; mains €7-10; ⊗7am-9pm Mon-Sat) A bit of Turin disconnected and relocated 150km to the south, this roaring-'20s, tiled art deco showpiece was (and is) a favourite hang-out of the literati. You can sink your espresso at street level or disappear upstairs amid the velvet seats and mirrors for coffee, cake and an *aperitivo* buffet.

Cambi Cafe   BAR, CAFE
(Via Falamonica 9; ⊗10am-11pm) Admire the pleasantly faded 17th-century frescoes of Bernardo Strozzi while sipping on your am cappuccino or your pm aperitif in this spectacular bar-cafe (it also serves dinner) encased in an old Doria palace. Exquisite!

Bar Berto   BAR, RESTAURANT
(Piazza delle Erbe 6; ⊗10.30am-1am Sun-Thu, to 2am Fri & Sat) Rambunctious Piazza delle Erbe is *the* place to enjoy an alfresco drink after dark. The tables of various bars merge in the cobbled square, but the beers and aperitifs that come out of Bar Berto are particularly tempting.

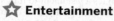 **Entertainment**

At the western end of the Porto Antico, the Magazzini del Cotone (one-time cotton warehouses) have been converted into an entertainment area with a multiplex cinema, games arcade and shops.

Teatro Carlo Felice   THEATRE
(☑010 538 12 24; www.carlofelice.it; Passo Eugenio Montale 4) Take in a play or opera at Genoa's stunning four-stage opera house.

Teatro della Tosse   THEATRE
(www.teatrodellatosse.it; Piazza Renato Negri 4) Casanova trod the boards of the city's oldest theatre, which dates from 1702.

🛍 **Shopping**

Heading southwest, elegant Via Roma, with its art nouveau boutiques and adjacent glass-covered **Galleria Mazzini**, is Genoa's most exclusive designer-shopping street. It links Piazza Corvetto with Piazza de Ferrari.

ℹ **Information**

Ospedale San Martino (☑010 55 51; Largo Rosanna Benci 10) Hospital.
Police station (☑010 5 36 61; Via Armando Diaz 2)
Main post office (Via Dante 4; ⊗8am-6.30pm Mon-Sat)
Post office (Stazione Principe; ⊗8am-6.30pm Mon-Fri, to 12.30pm Sat)
Tourist offices Airport (☑010 601 52 47; ⊗10am-1pm & 1.30-6.30pm); Via Garibaldi (☑010 557 29 03; Via Garibaldi 12r; ⊗9am-6.30pm); Piazza Ferrari (next to Teatro Carlo Felice; ⊗9am-1pm & 2.30-6.30pm)

ℹ **Getting There & Away**

AIR
Regular domestic and international services, including Ryanair flights to London Stansted, use **Cristoforo Colombo Airport** (☑010 6 01 51; www.airport.genova.it), 6km west of the city in Sestri Ponente.

BOAT
Ferries sail to/from Spain, Sicily, Sardinia, Corsica and Tunisia from the **international passenger terminal** (Terminal Traghetti; www.porto.genova.it; Via Milano 51). Only cruise ships

use the 1930s passenger ship terminal on Ponte dei Mille.

Fares listed here are for one-way, low-/high-season deck-class tickets. Ferry operators based at the international passenger terminal include the following:

From June to September, **Cooperativa Battellieri del Golfo Paradiso** (www.golfoparadiso.it) operates boats from Porto Antico to Camogli (one way/return €10/15), Portofino (€12/20) and Porto Venere (€20/35).

Consorzio Liguria Via Mare (www.liguriaviamare.it) runs a range of seasonal trips to Camogli, San Fruttuoso and Portofino; Monterosso in the Cinque Terre; and Porto Venere.

Grandi Navi Veloci (GNV; ☎010 209 45 91; www.gnv.it) Ferries to Sardinia (Porto Torres, €65, year-round) and Sicily (Palermo, €69, year-round). Also ferries to Barcelona, Tunis (Tunisia) and Tangier (Morocco).

Moby Lines (☎199 30 30 40; www.mobylines.it) Ferries year-round to Corsica (Bastia, €39) and Sardinia (Olbia, €72).

BUS

Buses to international cities depart from Piazza della Vittoria, as do buses to/from Milan's Malpensa airport (€16, two hours, 6am and 3pm) and other interregional services. Tickets are sold at **Geotravels** (Piazza della Vittoria 57) and **Pesci Viaggi e Turismo** (Piazza della Vittoria 94r).

TRAIN

Genoa's Stazione Principe and Stazione Brignole are linked by train to the following destinations.

TO	FARE (€)	DURATION (HR)	FREQUENCY
Milan	19.50	1½	up to 8 daily
Pisa	26	2	up to 8 daily
Rome	60.50	5	6 daily
Turin	19	1¾	7–10 daily

Stazione Principe tends to have more trains, particularly going west to San Remo (€16.50, two hours, five daily) and Ventimiglia (€13.20, 2¼ hours, six daily).

ⓘ Getting Around

TO/FROM THE AIRPORT

The **AMT** (www.amt.genova.it) line 100 runs between Stazione Principe and the airport at least every hour from 5.30am to 11pm (€4, 30 minutes). Tickets can be bought from the driver.

A taxi to or from the airport will cost around €15.

PUBLIC TRANSPORT

AMT operates buses throughout the city and there is an **AMT information office** (Via d'Annunzio 8; ☉7.15am-6pm Mon-Fri, 7am-7pm Sat & Sun) at the bus terminal. Bus line 383 links Stazione Brignole with Piazza de Ferrari and Stazione Principe. A ticket valid for 90 minutes costs €1.50. Tickets can be used on main-line trains within the city limits, as well as on the currently expanding **metro** (www.genovametro.com), which has numerous stations across the city.

Around Genoa

Nervi

A former fishing village engulfed by Genoa's urban sprawl, modern Nervi classifies itself as a 'resort' – though with plenty of ritzier Riviera competition, it's rarely top of anyone's holiday list. Its saving graces are its bounty of museums and galleries, and the 2km cliffside promenade, the Passeggiata Anita Garibaldi.

◉ Sights

All four of Nervi's museums and galleries can be accessed in a combined ticket (€10) or they're included on the Genoa Museum Card.

Galleria d'Arte Moderna ART GALLERY
(Via Capolungo 3; adult/reduced €6/5; ☉10am-7pm Tue-Sun) This museum, which is the most celebrated of the four, displays works by 19th- and 20th-century artists such as Filippo De Pisis, Arturo Martini and Rubaldo Merello.

ⓘ MAKING THE MOST OF YOUR EURO

Easily the best way to get around the Cinque Terre is with a **Cinque Terre card**.

Two versions of the card are available: with or without train travel. Both include unlimited use of walking paths and electric village buses, as well as cultural exhibitions. Without train travel, a basic one-/two-day card for those aged over four years costs €5/9. A card that also includes unlimited train trips between the towns costs €10/19. A family card for two adult and two children (under 12) costs €26 including train travel.

Both versions of the card are sold at all Cinque Terre park information offices.

BREAKING FOCACCIA WITH THE LOCALS

Spend a week breaking bread in the bars and bakeries of the Ligurian coast and you'll quickly ascertain that no two focaccias are alike. The classic focaccia, called 'alla genovese', is a simple oven-baked flat-bread made with flour, yeast, water, salt and oil (and topped with salt, olive oil and sometimes rosemary), but various regional variations crop up only a short train ride away. To the east, the galletta di Camogli from the town of Camogli is a crisp focaccia more akin to a biscuit, which was supposedly invented for the town's sailors to take on long sailing voyages. In nearby Recco, the delicious focaccia col formaggio spreads mild creamy cheese (usually crescenza) between two thin slices of bread made without yeast. It traces its roots back to the Saracen invasions of the Early Middle Ages. San Remo, on the Riviera di Ponente, has concocted sardenara, a pizza-like focaccia with a wheat-flour base topped with tomatoes, onions, capers and – as the name implies – sardines. Inland, in the Valle Stura, focaccine revzora is a polenta-like bread made with cornmeal in a wood-burning oven.

Raccolte Frugone   ART GALLERY

(Via Capolungo 9; adult/reduced €4/2.80; ⊙9am-7pm Tue-Fri, 10am-7pm Sat & Sun) More 19th- and early-20th-century Italian art, including Edoardo Rubino's sensual marble nude Il Risveglio (the Awakening) is displayed here in the Villa Grimaldi Fassio, overlooking the leafy, squirrel-filled Parchi di Nervi.

Wolfsoniana   MUSEUM

(www.wolfsoniana.it; Via Serra Gropallo 4; adult/reduced €5/4; ⊙10am-7pm Tue-Sun) Some 18,000 items from the period 1880–1945 are displayed in the Wolfson Collection. On show are items documenting this turbulent time in Italy's history, including advertising and propaganda posters, along with architectural drawings, paintings and furnishings.

Museo Giannettino Luxoro   MUSEUM

(Via Mafalda di Savoia 3; adult/reduced €4/2.80; ⊙9am-1pm Tue-Fri, 10am-1pm Sat) Going back earlier in time, this place has a rich collection of 18th-century clocks, silverware, ceramics and furniture, displayed in a splendidly restored villa. The entrance fee also includes entry to the Raccolte Frugone.

✖ Eating

Chandra Bar   INTERNATIONAL €

(Passeggiata Garibaldi 26r; €18-25; ⊙3pm-2am Tue-Sat, 11.30am-2am Sun) Situated on the seafront promenade, the Chandra serves up pasta and daily specials of freshly caught fish occasionally spiced up with Thai and Brazilian inflections. Also has live music.

❶ Getting There & Away

Nervi is 7km east of Genoa and is best reached by frequent trains from Stazione Brignole and Stazione Principe (€1.50, 20 to 25 minutes).

Pegli

Roughly 9km west of Genoa's centre, flower-filled parks make Pegli a peaceful spot to retreat from the urban tumult. Like Nervi, this former seafront village now lies within the city boundaries of Genoa and, again like Nervi, it has yet more museums. A combined ticket for all of the following sights costs €8.

◉ Sights

Museo di Archeologia Ligure   MUSEUM

(www.museoarcheologicogenova.it; Villa Pallavicini, Via Pallavicini 11; admission €5; ⊙9am-7pm Tue-Fri, 10am-7pm Sat & Sun) This museum in the striking Villa Pallavicini holds displays of locally excavated artefacts from prehistoric times through to the Roman period, as well as a collection of Egyptian antiquities.

Museo Navale   MUSEUM

(www.museonavale.it; Villa Doria, Piazza Bonavino 7; admission €5; ⊙9am-1pm Tue-Fri, 10am-6pm Sat, to 1pm Sun) Maritime matters are covered in a former residence of the Doria clan, with an exhibition of models, photographs and other reminders of the days from the 15th to the 19th centuries, when Genoa sported a significant sea force.

Parco Villa Pallavicini   PARK

(Via Pallavicini; admission €3.50; ⊙9am-7pm Apr-Sep, to 5pm Oct-Mar) Pallavicini is a manicured park with formal lawns, lakes and a glasshouse that is an epitome of the lush Italian Riviera landscape. The neighbouring **Giardino Botanico** (admission €3.50; ☺ 9am-12.30pm Tue-Sun) is home to a small collection of exotic plants.

❶ Getting There & Away

Frequent trains from Genoa's Stazione Brignole and Stazione Principe (€1.50, 20 to 25 minutes) travel to Pegli.

Riviera di Levante

Running claustrophobically from Genoa's eastern sprawl, you're quickly apprehended by the deep blue waters of the Mediterranean, fringed by some of Italy's most elite resorts, including jet-set favourite Portofino. Anything but off the beaten track, this glittering stretch of coast is hugely popular but never tacky. Heading further east, swanky resorts battle bravely with increasingly precipitous topography.

Camogli

POP 5621

This still-authentic fishing village, 25km east of Genoa, has *trompe l'œil* decorating its alleys and cobbled streets, beneath a canopy of umbrella pines and voluptuous olive groves.

Camogli's name means 'house of wives', hailing from the days when the women ran the village while their husbands were at sea. Fishing traditions continue here, especially during the second weekend in May when fishers celebrate the **Sagra del Pesce** (Fish Festival) with a big fry-up – hundreds of fish are cooked in 3m-wide pans along the busy waterfront.

◉ Sights & Activities

From the main esplanade, Via Garibaldi, boats sail to the **Punta Chiappa**, a rocky outcrop on the Portofino promontory where you can swim and sunbathe like an Italian.

A trail from the train station leads along Via Nicolò Cuneo and up countless steps to the church of **San Rocco di Camogli** (follow the two red dots). From here the path continues 3km to the clifftop **batterie**, a WW2 German anti-aircraft gun emplacement.

⌂ Sleeping

Delve down the lanes away from the water to escape the lunchtime crowd and search for some of the town's extra-crunchy focaccia. The local accommodation rewards those looking for a splurge.

Hotel Cenobio dei Dogi   HOTEL €€€
(☎ 0185 72 41; www.cenobio.com; Via Cuneo 34; s/s €180/290; ▣✳☎▨) Welcome to Riviera luxury. The Cenobio's name means 'gathering place of the doges', and yes, the Genovese dukes used to holiday here eons ago – sensible souls! Choose from one of 105 refined rooms that still manage to feel intimate.

❶ Information

Tourist Office (www.camogli.it; Via XX Settembre 33; ☺ 9am-12.30pm & 3.30-6pm Mon-Sat, to 1pm Sun) Has a list of diving schools and boat-rental operators.

❶ Getting There & Away

Camogli is on the Genoa–La Spezia train line, with regular connections to Santa Margherita (€2.10, five minutes) and Rapallo (€2.10, 10 minutes).

The **Cooperativa Battellieri del Golfo Paradiso** (www.golfoparadiso.it) runs boats year-round to Punta Chiappa (one way/return €5/9) and San Fruttuoso (€8/12). Between June and September there are services to Genoa's Porto Antico (€10/15), Portofino (€10/17) and the Cinque Terre (€20/28).

San Fruttuoso

The yin to Portofino's yang, San Fruttuoso is a slice of ancient tranquillity preserved amid some of Italy's ritziest coastal resorts. There are no roads here – thank heavens! Access is either by boat or on foot.

◉ Sights

Abbazia di San Fruttuoso di Capodimonte   CHURCH
(adult/reduced €5/3; ☺ 10am-5.45pm Jun–mid-Sep) The hamlet's extraordinary Benedictine abbey was built as a final resting place for Bishop St Fructuosus of Tarragona (martyred in Spain in AD 259). It was rebuilt in the mid-13th century with the assistance of the Doria family. The abbey fell into decay with the decline of the religious community, and in the 19th century it was divided into small living quarters by local fishers.

In 1954 a bronze **statue** of Christ was lowered 15m to the seabed, offshore from the abbey, to bless the waters. Dive to see it or view it from a boat if the waters are calm – the Cooperativa Battellieri del Golfo

Paradiso can provide details. Replicas were lowered in St George's harbour in Grenada, in 1961, and off Key Largo in Florida in 1966.

ℹ️ Getting There & Away

San Fruttuoso's isolation is maintained by its lack of road access. You can walk in on foot from Camogli (a tricky, rocky hike with metal hand supports) or Portofino, a steep but easier 5km cliffside walk. Both hikes take about 2½ hours one way. Alternatively, you can catch a boat from Camogli (one way/return €8/12) or Punta Chiappa (€5/9).

Portofino

POP 493

Even the trees are handsome in Portofino, a small but perfectly coiffured coastal village that sits on its own peninsula like a Milanese model glued to the catwalk. Spending the night here might stretch the wallets of mere mortals, but it's worth splashing out on an expensive cappuccino next to Portofino's yacht-filled harbour, logging the ubiquity of Ferrari key-rings and Gucci handbags.

◉ Sights

Castello Brown CASTLE
(www.portofinoevents.com; Via alla Penisola 13a; admission €5; ⊙ vary) From the sublime harbour, a flight of stairs signposted 'Salita San Giorgio' leads past the Chiesa di San Giorgio to Portofino's unusual castle, a 10-minute walk altogether (confirm the opening times with the tourist office before setting out, as the castle often hosts private events). The Genoese-built castle saw action against the Venetians, Savoyards, Sardinians and Austrians, and later fell to Napoleon.

In 1867 it was transformed by the British diplomat Montague Yeats Brown into a private mansion. The fabulous tiled staircase is one of the showpieces of the neo-Gothic interior, while there are great views from the garden. For a better outlook, continue for another 400m or so along the same track to the lighthouse.

🏃 Activities

If you're feeling flush, chat to the boat-taxi operators in the harbour about snorkelling and sightseeing trips, from €25.

Parco Naturale Regionale di Portofino HIKING
(www.parks.it/parco.portofino) 🥾 Unbeknown to the soft-top-sportscar drivers who zoom

in via the sinuous road from Santa Margherita, the Portofino peninsula is criss-crossed with 60km of narrow trails, many of them surprisingly remote and all of them free of charge. The tourist office has maps.

A good but tough day hike (there are exposed sections) is the 18km coastal route from Camogli to Santa Margherita via San Fruttuoso and Portofino. There are handy train connections at both ends.

🛏️ Sleeping

Warning: staying the night can severely damage your credit card!

Eden BOUTIQUE HOTEL €€€
(☑ 0185 26 90 91; www.hoteledenportofino.com; Vico Dritto 18; d €140-290; P ❄️) You've arrived in heaven, so you might as well stay there. Eden is an apt word for this residential-like hotel, on the quiet cobbled side streets a stone's throw from Portofino's idyllic harbourfront. It does a good job at looking posh without being too pretentious.

Hotel Splendido LUXURY HOTEL €€€
(☑ 0185 26 78 01; www.hotelsplendido.com; Salita Baratta 16; d €770; P ❄️ @ 🛜 🏊) The megarich, or those intent on blowing their life's savings, check into this bastion of whimsy and wisteria to follow in the footsteps of the Duke of Windsor, Frank Sinatra and countless other zillionaires. Ordinary Joes can freely wander round the columns and cupolas while nurturing fanciful dreams.

🍴 Eating & Drinking

Portofino favours Serie A footballers and lottery winners, though the average traveller can usually rustle up sufficient cash (€5) for a harbourside cappuccino.

Ristorante Puny LIGURIAN €€
(☑ 0185 26 90 37; Piazza Martiri dell'Olivetta; €35-40; ⊙ noon-3pm & 7-11pm Wed-Fri) Portofino's haughtiness doesn't seem to extend to Puny, whose owners treat everyone like they're a visiting celeb (half of the clinetele probably are!). The food sticks loyally to Ligurian specialities, especially seafood, and the harbourside location is exquisite. Now, if only the portions were bigger...

Pizzeria Il Portico PIZZERIA €€
(Via Roma 21; €20-25; ⊙ closed Tue) Wander a block from the harbour and pizza margheritas can be procured for €6. At Il Portici, diners can enjoy dishes such as octopus salad,

vongole (clams) and Genovese specials on chequered tablecloths outside.

❶ Information

Tourist Office (www.apttigullio.liguria.it; Via Roma 35; ⊙10am-1pm & 1.30-4.30pm Tue-Sun) Has free trail maps for the Parco Naturale Regionale di Portofino and information on mountain-bike rental, as well as seasonal sail- and motorboat rental.

❶ Getting There & Around

By far the best way is to walk. A designated path tracks the gorgeous coastline for 3km.

ATP (www.atp-spa.it) bus 882 runs to Portofino from outside the tourist office in Santa Margherita (€1.50, every 30 minutes).

From April to October, **Servizio Marittimo del Tigullio** (www.traghettiportofino.it) runs daily ferries from Portofino to/from San Fruttuoso (€8/11.50), Rapallo (€7.50/11) and Santa Margherita (€6/9).

Motorists must park at the village entrance, with obligatory parking fees starting from €4.50 per hour (cash only).

Santa Margherita

POP 10,035

After the chaos of Genoa, Santa Margherita materialises like a calm Impressionist painting. You wouldn't want to change a single detail of its picture-perfect seaside promenade, where elegant hotels with Liberty facades overlook million-dollar yachts in this favourite fishing-village-turned-wealthy-retirement-spot. Fortunately, unlike in Portofino, you don't have to be a millionaire to stay here.

◉ Sights & Activities

Santa Margherita's idyllic position in a sheltered bay on the turquoise Golfo di Tigullio makes it a good base for sailing, water-skiing and scuba diving. Those feeling less active can simply stretch out on its popular beach.

Villa Durazzo   VILLA, GARDEN
(www.villadurazzo.it; Piazzale San Giacomo 3; ⊙9am-1pm & 2.30-6.30pm) **FREE** Villa Durazzo is Santa Margherita personified: an exquisite mansion and gardens that are linked to a 16th-century castle overlooking the sea. You can take an aromatic stroll among lemon trees, hydrangea and camellia hedges, and other flora typical of the town's hot climate in the lavish Italian gardens.

The house is usually open and sometimes serves free canapés and wine on its lovely coffee terrace.

Santuario di Nostra Signora della Rosa   CHURCH
(Piazza Caprera) You'll gasp audibly when entering Santa Margherita's small yet lavish baroque church, not just at the truly dazzling array of gold leaf, frescoes, chandeliers and stained glass, but also at the sheer serendipity of seeing it in this relatively humble seaside town. A little slice of heaven on earth.

🛏 Sleeping

Hotel Europa   HOTEL €
(☑0185 28 71 87; www.hoteleuropa-sml.it; Via Trento 5; d from €75; ❄@🖨) Amid the *trompe l'œil* and ritzy F Scott Fitzgerald–style romance sits the humble Europa, whose clean, functional rooms provide a perfectly comfortable way of staying economically on this rather plush section of the Italian Riviera.

Lido Palace Hotel   HOTEL €€
(☑0185 28 58 21; www.lidopalacehotel.com; Via Doria 3; s €110-140, d €140-200; P❄🖨) Right on the waterfront and oozing old-school refinement, this Liberty-style grande dame offers the quintessential Santa Margherita experience. Rooms are generously proportioned and the breakfast buffet is bountiful. The restaurant has an outdoor terrace with elevated views and there are half- and full-board options.

🍴 Eating & Drinking

Ristorante-Pizzeria Da Emilio   PIZZERIA, SEAFOOD €
(☑0185 29 34 04; Piazza Martiri della Libertà 20; meals €20; ⊙lunch & dinner) Friendly *camerieri* (waiters) offer veal in lemon sauce and mixed fish dishes under the awning of this sea-drive classic, handily located near those hard-working fishing vessels whose catch keeps the business afloat.

Pasticceria Oneto   CAFE, CHOCOLATES €
(Via Partigiani d'Italia 3; cakes from €1.50; ⊙8am-8pm) Busy café populated by un-ritzy locals who pop in for sinful boxes of chocolates and brioches that are fresher than fresh. Join them to eavesdrop on the local gossip.

ℹ Information

Tourist Office (www.apttigullio.liguria.it; Piazza Vittorio Veneto; ⊙9.30am-12.30pm & 2.30-5.30pm Mon-Sat) Has a raft of information about water sports along the gulf.

Parco Naturale Regionale di Portofino (www.parks.it/parco.portofino; Viale Rainusso 1) Maps and information on hiking.

ℹ Getting There & Around

ATP Tigullio Trasporti (www.tigulliotrasporti.it) runs buses to/from Portofino (every 20 minutes) and Camogli (every 30 minutes).

By train, there are hourly services to/from Genoa (€3.40, 35 minutes) and La Spezia (€6.20, 1½ hours).

Servizio Marittimo del Tigullio (www.traghettiportofino.it; Via Palestro 8/1b) runs seasonal ferries to/from Cinque Terre (one way/return €17.50/25.50), Porto Venere (€22/33), San Fruttuoso (€10/15), Portofino (€6/9) and Rapallo (€4/5).

Rapallo
POP 30,571

WB Yeats, Max Beerbohm and Ezra Pound all garnered inspiration in Rapallo and it's not difficult to see why. With its bright-blue changing cabins, palm-fringed beach and diminutive 16th-century castle perched above the sea (hosting temporary art exhibitions), the town has a refined and nostalgic air. That's not to say it isn't friendly. Rapallo's compactness gives it a less elite atmosphere than its jet-set neighbours. It's at its busiest on Thursdays, when market stalls fill central Piazza Cile.

⊙ Sights

Rapallo's seafront promenade – Lungomare Vittorio Veneto – is an unwitting street theatre of the beautiful and the damned. It's worth checking inside the picturesque, impossible-to-miss **castle**, where temporary exhibitions are sometimes held.

Cable Car   CABLE CAR
(Piazzale Solari 2; one way/return €5.50/8; ⊙9am-12.30pm & 2-6pm) When you've had your fill of the promenade poseurs, rise above them in a 1934-vintage cable car up to **Santuario Basilica di Montallegro** (612m), a sanctuary built on the spot where, on 2 July 1557, the Virgin Mary was reportedly sighted. Walkers and mountain bikers can follow an old mule track (5km, 1½ hours) to the hilltop site.

🛌 Sleeping

Hotel Italia e Lido   HOTEL €€
(☑0185 504 32; www.italiaelido.com; Lungomare Castello 1; s €50-110, d €80-210; @ 🅿 🖥 🏠) Smack bang opposite the castle on Rapallo's waterfront and known for its family-friendliness, this slim and handsome hotel offers all sorts of interesting extras, including a private slice of beach and lifeguards who'll teach your kids swimming in the summer. Many of the sunny rooms have balconies and there's a decent restaurant on-site.

Hotel Miro   HOTEL €€
(☑0185 23 41 00; www.hotelmirorapallo.it; Lungomare Vittorio Veneto 32; s €60-120, d €75-135; 🅿 ❄) Right on the seafront, this charming boutique hotel with an occluded entrance behind a promenade cafe has retained much of its historical character, with canopied beds and floral-print wallpaper.

🍴 Eating

Behind rows of parked scooters, the waterfront has plenty of places to eat, drink and snack.

Antica Cucina Genovese   TRADITIONAL ITALIAN €€
(Via Santa Maria del Campo 133; €18-30; ⊙noon-2.30pm & 7pm-2am) Slightly outside the city centre but worth the trip. Handmade pasta dishes include a huge variety of vegetarian options, such as chestnut ravioli with pesto, as well as vegan fare, such as potato and mushroom stew.

Ristorante Eden   SEAFOOD €€€
(☑0185 505 53; www.ristoranteeden.com; Via Diaz 5; €45-50; ⊙lunch & dinner Thu-Tue) By consensus the best fish restaurant in Rapallo and possibly even the Ligurian coast, Eden serves whatever the market's offering on any given day. Rest assured your octopus, calamari, clams or anchovies will be cooked skilfully and complemented, if you wish, by fine homemade pasta. The only catch is the price.

ℹ Information

Tourist Office (www.apttigullio.liguria.it; Lungo Vittorio Veneto 7; ⊙9.30am-12.30pm & 2.30-5.30pm Mon-Sat) Details of walks in the area, plus maps.

ℹ Getting There & Away

Trains run along the coast to Genoa (€3.40, 40 minutes) and La Spezia (€6.30, one hour).

Servizio Marittimo del Tigullio (www.traghettiportofino.it) runs boats to/from Santa Margherita (one way/return €4/5), Portofino (€7.50/11), San Fruttuoso (€10/15), Genoa (€14/20), the Cinque Terre (€17.50/25.50) and Porto Venere (€22/33). Not all operate daily, and many are seasonal – the website posts updated schedules.

Cinque Terre

If you ever get tired of life, bypass the therapist and decamp immediately to Cinque Terre. Here five crazily constructed fishing villages, set amid some of the most dramatic coastal scenery on the planet, ought to provide enough to bolster the most jaded of spirits. A Unesco World Heritage Site since 1997, Cinque Terre isn't the undiscovered Eden it was, but frankly, who cares? Sinuous paths tempt the antisocial to traverse seemingly impregnable cliffsides, while a 19th-century railway line cut through a series of coastal tunnels ferries the less brave from village to village. Thankfully cars – those most ubiquitous of modern interferences – were banned over a decade ago.

Rooted in antiquity, Cinque Terre's five villages date from the early medieval period. Monterosso, the oldest, was founded in AD 643, when beleaguered hill dwellers moved down to the coast to escape from invading barbarians. Riomaggiore came next, purportedly established in the 8th century by Greek settlers fleeing persecution in Byzantium. The others are Vernazza, Corniglia and Manarola. Much of what remains in the villages today including several castles and a quintet of illustrious parish churches, dates from the late High Middle Ages,

Buildings aside, Cinque Terre's unique historical feature are the steeply terraced cliffs bisected by a complicated system of fields and gardens that have been hacked, chiselled, shaped and layered over the course of nearly two millennia. So marked are these artificial contours that some scholars have compared the extensive *muretti* (low stone walls) to the Great Wall of China in their grandeur and scope.

In October 2011 flash floods along the Ligurian coast wreaked havoc in Vernazza and Monterosso, burying historic streets and houses under metres of mud and killing half-a-dozen people. As of 2013, most businesses are open again, but check the status of the Sentiero Azzurro (blue walking trail) before you set out.

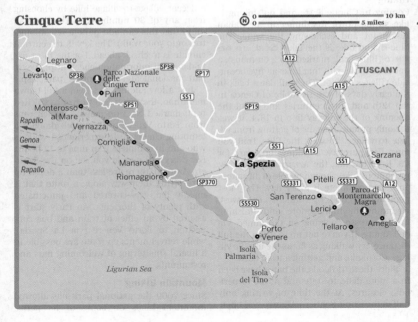

Cinque Terre

THE SANCTUARY WALKS

Each of Cinque Terre's villages is associated with a sanctuary perched high on the cliff-sides above the azure Mediterranean. Reaching these religious retreats used to be part of a hefty Catholic penance, but these days the walks through terraced vineyards and across view-splayed cliffs are a lot less onerous.

Monterosso to Santuario della Madonna di Soviore From Via Roma in the village, follow trail 9 up through forest and past the ruins of an old hexagonal chapel to an ancient paved mule path that leads to Soviore, Liguria's oldest sanctuary dating from the 11th century. Here you'll find a bar, restaurant and views as far as Corsica on a clear day.

Vernazza to Santuario della Madonna di Reggio From underneath Vernazza's railway bridge, follow trail 8 up numerous flights of steps and past 14 sculpted Stations of the Cross to this 11th-century chapel with a Romanesque facade.

Corniglia to Santuario della Madonna delle Grazie This sanctuary can be approached from either Corniglia (on trail 7b) or Vernazza (trail 7), though the latter is better. Branch off the Sentiero Azzurro and ascend the spectacular Sella Comeneco to the village of San Bernardino, where you'll find the church with its adored image of Madonna and child above the altar.

Manarola to Santuario della Madonna delle Salute The pick of all the sanctuary walks is this breathtaking traverse (trail 6) through Cinque Terre's finest vineyards to a diminutive Romanesque-meets-Gothic chapel in the tiny village of Volastra.

Riomaggiore to Santuario della Madonna di Montenero Trail 3 ascends from the top of the village, up steps and past walled gardens to a restored 18th-century chapel with a frescoed ceiling, which sits atop an astounding lookout next to the park's new cycling centre.

Activities

Hiking

Coming to Cinque Terre and not hiking is like sitting down for dinner in an Italian restaurant and eschewing the wine. The blue-riband hike is the 12km **Sentiero Azzurro** (Blue Trail; marked No 2 on maps), a one-time mule path that links all five oceanside villages by foot. The trail dates back to the early days of the Republic of Genoa in the 12th and 13th centuries and, until the opening of the railway line in 1874, it was the only practical means of getting from village to village. To walk the Blue Trail you must first purchase a Cinque Terre card for €5. Far from flat, the Azzurro is a narrow, precipitous hike, though people of all shapes and sizes complete it every day. The most popular direction of traffic is east–west, beginning in Riomaggiore and finishing in Monterosso, starting on the famed Via dell'Amore. If you're not up to going the full distance, try walking as far as the middle village, Corniglia, and getting a train back.

Since the 2011 floods, the paths have been in a more delicate state and prone to periodic closures. At the time of writing only half of the iconic Sentiero Azzurro was open.

However, Cinque Terre has a whole network of spectacular trails and you can still plan a decent village-to-village hike by choosing from any of 30 numbered paths (bear in mind that this can add quite a few kilometres onto your walk). The key in the current climate is to check ahead. For the most up-to-date trail information check http://www.parconazionale5terre.it/sentieri_parco.asp.

Just a few kilometres shy of a full-blown marathon, the 38km **Sentiero Rosso** (Red trail; marked No 1 on maps) – which runs from Porto Venere to Levanto – dangles a tempting challenge to experienced walkers who aim to complete it in nine to 12 hours. For every 100 people you see on the Sentiero Azzurro, there are less than a dozen up here plying their way along a route that is mainly flat, tree-covered and punctuated with plenty of shortcuts. An early start is assured by an efficient train and bus connection to Porto Venere (via La Spezia), while refreshments en route are possible in a liberal smattering of welcoming bars and restaurants.

Mountain Biking

Since 2009 the national park has allowed mountain bikes on some of its paths, though it's still very much a niche sport. The starting point of most of the paths is the **Santuario della Madonna di Montenero**, accessible by road or *sentiero* (trail) No 3 above Riomaggiore.

Courses

Arbaspàa COOKING
(☎0187 76 00 83; www.arbaspaa.com; courses €129) Prepare Ligurian specialities in a farmhouse near the town of Levanto. Cooking lessons are available on Monday from March to October.

Information

Online information is available at www.cinqueterre.it and www.cinqueterre.com.

Parco Nazionale (www.parconazionale5terre.it; ⏲7am-8pm) Offices in the train stations of all five villages and also in La Spezia station.

Getting There & Around

BOAT

In summer the **Cooperativa Battellieri del Golfo Paradiso** (www.golfoparadiso.it) runs boats to the Cinque Terre from Genoa (one way/return €18/33). Seasonal boat services to/from Santa Margherita (€17.50/25.50) are handled by the **Servizio Marittimo del Tigullio** (www.traghettiportofino.it).

From late March to October, La Spezia–based **Consorzio Marittimo Turistico Cinque Terre Golfo dei Poeti** (www.navigazionegolfodeipoeti.it) runs daily shuttle boats between all of the Cinque Terre villages (except Corniglia), costing €8 one way, including all stops, or €15 for an all-day ticket.

CAR & MOTORCYCLE

Private vehicles are not allowed beyond village entrances. If you're arriving by car or motorcycle, you'll need to pay to park in designated car parks. In some villages, minibus shuttles depart from the car parks (one way/return €1.50/2.50) – park offices have seasonal schedules.

TRAIN

Between 6.30am and 10pm, one to three trains an hour trundle along the coast between Genoa and La Spezia, stopping at each of the Cinque Terre's villages. Unlimited 2nd-class rail travel between Levanto and La Spezia is covered by the Cinque Terre card.

Monterosso

POP 1527

The most accessible village by car and the only Cinque Terre settlement to sport a tourist beach, Monterosso is the furthest west and least quintessential of the quintet (it was briefly ditched from the group in the 1940s). Noted for its lemon trees and anchovies, the village is split into two parts (old and new) linked by an underground tunnel that burrows beneath the blustery San Cristoforo promontory. Monterosso was badly hit by the 2011 floods, but has recovered remarkably quickly. Most businesses in town are open again, although trails are still experiencing closures. Check ahead on http://www.parconazionale5terre.it/sentieri_parco.asp.

Sights

Convento dei Cappuccini CHURCH
Monterosso's most interesting church and convent complex is set on the hill that divides the old town from the newer Fegina quarter. The striped church, the **Chiesa di San Francesco**, dates from 1623 and has a painting attributed to Van Dyck *(Crocifissione)* to the left of the altar.

Nearby, the ruins of an old castle have been converted into a cemetery.

Sleeping

Unlike the other four towns, Monterosso has a credible stash of hotels to choose from.

★**Hotel Pasquale** HOTEL €€
(☎0187 81 74 77; www.hotelpasquale.it; Via Fegina 4, Monterosso; s €90-145, d €155-200; ❄📶) On the cusp of the old quarter, this small-is-beautiful harbourside hotel is full of weird nooks and crannies built right into the cliffside (with exposed rock to prove it). Rooms have a luxurious, boutique sheen missing elsewhere in Cinque Terre and the owners are lovely.

La Poesia B&B €€
(☎0187 81 72 83; www.lapoesia-cinqueterre.com; Via Genova 4, Monterosso; d €90-180; ❄📶) Shoehorned up a backstreet in the older part of town, La Poesia's three rooms (named Clizia, Annetta and Aspasia after the women to which Nobel Prize–winning poet Eugenio Montale dedicated his poems) occupy an early-17th-century house. Breakfast is served on a terrace surrounded by lemon trees and the house has a regal quality that sets it apart from the competition.

Hotel La Spiaggia HOTEL €€
(☎0187 81 75 67; www.laspiaggiahotel.com; Via Lungomare 98, Monterosso; s/d €155/170; ❄📶)

ANDREW PEACOCK / GETTY IMAGES ©

1. Hiking past vineyards between Manarola and Corniglia
2. Colourful houses in village of Manarola (p189) 3. Vernazza
(p188) 4. Riomaggiore (p190)

CHRISTOPHER GROENHOUT / GETTY IMAGES ©

Cinque Terre

Climb above the crowds on Cinque Terre's terraced cliffs and you might have to pinch yourself to check you're still in the 21st century. Rooted in antiquity and bereft of modern interferences, these five historic fishing villages have embellished the Ligurian coastline with subtle human beauty and a fascinating medieval heritage.

Terraced Fields

Cinque Terre's cleverly cultivated cliff terraces are so old no one truly knows who built them. Held in place by hundreds of kilometres of dry stone walls they add a strange human beauty to a stunning natural landscape.

Sentiero Azzurro

The region's main highway, the famed 'blue trail', is a sinuous footpath that contours Cinque Terre's precipitous coastline. For over a millennium, it has guided farmers, pilgrims, invasion-thwarters and happy wanderers. Nowadays, tourists can drink in its exquisite views.

Manarola

Grapes grow abundantly on Cinque Terre's terraced plots especially around the village of Manarola. The area's signature wine is the sweet white Sciacchetrà, a blend of Bosco, Albarola and Vermentino grapes best sampled with cheese or sweet desserts.

Riomaggiore

Choosing your favourite Cinque Terre village is like choosing your favourite type of pasta – they're all good! The pleasantly mildewed medieval village of Riomaggiore is perhaps the most famous courtesy of its position at the start of the Sentiero Azzurro.

Vernazza

Guarding the best natural harbour in the five towns, Vernazza's tightly clustered streets and lanes were devastated by flooding and mudslides in 2011, but its recovery has been as remarkable as it has been rapid.

Book early (up to six months in advance): La Spiaggia is right on Monterosso's *spiaggia* (beach) in the new part of town and its 19 rooms, terrace, garden and restaurant get busy.

Eating

Along the seafront, restaurants dish up local anchovies straight out of the sea, served fried, raw (with lemon juice), pickled in brine or in a *tian* (baked with potatoes and tomatoes). To wash them down, stop in at one of several wine bars throughout the village.

La Cantina del Pescatore
SNACKS €

(Via V Emanuele 19, Monterosso; snacks €4-9; 📶) Try the pesto on toast, salads, hot dogs (for kids) and local wine. You can also buy local food and wine includng excellent jam, spreads and *limoncino* liqueur at this ultra-friendly restaurant-enoteca, making it worthwhile for a snack lunch. There's free wi-fi.

Ristorante Belvedere
ITALIAN, SEAFOOD €€

(📞 0187 81 70 33; www.ristorante-belvedere.it; Piazza Garibaldi 38, Monterosso; €30; ⊙ lunch & dinner Wed-Mon) As good a place as any to try all the local bounty, especially seafood, such as octopus, prawns, clams and those famous anchovies. It abuts the seafront in the old town and has a inclusive, unpretentious atmosphere.

Vernazza
POP 987

Guarding the only secure landing point on the Cinque Terre coast, Vernazza's small, quintessential Mediterranean harbour guards what is perhaps the quaintest of the five villages. Lined with little cafes, Vernazza's main cobbled street, Via Roma, links seaside Piazza Marconi with the train station. Side streets lead to the village's trademark Genoa-style *caruggi*.

◉ Sights

Piazza Matteotti and the harbour are a delight. There's a tiny sandy beach here and swimming is possible.

Chiesa di Santa Margherita d'Antiochia
CHURCH

(Piazza Matteotti, Vernazza) The waterfront is framed by a small Gothic-Ligurian church built in 1318 after a murky legend about the bones of St Margaret being found in a wooden box on a nearby beach. It is notable for its 40m-tall octagonal tower.

Castello Doria
CASTLE

(admission €1.50; ⊙ 10am-7pm) The oldest surviving fortification in Cinque Terre dates from around 1000. Today it is a collection of ruins with some astounding views. Climb up through the winding *caruggi* to the entrance.

🛏 Sleeping & Eating

Gianni Franzi
SEAFOOD, GUESTHOUSE €€

(📞 0187 82 10 03; www.giannifranzi.it; Piazza Matteotti 5, Vernazza; meals €22-30, s/d €70/100; ⊙ mid-Mar–early Jan) Traditional Cinque Terre seafood (mussels, seafood, ravioli and lemon anchovies) has been served up in this harbourside trattoria since the 1960s. More recently, they've been renting rooms with views, all of which share a communal terrace. Cheaper single rooms with a shared bathroom go for €45.

Batti Batti
SNACKS €

(Via Roma 3, Vernazza; focaccia €3-5) The bastion of that cheap Cinque Terre trademark – focaccia – Batti Batti knocks out the best slices in the village (some would say in the whole Cinque Terre). There's pizza slices too.

Gambero Rosso
SEAFOOD €€

(www.ristorantegamberorosso.net; Piazza Marconi 7, Vernazza; €30-35; ⊙ noon-3pm & 7-10.30pm Fri-Wed) If you've subsisted on focaccia, splash out here on Gambero's house special for dinner: *tegame di Vernazza* (anchovies with baked potatoes and tomatoes).

Corniglia
POP 600

Corniglia is the 'quiet' middle village that sits atop a 100m-high rocky promontory surrounded by vineyards. It is the only Cinque Terre settlement with no direct sea access (steep steps lead down to a rocky cove). Narrow alleys and colourfully painted four-storey houses characterise the ancient core, a timeless streetscape that was name-checked in Boccaccio's *Decameron*. To reach the village proper from the railway station you must first tackle the **Lardarina**, a 377-step brick stairway.

◉ Sights

Centrally located Corniglia is the only place where you can see all five settlements in the same panorama.

La Torre
LOOKOUT

This medieval lookout is reached by a stairway that leads up from the diminutive main square (Piazza Taragio).

Belvedere Santa Maria
LOOKOUT

Follow Via Fieschi through the heart of the village and you'll eventually reach a dead-end at this heart-stopping lookout with sweeping sea views.

Guvano Beach
BEACH

This hard-to-find, clothing-optional beach is situated between Corniglia and Vernazza. Getting there involves walking through an abandoned railway tunnel – ask a local for directions.

Sleeping & Eating

As elsewhere in the Cinque Terre, fish is the mainstay of Corniglia's restaurants – you can't go wrong by asking for whatever's fresh.

Ostello di Corniglia
HOSTEL €

(☎0187 81 25 59; www.ostellocorniglia.com; Via alla Stazione 3, Corniglia; dm/d €24/60; ☎) One of only two hostels in Cinque Terre Ostello di Corniglia is perched at the top of the village and has two eight-bed dorms and four doubles (with private bathroom). Prices are negotiable. There's a lockout from 1pm to 3pm.

Case di Corniglia
RENTAL ROOMS €

(☎0187 81 23 42; www.casedicorniglia.com; Via alla Stazione 19, Corniglia) These rent-a-rooms are spread over two buildings in the village's main street. Good for families or groups.

Caffe Matteo
CAFE €

(Piazza Taragio, Corniglia; meals €7; ☉8am-10pm) While the rest of Corniglia siestas, the Matteo stays open all day, its chairs spilling into the tiny main square. Don't leave without trying the pesto lasagne.

Manarola

POP 850

Bequeathed with more grapevines than any other Cinque Terre village, Manarola is famous for its sweet Sciacchetrà wine. It's also awash with priceless medieval relics, supporting claims that it is the oldest of the five. Due to its proximity to Riomaggiore (852m away), the village is heavily trafficked, especially by Italian school parties. The spirited locals speak an esoteric local dialect known as Manarolese.

◉ Sights

Piazzale Papa Innocenzo IV
PIAZZA

At the northern end of Via Discovolo, you'll come upon this small piazza dominated by a bell tower that was once used as a defensive lookout. Opposite, the **Chiesa di San Lorenzo** dates from 1338 and houses a 15th-century polyptych.

If you're geared up for a steep walk, from nearby Via Rollandi you can follow a path that leads through vineyards to the top of the mountain.

Punta Buonfiglio
LOOKOUT

Manarola's prized viewpoint is on a rocky promontory on the path out of town (Sentiero Azzurro) towards Corniglia where walkers stop for classic photos of the village. A rest area has been constructed here. Nearby are the ruins of an old chapel once used as a shelter by local farmers.

Sleeping & Eating

Ostello 5 Terre
HOSTEL €

(☎0187 92 00 39; www.hostel5terre.com; Via Riccobaldi 21, Manarola; dm €20-23, d €55-65, q €88-100; @☎) This hostel rents out mountain bikes, kayaks, Nordic-walking poles and snorkelling gear. Its single-sex, six-bed dorms come with their own bathrooms, and there's English-language satellite TV, PlayStation and a book exchange. Lockout times are 10am to 4pm (or 5pm June to August).

★ La Torretta Charme & Relax
B&B €€€

(☎0187 92 03 27; www.torrettas.com; Vico Volto 20, Manarola; r/ste €170/250 inc breakfast; ☎) Adding a splash of decadence to Cinque Terre's otherwise quaint collection of B&Bs, this small slice of Zen-like luxury can't be far from most people's idea of perfection. Everything from the romantic terrace to the breakfast in bed and the flowers on your bedspread are carefully thought out and designed to make your stay unforgettable. Spectacular!

Marina Piccola
SEAFOOD €

(☎0187 76 20 65; www.hotelmarinapiccola.com; Via Lo Scalo 16, Manarola; mains €16, s/d €90/120, half-/full-board per person €90/105; ☉noon-10.30pm Wed-Mon; ☎) A shoal of fish dishes and the house speciality, *zuppa di datteri* (date soup), are served up here along with sea views. If you want to stay, the 'little marina' has good deals for half- and full-board.

Cinque Terre Gelateria & Creperia

GELATO €

(Via Discovolo, Manarola; ⏰11am-8pm) It's all subjective, but if you did a snap survey of Cinque Terre's best ice-cream joints, this would be the likely winner.

Riomaggiore

POP 1712

Cinque Terre's easternmost village, Riomaggiore is the largest of the five and acts as its unofficial HQ (the main park office is based here). Its peeling pastel buildings tumble like faded chocolate boxes down a steep ravine to a tiny harbour – the region's favourite postcard view – and glow romantically at sunset. The famous Sentiero Azzurro coastal path starts here. The first hideously busy section to Manarola is called the Via dell'Amore.

◉ Sights & Activities

Outside the train station near the water's edge, murals depict the backbreaking work of Cinque Terre farmers, who, over the centuries, built the Cinque Terre with their bare hands. The village also has a couple of small churches and a ruined castle on a headland overlooking the settlement.

Torre Guardiola

NATURE RESERVE

(admission €1.50; ⏰9am-1pm & 4-7pm Feb-Jul, Sep & Oct, to 1pm Aug) 🌿 Birdlife and local flora can be seen from a nature observation and birdwatching centre on a promontory of land just east of Riomaggiore. The building was a former naval installation in WWII, known as La Batteria Racchia. Today there's a small bar and panels explaining the surrounding flora.

The Torre is reachable via a trail that starts just west of Fossola Beach.

Fossola Beach

BEACH

This small pebbly beach is immediately southeast of Riomaggiore marina. It's rugged but secluded. Swimmers should be wary of rocks and currents.

Cooperative Sub 5 Terre

DIVING

(☑0187 92 00 11; www.5terrediving.it; Via San Giacomo, Riomaggiore; ⏰vary seasonally) 🌿 To dive or snorkel in the translucent waters of the protected marine park, contact this outfit in the subway at the bottom of Via Colombo. It also rents out canoes and kayaks.

🛏 Sleeping

B&Bs and a handful of hotels are situated in the village, but the town's forte is room- and apartment-rental agencies.

La Casa di Venere

RENTAL ROOMS €

(☑338 329 71 53; www.lacasadivenere.com; Via Colombo 194, Riomaggiore; d €60-120 tr/qu €150/180) This agency offers some of the cheapest harbourside rooms. All are clean, bright and modern, and some have to-die-for views.

Hotel Zorza

HOTEL €

(www.hotelzorza.com; Via Colombo 231, Riomaggiore; d from €90; ❄🐱🔊) One of the few hotels in the five villages, the Zorza is a little sleepier than your average big-town affair. The reception shuts down at 7pm-ish, but opens in the morning for a decent breakfast. Well-kept middle-ranking rooms are spread across the sinuous 17th-century house of a former wine-grower.

Edi

RENTAL ROOMS €€

(☑0187 76 08 42; Via Colombo 111, Riomaggiore; r €60-180) This rental agency on the main drag has five rooms and seven two- to four-bed apartments for rent, many with sea views. It also operates the village laundry next door.

🍴 Eating

Riomaggiore has the best selection of restaurants in the five villages.

★ Dau Cila

MODERN ITALIAN €€

(☑0187 76 00 32; www.ristorantedaucila.com; Via San Giacomo 65, Riomaggiore; mains €18; ⏰8am-2am Mar-Oct) Perched within pebble-lobbing distance of Riomaggiore's snug harbour (which is crammed with fishing nets and overturned boats), Dau Cila is an obvious place to tuck into the local seafood. It also has the best wine cellar in town.

You can pair the best local stuff with cold plates such as smoked tuna with apples and lemon, or lemon-marinaded anchovies with pears and Parmesan.

La Lampara

MODERN ITALIAN €€

(Via Malborghetto 2, Riomaggiore; meals €25; ⏰7am-midnight) There are always lots of tourists here, but you won't feel like one as the service is so genuinely personable. Fish dishes predominate, though the pizza and pasta al pesto are also formidable.

Around Cinque Terre

La Spezia

POP 95,641

It's an understandable oversight. Situated minutes to the east of Cinque Terre by train, the hard-working port town of La Spezia is routinely overlooked. If you happen to get delayed, give it a once-over: it's home to Italy's largest naval base, where echoes of Genoa ring through the narrow winding streets of the Old Town. Not surprisingly, La Spezia has some cosy trattorias showcasing the Ligurian delicacies of wine, bread and pesto sauce.

La Spezia's bustle peaks on 19 March, the feast day of the city's patron saint, San Giuseppe (St Joseph). Celebrations see a giant market fill the port and surrounding streets, and the naval base (off-limits the rest of the year) open to the public.

◉ Sights

Museo Amedeo Lia   MUSEUM
(www.museola.spezianet.it; Via Prione 234; adult/reduced €7/4.50; ⊙10am-6pm Tue-Sun) This fine-arts museum in a restored 17th-century friary is La Spezia's star attraction. The collection covers the 13th to 18th centuries and includes paintings by masters such as Tintoretto, Montagna, Titian and Pietro Lorenzetti. Also on show are Roman bronzes and ecclesiastical treasures, such as Limoges crucifixes and illuminated musical manuscripts.

Castello di San Giorgio   CASTLE
(http://museodelcastello.spezianet.it; Via XXVII Marzo; adult/reduced €5.50/4; ⊙9.30am-12.30pm & 5-8pm Wed-Mon) An assortment of local archaeological artefacts from prehistoric to medieval times is on display at this lofty castle.

⌘ Sleeping & Eating

There are several cheap hotels around the train station, but they tend to be scruffy. The waterfront has plenty of relaxed places to wine and dine.

Albergo Birillo   HOTEL €
(☑0187 73 26 66; www.albergobirillo.it; Via Dei Mille 11/13; s €40-80, d €60-100; ☞) This homey haven has rather tight-fitting rooms, which are made up for by the ultrafriendly owners, who'll fill you in on the town's hidden attractions. A few blocks from Via Prione and near plenty of good eateries, it makes an economical alternative to digs in Cinque Terre.

Vicolo Intherno   MODERN ITALIAN €€
(Via della Canonica 22; meals €25; ⊙noon-3pm & 7-11pm Tue-Sat) ✐ Take a seat around chunky wooden tables beneath beamed ceilings at this Slow Food–affiliated restaurant and wash down the *torte di verdure* (Ligurian vegetable pie) or stockfish with local vintages.

❶ Information

Cinque Terre Park Office (☑0187 74 35 00; internet access per 10min €0.80; ⊙7am-8pm) Inside La Spezia's train station.

Tourist Office (www.aptcinqueterre.sp.it; Viale Giuseppe Mazzini 47; ⊙9am-1pm & 2.30-5.30pm Mon-Sat, to 1pm Sun)

❶ Getting There & Away

Buses run by **Azienda Trasporti Consortile** (ATC; www.atclaspezia.it) are the only way to reach Porto Venere (€1.50, approximately every 30 minutes) and Lerici (€1.50, approximately every 15 minutes). Catch buses on Via Domenico Chiodo close to the intersection with Via del Prione.

La Spezia is on the Genoa–Rome railway line and is also connected to Milan (€26.50, three hours, four daily), Turin (€27.50, 3½ hours, several daily) and Pisa (€5.20, 50 minutes, almost hourly). The Cinque Terre and other coastal towns are easily accessible by train and boat.

Porto Venere

POP 3942

If Cinque Terre were ever to pick up an honorary sixth member, Porto Venere would surely be it. Perched on the Gulf of Poets' western promontory, the village's sinuous seven- and eight-storey harbourfront houses form an almost impregnable citadel around the muscular Castello Doria. The Romans built Portus Veneris as a base en route from Gaul to Spain, and in later years the Byzantines, Lombards, Genovese and Napoleon all passed through here. Cinque Terre's marathon-length Sentiero Rosso (Red trail) to Levanto starts here, just behind the castle. Hikers, take a deep breath...

◉ Sights

Outside the hectic summer season, Porto Venere is something of a ghost town – and all the more alluring for it.

Castello Doria   CASTLE
(admission €2.20; ⊙10.30am-1.30pm & 2.30-6pm) No one knows when the original castle was built, though the current structure –

a formidable example of Genoese military architecture – dates from the 16th century. A highly strategic citadel in its time, it once stood on the front line with Genoa's maritime feud with Pisa. There are magnificent views from its ornate terraced gardens.

Chiesa di San Pietro
CHURCH

This wind- and wave-lashed church, built in 1198 in Gothic style, stands on the ruins of a 5th-century palaeo-Christian church. Before that it was a Roman temple dedicated to the goddess Venus (born from the foam of the sea), from whom Porto Venere takes its name.

Grotta Arpaia
CAVE

At the end of the quay, a Cinque Terre panorama unfolds from the rocky terraces of Grotta Arpaia, a former haunt of Lord Byron, who once swam across the gulf from Porto Venere to Lerici to visit his mate Shelley. Traces of a pagan temple have been uncovered on the quay, inside the black-and-white-marble Chiesa di San Pietro, which was built in 1277.

Just off the promontory lie the tiny islands of Palmaria, Tino and Tinetto.

🛏 Sleeping & Eating

A half-dozen or so restaurants line Calata Doria, by the sea. A block inland, Porto Venere's main old-town street, Via Cappellini, has several tasty choices.

Albergo Genio
HOTEL €€

(☑0187 79 06 11; www.hotelgenioportovenere.com; Piazza Bastreri 8; s €80-95, d €100-125; ☺mid-Feb–mid-Jan; P❄) From Piazza Bastreri, scale the spiral stairs in the round tower to reach this charming seven-room hotel. In summer breakfast is served alfresco beneath the vines. Some rooms are equipped with air-conditioning.

La Lanterna
B&B €

(☑0187 79 22 91; www.lalanterna-portovenere.it; Via Capellini 109; d €75-100; ❄) Down by Porto Venere's picturesque harbourfront, this little guesthouse has just two airy rooms (there's also an option of a four-person apartment on request). Breakfast isn't included, but can be arranged; otherwise stroll to a nearby cafe.

ℹ Information

Tourist Office (www.portovenere.it; Piazza Bastreri 7; ☺10am-noon & 3-8pm Jun-Aug, to 6pm Thu-Tue Sep-May) Sells a couple of useful maps and walking guides in English.

ℹ Getting There & Away

Porto Venere is served by daily buses from La Spezia.

From late March to October, **Consorzio Marittimo Turistico Cinque Terre Golfo dei Poeti** (☑0187 732987; www.navigazionegolfodeipoeti.it) sails from Porto Venere to/from Cinque Terre villages (one way with all stops €16, return €24 to €26) and runs boat excursions to the islands of Palmaria, Tino and Tinetto (€10), as well as services to La Spezia and Lerici (call for seasonal information).

Lerici & Around
POP 10,447

Magnolia, yew and cedar trees grow in the 1930s public gardens at Lerici, an exclusive retreat of pool-equipped villas clinging to the cliffs along its beach. In another age Byron and Shelley sought inspiration here.

◎ Sights & Activities

From Lerici a scenic 3km coastal stroll leads northwest to San Terenzo, a seaside village with a sandy beach and medieval castle. The Shelleys stayed at the waterfront Villa Magni (closed to visitors) in the early 1820s and Percy drowned here when his boat sank off the coast in 1822 on a return trip from Livorno.

Another coastal stroll, 4km southeast, takes you past magnificent little bays to Tellaro, a fishing hamlet with pink-and-orange houses cluttered about narrow lanes and tiny squares. Sit on the rocks at the Chiesa San Giorgio and imagine an octopus ringing the church bells – which, according to legend, it did to warn the villagers of a Saracen attack.

Castello di Lerici
CASTLE, MUSEUM

(www.castellodilerici.it; Piazza San Giorgio 1; admission €6/4; ☺10.30am-1.30pm & 5-9pm Tue-Sun) For outstanding views make your way on foot or by public lift to Lerici's symbolic 12th-century castle, once taken by the Pisans but today given over to a rather bizarre collection of dinosaurs in its Museo Geopaleontologico (fossils have been found near here).

🛏 Sleeping & Eating

Locanda Miranda
INN, GASTRONOMIC €€

(☑0187 96 40 12; Via Fiascherina 92; d €120, with half-board €180, set menus €40-60; P) Tellaro is home to this gourmet hideaway, an exquisite seven-room inn with art- and antiques-decorated rooms, and a Michelin-starred restaurant specialising exclusively in seafood (not for vegetarians or carnivores!).

ℹ Information

Tourist Office (Via Biaggini 6; ⊙9am-1pm & 2.30-5.30pm Mon-Sat, to 1pm Sun) Can advise on walking and cycling in the area, as well as accommodation.

Riviera di Ponente

Curving west from Genoa to the French border, the Ponente stretch of the Ligurian coast is more down-to-earth than the flashy Rivieria di Levante. As a result it shelters some unlikely escape hatches, particularly along the stretch of coast from Noli to Finale Ligure.

Savona

POP 62,494

Behind Savona's sprawling port facilities, the city's unexpectedly graceful medieval centre is well worth getting off the train to check out. Among the old-town treasures to survive destruction by Genoese forces in the 16th century are the baroque **Cattedrale di Nostra Signora Assunta** (Piazza Cattedrale) and the lumbering **Fortezza del Priamàr** (Piazza Priamar). This imposing fortress guards a couple of sculpture museums and the **Civico Museo Storico Archeologico** (Piazza Priamar; admission €2.50; ⊙10.30am-3pm Wed-Mon), which displays archaeological finds.

Art aficionados won't want to miss the **Pinacoteca Civica Savona** (Piazza Chabrol 1/2; admission €4; ⊙9.30am-1pm Mon-Sat, 3.30-6.30pm Thu-Sat, 10am-1pm Sun), which has an important collection of religious paintings, including a Madonna and child by Taddeo di Bartolo, dating from the 14th to the 15th centuries, and two Picassos.

Six- to seven-hour **whale-watching trips** (www.whalewatchliguria.it; tickets €35) depart Savona at 10am from July to September.

🛏 Sleeping & Eating

The tourist office can help book accommodation, both in the city and the coastal towns to the west.

Villa de' Franceschini HOSTEL €
(☎019 26 32 22; www.ostello-de-franceschini.com; Via alla Strà 'Conca Verde' 29; dm/d €16/38; ⊙mid-Mar–Oct; P@) Savona has one of Liguria's few hostels; it's 3km from the train station in a sprawling park.

Mare Hotel HOTEL €€
(☎019 26 32 77; www.marehotel.it; Via Nizza 41; d from €135; ❄@☎⊠) If you're not youth hostel fodder, go to the opposite end of the spectrum and book a room in the four-star beachfront Mare with its infinty pool and classy restaurant. It's 2km west of the station – regular buses run there.

Vino e Farinata TRADITIONAL ITALIAN €
(Via Pia 15; meals €17-20; ⊙11am-10pm Tue-Sat) To enter this place in the cobbled centre, you'll have to walk past the two ancient chefs: one shovelling fish into a wood-fired oven and the other mixing up batter in a barrel-sized whisking machine. The result: Ligurian *farinata*, the menu staple in this very local restaurant that also hordes some excellent wines.

ℹ Information

Tourist Office (Via Paleocapa 76r; ⊙9am-12.30pm & 3-6pm Mon-Sat, to 12.30pm Sun) A short stroll from Savona's sandy beach.

ℹ Getting There & Around

SAR (☎0182 2 15 44) and **ACTS** (www.tpllinea.it) buses, departing from Piazza del Popolo and the train station, are the best options for reaching points inland.

Trains run along the coast to Genoa's Stazione Brignole (€3.40, 45 minutes, almost hourly) and San Remo (€8, 1¾ hours, eight daily).

Corsica Ferries (www.corsica-ferries.fr) runs up to three boats daily between Savona's Porto Vado and Corsica.

Finale Ligure

POP 11,669

Set amid lush Mediterranean vegetation, this township comprises several districts. **Finale Ligure** has a wide, fine-sand beach; the walled medieval centre, known as **Finalborgo**, is a knot of twisting alleys set 1km back from the coast on the Pora river. **Finale Marina** sits on the waterfront, while the more residential **Finale Pia** runs along the Sciusa river in the direction of Genoa.

Each year in March, Finalborgo's cloisters are home to the **Salone dell'Agroalimentare Ligure**, where local farmers and artisan producers display delicacies and vintages.

🛏 Sleeping & Eating

The promenade along Via San Pietro and Via Concezione is crammed with eateries.

Hotel Florenz　　　　　　　　　HOTEL €
(📞 019 69 56 67; www.florenz.it; Via Celesia 1; s/d €67/106; ⊘ closed Nov & Feb; P @ 🐕 🛏) This rambling 18th-century former convent just outside Finalborgo's village walls (800m from the sea) is one of the area's most atmospheric spots to sleep.

Osteria ai Cuattru Canti　　　OSTERIA €
(Via Torcelli 22; set menus €20; ⊘ noon-2pm & 8-10pm Tue-Sun) Delicious Ligurian cuisine is cooked up at this rustic place in Finalborgo's historic centre.

ⓘ Information

Tourist Office (Via San Pietro 14; ⊘ 9am-12.30pm & 3-6.30pm Mon-Sat year-round, 9am-noon Sun Jul & Aug) From the train station on Piazza Vittorio Veneto, at Finale Marina's western end, walk down Via Saccone to the sea and this office.

ⓘ Getting There & Away

SAR (📞 0182 2 15 44) buses yo-yo every 30 minutes to/from Finale Ligure and Savona (€2.20, 50 minutes), stopping en route in Finalborgo (€1, five minutes) and Noli (€1.30, 20 minutes).

San Remo
POP 56,879

Fifty kilometres east of Europe's premier gambling capital lies San Remo, Italy's wannabe Monte Carlo, a sun-dappled Mediterranean resort with a casino, a clutch of ostentatious villas and lashings of Riviera-style grandeur. Known colloquially as the City of Flowers for its colourful summer blooms, San Remo also stages an annual music festival (the supposed inspiration for the Eurovision Song Contest) and the world's longest professional one-day cycling race, the 298km Milan–San Remo classic.

During the mid-19th century the city became a magnet for regal European exiles, such as Empress Elizabeth of Austria and Tsar Nicola of Russia, who favoured the town's balmy winters. Swedish inventor Alfred Nobel maintained a villa here, and an onion-domed Russian Orthodox church reminiscent of Moscow's St Basil's Cathedral still turns heads down by the seafront.

Beyond the manicured lawns and belle époque hotels, San Remo hides a little-visited old town, a labyrinth of twisting lanes that cascade down the Ligurian hillside. Curling around the base is a 25km bike and walking path that tracks the coast as far as Imperia,

following the course of a former railway line and passing through the town's two character-filled harbours.

◉ Sights

Chiesa Russa Ortodossa　　　CHURCH
(Via Nuvoloni 2; admission €1; ⊘ 9.30am-noon & 3-6pm) Non-Catholic churches are rare in Italy, so make the most of this multicoloured classic which was built for the Russian community that followed Tsarina Maria to San Remo in 1906. The Russian Orthodox church – with its onion domes and pale-blue interior – was designed by Alexei Shchusev, who later planned Lenin's mausoleum in Moscow.

These days it's used as an exhibition space for Russian icons.

Il Casinò Municipale　　　　　CASINO
(www.casinosanremo.it; Corso degli Inglesi) San Remo's belle époque casino (one of only four in Italy) was dealing cards when Vegas was still a waterhole in the desert. The building dates from 1905 and was designed by Parisian architect Eugenio Ferret. Slot machines (over 400 of them) open at 10am; other games (roulette, blackjack, poker etc) kick off at 2.30pm.

Dress smart-casual and bring ID.

Museo Civico　　　　　　　　MUSEUM
(Corso Matteotti 143; ⊘ 9am-noon & 3-6pm Tue-Sat) FREE Housed in the 15th-century Palazzo Borea d'Olmo, several rooms in this museum, some with fine frescoed ceilings, display local prehistoric and Roman archaeological finds, paintings and temporary exhibitions.

Highlights include Maurizio Carrega's *Gloria di San Napoleone* (painted in 1808 as a sycophantic homage to the Corsican despot of the same name) and bronze statues by Franco Bargiggia.

Villa Ormond　　　　　　　　GARDEN
(Corso Felice Cavallotti 51; ⊘ gardens 8am-7pm) FREE Just a short stroll east of town the peaceful Japanese gardens of this elegant villa are worth a visit.

Villa Nobel　　　　　　　　　MUSEUM
(Corso Felice Cavallotti 112; admission adult/reduced €4/3; ⊘ 10am-12.30pm Tue-Sun, 3-6pm Fri-Sun) The Moorish Villa Nobel houses a museum dedicated to Swedish inventor Alfred Nobel, who established the Nobel Prize while living here.

San Remo

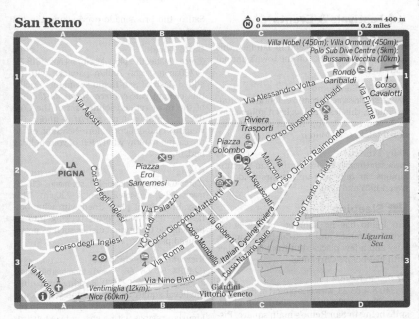

Bussana Vecchia   HISTORIC SITE

Ten kilometres northeast of San Remo lies an intriguing artists' colony. On Ash Wednesday 1887, an earthquake destroyed the village of Bussana Vecchia and survivors were eventually forced to abandon it. It remained a ghost town until the 1960s, when artists moved in and began rebuilding the ruins using the original stones from the rubble.

After successfully standing up to authorities who wanted to remove them, a thriving community of international artists remains in residence today. To get there take a bus to Bussana, 5km east of San Remo, and walk up (30 minutes).

🏃 Activities

Parco Costiero della
Riviera dei Fiori   CYCLING

🖋 As befits a city that hosts professional cycling's greatest Spring Classic, San Remo has a 25km *pista ciclabile* (cycling path) through what is known as the Parco Costiero della Riviera dei Fiori. The path – which runs along the route of a former railway line – connects Ospedaletti to San Lorenzo al Mare via San Remo and eight other seaside towns.

San Remo

◉ Sights

1 Chiesa Russa Ortodossa	A3
2 Il Casinò Municipale	A3
3 Museo Civico	C2
Palazzo Borea D'Olmo	(see 3)

🛏 Sleeping

4 Hotel Eletto	B3
5 Hotel Liberty	D1
6 Pisolo Resort	C2

🍴 Eating

7 Caffè Ducale	C2
8 Cuvea	D1
9 Ristorante Urbicia Vivas	B2

Bike hire outlets and refreshment/rest stops are set up along the route including at San Remo's old train station, Stazione Vecchia.

Polo Sub Dive Centre   DIVING

(www.polosubsanremo.com; Via Lungomare) Polo Sub Dive Centre offers diving for €35 per immersion from the Darsena Porto in Taggia, 5km to the east.

Festivals & Events

Corso Fiorito FLOWER
Held over the last weekend in January, this colourful parade kicks off the town's annual festivities.

Festival di San Remo MUSIC
(www.festivaldisanremo.com) Celebrating Italian music, this festival has been going since 1951, and attracts top Italian and international talent each March.

Rally Storico CAR RALLY
(www.sanremorally.it) In April, San Remo's famous car rally revs up for cars made between 1931 and 1981.

Sleeping

San Remo has no shortage of hotels, although summer and festival times can be busy and a few places shut from September until just before Christmas.

★ **Pisolo Resort** B&B €
(☎340 874 83 23; www.pisoloresort.it; Piazza Colombo 29; s/d €70/90; ❄📶) Hard to find despite being in San Remo's main square, Pisolo offers a divine quintet of modern rooms (three overlook the square). The accommodation is deluxe with careful attention to detail – bank on a basket of breakfast snacks, a coffee machine, modern air-con and your own personal slippers.

Hotel Liberty HOTEL €
(☎0184 50 99 52; www.hotellibertysanremo.com; Rondò Garibaldi 2; s €50-60, d €70-100; P❄) Equipped with young owners, this 10-room hotel is set in a Liberty-style villa off a small traffic circle about 100m from the train station. The small but clean rooms are quiet and infused with faded elegance, while most sights of note are only footsteps away.

Hotel Eletto HOTEL €€
(☎0184 53 15 48; www.elettohotel.it; Corso G Matteotti 44; s €80-95, d €90-135; P❄) Let the Parisian art nouveau entrance canopy lure you to a friendly reception desk where they'll direct you upstairs to clean, soundproofed rooms in a central location.

Eating & Drinking

Cheap trattorias fill the old-town alleys around Piazza Eroi Sanremesi and open-air snack bars stud the length of Corso Nazario Sauro, the promenade overlooking the old port.

Caffè Ducale CAFE €
(Corso Matteotti 145; lunch menus €18-22; ⏰7.30am-midnight) Italian panache with an added dash of San Remo swankiness make this elegant cafe-*enoteca–salon de thé* one of the most refined joints east of the Côte d'Azur. Enjoy a few *aperitivi* under the weighty chandeliers before heading off to the casino to blow what's left of your holiday budget.

Cuvea TRADITIONAL ITALIAN €
(Corso Giuseppe Garibaldi 110; set menus €16-22, mains €8-9; ⏰noon-2.30pm & 7-10pm) This cosy, brightly lit place lined with wine bottles overflows with locals tucking into its homemade traditional dishes such as pesto-doused pasta.

Ristorante Urbicia Vivas LIGURIAN €€
(☎0184 57 55 66; www.ristoranteurbiciavivas.it; Piazza Dolori 5; €25-32) Basking in a quiet medieval square in San Remo's remarkable old town, Urbicia is slavishly faithful to old Ligurian recipes with a strong bias towards seafood. Top ratings are reserved for the subtle ravioli filled with sea bass.

Information

Tourist Office (www.rivieradeifiori.org; Largo Nuvoloni 1; ⏰8.30am-7pm Mon-Sat, 9am-1pm Sun)

Getting There & Away

Riviera Trasporti (Piazza Colombo 42) buses leave regularly from the **bus station** for the French border, and destinations east along the coast and inland.

From San Remo's underground train station there are trains to/from Genoa (€9.80, 2½ hours, hourly), Ventimiglia (€2.70, 15 minutes, hourly) and stations in between.

Ventimiglia

POP 25,693

Long before the French–Italian border bore any significance, Ventimiglia harboured a stoic Roman town known as Albintimulium, which survived until the 5th century AD, when it was besieged by the Goths.

Sights

On a hill on the western bank of the Roia river, Ventimiglia's medieval town is crowned with a 12th-century cathedral (Via del Capo). The town itself is largely residential.

Area Archeologica ARCHAEOLOGICAL SITE
(⊘3-5.30pm Sat & Sun) FREE Sandwiched between the road and the railway line on the eastern edge of town, these Roman ruins bear testimony to Ventimiglia's Roman romance and include the remains of an amphitheatre and baths dating from the 2nd and 3rd centuries AD.

Market MARKET
(⊘8am-3pm or 4pm) These days Ventimiglia is better known as a border town, with a huge Friday market when hundreds of stalls sell food, clothes, homewares, baskets and everything else under the sun. The market is concentrated on Piazza della Libertà, near the river, and is popular with French day trippers.

Giardini Botanici Hanbury GARDEN
(www.giardinihanbury.com; Corso Montecarlo 43; adult/reduced €7.50/4.50; ⊘9.30am-6pm) 🖉 Established in 1867 by English businessman Sir Thomas Hanbury, the 18-hectare Villa Hanbury estate is planted with 5800 botanical species from five continents, including cacti, palm groves and citrus orchards. Today it's a protected area, under the care of the University of Genoa.

Take bus 1a from Via Cavour in Ventimiglia; the bus continues on to the Ponte San Lodovico frontier post, from where you can walk down to the Balzi Rossi caves and beach on the French border.

🍽 Sleeping & Eating

Cheap, cheerful eateries congregate around Via Cavour.

Hotel Seagull HOTEL €
(📞0184 35 17 26; www.seagullhotel.it; Passeggiata Marconi 24; s/d from €55/75; 🅿�🛜) A 10-minute stroll along the seafront from Ventimiglia's town centre, this family-run hotel has simple but appealing sky-blue-and-white rooms, a fragrant garden and a breezy terrace.

ℹ Information

Tourist Office (Lungo Roja Rossi; ⊘9am-12.30pm & 3.30-7pm Mon-Sat Jul & Aug, 9am-12.30pm & 3-6.30pm Mon-Sat Sep-Jun) Just steps from the train station.

ℹ Getting There & Away

From the **train station** (Via della Stazione), Corso della Repubblica leads to the beach. Trains connect Ventimiglia with Genoa (€13.20, two to 3½ hours, hourly), Nice (50 minutes, hourly) and other destinations in France.

PIEDMONT

POP 4.36 MILLION

Italy's second-largest region is arguably its most elegant: a purveyor of Slow Food and fine wine, regal *palazzi* and an atmosphere that is superficially more *français* than *italiano*. But dig deeper and you'll discover that Piedmont has 'Made in Italy' stamped all over it. Emerging from the chaos of the Austrian wars, the unification movement first exploded here in the 1850s, when the noble House of Savoy provided the nascent nation with its first prime minister and its dynastic royal family.

Most Piedmont journeys start in grandiose Turin, famous for football and Fiats. But beyond the car factories, Piedmont is also notable for its food – everything from Arborio rice to white truffles – and pastoral landscapes not unlike nearby Tuscany.

The region's smaller towns were once feuding fiefdoms that bickered over trade and religion. Today the biggest skirmishes are more likely to be over cheese recipes and wine vintages. Traditionally, Asti and Alba stand tallest in the culinary stakes, while understated Cuneo uses its long-standing chocolate obsession to help fuel outdoor adventures in the nearby Maritime Alps.

Turin

POP 911,800 / ELEV 240M

There's a whiff of Paris in Turin's elegant boulevards and echoes of Vienna in its art nouveau cafes, but make no mistake – this city is anything but a copycat. The innovative Torinese gave the world its first saleable hard chocolate, perpetuated one of its greatest mysteries (the Holy Shroud), popularised a best-selling car (the Fiat) and inspired the black-and-white stripes of one of the planet's most iconic football teams (Juventus).

But more important than any of this is Turin's role as instigator of the modern Italian state. Piedmont, with its wily Torinese president, the Count of Cavour, was the

Piedmont

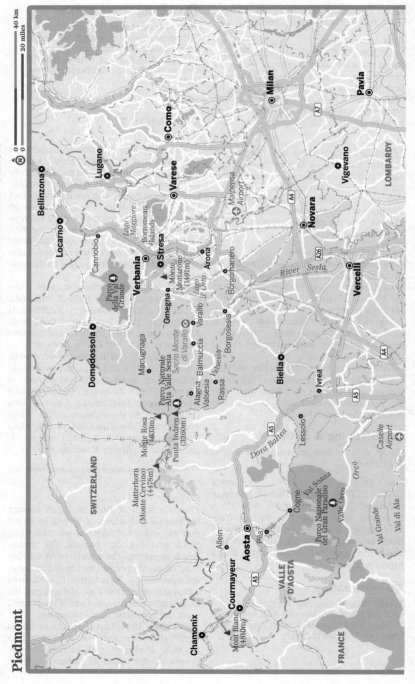

N
0   40 km
0   20 miles

Milan
Pavia
A7
Como
Lugano
Varese
A4
Vigevano
LOMBARDY
Bellinzona
Malpensa
Airport
Locarno
Cannobio
Lago
Maggiore
Borromean
Islands
Novara
Stresa
Verbania
Monte
Mottarone
(1491m)
Arona
A26
Borgomanero
River Sesia
Parco
della Val
Grande
Lago
d'Orta
Vercelli
Domodossola
Omegna
Sacro Monte
di Varallo
Varallo
Borgosesia
A4
Macugnaga
Parco Naturale
Alta Valle Sesia
Balmuccia
Valsesia
Biella
Alagna
Valsesia
Rassa
Ivrea
A5
Monte Rosa
(4633m)
Punta Indren
(3260m)
SWITZERLAND
Lessolo
Matterhorn
(Monte Cervino)
(4478m)
Caselle
Airport
Dora Baltea
Orco
Allein
Aosta
Pila
Cogne
Val Soana
Val Grande
Parco Nazionale
del Gran Paradiso
Valle Orco
Val di Ala
VALLE
D'AOSTA
Courmayeur
Mont Blanc
(4810m)
Chamonix
FRANCE

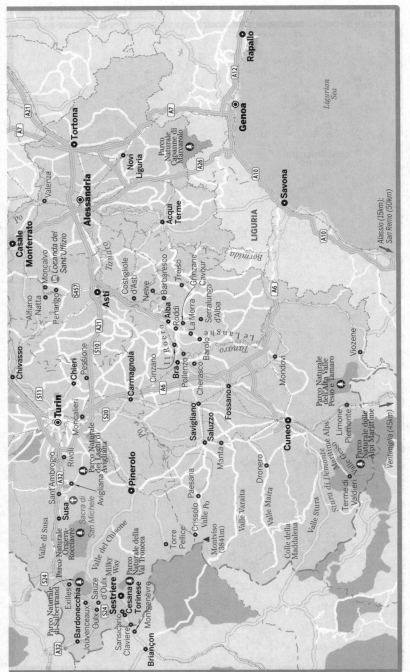

Turin

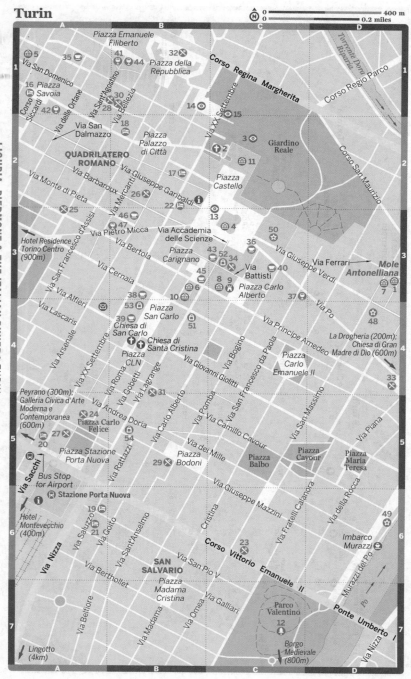

Piazza Emanuele Filiberto

Corso Regina Margherita

Torrente Dora Riparia

Corso Regio Parco

Via San Domenico

5

35

41

32

Piazza della Repubblica

16 Piazza Savoia

Via Sant'Agostino

30

14

15

Corso San Maurizio

42

28

Via della Orfane

18

Via San Dalmazzo

Piazza Palazzo di Città

2

3

11

Giardino Reale

QUADRILATERO ROMANO

Via Giuseppe Garibaldi

17

Piazza Castello

Via Barbaroux

Via Monte di Pieta

26

22

13

Piazza Carignano

Via Pietro Micca

Via Accademia delle Scienze

4

50

36

Mole Antonelliana

Via Giuseppe Verdi

Via Ferrari

7 1

Hotel Residence Torino Centro (900m)

Via San Francesco d'Assisi

25

46

47

Via Bertola

43 52 34

Via Battisti

40

Via Po

48

45

38

53

10

8 9

6

Piazza Carlo Alberto

37

Piazza San Carlo

51

39

Chiesa di San Carlo

Chiesa di Santa Cristina

Piazza CLN

Via Roma

Via Lagrange

Via Gobetti

31

Via Bogino

Via Giovanni Giolitti

Piazza Carlo Emanuele II

La Drogheria (200m); Chiesa di Gran Madre di Dio (600m)

33

Peyrano (300m); Galleria Civica d'Arte Moderna e Contemporanea (600m)

24

Piazza Carlo Felice

54

Via Andrea Doria

Via Carlo Alberto

Via Pomba

Via San Francesco da Paola

Via Principe Amedeo

27 20

Piazza Stazione Porta Nuova

Via Sacchi

Bus Stop for Airport

Stazione Porta Nuova

29

Piazza Bodoni

Via dei Mille

Piazza Balbo

Piazza Cayour

Piazza Maria Teresa

Via Piana

Via Camillo Cavour

Via San Massimo

Via della Rocca

49

Hotel Montevecchio (400m)

19

21

Via Saluzzo

Via Guito

Via Sant'Anselmo

Via Nizza

SAN SALVARIO

Via San Pio V

Via Giuseppe Mazzini

Via Fratelli Calandra

Imbarco Murazzi

Corso Vittorio Emanuele II

23

Lingotto (4km)

Via Belfiore

Via Berthollet

Via Madama

Via Galliari

Via Omea

Piazza Madama Cristina

Cristina

Parco Valentino

12

Murazzi del Po

Ponte Umberto I

Via Nizza

Borgo Medievale (800m)

Turin

◎ Top Sights

1 Mole Antonelliana	D3

◎ Sights

2 Duomo di San Giovanni	C2
3 Giardino Reale	C2
4 Museo Civico d'Arte Antica	C3
5 Museo della Sindone	A1
6 Museo Egizio	B3
7 Museo Nazionale del Cinema	D3
8 Museo Nazionale del Risorgimento Italiano	C3
9 Palazzo Carignano	C3
10 Palazzo dell'Accademia delle Scienze	B3
Palazzo Madama	(see 4)
11 Palazzo Reale	C2
12 Parco Valentino	C7
13 Piazza Castello	C3
14 Porta Palatina	B1
15 Roman Amphitheatre	C1

◎ Sleeping

16 Ai Savoia	A1
17 Hotel Chelsea	B2
18 Hotel Dogana Vecchia	B2
19 Hotel Due Mondi	A6
20 Hotel Roma e Rocca Cavour	A5
21 Hotel Urbani	A6
22 Townhouse 70	B2

◎ Eating

23 Alberto Marchetti	C6
24 Brek	A5
25 È Cucina	A3
26 Gofri Piemontéisa	B2
27 Grom	A5
28 Il Giglio	A1
29 Kipling Restaurant	B5
30 L'Acino	B1
31 Perino Vesco	B4
32 Porta Palazzo	B1
33 Porto di Savona	D4
34 Sfashion	C3

◎ Drinking & Nightlife

35 Al Bicerin	A1
36 Caffè Mulassano	C3
37 Caffè Nazionale	C3
38 Caffè San Carlo	B3
39 Caffè Torino	B4
40 Fiorio	C3
41 I Tre Galli	B1
42 Lobelix	A1
43 Mood	C3
44 Pastis	B1
45 Pepino	B3
46 San Tommaso 10	B3
47 Società Anonima	B3

◎ Entertainment

48 Cinema Massimo	D4
49 Phuddhu Bar	D6
50 Teatro Regio Torino	C3

◎ Shopping

51 Guido Golbino	B4
52 Libreria Luxemburg	C3
53 Paissa	B4
54 Pastificio Defilippis	B5

engine room of the Risorgimento (literally 'the Resurgence', referring to Italian unification). Turin also briefly served as Italy's first capital and donated its monarchy – the venerable House of Savoy – to the newly unified Italian nation in 1861.

More recently, the 2006 Winter Olympics sparked an urban revival in the city, which has spread to its culture and, most deliciously, its cuisine.

History

Whether the ancient city of Taurisia began as a Celtic or Ligurian settlement is unknown: it was destroyed by Hannibal in 218 BC. The Roman colony of Augusta Taurinorum was established here almost two centuries later. In succeeding years, Goths, Lombards and Franks tramped through the city. In 1563 the Savoys abandoned their old capital of Chambéry (now in France) to set up court in Turin, which shared the dynasty's fortunes thereafter. The Savoys annexed Sardinia in 1720, but Napoleon virtually put an end to their power when he occupied Turin in 1798. Turin was occupied by Austria and Russia before Vittorio Emanuele I restored the House of Savoy and re-entered Turin in 1814. Nevertheless, Austria remained the true power throughout northern Italy until the Risorgimento in 1861, when Turin became the nation's inaugural capital. Its capital status lasted only until 1864, and the parliament had already moved to Florence by the time full-sized chambers were completed.

Turin adapted quickly to its loss of political significance, becoming a centre for industrial production during the early 20th century. Giants such as Fiat lured hundreds of thousands of impoverished southern Italians to Turin and housed them in vast company-built and -owned suburbs. Fiat's owners, the Agnelli family (who also happen to own the Juventus football club, Turin's local newspaper and a large chunk of the national daily *Corriere della Sera*), remain one of Italy's most powerful establishment forces. Fiat's fortunes declined later in the 20th century, however, and only revived around a decade ago.

The highly successful 2006 Winter Olympics were a turning point for the city. The Olympics not only ushered in a building boom, including a brand-new metro system, but also transformed Turin from a staid industrial centre into a vibrant metropolis. Turin was European Capital of Design in 2008, hosting conferences and exhibitions, and the national focus of celebrations of the 150th anniversary of the Risorgimento in 2011.

◉ Sights

Got a week? You might need it to see all the sights Turin has to offer. The time-poor can concentrate on a trio of highlights: the Museo Egizio, the Mole Antonelliana and the Museo Nazionale dell'Automobile.

★ **Mole Antonelliana**   MUSEUM
(Via Montebello 20) The symbol of Turin, this 167m tower with its distinctive aluminium spire appears on the Italian two-cent coin. It was originally intended as a synagogue when construction began in 1862, but was never used as a place of worship. In the mid-1990s, the tower became home to the

multi-floored **Museo Nazionale del Cinema** (www.museonazionaledelcinema.org; Via Montebello 20; adult/reduced €9/7, incl panoramic lift €12/9; ⊙ 9am-8pm Tue-Fri & Sun, to 11pm Sat).

The museum takes you on a fantastic tour through cinematic history, from the earliest magic lanterns, stereoscopes and other optical toys to the present day. Movie memorabilia on display includes Marilyn Monroe's black lace bustier, Peter O'Toole's robe from *Lawrence of Arabia* and the coffin used by Bela Lugosi's Dracula. At the heart of the museum, the vast Temple Hall is surrounded by 10 interactive 'chapels' devoted to various film genres. The Mole's glass **panoramic lift** whisks you 85m up through the centre of the museum to the Mole's roof terrace in 59 seconds. Fair warning if you're even slightly prone to vertigo: it's suspended only by cables, so when you look out it's as if you're free-floating in space. The 360-degree views from the outdoor viewing deck are dazzling by day or night.

Museo della Sindone   MUSEUM
(www.sindone.org; Via San Domenico 28; adult/reduced €6/5; ⊙ 9am-noon & 3-7pm) Encased in the crypt of Santo Sudario church, this fascinating museum documents one of the most studied objects in human history: the Holy Shroud. Whatever your position on the shroud's authenticity, its story unfolds like a

---

TURIN IN...

Two Days

Two-day tourists will want to start early with a wake-up coffee at a historic coffeehouse and pint-sized **Caffè Mulassano** (p209) is a good bet. Flip a euro to decide which museum to visit first – the **Museo Nazionale del Cinema** (p202) or the **Museo Egizio** (p203). Check out Slow Food–affiliated baker **Andrea Perino** (p207) for lunch and walk it off with a *passeggiata* (stroll) in **Parco Valentino** (p204) beside the Po river. On day two visit whichever museum you missed yesterday before going for aperitifs at **I Tre Galli** (p208) and dinner at **L'Acino** (p208).

Four Days

If you have two more days, there are a couple more prestigious museums you should add to your itinerary: the **Museo della Sindone** (p202), outlining the history of the Holy Shroud, and the **Museo Nazionale del Risorgimento Italiano** (p203). Be sure to stop afterwards for coffee in **Fiorio** (p209) and chocolate in **Al Bicerin** (p209).

One Week

A week in Turin will enable you to get out to the outlying sights such as the **Basilica di Superga** (p205) and the massive **Reggia di Venaria Reale** (p204). Be sure to also visit **Lingotto** (p205) and its Eataly supermarket and refurbished **Museo Nazionale dell'Automobile** (p205). For a night-time treat check the next Verdi opera at the **Teatro Regio Torino** (p210).

gripping suspense mystery, with countless plots, subplots and revelations.

Of particular interest is the story of the shroud post-1898, when camera technology allowed people to see much clearer photographic negatives of the cloth for the first time.

Museo Nazionale del Risorgimento Italiano   MUSEUM

(www.museorisorgimentotorino.it; Via Accademia delle Scienze 5; adult/reduced €10/8; ⊙9am-6pm Tue-Sun) If only school history lessons had been this interesting. After extensive renovations, this legendary museum reopened in 2011 with an astounding 30-room trajectory covering the background and details of Italian unification in the very building (the baroque Palazzo Carignano) where many of the key events happened.

Not only was this the birthplace of Carlo Alberto and Vittorio Emanuele II, but it was also the seat of united Italy's first parliament from 1861 to 1864. Unmissable!

Museo Egizio   MUSEUM

(Egyptian Museum; www.museoegizio.org; Via Accademia delle Scienze 6; adult/reduced €8/6; ⊙8.30am-7.30pm Tue-Sun) 'The road through Memphis and Thebes passes through Turin' trumpeted French hieroglyphic decoder Jean-François Champollion in the early 19th century, and he wasn't far wrong. Opened in 1824, this legendary museum in the Palazzo dell'Accademia delle Scienze (Via Accademia delle Scienze 6) houses the most important collection of Egyptian treasure outside Cairo.

Two of many highlights include a statue of Ramesses II (one of the world's most important pieces of Egyptian art) and over 500 items found in the tomb of royal architect Kha and his wife, Merit (from 1400 BC), in 1906. The museum is in the process of a five-year refurbishment that should be complete in 2014.

Duomo di San Giovanni   CATHEDRAL

(Piazza San Giovanni) Turin's cathedral was built between 1491 and 1498 on the site of three 14th-century basilicas and, before that, a Roman theatre. Most ignore the fairly plain interior and focus on a far bigger myth: the church is home to the famous Shroud of Turin (alleged to be the burial cloth in which Jesus' body was wrapped). A copy of the cloth is on permanent display to the left of the cathedral altar.

To get the full story you . the Museo della Sindone. 'ı Romanesque-style bell tower loc than it really is; it was designed by ى and built in 1723. Just to the north lie remains of a 1st-century Roman amphithe atre, while a little further to the northwest lies Porta Palatina, the red-brick remains of a Roman-era gate.

Piazza Castello   PIAZZA

Turin's central square shelters a wealth of museums, theatres and cafes. Essentially baroque, the grand piazza was laid out from the 14th century to serve as the seat of dynastic power for the House of Savoy.

Museo Civico d'Arte Antica   MUSEUM

(www.palazzomadamatorino.it; Piazza Castello; adult/reduced €10/8; ⊙10am-6pm Tue-Sat, to 7pm Sun) The piazza is dominated by Palazzo Madama (Piazza Castello), a part-medieval, part-baroque castle built in the 13th century on the site of the old Roman gate. It was named after Madama Reale Maria Cristina, the widow of Vittorio Amedeo I (Duke of Savoy, 1630-37), who lived here in the 17th century. Today, part of the palace houses this expansive museum, which contains four floors of works that document the city's artistic movements after Italian unification.

Palazzo Reale   MUSEUM

(Piazza Castello; adult/reduced €10/5; ⊙8.30am-7.30pm Tue-Sun) Statues of the mythical twins Castor and Pollux guard the entrance to this eye-catching palace and, according to local legend, also watch over the border between the sacred ('white magic') and diabolical ('black magic') halves of the city that date back to Roman times. Built for Carlo Emanuele II around 1646, its lavishly decorated rooms house an assortment of furnishings, porcelain and other knick-knacks. The surrounding Giardino Reale (Royal Garden; ⊙9am-1hr before sunset) FREE, north and east of the palace, was designed in 1697 by André le Nôtre, who also created the gardens at Versailles.

The Palazzo Reale ticket allows you to view the Galleria Sabauda, the personal art collection of the Savoy monarchy, which was amassed over 400 years and includes gems by Van Dyck, Rubens and Lippi. Since 2012, the collection has been housed in the Manica Nuova, the newer wing of the Palazzo Reale. Access is also allowed into the Armeria Reale, another wing of the palace

... need to visit
... e separate
... ks older
... varra
... he

...ARIA REALE

...atious, regal, yet strangely under-publicised, the Reggia di Venaria ...ed palace complex built as a glorified hunting lodge by the frivolous ...o Emanuele II in 1675, is Italy's proverbial Versailles. Sure, it may not ...ublicity of its über-famous French counterpart (restoration work only ..., but this is one of the largest royal residences in the world, rescued ...ades of neglect by a €235 million 10-year-long restoration project.

Among the jewels bequeathed by its erstwhile royal rulers are a vast garden complex, a glittering **stag fountain** (with water shows), a Louis XIV-worthy **Grand Gallery**, plus the attached **Capella di Sant'Uberto** and **Juvarra stables**. The last three were all designed by the great Sicilian architect Filippo Juvarra in the 1720s.

To enjoy the permanent exhibition alone, you'll need to walk 2km through the aptly-named *Theatre of History and Magnificence*, a museum trajectory that relates the 1000-year history of the Savoy clan bivouacked in their former royal residential quarters and taking in the aforementioned gallery and church. On top of this are numerous high-profile temporary exhibitions, regular live concerts, an on-site cafe and restaurant, and an adjacent **borgo** (old village), now engulfed by Turin's suburbs, that's full of cosy places to eat and drink. Take note, there's a lot to digest and you'll need the best part of a day to see it. You can reach the palace complex (10km northwest of the city centre) on bus 11 from Porta Nuova station.

full of impressive muskets, spears and suits of armour.

Galleria Civica d'Arte Moderna e Contemporanea   ART GALLERY
(GAM; www.gamtorino.it; Via Magenta 31; adult/reduced €10/8; ⊙10am-6pm Tue-Sun) Italy can sometimes feel strangely light on modern art, until you come to Turin. GAM has an astounding 45,000 works in its vaults dedicated to 19th- and 20th-century artists, including De Chirico, Otto Dix and Klee. It cleverly hires art experts to reconfigure its permanent displays on a regular basis. You never know what you're going to get.

Museo d'Arte Contemporanea   ART GALLERY
(www.castellodirivoli.org; Piazza Mafalda di Savoia; adult/reduced €6.50/4.50; ⊙10am-5pm Tue-Fri, to 7pm Sat & Sun) Works by Frank Ackermann, Gilbert and George, and Frank Gehry would have been beyond the wildest imagination of the Savoy family, who once resided in the 17th-century **Castello di Rivoli**, where the cutting edge of Turin's contemporary art scene has been housed since 1984.

The castle is west of central Turin in the town of Rivoli (not to be confused with the city's Rivoli metro station). Take the metro to Paradiso station and then bus 36 to Rivoli bus station. Journey time is about one hour. Otherwise, take the metro to the Fermi stop, from where there's a free daily shuttle – see the website for shuttle schedules.

Parco Valentino   PARK
(⊙24hr; ⛴) Opened in 1856, this 550,000-sq-metre French-style park kisses the banks of the Po and and is filled with joggers, promenaders and lovers night and day. Walking southwest along the river brings you to **Castello del Valentino** (closed to the public), a mock chateau built in the 17th century.

Borgo Medievale   HISTORIC PARK
(Parco Valentino; ⊙9am-8pm Apr-Sep; ⛴) FREE One of Parco Valentino's more esoteric sights is this faux medieval village, built for the Italian General Exhibition in 1884. Its centrepiece is the **Rocca** (Viale Virgilio 107; adult/reduced €5/4; ⊙9am-5pm Tue-Sat, to 6pm Sun), a mock, scaled-down castle. Real historians might want to spare their change for the real thing (there's no shortage of medieval villages in Italy), though kids might enjoy the kitsch.

Chiesa di Gran Madre di Dio   CHURCH
(Piazza Vittorio Veneto) Framing the exquisite view southeast over Piazza Vittorio Veneto towards the Po river, this church was built in the style of a mini-Pantheon from 1818 to 1831 to commemorate the return of Vittorio Emanuele I from exile. It's small and rounded inside; some claim it's yet another secret repository for the Holy Grail.

In 1969 the church was memorably featured in the film *The Italian Job* when Michael Caine and his gang drove their Mini Coopers down the front staircase.

Lingotto   LANDMARK
(www.lingottofiere.it; Via Nizza 294) Around 3km south of the city centre is the **Lingotto Fiere**, Turin's former Fiat factory, which was redesigned by architect Renzo Piano into a congress and exhibition centre. In addition to two striking NH hotels, it houses congress facilities and the precariously perched 'treasure chest' rooftop gallery **Pinacoteca Giovanni e Marella Agnelli** (www.pinacoteca-agnelli.it; Via Nizza 230; adult/reduced €4/2.50; ⊘10.30am-7pm Tue-Sun), with masterpieces by Canaletto, Renoir, Manet, Matisse and Picasso, among others.

Lingotto is on Turin's most recent metro line and is easily accessible from the city centre.

⭐**Museo Nazionale dell'Automobile**   MUSEUM
(⊘011 67 76 66; www.museoauto.it; Corso Unità d'Italia 40; adult/reduced €8/6; ⊘10am-7pm Wed, Thu & Sun, to 9pm Fri & Sat, to 2pm Mon, 2-7pm Tue; Ⓜ Lingotto) Reopened after extensive renovations in 2012, and now befitting of a city that is the HQ of one of the world's leading car manufacturers (the 'T' in Fiat stands for 'Torino'), this dashing museum pays homage to the motor car and is anchored by a precious collection of over 200 automobiles – everything from an 1892 Peugeot to a 1980 Ferrari 308 (in red, of course).

Displaying an only-in-Italy panache for interior design, the museum – rather than leaving you to gawp helplessly at boring engines – takes you on a rollercoaster journey spread over three floors; the first part a car chronology, the second a more technical look at car design, and the third a self-critical assessment of issues such as pollution and congestion. Don't worry if you hate cars, you'll love this museum. Located roughly 5km south of the city centre.

Basilica di Superga   BASILICA
(www.basilicadisuperga.com; Strada della Basilica di Superga 73) **FREE** In 1706 Vittorio Amedeo II promised to build a basilica to honour the Virgin Mary if Turin was saved from besieging French and Spanish armies. Like a religious epiphany, the city was saved and architect Filippo Juvarra built the church on a hill across the Po river.

Basilica di Superga became the final resting place of the Savoy family, whose lavish tombs make for interesting viewing, as does the dome here.

In 1949 the basilica gained less welcome fame when a plane carrying the entire Turin football team crashed into the church in thick fog, killing all on board. Their tomb rests at the rear of the church. To get here take tram 15 from Piazza Vittorio Veneto to the Sassi–Superga stop on Corso Casale, then walk 20m to **Stazione Sassi** (Strada Comunale di Superga 4), from where an original 1934 **tram** (one way €4-6, return €6-9; ⊘from Sassi 9am-noon & 2-8pm Mon & Wed-Fri, 9.30am-12.30pm & 2.30-8.30pm Sat & Sun, 30min later from Superga) rattles the 3.1km up the hillside in 18 minutes every day except Tuesday.

🍴 Courses

Eataly   COOKING
(www.eatalytorino.it; from €20) ✏ Food sampling, tasting, and becoming a chef, sommelier secrets and cookery workshops all take place at Turin's famous Slow Food supermarket.

☞ Tours

Turismo Bus Torino   BUS TOUR
(1-day ticket adult/reduced €15/7.50; ⊘10am-6pm) This hop-on, hop-off bus service serves over a dozen different points around central Turin and has on-board staff providing information. Tickets are sold on board; information is available from the **Gruppo Torinese Trasporti** (GTT; www.torino.city-sightseeing.it; Piazza Castello; €15 for 24 hrs; ⊘10am-6pm).

Navigazione sul Po   BOAT TOUR
(return fare €4) Grupo Torinese Transporti operates boat trips on the Po. Boats to the Borgo Medievale in Parco Valentino and on to Moncalieri depart from **Imbarco Murazzi** (Murazzi del Po 65) four to seven times daily except Mondays.

Somewhere   WALKING TOUR
(www.somewhere.it) Turin's 'black and white magic' is illuminated on quirky walking tours with Somewhere. The company also runs other tours on lesser-known aspects of the city, such as 'Underground Turin'. Tours cost around €25; confirm departure points when booking.

🎆 Festivals & Events

The tourist office has details of these and other events.

Salone Internazionale del Gusto   FOOD
(www.salonedelgusto.it) ✏ Every October in even-numbered years, foodies roll into town

for this festival organised by Slow Food, with traditional producers from around the world showcasing their wares in a huge market at Lingotto Fiere. A day's entry costs €20, after which tastings cost between €1 and €5.

Cioccolatò
FOOD

(www.cioccola-to.it) Turin's famous chocolate is the focus of celebrations during March.

Salone Internazionale del Libro di Torino
BOOK FAIR

(http://en.salonelibro.it) Held every May, Turin's book fair is one of the most important in Europe.

Torino Film Festival
FILM

(www.torinofilmfest.org) Currently headed up by Palme d'Or winner Nanni Moretti, the festival takes place in November.

🛏 Sleeping

⭐ Hotel Residence Torino Centro
HOTEL €

(☎ 011 433 82 23; www.hoteltorinocentro.it; Corso Inghilterra 33; d/tr €84/105; P ✳ 🛜) The best player in the field by a good stretch is this chic, upgraded convent right behind the Porta Susa train station. Smart modern furnishings combine with old mosaic floors in huge rooms with the mod cons. Service is professional and efficient and there's a funky coffee bar (Coffee Lab Inghiliterra) downstairs in which to enjoy a complimentary breakfast.

Best bargain in Turin!

Hotel Urbani
HOTEL €

(☎ 011 669 90 47; www.hotelurbani.it; Via Saluzzo 7; s/d €56/76; @ 🛜) More urban than urbane, the Urbani is a two-minute suitcase drag from the main Porta Nuova train station and is clean, efficient and economical for a three star, even if its compact, business-like rooms pull few surprises. Breakfasts are hearty and staff never miss a *buongiorno*. Wi-fi costs €4 a day extra.

Hotel Dogana Vecchia
HOTEL €

(☎ 011 436 67 52; www.hoteldoganavecchia.com; Via Corte d'Appello 4; s/d €80/95; P) Mozart, Verdi and Napoleon are among those who have stayed at this historic three-star inn. Renovations have fortunately preserved its old-world charm, and its location in the Quadrilatero Romano is hard to beat.

Hotel Due Mondi
HOTEL €

(☎ 011 650 50 84; www.hotelduemondi.it; Via Saluzzo 3; s/d €55/69; ✳ @ 🛜) A close-to-the-station bargain, the Due Mondi equips its small rooms with bright, laminated floors, comfortable furnishings and ingenious shower-sauna cubicles. Most rooms have wi-fi, there's a cosy sitting area downstairs, and a classy restaurant next door lures you in with tasty-looking food trolleys. With such elegant diversions, the slightly seedy surroundings barely register.

Ostello Torino
HOSTEL €

(☎ 011 660 29 39; www.ostellotorino.it; Via Giordano Bruno 191; dm/s/tw shared bathroom €17/25/42; ☽ mid-Jan–mid-Dec; ✳ @) Turin's 76-bed HI hostel, 1.8km from Stazione Porta Nuova, can be reached by bus 52 (bus 64 on Sunday) from the train station. Facilities are good (including online computers, wi-fi, and dinner Monday to Saturday for €10) and breakfast's included, but there's an afternoon lockout.

Ai Savoia
BOUTIQUE HOTEL €€

(☎ 339 125 77 11; www.aisavoia.it; Via del Carmine 1b; r €95-125; P) Occupying an 18th-century town house, this little treasure seems like something out of a small town rather than a big city. The classical decor of each of its three rooms is ornate without being over-wrought, and staff are friendly and obliging.

Townhouse 70
BOUTIQUE HOTEL €€

(☎ 011 19 70 00 03; www.townhouse.it; Via XX Settembre 70; r from €115; @ 🛜) Small Milan-founded hotel chain whose classy interior is best described with adjectives such as 'chic', 'elegant', 'boutique' and 'suite'. If you like to invest your euros in fluffy bathrobes and receptionists in suits who'll call you 'sir' or 'madam', this is your ideal stopover.

Hotel Chelsea
HOTEL €€

(☎ 011 436 01 00; www.hotelchelsea.it; Via XX Settembre 79e; s/d/tr €110/160/180; P @) A stone's throw from Turin's main square, Piazza Castello, the Chelsea has modern, softly lit rooms with coordinated bedspreads and drapes. The romantic downstairs restaurant, La Campana, serves Pugliese cuisine.

Hotel Montevecchio
HOTEL €€

(☎ 011 562 00 23; www.hotelmontevecchio.com; Via Montevecchio 13; s €45-95, d €65-140; @ 🛜) In a quiet residential area yet just 300m from Stazione Porta Nuova, this two-star hotel has colourful, stencilled rooms in sunset shades, an above-average buffet breakfast and a guest laundry.

Hotel Roma e Rocca Cavour HOTEL €€

(☑ 011 561 27 72; www.romarocca.it; Piazza Carlo Felice 60; s/d €77/110; P ❋) If you've stayed in too many cramped hotel rooms, you'll love this c 1854 hotel opposite the Porta Nuova train station. Hallways are wide, ceilings are high and antique-furnished rooms are sumptuously proportioned, especially the flowing 'comfort' rooms.

NH Lingotto +
Lingotto Tech LUXURY HOTEL €€€

(☑ 011 664 20 00; www.nh-hotels.com; Via Nizza 262; NH Lingotto d €270-300, NH Lingotto Tech d €390-410; P ❋ ☎) Stay in luxury in the old Fiat factory with a few unusual perks thrown in – the 1km running track on the roof is Fiat's former testing track and featured in the film *The Italian Job*. Newly acquired by the NH chain, this giant hotel is in Lingotto and its ex-factory status means rooms are huge and bright with large windows.

There's a slick restaurant, professional service and complimentary use of an on-site gym.

✗ Eating

Where Italy rubs up against France, you're bound to get some exciting culinary fusion, though much of Turin's inspiration (and ingredients) comes from its own hinterland – Piedmont. Specialities include *risotto alla piemontese* (risotto with butter and cheese), *finanziera* (sweetbreads, mushrooms and chicken livers in a creamy sauce) and panna cotta (a creamy dessert, literally cooked cream).

The San Salvario neighbourhood, in the southeastern part of the city, has a host of multicultural eateries, particularly around Piazza Madama Cristina, as well as some of the city's best pizzerias and pubs.

Sfashion PIZZERIA €

(☑ 011 516 00 85; Via Cesare Battisti 13; pizzas/mains from €6/8.50; ☺ 8am-midnight) Best pizza in Turin? Mention Sfashion and you'll get more than a few takers. Naples-thick and with wonderfully rustic ingredients (and not too much cheese), they fly like hot bullets from the ovens of comic Torinese TV presenter Piero Chiamretti, whose funky postmodern city-centre set-up pitches retro toys amid an outlandish interior. The other in-house classic is mussels in tomato sauce.

Perino Vesco BAKERY €

(☑ 011 068 60 56; www.perinovesco.it; Via Cavour 10; snacks from €4; ☺ 9.30am-7.30pm Mon-Sat) Ligurians missing their daily bread fix needn't worry. The fresh focaccia has followed you to Turin courtesy of cult Slow Food Torinese baker Andrea Perino, who knocks out generous portions of tasty snacks at this bakery-cum-cafe.

Gofri Piemontéisa SNACKS €

(www.gofriemiassepiemontesi.it; Via San Tommaso 4a; ☺ 11.30am-7.30pm Mon-Sat) *Gofri* are thin waffles made from flour, water and yeast, cooked in hot irons. This traditional dish from the mountainous regions of northern Piedmont has been reinvented as tasty fast food by a local chef. Try the house *gofre* with ham, soft cheese and rocket or one of the equally delicious *miasse* (corn-based crêpes).

Eataly CAFE, DELI €

(www.eatalytorino.it; Via Nizza 230; ☺ 10am-8pm Tue-Sun) Adjacent to the Lingotto congress centre is the Slow Food Movement's supermarket. Set in a vast converted factory, it houses a staggering array of sustainable food and beverages, with a separate area for each, including cheeses, breads, meats, fish, pasta, chocolate and much more.

The best time to visit is around 12.30pm to 2.30pm, when each area has its own little restaurant serving lunch.

Grom GELATO €

(www.grom.it; Piazza Pietro Paleocapa; ☺ 11am-midnight Sun-Thu, to 1am Fri & Sat) If you haven't heard of Grom, you haven't been in Turin long. The Slow Food–championed, artisan ice cream chain founded their first store right here in 2003, promising to put the same care and attention into ice cream production as oenologists put into wine. Long queues testify to a burgeoning legend.

Alberto Marchetti ICE CREAM €

(☑ 011 839 08 79; www.albertomarchetti.it; Corso Vittorio Emanuele II 24; ☺ noon-11pm Tue-Sat, 11am-10pm Sun) Riding in the slipstream of the Grom ice-cream phenomenon, Alberto Marchetti is a master of quality, managing every part of his ice-cream making process, from fruit selection to the type of milk used. Better than Grom? You decide.

Brek BUFFET €

(www.brek.com; Piazza Carlo Felice 18; buffets from €10; ☺ 8.30am-11pm) Only Italians could take

APERICENAS

Who needs *cena* (dinner) when you've got bar snacks the size of...well...dinners? Turin's answer to the aperitif is the *apericena*, where bar-side buffets resemble full-blown meals and hard-up backpackers can bypass the cheap pizza joints in favour of posher Piedmontese snacks accompanied by a decent glass of wine. Turin's best and most economical *apericenas* can be procured along Via Po and in Piazza Vittorio Veneto. Here, places such as **Caffè Nazionale** (Via Po 18) serve up excellent pasta concoctions, artichoke pies, risotto and all sorts of other goodies. Another nexus is the Quadrilatero quarter, where the buffet at **I Tre Galli** (www.3galli.com; Via Sant'Agostino 25; ⊙12.30pm-2.30pm & 6.30pm-midnight Mon-Wed, to 2am Thu-Sat) should take the sting out of your early evening appetite without ruining it. Expect to pay between €5 to €10 for an *apericena* (a drink plus full licence to raid the buffet).

'fast food' and make it both credible *and* edible. Brek is a small self-service restaurant chain where you can pick up fresh pasta, pizza, sausages, salads and desserts. Inside, the ambience is far from plastic. Indeed, you might even be inclined to linger awhile in the plant-bedecked outdoor courtyard.

★ **L'Acino** PIEDMONTESE €€
(☑ 011 521 70 77; Via San Domenico 2A; meals €30-35; ⊙7.30pm-midnight Mon-Sat) Half a dozen tables and a legion of enamoured followers mean this inviting restaurant is hard to get into. Book ahead or arrive on the stroke of 7.30pm (it doesn't open for lunch) if you want to get your taste buds around snails, tripe and beef stew cooked in Roero wine. Overtures are provided by classic Piedmontese pasta staples.

È Cucina FUSION €€
(www.cesaremarretti.com; Via Bertola 27a; meals €20-30) Here's an interesting Torinese culinary concept: haute cuisine at everyman prices. The meals at this sleek restaurant are courtesy of Bolognese chef Cesare Marretti and his creative scope is breathtaking. There is no printed menu; waitstaff will merely tell you it's a *sorpesa* (surprise). You pay for the number of courses you consume.

It's impossible to list or rank the pot-luck dishes. Bank on artichokes with prawns, eggplants overlaid with avocado cream, pears atop salmon, and plenty more.

Porto di Savona TRATTORIA €€
(Piazza Vittoria Veneto 2; meals €25; ⊙12.30-2.30pm & 7.30-10.30pm) An economical, unpretentious trattoria, it has a deserved reputation for superb *agnolotti al sugo arrosto* (Piedmontese ravioli in a meat gravy), and *gnocchi di patate al gorgonzola*. The mains – including *bollito misto alla piemontese*

(boiled meat and vegetable stew) – are equally memorable. Be patient: the food takes a while to arrive, probably because it's 100% homemade and 100% Piedmontese.

Il Giglio SEAFOOD €€
(☑ 011 436 50 21; Via San Domencia 4; meals €30; ⊙7.30-11.30pm Mon-Sat, 12.30-2pm Fri & Sat) Making a surprise appearance in landlocked Piedmont is fish specialist Il Giglio, where 'sausage' is a swear-word and 90% of the menu comes from the sea. The gregarious, table-hopping owner breezes around, juggling plates of prawns, calamari and sea bass.

Kipling Restaurant ITALIAN, FUSION €€
(☑ 011 817 26 16; www.kiplingrestaurant.com; Via Mazzini 10; meals €25-30; ⊙noon-12.30am) It's rare that a visitor to Italy can be tempted away from the plump fruits of traditional cooking, but worth an away-day from the trusty trattorias is the stylish modern Kipling, which keeps 50% of its menu *italiano* and uses the other half to showcase Indian, Mexican and Chinese influences.

A bookcase of Lonely Planet guidebooks near the entrance hints at the global ambitions. Juventus soccer players often come here for lunch.

Combal Zero MODERN, FUSION €€€
(☑ 011 956 52 25; www.combal.org; Piazza Mafalda di Savoia; 5-course tasting menu €110; ⊙Tue-Sat) If you're counting Michelin stars or revel in ultra-weird food experiences, you need to make the trip out to the Castello di Rivoli, where Combal Zero shares digs with the Museo d'Arte Contemporanea – quite appropriate as it turns out, considering resident chef Davide Scabin is something of a Jackson Pollock of modern cooking.

His latest creation, *cyber-elio Campari*, involves inhaling from a helium balloon, taking a slug of Campari and then biting on a soda-water capsule. Delicious – no? Bookings are essential.

Self-catering

Porta Palazzo MARKET €

(Piazza della Repubblica; ☉ 8.30am-1.30pm Mon-Fri, to 6.30pm Sat) Europe's largest open-air food market has literally hundreds of food stalls. Pick up a picnic.

🍷 Drinking & Nightlife

In Turin, drinking can also mean eating. *Aperitivi* and more substantial *apericenas* are a Turin institution. As in Milan, if you're on a tight budget, you can fill up on a generous buffet of bar snacks for the cost of a drink. The main drinking spots are the riverside area around Piazza Vittoria Veneto and in the Quadrilatero Romano district.

Turin's historical cafes have their rivals – Trieste and Rome to name but two – but it's splitting hairs really. These are evocative places full of literary legend, architectural excellence, aromatic coffee and the city's best gossip – and gossipers. Then there's the chocolate, either liquid or solid, a speciality unto itself.

★ Caffè Mulassano CAFE

(Piazza Castello 15; ☉ 7.30am-10.30pm) With dozens of customers and only five dwarf-sized tables, the art nouveau Mulassano is where regulars sink white-hot espresso *in piedi* (standing) while discussing Juventus' current form with the knowledgeable bow-tied barista.

Caffè San Carlo CAFE

(Piazza San Carlo 156; ☉ 8am-midnight Tue-Fri, to 1am Sat, to 9pm Mon) Perhaps the most gilded of the gilded, this glittery cafe dates from 1822. You'll get neckache admiring the weighty chandelier and heartache contemplating your bill (a hefty €4.50 for a cappuccino).

Fiorio CAFE

(Via Po 8; ☉ 8.30am-1am Tue-Sun) Garner literary inspiration in Mark Twain's old window seat as you contemplate the gilded interior of a cafe where 19th-century students once plotted revolutions and the Count of Cavour deftly played whist. The bittersweet hot chocolate ain't bad either.

Al Bicerin CAFE, CHOCOLATE

(Piazza della Consolata 5; ☉ 8.30am-7.30pm Mon, Tue, Thu & Fri, 8.30am-1pm & 3.30-7.30pm Sat & Sun) Established in 1763 beneath a 14th-century bell tower, this cafe takes its name from *bicerin,* a caffeine-charged hot drink of chocolate, coffee and cream. Tasting one is a Torinese rite of passage.

Mood CAFE

(www.moodlibri.it; Via Battisti 3e; ☉ cafe 8am-9pm Mon-Sat, bookshop 10am-9pm Mon-Sat) Are you bluesy, deflated, in dire need of a caffeine injection? Any mood suits this coffee shop–cocktail bar–bookshop combo, as long as you can find room among the wilting shoppers and students flicking through Dante. The interior's slavishly hip, all polished concrete and shiny laminate.

LIGURIA, PIEDMONT & THE ITALIAN RIVIERA TURIN

DON'T MISS

WORSHIP AT THE SHRINES OF FOOTBALL

After paying your respects to the Holy Shroud, find time to tap into Italy's other religion: *calcio* (football). Its cathedral is the **Juventus Stadium**, inaugurated in 2011 as the home ground to the legendary *bianconeri*, Italy's most successful football club. The state-of-the-art ground has a **Juventus Museum** (www.juventus.com; Strada Comunale di Altessano 131; museum €10, incl stadium vist €18; ☉ 10.30am-6.30pm Mon & Wed-Fri, to 7.30pm Sat & Sun) that will blind you with its silverware (28 league titles – and the rest!) and proudly recount how it was all amassed.

On the other side of town, the **Stadio Olimpico** (which hosted the 2006 Winter Olympics) is home to Turin's other team, Torino FC. Until 2011, Torino shared their ground with Juventus, but now they've got the place to themselves except when they play the *bianconeri* in the hotly fought *Derby della Mole*. The Stadio Olimpico also offers a stadium tour and hosts a more general sports museum, the **Museo dello Sport** (www.olympicstadiumturin.com; Corso Agnelli; museum €10, incl stadium €14; ☉ 10am-6pm).

To get to the Juventus Stadium from the city centre, catch bus 72 from the corner of Via XX Settembre and Via Bertola. To get to the Stadio Olimpico, take tram No 4 from Porta Nuova train station and get off after eight stops.

Società Anonima BAR, CAFE
(Via Pietro Micca 12; ⊙ 7am-11pm; 🛜) More cool-contemporary than stuffy-traditional, SA's clientele is all-over-the-map, rather like its eclectic furniture which doffs a libertine cap to every genre from Louis XV to Ikea. Working stiffs drop by for a breakfast cappuccino; live DJs rock the rafters after 9pm.

Pastis WINE BAR
(Piazza Emanuele Filiberto 9; ⊙ 9am-3.30pm & 6pm-2am) This boldly painted cafe-bar is where Torinese office workers go for a two-hour lunch break – spicy meatballs with an obligatory glass of wine.

La Drogheria BAR
(www.la-drogheria.it; Piazza Vittorio Veneto 18; ⊙ 10am-2am) Occupying the space of an old pharmacy, La Drogheria's sofas are coveted by a studenty crowd who enjoy cheap drinks and *aperitivi* fare before hitting the Murazzi nightlife.

Lobelix BAR
(Via Corte d'Appello 15f; ⊙ 7pm-3am Mon-Sat) Beneath the trees on Piazza Savoia, the terrace here is a favourite place for an *aperitivo* – Lobelix' buffet banquet is one of Turin's most extravagant.

Caffè Torino CAFE
(Piazza San Carlo 204; ⊙ 7.30am-1am) This chandelier-lit showpiece opened in 1903. A brass plaque of the city's emblem, a bull ('Torino in Italian means 'little bull'), is embedded in the pavement out the front; rub your shoe across it for good luck.

San Tommaso 10 CAFE
(Via San Tommaso 10; ⊙ 8am-midnight Mon-Sat) The Lavazza family started roasting coffee here in 1900. Now modernised, the cafe offers a staggering variety of flavours as well as an excellent restaurant. Caffeine fiends can buy espresso machines.

Pepino CAFE, CHOCOLATE
(Piazza Carignano 8; ⊙ 8.30am-8pm Sun-Thu, to midnight Fri & Sat) Chocolate in all its guises is available at Pepino, where ice cream dipped in chocolate on a stick was invented in 1937. Longer opening hours in summer.

☆ Entertainment

Most clubs open from 9pm to late and cover charges vary depending on the night. Turin's clubbing district centres on Murazzi del Po (also called Lungo Po Murazzi), the arcaded riverside area stretch-ing between Ponte Vittorio Emanuele I and Ponte Umberto I – follow the crowds (and the music).

Teatro Regio Torino THEATRE
(✎ 011 881 52 41; www.teatroregio.torino.it; Piazza Castello 215; ⊙ ticket office 10.30am-6pm Tue-Fri, to 4pm Sat & 1hr before performances) Sold-out performances can sometimes be watched free on live TV in the adjoining Teatro Piccolo Regio, where Puccini premiered *La Bohème* in 1896. Tickets start at €48.

Hiroshima Mon Amour CLUB
(www.hiroshimamonamour.org; Via Bossoli 83; admission free-€15) This legendary dance club plays everything from folk and punk to tango and techno.

Phuddhu Bar CLUB
(Murazzi del Po; ⊙ 7pm-3am) Drum and bass music on Friday and Saturday nights with DJs are par for the course in this *Murazzi* club on the riverside.

Cinema Massimo CINEMA
(Via Giuseppe Verdi 18; admission €7) Near the Mole Antonelliana, the cinema offers an eclectic mix of films, mainly in English or with subtitles. One of its three screens only shows classic films.

🛍 Shopping

Via Roma's arcaded walkways shelter the city's most expensive fashion boutiques, while those along pedestrianised Via Garibaldi are more affordable. Via Po has some great secondhand record shops, and vintage and alternative clothes.

★ Guido Golbino CHOCOLATE
(www.guidogolbino.it; Via Lagrange 1; ⊙ 10am-8pm Tue-Sun, 3-8pm Mon) Chocolate heaven even by Turin standards, Guido's is currently the Torinese chocolatier of choice. This outlet has a slim little seating area tucked away behind its delectable chocolate shop where you can sit down to sample fondues, *giandujas* (hazelnut chocolates), and other such belt-looseners.

Peyrano CHOCOLATE
(www.peyrano.com; Corso Vittorio Emanuele II 76) Creator of *Dolci Momenti a Torino* (Sweet Moments in Turin) and *grappini* (chocolates filled with grappa), Peyrano has been in operation since 1912. After changing hands in 2002, it went under during the recent economic crisis, but was

quickly bought back by its original family owners.

Libreria Luxemburg — BOOKS
(Via Battisti 7) This British bookshop is well stocked with light and heavy lit plus a full stash of Lonely Planet guides. There are also daily British newspapers.

Pastificio Defilippis — FOOD
(Via Lagrange 39; ⏱8.30am-1pm & 4-7.30pm Mon-Sat) Nose through the open doorway of this 1872 establishment to watch the family making dozens of varieties of pasta; you can buy it here to cook later or sit down to eat it.

Paissa — FOOD
(www.paissa.it; Piazza San Carlo 196) This wonderful old-fashioned emporium in Piazza San Carlo, complete with ladders and a heavy wooden counter, is where you can buy everything Turin is famous for, including *grissini* (breadsticks), wine and chocolates.

ℹ Information

A bank, ATM and exchange booth can all be found within Stazione Porta Nuova; others are dotted throughout the city. A 24-hour automatic banknote-change machine can be found outside **Unicredit Banca.** (Piazza CLN)

Farmacia Boniscontro (🖉011 53 82 71; Corso Vittorio Emanuele II 66; ⏱3pm-12.30am) Night pharmacy.

Ospedale Mauriziano Umberto I (🖉011 5 08 01; Largo Turati 62) Hospital.

Pharmacy (🖉011 518 64 67; Stazione Porta Nuova; ⏱7am-7.30pm)

Police Station (🖉011 5 58 81; Corso Vinzaglio 10)

Post Office (Via Alfieri 10; ⏱8.30am-7pm Mon-Fri, to 1pm Sat)

Tourist Office (🖉011 53 51 81; www.turismotorino.org; Piazza Castello; ⏱9am-6pm) Central, multilingual, open daily.

Stazione Porta Nuova Tourist Office (🖉011 53 51 81; Stazione Porta Nuova; ⏱9am-6pm) The office at Stazione Porta Nuova offers a free accommodation and restaurant booking service.

ℹ Getting There & Away

AIR
Turin's **Caselle** (TRN; www.turin-airport.com) airport, 16km northwest of the city centre in Caselle, has connections to European and national destinations. Budget airline Ryanair operates flights to London Stansted, Barcelona and Ibiza. Alitalia links to half a dozen Italian cities.

BUS
Most international, national and regional buses terminate at the **bus station** (Corso Castelfidardo), 1km west from Stazione Porta Nuova along Corso Vittorio Emanuele II. You can also get to Milan's Malpensa airport from here.

TRAIN
Regular daily trains connect Turin's **Stazione Porta Nuova** (Piazza Carlo Felice) to the following destinations:

TO	FARE (€)	DURATION (HR)	FREQUENCY
Milan	11.20	1¾	28
Aosta	8.40	2	21
Venice	56	4½	17
Genoa	11.20	2	16
Rome	from 57.50	7	11

Most also stop at the space-age new **Stazione Porta Susa** (Corso Inghilterra) terminal. Some trains also stop at **Stazione Torino Lingotto** (Via Pannunzio 1), though it's generally more convenient to travel between the city centre and Lingotto by metro.

ℹ Getting Around

TO/FROM THE AIRPORT
Sadem (www.sadem.it) runs buses to the airport from Stazione Porta Nuova (40 minutes), also stopping at Stazione Porta Susa (30 minutes). Buses depart every 30 minutes between 5.15am and 10.30pm (6.30am and 11.30pm from the airport). Single tickets cost €5 from **Confetteria Avvignano** (Piazza Carlo Felice 50), opposite where the bus stops, or €5.50 if bought on the bus.

A taxi between the airport and the city centre will cost around €35 to €40.

ℹ TURIN BIKE-SHARING

Turin's ever-expanding bike-sharing scheme, **[To]Bike** (www.tobike.it), was inaugurated in 2010 and is now one of the largest in Italy, with over 18,000 subscribers and 116 stations storing bright-yellow *biciclette*. Temporary usage can be procured for €8 a week or €5 a day, after which the first 30 minutes are free. You'll then pay 80c, €1 and €2 for subsequent 30-minute sessions. To buy an access card, drop by Via Santa Chiara 26F or register online.

LIGURIA, PIEDMONT & THE ITALIAN RIVIERA TURIN

CAR & MOTORCYCLE

Major car-rental agencies have offices at Stazione Porta Nuova and the airport.

PUBLIC TRANSPORT

The city boasts a dense network of buses, trams and a cable car run by the Gruppo Torinese Trasporti (p205), which has an **information office** (☉7am-9pm) at Stazione Porta Nuova. Buses and trams run from 6am to midnight and tickets cost €1 (€13.50 for a 15-ticket carnet and €3.50 for a one-day pass).

Turin's single-line **metro** (www.metrotorino.it) runs from Fermi to Lingotto. It first opened for the Winter Olympics in February 2006. It was extended to Stazione Porta Nuova in October 2007 and Lingotto in March 2011. The line is currently being extended south to Piazza Bengazi, two stations south of Lingotto. Tickets cost €1.50.

TAXI

Call **Centrale Radio** (☎ 011 57 37) or **Radio Taxi** (☎ 011 57 30).

The Milky Way

Neither a chocolate bar nor a galaxy of stars, Piedmont's Milky Way (Via Lattea) consists of two parallel valleys just west of Turin that offer top-notch skiing facilities. The more northern of the two, Valle di Susa, meanders past a moody abbey, the old Celtic town of Susa and pretty mountain villages. Its southern counterpart, the Valle di Chisone, is pure ski-resort territory. The valleys hosted many events at the 2006 Winter Olympics, and the facilities and infrastructure are state of the art.

⊙ Sights

Brooding above the road 14km from Turin is the Sacra di San Michele (admission €4; ☉9.30am-12.30pm & 2.30-6pm Tue-Fri, 9.30am-noon & 2.40-6.30pm Sat & Sun Apr-Sep, closes earlier in winter), a Gothic-Romanesque abbey that has kept watch atop Monte Pirchiriano (962m) since the 10th century. Look out for the whimsical 'Zodiac door', a 12th-century doorway sculpted with putti (cherubs) pulling each other's hair. To reach the abbey, get off at Sant'Ambrogio station and hike up a steep path for 1½ hours. Alternatively, there's a special bus from Avigliana train station six times a day from May to September. Concerts are held on Saturday evenings in summer; ask for details at the tourist office in Avigliana (population 10,500), 12km west.

A Druid well remains as testimony to the Celtic origins of Susa (population 6580, ele-

---

GOURMET PIEDMONT

Arguably Italy's most culinary progressive region, Piedmont has challenged the hegemony of the nation's pizza and spaghetti monopoly in recent years and come up with some gourmet alternatives. The Slow Food movement (founded in Bra) now has chapters in over 150 countries, Oscar Farinetti's Eataly food market (from Turin) is hugely successful in New York, while artisan ice-cream maker, Grom (also from Turin) has branches in Tokyo, New York and Paris. Then there's the region's ever-expanding stash of acclaimed Michelin star restaurants, which has practically formed a constellation.

Eschewing the habits of their southern cousins, the Piedmontese have always had a different approach to food. They have long preferred risotto over pizza, butter over olive oil, and egg pasta over durum wheat spaghetti. Gastronomically, favourite dishes call upon precious local ingredients (white truffles, Arborio rice, hazelnuts and Castelmagno cheese among them), and are supported by a weighty wine culture (the region nurtures two of Italy's finest wines: Barolo and Barbaresco).

Classic trattoria dishes in Piedmont include *agnolotti al plin* (meat ravioli in beef broth and butter), *risotto al barolo* (sometimes served with sausages), and *vitello tonnato* (cold veal with a tuna-flavoured cream topping). Sitting improbably alongside them are the high-art hipster offerings of the new breed fanned by a mixture of international influences, the locavore traditions of Eataly, and the molecular gastronomy of Spaniard Ferran Adrià. Ristorante Piazza Duomo in Alba serves a dish called 'salad 41' named after the number of different leaves it contains, while Davide Scabin at Turin's Combal Zero offers a plate called 'virtual oysters' (it tastes like oysters but is made from watermelon, anchovies and almonds), and another called 'hambook' (prosciutto and melon gel served in a hollowed-out book). Weird, playful and intentionally funny, it's a long way from Neapolitan pizza.

vation 503m) before it fell under the Roman Empire's sway. Susa's Roman ruins make for an interesting stop on the way to the western ski resorts. In addition to the remains of a Roman aqueduct, a still-used amphitheatre and the triumphal Arco d'Augusto (dating from 9 BC), you can visit the town's early-11th-century cathedral.

Also worth a brief stop is the forbidding Forte di Exilles (www.fortediexilles.com; admission €10/8; ⊙10am-7pm Tue-Sun Apr-Sep, to 2pm Oct-Mar), overlooking the quiet village of Exilles, 15km west of Susa. Its military role only ended in 1943.

🏃 Activities

Skiing

The prestigious Via Lattea (www.vialattea. it) ski domain embraces 400km of pistes and five interlinked ski resorts: Sestriere (2035m), Sauze d'Oulx (1509m), Sansicario (1700m), Cesana Torinese (1350m) and Claviere (1760m) in Italy; and Montgenèvre (1850m) in neighbouring France. Its enormous range of slopes and generally reliable snow conditions provide for skiers and boarders of all abilities. A single daily ski pass costing €34 covers the entire Milky Way, including the French slopes.

Built in the 1930s by the Agnelli clan of Fiat fame, Sestriere (population 885) ranks among Europe's most glamorous ski resorts due to its enviable location in the eastern realms of the vast Milky Way ski area.

The tourist offices have mountains of information on every conceivable summer and winter sport, including heli-skiing, bobsledding, golfing on Europe's highest golf course, walking, free-climbing and mountain biking.

Cross-country skiing in the area is centred on Bardonecchia (population 3084, elevation 1312m), the last stop in Italy before the Fréjus Tunnel.

Hiking

Avigliana's tourist office has route maps and information on summertime walking and mountain biking, including the protected lakes and marshlands in the Parco Naturale dei Laghi di Avigliana (www.parks.it/parco.laghi.avigliana) on the town's western fringe. From Avigliana, experienced walkers can tackle a strenuous climb or take a 30km circular bike trail to the Sacra di San Michele abbey.

Rafting

Rafting and kayaking trips from Cesana Torinese are organised through OK Adventure (www.okadventure.it; 3hr trips €40-50).

🛏 Sleeping & Eating

Many hotels shut outside winter and summer. The area's tourist offices can make hotel reservations.

Sestriere's central square, Piazza Fraiteve, is loaded with places to eat and drink, including the perennially popular pizzeria Pinky (Piazza Fraiteve 5n; pizzas €4-6) and the trendier Napapijri (Piazza Agnelli 1; meals €17-18).

Casa Cesana　　　　　　　　　HOTEL €
(☎0122 8 94 62; www.hotelcasacesana.com; Viale Bouvier, Cesana Torinese; d €55, half-board €70; 🅿❋) Right across from Cesana Torinese's ski lift, this timber chalet was built for the 2006 Olympics. Its rooms are light-filled and spotless, there's a well-patronised restaurant open to nonguests (set menus around €18), and its bar is one of the area's liveliest.

Hotel Susa Stazione　　　　　HOTEL €
(☎0122 62 22 26; www.hotelsusa.it; Corso Stati Uniti 4/6, Susa; s/d €59/88; 🅿) A handy all-round base for the area and located directly opposite Susa's train station, this cycle-friendly hotel has 12 uniform rooms with private bathrooms, plus a restaurant (set menu €20). Staff hand out maps and itinerary proposals.

ℹ Information

There are numerous tourist offices in the valleys.
Tourist Office Avigliana (☎011 936 60 37; Piazza del Popolo 2, ⊙9am-1pm & 2-6pm Mon-Fri) Cesana Torinese (Piazza Vittorio Amedeo 3, ; ⊙9am-12.30pm & 2.30-7pm) Sestriere (www.sestriere.it; Via Louset; ⊙9am-12.30pm & 2.30-7pm).

ℹ Getting There & Away

The main Italy–France motorway and railway line roar along the Valle di Susa, making the area easily accessible by both public transport and car (though motorists should keep change on hand for the numerous tolls).
Sapav buses (www.sapav.it) link Susa with Avigliana (€3.05, 35 minutes), Oulx (€2.25, 45 minutes), Turin (€3.95, 1¼ hours) and the Milky Way resorts. From Sestriere, buses serve Cesana Torinese (€1.75, 25 minutes), Oulx (€2.25, 45 minutes) and Turin (€5.77, two to three hours) up to five times daily.

Southern & Eastern Piedmont

Gourmets on the rebound from an Emilia-Romagna food tour (fattened up with balsamic vinegar and Parmesan) might think it couldn't get any better. But it can and it does. The rolling hills, valleys and townships of southern and eastern Piedmont are northern Italy's specialist pantry, weighed down with sweet hazelnuts, rare white truffles, Arborio rice, delicate veal, subtle cheeses and Nebbiolo grapes that metamorphose into Barolo and Barbaresco wines. Out here in the damp Po river basin, they give out Michelin stars like overzealous schoolteachers give out house points, and with good reason. The food is sublime, steeped in traditions as old as the towns that fostered them. There's Bra, home of the Slow Food Movement; Pollenzo, host to a University of Gastronomic Sciences; Asti, replete with truffles and wine; and Alba, home of Barolo wines.

Many trace the gourmet routes in a car, but to compensate for the calorific overload, there are also excellent walking and cycling opportunities.

South of Cuneo, and forgotten by most, are the Maritime Alps, a one-time hunting ground for Savoy kings that's now open to hikers.

Cuneo & Around

POP 55,464 / ELEV 543M

Cuneo is a condensed version of Turin without the clamour. There is a raft of reasons why you should drop by here, not least being the food, the bike friendliness, the great hiking possibilities in the nearby Maritime Alps, and the city's signature rum-filled chocolates.

Sitting on a promontory of land between two rivers, Cuneo enjoys excellent Alpine views framed by the high pyramid-shaped peak of Monte Viso (3841m) in the Cottian Alps.

⊙ Sights

The city's Napoleonic avenues give it an almost French air.

Piazza Galimberti   PIAZZA
Arriving in Cuneo's gargantuan main piazza, you'd think you just touched down in a capital city. The outsized square was finished in 1884 and sits aside an older

portico-embellished town founded in 1198. Some of the heavier arches date back to the Middle Ages.

Museo Civico di Cuneo   MUSEUM
(Via Santa María 10; admission €2.60; ⊙ 9am-1pm & 3-5.30pm Tue-Thu, to 7pm Fri & Sat) Cuneo has some wonderfully dark and mysterious churches. The oldest is the deconsecrated San Francisco convent and church, which today hosts this museum tracking the history of the town and province.

🏃 Activities

To the southwest lie the Maritime Alps, a rugged outdoor adventure playground where French and Italian influences mix.

The best-equipped ski town is **Limone Piemonte** (www.limonepiemonte.it), 20km south of Cuneo and reachable by regular trains (€2.50, 40 minutes). Limone has been a ski station since 1907 and maintains 15 lifts and 80km of runs, including some put aside for Nordic skiing. The town (population 1600) has numerous hotels and ski-hire shops. See the website for details.

🛏 Sleeping

★**Hotel Royal Superga**   HOTEL €
(☑ 0171 69 32 23; www.hotelroyalsuperga.com; Via Pascal 3; s/d €86/109; 🅿 ❋ @ 🛜) For 'Superga' read 'superb'. This appealing old-fashioned hotel, hidden off a corner of Piazza Galimberti, mixes some regal touches with a raft of complimentary items. Bank on free wi-fi, free DVDs to watch in your room, interesting books to peruse downstairs, and free city bikes for guests. Breakfast (included) is a delicious spread made from organic produce.

Friendly, professional staff go way beyond the call of duty.

Hotel Ligure   HOTEL €
(☑ 0171 63 45 45; www.ligurehotel.com; Via Savigliano 11; s €55-65, d €75-85; 🅿 ❋ 🛜) In the heart of the old town, this two-star hotel has a handful of apartments, each with its own kitchen (minimum seven-night stay). If you're just passing through, its freshly spruced-up hotel rooms (with breakfast) are simple but spotless. Friendly trilingual service adds further kudos.

Hotel Palazzo Lovera   HOTEL €€
(☑ 0171 69 04 20; www.palazzolovera.com; Via Roma 37; s €85-115, d €120-140; 🅿 ❋ 🛜) A French king and an Italian pope have stayed here, hinting at the Loverna's stately past.

Rooms are comfortable if not lavish, but the value for money comes with rare small-town Italian extras, such as a gym, sauna and two affiliated restaurants, one of which (Delle Antiche Contrade) has a deserved Michelin star.

✖ Eating & Drinking

Typically for Piedmont, Cuneo has some standout places to wine and dine.

★ 4 Ciance PIEDMONTESE €

(✆0171 48 90 27; www.4cianceristorante.it; Via Dronero 8C; two-course menu with wine €22; ⊘lunch & dinner) Cuneo, like Alba, is one of Piedmont's curiously under-praised culinary powerhouses, and it has grown more powerful since the opening of the new 4 Ciance, where the love of local food is evident in every forkful, and the warm, unpretentious staff serve earthy but poshly presented food at decidedly un-posh prices.

Everything is homemade, including the bread, and the wine list is superb.

Arione CHOCOLATE €

(www.arione-cuneo.com; Piazza Galimberti 14; ⊘8am-8pm Tue-Sat, 8am-1pm & 3.30-8pm Sun) This 1920s-vintage chocolatier invented the *Cuneesi al Rhum* – a large, rum-laced praline wrapped in cellophane. The chocolates came to the attention of Hemingway, who made a detour from Milan en route to Nice in 1954 to try them – there's a photograph of his visit in the window.

Bar Gelateria Corso CAFE, GELATO €

(Corso Nizza 16; snacks €2-5; ⊘7am-1am Thu-Tue) Go-to cafe for gelato, gossip and cups of ultra-thick hot chocolate.

Osteria della Chiocciola GASTRONOMIC €€

(✆0171 6 62 77; Via Fossano 1; meals €28-33; ⊘12.30-11pm Mon-Sat) ✐ The lack of outside signage reflects an inner confidence at Chiocciola's, where seasoned cooks perform small miracles. Although the restaurant is Slow Food affiliated, the time-poor can still stop by for a glass of wine with cheese and salami on the ground floor. Upstairs, in a buttercup dining room, dawdlers can choose from the handwritten menu's alchemy of flavours.

Delle Antiche Contrade GASTRONOMIC €€€

(✆0171 48 04 88; www.antichecontrade.it; Via Savigliano 11; meals €60; ⊘lunch Tue-Sun, dinner Tue-Sat) This former 17th-century postal station is the culinary workshop of Ligurian chef Luigi Taglienti, who melds the fish of his home region with the meat and pasta of his adopted one. The result: a Michelin star. Those with bottomless wallets can bag a personal table overlooking the kitchen action for €130 per head.

❶ Information

Tourist Office (www.comune.cuneo.it; Via Roma 28; ⊘9.30am-12.30pm & 3-6.30pm Mon-Sat)

❶ Getting There & Away

Regular trains run from Cuneo's central train station, at Piazzale Libertà, to Turin (€5.90, 1¼ hours, up to eight daily), San Remo (€8, 2¼ hours, three daily) and Ventimiglia (€7, two hours, around four daily), as well as Nice (€15, 2¾ hours, at least six daily) in France. A second train station for the Cuneo–Gesso line serves the small town of Mondovì, from where there are connections to Savona and Genoa.

Saluzzo

POP 16,877 / ELEV 395M

Like Asti and Alba, Saluzzo was once a powerful city-state and its historical importance – while now diminished – has left a stirring legacy etched in red terracotta bricks.

The town is divided into 'old' and 'new' quarters, and the two sections are a short walk apart. Once a medieval stronghold, the town maintained its independence until the Savoys won it in a 1601 treaty with France. One of its better-known sons was the Italian writer Silvio Pellico (1788–1854). Imprisoned for his patriotism against the Austrian occupation, he wrote parts of his novel *Le Mie Prigioni* (My Prisons) by cutting himself and using his blood as ink. A second well-known local is General Carlo dalla Chiesa (1920–82), whose implacable pursuit of the Mafia led to his assassination.

◉ Sights

Torre Civica LANDMARK

(Via San Giovanni; admission €2, incl Museo Civico di Casa Cavassa €6; ⊘10.30am-12.30pm & 2.30-6.30pm Fri-Sun) The burnt-red-tiled rooftops of Saluzzo's old town make a timeless picture from the loggia beneath the 15th-century belfry, which is reached by a steep flight of steps.

La Castiglia CASTLE

(Piazza Castello; adult/reduced €5/2.50) Saluzzo's medieval rulers meted out justice from

OFF THE BEATEN TRACK

HIKING IN THE MARITIME ALPS

Northern Italy, crowded? Not if you bring your hiking boots. Shoehorned between the rice-growing plains of Piedmont and the sparkling coastline of Liguria lie the brooding Maritime Alps – a small pocket of dramatically sculpted mountains that rise like stony-faced border guards along the frontier of Italy and France. Smaller yet no less majestic than their Alpine cousins to the north, the Maritimes are speckled with mirror-like lakes, foraging ibexes and a hybrid cultural heritage that is as much southern French as northern Italian.

Despite their diminutive size, there's a palpable wilderness feel to be found among these glowering peaks. Get out of the populated valleys and onto the imposing central massif and you'll quickly be projected into a high-altitude Shangri La. Whistling marmots scurry under rocky crags doused in mist above a well-marked network of mountain trails where the sight of another hiker – even in peak season – is about as rare as an empty piazza in Rome. This is Italy at its most serene and serendipitous. Not 20km to the south lie the swanky resort towns of Portofino and San Remo, where martini-supping celebrities wouldn't be seen dead without their expensive handbags and private yachts. Yet up here in the high country that straddles the invisible border between Italy and France, all you need is a map, a decent pair of shoes and enough cheese and ciabatta to keep you going until dinnertime.

The main trailheads lie to the south of the city of Cuneo in a couple of ruggedly attractive regional parks: the **Parco Naturale delle Alpi Marittime** and the **Parco Naturale dell'Alta Valle Pesio e Tamaro**. The Lago di Valscura Circuit (21km) starts in the airy spa of **Terme di Valdieri** and follows an old military road via the Piano del Valasco to an icy lake near the French border. It loops back past the Rifugio Questa before descending via the same route. For a two-day hike try the Marguareis Circuit (35km), which begins in the small ski centre of Limone Piemonte and tracks up across cols and ridges to the **Rifugio Garelli** (☎ 0171 73 80 78; dm €36; ☺ Jun-Sep). Day two involves looping back through a small segment of France to your starting point in Limone. For more information on both hikes check out Lonely Planet's *Hiking in Italy* guide or consult the APT offices in either Terme or Limone.

the 13th-century Castello dei Marchesi atop Saluzzo's old town. It is open Sundays only from 3pm to 7pm. Enquire at the tourist office about guided tours.

Museo Civico di Casa Cavassa MUSEUM
(www.casacavassa.it; Via San Giovanni 5; adult/reduced €5/2.50, admission incl Torre Civica €6; ☺ 10am-1pm & 3-5pm Tue & Wed, to 7pm Thu-Sun) This fine example of a 16th-century noble residence contains a valuable 1499 gold-leaved painting, *Nostra Signora dell Grazie* (Our Lady of Mercy), by Hans Klemer.

🛏 Sleeping & Eating

Albergo Ristorante Persico HOTEL €
(☎ 0175 4 12 13; www.albergopersico.net; Vicolo Mercati 10; s/d €45/67; ⓟ ✳ @ ⓢ) This simple but comfy hotel is tucked just off Piazza Cavour in Saluzzo's new town. Discounted half-board options are also available; the restaurant (closed Monday) has regional menus ranging from €15 to

€25 for nonguests. Free wi-fi is available in the lobby.

Perpöin HOTEL, INTERNATIONAL €
(☎ 0175 4 23 83; www.hotelsaluzzo.com; Via Spielberg 19-27; s €40-70, d €70-100, set menus €12-25; ⓟ) Enjoy hearty home cooking (and fresh-from-the-oven Nutella-filled croissants at breakfast) at this family-run hotel-restaurant in the new town's centre. There is no hotel reception (the building is a maze of corridors), so call ahead to confirm your arrival.

Le Quattro Stagioni MEDITERRANEAN €€
(Via Volta 21; ☺ lunch & dinner Wed-Mon) As the name implies, the food changes with the season at this bodega-cum-restaurant situated in a street of dark porticoes and obscure arcades. The smell of fruity wine through the doorway provides the initial temptation, but just wait till you get inside for crusty pizza and al dente pasta. There's a pleasant *giardino* (garden) attached.

ℹ️ Information

Tourist Office (www.comune.saluzzo.it; Piazza Risorgimento; ⏱ 9am-12.30pm & 3-6.30pm Mon-Sat, 9am-noon & 3-7pm Sun)

ℹ️ Getting There & Away

Buses from Saluzzo run to/from Turin (€3.50, 1½ hours, hourly). Otherwise, take a train to Savigliano (€1.70, 30 minutes, up to six daily), from where there are connections for Turin.

Alba

POP 31,272 / ELEV 172M

In the gastronomic heaven that is Italy, Alba is a leading player courtesy of its black truffles, dark chocolate and wine – including the incomparable Barolo, the Ferrari of reds. Eschewing the modern penchant for junk food, this once-powerful city-state has redirected its energy into showcasing the fine art of *real* cooking, with ingredients plucked from within spear-throwing distance of your restaurant table. All becomes clearer at the annual truffle fair and the equally ecstatic *vendemmia* (grape harvest).

The vine-striped Langhe Hills radiate out from the town like a giant undulating vegetable garden, replete with grapes, hazelnut groves and fine wineries. Exploring Alba's fertile larder on foot or with two wheels is a rare pleasure.

👁️ Sights

A historical heavyweight, Alba enjoyed prosperity that reached its apex in the Middle Ages and lasted until 1628, when Savoy took control. At its peak Alba sported more than 100 towers. A less illustrious four remain.

Cattedrale di San Lorenzo CATHEDRAL
(Piazza Duomo) There's been a cathedral here since the 12th century, though the current terracotta-brick affair is mostly a result of an almost complete neo-Gothic 19th-century makeover. The intricate choir stalls date from 1512.

Museo Civico Archeologico ' Federico Eusebio' MUSEUM
(Via Vittorio Emanuele II; admission €3; ⏱ 3-6pm Tue-Fri, to 7pm Sat, 10am-1pm & 2-7pm Sun) Worth a peek for those keen to sober up between wine-tasting excursions, the city museum was founded in 1887. It has archaeological and natural history sections.

Centro Culturale San Giuseppe CULTURAL CENTRE
(☎ 0173 29 61 63; www.centroculturalesangiuseppe. it; Piazza Vernazza 6) Those who can prise themselves away from all-day wine-tasting or ridiculously elongated lunches, head to this converted church turned cultural center for concerts (choir and chamber music), art expos or a hike up 134 steps to the 36m bell-tower (€1). In the basement, 2nd-century archaeological remains from the vanquished Roman Empire have been uncovered.

👉 Tours

Consorzio Turistico Langhe Monferrato Roero TOURS
(☎ 0173 36 25 62; www.tartufoevino.it; Piazza Risorgimento 2) The Alba-based consortium organises a wide variety of tours and courses unique to the Alba region and its gastronomy. Truffle hunting can be arranged seasonally for white (September to December) or black (May to September) truffles for €80 per person. Alternatively, you can tour a hazelnut farm for €30 year-round, or take part in a four-hour cooking course for €130.

There are various wine-themed excursions, including a guided tour of a Barolo winery for €55. If your appetite is sated, join 'Lens on the Langhe', a tour with a professional photographer (€60 to €90). All tours can be booked up to a day in advance at Alba's tourist office.

🎎 Festivals & Events

Truffle Festival FOOD
🍄 The countryside around Alba contains precious white truffles and they change hands for ridiculous amounts of money at this annual festival, held every weekend in October.

🛏️ Sleeping

⭐ **Hotel Langhe** HOTEL €
(☎ 0173 36 69 33; www.hotellanghe.it; Strada Profonda 21; d/ste €78/160; 🅿 ❄ 🛜) Two kilometres from the city centre but worth every step (even if you're walking it), Hotel Langhe sits on the cusp of the vineyards that push up against Alba's suburbs and manages to ignite feelings of bucolic bliss despite its proximity to the urban core.

The layout is sublime: a wine conservatory, a bright breakfast area and downstairs rooms with French windows that open onto a sunny forecourt.

1. Man examining a large white truffle **2.** Truffle hunter with dog, Alba **3.** Inspecting truffles **4.** Black truffle appetiser

2

Truffles: Food of the Gods

One of the world's most mystical, revered foodstuffs, truffles are Italy's gastronomic gold. Roman emperor Nero called them the 'food of the gods', while composer Rossini hailed them as the 'mushrooms of Mozart'.

Hunting them out is a specialist activity. Truffles – subterranean edible fungi, similar to mushrooms, that colonise the roots of certain tree species – are notoriously hard to find. The most prized variety is the white truffle from the Alba region in Piedmont. Other slightly less aromatic white truffles are found in Tuscany, while black truffles are most prevalent in Umbria and Le Marche. White truffles are harvested from early October to December; black truffles are available from November to March.

The season is crowned in the Umbrian town of Norcia during late February and early March with a boisterous black-truffle festival. Italy's biggest truffle festival is held in Alba every weekend in October, while other notable extravaganzas enliven the Tuscan towns of San Miniato and San Giovanni d'Asso, near Siena, during the second half of November.

4

JOINING A TRUFFLE HUNT

Alba Tourist Office (www.langheroero. it) Organises culinary-biased excursions, including truffle hunts during the season.

I Viaggi del Tartufo (www.viaggidel-tartufo.com) Alba-based tour operator offering truffle-hunt demos in white-truffle heartland.

Assotartufi San Giovanni (www.as-sotartufi.it) Organises hunts year-round in San Giovanni d'Asso, southern Tuscany.

Barbialla Nuova (www.barbiallanuova.it) An *agriturismo* (farm stay accommodation) known for its truffle hunts near the town of San Miniato in Tuscany.

Love Umbria (www.love-umbria.com) Agency offering culinary tours of Umbria, including truffle-hunting weekends around Norcia.

LOCAL KNOWLEDGE

CHERASCO & ITS SNAILS

Within the Langhe's lush wine country, Cherasco, 23km west of Alba, is best known for *lumache* (snails). The town is home to the **Istituto Internazionale di Elicicoltura** (International Institute for Heliciculture; ☑ 0172 48 92 18; www.lumache-elici.com; Via Vittorio Emanuele 55), which provides technical advice for snail breeders (heliciculture is edible-snail breeding). Snails in this neck of the woods are dished up *nudo* (shell-less). They can be pan-fried, roasted, dressed in an artichoke sauce or minced inside ravioli. Piedmont dishes made with snails include *lumache al barbera* (snails simmered in Barbera red wine and ground nuts) and *lumache alla piemontese* (snails stewed with onions, nuts, anchovies and parsley in a tomato sauce).

Traditional trattorias serving such dishes include **Osteria della Rosa Rossa** (☑ 0172 48 81 33; Via San Pietro 31; set menus €30-35; ☺ noon-2pm & 7-11pm Fri-Tue). Reservations are required.

Casa Bona   B&B, APARTMENTS €

(☑ 0173 29 05 35; Corso Nino Bixio 22; r €85; ℗ 🛜) Disregard the unremarkable building. Extraordinary personal service and slick interior furnishings will make Casa Bona a holiday highlight. The collection of several apartments with kitchens, bedrooms and bathrooms are fabulous (you even get your own stove-top espresso maker).

But, the clincher is owner Massimo, who will drop by with homemade cakes and go out of his way to make your stay memorable. No credit cards.

🍴 Eating & Drinking

The key to finding out about Alba's fantastic cuisine is not by counting Michelin stars, but by word of mouth. Here lie some of the best grandma-in-the-kitchen places north of Sicily.

★ Osteria dei Sognatori   OSTERIA €

(Via Macrino 8b; meals €12-20; ☺ noon-2pm & 7-11pm Thu-Tue) Menu? What menu? You get whatever's in the pot at this rustic beneath-the-radar place and it's always delicious. Bank on homemade pasta in a nutty pesto-like sauce and the best breadsticks in Italy. Walls are bedecked with football memorabilia and B&W snaps of bearded wartime partisans.

Vincafé   WINE BAR €

(www.vincafe.com; Via Vittorio Emanuele II 12; set menus €10-25) It's hip, but by no means exclusive. Anyone can sup on a glass of wine here, as long as you can squeeze through the door (it's small and popular) and have the time or expertise to sift through a list of over 350 varieties. If in doubt, choose Barolo.

Downstairs, in a cool vaulted stone cellar, the restaurant serves up huge healthy salads and pasta.

**Locanda Cortiletto
D'Alba**   TRADITIONAL ITALIAN €€

(www.cortilettodalba.com; Corso M Coppino 27; meals €20-30; ☺ noon-midnight) The Cortiletto is one of those secluded ring-the-front-door-bell kind of places where you're welcomed like a family friend and served like a Savoy king. Seating is on an upstairs terrace or in a downstairs wine cellar, and menu items never stray far from the Langhe hinterland. Think *plin* (ravioli) sautéed in sage and butter, cheese fondue or veal cooked in Nebbiolo wine.

It has five lovely colour-themed rooms upstairs that are rented out from €80 a double.

Piazza Duomo-La Piola   GASTRONOMIC €€€

(☑ 0173 44 28 00; www.piazzaduomoalba.it; Piazza Risorgimento 4; meals €20-30, set menus €60-80; ☺ 12.30-2pm & 7.30-10pm Tue-Sat) The best of both worlds are bivouacked in this two-in-one, suit-all-budgets culinary extravaganza in Alba's main square. Downstairs, La Piola sports local blackboard specials, such as *vitello tonnato,* that change daily and allow diners to create their own plates. Upstairs, the theme goes more international in chef Enrico Crippa's Michelin-starred Piazza Duomo, where you can eat creative food beneath colourful wall frescoes painted by contemporary artist Francesco Clemente.

❶ Information

Tourist Office (www.langheroero.it; Piazza Risorgimento 2; ☺ 9am-6.30pm Mon-Fri, 10am-6.30pm Sat & Sun) In the town's historic centre, this office sells walking maps and has internet access.

ℹ️ Getting There & Around

From the **bus station** (Corso Matteotti 10) there are frequent buses to/from Turin (€4.50, 1½ hours, up to 10 daily) and infrequent buses to/from Barolo (€2.20, 25 minutes, two daily) and other surrounding villages.

From Alba's **train station** (Piazza Trento e Trieste) regular trains run to/from Turin (€4.85 via Bra/Asti, 1½ hours, hourly).

The irregularity of buses makes touring the Langhe better by car or bike. For bike hire (from €20 a day) book through the tourist office. Car hire goes from about €35 per day or the tourist office can hook you up with a driver (prices vary).

Barolo Region

Wine lovers rejoice! This tiny, 1800-hectare parcel of undulating land immediately south-west of Alba knocks out what is arguably the finest *vino* in Italy. Unbiased laypersons call it Barolo (after the eponymous village where it is produced), but everyone else hails it as the 'wine of kings' and discusses its velvety truffle-scented flavours with an almost religious reverence.

BAROLO
POP 750

A wine village for centuries, Barolo is no uppity New World viticultural wannabe. The settlement dates from the 13th century and references to wine production have been commonplace since the late 1600s.

◉ Sights & Activities

Castello Falletti   CASTLE
(www.baroloworld.it; Piazza Falletti; ⊙ Enoteca Regionale del Barolo 10am-12.30pm & 3-6.30pm Fri-Wed) Barolo village is lorded over by a castle once owned by the powerful Falletti banking family. Its origins lie in the 10th century, though most of the current structure dates from the 1600s. Today the castle hosts the Museo del Vino a Barolo and, in its cellars, the **Enoteca Regionale del Barolo**, organised and run by the region's 11 wine-growing communities.

The *enoteca* (wine bar) has Barolo wines available for tasting each day, costing €2 for one or €6 for five.

★ Museo del Vino a Barolo   MUSEUM
(www.wimubarolo.it; Castello di Barolo; adult/reduced €8/6; ⊙10.30am-7pm, closed Jan-Feb) This isn't just a museum about wine. It is a rollercoaster jaunt through a medieval castle that tells the story of viticulture through light, film, and the wild and creative imagination of Swiss designer François Confino (who also designed Turin's Cinema museum).

It would be a tour de force in any city, but popping up improbably in the tiny village of Barolo leaves many visitors pinching themselves to check they're not having alcohol-induced hallucinations. Eight euros well spent.

Museo dei Cavatappi   MUSEUM
(Piazza Castello 4; adult/reduced €4/3; ⊙10am-1pm & 2pm-6.30pm Fri-Wed) This is a rather expensive way to view the evolution of corkscrews (decorative, miniature, multipurpose etc) throughout history. There's also a display of old (empty) Barolo bottles and an equally pricey shop.

🛏️ Sleeping & Eating

★ Hotel Barolo   HOTEL **€**
(🖊️0173 5 63 54; www.hotelbarolo.it; Via Lomondo 2; s/d €70/100; 🅿️@❄️) Overlooked by the famous *enoteca*-castle, Hotel Barolo is the ultimate place to sit back on the terrace with a glass of you know what, contemplating the 18th-century Piedmontese architecture that guards its shimmering swimming pool. You don't have to go far for a good meal – the on-site Ristorante Brezza has been serving up truffles and the like for four generations.

The family has been making wine since 1885.

Trattoria della Posta di Barolo   PIEDMONTESE **€€**
(Piazza Municipio 4; €30) Part *enoteca* (wine bar), part B&B, part one of the village's cosiest restaurants, the Posta's cavernous but elegant interior fairly smells of Barolo. If you don't have it in your glass (are you mad?) try it in your risotto or on your meat, both divine.

LA MORRA
POP 2668

Atop a hill surrounded by vines with the Alps as a backdrop, La Morra is quieter than Barolo, though no less beguiling. It could be Tuscany, until you taste the *vino*, which could only be one thing – the wine of kings!

Villa Carita B&B   B&B **€€**
(🖊️0173 50 96 33; www.villacarita.it; Via Roma 105; s/d/ste €90/120/150; 🅿️) When you dream of Italy, the chances are that somewhere in that dream is a room with a view across sun-dappled vineyards. This B&B not only has 'blink to be sure you're not still dreaming'

WINE-TREKKING

The three main villages of the diminutive Barbaresco wine region – Barbaresco, Neive and Treiso – lie several kilometres east, northeast and southeast (respectively) of Alba; however, by combining a short bus ride with a little leg work you can make a wine-tasting tour of all three without ever having to get behind the wheel of a car. Start by catching the hourly Asti-bound bus from outside Alba train station. The bus stops in Neive, one of Piedmont's prettiest villages, studded with baroque palaces and criss-crossed by a web of footpaths. The village proper lies a little uphill from the bus station and is accessed by passing beneath the arch of San Rocco. Despite its obvious Barbaresco bias, Neive is known as the village of 'four wines', meaning there's a quadruple-whammy of tasting opportunities to enjoy. Line up the Barbaresco, Dolcetto, Barbera and Moscato bottles in the Bottega dei Quattro Vini (p223). If you walk south from Neive for 6km on the **Sentiero delle Rocche dei Sette Fratelli**, you'll end up in Treiso, the region's highest village, which is known for its lighter-bodied Barbaresco. Imbibe the flavours at the **Bottega dei Grandi Vini di Treiso** (Piazza Baracco; ☉ 10am-1pm & 2-7pm Thu-Mon). Equally enticing is the shorter 5km trek northwest from Neive over gentle vine-striped hills on the **Sentiero Barbaresco** to Barbaresco village. Producing 45% of the region's wine, tiny Barbaresco has over a dozen *cantine* (wine cellars), two *enoteche* (wine bars/shops) and a Michelin-starred restaurant called **Antinè** (☑ 0173 63 52 94; www.antine.it; Via Torino 34; meals €50; ☉ 11.30am-2.30pm & 6.30-10.30pm Thu-Tue). Stay for the afternoon and you'll find ample opportunity to taste, pair, discuss and get mildly inebriated on the local plonk, though you might want to save enough energy to re-trace your footsteps to Neive afterwards. Alternatively, you can trek directly back to Alba (approximately 5km) along a path that roughly tracks the Tanaro river. Helpful walking maps of the area can be purchased from the tourist office in Alba for €5.

daytime views from every room (and its panoramic terrace), but also romantic night-time views of the village lights.

Tucked below the main building, one room and one suite are hidden in the hillside with their own private terraces.

Ristorante Bovio　　　　　　GASTRONOMIC
(☑ 0173 59 03 03; www.ristorantebovio.it; Via Alba 17; mains €18-20; ☉ 12.30-2pm & 7.30-9:15pm Fri-Tue) Local food alchemists, the Bovio family have recently moved digs from Belvedere to this elegant view-splayed building perched atop La Morra's ancient hill. They still serve the legendary risotto al Barolo, Barbera-cooked steak and a wicked chocolate temptation, all of which do their best to distract you from the vistas, as does the bewildering decision of choosing among more than 1000 wines.

Barbaresco Region

Same grape, different flavour! Only a few kilometres separate Barolo from Barbaresco, the home of the renowned wine of the same name, but a rainier microclimate and fewer ageing requirements have made the latter

into a softer, more delicate red that plays 'queen' to Barolo's 'king'.

BARBARESCO
POP 650

The village of Barbaresco is surrounded by vineyards and characterised by its 30m-high, 11th-century tower, visible from miles around. There are over 40 wineries and two *enotecas* in the area.

Activities

⭐**Enoteca Regionale del Barbaresco**　　　　　　WINE TASTING
(Piazza del Municipio 7; ☉ 9.30am-6pm Thu-Tue) Blasphemous as it may seem, you can worship Barbaresco wines at this intimate *enoteca* housed inside a deconsecrated church, with wines lined up where the altar once stood. It costs €1.50 per individual tasting; six Barbaresco wines are available to try each day.

Sentiero dei Barbaresco　　　　　　HIKING
Various trails surround the village, including this 13km loop through the undulating vineyards. The *enoteca* and info centre have maps.

🛌 Sleeping & Eating

The village has four fine restaurants, one of which – Antinè – has a Michelin star.

Casa Boffa   PENSION €
(☑ 0173 63 51 74; www.boffacarlo.it; Via Torino 9a; s/d/tr €70/85/105; 🛜) In a lovely house in the centre of the village, Boffa offers four modern, minimalist rooms and one suite above a stunning terrace with limitless Langhe valley views. There's a bright breakfast room downstairs and an *enoteca* open for tasting (11am to 6pm daily except Wednesday).

Ristorante Rabayà   TRADITIONAL ITALIAN €€
(☑ 0173 63 52 23; Via Rabayà 9; set menus €30-45; ⊙lunch Fri-Wed, closed mid-Feb–early Mar) 🍴 One in a quartet of Barbaresco restaurants, the Rabayà on the fringe of the village is first rate, with the ambience of dining at a private home. Its antique-furnished dining room has a roaring fire, but when the sun's shining there's no better spot than its terrace set high above the vineyards.

Try Rabayà's signature rabbit in Barbaresco, followed by a platter of local cheese.

NEIVE
POP 2930

Ping-ponged between Alba and Asti during the Middle Ages, Neive is a quieter proposition these days, its hilltop medieval layout earning it a rating as one of Italy's *borghi più belli* (most beautiful towns). Come here to taste the village's four legendary wines – Dolcetto d'Alba, Barbaresco, Moscato and Barbera d'Alba – amid sun-dappled squares and purple wisteria.

🏃 Activities

The tourist office has a list of six different local day hikes, ranging from 12.5km to 20km in distance.

Bottega dei Quattro Vini   WINE TASTING
(www.bottegadei4vini.com; Piazza Italia 2; ⊙vary) 🍴 This two-room shop was set up by the local community to showcase the four DOC wines produced on Neive's hills. Inside you can sample wines by the glass (€1.80 to €4.50), accompanied by cold local specialities (€3.50 to €10).

🛌 Sleeping & Eating

La Contea   PENSION €
(☑ 0173 67 12 6; www.la-contea.it; Piazza Cocito 8; s/d €70/100; 🛜) *Enoteca,* shop, restaurant and small hotel, the family-run La Contea

has been part of Neive's fabric for eons. Chefs pluck fresh herbs from their window boxes to embellish dishes such as rabbit, *ravioli al plin*, and *brasato al Barbaresco*. The rooms are traditional and comfortable.

ℹ️ Getting There & Away

Neive is on the train line between Alba and Asti. Train services were suspended at last visit, but hourly buses to and from Alba (€1.50) run from outside Alba's train station.

Bra & Pollenzo
pop 29,796

Home to some of the best gastronomic alchemy in Italy, Bra is the small, unassuming Piedmontese town where the Slow Food Movement first took root in 1986. The initial manifesto ignited a global crusade against fast food. The backlash worked and Bra happily broadcasts its success. There are no cars and no supermarkets in this refreshingly laid-back town's historic centre, where small, family-run shops (which shut religiously for a 'slowdown' twice a week) are replete with organic sausages, handcrafted chocolates and fresh local farm produce.

👁 Sights

Churches   CHURCH
Bra's sloping main square contains some stately baroque architecture best exemplified in the **Chiesa di San Andrea** (Piazza Caduti), designed by Bernini. The **Santuario della Madonna dei Fiori** (Viale Madonna dei Fiori) mixes baroque with neoclassical and is devoted to the Madonna, who supposedly appeared here in 1336, while the elegantly domed **Chiesa di Santa Chiara** (Via Craveri) is a jewel of Piedmontese Rococo.

Museo Civico Artistico-Storico   MUSEUM
(Palazzo Traversa, Via Parpera 4; ⊙ 3-6pm Tue-Thu, 10am-noon & 3-6pm Sat & Sun 2nd weekend of month) 𝗙𝗥𝗘𝗘 Bra's history began long before its 1986 Slow Food epiphany and is exhibited in the Palazzo Traversa. Displays include Roman artefacts, 18th-century paintings and medieval weaponry.

Università di Scienze Gastronomiche   UNIVERSITY
(University of Gastronomic Sciences; www.unisg.it; Piazza Vittorio Emanuele 9) 🍴 Another creation of Carlo Petrini, founder of the Slow Food Movement, this university, established in the

village of Pollenzo (4km southeast of Bra) in 2004, occupies a former royal palace, and offers three-year courses in gastronomy and food management.

Next door is the **Albergo Dell'Agenzia** (s €155, d €195-240) and the **Banca del Vino** (www.bancadelvino.it; Piazza Vittorio Emanuele II 13), a wine cellar-'library' of Italian wines. Free guided tastings are available by reservation.

🛏 Sleeping & Eating

★ **Albergo Cantine Ascheri**   HOTEL €€
(☑0172 43 03 12; www.ascherihotel.it; Via Piumati 25; s/d €105/140; P🐾@) Built around the Ascheri family's 1880-established winery, incorporating wood, steel mesh and glass, this ultra-contemporary hotel includes a mezzanine library, 27 sun-drenched rooms and a vine-lined terrace overlooking the rooftops. From the lobby you can see straight down to the vats in the cellar (guests get a free tour). It's just one block south of Bra's train station.

Osteria del Boccondivino   OSTERIA €€
(☑0172 42 56 74; www.boccondivinoslow.it; Via Mendicità Istruita 14; set menus €26-28; ⊙noon-2.30pm & 7-10pm Tue-Sat) 🌿 Up on the 1st floor of the recessed courtyard of the Slow Food Movement's headquarters, this homey little eatery lined with wine bottles was the first to be opened by the emerging organisation back in the 1980s. The food is predictably fresh and excellent, and the local Langhe menu changes daily.

❶ Information

Tourist Office (www.comune.bra.cn.it; Via Moffa di Lisio 14; ⊙9am-1pm & 3-6pm Mon-Fri, to noon Sat & Sun Mar-Nov) Has information on both towns and the region.

❶ Getting There & Away

From the train station on Piazza Roma, trains link Bra with Turin (€3.95, 45 minutes), via Carmagnola, while buses connect Bra with Pollenzo (€1, 15 minutes, Monday to Saturday morning).

Asti

POP 75,910 / ELEV 123M

Just 30km apart, Asti and Alba were fierce rivals in medieval times when they faced off against each other as feisty, independent strongholds ruled over by feuding royal families. These days the two towns are united by viticulture rather than divided by factionalism. Asti – by far the bigger town – produces the sparkling white Asti Spumante wine made from white muscat grapes, while Alba concocts Barolo and Barbaresco.

◉ Sights & Activities

Asti's largely pedestrianised centre is attractive, though less intimate than Alba's.

Torre Troyana o Dell'Orologio   LANDMARK
(Piazza Medici; admission free; ⊙10am-1pm & 4-7pm Apr-Sep, 10am-1pm & 3-6pm Sat & Sun Oct) 🆓 During the late 13th century the region became one of Italy's wealthiest, with 150-odd towers springing up in Asti alone. Of the 12 that remain, only this one can be

---

FOOD THAT'S CLOSE TO ITS ROOTS

'Fresh, local and sustainable' has always been a powerful mantra in fertile Piedmont, where small-scale food producers and family restaurant owners were preaching ethical farm-to-table culinary practices long before today's generation of celebrity chefs made it trendy. Not coincidentally, the Slow Food movement was the 1980s brainchild of a group of disenchanted Italian journalists from the Piedmontese town of Bra, who went on to ignite a global crusade against the fast-food industry whose plastic tentacles were threatening to engulf Italy's centuries-old gastronomic heritage. The movement rapidly morphed, inspiring a fresh generation of homegrown back-to-the-landers. Grom, the Slow Food artisan ice-cream chain, was founded in 2003 in Turin by Federico Grom and his wine-making friend Guido Martinetti with the slogan 'come una volta', promising ice cream 'like it once was'. Since then it has sprouted over 60 branches, with outlets in New York City, Tokyo and Paris. Four years later, Alba-born Oscar Farinetti opened his first multi-faceted food market, Eataly in Turin's Lingotto district, promising to spread the love of cooking, gastronomy and alti cibi (high food). He did. Eataly now has branches in Rome, New York City, Chicago and Tokyo. What next? Look out for Turin's artisan baker Andrea Perino, and new ice cream maker Alberto Marchetti. Food around the world is slowly going back to its roots and Piedmont is playing a leading role.

climbed. Troyana is a 38m-tall tower that dates from the 12th century. The clock was added in 1420.

Cattedrale di Santa Maria Assunta
CATHEDRAL

(Piazza Cattedrale) Rising above Asti's historic core is the enormous belfry of this 13th-century Romanesque-Gothic cathedral. Its grandly painted interior merits a peek.

Palazzo Mazzetti
MUSEUM

(www.palazzomazzetti.it; Corso Alfieri 357; ⊙10.30am-6.30pm Tue-Sun) FREE This 18th-century residence of the Mazzetti family houses the civic museum and an information office. Downstairs you'll find Roman artefacts and a scale model of the city. Upstairs there are Italian paintings from the 17th to the 19th centuries.

Enoteca Boero di Boero Mario
WINE TASTING

(Piazza Astesano 17; ⊙9am-noon & 3-8pm daily, closed Mon morning) Roll up your sleeves and get down to Asti's most pleasurable activity – wine tasting. This small, unassuming *enoteca* (wine bar) lines up the glasses morning and afternoon for free tastings administered with expert evaluations from the owner. Don't miss the Barbera d'Asti and the sparkling Moscato.

☆ Festivals & Events

Palio d'Asti
HORSE RACING

Held on the third Sunday of September, this bareback horse race commemorates a victorious battle against Alba during the Middle Ages and draws over a quarter of a million spectators from surrounding villages. (Alba answers with a tongue-in-cheek donkey race on the first Sunday in October).

Douja d'Or
FOOD

This 10-day festival (a *douja* is a terracotta wine jug unique to Asti), held in early September, is complemented by the Delle Sagre food festival on the second Sunday of September.

⌸ Sleeping & Eating

Outside the town centre, there are some lovely spots to sleep in the nearby Monferrato vineyards – ask Asti's tourist offices for a list of properties, including *agriturismi* (farm-stay accommodation).

Fresh food, clothes and all sorts of household paraphernalia are sold at Asti's Wednesday and Saturday morning markets on Piazza Alfieri and Piazza Campo del Palio.

Hotel Palio
HOTEL €€

(☑0141 3 43 71; www.hotelpalio.com; Via Cavour 106; s/d €85/115; P❄@✿) Wedged between the train station and the old town, the Palio's utilitarian exterior belies plusher facilities inside. Reflecting Asti's juxtaposition of old and new, the hotel broadcasts chic, smart rooms with satellite TV and wi-fi, along with an atmospherically decorated inner sanctum. The owners also run the Ristorante Falcon Vecchia, one of Asti's oldest, which opened in 1607.

★ Osteria La Vecchia Carrozza
OSTERIA €

(Via Caducci 41; meals €18-25; ⊙lunch & dinner Mon-Sat) You could be sharing the room with a quartet of nuns or a birthday party of celebrating college graduates at this local spot. Bedecked with white tablecloths and polished wine glasses, it's characterised by plenty of down-to-earth Piedmontese ambience. This being Asti, the food is infused with truffles, Barolo wine and a formidable *agnolotti di astigiana*.

Ristorante Rué
PIEDMONTESE €€

(Via Giuliani 3; meals €25; ⊙closed dinner Sun & lunch Mon) Small restaurant with a plain interior down a narrow backstreet that knocks out some flavorsome regional classics, particularly if you opt for the daily specials – anything from rabbit to spinach pie.

❶ Information

Tourist Office (www.astiturismo.it; Piazza Alfieri 29; ⊙9am-1pm & 2.30-6.30pm) Has details of September's flurry of wine festivals.

❶ Getting There & Away

Asti is on the Turin–Genoa railway line and is served by hourly trains in both directions. Journey time is 30 to 55 minutes to/from Turin (€4.35), and 1¾ hours to/from Genoa (€7.60). To get to Alba you must take a bus.

Monferrato Region

Vineyards fan out around Asti, interspersed with castles and celebrated restaurants. Buses run from Asti to many of the villages; Asti's tourist offices can provide schedules.

A land of literary giants (contemporary academic and novelist Umberto Eco and 18th-century dramatist Vittorio Alfieri hail from here) and yet another classic wine (the intense Barbera del Monferrato), the Monferrato area occupies a fertile triangle of terrain between Asti, Alessandria and its historical capital, Casale Monferrato (population 38,500).

◉ Sights

The tiny hamlet of Moncalvo (population 3320), 15km north of Asti along the S457, makes a perfect photo stop, with a lookout above its castle, where you'll also find an information office (Piazza Antico Castello; ☺ Sat & Sun, hours vary) and wine tasting.

Many producers conduct cellar tours; the Consorzio Operatori Turistici Asti e Monferrato (www.terredasti.it; Piazza Alfieri 29) in Asti has a detailed list of tours and can provide directions.

🛏 Sleeping & Eating

Tenuta del Barone AGRITURISMO €
(☏ 0141 91 01 61; www.tenutadelbarone.com; Via Barone 18, Penango; s/d €50/75; P ⊗) ✈ This family farm dating from 1550 has been converted into a cheery B&B, where you can sleep in the old stables and feast on huge amounts of homemade food (dinner excluding wine €25). Medieval-cooking courses and wine tasting are often available. Penango, 2km from Moncalvo, is signposted from Moncalvo's southern end.

Tenuta Castello di Razzano BOUTIQUE HOTEL €€
(☏ 0141 92 21 24; www.castellodirazzano.it; Frazione Casarello 2, Alfiano Natta; r €115-150; P ✻ @) ✈ You can visit this rambling castle just to tour its working winery and take part in a personal, seated wine tasting (from €6 for five wines and food snacks). But to soak up the antiques-filled castle's atmosphere, you'll want to stay in one of its rooms (the size of small apartments), roam its historic halls or curl up in its book-lined reading room.

The Museo Artevino Razzano (admission €10) bills itself as a museum of art and wine. Entrance is by appointment only. Alfiano Natta is 6km west of Moncalvo.

Locanda del Sant'Uffizio LUXURY HOTEL €€
(☏ 0141 91 62 92; www.relaissantuffizio.com; Strada Sant'Uffizio 1; d/ste €130/220, restaurant lunch/dinner menus €23/55; P ✻ @ ✺) This knockout, restored 17th-century convent (and sleek wellness centre) is set in 4 hectares of vineyards. Many of the convent's rooms – some

with original frescoes – reflect the colour of the flowers after which they are named. Bike rental is free, and a pick-up service from Asti can be arranged.

Sant'Uffizio has a small, elegant restaurant, which is open to nonguests, though you'll need to book ahead. The *locanda* (inn) is 3.3km south of Moncalvo.

Varallo & the Valsesia

Situated 66km northwest of Vercelli in northern Piedmont, Varallo guards the amazing Sacro Monte di Varallo (www.sacromontedivarallo.it; ☺7.30am-6.30pm) FREE, the oldest of Italy's nine Sacri Monti (Sacred Mountains), which were inscribed communally as a Unesco World Heritage Site in 2003. The complex consists of an astounding 45 chapels, with 800 religious statues depicting the Passion of Christ set on a rocky buttress high above Varallo on the slopes of Monte Tre Croci. It was founded in 1491 by a Franciscan friar whose aim was to reproduce a version of Jerusalem as a substitute pilgrimage site for local worshippers. The complex is anchored by a basilica dating from 1614, and the subsequent chapels follow the course of Christ's life told through frescoes and life-size terracotta statues. Some of the scenes are macabre. The Monte is accessed via a winding walking path from Piazza Ferrari in town.

Beyond Varallo, the Sesia river heads spectacularly north to the foot of the Monte Rosa massif. Alpine slopes climb sharply, offering numerous walking, cycling and white-water-rafting possibilities. The valley's last village, Alagna Valsesia, is an ancient Swiss-Walser settlement-turned-ski-resort, which is part of the Monte Rosa Ski Area (p231). It is well known for its off-piste runs. From the town a cable car climbs to Punta Indren (3260m), from where fit walkers or climbers can strike out for the highest *rifugio* (mountain chalet) in Europe, the Capanna Regina Margherita (☏0163 9 10 39; dm €85), perched atop Punta Gnifetti on the Swiss–Italian border at an astounding 4554m. The ascent requires glacier travel, but non-experts can hire a guide through Corpo Guide Alagna (www.guidealagna.com; Piazza Grober 1). Costs are €300 for a four person group for the five-day excursion (June to September).

VALLE D'AOSTA

POP 126,620

While its Dolomite cousins exhibit notable German tendencies, Aosta's nuances are French. The result is a curious hybrid culture known as Valdostan, a historical mix of French Provençal and northern Italian that has infiltrated the food (polenta, spicy sausages and the famous *fontina* cheese) and ensured the survival of an esoteric local language, Franco-Provençal or Valdôtain, a dialect still used by approximately 55% of the population.

Comprising one large glacial valley running east–west, which is bisected by several smaller valleys, the semi-autonomous Val d'Aosta is overlooked by some of Europe's highest peaks, including Mont Blanc (4810m), the Matterhorn (Monte Cervino; 4478m), Monte Rosa (4633m) and Gran Paradiso (4061m). Not surprisingly, the region offers some of the best snow facilities on the continent, with opportunities for skiers to descend hair-raisingly into France and Switzerland over lofty glaciers or traverse them in equally spectacular cable cars.

When the snow melts, the hiking is even more sublime, with access to the 165km Tour du Mont Blanc, Parco Nazionale del Gran Paradiso, and Aosta's two blue-riband, high-altitude trails: the Alte Vie 1 and 2.

Aosta's roots are Roman – the eponymous town guards some significant ruins – while annexation by the House of Savoy in the 11th century led to the building of numerous medieval castles. In the 12th and 13th centuries, German-speaking Walsers from Switzerland migrated into the Val di Gressoney and a handful of villages still preserve the vernacular language and architecture.

Aosta

POP 35,078 / ELEV 565M

Jagged Alpine peaks rise like marble cathedrals above the town of Aosta, a once-important Roman settlement that has sprawled rather untidily across the valley floor since the opening of the Mont Blanc tunnel in the 1960s. Bounced around between Burgundy (France) and Savoy (Italy) in the Middle Ages, the modern town remains bilingual, with a culture that is Valdostan, a factor best reflected in its musical local dialect and simple but hearty cuisine.

⊙ Sights

Chiesa di Sant'Orso   CHURCH

(Via Sant'Orso; ⊙9am-7pm) Aosta's most intriguing church is part of a still-operating monastery. The church dates back to the 10th century but was altered on several occasions, notably in the 15th century, when Giorgio di Challant of the ruling family ordered the original frescoes to be painted over and a new, lower roof installed.

All was not lost: the renovations left the upper levels of the frescoes intact above the new roofline. You can ask the warden to unlock the door, letting you clamber up a narrow flight of wooden steps into the cavity between the original and the 15th-

---

INTO THE VALLEYS

While the rest of the Valle d'Aosta leans culturally towards France, the three valleys of Ayas, Gressoney and Sesia (the latter in Piedmont) are home to an 800-year-old Walser tradition. The German-descended Walsers migrated from Switzerland's Valais region in the 13th century, and their community has survived intact; many of the people who live in this rugged region still speak German (and Tich dialect) as a mother tongue and inhabit traditional Walser wood-slatted houses built on short stilts.

The main nexus in the **Valsesia** is Alagna Valsesia (1191m), a small ski resort at the valley head. To reach it you'll need to get a bus from Turin to Varallo (2¼ hours, two daily), where you can connect with buses to Alagna Valsesia.

To the west the **Valle d'Ayas** harbours its own ski resort, Champoluc (population 500, elevation 1560m), a storybook spot saved from tourism overload by the difficult road twisting from the A5 exit at Verrès around some tortuous hairpin bends. Verrès is on the main Turin–Aosta train line and is the dropping-off point for the Ayas. From here regular buses ply the road to Champoluc (€3, one hour, nine daily).

The main villages in the **Val di Gressoney** are pretty lakeside Gressoney-St-Jean (population 816, elevation 1385m), and **Gressoney-La-Trinité** (population 306, elevation 1637m), a few kilometres north – both Walser strongholds.

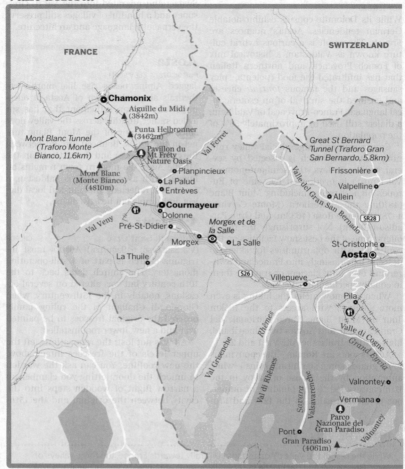

century ceilings to view the well-preserved remnants. The interior and the magnificently carved choir stalls are Gothic, but excavations have unearthed the remains of an earlier church. Beneath the altar, protected by glass, is a 12th-century mosaic, which was only discovered in 1999 when the church's heating system underwent maintenance.

The monastery's beautiful Romanesque cloister, with ornately carved capitals representing biblical scenes, is to the right of the church.

Museo Archeologico
Regionale MUSEUM
(Piazza Roncas 12) FREE Small and free, Aosta's city museum does an excellent job of detailing the city's Roman history. There's a scale model of Aosta's Roman layout plus various antediluvian remains. An otherwise boring coin collection has been laid out chronologically, allowing you to plot the reigns and coin profiles of each Roman emperor.

Roman Ruins ARCHAEOLOGICAL SITE
(⊙ Torre dei Fromage vary depending on exhibition) FREE While Aosta's splayed suburbs can be a little hard on the eye, its 2000-year-old

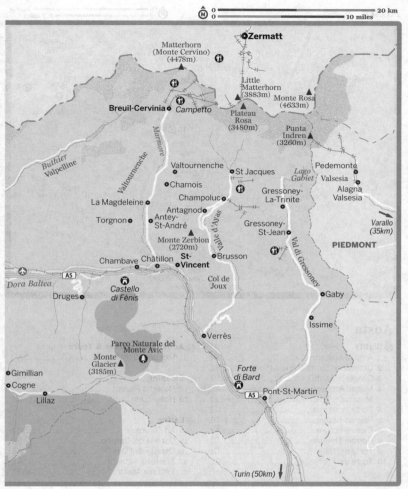

central district is awash with Roman ruins. The grand triumphal arch, **Arco di Augusto** (Piazza Arco di Augusto), has been strung with a crucifix in its centre since medieval times. From the arch, head east across the Buthier river bridge to view the cobbled **Roman bridge** – in use since the 1st century AD.

Backtracking west 300m along Via Sant'Anselmo brings you to **Porta Praetoria**, the main gate to the Roman city. Heading north along Via di Bailliage and down a dust track brings you to Aosta's **Roman theatre** (Via Porta Praetoria; ⏰9am-7pm Sep-Jun, to 8pm Jul & Aug). Part of its 22m-high facade is still intact. In summer, performances are held in the better-preserved lower section. Further north, the forbidding **Torre dei Balivi**, a former prison, marks one corner of the Roman wall and peers down on the smaller **Torre dei Fromage** – named after a family rather than a cheese. It's closed to the public except during temporary art exhibitions – the tourist office has a program. All that remains of the **Roman forum**, another couple of blocks west, beneath Piazza Giovanni XXIII, is a colonnaded underground walkway known as **Criptoportico**.

Aosta

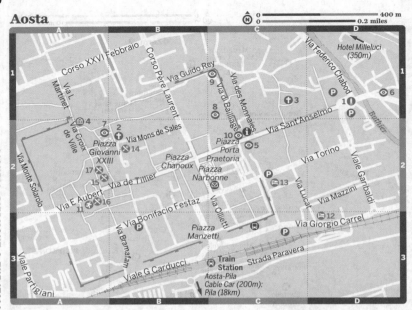

Aosta

◎ Sights

1	Arco di Augusto	D1
2	Cattedrale Santa Maria Assunta	B2
3	Chiesa di Sant'Orso	C1
4	Museo Archeologico Regionale	A2
	Museo del Tesoro	(see 2)
5	Porta Praetoria	C2
6	Roman Bridge	D1
7	Roman Forum	A2
8	Roman Theatre	C1
9	Torre dei Balivi	C1
10	Torre dei Fromage	C2

⊕ Activities, Courses & Tours

| 11 | Meinardi Sport | A2 |

⊟ Sleeping

| 12 | Hotel Le Pageot | D3 |
| 13 | Hotel Turin | C2 |

⊗ Eating

14	Ad Forum	B2
15	Osteria del Calvino	A2
16	Osteria dell'Oca	A2
17	Trattoria Aldente	A2
	Vecchia Aosta	(see 5)

Cattedrale Santa Maria Assunta
CATHEDRAL

(Piazza Giovanni XXIII; ⊗ 6.30am-noon & 3-7pm)
The neoclassical facade of Aosta's **cathedral**
belies the impressive Gothic interior. Inside,
the carved 15th-century walnut-wood choir
stalls are particularly beautiful. Two mosaics
on the floor, dating from the 12th to the 13th
centuries, are also worth studying, as are the
religious art treasures displayed in the lovingly attended **Museo del Tesoro** (admission
€2.10; ⊗9-11.30am & 3-5.30pm Mon-Sat, 8.30-
10am & 10.45-11.30am Sun).

🏃 Activities

Skiing

The nearest skiing to the town of Aosta is
the 1800m-high resort of **Pila** (www.pila.it;
half-/full-day pass €25/34; ⊗mid-Dec–mid-Apr),
accessible by the Aosta–Pila cable car from
town or a zigzagging 18km drive south. Its
70km of runs, served by 13 lifts, form one
of the valley's largest ski areas. Its highest slope, in the shadow of Gran Paradiso,
reaches 2700m and sports an ace snow
park with a half-pipe, jump and slide, and
freestyle area for boarders and freestyle skiers. The ski station is a village of sorts, but

services such as the tourist office, police and medical services are handled from Aosta.

Hiking & Mountain Biking

The lower slopes leading down from Pila into the Dora Baltea valley provide picturesque walks and rides. Mountain bikes can be transported for free on the Aosta–Pila cable car (one way/return €3/5; ☺8am-12.15pm & 2-5pm or 6pm Jun-Aug) and mountain bikers can buy a one-day pass (transport only; €13), allowing unlimited use of the cable car and chairlifts.

Walking clubs can organise treks and provide guides:

Club Alpino Italiano   HIKING
(CAI; www.caivda.it; Corso Battaglione Aosta 81; ☺6.30-8pm Tue, 8-10pm Fri) West of the city centre.

Meinardi Sport   OUTDOOR EQUIPMENT
(Via E Aubert; ☺3-7.30pm Mon, 9am-12.30pm & 3-7.30pm Tue-Sat) A well-stocked sports shop with walking supplies and maps.

Wine & Cheese Tasting

Morgex et de La Salle   WINE TASTING
(www.caveduvinblanc.com; Chemin des Iles 31)
🖉 The Valle d'Aosta is home to vineyards producing sought-after wines that are rarely available outside the region, including those from Europe's highest vineyard, named after the two villages that are strung together by its vines. Aosta's tourist office has a free,

comprehensive booklet in English with information on cellars you can tour and taste. The vineyard is 25km west of Aosta.

Take the A5 then branch off onto SS26.

Valpelline Visitors' Centre   CHEESE TASTING
(www.fontinacoop.it; Frissonière; ☺8.30am-12.30pm & 2.30-6.30pm Mon-Fri, 9am-noon & 3-6pm Sat & Sun) **FREE** In a country where cheese can inspire feuds and debates, if not all-out wars, it's a good idea to get the lowdown on the local curds – in this case *fontina* – before you state an opinion . You can learn more about Aosta's signature cheese, the history, *terroir* (the land) and production of *fontina* and other Aostan cheeses at this museum-cum-visitors centre. You'll need wheels to get here from Aosta. Follow the SR28 for 7km north to Valpelline, turn east towards Ollomont and after 1.5km turn west along a mountain road to Frissonière.

★ Festivals & Events

Fiera di Sant'Orso   WOODCARVING
For over 1000 years the annual winter wood fair has been held on 30 and 31 January around Porta Praetoria, in honour of the town's patron saint, who made wooden shoes for the poor (hence the many wooden shoes you'll see in craft shops around town). Woodcarvers from all over the valley gather to display their works and present an item to the saint at the Chiesa di Sant'Orso.

LIGURIA, PIEDMONT & THE ITALIAN RIVIERA AOSTA

SKIING IN THE VALLE D'AOSTA

The Aosta Valley allows access to three of Europe's most prestigious ski areas – Courmayeur, Breuil-Cervinia and Monte Rosa – plus numerous smaller runs.

Courmayeur (www.courmayeur.com) is dominated by spectacular Mont Blanc vistas and allows access to legendary runs such as the Vallée Blanche. Down below, the pretty Alpine town hosts a chilled, non-glitzy après-ski scene. Breuil-Cervinia (www.cervinia.it), in the shadow of the Matterhorn, is set at a higher altitude and has more reliable late-season snow. There are good intermediate runs and kids' facilities here, but the resort is ugly and rather tacky in places. On the brighter side, you can ski across into Zermatt in Switzerland.

The three valleys to the east are home to the Monte Rosa ski area (www.monterosa-ski.com). Champoluc anchors the Valle d'Ayas, Gressoney lights up the Val d'Gressoney and Alagna Valsesia is the focal point in the Valsesia. These valleys have a less manic resort scene and harbour some quiet Walser villages. The skiing, however, is white-knuckle, with plenty of off-piste and heli-skiing possibilities, particularly in the Valsesia.

The best of the smaller resorts is Pila (p230), easily accessible by cable car from Aosta town, while the pristine Valle di Cogne, in Parco Nazionale del Gran Paradiso, is an idyllic place to enjoy cross-country skiing in relative solitude.

A lift pass covering the entire Valle d'Aosta costs €111/241 for three/seven days; add on access to Zermatt and you'll be parting with €171/285. For up-to-date prices and pass variations see www.skivallee.it.

🛏 Sleeping

Bar the magnificent (if expensive) Hotel Milleluci, you probably won't be tweeting your mates about the wonders of Aosta's hotel scene. But with hiking and skiing on the agenda, you won't be spending much time in your room anyway.

Hotel Turin   HOTEL €

(☎0165 4 45 93; www.hotelturin.it; Via Torino 14; s/d €52/84; ⓟ🅰) A modern, boxy glass-and-steel affair, the Turin is a handy suitcase-drag from the train station and a short distance to carry your gear to the cable car.

Hotel Le Pageot   HOTEL €

(☎0165 3 24 33; www.lepageot.info; Via Giorgio Carrel 31; s/d €70/110; ⓟ🅰) Next to the bus stop, the no-frills, family-run and clean Le Pageot will suit hikers and skiers on a budget even if it doesn't win any architectural or interior design awards.

★ Hotel Milleluci   LUXURY HOTEL €€€

(☎0165 4 42 74; www.hotelmilleluci.com; Loc Porossan 15; r €170-220; ⓟ❄🅰❄) Old wooden skis, traditionally carved wooden shoes, claw-foot baths, indoor and outdoor pools, Jacuzzi, sauna and gym, and sumptuous breakfasts make this large, family-run converted farmhouse seem more like a palace. Set on a hillside its balconied rooms look out to the eponymous 'thousand lights' twinkling from Aosta below.

🍴 Eating

Traditional dishes include *seupa valpellinentze* (a thick soup of cabbage, bread, beef broth and *fontina*) and *carbonada con polenta* (soup traditionally made with chamois, though these days usually beef). Open-air cafe terraces spring up on Piazza Chanoux in summer.

Osteria del Calvino   PIZZERIA €

(Via Croix de Ville 24; meals $18-25; ⊘noon-2.30pm & 7-10.15pm Tue-Sun) This three-floor wine bar, restaurant and pizzeria delivers the goods on all fronts thanks to congenial service and good, simple food.

★ Trattoria Aldente   VALDOSTAN, ITALIAN €€

(☎0165 19 45 96; Via Croce de Ville 34; meals €26-28; ⊘noon-2.30pm & 7-10.30pm) Al dente pasta is guaranteed in this bistro-like trattoria , whose alluring menu of Valdostan and wider Italian dishes is enhanced by an equally alluring interior (the back seating section resembles a cozy cave on snowy days).

Osteria dell'Oca   VALDOSTAN €€

(☎0165 23 14 19; www.ristoranteosteriadelloca.com; Via E Aubert15; meals €25-32; ⊘12.30-2.30pm & 7.30-10.30pm Tue-Sun) *Oca* means 'goose' and there are plenty of them in this quaint perch under an archway off Via E Aubert, both on the menu and reproduced in china around the room. This is Valdostan food heaven. Forget your standard *primi* (first courses) and *secondi* (mains), and dig into veal stew spooned over polenta, or sausages covered in *fontina*.

Dessert cakes are displayed on the bar by the door in case you have the audacity to think about leaving without trying one.

Ad Forum   MODERN ITALIAN €€

(☎0165 4 00 11; Via Mons de Sales 11; meals €22-30; ⊘noon-2.30pm & 7-10.45pm Tue-Sun) Another fantastic Aosta restaurant setting, this time in a stylish garden (and interior rooms) built on part of the remains of the Roman forum. Conceptual dishes such as risotto with strawberries and Spumante, or lasagnetta with pear and blue cheese, come in generous portions, and you get an equally tasty complimentary aperitif while you wait.

The attached *enoteca* has an excellent line-up of wines.

Vecchia Aosta   TRADITIONAL ITALIAN €€

(☎0165 36 11 86; Piazza Porta Praetoria 4; set menus €30-35; ⊘12.15-2.30pm & 7.30-10pm) Maybe it's the French influence, but Aosta restaurants such as the Vecchia score consistently highly when it comes to culinary creativity. Grafted onto a section of the old Roman wall, the Vecchia's setting is sublime and the waiters are highly knowledgable. Take their advice and go for the lamb – it's a real holiday highlight.

🛍 Shopping

Craft shops in town sell traditional Valdostan objects made by certified local artisans. Unique items to look out for include a *grolla* (a large wooden goblet whose name is derived from the word 'grail' in reference to the Holy Grail, which is said to have passed through the village and been copied by local artisans). Another Valdostan tradition is the *coppa dell'amicizia* (friendship cup), a wooden bowl filled with coffee, laced with citrus rind and strong grappa and set alight. The 'cup' has anything from two to 15 mouthpieces, out of which friends take turns drinking as it's passed around.

ℹ Information

Banks abound on and around Piazza Chanoux.

Aosta Tourist Office (www.lovevda.it; Piazza Porta Praetoria 3; ⊗9am-7pm; 🕾) Housed in the old Roman gateway to the city.

Farmacia Centrale (☑0165 26 22 05; Piazza Chanoux 35; ⊗8.30am-12.30pm & 3.30-7.30pm Mon-Fri) Pharmacy.

Hospital (Ospedale Regionale; ☑0165 30 41; Viale Ginevra 3)

Police Station (☑0165 26 21 69; Corso Battaglione Aosta 169) West of the town centre.

Post Office (Piazza Narbonne; ⊗8.15am-6pm Mon-Fri, to 1pm Sat)

ℹ Getting There & Away

Buses operated by **Savda** (www.savda.it) run to Milan (1½ to 3½ hours, two daily), Turin (two hours, up to 10 daily) and Courmayeur (€3.50, one hour, up to eight daily), as well as to French destinations, including Chamonix. Services leave from Aosta's **bus station** (Via Giorgio Carrel), virtually opposite the train station. To get to Breuil-Cervinia, take a Turin-bound bus to Châtillon (30 minutes, eight daily), then a connecting bus (one hour, seven daily) to the resort.

Aosta's train station, on Piazza Manzetti, is served by trains from most parts of Italy. All trains to Turin (€8.40, two to 2½ hours, more than 10 daily) change at Ivrea.

Aosta is on the A5, which connects Turin with the Mont Blanc tunnel and France. Another exit road north of the city leads to the Great St Bernard tunnel and on to Switzerland.

Courmayeur

POP 2923 / ELEV 1224M

Flush up against France and linked by a dramatic cable-car ride to its cross-border cousin in Chamonix, Courmayeur is an activity-oriented Aosta village that has grafted upmarket ski facilities onto an ancient Roman base. Its *pièce de résistance* is lofty Mont Blanc, Western Europe's highest mountain – 4810m of solid rock and ice that rises like an impregnable wall above the narrow valleys of northwestern Italy.

In winter Courmayeur is a fashion parade of skiers bound for the high slopes above town that glisten with plenty of late-season snow. In summer it wears a distinctly different hat: the Società delle Guide Alpine di Courmayeur is bivouacked here and the town is an important staging post on three iconic long-distance hiking trails: the Tour du Mont Blanc (TMB), Alta Via 1 and Alta Via 2.

◎ Sights

★ **Funivie Monte Bianco**　　　CABLE CAR
(www.montebianco.com; return €35, Pavillon du Mt Fréty return €16; ⊗8.30am-12.40pm & 2-4.30pm) Ears pop, eyes widen, mouths gasp. Technically, the Mont Blanc cable car might not be the world's highest, but it's surely the most spectacular. This astounding piece of engineering climbs three-quarters of the way up Western Europe's highest mountain before heading (over multiple glaciers) into France. The cable car departs every 20 minutes from the village of La Palud, 15 minutes from Courmayeur's main square by a free bus service.

First stop is the 2173m-high midstation Pavillon du Mt Fréty, where there's a restaurant and the Mt Fréty Nature Oasis. At the top of the ridge is Punta Helbronner (3462m). Take warm clothes and sunglasses for the blinding snow, and head up early in the morning to avoid the heavy weather that often descends here in the early afternoon. At Punta Helbronner a small, free museum displays crystals found in the mountains.

From Punta Helbronner another cable car (from late May to late September, depending on the weather conditions) takes you on a breathtaking 5km transglacial ride across the Italian border into France to the Aiguille du Midi (3842m), from where the world's highest cable car transports you down to Chamonix. The total journey from Courmayeur to Chamonix costs €50, and includes a bus back through the Mont Blanc tunnel. It's worth every penny.

Pavillon du Mt Fréty
Nature Oasis　　　NATURE RESERVE
🖋 A protected zone of 1200 hectares tucked between glaciers, this nature oasis is accessible from the Pavillon du Mt Fréty at the mid-station of the Funivie Monte Bianco.

You can take a walk through the flower-filled Alpine garden, Giardino Botanico Alpino Saussurea (admission €2; ⊗9.30am-6pm Jul-Sep) in summer (it's blanketed by snow in winter) and enjoy numerous other trails, including the Sentiero Francesco e Giuditta Gatti, where you have a good chance of spotting ibexes, marmots and deer.

Museo Alpino Duca degli Abruzzi　MUSEUM
(Piazza Henry 2; admission €3; ⊗9am-noon & 3.30-6.30pm Thu-Tue, 3.30-6.30pm Wed) Courmayeur guiding association's dramatic history unfolds in this small but inspiring museum that tracks the heroic deeds of erstwhile alpinists.

🏃 Activities

Courmayeur is an outdoor-activity heaven. Few come here to idle.

Società delle Guide Alpine di Courmayeur
MOUNTAINEERING

(www.guidecourmayeur.com; Strada del Villair) Founded in 1859, this is Italy's oldest guiding association. In winter its guides lead adventure seekers off-piste, up frozen waterfalls and on heli-skiing expeditions. In summer, rock climbing, canyoning, canoeing, kayaking and hiking are among its many outdoor activities.

Terme di Pré-Saint-Didier
SPA

(☑ 0165 86 72 72; www.termedipre.it; Allée des Thermes; admission €34-49; ☺ 9.30am-9pm Mon-Thu, 8.30am-11pm Fri & Sat, to 9pm Sun) Bubbling a natural 37°C from the mountains' depths, the thermal water at Pré-Saint-Didier has been a source of therapeutic treatments since the bath-loving Romans stopped past. A spa opened in 1838, though the present renovated building dates from the 1920s. Admission includes use of a bathrobe, towel and slippers, plus freshly squeezed juices, fruit and herbal teas.

In addition to saunas, whirlpools and waterfalls, there's an indoor-outdoor thermal pool. It's lit by candles and torches on Saturday nights, when it is spectacular amid the snow and stars. Before leaving the spa, head 50-odd metres beyond the car park in the opposite direction to the village, where a little Roman bridge arcs over the trout-filled river.

Skiing

Courmayeur offers some extraordinary skiing in the spectacular shadow of Mont Blanc. The two main ski areas – the Plan Checrouit and Pré de Pascal – are interlinked by various runs (100km worth) and a network of chairlifts. Three lifts leave from the valley floor: one from Courmayeur itself, one from the village of Dolonne and one from nearby Val Veny. They are run by Funivie Courmayeur Mont Blanc (www.courmayeur-montblanc.com; Strada Regionale 47). Queues are rarely an issue.

Skiing lessons starting at around €40 an hour are available from the Scuola di Sci Monte Bianco (www.scuolascimontebianco.com; Strada Regionale 51), founded in 1922. It also offers cross-country and telemark lessons for similar rates.

Vallée Blanche
SKIING

This is an exhilarating off-piste descent from Punta Helbronner across the Mer de Glace glacier into Chamonix, France. The route itself is not difficult (anyone of intermediate ability can do it), but an experienced guide is essential to steer you safely round the hidden crevasses.

All up, the 24km Vallée Blanche takes around four to five hours, allowing time to stop and take in the view.

Toula Glacier
SKIING

Only highly experienced, hard-core skiers need apply for this terrifying descent, which also takes off from Punta Helbronner and drops for six sheer kilometres to La Palud. A guide is essential. It's usually easy to join in with a guide-led group.

Hiking

In July and August Courmayeur's cable cars whisk walkers and mountain bikers up into the mountains; transporting a bike is free.

Tour du Mont Blanc
WALKING TRAIL

For many walkers (some 30,000 each summer), Courmayeur's trophy hike is the Tour du Mont Blanc (TMB). This 169km trek cuts across Italy, France and Switzerland, stopping at nine villages en route. Snow makes it impassable for much of the year. The average duration is anything from one week to 12 days; smaller sections are also possible.

It's possible to undertake the hike without a guide but, if you're unfamiliar with the area, hooking up with a local guide is a good idea as the route traverses glacial landscapes. Easy day hikes will take you along the TMB as far as the Rifugio Maison Vieille (one hour, 50 minutes) and Rifugio Bertone (two hours). Follow the yellow signposts from the Piazzale Monte Bianco in the centre of Courmayeur.

Mountain Biking

Mountain bikes can be hired for around €15 per day at Noleggio Sci e Mountain Bike (Stada Regionale 17).

🛏 Sleeping

Ask the tourist office for a list of *rifugi* (mountain huts), usually open from late June to mid-September.

Hotel Bouton d'Or
HOTEL €€

(☑ 0165 84 67 29; www.hotelboutondor.com; Strada Statale 26/10; s €80-95, d €130-175; P❄@☎👪) Is it a dream? You open your eyes and there before you is the imposing hulk of Mont Blanc. There can't be many hotels where the view is this good, the rooms this clean or the service this attentive.

To top it all, Bouton d'Or is in the centre of Courmayeur and sports a sauna, breakfast, a shuttle to the cable car and a lounge full of interesting Alpine paraphernalia.

Hotel Triolet
HOTEL €€

(☎0165 84 68 22; www.hoteltriolet.com; Strada Regionale 63; s €80-100, d €130-160; P ✳ 🛜 🌊) Triolet is a tad more elegant than your average ski digs. It's smaller, too, with only 20 rooms, allowing service to remain personal as well as affable. Aside from the usual ticklist, there's a pleasant spa (Jacuzzi, steam room, sauna), ski lockers and a vista-laden breakfast room.

Mont Blanc Hotel Village
LUXURY HOTEL €€€

(☎0165 86 41 11; www.hotelmontblanc.it; La Croisette 36; s/d €290/320; P ✳ @ 🌊) On the hillside of La Salle, 10km east of Courmayeur, this haven of luxury has beautiful stone-and-wood rooms, many with enormous balconies with views across the valley. A series of cave-like nooks conceals spa treatment rooms and steaming saunas. Half-board is available; meals are provided in the hotel's standard restaurant.

To truly dine in style, guests and non-guests can head to the hotel's second, gastronomic restaurant.

✗ Eating

Quality food shops and restaurants line Via Roma.

Petit Bistrot
INTERNATIONAL €

(Via Marconi 6; crepes €5-7) A crêpe window lures you at this cafe-cum-restaurant where Valdostan classics (eg *talgiere di lardo* – sliced salami) mingle with more cross-over snacks (hamburgers with rocket and Parmesan).

Pan Per Focaccia
SNACKS €

(Via dei Giardini 2a; foccaccia €2-5) Tucked down a side street is this cosy mountain nook offering cheap crêpes and fresh-from-the-oven focaccia, which you can enjoy perched on a wooden stool inside.

La Terrazza
INTERNATIONAL €€€

(Via Circonvalazione 73; meals €35-45; ⊙ lunch & dinner) This lively, central bar-restaurant-pizzeria has the full gamut of pizzas, steaks and après-ski nosh. True to the local spirit there are also plenty of Valdostan dishes, including polenta, spicy sausage, fondue and pasta with the celebrated *fontina* cheese.

ⓘ Information

Ambulance (☎0165 84 46 84)

Centro Traumatologico (☎0165 84 46 84; Strada dei Volpi 3) Medical clinic. The nearest hospital is in Aosta.

Tourist Office (www.courmayeur.net; Piazzale Monte Bianco 13; ⊙9am-12.30pm & 3-6.30pm)

ⓘ Getting There & Away

Three trains a day from Aosta terminate at Pré-St-Didier, with bus connections (20 to 30 minutes, eight to 10 daily) to **Courmayeur bus station** (Piazzale Monte Bianco), outside the tourist office. There are up to eight direct Aosta–Courmayeur buses daily (€3.50, one hour), and long-haul buses serve Milan (€15.50, 4½ hours, three to five daily) and Turin (€9, 3½ to 4½ hours, two to four daily).

Immediately north of Courmayeur, the 11.6km Mont Blanc tunnel leads to Chamonix (France). At the Italian entrance, a plaque commemorates Pierlucio Tinazzi, a security employee who died while saving at least a dozen lives during the 1999 disaster when a freight truck caught fire in the tunnel.

Parco Nazionale del Gran Paradiso

Italy's oldest national park is also one of its most diverse – and aptly named. Gran Paradiso, formed in 1922 after Vittorio Emanuele II gave his hunting reserve to the state (ostensibly to protect the endangered ibex), is a veritable 'grand paradise'. What makes it special is a tangible wilderness feel (rare in Italy). The park's early establishment preceded the rise of the modern ski resort; as a result, the area has (so far) resisted the lucrative lure of the tourist trade with all its chairlifts, dodgy architecture and après-ski clubs.

Gran Paradiso incorporates the valleys around the eponymous 4061m peak, three of which are in the Valle d'Aosta: the Valsavarenche, Val di Rhêmes and the beautiful Valle di Cogne. On the Piedmont side of the mountain, the park includes the valleys of Soana and Orco.

The main stepping stone into the park is tranquil **Cogne**, a refreshing antidote to overdeveloped Breuil-Cervinia on the opposite side of the Valle d'Aosta. Aside from its plethora of outdoor opportunities, Cogne is known for its lace-making; you can buy the local fabrics at a charming craft and antique shop, **Le Marché Aux Puces** (Rue Grand Paradis 4; ⊙ closed Wed).

◉ Sights

Giardino Alpino Paradisia   GARDEN
(adult/reduced €3/1.50; ⊙10am-5.30pm Jun–mid-Sep, to 6.30pm Jul & Aug) ✐ The park's amazing biodiversity, including butterflies and Alpine flora, can be seen here in summer, in the tiny hamlet of Valnontey, 3km south of Cogne. Guided nature walks from July to September are organised by the **Associazione Guide della Natura** (www.guidenaturacogne.net; Piazza Chanoux 36; ⊙9am-noon Mon, Wed & Sat).

🏃 Activities

Gran Paradiso is one of Italy's best walking areas, with over 700km of trails linked by a network of *rifugi*. The tourist office has free winter and summer trail maps.

Skiing

Despite a (welcome) dearth of downhill-ski facilities, 80km of well-marked **cross-country skiing trails** (admission per day €5) line the unspoilt Valle di Cogne. Try trail 23 up to Valnontey and **Vermiana**, or head east to Lillaz. Alas, there are still 9km of downhill slopes. A one-day ski pass covering the use of Cogne's single cable car, chairlift and drag lift costs €23. Skiing lessons are offered by the **Società Guide Alpine di Cogne** (www.guidealpinecogne.it; Piazza Chanoux 1). If you want something more esoteric, they also offer **ice-climbing** expeditions on the Lillaz waterfall.

Walking

Easy walks around Cogne include the 3km stroll (wheelchair accessible) to the village of Lillaz on trail 23, where there is a geological park and a waterfall that drops 150m in three stages. Trails 22 and 23 will also get you to the village of Valnontey, where you can continue up the valley to the hamlet of Vermiana (1½ hours one way). Trail 8 from Cogne leads to another waterfall (Pila) via the village of Gimillian.

A moderately strenuous hike from Valnontey is to the **Rifugio Sella** (☎0165 74310; www.rifugiosella.com; dm €17), a former hunting lodge of King Vittorio Emanuele II. From the town bridge, follow the Alta Via 2 uphill for two to 2½ hours. More adventurous hikers can continue along the exhilarating Sella–Herbetet Traverse (15km), a seven-hour loop that will drop you back in Valnontey. You'll need a head for heights and a good map.

Climbing

The main point of departure for the Gran Paradiso peak is Pont in the Valsavarenche. Technically it's no Mont Blanc and can be completed in a day, but you'll need a guide (a two-day ascent for two people starts at €500). Contact the Società Guide Alpine di Cogne (p236).

Horse Riding

Horse riding (per hr €25) through the mountain meadows and 45-minute **horse-and-**

WORTH A TRIP

FORTE DI BARD

Shakespearean in stature and gazing down over a poetry-inspiring valley, the Bard of Aosta is a large, imposing fortress set on a rocky escarpment at the jaws of the Valle d'Aosta. Plucky Italian soldiers, outnumbered 100 to one, fought off Napoleon's army from its lofty battlements for two weeks in 1800. The French emperor was so piqued he razed the fortress to the ground. The contemporary **Forte di Bard** (www.fortedibard. it; ⊙10am-6pm Tue-Fri, to 7pm Sat & Sun) **FREE** thus dates from the 1830s and was completely restored in 2006. Replete with history and punctuated with epic views, it makes a great day out from the standard Aostan skiing or hiking trips (it's 70 minutes from Aosta by regular bus). Entrance to the main fort is free. To reach the inner sanctum, perched high above the valley, ride up a series of super-modern elevators. For no cost you can admire the seductive Alpine views and gain access to the **Valley culture rooms**, which offer interesting nuggets of information on Aosta's history and culture. To enjoy a full day out it is worth investing in a ticket for the **Museo delle Alpi** (adult/reduced €8/6), a clever, interactive museum that takes you on an educational journey across the entire Alps. The standout feature is the *Flight of the Eagle* cinema section, which simulates the feeling of flying over valleys, villages, lakes and snow-capped peaks. Also worth a visit are the fort's **prisons** (adult/reduced €4/2), which were still in use right up until the end of WW2. There's a handy on-site cafe and restaurant, and various shops scattered around the fortifications. Music concerts are held here in the summer.

carriage rides (per carriage of up to 4 people €40) are run by Le Traîneau Equestrain Tourism Centre (☑ 333 3147248; www.letraine-au.too.it; ⊙ 10am-12:30pm, 2-7pm) in Valnontey.

🛏 Sleeping & Eating

Wilderness camping is forbidden in the park, but there are 11 *rifugi*.

Hotel Sant'Orso   HOTEL €

(☑ 0165 7 48 21; www.cognevacanza.com; Via Bourgeois 2; s/d €73/84, s/d half-board €109/121; ⊙ spring & autumn closures vary; ℗⛱🍴) Cogne personified (ie, tranquil, courteous and understated), the Sant'Orso is nonetheless equipped with plenty of hidden extras. Check out the restaurant, small cinema, sauna, kids room and terrace. And you can start your cross-country skiing pretty much from the front door. The owners also run the Hotel du Gran Paradis nearby.

Camping Lo Stambecco   CAMPGROUND €

(☑ 0165 7 41 52; www.campinglostambecco.com; camping per person/tent/car €7/5/3; ⊙ May-Sep; ℗) Pitch up under the pine trees in the heart of the park at this well-run and friendly site.

Hotel Ristorante
Petit Dahu   TRADITIONAL ITALIAN €€

(☑ 0165 7 41 46; www.hotelpetitdahu.com; s/d half-board €74/146, menus €35; ⊙ closed May & Oct; ℗) Straddling two traditional stone-and-wood buildings, this friendly, family-run spot has a wonderful restaurant (also open to nonguests; advance bookings essential) preparing rustic mountain cooking using wild Alpine herbs. It also has accommodation (singles €36 €50, doubles €72-€100).

★ Hotel Bellevue   LUXURY HOTEL €€€

(☑ 0165 7 48 25; www.hotelbellevue.it; Rue Grand Paradis 22; s/d €220/240, 2-person chalets €250-320; ⊙ mid-Dec–mid-Oct; ℗⛱) This green-shuttered mountain hideaway evokes its 1920s origins with romantic canopied timber 'cabin beds' and claw-foot baths. There are open fireplaces in some rooms. Afternoon tea is included in the price, as is use of the health spa, and you can also rent mountain bikes and snowshoes.

Its four restaurants include a Michelin-starred gourmet affair (closed Wednesday), a cheese restaurant (closed Tuesday) with cheese from the family's own cellar, a lunch-time terrace restaurant and a brasserie (closed Monday) on the village's main square, a few moments' stroll away.

ℹ Information

Consorzio Gran Paradiso Natura (www.granparadisonatura.it; Loc Trépont 91)
Tourist Office (www.cogne.org; Piazza Chanoux 36; ⊙ 9am-12.30pm & 2.30-5.30pm Mon-Sat).

ℹ Getting There & Around

Up to seven buses run daily to/from Cogne and Aosta (50 minutes). Cogne can also be reached by cable car from Pila.

Valley buses (up to 10 daily) link Cogne with Valnontey (€0.90, five minutes) and Lillaz (€0.90, five minutes).

Valtournenche

One of Europe's most dramatic mountains, the Matterhorn (4478m) frames the head of Valtournenche. Byron once stood here and marvelled at 'Europe's noble rock'. Today he'd also see one of the Alps' ugliest ski resorts, Breuil-Cervinia. However, Cervinia's ski facilities are second to none; you can hit the snow year-round up here and even cross into Zermatt, Switzerland.

🏃 Activities

Plateau Rosa (3480m) and the Little Matterhorn (3883m) in the Breuil-Cervinia ski area offer some of Europe's highest skiing, while the Campetto area has introduced the Valle d'Aosta to night skiing. A couple of dozen cable cars, four of which originate in Breuil-Cervinia, serve 200km of downhill pistes. A one-day ski pass covering Breuil-Cervinia and Valtournenche costs €36.

Contact Breuil-Cervinia's Scuola di Sci del Breuil Cervinia (www.scuolascibreuil.com) or Scuola Sci del Cervino (www.scuolacervino.com) for skiing and snowboarding lessons, and its mountain-guide association Società Guide del Cervino (www.guidedelcervino.com; Via J Antoine Carrel 20) to make the most of the wild off-piste opportunities.

Between July and September several cable cars and lifts to Plateau Rosa continue to operate, allowing year-round skiing on the Swiss side of the mountain. A one-day international ski pass costs €50.

ℹ Getting There & Away

Savda (☑ 0165 36 12 44) operates buses from Breuil-Cervinia to Châtillon (one hour, seven daily), from where there are connecting buses to/from Aosta.

Milan & the Lakes

Best Places to Eat

➡ Trattoria del Nuovo Macello (p254)

➡ Gatto Nero (p275)

➡ Osteria Le Servite (p287)

➡ Osteria al Bianchi (p293)

➡ Dal Pescatore (p297)

Best Places to Stay

➡ Maison Borella (p252)

➡ Hotel Pironi (p266)

➡ Hotel Silvio (p274)

➡ Residence Filanda (p286)

➡ Armellino (p297)

Why Go?

Sprawling between the Alps and the Po valley, Lombardy (Lombardia) has a varied landscape: industrious cities, medieval hill towns and lakeside resorts are interspersed with powdered slopes, lemon groves, vineyards and rice paddies.

Dominating is Lombardy's capital and Italy's economic powerhouse, Milan. Home to the nation's stock exchange, one of Europe's biggest trade-fair grounds and an international fashion hub, it is Italy's second-largest metropolis.

Sparkling, glacial lakes are strung along the north of the region like a glittering necklace. Wedding-cake villas set in tiered gardens adorn elegant towns and coquettish villages along the shores. Further north still, the Valtellina and the Orobie Alps stretch into dramatic national parks, which hide sharp-sided valleys and wildly wooded mountain slopes.

South of the main chain of lakes, cities steeped in history include medieval Bergamo, the age-old violin-making centre of Cremona and the Renaissance city of Mantua.

When to Go
Milan

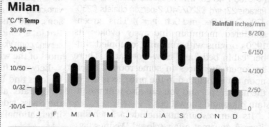

May & Jun Spring flowers, mild weather and concerts in Cremona herald the start of summer.

Sep As many as 350 vessels turn out for the Centomiglia, Lago di Garda's prestigious regatta.

Dec Winter warmers include the Feast of St Ambrogio and opera at La Scala.

Expo 2015

In 1851 the world's first Expo took place in London, exhibiting the 'Works of Industry of All Nations'. It featured 25 countries and from the profits emerged the Victoria & Albert Museum, the Science Museum and the Natural History Museum. With 128 countries already signed up, Milan is looking forward to hosting one of the biggest Expos yet, starting on 1 May 2015 (www.expo2015.org). Costing a cool €13.5 billion; the six-month shindig is estimated, by Bocconi University, to achieve €25 billion in investment and create more than 200,000 jobs. It's a bold vision and one that the precarious Italian government is counting on to lift the country out of its economic doldrums. If you plan on visiting the city during the event (May to October 2015); book everything well in advance as there'll be 20 million other people looking to do the same.

SEASON MATTERS

Around the lakes prices can fluctuate considerably depending on the season, with Easter, summer and the Christmas/New Year period being the typical peak tourist times. Indeed, many lakeside hotels only open from Easter to October, going into hibernation once the colder weather sets in. In Verona the opera season runs from June to September and puts pressure on prices and availability.

Milan is a case of its own, with price variations linked to the trade-fair and events calendar – the bigger the fair, the higher the price and the greater the degree of difficulty in locating a room. During the Salone Internazionale del Mobile (April) prices can increase by as much as 200%, with hotel rooms evaporating in a 100km radius of the city. August, on the other hand, is low season for Milan as everyone escapes to the lakes for their annual holidays.

Getting Away From It All

➡ Get some green with a picnic and sunbathing in Parco Sempione (p247).

➡ Lose yourself in a crowd of determined bargain hunters at Luino's weekly flea market (p267).

➡ Tour lakes under your own steam with kayaks from Bellagio Water Sport (p274).

➡ Find Lorenzo Lotto with a church crawl around some of Bergamo's finest masterpieces (p292).

➡ Research rock art along the Unesco heritage protected valley, Valle Camonica (p277).

➡ Barge and cycle down the Mincio River on a week-long tour with Avemaria (p295).

DON'T MISS

Reserve ahead for fascinating behind-the-scenes tours of La Scala's costume and craft **workshops** (Map p244; ☎390 243353521; www.teatroallascala.org; Via Bergognone 34; €5; Ⓜ Porto Genova).

Top Tours & Courses

➡ Bike & the City (p251) Get to know Milan with a local

➡ Bellagio Cooking Classes (p274) Learn to cook with local housewives

➡ Visit Mantua (p297) Take a personal tour of Renaissance Mantua

Advance Planning

➡ **3 months** Book tickets for operas in Milan and Verona

➡ **2 months** Buy tickets for *The Last Supper* and Serie A football matches

➡ **1 month** Plan activities and book guides and courses

➡ **1 week** Check out events in *Corriere della Sera*

Resources

➡ **Cenacolo Vinciano** (www.cenacolovinciano.org) Booking for *The Last Supper*

➡ **Milan is Tourism** (www.turismo.milano.it)

➡ **Navigazione Laghi** (☎800 55 18 01; www.navigazionelaghi.it) For ferries on Lago Maggiore, Como and Garda

MILAN & THE LAKES

Milan & the Lakes Highlights

1 Admiring Milanese inventiveness in the **Quadrilatero d'Oro** (p259) and da Vinci's ground-breaking mural, *The Last Supper* (p247).

2 Strolling Lago Maggiore's most spectacular island gardens **Isola Bella** (p265) and **Isole di Brissago** (p266).

3 Taking the slow boat to Switzerland from Cannobio to **Locarno** (p266).

4 Touring Lago di Como in your own **cigarette boat** (p274) or **kayak** (p274).

5 Staying on after the crowds have gone and having timeless **Bellagio** all to yourself (p273).

6 Catching a boat or catamaran, or windsurfing beneath snowcapped peaks in **Riva del Garda** (p283).

7 Being among the first to visit Cremona's **Museo del Violino** (p298) and Bergamo's renovated **Accademia Carrara** (p289).

8 Marvelling at frescoes of Olympian gods and Renaissance dukes in Mantua's **Palazzo Ducale** (p294) and **Palazzo Te** (p295).

9 Dining on Lombardy's most refined cooking at the award-winning Canneto sull'Oglio restaurant **Dal Pescatore** (p297).

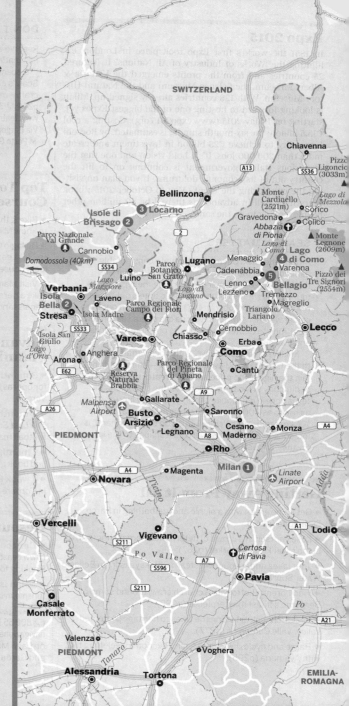

MILAN

POP 1.3 MILLION

Milan is Italy's city of the future, a fast-paced metropolis with New World qualities: ambition, aspiration and a highly individualistic streak. In Milan appearances really do matter and materialism requires no apology. The Milanese love beautiful things, luxurious things, and it is for that reason perhaps that Italian fashion and design maintain their esteemed global position.

But like the models that stalk the catwalks, many consider Milan to be vain, distant and dull. And it is true that the city makes little effort to seduce visitors. But this superficial lack of charm disguises a city of ancient roots and many treasures, that, unlike in the rest of Italy, you'll often get to experience without the queues. So while the Milanese may not have time to always play nice, jump in and join them in their intoxicating round of pursuits, be that precision shopping, browsing edgy contemporary galleries or loading up a plate with local delicacies while downing an expertly mixed negroni cocktail.

History

Celtic tribes settled along the Po river in the 7th century BC, and the area encompassing modern-day Milan has remained inhabited since. In AD 313, Emperor Constantine made his momentous edict granting Christians freedom of worship here. The city had already replaced Rome as the capital of the empire in 286, a role it kept until 402.

A *comune* (town council) was formed by all social classes in the 11th century, and, from the mid-13th century, government passed to a succession of dynasties – the Torrianis, Viscontis and, finally, the Sforzas. It fell under Spanish rule in 1525 and Austrian rule in 1713. Milan became part of the nascent Kingdom of Italy in 1860.

Benito Mussolini, one-time editor of the socialist newspaper *Avanti!*, founded the Fascist Party in Milan in 1919. He was eventually strung up here by partisans after he sought to escape to Switzerland in 1945. Mussolini joined Germany in WWII in 1940. By early 1945, Allied bombings had destroyed much of central Milan.

At the vanguard of two 20th-century economic booms, Milan cemented its role as Italy's financial and industrial capital. Immigrants poured in from the south and were later joined by others from China, Africa, Latin America, India and Eastern Europe, making for one of the least homogenous cities in Italy. Culturally, the city was the centre of early Italian film production, and in the 1980s and '90s it ruled the world as the capital of design innovation and production. Milan's self-made big shot and media mogul, Silvio Berlusconi, made the move into politics in the 1990s and was then elected prime minister three more times – scandal and economic armageddon finally forced him from office in 2011.

The city's next big date with destiny is Expo 2015, when Milan is hoping to wow 20 million visitors with a world exposition based on the theme 'Feeding the Planet, Energy for Life'.

⊙ Sights

Milan's runway-flat terrain and monumental buildings are defined by concentric ring roads that trace the path of the city's original defensive walls. Although very little remains

---

ADOPT A SPIRE

The building of Milan's cathedral was such an epic feat that it necessitated the creation of a factory responsible for all operational activities and construction. That factory is the Fabbrica del Duomo, Italy's oldest company. It has overseen the work of the Duomo's construction from 1387 until January 1965 (the inauguration of the last gate).

Today it continues the enormous task of maintaining the cathedral. This is no mean feat when 5 million people (and 40% of all visitors to Milan) pass through the bronze doors each year, not to mention new austerity measures that slashed 30% off Italy's culture budget.

But now you, too, can chip in with the Fabbrica's latest inspired idea, **Adopt a Spire** (www.getyourspire.com). This crowd-sourced campaign aims to raise some €25 million in order to restore 134 of the cathedral's fabulous spires. Major donors (contributing €100,000 or more) will even have their names engraved on the spires, but you can donate as little as €10.

of the walls, ancient *porta* (gates) act as clear compass points. Almost everything you want to see, do or buy is contained within these city gates.

★ Duomo
CATHEDRAL

(Map p250; www.duomomilano.it; Piazza del Duomo; adult/reduced Battistero di San Giovanni €4/2, terraces stairs €7/3.50, terraces lift €12/6, treasury €2; ⏰ 7am-6.45pm, roof terraces 9am-6pm, baptistry 9.30am-5pm, treasury 9.30am-5pm Mon-Sat; Ⓜ Duomo) A vision in pink Candoglia marble, Milan's cathedral aptly reflects the city's creativity and ambition. Its pearly-white facade, adorned with 135 spires and 3200 statues, rises like the filigree of a fairy-tale tiara, wowing the crowds with extravagant detail. The vast interior is no less impressive, with the largest stained-glass windows in Christendom, while below is the early Christian baptistry and crypt, where the remains of the saintly Carlo Borromeo are on display in a rock crystal casket.

Begun by Giangaleazzo Visconti in 1387, the cathedral's design was originally considered unfeasible. Canals had to be dug to transport the vast quantities of marble to the centre of the city and new technologies were invented to cater for the never-before-attempted scale. There was also that small matter of style. The Gothic lines went out of fashion and were considered 'too French', so it took on several looks as the years, then centuries, dragged on. Its slow construction became the byword for an impossible task (*fabrica del Dom* in the Milanese dialect). Indeed, much of its ornament is 19th-century neo-Gothic, with the final touches only applied in the 1960s. Crowning it all is a gilded copper statue of the Madonnina (Little Madonna), the city's traditional protector.

The most spectacular view, though, is through the innumerable marble spires and pinnacles that adorn the rooftop. On a clear day you can see the Alps.

★ Museo del Novecento
ART GALLERY

(Map p250; ☑ 02 8844 4072; www.museodelnovecento.org; Piazza del Duomo 12; adult/reduced €5/3; ⏰ 9.30am-7.30pm Tue-Sun, 2.30-7.30pm Mon; Ⓜ Duomo) Overlooking the Piazza del Duomo, with fabulous views of the cathedral, is Mussolini's Arengario (Map p250; Ⓜ Duomo), from where he would harangue huge crowds in the glory days of his regime. Now it houses Milan's museum of 20th-century art. Built around a futuristic spiral

ramp (an ode to the Guggenheim), the lower floors are cramped, but the heady collection, which includes the likes of Boccioni, Campigli, De Chirico and Marinetti, more than distracts.

Afterwards, dine in the 3rd-floor bistro (Map p250; ☑ 02 7209 3814; www.giacomoarengario.com; Via Guglielmo Marconi 1; meals €30-40; ⏰ noon-midnight; Ⓜ Duomo) overlooking the Duomo.

Palazzo Reale
MUSEUM, PALACE

(Map p250; www.comune.milano.it/palazzoreale; Piazza del Duomo 12; exhibitions €5-12, Museo della Reggia free; ⏰ exhibitions 2.30-7.30pm Mon, 9.30am-7.30pm Tue, Wed, Fri & Sun, 9.30am-10.30pm Thu & Sat, museo 9.30am-5.30pm Tue-Sun; Ⓜ Duomo) Empress Maria Theresa's favourite architect Giuseppe Piermarini gave this town hall and Visconti palace a neoclassical overhaul in the late 18th century. The supremely elegant interiors were all but destroyed by WWII bombs; the Sala delle Cariatidi remains unrenovated as a reminder of war's indiscriminate destruction. Now blockbuster shows wow the crowds with artists as diverse as Titian, Bacon and Dario Fo.

Teatro alla Scala
OPERA HOUSE

(La Scala; Map p250; www.teatroallascala.org; Via Filodrammatici 2; Ⓜ Cordusio, Duomo) Giuseppe Piermarini's grand 2800-seat theatre was inaugurated in 1778 with Antonio Salieri's *Europa Riconosciuta*, replacing the previous theatre, which burnt down in a fire after a carnival gala. Costs were covered by the sale of *palchi* (private boxes), of which there are six gilt-and-crimson tiers. When rehearsals are not in session you can stand in boxes 13, 15 and 18 for a glimpse of the jewel-like interior.

MILAN & THE LAKES

Milan

1 km
0.5 miles

La Cucina Italiana (700m); Orio al Serio (48km)

Casa Boschi di Stefano (500m)

Lima

Corso Buenos Aires

Airport Buses
Caiazzo

Via Brianza

Viale Brianza

Via Schiaparelli

Via Dom Scarletti

Via Dom Vitruvio

Via Tadino

Via Panfilo Castaldi

Porta Venezia

Viale Luigi Majno

Via Lambro

Via Poerio

Viale Piave

Stazione Centrale

Piazza Duca d'Aosta

Via Tonale

Sondrio

Torre Pirelli

Centrale FS

Via Fabio Filzi

Via Vittor Pisani

Via Mauro Macchi

Via Felice Casati

Via San Gregorio

Viale Tunisia

Via Vittorio Veneto

Bastioni di Porta Venezia

Palestro

Via Senato

Gioia

Via Melchiorre Gioia

Via Generale Gustavo Fara

Via G Galilei

Giardini Pubblici

Piazza Fatebenefratelli Cavour

Via Fatebenefratelli

Zara

Piazzale Lagosta

ISOLA

Via Sebenico

Via F Confalonieri

Via Gaetano De Castillia

Via Borsieri

Via Pollaiuolo

Via Pastrengo

Piazza Fidia

Stazione Porta Garibaldi

Garibaldi

Piazza Sigmund Freud

Piazzale XXV Aprile

Viale Pasubio

Viale F Crispi

Corso di Porta Nuova

Republica

Turati

BRERA

Via Brera

Via Pontaccio

Via Marsala

Via Solferino

Lanza

Largo La Foppa

Moscova

Via Ceresio

Via Donato Bramante

Viale Montello

Via Legnano

Viale Elvezia

Piazzale Cimitero Monumentale

Cimitero Monumentale

Via Tazzoli

Via G Pepe

Via Paolo Sarpi

Via Luigi Canonica

Via Melzi d'Eril

Viale Emilio Alemagna

Parco Sempione

Viale Gadio

Piazza Sempione

Via Canova

Via Mario Pagano

Corso Sempione

Via Fratelli Induno

Via Giulio Cesare Procaccini

Via Messi

Via Losanna

Via Fauché

Via Censio

Piazza Gerusalemme

Expo 2015 (850m); Fieramilanocity (850m); Malpensa (46km)

Via Piero della Francesca

MILAN & THE LAKES

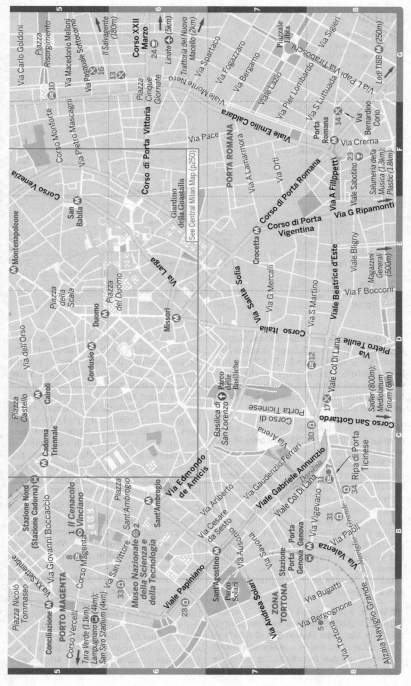

Piazza Nicolò Tommaseo

Conciliazione Ⓜ

PORTO MAGENTA

Via XX Settembre

Corso Vercelli

Tara Verde (1.1km);
Lampugnano Ⓜ (4km);
San Siro Stadium (4km)

Stazione Nord
(Stazione Cadorna) Ⓜ

Via Giovanni Boccaccio

8 1 Il Cenacolo
🍴 Vinciano

Corso Magenta

Via San Vittore

Museo Nazionale
della Scienza e
della Tecnologia

33 🏨

28 ⓘ

Viale Papiniano ⓘ

Sant'Agostino Ⓜ

Parco
Solari

ZONA
TORTONA

Via Andrea Solari

Via Bergognone

Via Bugatti

Via Tortona

Alzaia Naviglio Grande

Via Carlo Goldoni

Piazza
Risorgimento

Via Macedonio Melloni

Il Salvagente
(180m)

Via Pasquale Sottocorno

10 🏨

16 ⓘ

13 ⊗

Corso XXII
Marzo

24 🍴

Lin"ate (5km)

Trattoria del Nuovo
Macello (2km)

Via Monte Nero

Via Spartaco

Via Fogazzaro

Via Bergamo

Via Pier Lombardo

Piazzale
Libia

Via L Papi/Via Tiraboschi

Via Sigieri

Lodi TIBB Ⓜ (250m)

Via S Luttuada

Via
Bernardino
Corio

14 ⊗

Via Crema

Porta
Romana

PORTA ROMANA

Viale Emilio Caldara

Corso di Porta Vittoria

Piazza
Cinque
Giornate

Via Pace

Giardino
della Guastalla

See Central Milan Map (p250)

Via A Lamarmora

Via Orti

Corso di Porta Romana

Via A Filippetti

Viale Sabotino

Salumeria della
Musica (1.3km);
Plastic (1.8km)

23 ⓘ

Via G Ripamonti

Corso di Porta
Vigentina

Crocetta Ⓜ

Via G Mercalli

Via Santa
Sofia

Via S Martino

Corso Italia

Viale Beatrice d'Este

Viale Bigny

Magazzini
Generali
(500m)

Via F Bocconi

Via S Vittore

Corso Venezia

Montenapoleone Ⓜ

Via dell'Orso

Piazza
della
Scala

Piazza
Castello

Piazza
Castello Ⓜ

Cairoli Ⓜ

Cadorna
Triennale Ⓜ

Piazza
del Duomo

Duomo Ⓜ

Cordusio Ⓜ

Via Larga

San
Babila Ⓜ

Missori Ⓜ

12 ⓘ

Viale Col Di Lana

Via Pietro Teulie

Via Pietro Mascagni

Corso Monforte

Corso di Porta Vittoria

Sadler (800m);
Mediolanum
Forum (6km)

17 ⊗

Corso San Gottardo

Viale Gabriele Annunzio

Via Gaudenzio Ferrari

Via Ariberto

Via Cesare
da Sesto

Via Edmondo
de Amicis

Parco
delle
Basiliche

Basilica di
San Lorenzo ✚

Corso di
Porta Ticinese

Via Arena

30 ⓘ

Ripa di Porta
Ticinese

Darsena

7

11 ⓘ

34 🍴

Sant'Ambrogio Ⓜ

Sant'Ambrogio

Piazza
Sant'Ambrogio

Via Savona

Via Ausonio

Porta
Genova Ⓜ

Stazione
Porta
Genova Ⓜ

Via Vigevano

Via Valenza

Via Paoli

Via Col Di Lana

Naviglio Grande

31 ⓘ

Milan

In the theatre's museum (La Scala Museum; Map p250; ☏ 02 4335 3521; Largo Ghiringhelli 1; admission €6; ⊗9am-12.30pm & 1.30-5.30pm), harlequin costumes and a spinet inscribed with the command 'Inexpert hand, touch me not!' hint at centuries of Milanese musical drama, on and off stage.

★**Pinacoteca di Brera**　　　　GALLERY
(Map p250; ☏02 7226 3264; www.brera.benicul-turali.it; Via Brera 28; adult/reduced child €6/3; ⊗8.30am-7.15pm Tue-Sun; Ⓜ Lanza) Located upstairs from the centuries-old Accademia di Belle Arti (still one of Italy's most prestigious art schools); this gallery houses Milan's most impressive collection of old masters, much of the bounty 'lifted' from Venice by Napoleon. Rembrandt, Goya and van Dyck all have a place in the collection, but you're here to see the Italians: Titian, Tintoretto, glorious Veronese; ground-breaking Mantegna, the Bellini brothers and a Caravaggio.

★**Museo Poldi Pezzoli**　　　　MUSEUM
(Map p250; ☏02 79 48 89; www.museopoldipez-zoli.it; Via Alessandro Manzoni 12; adult/reduced €9/6; ⊗10am-6pm Wed-Mon; Ⓜ Montenapoleone) Inheriting his vast fortune at the age of 24, Gian Giacomo Poldi Pezzoli also inherited his mother's love of art; and during extensive European travels he was inspired by the 'house museum' that was later to become London's V&A (Victoria and Albert Museum). As his collection grew, Pezzoli had the idea of transforming his apartments into a series of historically themed rooms based on the great art periods of the past (the Middle Ages, early Renaissance, baroque and rococo). Although crammed with a collection of big ticket artworks, including Botticelli, Bellini and the beautiful *Portrait of a Woman* by Pollaiuolo, these Sala d'Artista are exquisite works of art in their own right.

Castello Sforzesco　　　CASTLE, MUSEUM
(Map p250; ☏02 884 63 700; www.milanocastello.it; Piazza Castello; ⊗7am-7pm summer, to 6pm winter; Ⓜ Cairoli) Originally a Visconti fortress, this iconic red-brick castle was later home to the mighty Sforza dynasty who ruled Renaissance Milan. The castle's defences were designed by the multitalented Leonardo da Vinci; Napoleon later drained the moat and removed the drawbridges. Today it shelters seven specialised museums, which gather together intriguing fragments of Milan's cultural and civic history, Lombard Gothic masterpieces and Michelange-

lo's final work, the shockingly modern, *Rondanini Pietà*.

Situated behind the castle, Parco Sempione (Map p250; ⊙ 6.30am-nightfall; M Cadorna, Cairoli) FREE is the green lung of the city landscaped with winding paths and ornamental ponds, and overlooked by Giò Ponti's spindly, 1933 Torre Branca tower (Map p244; ✆ 02 331 41 20; lift €4; ⊙ 9.30am-midnight Tue & Thu, 10.30am-12.30pm, 4-6.30pm & 9.30pm-midnight Wed, 2.30-6pm & 9.30pm-midnight Fri, 10.30am-2pm, 2.30-7.30pm & 9.30pm-midnight Sat & Sun May–mid-Oct, shorter hours in winter; M Cadorna).

★ The Last Supper
(Il Cenacolo Vinciano)   MURAL
(Map p244; ✆ 02 8942 1146; www.architettonici milano.lombardia.beniculturali.it; adult/reduced €6.50/3.25, booking fee €1.50; M Cadorna-Triennale) Milan's most famous mural, Leonardo da Vinci's *The Last Supper* (*Il Cenacolo*), is hidden away on a wall of the refectory adjoining the Basilica di Santa Maria delle Grazie (Corso Magenta; ⊙ 8.30am-7pm Tue-Sun; M Conciliazione, Cadorna) FREE. Depicting Christ and his disciples at the dramatic moment when Christ reveals he is aware of the betrayal afoot, it is a masterful psychological study and one of the world's most iconic images.

Restoration of *Il Cenacolo* was completed in 1999 after more than 22 years' work. The mural was in a lamentable state after centuries of damage. Da Vinci himself is partly to blame: his experimental mix of oil and tempera was applied between 1495 and 1498, rather than within a week as is typical of fresco techniques. The Dominicans didn't help matters in 1652 by raising the refectory floor, hacking off a lower section of the scene, including Jesus' feet. The most damage was caused by restorers in the 19th century, whose alcohol and cotton-wool technique removed an entire layer. But its condition does nothing to lessen its astonishing beauty. Stare at the ethereal, lucent windows beyond the narrative action and you'll wonder if da Vinci's uncharacteristic short-sightedness wasn't divinely inspired.

When he was at work on the masterpiece a star-struck monk noted that he would sometimes arrive in the morning, stare at yesterday's effort, then promptly call it quits for the day. Your visit too will be similarly brief (15 minutes) unless you invest in Tickitaly's (www.tickitaly.com; guided tour €69; ⊙ 7.15pm & 8pm) guided, after-hours tour which allows an extended 30-minute visit.

★ Museo Nazionale della
Scienza e della Tecnologia   MUSEUM
(Map p244; ✆ 02 48 55 51; www.museoscienza. org; Via San Vittore 21; adult/child €10/7, submarine tour €8; ⊙ 9.30am-5pm Tue-Fri, to 6.30pm Sat, Sun & holidays; M Sant'Ambrogio) Kids, would-be inventors and geeks will go goggle-eyed at Milan's impressive museum of science and technology, the largest of its kind in Italy. It is a fitting tribute in a city where arch-inventor Leonardo da Vinci did much of his finest work. The 16th-century monastery, where it is housed, features a collection of more than 10,000 items, including models based on da Vinci's engineering sketches, halls devoted to the sciences of physics, astronomy and horology, and outdoor hangars housing steam trains, planes, full-sized galleons and Italy's first submarine.

★ Chiesa di San Maurizio   CHAPEL, CONVENT
(Map p250; Corso Magenta 15; ⊙ 9am-noon & 2-5.30pm Tue-Sun; M Cadorna-Triennale) The 16th-century royal chapel and convent of San Maurizio is Milan's hidden crown jewel, every inch of it covered in Bernardino Luini's breathtaking frescoes. Many of them immortalise the star of Milan's literary scene at the time, Ippolita Sforza, and her family. Duck through a small doorway on the left to enter the secluded convent hall where blissful martyred women saints bear their tribulations serenely – note Santa Lucia calmly holding her lost eyes, and Santa Agata casually carrying her breasts on a platter.

Civico Museo Archeologico   MUSEUM
(Map p250; ✆ 02 8844 5208; Corso Magenta 15; adult/child €2/1; ⊙ 9am-5.30pm Tue-Sun; M Cadorna-Triennale) Adjoining the church of San Maurizio is the 9th-century Monastero Maggiore, once the most important Benedictine convent in the city and now the backdrop for the archaeological museum. Accessed via a cloister where fragments of the city's Roman walls can be seen, and through the 3rd-century frescoed Ansperto Tower, it provides great insight into old Mediolanum with well-curated collections of Etruscan, Greek, Roman, Gothic and Lombard artefacts.

Fashion

Northern Italian artisans and designers have been dressing and adorning Europe's affluent classes since the early Middle Ages. At that time Venetian merchants imported dyes from the East and Leonardo da Vinci helped design Milan's canal system, connecting the wool merchants and silk weavers of the lakes to the city's market places. Further south, Florence's wool guild grew so rich they were able to fund a Renaissance.

Global Powerhouses

In the 1950s Florence's fashion houses, which once produced only made-to-measure designs, began to present seasonal collections to a select public. But Milan literally stole the show in 1958, hosting Italy's first Fashion Week. With its ready factories, cosmopolitan workforce and long-established media presence, Milan created ready-to-wear fashion for global markets.

Recognising the enormous potential of mass markets, designers such as Armani, Missoni and Versace began creating and following trends, selling their 'image' through advertising and promotion. In the 1980s Armani's power suits gave rise to new unisex fashions, Dolce & Gabbana became a byword for Italian sex appeal and Miuccia Prada transformed her father's ailing luxury luggage business by introducing democratic, durable totes and backpacks made out of radical new fabrics (like waterproof Pocono, silk faille and parachute nylon).

Fashion Mecca Milan

Milan's rise to global fashion prominence was far from random. No other Italian

1. Window display at Valentino, Rome
2. Display of ties, Milan
3. Shopper browsing, Milan

RICHARD I'ANSON / GETTY IMAGES ©

LONELY PLANET IMAGES / GETTY IMAGES ©

PAOLO CORBELLI / GETTY IMAGES ©

city, not even Rome, was so well suited to take on this mantle. First, thanks to its geographic position, the city had historically strong links with European markets. It was also Italy's capital of finance, advertising, television and publishing, with both *Vogue* and *Amica* magazines based there. What's more Milan always had a fashion industry based around the historic textile and silk production of upper Lombardy. And, with the city's postwar focus on trade fairs and special events, it provided a natural marketplace for the exchange of goods and ideas.

As a result, by 2011 Milan emerged as Italy's top (and the world's fourth-biggest) fashion exporter. Six of the world's top 10 fashion houses are Italian, and four of those are based in Milan. The Quadrilatero d'Oro, that 'Golden Quad', is now dominated by more than 500 fashion outlets in an area barely 6000 sq metres. Such is the level of display, tourists now travel to Milan to 'see' the fashion.

FASHION WEEKS

The winter shows are held in January (men) and February (women) and the spring/summer events are in June (men) and September (women). You'll enjoy the full carnival effect as more than 100,000 models, critics, buyers and producers descend on the city to see 350-plus shows.

For a full timetable check out www.cameramoda.it or http://milanfashionweeklive.com.

Central Milan

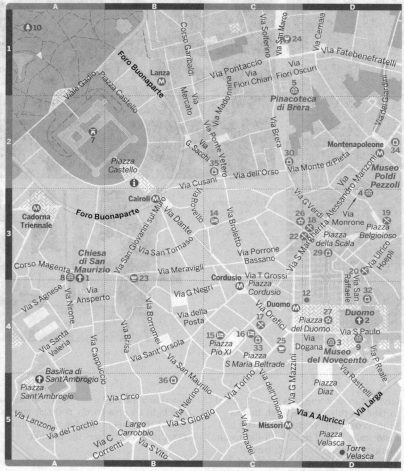

Villa Necchi Campiglio   HOUSE MUSEUM
(Map p250; ☑02 7634 0121; www.casemuseo.
it; Via Mozart 14; adult/child €8/4; ⊙10am-6pm
Wed-Sun; Ⓜ San Babila) Set in a beautiful garden with tall magnolia trees, this villa is a
symbol of Milan's modernist imaginings in
the early 1930s. Designed by Rationalist architect Piero Portaluppi for Pavian heiresses
Nedda and Gigina Necchi, the house blends
Art Deco and Rationalist styles. Quotidian
details are as enthralling as the sleek architectural lines and big ticket artworks by Morandi and de Chirico.

🏃 Activities

Navigli Lombardi   BOAT TOUR
(Map p244; ☑02 9227 3118; www.naviglilombardi.it;
Alzaia Naviglio Grande 4; adult/concession €12/10;
Ⓜ Porta Genova, 🚊3) From April to mid-
October you can take a boat tour along the
Naviglio Grande for views of the churches,
farms and villas that line its banks.

Spiga 8 Spa at Hotel Baglioni   SPA
(Map p250; ☑02 4547 3111; www.baglionihotels.
com; Via della Spiga 8; Ⓜ San Babila) Spiga 8 Spa
has a minimalist all-white aesthetic and a

menu of treatments that seem good enough to eat, such as the chocolate facial.

Tours

Autostradale   GUIDED TOUR
(Map p250; ☏ 02 720 01 304; www.autostradale.it; ticket €60; ☺ 9.30am Tue-Sun Sep-Jul) The tourist office sells tickets (good for the whole day) for Autostradale's three-hour city bus tours, including admission to *The Last Supper*, Castello Sforzesco and La Scala's museum. Tours depart from the taxi rank on the western side of Piazza del Duomo.

Bike & the City   BIKE TOUR
(Map p244; ☏ 346 9498623; www.bikeandthecity.it; day/sunset tour €35/30; ☺ morning/afternoon/sunset tour 9.30am/3.30pm/6.30pm) Make friends while you get the inside scoop on city sights on these leisurely, four-hour bike tours.

✾ Festivals & Events

Milan has two linked trade-fair grounds, collectively known as **Fiera Milano** (www.fieramilano.it). The older of the two, **Fieramilanocity**, is close to the centre (metro line 2, Lotto Fieramilanocity stop), while the main grounds, **Fieramilano**, are west of town in the satellite town of Rho (metro line 2, Rho Fiera stop). The furniture fair, fashion shows and most large trade fairs take place here.

Carnevale Ambrosiano   CULTURAL
(☺ February) The world's longest carnival, this event culminates with a procession to the Duomo.

Salone Internazionale del Mobile   FAIR
(www.cosmit.it) The world's most prestigious (and profit-driven) furniture fair is held annually in April at Fieramilano (in Rho), with satellite exhibitions in Zona Tortona. Alongside the Salone runs the **Fuorisalone** (http://fuorisalone.it), literally, the outdoor lounge, which incorporates the dozens of spontaneous design-related events, parties, exhibits and shows that animate the entire city.

Cortili Aperti   CULTURE
For one May Sunday, the gates to some of the city's most beautiful private courtyards are flung open. Print a map and make your own itinerary.

Festa del Naviglio   CULTURAL
Parades, music and performances during the first 10 days of June.

La Bella Estate   MUSIC
(www.comune.milano.it) Concerts in and beyond town from June to August. Check the town hall's website.

Festa di Sant'Ambrogio & Fiera degli Obei Obei   RELIGIOUS
The feast day of Milan's patron saint (7 December) is celebrated with a large Christmas fair. It goes by the name Obej! Obej! (pronounced o-bay, o-bay).

Central Milan

🛏 Sleeping

Great-value accommodation is hard to come by in Milan and downright impossible to find during the Salone del Mobile furniture fair, the fashion shows and other large fairs. That said, booking ahead and shopping around can yield some surprisingly good results. The tourist office distributes *Milano Hotels,* which lists more than 350 options.

Ostello Burigozzo 11
HOSTEL €

(Map p244; ☎02 5831 4675; www.ostelloburigozzo11.com; Via Burigozzo 11; dm/s/d €21/50/80; P◉@🛜; ◉9, 29, 30) A spartan but spotless hostel decked out with a dash of design brio. Bunks are in single-sex dorms (each with their own shower), but doubles, triples and quads are also available.

Euro Hotel
HOTEL €

(Map p244; ☎02 3040 4010; www.eurohotelmilano.it; Via Giuseppe Sirtori 24; d €75-120; P◉@🛜◉; ◉Porta Venezia) This large, well-serviced hotel near Porta Venezia offers a huge variety of comfortable, modern rooms and efficient service. It is popular with groups and fills up fast during events and fairs. Book ahead online for the best rates.

★ Maison Borella
BOUTIQUE HOTEL €€

(Map p244; ☎02 5810 9114; www.hotelmaisonborella.com; Alzaia Naviglio Grande 8; d €140-220; ◉@🛜; ◉Porta Genova) With geranium-clad balconies overhanging the Naviglio Grande, and striking black, white and grey decor and pinstriped bedlinen, Maison Borella brings a much-needed touch of class to Navigli and is, amazingly, the first canal-side hotel. The hotel is a converted house arranged around an internal courtyard, and its historic rooms feature parquet floors, beamed ceilings and elegant *boiserie* (sculpted panelling).

Foresteria Monforte
B&B €€

(Map p244; ☎02 7631 8516; www.foresteriamonforte.it; Piazza del Tricolore 2; d €150-250; ◉@🛜; ◉San Babila) The three classy rooms in this upmarket B&B have Philippe Starck chairs, flat-screen TVs and a communal kitchen. Ceilings are high, rooms are filled with natural light and bathrooms are dizzyingly contemporary. About a 1.5km walk from the Duomo.

Hotel Gran Duca di York
HOTEL €€

(Map p250; ☎02 87 48 63; www.ducadiyork.com; Via Moneta 1; d €160-205; ◉@🛜◉; ◉Duomo) This lemon-yellow *palazzo* (mansion), literally a stone's throw from the *duomo*, was once a residence for scholars working in the nearby Ambrosiana library. Now it offers smiley service and 33 small, breezy rooms (some with balconies) with plump beds and neat, marble bathrooms. Our advice is to skip the rather dull breakfast and opt for five-star pastries at Princi a few blocks away.

Tara Verde
B&B €€

(☎ 02 3653 4959; www.taraverde.it; Via Delleani 22; d €110-120; ❀ @ ☎; Ⓜ De Angeli) This painted *palazzo* in a quiet residential street offers three exotically coloured rooms in rag-rolled lime green, lemon yellow or raspberry. Owner Roberta has a designer's eye for the details: luggage racks, orthopaedic mattresses and complimentary minibars.

Antica Locanda Leonardo
HOTEL €€

(Map p244; ☎ 02 4801 4197; www.anticalocandaleonardo.com; Corso Magenta 78; s €80-120, d €90-200; ❀ @ ☎; Ⓜ Conciliazione) Rooms here exude homey comfort, from the period furniture and parquet floors to the plush drapes. Take breakfast in the quiet, scented interior garden of this 19th-century residence.

Hotel Spadari Duomo
DESIGN HOTEL €€€

(Map p250; ☎ 02 7200 2371; www.spadarihotel.com; Via Spadari 11; d €185-345; ❀ ☎; Ⓜ Duomo) The rooms at the Spadari, Milan's original design hotel, are miniature galleries showcasing the work of emerging artists. The hotel itself is the creation of respected architect-engineers Urbano Pierini and Ugo La Pietra, who designed every inch of the 'look' down to the sinuous pale-wood furniture.

Alle Meraviglie
HOTEL €€€

(Map p250; ☎ 02 805 10 23; www.allemeraviglie.it; Via San Tomaso 6; d €225-295; Ⓟ ❀ ☎; Ⓜ Cairoli) There are just six soothing rooms at this boutique hotel in a pretty side street in the city centre. Each is uniquely decorated with beautiful fabrics and fresh flowers, and there are no TVs. Indeed, there is a pleasingly hushed atmosphere about this retreat from the daily hustle outside.

3Rooms
B&B €€€

(Map p244; ☎ 02 62 61 63; www.10corsocomo.com; Corso Como 10; d €270-340; Ⓟ ❀ @ ☎; Ⓜ Garibaldi) Can't drag yourself and your shopping bags away from concept shop Corso Como? You don't have to – the villa's three guest rooms let you sleep amid Eames bedspreads, Arne Jacobsen chairs and Saarinen leather.

Thrown in are some vintage items and a few pieces of artwork.

✕ Eating

Milan's dining scene is much like its fashion scene, with new restaurant openings hotly debated and seats at Michelin-starred tables hard to come by. Whether it's dyed-in-tradition or fusion cuisine, you'll eat some of Italy's most innovative and sophisticated food here.

Milan's provincial specialities include polenta, *risotto alla milanese* (saffron and bone-marrow risotto), *busecca* (sliced tripe boiled with beans) and *costoletta alla milanese* (breaded veal). Milan is also the home of *panettone* (yeast-risen sweet bread), now internationally popular at Easter and Christmas.

Reservations are required for most popular restaurants and essential for top-end establishments.

Latteria di San Marco
TRATTORIA €

(Map p244; ☎ 02 659 76 53; Via San Marco 24; meals €18-25; ☺ 7-11pm Mon-Fri; ❀; Ⓜ Moscova) If you can snare a seat in this tiny and ever-popular restaurant, you'll find old favourites like *spaghetti alla carbonara* mixed in with chef Arturo's own creations, such as *polpettine al limone* (little meatballs with lemon) or *riso al salto* (risotto fritters) on the ever-changing, mostly organic menu.

Trattoria da Pino
MILANESE €

(Map p250; ☎ 02 7600 0532; Via Cerva 14; meals €20-25; ☺ noon-3pm Mon-Sat; Ⓜ San Babila) In a city full of models in Michelin-starred restaurants, working-class da Pino's offers the perfect antidote. Sit elbow-to-elbow at long cafeteria-style tables and order up bowls of *bollito misto* (mixed boiled meats), handmade pasta and curried veal nuggets.

LOCAL KNOWLEDGE

BEHIND THE SCENES AT LA SCALA

To glimpse the inner workings of La Scala visit the Ansaldo Workshops (p239), where the stage sets are crafted and painted, and where some 800 to 1000 new costumes are handmade each season. Tours must be booked in advance and are guided by the heads of each creative department.

NAVIGLI MARKETS

Overlooking the Darsena, once the city's main port, is the **Mercato Comunale** (Food Market; Map p244; Piazza XXIV Maggio; ⊙8.30am-1pm Mon, 8.30am-1pm & 4-7.30pm Tue-Fri, 8.30am-1.30pm & 3.30-6.30pm Sat; Ⓜ Porta Genova, 🚃 3), this is the city's main covered market, selling fresh fruit, vegetables and fish. Northwest, Viale Gabriele d'Annunzio merges into Viale Papiano, where the city's main **flea market** (Map p244; Viale Papiniano; ⊙8am-2pm Tue, to 5pm Sat) operates. It's at its best on Saturday morning.

The city's most scenic market, the **Mercatore Antiquario di Navigli** (Map p244; www.naviglilive.it; ⊙9am-6pm last Sun of month; Ⓜ Porta Genova), sets up along a 2km stretch of the Naviglio Grande. With more than 400 well-vetted antique and secondhand traders, it provides hours of treasure-hunting pleasure.

Luini
PASTRIES & CAKES €

(Map p250; www.luini.it; Via Santa Radegonda 16; panzerotti €2.50; ⊙10am-3pm Mon, to 8pm Tue-Sun; 🏫; Ⓜ Duomo) *Panzerotti* is Milanese for yummy at this historic purveyor of pizza-dough pastries stuffed with cheese, spinach, tomato, pesto and prosciutto.

★ Trattoria del Nuovo Macello
MILANESE €€

(☏02 5990 2122; www.trattoriadelnuovomacello.it; Via Cesare Lombroso 20; meals €28-50; ⊙noon-2.15pm & 8-10.30pm Mon-Fri, 8-10.30pm Sat) A real Milanese will tell you that those thin, battered 'elephant ears' that currently masquerade as *cotoletta alla Milanese* (Milanese schnitzel) are a poor imitation of the real deal. For authentic Milanese *cotoletta* take a taxi ride out to the old meat district, Nuovo Macello, where you'll be presented with a thick, juicy slab of veal on the bone, cooked slowly to perfection in butter.

Al Bacco
MILANESE €€

(Map p244; ☏02 5412 1637; Via Marcona 1; meals €25-30; ⊙dinner Mon-Sat) One-time pupil to the famous chef Claudio Sadler, Andrea now has his own Slow Food–recommended restaurant where he prepares Milanese classics with love. Try the homemade pasta with fava beans, pancetta and pecorino, or the rabbit with Taggiasche olives.

Dongiò
CALABRESE €€

(Map p244; ☏02 551 13 72; Via Bernardino Corio 3; meals €30-40; ⊙noon-2.30pm & 7.30-11.30pm Mon-Fri, 7.30-11.30pm Sat; 🏫; Ⓜ Porta Romana) One of the best value-for-money restaurants in Milan, this big-hearted Calabrese trattoria serves the spicy flavours of the south on delicious homemade pasta. Starters include bountiful platters of southern salami and piquant cheeses. Reservations recommended.

Sushi Koboo
JAPANESE €€

(Map p244; ☏02 837 26 08; www.sushi-koboo.com; Viale Col di Lana 1; meals €20-35; ⊙noon-2.30pm & 7.30-11.30pm Tue-Sun; 🚃 3, 9) Elegant Sushi Koboo serves delectable sushi, sashimi and tempura at a traditional *kaiten* (conveyor belt) and tables in several stylish restaurant rooms. The atmosphere is warm and welcoming, with tables aglow beneath large, moonlike light fittings. If you're with a group order the mixed sushi boat, which actually comes in a handcrafted vessel.

L'Antico Ristorante Boeucc
MILANESE €€€

(Map p250; ☏02 7602 0224; www.boeucc.com; Piazza Belgioioso 2; meals €60-80; ⊙lunch & dinner Mon-Fri, lunch Sun; Ⓜ Duomo) Set in the basement of the grand-looking neoclassical Palazzo Belgioioso, Milan's oldest restaurant has been entertaining diners since 1696. Vaulted dining rooms and service reminiscent of more regal times lend your evening meal a sense of theatre. From *crespelle al prosciutto* (a kind of cross between pasta and crêpe with ham) you might move on to a *trancio di salmone al pepe verde* (slice of salmon with green pepper).

Ristorante Da Giacomo
SEAFOOD €€€

(Map p244; ☏02 7602 3313; www.giacomomilano.com; Via Pasquale Sottocorno 6; meals €40-60; 🚃 9, 23) This sunny Tuscan restaurant with its custard-coloured walls and mint-green panelling serves an unpretentious menu featuring mainly fish and shellfish. Start with a slice of sardine and caper pizza and follow with the fresh linguine with scampi, and zucchini flowers.

🍷 Drinking & Nightlife

Milanese bars are generally open until 2am or 3am, and virtually all serve *aperitivi*. The Navigli canal district, the cobbled backstreets of Brera, and swish Corso Como and its surrounds are all great areas for a drink, Milan-style. Clubs are generally open until 3am or 4am Tuesday to Sunday; cover charges vary from €10 to upwards of €25. Door policies can be formidable as the night wears on.

Princi
CAFE

(Map p250; ☑ 02 87 47 97; www.princi.it; Via Speronari 6; ⊙ Mon-Sat) Coffee bar with artisanal pastries, bread and pizza.

Caffeteria degli Atellani
CAFE, BAR

(Map p244; ☑ 02 3653 5959; www.atellani.it; Via della Moscova 28; ⊙ 8.30am-9.30pm Mon-Fri, 9.30am-7.30pm Sat & Sun; ☎; Ⓜ Moscova, Turati) Cafe Atellani's glasshouse design is modelled on a tropical greenhouse and overlooks a tranquil garden. Inside, the sleek bar is lined with an extensive selection of Italian wines, which you can enjoy after a browse in the cinema bookshop.

Torrefazione Il Caffè Ambrosiano
CAFE

(Map p244; ☑ 02 2952 5069; http://torrefazioneambrosiano.it; Corso Buenos Aires 20; ⊙ 7am-8pm; Ⓜ Porta Venezia) No seating, just the best coffee in Milan. There's also a branch (Map p244; Corso XXII Marzo 18; ⊙ 7am-8pm; 🚌 9, 23) on Corso XXII Marzo.

Marchesi
CAFE

(Map p250; ☑ 02 876 730; www.pasticerriamarchesi.it; Via Santa Maria alla Porta 11a; ⊙ Mon-Sat; Ⓜ Cardusio, Cairoli) Perfect-every-shot coffee since 1824.

Pandenus
BAR

(Map p244; ☑ 02 2952 8016; www.pandenus.it; Via Alessandro Tadino 15; cocktails €8, brunch €20; ⊙ 7am-10pm; ☎; Ⓜ Porta Venezia) Originally a bakery, Pandenus was named after the walnut bread that used to emerge from its still-active oven. Now the focaccia, *pizzetta* and bruschetta on its burgeoning *aperitivo* bar are some of the best in town. Given its proximity to the Marconi Foundation (which is dedicated to contemporary art) expect a good-looking, arty crowd.

10 Corso Como
BAR

(Map p244; ☑ 02 2901 3581; www.10corsocomo.com; Corso Como 10; ⊙ 12.30pm-midnight Mon-Fri, 11.30am-1.30am Sat & Sun; Ⓜ Garibaldi) A picture-perfect courtyard, world-class people-watching and an elegant *aperitivo* scene lit at night by a twinkling canopy of fairy lights make Corso Como the best lifestyle concept bar in Milan.

Living
BAR

(Map p244; ☑ 02 3310 0824; www.livingmilano.com; Piazza Sempione 2; ⊙ 8am-2am Mon-Fri, 9am-2am Sat & Sun; Ⓜ Moscova) Living has one of the city's prettiest settings, with a corner position and floor-to-ceiling windows overlooking the Arco della Pace (Map p244). The bounteous *aperitivo* spread draws a crowd of smart-casual 20- and 30-somethings. Their sister bar, Refeel (Map p244; ☑ 02 5832 4227; www.refeel.it; Viale Sabotino 20; ⊙ 7am-2am Mon-Sat, noon-4pm Sun; Ⓜ Porta Romana), in Porta Romana, is also worth a trip.

N'Ombra de Vin
WINE BAR

(Map p250; ☑ 02 659 96 50; www.nombradevin.it; Via San Marco 2; ⊙ 9am-midnight Mon-Sat; Ⓜ Montenapoleone) This *enoteca* is set in a one-time Augustine refectory. Tastings can be had all day and you can also indulge in food such as *carpaccio di pesce spade agli agrumi* (swordfish carpaccio prepared with citrus) from a limited menu.

Vinile
BAR

(Map p244; www.vinilemilano.com; Via Alessandro Tadino 17; ⊙ 11am-midnight; Ⓜ Porta Venezia) Calling all comic connoisseurs and geeks, Vinile serves a limited-production wine list and artisanal cold cuts in the midst of an impressive collection of *Star Wars* and Marvel memorabilia. Check out their Facebook page for community art and music events.

Plastic
NIGHTCLUB

(☑ 02 73 39 96; Via Gargano 15; ⊙ 11pm-4am Fri-Sun mid-Sep-Jun; Ⓜ Lodi TIBB) Friday's London Loves takes no prisoners with an edgy, transgressive indie mix and Milan's coolest kids.

DON'T MISS

FEELING PECKISH?

Forget *The Last Supper*: gourmands head to the food and wine emporium Peck (Map p250; ☑ 02 802 31 61; www.peck.it; Via Spadari 7-9; ⊙ 3-7.30pm Mon, 8.45am-7.30pm Tue-Sat; Ⓜ Duomo). This Milanese institution first opened its doors as a deli in 1883. Since then, it's expanded to a restaurant-bar upstairs and an *enoteca* (wine bar). The Aladdin's cave–like food hall is the best in Milan, stocked with some 3200 variations of *parmigiano reggiano* (Parmesan) at its cheese counter, just for starters.

MILAN'S BRIGHTEST MICHELIN STARS

Milan's most important contemporary Italian restaurants are equally fashion- and food-oriented:

Cracco (Map p250; ☎02 87 67 74; www.ristorantecracco.it; Via Victor Hugo 4; meals €130-160; ⏲7.30-11pm Mon & Sat, 12.30-2.30pm & 7.30-11pm Tue-Fri ; Ⓜ Duomo) Star chef Carlo Cracco conjures up exemplary deconstructive *alta cucina* (haute cuisine) in a formal contemporary environment.

Il Marchesino (Map p250; ☎02 7209 4338; www.ilmarchesino.it; Via Filodrammatici 2; meals €50-80, tasting menu €110; ⏲8am-1am Mon-Sat; Ⓜ Duomo) Gualtiero Marchesi, Italy's most revered chef, presides over an elegant modern dining room at La Scala.

Sadler (☎02 87 67 30; www.sadler.it; Via Ascanio Sforza 77; meals €120; ⏲7.30-11pm Mon-Sat; Ⓜ Romolo, 🚊3) On the Milanese scene since 1995, Claudio Sadler's culinary wisdom remains undisputed.

Trussardi alla Scala (Map p250; ☎02 8068 8201; www.trussardiallascala.com; Piazza della Scala 5; meals €120; ⏲7.30am-11pm Mon-Fri, dinner Sat; Ⓜ Duomo) Gualtiero Marchesi alumni, Andrea Berton, runs the kitchen of this subdued sexy dining room overlooking La Scala.

If you're looking fab, club art director Nicola Guiducci's private Match à Paris on Sunday mashes French pop, indie and avant-garde sounds. You'll find it just south of the Lodi metro stop just off Viale Brenta.

Il Gattopardo NIGHTCLUB
(Map p244; ☎02 3453 7699; www.ilgattopardocafe.it; Via Piero della Francesca 47; ⏲6pm-4am Tue-Sat Sep-Jun; 🚊1, 14, 19, 33) This gorgeous champagne-coloured space in a deconsecrated church is filled with candles and baroque-style furniture. Gattopardo's clientele is equally aesthetically blessed. The only way in is with advance booking.

Magazzini Generali NIGHTCLUB
(☎02 539 39 48; www.magazzinigenerali.it; Via Pietrasanta 14; ⏲11pm-4am Wed-Sat Oct-May; Ⓜ Lodi TIBB, 🚊24) When this former warehouse is full of people working up a sweat to an international indie act, there's no better place to be in Milan. Most gigs are under €20, and there's free entry on other nights when DJs get the party started.

☆ Entertainment

Most big names that play Milan do so at major venues outside the city centre, which run shuttle buses for concerts. They include **Mediolanum Forum** (☎02 48 85 71; www.forumnet.it; Via Giuseppe di Vittorio 6; Ⓜ Assago Milanofiori) and the San Siro Stadium (p256).

La Salumeria della Musica CLUB
(☎02 5680 7350; www.lasalumeriadellamusica.com; Via Pasinetti 4; ⏲9pm-2am Mon-Sat Sep-Jun; 🚊24) The 'delicatessen of music' is a firm favourite with Milan's alternative scene. Come here for new acts, literary salons, cultural events and jazz. Shows start around 10.30pm, and if you get the munchies you can grab a plate of cheese and cold cuts.

Blue Note JAZZ
(Map p244; ☎02 6901 6888; www.bluenotemilano.com; Via Borsieri 37; tickets €20-35; ⏲Tue-Sun Sep-Jul; Ⓜ Zara, Garibaldi) Top-class jazz acts perform here from around the world; get tickets by phone, online or at the door from 7.30pm. It also does a popular easy-listening Sunday brunch (€35 or €55 for two adults and two children).

Teatro alla Scala OPERA
(Map p250; ☎02 8 87 91; www.teatroallascala.org; Piazza della Scala; Ⓜ Duomo) You'll need perseverance and luck to secure opera tickets at La Scala (€13 to €210, up to €2000 for opening night), which go on sale two months in advance of performances at the **box office** (Map p250; Galleria del Sagrato, Piazza del Duomo; ⏲noon-6pm; Ⓜ Duomo). On performance days, 140 tickets for the gallery are sold two hours before the show (one ticket per customer). Queue early.

The opera season runs from November through July, but you can see theatre, ballet and concerts at Teatro alla Scala year-round, with the exception of August.

San Siro Stadium FOOTBALL
(Stadio Giuseppe Meazza; ☎02 404 24 32; www.sansiro.net; Via dei Piccolomini 5, museum admission €7, plus guided tour adult/reduced €13/10; ⏲nonmatch days 10am-6pm; Ⓜ Lotto) The city's

two football clubs are the 1899-established AC Milan, owned by former prime minister Silvio Berlusconi, and the 1908-established FC Internazionale Milano (aka 'Inter'). They play at the stadium on alternate Sundays during the season. Guided tours of the stadium, built in the 1920s, take you behind the scenes to the players' locker rooms and include a visit to the **Museo Inter e Milan** (☑ 02 404 2432; www.sansiro.net; Gate 21, Via Piccolomini 5; museum & tour adult/concession €13/10; ⊙ 10am-6pm, tours every 20 mins; ♠; Ⓜ Lotto, ☐ 16, shuttle from Piazzale Lotto to the stadium), a shrine of memorabilia, papier-mâché caricatures of players, and film footage. Take tram 24, bus 95, 49 or 72, or the metro to the Lotto stop, from where a free bus shuttles to the stadium.

🔒 Shopping

Beyond the hallowed streets of the Quadrilatero d'Oro, designer outlets and chains can be found along Corso Buenos Aires and Corso Vercelli; younger, hipper labels along Via Brera and Corso Magenta; while Corso di Porta Ticinese and Navigli are home of the Milan street scene and subculture shops. For cutting-edge talent and great bargains venture down the up-and-coming Via Tortona.

★ **Spazio Rossana Orlandi**   HOME, GARDEN
(Map p244; ☑ 02 467 44 71; www.rossanaorlandi. com; Via Matteo Bandello 14; ⊙ 3.30-7.30pm Mon, 10am-7.30pm Tue-Fri; Ⓜ Conciliazione) Installed in a former tie factory in the Magenta district, finding this iconic interior design studio is a challenge in itself. Once inside though, you'll find it hard to leave this dream-like treasure trove, stacked with vintage and contemporary limited-edition pieces from young and upcoming artists.

Monica Castiglioni   JEWELLERY
(Map p244; ☑ 02 8723 7979; www.monicacastiglioni.com; Via Pastrengo 4; ⊙ 11am-8pm Thu-Sat; Ⓜ Garibaldi) Located in the up-and-coming neighbourhood of Isola, Monica's studio turns out organic and industrial-style jewellery in bronze, silver and gold. Deeply rooted in Milan's modernist traditions, these are statement pieces and well priced for the quality.

La Vetrina Di Beryl   SHOES
(Map p244; ☑ 02 654278; Via Statuto 4; Ⓜ Moscova) Barbara Beryl's name was known to cultists around the world way before 'Manolo' shoes became a byword for female desire. Stumbling upon this deceptively nondescript shop is like chancing upon the shoe racks at a *Vogue Italia* photo shoot.

Borsalino Outlet   ACCESSORIES
(Map p250; ☑ 02 8901 5436; www.borsalino.com; Galleria Vittorio Emanuele II 92; ⊙ 3-7pm Mon, 10am-7pm Tue-Sat; Ⓜ Duomo) The iconic Alessandrian milliner has worked with design greats such as Achille Castiglioni, who once designed a pudding-bowl bowler hat. This outlet in Galleria Vittorio Emanuele II stocks seasonal favourites. Otherwise you can visit the **main showroom** (Map p250; ☑ 02 7601 7072; www.borsalino.com; Via Sant'Andrea 5; Ⓜ Montenapoleone).

Pellini   JEWELLERY, ACCESSORIES
(Map p250; ☑ 02 7600 8084; www.pellini.it; Via Alessandro Manzoni 20; ⊙ 3.30-7.30pm Mon, 9.30am-7.30pm Tue-Sat Sep-Jul; Ⓜ Montenapoleone) For unique, one-off costume jewellery pieces, bags and hair pieces, look no further than Donatella Pellini's boutique. Granddaughter of famous costume designer Emma Pellini, the Pellini women have been making jewellery for three generations, and their fanciful, handmade creations are surprisingly affordable.

G Lorenzi   HOMEWARES, DESIGN
(Map p250; ☑ 02 7602 2848; www.lorenzi.it; Via Monte Napoleone 9; ⊙ 3-7.30pm Mon, 9am-12.30pm & 3-7.30pm Tue-Sat; Ⓜ San Babila) One of Milan's extant early-20th-century gems, G Lorenzi specialises in the finest-quality grooming and kitchen paraphernalia. There are things here – handcrafted pocket knives set into stag antlers, say – so fine and functional that they stand as classic examples of utilitarian design.

ⓘ WHAT'S ON

The tourist office stocks several entertainment guides in English: *Milano Mese, Hello Milano* (www.hellomilano. it) and *Easy Milano* (www.easymilano. it). The free Italian newspapers distributed on the metro are also handy for what's-on listings.

    For club listings, check out *Vivi Milano* (http://milano.corriere.it), which comes out with the *Corriere della Sera* newspaper on Wednesday; *La Repubblica* (www.repubblica.it) is also good on Thursday. Another source of inspiration is *Milano2night* (http:// milano.2night.it).

VINTAGE FINDS

Il Salvagente (🏠 02 7611 0328; www. salvagentemilano.it; Via Fratelli Bronzetti 16; ⏰10am-7pm Tue-Sat, 3-7pm Mon; 🚌60, 62 & 92) A basement room crammed with heavily discounted big brand names.

Cavalli e Nastri (Map p250; 🏠 02 7200 0449; www.cavallienastri.com; Via Brera 2; ⏰10am-7pm; Ⓜ Montenapoleone) Legendary early and mid-20th-century Italian fashion house names.

Vintage Delirium (Map p250; 🏠02 8646 2076; www.vintagedeliriumfj.com; Via Sacchi 3; ⏰10am-1pm & 2-7pm Mon-Fri Sep-Jul; Ⓜ Cairoli) Pristine woollens, 1930s eveningwear from Chanel and Neapolitan silk ties from the 1960s.

Superfly (Map p244; 🏠339 579 2838; www.superflyvintage.com; Ripa di Porta Ticinese 27; ⏰11am-8pm Tue-Sat, 3-7pm Sun; Ⓜ Porta Genova, 🚌2, 3) Disco diva vintage finds from the 1970s.

10 Corso Como   FASHION
(Map p244; 🏠 02 2900 2674; www.10corsocomo. com; Corso Como 10; ⏰10.30am-7.30pm Tue & Fri-Sun, to 9pm Wed & Thu, 3.30-7.30pm Mon; Ⓜ Garibaldi) It might be the world's most hyped 'concept shop', but Carla Sozzani's selection of desirable things (Lanvin ballet flats, Alexander Girard wooden dolls, a demi-couture frock by a designer you've not read about *yet*) makes 10 Corso Como a tempting shopping experience. Next to the gallery upstairs is a bookshop with art and design titles.

La Rinascente   DEPARTMENT STORE
(Map p250; 🏠02 8 85 21; www.rinascente.it; Piazza del Duomo; ⏰10am-midnight; Ⓜ Duomo) Italy's most prestigious department store doesn't let the fashion capital down – come for Italian diffusion lines, French lovelies and LA upstarts. The basement also hides an amazing homewares department. Take away edible souvenirs from the 7th-floor food market (and peer across to the Duomo while you're at it).

Wait and See   FASHION
(Map p250; 🏠02 7208 0195; www.waitandsee; Via Santa Marta 14; ⏰3.30-7.30pm Mon, 10.30am-7.30pm Tue-Sat; Ⓜ Missori) With collaborations with Missoni, Etro and Molinari under her belt, Uberta Zambeletti launched her own

collection in 2010. Quirky Wait and See indulges her eclectic tastes showcasing unfamiliar brands alongside items exclusively designed for the store, such as gorgeous Raptus & Rose dresses.

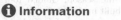 Information

EMERGENCY

Police station (🏠02 6 22 61; Via Fatebene-fratelli 11; Ⓜ Turati, Montenapoleone)
Tourist police (🏠02 863 701) English-speaking service for tourist complaints.

MEDICAL SERVICES

24-Hour Pharmacy (🏠02 669 09 35; Galleria delle Partenze, Stazione Centrale; Ⓜ Centrale FS) Located on 1st floor of the central station.
Hospital (Ospedale Maggiore Policlinico; 🏠02 5503 3137; www.policlinico.mi.it; Via Francesco Sforza 35; Ⓜ Crocetta)
Milan Clinic (🏠02 7601 6047; www.milan-clinic.com; Via Cerva 25; Ⓜ San Babila) English-speaking doctors.

TOURIST INFORMATION

Milan Tourist Office (Map p250; 🏠02 7740 4343; www.turismo.milano.it; Piazza Castello 1; ⏰9am-6pm Mon-Fri, 9am-1.30pm & 2-6pm Sat, to 5pm Sun; Ⓜ Duomo)
Stazione Centrale Tourist Office (Map p244; 🏠02 7740 4318; opposite platform 13, Stazione Centrale; ⏰9am-6pm Mon-Fri, 9am-1.30pm & 2-6pm Sat, to 5pm Sun)
Linate Airport Information Desk (🏠02 7020 0443; Linate Airport, Arrivals, Ground Floor; ⏰7.30am-11.30pm)
Malpensa Airport Information Desk (🏠02 5858 0080; Malpensa Airport, Terminal B, Ground Floor; ⏰8am-8pm)

🚍 Getting There & Away

AIR

Orio al Serio Airport (🏠035 32 63 23; www. sacbo.it)
Linate Airport (🏠02 232323; www.sea-aeroportimilano.it) Located 7km east of the city century; domestic and some European flights.
Malpensa Airport (🏠02 232323; www.sea-aeroportimilano.it) About 50km northwest of the city; northern Italy's main international airport.

BUS

National and international buses depart from **Lampugnano bus station** (Via Giulia Natta) (next to the Lampugnano metro stop), 5km west of central Milan. The main national operator is Autostradale (p259). Tickets can be purchased at the main tourist office.

CAR & MOTORCYCLE

The A1, A4, A7 and A8 converge from all directions on Milan.

TRAIN

International, high-speed trains from France, Switzerland and Germany arrive in Milan's **Stazione Centrale** (Piazza Duca d'Aosta). The ticketing office and left luggage are located on the ground floor and the tourist information booth (p258) is opposite platform 13. For regional trips, skip the queue and buy your tickets from the multilingual, touch-screen vending machines, which accept both cash and credit card. Daily international and long-distance destinations include:

Florence (€19 to €50, 1½ to 3½ hours, hourly)

Geneva (€78, four hours, three daily)

Munich (€99 to €130, 7½ to 8½ hours, seven daily) via Verona, Bologna or Venice

Paris (from €80, 7½ to nine hours, three daily) via Geneva, Lausanne, Basel or Dijon

Rome (€55 €58, three hours, half hourly)

Venice (€18.50 to €37, 2½ to 3½ hours, half hourly)

Vienna (from €80, 11 to 14 hours overnight, two daily)

❶ Getting Around

TO/FROM THE AIRPORT
Bus

Air Bus (Map p244; www.atm-mi.it) Coaches, run by ATM, depart from the Piazza Luigi di Savoi, next to Stazione Centrale, for **Linate Airport** (adult/child €5/2.50, 25 minutes) every 30 minutes from 6am to 11pm.

Autostradale (Map p244; ☑02 720 01 304; www.autostradale.it) Runs buses from **Orio al Serio Airport** (adult/child €5/3.50; one hour) every 30 minutes between 2.45am and 11.30pm from Piazza Luigi di Savoia.

Malpensa Shuttle (Map p244; ☑02 585 83 185; www.malpensashuttle.it; ticket €10)

Coaches depart from Piazza Luigi di Savoi, next to Stazione Centrale, every 20 minutes from 3.45am to 12.30am, taking 50 minutes to reach **Malpensa Airport**.

Taxi

There is a flat fee of €90 to and from Malpensa Airport to central Milan. The drive should take 50 minutes outside peak traffic times. For travellers to Terminal 2, this might prove the quickest option. The taxi fare to Linate Airport is between €10 and €20.

Train

Malpensa Express (☑02 7249 4494; www.malpensaexpress.it) Coaches depart Malpensa Airport every 30 minutes from Terminal 1 for Stazione Centrale (adult/child €10/5, 50 minutes) and Cadorna Nord (Stazione Nord; www.ferrovienord.it; Piazza Luigi Cadorna (adult/child €11/5, 30 minutes) between 5.25am and 11.40pm. Passengers arriving or departing from Terminal 2 will need to catch the free shuttle bus to Terminal 1 train station.

BICYCLE

BikeMi (www.bikemi.it) is Milan's public bike network. Daily, weekly or annual passes are available, and you can pick up and drop off bikes at different stations. Get passes online or at an **ATM Info Point** (☑800 80 81 81; www.atm.it; ⊙7.45am-7.15pm Mon-Sat).

CAR & MOTORCYCLE

It simply isn't worth having a car in Milan. Many streets have restricted access and parking is a nightmare. In the centre, street parking costs €1.50 per hour. To pay, buy a SostaMilano card from a tobacconist, scratch off the date and hour, and display it on your dashboard. Underground car parks charge between €25 and €40 for 24 hours.

PUBLIC TRANSPORT

ATM (☑800 80 81 81; www.atm.it) Runs the metro, buses and trams. The metro is the most

---

DON'T MISS

QUADRILATERO D'ORO

For anyone interested in the fall of a frock or the cut of a jacket, a stroll around the Quadrilatero d'Oro (Golden Quad; Map p250), the world's most fabled shopping district, is a must. This quaintly cobbled quadrangle of streets may have always been synonymous with elegance and money (Via Monte Napoleone was where Napoleon's government managed loans), but the Quad's legendary fashion status belongs firmly to Milan's postwar reinvention. During the boom years of the 1950s the city's fashion houses established ateliers in the area bounded by Via Monte Napoleone, Via Sant'Andrea, Via della Spiga and Via Alessandro Manzoni and by the 1960s Milan had outflanked Florence and Rome to become the country's haute couture capital. Nowadays, the world's top designers unveil their women's collections in February/March and September/October, while men's fashion hits the runways in January and June/July.

ℹ MAPS & PASSES

Bus and tram route maps are available at ATM Info points. Otherwise download the IATM app. There are several good money-saving passes available for public transport:

One-day ticket Valid 24 hours, €4.50

Three-day ticket Valid 72 hours, €8.25

Carnet of 10 tickets Valid for 90 minutes each, €13.80

convenient way to get around and consists of three main lines and the blue Passante Ferroviario, which run from 6am and 12.30am, after which a night service runs to 2.30am. A ticket costs €1.50 and is valid for one metro ride or up to 90 minutes' travel on ATM buses and trams. Tickets are sold at metro stations, tobacconists and newspaper stands. Tickets must be validated on trams and buses.

M1 (red) Connects Duomo, Corso Venezia, Castello Sforzesco and the Fiera.

M2 (green) Connects Porta Garibaldi, Brera and Navigli.

M3 (yellow) Connects the Quadrilatero d'Oro with Porta Romana.

TAXI

Taxis are only available at designated taxi ranks; you cannot flag them down. Alternatively, call ☑ 02 40 40, ☑ 02 69 69 or ☑ 02 85 85. The average short city ride costs €10. Be aware that when you call for a cab, the meter runs from receipt of call, not pick up.

Around Milan

Pavia

POP 68,350

Founded by the Romans as a military garrison, Pavia has long been a strategic city both geographically and politcally. It sits at the centre of an agricultural plain (hence its ugly periphery), is an important provincial player with strong Lega Nord leanings, and its university (founded in the 14th century) is one of the best in Italy. Aside from its buzzy, student atmosphere, Pavia has a lovely historic centre and is the location of the extraordinary Carthusian monastery, the Certosa di Pavia.

★ **Certosa di Pavia** (Pavia Charterhouse; ☑ 0382 92 56 13; www.certosadipavia.com; Viale Monumento; donations appreciated; ⊙ 9-11.30am & 2.30-5.30pm Tue-Sun) is one of the Ital-

ian Renaissance's most notable buildings. Giangaleazzo Visconti of Milan founded the monastery, 10km north of Pavia, in 1396 as a private chapel and mausoleum for the Visconti family. Construction proceeded in a stop-start fashion until well into the 16th century, making this a prime example of the transition from Gothic to Renaissance.

While the interior is predominantly Gothic, the exterior is Renaissance. The church is fronted by a spacious courtyard and flanked by a small cloister, which itself leads to a much grander second cloister, under whose arches are 24 cells, each a self-contained living area for one monk. Several cells are open to the public. In the chapels you'll find frescoes by, among others, Bernardino Luini and the Umbrian master, Il Perugino.

Sila (☑ 199 153155; www.sila.it) bus 175 (Pavia–Binasco–Milano) runs services from Pavia bus station (Via Trieste) and Certosa di Pavia (15 minutes, at least seven daily).

Plenty of direct trains from Stazione Centrale link Pavia with Milan (€3.80, 25 to 40 minutes).

Monza

POP 120,000

Known to many as the home of a classic European Formula One track (where high-speed races have been held annually in September since 1950), Monza is sadly overlooked by visitors to Milan, but history and architecture buffs are rewarded.

Monza racetrack (☑ 039 2 48 21; www.monzanet.it; Via Vedano 5, Parco di Monza; race tickets adult €10-20, reduced €8-14, use of circuit €45; ⊙ 8am-1pm & 2.30-6.30pm Mar-Sep, 8am-1pm & 2-6pm Oct-Feb), which you can actually drive on most days in winter, is worth visiting, as is the Gothic **Duomo** (☑ 039 38 94 20; www.duomomonza.it; Piazza Duomo; corona ferrea adult/reduced €4/3; ⊙ 9am-noon & 2-6pm), with its white and green banded facade, which contains a key early-medieval treasure, the **Corona Ferrea** (Iron Crown), fashioned according to legend with one of the nails from the Crucifixion. Charlemagne, King of the Franks and the first Holy Roman Emperor, saw it as a symbol of empire and he was not alone. Various other Holy Roman Emperors, including Frederick I (Barbarossa) and Napoleon, had themselves crowned with it. The crown is on show in the chapel (Tuesday to Sunday only) dedicated to the Lombard queen Theodolinda. Next door, the **Museo e Tesoro del Duomo** (☑ 039 32 63 83; www.

museoduomomonza.it; Piazza del Duomo; adult/reduced €6/4, with Corono Ferrea €8/6; ⊙ 9am-1pm & 2-6pm Tue-Sun) contains one of the greatest collections of early religious art in Europe.

The **Parco di Monza** (Porta Monza, Viale Cavriga; ⊙ 7am-7pm) sits on the Lambro river and incorporates not only the Autodromo, but a horse-racing track, a golf course, tennis courts, a 50m Olympic **swimming pool** (☑ 039 248 22 32; Porta Santa Maria delle Selve, Via Vedano; adult/reduced €8/3; ⊙ 10am-7pm Jun-Aug), horse-riding tracks and cycle paths. You can hire bikes at the Porta di Monza entrance (€3 per hour).

Frequent trains connect Milan's Porta Garibaldi station with Monza (€2.10, 15 to 20 minutes), 23km to the north, making this an easy half-day trip.

THE LAKES

Writers from Goethe and Stendhal to DH Lawrence and Hemingway have all lavished praise on the Italian lakes, which are dramatically ringed by snow-powdered mountains.

The westernmost of the main lakes, Lago d'Orta, is entirely within Piedmont. The three big ones are, west to east, Lago Maggiore, with its spectacular Borromean Islands; Lago di Como, closed in by densely wooded mountains; and Lago di Garda, the biggest and the busiest. Its southeast corner (in the Veneto region) has Disney-style family amusement parks, including Italy's largest, Gardaland. The northern reaches of Lago di Garda extend into the Alpine region of Trentino–Alto Adige.

Lago Maggiore

By train or by road, travellers traversing the Alps from Switzerland at the Sempione Pass wind down from the mountains and sidle up to the western shore of Lago Maggiore. The star attractions are the Borromean Islands, which, like a fleet of fine vessels, lie at anchor in the Borromean Gulf. More than Como and Garda, Lago Maggiore retains the belle époque air of its 19th-century heyday when the European *haute bourgeoisie* flocked to buy and build grand lakeside villas and establish a series of extraordinarily rich gardens.

The northern end of the lake, where it narrows between the mountains and enters Switzerland, is the prettier, more secluded end. And it's well worth taking the delightful drive south along the SS34 and SS33.

ℹ Getting There & Around

BOAT

Car Ferries Connect Verbania Intra and Laveno. Ferries run every 20 minutes; one-way transport costs from €6.90 to €11.50 for a car and driver or €4.30 for a bicycle and cyclist

Navigazione Lago Maggiore (☑ 800 551801; www.navigazionelaghi.it) Operates ferries and hydrofoils. There are ticket booths in each town next to the embarkation quay; the main office is in Arona. Day passes cost from €15.50/8.80 to €21.50/11.80 per adult/child, depending on the departure port, and include the Swiss town of Locarno as a stop

BUS

SAF (☑ 0323 55 21 72; www.safduemila.com) offers a daily service from Stresa to Milan (€8.75, 1½ hours), and also serves Verbania Pallanza (€2.25, 20 minutes) and Arona (€2.25, 20 minutes), departing from the waterfront.

TRAIN

Stresa is on the Domodossola–Milan train line. Domodossola, 30 minutes northwest, is on the Swiss border, from where the train line leads to Brig and on to Geneva.

Stresa

POP 5230

Facing due east across the lake, Stresa has a ringside view of the fiery orange sun rising up over the water. Since the 18th century, the town's easy accessibility from Milan has made it a favourite for artists and writers seeking inspiration. Hemingway was one of many; he arrived in Stresa in 1918 to convalesce from a war wound. A couple of pivotal scenes towards the end of his novel *A Farewell to Arms* are set at the Grand Hôtel des Iles Borromées, the most palatial of the hotels garlanding the lake.

⊙ Sights & Activities

People stream into Stresa to meander along its promenade and visit the Borromean Islands. The pebble beach just west of the main ferry dock is good for a sunbathe.

Parco della Villa Pallavicino   ZOO
(☑ 0323 3 15 33; www.parcozoopallavicino.it; adult/child €9.50/6.50; ⊙ 9am-6pm Mar-Oct) Barely 1km southeast of Stresa along the SS33 road, exotic birds and animals roam relatively freely at the child-friendly Parco della Villa Pallavicino. Forty species of animal, including llamas, Sardinian donkeys, flamingos and toucans keep everyone amused.

FLAVIO VALLENARI / GETTY IMAGES ©

1. Lago di Garda (p279)
Gardone Riviera's villas and architecture make for an elegant holiday spot.

2. Villa Carlotta (p275)
This 17th-century villa is a must-see for any visitor to Lago di Como.

3. Lago di Como (p269)
Pastel-coloured houses rise steeply up the hillside in pretty Varenna.

4. Lago Maggiore (p261)
The villa and gardens on Isola Bella, one of the Borromean Islands, were built to look like a ship.

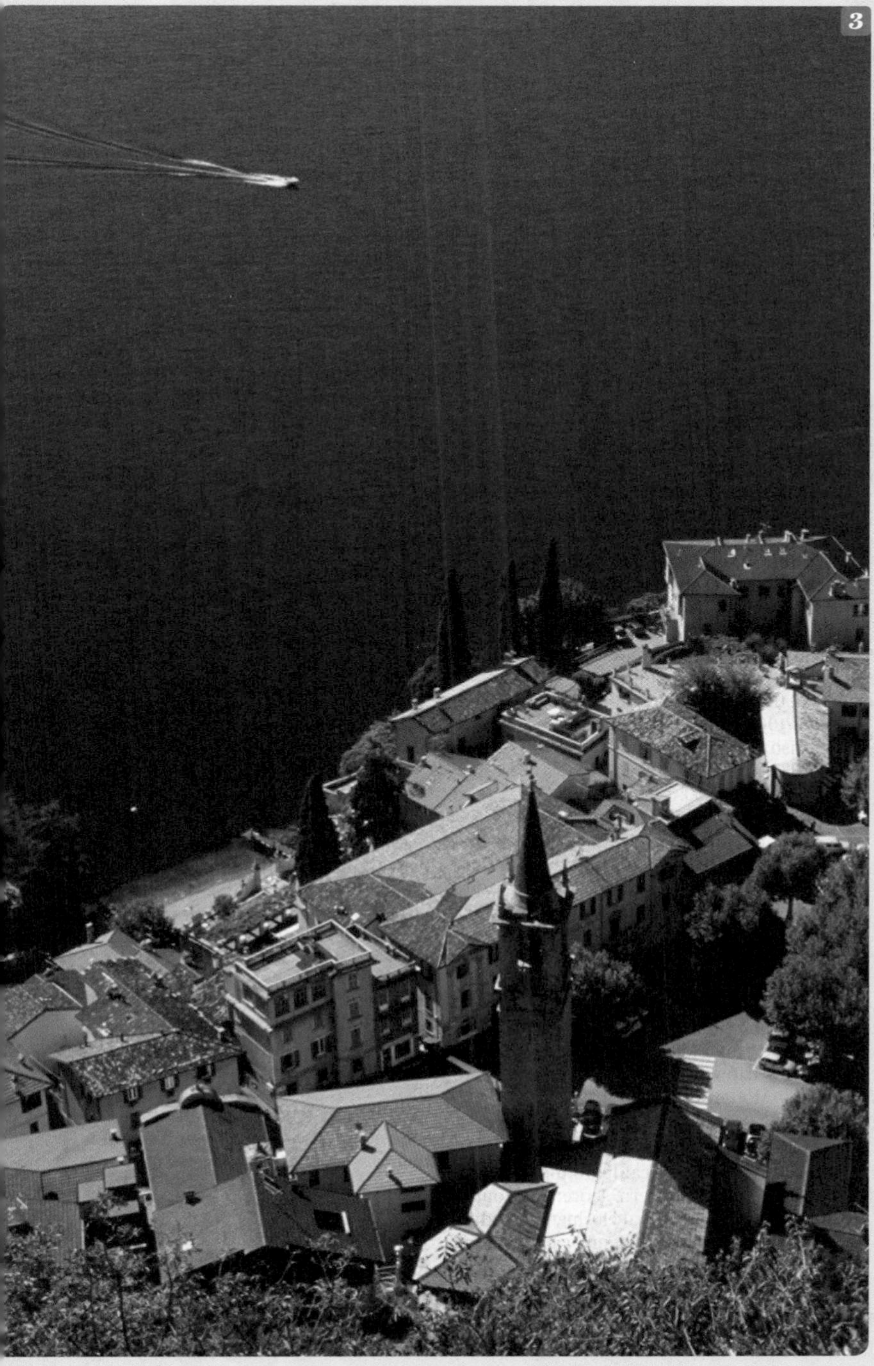

RELIGIOUS IMAGES/ UIG / GETTY IMAGES ©

ⓘ LAGO MAGGIORE EXPRESS

The **Lago Maggiore Express** (www.lagomaggioreexpress.com; adult/child 1-day pass €32/16, 2-day €42/21) is a picturesque day trip you can do under your own steam. It includes train travel from Arona or Stresa to Domodossola, from where you get the charming Centovalli (Hundred Valleys) train to Locarno in Switzerland and a ferry back to Stresa. The two-day version is better value if you have the time. Tickets are available from the Navigazione Lago Maggiore ticket booths at each port.

Funivia Stresa–Mottarone   CABLE CAR

(☎0323 3 02 95; www.stresa-mottarone.it; Piazzale della Funivia, Mottarone; return adult/child €18/12, to Alpino station €12.50/8.50; ⊙9.30am-5.30pm Apr-Oct, 8.10am-5.30pm Nov-Mar; ⛴Stresa) Captivating views of the lake unfold during a 20-minute cable-car journey to the top of 1491m-high Monte Mottarone. Cars depart every 20 minutes in summer. On a clear day you can see Lago Maggiore, Lago d'Orta and Monte Rosa, on the Alpine border with Switzerland.

At the Alpino midstation (803m), more than 1000 Alpine and sub-Alpine species flourish in the **Giardino Botanico Alpinia** (☎0323 3 02 95; www.giardinoalpinia.it/info.htm; adult/child €3/2.50; ⊙9.30am-6pm Apr-Oct), a botanical garden dating from 1934.

The mountain itself offers good biking trails as well as walking opportunities. **Bicicò** (☎0340 357 21 89; www.bicico.it; half-/full-day rental €23/28, half-/full-day guide €80/150; ⊙9.30am-12.30pm & 1.30-5.30pm) rents out mountain bikes at the Stresa cable-car station. Rates include a helmet and road book detailing panoramic descents (accessible to pretty much anyone who can ride a bike) from the top of Mottarone back to Stresa. A one-way trip with a bike on the cable car to Alpino/Mottarone costs €9/12.

🛏 Sleeping & Eating

There are some 40 campgrounds up and down the lake's western shore; the tourist office has a list. Seasonal closings (including hotels) are generally November to February, but this can vary, so it's always best to check ahead.

Hotel Elena   HOTEL €

(☎0323 3 10 43; www.hotelelena.com; Piazza Cadorna 15, Stresa; s/d €60/85; ℙ) Adjoining a cafe, the old-fashioned Elena is slap-bang on Stresa's central square. Wheelchair access is available, and all of Elena's comfortable rooms, with parquet floors, have a balcony, many overlooking the square.

Casa Kinka   B&B €€

(☎0323 3 24 43; www.casakinka.it; Strada Comunale Lombartino 21, Magognino; s/d €90/130; ⊙Mar-Oct; ℙ@) This lovely B&B is set on a rise high above Stresa, about 6km out of town. The friendly owners have two comfortable rooms. You can sit back on a sun lounger on the garden lawn and gaze down over the lake. To get here from Stresa, follow the road for Mottarone and turn off towards Vedasco.

Villa Aminta   HOTEL €€€

(☎0323 93 38 18; www.villa-aminta.it; Via Sempione Nord 123; d €295-440; ℙ❄🛜🏊) Stay in turn-of-the-century style at fairy-tale Villa Aminta, which offers picture-perfect views of Isola Bella. Rooms decked out with Murano chandeliers, silk curtains and acres of gilt and velvet resemble the baroque opulence of the Borromeo Palace. The hotel also has its own private beach, heated pool, fitness centre and a regular shuttle service into Stresa.

La Botte   PIEDMONTESE €€

(☎0323 3 04 62; Via Mazzini 6; meals €25-30; ⊙noon-2pm & 6.30-9pm Fri-Wed) A traditional *osteria* (casual eatery presided over by a host) just in from the lakefront, with simple, dark timber furniture and decades of accumulated baubles hanging on the walls. The grilled polenta or risotto with blue cheese and pears are fine ways to get things going.

Piemontese   ITALIAN €€

(☎0323 3 02 35; www.ristorantepiemontese.com; Via Mazzini 25; set menu from €28, meals €35-45; ⊙12.30-2pm & 6.30-9.30pm) Refined surrounds and high-quality cooking dominate this well-regarded place. Try the polenta with cheese fondue and air-dried beef, or the *menu di mezzogiorno* (lunchtime set menu).

ⓘ Information

Tourist Office (☎0323 3 13 08; www.stresaturismo.it; Piazza Marconi 16; ⊙10am-12.30pm & 3-6.30pm mid-Mar–mid-Oct, shorter weekend hrs in winter)

Borromean Islands

The Borromean Gulf forms Lago Maggiore's most beautiful corner, and the Borromean Islands can be reached from various points around the lake, although Stresa and Baveno offer the best access.

ISOLA BELLA

Isola Bella took the name of Carlo III's wife, the *bella* Isabella, in the 17th century, when its centrepiece, **Palazzo Borromeo** (☑0323 3 05 56; www.isoleborromee.it; adult/child €13/5.50, combined ticket with Isola Madre €18/8, Galleria dei Quadri €3; ☉9am-5.30pm Apr–mid-Oct), was built for the Borromeo family. Construction of the villa and gardens was thought out in such a way that the island would have the appearance of a ship, with the villa at the prow and the gardens dripping down 10 tiered terraces at the rear. Well-known guests have included Napoleon and Josephine in 1797 (you can see the bed they slept in), and Prince Charles and Princess Diana in 1985. A separate ticket gives you access to the **Galleria dei Quadri** (Picture Gallery; admission €3), a series of halls covered from top to bottom with the Borromeo art collection which includes Rubens, Titian, Paolo Veronese and Andrea Mantegna.

Below ground a 3000-year-old fossilised boat is displayed in the palace grottoes, which themselves are studded with pink marble, lava stone and pebbles from the lake bed. Outside, white peacocks strut through one of the finest examples of baroque Italian garden design.

Elvezia (☑0323 3 00 43; meals €30-35; ☉noon-2pm & 6.30-9pm Tue-Sun Mar-Oct, Fri-Sun only Nov-Feb) is the place for authentic family cooking.

ISOLA MADRE

All of Isola Madre is taken up by the fabulous 16th- to 18th-century **Palazzo Madre** (☑0323 3 05 56; adult/child incl gardens €11/5.50, combined ticket with Isola Bella €18/8; ☉9am-6pm Mar-Oct) and its gardens. The latter is brimming with azaleas, rhododendrons, camellias and hibiscus and is home to white peacocks and vibrant-coloured Chinese pheasants. Palace highlights include a neoclassical puppet theatre designed by a scenographer from Milan's La Scala, and a 'horror' theatre with a cast of devilish marionettes.

ISOLA SUPERIORE (PESCATORI)

Lacking any real sights, tiny 'Fishermen's Island' retains much of its original village atmosphere. Apart from an 11th-century apse and a 16th-century fresco in the **Chiesa di San Vittore**, there isn't anything to see; hence many visitors make it their port of call for lunch. Restaurants cluster around the boat landing, all serving grilled fish fresh from the lake from around €15.

If you want to stay on the island, **Albergo Belvedere** (☑0323 3 22 92; www.belvedere-isolapescatori.it; Isola Superiore; r €99-199; ✸) has rooms with balconies overlooking the lake.

Verbania

POP 31,200

North of Stresa, Verbania is the biggest town on the lake and is split into three districts. Verbania Pallanza is the most interesting, with a tight web of lanes in its old centre, while Verbania Intra has a pleasant waterfront and handy car ferries to Laveno on the eastern shore. Running north from Pallanza, Via Vittorio Veneto has a jogging and cycling path that follows the lakefront.

The city's highlight is the spectacular grounds of the late-19th-century **Villa Taranto** (☑0323 40 45 55; www.villataranto.it; Via Vittorio Veneto 111, Verbania Pallanza; adult/child €10/5.50; ☉8.30am-6.30pm; ☑Villa Taranto). In 1931, royal archer and Scottish captain Neil McEacharn bought the villa from the Savoy family and started to plant some 20,000 species over a 30-year period. With its rolling hillsides of purple rhododendrons and camellias, acres of tulip flowers and hothouses full of equatorial lilies, it is considered one of Europe's finest botanical gardens. During the last week in April tens of thousands of tulips erupt in magnificent multicoloured bloom for **Settimana del Tulipano**, while in spring and autumn Verbanis hosts the Camellia Show (www.camelieinmostra.it).

Overlooking Pallanza's cute port and the Isolino San Giovanni, the neo-Gothic **Ristorante Milano** (☑0323 55 68 16; www.ristorantemilanolagomaggiore.it; Corso Zanitelli 2, Verbania Pallanza; meals €60-70; ☉noon-2pm & 7-9pm Wed-Sun, noon-2pm Mon) sits lakeside amid a shady gravel-and-lawn garden. It serves a contemporary menu including lake perch and char with seasonal vegetables. **Caffè Bolongaro** (☑0323 50 32 54; Piazza Garibaldi 9; pizzas €4.50-8), on the waterfront in Pallanza, serves good pizza.

Verbania's **tourist office** (☏ 0323 50 32 49; www.verbania-turismo.it; Corso Zanitello 6-8; ☺ 9am-1pm Mon-Fri) is on the waterfront in Verbania Pallanza.

Set in a lovely 19th-century building on the lakefront promenade, **Hotel Belvedere** (☏ 0323 50 32 02; www.pallanzahotels.com; Viale Magnolie 6, Verbania Pallanza; d without/with lake view from €99/110; ❈ ☎) makes an excellent Maggiore base.

Cannobio

POP 5230

Sheltered by a high mountain and sitting at the foot of the Cannobino valley, the medieval hamlet of Cannobio, located 5km from the Swiss border, is a dreamy place. Although there are no specific sites in the town, its restaurants and hotels are some of the best on the lake. And on Sunday its lakeside market attracts visitors from Switzerland.

The **tourist office** (☏ 0323 7 12 12; www.pro-cannobio.it; Via Giovanola 25; ☺ 9am-noon & 4-7pm Mon-Sat, 9am-noon Sun & holidays) is just inland off the main lakeside road.

Activities

Cannobio has an active sailing and windsurfing school, **Tomaso Surf & Sail** (☏ 0323 7 22 14; www.tomaso.com; Via Nazionale 7), next to a gritty beach at the village's northern end. You can also hire small sailing boats here

(€120 per day) and make a nice excursion to the ruined **Castelli della Malpaga**, located on two rocky islets to the south of Cannobio.

Alternatively, remain landbound and explore the wild beauty of the Val Cannobino by car or bike. The route meanders along the scenic SP75, winding its way 28km beside the surging Torrente Cannobino stream, into the heavily wooded hills to Malesco in Valle Vigezzo. Just 2.5km along the valley, in Sant'Anna, the Torrente Cannobino powerfully forces its way through a narrow gorge known as the **Orrido di Sant'Anna**, crossed at its narrowest part by a Romanesque bridge. A further 7km on, a steep 3km side road consisting of hairpin bends leads up to the central valley's main town, **Falmenta**. Hire mountain bikes in Cannobio from **Cicli Prezan** (☏ 0323 7 12 30; www.cicliprezan.it; Viale Vittorio Veneto 9; per hr/day €5/15; ☺ 8.30am-noon & 3-7pm Mon-Sat, 8.30pm-noon Sun)

Sleeping & Eating

★ **Hotel Pironi** HOTEL €€

(☏ 0323 7 06 24; www.pironihotel.it; Via Marconi 35, Cannobio; s €110-120, d €150-190; ℗ ❈ ❈) In a 15th-century mini-monastery (later home of the noble Pironi family) high in Cannobio's cobbled maze, Hotel Pironi is a charming choice. Behind its thickset stone walls lurks a beautifully restored excursion into the past, with antiques sprinkled about, frescoed vaults, exposed timber beams, stairs

---

WORTH A TRIP

INTO SWITZERLAND

With its much vaunted 2300 hours of sunshine a year, **Locarno** (pop 15,300) and its equally pretty neighbour **Ascona** (pop 5450) have long been beloved of Mitteleuropeans seeking class and culture in the sun. Take the Centovalli railway from Domodossola or arrive aboard a ferry from Cannobio, and you'll soon see what all the fuss is about.

Stride out and about in Locarno's handsome Italianate piazzas or join the sunglasses crowd on the flower-filled *lungolago* (lakeside promenade); catch the **funicular** (adult one way/return Sfr4.80/7.20, child Sfr2.20/3.60; ☺ 7am-8pm) up to the Santuario della Madonna del Sasso for Bramantino's *Flight into Egypt*; or head up, up and away on the chairlift up to **Cimetta** (1672m) for panoramic views and gentle hikes. Stay overnight at hip **Caffe dell'Arte** (☏ +41 091 751 9 333; www.caffedellarte.ch; Via Cittadella 9, Locarno; ☺ 8.30am-9pm Tue-Sat; ☎ Locarno) and spend a day or two exploring modern art at the **Museo Comunale d'Arte Moderna** (☏ 091 759 81 40; www.museoascona.ch; Via Borgo 34; adult/reduced Sfr7/5; ☺ 10am-noon & 3-6pm Tue-Sat, 10.30am-12.30pm Sun Mar-Dec) in nearby pastel-hued Ascona, or take a ferry and picnic amid the exotic blooms on the island garden of **Isole di Brissago** (☏ 091 791 43 61; www.isolebrissago.ch; Via Borgo 34; adult/child Sfr8/2.50; ☺ 9am-6pm Apr–late-Oct).

In August, the cinema world descends on Locarno for one of Europe's top film festivals, **Festival Internazionale di Film**, when every night Piazza Grande is transformed into a massive outdoor theatre beneath the stars.

LUINO

The otherwise sleepy town of Luino hosts Lago Maggiore's biggest **market** (Market; ⊙8.30am-4.30pm Wed) on Wednesdays. This is no ordinary local flea market but rather an enormous bazaar that snakes off into the surrounding streets wth all manner of trash and treasure, not to mention some good street food. The records show that an important weekly market was first held here in 1535. Today more than 350 stands are set up in the old town centre, with everything from local cheese to second-hand fashion on sale. Bargain-hunters come from as far away as the Netherlands.

climbing off in odd directions, a frescoed breakfast room and an assortment of tastefully decorated rooms, some with lake views.

Lo Scalo　　　　　　MODERN ITALIAN €€
(☑0323 7 14 80; www.loscalo.com; Piazza Vittorio Emanuele III 32, Cannobio; meals €35-45; ⊙11.30am-2.30pm & 6-9pm Wed-Sun, 6-9pm Tue; ☑Cannobio) The pick of the restaurants along the main promenade, Lo Scalo has a fine setting. The cooking is sophisticated and clean, featuring dishes such as ribbonthin *tagliolini* pasta with black truffles and mountain butter.

Santa Caterina del Sasso

The monastery of **Santa Caterina del Sasso** (www.santacaterinadelsasso.com; ⊙8.30am-noon & 2.30-6pm Apr-Sep, to 5pm Mar, closed weekdays Nov-Feb) is spectacularly located at Leggiuno, clinging to the high rocky face of the southeast shore of Lago Maggiore. It is reached by a spiralling staircase, 267 steps from the road above and 80 steps from the lake below (there is also a lift). Father Roberto Comolli, the only Carmelite monk who still lives here, is the spiritual guide of the seven oblates of St Benedict who keep the candles lit in the frescoed 13th- and 14th-century chapels. A few ferries from Stresa dock here between March and October (return €6.80). Otherwise, by car or bus it's 5.6km south of Laveno (watch for the signs for Leggiuno and then a sign for the convent, 1km in off the main road).

Arona

POP 14,600

It was in Arona that the son of the Count of Arona and Margherita de' Medici, who would go on to be canonised San Carlo Borromeo (1538–84), was born. His birthplace, the Rocca Borromea castle, was destroyed in 1801 on Napoleon's orders, its stone used to pave the Via del Sempione. In 1610 San Carlo was declared a saint and his cousin, Federico, ordered the creation of a *sacro monte* (sacred mountain), with 15 chapels lining a path uphill to a church dedicated to the saint. The church and three of the chapels were built, along with a special extra atop the **Sacro Monte di San Carlo** (☑0322 24 96 69; Piazza San Carlo, Arona; admission €4; ⊙9am-12.30pm & 2.30-6pm Mar-Oct, to 4.30pm Sat & Sun Nov-Feb; ☑Arona): a hollow 35m bronze-and-copper statue of the saint, commonly known as the Sancarlone (Big St Charles). It can be climbed, affording a spectacular view from the top (children under six years old are not permitted).

To reach the hill, walk or drive 2km west from Piazza del Popolo, Arona's most charming piazza.

Lago d'Orta

Shrouded by thick, dark-green woodlands, little Lago d'Orta measures 13.4km in length and just 2.5km wide. It's separated from its bigger and better-known eastern neighbour, Lago Maggiore, by Monte Mottarone.

⊙ Sights

The focal point of the lake is the medieval village of **Orta San Giulio** (population 1170), often referred to simply as Orta. Its cream-coloured houses are roofed with thick slate tiles, and the central square, Piazza Motta, is overlooked by the Palazotto, a frescoed 16th-century building borne up on stilts above a small loggia. Just across the water sits **Isola San Giulio**. The island is dominated at its south end by the 12th-century **Basilica di San Giulio** (⊙9.30am-6.45pm Tue-Sun, 2-5pm Mon Apr-Sep, 9.30am-noon & 2-5pm Tue-Sun & 2-5pm Mon Oct-Mar), full of frescoes that alone make a trip to the island worthwhile. You may find the island's only snack restaurant open on busy weekends. Regular ferries (€2.85 return) and private boats (€8 return) make the five-minute crossing.

For more serenity, head up to **Sacro Monte**, a hillside dotted with 20 small chapels dedicated to St Francis of Assisi. The parklands here are a great spot for a picnic: pick up picnic fare at Orta San Giulio's Wednesday market. Between March and September a **tourist train** (www.trenino-diorta.it/ita; one way/return €2.50/4; ⊙9am-7pm May-Sep, 9am-5.30pm Mar, Apr & Oct, 9.30am-5.30pm rest of year) shuttles between the town centre and the Sacro Monte.

🍴 Sleeping & Eating

★Locanda di Orta   HOTEL €
(☑0322 90 51 88; www.locandaorta.com; Via Olina 18; s/d/ste from €60/70/150; 🖥) This new place is outrageously good value, effortlessly combining medieval touches with modern design flair. Most of the rooms have exposed stone walls, which nicely offset the contemporary decor. They also offer packages that include dinner and boat tickets to Isola San Giulio.

Piccolo Hotel Olina   HOTEL €
(☑0322 90 56 56; www.ortainfo.com; Via Olina 40, Orta San Giulio; s €64-75, d €90-105; 🌸) Artistically decorated with bright colours and light-wood furniture, this ecofriendly hotel in Orta San Giulio's medieval heart is a gem. It also has a fine, somewhat avant-garde restaurant downstairs, and it has other hotel options scattered around the old town if they're full.

Enoteca Al Boeuc   PIEDMONTESE €
(☑339 584 00 39; http://alboeuc.beepworld.it; Via Bersani 28, Orta San Giulio; meals €15-20; ⊙11.30am-3pm & 6.30pm-midnight Wed-Mon) This candlelit stone cavern has been around since the 16th century, and in its present incarnation, you'll be served light meals (*bruschette*, charcuterie and *bagna cauda*, an anchovie and garlic dip), to be savoured with fine wines by the glass.

Ristorante Sant'Antonio   ITALIAN €€
(☑0322 91 19 63; Tortirogno; meals €25-30; ⊙noon-2pm & 7-9.30pm Wed-Sun) About 1.5km north of Orta on the main road, this family-run place has a winning combination of lakeside tables and simple, non-nonsense cooking. Not surprisingly, it's deservedly popular. While the occasional meat dish appears, fish is the name of the game.

Agriturismo Cucchiaio di Legno   AGRITURISMO €€
(☑0322 90 52 80; www.ilcucchiaiodilegno.com; Via Prisciola 10, Località Legro; set menu €24; ⊙6-9pm Thu & Fri, noon-2.30pm Sat & Sun) This honest-to-goodness *agriturismo* restaurant cooks up delicious local dishes including risotto, fish straight out of the lake, and salami and cheese from the surrounding valleys. It's about 800m from the Orta Miasino train station.

🛍 Shopping

Alessi   OUTLET STORE
(☑0323 86 86 48; www.alessi.com; Via Privata Alessi 6, Omegna; ⊙9.30am-6pm Mon-Sat, 2.30-6pm Sun) Established in the small town of Omegna on Lake Orta in 1921, Alessi went on to transform modern kitchens with humorous, ultra-cool utensils designed by a pantheon of great-name architect-designers, including most recently, Zaha Hadid. Go mad in their huge factory outlet, where the whole range is on offer along with end-of-line deals.

Information

Tourist Office   TOURIST INFORMATION
(☑0322 90 51 63; www.comune.ortasangiulio.no.it; Via Panoramica; ⊙9am-1pm & 2-6pm Wed-Sun Apr-Oct, 8.30am-1.30pm & 2.30-5.30pm Sat & Sun Nov-Mar) Orta San Giulio's tourist office has information on the lake.

Pro Loco   TOURIST INFORMATION
(☑0322 9 01 55; Via Bossi 10; ⊙11am-1pm & 2-6pm Mon & Wed-Fri, 10am-1pm & 2-6pm Sat & Sun) Located in the centre of town.

ℹ Getting There & Around

BOAT
Navigazione Lago d'Orta (☑0322 84 48 62; www.navigazionelagodorta.it) Operates ferries from Piazza Motta, including Isola San Giulio (one-way/return €2/2.85). A day ticket for unlimited travel costs €8.50.

BUS
From June to September three daily buses run from Orta to Stresa (€4).

TRAIN
Orta Miasino train station is 3km from the centre of Orta San Giulio. From Milan there are trains from Stazione Centrale (change at Novara; €6.50, two hours).

Lago di Como

Set in the shadow of the snow-covered Rhaetian Alps and hemmed in on both sides by steep, wooded hills, Lago di Como (also known as Lake Lario) is the most spectacular and least visited of the three major lakes. Shaped like an upside-down letter Y, its winding shoreline is scattered with villages, including delightful Bellagio, which sits at the centre of the two southern branches on a small promontory. Where the southern and western shores converge is the lake's main town, Como.

In May and June, watch out for musical concerts at some of Lago di Como's finest villas as part of the Lake Como Festival (www.lakecomofestival.com).

ⓘ Getting There & Around

BOAT

Navigazione Lago di Como (☑ 800 551801, 031 57 92 11; www.navigazionelaghi.it; Piazza Cavour) ferries and hydrofoils criss-cross the lake, departing year-round from the jetty at the northern end of Como's Piazza Cavour. One-way fares range from €2.50 (Como–Cernobbio) to €12.60 (Como–Lecco or Como–Gravedona). Hydrofoil fast services entail a supplement of €1.40 to €4.90.

Car ferries link Cadenabbia on the west shore with Varenna on the eastern shore and Bellagio.

BUS

ASF Autolinee (☑ 031 24 72 47; www.sptlinea. it) operates regular buses around the lake, which depart from the bus station on Piazza Giacomo Matteotti. Key routes include Como–Colico (€5.90, 1½ hours, three to five daily), via all the villages on the western shore, and Como–Bellagio (€3.20, one hour 10 minutes, hourly). Further afield, buses link Como with Bergamo (€5.90, 2¼ hours, up to six daily).

CAR

From Milan, take the A9 motorway and turn off at Monte Olimpino for Como. The SS36 leads east to Lecco while the SS233 heads west to Varese. The roads around the lake are terribly scenic, but also windy, narrow and busy in summer.

TRAIN

Como's main train station (Como San Giovanni) is served from Milan's Stazione Centrale and Porta Garibaldi station (€4.55 to €13, 30 minutes to one hour, hourly); some continue on to Switzerland. Trains from Milan's Stazione Nord (€4.10, one hour) use Como's lakeside Stazione FNM (aka Como Nord Lago). Trains from Milan to Lecco continue north along the eastern shore. If you're going to Bellagio, it is better to continue on the train to Varenna and make the short ferry crossing from there.

Como

POP 85,300

With its charming historic centre, 12th-century city walls and self-confident air, Como is an elegant and prosperous town. Built on the wealth of the silk industry, it remains Europe's most important producer of silk products; you can buy scarves and ties here for a fraction of the cost elsewhere.

MILAN & THE LAKES LAGO DI COMO

COMO SILK

Incorporating both the production and processing of silk, Como manufacturers, especially those around Lecco, produced some of the world's finest, most durable silks. By the 18th and 19th centuries, Como was the third largest silk producing sector in the world (not far behind China and Japan) and silk constituted Italy's most important national export. So valuable was the trade that the export of silk represented a third of the value of all Italian exports.

Even after the devastating prebina epidemic of 1855 – which all but wiped out the Italian moth species necessitating the import of raw silk from the Far East – the Como weaving industry retained a significant world presence. It was only in the early 20th century, following the economic crash of 1929 and the advent of new synthetic fabrics, that the industry fell into terminal decline.

Today, raw silk is imported from China and only the finishing, dyeing and printing work is carried out in Como. Out of literally hundreds of silk houses only three big firms remain: **Seteria Ratti** (www.ratti.it), **Mantero** (www.mantero.com) and **Canepa** (www. canepa.it). They still employ nearly one third of the Como population while Como's Istituto Tecnico Industriale di Setificio, founded in 1869, continues to turn out world-class designers, printers and chemical-dyeing experts.

Como

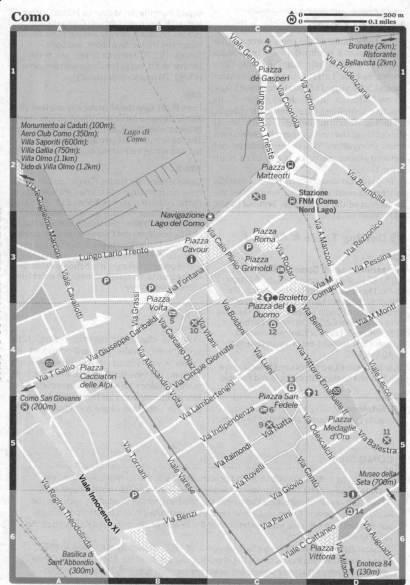

N 0 —————— 200 m
0 —————— 0.1 miles

Brunate (2km);
Ristorante
Bellavista (2km)

Monumento ai Caduti (100m);
Aero Club Como (350m);
Villa Saporiti (600m);
Villa Gallia (750m);
Villa Olmo (1.1km);
Lido di Villa Olmo (1.2km)

Lago di
Como

Piazza
de Gasperi

Piazza
Matteotti

Stazione
FNM (Como
Nord Lago)

Navigazione
Lago del Como

Piazza
Cavour

Piazza
Roma

Piazza
Grimoldi

Piazza
Volta

Broletto
Piazza del
Duomo

Piazza
Cacciatori
delle Alpi

Como San Giovanni
(200m)

Piazza San
Fedele

Piazza
Medaglie
d'Oro

Museo della
Seta (700m)

Basilica di
Sant'Abbondio
(300m)

Piazza
Vittoria

Enoteca 84
(130m)

Lungo Lario Trento

Lungo Lario Trieste

MILAN & THE LAKES LAGO DI COMO

◉ Sights & Activities

Como's lakeside location is stunning and flower-laden; lakeside promenades make for pleasant walks to the various sights. The tourist office has walking and cycling information.

Villa Olmo   VILLA, MUSEUM
(☎ 031 57 61 69; www.grandimostrecomo.it; Via Cantoni 1; adult/reduced €10/8; ⊙ villa during exhibitions 9am-12.30pm & 2-5pm Mon-Sat; gardens 7.30am-7pm Sep-May, 7.30am-11pm Jun-Aug) Set grandly facing the lake, the creamy facade

Como

of neoclassical Villa Olmo is one of Como's landmarks. The extravagant structure was built in 1728 by the Odescalchi family, related to Pope Innocent XI. If there's an art exhibition inside, you'll get to admire the sumptuous Liberty-style interiors. Otherwise, you can enjoy the Italianate and English gardens, which are open all day.

Almost as nice as the gardens is the lakeside stroll from Piazza Cavour. Follow Passeggiata Lino Gelpi along the water, passing the **Monumento ai Caduti** (War Memorial; Viale Puecher 9), a memorial to those killed in WWI and a classic example of Fascist-era architecture; it dates to 1931. You'll pass a series of mansions and villas, including **Villa Saporiti** and the adjacent **Villa Gallia**, both now owned by the provincial government.

During summer the **Lido di Villa Olmo** (www.lidovillaolmo.it; Via Cernobbio 2; adult/reduced day €6/4, half-day €4.50/2.50; ⊙9am-7pm mid-May–Sep), an open-air swimming pool and lakeside bar, is open to the public.

Duomo   CATHEDRAL
(Piazza del Duomo; ⊙8am-noon & 3-7pm) Although largely Gothic, elements of Romanesque, Renaissance and baroque styles can also be seen in Como's imposing, marble-clad *duomo*. The cathedral was built between the 14th and 18th centuries, and is crowned by a high octagonal dome.

Next door, the polychromatic Broletto, or medieval town hall, is unusual in that it butts right up against the church and is rather overwhelmed by it.

Basilica di Sant'Abbondio   BASILICA
(Via Regina; ⊙8am-6pm Apr-Sep, to 4pm Oct-Mar) About 500m south of the city walls and just beyond the busy and rather ugly Viale Innocenzo XI is the remarkable 11th-century Romanesque Basilica di Sant'Abbondio. Aside from its proud, high structure and impressive apse decorated with a beautiful geometric relief around the outside windows, the highlight is the remarkable fresco series inside the apse depicting scenes from the life of Christ.

Basilica di San Fedele   BASILICA
(Piazza San Fedele; ⊙8am-noon & 3.30-7pm) The circular layout of the originally 6th-century Basilica di San Fedele, with three naves and three apses, has been likened to a clover leaf. Its 16th-century rose window and precious 16th- and 17th-century frescoes add to its charm. The facade is the result of a 1914 remake but the apses are the real deal, featuring some eye-catching sculpture on the right side.

Museo della Seta   MUSEUM
(Silk Museum; ☑031 30 31 80; www.museosetacomo.com; Via Castelnuovo 9; adult/child €10/4; ⊙9am-noon & 3-6pm Tue-Fri) Housed in the bowels of the predictably ugly 1970s buildings of the Istituto Tecnico Industriale di Setificio textile technical school (where tomorrow's silk-makers and designers learn their trade), the Museo della Seta unravels the town's silk history, with early dyeing and printing equipment on display.

Funicolare Como-Brunate   FUNICULAR
(☑031 30 36 08; www.funicolarecomo.it; Piazza de Gasperi 4, Como; adult one way/return €2.90/5.25, child €1.90/3.20; ⊙half-hourly departures 8am-midnight mid-Apr–mid-Sep, to 10.30pm mid-Sep–mid-Apr) Northeast along the waterfront, past Piazza Matteotti and the train station, is the Como–Brunate cable car, which was built in 1894. It takes seven minutes to reach hilltop **Brunate** (720m), a quiet village offering splendid views. In **San Maurizio**, a 30-minute, steep walk from Brunate's funicular stop scales 143 steps to the top of the lighthouse, built in 1927 to mark the centenary of Alessandro Volta's death. The Como tourist office can provide a map with suggested walks.

MILAN & THE LAKES LAGO DI COMO

Come to Bruante at sunset and make a night of it with dinner on the terrace of **Ristorante Bellavista** (☎031 22 10 31; Piazza di Bonacossa 2, Brunate; meals €30-35; ◷noon-2.30pm & 6.30-9.30pm Wed-Mon).

★**Aero Club Como**   SEAPLANE TOURS
(☎031 57 44 95; www.aeroclubcomo.com; Viale Masia 44, Como; 2 people €140; ▣Como) For a touch of Hollywood glamour, take one of the 30-minute seaplane tours from the Aero Club and buzz Bellagio. Longer excursions over Lago Maggiore and Lago Lugano are also possible. During summer you'll need to reserve at least three or four days in advance.

🛏 Sleeping

Le Stanze del Lago   APARTMENT €
(☎339 5446515; www.lestanzedellago.com; Via Rodari 6; 2-/4-person apt €100/130; ▣) Five cosy apartments, nicely decked out in modern but understated fashion, make for a good deal in the heart of Como. For stays of five days or longer you can use the kitchen too. All apartments feature a double bed, sofa bed, timber ceiling and tiled floor.

★**Avenue Hotel**   BOUTIQUE HOTEL €€
(☎031 27 21 86; www.avenuehotel.it; Piazzole Terragni 6; d/ste from €170/220; ▣ 🛜) Combining a quiet location deep in the old town with ultra-modern rooms in which bold colours offset a minimalist white background, Avenue Hotel is deservedly popular. The free bicycle rental is a nice touch, as is the laptop safe box and flat-screen TVs. The service, too, is warm but discreet.

Albergo Firenze   HOTEL €€
(☎031 30 03 33; www.hotelfirenzecomo.it; Piazza Volta 16; s €92, d without/with piazza view €125/145; ▣ 🛜) Tucked above a women's fashion boutique on Piazza Volta, this attractive hotel has bright, spotless rooms, including several with access for wheelchairs. Don't be put off by the somewhat gloomy reception area, but do pay extra for a superior room with a piazza view because those out the back are a little dark.

🍴 Eating

Self-caterers can stock up on fresh fruit and vegetables at Como's **food market** (◷8.30am-1pm Tue & Thu, to 7pm Sat) outside Porta Torre.

★**Natta Café**   CAFE €
(☎031 26 91 23; Via Natta 16; meals €10-15; ◷9.30am-3.30pm Mon, 9.30am-midnight Tue-Thu, 9.30am-2am Fri, 11.30am-2pm Sat; 🛜) This funky space, in the old town but ever-so-slightly removed from the busier thoroughfares, is Como's antidote to traditional trattorias and *osterie*. A funky cafe with free wifi, it serves up light meals that change regularly, baguettes, salads, wine by the glass and well-priced cocktails (€5 to €8). It's a lovely, laid-back little spot.

Gelateria Ceccato   GELATO €
(☎031 2 33 91; Lungo Lario Trieste 16; gelato €1.50-4; ◷noon-midnight) For generations, Comaschi have turned to Ceccato for their Sunday afternoon gelato (located inside the Palace Hotel) and then embarked on a ritual *passeggiata* (evening stroll) with the dripping cones along the lakeshore.

Enoteca 84   ITALIAN €
(☎031 27 04 82; Via Milano 84; meals €20-25; ◷noon-2.30pm & 7-10pm Fri & Sat, noon-2.30pm Mon-Thu) Down one side of this minuscule locale are lined-up tables; down the other are shelves of fine wine. The menu changes often, and ranges from platters of cold meats and cheeses to such Lombard classics as *pizzoccheri artigianali* (handmade buckwheat tagliatelle).

★**Osteria del Gallo**   ITALIAN €€
(☎031 27 25 91; www.osteriadelgallo-como.it; Via Vitani 16; meals €25-30; ◷12.30pm-3pm Mon, to 9pm Tue-Sat) This ageless *osteria* is a must. Cheerful green and white gingham is draped over the little timber tables. All around are shelves of wine and other goodies. The menu is recited by staff (in French if you wish) and might include an entrée of giant ravioli, followed by lightly fried lake-fish fillets. Otherwise, pop by for a glass of wine.

Trattoria dei Combattenti   TRATTORIA €€
(☎031 27 05 74; www.trattoriadeicombattenti.com; Via Balestra 5/9; meals €30-35; ◷12.15-2.30pm & 7.30-10.15pm Tue-Sat, 12.15-2.30pm Sun & Mon; ▣) Set off a lovely cobblestone lane just inside the old city walls, this popular trattoria has inside timber tables with muted decor, an inner courtyard or a sunny gravel yard at the front. Opt for an *insalatone* (€9) if you want a 'big salad', or the two-course €14 set lunch. Grilled meats take a prominent place.

🛍 Shopping

A **craft and antiques market** (Piazza San Fedele; ⊙9am-7pm Sat) fills the piazza in front of the Basilica di San Fedele from 9am to 7pm every Saturday.

A Picci   SILK
(☑031 26 13 69; Via Vittorio Emanuele II 54, Como; ⊙3-7.30pm Mon, 9am-12.30pm & 3-7.30pm Tue-Sat; ▣Como) Open since 1919, this is the last remaining silk shop in town dedicated to selling Como-designed-and-made silk products such as ties, scarves, throws and sarongs. Products are grouped in price categories (starting at €15 for a tie) reflecting the skill and craft involved in each piece. Sales assistants are happy to advise on colours and styles. If it's a gift, they'll also wrap it for you.

ℹ Information

Post Office (Via T Gallio 6; ⊙8.30am-7pm Mon-Fri, 8.30am-12.30pm Sat) Has currency exchange. There is also a branch in the old town (Via Vittorio Emanuele II, 113; ⊙8.30am-7pm Mon-Fri, to 12.30pm Sat).

Tourist Office (☑031 26 97 12; www.lakecomo.org; Piazza Cavour 17; ⊙9am-1pm & 2-5pm Mon-Sat) There is an information kiosk (⊙10am-1pm & 2-5pm) next to the Duomo, and another at the train station (⊙10am-1pm & 2-5pm).

Triangolo Lariano

The mountainous territory between Como and Lecco in the south and Bellagio in the north is called the Triangolo Lariano, or the Lario Triangle. Lakeside villages **Torno**, **Careno** and **Lezzeno** line the Como–Bellagio road, and hiking trails abound.

The classic trail is known as the **Dorsale** (Ridge) and zigzags for 31km across the interior of the 'triangle' from the Brunate funicular station in Como to Bellagio. The standard trail, which follows old mule tracks, takes about 12 hours and is usually done in two stages. A more challenging route is the **Dorsale Creste** trail, which follows a series of mountain crests. Several *rifugi* (mountain huts), including the alpine chalet **Agriturismo Munt de Volt** (☑031 91 88 98; www.muntdevolt.altervista.org; Via Monti di Là 3, Pian del Tivano; r per person €20), can be found along the way at **Pian del Tivano**.

Another option is to walk the 32km **Strada Regia** (Royal Way), a partly stone-paved path that links Como to Bellagio by way of Torno and Lezzeno. The easiest stretch connects Torno and Pognana Lario (about five hours). Ask at the Como tourist office for the fine *Carta dei Sentieri* (Trail Map, 1:25,000).

Bellagio

POP 3080

It's impossible not to be charmed by Bellagio's waterfront of bobbing boats, or its maze of steep stone staircases, dark cypress groves and showy rhododendron-filled gardens. Although summers and weekends teem with visitors, if you turn up on a weekday outside high season, you'll have the little village almost to yourself.

Bellagio's **tourist office** (☑031 95 02 04; Piazza Mazzini; ⊙9am-12.30pm & 1-6pm Mon-Sat, 10am-2pm Sun), next to the boat landing stage, has information on water sports, mountain biking and other lake activities. Otherwise, **PromoBellagio** (☑031 95 15 55; www.bellagiolakecomo.com; Piazza della Chiesa 14; ⊙9.30am-1pm Mon, 9.30-11am & 2-4pm Tue, Thu & Fri, 9.30-11am & 2-3.30pm Wed, 10-11am & 2-3.30pm Sat & Sun, shorter hours in winter), in the basement of an 11th-century watchtower, also has information.

⊙ Sights & Activities

Before setting out to explore the town, pick up the three self-guided walking tour brochures from the tourist office.

Villa Serbelloni   VILLA, GARDEN
(☑031 95 15 55; Via Garibaldi 8; adult/child €9/5; ⊙tours 11.30am & 3.30pm Tue-Sun Apr-Oct) The lavish gardens of Villa Serbelloni cover much of the promontory on which Bellagio sits. The villa has seen plenty of illustrious people, such as Austria's Emperor Maximilian I and Queen Victoria, and now the house is owned by the Rockefeller Foundation and is closed to the public.

Guided garden tours, however, are possible; tickets are sold at the PromoBellagio office in the Torre di Defensa Medievale near the church.

Villa Melzi D'Eril   VILLA, GARDEN
(☑339 4573838; www.giardinidivillamelzi.it; Lungo Lario Manzoni; adult/child €6.50/4; ⊙9.30am-6.30pm late-Mar–Oct) Garden-lovers can stroll the grounds of neoclassical Villa Melzi d'Eril, built in 1808 for one of Napoleon's associates and coloured by flowering azaleas and rhododendrons in spring. The gardens, adorned with statues scattered about,

formed the first English-style park on Lago di Como.

Barindelli's
BOAT TOUR

(📞 338 2110337; www.barindellitaxiboats.com; Piazza Mazzini; 1hr-long tour €140) For a touch of George Clooney glamour, consider taking a tour in one of Barindelli's slick, mahogany cigarette boats. They offer hour-long sunset tours for groups of up to 12 people around the Bellagio headland, which are well worth the cost. They can also tailor outings around the lake; consider making a night of it and using the boat as a taxi service for a top-class dinner.

Bellagio Water Sports
KAYAKING

(📞 340 394 93 75; www.bellagiowatersports.com) Kayak tours (including to Villa Balbianello) and rental are possible from this experienced outfit in Pescallo.

Courses

Bellagio Cooking Classes
COOKING

(📞 333 786 00 90; www.gustoitalianobellagio.com; Salita Plinio 5; per person €60-75) A wonderful way to really get to know Bellagio, these cooking classes have a personal touch – they take you to the local shops to buy the food and local women lead the classes. Classes are small (a miminum of two, maximum of five).

🛏 Sleeping

For such a prime spot, there are a surprising number of affordable places to sleep and eat.

Residence La Limonera
APARTMENT €

(📞 031 95 21 24; www.residencelalimonera.com; Via Bellosio 2; studios €80-105, 4-person apt €90-170;

@ 🛜 ♿) This elegant villa is perched high up in the town in an old lemon grove. It has been divided into 11 spacious and thoughtfully furnished self-catering apartments for two to four people.

★ Hotel Silvio
HOTEL €€

(📞 031 95 03 22; www.bellagiosilvio.com; Via Carcano 10-12, Bellagio; d from €180; ⊙ Mar–mid-Nov & Christmas; P ❋ ♿) Located above the small fishing hamlet of Loppia, a short walk from the centre of Bellagio through the gorgeous Villa Melzi gardens, this family-run hotel is Bellagio's best-value accommodation. From the contemporary Zen-like lakefront rooms you look out over the 10th-century church of Santa Maria and across to Villa Carlotta on the western shore. The hotel restaurant with its outdoor terrace is well regarded locally (meals €30 to €40).

🍴 Eating & Drinking

★ Ittiturismo Da Abate
LARIAN, SEAFOOD €€

(📞 338 584 38 14; www.ittiturismodabate.it; Frazione Villa 4, Lezzeno; meals €25-35; ⊙ 7-10.30pm Tue-Sat, noon-2.30pm & 7-10.30pm Sun; P 🛃; 🚌 Lezzeno) Da Abate is located just 8km south of Bellagio in the hamlet of Lezzeno. Run by Claudio and Giuseppe, it is one of the few fish farms left on the lake and is Slow Food recommended. Sample traditional fish specialities such as *lavarello* in balsamic vinegar and the robust-flavoured *missoltino* (fish dried in salt and bay leaves).

Terrazza Barchetta
ITALIAN €€

(📞 031 95 13 89; www.ristorantebarchetta.com; Salita Mella 13; meals €40-45; ⊙ noon-2.30pm & 7-10.30pm) Barchetta's intimate terrace in Bellagio's old town is a fine place for a meal.

MADONNA DEL GHISALLO

In the high-country village of **Magreglio** (497m), 7km south of Bellagio, stands a simple 17th-century church known as the **Santuario della Madonna del Ghisallo**. But this is not just any old high-mountain chapel.

The road up has frequently been included as a classic stage of the Giro d'Italia cycle race, and is known to professional and amateur cyclists alike. The sanctuary long ago became a symbolic finishing line for cyclists, who began leaving mementoes there. The place's importance for two-wheeled enthusiasts was such that Pope Pius XII declared the Madonna del Ghisallo the patron of cyclists. The gifts and tokens left at the sanctuary down the years became so numerous that it was decided to open the nearby **Museo del Ciclismo** (📞 031 96 58 85; www.museodelghisallo.it; Via Gino Bartali 4; adult/child €6/3; ⊙ 9.30am-5.30pm Tue-Sun Apr-Oct, 9.30am-5.30pm Sat & Sun Nov-Mar) to contain the overflow. The museum is devoted to all aspects of the business of cycling, with 100 film clips of great moments in Italian cycling, memorabilia (including many bicycles) and temporary exhibitions – ample reward for the punishing climb.

The restaurant has been around since 1887, which is plenty of time to have perfected dishes such as perch in a pistacchio crust or guinea fowl with whisky and mushroom sauce.

Bar Rossi   CAFE, BAR
(☑ 031 95 01 96; Piazza Mazzini 22-24, Bellagio; snacks €2-6; ☻ 7.30am-midnight Apr-Sep, to 10.30pm Oct-Mar) Have at least one coffee in art nouveau Bar Rossi.

Western Shore

The western shore gets the most sunshine on the lake. For this reason it's lined with lavish villas, where high-fliers, Arab sheiks and film stars reside. The shore stretches 75km from Como north to Sorico; from here you can continue north into Switzerland or east into Trentino-Alto Adige through the Valtellina valley.

CERNOBBIO TO LENNO

Ocean's 11 may have been shot at Bellagio's Vegas namesake, but scenes from *Ocean's 12* were filmed in the Lago di Como village of Cernobbio, at the 19th-century **Villa Erba** (Largo Luchino Visconti; closed to the public). Cernobbio is also home to the lake's most magnificent hotel, **Villa d'Este** (☑ 031 34 81; www.villadeste.it; Via Regina 40; ☻ 10.30-11.30am & 3.30-4pm Mar-Nov). But if you don't have a cool €800 to €950 to spend a night you won't get a glimpse of its palatial interiors. Garden visits are possible though in pre-booked groups of 10 people or more. The other reason to come to Cernobbio is to make the gourmet pilgrimage to romantic **Gatto Nero** (☑ 031 51 20 42; www.gattonerocernobbio.com; Via Monte Santo 69, Rovenna, Cernobbio; meals €60-70; ☻ noon-2pm & 7.30-10pm Wed-Sun, 7.30-10pm Tue), situated in a peerless position above the lake.

If you're driving, follow the lower lakeside road (Via Regina Vecchia) north from Cernobbio, which skirts the lake shore past a fabulous row of 19th-century villas (all private) around **Moltrasio**. A few kilometres north is the villa-lined hamlet of **Laglio**, home to *Ocean's* star George Clooney (he owns Villa Oleandra). In both places you can stop and wander down the cobbled lanes to the lake. Or live the celebrity lifestyle and book into gorgeous **Relais Regina Teodolinda** (☑ 031 40 00 31; www.relaisreginateodolinda.it; Via Vecchia Regina 58, Laglio; r €180-520; P ❋ @ ☎ ☱).

Finally, in Lenno, **Villa Balbianello** (☑ 0344 5 61 10; www.fondoambiente.it; Via Comoedia 5, Località Balbianello; villa & gardens adult/child €13/7, with prior reservation €10/5, gardens only €7/3; ☻ 10am-6pm Tue & Thu-Sun mid-Mar–mid-Nov) takes the prize for the lake's most dramatically situated gardens, dripping down the sides of the high promontory like melting ice cream. Scenes from *Star Wars: Episode II* and 2006's James Bond remake, *Casino Royale*, were shot here. The villa itself was built by Cardinal Angelo Durini in 1787. Now it houses a curious collector's museum of all sorts. If you want to see inside, you must join a guided tour (generally in Italian) by 4.15pm. Visitors are only allowed to walk the 1km from the Lenno landing stage to the estate on Tuesdays and weekends; other days, you have to take a **taxi boat** (☑ 0349 229 09 53; www.taxiboatlecco.com; return €7) from Lenno.

TREMEZZO
POP 1260

Tremezzo is high on everyone's list for a visit to the 17th-century **Villa Carlotta** (☑ 0344 4 04 05; www.villacarlotta.it; Via Regina 2; adult/reduced €9/5; ☻ 9am-5pm Easter-Sep, 10am-4pm mid-Mar–Easter & Oct–mid-Nov; ☲ Cadenabbia), where the botanic gardens overflow with orange trees knitted into pergolas, and some of Europe's finest rhododendrons, azaleas and camellias. The villa, which is decorated with paintings and fine alabaster-white sculptures (especially those by Antonio Canova), takes its name from the Prussian princess who was given the palace in 1847 as a wedding present from her mother.

Tremezzo's **tourist office** (☑ 0344 4 04 93; Via Statale Regina; ☻ 9am-noon & 3.30-6.30pm Wed-Mon Apr-Oct) adjoins the boat jetty.

★ **Hotel La Perla**   HOTEL €€
(☑ 034 44 17 07; www.laperlatremezzo.com; Via Romolo Quaglino 7, Tremezzo; d €125-145, with lake view €140-160, family ste €185-235; ❋ ☎ ☱) It's rare that hotels are so universally acclaimed as this one. Rooms are immaculate, service is warm and friendly, and the vantage point from Tremezzo is one of Lago di Como's loveliest. It's all housed in an artful reconstruction of a 1960s villa; definitely pay extra for a room with a view.

Al Veluu   LARIAN, INN €€€
(☑ 0344 4 05 10; www.alveluu.com; Via Rogaro 11, Tremezzo; meals €50-70; ☻ Wed-Mon; ☕ ; ☲ Cadenabbia) Situated on the steep hillside above

MILAN & THE LAKES LAGO DI COMO

the lake, Al Veluu offers panoramic views and home-cooked dishes based on seasonal produce from the mountains and the lake. The terrace is a great place to view the Ferragosto fireworks on 15 August. Upstairs there are two comfortable suites (€130-250 per night, €850-1200 per week) each sleeping four people. The inn offers a pick-up from the dock.

CADENABBIA & MENAGGIO

North of Tremezzo, Cadenabbia is a key transport hub serviced by car ferries. Given its lack of sights, it offers some good-value accommodation, such as the unpretentious **Alberghetto della Marianna** (☑ 0344 4 30 95; www.la-marianna.com; Via Regina 57, Cadenabbia di Griante; d €80-95; ❋ 🖀), which has homely rooms with brass beds, parquet floors and small balconies. The attached restaurant, **La Cucina di Marianna** (☑ 0344 4 31 11; www.lamarianna.com; Via Regina 57, Cadenabbia; menus €21-50; ⊙ Wed-Sun; 🖪; 🖫 Bellagio, Varenna), is also a good place to eat.

A further 3km north, Menaggio (population 3260) has a cute cobbled centre and a central square lined with cafes, which is perfect for lake-gazing. Menaggio is the jumping-off point for **Lago di Piano** in the Val Menaggio, a remote valley connecting Lago di Como with Lago di Lugano, which straddles the Italian–Swiss border to the west. Menaggio's **tourist office** (☑ 0344 3 29 24; www.menaggio.com; Piazza Garibaldi 3; ⊙ 9am-12.30pm & 2.30-6pm Apr-Oct, closed Wed & Sun Nov-Mar) has brochures on walking and biking.

ALTO LARIO

Beyond Menaggio, the northern stretch of the lake is known as the Alto Lario (Upper Lario). It is far less touristed than the southern shore and is wonderfully scenic. At Rezzonico there is a quiet pebble beach lined with wooden seats.

The towns of Dongo, Gravedona and Sorico once formed the independent republic of the Tre Pievi (Three Parishes) and were a hotbed of Cathar heresy. Now they're more popular with watersports enthusiasts than Inquisitors. Gravedona (pop 2750), the largest of the three, sits on a gently curved bay with views across to Mount Legnone. **Comolakeboats** (☑ 333 401 49 95; www.comolakeboats.it; Via Antica Regina 26) hires out inflatable boats (€65 for two hours) and organises waterskiing (€55 for 30 minutes) and wakeboarding (€50 for 30 minutes).

Up on the plateau at Peglio, the **Chiesa di Sant'Eusebio e Vittore** (Peglio; ⊙ 3-6pm Sat-Sun & Thu Jul-Sep) offers lake views and masterly frescoes by 17th-century Milanese painter Giovan Mauro della Rovere, better known as Il Fiammenghino ('Little Fleming'). He sought refuge here after murdering a man and did penance painting the vivid *Last Judgement*.

Sorico, the most northerly of the three towns, guards the mouth of the River Mera, which flows into shallow **Lake Mezzola**, once part of Lago di Como and now a bird-breeding nature reserve. Follow the path of the river to the tiny **Oratorio di San Fedelino**, with its 1000-year-old fresco of Christ and the Apostles. It's only accessible on foot or by boat from Sorico.

Valtellina

From the north end of Lago di Como, the Valtellina valley cuts a broad swathe along the course of the Adda river, between the Swiss mountain frontier to the north and the Orobie Alps to the south. The steep northern flank is carpeted by nebbiolo grapes, which yield a light red wine. Both body and alcohol content improve with altitude so generations of Valtenesi built upwards, carrying the soil in woven baskets to high mountain terraces. Their reward: a DOC classification (a regional quality classification) for Valtellina Superiore since 1968. In Sondrio, the hub of the valley, it's possible to visit the cellars of **Pellizzatti Perego** (www.arpepe.com; Via Buon Consiglio, Sondrio), and in Chiuri, **Nino Negri** (www.ninonegri.it; Via Ghibellini 3). You'll also find the valley's **tourist office** (☑ 0342 21 59 21; www.valtellina.it; Piazzale Bertacchi 77, Sondrio; ⊙ 9am-12.30pm & 3.30-6.30pm Mon-Fri, 9am-noon Sat) in Sondrio.

The prettiest town in the valley is **Tirano**, where mule trains once came from Venice and Brescia, and which is now the departure point for the **Trenino Rosso del Bernina** (☑ 0342 70 62 63; www.treninorosso.it; one way/return €24.50/49), a gravity-defying rail track that crests Europe's highest Alpine pass at 2253m on the way to St Moritz in Switzerland.

Located in the heart of the Valtellina's finest vineyards in Bianzone is Anna Bertola's charming Alpine chalet, **Altavilla** (☑ 0342 72 03 55; www.altavilla.info; Via ai Monti 46, Bianzone; meals €30; ⊙ noon-2.30pm & 7-10pm Tue-Sun, daily Aug; 🅿 🖀 🖪), one of the gastronomic treats of the region. Expect traditional mountain dishes such as *sciàtt* (buckwheat pancakes stuffed with Bitto cheese), *piz-zocheri* (buckwheat pasta) and venison. Rooms are also available (singles €25 to €50, doubles €55 to €70).

Eastern Shore

Lago di Como's shadier eastern shore has a wilder feel to it. The main town is Lecco (pop 47,800), with a winding waterfront, but there's little of specific interest; otherwise the key attraction is pretty Varenna situated a short hop across the water from Bellagio. If driving, skip the motorway and meander along the SS36 from Colico south to Lecco. At the northern end of the lake, 3km south of Colico, a side road leads 2km from the SP72 to this Cistercian abbey (☑ 0341 94 03 31; www.cistercensi.info/piona; ☉ 7am-7.30pm), set scenically on a promontory stretching out into the lake. The present church is Romanesque, but the highlight (apart from the setting) is the 13th-century cloister and the incomparable views across the lake to Gravedona.

VARENNA
POP 810

Villa-studded Varenna sits across the lake from Bellagio and vies with its better-known neighbour for the title of prettiest village on the lake. Its pastel-coloured houses rise steeply up the hillside and its gardens and walkways burst with flowers and birdsong. A series of lanes and stairways slither down the hill to the water's edge. About halfway down is Varenna's main street, the pedestrianised Via XX Settembre. Higher up, the SP72 passes the town's two most luxurious villas and the cobbled main square, Piazza San Giorgio, before scooting on north.

Those arriving by ferry land at Piazzale Martiri della Libertà. From here, a 15- to 20-minute stroll follows a flower-laden shoreline pathway up to Piazza San Giovanni and the town's two main attractions, the gardens of Villa Cipressi (☑ 0341 83 01 13; www.hotelvillacipressi.it; Via IV Novembre 22; adult/child €4/2; ☉ 9am-7pm Mar-Oct), surrounding a luxury hotel, and, 100m further south, Villa Monastero (☑ 0341 29 54 50; www.villamonastero.eu; Via IV Novembre; villa & gardens adult/reduced €8/4, gardens only €5/2; ☉ gardens 9am-7pm, villa 2-7pm Fri, 9am-7pm Sat & Sun Mar-Oct, closed Nov-Feb), a former convent turned into a vast residence by the Mornico family in the 17th century.

From the north end of Varenna, you can make a steep half-hour hike up an old mule path (or drive 3km on the SP65) to the hillside hamlet of Vezio. It is dominated by the 13th-century Castello di Vezio (www.castellodivezio.it; adult/child €4/2; ☉ 10am-6pm Mar-Oct), once part of a chain of early-warning medieval watchtowers. From here you can gaze down on the terracotta rooftops of Varenna, and at 4pm on Tuesday, Wednesday, Saturday and Sunday they host a falconry display.

The top sleeping option in Varenna is Albergo Milano (☑ 0341 83 02 98; www.varenna.net; Via XX Settembre 35, Varenna; s €115-125, d €140-180; ✳ @ 🛜), nestled half-way up the slope and offering 12 rooms with magnificent lake views and a super cocktail terrace. There's also a good on-site restaurant.

Eating choices include Osteria Quattro Pass (☑ 0341 81 50 91; www.quattropass.com; Via XX Settembre 20; meals €35-40; ☉ noon-3pm & 6.30-9.30pm daily Jun-Aug, Thu-Sun only Sep-May), situated back from the waterfront, and Ristorante La Vista (☑ 0341 83 02 98; www.varenna.net/eng/ristorante-lavista.php; Via XX Settembre 35; 3-/4-course set menus €38/45, meals €35-40; ☉ 7-10pm Wed-Sat & Mon mid-Mar–late Oct) with a terrace and nouvelle lake cuisine for diehard romantics.

MILAN & THE LAKES LAGO DI COMO

WORTH A TRIP

VALLE CAMONICA

Northeast of Lago d'Iseo, the Valle Camonica is dotted with Unesco-heritage rock carvings concentrated in several sites around the small town of Capo di Ponte (www.capodiponte.eu). The main site is the Parco Nazionale delle Incisioni Rupestri (☑ 0364 4 21 40; www.arterupestre.it; Località Naquane; admission €4; ☉ 9am-5.30pm Mar-Oct, to 4pm Nov-Feb), a 30-hectare open-air museum containing rock engravings dating as far back as the Bronze Age. Colour-coded paths lead you past vast rock slabs that seem to have been created specifically for people to clamber around and chisel in their artistic vision of animals (among them an extravagantly antlered deer) and fellow villagers. Especially rich is Rock No 1 (aka Roccia Grande). If driving, you'll be charged €2 to park at the start of the path.

WINE ROADS

South of Lago d'Iseo and stretching towards Brescia are the flourishing vineyards of the **Franciacorta wine region** (www.stradadelfranciacorta.it). It is perfect cycling country, with no high-rises and plenty of villages to explore. In the Middle Ages, monks living in the area were granted privileges to work the land. These 'franchises', or *franchae curtes*, were exempt from taxes, from whence originated the name. The Iseo and Brescia tourist offices can provide brochures and help book visits to wineries (essential on weekdays).

You can pick up the wine route at **Paràtico**, which lies at the region's northwestern tip. The quaint villages of **Nigoline Bonomelli**, **Colombaro**, **Timoline** and **Borgonato** form the heart of the comune of Corte Franca and are home to most of the prestigious winemakers in the area. Just to the north of them is **Provaglio d'Iseo**, the location of the 11th-century **Monastero San Pietro in Lamosa** (www.sanpietroinlamosa.org) which was founded by the Cluniac monks who first started to cultivate the region. The complex sits above a 2-sq-km protected **wetland** (www.torbiere.it), formed from 18th-century peat beds. In late spring the beds are smothered in water lilies.

If you're driving through the region, book yourself in to the **Ristorante Gualtiero Marchesi** (www.marchesi.it; meals €150-200; ⊙ noon-2.30pm & 7.30-10pm Tue-Sat, noon-2.30pm Sun), set in the luxurious country estate of the L'Albereta Hotel in Erbusco, and presided over by Gualtiero Marchesi, one of the best-known names in contemporary Italian dining.

The route ends at **Rodengo-Saiano**, where you'll find another impressive monastic complex, the **Abbazia di San Nicola** (www.benedettiniabbaziaolivetana.org).

Varenna's **tourist office** (☑ 0341 83 03 67; www.varennaitaly.com; Via del IV Novembre 7; ⊙ 9.30am-12.30pm & 2-6.30pm Tue-Sat, 9.30am-12.30pm Sun Jul, shorter hours rest of year) offers information on the lake's entire eastern shore.

Lago d'Iseo

Cradled in a deep glacial valley, less than 50km from both Bergamo and Brescia, Lago d'Iseo (aka Sebino) is one of the least known of the Lombard lakes. Shut in by soaring mountains, it is a magnificent sight. To the lake's north stretches the **Valle Camonica**, renowned for its Stone Age rock carvings. To the south stretches the rolling **Franciacorta** wine country, and to the west the picture-book-pretty **Lake Endine**.

With the exception of the south shore, the road closely hugs the water on its circuit around the lake and is especially dramatic south of Lovere.

◉ Sights & Activities

At the lake's southwest edge, the sun sets directly in front of the lakefront promenade in **Iseo** (population 9200). It's a pleasant spot with a string of squares just behind the waterfront and a public beach where you can hire canoes and paddle boats. **Iseobike** (☑ 340 3 96 20 95; www.iseobike.com; Via Colomb-

era 2; bike rental per hour/day €4.50/12, helmet €3; ⊙ 9.30am-12.15pm & 2.30-7pm May-Aug, Fri-Sun only Sep-Apr) hires out bikes and can put together tailor-made cycling tours around the lake into the Franciacorta wine region.

Directly west of Iseo is **Sarnico** (population 6650), with its lovely Liberty villas, many of which were designed by Giuseppe Sommaruga. Among them, his lakeside Villa Faccanoni (Via Veneto) is the most outstanding. The heart of the old town, known as La Contrada, straggles back from the Oglio river. It is perfect for a wander along the riverside after a morning coffee.

North of Iseo, rising out of the lake, **Monte Isola** (population 1800), Europe's largest lake island at 4.28 sq km, is easily the lake's most striking feature. Francesco Sforza granted the islanders special fishing rights in the 15th century and the island is still dotted with fishing villages. From Carzano, in the northeast (where boats land), you can climb rough stairs to the summit (599m). A 15km trail allows you to walk or cycle around the island (no cars are permitted).

On the northwest tip of the lake, the port town of **Lovere** (population 5600) is a working harbour with a higgledy-piggledy old centre and a wealth of walking trails in the hills behind it. At the waterfront you'll find the **Accadamia Tadini** (☑ 035 96 27 80; www.accademiatadini.it; Via Tadini 40; adult/concession €7/5; ⊙ 3-

7pm Tue-Sat, 10am-noon & 3-7pm Sun & holidays May-Sep, 3-7pm Sat, 10am-noon & 3-7pm Sun & holidays Apr & Oct), home to a considerable art collection with works by Jacopo Bellini, Giambattista Tiepolo and Antonio Canova. Short drives out of Lovere to nearby villages like **Bossico** and **Esmate** bring you to marvellous lookout points high above the lake.

Sleeping & Eating

Hotel Milano HOTEL €
(030 98 04 49; www.hotelmilano.info; Lungolargo Marconi 4, Iseo; s €42-47, d €84-92) One of only two hotels in the centre of Iseo, the lakefront Milano is an excellent deal. It's definitely worth paying fractionally more for the pleasant rooms with lake views (one-week minimum stay mid-July to mid-August) – so you have a front row seat for sunset behind the mountains over the lake.

Ristorante Monte Isola ITALIAN €€
(030 982 52 84; www.ristorantemonteisola.it; Località Carzano 144, Carzano; meals €25-35; noon-3pm Tue, noon-3pm & 7-10pm Wed-Sun) It's worth jumping on a boat in Sale Marasino just to get across to this restaurant on Monte Isola, where simply prepared lake fish is served with endless views across the water.

Information

Iseo Tourist Office (030 98 02 09; www.agenzialagoiseofranciacorta.it; Lungolago Marconi 2, Iseo; 10am-12.30pm & 3.30-6.30pm Easter-Sep, 10am-12.30pm & 3-6pm Mon-Fri, 10am-12.30pm Sat Oct-Easter)

Sarnico Tourist Office (035 4 20 80; www.prolocosarnico.it; Via Lantieri 6, Sarnico; 9.30am-12.30pm & 3-6.30pm Tue-Sat, 9.30am-12.30pm Sun)

Getting There & Around

Navigazione sul Lago d'Iseo (035 97 14 83; www.navigazionelagoiseo.it) From April to September regular services run the length of the lake from Lovere and Sarnico in the south to Pisogne (€6.65, two to three hours) in the north.

Small boats make the quick crossing (10 minutes, every half-hour) from Sale Marasino and Sulzano, on the east shore, respectively to Carzano and Peschiera Maraglio on Monte Isola (€2.20/3.60 one way/return).

SAB (035 28 90 00; www.sab-autoservizi.it) Runs buses (Line E) between Sarnico and Bergamo (€3.30, 50 minutes). Line C runs via Lake Endine to Lovere and on to Boario in the Valle Camonica.

Iseo Train Station Links Iseo with Brescia (€3.25, 30 minutes, hourly), where you can connect to Bergamo.

Lago di Garda

Poets and politicians, divas and dictators, they've all been drawn to Lago di Garda. At 370 sq km it is the largest of the Italian lakes, straddling the border between Lombardy and the Veneto, with soaring mountains to the north and softer hills to the south. Vineyards, olive groves and citrus orchards range up the slopes, while villages sit around a string of natural harbours. In the southwest corner, Desenzano del Garda has good transport connections.

Garda is the most developed of the lakes and, despite a plethora of accommodation, booking ahead is advised.

Getting There & Around

AIR

Verona-Villafranca Airport (045 809 56 66; www.aeroportoverona.it) Verona's airport is most convenient for the lake. Regular trains connect Verona with Peschiera del Garda (€2.85, 15 minutes) and Desenzano del Garda (€3.80, 25 minutes).

BOAT

Navigazione Lago di Garda (800 551801; www.navigazionelaghi.it; Piazza Matteotti 2, Desenzano del Garda) Operates ferries year-round. A one-day ticket allowing unlimited travel in the Alto Garda (Upper Garda) costs €24.30/17.60 per adult/child, while the Basso Garda (Lower Garda) ticket costs €27.40/16.40 per adult/child.

MILAN & THE LAKES LAGO DI GARDA

LAGO DI GARDA'S BEST BEACHES

Rocca di Manerba A designated a nature reserve 10km south of Salò.

Parco la Fontanella A white-pebble beach north of Gargnano, backed by olive groves.

Campione del Garda A ciff-backed beach north of Gargnano where windsurfers set sail.

Riva del Garda A family-friendly landscaped waterfront running for 3km.

Punta San Vigilio A cypress-lined headland curling into the lake 3km north of Garda.

Motorists can cross the lake using the car ferry between Toscolano-Maderno and Torri del Benaco, or seasonally between Limone and Malcesine. A car costs €10.70 one way.

BUS

APTV (☎045 805 78 11; www.aptv.it) Connects Desenzano del Garda train station with Riva del Garda (€4.70, two hours, up to six daily). Peschiera del Garda train station is on the Riva del Garda–Malcesine–Garda–Verona APTV bus route, with hourly buses to both Riva (€4.10, one hour 40 minutes) and Verona (€3.20, 30 minutes).

Trasporti Brescia (☎030 440 61; www. trasportibrescia.it; Via Cassale 3/a, Brescia) Operates services from Brescia up the western side of the lake to Riva del Garda.

Trentino Trasporti (☎0461 821 000; www.tte-servizio.it) Connects Riva del Garda with Arco (20 minutes) and Trento (€4.20, 1¾ hours).

CAR

Lake Garda lies north of the A4 Milan–Venice autostrada, and just west of the A22 Modena–Trento route. A single-lane road circles the lake shore and is heavy with traffic in summer. Local tourist offices can advise on car hire.

TRAIN

Desenzano del Garda and Peschiera del Garda are on the Milan–Venice train line.

Sirmione

POP 7420

Sitting on an impossibly narrow peninsula on the southern shore, Sirmione is Garda's most picturesque village. Throughout the centuries it has attracted the likes of Roman poet Catullus and Maria Callas, and today thousands follow in their footsteps.

The **tourist office** (☎030 91 61 14; Viale Marconi 8; ☺9am-12.30pm & 3-6pm Mon-Fri, 9am-12.30pm Sat) adjoins the bus station. Motorised vehicles are banned beyond this point, except for those with a hotel booking.

◎ Sights & Activities

To get even the slightest glimpse of Sirmione's legendary natural beauty, come out of season (April or October) or in the evening when most day trippers have departed. Then you can snap the Rocca Scaligera without dozens of gelati-licking visitors in the foreground and stroll around the 4km peninsula along the panoramic pathway.

From the jetty near the castle, boat trips around the lake can be arranged.

Rocca Scaligera CASTLE
(Castello Scaligero; adult/reduced €4/2; ☺8.30am-7pm Tue-Sun) Expanding their influence northwards, the Scala family built this enormous square-cut castle right at the entrance to the island. It guards the only footbridge into Sirmione, looming over it with impressive crenellated turrets and towers. There's not a lot inside, but the climb to the top (146 steps to the top of the tower) affords beautiful views over Sirmione's rooftops and the enclosed harbour.

Grotte di Catullo HISTORIC SITE
(☎030 91 61 57; adult/reduced €4/2; ☺8.30am-8pm Tue-Sat, 9.30am-6.30pm Sun Mar-Oct, 8.30am-2pm Tue-Sun Nov-Mar) Occupying 2 hectares at Sirmione's northern tip, this ruined, 1st-century AD Roman villa is a picturesque complex of teetering stone arches and tumbledown walls, some three storeys high. It's the largest domestic Roman villa in northern Italy and wandering its terraced hillsides offers fantastic views.

★ **Aquaria** SPA
(☎030 91 60 44; www.termedisirmione.com; Piazza Don Angelo Piatti; pools day/evening €33/27, treatments from €25; ☺pools 2-10pm Mon, 10am-10pm Tue-Sun Mar-Dec, hours vary Jan & Feb) Sirmione is blessed with a series of offshore thermal springs that pump out water at a natural 37°C. At the Aquaria spa you can wallow in two thermal pools – the outdoor one is set right beside the lake. Bring along your swimsuit and flip-flops (thongs); towels and robes will be provided. Swimsuits are also available for purchase.

Other treatments – including mud sessions (€50) and massages (€80) – have to be booked in advance.

🛏 Sleeping & Eating

An inordinate number of hotels are crammed into Sirmione, many of which close from the end of October to March. Four campgrounds lie near the town and the tourist office can advise on others around the lake.

Hotel Marconi HOTEL €€
(☎030 91 60 07; www.hotelmarconi.net; Via Vittorio Emanuele II 51, Sirmione; s €45-75, d €80-135; P ❄) Blue-and-white striped umbrellas line the lakeside deck at this stylish, family-run hotel. The restrained rooms are all subtle shades and crisp fabrics, and the breakfasts and homemade pastries are a treat.

La Fiasca

TRATTORIA €€

(✆030 990 61 11; www.trattorialafiasca.it; Via Santa Maria Maggiore; meals €30; ⊙noon-2.30pm & 7-10.30pm Thu-Tue) Serving up the kind of sauces you can't help dunking your bread into, this authentic trattoria is tucked away in a back street just off the main square. The atmosphere is warm and bustling, and the dishes are packed with traditional Lake Garda produce: tagliatelle with perch and porcini, and duck with cognac and juniper.

Desenzano del Garda

POP 26,900

An easygoing commuter town 9km southwest of Sirmione, Desenzano del Garda is known as the *porta del lago* (gateway to the lake). It's not as pretty as some of its counterparts, but its ancient harbour, broad promenades and vibrant Piazza Matteotti make for pleasant wanderings. It is also a hub for nightlife in the summer.

Desenzano's best-known site is its well-preserved Roman mosaics at the **Roman Villa** (✆030 914 35 47; Via Crocifisso 2; adult/reduced €2/1; ⊙8.30am-7pm Mar-Oct, to 5pm Nov-Feb). Built 2000 years ago, the villa was remodelled in the 2nd century, with most of the mosaics being added in the 4th century. Wooden walkways lead directly over vivid scenes of chariot-riding, grape-gathering cherubs.

For more information on the town, consult the main **tourist office** (✆030 914 15 10; Via Porto Vecchio 34; ⊙9am-12pm & 3-6pm Mon-Sat). For a light lunch and excellent aperitivo head to **Caffe Italia** (✆030 914 12 43; www.ristorantecaffeitalia.it; Piazza Malvezzi 19; meals €25-35; ⊙12.30-2.30pm & 7.30-10.30pm).

The Valtenesi

The Valtenesi stretches languidly between Desenzano and Salò, its rolling hills etched with vine trellises and flecked with olive groves. The main lake road heads inland, allowing for gentle explorations of an array of wineries and small towns, including Padenghe sul Garda, Moniga del Garda, Manerba del Garda and San Felice del Benaco.

◉ Sights & Activities

The Valtenesi is perfect cycling country, so pick up a bike from **Cicli Mata** (✆0365 55 43 01; www.matashop.it; Via Nazionale 63, Raffa di Puegnago; half-/full-day €18/25; ⊙9am-1pm & 2.30-7.30pm Tue-Sat, 2.30-7.30pm Sun & Mon)

LAGO DI GARDA FOR KIDS

One lake, theme parks galore, packed with enough rides and stunt shows to thrill all day.

➡ **Gardaland** (✆045 644 97 77; www.gardaland.it; Via Dema 4, Castelnuovo del Garda; adult/reduced €37.50/31; ⊙10am-11pm mid-Jun–mid-Sep, 10am-6pm Apr–mid-Jun & last 2 weeks Sep, 10am-6pm Sat & Sun Oct, late Dec & early Jan)

➡ **CanevaWorld** (✆045 696 99 00; www.canevaworld.it; Via Fossalta 1; adult/reduced €25/19)

➡ **Aquaparadise** (adult/child €24/19; ⊙10am-7pm Jul & Aug, 10am-6pm mid-May–Jun & Sep)

➡ **Movieland** (⊙10am-6pm Easter–mid-Sep, to 6pm Sat & Sun Apr & Oct)

---

and select a route on the community website www.pisteciclabili.com. Another good resource is the mobile app, **Garda Bello e Buono** (www.gardabelloebuono.it), which you can download for iPhones and Android.

★ **Parco Archeologico Rocca di Manerba**

NATURAL RESERVE

(www.parcoroccamanerba.net; ⊙10am-8pm Apr-Sep, to 6pm Thu-Sun Oct-Mar) FREE Protected by Unesco and now a natural reserve, the 'rock of Minerva' (so named after a long-gone Roman temple dedicated to Minerva) juts out scenically into the lake just north of Moniga del Garda. Now all that remains are the ruins of a medieval castle and a restful nature reserve of evergreen woods criss-crossed with cycling and walking trails.

Santuario della Madonna del Carmine

MONASTERY

(✆0365 6 20 32; www.santuariodelcarmine-sanfelice.it; Via Fontanamonte 1, San Felice del Benaco; ⊙7am-noon & 3-6pm) FREE In the tiny village of San Felice del Benaco you'll find the frescoed sanctuary of the Madonna del Carmine, which dates from 1452. The simple Gothic-Romanesque exterior does little to prepare you for the technicolour frescoes inside. Although their provenance is unknown, a number of them are thought to be the work of Mantegna, Paolo Uccello and Vicenzo Foppa, such is their quality and depth of perspective.

TASTING OLIVE OIL

Lago di Garda's microclimate resembles the Mediterranean's, ensuring ideal olive-growing conditions. The lake's banks produce a tiny 1% of Italy's olive oil, but the product is renowned for being light, soft and sweet. Some 15 varieties of olive are grown here; the local black fruit produces subtler tasting oil, while the green olives are spicier.

Comincioli (☎ 0365 65 11 41; www.comincioli.it; Via Roma 10, Puegnago del Garda; ☉ by reservation 9.30am-noon & 2.30-7pm Mon-Sat) ✐ **FREE** set in the Valtanesi hills, is the perfect place for a tutored tasting in the lake's oil. The same family has been harvesting olives for 500 years and their Numero Uno oil is considered one of the best olive oils in Italy.

You can stay overnight in the adjoining complex (www.carminesanfelice.it).

La Basia HORSE RIDING
(☎ 0365 55 59 58; www.labasia.it; Via Predefitte 31, Puegnago del Garda; half-hr/1hr lesson €15/25) Situated just above the Viale Panoramico between Puegnago and Salò is Elena Parona's extensive vineyard and riding school. While parents sample wines and wild honey on the terrace, kids can enjoy structured riding lessons or rides in the surrounding vineyards. Between March and September, you can also bed down in one of their family-sized apartments (€345-550 per week).

🛏 Sleeping & Eating

★ **Campeggio Fornella** CAMPGROUND €
(☎ 0365 6 22 94; www.fornella.it; Via Fornella 1, San Felice del Benaco; pitches €13-37, bungalows €45-198; 🅿 ❋ @ 🎇 🐕) This luxury, 4-star campground comes complete with private beach, lagoon pool, spa, children's club, boat centre, restaurant, bar and pizzeria. All you have to do is pick a scenic pitch, mobile home or bungalow.

La Dispensa MODERN ITALIAN €€
(☎ 0365 55 70 23; Piazza Municipio 10, San Felice del Benaco; meals €25-40; ☉ 7-11.30pm) This fun and colourful wine bar and restaurant (with accompanying shop, VinoeLino) offers a mouthwatering modern Italian menu with a focus on sensational fish and charcuterie platters. Ingredients are top-notch, locally sourced and sometimes come accompanied by live jazz.

Salò

POP 10,400

Wedged between the lake and precipitous mountains, Salò exudes an air of grandeur. Its long waterfront promenade is lined with ornate buildings and palm trees, while the graceful bell tower of its 15th-century cathedral overlooks picturesque lanes.

In 1943 Salò was named the capital of the Social Republic of Italy as part of Mussolini and Hitler's last-ditch efforts to organise Italian Fascism in the face of advancing allied forces. This episode, known as the Republic of Salò, saw more than 16 public and private buildings in the town commandeered and turned into Mussolini's ministeries and offices. Strolling between the sites is a surreal tour of the dictator's doomed ministate. The tourist office has an English-language map and booklet featuring significant locations.

It's not often that you get to explore a private island in the company of its aristocratic owners, but you can at the tiny, comma-shaped **Isola del Garda** (☎ 328 384 92 26; www.isoladelgarda.com; tour incl boat ride €25-30; ☉ Apr-Oct) just off Salò. The sumptuous neo-Gothic Venetian villa is owned by Contessa Cavazza, and your visit is likely to be guided by a member of her family. The two-hour tour takes in a clutch of opulent rooms, some with a disarming real-life family feel.

Boats to Isola del Garda depart from Salò, Gardone Riviera, Garda and Sirmione, but they only leave each location once or twice a week. On your return to Salò, nab a lakeside table at **Ristorante Papillon** (☎ 0365 4 14 29; www.ristorantepapillon.it; Lungolago Zanardelli 69/70; pizza €8-14; ☉ 8am-10pm Tue-Sun; 🐕) for surprisingly good thin-crust pizza.

Salò is a good place to base yourself. Why not check in to Mussolini's former Foreign Ministry the Villa Simonini, which has now been converted into the lovely **Hotel Laurin** (☎ 0365 2 20 22; www.laurinhotelsalo.com; Viale Angelo Landi 9; d €155-250; 🅿 ❋ @ 🛜 🎇).

Gardone Riviera

POP 2700

Gardone's glory days were in the late 19th and early 20th centuries, and today the resort's opulent villas and ornate architecture make it one of the lake's most elegant holiday spots. About 12km north of Gardone is **Gargnano** (population 3050), a tiny harbour that fills with million-dollar yachts come September when sailing fans gather for the **Centomiglia**, the lake's most prestigious sailing regatta.

The **tourist office** (☑ 0365 374 87 36; Corso della Repubblica 8; ☺ 9am-12.30pm & 2.30-6pm Mon-Sat) stocks information on activities.

◎ Sights

★ **Il Vittoriale
degli Italiani** MUSEUM
(☑ 0365 29 65 11; www.vittoriale.it; Piazza Vittoriale; gardens & museums adult/reduced €16/12; ☺ grounds 8.30am-8pm Apr-Sep, to 5pm Oct-Mar, museums to 7pm Tue-Sun Apr-Sep, 9am-1pm & 2-5pm Tue-Sun Oct-Mar) Poet, soldier, hypochondriac and proto-Fascist, Gabriele d'Annunzio (1863–1938) defies easy definition, and so does his estate. Bombastic, extravagant and unsettling, it's home to every architectural and decorative excess imaginable and the decor helps shed light on the eccentric man. In the 1920s d'Annunzio became a strong supporter of Fascism and Mussolini, while his affairs with wealthy women were legendary.

In his main house, the **Prioria**, black velvet drapes and stained-glass windows cast an eerie light on gloomy rooms (he had an eye condition that made exposure to sunlight painful) crammed with classical figurines, leather-bound books, leopard skins, gilded ornaments, lacquer boxes and chinoiserie. Highlights include the bronze tortoise that sits on the guests' dining table (in admonition of overeaters, it was cast from a pet that died of overeating); the bright blue bathroom suite with over 2000 pieces of bric-a-brac; his spare bedroom where he would retire to lie in on a coffin-shaped bed and contemplate death; and his study with its low lintel – designed so visitors would have to bow as they entered. Guided visits, in Italian only, tour the house every 10 minutes and last half an hour.

**Giardino Botanico
Fondazione André Heller** GARDEN
(☑ 336 41 08 77; www.hellergarden.com; Via Roma 2; adult/child €10/5; ☺ 9am-7pm Mar-Oct) Gardone's heyday was due in large part to its consistently mild climate, and this mildness benefits the thousands of exotic blooms that fill artist André Heller's sculpture garden. Laid out in 1912 by Arturo Hruska, a dentist who did rather well tending to European royalty, the garden is zoned into pocket-sized climate zones and dotted with 30 pieces of contemporary sculpture, including pieces by Keith Haring and Roy Lichtenstein.

🛏️ Sleeping & Eating

Locanda Agli Angeli HOTEL €€
(☑ 0365 2 09 91; www.agliangeli.com; Via Dosso 7; s €45-70, d €80-180; P ⊠) A delightful renovation has produced an 18th-century *locanda* (inn) of old polished wood, gauzy curtain fabrics and bursts of lime, orange and aquamarine. The terrace has a compact pool and views across rooftops and the lake beyond. The restaurant is also good, serving classic Lake Garda cooking (meals €25–35).

Riva del Garda

POP 15,800

Even on a lake blessed with dramatic scenery, Riva del Garda still comes out on top. Encircled by towering rock faces and a looping strip of beach, its appealing centre is a medley of elegant architecture, maze-like streets and wide squares. Riva lies across the border from Lombardy in the Alpine region of Trentino-Alto Adige; for centuries the town's strategic position saw it fought over by the competing powers of the bishops of Trento, the republic of Venice, Milan's Viscontis and Verona's Della Scala families. It remained part of Austria until 1919, subsequently saw fierce fighting in the Italian wars of independence, and was home to anti-Nazi resistance groups in WWII.

The **tourist office** (☑ 0464 55 44 44; www.gardatrentino.it; Largo Medaglie d'Oro; ☺ 9am-7pm May-Sep, to 6pm Oct-Apr) advises on everything from climbing and paragliding to wine tasting and markets.

◎ Sights & Activities

Riva makes a natural starting point for a host of activities, including hiking and biking trails around Monte Rocchetta (1575m). More gentle pursuits are possible along the gorgeous landscaped lakefront: swimming,

Design

Better living by design: what could be more Milanese? From the cup that holds your morning espresso to your bedside light, there's a designer responsible and almost everyone in Milan will know their name. Design here is a way of life.

Modern Italian Design

The roots of Italian design stretch back to early-20th-century Milan, with the development of the Fiera trade fair, the rebuild of the Rinascente department store (Giorgio Armani started there as window dresser), the founding of architectural and design magazines *Domus* and *Casabella* and the opening of the Triennale in 1947. Where elaborate French rococo and ornate Austrian art nouveau had captured the imagination of a genteel prewar Europe, the dynamic deco style of Italian futurism was a perfect partner for the industrial revolution and Fascist philosophies.

Fascist propaganda co-opted the radical, neoclassical streamlining that futurism inspired and Italy implemented these ideas into architecture and design. Modern factories had to aid the war effort and fascist tendencies towards centralised control boosted Italian manufacturing. Through an inherent eye for purity of line, modern Italian design found beauty in balance and symmetry. This refreshing lack of detail appealed to a fiercely democratising war-torn Europe where minimalism and utility came to represent the very essence of modernity.

'From the Spoon to the City'

Milan's philosopher-architects and designers – Giò Ponti, Vico Magistretti,

1. Coffee cups and saucers at Spazio Rossana Orlandi (p257), Milan 2. Vintage 1935 Alfa Romeo Spider 3. Vespas

PAOLO CORDELLI / GETTY IMAGES ©

CAR CULTURE / GETTY IMAGES ©

DAVID BORLAND / GETTY IMAGES ©

Gae Aulenti, Achille Castiglioni, Ettore Sottsass and Piero Fornasetti – saw their postwar mission as not only rebuilding the bombed city but redesigning the urban environment. A defining statement came from Milanese architect Ernesto Rogers, who said he wished to design 'everything, from the spoon to the city'.

Far from being mere intellectual theorists, this cadre of architect-designers benefited from a unique proximity to artisanal businesses located in Brianza province, north of Milan. This industrial district grew from rural society and thus retained many specialist peasant craft skills. While these production houses remained true to the craft aspect of their work, they were able to use modern sales and production techniques via the central marketplace of the Triennale. This direct connection between producer and

marketplace allowed Milanese designers to create a happy symbiosis between creativity and commercialism, ultimately fine-tuning Italian design to achieve the modernist ideal of creating beautiful, *useful* objects.

DESIGN CLASSICS

Alessi Crafted kitchen utensils designed by big-name architect-designers.

Vespa 1946 Piaggio mini-motor scooter that transformed the lives of urbanites.

Cassina 'Masters' collection Furniture by Le Corbusier, Frank Lloyd Wright and Giò Ponti.

Alfa Romeo This legendary roadster, launched in 1910, is the most famous product from Milanese petrolheads.

ACTIVITIES AROUND RIVA

Although you can ride, cycle, hike and sail your way around Garda, the real hub of the lake's activities is the triangle of towns Riva del Garda, Arco and Torbole.

Watersports

Fleets of operators provide equipment hire and tuition along the lakefront in Riva and Torbole. One of the largest is **Surfsegnana** (☑ 0464 50 59 63; www.surfsegnana.it; Foci del Sarca, Torbole), which operates from Lido di Torbole and Porfina Beach in Riva. It runs lessons in windsurfing (€72), kitesurfing (€110) and sailing (€75), as well as hiring out the windsurf kit (€40 per half-day), sail boats (€32 to €52 per hour) and kayaks (€9/14 for 1-/2-person kayaks). Other operators include www.sailingdulac.com, www.pierwindsurf. it and www.vascorenna.com.

Climbing

Surrounded by perfect waves of limestone, Arco is one of Europe's most popular climbing destinations and is the location of the **Rockmaster festival** (www.rockmasterfestival.com) in September.

With hundreds of routes of all grades to choose from, Arco climbs are divided between short, bolted, single-pitch sports routes and long, Dolomite-style climbs, some extending as much as 1400m. The 300m **Zanzara** is a world classic, a 7a+ climb directly above the Rockmaster competition wall.

For information on climbing courses and routes contact www.friendsofarco.it. **Guide Alpine Arco** (www.guidealpinearco.com) is another good resource.

Canyoning

Thanks to glacial meltwaters, which have worn smooth the limestone mountains surrounding Riva and the Val di Ledro, canyoning here is a fantastic experience offering lots of slides, jumps and abseiling. Both Friends of Arco and Guide Alpine Arco arrange trips to the Palvico and Rio Nero gorges in the Val di Ledro (€69 each) and the Vione canyon in Tignale (€125), as does **Canyon Adventures** (www.canyonadv.com).

---

sunbathing and cycling the 3km lakeside path to Torbole. Windsurfing schools hire out equipment on Porfina Beach.

Museo Alto Garda   MUSEUM
(La Rocca; ☑ 0464 57 38 69; www.museoaltogarda. it; Piazza Cesare Battisti 3; adult/child €3/1.50; ◎10am-6pm Tue-Sun Mar-Nov, to 5pm Dec-Feb) Housed in Riva's stunted medieval castle, known locally as La Rocca, the civic museum features a modest selection of local archaeology, frescoes from Roman Riva, historical documents and paintings. Perhaps the most revealing exhibits are the antique maps dating from 1579 and 1667 and a 1774 *Atlas Tyrolensis*, which evocatively convey the area's shifting boundaries.

Cascata del Varone   WATERFALL
(www.cascata-varone.com; adult/reduced €5.50/2.50; ◎9am-7pm May-Aug, to 6pm Apr & Sep, to 5pm Mar & Oct) This 100m waterfall thunders down sheer limestone cliffs through an immense, dripping gorge. Walkways lead 50m into the mountain beside the crashing torrent, and strolling along them is like walking in a perpetual thunderstorm. You'll find it signposted 3km northwest of Riva's centre.

🛏 Sleeping & Eating

Hotel Garni Villa Maria   APARTHOTEL €
(☑ 0464 55 22 88; www.garnimaria.com; Viale dei Tigli, Riva del Garda; s €35, d €60-100, apt €280-340; P ❀ ❀ ⓐ) A small, spruce hotel with a Scandinavian vibe sporting all-white linens, sleek modern bathrooms and zesty lime green and orange accents. Situated just outside Riva's historic town centre, it has balconied rooms offering views of soaring mountains.

★ **Residence Filanda**   APARTHOTEL €€
(☑ 0464 55 47 34; www.residencefilanda.com; Via Sant'Alessandro, 51 ; d €105-135, qd €165-210; P ❀ @ ❀ ⓐ) Located 2km outside Riva, this bright, burnt-orange residence situated amid olive groves is a haven for families. Rooms and apartments overlook lush grounds that incorporate a heated pool, tennis and volleyball courts and a hectare of child-friendly gardens. Facilities are top-

notch, too, with fully equipped kitchenettes, a laundrette and all the necessary paraphernalia for young children.

Lido Palace — LUXURY HOTEL €€€

(☑ 0464 02 18 99; www.lido-palace.it; Viale Carducci 10, Riva del Garda; d €270-380, ste €450-550; P ✳ @ 🖥 ⚊) If you're going to splash the cash, this is the place to do it. Riva's historic Lido palace dates back to 1899 and is an absolute stunner. Sensitive renovations have installed uncompromisingly modern interiors within the grand Liberty-style palace, complete with a Michelin-starred restaurant, peerless views over lawns and lake, and sumptuous spa facilities (open to non-hotel guests by reservation).

★ Cristallo Caffè — GELATO €

(☑ 0464 55 38 44; www.cristallogelateria.com; Piazza Catena 11; cones €2.50; ☉ 7-1am) Over 60 flavours of artisanal ice cream served in giant sundaes. This is also a good spot for a spritz with views across the lake.

★ Osteria Le Servite — OSTERIA, GARDESE €€

(☑ 0464 55 74 11; www.leservite.com; Via Passirone 68, Arco; meals €30-45; ☉ 7-10.30pm Tue-Sun Apr-Sep, 7-10.30pm Thu-Sun Oct-Mar; P 👪) Tucked away amid Arco's vineyards is this elegant little *osteria* where Alessandro and his wife serve *mimosa* gnocchi, tender *salmerino* and pork fillet with grape must. In summer you can sit out on the patio sipping small-production DOC Trentino wines.

Trattoria Piè di Castello — TRENTINO €€

(☑ 0464 52 10 65; www.piedicastello.it; Via al Cingol Ros 38, Tenno; meals €20-25; ☉ noon-2.30pm & 7-10pm Wed-Mon; P 👪) Come here for the typical Trentino dish, *carne salata*: salted beef tenderised in herb-infused brine in a ceramic dish and served with various pickled side dishes. It's been around since the Middle Ages.

Malcesine

POP 3650

With the lake lapping right up to the tables of its harbourside restaurants and the vast ridge of Monte Baldo looming behind, Malcesine is another Garda hot spot. Like Riva del Garda and Torbole, it is a windsurfing centre and its streets are cobbled with thousands of lake pebbles. The whole affair is crowned by the chalky-white Castello Scaligero, where Goethe was temporarily imprisoned after being mistaken for a spy.

Malcesine's cable car, Funivia Malcesine-Monte Baldo (☑ 045 740 02 06; www.funiviedelbaldo.it; Via Navene Vecchia; adult/reduced return €19/15; ☉ 8am-7pm Apr-Aug, to 6pm Sep, to 5pm Oct) whisks you 1760m above the lake in rotating, glass cabins. The mountain is actually part of a 40km-long chain, and the ridges are the starting point for mountain-biking tours and paragliding, as well as skiing in winter. Getting off the cable car at the intermediate station of San Michele (one way/return €5/7) is the starting point for some excellent hikes. The hour-long walk back to Malcesine along quiet roads and rocky mountain paths reveals a rural world far from the throngs at the lake. Hire bikes at Bikextreme (☑ 045 740 0105; www.bikextreme-malcesine.com; Via Navene Vecchia 10; bikes per day €15-30) and check into Rifugio Monte Baldo for more extended mountain explorations.

Olives harvested around Malcesine are milled into extra-virgin olive oil by Consorzio Olivicoltori di Malcesine (☑ 045 740 12 86; Via Navene 21; ☉ 9am-1pm & 4.30-7pm) FREE. The oil is renowned for its light, fruity taste with traces of almonds. Prices of the cold-pressed extra virgin DOP olive oil range start at €11 for 0.5L.

To escape the crowds head up to Michelin-starred Vecchia Malcesine (☑ 045 740 04 69; www.vecchiamalcesine.com; Via Pisort 6; meals

---

WORTH A TRIP

LAGO DI LEDRO

From Riva, follow first the SP37 and then the SS240 as they wind their way west up the mountains, past olive groves and vine-lined terraces. Around 11km from Riva the road flattens and Lago di Ledro comes into view. Only 2.5km long and 2km wide, this diminutive lake sits at an altitude of 650m, set in a gorgeous valley beneath tree-covered mountains. Molina di Ledro is at the lake's eastern end, where tiny thatched huts line up beside a string of beaches and boat-hire pontoons. Stay at the glass-and-timber ecolodge Hotel Elda (☑ 0464 59 10 40; www.hotelelda.com; Via 3 Giugno 3; s €70-120, d €94-160; P @ ⚊ 👪) 🍴.

€45-100; ☺ noon-2.30pm & 7-10.30pm Thu-Tue) for artful food and 'meteorite' chocolates filled with Garda olive oil. Otherwise, **Speck Stube** (☑ 0457 40 11 77; www.speckstube.com; Via Navene Vecchia 139, Campagnola; meals €8-20; ☺ noon-midnight Mar-Oct; P ➠) is a fun barbeque place on the outskirts of town.

The **tourist office** (☑ 045 740 00 44; www.malcesinepiu.it; Via Capitanato 6; ☺ 9.30am-12.30pm & 3-6pm Mon-Sat, 9.30am-12.30pm Sun) has information on windsurfing, sailing, walking and skiing.

Garda & Punta San Vigilio

Situated in the shade of the Rocca del Garda is the 10th-century fishing village that gave the lake its name. Sadly, the picturesque town is now cut through by the main perimeter road around the lake, making summer traffic overwhelming. Out of season, Garda's perfectly curved bay and fine shingle beaches make it a great lunch spot. Boat trips to Isola del Garda (p282) leave from Garda (in front of Hotel Miralago) on Wednesday morning.

Three kilometres north, the leafy headland of **Punta San Vigilio** curves out into the lake, sheltering the best beach on the eastern shore. The privately owned **Parco Baia delle Sirene** (☑ 045 725 58 84; www.parcobaiadellesirene.it; Punta San Vigilio; adult/child €9/6, reduced admission after 4.30pm; ☺ 10am-7pm Apr-May, 9.30am-8pm Jun-Aug) rents sun lounges beneath the trees. Prices range from €5 to €9 per adult (€4 to €6 per child) per day between April and October.

The tiny headland is home to the plush **Locanda San Vigilio** (☑ 045 725 66 88; www.punta-sanvigilio.it; Punta San Vigilio; d €270-375, ste €440-890; P ❄ @ ❄), where you can dine elegantly overlooking the water from the restaurant's open-sided loggia.

Bardolino

More than 70 vineyards and wine cellars (many within DOC and even DOCG boundaries) grace the gentle hills that roll east from Bardolino on the east shore of Garda. They produce an impressive array of pink Chiaretto, ruby Classico, dry Superiore and young Novello.

One of the most atmospheric ways to savour their flavours is a tutored tasting at **Guerrieri Rizzardi** (☑ 045 721 00 28; www.guerrieri-rizzardi.com; Via Verdi 4; tastings €15; ☺ 5pm Wed May-Oct). After a tour of wine cellars full of cobweb-laced bottles, relaxed

tastings take place in the walled kitchen garden. Alternatively, settle in for a meal of local delicacies accompanied by wines, recommended by the sommelier-owner of **Il Giardino delle Esperidi** (☑ 045 621 04 77; Via Goffredo Mameli 1; meals €35-50; ☺ 7-10pm Wed-Fri & Mon, noon-2.30pm & 7-10pm Sat & Sun).

Bardolino is at its most Bacchic during the **Festa dell'Uva e del Vino** in early October, when the town's waterfront fills with food and wine stands. The **tourist office** (☑ 045 721 00 78; www.tourism.verona.it; Piazzale Aldo Moro; ☺ 9am-1pm & 2-6pm Mon-Sat, 10am-4pm Sun Sep-May, 9am-7pm late-Jun-Aug) stocks a map of producers on the Bardolino **Strada del Vino** (www.stradadelbardolino.com).

THE PO PLAIN

The Lombard Plains, otherwise known as the Po or Padan Plain, spread out east and west of Milan, extending some 650km from Turin and Cuneo in the west to Mantua and Modena in the east. To the north, the western Alps and the great lakes drain into the valley via the Ticino, Adda, Oglio and Mincio rivers.

Sitting on the Milan–Aquileia trade route, between the western Alps and the Gulf of Trieste, the region has been politically and economically significant since the Roman era, when Julius Caesar granted citizenship to the people of the valley in 49 BC. When Napoleon conquered northern Italy in the late 18th century he found the valley dotted with prosperous towns such as Bergamo, Brescia and Mantua, which continue to power a great deal of Italy's agriculture and light industry.

Bergamo

POP 119,600

Split into a more modern Lower Town (Città Bassa) and a captivating Upper Town (Città Alta) that incorporates an attractive ensemble of medieval, Renaissance and baroque architecture, Bergamo is one of northern Italy's most attractive and interesting cities. With its privileged position at the foot of the pre-Alps between the Brembo and Serio river valleys, Bergamo has long been appreciated not only as a key trade centre (textiles and metals in particular) but also as a handy lookout over the Lombard plains.

Although Milan's skyscrapers to the southwest are visible on a clear day, historically Bergamo was more closely associated with

Venice, which controlled the city for 350 years (1428–1797) until Napoleon arrived.

◉ Sights

The Città Alta is a tangle of medieval streets, protected by 5km of Venetian walls. The Upper Town's beating heart is the cafe-clad Piazza Vecchia (Old Square), lined by elegant architecture that is a testament to Bergamo's long and colourful history. The Renaissance square was created by bulldozing the huddle of medieval housing that once stood there, creating what Le Corbusier called 'the most beautiful square in Europe'.

A funicular carries you from the western edge of the Upper Town up to the quaint quarter of San Vigilio, which offers some stunning views. On the plain below sprawls the modern Città Bassa, where you'll find the better dining options.

Palazzo Nuovo HISTORIC BUILDING
The white, porticoed Palazzo Nuovo defines the northern side of Piazza Vecchio. Designed in 1611 by a brilliant architectural mind from Vicenza, Vincenzo Scamozzi (1548–1616), it was not completed until 1928. Long the seat of the town hall, it has been the Angelo Mai library since 1873 and is the repository of Giovannino de'Grassi's rare, Gothic Sketch Book.

Palazzo del Podestà HISTORIC BUILDING
On the northwest side of Piazza Vecchio is the Palazzo del Podestà, the long home to Venice's representative in Bergamo.

Palazzo della Ragione HISTORIC BUILDING
This 12th-century palace at the southern end of the piazza displays the lion of St Mark as a reminder of Venice's long reign here. It's an early-20th-century replica of the 15th-century original, which was torn down when Napoleon took over in 1797. Note the sun clock in the pavement beneath the arches and the curious Romanesque and Gothic animals and busts decorating the pillars of the arches. At the time of writing the palazzo was acting as a temporary exhibition space for artworks from the Carrara collection.

Torre del Campanone TOWER
(adult/child €3/free; ⊙9.30am-6pm Tue-Fri, 9.30am-8pm Sat & Sun Apr-Oct, 9.30am-1pm & 2.30-6pm Tue-Fri, 9.30am-6pm Sat & Sun Nov-Mar) The square-based Torre del Campanone in Piazza Vecchio tolls the old 10pm curfew. Originally raised in the 12th century and partly used as a jail in the 14th century, it has undergone numerous alterations. Take the wheelchair-accessible lift to the top for splendid views.

Duomo CATHEDRAL
(☑035 21 02 23; Piazza del Duomo; ⊙7.30-11.45am & 3-6.30pm) Located in Piazza del Duomo – the core of Bergamo's spiritual life. Roman remains were discovered during renovations of the modest and mostly baroque *duomo*. A rather squat maroon cathedral, it has a brilliant white facade.

Basilica di Santa Maria Maggiore BASILICA
(Piazza del Duomo; ⊙9am-12.30pm & 2.30-6pm Apr-Oct, shorter hourrs Nov-Mar) An intriguing Romanesque basilica next door to the *duomo*. Gothic additions were grafted onto its whirl of Romanesque apses, which begun in 1137. Influences come from afar, with the dual-colour banding (black and white, and rose and white) typical of Tuscany and an interesting trompe l'œil pattern on part of the facade.

What stands out, however, is the Renaissance chapel of Bartolomeo Colleoni (c 1400–1475), the **Cappella Colleoni** (⊙9am-12.30pm & 2-6.30pm Mar-Oct, 9am-12.30pm & 2-4.30pm Tue-Sun Nov-Feb), which was ostentatiously added to the side fronting the square between 1472 and 1476. Built as a mausoleum for the Bergamasche mercenary commander, who led Venice's armies in campaigns across northern Italy, it is decorated with frescos by Venetian rococo master Giambattista Tiepolo (1696–1770). Bartolomeo lies buried inside in a magnificent tomb.

Detached from the main body of the church is the octagonal **baptistery**, built in 1340 but moved to its present spot in 1898.

★ **Accademia Carrara** ART GALLERY
(☑035 39 96 40; www.accademiacarrara.bergamo.it; Piazza Carrara 82a) Just east of the old city walls is one of Italy's great art repositories, although it has been closed for major renovations since 2007. The reopening has been pushed back numerous times over the years, but May 2014 was the latest target at the time of our visit. Until it reopens, a selection of its masterpieces is on show in Palazzo della Ragione.

Founded in 1780, it contains an exceptional range of Italian masters. Raphael's *San Sebastiano* is a highlight, but other artists represented include Botticelli, Canaletto, Mantegna and Titian.

Galleria d'Arte Moderna e Contemporanea ART GALLERY
(GAMeC; ☑035 27 02 72; www.gamec.it; Via San Tomaso 53; ⊙10am-1pm & 3-7pm Tue-Sun) FREE

Bergamo

400 m
0.2 miles

COLLE APERTO

Monte San Vigilio (400m)

Via F Cavagnis

Via Tre Armi

Largo Colle Aperto

Piazza della Cittadella

Bus No 1 to Train Station

Via Baioni

Via Nazario Sauro

Morla

Via Mairoda Porte

Via della Boccola

Via della Fara

Piazzale della Fara

Ex-Convento di Sant'Agostino

Piazzale Brigata Legnano

Via Solata

Via San Lorenzo

Via della Fara

Piazza Mercato del Fieno

Piazza Vecchia

Piazza del Duomo

Piazza San Salvatore

Piazza Arena

Citadel

Via Mascheroni

Via Bartolomeo Colleoni

Via Tassis

Piazza Via Bartolomeo Colleoni

Via Gombito

Via alla Rocca

Youth Hostel (Ostello)

Bus No 3 to Youth Hostel (Ostello)

Piazza Mercato delle Scarpe

Cappella Colleoni

Piazza Giuliani

Via Arena

Viale delle Mura

Via Rosate

Via Giacomo Donizetti

Via Giacomo

Via di Sal...

Via San Tomaso

Via della Noca

Via Porta Dipinta

CITTÀ ALTA (UPPER TOWN)

Viale delle Mura

Viale Vittorio Emanuele II

Nuovo Ostello di Bergamo (2.3km)

Piazza Giacomo Carrara

Accademia Carrara 1

6

CITTÀ BASSA (LOWER TOWN)

Via San Giovanni

Chiesa del Santo Spirito (250m); Orio al Serio (5km)

Via Pignolo

Via Monte Ortigara

Chiesa di San Bernardino (1km)

Ristorante a Modo (180m); ATB Infopoint (1km); (1.2km); Città Bassa Tourist Office (1.2km)

17
4
7
8 10 12 11 15 13 16
2 3 14 9 5

Bergamo

Facing across the square from the Accademia Carrara is this gallery, which displays the academy's small permanent collection of modern works by Italian artists such as Giacomo Balla, Giorgio Morandi, Giorgio de Chirico and Filippo de Pisis. A contribution from Vassily Kandinksy lends an international touch. Admission prices and opening hours vary for temporary exhibitions.

La Rocca   FORTRESS
(Piazzale Brigata Legnano; adult/child €3/free; ◷9.30am-1pm & 2.30-6pm Tue-Fri, 9.30am-7pm Sat & Sun Jun-Sep, 9.30am-1pm & 2.30-6pm Tue-Sun Oct-May) This impressive fortress houses part of the city's **history museum** and is surrounded by a park with lovely views over lower Bergamo. The views are even better from the tower summit.

🛏 Sleeping

Nuovo Ostello di Bergamo   HOSTEL €
(☑035 369 23 76; www.ostellodibergamo.it; Via Galileo Ferraris 1, Monterosso; dm/s/d €18/35/50; ℗@) Bergamo's state-of-the-art HI hostel is about 4km north of the train station. Its 27 rooms offer views of Bergamo's Città Alta. Take bus 6 from Largo Porta Nuova near the train station (get off at the Leonardo da Vinci stop) or **bus 3** for Ostello from the Città Alta.

★**Hotel Piazza Vecchia**   HOTEL €€
(☑035 428 42 11; www.hotelpiazzavecchia.it; Via Bartolomeo Colleoni 3; s/d from €120/145; ❅@🌐) Carved out of a 13th-century building a few steps off Piazza Vecchia, this charming hotel's 13 rooms are all quite different. All have parquet floors and a bath set in stone, but decor varies. Some have exposed beams, some a balcony, some a king-size bed.

Albergo Il Sole   HOTEL €€
(☑035 21 82 38; www.ilsolebergamo.com; Via Bartolomeo Colleoni 1; s/d €70/90) The picture windows and colourful bedspreads at Il Sole lend a countryfied air to its otherwise fairly straightforward but immaculately maintained rooms.

✖ Eating

The Bergamaschi like their polenta and even named a classic sweet after it: *polenta e osei* are pudding-shaped cakes filled with jam and cream, topped with icing and chocolate birds. Bergamo's other famous dish is *casonsèi*, aka *casoncelli* (a kind of ravioli stuffed with spicy sausage meat).

Il Fornaio   PIZZA, BAKERY €
(Via Bartolomeo Colleoni 1; pizza slices €1.10-2; ◷8am-8pm Mon-Sat, 7.30am-8pm Sun; ➕) Bergamo's best coffee is the attraction here, plus hot-to-trot pastries and pizza.

Polentone   ITALIAN €
(☑348 804 60 21; Piazza Mercato delle Scarpe 1, Città Alta; meals €10-15; ◷11.30am-3.30pm & 6-9.30pm Mon-Thu, to 1am Fri, 11.30am-1am Sat, 11.30am-9pm Sun) Styling itself as Italy's first polenta takeaway, Polentone serves up steaming bowls of polenta with sauces such as wild boar, venison and other unusual tastes. Choose between *gialla* (simple, corn polenta) or *taragna* (with cheese and butter). It's under the arches opposite the Upper Town Funicular Stop.

Ristorante a Modo   MODERN ITALIAN €€
(☑035 21 02 95; www.ristoranteamodo.com; Viale Vittorio Emanuele II 19; meals €35; ◷noon-3pm & 8pm-midnight Mon-Sat) Inventive takes on modern Italian cooking make this our pick of the restaurants in the Lower Town. Try their ravioli stuffed with pumpkin or walnuts, or seabass carpaccio with crustaceans of the day. The weekday lunch menu is excellent value at €13/17/22 for one/two/three courses.

La Cantina di Via Colleoni   BERGAMESE €€
(☑035 21 58 64; www.lacantinadiviacolleoni.it; Via Bartolomeo Colleoni 5; meals €25-30; ◷10am-3pm &

IN SEARCH OF LORENZO LOTTO

One of the great names of the late Venetian Renaissance, Lorenzo Lotto worked for 12 years in and around Bergamo from 1513. Many of his stunning masterpieces – depictions of *sacra conversazione* (sacred conversations) between Madonna and saints – remain in situ in Bergamo's churches:

Chiesa dei Santi Bartolomeo e Stefano (Largo Bortolo Belotti 1; ⊙7.30am-noon & 3.30-7.15pm Mon-Fri, to 8pm Sat, to 10pm Sun) Lotto's largest altarpiece (pala) is the Pala Martinengo (c 1513–1516) where his Madonna sits in a Bramante-esque temple framed by saints and overlooked by a Mantegna-inspired oculus.

Chiesa del Santo Spirito (Church of the Holy Spirit; Via Torquato Tasso) Gone is the classical temple and in its place a Venetian-inspired countryside and colour palette define the Pala di Santo Spirito (1521), while the Madonna sits beneath a garland of energetic, winged *putti* (cherubs).

Chiesa di San Bernardino (Via San Bernardino) Lotto's final, stylistically-evolved Pala di San Bernardino (1521) depicts the Madonna beneath a dynamic, foreshortened canopy deep in intense conversation with her saintly companions.

Chiesa di San Michele al Pozzo (St Michael at the Well; Via Porta Dipinta, Città Alta; ⊙9am-5pm) There's no Lotto altarpiece here, just an entire fresco-cycle devoted to the Storie della Vergine (Stories of the Virgin Mother; 1525)

6pm-midnight) Still going strong after 10 years, this laid-back and casual eatery and bar serves up fine local dishes (such as cured meats, local cheeses and *casoncelli* in a warm, brick-lined space and with a carefully chosen and very cool musical soundtrack. There's an excellent lunch *menu Bergamasco* (Bergamo menu) for €15.

★ **Colleoni & Dell'Angelo** ITALIAN €€€ (☑035 23 25 96; www.colleonidellangelo.com; Piazza Vecchia 7, Città Alta; meals €50-60, tasting menus €75; ⊙noon-2.30pm & 7pm-10.30pm Tue-Sun) Piazza Vecchia provides the ideal backdrop to savour inventive local cuisine. Grab an outside table in summer or opt for the noble 15th-century interior, with its polished tile floors, spotless linen and the odd suit of armour standing around. Classic dishes range from the strictly local chickpea soup with cod tripe to national favourites such as grilled turbot with Sicilian lemon peel or *tagliolini* with king crab.

ℹ Information

Airport Tourist Office (☑035 32 04 02; www.turismo-bergamo.it; Airport arrivals hall; ⊙8am-9pm)
Città Alta Tourist Office (☑035 24 22 26; www.turismo-bergamo.it; Via Gombito 13; ⊙9am-5.30pm)
Città Bassa Tourist Office (☑035 21 02 04; www.turismo.bergamo.it; Piazza Gugliemo Marconi; ⊙9am-12.30pm & 2-5.30pm) Province-wide information, including Alpine activities. Check out www.apt.bergamo.it too.

ℹ Getting There & Away

AIR
Orio al Serio (☑035 32 63 23; www.sacbo.it) Bergamo's airport, 4km southeast of the train station.

BUS
Bus Station (☑035 28 90 00, 800 139392; www.bergamotrasporti.it) Located just off Piazza Gugliemo Marconi. SAB (☑035 28 90 00; www.sab-autoservizi.it) operates services to Brescia, Mantua and the lakes.

TRAIN
Train Station (☑035 24 79 50; Piazza Guglielmo Marconi) Services to Milan (€5.25, 65 minutes), Lecco (€3.45, 40 minutes) and Brescia (€4.55, one hour, with connections for Lake Garda and Venice).

ℹ Getting Around

TO/FROM THE AIRPORT
ATB (☑035 23 60 26; www.atb.bergamo.it) Every 20 minutes from Bergamo bus and train stations (€2.10, 15 minutes). Direct buses also connect the airport with Milan and Brescia.

PUBLIC TRANSPORT
ATB's **bus 1** connects the train station with the funicular to the Upper Town and Colle Aperto (going the other way not all buses stop at the station but at the Porta Nuova stop). From Colle Aperto, either bus 21 or a funicular continues uphill to San Vigilio. Buy tickets, valid for 75 minutes' travel on buses, for €1.25 from machines at the train and funicular stations or at newspaper stands.

Brescia

POP 193,900

Urban sprawl, a seedy bus and train station, and the odd 1960s skyscraper don't hint at Brescia's fascinating old town, which serves as a reminder of its substantial history. Its narrow streets are home to some of the most important Roman ruins in Lombardy and an extraordinary circular Romanesque church. The town is dominated by the Colle Cidneo hill, on top of which sit Bresica's rambling castle; the grounds make for a pleasant stroll.

◎ Sights

Museo della Città   MUSEUM, MONASTERY
(City Museum; ☑ 030 297 78 34; www.bresciamusei.com; Via dei Musei 81b; admission adult/child €10/free, temporary exhibitions extra; ☉ 10.30am-7pm Tue-Sun mid-Jun–Sep, shorter hours rest of year) The **Monastero di Santa Giulia & Basilica di San Salvatore** is Brescia's single most intriguing sight. Inside this rambling church and convent complex, the Museo della Città houses collections that run the gamut from prehistory to the age of Venetian dominance. The star piece of the collections is the 8th-century Croce di Desiderio, an extraordinary cross encrusted with jewels.

The building of the monastery, which started as early as the 8th century, absorbed two *domus* (Roman houses), which were left standing in what would become the monks' garden (Ortaglia) near the north cloister. The remains have thus come to be known as the **Domus dell'Ortaglia** and have been protected by the monastery walls through the centuries. Raised walkways allow you to wander round the **Domus di Dioniso** (so called because of a mosaic of Dionysius, god of the grapevine) and the **Domus delle Fontane** (so called because of two marble fountains in it). The beautiful floor mosaics and colourful frescoes are real highlights.

Piazza Paolo VI   PIAZZA
The 11th-century **Duomo Vecchio** (Old Cathedral; Piazza Paolo VI; ☉ 9am-noon & 3-6pm Wed-Sat, 9-10.45am & 3-6pm Sun) is a rare example of a circular-plan Romanesque basilica, built over a 6th-century church. Interesting features include fragmentary floor mosaics and the elaborate 14th-century sarcophagus of Bishop Berado Maggi.

Next door, the **Duomo Nuovo** (New Cathedral; Piazza Paolo VI; ☉ 7.30am-noon & 4-7pm Mon-Sat, 8am-1pm & 4-7pm Sun), dating from 1604, dwarfs its neighbour but is of less interest.

Museo Mille Miglia   MUSEUM
(☑ 030 336 56 31; www.museomillemiglia.it; Viale della Rimembranza 3; adult/reduced €7/5; ☉ 10am-6pm) The Mille Miglia was an annual classic Italian car race held between 1927 and 1957. It started and ended in Brescia and took around 16 hours to complete over 1000 miles. The colourful museum is loaded with some of the great cars to cross the finish line.

The museum is housed outside central Brescia in the sprawling 11th-century Monastero di Sant'Eufemia della Fonte.

🛏 Sleeping & Eating

Risotto, beef dishes and *lumache alla Bresciana* (snails cooked with Parmesan cheese and fresh spinach) are common in Brescia. Via Beccaria is the small but fiercely pumping heart of the evening action. Corso Cavour, Via Gabriele Rosa and Piazza Paolo VI are lined with casual dining options.

★**Albergo Orologio**   BOUTIQUE HOTEL **€€**
(☑ 030 375 54 11; www.albergoorologio.it; Via Beccaria 17; s €85-150, d €110-200; ❄ @ ☎) Located right by the clock tower in the pedestrianised old town, this boutique hotel has fine art and artefacts, soft gold, brown and olive furnishings and terracotta floors. It has just 16 rooms carved out of a medieval building, which combine warmth in the decor with contemporary design in the bathrooms.

★**Osteria al Bianchi**   OSTERIA **€**
(☑ 030 29 23 28; www.osteriaalbianchi.it; Via Gasparo da Salò 32; meals €20-25; ☉ 9am-2pm & 4.30pm-midnight Thu-Mon) Crowd inside this classic old bar and be tempted by the *pappardelle al Taleggio e zucca* (broad ribbon pasta with Taleggio cheese and pumpkin), followed by anything from *brasato d'asino* (braised donkey) to local speciality *pestöm* (minced pork meat served with polenta).

❶ Information

Info Point (☑ 030 240 03 57; www.bresciatourism.it; Via Trieste 1; ☉ 9.30am-1pm & 1.30-5.30pm) The city's main tourist office. There's another, smaller Info Point (☑ 030 837 85 59; Piazzale Stazione) at the station.

❶ Getting There & Around

Bus Station (☑ 030 4 49 15; Via Solferino) SAIA Trasporti (☑ 800 883999, 030 288 99 11; www.saiatrasporti.it) serves destinations

MILAN & THE LAKES BRESCIA

throughout the province including Desenzano del Garda and Mantua. Some leave from another station off Via della Stazione.

Train Station (☑030 4 41 08; Viale della Stazione 7) Situated on the Milan–Venice line, with regular services to Milan (€7 to €20.50, 45 minutes to 1¼ hours) and Verona (€6.25, 40 minutes). There are also secondary lines to Cremona and Bergamo.

Mantua

POP 46.600

As serene as the three lakes it sits beside, Mantua is home to sumptuous ducal palaces and a string of atmospheric, cobbled squares. Settled by the Etruscans in the 10th century, Mantua and its surrounding farmland has long been prosperous. The Latin poet Virgil was born just outside the modern town in 70 BC, Shakespeare's Romeo heard of Juliet's death here and Verdi set his tragic 19th-century opera, *Rigoletto*, in Mantua's melancholy streets. In 1328 the city fell to the fast-living, art loving Gonzaga dynasty, under whose rule it flourished until the Austrians seized control in 1708. Even now, and despite a worrying wobble caused by an earthquake in 2012, the city preserves its antique timeline in its art and architecture.

◉ Sights

The tight-knit centre of Mantua is like an al fresco architectural museum, the interlocking piazzas a series of medieval and Renaissance rooms, comprising from north to south: Piazza Sordello, Piazza Broletto, Piazza delle Erbe and Piazza Mantegna. All four fill with market stalls at the weekends, and come early evening waves of promenading Mantuans ebb and flow between them.

★**Palazzo Ducale**   PALACE
(☑0376 22 48 32, bookings 041 241 18 97; www.mantovaducale.benicultura.it; Piazza Sordello 40; adult/reduced €6.50/3.25; ⊙8.15am-7.15pm Tue-Sun) For more than 300 years the enormous Palazzo Ducale was the seat of the Gonzaga – a wealthy family who rose to power in the 14th century to become one of Italy's leading Renaissance families. At the height of their power, its 500-plus rooms, three squares and 15 courtyards were adorned with more than 2000 artworks. Sadly the collection was auctioned off by Vicenzo II to Charles I of England in 1627, just prior to the collapse of the family's fortunes in 1630.

The tour of the palace, for which you should budget several hours, takes you through just 40 of the palace's finest rooms. The biggest draw, however, is the mid-15th-century fresco by Mantegna, the **Camera degli Sposi** (Bridal Chamber). Executed between 1465 and 1474, the room, which is entirely painted, shows the Marquis, Lodovico, going about his courtly business with family and courtiers in tow. Most playful of all is the trompe l'œil oculus which features barebottomed *putti* balancing precariously on a painted balcony, while smirking courtly pranksters appear ready to drop a large potted plant on gawping tourists below.

Other palace highlights are Domenico Morone's *Expulsion of the Bonacolsi* (1494), in Room 1, depicting the Gonzaga *coup d'etat* of 1328; and Rubens' vast *Adoration of the Magi* in the **Sala degli Arcieri** (Room of Archers), which Napoleonic troops brutally dismembered in 1797. In the **Sala del Pisanello** fascinating preliminary sketches of Pisanello's frescoes of Arthurian knights remain, while the cream-and-gold **Galleria degli Specchi** (Gallery of Mirrors) is actually a complete 17th-century Austrian reworking – under the Gonzaga the gallery housed prized paintings, including Caravaggio's radical *Death of the Virgin* (now in the Louvre).

Last, but not least, Rooms 34 to 36, the **Stanze degli Arazzi**, house some of the only original artworks commissioned by the family: nine 16th-century Flemish tapestries reproduced from Raphael's original designs for the Sistine Chapel. Woven in Brussels using the finest English wool, Indian silk and Cypriot gold and silver thread, they represent the cosmopolitan sophistication of the Gonzaga court at the height of its power.

Basilica di Sant'Andrea   BASILICA
(☑0376 32 85 04; Piazza Andrea Mantegna; ⊙8am-noon & 3-7pm Mon-Fri, 10.30am-noon & 3-6pm Sat, 11.45am-12.15pm & 3-6pm Sun) This towering basilica safeguards the golden vessels said to hold earth soaked with the blood of Christ. Longinus, the Roman soldier who speared Christ on the cross, is said to have scooped up the earth and buried it in Mantua after leaving Palestine. Today, these containers rest beneath a marble octagon in front of the altar and are paraded around Mantua in a grand procession on Good Friday.

Ludovico II Gonzaga commissioned Leon Battista Alberti to design the suitably monumental basilica to house the relic in 1472. Its vast, arched interior is free from pillars and has just one sweeping central aisle, which is covered with frescoes, gilded ceiling blocks and columns cleverly painted to look like carved stone.

The first chapel on the left contains the tomb of court painter Andrea Mantegna, the man responsible for the splendours in the Palazzo Ducale's Camera degli Sposi. The chapel is beautifully lit and contains a painting of the Holy Family and John the Baptist, attributed to Mantegna and his school.

★ Palazzo Te
PALACE

(☑ 0376 32 32 66; www.palazzote.it; Viale Te; adult/reduced €8/5; ☉ 1-6pm Mon, 9am-6pm Tue-Sun) Hardly more modest in scale than the Palazzo Ducale, Frederico II's (1500–1540) suburban villa is decorated in playboy style with stunning frescoes and encoded symbols. A Renaissance pleasure-dome, it is the finest work of Mannerist architect Giulio Romano.

Having escaped a prison sentence for designing pornographic prints, Romano was the perfect choice for the commission. Using the trompe l'oeil technique, he eschewed the cool classicism of the past in favour of a fanciful Mannerist scheme of wildly distorted perspectives, pastel colours and esoteric symbols.

The second room, the Camera delle Imprese (Room of the Devices) sets the scene with a number of key symbols: the salamander, the symbol of Federico; the eagles of the Gonzaga standard; and Mt Olympus, the symbol of Charles V, Holy Roman Emperor, from whom the Gonzaga received their titles. The purpose of Renaissance devices was to encode messages so that visitors to the palace could 'read' the political and personal power structures. Federico's device, the salamander, is accompanied by the quote: *quod hic deest, me torquet* (what you lack, torments me), alluding to his uncontrollably passionate nature when compared to the cold-blooded salamander.

The culmination of the villa's narrative comes together in the Camera dei Giganti (Chamber of the Giants), a domed room frescoed with towering figures of the rebellious giants (disloyal subjects) clawing their way up Mt Olympus (symbol of Charles V) only to be laid low by Jupiter's (Charles') thunderbolt. As the viewer you are both spectator and participant; standing in the centre of the scene, the worried faces of Olympian gods stare down at you – would-be presumptuous giant or loyal subject?

The symbolism was not lost on Emperor Charles V, who visited the palace in 1530 and afterwards raised Federico up from a marquis to a duke.

Activities

On a sunny day the people of Mantua head for the waterfront. The shore of Lago di Mezzo, complete with the child-friendly Parco della Scienza (outdoor science park), is the most crowded; the quieter path beside Lago Superiore meanders through reed beds before petering out, while the shore of Lago Inferiore brings broad views. At all three you'll find waterside snack bars.

La Rigola
CYCLING

(☑ 0376 36 66 77; Via Trieste 7; per day from €10) Hire bikes here, and the tourist office (p298) stocks the excellent, English-language booklet, *Mantova in Bici*, detailing cycling itineraries around the lakes, along the Po river and in the Parco del Mincio (www.parcodelmincio.it).

Tours

Boat Tours
BOAT TOUR

One- to two-hour tours on Lake Superiore are offered by two competitor companies between April and October: Navi Andes (☑ 0376 32 45 06; www.naviandes.com; Lago di Mezzo jetty; Mon-Sat €9, Sun €10; 1½ hours) and Motonavi Andes (☑ 0376 36 08 70; www.motonaviandes.it; Via San Giorgio 2), although the shop is located in town, the embarkation point for Motonavi Andes tours is near Parco della Scienza. They skirt lotus flowers, reed beds and heron roosts, and provide great city views.

Both companies also offer longer trips to San Benedetto Po (one way/return Mon-Sat €13.50/19, Sun €15.50/20; 2½ hours one way)

AVEMARIA BIKE & BOAT

Peak out of your porthole at cormorants sunning themselves on branches as you glide from Mantua down the Mincio and Po rivers to Ferrara or Venice. Avemaria (☑ 0444 32 36 39; www.avemariaboat.com; Contrà Manin, Vicenza; per person weekend €160-250, week €955; 🖥👤) ∥ is a barging hotel offering 4-day or week-long cultural itineraries exploring the peaceful nooks and crannies of the delta. Onboard, 40 unisex bikes (child seats available on request) make for easy hop-on, hop-off explorations while the rooftop sundeck provides a superlative terrace for cocktails and romantic dining.

Mantua

0 — **200 m**
0 — **0.1 miles**

Lago di Mezzo

Lago Inferiore

Lago Superiore

Boats of Navi Andes

Boat tours of Lago Superiore

Peschiera del Garda (36km)

Porta Mulini

Viale Mincio

Viale Mincio

Bike Trail

Parco della Scienza

Embarkation Point for Motonavi Andes

Boats to San Benedetto

Boats to San Benedetto Po & Venice

Porta San Giorgio

Verona (38km)

Boats to San Benedetto Po

Via Legnago

Lungolago del Gonzaga

Piazza Castello

Palazzo Ducale **1**

Piazza Santa Barbara

Piazza Arche **6**

La Rigola (330m)

Cattedrale

Piazza Sordello

3

Torre della Gabbia

Piazza Broletto

Via dell'Accademia

Via Ardigo

Piazza Concordia

9 **4**
5
10
Via Broletto
Piazza Mantegna **2**
Piazza delle Erbe

Via G Bertani

Via Cavour

Vicolo Alberto

Vicolo Nazione

8

Via Roma

Palazzo Te (1.1km)

Corso del Sogliari

Via Ippolito Nievo

Corso Umberto I

Piazza Virgiliana

Via Fratelli Cairoli

Via Cappuccine

Via Dario Tassoni

Via Due Catene

Via Finzi

Via Domenico Fernelli

Via Giovanni Arrivabene

Via Trento

Via Concezione

Piazza San Giovanni

Piazza d'Arco **7**

Via A Scarsellini

Via Fratelli Bandiera

Via Marangoni

Corso Vittorio Emanuele II

Piazza Cavallotti

Via Porto

Via XXV Aprile

Via Alberto Pitentino

Sottoriva

Bike Trail

Train Station

Piazza Don Leoni

Via Solferino e San Martino

Dal Pescatore (38km)

Mantua

through the Mincio park. The trip leaves Mantua from the jetty on Lungolago dei Gonzaga.

★ **Visit Mantua**　　　　WALKING TOUR
(☎347 402 20 20; www.visitmantua.blogspot.co.uk) Get the insider view of Renaissance dukes and duchesses with Lorenzo Bonoldi's fascinating conversational tours of Mantua's highlight palaces.

🎉 Festivals & Events

Mantova Jazz　　　　MUSIC
This annual jazz fest runs from late March to early May. Check out the Mantova Jazz Facebook page for details of venues.

🛏 Sleeping

★ **Armellino**　　　　B&B €
(☎346 314 80 60; www.bebarmellino.it; Via Cavour 67; s €65, d €75-85; @🔲⏸) Enjoy a touch of ducal splendour in Antonella and Massimo's fabulous *palazzo*. Grand rooms are furnished with 18th-century antiques and retain their original wooden floors, fireplaces and ceiling frescoes. Not all bedrooms have a bathroom, but this place has the feel of an exclusive private apartment rather than a B&B.

C'a delle Erbe　　　　B&B €€
(☎0376 22 61 61; www.cadelleerbe.it; Via Broletto 24; d €130-160; ❄🔲) With an unbeatable location in the heart of old Mantua, this 16th-century townhouse teams exposed brick walls with contemporary design and modern art. Ask for the room with the balcony overlooking Piazza delle Erbe.

🍽 Eating

Mantua's most famous dish is melt-in-your-mouth *tortelli di zucca* (pumpkin-stuffed cushions of pasta). Pork also features heavily on the menu; look out for *salumi* (salt port), *prosciutto crudo* (salt-cured ham) and *risotto alla pilota* (risotto with minced pork). Many dishes are accompanied by a sweet mustard, *mostarda di mele* or *mantovana* (made with apples or pears).

Pick up sweet local treats from **Bar Caravatti** (☎0376 32 78 26; Portici Broletto 16; ⏰7am-8.30pm) and picnic fare from **Zapparoli** (☎0376 32 33 45; Via Cavour 49; ⏰8.15am-1pm & 4.30-7.30pm Tue-Sun, 8.15am-1pm Mon).

MILAN & THE LAKES MANTUA

WORTH A TRIP

DAL PESCATORE

Petals of egg pasta frame slices of guinea fowl caramelized in honey saffron, while silky tortellini are stuffed to bursting with pumpkin, nutmeg, cinnamon and candied mostarda. You can practically eat the Mantuan countryside in Nadia Santini's internationally-acclaimed restaurant **Dal Pescatore** (☎0376 72 30 01; www.dalpescatore.com; Località Runate, Canneto sull'Oglio; meals €150-250; ⏰noon-4pm & 7.30-late Thu-Sun, 7.30-late Wed; 🅿). What's even more surprising is that Italy's best female chef (2013) is entirely self-taught and has only ever cooked in this singular restaurant, originally the modest trattoria of her husband's family. Beneath the tutelage of her now 84-year-old mother-in-law, who still cooks in the kitchen, Nadia learnt to cook Mantuan cuisine deftly and creatively. Despite her background in food science the food isn't remotely high-tech, but rather quietly brilliant, focusing on the essentials and balancing simplicity with the very finest natural produce.

The restaurant is located 40km west of Mantua in a green glade beside the Oglio river. Nearby, **9 Muse B&B** (☎335 800 76 01; www.9muse.it; Via Giordano Bruno 42/a, Canneto sull'Oglio; s/d €45/75; 🅿❄@⏸) provides elegant and charming accommodation.

CREMONA'S VIOLINS

It was in Cremona that master craftsman Antonio Stradivari lovingly put together his first Stradivarius violins, helping establish a tradition that continues today. The Stradivarius violin is typically made from spruce (the top), willow (the internal blocks and linings) and maple (the back, ribs and neck), and is prized for its unique sound, attributed to the density of the wood and possibly the unique treatment and varnish.

But Stradivari was by no means the only master craftsman in Cremona. Other great violin-making dynasties that started here include the Amati and Guarneri families, and even today some 100 violin-making workshops cluster in the streets around the Piazza del Comune.

Long overdue, but worth the wait, is the brand new, state-of-the-art **Museo del Violino** (☑ 037 2 80 18 01; www.museodelviolino.org; Piazza Marconi; adult/reduced €10/7; ☉ 10am-6pm Tue-Sun), which brings together the city's historic collection of violins, presenting them alongside the tools of the trade and placing them in the context of the development of the craft and the evolving popularity of the instrument internationally. The complex also features a specially engineered auditorium, which will play host to Cremona's numerous classical music events.

To hear Cremona's violins in action, head to the 19th-century **Teatro Amilcare Ponchielli** (☑ 0372 02 20 01; www.teatroponchielli.it; Corso Vittorio Emanuele II 52), whose season runs from October to June.

Osteria delle Quattro Tette
MANTUAN €

(☑ 0376 32 94 78; Vicolo Nazione 4; meals €10-15; ☉ 12.30-2.30pm Mon-Sat) Take a pew at wooden tables beneath echoing barrel-vaulted ceilings and order up pumpkin pancakes, pike in sweet salsa or *risotto alla pilota*. It is rustic and extremely well priced.

Fragoletta Antica
MANTUAN €€

(☑ 0376 32 33 00; www.fragoletta.it; Piazza Arche 5; meals €35; ☉ noon-3pm & 7-11.30pm Tue-Sun; 🖼) Diners eagerly tuck into Slow-Food accredited *culatello di Zibello* (lard) at this friendly local trattoria. Other Mantuan specials such as *risotto alla pilota* and perfectly seasoned steaks feature on the menu. Dine in the back room with its bright homemade art amid stacks of wine crates.

★ Il Cigno
MANTUAN €€€

(☑ 0376 32 71 01; www.lesoste.it; Piazza d'Arco 1; meals €55-65; ☉ 12.30-2.30pm & 7-11pm Wed-Sun, closed Aug) The building is as beautiful as the food: a lemon-yellow facade dotted with faded olive-green shutters, and dining rooms adorned with Venetian glassware. Inside, Mantua's gourmets tuck into risotto with spring greens, poached cod with polenta or gamey guinea fowl with spicy Mantuan *mostarda*.

ⓘ Information

Tourist Office (☑ 0376 43 24 32; www.turismo.mantova.it; Piazza Mantegna 6; ☉ 9am-1.30pm & 2.30-6pm Mon-Fri, 10am-6pm Sat & Sun)

ⓘ Getting There & Around

Bus Station (☑ 0376 23 03 46; www.apam.it; Piazza Don Leoni; ☉ 7.30am-12.45pm & 3-5.45pm Thu-Tue, 7.30am-12.45pm Wed & Sat) Runs buses to Sabbioneta, San Benedetto Po and Brescia. Most leave from Piazza Don Leoni, but some leave from Viale Risorgimento.

A new express service also operates from Piazza Sordello and Piazza don Leoni for Verona airport (adult/child €5/free, 45 minutes, four daily).

Train Station (Piazza Don Leoni) Regular services to Cremona (€5.80, 40 to 60 minutes), Milan (€11.05, two hours), Verona (€3.45, one hour) and Peschiera del Garda (€5.40, 1½ hours, via Verona).

Cremona

POP 72,200

A wealthy, independent city-state for centuries, Cremona is best known for its violin making.

⊙ Sights

Piazza del Comune
PIAZZA

This beautiful square is considered one of the best-preserved medieval squares in all of Italy. To divide the secular and spiritual, Church buildings were erected on the eastern side of Piazza del Comune, and those concerned with secular affairs were across the way.

The business of city government was, and still is, carried out in the 13th-century **Palazzo Comunale** (Piazza del Comune). On the central pillar of the main facade, a marble *arengario* (balcony from which decrees were read and speeches given) was added in 1507. South across a lane is the **Loggia dei Militi** (Piazza del Comune), a delightful little Gothic gem built in 1292.

Duomo
CATHEDRAL

(☑0372 2 73 86; www.cattedraledicremona.it; Piazza del Comune; ⊗7.30am-noon & 3.30-7pm) Cremona's stately cathedral started out as a Romanesque basilica, but by the time it was finished in 1190 it was heavily overtaken by Gothic modishness. The central nave and apse flaunt frescoes of the lives of the Virgin Mary and Christ; the *Storie di Cristo* (Stories of Christ) by Pordenone stands out.

The cathedral's most prized possession is the Sacra Spina (Holy Thorn), allegedly from the Crown of Thorns worn by Jesus Christ. It's kept behind bars in the **Capella delle Reliquie.**

Torrazzo
TOWER

(Piazza del Comune; adult/child €5/4, incl baptistry €6/5; ⊗10am-1pm & 2.30-6pm Tue-Sun Mar-Nov) The 111m-tall bell tower is connected to the duomo by a Renaissance loggia, the **Bertazzola**. It is fronted by a beautiful zodiacal clock, 8m wide and installed in 1583. A total of 502 steps wind up to the top of the tower for views across the city.

Chiesa di Sant'Agostino
CHURCH

(Piazza Sant'Agostino) Inside the Chiesa di Sant'Agostino, the **Cappella Cavalcabò** (third chapel on the right) is a stunning late-Gothic fresco cycle by Bonifacio Bembo and his assistants. One of the altars is graced with a 1494 painting by Pietro Perugino, *Madonna in trono e santi* (The Madonna Enthroned with Saints).

Chiesa di San Sigismondo
CHURCH

(Largo Visconti) A couple of kilometres outside the old city, the Chiesa di San Sigismondo (1463–1492) was built to commemorate the wedding of Francesco Sforza to Bianca Maria Visconti in 1441. The 16th-century fresco cycle is a great example of Mannerism

📷 Festivals & Events

Festival di Cremona Claudio Monteverdi
MUSIC

(www.teatroponchielli.it) A month-long series of concerts centred on Claudio Monteverdi and other baroque-era composers in early May to early June.

Festa del Torrone
FOOD

(www.festadeltorronecremona.it) A late-autumn weekend dedicated to tastings of Cremona speciality *torrone* (nougat).

🛏 Sleeping & Eating

Albergo Duomo
HOTEL €

(☑0372 3 52 42; www.hotelduomocremona.com; Via Gonfalonieri 13; s/d €60/85; 🅿❋🛜) Just a few steps from Cremona's cathedral, Albergo Duomo was given a complete overhaul in 2013 and now offers well-priced rooms with contemporary flair.

Delliarti Design Hotel
DESIGN HOTEL €€

(☑0372 2 31 31; www.hoteldellearti.com; Via Bonomelli 8; s/d from €109/139; ❋🛜) This high-tech vision of glass, concrete and steel has rotating displays of contemporary paintings and photos, a Turkish bath, a gym and suitably chic rooms with clean lines, bold colours and artistic lighting. For those who want to feel like they never left the fashion crowd in Milan, this could be the place.

★Hosteria '700
CREMONESE €€

(☑0372 3 61 75; www.hosteria700.it; Piazza Gallina 1; meals €30-35; ⊗noon-3pm & 7.30-10pm Wed-Mon) Behind the dilapidated facade lurks a sparkling gem. A series of vaulted rooms, some with ceiling frescoes, winds off from the entrance. There is something noble about the atmosphere, with the antique cupboards and dark timber tables and chairs. The hearty Lombard cooking also comes in at a refreshingly competitive cost.

La Sosta
OSTERIA €€

(☑0372 45 66 56; www.osterialasosta.it; Via Vescovo Sicardo 9; meals €30-35; ⊗12.15-2.30pm & 7.15-10pm Tue-Sat, 12.15-2.30pm Sun) Surrounded by violin-makers' workshops, this is a beautiful place to feast on regional delicacies such as local cheeses and baked snails

ℹ Information

Tourist Office (☑0372 40 63 91; www.turismocremona.it; Piazza del Comune 5; ⊗9am-1pm & 2-5pm Sep-Jun, closed Sun afternoon Jul & Aug)

ℹ Getting There & Away

Train Station (Via Dante) The city can be reached by train from Milan (from €7, one to two hours, several daily) and Brescia (€5.25, one hour, hourly).

Trento & the Dolomites

Why Go?

While they're not Italy's tallest mountains, the Dolomites' red-hued pinnacles are the country's most spectacular, drawing a faithful fan club of hikers, skiers, poets and fresh-air fanciers for at least the last few centuries.

Protected by seven natural parks, the two semi-autonomous provinces of Trentino and Alto Adige offer up a number of stunning wilderness areas, where adventure and comfort can be found in equal measure. Wooden farmhouses dot vine- and orchard-covered valleys and the region's cities – the southerly enclave of Trento, the Austro-Italian Bolzano and the very Viennese Merano – are easy to navigate, cultured and fun. From five-star spa resorts to the humblest mountain hut, multi-generational hoteliers combine genuine warmth with extreme professionalism.

Nowhere are the oft-muddled borders of Italy's extreme north reflected more strongly than on the plate: don't miss out on tasting one of Europe's fascinating cultural juxtapositions.

Best Places to Eat

➡ Löwengrube (p320)

➡ Scrigno del Duomo (p306)

➡ Acherer Patisserie & Blumen (p331)

➡ Paradeis (p324)

Best Places to Stay

➡ Miramonti (p323)

➡ Gasthof Grüner Baum (p325)

➡ Park Hotel Azalea (p315)

➡ Chalet Fogajard (p313)

When to Go
Bolzano

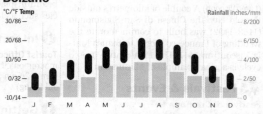

Jan Grab a bargain on the slopes after the Christmas high.

Jul Hit the high-altitude trails and mountain huts of the Alta Vie.

Dec Get festive at Tyrolean Christmas markets in Bolzano, Merano and Bressanone.

Seasons

The ski season runs from early December to early April, high season hits mid-December to January 6, the last two weeks of February and any early Easter. Summer rates plummet, apart from August. Many resorts shut in April/May and October/November, while *rifugi* (mountain huts) open from late June to September, the prime hiking season.

Language

Trentino's first language is Italian but head north to Alto Adige (Südtirol) and you'll find 75% of the population are German speakers, a legacy of the region's Austro-Hungarian past. The Ladin language is spoken in both provinces, across five eastern Dolomiti valleys; it's a direct descendant of provincial Latin.

TRENTINO

Trento

POP 117,300 / ELEV 194M

Trento rarely makes the news these days, but that wasn't the case in the mid-16th century. During the tumultuous years of the Counter-Reformation, the Council of Trent convened here, dishing out far-reaching condemnations to uppity Protestants. Modern Trento is far from preachy; instead it's quietly confident, liberal and easy to like. Bicycles glide along spotless streets fanning out from the atmospheric, intimate Piazza del Duomo, students clink spritzes by Renaissance fountains and a dozen historical eras intermingle seamlessly amid stone castles, shady porticoes and the city's signature medieval frescoes. While there's no doubt you're in Italy, Trento does have its share of Austrian influence: apple strudel is ubiquitous and beer halls not uncommon. Set in a wide glacial valley guarded by the crenulated peaks of the Brenta Dolomites, amid a patchwork of vineyards and apple orchards, Trento is a perfect jumping-off point for hiking, skiing or wine tasting. And road cycling is huge: 400km of paved cycling paths fan out from here.

◉ Sights

Helpful plaques indicate which historical era various buildings belong to – often several at once in this many-layered city.

Castello del Buonconsiglio MUSEUM
(🖉0461 23 37 70; www.buonconsiglio.it; Via Clesio 5; adult/reduced/family €8/5/7; ⊙9.30am-5pm Tue-Sun) Guarded by hulking fortifications, Trento's bishop-princes holed up here until Napoleon's arrival in 1801. Behind the walls are the original 13th-century castle, the Castelvecchio, and the Renaissance residence Magno Palazzo, which provides an atmospheric backdrop for a varied collection of artefacts.

Duomo CATHEDRAL
(Cattedrale di San Vigilio; ⊙6.30am-6pm) Once host to the Council of Trent, this dimly lit Romanesque cathedral displays fragments of medieval frescoes inside its transepts. Two colonnaded stairways flank the nave, leading, it seems, to heaven. Built over a 6th-century temple devoted to San Vigilio, patron saint of Trento, the foundations form part of a **palaeo-Christian archaeological area** (10am-noon & 2.30-5.30pm Mon-Sat, admission €1.50 or included with Museo Diocesano entrance).

Museo Diocesano Tridentino MUSEUM
(Palazzo Pretorio; 🖉0461 23 44 19; Piazza del Duomo 18; adult/reduced €5/3 incl Duomo's archaeological area; ⊙9.30am-12.30pm & 2.30-5.30pm Wed-Mon) Sitting across the square from the *duomo*, this former bishop's residence dates from the 11th century. It now houses one of Italy's most important ecclesiastical collections with enormous documentary paintings of the Council of Trent, along with Flemish tapestries, exquisite illustrated manuscripts, vestments and some particularly opulent reliquaries.

Piazza del Duomo PIAZZA
Trento's heart is this busy yet intimate piazza, dominated, of course, by the *duomo*, but also host to the **Fontana di Nettuno**, a flashy late-baroque fountain rather whimsically dedicated to Neptune. Intricate, allegorical frescoes fill the 16th-century facades of the **Casa Cazuffi-Rella**, on the piazza's northern side.

Tridentum La Città Sotterranea ROMAN SITE
(🖉0461 23 01 71; Piazza Battisti; adult/reduced €2.50/1.50; ⊙9am-noon & 2-5.30pm Oct-May, 9.30am-1pm & 2-6pm Tue-Sun Jun-Sep) Explore Roman Tridentum's city walls, paved streets, tower, domestic mosaics and a workshop. The site was discovered less than two decades ago, during restoration works on the nearby theatre.

ento
the
Dolomites
Highlights

1 Working up a high-altitude appetite on the slopes, then hit the fine-dining hot spot of **Alta Badia** (p328).

2 Being enchanted by the endless green pastures of the **Alpe di Siusi** (p327).

3 Testing your mettle on a vertiginous **via ferrata** in the Brenta Dolomites (p308).

4 Sipping a Veneziana *spritz* on a frescoed piazza in **Trento** (p301).

5 Floating away beneath palm trees and snowy peaks at **Terme Merano** (p322).

6 Uncovering excellent contemporary art collections in **Rovereto** (p307), **Bolzano** (p317) and **Merano** (p322).

7 Discovering Italy's most elegant white wines along the **Weinstrasse** (p324).

8 Getting high above Bolzano's pretty streets on one of its three **cable cars** (p317).

9 Feasting your way through schnitzel and *spätzle*, strudel and *knödel* in the **Val Pusteria** (p330).

10 Mountain biking the apple-clad hills of the **Val di Sole** (p314).

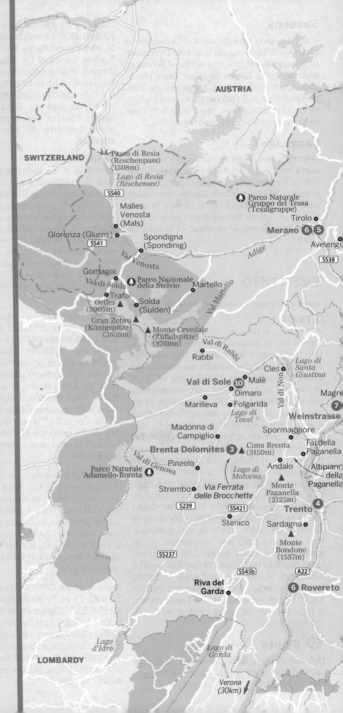

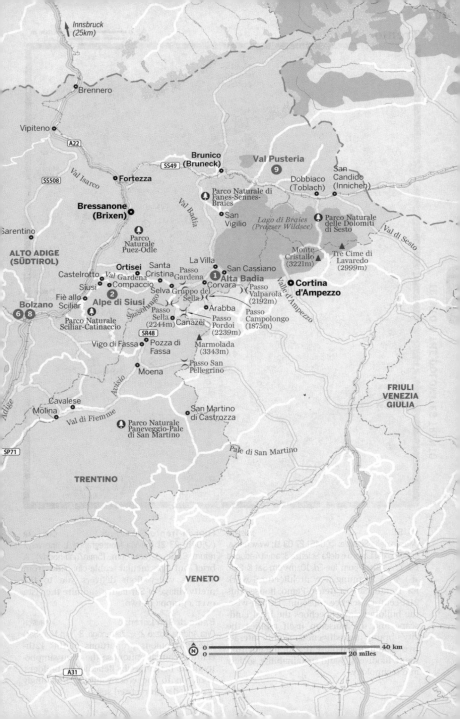

Trento

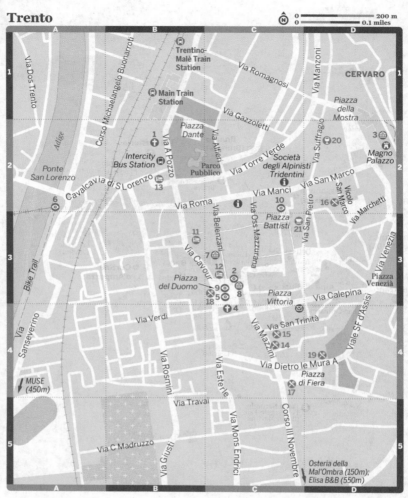

MUSE

MUSEUM

(Museo della Scienze; ☎ 0461 27 03 11; www.muse.
it; Corso del Lavoro e della Scienza 3; adult/reduced
€9/7; ☉ 10am-6pm Tue-Fri, 10am-7pm Sat & Sun;
👶) 🌿 A stunning new architectural work
for Trento, care of Renzo Piano, houses this
21st-century science museum. Design-wise,
the building cleverly echoes the local landscape and the museum itself typifies the
city's brainy inquisitiveness. Highly interactive exhibitions explore the Alpine environment, biodiversity and sustainability, society
and technology.

Funivia Trento-Sardagna

CABLE CAR

(☎ 0461 23 21 54; Via Montegrappa 1; one way/
return €3/5; ☉ 7am-10pm, 15min/half-hourly) A
brief but spectacular cable-car ride from
Trento's valley floor delivers you to the
pretty village of Sardagna – admire the vista
over a grappa or two.

Badia di San Lorenzo

CHURCH

(Via Andrea Pozzo 2; ☉ 7am-noon, 3-7pm Mon-Sat)
The harmonious proportions of this 12th-
century church epitomise the calm simplicity of its Bergameschi Benedictine builders.
Look up to the cross-vaulting, touchingly
festooned with rust-red stars.

Trent

Galleria Civica di Trento   ART GALLERY

(☎0461 98 55 11; www.mart.tn.it/galleriacivica; Via
Belenzani 46; ⊙Tue-Sun 10am-6pm) FREE This
new city gallery project space steps into
the breach while the future of the Trento
campus of MART (Museo di Arte Moderna
e Contemporanea di Trento e Rovereto) remains uncertain.

🏃 Activities

The small ski station of **Vaneze di Monte**
(1350m) is a 17km winding drive from Trento and is connected by cable car to its higher
counterpart, **Vasòn**, and the gentle slopes
of **Monte Bondone** (www.montebondone.it).
Criss-crossed by 37km of cross-country ski
trails and nine downhill runs in winter,
Monte Bondone's pristine slopes are also
home to the **Giardino Alpine Botanico**
(Botanical Alpine Gardens; ☎0461 94 80 50; www.
mtsn.tn.it/Viote_giardino_botanico; Viote de Monte
Bondone; adult/reduced €3.50/2.50; ⊙9am-5pm
Jun & Sep, 9am-6pm Jul & Aug), with a collection of Alpine plants from across Europe, as
well as an indigenous nature trail. On weekends between December and March, Skibus
Monte Bondone, run by Trentino Trasporti,
wends its way from Trento to Vason and Viote (free with TrentoRovereto card, one way
€3, 7-day pass €15).

For suggested walking itineraries, and
information on *vie ferrate* (trails with permanent cables and ladders) and *rifugi*
(mountain huts), visit the local **Società
degli Alpinisti Tridentini** (SAT; ☎0461 98 28
04; www.sat.tn.it; Palazzo Saracini Cresseri, Via Manci 57; ⊙9am-noon & 3-7pm Mon-Fri, afternoons only
in winter), staffed by friendly mountaineers.

☞ Tours

The tourist office runs two-hour multilingual walking tours (€6) every Saturday,
visiting Castello del Buonconsiglio at 10am
or around the town centre at 3pm.

🛏 Sleeping

Central hotels book out in early June, when
the **Festival Economia** (2012.festivalecono-
mia.eu) comes to town, and during other
conferences. **Agritur Trentino** (☎0461 23
53 23; www.agriturismotrentino.com; Via Aconcio
13; ⊙9am-noon Mon-Fri) can put you in touch
with rural B&Bs and *agriturismi* (farm stay
accommodation), often only a short drive
from the centre.

★Elisa B&B   B&B €

(☎0461 92 21 33; www.bbelisa.com; Viale Rovereto 17; s/d €60/90; ❇🅿🛜) This is a true B&B
in an architect's family home, with three
private, stylish rooms and charming hosts
who dispense organic breakfasts (home-
baked cakes, freshly squeezed juice, artisanal cheese, eggs), along with invaluable
local tips. It's located in a quiet, residential
neighbourhood, a pleasant stroll from the
city centre, with lots of eating, shopping and
drinking options along the way.

Hotel Venezia   HOTEL €

(☎0461 23 41 14; www.hotelveneziatn.it; Piazza
del Duomo 45; with/without bathroom s €44/57
d €60/80; 🛜) Rooms in this friendly place
overlook the Piazza del Duomo, pretty Via
Belanzani or a quiet inner courtyard. The
hotel has been recently remodelled including flash bathrooms, while prices remain the
same.

Ostello Giovane Europa
HOSTEL €

(☑0461 26 34 84; www.gayaproject.org; Via Torre Vanga 9; dm/s/d €16/27/45; ⊘reception closed 10am-2pm) This squeaky-clean hostel is bang in the middle of town and just a few minutes' walk from the main train station (convenient, yes, but also, at times, noisy). Rooms are comfortable and upper floors have mountain views; the mansard-roofed family room on the top floor is particularly spacious.

Albergo Accademia
HOTEL €€

(☑0461 23 36 00; www.accademiahotel.it; Vicolo Colico 4/6; s €100, d €165; [P][❄][@]) Elegant small hotel in a historic medieval house with rooms that are modern and airy (if a little on the staid side). Suites are luxuriously spacious, including one with a large private terrace and sauna.

✗ Eating & Drinking

Trento's table is a hearty one and draws many of its ingredients – beef, game, cheese, mushrooms – from its fertile hinterland. There's a lot of cross-cultural traffic too: *cotoletta* (schnitzel) and *canederli* (dumplings) are decidedly northern, polenta and asparagus evoke the Veneto and Garda's olive oil conjures the Mediterranean. Bakeries brim with apple strudel, but don't overlook the local carrot cake. Wines to look out for include Trento DOC, a sparkling made from chardonnay grapes, the white Nosiola and the extremely drinkable red, Teroldego Rotaliano DOC. Trentino's smartly bottled Surgiva mineral water is considered one of Italy's best, for taste and purity

Uva et Mente
PIZZERIA €

(☑0461 190 31 62; Via Dietro le Mura A 35; pizzas €7, meals €15-30; ⊘noon-midnight Tue-Sun) A young, friendly team keep the crowds smiling in the bustling basement space or out on the sunny terrace, with steaks, pastas and risottos making the most of fresh, regional ingredients. There's a €10 lunch deal and a dedicated beer menu, but good pizza is the highlight; a bonus, they can be ordered wholemeal or gluten-free.

Al Tino
TRENTINO €

(☑0461 98 41 09; Via San Trinita 10; meals €20; ⊘6.45-9.30pm Mon-Sat) Al Tino has a sweet, old-fashioned dining room and service to match, with a menu dedicated to traditional dishes such as barley soup, *canederli in brodo* (dumplings in broth) and pork chops.

Pedavena
BREWERY €

(☑0461 98 62 55; Piazza di Fiera 13; meals €18-30; ⊘Wed-Mon 9am-midnight, Fri & Sat to 1am) Proudly crowd-pleasing and perennially popular, this sprawling 1920s beer hall (complete with fermenting brew in the corner) serves up the comfort food you'd expect: bratwurst, schnitzel and steaming plates of polenta with mushroom stew and slabs of melty white *tosella* cheese.

Scrigno del Duomo
GASTRONOMIC €€

(☑0461 22 00 30; www.scrignodelduomo.com; Piazza del Duomo 29; meals €35, degustation from €50; ⊘wine bar 11am-2.30pm & 6-11pm, dining room 12.30-2.30pm & 7.30-10pm Tue-Sun, dinner only Sat) Trento's culinary and social epicentre is discreetly housed in a building dating back to the 1200s. Take the stairs down to the formal restaurant, with its glassed-in Roman-era cellar, for degustation dining. Or stay upstairs underneath the beautiful painted wooden ceiling for simple, stylishly done local specialities – stuffed rabbit, lake fish, asparagus lasagne with *puzzone* cheese from Moena, thyme-scented crème brûlée – many made with '0km-sourced produce. A wine at the bar, with generous helpings of Scrigno's baton-like *grissini* (Turin-style breadstick), parmesan chunks and olives, is always a pleasure and the staff's advice on the list is spot on.

Ai Tre Garofani
MODERN TRENTINO €€

(☑0461 23 75 43; Via Mazzini 33; meals €38; ⊘Mon-Sat 12.30-2pm & 7.30-10pm) While the low-beamed ceiling and deep drapery give a traditional vibe, the staff here deliver a dining experience full of new ideas and local flavours. Diners are welcomed with an *amuse-bouche* (perhaps a deer and yoghurt mousse) and house-made breads – milk and potato, spelt and seeded. Mountain pine mugo scents a tagliatelle, while a hazelnut crusted hare is accompanied by a dark cocoa sorbet and bitter-sweet roots and leaves. Wines are well chosen and, of course, local.

Il Cappello
TRENTINO €€

(☑0461 23 58 50; www.osteriailcappello.it; Piazzetta Lunelli 5; meals €35; ⊘Tue-Sat noon-2.30pm & 7-10pm, Sun noon-3pm, Mon 7-10pm) This intimate dining room has an unexpectedly rustic feel, with wood beams and a terrace seat in a quiet courtyard. The menu is Trentino to the core, and simple presentation makes the most of good local produce. The wine list is also notable.

Casa del Caffe
CAFE

(Via San Pietro 38; ⊘Mon-Sat 7.30am-12.30pm & 3pm-7.30pm) Follow your nose to this coffee bar and chocolate shop for Trento's best espresso. Beans are roasted on the premises and the crowded shelves feature some of the country's best boutique products.

Osteria della Mal'Ombra
BAR

(www.osteriadellamalombra.com; Corso III Novembre 43; ⊘8.30am-2.30pm & 3.30pm-midnight Mon-Fri, 4pm-1am Sat) Join the locals for good wine and grappa, possibly some spirited political debate and music on Tuesdays.

Cafe de la Paix
BAR

(www.cafedelapaix.org; Passaggio Teatro Osele, (off Via Suffragio); ⊘Mon-Sat 10am-midnight, Sun 5.30pm-midnight) With its vintage aesthetic and laidback staff, this hideaway bar is a departure from Trento's conservative norm. Students start the day here with toast (€2), and the party gets going later with an international menu of snacks, well-priced wine and a rock-and-roll soundtrack.

ℹ Information

Hospital (☏0461 90 31 11; Largo Medaglie d'Oro 9)
Police Station (☏0461 89 95 11; Piazza della Mostra 3)
Post Office (Piazza Vittoria; ⊘8am-6.30pm Mon-Fri, to 12.30pm Sat)
Tourist Office (☏0461 21 60 00; www.apt.trento.it; Via Manci 2; ⊘9am-7pm)

ℹ Getting There & Away

TRAIN

Trento is well connected. Regular trains leave the main train station (Piazza Dante) for the following destinations:
Bologna (€14, 3¼ hours, every two hours)
Bolzano (€6.40, 30 minutes, four per hour)
Venice (€10, 2½ hours, hourly)
Verona (€7.10, one hour, every 30 minutes)

Next door to the main station, the Trento–Malè train line goes to Cles (€3.70, 1¼ hours) and Malé (€4.40, 1½ hour) in the Val di Non.

BUS

Trentino Trasporti (☏0461 82 10 00; www.ttesercizio.it)
The local bus company runs buses from the InterCity bus station (Via Andrea Pozzo), to and from Madonna di Campiglio, San Martino di Castrozza, Molveno, Canazei and Rovereto.

Rovereto

POP 37,500

In the winter of 1769, Leopold Mozart and his soon-to-be-famous musical son visited Rovereto and found it to be 'rich in diligent people engaged in viticulture and the weaving of silk'. The area is no longer known for silk, but still produces some outstanding wines, including the inky, cherry-scented Marzemino (the wine's scene-stealing appearance in *Don Giovanni* suggests it may have been a Mozart family favourite). Those on a musical pilgrimage come for the annual Mozart Festival (www.festivalmozartrovereto.it) in August. The town that Mozart knew still has its haunting, tightly coiled streets, but it's the shock of the new that now lures most: Rovereto is home to one of Italy's best contemporary and 20th-century art museums.

◎ Sights

★ **Museo di Arte Moderna e Contemporanea Rovereto**
ART GALLERY

(MART; ☏0464 43 88 87; english.mart.trento.it; Corso Bettini 43; adult/reduced €11/7, incl Casa del Depero €13/9; ⊘10am-6pm Tue-Thu, Sat & Sun, to 9pm Fri) The four-floor, 12,000-sq-m steel, glass and marble behemoth, care of the Ticinese architect Mario Botta, is both imposing and human, with mountain light filling a central atrium from a soaring cupola. It's home to some huge 20th-century works, including Warhol's *Four Marilyns* (1962), several Picassos and a clutch of contemporary art stars, including Bill Viola, Kara Walker, Arnuf Rainer and Anslem Keifer. Italian work is, naturally, well represented, with pieces from Giacomo Balla, Giorgio Morandi, Lucio Fontana and Piero Manzoni. Temporary exhibitions cast a broad net, from easygoing shows of Monet or Modigliani to cutting-edge contemporary surveys.

SKI TRENTINO

➡ Val di Fassa (p316)

➡ Val di Fiemme (p315)

➡ Val di Non (p313)

➡ Andalo & Fai della Paganella (p308)

➡ Folgarida-Marilleva (p314)

➡ Madonna di Campiglio & Pinzolo (p312)

➡ Monte Bondone (p305)

Casa del Depero   MUSEUM

(☑ 0424 60 04 35; Via Portici 38; adult/reduced €7/4, incl MART admission €13/9; ⊙ 10am-6pm Tue-Sun) The futurists were never afraid of a spot of self-aggrandisement and local lad Fortunato Depero was no exception. This self-designed museum was first launched shortly before his death in 1960, and was then restored and reopened by MART in recent years. The obsessions of early-20th-century Italy mix nostalgically, somewhat unnervingly, with a historic past – bold tapestries and machine-age-meets-troubadour-era furniture decorate a made-over medieval town house.

Church of San Marco   CHURCH

(Piazza San Marco; ⊙ 8.30am-noon & 2-7pm) It was here that the 13-year-old Wolfgang Mozart wowed the Roveretini.

🍷 Drinking & Nightlife

Osteria del Pettirosso   WINE BAR

(www.osteriadelpettirosso.com; Corso Bettini 24; ⊙ Mon-Sat 10am-11pm) There's a moody downstairs dining room but most people come here for the blackboard menu of wines by the glass, many from small producers, a plate of cheese (€7) or a couple of *crostone all lardo* (toasts with cured pork fat; €2.50).

ℹ Information

Tourist Office (☑ 0464 43 03 63; www.visitrovereto.it; Piazza Rosmini 16; ⊙ 9am-1pm & 2-6pm Mon-Sat, 10am-4pm Sun) The tourist office has lots of information on Rovereto, town maps and details of cycling trails.

ℹ Getting There & Away

Rovereto is around 15 minutes by train from Trento on the Bologna–Brennero line, or a pleasantly rural bus ride (€2.90, 45 minutes).

ℹ TRENTOROVERETO CARD

Available from the tourist office and some museums, this card (adult plus one child €20, 48 hours) gets you free entry to all city and regional museums, the Botanical Alpine Gardens as well as wine tastings and walking tours, bike hire and free public transport – including the Trento–Sardagna cable car and regional trains and buses. Register online and the card lasts a further three months, free transport aside.

Brenta Dolomites

The Brenta group lies like a rocky island to the west of the main Dolomite range. Protected by the Parco Naturale Adamello-Brenta, these sharp, majestic peaks are well known among mountaineers for their sheer cliffs and tricky ascents and are home to some of the world's most famous *vie ferrate* routes, including the Via Ferrata delle Bocchette, pioneered by trailblazing British climber Francis Fox Tuckett in the 1860s.

On the eastern side of the Brenta group is the Altipiano della Paganella, a high plateau offering some skiing and a range of outdoor adventures. On the densely forested western side is the glitzy resort of Madonna di Campiglio. The wiggly S421, S237 and S239 linking the two make for some scenic driving. Regular bus connections with Trento are plentiful in the high seasons.

While the Superskirama (www.skirama.it; 1/3/7-days €47/136/277) pass covers the Brenta, separate passes are also available. Skiarea passes cover Madonna di Campiglio, Pinzolo and Folgarida-Marilleva (1/3/7-days €46/131/266); specific Madonna di Campiglio or Pinzolo passes are a few euros cheaper. Paganella passes cost €37/95/165, or there is a 5-day pass (€170) that includes a free day in one other Brenta resort.

Altipiano Della Paganella

POP 5000 / ELEV 2098M

Less than an hour's drive northwest of Trento, this dress-circle plateau looks out onto the towering Brenta Dolomites. The Altipiano incorporates five small villages: ski resort Fai della Paganella, touristy Andalo, lakeside Molveno and little Cavedago and Spormaggiore.

◉ Sights & Activities

Parco Naturale Adamello Brenta   PARK

(http://www.parks.it/parco.adamello.brenta) Parco Naturale Adamello Brenta is a wild and beautiful park encompassing more than 80 lakes and the vast Adamello glacier which was once home to the Alps' only brown bears. Although this became a protected area in 1967, by then bear numbers had dwindled to just three. Beginning in 1999, park authorities set about reintroducing Alpine brown bears from Slovenia. The first cubs were born in the park in 2002 and more are to be born every winter.

Bears aside, the 620-sq-km park – Trentino's largest protected area – is home to ibexes, red deer, marmots, chamois and 82 bird species, along with 1200 different mountain flowers, including two (Nigritella luschmannie and Eryshimum auranthiacum) that are unique to the area. This wildlife thrives around the banks of Lago di Tovel, set deep in a forest some 30km north of Spormaggiore in the park's heart. An easy one-hour walking trail encircles the once-red lake. The lakeside visitors' centre has extensive information on other walks.

Casa dell'orso
Spormaggiore   ANIMAL RESERVE
(☑0461 65 36 22; Via Alt Spaur 6; adult/reduced €6/5, incl park admission; ⊙10am-1pm & 2-6.30pm Tue-Sun Jun-Sep, book for other periods) This is the top place to see the Parco Naturale Adamello Brenta's 20-odd population of brown bears. There are cute displays for kids, and you can book to see the bears in winter dormancy via infrared camera. It's 15km northeast of Molveno.

Funivie Molveno Pradel   CABLE CAR
(one way/return €4/7.20) From the top of Molveno village, a two-seater cable car transports you in two stages up to Pradel (1400m) from where trail No 340, a pleasant and easy one-hour walk, leads to the Rifugio Croz dell'Altissimo at 1430m. Several other trails, of varying difficulty, start from there.

Paganella Ski Area   SKIING
The Paganella ski area is accessible from Andalo by cable car and Fai della Paganella by chairlift. It has two cross-country skiing trails and 50km of downhill ski slopes, ranging from beginner-friendly green runs to the heart-lurching black.

Gruppo Guide Alpine
Dolomiti di Brenta   HIKING, ROCK CLIMBING
(☑0461 58 53 53; guidealpine@visitdolomitipaganella.it) Organises rock climbing and guided walks in summer and ski-mountaineering, ice climbing and snowshoeing excursions in winter.

🛏 Sleeping & Eating
The plateau's five villages have a huge stock of hotels; alternatively, check with the tourist offices for details of the equally numerous farm-stays and self-catering apartments.

HIKING HIGHS
➡ Alpe di Siusi, Sciliar and Catinaccio group (p327)

➡ Brenta Dolomites (p308)

➡ Gruppo del Sella (p316)

➡ Sesto Dolomites (p330)

➡ Val di Genova/Adamello group (p312)

Agriturismo Florandonole   AGRITURISMO €
(☑0461 58 10 39; www.florandonole.it; Via ai Dossi 22, Fai della Paganella; d €100; 🅿🐾🐕) 🍃 This modern farmhouse may look nondescript from the outside. Inside, however, smart local wood furniture and crisp goosedown duvets give this place a luxury feel. If the views over fields towards the Brenta Dolomites or Paganella ranges beckon, grab a complimentary mountain bike. This is also a working honey farm, with hives, production facilities and a shop to explore.

Camping Spiaggia   CAMPGROUND €
(☑0461 58 69 78; www.campingmolveno.it; Via Lungolago 25, Molveno; camping 2 people, car & tent €43; ⊙reception 9am-noon & 2-7pm year-round; 🅿@🏊) These pleasant sites on the shores of Lago di Molveno come with free use of the neighbouring outdoor pool, tennis court and table tennis. It's an easy stroll into Molveno's bustling village centre, and entertainment and water sports are on tap in high summer.

Al Penny   TRENTINO €€
(☑0461 58 52 51; Viale Trento 23, Andalo; meals €28; ⊙11am-2.30pm & 5pm-midnight) First impressions may clock the decor as a little too Alpine-for-dummies, but this is a genuinely cosy spot. A glass of warming Marzemino sets the scene, then out come authentic and tasty Trentino specialities – venison *ragù* (meat and tomato sauce) with pine nuts, *taiadele smalzade* (pan-fried fat noodles) or mushroom *canederli*, all served with homemade bread.

ℹ Information
All these tourist offices share a website (www.visitdolomitipaganella.it).

Andalo Tourist Office (☑0461 58 58 36; Piazza Dolomiti 1; ⊙9am-12.30pm & 3-6.30pm Mon-Sat, 9.30am-12.30pm Sun) The main office with good information for both winter and summer activities.

FRANK FELL / GETTY IMAGES ©

RUTH EASTHAM & MAX PAOLI / GETTY IMAGES ©

GLENN VAN DER KNIJFF / GETTY IMAGES ©

1. Alpe di Siusi (p327)
Cows grazing in Europe's largest plateau in the Dolomites.

2. Cortina d'Ampezzo (p400)
Cyclists pass by this fashionable town, which is icy in winter and a great base for hiking in summer.

3. Bolzano (p317)
The provincial capital of Alto Adige boasts daily street markets bursting with local produce.

4. Val Pusteria (p330)
This narrow valley is the gateway to Tre Cime, suitable for inexperienced walkers to explore.

Fai della Paganella Tourist Office (☑ 0461 58 31 30; Via Villa; ☺ 9am-12.30pm & 3-6.30pm Mon-Sat, 9.30am-12.30pm Sun)

Guardia Medica Notturna (☑ 0461 58 56 37; Piazza Centrale 1, Andalo; ☺ 8pm-8am) After-hours medical call-out service.

Molveno Tourist Office (☑ 0461 58 69 24; Piazza Marconi; ☺ 9am-12.30pm & 3-6.30pm Mon-Sat, 9.30am-12.30pm Sun)

ⓘ Getting There & Around

Free ski buses serve the area in winter.

Trentino Trasporti (☑ 0461 82 10 00; www.tte-sercizio.it) Runs buses between all five villages and Trento (€3.10 to €4.40, 1-2½ hours, up to nine daily) and services to Madonna di Campiglio (€5.10) and Riva del Garda (€6.20) on Lago di Garda; tourist offices have timetables.

Madonna Di Campiglio & Pinzolo

POP 700 / ELEV 1522M

Let there be no doubt, this is the Dolomites' bling belt, where ankle-length furs are standard après-ski wear and the formidable downhill runs often a secondary concern to the social whirl. Austrian royalty set the tone in the 19th century, in particular Franz Joseph and wife Elisabeth (Sissi). This early celeb patronage is commemorated in late February, when fireworks blaze and costumed pageants waltz through town for the annual Habsburg Carnival. Despite the traffic jams and mall-like hotel complexes, the central village square has retained something of its essence, overlooked by a pretty stone church and the jutting battlements of the Brenta Dolomites beyond. In summer

this is an ideal base for hikers and *vie fer-rate* enthusiasts.

Pinzolo (pop 2000, elev 800m), in a lovely valley 16km south, has a lively historic centre and quite a few less tickets on itself.

⊙ Sights & Activities

Chiesa di San Vigilio   CHURCH
Pinzolo's beautifully sited 16th-century Chiesa di San Vigilio merits a visit for its *danza macabra* (dance of death) decor.

Val di Genova   VALLEY
North of Pinzolo is the entrance to the Val di Genova, often described as one of the Alps' most beautiful valleys. It's great walking country, lined with a series of spectacular waterfalls. Four mountain huts strung out along the valley floor make overnight stays an option – Pinzolo's tourist office has details.

**Funivie Madonna
di Campiglio**   CABLE CAR
(☑ 0465 44 77 44; www.funiviecampiglio.it) A network of cable cars take skiers and boarders from Madonna to its numerous ski runs and a snowboarding park in winter and to walking and mountain-biking trails in summer. In Campo Carlo Magno, 2km north of Madonna, the Cabinovia Grostè takes walkers to the Passo Grostè (2440m). Brenta's most famous *via ferrata*, the Via Bocchetta di Tuckett (trail No 305), leaves from the cable-car station.

Funivia Pinzolo   CABLE CAR
(☑ 0465 50 12 56; www.doss.to; Via Nepomuceno Bolognini 84; one-way/return €8/11; ☺ 8.30am-12.30pm & 2-6pm mid-Dec–Apr & Jun–mid-Sep) This cable

---

IRON WAYS

During WWI, the Italian army was engaged in a lengthy conflict against their Austrian foes on a vertiginous battlefront that sliced across the Dolomites, and the scars of this brutal campaign are still etched indelibly over the Alpine landscape.

In order to maximise ease of movement up in the rugged, perilous peaks, the two armies attached ropes and ladders across seemingly impregnable crags in a series of fixed-protection climbing paths known as *vie ferrate* (iron ways). Renovated with steel rungs, bridges and heavy-duty wires after the war, the *vie ferrate* evolved into a cross between standard hiking and full-blown rock climbing, allowing non-mountaineers, with the right equipment, to experience such challenging terrain.

Madonna di Campiglio and Cortina d'Ampezzo are the gateways to the most spectacular routes, but *vie ferrate* exist all over the Dolomites.

From mid-June to mid-September, a network of mountain huts offering food and accommodation line the route – Tourism Südtirol (www.trekking.suedtirol.info) maintains a comprehensive list. Tourist offices can provide maps and details of skill level required, and descriptions of each route can be found at www.dolomiti-altevie.it.

car climbs to the 2100m-high Doss del Sabion, stopping at midstation Pra Rodont en route. Mountain bike hire is available.

Sleeping & Eating

Budget beds in Madonna are non-existent in winter, and most midrange hotels insist on at least half-board and minimum stays during high season. Commuting to the ski fields from the Val di Sole is a doable alternative, and Pinzolo has a few more affordable options.

Camping Parco Adamello CAMPGROUND € (☑ 0465 50 17 93; www.campingparcoadamello.it; Località Magnabò, Pinzolo; camping 2 people, car & tent €40; ☺ year-round; ℗) Beautifully situated within the national park 1km north of Pinzolo, this campground is a natural starting point for outdoor adventures such as skiing, snowshoeing, walking and biking. There are also weekly apartment rentals.

Chalet Fogajard AGRITURISMO €€ (Località Fogajard 36, Madonna di Campiglio; d €190 half board; 🐾) 🍴 If you're looking for a mountain retreat, this six-room Alpine idyl will fit the bill. Its remote location, down a steep dirt track way south of Madonna's resort row, is stupefyingly beautiful and blissfully silent. Rooms have a craft ethos that seems from an other era and an atmospheric dining room delivers hearty, wholesome, locally sourced meals. With uninterrupted views of a deep, wooded valley and the jagged Brenta peaks beyond, balcony rooms are worth the extra euros.

Hotel Chalet Del Brenta HOTEL €€ (☑ 0465 44 31 59; www.hotelchaletdelbrenta.com; Via Castelletto Inferiore 4, Madonna di Campiglio; d €140; ℗✳🛜🍴) This large place offers smart, comfortable rooms, all with balconies, and the full-range of resort services, including a kids' club. It's in one of Madonna's most picturesque streets, close to the village but quiet and there's a speedy shuttle service to the lifts.

Chalet La Dolce Vita DESIGN HOTEL €€€ (☑ 0465 44 31 91; www.dvchalet.it; Via Castelletto Inferiore 10, Madonna di Campiglio; d €300; ℗✳🛜🍴) This is the latest entry in the Madonna ultraluxe hotel stakes, with friendly staff and a quiet, wooded setting. The bar keeps the Milanese fashion set happy come *aperitivo* hour, and upstairs, guests are cocooned in beautiful, earthy rooms.

ℹ Information

Madonna Tourist Office (☑ 0465 44 75 01; www.campigliodolomiti.it; Via Pradalago 4; ☺ 9am-12.30pm & 3-7pm Mon-Sat, 10am-1pm Sun) Madonna's tourist office teams up with the Parco Naturale Adamello-Brenta in high summer to run guided thematic walks.

Pinzolo Tourist Office (☑ 0465 50 10 07; www.campigliodolomiti.it; Piazzale Ciciamimo; ☺ 9am-1pm & 2-6pm Wed-Mon)

Tourist Medical Service (☑ 0465 44 08 81; Centro Rainalter, Madonna; ☺ 8am-8pm early Dec–Easter)

ℹ Getting There & Away

Madonna di Campiglio and Pinzolo are accessible by bus from Trento (€9, 1½ hours, five daily), Brescia (€13, 1½ hours) and Milan (€24, 3¾ hours, one daily). A private transfer service also operates year round; see the tourist office website for details.

Flyski (☑ 0461 39 11 11; www.flyskishuttle.com; one way/return €19/32) From mid-December to mid-April the Flyski shuttle runs weekly services to and from Madonna and Pinzolo from Verona, Bergamo, Treviso and Venice airports .

Val di Non, Val di Sole & Val di Rabbi

Sandwiched between the Brenta group and Parco Nazionale dello Stelvio, these Italian-speaking farming valleys are an easy train ride from Trento.

Val di Non

The first thing you notice about Val di Non is the apple trees – their gnarly, trellised branches stretch for miles, and in spring their fragrant blossoms scent the air. Craggy castles dot the surrounding rises, including the stunning Castel Thun (☑ 0461 49 28 29; adult/reduced €6/4; ☺ 10am-5pm Tue-Sun). The valley is centred on Cles, whose tourist office (☑ 0463 422 88 83; Corso Dante 30; ☺ 9am-12.30pm & 3-6pm Mon-Sat, 9am-noon Sun Jul & Aug) is just off the main road through town. In the town's historic centre is Antica Trattoria (☑ 0463 42 16 31; www.anticatrattoriacles.it; via Roma 13, Cles; meals €38; ☺ noon-2.30pm & 7-10pm Sun-Fri), a fabulously atmospheric place with a modern take on Trentino specialities.

Italy's apple giant, Melinda, is a valley girl. A couple of villages on from Cles, near Mollaro, Melinda Mondo (☑ 0463 46 92 99; www.melinda.it; Via della Cooperazione 21;

WINTER WONDERLAND

The jagged peaks of the Dolomites, or Dolomiti, span the provinces of Trentino and Alto Adige, jutting into neighbouring Veneto. Europeans flock here in winter for highly hospitable resorts, sublime natural settings and extensive, well-coordinated ski networks. Come for downhill, cross-country and snowboarding or get ready for *sci alpinismo*, an adrenaline-spiking mix of skiing and mountaineering, freeride and a range of other winter adventure sports.

The **Sella Ronda**, a 40km circumnavigation of the Gruppo di Sella range (3151m, at Piz Boé) – linked by various cable cars and chairlifts – is one of the Alps' iconic ski routes. The tour takes in four passes and their surrounding valleys; Alto Adige's Val Gardena, Val Badia, Arabba (in the Veneto) and Trentino's Val di Fassa. Experienced skiers can complete the clockwise (orange) or anticlockwise (green) route in a day.

The region's two flexible passes are **Dolomiti Superski** (www.dolomitisuperski.com; high season 3-/6-day pass €144/254), covering the east, with access to 450 lifts and some 1200km of ski runs, spread over 12 resorts, and Superskirama (p308), covering the western Brenta Dolomites, with 150 lifts, 380km of slopes and eight resorts.

⊙ 8.30am-12.30pm & 3-7pm Mon-Sat Oct-Jul, 9am-noon Sun Jul), conducts tours of the orchards and processing plants and has a cheery shop selling apples and all sorts of apple-related products. Look out for the big cheese next door, the home of **Trentingrana**, Trentino's sweet, subtle 'Parmesan-style' Grana.

Val di Sole

Leaving Cles in the rear-view mirror, the apple orchards draw you west into the aptly named Val di Sole (Valley of the Sun) tracing the course of the foaming river Noce, with its charming main town of **Malè**. This valley is renowned for the full complement of outdoor pursuits, and is popular with young Trentini. The Noce offers great rafting and fishing.

In winter, the valley can provide good alternative accommodation to the Brenta resorts.

🏃 Activities

Centro Rafting Val di Sole   RAFTING
(☑ 0463 97 32 78; www.rafting center.it; Via Gole 105, Dimaro; ⊙ Jun-Sep) Runs rafting trips (from €67), as well as kayaking, canyoning, Nordic walking and other adventures.

Cicli Andreis   CYCLING
(☑ 0463 90 28 22; www.andreissnc.com; Via Conci 19, Malè; ⊙ 8.30am-noon & 3-7pm Mon-Sat) Offering a huge range of bikes for hire, and friendly, knowledgeable service, Cicli Andreis is handily located just off Malè's main street. Daily/weekly mountain bike rental costs from €18/55.

Dolomiti di Brenta Bike   BICYCLE TRAIL
(www.dolomitibrentabike.it) Sole guards a flattish 35km section of the Brenta Dolomite Bike Loop and there is a special bike train June to September, allowing cyclists to step on and alight when they wish.

🛏 Sleeping

Agritur il Tempo delle Mele   FARMSTAY €
(☑ 0463 90 13 89; www.agriturdellemele.it; Via Strada Provinciale 65, Caldes; s/d €70/94; 🅿 🐾 🛜 🌐)
Has bright, comfortable, modern rooms and easy access to the Folgarida-Marilleva and Pejo 3000 ski areas, from where you can ski on to Madonna di Campiglio.

Dolomiti Camping Village   CAMPGROUND €
(☑ 0463 97 43 32; www.campingdolomiti.com; Via Gole 105, Dimaro; camping 2 people, car & tent €44, apt €75; ⊙ mid-May–mid-Oct & Dec-Easter; 🅿 @ 🐾 🌐) Riverside and adjacent to the rafting centre, the well-kept campsites and bungalows come with access to a wellness centre, indoor and outdoor pools, volleyball courts and trampolines.

ℹ Information

Malè Tourist Office (☑ 0463 90 12 80; www.valdisole.net; Piazza Regina Elena 19; ⊙ 4-7pm Mon-Sat) Has good information on the entire valley and can advise you on ski facilities and walking trails in nearby Stelvio.

Val di Rabbi

Narrow, deep green Val di Rabbi is a refreshingly tranquil and picturesquely rustic Alpine valley that provides the best southern entry into Parco Nazionale dello Stelvio. Europeans come here for the supposedly curative Antica Fonte spring waters; the **Terme di Rabbi** (☏0463 98 30 00; www.termedirabbi.it; Località Fonti di Rabbi 162; ☺8.30am-noon & 4-8pm Mon-Sat, 5-7pm Sun Jul & Aug) offers a wide range of traditional treatments and is administered by the suitably grand **Grand Hotel Rabbi** (☏0463 98 30 50; www.grandhotelrabbi.it; Fonti di Rabbi 153; half-board d €90-140; ☺May-Sep; P ✶). Next door is a small **visitors' centre** (☏0463 98 51 90; ☺ 8.30am-1pm & 3-7pm Thu-Tue Jun-Sep, 9am-noon & 2-5pm Oct-May) and the starting point for a network of paths into Stelvio, some of which connect to Val Martello in Alto Adige. Regular buses head up the valley from outside Malè train station.

❶ Getting There & Around

The Folgarida-Marilleva and Daolasa-Commezzadura **cable cars** ferry skiers and walkers up the mountainside from the train stations, and provide lockers.

Free ski buses loop around the area in winter; tourist offices have the schedules.

Ferrovia Trento-Malè (☏0463 90 11 50) Ferrovia Trento-Malè has frequent services to Cles (€2.90, 45 min+utes) and Malè (€5, 1½ hours, eight daily) and continue to Dimaro and Marilleva.

Trentino Transporti (www.ttesercizio.it) Buses connect Rabbi and Madonna di Campiglio with Malè.

Val di Fiemme

In a region where few valleys speak the same dialect, let alone agree on the same cheese recipe, the Val di Fiemme stands out. In the 12th century, independently minded local noblemen set up their own quasi-republic here, the Magnificent Community of Fiemme, and the ethos and spirit of the founders lives on.

From Cavalese, skiers can take a cable car up to the **Cermis ski area** (2229m), part of the extensive Dolomiti Superski region. There is a Fiemme-Obereggen pass (1/3/7-days €42/120/227), or Dolomiti Superski passes can be used. Cavalese's tourist office acts as a contact point for local alpine guide groups who organise, among other things, mountaineering ascents on Pale di San Martino, Cima della Madonna and Sass Maor, a 120km-long high-altitude skiing excursion.

◎ Sights

Palazzo Vescovile   PALACE
(Piazza Battisti) The modern day Magnificent Community of Fiemme is headquartered in the wonderfully frescoed Palazzo Vescovile in Val di Fiemme's main town of Cavalese. The building is well worth an admiring look.

⌁ Sleeping & Eating

Agritur la Regina dei Prati   AGRITURISMO €
(www.lareginadeiprati.it; Via Margherita Dellafiore 17, Masi di Cavalese; s/d €50/85; P ✶ ☎ 🖢) Across the river in a village 'suburb' of Cavalese, this is a relaxed, family-run place with spacious contemporary rooms with nice extras like heated floors and balconies. The rustic setting is magnificent, and you can ski in during winter.

★ Park Hotel Azalea   SPA HOTEL €€
(☏0462 34 01 09; www.parkhotelazalea.it; Via delle Cesure 1; half-board d €90-180; P ☎ 🖢) ✎ This hotel combines impeccable eco-credentials, super stylish interiors and a warm, welcoming vibe. Rooms are individually decorated and make use of soothing, relaxing colours; some have mountain views, others look across the village's pretty vegetable gardens. Children's facilities eschew plastic and tat for wood and natural textiles, and there are little daily extras like a groaning afternoon tea spread (all organic of course).

El Molin   GASTRONOMIC €€€
(☏0462 34 00 74; www.elmolin.info; Piazza Battisti 11, Cavalese; meals €20-30, degustations €70-110; ☺Wed-Mon noon-2.30pm & 7-11pm) A legend in the valley, this Michelin-starred old mill sits at the historic heart of Cavalese. Downstairs, next to the old waterwheels, you will find playful gastronomic dishes featuring local, seasonal ingredients. Streetside, the wine bar does baked-to-order eggs with Trentingrana or truffles, burgers, hearty mains and creative desserts.

RESOURCES

➜ Find a mountain guide at www.bergfuehrer-suedtirol.it.

➜ Lonely Planet's *Hiking in Italy* details five classic Dolomites hikes.

➜ **Cicerone** (www.cicerone.co.uk) publishes specialist route guides.

PALE DI SAN MARTINO

Pink blends seamlessly with green in the Pale di San Martino (elevation 1467m), where the luminous Dolomite mountains rise like ghosts above the ancient forest of Paneveggio, whose wood is made into prized violins. The mountains are embraced by the **Parco Naturale Paneveggio-Pale di San Martino** (📞 0439 76 88 59; http://parcopan.org; Via Laghetto, San Martino), home to roe deer, chamois, marmots, wild fowl and birds of prey such as the golden eagle. At the park's impressive headquarters in the 1853-built **Villa Welsperg** (📞 0439 6 48 54; www.parcopan.org; Via Castelpietra 2; ⊙ 9.30am-12.30pm & 3-6pm summer, 2-5pm winter), suspended aquariums illustrate the park's water life.

At the park's feet huddles **San Martino di Castrozza**, a small but popular ski resort and walking spot, accessible via bus from Trento.

ℹ Information

Val di Fiemme Tourist Office (📞 0462 24 11 11; www.visitfiemme.it; Via Bronzetti 60; ⊙ 9am-noon & 3.30-7pm Mon-Sat)

Val di Fassa

Val di Fassa is Trentino's only Ladin-speaking valley, framed by the stirring peaks of the **Gruppo del Sella** to the north, the **Catinaccio** to the west and the **Marmolada** (3342m) to the southeast. The valley has two hubs: **Canazei** (pop 1866, elev 1465m), beautifully sited but verging on overdevelopment, and the pretty riverside village of **Moena** (pop 2690, elev 1114m), more down to earth and increasingly environmentally conscious. Fassa is the nexus of Italy's cross-country skiing scene. Italian cross-country champ Christian Zorzi hails from Moena and the town also plays host to the sport's most illustrious mass-participation race, the annual **Marcialonga** (www.marcialonga.it).

Dolomiti Superski passes are valid; alternatively there are separate 1/3/7-day passes for either the Val di Fassa/Carezza or the Tre Valli (€42/125/230) covering the Moena area and San Pellegrino valley.

◉ Sights & Activities

Variety is the spice of life for skiers here, with 120km of downhill and cross-country runs as well as challenging Alpine tours and the Sella Ronda ski circuit. In summer, you can ski down the Marmolada glacier.

The Gruppo del Sella is approached from **Passo Pordoi**, where a cable car travels to almost 3000m. The best approach to the Catinaccio group is from **Vigo di Fassa**, 11km southwest of Canazei near Pozza di Fassa; a cable car climbs to an elevation of 2000m, dropping you off near the cheerful mountain hut Baita Checco.

For gentler summertime rambles, ask at the tourist office for the brochure *Low-Level Walks in the Fassa Valley*, which outlines 29 walks (1.5km to 8km long), including visits to historic Ladin landmarks.

🛏 Sleeping, Eating & Drinking

Garnì Ladin   B&B €
(📞 0462 76 44 93; www.ladin.it; Strada de la Piazedela 9, Vigo di Fassa; s/d €70/100; 🅿 🛜) Right in the middle of villagey Vigo di Fassa, midway between Moena and Canazei, the rooms here are full of sweetly kitsch Ladin-alia while having ultramodern bathrooms.

Villa Kofler   DESIGN HOTEL €€
(📞 0462 75 04 44; www.villakofler.it; Via Dolomiti 63, Campitello di Fassa; d €160-220; 🅿 🛜) 🖊 An intimate hotel in a valley of giants, just outside of the Canazei bustle; choose from rooms that range across various current design trends and tastes. There's a little gym, a library and, bliss, in-room infrared saunas.

El Paél   TRENTINO €€
(📞 0462 60 14 33; www.elpael.com; Via Roma 58, Canazei; meals €25-35; ⊙ noon-2.30pm & 6.30-10pm Tue-Sun) This *osteria tipica trentina* cooks up traditional Ladin specialities of the valley – nettle dumplings, asparagus with liquorice sauce, and venison with steamed pumpkin.

Malga Panna   GASTRONOMIC €€€
(📞 0462 57 34 89; www.malgapanna.it; Via Costalunga 29, Moena; degustations from €65; ⊙ 12.30-2pm & 7.30-10pm) Fine-dining interpretations of mountain food stay true to their culinary roots and are served in an evocatively simple setting. Expect to encounter the flavours of Alpine herbs and flowers and lots of game.

Kusk La Locanda
BAR

(Via dei Colli 7, Moena; ⊙8am-2am Wed-Mon) Legendary throughout the Val di Fassa for après-ski, this four-way split between a pizzeria, American bar, trash disco and Italian restaurant still manages to maintain a Ladin cosiness.

ⓘ Information

Canazei Tourist Office (✆0462 60 96 00; www.fassa.com; Piazza Marconi 5; ⊙8.30am-noon, 2.30-6pm Mon-Sat, 10am-12.30pm Sun)
Moena Tourist Office (✆0462 60 97 70; www.fassa.com; Piazza del Navalge 4; ⊙8.30am-noon, 2.30-6pm Mon-Sat, 10am-12.30pm Sun)

ⓘ Getting There & Away

Free ski buses also serve the region in winter.
Trentino Trasporti (✆0461 82 10 00; www.ttesercizio.it) Runs buses to the Val di Fassa from Trento year-round (€6.10, 1½ to 2½ hours).
SAD (www.sad.it) Buses from Bolzano and the Val Gardena from June to mid-September.

ALTO ADIGE (SÜDTIROL)

Bolzano (Bozen)

POP 104, 000 / ELEV 265M

The provincial capital of Alto Adige (Südtirol, or South Tyrol) is anything but provincial. Once a stop on the coach route between Italy and the flourishing Austro-Hungarian Empire, this small city is worldly and engaged, a long-time conduit between cultures. Its quality of life – one of the highest in Italy – is reflected in its openness, youthful energy and an all-pervading greenness. A stage-set-pretty backdrop of rotund green hills sets off rows of pastel-painted town houses. Bicycles ply riverside paths and wooden market stalls are laid out with Alpine cheese, speck (cured ham) and dark, seeded loaves. German may be the first language of 95% of the region, but Bolzano is an anomaly. Today its Italian-speaking majority – a legacy of Mussolini's brutal Italianisation program of the 1920s and the more recent siren call of education and employment opportunities – looks both north and south for inspiration.

⊙ Sights

★**Museo Archeologico dell'Alto Adige**
MUSEUM

(✆0471 32 01 00; www.iceman.it; Via Museo 43; adult/reduced €9/7; ⊙10am-6pm Tue-Sun) The star of the Museo Archeologico dell'Alto Adige is Ötzi, the Iceman, with almost the entire museum being given over to the Copper Age mummy. Kept in a temperature-controlled 'igloo' room, he can be viewed through a small window (peer closely enough and you can make out faintly visible tattoos on his legs). Ötzi's clothing – a wonderful get-up of patchwork leggings, rush-matting cloak and fur cap – and other belongings are also displayed. Various exhibitions explore his discovery, the world he lived in and his untimely death.

Messner Mountain Museum
MUSEUM

(MMM; ✆0471 63 31 45; www.messner-mountain-museum.it; Via Castel Firmiano 53; adult/reduced €9/7; ⊙10am-6pm Tue-Sun Mar-Nov) The imposing Castel Firmiano, dating back to AD 945,

TRENTO & THE DOLOMITES BOLZANO (BOZEN)

THE ICEMAN COMETH

When Austrian hikers stumbled upon a human corpse wedged into a melting glacier on Hauslabjoch Pass in 1991, they assumed they'd found the remains of an unfortunate mountaineer caught in a winter storm. But when the mummified body was removed and taken to a morgue, it was discovered to be over 5300 years old.

The male corpse – subsequently nicknamed Ötzi, or the Iceman – is the oldest mummified remains ever found in Europe, dating from an ancient Copper Age civilisation that lived in the Dolomites around the same time as ancient Egypt's founding. What Ötzi was actually doing 3200m up a glaciated mountainside, 52 centuries before alpinism became a serious sport, is still a matter of some debate.

Though initially claimed by the Austrian government, it was later ascertained that Ötzi had been unearthed 100m inside the Italian border on the Schnalstal glacier. After a brief diplomatic impasse and stabilisation work in Innsbruck, the mummy was returned to Italy, where it has been on display in Bolzano's Museo Archeologico dell'Alto Adige since 1998.

Bolzano

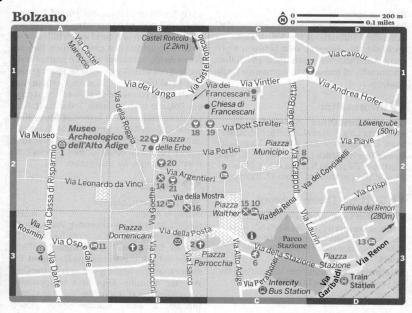

Bolzano

◎ Top Sights
1 Museo Archeologico dell'Alto Adige A2

◎ Sights
2 Cathedral...B3
3 Chiesa dei Domenicani........................B3
4 Museion..A3

◈ Activities, Courses & Tours
5 Alpine Information Office.....................C1
6 Bike Rental Stall.................................C3
7 Club Alpino Italiano.............................B2

◎ Sleeping
8 Hotel Feichter.....................................C2
9 Hotel Figl..C2
10 Hotel Greif...C2

11 Kolpinghaus Bolzano A3
12 Residence Fink...................................B2
13 Youth Hostel Bolzano.........................D3

◈ Eating
Gasthaus Fink...............................(see 12)
14 Vögele...B2
15 Walthers'...C2
16 Zur Kaiserkron...................................B2

◈ Drinking & Nightlife
17 Batzen-bräu.......................................D1
18 Enovit...B2
19 Fischbänke...C2
20 Hopfen & Co.......................................B2
21 Il Baccaro...B2
22 Nadamas..B2

is the centrepiece of mountaineer Reinhold Messner's five museums. Based around humankind's relationship with the mountains across all cultures, the architecture itself suggests the experience of shifting altitudes, and requires visitors to traverse hundreds of stairs and mesh walkways. The collection is idiosyncratic, but when it works, it's heady stuff. The museum is on the BoBus route; in winter catch a taxi (suburban trains go to Ponte Adige/Sigmundskron but beware the long walk up a truck-laden road). Messner's other museums are scattered across the region, including Ortles.

Museion   ART GALLERY
(☎0471 22 34 13; www.museion.it; Via Dante 2; adult/reduced €6/4, Thu from 6pm free; ⊙10am-6pm Tue-Sun, to 10pm Thu) The city's contemporary art space is housed in this huge multifaceted glass cube, a surprising architectural assertion that beautifully vignettes

the old-town rooftops and surrounding mountains from within. There's an impressive permanent collection of international art work; temporary shows are a testament to the local art scene's vibrancy, or often highlight an ongoing dialogue with artists and institutions from Austria and Germany. The river-facing cafe has a terrace perfect for a post-viewing spritz.

Castel Roncolo   CASTLE
(Schloss Runkelstein; ✍ 0471 32 98 08; www.runkelstein.info; Via San Antonio 15; adult/child €8/5.50; ⊙ 10am-6pm Tue-Sun) This stunningly located castle was built in 1237 but is renowned for its 14th-century frescoes. These are particularly rare, with themes that are drawn from secular literature, including the tale of Tristan and Isolde, as well as depictions of day-to-day courtly life. BoBus runs here or catch suburban bus 12 or 14.

Chiesa dei Domenicani   CHURCH
(Piazza Domenicani; ⊙ 9.30am-6pm Mon-Sat) The cloisters and chapel here feature touching, vibrant 14th-century frescoes by the Giotto school.

Cathedral   CATHEDRAL
(Piazza Parrocchia; ⊙ 9.30am-5.30pm Mon-Sat) This splendid Gothic cathedral is Bolzano's most emblematic building, its imposing spires backed by the equally Gothic peaks of the not-so-distant Dolomites.

🏃 Activities

Bolzano's trio of cable cars whisk you up out of the city, affording spectacular views over the city and valley floor, then of terraced vineyards, tiny farms, ancient mountain chapels and towering peaks beyond. The respective villages are delightful destinations in themselves or jumping off points for rambles or serious hikes.

Funivia del Renon   CABLE CAR
(Via Renon; one way/return €6/10) The journey over the Renon (Ritten) plateau to Soprabolzano (Oberbozen) runs along the world's longest single track, stretching for 4.56km, passing over eerie red earth pyramids.

Funivia del Colle   CABLE CAR
(Via Campegno 4; one way/return €5/6.50) This is the world's oldest cable car, dreamt up by a canny inn-keeper in 1908.

Funivia San Genesio   CABLE CAR
(Via Sarentino; one way/return €3.50/6) An ultra-steep ascent takes you to the beautiful terraced village of San Genesio (Jenesien), where there are roof-of-the-world views and forest trails to follow.

Salewa Cube   ROCK CLIMBING
(✍ 0471 188 6867; www.salewa-cube.com; Via Waltraud-Gebert-Deeg, Bolzano Sud; daily entrance €12/10; ⊙ 9am-11pm) Part of the outdoor clothing empire's HQ, this is Italy's largest indoor climbing centre. There are over 2000m of climbing surface and 180 different routes. In good weather the enormous entrance is open, so climbing has an outdoor feel. On the BoBus route, or take bus 10A/B from the centre.

Bike Rental Stall   BICYCLE RENTAL
(✍ 0471 99 75 78; Via della Stazione 2; ⊙ 7.30am-7.45pm Easter-Oct) Bicycles can be picked up at the open-air bike rental stall near the train station. Rental is free, but bikes must be returned overnight and you'll need cash for a deposit and ID.

☞ Tours

The tourist office organises seasonal guided walks and gentle treks (in Italian and German). For serious hiking information, contact one of the local walking associations.

Club Alpino Italiano   WALKING TOUR
(✍ 0471 97 81 72; Piazza delle Erbe 46; ⊙ 11am-1pm & 5-7pm Wed, 1-5pm Tue, Thu & Fri)

Alpine Information Office   WALKING TOUR
(Alpenverein Südtirol; ✍ 0471 81 41 55; www.alpenverein.it; Galleria Vintler 16)

🛏 Sleeping

Hotel Figl   HOTEL €
(✍ 0471 97 84 12; www.figl.net; Piazza del Grano 9; s/d €100/120; ❄ @) Affable staff and a busy

---

ℹ BOLZANO BOZEN CARD

This **card** (adult/child €28/16) grants you entry to most city and regional museums. Transport on local buses, regional trains and Bolzano's three cable cars are included, as well as bike hire, city tours and national park excursions. It's available from the tourist office. It also covers the summer BoBus, an hourly shuttle service to the city's outlying sites and cable cars.

DON'T MISS

BEER & SAUSAGE

In Canazei, look out for the fork-wielding Ladin sausage cook; his roadside stall, just off Piazza Marconi, draws queues of ravenous skiers all winter long.

downstairs bar lend this place a home-away-from-home feel. Mod-Euro rooms are fabulously cosy and look out over a pretty square or town rooftops. Business travellers and long-stay guests can negotiate discounts.

Youth Hostel Bolzano   HOSTEL €

(Jugendherberge Bozen; ☎ 0471 30 08 65; bozen.jugendherberge.it; Via Renon 23; dm/s €22/28; 🛜) The three- and four-bed dorms in this airy and friendly hostel are well designed and configured for privacy. Singles can squeeze in a foldout if needed. Rooms at the back have balconies, but sadly no longer any view.

Hotel Feichter   HOTEL €

(☎ 0471 97 87 68; www.hotelfeichter.it; Via Grappoli 15; s/d €60/90) This central and totally Tyrolean hotel has simple, cosy rooms, many with balconies or little breakfast nooks.

Kolpinghaus Bolzano   HOSTEL €

(☎ 0471 308400; www.kolpingbozen.it; Largo Kolping 3; s/tw €65/99; ❇🛜) This big Catholic hostel has comfortable rooms; the singles are particularly spacious and have polished floorboards. There are storage and repair facilities for cyclists and they'll provide lunch for an extra €10. Note that there are no doubles, only twins.

Hotel Greif   DESIGN HOTEL €€

(☎ 0471 31 80 00; www.greif.it; Piazza Walther; s/d €117/176; ❇🛜) Tumbling golden text courtesy of the troubled poet Ezra Pound greets you in the stairwell (this was, it seems, an 'art hotel' long before its modern makeover). Rooms here are generously proportioned, full of light and richly draped; all include a bath. Guests can use the lush gardens at parent Parkhotel Laurin, just down the lane, for cocktails or a swim.

Residence Fink   APARTMENTS €€

(☎ 335 7189411; www.residence-fink.it; Via della Mostra 9; apt €80-200; 🛜) If you don't need hotel facilities or service, these stylish, atmospheric apartments can't be beaten for their living-like-a-local position and facilities.

They range in size from studios to those with enough room for eight people.

 Eating

Redolent of rural mountain life one minute, Habsburg splendour the next, Bolzano's restaurants (often in the guise of a wood-panelled stube) are a profound reminder of just how far north you've come. Goat or rabbit is roasted, bone-warming broths hide *canederli*, venison finds its way into gulasch, and speck (the region's IGP cured ham, cold-smoked and juniper- and pepper-scented) turns up in everything bar dessert. Window displays in the city's many *konditorei* (pastry shops) brim with Sachertorte, cheese strudels, *krapfen* (doughnuts) and earthy buckwheat-and-berry cakes. Bakers ply dark, dense seed-studded breads, including *schüttelbrot*, a crispy spiced rye flat bread. Pick up produce from the daily street market on Piazza delle Erbe.

Gasthaus Fink   SÜDTIROLEAN €

(☎ 0471 97 50 47; Via della Mostra 9; meals €24; ☉ lunch & dinner Thu-Mon, lunch only Wed) Fink's dining room is a calm, contemporary take on *stube* style, with fresh flowers on the tables and young attentive staff. Fill up on local comfort food, cooked with care. A great lunch choice, with pastas under €10.

Vögele   SÜDTIROLEAN €

(☎ 0471 97 39 38; Via Goethe 3; meals €19-24; ☉ 9am-1am) Dating back to 1277 and owned by the same family since 1840, this multi-level antique-stuffed restaurant is well loved for its schnitzels, steaks and suckling pig. The attached bar is pleasantly rowdy too.

★ Löwengrube   MODERN SÜDTIROLEAN €€

(☎ 0471 98 00 32; www.loewengrube.it; Piazza Dogana 3; meals €45; ☉ 10am-midnight Mon-Sat) A glorious 16th-century *stube* is the suprise design element in an otherwise supermodern fit out at Bolzano's hottest 'new' restaurant. The menu ranges across local and Mediterranean dishes, and its combinations and presentation push boundaries, as well as borders; staff are knowledgeable and obliging. Don't miss a peek at the cellar (dating back to 1280), it holds a vast collection that honours international name vineyards as well as local micro-producers (drink in with a modest corkage of €10).

Zur Kaiserkron   MODERN SÜDTIROLEAN €€

(☎ 0471 98 02 14; www.kaiserkron.bz; Piazza della Mostra 2; meals €40; ☉ noon-2.30pm & 7-9.30pm

Mon-Sat) Sweetly efficient staff greet you at the door of a calm and elegant dining room. Refined but unfussy takes on regional favourites fill the menu, and the excellent produce is allowed to shine. It's tempting to just choose from their interesting starters and pastas but meaty mains are particuarly well executed. Hyperlocal labels star on the winelist.

Walthers'   MODERN ITALIAN €€
(🖉0471 98 25 48; www.walthers.it; Piazza Walther 6; meals €27; ⊙8am-1am Mon-Sat, to 7pm Sun) Take your spritz out onto the piazza terrace, then head inside to the low-lit back room to dine on bold-flavoured, appetite-appeasing dishes that roam from Sicily to Bolzano's backyard. A lively crowd and the management's penchant for Prince and Blondie can see a quick meal turn into a big night out.

Drinking & Nightlife

Bolzano after dark will come as a surprise after sophisticated but snoozy Trento. The pristine city centre may be hushed at 8pm, but it's a different story 'round midnight. Follow the locals heading for Piazza delle Erbe or the beer halls – including local Forst and the Bavarian Paulaner – along Via Argentieri and Via Goethe.

Enovit   WINE BAR
(Via Dott Streiter 30; ⊙ 10am-1pm & 3.30-8.30pm Mon-Fri, 10am-1pm Sat) An older, well-dressed lot frequents this warm, woody corner bar and shop for expertly recommended, generously poured local wine by the glass. If there's a crowd, and on Fridays there *always* is, it kicks on past closing.

Il Baccaro   WINE BAR
(Via Argentieri 17; ⊙9am-8pm Mon-Fri, to 3pm Sat) Scurry down the cobbled passageway and poke your nose into this wonderful wine burrow, with a good blackboard selection of regional or Friulian wines and delightful hosts. *Stuzzichini* (snacks) are a euro or two and are made to order.

Hopfen & Co   SÜDTIROLEAN, PUB
(🖉0471 30 07 88; Piazza delle Erbe 17; ⊙9.30am-1am Mon-Sat) The dark bar is the perfect stage set for sampling the cloudy, unfiltered beer that's brewed on the premises. This venerable 800-year-old inn also serves up hearty portions of traditional dishes like sauerkraut and sausages cooked in ale (meals €18).

Fischbänke   WINE BAR
(Via Dott Streiter 26; ⊙noon-sunset Mon-Fri) Local wines and bruschetta (from €6) care of bon vivant Cobo at the old outdoor fish market; pull up a stool at one of the original marble-slab counters.

Batzen-bräu   PUB
(🖉471 05 09 50; www.batzen.it; Via Andreas-Hofer 30; ⊙10am-midnight) A mash of traditional and contemporary architecture makes for many different moods as you elbow your way from one end to the next. A beer garden is welcome during flash Bolzano heatwaves and a basement theatre space turns into a nightclub on weekends.

Nadamas   BAR
(Piazza delle Erbe 43; ⊙ 9am-1am Mon-Sat) Bolzano's party reputation got started at this Piazza delle Erbe veteran. If you can make it through the animated front-bar crowd, there are tables and a tapas menu out back.

ℹ Information

Hospital (🖉0471 90 81 11; Via Böhler) Out of the centre of Bolzano towards Merano.

Police Station (🖉0471 94 76 80, 0471 94 76 11; Via Marconi 33)

Tourist Office (🖉0471 30 70 00; www.bolzano-bozen.it; Piazza Walther 8; ⊙9am-7pm Mon-Fri, 9.30am-6pm Sat)

ℹ Getting There & Around

AIR
Bolzano Airport (Aeroporto di Bolzano; 🖉0471 25 52 55; www.abd-airport.it) Bolzano's wee airport is served by twice-weekly flights from Rome and, seasonally, from Olbia.

BUS
SAD (🖉0471 45 01 11; www.sad.it) Local SAD buses leave from the bus station for destinations throughout the province, including hourly routes to Val Gardena, Brunico and Merano. SAD buses also head for resorts outside the province, including Cortina d'Ampezzo.

TRAIN
Train Station (Piazza Stazione) Bolzano's train station is connected by hourly trains with Merano (€5, 40 minutes), Trento (€6.75, 30 minutes) and Verona (€8, 2½ hours), with less-frequent connections to Bressanone (€6, 25 minutes) and Brunico (€11.50, 1½ hours) in the Val Pusteria. Deutsche Bahn trains run to Innsbruck and Munich via Brennero.

Merano (Meran)

POP 38,200 / ELEV 325M

With its leafy boulevards, birdsong, oleander and cactus, Merano feels like you've stumbled into a valley Shangri-La. Long lauded for its sunny microclimate, this poignantly pretty town (and one-time Tyrolean capital) was a Habsburg-era spa, the hot destination of its day, favoured by the Austrian royals, Freud, Kafka and Pound. The Jugendstil (art nouveau) villas, recuperative walks and the grand riverside Kurhaus of this era fan out from its intact medieval core. The city's therapeutic traditions have served it well in the new millennium, with spa hotels drawing a new generation of health-conscious visitors and a booming organics movement in the surrounding valleys.

German is widely used here, sausage and beer stalls dot the streets and an annual open-air play celebrates Napoleonic-era Tyrolean freedom fighter Andreas Hofer; despite the palm trees, you're far closer to Vienna than Rome.

Sights

Castel Trauttmansdorff   GARDEN
(www.trauttmansdorff.it; Via San Valentino 51a; garden & museum adult/reduced €10.80/7.90; ⊙9am-6pm Apr-Nov, to 11pm Fri summer) You could give over an entire day to these beautiful botanical gardens a little outside Merano. Exotic cacti and palms, fruit trees and vines, beds of lilies, iris and tulips all cascade down the hillside surrounding a mid-19th-century castle where Sissi – Empress Elisabeth – spent the odd summer. Inside, Touriseum charts two centuries of travel in the region, exploring the changing nature of our yearning for the mountains. There's a restaurant and a cafe by the lily pond.

SKI ALTO ADIGE

➡ Alta Badia (p328)

➡ Plan de Corones (p330)

➡ Plose-Bressanone (p331)

➡ Val Gardena (p326)

➡ Alpe di Siusi (p327)

➡ Merano 2000 (p322)

➡ Solda (p325)

➡ Valli di Tures/Aurina (p330)

Kunst Meran   ART GALLERY
(⌖0473 21 26 43; www.kunstmeranoarte.org; Via Portici 16; adult/reduced €5/4; ⊙10am-6pm Tue-Sun, 11am-7pm summer) Shows of high-profile international and regional artists are installed in this contemporary gallery, a thoughtful refiguring of a skinny medieval town house. Look out for monthly talks over *aperitivo*.

Castel Tirolo   MUSEUM
(Schlosstirol; ⌖0473 22 02 21; www.schlosstirol.it; admission €6; ⊙10am-5pm Tue-Sun mid-Mar–Dec, to 6pm Aug) The ancestral seat of the counts of Tyrol is home to a dynamically curated museum of Tyrolean history, including, in the keep, the turbulent years of the 20th century. The castle can be reached by taking the chairlift from Merano to Tirolo (Dorf Tirol). Book ahead for tours in English.

Activities

Some 6km east of town, a cable car (Via Val di Nova) carries winter-sports enthusiasts up to Piffling in Merano 2000 (www.hafling-meran2000.eu), with 30km of (mostly beginner) slopes. Bus 1B links Merano with the valley station. A chairlift (Via Galilei; one way/return €2.70/4; ⊙9am-6pm Apr-Nov, to 7pm summer) runs to the village of Tirolo (Dorf Tirol). The tourist office has details of the many other cable cars and lifts that ring the town.

The promenade or *passeggiata* (evening stroll) has long been a Merano institution. Fin-de-siècle-era walks trace the river, traverse pretty parks and skirt Monte Benedetto (514m). A winter and summer pair follow opposing sides of the river, one shady, one sunny. The Gilfpromenade follows 24 poems carved on wooden benches (also handy for a breather). The Tappeiner meanders above the town for 4km. The tourist office offers guides in summer, or can give you a detailed map; all routes have helpful signage.

Terme Merano   THERMAL BATHS
(⌖0473 25 20 00; www.thermemeran.it; Piazza Terme 1; bathing pass 2hr adult/child €12/8, all day €18/11; ⊙9am-10pm) Bolzano-born Matteo Thun's dream commission – a modern redevelopment of the town's thermal baths – was reopened in 2005. It houses 13 indoor pools and various saunas within a massive glass cube; there's another 12 outdoor pools open in summer. Swim through the sluice and be met by a vision of palm-studded gardens and snow-topped mountains beyond. The

MOUNTAIN MAGIC

The culture of the 'cure' is no passing fad in Alto Adige. Spas have done a roaring trade here for over two hundred years and wellness continues to be been taken very seriously – many Europeans can claim spa visits on national health insurance.

Local spa treatments use ingredients from field and forest – pine, honey, apples, grapes and whey – stirred, pounded or powdered into packs, scrubs, massage oils or topping up soaking tubs. The most curious, and intrinsically Tyrolean, is the hay bath, where spa-goers are cocooned in aromatic Alpine grasses, flowers and herbs. The mulch slowly heats the body while releasing a potent mix of medicinal oils. Curative? Perhaps... Relaxing? Absolutely.

Boutique manufacturers of body-care products and herbal tisanes, based around folk traditions and incorporating Alpine botanicals, are also a booming local industry; pharmacies throughout the region offer a staggering range.

front desk can give first-timers a rundown on the potentially baffling change-room routine. See the website for details of the excellent wellness centre.

Sleeping

Youth Hostel Merano HOSTEL €
(☑ 0473 20 14 75; meran.jugendherberge.it; Via Carducci 77; dm/s €22/24.50; P @ 🛜 ♿) A five-minute stroll from both the train station and the riverside promenade, this hostel is bright and modern, with a sunny terrace and other down-time extras. It has 59 beds, either singles or en suite dorms.

★ **Miramonti** BOUTIQUE HOTEL €€
(☑ 0473 27 93 35; www.hotel-miramonti.com; Via Santa Caterina 14, Avelengo; d €170; P ✳ ♿ ♿)
🌿 This extraordinary small hotel, fifteen minutes drive from town, nestles on the side of a mountain at 1,230m. Rooms are vast, cosy and have awe-inspiring views – such a potent mix, it's hard not to retreat entirely. But you'll be coaxed downstairs by the spa facilities, a sun terrace with lambskins and blankets, or a spot of 'forest therapy' in the nearby woods. The glass-walled **Panorama** restaurant welcomes non-guests, and serves adventurous, beautifully presented dishes using local produce. The entire young team exemplify Südtirolean hospitality, relaxed but attentive to every detail.

Hotel Aurora HOTEL €€
(☑ 0473 21 18 00; www.hotelaurora.bz; Passeggiata lungo Passirio 38; s/d €120/180; P ✳ 🛜) A traditional family hotel, just across the river from the Terme, is working some fresh ideas. 'New' rooms are Italian designed, bright and slick, but the parquetry-floored '60s originals do have their own charm (and

river-facing balconies). The corridors are littered with mid-century pieces that would do a Williamsburg loft proud.

Ottmanngut BOUTIQUE HOTEL €€€
(☑ 0473 44 96 56; www.ottmanngut.it; Via Verdi 18; s/d €115/230; 🛜) 🌿 This boutique hotel encapsulates Merano's beguiling mix of stately sophistication, natural beauty and gently bohemian back story. The remodelled townhouse has nine rooms scattered over three floors, and is set among terraced vineyards a scant five-minute walk from the centre. The interiors are thoughtful and textured: respectful of the building's storied past but refreshingly contemporary. Individually furnished, antique-strewn rooms evoke different moods, each highlighting the different landscape glimpsed from the window.

Imperial Art Hotel DESIGN HOTEL €€€
(☑ 0473 23 71 72; www.imperialart.it; Corso della Libertà 110; d €200-350; ✳ 🛜) Upstairs in what was once a belle époque coffee palace, this inconspicuous, supercomfortable hotel has 11 distinct artist-designed rooms – Tyrolean furniture morphs into neo-geo abstraction; velvet covers and dark-hued walls pay homage to the former Hotel Bristol; an armoire and walls emit an aluminium sheen.

Eating & Drinking

As befits a town dedicated to bodily pleasure, Merano has an excellent fine-dining scene, including the Michelin-starred **Sissi** and **Castel Fragsburg**. Via Portici brims with speck-dealing delis, *konditorei* line Corso della Libertà, and there are more late-night imbibing options, often squirreled down lanes, than you'd imagine.

TASTING TRAIL

Follow Alto Adige's Weinstraße – wine road – far enough south from Bolzano and you'll hit **Paradeis** (Alois Lageder; ☑ 0471 80 95 80; www.aloislageder.eu/paradeis; Piazza Geltrude 5, Magrè; ◷ 10am-8pm, dining room noon-4pm Mon-Sat, to 11pm Thu). Take a seat at the long communal table, crafted from the wood of a 250-year-old oak tree, at fourth-generation winemaker Alois Lageder's biodynamic *weinschenke/vineria* (winery) and start tasting. Book for lunch in the stunning dining room or linger over a bottle and plate of cheese in the pretty courtyard. Whites – highly finessed, Germanic in style, but shot through with the warmth and verve of an Italian summer – are the money here; over 70% of production is devoted to Pinot Grigio, chardonnay and Gewürztraminer. Even so, Lageder's Pinot Noir and local Lagrein are highly regarded.

If you're up for more tasting, or just a pleasant day's cycle, the Weinstraße begins north of Bolzano in Nals, meanders past Terlano (Terlan) through Upper Adige (Überetsch) and Lower Adige (Unterland) until it reaches Salorno (Salurn). Native grape varieties line the route: Lagrein, Vernatsch and local varietal Gewürztraminer, along with well-adapted imports Pinot Blanc, sauvignon, merlot and cabernet. For details of cellar doors, accommodation and bike trails see www.weinstrasse.com.

★ **Pur Südtirol** ARTISAN, WINE BAR €

(www.pursuedtirol.com; Corso della Libertà 35; plates from €7; ▣) This stylish regional showcase has an amazing selection of farm produce: wine, cider, some 80 varieties of cheese, speck and sausage, pastries and breads, tisanes and body care. Everything is hyperlocal (take Anton Oberhöller's chocolate, flavoured with apple, lemon balm or dark bread crisps). Specially commissioned wood, glass and textiles fill one corner of the shop. Stay for a coffee, glass of wine or the *bretteljause* – a plate of cured meat – at one of the communal tables.

Forsterbräu BREWERY €€

(☑ 0473 23 65 35; Corso della Libertà 90; meals €25; ◷ 10.30am-midnight) This brewery restaurant has a huge beer garden and a number of beautifully designed and cosy dining rooms. Come for a pint or heaped plates of *gulaschsuppe* (gulasch soup), trout and roast boar.

Kallmünz GASTRONOMIC €€€

(☑ 0473 21 29 17; www.kallmuenz.it; Piazza della Rena 12; meals €47, degustations €50-65; ◷ Tue-Sun) With rough rendered walls and a dark-beamed ceiling, the dining room here is theatrically simple, and the food too strikes a balance between flirtatious experimentation and letting great (mainly organic) local ingredients shine. Wine is from surrounding vineyards and is reasonably priced – follow the recommendations of the quad-

and quin-lingual black-clad staff, they don't disappoint.

Café Kunsthaus BAR, CAFE

(Via Portici 16; ◷ 9am-7pm Mon-Thu & Sun, 9am-1am Fri & Sat) You can while away the hours in this relaxed gallery cafe, then find yourself still here when the DJs begin and the beer and pizzas are doing the rounds. Note, evening access is from the back lane off Via Risparmio.

❶ Information

Ospedale Civile Tappeiner (☑ 0473 26 33 33; Via Rossini 5) For medical emergencies.

Tourist Office (☑ 0473 23 52 23; www.meran-info.it; Corso Libertà 35; ◷ 9am-6pm Mon-Sat, 10am-noon Sun)

❶ Getting There & Around

SAD buses leave Merano **bus station** (Piazza Stazione) for villages in the Gruppo del Tessa, Silandro and the valleys leading into the Parco Nazionale dello Stelvio and Ortles range.

Bolzano (€5, almost hourly) is an easy 40-minute trip from Merano train station (Piazza Stazione), while the Venosta/Vinschgau line heads west to Malles, from where you can catch buses to Switzerland or Austria.

Hire a bike and helmet next door to the **train station**; the **bikemobil card** (www.suedtirol-bike.it; 1/3/7 days €24/30/34, children half price; ◷ Apr-Nov) includes both rental and unlimited regional train travel. Bike trails track the 65km route between Bolzano, Merano and Malles.

Val Venosta (Vinschgau)

This north-western valley is prettily pastoral, dotted with orchards, farms and small-scale, often creative, industries including marble quarries and workshops. It may feel remote, nestled as it is within the embrace of towering, snowy alps, but for much of its history it was a vibrant border zone, long on the road to somewhere.

◉ Sights

Glorenza   VILLAGE
(Glurns) A walled medieval town, Glorenza was once a kingpin in the region's salt trade. Its pristine burgher houses, colonnaded shops, town gates, fortifications and ramparts were faithfully restored in the 1970s, and while it's certainly picturesque, it retains a comforting normalcy, with the road to Switzerland passing through its very centre.

Marienberg   MONASTERY
(www.marienberg.it; Malles; museum entrance adult/reduced €5/2.50; ⊙ 10am-7pm Mon-Sat, closed Jan, Feb & Nov) The beautiful Benedictine monastery of Marienberg, perched up some 1340m above Malles, has a museum dedicated to its eight centuries of monastic life, though the view and architecture are worth the drive up alone.

Lago di Resia   LAKE
Just before the Passo di Resia and Austrian border, is the deep blue Lago do Resia, a result of 1950s dam projects. This is a popular destination for sailing and kiteboarding in summer, and ice-fishing and snowkiting in winter, as well as a gateway to the Ski-paradies Reschenpass area. The drowned Romanesque church tower in the lake here might be the region's de rigueur roadside photo op, but is still oddly affecting.

🛏 Sleeping

Gasthof Grüner Baum   BOUTIQUE HOTEL €€
(☑ 0473 83 12 06; www.gasthofgruenerbaum. it; Piazza della Città 7, Glorenza ; d €116; Ⓟ ❋ 🛜) Gracious Gasthof Grüner Baum combines arresting contemporary architecture, authentic charm and quiet luxury – freestanding baths, antiques and handcrafted furniture are standard issue in the rooms.

❶ Getting There & Away

Val Venosta is serviced by the SüdtirolBahn Venosta line, from Merano; from Malles, Swiss Post buses run to Zernez across the border and SAD bus 273 runs to Nauders in Austria. Südtirol Express runs coaches to Zurich.

Part of the ancient Via Claudia Augusta forms an easy, and intriguing, 80km bicycle trail from Merano to Malles.

Parco Nazionale dello Stelvio

It's not quite Yellowstone, but 1346-sq-km Parco Nazionale dello Stelvio (☑ 0469 0 30 46; www.stelviopark.it) is northern Italy's, and the Alps', largest national park, spilling into the next-door region of Lombardy and bordering with Switzerland's Parco Nazionale Svizzero.

It's primarily the preserve of walkers who come for the extensive network of well-organised mountain huts and marked trails which, while often challenging, don't require the mountaineering know-how necessary elsewhere in the Dolomites. Stelvio's central massif is guarded over by Monte Cevedale (3769m) and Ortles (3905m), protecting glaciers, forests and numerous wildlife species, not to mention many mountain traditions and histories.

Ski facilities are rare, but Stelvio has a couple of well-serviced runs in Solda and the Passo dello Stelvio (2757m), both of which offer the novelty of year-round skiing. The latter is the second-highest pass in the Alps and is approached from the north from the hamlet of Trafoi (1543m) on one of Europe's most spectacular roads, a series of tight switchbacks covering 15km, with some very steep gradients. The road is also famous among cyclists, who train all winter to prepare for its gut-wrenching ascent, and often features in the Giro d'Italia. The hair-raising high pass is only open from June to September, and always subject to closures dependent on early or late snowfall.

Bormio

Lying immediately south of Passo dello Stelvio, Bormio (1125m) is actually in Lombardy, but acts as an unofficial HQ for the park. It's a popular ski resort, with proximity to some of Italy's highest runs. From October through May, Bormio is best approached from Sondalo in Lombardy, or via Tubre into Switzerland to take the Munt la Schera tunnel to Livigno. Cima Bianca rises just above the town, while nearby the year-round **Pista Stelvio** drops 1800m over 8km. The town's now very posh thermal springs have been famous since Roman times (Leonardo da Vinci liked a soak). Visit Bormio **tourist office** (☑0342 90 33 00; www.bormioonline.com; Via Roma 131b) for maps, weather forecasts and trekking advice.

Val di Solda

The village of **Solda** (Sulden; 1906m), reached by winding your way up the deep, dark valley of the same name, is surrounded by 14 peaks over 3000m high. This low-key ski resort becomes a busy base for walkers and climbers in summer. Challenging trails lead quickly to high altitudes, including trail No 28, which crosses the Passo di Madriccio (3123m) into the Val Martello.

Located – literally – inside a hill, the **Messner Mountain Museum – Ortles** (☑0473 61 32 66; www.messner-mountain-museum.it; adult/reduced €6/5; ☉2-6pm Wed-Mon, 1-7pm summer, closed May & Nov) articulates the theme of 'eternal ice'. Messner's **Yak & Yeti** (☑0473 61 35 77; Località Solda 55) restaurant, in a 17th-century farmhouse, is at the entrance.

Solda's **tourist office** (☑0473 61 30 15; www.ortlergebiet.it; ☉ 9am-noon & 3-6pm Mon-Fri, 9am-noon Sat) has information on activities and the Ortles tourism website has a comprehensive accomodation booking service. SAD buses connect Solda with Merano (via Spondigna), summer weekdays only.

Val Gardena (Gröden/ Gherdëina)

Despite its proximity to Bolzano, Val Gardena's historical isolation amid the turrets of Gruppo del Sella and Sassolungo has ensured the survival of many pre-mass-tourism traditions. Ladin is a majority tongue and this linguistic heritage is carefully maintained. The pretty and bustling villages are full of reminders of this distinct culture too, with folksy vernacular architecture and a profusion of woodcarving shops.

In recent times, the valley has become an 'everyman' ski area, with the emphasis firmly on classic runs and fine powder. The valley's main trilingual towns, **Ortisei** (St Ulrich; pop 5650, elev 1236m), **Santa Cristina** (pop 1900, elev 1428m) and **Selva** (Wolkenstein; pop 2580, elev 1563m) all have good facilities.

⊙ Sights

Museum de Gherdëina MUSEUM
(☑0471 79 75 54; www.museumgherdeina.it; Via Rezia 83, Ortisei; adult/reduced €7/4.50; ☉10am-noon & 2-6pm Mon-Fri, closed Mon in winter) Ortisei's Museum de Gherdëina has a particularly exquisite collection of wooden toys and sculptures.

🏃 Activities

In addition to its own good runs, the valley forms part of the Sella Ronda and the Dolomiti Superski area. Passes for Val Gardena–Alpe di Siusi cost €42/121/226 for 1/3/7 days.

Vallunga, near Selva, is one of the region's best spots for cross-country skiing. There are stunning trails around Forcella Pordoi and Val Lasties in the Gruppo del Sella, and on the Sassolungo.

This is also a walkers' paradise with endless possibilities, from the challenging **Alte Vie** of the Gruppo del Sella and the magnificent **Parco Naturale Puez-Odle**, to picturesque strolls including the **Naturonda**, a signposted nature-and-geology trail beginning at **Passo di Sella** (2244m).

In summer cable cars operate from all three towns. From Ortisei you can ascend to **Seceda**, which, at 2518m, offers an unforgettable view of the Gruppo di Odle, a cathedral-like series of mountain spires. From Seceda, trail No 2A passes through a typical Alpine environment – impossibly green, sloping pastures dotted with wooden *malghe* (shepherds' huts).

Both the Sella and Sassolungo walking trails can be reached from Val Gardena resorts, or Canazei, by bus to **Passo di Sella** or **Passo di Pordoi** – steel yourself for some hairpin bends. From Passo di Pordoi (2239m), a cable car takes you to Sasso Pordoi (2950m).

🛏 Sleeping & Eating

If you're looking to spend a week or more in the mountains, hotels offer weekly half-board deals that are more affordable than those in Alta Badia or Val di Fassa. Hotel restaurants here are often very good too.

Saslong Smart Hotel HOTEL €
(☑0471 77 44 44; www.saslong.eu; Strada Palua; d €80; ☎) Rooms are small but slick (Antonio Citterio had a hand in the design) and comfortable; the 'smart' concept keeps rates low by making daily cleaning and breakfast optional. Short stays do incur a fee, usually around €15 per night.

Charme Hotel Uridl
HOTEL €€

(☎0471 79 32 15; www.uridl.it; Via Chemun 43; half-board s/d €100/190; P✷@) Nestled behind the church in the original 'high' village, this is a friendly, character-filled hotel with bright, simple rooms, a heritage *stube*, and beautiful views back over the valley from its sunny garden.

Chalet Gerard
HOTEL €€€

(☎0471 79 52 74; www.chalet-gerard.com; Plan de Gralba; half-board s/d €150/260; ☎🌢) Stunning modern chalet with panoramic views, 10 minutes drive from Selva proper. Lots of cosy lolling by the (architect-designed) fire spots, a steam room and the option to ski in, plus super cute rooms. The restaurant is both romantic – all pine, felt and candlelight – and highly regarded.

ℹ Information

Ortisei Tourist Office (☎0471 77 76 00; www.valgardena.it; Via Rezia 1; ⊙8.30am-12.30pm & 2.30-6.30pm Mon-Sat, 9am-noon & 5-6.30pm Sun)

Santa Cristina Tourist Office (☎0471 77 78 00; www.catores.com; Via Chemun 9; ⊙8.30am-12.30pm & 2.30-6.30pm Mon-Sat, 9am-noon Sun)

Scuola di Alpinismo Catores (☎0471 79 82 23; www.catores.com; Piazza Stettenect 1; ⊙5.30-7pm) Offers botanical walks, climbing courses, glacier excursions and treks.

Selva Tourist Office (☎0471 77 79 00; www.valgardena.it; Via Mëisules 213; ⊙8am-noon & 3-6.30pm Mon-Sat, 9am-noon & 5-6.30pm Sun)

Medical Centre (☎Dolomiti Sportclinic, branches at Ortisei 0471 08 60 00, Ortisei 0471 79 77 85 and Selva 0471 79 42 66)

ℹ Getting There & Around

The Val Gardena is accessible from Bolzano and Bressonone by SAD buses year-round, and the neighbouring valleys in summer.

Regular buses connect the towns along the valley throughout the year, including a weekend night bus. In winter the **Val Gardena Ski Express** shuttles between villages and the lifts (7-day pass €7). Timetables are available at tourist offices.

In summer, the **Sella Ronda** can be navigated by bus, with services to Passo Gardena, Passo Campolongo, Passo Sella and Passo Pordoi. The **Val Gardena card** gets you unlimited regional transport and summer lifts (3/6 days €62/82).

Alpe di Siusi & Parco Naturale Sciliar-Catinaccio

There are few more jarring or beautiful juxtapositions than the undulating green pastures of the Alpe di Siusi – Europe's largest plateau – ending dramatically at the base of the towering Sciliar Mountains. To the southeast lies the jagged Catinaccio range, its German name 'Rosengarten' an apt description of the eerie pink hue given off by the mountains' dolomite rock at sunset. The two areas are protected in the Parco Naturale Sciliar-Catinaccio. Signposted by their onion-domed churches, the villages that dot the gentle valleys – including Castelrotto (Kastelruth), Fiè allo Sciliar (Völs am Schlern) and Siusi – are lovingly maintained and unexpectedly sophisticated.

🏃 Activities

The region is part of the Dolomiti Superski network, with downhill skiing, ski-mountaineering, cross-country skiing and snowshoe trails all possible.

The gentle slopes of the Alpe di Siusi are perfect hiking terrain for families with kids; average stamina will get you to the Rifugio Bolzano (☎0471 61 20 24; www.schlernhaus.it; ⊙Jun-Oct), one of the Alps' oldest mountain huts, which rests at 2457m, just under Monte Pez (2564m), the Sciliar's summit. Take the Panorama chairlift (one way/return €3.50/5) from Compaccio to the Alpenhotel, followed by paths S, No 5 and No 1 to the *rifugio;* from here it's an easy walk to Monte Pez (three hours total). The more jagged peaks of the Catinaccio group and the Sassolungo are nearby. These mountains are revered among climbers worldwide, and harbour several *vie ferrate* and loads of good bike trails. They're usually accessed from Vigo in Val di Fiemme.

Horses are a big part of local life and culture and there's nothing more picturesque than a local chestnut Haflinger pony galloping across endless pastureland. Riding stables can be found throughout the area.

The Seiser Alm cableway (www.seiseralmbahn.it; one way/return €9/13.50; ⊙8am-6pm mid-Dec–Mar & mid-May–Oct) is a dizzying 15-minute, 4300m trip (800m ascent) from Siusi to Compaccio. The road linking the two is closed to normal traffic when the cableway is open.

REINHOLD MESSNER

The man invariably venerated as the greatest mountaineer of them all, Reinhold Messner, is an Italian (albeit a German-speaking one) from the Alto Adige town of Bressanone (Brixen).

Messner grew up surrounded by the sharp, seductive peaks of the Dolomites. Scaling his first Alpine summit at the age of five, by his early 20s he was recognised as a rising star in the tough world of mountaineering. Derisive of the siege tactics employed by traditional Himalayan expeditions in the 1960s, Messner advocated a simpler Alpine-style approach to climbing that emphasised fast ascents with minimal equipment. By the '70s he had set his sights on Everest, confidently announcing his ambition to climb the mountain 'by fair means', that is, without supplementary oxygen.

The prophecy was heroically fulfilled in 1978 when Messner and Austrian Peter Habeler became the first men to summit the world's tallest peak without oxygen tanks, a feat that was considered physically impossible, if not suicidal, at the time. Unsatisfied with his team effort, Messner returned two years later and hacked his way up the mountain's north face to the summit, alone – a superhuman achievement.

The iron-willed Messner logged another record in 1986 when, at 42, he became the first person to scale all eight-thousanders (the 14 mountains in the world over 8000m). Shunning a well-earned retirement, he also took part in the first unassisted crossing of Antarctica.

These days Messner treks at a gentler pace, mainly in his home Dolomites. A retired Euro MP for the Italian Green Party, he now also tends to his quintet of museums that explore mountain life across the world.

🛏 Sleeping & Eating

Martina Breakfast Lodge　　　HOTEL €
(☑0471 70 6 361; www.martina-lodge.com; Via Panider 19, Castelrotto; d €110; P🖥🛜🗺💦) On the road just outside Castelrotto's historic centre, this newly renovated hotel has bright, modern rooms. Opt for one with a balcony and view over Sciliar and Bullaccia. Welcome extras include kitchens in the larger apartments, complimentary laundry facilities and a sauna.

★ Hotel Heubad　　　SPA HOTEL €€
(☑0471 72 50 20; www.hotelheubad.com; Via Sciliar 12, Fiè; s/d €99/180; P🖥@🗺💦) As if the views, pretty garden and lounge areas here weren't relaxing enough, the spa is known for its typically Tyrolean hay baths, which have been on offer since 1903 and give the hotel its name. Delightful service is courtesy of the founder's great- and great-great-grandchildren, while rooms are modern, light and spacious.

Schagaguler　　　HOTEL €€€
(☑0471 71 21 00; www.schgaguler.com; Via Dolomiti 2; half-board per person €99-170; P🖥🛜) Streamlined blond-wood rooms offer stunningly rustic vistas from the bathroom, the bedroom, the living room...Downstairs Vinbar Rubin is an urbane town hub.

ℹ Information

Castelrotto Tourist Office (☑0471 70 63 33; www.alpedisiusi.info; Piazza Kraus 1; ☉8am-noon & 2-6pm Mon-Fri, 8am-noon Sat)
Fiè allo Sciliar Tourist Office (☑0471 72 50 27; www.alpedisiusi.info; Via Bolzano 4; ☉8am-noon & 2-6pm Mon-Fri, 8am-noon Sat)
Siusi Tourist Office (☑0471 70 70 24; www.alpedisiusi.info; Via Sciliar 16; ☉8am-noon & 2-6pm Mon-Fri, 8am-noon Sat)

ℹ Getting There & Away

SAD (www.sad.it) Runs buses into the Alpe di Siusi from Bolzano, the Val Gardena and Bressanone.
Silbernagl (☑0471 70 74 00; www.silbernagl.it) Runs regular buses to the area from Castelrotto and Siusi.

Val Badia & Alpe di Fanes

For centuries Ladin legends have resonated across this mystical landscape, which inspired JRR Tolkien. Not surprisingly, the Badia valley and the adjoining high plains of Fanes are often touted as one of the most evocative places in the Dolomites. Since 1980 they have been protected as part of the Parco Naturale di Fanes-Sennes-Braies. Villages in the valley – **Colfosco**, **Pedraces**,

La Villa, San Cassiano (St Kassian) and Corvara – form the Alta Badia ski area. While undoubtedly upmarket, they remain relatively low key and brim with character.

Activities

The Alta Badia is located on the Sella Ronda, with the best access from Corvara, and forms part of the Dolomiti Superski network. Alta Badia passes for 1/3/7 days cost from €41/121/226. Of the Alta Badia's 130km of slopes, the Gran Risa, 4.5km north of Corvara in La Villa, is undoubtedly the most legendary.

In summer a cable car ascends into the Parco Naturale di Fanes-Sennes-Braies from the Passo Falzarego (2105m). Alternatively, pick up trail No 12, near La Villa, or trail No 11, which joins Alta Via No 1 at the Capanna Alpina, a few kilometres off the main road between Passo Valparola and San Cassiano. Either trail takes you up to the Alpe di Fanes and the two *rifugi*, Lavarella and Fanes.

Horse riding, mountain biking and hanggliding are other popular valley activities. Hotels often have loan bikes.

Tours

Alta Badia Guides GUIDES
(☏0471 83 68 98; www.altabadiaguides.com; Via Col Alt 94, Corvara; ☺5-7pm) Freeride, ski circuits and ice-climbing courses and tours, as well as snowshoe walks in winter. In summer they organise climbs, including *vie ferrate*, trekking and excursions to the natural parks and WWI sites.

Sleeping & Eating

These resorts are known for their discreet, luxurious hotels. Budget options are scarce, though shoulder season prices do drop dramatically. Residence apartments and mountain huts can be a good deal if booked well in advance. Alta Badia ups the Alpine ante with a number of fine-dining (and often Michelin-starred) restaurants. This gastronomic hot spot also hosts the Chef's Cup Food Festival (www.chefscup.it) in January and from July to September organic farmers markets take over village squares.

Garni Ciasa Urban HOTEL €
(www.garniurban.it; Via Pantansarè 35, Badia; d €85, apt €100) A simple, welcoming, family-run place, set in a blissfully peaceful spot right at the top of the village. The uncluttered, spacious rooms have spectacular views of Santa Croce and home-cooked dinners can be arranged. Note, the Urban of the name is the house saint, not a style or attitude!

Dolomit B&B B&B €€
(☏0471 84 71 20; www.dolomit.it; Via Colz 11, La Villa; d €125; [P][✳][@][✿][⬚]) Rooms here are very prettily decorated, as well as surprisingly spacious (baths! walk in wardrobes!). You might be right in the middle of town but the mountain views are still something to behold. The attached La Tor restaurant does Ladin dishes and pizza; its popularity with locals makes it a convivial spot year round.

Hotel Rezia HOTEL €€
(☏0471 84 71 55; www.hotelrezia.com; Via Cianins 3, La Villa; half-board d €180) This hotel is in a lovely bucolic position, just out of the village on

---

LADIN LANDS

According to one Val Gardena local in her 20s, to be Ladin is 'just a way of feeling...I've grown up speaking the language; I don't feel Italian, or South Tyrolean, I feel Ladin.' She is but one of 20,000 first-language Ladin speakers, almost half are the Val Gardena, the others spread across valleys in the neighbouring Val Badia and Val di Fassa as well as Arabba and Ampezzo near Cortina in the Veneto.

Children in these valleys are taught in Ladin, alongside German and Italian, and the Ladin cultural and linguistic identity is enshrined in EU law. The culture is underpinned by vibrant poetry as well as legends peopled by the good-natured *salvan* (a Dolomiti cousin of the gnome) and a further pantheon of fairies, giants and heroes. Encounter these folk traditions at various valley museums:

Museo Ladin (☏0474 52 40 20; www.museumladin.it; Tor 65, St Martin de Tor; adult/reduced €8/6.50; ☺10am-5pm Tue-Sat, 2-6pm Sun summer, 3-7pm Thu-Sat winter)

Museo Ladin de Fascia (☏0462 76 01 82; www.istladin.net; Località S. Giovanni, Vigo di Fassa; adult/reduced €5/3; ☺10am-12.30 & 3-7pm summer, 3-7pm winter)

Museum de Gherdëina (p326)

the road to San Cassiano. It's big and there's a recently added ultra-modern wing, but the place retains a very individual, very local feel.

Lagacio Mountain Residence
APARTHOTEL €€€

(✏️0471 84 95 03; www.lagacio.com; Strada Micurá de Rü 48, San Cassiano; apt €290; P❄️🛜📶) ✏️
A stylish residence hotel with a casual vibe. Pared-back apartments are decorated with wood, wool and leather; all have heated floors, big baths and balconies. Kitchens come with WMF gear, Nespresso machines and filtered mountain water. There are good spa facilites as well as guest-only bar. The breakfast buffet has Tyrolean and Italian cakes, DIY vegetable juices and fry-ups.

Delizius
DELI €

(✏️0471 84 01 55; www.delizius.it; Micurá de Rü 51, San Cassiano; ⊙8.30am-9pm) Specialist cheese and speck counters, well-priced local wine and grappa, plus an excellent selection of prepared meals – *canederli*, gulasch, lasagne – perfect for self-catering dinners.

Rifugio Scotoni
SÜDTIROLEAN €

(✏️0471 84 73 30; www.scotoni.it; Alpe Lagazuoi 2; meals €25; ⊙year-round) At 1985m there are stunning views, and the traditional food and mountain hospitality make this a quintessential Badia experience. Book ahead to stay in one of their cosy, blond-wood bunkrooms.

Stüa de Michil
GASTRONOMIC €€€

(Hotel La Perla; ✏️0471 83 10 00; www.hotel-laperla.it; Col Alt 105, Corvara; meals €100; ⊙7-9.30pm Mon-Sat) Stuffed with Alpine antiques and built entirely from wood, Stüa de Michil is intimate and ridiculously atmospheric. Beautifully presented dishes rework Ladin or Tyrolean traditions and use biodynamic ingredients. Rare wines are also a speciality.

St Hubertus
GASTRONOMIC €€€

(Hotel Rosa Alpina; ✏️0471 84 95 00; www.rosalpina.it; Micurá de Rü 20, San Cassiano; meals €100; ⊙7-10pm Wed-Mon) Part of the luxurious Rosa Alpina Hotel & Spa, this two-Michelin-starred restaurant is cosy and quietly elegant. The mountain beef cooked in salt and hay is a menu stalwart, as is suckling pig, though dishes also take a creative, delicate turn.

La Siriola
GASTRONOMIC €€€

(Hotel Ciasa Salares; ✏️0471 84 94 45; Pré de Vi 31, San Cassiano; meals €70; ⊙7.15-9.30pm Tue-Sun) A wonderful setting just outside the village, and a wide ranging menu. The wine by the glass selection is broader than most fine dining places, and they do a dessert degustation if you simply can't stand more deer or pork.

❶ Information

Full ski-pass prices, lift information and the location of ski-pass sales points can be found online (www.altabadia.org) or at tourist offices.

Corvara Tourist Office (✏️0471 83 61 76; Via Col Alt 36; ⊙8am-noon, 3-6pm)

La Villa Tourist Office (✏️0471 84 70 37; Via Colz 75; ⊙9am-noon & 3-6pm)

San Cassiano Tourist Office (✏️0471 84 94 22; Strada Micurá de Rü 24; ⊙8.30am-noon & 3-7pm Mon-Sat, 10am-noon & 4-6pm Sun)

❶ Getting There & Away

SAD (✏️800 84 60 47; www.sad.it) buses link the villages with Bolzano (2½ hours) and Brunico (1¼ hours) hourly or so. Summer services link Corvara with the Val Gardena, Passo di Sella and Passo di Pordoi, Canazei and the Passo Falzarego.

Val Pusteria (Pustertal)

Running from the junction of the Valle Isarco at Bressanone (Brixen) to San Candido (Innichen) in the far east, the narrow, verdant Val Pusteria is profoundly Tyrolean and almost entirely German-speaking.

Dobbiaco (Toblach) is the gateway to the ethereal Parco Naturale delle Dolomiti di Sesto, home of the much-photographed Tre Cime di Lavaredo ('Three Peaks' or, in German, Drei Zinnen). Down yet another deeply forested valley the jewel-like Lago di Braies (Pragser Wildsee) is just the spot for a peaceful lake-side stroll, and is home to a beautiful historic hotel, the Pragser Wildsee (www.lagodibraies.com; St. Veit 27, Prags; half-board d €170). Serious walkers tackle part of the Alta Via No 1 from here.

The Plan de Corones (Kronplaz) ski area (covered by Dolomiti Superski) is 4km to the south of bustling Brunico and can be reached by cable car. Ample green and blue runs are spectacularly set for beginners.

Bumping the Austrian and Veneto borders in the far northeast is a vast, wild territory, the Sesto Dolomiti. The Valle Campo di Dentro and Val Fiscalina are crisscrossed with spectacular walking and cross-country skiing trails; most around the Tre Cime are easy enough for inexperienced walkers and families. From the Val Fiscalina it's a long but gentle walk along trail No 102 to Rifugio Locatelli (2405m), from where you can see the Tre Cime di Lavaredo in all its glory.

Bressanone (Brixen)

Alto Adige's oldest city, dating to 901, might be the picture of small town calm, but has a grand ecclesiastical past and a lively, cultured side today. Stunning baroque architecture is set against a beguiling Alpine backdrop, a stately piazza leads into a tight medieval core, and pretty paths trace the fast-moving Isarco river.

◉ Sights

Museo Diocesano   MUSEUM
(🖉0472 83 05 05; www.hofburg.it; Piazza Palazzo Vescovile 2; adult/reduced €7/6; ◷10am-5pm Tue-Sun, summer & Dec–early Jan) This museum is far more interesting than most of its ilk, its magnificent palazzo home testament to the town's once-important religious standing; it's popular when the Christmas Market crowds arrive, due to its extensive 'crib' collection – nativity figures and dioramas.

🛏️ Sleeping

★Hotel Elephant   HISTORIC HOTEL €€
(🖉0472 83 27 50; www.hotelelephant.com; Via Rio Bianco 4; s/d €100/190; P❄️🛜🏊) This 15th-century inn marks the entrance to old Bressanone, and as the name suggests, once gave shelter to an Indian elephant, a gift on its way to Archduke Massimiliano of Austria. Inside are extremely comfortable rooms and serenely professional service, exquisite stained glass and museum-worthy paintings. An honour roll/guestbook features a staggering assortment of European royalty, signing off with the Duchess of Aosta.

Hotel Pupp   BOUTIQUE HOTEL €€
(🖉0472 26 83 55; www.small-luxury.it; Via Mercato Vecchio 36; d €180; P❄️🛜) Fabulously designed rooms are suite-sized, and come with Nespresso machines and wine-stocked fridges; some include a terrace with a hot tub.

🍴 Eating & Drinking

Oste Scuro   SUDTIROLEAN €€
(Restaurant Finsterwirt; 🖉0472 83 53 43; www.ostescuro.com; Vicolo del Duomo 3; meals €43; ◷11.45am-2.15pm & 6.45-9.15pm Tue-Sat, noon-3pm Sun) This place would be worth a visit for the décor alone, but the food here is seriously good. The menu doesn't shy from traditional dishes, but gets creative with generous use of local herbs and seasonal vegetables. Lunch menus are a steal at €15/20 but don't pass up the nut-infused digestives.

Pupp Konditorei Cafe   CAFE, PASTRIES & CAKES
(www.pupp.it; Via Mercato Vecchio 37; ◷7am-7pm Tue-Sat, 7am-noon Sun) In the Pupp family for almost a hundred years, this is a Bressanone favourite. The cosy velvet booths are perpetually filled with locals scoffing great coffee and cake. The poppyseed or walnut *potize* (stuffed brioche) are famous.

La Habana   WINEBAR
(Via Portici Maggiore 14; ◷ 8am-midnight) Smart hole-in-the-wall bar that caters equally well to workers sipping morning espresso, ladies who spritz mid-morning and students nursing a *hugo* (elderflower and sparkling wine).

Peter's Weinstube   WINEBAR
(Vinus; www.vinothekvinus.it; Via Mercato Vecchio 6; ◷ 10am-10pm Mon-Fri, 10am-7pm Sat) A classy, dark, low-ceilinged space with an extensive wine-by-the-glass list. There's a 'tavola calda' – a limited hot menu – on Wednesdays, Fridays and Saturdays (mains €20).

Brunico (Bruneck)

Brunico has a quintessentially Tyrolean historic centre and is worth a detour.

Right by the town gate, head to **Acherer Patisserie & Blumen** (🖉0474 41 00 30; www.acherer.com; Via Centrale; ◷8am-7pm Mon-Fri, to 5pm Sat & Sun), for apple strudel, cheesecakes and Sachertorte that may just be the region's best. If you'd like your cake with coffee, they'll happily plate it and you can waltz next door to **Wörtz Bäck** (Via Centrale 12; ◷ 8am-late Wed-Fri, to 7pm Mon, Tue & Sat), a friendly bar where locals gather for coffee, jugs of beer and wine, often all at once.

On the town's outskirts, visit local wool manufacturer **Moessmer** (Via Vogelweide; ◷9am-12.30pm & 2.30-6pm Mon-Fri, 9am-2.30pm Sat) for cashmere and Tyrolean tweeds from its outlet shop. **Hotel Blitzburg** (🖉0474 55 57 23; www.blitzburg.it; Via Europa 10; half-board d €140; P), in the new town, is a rambling old place with big, bright rooms and a nice mountain orientation.

ⓘ Information

Tourist office (🖉0474 55 57 22; www.bruneck.com; Piazza Municipio 7; ◷9am-12.30pm & 3-6pm Mon-Fri, 9am-noon Sat)

Bressanone is on the main Bolzano–Innsbruck line (25 minutes, €8). Regional Val Pusteria trains connect to this line at Fortezza (Franzensfeste), and run down the valley as far as SanCandido. SAD buses also connect Brunico (45 minutes, hourly) and Cortina (one hour, four daily) to San Candido.

Venice & the Veneto

Includes →

Best Places to Eat

Best Places to Stay

Why Go?

Pinch yourself, and you might expect to awaken from this dreamscape of pink palaces, teal waters and golden domes. Instead you're in Venice, and all five senses never felt so alert. Gondoliers call 'Ooooooeeee!' around canal bends, nostrils flare at fresh espresso wafting from 250-year-old cafes, mouths water at cascades of purple artichokes on Rialto market stalls, and everywhere, constantly, water gently laps at your feet.

Scan the Veneto coastline, and you might spot signs of modern life: beach resorts, malls and traffic. But look closer and you'll also discover stately villas on the Brenta Riviera, and newly restored masterpieces: Titians and Veroneses in Venice, Palladios and Tiepolos in Vicenza, and Giottos in Padua.

This calls for a toast with local *prosecco* (sparkling wine) or cult wines from Valpolicella and Soave. Elsewhere in Italy, *cin-cin* (cheers) will do – but in Veneto, raise your glass to *la bea vita* (the good life).

When to Go
Venice

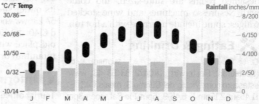

Jan & Feb Snow-covered gondolas, skiers on the Dolomites slopes and Carnevale partiers in Venice.

Apr–Jun Canalside dining, Vin-Italy toasts and Biennale openings (skip pricey Easter holidays).

Sep–Nov Venice Film Festival red carpets, wild duck pasta and palatial accommodation for less.

Navigating Venice

Although you can take a train or bus to the western edge of Venice, the only ways to navigate this city are on foot or by boat. Since 1171, the 117 islands that make up Venice have been loosely organised into six *sestieri* (districts): Cannaregio, Castello, San Marco, San Polo, Dorsoduro and Santa Croce. As you cross canals by footbridge, you may notice white signs informing you which *sestiere* you're entering. Directions to Piazza San Marco, the Rialto and Accademia are found on yellow signs – but the best adventures begin by ignoring those signs and wandering Venice's *calli* (lanes).

VENETO MYTHS...& REALITIES

Verona is the home of Romeo and Juliet...never mind that they're fictional characters. Lovelorn visitors still leave notes to Juliet on the door of a Renaissance house with a balcony.

There's nothing to see in Padua...except pivotal Giotto frescoes that are the missing link between medieval and Renaissance art, rare botanic gardens planted in 1545 where the Italian Resistance was plotted in WWII, and Galileo's anatomy theatre that revolutionised scientific methods.

Everyone drinks prosecco in the Veneto... when they're not wine tasting in Valpollicella or Soave, or sampling rarely exported Indicazione Geografica Tipica (IGT) blends at Venetian *enoteche* (wine bars) or Verona's annual VinItaly expo.

See one Palladian building and you've seen them all...other than Palladio's 24 Unesco-protected, soaring Veneto villas, three blinding-white Istrian stone churches with double the dazzle along Venice's Giudecca Canal, and the entire Greek metropolis inside Vicenza's Teatro Olimpico.

There's nowhere to stay in Venice...except for all those palaces converted to B&Bs and apartments that have become available in the decade since Venice loosened laws allowing families to open their homes to visitors.

Veneto's Best Freebies

➡ **Basilica di San Marco** (p337) Where East meets West under shimmering gold mosaic domes.

➡ **Padua's markets** Hawking the finest Veneto produce, much as it did in the Middle Ages.

➡ **Verona's wine country** Free and fabulous tastings by appointment at wineries.

➡ **Historical Vicenza** A Unesco-protected urban centre with Palladios at every turn.

DON'T MISS

Winter sports and summer fun are within easy reach of Venice. Skiers head for the Dolomites as soon as the snow sticks – but once it thaws, everyone hits Lido beaches.

Fast Facts

➡ Population: 4.85 million

➡ Area: 18,378 sq km

➡ Unesco World Heritage Sites: 30, including three cities (Vicenza, Venice and Verona), Venice's lagoon and the Dolomites

➡ Number of union-certified artisans in Venice: 2000

High-Season Hints

Don't miss Venice's Biennale and Verona's open-air opera – if only to dodge summer crowds. Broaden your accommodation and restaurant options by visiting cities on weekdays and Veneto countryside on weekends.

Resources

➡ **Veneto Regional Tourism** (www.veneto.to) Has information on what's happening around the Veneto, from dancing on the beaches to biking through the Dolomites.

VENICE & THE VENETO

Venice & the Veneto Highlights

1 Joining the collective gasp at the golden mosaic domes of Venice's **Basilica di San Marco** (p337).

2 Comparing Titian's radiant reds and Tintoretto's lightning-strike brush strokes at Venice's **I Frari** (p350) and **Scuola Grande di San Rocco** (p350).

3 Fleeing the crowds and escaping to **Lido beaches** (p359) and remote, outer islands aboard a traditional *bragozzo*.

4 Browsing backstreet **studios** (p376) for one-of-a-kind finds, handcrafted by some of Venice's 2000 registered artisans.

5 Villa-hopping by barge just like a 1600s Venetian socialite along the **Brenta Riviera** (p380).

6 Shouting 'Brava!' for opera-diva encores at Verona's outdoor **Roman Arena** (p390).

7 Seeing the Renaissance coming in Giotto's moving frescoes for **Capella degli Scrovegni** (p381).

8 Letting your spirits soar sampling one of Italy's boldest red wines, Amarone, at cutting-edge **Valpolicella wineries** (p395).

9 Hiking, climbing and dining on mountain-fresh fare amid the awesome snow-capped peaks of the **Cinque Torri** (p401).

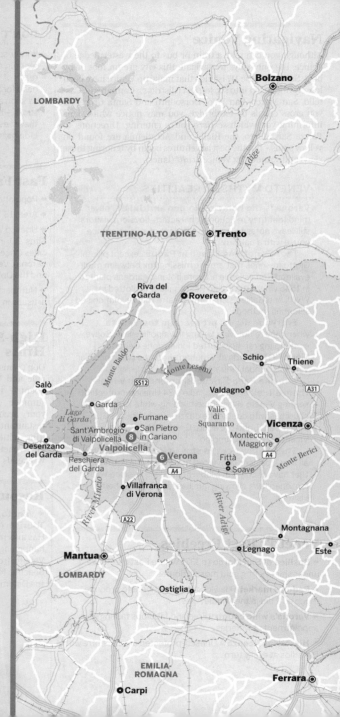

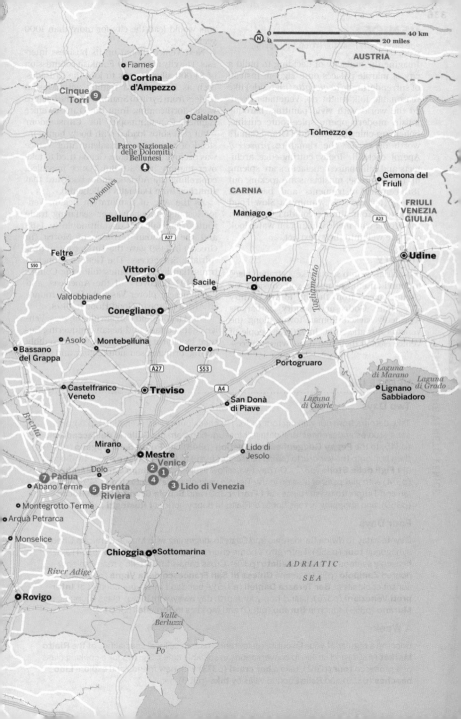

VENICE

POP 59,000 (CITY), 261,400 (TOTAL INCLUDING MAINLAND)

Imagine the audacity of deciding to build a city of marble palaces on a lagoon. Instead of surrendering to *acque alte* (high tide) like reasonable folk might do, Venetians flooded the world with vivid painting, baroque music, modern opera, spice-route cuisine, bohemian-chic fashions and a Grand Canal's worth of *spritz*: the signature *prosecco/*Aperol cocktail. Today cutting-edge architects and billionaire benefactors are spicing up the art scene, musicians are rocking out 18th-century instruments and backstreet *osterie* (taverns) are winning a Slow Food following. Your timing couldn't be better: the people who made walking on water look easy are well into their next act.

History

A malarial swamp seems like a strange place to found an empire, unless you consider the circumstances: from the 5th to 8th century AD, Huns, Goths and sundry barbarians repeatedly sacked Roman towns along the Veneto's Adriatic coast. In 726 the people of Venice elected their first doge, whose succes-sors would lead the city for more than 1000 years.

Next Venice shored up its business interests. The city accepted a Frankish commission of 84,000 silver marks to join the Crusades, even as it continued trading with Muslim leaders from Syria to Spain. When the balance wasn't forthcoming from the Franks, Venice claimed Constantinople 'for Christendom' – but sent ships loaded with booty home, instead of onward to Jerusalem. After Venice was decimated by plague, Genoa tried to take over the city in 1380. But Venice prevailed, controlling the Adriatic and a backyard that stretched from Dalmatia to Bergamo.

As the Age of Exploration began, Venice lost its monopoly over seafaring trade routes. The fall of Constantinople in 1453 and the Venetian territory of Morea (in Greece) in 1499 gave the Turks control over Adriatic Sea access. The Genovese opened transatlantic trade routes following Columbus' 1492 discovery of the Americas, and Portuguese explorer Vasco da Gama rounded Africa's Cape of Good Hope in 1498.

Once it could no longer rule the seas, Venice changed tack and began conquering Europe by charm. Venetian art was incredibly daring, bringing sensuous colour and sly so-

VENICE IN...

Two Days

Take detours from our walking tour (p362) to check out *cicheti* (Venetian tapas), artisans' studios and architectural details. Museum-hop from the **Gallerie dell'Accademia** (p345) to the **Peggy Guggenheim Collection** (p348) and **Punta della Dogana** (p349), then hop onto the *vaporetto* (small passenger ferry) to Giudecca for a romantic dinner at **I Figli delle Stelle** (p372). On day two, follow espresso in **Campo Santa Margherita** (p374) with glimpses of heaven in the Tiepolo ceilings at **Ca' Rezzonico** (p349), Titian and Tintoretto masterpieces at **I Frari** (p350) and **Scuola Grande di San Rocco** (p350), and shopping across Ponte di Rialto to happy hour at **I Rusteghi** (p373).

Four Days

Devote a day to divine Cannaregio and Castello, beginning with Museo Ebraico's Ghetto synagogue **tour** (p353), Tintoretto's home church of **Madonna dell'Orto** (p354) and heavenly seafood at **Anice Stellato** (p372). Cross canals to Castello's many-splendoured **Zanipolo** (p354), serene **Chiesa di San Francesco della Vigna** (p356) and sunset cocktails at **Bar Terazza Danieli** (p375) – but don't miss your concert at **Interpreti Veneziani** (p376). Island-hop your fourth day away, with blown-glass shopping in **Murano** (p359), lunch in **Burano** (p360) and mosaics in **Torcello** (p360).

A Week

Become a regular at your favourite restaurants, recognise local specialities at the **Rialto Market** (p367) and strike up conversations in sociable cafes. Sign up for a cooking class or a prosecco **tour** (p361), take a **bar crawl** (p373) with new friends and explore **Lido beaches** (p359) and Belle Epoque villas by **bike** (p359).

cial commentary even to religious subjects. By the end of the 16th century, Venice was known across Europe for its painting, catchy music and 12,000 registered prostitutes.

Venetian reputations did nothing to prevent Napoleon from claiming the city in 1797 and looting it of its art. By 1817 one-quarter of Venice's population was destitute. When Venice rallied to resist the Austrian occupation in 1848–49, a blockade left it wracked by cholera and short on food. Venetian rebels lost the fight but not the war: they became early martyrs to the cause of Italian independence, and in 1866 Venice joined the independent kingdom of Italy.

The once-glamorous empire gradually took on an industrious workaday aspect, with factories springing up on Giudecca and a roadway from the mainland built by Mussolini. Italian partisans joined Allied troops to wrest Veneto from Fascist control, but the tragedy of war and mass deportation of Venice's Jewish population in 1942–44 shook Venice to its moorings. Postwar, many Venetians left for Milan and other centres of industry.

On 4 November 1966, disaster struck: record floods poured into 16,000 Venetian homes, stranding residents in the wreckage of 1200 years of civilisation. But Venice's cosmopolitan charm was a saving grace: assistance from admirers poured in (from Mexico to Australia, from millionaires to pensioners) and Unesco coordinated some 27 international charities to redress the ravages of the flood.

Defying centuries of dire predictions, Venice has not yet become a Carnevale-masked parody of itself nor a lost Atlantis. The city remains relevant and realistic, a global launch pad for daring art and film, ingenious crafts, opera premieres and music revivals, even as it seeks sustainable solutions to rising water levels.

◉ Sights

◉ Piazza San Marco & Around

★ **Basilica di San Marco**   CHURCH
(St Mark's Basilica; Map p342; ☑041 270 83 11; www.basilicasanmarco.it; Piazza San Marco; ⊙9.45am-5pm Mon-Sat, 2-5pm Sun & holidays, baggage storage 9.30am-5.30pm; ⊛San Marco) **FREE** Creating Venice's architectural wonder took nearly 800 years and one saintly barrel of lard. In AD 828, wily Venetian merchants allegedly smuggled St Mark's corpse

---

ⓘ SPEEDY ENTRY TO THE BASILICA DI SAN MARCO

The grandest entrances to the Basilica di San Marco are with a crowd. Luckily, the queue moves quickly – the wait to enter is rarely over 15 minutes, even when the queue extends past the door to Palazzo Ducale. But to abbreviate your wait, consider these tips:

➡ Booking your visit **online** (www. venetoinside.com; booking fee €1) allows you to skip the queues and head directly into the central portal.

➡ Tour groups tend to arrive on the hour or half-hour, so arrivals at odd times usually mean shorter waits.

➡ The diocese offers **free guided tours** (⊙11am Mon-Sat Apr-Oct by reservation) explaining the theological messages in the mosaics, with expedited entry through the central portal.

---

out of Egypt in a barrel of pork fat to avoid inspection by Muslim customs authorities. Venice built a golden basilica around its stolen saint, whose bones were misplaced twice during construction (oops).

The front of the basilica ripples and crests like a wave, its five niched portals capped with shimmering mosaics. In the far-left portal, lunette mosaics dating from 1270 show St Mark's stolen body arriving at the basilica – a story reprised in 1660 lunette mosaics on the second portal from the right. Grand entrances are made through the central portal, under an ornate triple arch with Egyptian purple porphyry columns and 13th- to 14th-century reliefs of vines, virtues and astrological signs.

Blinking is natural upon your first glimpse of the basilica's glittering mosaics, many made with 24-carat gold leaf fused onto the glass. Just inside the narthex (vestibule) glitter the basilica's oldest mosaics: *Apostles with the Madonna*, standing sentry by the main door for over 950 years. The atrium's medieval **Dome of Genesis** depicts the separation of sky and water with surprisingly abstract motifs, anticipating modern art by 650 years. *Last Judgment* mosaics cover the atrium vault and the apocalypse looms large in vault mosaics over the gallery.

Mystical transfusions occur in the **Dome of the Holy Spirit**, where a dove's blood streams onto the heads of saints. In the

VENICE & THE VENETO VENICE

Venice

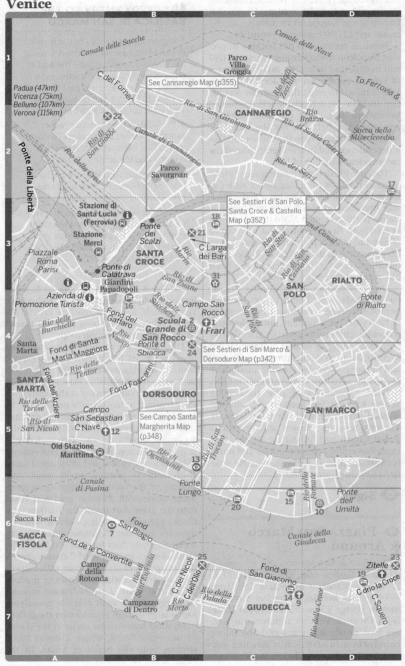

Padua (47km)
Vicenza (75km)
Belluno (107km)
Verona (115km)

Ponte della Libertà

Canale delle Sacche

Canale delle Navi

Parco
Villa
Groggia

C del Forner

See Cannaregio Map (p355)

Rio degli Zecchini

CANNAREGIO

Rio di San Girolamo

Rio Brazzo

Rio di Santa Caterina

Sacca della
Misericordia

Rio di San Giobbe

Canale di Cannaregio

Rio dei Serzi

Parco
Savorgnan

To Ferrovia &

Rio della Crea

See Sestieri di San Polo,
Santa Croce & Castello
Map (p352)

Stazione di
Santa Lucia
(Ferrovia)

Ponte
dei
Scalzi

Grand Canal

Stazione Merci

Rio di San Stae

SANTA
CROCE

Rio Marin

C Larga
dei Bari

Rio di San Cassiano

Piazzale
Roma
Parisi

Ponte di
Calatrava

Rio di San Zuane

SAN
POLO

RIALTO

Giardini
Papadopoli

Rio delle Succhere

Campo San
Rocco

Rio di San Polo

Ponte
di Rialto

Azienda di
Promozione Turista

Scuola 2
Grande di
San Rocco

I Frari

Rio delle
Burchielle

Fond del
Gaffaro

Rio
Nuovo

Ponte d
Sbiacca

See Sestieri di San Marco &
Dorsoduro Map (p342)

Santa
Marta

Fond di Santa
Maria Maggiore

Rio delle
Tentor

DORSODURO

SANTA
MARTA

Fond dell'Arzere

Fond Foscarini

See Campo Santa
Margherita Map
(p348)

SAN MARCO

Rio delle
Terese

Campo
San Sebastian
C Nave

Rio di San Trovaso

Rio di
San Nicolò

Old Stazione
Marittima

Rio di
Ognissanti

Rio della
Fornace

Ponte
dell'
Umiltà

Canale
di Fusina

Ponte
Lungo

Sacca Fisola

Fond
San Biagio

Canale della
Giudecca

SACCA
FISOLA

Fond de le Convertite

Campo
della
Rotonda

Rio di
San Eufemia

C del Nicolò
C dell'Olio

Rio della
Palada

Fond di
San Giacomo

Zitelle

C drio la Croce

Campazzo
di Dentro

Rio
Morto

GIUDECCA

Rio della Croce

C Squero

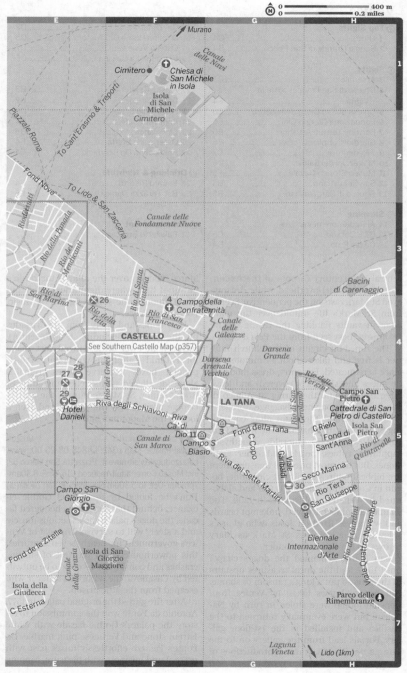

0 — 400 m
0 — 0.2 miles

Ⓝ

To Murano

Canale delle Navi

Cimitero

✝ Chiesa di San Michele in Isola

Isola di San Michele

Cimitero

Piazzale Roma

Fond Nove

To Sant'Erasmo & Treporti

To Lido & San Zaccaria

Rio dei Vetrai

Rio della Pignada

Rio del Mendicanti

Rio di Sen Marina

Canale delle Fondamente Nuove

Rio di Santa Giustina

Bacini di Carenaggio

Rio della Tetta

✖ 26

4 ✝ Campo della Confraternità

Rio di San Francesco

CASTELLO

Rio dei Greci

See Southern Castello Map (p357)

Canale delle Galeazze

Darsena Arsenale Vecchio

Darsena Grande

Rio delle Vergini

Campo San Pietro ✝

Cattedrale di San Pietro di Castello

Isola San Pietro

27 ❸ ❸ 28

29 ⊗❸

Hotel Danieli

Riva degli Schiavoni

Riva Ca' di Dio 11 🏛

🏛 3

LA TANA

Fond della Tana

C Copo

Rio di San Gerolamo

C Riello

Fond di Sant'Anna

Rio di Quintavelle

Campo S Biasio

Canale di San Marco

Riva dei Sette Martiri

✖ Viale Garibaldi

30 ⊗

Seco Marina

Rio Terà San Giuseppe

Campo San Giorgio

6 ◎ ✝ 5

Isola di San Giorgio Maggiore

❽ 8

Biennale Internazionale d'Arte

Viale Quattro Novembre

Rio dei Giardini

Fond de te Zitelle

Canale della Grazia

Isola della Giudecca

C Esterna

Parco delle Rimembranze

Laguna Veneta

Lido (1km)

E   F   G   H

Venice

central 13th-century **Cupola of the Ascension**, angels swirl overhead while dreamy-eyed St Mark rests on the pendentive. Scenes from St Mark's life unfold over the main altar, in vaults flanking the **Dome of the Prophets** (best seen from the Pala d'Oro).

The roped-off circuit of the church interior is free and takes about 15 minutes. Silence is requested. For entry, dress modestly (ie knees and shoulders covered) and leave large bags around the corner at Ateneo di San Basso's free one-hour baggage storage.

Tucked behind the main altar containing St Mark's sarcophagus is the Pala d'Oro, studded with 2000 emeralds, amethysts, sapphires, rubies, pearls and other gemstones. But the most priceless treasures here are biblical figures in vibrant cloisonné, begun in Constantinople in AD 976 and elaborated by Venetian goldsmiths in 1209. The enamelled saints have wild, unkempt beards and wide eyes fixed on Jesus, who glances sideways at a studious St Mark as Mary throws up her hands in wonder.

San Marco remained the doge's chapel until 1807, and the ducal treasures upstairs in the **Museo** put a king's ransom to shame. Gilt bronze horses taken by Venice from Constantinople were stolen in turn by Napoleon but were eventually returned to the basilica and installed in the 1st-floor gallery. Portals lead from the gallery on to the **Loggia dei Cavalli**, where reproductions of horses gallop off the balcony over Piazza San Marco. Hidden over the altar is the **doge's banquet hall**, where dignitaries wined and dined among lithe stucco figures of Music, Poetry and Peace.

Holy bones and booty from the Crusades fill the **Tesoro**, including a 10th-century rock-crystal ewer with winged feet made for Fatimid Caliph al-'Aziz-bi-llah. Velvet-padded boxes preserve doges' remains alongside alleged saints' relics, including St Roch's femur, St Mark's thumb, the arm St George used to slay the dragon and even a lock of the Madonna's hair.

★ Palazzo Ducale   MUSEUM
(Ducal Palace; Map p342; ☎848 08 20 00; www.palazzoducale.visitmuve.it; Piazzetta San Marco 52; incl Museo Correr adult/reduced €16/8; ⊗8.30am-7pm Apr-Oct, to 5.30pm Nov-Mar; ⛴San Zaccaria) Don't be fooled by its genteel Gothic elegance: behind that lacy, pink-chequered facade, the doge's palace shows serious muscle and a steely will to survive. The seat of Venice's government for nearly seven centuries, this powerhouse stood the test of storms, crashes and conspiracies – only to be outwitted by Casanova, the notorious seducer who escaped from the attic prison.

After fire gutted the original palace in 1577, Antonio da Ponte won the commission to restore the palace's Gothic facade with white Istrian stone and Veronese pink marble. Da Ponte's Palazzo effortlessly mixes past with present and business with pleasure, capping a graceful colonnade with medieval capitals depicting key Venetian guilds.

Climb the Scala dei Censori (Stairs of the Censors) to the Doge's Apartments, where the doge lived under 24-hour guard with a short commute to work up a secret staircase capped with Titian's painting of St Christopher. The Sala del Scudo (Shield Room) is covered with world maps that reveal the extents of Venetian power (and the limits of its cartographers) c 1483 and 1762. The New World map places California near Terra Incognita d'Antropofagi (Unknown Land of the Maneaters), aka Canada, where Cuzco is apparently located.

Head up Sansovino's 24-carat gilt stuccowork Scala d'Oro (Golden Staircase) and emerge into rooms covered with gorgeous propaganda. In Palladio-designed Sala delle Quattro Porte (Hall of the Four Doors), ambassadors awaited ducal audiences under a lavish display of Venice's virtues by Giovanni Cambi, Titian and Tiepolo.

Few were granted an audience in the Palladio-designed Collegio (Council Room), where Veronese's 1575–78 *Virtues of the Republic* ceiling shows Venice as a bewitching blonde waving her sceptre over Justice and Peace. Father-son team Jacopo and Domenico Tintoretto attempt similar flattery, showing Venice keeping company with Apollo, Mars and Mercury in their *Triumph of Venice* ceiling for the Sala del Senato (Senate Hall).

Government cover-ups were never so appealing as in the Sala Consiglio dei Dieci (Trial Chambers of the Council of 10; Room 20), where Venice's star chamber plotted under Veronese's *Juno Bestowing Her Gifts on Venice*, a glowing goddess strewing gold ducats. Over the slot where anonymous treason accusations were slipped in the Sala della Bussola (Compass Room; Room 21) is his *St Mark in Glory* ceiling.

The cavernous 1419 Sala del Maggior Consiglio (Grand Council Hall) features the doge's throne with a 22m-by-7m *Paradise* backdrop by Tintoretto's son Domenico where heaven is crammed with 500 prominent Venetians, including several Tintoretto patrons.

Museo Correr   MUSEUM
(Map p342; 041 4273 0892; http://correr.visit-muve.it/; Piazza San Marco 52; adult/reduced incl Palazzo Ducale €16/8; ⊙10am-7pm Apr-Oct, to 5pm Nov-Mar; San Marco) Napoleon filled his royal digs over Piazza San Marco with the riches of the doges, and took some of Venice's finest heirlooms to France as trophies. But the biggest treasure couldn't be lifted: Jacopo Sansovino's 16th-century Libreria Nazionale Marciana, covered with larger-than-life philosophers by Veronese, Titian and Tintoretto.

Venice successfully reclaimed many ancient maps, statues, cameos and weapons, plus four centuries of artistic masterpieces in the Pinacoteca. Not to be missed are Paolo Veneziano's 14th-century sad-eyed saints (room 25); Lo Schiavone's Madonna with a bouncing baby Jesus (room 31); Jacopo di Barbari's minutely detailed woodblock perspective view of Venice (room 32); an entire room of bright-eyed, peach-cheeked Bellini saints (room 36); and a wonderful anonymous 1784 portrait of champion rower Maria Boscola, five-time regatta winner (room 47).

VENICE & THE VENETO VENICE

STATE SECRETS REVEALED: ITINERARI SEGRETI

Discover state secrets in the Palazzo Ducale attic on a fascinating 75-minute guided tour (Secret Passages; 041 4273 0892; adult/reduced €20/14; ⊙tours in English 9.55am, 10.45am & 11.35am, in Italian 9.30am & 11.10am, in French 10.20am & noon). Head through a hidden passageway disguised as a filing cabinet in Sala del Consiglio dei Dieci (Chamber of the Council of 10), festooned with happy cherubim and Veronese's optimistic *Triumph of Virtue over Vice*. Suddenly you're in the cramped, unadorned Council of 10 Secret Headquarters, adjoining a trial chamber lined with top-secret file drawers.

Follow the path of the accused into the windowless interrogation room with a single rope, used until the 17th century to extract information. Next are the studded cells of the Piombi, Venice's notorious attic prison. In 1756 Casanova was condemned to five years' confinement here for corrupting nuns and spreading Freemasonry, but he escaped through the roof of his cell and walked confidently out through the front door, even pausing for a coffee on Piazza San Marco.

Sestiere di San Marco & Dorsoduro (Venice)

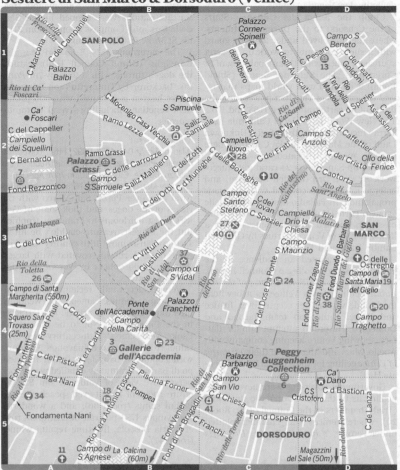

Torre dell'Orologio LANDMARK
(Clock Tower; Map p342; ☎ 041 4273 0892; www.museicivicivenezia ni.it; Piazza San Marco; adult/reduced with Museum Pass €12/7; ☉ tours in English 10am & 11am Mon-Wed, 2pm & 3pm Thu-Sun, in Italian noon & 4pm daily, in French 2pm & 3pm Mon-Wed, 10am & 11am Thu-Sun; ⊕ San Marco) Venice's gold-leafed timepiece, designed by Zuan Paolo Rainieri and his son Zuan Carlo in 1493–99, had one hitch: the clockworks required constant upkeep by a live-in clock-watcher until 1998. After a nine-year renovation, the clock's works are in independent working order and tours climb the steep stairs to the roof for giddy, close-up views of the bare-bottomed 'Do Mori' (Two Moors), who chime every hour.

Campanile TOWER
(Bell Tower; Map p342; www.basilicasanmarco.it; Piazza San Marco; admission €8; ☉ 9am-9pm Jul-Sep, to 7pm Apr-Jun & Oct, 9.30am-3.45pm Nov-Mar; ⊕ San Marco) The basilica's 99m-tall tower has been rebuilt twice since its initial construction in AD 888, and Galileo Galilei found it handy for testing his telescope in 1609. Critics called Bartolomeo Bon's 16th-century tower redesign ungainly, but when

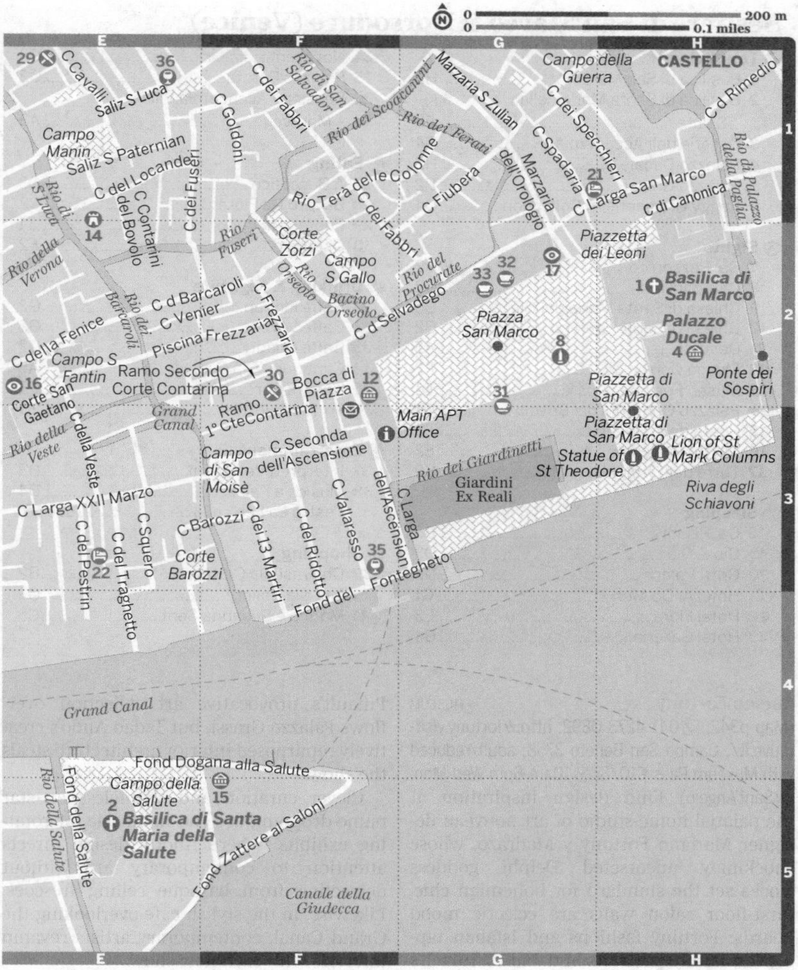

this version suddenly collapsed in 1902, Venetians rebuilt the tower as it was, brick by brick.

Teatro La Fenice THEATRE

(Map p342; ☎041 78 65 11; www.teatrolafenice.it; Campo San Fantin 1965; theatre visits adult/reduced €8.50/6, opera tickets from €40; ⏲tours 9.30am-6pm; Santa Maria del Giglio) Once its dominion over the high seas ended, Venice discovered the power of high Cs, hiring as San Marco choirmaster Claudio Monteverdi, the father of modern opera, and opening La Fenice (The Phoenix) in 1792. Rossini and Bellini staged operas here, making La Fenice the envy of Europe – until it went up in flames in 1836.

Venice without opera was unthinkable, and within a year the opera house was rebuilt. But La Fenice was again reduced to ashes in 1996; two electricians found guilty of arson were apparently behind on repairs. A €90-million replica of the 19th-century opera house reopened in 2003, and although those who had lobbied for Gae Aulenti's avant-garde design were disappointed, few disputed that the reprise performance of *La Traviata* was a sensation.

Sestiere di San Marco & Dorsoduro (Venice)

Museo Fortuny   MUSEUM

(Map p342; ☎ 041 4273 0892; http://fortuny.visit-muve.it/; Campo San Beneto 3758; adult/reduced with Museum Pass €10/8; ☺ 10am-6pm Wed-Mon; ⓢ Sant'Angelo) Find design inspiration at the palatial home-studio of art nouveau designer Mariano Fortuny y Madrazo, whose shockingly uncorseted Delphi goddess frocks set the standard for bohemian chic. First-floor salon walls are eclectic mood boards: Fortuny fashions and Isfahan tapestries, family portraits and James Turrell's sublime red-light installation.

If these salons inspire design schemes, visit Fortuny Tessuti Artistici (p358) in Giudecca, where textiles are still hand-printed according to Fortuny's top-secret methods.

★ **Palazzo Grassi**   MUSEUM

(Map p342; ☎ box office 199 13 91 39, 041 523 16 80; www.palazzograssi.it; Campo San Samuele 3231; adult/reduced €15/10, 72hr ticket incl Punta della Dogana €20/15; ☺ 10am-7pm Wed-Mon; ⓢ San Samuele) Grand Canal gondola riders gasp at the first glimpse of massive sculptures by contemporary artists like Thomas Houseago docked in front of Giorgio Masari's 1749 neoclassical palace. French billionaire François

Pinault's provocative art collection overflows Palazzo Grassi, but Tadao Ando's creatively repurposed interior architecture steals the show.

Clever curation and shameless art-star name-dropping are the hallmarks of rotating exhibits, where Ando's design directs attention to contemporary art without detracting from baroque ceiling frescoes. Likewise, in the stylish cafe overlooking the Grand Canal, contemporary artists revamp interiors with each new show.

Chiesa di Santo Stefano   CHURCH

(Map p342; www.chorusvenezia.org; Campo Santo Stefano; admission €3, with Chorus Pass free; ☺ 10am-5pm Mon-Sat; ⓢ Accademia) The freestanding **bell tower** behind it leans disconcertingly, but this brick Gothic church has stood tall since 1325. Credit for shipshape splendour goes to Bartolomeo Bon for the marble entry portal and to the Venetian shipbuilders who constructed the vast wooden *carena di nave* (ship's keel) ceiling that resembles an upturned Noah's Ark.

Enter the cloisters museum to see Canova's 1808 funerary stelae, Tullio Lombardo's wide-eyed 1505 saint, and three brooding

1575–80 Tintorettos: *Last Supper,* with a ghostly dog begging for bread; the gathering gloom of *Agony in the Garden;* and the abstract, mostly black *Washing of the Feet.*

Chiesa di Santa Maria del Giglio   CHURCH
(Santa Maria Zobenigo; Map p342; www.chorus venezia.org; Campo di Santa Maria del Giglio; admission €3, with Chorus Pass free; ⊙10am-5pm Mon-Sat; ⛴ Santa Maria del Giglio) Experience awe through the ages in this compact church with a 10th-century Byzantine layout, charmingly flawed maps of Venice territories c 1678 on the facade, and three intriguing masterpieces. Veronese's *Madonna with Child* hides behind the altar, Tintoretto's four evangelists flank the organ, and Peter Paul Rubens' *Mary with St John* in the **Molin Chapel** features a characteristically chubby baby Jesus.

⊙ Dorsoduro

★**Gallerie dell'Accademia**   GALLERY
(Map p342; ☑041 520 03 45; www.gallerie accademia.org; Campo della Carità 1050; ticket incl Palazzo Grimani adult/reduced €14/11; ⊙8.15am-2pm Mon, to 7.15pm Tue-Sun, last admission 45min before closing; ℗; ⛴Accademia) Hardly academic, these galleries contain more murderous intrigue, forbidden romance and shameless politicking than the most outrageous Venetian parties. The former Santa Maria della Carità convent complex maintained its serene composure for cen-

❶ **OUTSMARTING ACCADEMIA QUEUES**

To skip Accademia ticket-booth queues, book ahead online or by phone (booking fee €1.50). Otherwise, queues tend to be shorter in the afternoon. But don't wait too long: the last entry to the Accademia is 45 minutes before closing. Leave any large items behind, or you'll have to drop them off at the baggage depot (€0.50 per piece). Also available at the baggage depot is an audioguide (€5) that is mostly descriptive and largely unnecessary – it's better to avoid the wait and just follow your nose and the explanatory wall tags.

turies, but ever since Napoleon installed his haul of Venetian art trophies in 1807, there's been nonstop visual drama inside these walls.

Rooms 1–5 To guide you through the ocular onslaught, the gallery layout is loosely organised by style and theme from the 14th to 18th centuries, though recent restorations and works on loan have shuffled around some masterpieces. The grand gallery you enter upstairs features vivid early works that show Venice's precocious flair for colour and drama. Case in point: Jacobello Alberegno's late-14th-century *Apocalypse* (Room 1) shows the whore of Babylon riding a Hydra, babbling rivers of blood from her mouth.

VENICE & THE VENETO VENICE

❶ **MAKING THE MOST OF YOUR EURO**

These passes can help you save admission costs on Venetian sights.

➡ **Civic Museum Pass** (Musei Civici Pass; ☑041 240 52 11; www.visitmuve.it; adult/reduced €20/14) Valid for single entry to 11 civic museums for six months, or just the five museums around Piazza San Marco (adult/reduced €16/8). Purchase online or at participating museums.

➡ **Chorus Pass** (☑041 275 04 62; www.chorusvenezia.org; adult/reduced €10/7) Single entry to 11 Venice churches at any time within six months; on sale online or at church ticket booths.

➡ **Venice Card** (☑041 24 24; www.venicecard.com; adult/junior €39.90/29.90; ⊙call centre 8am-7.30pm) Combines the Museum Pass and Chorus Pass as well as reduced entry to the Guggenheim Collection and the Biennale, two public bathroom entries and discounts on concerts, temporary exhibits and parking. Purchase at tourist offices and at HelloVenezia booths at *vaporetto* (small passenger ferry) stops.

➡ **Rolling Venice** (☑041 24 24; www.hellovenezia.com; 14-29yr €4) Entitles young visitors to discounted access to monuments and cultural events, plus eligibility for a 72-hour public-transport pass for €18 rather than the regular price of €33. Identification is required for purchase at tourism offices or HelloVenezia booths.

Grand Canal

The 3.5km route of *vaporetto* (passenger ferry) No 1, which passes some 50 *palazzi* (mansions), six churches and scene-stealing backdrops featured in four James Bond films, is public transport at its most glamorous.

The Grand Canal starts with controversy: **Ponte di Calatrava 1** a luminous glass-and-steel bridge that cost triple the original €4 million estimate. Ahead are castle-like **Fondaco dei Turchi 2**, the historic Turkish trading-house; Renaissance **Palazzo Vendramin 3**, housing the city's casino; and double-arcaded **Ca' Pesaro 4**. Don't miss **Ca' d'Oro 5**, a 1430 filigree Gothic marvel.

Points of Venetian pride include the **Pescaria 6**, built in 1907 on the site where fishmongers have been slinging lagoon crab for 600 years, and neighbouring **Rialto Market 7** stalls, overflowing with island-grown produce. Cost overruns for 1592 **Ponte di Rialto 8** rival Calatrava's, but its marble splendour stands the test of time.

The next two canal bends could cause architectural whiplash, with Sanmicheli-designed Renaissance **Palazzo Grimani 9** and Mauro Codussi's **Palazzo Corner-Spinelli 10** followed by Giorgio Masari-designed **Palazzo Grassi 11** and Baldassare Longhena's baroque jewel box, **Ca' Rezzonico 12**.

Wooden **Ponte dell'Accademia 13** was built in 1930 as a temporary bridge, but the beloved landmark was recently reinforced. Stone lions flank **Peggy Guggenheim Collection 14**, where the American heiress collected ideas, lovers and art. You can't miss the dramatic dome of Longhena's **Chiesa di Santa Maria della Salute 15** or **Punta della Dogana 16**, Venice's triangular customs warehouse reinvented as a contemporary art showcase. The Grand Canal's grand finale is pink Gothic **Palazzo Ducale 17** and its adjoining **Ponte dei Sospiri 18**, currently draped in advertising.

Palazzo Grassi
French magnate François Pinault scandalised Paris when he relocated his contemporary art collection here, where there are galleries designed by Gae Aulenti and Tadao Ando.

Ca' Rezzonico
See how Venice lived in baroque splendour at this 18th-century art museum with Tiepolo ceilings, silk-swagged boudoirs and even an in-house pharmacy.

Ponte dell'Accademia

Peggy Guggenheim Collection

Chiesa di Santa Maria delle Salute

Punta della Dogana
Minimalist architect Tadao Ando creatively repurposed abandoned warehouses as galleries, which now host contemporary art installations from François Pinault's collection.

Ponte di Calatrava
With its starkly streamlined fish-fin shape, the 2008 bridge is the first to be built over the Grand Canal in 75 years.

Fondaco dei Turchi
Recognisable by its double colonnade, watchtowers, and dugout canoe parked at the Museo di Storia Naturale's ground-floor loggia.

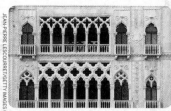

Ca' d'Oro
Behind the triple Gothic arcades are priceless masterpieces: Titians looted by Napoleon, a rare Mantegna and semiprecious stone mosaic floors.

2 3 **Palazzo Vendramin**

4 5

6 **Pescaria**

7 **Rialto Market**

Palazzo Grimani

10 9

Palazzo Corner-Spinelli

8 **Ponte di Rialto**

Ponte dei Sospiri

Palazzo Ducale 17 18

Ca' Pesaro
Originally designed by Baldassare Longhena, this palazzo was bequeathed to the city in 1898 to house the Galleria d'Arte Moderna and Museo d'Arte Orientale.

Ponte di Rialto
Antonio da Ponte beat out Palladio for the commission of this bridge, but construction costs spiralled to 250,000 Venetian ducats – about €19 million today.

Campo Santa Margherita

C Nuova
C d Caffettier
C d Forno
Fond Foscarini
Rio di Santa Margherita
C d della Chiesa
C d Magazen
C dell'Aseo
C d Saoneri
Scuola Grande dei Carmini
Rio Terà della Scoazzera
Campo Santa Margherita
C delle Botteghe
Rio Terà Canal
C d della Vida
Ponte dei Pugni
C delle Pazienze
Fond de la Squero
Rio di San Barnaba
Fond Gherardini
Campo San Barnaba
C del Lombardo Fondamenta della Toletta
C Lunga San Barnaba
Rio Malpaga
Rio Terà di Ognissanti
Fond di Borgo Fondamenta delle Eremite
C d Eremite
C Forno

Campo Santa Margherita

🍴 Eating
1	Do Farai	B2
2	Enoteca Ai Artisti	B3
3	Grom	B2
4	Pane Vino e San Daniele	A2
5	Ristorante La Bitta	B3

🍷 Drinking & Nightlife
6	Il Caffè Rosso	A1
7	Osteria alla Bifora	A1

🛍 Shopping
8	Ca' Macana	B2
9	Danghyra	B2

Rooms 6–10 Venice's Renaissance awaits around the corner in Room 6, featuring Titian and Tintoretto. Tintoretto's *Creation of the Animals* is a fantastical bestiary suggesting God put forth his best efforts inventing Venetian seafood (no argument here). Tintoretto's 1562 *St Mark Saving a Saracen from Shipwreck* is an action-packed blockbuster, with fearless Venetian merchants and an improbably muscular, long-armed saint rescuing a turbaned sailor. Artistic triumph over censorship dominates Room 10: Paolo Veronese's freshly restored *Feast in the House of Levi*, originally called *Last Supper* until Inquisition leaders condemned him for showing dogs, drunkards, dwarves, Muslims and Reformation-minded Germans cavorting with Apostles. He refused to change a thing, besides the title.

Rooms 11–19 As you enter Room 11, you'll notice a lighter baroque touch: gossipy Venetian socialites hang over balconies in 1743–45 lunettes by Tiepolo. These charming ceiling details originally hung in the Scalzi Church, and were narrowly salvaged after 1915 Austrian bombings.

Rooms 12–18 These rooms are currently undergoing restoration to showcase Canaletto's sweeping views of Venice and Giorgione's highly charged *La Tempesta* (The Storm).

Restored portrait galleries will feature larger-than-life Venetian characters: Lorenzo Lotto's soul-searching *Portrait of a Young Scholar*; and a saucy socialite in Giambattista Piazzetta's *Fortune-Teller*.

Rooms 20–24 Finales don't come any grander than the Accademia's final suite of rooms. Room 20 is currently undergoing restorations to accommodate Gentile Bellini and Vittore Carpaccio's Venetian versions of *Miracles of the True Cross*, thronged with multicultural merchant crowds. After careful restoration, the original convent chapel (Room 23) is a serene showstopper fronted by a Bellini altarpiece, with temporary shows in the centre.

★ Peggy Guggenheim Collection
MUSEUM

(Map p342; ☎ 041 240 54 11; www.guggenheim-venice.it; Palazzo Venier dei Leoni 704; adult/senior/reduced €14/11/8; ☽ 10am-6pm Wed-Mon; 🚤 Accademia) After tragically losing her father on the *Titanic*, heir Peggy Guggenheim befriended Dadaists, dodged Nazis and changed art history at her palatial home on the Grand Canal. The Palazzo Venier dei Leoni is a showcase for surrealism, futurism and abstract expressionism by some 200 breakthrough modern artists, including Peggy's ex-husband Max Ernst, and Jackson Pollock (among her many rumoured lovers).

Wander past bronzes by Moore, Giacometti and Brancusi, Yoko Ono's *Wish Tree* and a shiny black-granite lump by Anish Kapoor in the sculpture garden. The city of Venice granted Peggy an honorary dispensation to be buried here, beneath the Giacometti sculptures and alongside her dearly departed lapdogs in 1979. Through the gardens is a pavilion housing a sunny cafe, a bookshop and temporary exhibits highlighting modernist rebels.

Ca' Rezzonico
MUSEUM

(Museum of the 18th Century; Map p342; 🗹 041 241 01 00; www.visitmuve.it; Fondamenta Rezzonico 3136; adult/reduced €8/5.50; ⊙10am-6pm Wed-Mon Apr-Oct, to 5pm Nov-Mar; 🚊Ca' Rezzonico) Baroque dreams come true at Baldassare Longhena's Grand Canal palace, where a marble staircase leads to gilded ballrooms, frescoed salons and sumptuous boudoirs. Giambattista Tiepolo's Throne Room ceiling is a masterpiece of elegant social climbing, showing gorgeous Merit ascending to the Temple of Glory clutching the Golden Book of Venetian nobles' names – including Tiepolo's patrons, the Rezzonico family.

In the Pietro Longhi Salon, sweeping Grand Canal views are upstaged by the artist's winsome satires of society antics observed by disapproving lapdogs. Sala Rosalba Carriera features Carriera's wry social portraits, and Giandomenico Tiepolo's swinging court jesters add humour to Zianigo Villa frescoes.

Check at the front desk for chamber-music concerts in the trompe l'œil frescoed ballroom.

Punta della Dogana
GALLERY

(Map p342; 🗹 041 271 90 39; www.palazzograssi.it; adult/reduced €15/10, incl Palazzo Grassi €20/15; ⊙10am-7pm Wed-Mon; 🚊Salute) Fortuna, the weathervane atop Punta della Dogana, swung Venice's way in 2005, when bureaucratic hassles in Paris convinced billionaire art collector François Pinault to showcase his artworks in these long-abandoned customs houses. Originally built by Giuseppe Benoni in 1677 to ensure no ship entered the Grand Canal without paying duties, they now house massive, thought-provoking installations in front of cutaway views of passing ships.

★ Basilica di Santa Maria della Salute
CHURCH

(La Salute; Map p342; 🗹 041 241 10 18; www.seminariovenezia.it; Campo della Salute 1b; admission free, sacristy adult/reduced €3/1.50; ⊙9am-noon & 3-5.30pm; 🚊Salute) A monumental sigh of relief, this splendid domed church was commissioned by Venice's plague survivors as thanks for salvation. Baldassare Longhena's

uplifting design is an engineering feat that defies simple logic, and in fact the church is said to have mystical curative properties. Titian eluded the plague until age 94, leaving a legacy of 12 masterpieces now in Salute's sacristy.

Gesuati
CHURCH

(Church of Santa Maria del Rosario; Map p342; www.chorusvenezia.org; Fondamenta delle Zattere 918; admission €3, with Chorus Pass free; ⊙10am-5pm Mon-Sat) No matter the weather outside, the outlook is decidedly sunny inside this high-baroque church designed by Giorgio Massari. Luminous late-afternoon skies surrounding St Dominic in Tiepolo's 1737–39 ceiling frescoes are so convincing that you'll wonder whether you're wearing enough sunscreen. Striking a sombre note on the left side of the nave, Tintoretto's 1565 *Crucifixion* shows Mary fainting with grief, but in the 1730–33 *Saints Peter and Thomas with Pope Pius V,* Sebastiano Ricci's chubby cherubs provide heavenly comic relief with celestial tumbling routines.

Magazzini del Sale
ART GALLERY

(Map p338; 🗹 041 522 66 26; www.fondazionevedova.org; Zattere 266; donation suggested during shows; ⊙during shows 10.30am-6pm Wed-Mon; 🚊Zattere) A recent retrofit designed by Pritzker Prize–winning architect Renzo Piano transformed Venice's historic salt warehouses into Fondazione Vedova art galleries, commemorating pioneering Venetian abstract painter Emilio Vedova. Fondazione Vedova shows are often literally moving and rotating: powered by renewable energy sources, 10 robotic arms designed by Vedova and Piano move major modern artworks in and out of storage slots.

VENICE & THE VENETO VENICE

LOCAL KNOWLEDGE

SQUERO DI SAN TROVASO

The wood cabin (Map p338; Campo San Trovaso 1097; 🚊Zattere) along Rio di San Trovaso may look like a stray ski chalet, but it's one of Venice's three working *squeri* (shipyards), with refinished gondolas drying in the yard. When the door's open, you can peek inside in exchange for a donation left in the can by the door. To avoid startling gondola builders working with sharp tools, no flash photography is allowed.

San Polo & Santa Croce

★ **Scuola Grande di San Rocco**   MUSEUM
(Map p338; ☑ 041 523 48 64; www.scuolagrande-sanrocco.it; Campo San Rocco 3052, San Polo; adult €8, incl Scuola Grande dei Carmini €12; ⊙ 9.30am-5.30pm, Tesoro to 5.15pm; ⛴ San Tomà) Everyone wanted the commission to paint this building dedicated to the patron saint of the plague-stricken, so Tintoretto cheated: instead of producing sketches like rival Veronese, he gifted a splendid ceiling panel of patron St Roch, knowing it couldn't be refused or matched by other artists.

Old Testament scenes Tintoretto painted from 1575 to 1587 for the Sala Grande Superiore ceiling upstairs read like a modern graphic novel: you can almost hear the swoop! overhead as an angel dives to feed ailing Elijah. Against the shadowy backdrop of the Black Death, eerie lightning-bolt illumination strikes Tintoretto's subjects in New Testament wall scenes. When Tintoretto painted these scenes, Venice's outlook was grim indeed: the plague had taken 50,000 Venetians, including the great colourist Titian.

Downstairs in the assembly hall, Tintoretto tells Mary's life story, starting on the left wall with *Annunciation* and ending with dark and cataclysmic *Ascension* opposite. Gregorian chant concerts are occasionally performed here (ask at the counter), and you can practically hear their echoes in Tintoretto's haunting paintings.

TOUR THE ULTIMATE WALK-IN CLOSET

Fashion alert: by popular demand, Palazzo Mocenigo now opens its secret attic storeroom the last Friday of every month for fascinating tours through fashion history. Costume historians lead up to 15 people into the ultimate walk-in closet, and open cupboards to reveal 1700s cleavage-revealing, nude-coloured silk gowns, men's 1600s embroidered peacock frockcoats with exaggerated hips, and other daring fashions too delicate for permanent display. Reserve ahead for 11am and 2pm tours in Italian and English (☑ 041 270 03 70; tours €12).

★ **I Frari**   CHURCH
(Basilica di Santa Maria Gloriosa dei Frari; Map p338; www.chorusvenezia.org; Campo dei Frari 3004, San Polo; adult/reduced €3/1.50; ⊙ 9am-6pm Mon-Sat, 1-6pm Sun, last admittance 5.30pm; ⛴ San Tomà) This soaring Gothic church features marquetry choir stalls, Canova's pyramid mausoleum, Bellini's achingly sweet *Madonna with Child* triptych in the sacristy, and Longhena's creepy Doge Pesaro funereal monument hoisted by burly slaves bursting from ragged clothes like Incredible Hulks – yet visitors are inevitably drawn to the small altarpiece.

This is Titian's 1518 *Assumption*, in which a radiant Madonna in a Titian-red cloak reaches heavenward, steps onto a cloud and escapes this mortal coil. Titian outdid himself here, upstaging his own 1526 Pesaro Altarpiece near the entry. Titian was lost to the plague in 1576, but legend has it that strict rules of quarantine were bent to allow his burial near his masterpiece.

Museo di Storia Naturale di Venezia   MUSEUM
(Fondaco dei Turchi; Map p352; ☑ 041 275 02 06; msn.visitmuve.it; Salizada del Fontego dei Turchi 1730, Santa Croce; adult/reduced €8/5.50; ⊙ 10am-6pm Tue-Sun, to 5pm Tue-Fri Nov-May; ⛴ San Stae) Never mind the doge: insatiable curiosity rules Venice, and inside the Museum of Natural History it runs wild. The adventure begins upstairs with dinosaurs, then dashes through evolution to Venice's great age of exploration, when adventurers like Marco Polo fetched peculiar specimens from distant lands. Around every turn, scientific marvels await discovery in luminous new exhibits.

As you might expect from this lagoon city, the marine-biology exhibits are especially breathtaking. The most startling ceiling in Venice isn't a salon Tiepolo fresco but the *museo*'s 19th-century *wunderkammer* (cabinet of curiosities), covered with shark jaws, poisonous blowfish and other outrageous sea creatures.

Palazzo Mocenigo   MUSEUM
(Map p352; ☑ 041 72 17 98; http://mocenigo.visitmuve.it; Salizada di San Stae 1992, Santa Croce; adult/reduced €5/3.50; ⊙ 10am-5pm Tue-Sun Apr-Oct, to 4pm Nov-Mar; ⛴ San Stae) From 18th-century duchess *andrienne* (hip-extending dresses) to Anne Hathaway's megaruffled Versace Venice Film Festival ball gown, Palazzo Mocenigo's head-turning fashion will leave you feeling glamorous by association. Costume dramas unfold across the piano nobile of this swanky

Grand Canal palace, much as they did at 18th-century A-list Venetian parties held here. Necklines plunge in the **Red Living Room**, lethal corsets come undone in the **Contessa's Bedroom** and men's paisley knee-breeches reveal some leg in the **Dining Room**.

Ca' Pesaro   MUSEUM
(Galleria Internazionale d'Arte Moderna e Museo d'Arte Orientale; Map p352; ☏ 041 72 11 27; www.visitmuve.it; Fondamenta di Ca' Pesaro 2070, Santa Croce; adult/reduced €8/5.50; ⊙ 10am-6pm Tue-Sun Apr-Oct, to 5pm Nov-Mar; ⛴ San Stae) **FREE** Like a Carnevale costume built for two, the stately exterior of this Baldassare Longhena–designed 1710 *palazzo* (mansion) hides two quirky museums: **Galleria Internazionale d'Arte Moderna** and **Museo d'Arte Orientale**. The former highlights Venice's role in modern-art history, while the latter holds treasures from Prince Enrico di Borbone's epic 1887–89 shopping spree across Asia.

The modern art collection begins with flag-waving early Biennales, showcasing Venetian landscapes and Venetian socialites by Venetian painters (notably Giacomo Favretto). Savvy Venice Biennale organisers soon diversified, showcasing Gustav Klimt's 1909 *Judith II (Salome)* and Marc Chagall's *Rabbi of Vitebsk* (1914–22). The 1961 De Lisi Bequest added Kandinskys and Morandis to the modernist mix of de Chiricos, Mirós and

Moores, plus radical abstracts by postwar Venetian artists Giuseppe Santomaso and Emilio Vedova.

Climb the creaky attic stairs past a phalanx of samurai warriors, guarding a princely collection of Asian travel souvenirs. Prince Enrico di Borbone reached Japan when Edo

---

DON'T MISS

CHIESA DI SAN SEBASTIANO

Over three decades, this modest parish church (Map p338; www.chorusvenezia.org; Campo San Sebastiano 1687; admission €3, with Chorus Pass free; ⊙ 10am-5pm Mon-Sat) was covered by Paolo Veronese with floor-to-ceiling masterpieces. Veronese's horses rear over the frames of the coffered ceiling; the organ doors are covered with vivid Veronese masterworks; and in Veronese's *Martyrdom of Saint Sebastian* near the altar, the bound saint defiantly stares down his tormentors amid a Venetian crowd of socialites, turbaned traders and Veronese's signature frisky spaniel. Pay respects to Veronese, who chose to be buried here among his masterpieces, but don't miss Titian's *San Niccolo* and the Tintorettos in the glowing, newly restored sacristy.

THE ORIGINAL GHETTO

In medieval times this Cannaregio outpost housed a *getto* (foundry). But it was as the designated Jewish quarter from the 16th to 18th centuries that this area gave the word a whole new meaning. In accordance with the Venetian Republic's 1516 decree, Jewish lenders, doctors and clothing merchants were allowed to attend to Venice's commercial interests by day, while at night and on Christian holidays most were restricted to the gated island of **Ghetto Nuovo**. Unlike most European cities at the time, pragmatic Venice granted Jewish doctors dispensation for consultations. In fact, Venice's Jewish and Muslim physicians are credited with helping establish the quarantine on incoming ships that spared Venice the worst ravages of plague.

When Jewish merchants fled the Spanish Inquisition for Venice in 1541, there was no place to go in the Ghetto but up. Around **Campo del Ghetto Nuovo**, upper storeys housed new arrivals, synagogues and publishing houses. Despite a 10-year censorship order issued by the church in Rome in 1553, Jewish-Venetian publishers contributed hundreds of titles popularising new Renaissance ideas on religion, humanist philosophy and medicine. By the 17th century, Ghetto literary salons organised by the philosopher Sara Copio Sullam, Rabbi Leon da Modena and others brought leading thinkers of all faiths to the Ghetto.

After Napoleon lifted restrictions in 1797, some 1626 Ghetto residents gained standing as Venetian citizens. However, Mussolini's 1938 race laws were throwbacks to the 16th century, and in 1943 most Jewish Venetians were rounded up and sent to concentration camps; only 37 returned. Today few of Venice's 400-strong Jewish community actually live in the Ghetto, but their children come to Campo del Ghetto Nuovo to play, surrounded by the Ghetto's living legacy of bookshops, art galleries and religious institutions.

Sestiere di San Polo, Santa Croce & Castello (Venice)

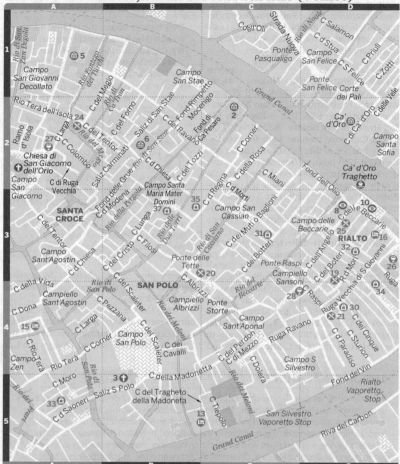

art was discounted in favour of modern Meiji, and Edo-era netsukes, screens and a lacquerware palanquin are standouts in his collection of 30,000 objets d'art.

Chiesa di San Polo CHURCH
(Map p352; www.chorusvenezia.org; Campo San Polo 2118, San Polo; admission €3, with Chorus Pass free; ⊙10am-5pm Mon-Sat; ☐San Tomà) Travellers pass this modest 9th-century Byzantine brick church without guessing that major dramas unfold inside. Under the **carena di nave ceiling**, Tintoretto's *Last Supper* shows apostles alarmed by Jesus' announce-

ment that one of them will betray him. Giandomenico Tiepolo's *Stations of the Cross* **sacristy** cycle shows onlookers tormenting Jesus, who leaps triumphantly from his tomb in the ceiling panel.

⊙ Cannaregio

Museo Ebraico MUSEUM
(Map p355; ☎041 71 53 59; www.museoebraico. it; Campo del Ghetto Nuovo 2902b; adult/reduced €3/2; ⊙10am-7pm Sun-Fri except Jewish holidays Jun-Sep, to 6pm Oct-May; ☐Guglie) At the Ghetto's heart, the Jewish Museum explores

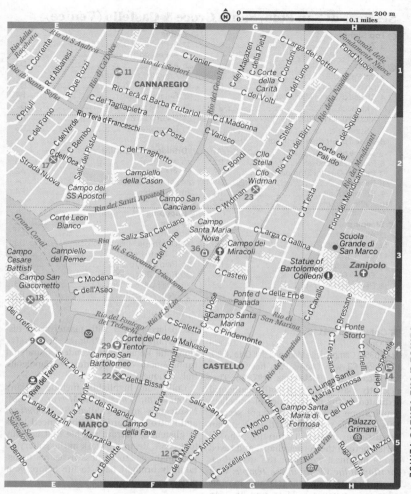

the history of Venice's Jewish community through everyday artefacts, and showcases its pivotal contributions to Venetian, Italian and world history. Opened in 1955, the museum has a small collection of finely worked silverware and other Judaica art objects, as well as early books published during the Renaissance. Entry to the museum is included with tickets for guided synagogue tours, and you can also enquire here about tours to the **Antico Cimitero Israelitico** (Old Jewish Cemetery) on the Lido.

Hour-long English-language **tours** (tours incl admission adult/reduced €8.50/7; ⏱ 4 tours daily from 10.30am) lead inside three of the Ghetto's seven tiny synagogues: the 1528 **Schola Tedesca** (German Synagogue), with a gilded, elliptical women's gallery modelled after an opera balcony; the 1531 **Schola Canton** (French Synagogue), with eight charming landscapes taken from biblical parables; and either the simple, darkwood **Schola Italiana** (Italian Synagogue) or the still-active **Schola Spagnola** (Spanish Synagogue), with interiors attributed to Baldassare Longhena.

Sestiere di San Polo, Santa Croce & Castello (Venice)

★ **Chiesa della Madonna dell'Orto**   CHURCH
(Map p355; Campo della Madonna dell'Orto 3520; admission €3, with Chorus Pass free; ⊙10am-5pm Mon-Sat; 🚹; 🚤Madonna dell'Orto) This elegantly spare 1365 brick Gothic cathedral dedicated to the patron saint of travellers remains one of Venice's best-kept secrets. This was the parish church of Venetian Renaissance master Tintoretto, who is buried here in the corner chapel and saved two of his finest works for the apse: *Presentation of the Virgin in the Temple,* with throngs of starstruck angels and mortals vying for a glimpse of Mary, and his 1546 *Last Judgment,* where lost souls attempt to hold back a teal tidal wave while an angel rescues one last person from the ultimate *acque alte.*

Ca' d'Oro   MUSEUM
(Map p352; ☑041 520 03 45; www.cadoro.org; Calle di Ca' d'Oro 3932; adult/reduced €6/3; ⊙8.15am-7.15pm Mon-Sat, 9am-12.30pm Sun; 🚤Ca' d'Oro) Along the Grand Canal, you can't miss 15th-century Ca' d'Oro's lacy **arcaded Gothic facade**, resplendent even without the original gold-leaf details that gave the palace its name (Golden House). Baron Franchetti donated to Venice this treasure-box palace packed with masterpieces displayed upstairs in **Galleria Franchetti**, alongside Renaissance wonders plundered from Veneto churches during Napoleon's Italy conquest.

Collection highlights include Titian's smouldering *Venus at the Mirror* (c 1550); Mantegna's arrow-riddled *St Sebastian*; and Pietro Lombardo's chubby-kneed Jesus in glistening Carrara marble that actually looks soft. Restorers work in the gallery, so you might get to witness treasures painstakingly brought back to life before your eyes.

◎ Castello

★ **Zanipolo**   BASILICA
(Chiesa dei SS Giovanni e Paolo; Map p352; ☑041 523 59 13; www.basilicasantigiovanniepaolo.it; Campo Zanipolo; adult/student €2.50/1.25; ⊙9am-6pm Mon-Sat, noon-6pm Sun; 🚤Ospedale) When the Dominicans began building Zanipolo in 1333 to rival the Franciscans' I Frari (p350), this barnlike church stirred passions more common to Serie A football than architecture. Both structures feature red-brick facades with high-contrast detailing, but since Zanipolo's facade remains unfinished, the Frari

Cannaregio (Venice)

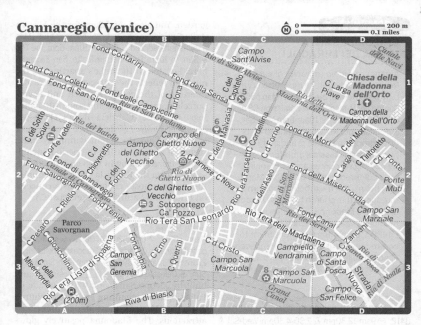

won a decisive early decision. Over the centuries, Zanipolo has at least tied the score with its pantheon of ducal funerary monuments and the variety of its masterpieces.

Built in classic Italian Gothic style, the basilica could accommodate virtually the entire population of 14th-century Castello and its walls are lined with the lavish tombs of 25 Venetian doges. In 1867 a fire destroyed paintings by Tintoretto, Palma di Giovanni, Titian and Bellini, but thankfully a second Bellini polyptych, on the second altar in the right aisle, survived intact. Rarest of all is the surviving 15th-century stained glass in the south transept. Created on Murano, it richly illuminates designs by Bartolomeo Vivarini and Girolamo Mocetto.

★ **Scuola di San Giorgio
degli Schiavoni**   CHURCH
(Map p357; ☎041 522 88 28; Calle dei Furlani 3259a; adult/reduced €5/3; ⊙2.45-6pm Mon, 9.15am-1pm & 2.45-6pm Tue-Sat, 9.15am-1pm Sun; ♿; ☒Pietà) In the 15th century, Venice annexed Dalmatia – an area roughly corresponding to the former Yugoslavia – and large numbers of Dalmatians, known as Schiavoni, emigrated to Venice. In a testament to Venetian pluralism, they were granted their own *scuola* (religious confraternity) in

Cannaregio (Venice)

1451. Around 1500, they began building their headquarters, making the brilliant decision to hire Vittore Carpaccio (also of Dalmatian descent) to complete an extraordinary cycle of paintings of Dalmatia's patron saints George, Tryphone and Jerome.

CHIESA DI SANTA MARIA DEI MIRACOLI

A minor *miracolo* (miracle) of early-Renaissance architecture, Pietro Lombardo's little marble chapel (Map p352; Campo dei Miracoli 6074; admission €3 or with Chorus Pass; ⏱10am-5pm Mon-Sat; 🚤Fondamenta Nuove) was ahead of its time, dropping Gothic grandiosity for human-scale classical architecture. By pooling resources and scavenging multicoloured marble from San Marco slag heaps, the neighbourhood commissioned this church to house Niccolò di Pietro's Madonna icon when it miraculously started weeping in c 1480. Completing this monument to community spirit, Pier Maria Pennacchi filled 50 ceiling panels with portraits of prophets dressed as Venetians.

Chiesa di San Giorgio dei Greci CHURCH
(Map p357; 🖉041 522 65 81; Campiello dei Greci 3412; ⏱9am-12.30pm & 2.30-4.30pm Wed-Sat & Mon, 9am-1pm Sun; 🚤Pietà) FREE Greek Orthodox refugees who fled to Venice from Turkey with the rise of the Ottoman Empire built a church here in 1536, with the aid of a special dispensation from Venice to collect taxes on incoming Greek ships. Nicknamed 'St George of the Greeks', the little church has an impressive iconostasis, and clouds of fine incense linger over services. Other fabulous works by the Venetian school of icon painters can be found in the Museo delle Icone (Museum of Icons; Map p357; 🖉041 522 65 81; www.istitutoellenico.org; Campiello dei Greci 3412; adult/student €4/2; ⏱10am-5pm; 🚤Pietà).

Palazzo Querini Stampalia MUSEUM
(Map p352; 🖉041 271 14 11; www.querinistampalia.it; Campiello Querini Stampalia 5252; 🚤Rialto, San Zaccaria) In 1869 Conte Giovanni Querini Stampalia made a gift of his ancestral *palazzo* to the city on the forward-thinking condition that its 700-year-old library operate late-night openings. Downstairs savvy drinkers take their *aperitivi* (predinner drinks with snacks) with a twist of high modernism in the Carlo Scarpa–designed garden, while the *palazzo*'s temporary contemporary shows add an element of the unexpected to the silk-draped salons upstairs.

Enter through the Mario Botta–designed QShop to get a free pass to the cafe and its garden. You also buy tickets for the Museo della Fondazione Querini Stampalia (Map p352; adult/reduced €10/8; ⏱10am-6pm Tue-Thu & Sun, to 10pm Fri & Sat; 🚤Rialto, San Zaccaria) here. Located in the duke's apartments, the museum reflects the 18th-century tastes and interests of the count: Meissen and Sèvres porcelain, marble busts and some 400 paintings. Of these, Gabriela Bella's (1730–99) *Scenes of Public Life in Venice* are the most engaging. They document winningly naive scenes of the city during the period, including the frozen lagoon in 1708 and the courtesans' race on the Rio de la Sensa. In summer the *palazzo* hosts chamber-music concerts on Friday and Saturday. Tickets cost €3.

Chiesa di San Francesco della Vigna CHURCH
(Map p338; 🖉041 520 61 02; www.sanfrancescodellavigna.it; Campo San Francesco della Vigna 2786; ⏱9.30am-12.30pm & 3-6pm Mon-Sat, 3-6pm Sun; 🚤Celestia, Ospedale) FREE Designed and built by Jacopo Sansovino with a facade by Palladio, this enchanting Franciscan church is one of Venice's most underappreciated attractions. The Madonna positively glows in Bellini's 1507 *Madonna and Saints* in the Cappella Santa, just off the flower-carpeted cloister, while swimming angels and strutting birds steal the scene in the delightful *Virgin Enthroned*, by Antonio da Negroponte (c 1460–70). Bring €0.20 to illuminate them.

Palladio and the Madonna are tough acts to follow, but father-son sculptors Pietro and Tullio Lombardo make their own mark in the Cappella Giustiniani with their fabulous 15th-century marble reliefs that recount the lives of Christ and an assortment of saints.

Out the back, the *campo* (field) makes a sociable setting for Venice's best annual block party, the Festa di Francesco della Vigna, with wine and rustic fare; it's usually held the third week in June.

Chiesa di San Zaccaria CHURCH
(Map p357; 🖉041 522 12 57; Campo San Zaccaria 4693; ⏱10am-noon & 4-6pm Mon-Sat, 4-6pm Sun; 🚤San Zaccaria) FREE When 15th-century Venetian girls showed more interest in sailors than saints, they were sent to the convent adjoining San Zaccaria. The wealth showered on the church by their grateful parents is evident. Masterpieces by Bellini, Titian, Tintoretto and Van Dyck crowd the walls. Bellini's altarpiece is such a treasure

Southern Castello (Venice)

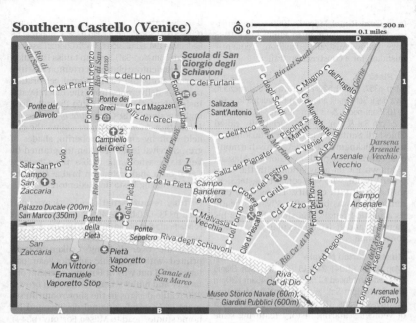

that Napoleon whisked it away to Paris for 20 years when he plundered the city in 1797.

Arsenale
HISTORIC BUILDING

(Map p338; ☎041 521 88 28; www.labiennale. org; Campo della Tana; adult €20, reduced €12-16; ☺10am-6pm Tue-Sun; 🚢Arsenale) Founded in 1104, the Arsenale soon became the greatest medieval shipyard in Europe, home to 300 shipping companies employing up to 16,000 people. Capable of turning out a new galley in a day, it is considered a forerunner of mass industrial production. Though it's closed to the public most of the year, arty types invade the shipyard during Venice's art and architecture Biennales, when it hosts exhibitions and special events.

Giardini Pubblici
GARDEN

(Map p338; www.labiennale.org; 🚢Giardini, Biennale) Venice's public gardens were laid out between 1808 and 1812 on the orders of Napoleon, who decided the city needed a little breathing space. Never mind that an entire residential district had to be demolished. A winning combination of formal gardens and winding pathways, the park now stretches from Via Garibaldi past the Biennale pavilions to Sant'Elena, making this the largest park in Venice.

Southern Castello (Venice)

◉ **Top Sights**

1 Scuola di San Giorgio degli
Schiavoni...B1

◉ **Sights**

2 Chiesa di San Giorgio dei Greci..........B2
3 Chiesa di San Zaccaria.........................A2
4 La Pietà..B2
5 Museo delle Icone.................................A1

⌂ **Sleeping**

6 Palazzo Schiavoni.................................B1
7 Palazzo Soderini...................................B2

✗ **Eating**

8 Al Covo...C2
9 Trattoria Corte Sconta.........................C2

✪ **Entertainment**

Concerts at La Pietà....................(see 4)

A large portion of the gardens is given over to the Biennale exhibition arena, hosting international art (odd years) and architecture (even years) events in 30 modernist pavilions, each allocated to a different nation. During the Art Biennale's June–September run, connoisseurs swarm national showcases ranging from Geza Rintel Maroti's 1909 secessionist-era Hungarian Pavilion to Philip Cox's 1988 boxy, yellow Australian Pavilion, frequently mistaken for a construction trailer.

La Pietà
CHURCH

(Map p357; ☑ 041 522 21 71; www.pietavenezia.it; Riva degli Schiavoni; admission €3, guided tour €5; ☉ 10.15am-noon & 3-5pm Tue-Fri, 10.15am-1pm & 2-5pm Sat & Sun; ☒ Pietà) Originally called Chiesa di Santa Maria della Visitazione but fondly nicknamed La Pietà, this harmonious church designed by Giorgio Massari is known for its association with the composer Vivaldi, who was concert master here in the early 18th century. Though the current church was built after Vivaldi's death, its acoustic-friendly oval shape honours his memory, and it is still regularly used as a concert hall.

Museo Storico Navale
MUSEUM

(Map p338; ☑ 041 244 13 99; Riva San Biagio 2148; adult/reduced €1.55/free; ☉ 8.45am-1.30pm Mon-Fri, to 1pm Sat; ☒; ☒ Arsenale) Maritime madness spans 42 rooms at this museum of Venice's seafaring history, featuring scale models of Venetian-built vessels as well as Peggy Guggenheim's not-so-minimalist gondola. On the ground floor, 'the barn', you'll find sprawling galleries of fearsome weaponry and 17th-century dioramas of forts and ports. Upstairs you can gawk at a sumptuous model of the *bucintoro*, the doge's gilded ceremonial barge, destroyed by Napoleonic troops in 1798.

⊙ Giudecca

Giudecca is probably derived from *zudega* (from *giudicato*, or 'the judged'), the name given to rebellious Venetian nobles banished to Giudecca. The banishments backfired: Giudecca became fashionable and Venetians built weekend garden villas on the island. However, many were abandoned during times of plague and war, and were eventually displaced by 19th-century industry.

Today Giudecca is entering its third act, with brick factories converted into artists' lofts and galleries taking over the Fondamenta San Biagio. *Vaporetti* (small passenger ferries) 41, 42, 82 and N make Giudecca an easy stop between San Marco and Dorsoduro.

Il Redentore
CHURCH

(Chiesa del SS Redentore; Map p338; Campo del SS Redentore 194; admission €3, with Chorus Pass free; ☉ 10am-5pm Mon-Sat) You can't miss Palladio's 1577 Il Redentore church, a triumph of white marble along the Grand Canal celebrating the city's deliverance from the Black Death. Inside above the portal, Paolo Piazza's strikingly modern 1619 *Gratitude of Venice for Liberation from the Plague* shows the city held aloft by angels in sobering shades of grey. Survival is never taken for granted by Venetians, who walk across the Giudecca Canal on a shaky pontoon bridge from the Zattere during Festa del Redentore.

Fortuny Tessuti Artistici
FACTORY OUTLET

(Map p338; ☑ 041 522 40 78; www.fortuny.com; Fondamenta San Biagio 805; ☉ 10am-1pm & 2-6pm Mon-Sat; ☒ Palanca) Marcel Proust waxed rhapsodic over Fortuny's silken cottons printed with boho-chic art nouveau patterns. Find out why at Fortuny's version of a factory and outlet where visitors can browse 260 textile designs in the showroom. To see more of Fortuny's original designs and his home studio, head to Museo Fortuny (p344).

⊙ Isola di San Giorgio Maggiore

Chiesa di San Giorgio Maggiore
CHURCH

(Map p338; ☑ 041 522 78 27; Isola di San Giorgio Maggiore; bell tower adult/reduced €3/2; ☉ 9am-12.30pm & 2.30-6.30pm Mon-Sat May-Sep, to 5pm Oct-Apr; ☒ San Giorgio Maggiore) Solar eclipses are only marginally more dazzling than Palladio's white Istrian marble facade. Begun in the 1560s, it owes more to ancient Roman temples than the baroque of Palladio's day. Inside, ceilings billow over a generous nave, with high windows distributing filtered sunshine. Two of Tintoretto's masterworks flank the altar, and a lift whisks visitors up the 60m-high **bell tower** for stirring Ventian panoramas – a great alternative to long lines at San Marco's campanile.

Behind the church, a defunct naval academy has been converted into a shipshape gallery by the **Fondazione Giorgio Cini** (Map p338; ☑ 041 220 12 15; www.cini.it; Isola di San Giorgio Maggiore; adult/reduced €10/8; ☉ guided tours in English & French 11am, 1pm, 3pm & 5pm Sat & Sun, in Italian 10am, noon, 2pm & 4pm Sat & Sun; ☒ San Giorgio Maggiore). After escaping the Dachau internment camp with his son Giorgio, Vittorio Cini returned to Venice on a mission to save San Giorgio Maggiore, which was a ramshackle mess in 1949. Cini's foundation restored the island into a cultural centre. In addition to its permanent collection of Old Masters and modern art, the gallery hosts important contemporary works, from Peter Greenaway to Anish Kapoor.

⊙ The Lido

Only 15 minutes by *vaporetto* 1, 51, 52, 61, 62, 82 or N from San Marco, the Lido has been the beach and bastion of Venice for centuries. In the 19th century it found a new lease of life as a glamorous bathing resort, attracting monied Europeans to its grand Liberty-style hotels. Thomas Mann's novel *Death in Venice* was set here, and you'll spot plenty of ornate villas that date from those decadent days. Walking itineraries around the most extravagant are available to download at www2.comune.venezia.it/lidoliberty.

Lido beaches, such as the Blue Moon complex, line the southern, seaward side of the island and are easily accessed from the *vaporetto* down the Gran Viale. To head further afield, hire a bike from Lido on Bike (☑ 041 526 80 19; www.lidoonbike.it; Gran Viale 21b; bikes per 90min/day €5/9; ☺ 9am-7pm mid-Mar–Oct; ⛴ Lido) and cycle south across the Ponte di Borgo to tiny Malamocco, a miniature version of Venice right down to the lions of St Mark on medieval facades.

At the southern tip of the island the Alberoni pine forest slopes down to the Lido's wildest, most scenic beach where marine birds fish in shallow sea pools. The majority of the beach is open to the public, but if you feel the need for a restaurant and sun loungers, head for the Bagni Alberoni (☑ 041 73 10 29; www.bagnialberoni.com; Strada Nuova dei Bagni 26; umbrella/sun lounger/deck chair €8/7/5; ☺ 8am-midnight Jun-Sep; ⛴ Lido).

The biggest event on the Lido social calendar is September's Venice Film Festival, when starlets and socialites attempt to blind paparazzi with Italian couture. Major events are held at the 1930s Palazzo del Cinema, which looks like a Fascist airport when stripped of its red carpet.

⊙ Isola di San Michele

Shuttling between Murano from the Fondamente Nuove, *vaporetti* 41 and 42 stop at Venice's city cemetery, established on Isola di San Michele under Napoleon. Until then,

❶ LIDO BEACHES

There are only three 'free' Lido beaches: the Blue Moon (Piazzale Bucintoro 1; ☺ 10am-6.30pm May-Sep; ♿; ⛴ Lido) complex, the San Nicolò beach to the north and the Alberoni beach at the southern end of the island. The rest of the shoreline is occupied by *stabilimenti*: privately managed sections of beach lined with wooden *capannas* (cabins), a relic of the Lido's 1850s bathing scene. Many of them are rented by the same families year in, year out or reserved for guests of the grand hotels. The *stabilimenti* also offer showers, sun loungers (€6 to €9), umbrellas (€11 to €16) and small lockers (€18.50 to €28). Rates drop a few euros after 2pm.

Venetians were buried in parish plots across town – not the most salubrious solution, as Napoleon's inspectors soon realised. Today, goths, incorrigible romantics and music lovers pause here to pay respects to Ezra Pound, Sergei Diaghilev and Igor Stravinsky.

⊙ Murano

Venetians have been working in crystal and glass since the 10th century, but due to fire hazards all glass-blowing was moved to the island of Murano in the 13th century. Woe betide the glass-blower with wanderlust: trade secrets were so jealously guarded that any glass-worker who left the city was accused of treason and subject to assassination. Today glass artisans ply their trade at workshops along Murano's Fondamenta dei Vetrai marked by *Fornace* (furnace) signs. To ensure glass you buy is hand-made in Murano and not factory-fabricated elsewhere, look for the heart-shaped seal guarantee.

Museo del Vetro   MUSEUM
(Glass Museum; ☑ 041 73 95 86; www.museo-vetro.visitmuve.it; Fondamenta Giustinian 8; adult/reduced €8/5.50; ☺ 10am-6pm Apr-Oct, to 5pm Nov-Mar; ⛴ Museo) Since 1861, Murano's glass-making prowess has earned pride of place in Palazzo Giustinian (the seat of the Torcello bishopric from 1659 until its dissolution). Downstairs are priceless 1500-year-old examples of iridescent Roman glass, but

A NORTHERN LAGOON BOAT TRIP

Whereas other cities sunk their history in foundations, Venice cast out across the lagoon's patchwork of shifting mudflats, so understanding something of the lagoon is integral to understanding Venice. Unesco recognised this by including the 550-sq-km (212-sq-mile) lagoon – the largest coastal wetland in Europe – in its designation of Venice as a World Heritage Site in 1987.

Rich in unique flora and fauna, the tidal *barene* (shoals) and salt marshes are part of the city's psyche. Between September and January more than 130,000 migrating birds nest, dive and dabble in the shallows; while year-round fishing folk tend their nets and traps, and city-council workers dredge canals and reinforce shifting islands of cordgrass and saltwort so essential to the lagoon's ecology.

Take a boat tour with Terra e Acqua (p361) and dock for wine tasting at the Sant'Erasmo *cantina*, tour the quarantine island of Lazzaretto Nuovo and explore Sant'Andrea, the finest fort in the lagoon. Then return to Venice as a rosy-tinted sunset frames the city's *campaniles* (bell towers).

upstairs Murano shows off in the frescoed **Salone Maggiore** (Grand Salon), with displays ranging from gold-flecked 17th-century winged aventurine goblets to a botanically convincing 1930s glass cactus.

◉ Burano

Venice's lofty Gothic architecture might leave you feeling slightly loopy, but Burano will bring you back to your senses with a reviving shock of colour. The 50-minute Laguna Nord (LN) ferry ride from the Fondamente Nuove is packed with photographers bounding into Burano's backstreets, snapping away at pea green stockings hung to dry between hot pink, royal blue and caution orange houses.

Burano is also famed for its handmade lace, which once graced the décolleté of European aristocracy. Unfortunately the ornate styles and expensive table coverings fell out of vogue in lean post-WWII times and the industry has since suffered a terminal decline. Some women still maintain the traditions, but few production houses remain – with the singular exception of **Emilia** (☑ 041 73 52 99; www.emiliaburano.it; Piazza Galuppi 205; ⬢ Burano), most of the lace for sale in local shops is of the imported, machine-made variety.

If you fancy a stroll, hop across the 60m bridge to Burano's even quieter sister island, **Mazzorbo**. Little more than a broad grassy knoll, Mazzorbo is a great place for a picnic or a long, lazy lunch at winery **Venissa** (☑ 041 527 22 81; www.venissa.it; Fondamenta Santa Caterina 3; ⊘ noon-3pm & 7-9.30pm Tue-Sun;

⬢ Mazzorbo) ⬤. The LN *vaporetto* also stops at Mazzorbo.

Museo del Merletto   MUSEUM
(Lace Museum; ☑ 041 4273 0892; www.visitmuve.it; adult/reduced €5/3.50; ⊘ 10am-6pm Tue-Sun Apr-Oct, to 4.30pm Nov-Mar; ⬢ Burano) Burano's newly renovated Lace Museum tells the story of a craft that cut across social boundaries, endured for centuries and evoked the epitome of civilisation reached during the Republic's heyday. From the triple-petalled corollas on the fringes of the Madonna's mantle in Torcello's 12th-century mosaics to Queen Margherita's spider web–fine 20th-century mittens, lace-making was both the creative expression of female sensitivity and a highly lucrative craft.

Bringing it all to life, a group of local lacemakers sit tatting and gossiping beneath pictures of the Lace School (where many of them learnt their craft), which was located here from 1872 to 1970.

◉ Torcello

On the pastoral island of Torcello, a three-minute T-line ferry-hop from Burano, sheep outnumber the 14 or so human residents. This bucolic backwater was once a Byzantine metropolis of 20,000, but of its original nine churches and two abbeys, only the striking brick **Chiesa di Santa Fosca** (⊘ 10am-4.30pm; ⬢ Torcello) and splendid mosaic-filled Santa Maria Assunta remain.

Basilica di Santa Maria Assunta   CHURCH
(Piazza Torcello; adult/reduced €5/4, incl museum €8/6; ⊘ 10.30am-6pm Mar-Oct, 10am-5pm Nov-

Feb; 🛳 Torcello) Life choices are presented in no uncertain terms in Santa Maria Assunta's vivid cautionary tale: look ahead to a golden afterlife amid saints and a beatific Madonna, or turn your back on her to face the wrath of a devil gloating over lost souls. In existence for more than a millennium, this cathedral is the lagoon's oldest Byzantine-Romanesque monument.

The restrained brick exterior (c 824) betrays no hint of the colourful scene that unfolds as you enter. The Madonna rises in the east like the sun above a field of corn poppies in the 12th-century apse mosaic, while the back wall vividly depicts the dire consequences of dodging biblical commandments. This extraordinary **Last Judgment mosaic** shows the Adriatic as a sea nymph ushering souls lost at sea towards St Peter while a sneaky devil tips the scales of justice, and the Antichrist's minions drag sinners into a hell populated with bloated gluttons and greedy, bejewelled merchants.

 Activities

A gondola ride is anything but pedestrian, with glimpses into *palazzi* courtyards and hidden canals otherwise invisible on foot. Official daytime rates are €80 for 40 minutes (six passengers maximum), and it's €100 between 7pm and 8am, not including songs (negotiated separately) or tips. Additional time is charged in 20-minute increments (day/night €40/50). You may negotiate a price break in low season, overcast weather or around midday, when other travellers get hot and hungry. Agree on a price, time limit and singing in advance to avoid surcharges. Gondole cluster at *stazi* (stops) along the Grand Canal, at the train station (📞 041 71 85 43), the Rialto (📞 041 522 49 04) and near major monuments (eg I Frari, Ponte Sospiri and Accademia), but you can also book a pick-up at a canal near you (📞 041 528 50 75).

 Tours

From April to October, **APT** (www.turismovenezia.it) tourist offices offer guided tours ranging from the classic gondola circuit (€40 per person) to a penetrating look at Basilica di San Marco (€21 per person) and a four-hour circuit of Murano, Burano and Torcello (€20 per person).

Laguna Eco Adventures   SAILING TOUR
(📞 329 722 62 89; www.lagunaecoadventures.com; 2-8hr trips per person €40-150) Explore the far reaches of the lagoon by day or hidden Venetian canals by night in a traditional *sampierota*, a narrow twin-sailed boat. Reserve ahead and note that trips are subject to weather conditions.

★ **Row Venice**   ROWING
(📞 345 241 52 66; www.rowvenice.com; 2hr lessons 1-2 people €80, 4 people €120) The next best thing to walking on water: rowing a *sandolo* (Venetian boat) standing up like gondoliers do, with Australian-Venetian rowing coach Jane Caporal.

★ **Terra e Acqua**   BOAT
(📞 347 420 50 04; www.veneziainbarca.it; day-long trips incl lunch for 9-12 people €380-460) Spot rare lagoon wildlife, admire architectural gems of Burano and Torcello, and moor for a tasty fish-stew lunch, all via *bragosso* (Venetian barge).

Venice Day Trips   CULTURAL TOUR
(📞 049 60 06 72; www.venicedaytrips.com; Via Saetta 18, Padua; semiprivate/private tours per person €165/275) Off-the-shelf and customised tours, ranging from cooking classes in Cannaregio and shopping tours along the Brenta to cheese-making on Monte Veronese and tutored wine tastings in Valdobbiadene and Valpolicella. Pick-up for excursions outside Venice is from the Isola di Tronchetto *vaporetto* stop.

Venicescapes   WALKING TOUR
(📞 041 520 63 61; www.venicescapes.org; 4-6hr tour incl book 2 adults US$250-290, additional adult US$60, under 18yr US$30) Intriguing walking tours run by a nonprofit historical society (proceeds support ongoing Venetian historical research) with themes such as 'A City of Nations', exploring multiethnic Venice through the ages.

Walks Inside Venice   WALKING TOUR
(📞 041 524 17 06; www.walksinsidevenice.com; per hour €75, for groups up to 6 people; ♿) Spirited tours run by three local women lead groups on afternoon treks through the city's hidden backstreets via paintings that show the Venetian love of colour, following the path of the plague through Venice, or on a family-friendly circuit.

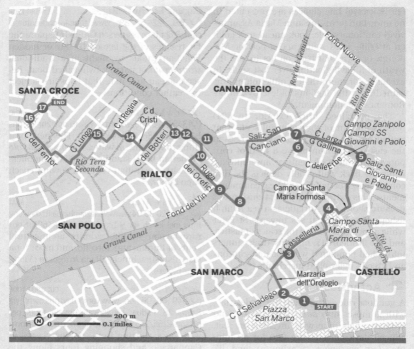

🏃 City Walk
Venice Labyrinth

START PIAZZA SAN MARCO
END CAMPO SAN GIACOMO DELL'ORIO
LENGTH 6KM/2 HOURS, EXCLUDING
LUNCH AND DRINKS

This adventure begins with the obligatory salute to ① **Basilica di San Marco** (p337). Duck under the ② **Torre dell'Orologio** (p342) and follow the *calle* veering right into ③ **Campo della Guerra**, where you'll hear Venetian gossip whispered over *spritz*. Pass over the bridge along Calle Casselleria into sunny ④ **Campo Santa Maria Formosa**. Straight ahead is Calle Santa Maria della Formosa; follow it to the left across two bridges to Salizada Santi Giovanni e Paolo, which leads left to the massive Gothic cathedral, ⑤ **Zanipolo** (p354).

Calle Larga Gallina leads over a bridge, after which turn left for a glimpse of heaven at Venice's small wonder, the marble-clad ⑥ **Chiesa di Santa Maria dei Miracoli** (p356). Backtrack over the bridge to browse through ⑦ **Campo Santa Maria Nova** to Salizada San Canciano, which you'll follow to

skinny ⑧ **Chiesa di San Bartolomeo**, lined with souvenir stalls. To the right is ⑨ **Ponte di Rialto**; stay on the right as you cross and duck towards happy-hour central, ⑩ **Campo Cesare Battisti**, and continue along the ⑪ **Grand Canal** to Venice's tastiest *campi*: produce-piled ⑫ **Campo Rialto Mercato** and the covered seafood market, ⑬ **Pescaria** (p367).

Turning left along Calle dei Botteri and then onto boutique-lined Calle di Cristi, you'll come to ⑭ **Campo San Cassian**, the site of the world's first public opera house. Cross the bridge to Calle della Regina, then head right to cross another bridge to sociable ⑮ **Chiesa di Santa Maria Mater Dominii**, with its cafes and ancient neighbourhood well. Turn left down Calle Lunga and over a bridge until it dead-ends, then jog left to Rio Tera Seconda and right again onto Calle del Tentor. Straight ahead, you'll see a medieval church, ⑯ **San Giacomo dell'Orio**, and your pick of Italy's best natural-process wines at ⑰ **Al Prosecco** (p374). *Cin-cin!*

Festivals & Events

Carnevale CARNIVAL
(www.carnevale.venezia.it) Masquerade madness stretches over two weeks in February before Lent. Tickets to La Fenice's masked balls start at €200, but there's a free-flowing wine fountain to commence Carnevale, public costume parties in every *campo*, and a Grand Canal flotilla marking the end of festivities.

La Biennale di Venezia CULTURE
(www.labiennale.org) In odd years the Art Biennale runs from June to October, while in even years the Architecture Biennale runs from September to November. The main venues are Giardini Pubblici pavilions and the Arsenale.

Festa del Redentore RELIGIOUS
(Feast of the Redeemer; www.turismovenezia.it) Walk across the Giudecca Canal to Il Redentore via a pontoon bridge on the third Saturday and Sunday in July, then watch the fireworks from the Zattere.

Venice International Film Festival FILM
(Mostra del Cinema di Venezia; www.labiennale.org/en/cinema) The only thing hotter than a Lido beach in August is the Film Festival's star-studded red carpet, usually rolled out from the last weekend in August through the first week of September.

Regata Storica BOAT RACE
(www.regatastoricavenezia.it) Never mind who's winning, just check out all the cool gear: 16th-century costumes, eight-oared gondolas and ceremonial barges feature in a historical procession (usually held in September), which re-enacts the arrival of the Queen of Cyprus.

Festa della Madonna della Salute CULTURE
(www.turismovenezia.it) If you'd survived a plague, you'd throw a party too. Every year since the 17th century, on 21 November Venetians cross a pontoon bridge across the Grand Canal to give thanks at Chiesa di Santa Maria della Salute.

Sleeping

The **APT tourist board** (www.turismovenezia.it) lists hundreds of B&Bs, *affittacamere* (rooms for rent) and apartments to rent in Venice proper. More can be found at **BB Planet** (www.bbplanet.it), www.guestinitaly.com and www.veniceapartment.com.

The best hotel rates are typically in November, early December, January and the period between Carnevale and Easter, but you might swing deals in July and August.

Piazza San Marco & Around

Giò & Giò B&B €
(Map p342; ☎347 366 50 16; www.giogiovenice.com; Calle delle Ostreghe 2439; d incl breakfast €90-150; ❄📶; ⛴Santa Maria del Giglio) Restrained baroque sounds like an oxymoron, but here you have it: burl-wood bedsteads, pearl grey silk draperies, polished parquet floors and spotlit art. Packaged breakfasts are available in the shared kitchen. Ideally located near Piazza San Marco along a side canal, next to the Gritti Palace; angle for rooms overlooking the gondola stop, and wake to choruses of '*Volare, oh-oh-oooooh*!'

Hotel Ai Do Mori HOTEL €
(Map p342; ☎041 520 48 17; www.hotelaidomori.com; Calle Larga San Marco 658; d €50-150; ❄📶; ⛴San Zaccaria) Artists' garrets just off Piazza San Marco, each snug as an Arsenale ship's cabin. Book ahead to score upper-floor rooms with sloped wood-beamed ceilings, parquet floors, wall tapestries and close-up views of basilica domes and the clock tower's Do Mori (bell-ringers) in action. Ask for No 11, with a private terrace – but pack light, because there's no lift.

Palazzo Paruta HOTEL €
(Map p342; ☎041 241 08 35; www.palazzoparuta.com; Campo Sant'Angelo 3824; d incl breakfast €90-320; ❄📶; ⛴Sant'Angelo) Kissing frogs won't get you princely palace surroundings like this: lantern-lit courtyard staircases beckon to silken boudoir bedrooms with mirrored bedsteads and Carrara marble en suite baths. Museum-worthy suites feature velvet-draped beds, stuccoed ceilings and parquet floors; ask for marble fireplaces and canal views. Breakfasts seduce gourmets with freshly squeezed juices, award-winning local cheeses and cured meats, fresh pastries, pancakes and eggs.

Hotel Flora HOTEL €
(Map p342; ☎041 520 58 44; www.hotelflora.it; Calle Bergamaschi 2283a; d incl breakfast €100-358; ❄📶👪; ⛴Santa Maria del Giglio) Down a lane from glitzy Calle Larga XXII Marzo, this ivy-covered retreat quietly outclasses brash designer neighbours with its delightful

GRITTI PALACE RESTORATION

Guests at the **Gritti Palace** (Map p342; ☎ 041 79 46 11; www.hotelgrittipalacevenice. com; Campo di Santa Maria del Giglio 2467; d €425-700, ste from €1100; ❄ ☎; ⛴ Santa Maria del Giglio) on the Grand Canal don't have to leave their balconies to go sightseeing: this landmark 1525 doge's palace reopened in 2013 after an extensive year-long restoration, from Rubelli silk damask lining top-floor suites to underfloor heating beneath terrazzo marble floors in the Gritti Epicurean School. Classic Venetian rooms have also been touched up gently, with restored antique fainting couches, stucco ceilings and bathrooms sheathed in rare marble. Rooms facing north and west lack Grand Canal views, but the level of luxury is consistent. Starwood manages operations, and chef Daniele Turco creates inspired Venetian trade-route cuisine for fabulous dockside meals.

tearoom, breakfasts around the garden fountain, and gym offering shiatsu massage. Guest rooms feature antique mirrors, fluffy duvets atop hand-carved beds, and tiled en suite baths with apothecary-style amenities; damask-clad superior rooms overlook the garden. Strollers and kids' teatime are complimentary; babysitting is available.

★ Novecento
BOUTIQUE HOTEL €€

(Map p342; ☎ 041 241 37 65; www.novecento. biz; Calle del Dose 2683/84; d €140-300; ❄ ☎; ⛴ Santa Maria del Giglio) World travellers put down roots in nine bohemian-chic rooms plush with Turkish kilim pillows, Fortuny draperies and 19th-century carved bedsteads piled with duvets. Linger over breakfasts in the garden under Indian parasols, go for a massage at sister property Hotel Flora, take a hotel-organised course in Venetian cooking or landscape drawing, or mingle with creative fellow travellers around the honesty bar.

🛏 Dorsoduro

B&B Dorsoduro 461
B&B €

(Map p338; ☎ 041 582 61 72; www.dorsoduro461. com; Rio Terà San Vio 461; d €70-120; ❄ ☎; ⛴ Accademia) Get to know Venice from the inside out at Sylvia and Francesco's home-style B&B, around the corner from Peggy Guggenheim's place. Your hosts' shared love of books, antique restoration and design is obvious in the bookshelf-lined breakfast room and three well-curated guestrooms, with Kartell lamps perched atop 19th-century poker tables. English-speaking violin-maker Francesco cooks tasty pancakes and dishes excellent Venice tips.

Hotel Galleria
INN €

(Map p342; ☎ 041 523 24 89; www.hotelgalleria.it; Campo della Carità 878a; d incl breakfast €110-220; ⛑; ⛴ Accademia) Smack on the Grand Canal alongside the Ponte dell'Accademia is this classic hotel in a converted 18th-century mansion. Book ahead, especially for rooms 7 and 9, small doubles overlooking the Grand Canal, and room 8, with Liberty furnishings and Grand Canal views. Most rooms share updated bathrooms; room 10 sleeps five, with an original frescoed ceiling and Grand Canal–facing windows.

★ Pensione Accademia Villa Maravege
INN €€

(Map p342; ☎ 041 521 01 88; www.pensioneaccademia.it; Fondamenta Bollani 1058; d €145-340; ❄ ☎ ⛑; ⛴ Accademia) Step through the ivy-covered gate of this 17th-century garden villa just off the Grand Canal, and you'll forget you're a block from the Accademia. All 27 guest rooms are recently restored and effortlessly elegant, with parquet floors, antique desks, creamy walls and snug, shiny modern bathrooms – some offer four-poster beds, wood-beamed ceilings and glimpses of the canal.

Pensione La Calcina
HOTEL €€

(Map p338; ☎ 041 520 64 66; www.lacalcina.com; Fondamenta Zattere ai Gesuati 780, Dorsoduro 780; s €90-170, d €110-310; ❄ ☎) An idyllic seaside getaway, this place has breakfasts on the roof terrace, an elegant canalside restaurant and 29 airy, parquet-floored guest rooms, several facing the Giudecca Canal and Palladio's Redentore church. Book ahead for rooms with en suites and/or views, especially room 2, where John Ruskin stayed while he wrote his classic (if inexplicably Palladio-bashing) 1876 *The Stones of Venice*.

Ca' Pisani
DESIGN HOTEL €€

(Map p342; ☎ 041 240 14 11; www.capisanihotel.it; Rio Terà Antonio Foscarini 979a; d €140-351; ❄ ☎; ⛴ Accademia) Sprawl out in style right behind the Accademia, and luxuriate in sleigh beds, jacuzzi tubs and walk-in closets. Mood lighting and soundproofed padded leather walls make downstairs deco rooms right for romance, while families appreciate top-floor rooms with sleeping lofts. Venetian winters require in-house Turkish steam baths, summers mean roof-terrace sunning, and patio breakfasts and wine-bar happy hours are ideal year-round.

🛏 San Polo & Santa Croce

Ca dei Polo
B&B €

(Map p338; ☑ 041 244 02 13; www.cadeipolo.com; Fondamenta dei Tolentini 203, Santa Croce; d incl breakfast €90-260; ☒ 🛜; 🚢 Piazzale Roma) A smart, stylish new option for quick getaways by car, bus or train – but breakfasts on the canalfront terrace and sunset toasts on the roof deck are valid reasons to linger. Custom Murano art-glass chandeliers grace sprawling suites and superior rooms like extraterrestrial lilies, and even smaller rooms have wood floors and design magworthy details, including bathrooms with excellent water pressure.

Ca' Angeli
BOUTIQUE HOTEL €

(Map p352; ☑ 041 523 24 80; www.caangeli.it; Calle del Traghetto de la Madonnetta 1434, San Polo; d incl breakfast €70-215; ☒ 🛜; 🚢 San Silvestro) Brothers Giorgio and Matteo inherited this Grand Canal palace and restored its Murano glass chandeliers, Louis XIV love seat and namesake 16th-century angels. Guest rooms feature beamed ceilings, antique carpets and big bathrooms; some have Grand Canal or secluded courtyard views. Hearty breakfasts are made with organic products and served on antique china in the dining room, overlooking the Grand Canal.

Pensione Guerrato
INN €€

(Map p352; ☑ 041 528 59 27; www.pensioneguerrato.it; Calle Drio la Scimia 240a, San Polo; d/tr/q incl breakfast €145/165/185; ☒ 🛜 📶; 🚢 Rialto Mercato) In a 1227 landmark that was once a hostel for knights headed for the Third Crusade, updated guest rooms haven't lost their sense of history – some have frescoes or glimpses of the Grand Canal. A prime Rialto Market location amid gourmet *bacari* (eateries) makes Pensione Guerrato the Holy Grail for visiting foodies, and newly restored apartments are equipped with kitchens. Wi-fi in lobby.

Domina Home Ca' Zusto
BOUTIQUE HOTEL €€

(Map p338; ☑ 051 639 18 01; www.dominavacanze.it; Campo Rielo 1358, Santa Croce; d incl breakfast €110-

210; ☒ 🛜 📶; 🚢 Riva di Biasio) Gothic goes pop at this palace, the stately Veneto-Byzantine exterior of which disguises a colourful wild streak. Designer Gianmarco Cavagnino winks at nearby Fondaco dei Turchi (Turkish trading house) and Fondazione Prada, with 22 mod-striped, harem-styled suites named after Turkish women. Pedestal tables flank baroque beds fit for pashas; amenities may include slippers, jacuzzis and iPod docks. Breakfast and wi-fi is in the '60s lounge.

★ Oltre il Giardino
BOUTIQUE HOTEL €€

(Map p352; ☑ 041 275 00 15; www.oltreilgiardino-venezia.com; Fondamenta Contarini, San Polo 2542; d incl breakfast €180-250; ☒ @ 📶; 🚢 San Tomà) Live the design-magazine dream in this garden villa brimming with historic charm and modern comforts: marquetry composer's desks and flat-screen TVs, candelabras and minibars, 19th-century poker chairs and babysitting services. Light fills six high-ceilinged bedrooms, and though sprawling Turquoise overlooks the canal and Green hides away in the walled garden, Grey has a sexy wrought-iron bedframe under a cathedral ceiling.

🛏 Cannaregio

★ Allo Squero
B&B €

(Map p352; ☑ 041 523 69 73; www.allosquero.it; Corte dello Squero 4692; d incl breakfast €80-130; 🛜 📶; 🚢 Fondamenta Nuove) Dock for the night at this historic gondola *squero* (shipyard), recently converted into a garden getaway. Gondolas passing along two canals are spotted from modern, sunny upstairs guest rooms, with terrazzo marble floors and sleek mosaic-striped ens uite baths, some with tubs. Hosts Andrea and Hiroko offer Venice-insider tips over cappuccino and pastry breakfasts in the fragrant, wisteria-filled garden. Cots and cribs available.

Ca' Pozzo
INN €

(Map p355; ☑ 041 524 05 04; www.capozzovenice.com; Sotoportego Ca' Pozzo 1279; d €90-190; ☒ @ 🛜; 🚢 Guglie) Recover from Venice's sensory onslaught at this minimalist-chic hotel near the Ghetto. Sleek contemporary guest rooms feature platform beds, abstract artwork and cube-shaped bathroom fixtures; some have balconies, two accommodate disabled guests, and sprawling 208 could house a Damien Hirst entourage. Laundry, concert-booking and ticket-printing services available; check the website for photography expeditions led by National Geographic photographers. Two-night minimum stay April to June.

★ Ca' Zanardi
BOUTIQUE HOTEL €€

(Map p338; ☑041 241 33 05; www.cazanardi.eu; Calle Zanardi 4132; d €130-300; ☎; ☒Madonna dell'Orto) Pristine 16th-century Venetian palace, international contemporary-art gallery, idyllic canalside garden: since Ca' Zanardi is all these things, calling it home for the weekend is a distinct privilege. Those thronelike chairs, tapestries and mercury-glass mirrors aren't decor but the original furnishings kept in the family over four centuries; drawing-room concerts and gala ballroom masquerades are still held here.

Domus Orsoni
B&B €€

(Map p355; ☑041 275 95 38; www.domusorsoni. it; Corte Vedei 1045; d incl breakfast €100-250; ✳@; ☒Guglie) Surprise: along a tranquil Ghetto lane and behind a rosy, historic facade is Venice's most original artists' retreat. Continental breakfasts are served in the palm-shaded garden near the Orsoni mosaic works, located here since 1885 – hence the custom mosaics glittering across walls, bathrooms and tables. Find artistic bliss in five guest rooms, or join Venetian crowds midtoast around the corner.

🛌 Castello

Foresteria Valdese
HOSTEL €

(Palazzo Cavagnis; Map p352; ☑041 528 67 97; www.foresteriavenezia.it; Castello 5170; dm €30-35, d €70-140, q €95-190; ☒; ☒Ospedale, San Zaccaria) Holy hostel: this rambling palace owned by the Waldensian church has 1st-

floor guest rooms with 18th-century frescoes by Bevilacqua, and one floor up guest rooms with canal views. Dorm beds are available only for families or groups; book well ahead. Rates include breakfast.

★ Palazzo Soderini
B&B €€

(Map p357; ☑041 296 08 23; www.palazzosoderini. it; Campo di Bandiera e Mori 3611; d incl breakfast €150-200; ✳☎; ☒Arsenale) Whether you're coming from cutting-edge art at the Biennale or baroque masterpieces at the Palazzo Ducale, this tranquil all-white B&B with a lily pond in the garden is a welcome reprieve from the visual onslaught of Venice. Minimalist decor emphasises spare shapes and clean lines, with steel-edged modern furniture and whitewashed walls. The three rooms have all the mod cons: TVs, wi-fi, minibars, air-con and heating. Book well ahead.

Palazzo Schiavoni
APARTHOTEL €€

(Map p357; ☑041 241 12 75; www.palazzoschiavoni. com; Fondamente dei Furlani 3288; d €155-263, 2-person apt €170-295, 4-person apt €210-380; ✳@☎☊; ☒San Zaccaria, Arsenale) Lie beneath your crown canopy and gaze at frescoed ceilings in this 18th-century *palazzo*. The impeccable refurbishment retains many period features while paying close attention to guest comforts. Rooms, reached via an elevator, are spacious and furnished with period reproductions, while apartments are kitted out with designer kitchens and generous living space. Perfect for families seeking a little *dolce vita* on a reasonable budget.

Aqua Palace
LUXURY HOTEL €€€

(Palazzo Scalfarotto; Map p352; ☑041 296 04 42; www.aquapalace.it; Calle de la Malvasia 5492; s €150-350, d €200-490; ✳@☎; ☒San Marco,

DON'T MISS

GOURMET CENTRAL: RIALTO DISTRICT

Rialto Market (Map p352; ☑041 296 06 58; ☉7am-2pm; ☒Rialto-Mercato) offers superb local produce next to the legendary **Pescaria** (Map p352; Rialto; ☉7am-2pm Tue-Sun; ☒Rialto), Venice's 600-year-old fish market. Nearby backstreets are lined with bakeries, *bacari* (bars) and two notable gourmet shops: **Aliani** (Map p352; ☑041 522 49 13; Ruga Vecchia di San Giovanni, San Polo 654; ☉8.30am-1pm & 5-7.30pm Tue-Sat; ☒Rialto Mercato), with cheeses, cured meats and gourmet specialities from balsamic vinegar aged 40 years to *bottarga* (dried fish-roe paste); and **Drogheria Mascari** (Map p352; ☑041 522 97 62; www.imascari.com; Ruga degli Spezieri 381, San Polo; ☉8am-1pm & 4-7.30pm Mon, Tue & Thu-Sat, 8am-1pm Wed; ☒Rialto), an emporium lined with copper-topped jars, spices and truffles galore, plus an entire back room of speciality Italian wines. For organic edibles and sustainably produced wines, visit **Rialto Biocenter** (Map p352; ☑041 523 95 15; www.rialtobiocenter.it; Calle della Regina, Santa Croce 2264; ☉8.30am-1pm & 4.30-8pm Mon-Thu, 8.30am-8pm Fri & Sat; ☒San Stae).

★ **Alaska** (Map p338; ☎ 041 71 52 11; Calle Larga dei Bari 1159, Santa Croce; gelati €1-2; ⏰ noon-8pm; ⚙; 🛥 Riva de Biasio) 🍃 Outlandish organic gelato, including house-roasted local pistachio and vaguely minty *carciofi* (artichoke).

Gelateria Suso (Map p352; ☎ 348 564 65 45; Calle della Bissa 5453; gelati €2-5; ⏰ 10am-10pm; ⚙; 🛥 Rialto) 🍃 Locally made and extra creamy with an ostentatiously rich 'Doge' gelato: fig sauce and walnuts swirled into mascarpone cream.

Grom (Map p348; ☎ 041 099 17 51; www.grom.it; Campo San Barnaba 2461; gelati €2.50-4; ⏰ 11am-midnight Sun-Thu, to 1am Fri & Sat; ⚙; 🛥 Ca' Rezzonico) Slow Food ingredients from across Italy (lemon from the Amalfi Coast and strawberries from Sicily), plus Fair Trade–certified chocolate and coffee.

San Zaccaria) With its exotic, spice-route vibe and burnished colour palate of gold, bronze and old grey, the Aqua Palace is a heady mixture of modern amenities and Eastern romance. Suites 'interpret' the distant past of Marco Polo, and with only 25 of them you can expect aristocratic proportions, acres of weighty fabric and bathrooms marbled within an inch of their lives. Complete with its own private gondola pier, this is the hotel for lovebirds.

🛏 Giudecca

Ostello Venezia   HOSTEL €
(Map p338; ☎ 041 523 82 11; www.ostellovenezia.it; Fondamenta delle Zitelle 86, Giudecca; dm €21-33, s €39-60, d €65-95; ✳ @ 🛜; 🛥 Zitelle) After a swish new refurbishment by Generator Venice in 2012, Giudecca's hostel rocks a sharp, contemporary interior including a fabulous new bar-restaurant. To claim that perfect bunk by the window, you'll need to arrive promptly at the 3.30pm opening. Sheets, blanket and a pillow are provided in the bunk price; the buffet breakfast is an extra €3.50.

Check-in is from 3.30pm to 10pm; check-out is at 9.30am. There's no curfew. Reserve ahead for one of two viewless private rooms.

Al Redentore di Venezia   APARTMENTS €
(Map p338; ☎ 041 522 94 02; www.alredentoredivenezia.com; Fondamenta Ponte Lungo 234a, Giudecca; 2-person apt €70-190, 4-person apt €205-270; ✳ 🛜 ⚙; 🛥 Redentore) Within the shadow of Il Redentore, these fully serviced apartments offer divine views across the water to San Marco at less than half the price of the Bauer a few doors down. But don't think they've skimped on the details: from the travertine-marble lobby, up the ash-clad staircase to the anallergic pillows and

high-end, courtesy bath products, Al Redentore has thought of it all.

🍴 Eating

Venice's cosmopolitan outlook makes local cuisine anything but predictable. Don't be surprised if some Venetian dishes taste vaguely Turkish or Greek rather than strictly Italian, reflecting Venice's preferred trading partners for over a millennium. Spice-route flavours from the Mediterranean and beyond can be savoured in signature Venetian recipes such as *sarde in saor*, traditionally made with sardines in a tangy onion marinade with pine nuts and sultanas.

🍴 Piazza San Marco & Around

Bacaro Da Fiore   CICHETI BAR, VENETIAN €
(Map p342; ☎ 041 523 53 10; www.dafiore.it; Calle delle Botteghe 3461; meals €10-15; ⏰ 5.30-9pm Wed-Mon; 🛥 San Samuele) Attached to a posh trattoria, this *cicheti* (Venetian tapas) counter wins Venetian loyalty with small plates of *baccala mantecato* (creamed cod), octopus-fennel salad, *arancini* (risotto balls), and Venetian *trippa* (tripe) to enjoy on a stool at the bar or in the *calle*. Even with gorgeous Denominazione di Origine Controllata (DOC; a type of trademark for a product from a specific region) Soave by the glass, meals cost a fraction of what you'd pay for table seating.

Enoteca al Volto   VENETIAN, CICHETI BAR €
(Map p342; ☎ 041 522 89 45; Calle Cavalli 4081; cicheti €2-4, meals under €25; ⏰ 10am-3pm & 5.30-10pm Mon-Sat; 🛥 Rialto) Join the bar crowd working its way through the vast selection of wine and *cicheti*, or come early for a table outdoors (in summer). Inside the snug backroom

CICHETI: VENICE'S BEST MEAL DEALS
....

Even in unpretentious Venetian *osterie* (casual taverns), most dishes cost a couple of euros more than elsewhere in Italy – not a bad mark-up, given fresh seafood and local produce is brought in by boat. But *cicheti,* Venetian bar snacks, are some of the best foodie finds in the country, served at the bar in Venetian *osterie* at lunch and about 6pm to 8pm. *Cicheti* range from basic €1 to €2 bar snacks (spicy meatballs, fresh tomato bruschetta) to wildly inventive small plates for €2 to €5: think white Bassano asparagus and plump lagoon shrimp wrapped in pancetta at All'Arco fennel and octopus salad fresh from the Pescaria at ProntoPesce; crostini (open-face sandwiches) piled with *sopressa* (soft local salami) with marinated radicchio at Dai Zemei. Many *bacari* (bar/ eateries) and *enoteche* (wine bars) also offer nightly *cicheti* spreads that could easily pass as dinner.

that looks like a ship's hold, tuck into seaworthy bowls of pasta with *bottarga* (dried fish roe), steak drizzled with aged balsamic vinegar, and housemade ravioli. Cash only.

Osteria da Carla
OSTERIA, CICHETI BAR €
(Map p342; ☑ 041 523 78 55; Frezzaria 1535; meals €20-25; ◉10am-9pm Mon-Sat; ⊛Vallaresso) Diners in the know duck into this hidden courtyard to feast on handmade ravioli with poppyseed, pear and sheep's cheese for the price of hot chocolate in Piazza San Marco. Expect a wait at lunch and happy hour, when *gondolieri* abandon ship for DOC Soave and *sopressa crostini* (soft salami on toast).

★ A Beccafico
ITALIAN €€
(Map p342; ☑ 041 527 48 79; www.abeccafico.com; Campo Santo Stefano 2801; meals €25-45; ◉noon-3pm & 7-11pm; ⊛Accademia) Far from clubby pubs lining Venice's alleyways, A Beccafico basks in the sunshine of Campo Santo Stefano and open Venetian admiration. Instead of cold seafood on toast, chef Adeli serves Sicily-size bowls of mussels under a bubbling, flaky crust. He defies Venice's cardinal rule never to mix lagoon seafood with cheese, serving squid-ink pasta with lemon zest and ricotta. Linger over feather-light

Pieoropan Soave Classico, and leave with a surprisingly full belly – and wallet.

✕ Dorsoduro

Impronta Café
ITALIAN €
(Map p338; ☑ 041 275 03 86; Calle Crosera 3815; meals €8-15; ◉7am-2am Mon-Sat; ⚐; ⊛San Tomá) Join Venice's value-minded jet set for *prosecco* and bargain polenta-salami combos, surrounded by witty architectural diagrams of cooking pots. When other restaurants close, Impronta stays open to accommodate late lunches, teatime with a wide tea selection, and midnight snacks of club sandwiches – yet somehow, the staff remains chipper and the bathroom spotless.

Pane Vino e San Daniele
ITALIAN €
(Map p348; ☑ 041 243 98 65; www.panevinovenice. com; Calle Lunga San Barnaba 2861; meals €15-30; ◉10am-2pm Tue-Sun; ⊛Ca' Rezzonico) Artists can't claim they're starving any more after a meal in this wood-beamed trattoria, a favourite of art students and professors alike. Settle in to generous plates of gnocchi laced with truffle cheese, Veneto game such as roast rabbit and duck, lavish appetisers featuring the namesake San Daniele cured ham, and Friulian house wines made by the Fantinel family owners.

Ristorante La Bitta
RISTORANTE €€
(Map p348; ☑ 041 523 05 31; Calle Lunga San Barnaba 2753a; meals €30-40; ◉dinner Mon-Sat; ⊛Ca' Rezzonico) The daily menu arrives on an artist's easel, and the hearty rustic fare looks like a still life and tastes like a carnivore's dream: steak comes snugly wrapped in bacon, and roast rabbit tops marinated rocket. This bistro focuses on local meats – *'bitta'* means 'mooring post' – and seats only 35. Reservations essential; cash only.

Do Farai
SEAFOOD, VENETIAN €€
(Map p348; ☑ 041 277 03 69; Calle del Cappeller 3278; meals €25-35; ◉11am-3pm & 7-10pm Mon-Sat; ⊛Ca' Rezzonico) Venetian regulars pack this hidden wood-panelled room hung with football-championship scarves and fragrant with mouthwatering seafood: pasta with shellfish and sweet prawns; herb-laced, grilled *orata* (bream); and Venetian *tris di saor sarde, scampi e sogliole* (sardines, prawns and sole in tangy Venetian *saor* marinade). Service is leisurely; bide your time with a Negroni *aperitivo*, or postprandial *sgropin* (*prosecco*-lemon sorbet).

Enoteca Ai Artisti
RISTORANTE €€€

(Map p348; ☑ 041 523 89 44; www.enotecaartisti. com; Fondamenta della Toletta 1169a; meals €40-50; ⊘ noon-4pm & 6.30-10pm Mon-Sat; ☻ Ca' Rezzonico) Indulgent cheeses, exceptional *nero di seppia* (cuttlefish ink) pasta, and tender *tagliata* (sliced steak) drizzled with aged balsamic vinegar atop rocket are paired with exceptional wines by the glass by your oenophile hosts. Sidewalk tables for two make great people-watching.

✕ San Polo & Santa Croce

★ All'Arco
VENETIAN €

(Map p352; ☑ 041 520 56 66; Calle dell'Ochialer 436; cicheti €1.50-4; ⊘ 8am-3.30pm Mon-Sat Sep-Jun, plus 6-9pm Mon-Sat Apr-Oct; ☻ Rialto-Mercato) Father-son maestri Francesco and Matteo invent Venice's best *cicheti* daily with Rialto Market finds. Behind marble counters, Francesco wraps poached Bassano white asparagus with seasoned pancetta, while Matteo creates *otrega* (butterfish) *crudo* with mint–olive oil marinade and Hawaiian red-clay salt.

ProntoPesce
SEAFOOD, CICHETI €

(Map p352; ☑ 041 822 02 98; www.prontopesce. it; Rialto Pescheria 319, San Polo; cicheti €3-8; ⊘ 9am-2.45pm & 7-11.30pm Tue-Sat; ☻ Rialto-Mercato) Alongside Venice's fish market, this designer deli serves artfully composed *crudi* (Venetian-style sushi), well-dressed seafood salads, legendary Saturday-only fish risotto (served at 1pm exactly) and superb shellfish stews in winter. Grab a stool and a (unfortunately) plastic glass of DOC Soave to have with *folpetti* (baby octopus) salad and plump prawn *crudi*, or enjoy yours dockside along the Grand Canal.

Dai Zemei
VENETIAN, CICHETI €

(Map p352; ☑ 041 520 85 46; www.ostariadaizemei. it; Ruga Vecchia San Giovanni 1045, San Polo; cicheti €1.50-4; ⊘ 9am-8pm Wed-Mon; ☻ San Silvestro) The *zemei* (twins) who run this closet-sized *cicheti* counter serve loyal regulars and well-informed foodie tourists small meals with outsized imagination: octopus salad and marinated rocket, duck breast drizzled with truffle oil, or crostini loaded up with tuna-leek salad.

★ Antiche Carampane
VENETIAN €€

(Map p352; ☑ 041 524 01 65; www.antichecarampane.com; Rio Terà delle Carampane 1911, San Polo; meals €30-45; ⊘ noon-2.30pm & 7-11pm Tue-Sat;

☻ San Stae) Hidden in the once-shady lanes behind Ponte delle Tette, this culinary indulgence is a trick to find. The sign proudly announcing 'no tourist menu' signals a welcome change: say goodbye to soggy lasagne and hello to silky, lagoon-fresh *crudi*, asparagus and *granseola* (lagoon crab) salad, cloudlike gnocchi, and San Pietro (whitefish) atop grilled *radicchio trevisano*.

Osteria La Zucca
MODERN ITALIAN €€

(Map p352; ☑ 041 524 15 70; www.lazucca.it; Calle del Tentor 1762, Santa Croce; meals €30-45; ⊘ 12.30-2.30pm & 7-10.30pm Mon-Sat; ☑; ☻ San Stae) Vegetable-centric, seasonal small plates bring Venetian spice-trade influences to local produce: zucchini with ginger zing, cinnamon-tinged pumpkin flan, and raspberry spice cake. Herbed roast lamb is respectable here too, but the island-grown produce is the breakout star. The snug wood-panelled interior gets toasty, so reserve canalside seats in summer.

Al Pesador
MODERN ITALIAN €€€

(Map p352; ☑ 041 523 94 92; www.alpesador. it; Campo San Giacometto 125, San Polo; cicheti €1.50-5, meals €40-55; ⊘ noon-3pm & 7-11pm Mon-Sat; ☻ Rialto-Mercato) Watch the world drift down the Grand Canal outside or canoodle indoors, but prepare to sit up and pay attention once the food arrives. Pesador reinvents Venetian cuisine with culinary finesse: *cicheti* feature mackerel with balsamic-vinegar *saor* marinade and paper-thin *lardo* crostini with mint oil, while *primi* (mains) include red-footed scallops kicking wild herbs across squid-ink gnocchi.

✕ Cannaregio

Dalla Marisa
VENETIAN €

(Map p338; ☑ 041 72 02 11; Fondamenta di San Giobbe 652b; set menus €15-35; ⊘ noon-3pm & 7-11pm Tue & Thu-Sat, noon-3pm Mon & Wed; ☻ Crea) At Dalla Marisa, you'll be seated where there's room and get no menu – you'll have whatever Marisa's cooking, but you'll be informed that the menu is meat- or fish-based when you book, and house wine is included in the price. Venetian regulars confess Marisa's *fegato alla veneziana* (Venetian calf's liver) is better than their grandmothers', while fish nights bring hauls of lagoon seafood grilled, fried and perched atop pasta and rocket.

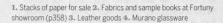

1. Stacks of paper for sale 2. Fabrics and sample books at Fortuny showroom (p358) 3. Leather goods 4. Murano glassware

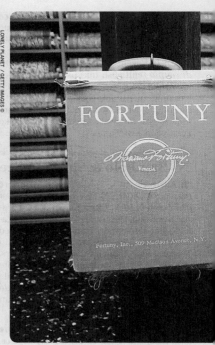

Venice for Shoppers

In Venice, shopping is really an educational experience. To find unique pieces, just wander the key artisan areas: San Polo around Calle dei Saoneri; Santa Croce around Calle Lunga and Calle del Tentor; San Marco along Frezzeria; Dorsoduro around the Peggy Guggenheim; and Murano.

Glass

Venetians have been working in crystal and glass since the 10th century. Trade secrets were so closely guarded that any glass worker who left the city was considered guilty of treason. To learn more head to the Museo del Vetro (p359).

Today, along Murano's Fondamenta dei Vetrai, centuries of tradition are upheld by Davide Penso, Nason Moretti, and Marina and Susanna Sent.

Paper

Embossing and marbling began in the 14th century as part of Venice's burgeoning publishing industry, but these bookbinding techniques and *ebru* (Turkish marbled paper) endpapers have taken on lives of their own. You can still watch a Heidelberg press in action at Veneziastampa (p377).

Textiles

Venetian lace was a fashion must for centuries, as Burano's Lace Museum (p360) attests. But the modern master of Venetian textiles is Fortuny, whose showroom on Giudecca features fabrics created using top-secret techniques.

TOP FIVE NON-TOURISTY SOUVENIRS

➡ **Pied à Terre** (p377) – *furlane* (gondolier shoes)

➡ **Veneziastampa** (p377) – calling cards with your own signature symbol

➡ **Cárte** (p376) – marbled-paper cocktail rings

➡ **Chiarastella Cattana** (p376) – strikingly original Venetian linens

Ai Promessi Sposi
VENETIAN €€

(Map p352; ☑ 041 241 27 47; Calle d'Oca 4367; meals €25-35; ⊙11.30am-3pm & 6-11pm Thu-Sun & Tue, 6-11pm Mon & Wed; ⛴Ca' d'Oro) Bantering Venetians thronging the bar are the only permanent fixtures at this newly revived neighbourhood *osteria*, where handwritten menus created daily feature fresh Venetian seafood and Veneto meats at excellent prices. Seasonal standouts include *seppie in umido* (cuttlefish in rich tomato sauce) and housemade tagliatelle with *anatra* (wild duck).

★ Anice Stellato
VENETIAN €€€

(Map p355; ☑ 041 72 07 44; Fondamenta della Sensa 3272; mains €18-23; ⊙noon-2pm & 7.30-11pm Wed-Sun; ⛴Madonna dell'Orto) 🖋 If finding this obscure corner of Cannaregio seems like an adventure, wait until dinner arrives: pistachio-encrusted lamb chops, succulent house-made prawn ravioli and lightly fried *moeche* (soft-shell crab) gobbled whole. Tin lamps and recycled paper place mats on communal tables keep the focus on local food and local company – all memorable. Book ahead.

Osteria Boccadoro
VENETIAN €€€

(Map p352; ☑ 041 521 10 21; www.boccadorovenezia.it; Campiello Widmann 5405a; meals €40-55; ⊙noon-3pm & 7-10pm Tue-Sun; ⛴Fondamenta Nuove) Birds sweetly singing in this *campo* are probably angling for your leftovers, but they don't stand a chance. Chef-owner Luciano's creative *crudi* are two-bite delights – tuna with blood orange, sweet prawn atop tart green apple – and fluffy gnocchi topped with spider crab are gone entirely too soon.

✖ Castello

Pasticceria Da Bonifacio
PASTRIES & CAKES €

(Map p338; ☑ 041 522 75 07; Calle degli Albanesi 4237; pastries €1.50-4; ⊙7am-8pm Fri-Wed; ⛴San Zaccaria) Pastry awards line the wall in this tiny bakery where gondoliers and Venetian housewives flock to devour the buttery, just-baked sweetness of almond croissants and take home boxes of Venetian specialities such as *zaletti* (cornmeal biscuits with sultanas). As afternoon wanes, the bakery turns into a makeshift bar as locals pop in for *spritz* and *mammalucchi* (deep-fried balls with candied fruit).

★ Osteria alla Staffa
MODERN VENETIAN €€

(Map p338; ☑ 041 523 91 60; Calle dell'Ospedale 6397a; meals €20-35; ⊙11.30am-3pm & 6-11pm; ⛴Ospedale) With fish fresh from the Rialto every morning and a preference for organic veg and cheese, Alberto's takes on Venetian classics have flavourful foundations. But this is home cooking with a twist: the seafood selection looks like a modernist masterpiece with its creamy, coiffed *baccalà* (cod) bedded on a rich, red radicchio leaf and baby octopus set like lagoon flowers against a splash of apricot salmon.

Trattoria Corte Sconta
MODERN VENETIAN €€€

(Map p357; ☑ 041 522 70 24; Calle del Pestrin 3886; meals €50-65; ⊙12.30-2.30pm & 7-9.30pm Tue-Sat, closed Jan & Aug; ⛴Arsenale) Well-informed visitors and celebrating locals seek out this vine-covered *corte sconta* (hidden courtyard) for its trademark seafood antipasti and imaginative house-made pasta. Inventive flavour pairings transform the classics: clams zing with the hot, citruslike taste of ginger; prawn and courgette linguine is recast with an earthy dash of saffron; and the roast eel loops like the Brenta river in a drizzle of balsamic reduction.

Al Covo
VENETIAN €€€

(Map p357; ☑ 041 522 38 12; www.ristorantealcovo.com; Campiello della Pescaria 3968; meals €55-80; ⊙12.45-2pm & 7.30-10pm Fri-Tue; ⛴Arsenale) For years Diane Rankin and Cesare Benelli have dedicated themselves to the preservation of heritage products and lagoon recipes, which has placed them firmly on the gourmet map. Only the freshest seasonal fish gets the Covo treatment, accompanied by artichokes, aubergines, *cipollini* onions and mushrooms from the lagoon larders of Sant'Erasmus, Vignole, Treporti and Cavallino.

✖ Giudecca

★ I Figli delle Stelle
ITALIAN €€

(Map p338; ☑ 041 523 00 04; www.ifiglidellestelle.it; Zitelle 70; meals €30-40; ⊙12.30-2.30pm & 7-10pm Tue-Sun, closed mid-Nov–mid-Mar; ⛴Zitelle) Beware of declarations of love at one of Venice's most romantic restaurants: are you sure that's not Pugliese chef Luigi's velvety pasta and soup talking? A creamy fava-bean mash with biting chicory and fresh tomatoes coats the tongue in a naughty way, and the mixed grill for two with langoustine, sole and fresh sardines is quite a catch.

La Palanca VENETIAN €€

(Map p338; ☑ 041 528 77 19; Fondamenta al Ponte Piccolo 448; meals €20-30; ⏱ 8am-8.30pm Mon-Sat; ☷ Palanca) Lunchtime competition for canalside tables is stiff, but the views of the Zattere make *tagliolini ai calamaretti* (narrow ribbon pasta with tiny calamari) and tuna steak with balsamic vinegar taste even better. At €7 to €9 for plates of pasta, you'll be forking out half what diners pay along the waterfront in San Marco. Dinner is not served, but you can get *cicheti* at the bar.

✕ The Lido

★ Le Garzette FARMSTAY €€

(☑ 041 712 16 53; www.legarzette.it; Lungomare Alberoni 32, Lido; meals €35-45; ⏱ 12.30-2.30pm & 7-10.30pm mid-Jan–mid-Dec; ⊞; ☷ Lido) ✎ Nestled amid gardens overflowing with red radicchio, astringent fennel and dark-green courgettes is the rust-red *agriturismo* (farm-stay accommodation) of Renza and Salvatore. Choose between a meat or a fish menu and wait for the parade of organic dishes: crepes filled with juicy asparagus, lightly fried Malamocco artichokes and mouthwatering pear tart made with farm eggs.

La Favorita SEAFOOD €€

(☑ 041 526 16 26; Via Francesco Duodo 33; meals €35-50; ⏱ 12.30-2.30pm & 7.30-10.30pm Wed-Sun, 7.30-10.30pm Tue, closed Jan–mid-Feb; ☷ Lido) For long, lazy lunches, bottles of fine wine and impeccable service, look no further than La Favorita. The menu is as elegant as the surroundings, giant *rhombo* (turbot) simmered with capers and olives, spider-crab *gnochetti* (mini-gnocchi) and classic fish risotto. Book ahead for the wisteria-filled garden and well ahead during the film festival, when songbirds are practically outsung by the ringtones of movie moguls.

🍷 Drinking & Nightlife

The usual 'rules' don't seem to apply to drinking in Venice. Don't mix spirits and wine? Venice's classic cocktails suggest otherwise; try a *spritz*, made with *prosecco*, soda water and bittersweet Aperol or bitter Campari. No girly drinks? Tell that to burly boat-builders enjoying frothy *prosecco*.

🍷 Piazza San Marco & Around

★ I Rusteghi WINE BAR

(Map p352; ☑ 041 523 22 05; www.osteriairusteghi. com; Corte del Tentor 5513; mini-panini €2-5; ⏱ 10.30am-3pm & 6-11.30pm Mon-Sat; ☷ Rialto) Honouring centuries of Venetian *enoteca* (wine bar) tradition, fourth-generation sommelier Giovanni d'Este will open any bottle on his shelves to pour you an *ombra* (half-glass of wine) – including collector's wines such as Cannubi Barolo. Request *'qualcosa di particolare'* (something exceptional) and Giovanni will reward you with a sensual Ribolla Gialla to pair with truffle-cheese mini-panini and platters of Spanish and Veneto ham.

Harry's Bar BAR

(Map p342; ☑ 041 528 57 77; Calle Vallaresso 1323; cocktails €12-22; ⏱ 10.30am-11pm; ☷ San Marco) Aspiring auteurs hold court at bistro tables well scuffed by Ernest Hemingway, Charlie Chaplin, Truman Capote and Orson Welles, enjoying the signature €16.50 bellini (Giuseppe Cipriani's original 1948 recipe: white-peach juice and *prosecco*) with a side of reflected glory. Upstairs is one of Italy's most unaccountably expensive restaurants – stick to the bar to save finances for your breakthrough film.

Torino@Notte BAR

(Map p342; ☑ 041 522 39 14; Campo San Luca 4592; ⏱ 7pm-1am Tue-Sat; ☷ Rialto) Free-form, eclectic and loud, Torino adds an element of the unexpected to otherwise staid San Marco. By day it's a cafe, but after 7pm locals roll in for €2 to €5 drinks and marathon DJ sessions

VENICE & THE VENETO VENICE

PUB CRAWL, WITH FRIENDS

Why drink alone? To help visitors navigate Venice's vast *cicheti* (bar snacks) menu and confusing backstreets, **Venice Urban Adventures** (www.urbanadventures.com; cicheti tours €52) offers intimate tours of happy-hour hot spots led by knowledgable, enthusiastic, English-speaking local foodies. Tours run €52 per person (with up to 12 participants), covering *ombre* (wine by the glass) and *cicheti* in five (yes, five) *bacari* and a tipsy Rialto gondola ride. Departure points vary seasonally; consult website.

of vintage reggae and soul on vinyl. Stop by Friday and Saturday after 9pm for a late bite or nightcap with live jazz, blues or rock.

🍷 Dorsoduro

★ Cantinone Già Schiavi
BAR

(Map p342; ☑ 041 523 95 77; Fondamenta Nani 992; ⊗ 8.30am-8.30pm Mon-Sat; ⛴ Zattere) Regulars gamely pass along orders to timid newcomers, who might otherwise miss out on tuna-leek *cicheti* with top-notch house Soave, or *pallottoline* (minibottles of beer) with generous *sopressa* (soft salami) *panini*. Chaos cheerfully prevails at this legendary canal-side spot, where Accademia art historians rub shoulders with San Trovaso gondola builders without spilling a drop.

Osteria alla Bifora
BAR

(Map p348; ☑ 041 523 61 19; Campo Santa Margherita 2930; ⊗ noon-3pm & 6pm-1am Wed-Mon; ⛴ Ca' Rezzonico) Other bars around this *campo* cater to *spritz*-pounding students, but this chandelier-lit medieval wine cave sets the scene for gentle flirting over big-hearted Veneto mer-

---

HISTORIC CAFES

In prime tourist zones, the price of coffee at a table seems more like rent, so take your coffee standing or splash out for architecturally splendid cafes in the Museo Correr, Palazzo Querini Stampalia or Piazza San Marco.

Historic baroque cafes around Piazza San Marco, such as **Caffé Florian** (Map p342; ☑ 041 520 56 41; www.caffeflorian.com; Piazza San Marco 56/59; drinks €6.50-16; ⊗ 10am-midnight Thu-Tue; ⛴ San Marco) and **Caffé Quadri** (Map p342; ☑ 041 522 21 05; www.alajmo.it; Piazza San Marco 120; drinks €6-25; ⊗ 9am-11.30pm; ⛴ San Marco), serve coffee and hot chocolate with live orchestras – though your heart might beat a different rhythm once you get the bill, with orchestra surcharge. Hint: **Caffe Lavena** (Map p342; ☑ 041 522 40 70; www.lavena.it; Piazza San Marco 133/4; drinks €1-12; ⊗ 9.30am-11pm; ⛴ San Marco) offers a €1 espresso at the counter. But this is Venice, and decadence is always in order – might as well order *caffe correto* (espresso 'corrected' with liquor), and tango with a stranger.

---

lot. Cured-meat platters are carved to order on that Ferrari-red meat slicer behind the bar, there are place mats to doodle on and new-found friends aplenty at communal tables.

Il Caffè Rosso
CAFE, BAR

(Map p348; ☑ 041 528 79 98; Campo Santa Margherita 2963; ⊗ 7am-1am Mon-Sat; ⛴ Ca' Rezzonico) Sunny piazza seating speeds recovery from last night's revelry, with espresso that opens eyes like a pull cord on venetian blinds – until the cycle begins again at 6pm, with standing-room-only happy-hour crowds. Locals affectionately call this red shopfront *'al rosso'*, and its inexpensive *spritz* generously splashed with scarlet Aperol gives visitors and locals alike an instant flush of Venetian colour.

🍷 San Polo & Santa Croce

★ Al Prosecco
WINE BAR

(Map p352; ☑ 041 524 02 22; www.alprosecco.com; Campo San Giacomo dell'Orio, Santa Croce 1503; ⊗ 9am-10.30pm Mon-Sat, to 8pm winter; ⛴ San Stae) ✐ The urge to toast sunsets in Venice's loveliest *campo* is only natural – and so is the wine at Al Prosecco. This forward-thinking bar specialises in *vini naturi* (natural-process wines) – organic, biodynamic, wild yeast fermented – from the €3.50 unfiltered 'cloudy' *prosecco* to the silky €5 Veneto Venegazzú that trails across the tongue and lingers in the imagination.

Al Mercà
WINE BAR

(Map p352; ☑ 393 992 47 81; Campo Cesare Battisti 213, San Polo; ⊗ 9.30am-2.30pm & 6-9pm Mon-Sat; ⛴ Rialto) Discerning drinkers throng this cupboard-sized bar crammed with *cicheti* and 60 different wines, including top-notch *prosecco* and DOC wines by the glass (€2 to €3.50). Arrive by 6.30pm for meatballs and mini-*panini* (€1 to €2) and easy bar access, or mingle with crowds stretching to the Grand Canal docks – there's no seating, and it's elbow room only at Venice's friendliest bar counter.

Cantina Do Spade
PUB

(Map p352; ☑ 041 521 05 83; www.cantinadospade.it; Calle delle Do Spade 860, San Polo; ⊗ 10am-3pm & 6-10pm; ⛴ Rialto) Since 1488 this bar has kept Venice in good spirits, and the laid-back young management extends warm welcomes to *spritz*-sipping Venetian regulars and visiting connoisseurs drinking double-malt Dolomite beer and bargain Venetian

LA SERRA DEI GIARDINI

Order the signature pear bellini and sit back amid the hothouse flowers in Napoleon's 1894 greenhouse. Originally intended to house the palms used in Biennale events, it rapidly expanded into a community hub and a centre for propagation: many plants grown here went to adorn the municipal flowerbeds of the Lido and the ballrooms of aristocratic *palazzi* (mansions). Restored in 2010 by the Nonsoloverde social co-operative, **La Serra** (Serra dei Giardini; Map p338; ☎ 041 296 03 60; www.serradeigiardini.org; Viale Giuseppe Garibaldi 1254; snacks €4-15; ☺ 11am-8pm Tue-Fri, 10am-9pm Sat & Sun; ☎ ⓘ; ⓖ Giardini) now hosts events and workshops from gardening and paper-making to yoga and tango classes.

Downstairs, light snacks and cakes are available in the cafe alongside unique microbrews, herbal tisanes and Lurisia sodas flavoured with Slow Food Presidia products.

DOC cab franc. Come early for market-fresh *fritture* (batter-fried seafood; €2 to €6) and stick around for local gossip (free).

Cannaregio

★ **Al Timon**   WINE BAR
(Map p355; ☎ 041 524 60 66; Fondamenta degli Ormesini 2754; ☺ 11am-1am Thu-Tue, 6pm-1am Wed; ⓖ Guglie) Find a spot on the boat moored out front along the canal and watch the motley parade of drinkers and dreamers arrive for seafood crostini and quality organic and DOC wines by the *ombra* or carafe. Folk singers play sets canalside when the weather obliges; when it's cold, regulars scoot over to make room for newcomers at indoor tables.

Agli Ormesini   PUB
(Da Aldo; Map p355; ☎ 041 71 58 34; Fondamenta degli Ormesini 2710; ☺ 8pm-1am Mon-Sat; ⓖ Madonna dell'Orto) While the rest of Venice is awash in wine, Ormesini offers more than 100 brews, including reasonably priced bottles of speciality craft ales and local Birra Venezia. The cheery, beery scene often spills into the street – but keep it down, or the neighbours will get testy.

Castello

Bar Terazza Danieli   BAR
(Map p338; ☎ 041 522 64 80; www.starwoodhotels.com; Riva degli Schiavoni 4196; cocktails €18-22; ☺ 3-6.30pm Apr-Oct; ⓖ San Zaccaria) Gondolas glide in to dock along the quay, while across the lagoon the white-marble edifice of Palladio's San Giorgio Maggiore turns from gold to pink in the waters of the canal: the late-afternoon scene from the Hotel Danieli's top-floor balcony bar

definitely calls for a toast. Linger over a *spritz* (€10) or cocktail – preferably the sunset-tinted signature Danieli cocktail of gin, apricot and orange juices, and a splash of grenadine.

Bacaro Risorto   BAR
(Map p338; Campo San Provolo 4700; cicheti €1.50-4; ☺ 9am-9pm Mon-Sat; ⓖ San Zaccaria) Just a footbridge from San Marco, this shoebox of a corner bar overflowing with happy drinkers offers quality wines and abundant *cicheti*, including crostini heaped with *sarde in saòr*, soft cheeses and melon tightly swaddled in prosciutto. Note that opening times are 'flexible.'

☆ Entertainment

To find out what's on the calendar in Venice during your visit, check listings in free mags distributed citywide and online: *VeNews* (www.venezianews.it), *Venezia da Vivere* (www.veneziadavivere.com), and *2Venice* (www.2venice.it).

Casinos

Casinò Di Venezia   CASINO
(Palazzo Vendramin-Calergi; Map p355; ☎ 041 529 71 11; www.casinovenezia.it; Palazzo Vendramin-Calergi 2040; admission €5, with €10 gaming-token purchase free; ☺ 11am-2.30am Sun-Thu, to 3am Fri & Sat; ⓖ San Marcuola) Fortunes have been won and lost since the 16th century inside this palatial casino. Slots open at 11am; to take on gaming tables, arrive after 3.30pm wearing your jacket and poker face. Ask your hotel concierge for free-admission coupons, and take the casino's free water-taxi ride from Piazzale Roma – bargains, unless you count your losses. You must be at least 18 to enter the casino.

ⓘ PURCHASING EVENT TICKETS

For blockbuster events like the Biennale or La Fenice operas, you'll need to book ahead online at the appropriate website or www.veniceconnected.com. Tickets may also be available at the venue box office, www.musicinvenice.com or from HelloVenezia (☑041 24 24; www.hello venezia.it; tickets €15-20), ticket outlets located near key *vaporetto* (small passenger ferry) stops.

Opera & Classical Music

★ Teatro La Fenice
OPERA

(Map p342; ☑041 78 65 11; www.teatrolafenice.it; Campo San Fantin 1965; theatre visits adult/reduced €8.50/6, opera tickets from €40; ☉tours 9.30am-6pm; ☒Santa Maria dei Giglio) Tours are possible with advance booking (☑041 24 24), but the best way to see La Fenice is with the *loggione* – opera buffs who pass judgment from the top-tier cheap seats. When the opera is in recess, look for symphonies and chamber-music concerts.

★ Palazzetto Bru Zane
CLASSICAL MUSIC

(Centre du Musique Romantique Française; Map p338; ☑041 521 10 05; www.bru-zane.com; Palazetto Bru Zane 2368, San Polo; adult/reduced €25/15; ☉box office 2.30-5.30pm Mon-Fri; ☒San Tomà) Pleasure palaces don't get more romantic than Palazzetto Bru Zane on concert nights, when exquisite harmonies tickle Sebastiano Ricci angels tumbling across stucco-frosted ceilings. Multiyear restorations returned the 1695–97 Casino Zane's 100-seat music room to its original function, attracting world-class musicians to enjoy its acoustics.

Interpreti Veneziani
CLASSICAL MUSIC

(Map p342; ☑041 277 05 61; www.interpretiveneziani.com; Chiesa San Vidal, Campo di San Vidal 2862; adult/reduced €25/20; ☉doors open 8.30pm; ☒Accademia) All the Vivaldi you've heard at weddings and on mobile ring tones is proved fantastically wrong by Interpreti Veneziani, which plays Vivaldi on 18th-century instruments as a soundtrack for living in this city of intrigue.

Concerts at La Pietà
LIVE MUSIC

(Map p357; ☑041 522 21 71; www.pietavenezia.org; Riva degli Schiavoni; adult/reduced €25/20; ☉concerts 8.30pm; ☒Pietà) With fine acoustics, soaring Tiepolo ceilings and a long associa-tion with Vivaldi, this church makes an ideal venue for live baroque music.

Musica a Palazzo
OPERA

(Map p342; ☑340 971 72 72; www.musicapalazzo.com; Palazzo Barbarigo-Minotto, Fondamenta Barbarigo o Duodo 2504; tickets incl beverage €60; ☉doors open 8pm; ☒Santa Maria del Giglio) During 1½ hours of selected arias from Verdi or Rossini, the drama progresses from receiving-room overtures to parlour duets overlooking the Grand Canal, followed by second acts in the Tiepolo-ceilinged dining room and bedroom grand finales.

🛍 Shopping

Venice's ultimate shopping triumphs are unique finds at surprisingly reasonable prices, handmade by artisans in Murano and backstreet studios.

★ Cárte
PAPER PRODUCTS

(Map p352; ☑320 024 87 76; www.cartevenezia.it; Calle dei Cristi 1731, San Polo; ☉11am-5pm Mon-Sat, to 3pm Nov-Mar; ☒Rialto-Mercato) Lagoon ripples swirl across marbled-paper statement necklaces and artist's portfolios, thanks to the steady hands and restless imagination of *carta marmorizzata* (marbled-paper) *maestra* Rosanna Corrò. After years restoring ancient Venetian books, Rosanna began creating her original beauties: aquatic marbled-paper cocktail rings, op-art jewellery boxes and hypnotically swirled handbags.

Ca' Macana
MASKS, COSTUMES

(Map p348; ☑041 277 61 42; www.camacana.com; Calle delle Botteghe 3172; mask-making workshops from €60; ☉10am-6.30pm Sun-Fri, to 8pm Sat, mask-making workshops 11am-1pm & 2-6pm Mon-Fri; ☒; ☒Ca' Rezzonico) Glimpse the talents behind the Venetian Carnevale masks that so impressed Stanley Kubrick that he ordered several for his film *Eyes Wide Shut*. Choose your papier-mâché persona from the selection of coquettish courtesan's eye-shades and chequered Casanova disguises – or invent your own at Ca' Macana's one- to two-hour mask-making workshops for individuals and families.

★ Chiarastella Cattana
ARTISANAL, HOMEWARES

(Map p342; ☑041 522 43 69; www.chiarastellacattana.it; Salizada San Samuele 3357; ☉10am-1pm & 3-7pm Mon-Sat; ☒San Samuele) Transform any home into a thoroughly modern *palazzo* with these locally woven, strikingly original Venetian linens. Whimsical cushions feature a chubby purple rhinoceros and grumpy scarlet elephants straight out of Pietro Longhi paintings, and hand-tasseled Venetian jacquard hand towels will dry your royal guests in style.

Danghyra
ARTISANAL, CERAMICS

(Map p348; ☑ 041 522 41 95; www.danghyra.com; Calle delle Botteghe 3220; ⊙10am-1pm & 3-7pm Tue-Sun; ⧢San Tomà) Spare white bisque cups seem perfect for a Zen tea ceremony, but look inside: that iridescent lilac glaze is pure Carnevale. Danghyra's striking ceramics are hand-thrown in Murano with a magic touch – her platinum-glazed bowls make the simplest pasta dish appear fit for a modern doge.

Fiorella Gallery
FASHION

(Map p342; ☑ 041 520 92 28; www.fiorellagallery.com; Campo Santo Stefano 2806; ⊙9.30am-1.30pm & 3.30-7pm Tue-Sat, 3-7pm Mon; ⧢Accademia) Groupies are the only accessory needed to go with Fiorella's silk-velvet smoking jackets in louche lavender and oxblood, printed by hand with skulls, peacocks or a Fiorella signature: wide-eyed rats. Shock frockcoats starting in the mid-three figures make Alexander McQueen seem retro. Hours are approximate.

★ Gilberto Penzo
ARTISANAL, BOATS

(Map p352; ☑ 041 71 93 72; www.veniceboats.com; Calle 2 dei Saoneri 2681, San Polo; ⊙9am-12.30pm & 3-6pm Mon-Sat; ☖; ⧢San Tomà) Anyone fascinated by the models at Museo Storico Navale will go wild here, amid handmade wooden models of all kinds of Venetian boats, including some that are seaworthy (or at least bathtub worthy). Signor Penzo also creates kits so kids can have a crack at it themselves.

★ Marina e Susanna Sent
ARTISANAL, GLASS

(Map p342; ☑ 041 520 81 36; www.marinaesusannasent.com; Campo San Vio 669; ⊙10am-1pm & 3-6.30pm Tue-Sat, 3-6.30pm Mon; ⧢Accademia) Wearable waterfalls and unpoppable soap-bubble necklaces are Venice style signatures, thanks to the Murano-born Sent sisters. Defying centuries-old beliefs that women can't handle molten glass, their minimalist art-glass statement jewellery is featured in museum stores worldwide. See new collections at this flagship, their Murano studio (☑041 527 46 65; www.marinaesusannaset.com; Fondamenta Serenella 20; ⊙Sep-Jul; ⧢Colonna), or the San Marco branch (Ponte San Moise 2090).

Pied à Terre
ARTISANAL, SHOES

(Map p352; ☑041 528 55 13; www.piedaterre-venice.com; Sotoportego degli Oresi 60, San Polo; ⊙10am-1pm & 3-7pm Tue-Sat, 3-7pm Mon; ⧢Rialto) Pied à Terre's colourful *furlane* (slippers) are handcrafted with recycled bicycle-tyre treads. Choose from velvet, brocade or raw silk in vibrant shades of lemon and ruby, with optional piping. Don't see your size? Shoes can be custom-made and shipped.

Spilli Lab & Shop
CLOTHING

(Map p352; ☑340 276 72 96; Ponte dei Miracoli 6091; ⊙9.30am-12.30pm & 3.30-7.30pm Tue-Sun, 3.30-7.30pm Mon; ⧢Fondamente Nuove) Glamour comes easily at Spilli Lab & Shop, a Venetian design showcase with embroidered tunic dresses, graphite wool wrap-dresses and broad-brimmed fedoras. Alessia Sopelsa has an eye for luxe textures and original details – yet everything here is surprisingly affordable.

Veneziastampa
PAPER PRODUCTS

(Map p352; ☑041 71 54 55; www.veneziastampa.com; Campo Santa Maria Mater Domini 2173, Santa Croce; ⊙8.30am-7.30pm Mon-Fri, 9am-12.30pm Sat; ⧢San Stae) Mornings are best to catch the 1930s Heidelberg machine in action – but whenever you arrive, you'll find mementos hot off the proverbial press. Veneziastampa recalls more elegant times, when postcards were gorgeously lithographed and Casanovas invited dates upstairs to 'look at my etchings'.

ⓘ Information

EMERGENCY

Ambulance (☑118)

Police station (☑113, 112) At Castello (☑041 271 5511; www.poliziadistato.it; Fondamenta di San Lorenzo 505) and Piazza San Marco (Piazza San Marco 63).

INTERNET ACCESS

Wi-fi access is widely available in hotels, and internet cafes are dispersed throughout the city. There is also a citywide **wi-fi service** (www.veniceconnected.com; 1hr/72hr/week €5/8/15).

MEDICAL SERVICES

Information on rotating late-night pharmacies is posted in pharmacy windows and listed in the free magazine *Un Ospite di Venezia*, available at the tourist office.

Ospedale Civile (☑041 529 41 11; Campo SS Giovanni e Paolo 6777) Venice's main hospital; for emergency care and dental treatment, ask for *pronto soccorso* (casualty).

VENICE & THE VENETO VENICE

ⓘ VAPORETTO DELL'ARTE

New in 2012, this **vaporetto** (⌨ 041 24 24; www.vaporettoarte.com; ⊙ every 30min 9am-7pm) provides a luxurious hop-on, hop-off ride down the Grand Canal. Unlike the public *vaporetti*, which can be jam-packed, the Vaporetto dell'Arte offers seating in plush red armchairs complete with seat-back monitors screening multilingual information about the attractions en route. Most people don't bother with these, as the view out the windows is far more arresting.

To get the best value from the service, buy the ticket in conjunction with your Venice Card, when the +ARTE add-on will only set you back €10. The ticket will then be valid for the same length of time as your Venice Card.

MONEY

There are ATMs spread throughout the city, with clusters near the Rialto and Piazza San Marco.

Travelex (⌨ 041 528 73 58; Piazza San Marco 142; ⊙ 9am-7pm Mon-Fri, 9am-6pm Sat, 9.20am-6pm Sun)

POST

There are post offices in every *sestiere*, with addresses and hours searchable at www. poste.it. The most convenient is in **Calle Larga de l'Ascension** (Map p342; Calle Larga de l'Ascension 1241; ⊙ 8.25am-1.25pm Mon-Fri, to 12.35pm Sat), just behind San Marco.

TOURIST INFORMATION

Tourist office (Azienda di Promozione Turistica; ⌨ 041 529 87 11; www.turismovenezia. it) At several locations, including Marco Polo Airport (Marco Polo airport, arrivals hall; ⊙ 9am-8pm), Piazzale Roma (Map p338; Piazzale Roma, ground fl, multistorey car park; ⊙ 9.30am-2.30pm; ⊛ Santa Chiara), Piazza San Marco (Piazza San Marco 71f; ⊙ 9am-7pm; ⊛ San Marco) and Stazione di Santa Lucia (Map p338; Stazione di Santa Lucia; ⊙ 9am-7pm Nov-Mar, 1.30-7pm Apr-Oct; ⊛ Ferrovia Santa Lucia).

ⓘ Getting There & Away

AIR

Most flights arrive at and depart from **Marco Polo airport** (VCE; ⌨ 041 260 92 60; www. veniceairport.it), 12km outside Venice, east of Mestre. Ryanair also uses **San Giuseppe airport** (⌨ 042 231 51 11; www.trevisoairport.it), about

5km southwest of Treviso and a 30km, one-hour drive from Venice.

BOAT

Anek (www.anek.gr) runs regular ferries between Venice and Greece, and Venezia Lines (p947) runs high-speed boats to and from Croatia and Slovenia in summer. However, consider big-ship transport carefully – long-haul ferries and cruise ships have an outsized environmental impact on tiny Venice and its fragile lagoon aquaculture. Take the lower-impact train instead, and Venice will be most grateful. Boats leave from the ferry terminal, near Piazzale Roma.

BUS

All buses leave from the **bus station** (Map p338) on Piazzale Roma.

Azienda del Consorzio Trasporti Veneziano (ACTV; ⌨ 041 24 24; www.actv.it) Runs buses to Mestre and surrounding areas.

Azienda Trasporti Veneto Orientale (ATVO; ⌨ 0421 59 46 71; www.atvo.it) Has services to destinations all over the eastern Veneto, including airport connections.

Eurolines (⌨ 041 538 21 18; www.eurolines. com) Operates a wide range of international routes.

CAR & MOTORCYCLE

The congested Trieste–Turin A4 passes through Mestre. From Mestre, take the Venezia exit. From the south, take the A13 from Bologna, which connects with the A4 at Padua.

Once over the Ponte della Libertà bridge from Mestre, cars must be left at the car park at Piazzale Roma or Tronchetto; expect to pay €20 or more for every 24 hours. Parking stations in Mestre are cheaper. Car ferry 17 transports vehicles from Tronchetto to the Lido.

Avis, Europcar and Hertz all have car-rental offices on Piazzale Roma and at Marco Polo airport. Several companies operate in or near Mestre train station, too.

Interparking (Tronchetto Car Park; ⌨ 041 520 75 55; www.veniceparking.it; Isola del Tronchetto; per 2/24hr €6/21; ⊙ 24hr) has the largest parking lot with the cheapest 24-hour rate; *vaporetti* connect directly with Piazza San Marco.

TRAIN

Prompt, affordable, scenic and environmentally savvy, trains are the preferred transport option to and from Venice. Trains run frequently to Venice's Stazione Santa Lucia (signed as Ferrovia within Venice). In addition, there are direct InterCity services to major points in France, Germany, Austria and Slovenia.

TO	FARE (€)	DURATION (HR)	FREQUENCY (PER HR)
Florence	26-45	2-3	1-2
Milan	19-38	2½-3½	2-3
Naples	64-123	5½-9	1
Padua	3.50	½-1	3-4
Rome	46-80	3½-6	1-2
Verona	7.50	1¾	3-4

ⓘ Getting Around

TO/FROM THE AIRPORT
Boat

Alilaguna (☑ 041 240 17 01; www.alilaguna. com; Marco Polo airport) operates several lines that link the airport with various parts of Venice, including the Linea Blu (Blue Line, with stops at Lido, San Marco, Stazione Marittima and points in between), the Linea Rossa (Red Line, with stops at Murano and Lido) and Linea Arancio (Orange Line, with stops at Stazione Santa Lucia, Rialto and San Marco via the Grand Canal). Boats to Venice cost €15 and leave from the airport ferry dock (an eight-minute walk from the terminal).

Bus

ATVO buses run to the airport from Piazzale Roma (€6, one hour, every 30 minutes 8am to midnight).

VAPORETTO

The city's main mode of public transport is *vaporetto* – Venice's distinctive water bus. Tickets can be purchased from the **HelloVenezia** (☑ 041 24 24; www.hellovenezia.it) ticket booths at most landing stations. You can also buy tickets when boarding; you may be charged double with luggage, though this is not always enforced.

Instead of spending €7 for a one-way ticket, consider a Venice Card, which is a timed pass for unlimited travel (beginning at first validation). Passes for 12/24/36/48/72 hours cost €18/20/25/30/35. A week pass costs €60. Swipe your card every time you board, even if you have already validated it upon initial boarding.

WATER TAXIS

The standard **water taxi** (Consorzio Motoscafi Venezia; Map p352; ☑ 041 240 67 11, 24hr 041 522 23 03; www.motoscafivenezia.it) between Marco Polo airport and Venice costs €110 one way and €32 per person in a shared taxi. Official rates start at €8.90 plus €1.80 per minute, plus €6 if they're called to your hotel and more for night trips, luggage and large groups. Prices can be metered or negotiated in advance.

THE VENETO

Most visitors to the Veneto devote all their time to Venice itself, which is perfectly understandable – until you discover the rich variety of experiences that await just an hour or two away.

First, there are the city-states Venice annexed in the 15th century: Padua (Padova), with its pre-Renaissance fresco cycles; Vicenza, with Palladio's peerless architecture; and Verona, with its sophisticated bustle atop ancient Roman foundations. All are easily reached by train from Venice.

Then there are the wines, in particular, Valpolicella's bold Amarones. In a party

---

VAPORETTO ROUTES

Here are key *vaporetto* lines and major stops, subject to seasonal change:

1 Piazzale Roma–Ferrovia–Grand Canal (all stops)–Lido and return

2 San Zaccaria–Redentore–Zattere–Tronchetto–Ferrovia–Rialto–Accademia–San Marco

5 San Zaccaria–Murano and return

41 Murano–Fondamente Nuove–Ferrovia–Piazzale Roma–Redentore–San Zaccaria–Fondamente Nuove–San Michele–Murano

42 Reverse direction to line 41

51 Lido–Fondamente Nuove–Ferrovia–Piazzale Roma–Zattere–San Zaccaria–Giardini–Lido

52 Reverse direction to line 51

N (all-stops night circuit, 11.30pm to 5am) Lido–Giardini–San Zaccaria–Grand Canal (all stops)–Ferrovia–Piazzale Roma–Tronchetto–Zattere–Redentore–San Giorgio–San Zaccaria

DM (Diretto Murano) Tronchetto–Piazzale Roma–Ferrovia–Murano and return

T Torcello–Burano (half-hourly service) and return (7am to 8.30pm)

VENICE & THE VENETO VENICE

mood? The hills around Conegliano produce Italy's finest bubbly: Prosecco Superiore. For harder stuff, charming Bassano del Grappa obliges with its own eponymous firewater.

On the rare day when the Adriatic wipes Venice clean of its mists, you can catch glimpses of the snowcapped Dolomites. It's hard to believe, but in less than two hours you can go from canals to the crisp Alpine clarity of Belluno and Cortina d'Ampezzo – land of idyllic hikes, razor-sharp peaks and the world's most fashion-conscious skiing.

Brenta Riviera

Every 13 June for 300 years, summer officially kicked off with a traffic jam along the Grand Canal, as a flotilla of fashionable Venetians headed to their villas along the banks of the Brenta. Every last ball gown and poker chair was loaded onto barges for dalliances that stretched until November. The party ended when Napoleon arrived in 1797, but 80 villas still strike elegant poses along the Brenta and four of them are now open as museums.

◉ Sights

Villa Foscari HISTORIC BUILDING
(☑ 041 520 39 66; www.lamalcontenta.com; Via dei Turisti 9, Malcontenta; adult/student €10/8; ☺ 9am-noon Tue & Sat, closed Nov-Apr) The most romantic Brenta villa, the Palladio-designed 1555–60 Villa Foscari got its nickname La Malcontenta from a grand dame of the Foscari clan who was reputedly exiled here for cheating on her husband – though these bright, highly sociable salons hardly constitute a punishment. The villa was abandoned for years, but Giovanni Zelotti's frescoes

BRENTA BY BIKE

Speed past tour boats along 150km of cycling routes along the Brenta Riviera. **Veloce** (☑ 346 84 71 14; www. rentalbikeitaly.com; Via Gramsci 85, Mira; touring/mountain bicycle per day €20/25; ☺ 8am-8pm) offers a pick-up and drop-off service at railway stations and hotels in many Veneto towns, including Padua, Venice and Mira. City and mountain bikes are available, along with GPS units preloaded with multilingual Brenta itineraries (€10).

have now been restored to daydream-inducing splendour.

Villa Widmann Rezzonico Foscari HISTORIC BUILDING
(☑ 041 560 06 90; Via Nazionale 420, Mira; adult/student €5/4; ☺ 10am-5pm Tue-Sun May-Sep, 10am-5pm Sat & Sun Nov-Feb) To appreciate both gardening and Venetian-style social engineering, stop just west of Oriago at Villa Widmann Rezzonico Foscari. Originally owned by Persian-Venetian nobility, the 18th-century villa captures the Brenta's last days of rococo decadence, with Murano sea-monster chandeliers and a frescoed grand ballroom with upper viewing gallery. Head to the gallery to reach the upstairs ladies' gambling parlour where, according to local lore, villas were once gambled away in high-stakes games.

Villa Pisani Nazionale HISTORIC BUILDING
(☑ 049 50 20 74; www.villapisani.beniculturali.it; Via Doge Pisani 7, Stra; adult/reduced €7.50/3.75, park only €4.50/2.25; ☺ 9am-7pm Tue-Sun Apr-Sep, to 5pm Nov-Mar) To keep hard-partying Venetian nobles in line, Doge Alvise Pisani provided a Versailles-like reminder of who was in charge. The 1774 Villa Pisani Nazionale is surrounded by huge gardens, a labyrinthine hedge-maze and pools to reflect the doge's glory. And if the walls of these 114 rooms could talk, they'd name-drop shamelessly. Here you'll find the bathroom with a tiny wooden throne used by Napoleon; the sagging bed where new king Vittorio Emanuele II slept; and, in historical irony, the reception hall where Mussolini and Hitler met in 1934 under Tiepolo's ceiling depicting the *Geniuses of Peace*.

Villa Foscarini Rossi HISTORIC BUILDING
(☑ 049 980 10 91; www.villafoscarini.it; Via Doge Pisani 1/2, Stra; adult/reduced €5/2.50; ☺ 9am-1pm & 2-6pm Mon-Fri, 2.30-6pm Sat & Sun Apr-Oct, 9am-1pm Mon-Fri Nov-Mar) Well-heeled Venetians wouldn't have dreamt of decamping to the Brenta without their favourite cobblers, sparking a local tradition of shoemaking. The contribution of Brenta cobblers is commemorated with a **Shoemakers' Museum** at this 18th-century villa, a multiroom dream wardrobe that includes 18th-century slippers, kicks created for trendsetter Marlene Dietrich, and heels handcrafted for Yves Saint Laurent.

👉 Tours

Seeing the Brenta by boat reveals an engineering marvel: the ingenious hydraulic locks system developed in the 15th century to prevent river silt from being dumped into the lagoon.

⭐ Il Burchiello
BOAT TOUR

(📞 049 876 02 33; www.ilburchiello.it; adult/reduced half-day cruise €55/45, full day from €94/55) This modern luxury barge lets you watch 50 villas drift by from velvet couches with a glass of *prosecco* in hand. Day cruises stop at Malcontenta, Widmann and Pisani villas; half-day tours cover two villas. Full-day cruises leave from Venice's Stazione Maritima (Tuesday, Thursday and Saturday) or Padua (Wednesday, Friday and Sunday), with bus transfers included.

🎊 Festivals & Events

Riviera Fiorita
CULTURE

(www.rivierafiorita.it) Party like it's 1527 with baroque costume parties at the Villa Pisani and Villa Widmann, historically correct country fairs that even have gelati in baroque-era flavours. Held on the first or second weekend in September.

🍴 Eating

Osteria Da Conte
MODERN VENETIAN €€

(📞 049 47 95 71; www.osteriadaconte.it; Via Caltana 133, Mira; meals €35-45; ⊙ 10am-4pm & 6-10pm Tue-Sat) This unlikely bastion of sophistication is lodged practically underneath an overpass. Da Conte has one of the best wine lists in the region, plus creative takes on classic lagoon cuisine, from roasted quail to ginger-infused langoustines.

ℹ️ Getting There & Around

ACTV's Venezia–Padova Extraurbane bus 53 leaves from Venice's Piazzale Roma about every half-hour, stopping at key Brenta villages en route to Padua. Local Venice–Padua train services stop at Dolo (€2.85, 25 minutes, one or two hour). By car, take SS11 from Mestre-Venezia towards Padua and take the A4 autostrada towards Dolo/Padua.

Padua

POP 214,900

Though under an hour from Venice, Padua seems a world away with its medieval marketplaces, Fascist-era facades and hip student population. As a medieval city-state and

home to Italy's second-oldest university, Padua challenged both Venice and Verona for regional hegemony. A series of extraordinary fresco cycles recalls this golden age – including Giotto's remarkable Capella degli Scrovegni, Menabuoi's heavenly gathering in the Bapistry and Titian's St Anthony in the Scoletta del Santo. For the next few centuries Padua and Verona challenged each other for dominance over the Veneto plains. But Venice finally settled the matter by occupying Padua permanently in 1405.

As a strategic military-industrial centre, Padua became a parade ground for Mussolini speeches, an Allied bombing target and a secret Italian Resistance hub based at the university. Once Padua was wrested from Fascist control in 1945, there was a new industrial zone east of the city within a year, the university was back in session and the puzzlework that is Padua began anew.

◉ Sights

⭐ Cappella degli Scrovegni
CHURCH

(📞 049 201 00 20; www.cappelladegliscrovegni.it; Piazza Eremitani 8; adult/reduced €13/8; ⊙ 9am-7pm Mon, to 10pm Tue-Sun Mar-Oct, 9am-7pm Nov-Dec, by reservation only) Dante, da Vinci and Vasari all honour Giotto as the artist who ended the Dark Ages with his 1303–05 frescoes. Giotto's moving, modern approach changed how people saw themselves: not as lowly vassals but as vessels for the divine, however flawed. This humanising approach was especially well suited to the chapel Enrico Scrovegni commissioned in memory of his father, who as a moneylender was denied a Christian burial.

Previously medieval churchgoers had been accustomed to blank stares from saints perched on high, golden thrones, but Giotto introduced biblical figures as characters in

VENICE & THE VENETO PADUA

Padua

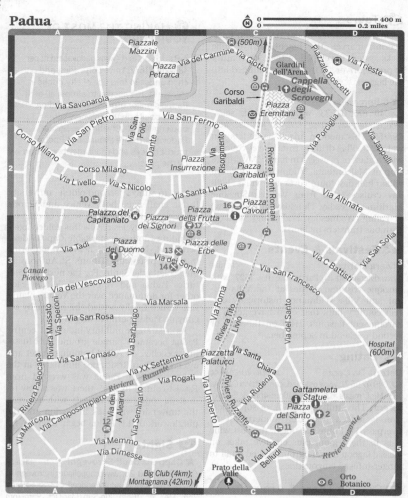

VENICE & THE VENETO PADUA

recognisable settings. Onlookers gossip as middle-aged Anne tenderly kisses Joachim, and Jesus stares down Judas as the traitor puckers up for the fateful kiss. A 10-minute introductory video provides some helpful insights before you enter the church itself.

Pick up prebooked tickets at the Musei Civici agli Eremitani, where you access the chapel. Chapel visits last 15 minutes, plus another 15 minutes for the video, though the 'double turn' night-session ticket (adult/reduced €12/6) allows a 30-minute stay in the church.

Musei Civici agli Eremitani MUSEUM
(☏049 8204 5450; Piazza Eremitani 8; adult/reduced €10/8; ☺9am-7pm Tue-Sun) The ground floor of this monastery houses artefacts dating from Padua's Roman and pre-Roman past. Upstairs, a rambling but interesting collection boasts a few notable 14th- to 18th-century works by Bellini, Giorgione, Tintoretto and Veronese. The showstopper is a crucifix by Giotto, showing a heartbroken Mary wringing her hands as Jesus' blood drips into the empty eye sockets of a human skull.

Padua

Palazzo del Bò　　　　　　HISTORIC BUILDING
(☑049 827 30 47; Via VIII Febbraio; adult/reduced €5/3.50; ⊙tours 9.15am, 10.15am & 11.15am Tue, Thu & Sat, 3.15pm, 4.15pm & 5.15pm Mon, Wed & Fri) This Renaissance *palazzo* is the seat of Padua's history-making university. Founded by renegade scholars from Bologna seeking greater intellectual freedom, the university has employed some of Italy's greatest and most controversial thinkers, including Copernicus, Galileo, Casanova and the world's first female doctor of philosophy, Eleonora Lucrezia Cornaro Piscopia (her statue graces the stairs). Guided tours cover Galileo's lecture hall and the world's first anatomy theatre.

Note there are only two tours per day from November to March.

Duomo　　　　　　　　　　CATHEDRAL
(☑049 66 28 14; Piazza del Duomo; baptistry adult/ reduced €2.80/1.80; ⊙7.30am-noon & 4-7.30pm Mon-Sat, 8am-1pm & 4-8.45pm Sun & holidays, baptistry 10am-6pm) Built from a much-altered design of Michelangelo's, the whitewashed symmetry of Padua's cathedral is a far cry from its rival in Piazza San Marco. The adjoining 13th-century baptistry, however, is a Romanesque gem frescoed with luminous

biblical scenes by Giusto de' Menabuoi. Hundreds of male and female saints congregate in the cupola, posed as though for a school graduation photo, exchanging glances and stealing looks at the Madonna.

Basilica di Sant'Antonio　　　　CHURCH
(Il Santo; www.basilicadelsanto.org; Piazza del Santo; ⊙6.20am-7.45pm Apr-Oct, to 7pm Nov-Mar) FREE Il Santo is the soul of Padua, a key pilgrimage site and the burial place of patron saint St Anthony of Padua (1193–1231). Begun in 1232, its polyglot style incorporates rising eastern domes atop a Gothic brick structure crammed with Renaissance treasures. Behind the high altar nine radiating chapels punctuate a broad ambulatory homing in on the Cappella del Tesoro (Treasury Chapel), where the relics of St Anthony reside.

You'll also notice dozens of people clustering along the right transept waiting their turn to enter the Cappella del Santo, where Anthony's tomb is covered with requests and thanks for the saint's intercession in curing illness and recovering lost objects. The chapel itself is a light-filled Renaissance confection lined with nine panels vividly depicting the story of Anthony's life in extraordinary relief sculptures. The panels are attributed to the Padua-born Lombardo brothers and were completed around 1510.

Other notable works include the lifelike 1360s crucifix by Veronese master Altichiero da Zevio in the frescoed Cappella di San Giacomo; the wonderful 1528 sacristy fresco of St Anthony preaching to spellbound fish by a follower of Girolamo Tessari; and 1444–50 high altar reliefs by Florentine Renaissance master Donatello (ask guards for access). Through the east door of the basilica you reach the attached monastery with its five cloisters. The oldest (13th century) is the Chiostro della Magnolia, so called because of the magnificent tree in its centre.

**Oratorio di San Giorgio
& Scoletta del Santo**　　　　CHURCH
(Piazza del Santo; admission €4; ⊙9am-12.30pm & 2.30-5pm Oct-Mar, to 7pm Apr-Sep) Anywhere else the fresco cycle of the Oratorio di San Giorgio and the paintings in the Scoletta del Santo would be considered highlights, but in Padua they must contend with Giotto's Scrovegni brilliance. This means you'll have Altichiero da Zevio and Jacopo Avanzi's jewel-like, 14th-century frescoes of St George, St Lucy and St Catherine all to yourself,

while upstairs in the *scoletta* (confraternity house) Titian paintings are seldom viewed in such tranquility.

Orto Botanico
GARDEN

(☑ 049 827 21 19; www.ortobotanico.unipd.it; Via dell'Orto Botanico 15; adult/reduced €4/3; ☺ 9am-1pm & 3-7pm Apr-Oct, 9am-1pm Mon-Sat Nov-Mar) South of Piazza del Santo, Padua's Orto Botanico is growing. Padua's Orto Botanico was planted in 1545 by Padua University's medical faculty to study the medicinal properties of rare plants, and served as a clandestine Resistance meeting headquarters in WWII. The oldest tree in here is nicknamed 'Goethe's palm'; it was planted in 1585 and mentioned by the great German writer in his *Voyage in Italy*.

🛌 Sleeping

The tourist office publishes accommodation brochures and lists dozens of B&Bs and hotels online.

Albergo Verdi
HOTEL €

(☑ 049 836 41 63; www.albergoverdipadova.it; Via Dondi dall'Orologio 7; s/d €70/100; ❄ @ ☎) With fresh orchids in the rooms and a bright, modern colour scheme, Albergo Verdi is a breath of fresh air in Padua's conservative hotel scene. Upper rooms benefit from lovely views over Piazza del Capitaniato, and the breakfast buffet groans with fresh fruit, pastries, cold meats, eggs and cheese.

Ostello Città di Padova
HOSTEL €

(☑ 049 875 22 19; www.ostellopadova.it; Via dei Aleardi 30; dm €19-23, d €76; ☺ reception 7.15-9.30am & 3.30-11.30pm; ☎) This central hostel has decent dorm rooms with four to six beds on a quiet side street. Sheets and wi-fi are free, but there is no open kitchen. Note there is an 11.30pm curfew, except when there are special events, and you must check out by 9.30am. Take bus 3, 8 or 12 or the city's new tram from the train station.

Belludi37
BOUTIQUE HOTEL €€

(☑ 049 66 56 33; www.belludi37.it; Via Luca Belludi 37; s €97, d €120-145; ❄ ☎) With its central location and mod decor the Belludi is the hotel of choice for many regular travellers to Padua. Although the black-and-brown rooms could do with a little freshening up, the generous-sized beds, free minibar and ample buffet breakfast more than compensate. Staff are always on hand with budget-friendly shopping advice and suggestions for biking itineraries and walking tours.

🍴 Eating

⭐ Godenda
MODERN ITALIAN €€

(☑ 049 877 41 92; www.godenda.it; Via Squarcione 4/6; meals €25-40; ☺ 10am-3pm & 6pm-2am Mon-Sat) Though hidden under an ancient portico, this local foodies' favourite is airy and modern with red-leather loungers, a long, sleek bar and a sultry jazz soundtrack. The seasonal menu offers creative takes on old Venetian classics such as venison and lentils with sauteed apples and there's an excellent selection of wines by the glass.

L'Anfora
OSTERIA €€

(☑ 049 65 66 29; Via dei Soncin 13; meals €25-30; ☺ 9am-11pm Mon-Sat) Preserving the long tradition of the university tavern, L'Anfora is perpetually filled with a raucous crowd of students and professors pressing home their points fuelled by an ample supply of *spritz* and snacks. On the chalkboard daily dishes feature no-frills *cucina casalinga* (home cooking) of the Veneto, from sardines in *saor* to *orecchiette* (little ears; pasta) with turnip greens and ricotta.

TO MARKET

One of the most enjoyable activities in Padua is browsing the markets in **Piazza delle Erbe** and **Piazza della Frutta**, which operate very much as they've done since the Middle Ages. Stalls in Piazza delle Erbe are dedicated to fresh fruit and vegetables and are tiered in terms of quality. Those with less choice products are on the outer perimeter, with better stalls nearer the Gothic **Palazzo della Ragione** (☑ 049 820 50 06; Piazza delle Erbe; adult/reduced €4/2; ☺ 9am-7pm Tue-Sun, to 6pm Nov-Jan). Beneath the arcades, known locally as **Sotto il Salone** (www.sottoilsalone. it), specialist butchers, cheesemakers, fishmongers, *salumerie* (smallgoods shops) and fresh pasta producers sell their wares, while on the other side of the *palazzo* (mansion), in Piazza della Frutta, stalls with nonlocal produce – spices, nuts, dried fruits, herbs and grains – cluster.

The markets are open all day, every day except Sunday, although the best time to go is before midday.

COLLI EUGANEI (EUGANEAN HILLS)

Southwest of Padua, the Euganean Hills feel a world away from the urban sophistication of Venice and the surrounding plains. To help you explore the walled hilltop towns, misty vineyards and bubbling hot springs, the Padua tourist office offers area maps, hiking and transport information online (www.turismotermeeuganee.it). Trains serve all towns except Arquà Petrarca.

Just south of Padua lie the natural-hot-spring resorts of Abano Terme and Montegrotto Terme. They have been active since Roman times, when the Patavini built their villas on Mt Montirone. The towns are uninspired, but the waters do cure aches and pains.

In the medieval village of Arquà Petrarca, look for the elegant little house (☑0429 71 82 94; Via Valleselle 4; adult/reduced €4/2; ☺9am-12.30pm & 3-7pm Tue-Sun Mar-Oct, 9am-12.30pm & 2.30-5.30pm Tue-Sun Nov-Feb) where great Italian poet Petrarch spent his final years in the 1370s.

At the southern reaches of the Euganei, you'll find Monselice, with its remarkable medieval castle; Montagnana, with its magnificent 2km defensive perimeter; and Este, with its rich architectural heritage and important archaeological museum (☑0429 20 85; www.atestino.beniculturali.it; Via Guido Negri 9c; adult/reduced €4/free; ☺8.30am-7.30pm). Este is also home to Este Ceramiche Porcellane (☑0429 22 70; www.esteceramiche.com; Via Zanchi 22a; ☺9am-noon & 2-5.30pm Mon-Fri), one of the oldest ceramics factories in Europe. It's been making tableware for Dior, Tiffany and Barneys for years, but here you can find some fabulous bargains in its outlet shop.

If you want to overnight, consider staying in one of the two apartments at Villa Vescovi (☑049 993 04 73; www.villadeivescovi.it; Luvigliano; villa tour adult/reduced €7/3.50, apartments €200; ☺10am-6pm Wed-Fri Apr-Oct, to 5pm Nov-Dec; ☎♿), one of the best preserved pre-Palladio Renaissance villas in the Veneto.

Trattoria al Prato
TRATTORIA €€

(☑049 66 24 29; Prato della Valle 4/5; meals €20-30; ☺12.15-2.30pm & 7.30-11pm Thu-Tue) Sit in the enclosed conservatory and enjoy the views of the Prato della Valle while you savour rabbit terrine and pumpkin puree or silky tagliatelle with *guanciale* (pig's cheek). Illicit lunch dates, well-fed business men and fur-clad female diners are your companions, testifying to the elegant and discreet service. The two-course, €10 set lunch is an absolute steal.

🍷 Drinking & Entertainment

Sundown isn't official until you've joined the crowds for a *spritz* in Piazza delle Erbe or Piazza dei Signori. Also note that Padua is the region's unofficial capital of gay and lesbian life.

★ Caffè Pedrocchi
CAFE

(☑049 878 12 31; www.caffepedrocchi.it; Via VIII Febbraio 15; ☺9am-10pm Sun-Wed, to 1am Thu-Sat) Since 1831 this neoclassical landmark has been a favourite of Stendhal and other pillars of Padua's cafe society. Divided into three rooms: red, white and green (the colours of the Italian flag), the Pedrocchi has long been a seat of intrigue and revolution.

The green room to the right of the bar was a 'no obligation' lounge where intellectuals could come and talk, while the white room bears a small plaque marking the spot where a bullet struck the wall in the 1848 student rebellion.

Enoteca Il Tira Bouchon
WINE BAR

(☑049 875 21 38; www.enotecapadova.it; Sotto il Salone 23/24) With a guiding French hand behind the bar you can be sure of an excellent *prosecco* or *spritz* at this traditional wine bar beneath the arcades of the Palazzo Ragione. Locals crowd in for *spunciotti* (a baked bread dough served with olive oil and cheese) and lively glasses of *prosecco*.

Big Club
NIGHTCLUB

(☑049 68 09 34; www.big-club.com; Via Armistizio 68; admission €7-12; ☺Fri-Sun 8.30pm-3am) Few clubs can boast the 30-year heritage of Padua's Big Club, which hosted big names from the London underground scene back in the '70s. These days the focus is on disco revival, and Latin American and Caribbean nights curated by resident DJ Lady Vega. There's an on-site wood-burning pizza oven to cater to famished punters.

ℹ Information

Hospital (☎049 821 11 11; Via Giustiniani 1) Main public hospital.

Police station (☎049 83 31 11; Piazzetta Palatucci 5)

Tourist office (☎049 875 20 77; www.turismopadova.it; ⊙9am-7pm Mon-Sat, to 12.30pm Sun) At the train station.

ℹ Getting There & Around

BUS

SITA (☎049 820 68 34; www.fsbusitalia.it) buses from Venice's Piazzale Roma (€4.10, 45 to 60 minutes, hourly) arrive at Piazzale Boschetti, 500m southeast of the train station. Check online for buses to Colli Euganei towns.

TRAIN

The easiest way to reach Padua from Venice (€4 to €19.50, 25 to 50 minutes, three or four per hour), Verona (€6 to €18, 40 to 90 minutes, two or three per hour), Vicenza (€3.50 to €15, 15 to 30 minutes, two or three per hour) and most other Italian destinations; the station is about 500m north of Cappella degli Scrovegni.

TRAM

It is easy to get to all the sights by foot from the train and bus stations, but a new single-branch tram running from the train station passes within 100m of all the main sights. Tickets (€1.20) are available at tobacconists and newsstands.

Vicenza

POP 115,900

When Palladio escaped an oppressive employer in his native Padua, few would have guessed the humble stonecutter would, within a few decades, transform not only his adoptive city but also the history of European architecture. By luck, a local count recognised his talents in the 1520s and sent him to study the ruins in Rome. When he returned to Vicenza, the autodidact began producing his extraordinary buildings that marry sophistication and rustic simplicity, reverent classicism and bold innovation. It's no wonder Vicenza and surrounding villas have been declared one grand Unesco World Heritage Site.

◉ Sights

The heart of historic Vicenza is **Piazza dei Signori**, where Palladio lightens the mood of government buildings with his trademark play of light and shadow. Dazzling white Piovene stone arches frame shady double arcades in the Basilica Palladiana while, across the piazza, white stone and stucco grace the exposed red brick colonnade of the 1571-designed **Loggia del Capitaniato**.

Two of Palladio's most extraordinary villas, La Rotonda and Villa Valmarana 'Ai Nani', lie a 20-minute walk south of the train station. Or you can catch local bus 8 (€1.50) in front of the station.

Basilica Palladiana   ART GALLERY
(☎0444 22 21 14; Piazza dei Signori; temporary exhibtions €9-12) The Palladian Basilica dominates the Piazza dei Signori, its enormous copper dome reminiscent of the hull of an upturned ship. Palladio himself called this city hall a 'basilica', modelled as it was on Roman structures that had inspired him. He was lucky to secure the commission in 1549 (it took his patron 50 years of lobbying the council), which involved radically restructuring the original, 15th-century *palazzo* and adding an ambitious double order of loggias.

Inside the awesome, 52m hall was where the Council of Four Hundred met. Now, after an extensive five-year restoration, it hosts internationally important temporary exhibitions. It's closed to the public when there are no exhibitions on.

**Gallerie di Palazzo
Leoni Montanari**   MUSEUM
(☎800 578875; www.gallerieditalia.com; Contrà di Santa Corona 25; adult/reduced €5/4; ⊙10am-6pm Tue-Sun) From the outside it looks like a bank, but a treasure beyond accountants' imagining awaits inside the Palazzo Leoni Montanari. Ascend past the nymphs along the extravagant stuccoed staircase to grand salons filled with Canaletto's misty lagoon landscapes and Pietro Longhi's 18th-century satires. Head upstairs to see Banca Intesa's superb collection of 400 Russian icons, gorgeously spotlit in darkened galleries in which recordings of soft Gregorian chants set the scene.

Chiesa di Santa Corona   CHURCH
(☎0444 22 28 11; Contrà di Santa Corona; ⊙9am-noon & 3-6pm Tue-Sun) **FREE** Built by the Dominicans in 1261 to house a relic from Christ's crown of thorns donated to the bishop of Vicenza by Louis IX of France, this Romanesque church also houses three light-filled masterpieces: Palladio's 1576 Valmarana Chapel in the crypt; Paolo Veronese's *Adoration of the Magi,* much praised by Goethe; and Giovanni Bellini's radiant

Vicenza

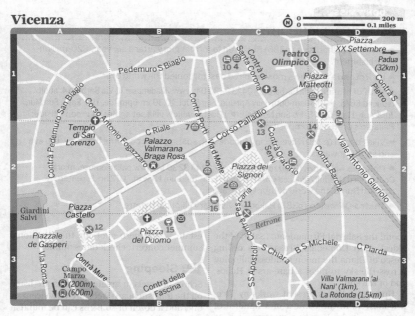

Baptism of Christ, where the holy event is witnessed by a trio of Veneto beauties and a curious red bird.

⭐ **Teatro Olimpico**   THEATRE
(☎0444 22 28 00; www.olimpicovicenza.it; Piazza Matteotti 11; adult/reduced incl Museo Civico €10/8; ⏰9am-5pm Tue-Sun) Behind a charming walled garden lies a Renaissance marvel: the Teatro Olimpico, which Palladio began in 1580 with inspiration from Roman amphitheatres. Vincenzo Scamozzi finished the elliptical theatre after Palladio's death, adding a stage set modelled on the ancient Greek city of Thebes, with streets built in steep perspective to give the illusion of a city sprawling towards a distant horizon.

Today, Italian performers vie to make an entrance on this gem of a stage; check the website for opera, classical and jazz performances.

Museo Civico   MUSEUM
(Palazzo Chiericati; ☎0444 22 28 11; www.musei civicivicenza.it; Piazza Matteoti 37/39; adult/ reduced incl Teatro Olimpico €10/8; ⏰9am-5pm Tue-Sun) This civic art museum is housed in one of Palladio's finest buildings, designed in 1550 with a colonnaded ground floor and double-height loggia. The frescoed ground floor includes the ultimate baroque party

Vicenza

◎ **Top Sights**
1 Teatro Olimpico D1

◎ **Sights**
2 Basilica Palladiana C2
3 Chiesa di Santa Corona C1
4 Gallerie di Palazzo Leoni
   Montanari C1
5 Loggia del Capitaniato B2
6 Museo Civico D1
7 Palladio Museum B2

🛏 **Sleeping**
8 Hotel Palladio C2
9 Ostello Olimpico D1
10 Relais Santa Corona C1

🍴 **Eating**
11 Al Bersagliere C2
12 Antico Ristorante agli Schioppi A3
13 Gastronomia Il Ceppo C2
14 Julien D2

🍷 **Drinking & Nightlife**
15 Osteria al Campanile B3
16 Pasticceria Sorarù C2

PALLADIAN HIGHLIGHTS

➡ **Basilica Palladiana** (p386) Restored to former glory after a six-year, €20-million refurbishment.

➡ **La Rotonda** Palladio's most inspired design, copied the world over.

➡ **Villa di Masèr** (Villa Barbaro; ☑ 0423 92 30 04; www.villadimaser.it; Via Barbaro 4; adult/reduced €6/5; ☉ 10.30am-6pm daily Apr-Jun, Sep & Oct, 10.30am-6pm Tue, Thu, Sat & Sun Mar, Jul & Aug, 11am-5pm Sat & Sun Nov-Feb; Ⓟ) Butter-yellow villa set against a green hillside; Palladio's prettiest composition.

➡ Villa Foscari (p380) River-facing facade with soaring Ionic columns that draw the eye and spirits upwards.

➡ **Palladio Museum** (Palazzo Barbarano; ☑ 0444 32 30 14; www.palladiomuseum.org; Contrà Porti 11; adult/reduced €6/4; ☉ 10am-6pm Tue-Sun) New in 2012 and created by Howard Burns, the world authority on Palladio.

➡ **Teatro Olimpico** (p387) Palladio's visionary elliptical theatre.

room: the Sala dal Firmamento (Salon of the Skies), with Domenico Brusasorci's ceiling fresco of Diana the moon goddess galloping across the sky to meet a bare-arsed Helios, god of the sun.

Upstairs galleries present works by Vicenza masters in the context of a handful of major works by Venetian masters such as Veronese, Tiepolo and Tintoretto.

La Rotonda
HISTORIC BUILDING

(☑ 049 879 13 80; www.villalarotonda.it; Via della Rotonda 45; villa/gardens €10/5; ☉ gardens 10am-noon & 3-6pm Tue-Sun mid-Mar–mid-Nov, to 5pm mid-Nov–mid-Mar, villa open Wed & Sat only) No matter how you look at it, this villa is a show-stopper: the namesake dome caps a square base, with identical colonnaded facades on all four sides. This is one of Palladio's most admired creations, inspiring variations across Europe and the USA, including Thomas Jefferson's Monticello.

Villa Valmarana 'Ai Nani'
HISTORIC BUILDING

(☑ 0444 32 18 03; www.villavalmarana.com; Stradella dei Nani 8; adult/reduced €9/6; ☉ 10am-12.30pm & 3-6pm Tue-Sun Mar-Oct, 10am-12.30pm Tue-Fri, 10am-12.30pm & 2.30-4.30pm Sat & Sun Nov-Jan) From La Rotonda, a charming footpath leads about 500m to the elegantly neoclassical Villa Valmarana 'ai Nani', the interior of which shelters 1757 frescoes by Giambattista Tiepolo and his son Giandomenico. Giambattista painted the Palazzina wing with his signature mythological epics, while his son painted the Foresteria with rural, carnival and Chinese themes.

Nicknamed after the 17 statues of gnomes ('ai Nani') around the perimeter walls, this estate is a superb spot for the occasional summer concert; check dates online.

🛏 Sleeping

Scores of hotels in greater Vicenza are listed on the tourism board website (www.vicenzae. org) and a dozen or so B&Bs can be found at www.vitourism.it.

Ostello Olimpico
HOSTEL €

(☑ 0444 54 02 22; www.ostellovicenza.com; Via Antonio Giuriolo 9; dm/s/d €20/29/50; ☉ reception 7.30-9.30am & 3.30-11.30pm; ☞) A convenient HI youth hostel set in a fine building by the Teatro Olimpico. There is no curfew and wi-fi is free.

Hotel Palladio
HOTEL €€

(☑ 0444 32 53 47; www.hotel-palladio.it; Contrà Oratorio dei Servi 25; s/d €110/170; Ⓟ ✳ @ ☞) The top choice in central Vicenza, this four-star hotel boasts well-appointed rooms done up in whitewashed minimalism, while preserving key details of the Renaissance *palazzo* it occupies.

Relais Santa Corona
HOTEL €€

(☑ 0444 32 46 78; www.relaissantacorona.it; Contrà Santa Corona 19; s/d €100/150; Ⓟ ✳ @ ☞) This boutique bargain offers stylish stays in an 18th-century palace ideally located on a street dotted with landmarks. Guest rooms are soothing and soundproofed, with excellent mattresses, minimal-chic decor and free wi-fi.

✗ Eating

Gastronomia Il Ceppo
DELI €

(☑ 0444 54 44 14; www.gastronomiailceppo.com; Corso Palladio 196; prepared dishes per 100g €3-

5; ☺8am-1pm & 3.30-7.45pm Mon, Tue & Thu-Sat, 8am-1pm Wed) San Daniele hams dangle over the vast glass counter, which is filled with ready-made specialities like fresh seafood salads, house-made pastas and cheeses. Ask counter staff to pair your food selections with a local wine from their shelves for a dream picnic at La Rotonda.

Julien
MODERN ITALIAN €€

(☑0444 32 61 68; Contrà Jacopo Cabianca 13; meals €18-25; ☺8.30am-2am) It's cool, it's crowded and with its floor-to-ceiling windows it is where Vicenza's hipsters gather to see and be seen. Fusion food includes basmati rice with shrimp and courgette, Caesar salads and grilled steaks, but you're not here for the food. Do as the locals do and grab yourself a cocktail and spend the evening grazing *aperitivo*.

Al Bersagliere
OSTERIA €€

(☑0444 32 35 07; Contrà Pescaria 11; meals €25-35; ☺12.30-2pm & 7.30-10pm Tue-Sat, 12.30-2pm Sun) Savour the taste of summer in Maria's *datterino* tomato and mozzarella salad or nurse a glass of Recioto with your stuffed quails or guinea-fowl pasta – Bersagliere's kitchen is first class, although the bill is surprisingly democratic. What's more, the exposed-brick interior with its hanging mezzanine is stylish and intimate.

Antico Ristorante agli Schioppi
OSTERIA €€

(☑0444 54 37 01; www.ristoranteaglischioppi.com; Contrà Piazza del Castello 26; meals €30-40; ☺dinner Mon, lunch & dinner Tue-Sat) Tucked under an arcade just off Piazza del Castello lies one of the city's simplest and best restaurants. The owners are devotees of locally sourced products, from wild forest greens to baby river trout, but without any pretensions about it; it's just what they know best.

🍷 Drinking & Nightlife

★ Osteria al Campanile
BAR

(☑0444 54 40 36; Piazza della Posta; ☺9am-2pm & 5-9pm) Owned by the same family for over three generations, the antique wooden bar of Al Campanile is one of Vicenza's historic watering holes, tucked beneath the Roman belltower by the cathedral. As you'd expect from local experts their cellar is stocked with unusual vintages such as the light red Tai Rosso and the sparkling Durelio.

Pasticceria Sorarù
CAFE

(☑0444 32 09 15; Piazzetta Palladio; ☺7.30am-12.30pm & 3.30-7.30pm Thu-Tue) Drink in the history at this marble-topped bar serving bracing espresso and pastries made on the premises. There are also tempting jars of sweets stashed on the elaborately gilded shelves. A few outdoor tables offer views of one of Italian's finest piazzas.

ℹ Information

Police station (☑0444 33 75 11; Viale G Mazzini 213)

Post office (Contrà Garibaldi 1; ☺8.30am-6.30pm Mon-Fri, to 1pm Sat)

Tourist office (☑0444 32 08 54; www.vicenzae.org; Piazza Matteotti 12; ☺9.30am-6pm Mon-Thu, to 7.30pm Fri-Sun) A good source of information on villas in the surrounding countryside.

ℹ Getting There & Away

Large car parks are located near Piazza Castello and the train station.

BUS

FTV (☑0444 22 31 15; www.ftv.vi.it) buses leave for outlying areas from the bus station, located next to the train station.

TRAIN

Three to four trains arrive hourly from Venice (€5.20 to €19.50, 30 minutes to 1¼ hours), Padua (€3.50 to €15, 15 to 40 minutes) and Verona (€4.70 to €16, 30 minutes to 60 minutes).

Verona

POP 263,950

Shakespeare placed star-crossed lovers Romeo Montague and Juliet Capulet in Verona for good reason: romance, drama and fatal family feuding have been the city's hallmark for centuries. From the 3rd century BC Verona was a Roman trade centre with ancient gates, a forum (now Piazza delle Erbe) and a grand Roman arena, which still serves as one of the world's great opera venues. In the Middle Ages the city flourished under the wrathful Scaligeri clan, who were as much energetic patrons of the arts as they were murderous tyrants. Their elaborate Gothic tombs, the Arche Scaligere, are just off Piazza dei Signori.

Under Cangrande I (1308–28) Verona conquered Padua and Vicenza, with Dante, Petrarch and Giotto benefitting from the city's patronage. But the fratricidal rage of

Verona

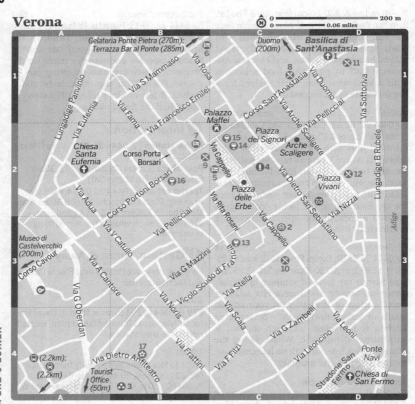

Cangrande II (1351–59) complicated matters, and the Scaligeri were run out of town in 1387. Venice took definitive control in 1404, ruling until Napoleon's arrival in 1797.

The city became a Fascist control centre from 1938 to 1945, a key location for Resistance interrogation and transit point for Italian Jews sent to Nazi concentration camps. Today, as the city grapples with its changing identity as an international commercial centre, it has become a Lega Nord (Northern League) stronghold. Yet the city is a Unesco World Heritage Site and a cosmopolitan crossroads, especially in summer when the 2000-year-old arena hosts opera's biggest names.

◉ Sights

Roman Arena   ARCHAEOLOGICAL SITE
(☑ 045 800 32 04; www.arena.it; Piazza Brà; opera tickets €21-220, adult/reduced €6/4.50, or with VeronaCard; ⊗ 8.30am-7.30pm Tue-Sun, 1.30-

7.30pm Mon; ⊡) This Roman-era arena, built of pink-tinged marble in the 1st century AD, survived a 12th-century earthquake to become Verona's legendary open-air opera house, with seating for 30,000 people. You can visit the arena year-round, though it's at its best during the June-to-August opera season. The **ticket office** (☑ 045 800 51 51; Via Dietro Anfiteatro 6b) is just outside.

Museo di Castelvecchio   MUSEUM
(☑ 045 806 26 11; Corso Castelvecchio 2; adult/reduced €6/4.50, or with VeronaCard; ⊗ 8.30am-7.30pm Tue-Sun, 1.30-7.30pm Mon; ⊡) Bristling with battlements along the River Adige, Castelvecchio was built in the 1350s by Cangrande II. The fortress was so severely damaged by Napoleon and then WWII bombings that many feared it was beyond repair. But instead of erasing the past with restorations, Carlo Scarpa reinvented the building, constructing bridges over exposed foundations,

Verona

filling gaping holes with glass panels, and balancing a statue of Cangrande I above the courtyard on a concrete gangplank.

Scarpa's revived Castelvecchio makes a fitting home for Verona's largest museum, with a diverse collection of statuary, frescoes, jewellery, medieval artefacts, and paintings by Pisanello, Giovanni Bellini, Tiepolo and Veronese.

Basilica di San Zeno Maggiore BASILICA
(www.chieseverona.it; Piazza San Zeno; adult/child €2.50/free, combined Verona church ticket €6 or with VeronaCard; ⊙8.30am-6pm Tue-Sat, 12.30-6pm Sun Mar-Oct, 10am-1pm & 1.30-5pm Tue-Sat, 12.30-5pm Sun Nov-Feb) A masterpiece of Romanesque architecture, the striped brick and stone basilica was built in honour of the city's patron saint. Enter through the flower-filled cloister into the nave – a vast space lined with 12th- to 15th-century frescoes. Painstaking restoration has revived Mantegna's 1457-59 *Majesty of the Virgin* altarpiece, painted with such astonishing perspective that you actually believe there are garlands of fresh fruit hanging behind the Madonna's throne.

Duomo CATHEDRAL
(☑045 59 28 13; www.chieseverona.it; Piazza Duomo; adult/reduced €2.50/2, or with VeronaCard; ⊙10am-5.30pm Mon-Sat, 1.30-5.30pm Sun Mar-Oct, 10am-1pm & 1.30-5pm Tue-Sat, 1.30-5pm Sun Nov-Feb) Verona's 12th-century cathedral is a striking, striped Romanesque building, with bug-eyed statues of Charlemagne's paladins Roland and Oliver, crafted by medieval master Nicolò, on the west porch. Nothing about this sober facade hints at the extravagant 16th- to 17th-century frescoed interior with angels aloft amid trompe l'œil architecture. At the left end of the nave is the **Cartolari-Nichesola Chapel**, designed by Renaissance master Jacopo Sansovino and featuring a vibrant Titian *Assumption*.

Torre dei Lamberti TOWER
(☑045 927 30 27; adult/reduced €6/4.50; ⊙8.30am-7.30pm) For superb views of Verona, take the lift or your feet up this 84m-high tower, built in stages from the 12th century (with a slight setback in 1403 when lightning knocked its top off). Sporting an octagonal bell tower, its two bells retain their ancient names: Rengo once called meetings of the city council, while Marangona warned citizens of fire.

★ Basilica di Sant'Anastasia BASILICA
(www.chieseverona.it; Piazza di Sant'Anastasia; adult/reduced €6/2, or with VeronaCard; ⊙9am-6pm Tue-Sat, 1-6pm Sun Mar-Oct, 1.30-5pm Tue-Sat, 1-5pm Sun Nov-Feb) Dating from the 13th to 15th centuries, the Gothic Chiesa di Sant'Anastasia is Verona's largest church and a showcase for local art. The multitude of frescoes is overwhelming, but don't overlook Pisanello's storybook-quality fresco *St George Setting out to Free the Princess from the Dragon* in the **Pisanelli Chapel**, or the 1495 holy water font featuring a hunchback carved by Paolo Veronese's father, Gabriele Caliari.

★ Giardino Giusti GARDEN
(☑045 803 40 29; Via Giardino Giusti 2; adult/reduced €6/5; ⊙9am-8pm Apr-Sep, to 7pm Oct-

VENICE & THE VENETO VERONA

> **ℹ MAKING THE MOST OF YOUR EURO**
>
> **VeronaCard** (www.veronacard.it; 2/5 days €15/20), available at tourist sights as well as tobacconists, grants access to most major monuments and churches, plus unlimited use of town buses.

WORTH A TRIP

BASSANO DEL GRAPPA, ASOLO & PALLADIO'S VILLA MASER

A road trip north from Vicenza takes you through one of Italy's most sophisticated stretches of countryside. You can visit all the key sites, even with a latish start and leisurely lunch.

Head first to Bassano del Grappa, which sits with charming simplicity on the banks of the Brenta river as it winds its way free from Alpine foothills. Located 35km northeast of Vicenza, the town is famous above all for its namesake spirit, a fiery distillation of winemaking leftovers: skins, pulp, seeds and stems. The town's most important structure is the **Ponte degli Alpini** (aka Ponte Vecchio), the covered bridge designed by Palladio. At the **Poli Museo della Grappa** (⏩ 0424 52 44 26; www.poligrappa.com; Via Gamba 6; ⊙ 9am-7.30pm) **FREE**, you can drink in four centuries' history of Bassano's signature grappa (including a free tasting). Before heading out of town, have lunch at the brightly contemporary **Ristorante Al Ponte** (⏩ 0424 21 92 74; www.alpontedibassano.com; Via Volpato 60; meals €35-50; ⊙ lunch Wed-Sun, dinner Tue-Sun), with its garden seating and perfect river views.

About 17km east of Bassano rises **Asolo**, known as the 'town of 100 vistas' for its panoramic hillside location, once the haunt of Romans and Veneti and a personal gift from Venice to Caterina, 15th-century queen of Cyprus, in exchange for her abdication. A historical hit with writers, including Pietro Bembo, Gabriele d'Annunzio and Robert Browning, its highbrow heritage outstrips its small size.

Another 5km east lies **Villa Maser** (⏩ 423 92 30 04; www.villadimaser.it; adult/reduced €6/5; ⊙ 10am-6pm Tue-Sun Apr-Jun & Sep-Oct, 10.30am-6pm Tue, Thu, Sat & Sun Mar, Jul & Aug, 11am-5pm Sat & Sun Nov-Feb), where Palladio and Paolo Veronese conspired to create the Veneto countryside's finest monument to *la bella vita* (the beautiful life). Palladio set the arcaded yellow villa into a verdant hillside with a fanciful grotto out the back. Inside Paolo Veronese nearly upstages his collaborator with wildly imaginative trompe l'œil architecture of his own. Vines climb the walls of the Stanza di Baccho; an alert watchdog keeps one eye on the painted door of the Stanza di Canuccio (Little Dog Room); and in a corner of the frescoed grand salon, the painter has apparently forgotten his spattered shoes and broom.

Mar; ♿) Across the river from the historic centre, these sculpted gardens, considered a masterpiece of Renaissance landscaping, are well worth seeking out. Named after the noble family that has tended them since opening them to the public in 1591, they have lost none of their charm. The vegetation is an Italianate mix of the manicured and natural, graced by soaring cypresses, one of which the German poet Goethe immortalised in his travel writings.

☆ Festivals & Events

VinItaly   WINE
(www.vinitaly.com) Held in April, the country's largest wine expo is open only to food and wine professionals. The event includes tastings, presentations about winemaking and unmatched insight into the breadth and depth of Italian wines.

Estate Teatrale Veronese   THEATRE, JAZZ
(www.estateteatraleveronese.it) One of the best ways to experience Verona's 1st-century-BC

Roman amphitheatre is during the summer festival, when a program of theatre (with a clear preference for Shakespeare and Goldoni), dance and jazz are performed at the archaeological site overlooking the city.

🛏 Sleeping

Cooperativa Albergatori Veronesi (⏩ 045 800 98 44; www.veronabooking.com) offers a no-fee booking service for two-star hotels. For homestyle stays outside the city centre, check **Verona Bed & Breakfast** (www.bedand breakfastverona.com).

Villa Francescatti   HOSTEL €
(⏩ 045 59 03 60; www.ostelloverona.it; Salita Fontana del Ferro 15; dm €18-20; ⊙ 7am-11.30pm) This HI youth hostel is housed in a 16th-century villa on a garden estate a 20-minute walk from central Verona. Rooms are off limits 9am to 5pm, and dinners require a reservation. Catch bus 73 (weekdays) or bus 90 (Sunday and holidays) from the train station. There's a strict 11.30pm curfew.

★ Corte delle Pigne
B&B €

(☑ 333 7584141; www.cortedellepigne.it; Via Pigna 6a; s €60-90, d €90-130, tr & q €110-150; P ❄ 🛜 🛁) The toast of the historic centre, this three-room B&B is arranged around the quiet internal courtyard of a historic villa. Personal touches are everywhere: a communal sweet jar, luxury toiletries and even a jacuzzi for one lucky couple.

Albergo Aurora
HOTEL €€

(☑ 045 59 47 17; www.hotelaurora.biz; Piazza XIV Novembre 2; s €90-135, d €100-160; ❄) Right off bustling Piazza delle Erbe yet cosy and blissfully quiet, this hotel has spacious, unfussy doubles, some with city views. There are cheaper single rooms with shared bathroom (€58 to €80). Head to the sunny terrace for drinks overlooking the piazza.

Hotel Gabbia d'Oro
HOTEL €€€

(☑ 045 59 02 93; www.hotelgabbiadoro.it; Corso Porta Borsari 4a; d from €220; P ❄ @ 🛜) One of the city's top addresses and also one of its most romantic, the Gabbia d'Oro features luxe rooms inside an 18th-century *palazzo* that manage to be both elegant and cosy. The rooftop terrace and central location are icing on the wedding cake.

Eating

Verona's historic centre teems with *osterie* and wine bars serving hearty country cooking with its emphasis on meats and thick sauces. For picnic supplies, pick up fresh fruit and veg from market stalls in Piazza delle Erbe. Nearby De Rossi (☑ 045 800 24 89; Corso Porta Borsari 3) sells fresh bread, pastries and plump olives, and mounds of homemade gnocchi. For meats and cheese, stroll 50m northeast to Albertini (☑ 045 803 10 74; Corso Sant'Anastasia 41).

Gelateria Ponte Pietra
GELATO €

(☑ 340 4717294; Via Ponte Pietra 23; ⏱ 2.30-10pm Jun-Aug, to 7.30pm Sep-Oct & Mar-May, closed Nov-Feb) Impeccable gelato is made on the premises, with flavours like *bacio bianco* (white chocolate and hazelnut), candied orange with cinnamon, and *mille fiori* (cream with honey and bits of pollen gathered from local hillsides).

Osteria Sottoriva
OSTERIA €

(☑ 045 801 43 23; Via Sottoriva 9a; meals €15-20; ⏱ 11am-10.30pm Thu-Tue) The last of the historic *osterie* that once lined this riverside alley, Sottoriva still draws local crowds to rough-hewn tables under the arcade, with wine by the glass at fair prices, and traditional pork sausages and horse meatballs.

La Taverna di Via Stella
VERONESE €€

(☑ 045 800 80 08; www.tavernadiviastella.com; Via Stella 5c; meals €20-30; ⏱ 11.30am-2.30pm & 6.30-11pm Thu-Sun & Tue, 11.30am-2.30pm Mon) Brush past the haunches of prosciutto dangling over the deli bar and make your way into a dining room, decorated Tiepolo-style with rustic murals of chivalric knights and maidens. This is the place you'll want to sample traditional Veronese dishes such as *pastissada* (horse stew), *bigoli* (a type of pasta) with duck *ragù* (meat and tomato sauce) and Denominazione di Origine Protetta (DOP; guarantees that a product and its production have been carried out in a strictly defined geographic area) Lessinia cheeses from Monte Veronese.

★ Pescheria I Masenini
SEAFOOD €€€

(☑ 045 929 80 15; www.imasenini.com; Piazzetta Pescheria 9; meals €50; ⏱ 12.30-2pm Wed-Sun, 7.30-10pm Tue-Sun) Located on the piazza where Verona's Roman fish market once held sway, Masenini quietly serves up Verona's most imaginative, modern fish dishes. Mullet tartare comes in a fresh tomato and basil purée, octopus is roasted with broccoli and anchovies, and scallops come gratinated with baked endives.

ROMEO & JULIET IN VERONA

Shakespeare had no idea what he'd start when he set his (heavily derivative) tale of star-crossed lovers in Verona, but the city has seized the commercial possibilities with both hands – everything from *osterie* (taverns) and hotels to embroidered kitchen aprons get the R&J branding. While the play's depiction of feuding families has genuine provenance, the lead characters themselves are fictional. Undaunted, in the 1930s the authorities settled on a house in Via Cappello (think Capulet) as Juliet's and added a 14th-century-style balcony and a bronze statue of our heroine. You can squeeze through the crowds at Casa di Giulietta (Juliet's House; ☑ 045 803 43 03; Via Cappello 23; adult/reduced €6/4.50 or with VeronaCard; ⏱ 8.30am-7.30pm Tue-Sun, 1.30-7.30pm Mon) onto the balcony itself, or see the circus from the square below, a spot framed by a slew of scribbled love graffiti.

VERONA'S OPERA FESTIVAL

On balmy summer nights, when 14,000 music lovers fill the Roman Arena and light their candles at sunset, expect goosebumps even before the performance starts. The festival (☎ 045 800 51 51; www.arena.it; Via Dietro Anfiteatro 6), which runs from mid-June to the end of August, was started in 1913 and is now the biggest open-air lyrical music event in the world. It draws international stars, and the staging is legendary – highlights have included Franco Zeffirelli's lavish productions of *Carmen* and *Aida*.

Prices rise at weekends and range from €21 to €25 on unreserved stone steps and €183 to €198 on the central gold seats. Performances start around 9pm with locals booking their dinner table for after the show. Tucking into a preshow picnic on the unreserved stone steps is fine, so decant that wine into a plastic bottle (glass and knives aren't allowed), arrive early, rent a cushion and prepare for an utterly unforgettable evening.

Drinking & Nightlife

Piazza delle Erbe is ringed with cafes and bars and fills with a fashionable drinking crowd come early evening. Most of them gather outside historic **Caffe Filippini** (☎ 045 800 45 49; Piazza delle Erbe 26; ⊙ 4pm-2am daily Jun-Aug, Thu-Tue Sep-May) and hip **Casa Mazzanti** (☎ 045 800 32 17; www.casamazzanticaffe.it; Piazza delle Erbe 32; ⊙ 8am-2am).

★ **Osteria del Bugiardo**　　WINE BAR
(☎ 045 59 18 69; Corso Porta Borsari 17a; ⊙ 11am-11pm, to midnight Fri & Sat) On busy Corso Porta Borsari, traffic converges at Bugiardo for glasses of upstanding Valpolicella bottled specifically for the *osteria*. Polenta and *sopressa* make worthy bar snacks for the powerhouse Amarone.

Antica Bottega del Vino　　WINE BAR
(☎ 045 800 45 35; www.bottegavini.it; Vicolo Scudo di Francia 3; 3 tasting plates €27; ⊙ noon-11pm) Wine is the primary consideration at this historic, wood-panelled wine bar. The sommelier will gladly recommend a worthy vintage for your lobster *crudo* salad, Amarone risotto or suckling pig – some of the best wines here are bottled specifically for the *bottega*. Note it sometimes closes in November and February.

Terrazza Bar al Ponte　　BAR
(☎ 045 927 50 32; www.terrazzabaralponte.eu; Via Ponte di Pietra 26; ⊙ 9am-2am) Join hip, young locals for *spritz* beneath the giant chandelier in this retro-cool bar. Come early enough and you might even nab a table on the tiny terrace overlooking the river and the Ponte Pietra.

ⓘ Information

Ospedale Borgo Trento (☎ 045 807 11 11; Piazza A Stefani) Hospital northwest of Ponte Vittoria.

Police station (☎ 113; Lungadige Galtarossa 11) Near Ponte Navi.

Tourist office (www.tourism.verona.it) At the airport (☎ 045 861 91 63; Verona-Villafranca airport; ⊙ 10am-4pm Mon & Tue, to 5pm Wed-Sat) and on Via degli Alpini (☎ 045 806 86 80; Via degli Alpini 9; ⊙ 9am-7pm Mon-Sat, 10am-4pm Sun). Extremely knowledgable and helpful.

ⓘ Getting There & Around

AIR

Verona-Villafranca airport (www.aeroportoverona.it) is 12km outside town and accessible by ATV Aerobus to/from the train station (€6, 15 minutes, every 20 minutes 6.30am to 11.30pm). A taxi costs €30. Flights arrive from all over Italy and some European cities, including Amsterdam, Barcelona, Berlin, Brussels, Dusseldorf, London and Paris.

BUS

The main intercity bus station is in front of the train station in the Porta Nuova area. Buses run to Padua, Vicenza and Venice.

Azienda Trasporti Verona (AVT; ☎ 045 805 79 22; www.atv.verona.it) city buses 11, 12, 13 and 14 (bus 91 or 92 on Sunday and holidays) connect the train station with Piazza Brà. Buy tickets from newsagents and tobacconists before you board the bus (tickets valid for one hour, €1.50).

TRAIN

There are at least three trains hourly to Venice (€7.50 to €23, 1¼ to 2½ hours), Padua (€6 to €18, 40 to 90 minutes) and Vicenza (€4.70 to €16, 30 minutes to one hour). There are also regular services to Milan (€11.50 to €21.50, 1½ to two hours) and Florence (€24 to €57, 1½ to three hours) and points south, as well as direct international services to Austria and Germany.

Verona's Wine Country

A drive through Verona's hinterland is a lesson in fine wine. To the north and northwest are Valpolicella vineyards, which predate the arrival of the Romans, and east on the road to Vicenza lie the white-wine makers of Soave.

Soave

Southeast of Verona, Soave serves its namesake DOC white wine in a story-book setting. The town may be entirely encircled by medieval fortifications, including 24 bristling watchtowers, but these days strangers are more than welcome to taste the good stuff across from the old-town church at Azienda Agricola Coffele (☑ 045 768 00 07; www.coffele.it; Via Roma 5; ⊙ 9am-12.30pm & 2.30-6.30pm Mon-Sat & by appt).

The more adventurous can climb up to Soave's medieval castle (☑ 045 768 00 36; www.castellodisoave.it; admission €6; ⊙ 9am-noon & 3-6.30pm Tue-Sun Apr-Oct, 9am-noon & 2-4pm Oct-Mar) and enjoy spectacular views over the surrounding countryside from the upper ramparts. If you have a car, strike out for Suavia (☑ 045 767 50 89; www.suavia.it; Via Centro 14, Fittà; ⊙ 9am-1pm & 2.30-6.30pm Mon-Fri, 9am-1pm Sat & by appt; ☏), a trailblazing winery in Fittà (about 8km north of Soave) run by the three Tessari daughters. Here, using sun-ripe Garganega grapes, the often light Soave is transformed into something altogether more complex with accents of licorice, aniseed and fennel.

Just outside the medieval walls of Soave, Locanda Lo Scudo (☑ 045 768 07 66; www.lo scudo.vr.it; Via Covergnino 9, Soave; meals €35-45, s/d €75/110; ⊙ 12.30-2.30pm & 7-10.30pm Tue-Sat Sep-Jul) is half country inn and half high-powered gastronomy. Book in here for daily fish specials and risotto made with Verona's zesty Monte Veronese cheese. Above the restaurant there are four lovely rooms.

To reach Soave, hop onto the Milan–Venice train to San Bonifacio (€2.85, 20 minutes) and catch the local ATV bus 30 (€1.80, 10 minutes, about two hourly), or exit the A4 autostrada at San Bonifacio and follow the Viale della Vittoria 2km north into town.

Valpolicella

The 'valley of many cellars', from which Valpolicella gets its name, has been in the business of wine production since the ancient Greeks introduced their *passito* technique (the use of partially dried grapes) to create the blockbuster flavours we still enjoy in the region's Amarone and Recioto wines.

Situated in the foothills of Monte Lessini, the valleys benefit from a happy microclimate created by the enormous body of Lake Garda to the west and cooling breezes from the Alps to the north. No wonder Veronese nobility got busy building weekend retreats here. Many of them, like the extraordinary Villa della Torre, still house noble wineries, while others like Villa Spinosa (☑ 045 750 00 93; www.villaspinosa.it; Via Colle Masua 12, Negrar; apt per 2/4/6 people €110/235/300; ☏) and the fabulous, family- and foodie-friendly Agriturismo San Mattia (☑ 045 91 37 97; www.agriturismosanmattia. it; Via Santa Giuliana 2, Verona; s €60-70, d 85-105, apt per wk €500-1150; ☏ ☐) ☏ provide comfortable accommodation.

◉ Sights

Seven *comuni* compose the DOC quality-controlled area: Pescantina, San Pietro in Cariano, Negrar, Marano di Valpolicella, Fumane, Sant'Ambrogio di Valpolicella and Sant' Anna d'Alfaedo.

To reach them, follow the SS12 northwest out of Verona, veer north onto SP4 and follow the route west towards San Pietro in Cariano, the region's main hub. Alternatively, APT bus 3 departs Verona's Porta Nuova for San Pietro about every half-hour (€2.60, 40 minutes). For tourist information, biking and hiking itineraries visit the Valpolicella tourist office (☑ 045 770 19 20; www.valpolicellaweb.it; Via Ingelheim 7; ⊙ 9am-12.30pm Mon-Fri, 3-6pm Tue & Thu-Sun, 9.30am-12.30pm Sat & Sun).

VENICE & THE VENETO VERONA'S WINE COUNTRY

---

❶ WINE TOURS

If you don't want to bother renting a car, Pagus (☑ 045 751 44 28; www. pagusvalpolicella.net) offers half- and full-day tours of Valpolicella and Soave, leaving regularly from Verona. Tours include visits to unusual, rural sites, impromptu rambles, lunches in local restaurants and, of course, wine tastings. Tours can also be customised.

DON'T MISS

TOP TIPPLES

➜ Allegrini ([☎] 045 683 20 11; www.allegrini.it; Via Giare 9/11, Fumane; tours €12-60; ◷ by appt; [P]) Valpolicella aristocracy, the Allegrini family have been producing grand crus from Corvinia and Rondinella grapes since the 16th century.

➜ Fratelli Vogadori ([☎] 328 941 72 28; www.amaronevalpolicella.org; Via Vigolo 16, Negrar; ◷ by appt) ✎ Producing just 10,000 bottles, the eponymous Vogadori brothers use organic methods and unusual native varieties such as Oseleta and Negrara.

➜ ★ Massimago ([☎] 045 888 01 43; www.massimago.com; Via Giare 21, Mezzane di Sotto; ◷ 9am-3.30pm Mon-Fri) Breaking the traditional mould, Camilla Chauvet concentrates on a limited range of lighter, more modern Valpolicellas at her winery-cum-*relais*, including a rosé and an unusual sparkling variety.

➜ Tezza ([☎] 045 55 02 67; www.tezzawines.it; Stradella Maioli, Valpantena; ◷ by appt) In the sheltered Valpantena valley, the Tezza brothers use a mixture of traditional and modern methods to produce their intense, tannic, dry wines.

➜ Valentina Cubi ([☎] 045 770 18 06; www.valentinacubi.it; Località Casterna 60, Fumane; ◷ by appt) ✎ This teacher-winemaker is blazing a trail with one of the few certified organic wineries in the region. The San Cero is one of few 'natural' Valpolicellas, which includes no sulphates at all.

Villa della Torre HISTORIC BUILDING
(www.villadellatorre.it; Via della Torre 25, Fumane; guided tour of the villa/with wine tasting/with lunch €10/30/60; [P]) The jewel in the Allegrini crown, this historic villa dates to the 16th century and was built by intellectual and humanist Giulio della Torre. Star-chitects such as Giulio Romana (of Palazzo Te fame), Michele Sanmicheli and Bartolomeo Ridolfo all contributed to its construction, and now Allegrini wine tastings are held in the peristyle or in front of Ridolfo's gaping-mouthed, monstrous fireplaces.

Pieve di San Giorgio CHURCH
(San Giorgio, Valpolicella; ◷ 7am-6pm) [FREE] In the tiny hilltop village of San Giorgio a few kilometres northwest of San Pietro in Cariano, you'll find this fresco-filled, cloistered 8th-century Romanesque church. Not old enough for you? In the little garden to its left you can also see a few fragments of an ancient Roman temple.

✗ Eating

★ **L'Antica Osteria Le Piere** OSTERIA €
([☎] 045 884 10 30; Via Nicolini 43, Mizzole; meals €15; ◷ noon-2.30pm & 7-10pm) In this large stone mansion in the village of Mizzole, self-trained chef Maurizio Poerio serves hearty three-course lunches to villagers and vineyard workers. Seasonal wild asparagus, pumpkin, wild game and smoky cured ham accompany a 250-bottle wine list. And Mau-

ro promises he'll open any one of them to serve by the glass.

Trattoria Caprini TRATTORIA €€
([☎] 045 750 05 11; www.trattoriacaprini.it; Via Zanotti 9, Negrar; meals €25-30; ◷ noon-2.30pm & 7-10pm Thu-Mon) This family-run trattoria in the centre of Negrar serves heart-warming home cooking. Many items on the menu are homemade, including the delicious *lasagnetta*, with hand-rolled pasta and a *ragù* of beef, tomato, porcini and finferli mushrooms. Downstairs, beside the fire of the old *pistoria* (bakery), you can sample some 200 Valpolicella labels.

Prosecco Country

In the foothills of the Alps, Conegliano (pop 34,250) and Valdobbiadene (pop 10,700) are the toast of the Veneto. Their vine-draped hillsides produce *prosecco*, a dry, crisp white wine made in *spumante* (bubbly), *frizzante* (sparkling) or still varieties.

To explore the region properly you'll need a car of your own. The A27 heads directly north from Mestre to Conegliano, and two or three trains per hour leave from Venice to Conegliano (€4.15, one hour).

◉ Sights & Activities

Plot a tasting tour along the Strada di Prosecco (Prosecco Rd; www.coneglianovaldobbiadene.it) from Conegliano to Valdobbiadene and drop into friendly, family-run wineries like **Azienda Agricola Barichel** (☑0423 97 57 43; www.barichel.net; Via Zanzago 9, Valdobbiadene) and **Azienda Agricola Frozza** (☑0423 98 70 69; www.frozza.it; Via Martiri 31, Colbertaldo di Vidor) where you can pick up bottles of top-quality bubbly for between €4 and €7. Conegliano's **tourist office** (☑0438 212 30; Via XX Settembre 61, Conegliano; ⊙9am-12.30pm Tue-Sun, 3-6pm Thu-Sun) can also supply information and help book visits.

In Conegliano itself, don't miss the eye-catching **Scuola dei Battuti**, covered inside and out with 16th-century frescoes by Ludovico Pozzoserrato. This building was once home to a religious lay group known as *battuti* (beaters) for their enthusiastic self-flagellation. Enter the **Duomo** through the *scuola* to discover early works by Veneto artists, notably a 1492–93 altarpiece by local master Cima da Conegliano.

Sleeping & Eating

Azienda Agricola Campion FARMSTAY € (☑0423 98 04 32; www.campionspumanti.it; Via Campion 2, San Giovanni di Valdobbiadene; s €45, d €65-75; ⊙tasting room 9am-noon & 3-7pm; P❄❄) Why not quit worrying about the challenges of *prosecco* tasting and driving and instead bed down at this farm-stay amid 14 hectares of vines in the heart of Valdobbiadene. The four charming rooms have been converted from farm buildings, and have been renovated in a warm rustic style.

★**Agriturismo Da Ottavio** AGRITURISMO € (☑0423 98 11 13; Via Campion 2, San Giovanni di Valdobiaddene; meals €15-20; ⊙noon-3pm Sat, Sun & holidays, closed Sep;) *Prosecco* is typically drunk with *soppressa*, a fresh local salami, as the sparkling *spumante* cleans the palate and refreshes the mouth. There's no better way to test this than at Da Ottavio, where everything on the table, *soppressa* and *prosecco* included, is homemade by the Spada family.

Veneto Dolomites

The spiked peaks and emerald-green valleys of the Venetian Dolomites are encompassed within the 31,500-hectare Parco Nazionale dell Dolomiti Bellunesi, just north of the Piave river and the historic town of Belluno. Further north, fashion-conscious snow bunnies flock to Cortina d'Ampezzo for excellent skiing and hiking in the Cinque Torri and the Parco Naturale di Fanes-Sennes-Braies. The latter sits in the neighbouring region of Trentino-Alto Adige (p300).

Belluno

POP 35,500 / ELEV 390M

Perched on high bluffs above the Piave river and backed majestically by the snow-capped Dolomites, Belluno makes a scenic and strategic base to explore the surrounding mountains. The historical old town is its own attraction, with easy walks past Renaissance-era buildings. And you'll be happy to fuel up for tramps in the nearby mountains on the city's mountain-based cuisine and some of Italy's most remarkable cheeses, including Schiz (semisoft cow's milk cheese, usually fried in butter) and the flaky, butter-yellow Malga Bellunense.

◉ Sights & Activities

Belluno's main pedestrian square is the **Piazza dei Martiri** (Martyrs' Sq), named after the four partisans hanged here in WWII. Nearby, the **Piazza del Duomo** is framed by the early-16th-century Renaissance **Cattedrale di San Martino**, the 16th-century **Palazzo Rosso** and the **Palazzo dei Vescovi**, with a striking 12th-century tower.

Parco Nazionale delle Dolomiti Bellunesi PARK (www.dolomitipark.it) Northwest of Belluno, this magnificent national park offers trails for hikers at every level, wildflowers in spring and summer and restorative gulps of crisp mountain air year-round. Between late June and early September, hikers walking six **Alte Vie delle Dolomiti** (high-altitude Dolomites walking trails) pass Belluno en route to mountain refuges. Route 1 starts in Belluno and, in about 13 days, covers 150km of breathtaking mountain scenery to **Lago di Braies** in Val Pusteria to the north. For more information about other hikes of all lengths and levels of difficulty, including themed itineraries and maps, check out www.parks.it/parco.nazionale.dol.bellunesi/Eiti.php.

Sleeping & Eating

To explore hotel, B&B, camping and *agriturismo* (farm stay accommodation) options in Belluno, the Parco Nazionale and beyond, check www.infodolomiti.it.

Shakespeare's Veneto

There is much debate about whether Shakespeare ever visited Italy, but his Italian plays are full of local knowledge. Venetian writer, architect and presenter Francesco da Mosto spoke to *Lonely Planet Traveller* magazine about the playwright's favourite Italian cities.

Verona

Verona was not thought of as a city of romance before *Romeo and Juliet* – in fact, not many people would have heard of it as it was very much in the shadow of Venice at that time. We don't know whether Romeo and Juliet existed, although Italian poet Dante did mention two feuding families, called the Montecchi and the Cappelletti. The famous balcony where Romeo is said to have declared his love to Juliet is close

to Verona's main promenade – although since the balcony was apparently added to a suitably old house in 1936, it's doubtful it is the original! My favourite site in Verona is Juliet's tomb. People go there to pay tribute to Juliet and Shakespeare – even Dickens visited.

Padua

The University of Padua was one of the first in the world, and in Shakespeare's time, the city was very well known as a centre of learning throughout Europe – Galileo (of telescope fame) and Casanova (of sexual-conquest fame) are both alumni. Shakespeare used its reputation, rather than actual locations, as a backdrop to *The Taming of the Shrew* – apart from the university, he rarely mentions specific sites. The best way to experience Shakespeare's Padua is

1. Piazza San Marco and Palazzo Ducale (p340) **2.** Juliet's balcony, Casa di Giulietta (p393), Verona **3.** Medieval Padua (p381)

by having a stroll around the university. It feels like a little world unto itself, detached from the rest of the city. There is a marvellous wooden anatomical amphitheatre in the Medical School that was built in the 16th century, where they dissected humans and animals for the students. The life of the university runs through the city. It's lovely to walk through the portico walkways that run under the houses, and into the Prato della Valle, one of the main city squares.

Venice

Shakespeare set *Othello* in Venice, and *The Merchant of Venice* mentions the Rialto Market area several times. He even talked about gondolas and 'the tranect', which could refer to the *traghetto* ferry, which transported people from Venice to the mainland. If he did visit,

Shakespeare would have spent his time wandering the streets, eavesdropping on people's conversations and observing the goings-on in shops and at the market. A walk to the Rialto is certainly evocative of that time. The Palazzo Ducale, with its magnificent Gothic facades and huge council hall, is probably what Shakespeare had in mind as the setting for the final courtroom scene in *The Merchant of Venice*, while the two bronze figures on top of the Torre dell'Orologio clock tower in Piazza San Marco are known as 'i Mori', or 'the Moors', which is a key reference in *Othello*.

PROSECCO LOWDOWN

What are the origins of prosecco? *Prosecco* can be traced back to the Romans. It was then known as 'Pucino' and was shipped direct to the court of Empress Livia from Aquileia, where it was produced with grapes from the Carso. During the Venetian Republic the vines were transferred to the Prosecco DOCG (quality-controlled) area, a small triangle of land between the towns of Valdobbiadene, Conegliano and Vittorio Veneto.

Describe the character of a good prosecco Straw yellow in colour with sparkling greenish reflections. The naturally formed bubbles are tiny, numerous and long-lasting in your glass. It's fragrant with fresh notes of white fruits and fresh grass. It pleases your mouth with its crispness and aromaticity. Keep in mind that these characteristics are not long-lasting – *prosecco* is meant to be drunk young.

Prosecco and the social scene Here in the Veneto we drink *prosecco* like water – sometimes it's even cheaper than water!

Mario Piccinin, sommelier and guide for Venice Day Trips (p361)

★ **Alla Casetta**   B&B €

(☑ 0439 428 91; www.allacasetta.com; Via Strada delle Negre 10, Cesiomaggiore; s €40-45, d €56-64; P @ ⊕) It might take the navigation skills of an Alpinist to find this patch of paradise on the Caorame river, but once you're installed you probably won't want to leave. It is home to superhosts Christian and Amy, who are happy to hand-draw maps of hiking and biking routes (the Alta Via 2 and Via Claudia Augusta bike trail are nearby), steer you in the direction of the nearest *malga* (cheese-making hut) and point out the choicest fishing and kayaking spots on the river.

Ostello Imperina   HOSTEL €

(☑ 0437 624 51; www.ostellodelledolomiti.it; Località Le Miniere; dm €25, half/full board €45/60; ☺ 7.30am-10pm Apr-Oct) The area's only youth hostel lies inside the Parco Nazionale delle Dolomiti Bellunesi, 35km northwest of Belluno at Rivamonte Agordino. Book ahead in summer. To get there, take the Agordo bus (50 minutes) from Belluno.

Al Borgo   TRADITIONAL ITALIAN €€

(☑ 0437 92 67 55; www.alborgo.to; Via Anconetta 8, Belluno; meals €30-40; ☺ noon-2.30pm Mon, noon-2.30pm & 7-10pm Wed-Sun) If you have wheels or strong legs, seek out this delightful restaurant in an 18th-century villa in the hills about 3km south of Belluno. Considered Belluno's best, the kitchen produces everything from homemade salami and roast lamb to artisanal gelato. Wines are also skilfully chosen.

Ristorante Terracotta   BELLUNESE €€

(☑ 0437 29 16 92; www.ristoranteterracotta.it; Borgo Garibaldi 61, Belluno; lunch menu €16, meals €30-40; ☺ 7-10.30pm daily, noon-2.30pm Thu-Mon) Having come down from the mountains, the Larese family have now converted a historic home in the heart of Belluno where they serve their signature seasonal menu with care and attention. The intimate dining room opens out onto a small courtyard in summer and the young chef reinterprets traditional dishes with great flair. Try the venison carpaccio with mustard ice cream and cranberries.

❶ Information

Tourist office (☑ 0437 94 00 83; www.infodolomiti.it; Piazza Duomo 2; ☺ 9am-12.30pm daily, 3.30-6.30pm Mon-Sat)

❶ Getting There & Away

By car, take the A27 from Venice (Mestre) – it's not the most scenic route, but avoids traffic around Treviso.

BUS

In front of the train station, **Dolomiti Bus** (☑ 0437 21 71 11; www.dolomitibus.it) offers regular service to Cortina d'Ampezzo, Conegliano and smaller mountain towns.

TRAIN

Services from Venice (€7, two to 2½ hours, five to 10 daily) run here via Treviso and/or Conegliano. Some require a change, which can add another hour.

Cortina d'Ampezzo

POP 5900 / ELEV 1224M

The Italian supermodel of ski resorts, Cortina d'Ampezzo is fashionable, pricey, icy and undeniably beautiful. The town's stone church spires and pleasant piazzas are framed by magnificent Alps. It doubles as a slightly less glamorous but still stunning summertime base for hiking, biking and rock climbing.

Activities

Winter crowds arrive in December for top-notch downhill and cross-country skiing and stay until late March or April, while from June until October summertime adventurers hit Cortina for climbing and hiking. Two cable cars whisk skiers and walkers from Cortina's town centre to a central departure point for chairlifts, cable cars and trails. Lifts usually run from 9am to 5pm daily mid-December to April and resume June to October.

Ski and snowboard runs range from bunny slopes to the legendary Staunies black mogul run, which starts at 3000m. The Dolomiti Superski pass provides access to 12 runs in the area, and are sold at Cortina's **ski pass office** (☑ 0436 86 21 71; www.dolomitisuperski.com; Via G Marconi 15; 1-/2-/3-/7-day pass €45/90/133/248; ☺ hours vary). Discounts are available for seniors, under 16s, families and season passes. You can also get better deals if you purchase passes online, in advance.

Other winter adventures in Cortina include dog sledding, ice climbing and skating at the **Olympic Ice Stadium** (☑ 0436 88 18 11; Via dello Stadio 1; adult/child incl skate rental €10/9; ☺ hours vary), built for the 1956 Winter Olympics. In the nearby Cinque Torri you can try your hand at **snowkiting** (www.kite4freedom. it) and, in summer, rock climbing.

Gruppo Guide Alpine Cortina (☑ 0436 86 85 05; www.guidecortina.com; Corso Italia 69a) runs rock-climbing courses (three-day climbing course including gear rental €260), mountain climbing and guided nature hikes (prices vary). In winter it also offers courses in off-trail skiing, snowshoeing and more.

🛏 Sleeping

For additional sleeping options, consult www.infodolomiti.it. Note that prices vary widely with the seasons, and spike wildly at the Christmas holidays. Many places close in April, May and/or November.

International Camping
Olympia   CAMPGROUND €
(☑ 0436 50 57; www.campingolympiacortina.it; Località Fiames 1; camping adult/child from €6/3, tent & car €7-9; ☺ May-Oct; ☏ 🖳) Sleep beneath towering pines 4km north of Cortina in Fiames, with free shuttles to town and on-site pizzeria, market, laundry and sauna.

Hotel Montana   HOTEL €
(☑ 0436 86 21 26; www.cortina-hotel.com; Corso Italia 94, Cortina d'Ampezzo; s €46-78, d €85-175; @) Right in the heart of Cortina, this friendly, vintage 1920s Alpine hotel offers simple but well-maintained rooms. In winter there's a seven-night minimum (€320 to €560 per person), but call for last-minute cancellations. Reception areas double as gallery space for local artists.

Baita Fraina   INN €
(☑ 0436 36 34; www.baitafraina.it; Via Fraina 1, Cortina d'Ampezzo; d Jan-Nov €60-100, Dec €100-140; ☺ closed May & Nov; ☏) Reserve ahead in high season at this beloved, Swiss-style inn with simple but spotless rooms of knotty pine. The fine restaurant has a menu inspired by local ingredients, from mountain herbs to wild game.

CINQUE TORRI

At the heart of the Dolomites, just 16km west of Cortina at the confluence of the Ampezzo, Badia and Cordevole valleys, is the gorgeous area of **Cinque Torri** (www.5torri.it). It is accessible from Cortina by bus: a ski shuttle in winter (free to ski-pass holders) and a Dolomiti Bus service in summer, which connect with the lifts at **Passo Falzarego**.

Hard though it is to believe, some of the fiercest fighting of WWI took place in these idyllic mountains between Italian and Austro-Hungarian troops. Now you can wander over 5km of restored trenches in an enormous open-air museum between Lagazuoi and the Tre Sassi fort. Guided tours are offered by the Gruppo Guide Alpine, and in winter you can ski the 80km **Great War Ski Tour** with the Dolomiti Superski pass. En route, mountain refuges like **Rifugio Scoiattoli** (☑ 333 814 69 60; www.5torri.it/rifugio-scoiattoli; Località Potor, 2255m; meals €15-25, half board per person €55; ☺ 9am-9pm) and **Rifugio Averau** (☑ 0436 46 60; www.5torri.it/rifugio-averau; Forcella Averau, 2413m; meals €35; ☺ 9am-10pm; 🖳) provide standout lunches with spectacular views.

Eating

Cortina's pedestrian centre is ringed with pizzerias and cafes, which are your best bets for reasonable eats. The real culinary action takes place on the surrounding slopes, where a network of *rifugi* (mountain huts) cook up some of the heartiest and homiest gourmet cuisine in the Alps.

★ Agriturismo El Brite de Larieto AGRITURISMO €
(☎368 700 80 83; www.elbritedelarieto.it; Passo Tre Croci, Località Larieto; meals €20; ⏲noon-3pm & 7-10pm high season, Sat & Sun only low season; 👪) Located 5km northwest of Cortina off the SS48 towards Passo Tre Croci, this idyllic farm enjoys a wonderfully sunny situation in the midst of thick larch forest. It produces all its own dairy products, vegetables and even many of the cuts of meat on the menu and you can expect some sensational home cooking. The mountain dumplings stuffed with cheese, artichoke or beetroot are a real highlight.

Ristorante Da'Aurelio GASTRONOMIC €€
(☎0437 72 01 18; www.da-aurelio.it; Passo Giau 5, Colle Santa Lucia; meals €30-45, tasting menu €55) Located at an altitude of 2175m, on the road between Cortina and Selva (SP638), elegant Da'Aurelio serves *haute* mountain cuisine in a classic chalet-style restaurant. Part of the **Alto Gusto** (www.ristorantealtogusto.eu) network of gourmet chefs, Luigi Dariz produces startling flavours from the freshest mountain ingredients, such as his rich, yellow egg with fragrant finferli mushrooms and the rack of lamb crusted with mountain herbs.

The restaurant offers two comfortable rooms, which are worth considering if you're indulging in the tasting menu.

Il Meloncino TRADITIONAL ITALIAN €€€
(☎0436 44 32; www.ilmeloncino.it; Locale Rumerlo 1, Cortina d'Ampezzo; meals €45-60; ⏲noon-2.30pm & 7-10pm Wed-Mon) With a rustically elegant dining room and spectacular terrace, Il Meloncino is one of the few finer restaurants that stays open almost year-round (though it does close for part of May and June). The roasted boar and venison-stuffed ravioli in a hazelnut sauce are as jaw-dropping as the Alpine views.

Information

Tourist office (☎0436 32 31; www.infodolomiti.it; Piazzetta San Francesco 8; ⏲9am-12.30pm & 3.30-6.30pm Mon-Sat)

Getting There & Away

The following companies operate services out of Cortina's **bus station** (Via G Marconi).

Cortina Express (☎0437 86 73 50; www.cortinaexpress.it) Daily direct services to Mestre train station (€20, 2¼ hours) and Venice airport (two hours).

Dolomiti Bus (☎0437 21 71 11; www.dolomitibus.it) For smaller mountain towns, Belluno and other Veneto locales.

SAD Buses (☎0471 45 01 11; www.sad.it) Services to nearby towns, Bolzano and other Alto Adige destinations.

The nearest train station is in Calalzo di Cadore, 35km south of Cortina. A convenient bus service departs every hour from outside the station, taking you straight to the centre of Cortina.

Friuli Venezia Giulia

Includes ➡

Best Places to Eat

➡ La Frasca (p415)

➡ La Subida (p415)

➡ Salumare (p410)

Best Places to Stay

➡ L'Albero Nascosto (p409)

➡ Palazzo Lantieri (p414)

➡ Albergo Diffuso Sauris (p427)

Why Go?

With its triple-barrelled moniker, Friuli Venezia Giulia's multifaceted nature should come as no surprise. Cultural complexity is cherished in this small, little-visited region, tucked away on Italy's far northeastern borders with Austria and Slovenia. Friuli Venezia Giulia's landscapes offer profound contrasts too, with the foreboding, perpetually snowy Giulie and Carnic Alps in the north, idyllic grapevine-filled plains in the centre, the south's beaches, Venetian-like lagoons and curious, craggy karst encircling Trieste.

While there's an amazing reserve of often uncrowded historical sights, from Roman ruins to Austro-Hungarian palaces, this is also a fine destination for simply kicking back with the locals, tasting the region's world-famous wines and discovering a culinary heritage that will broaden your notions of the Italian table. Serene, intriguing Trieste and friendly, feisty Udine make for great city time – they're so easy and welcoming you'll soon feel as if you're Friulian, Venezian or Giulian too.

When to Go
Trieste

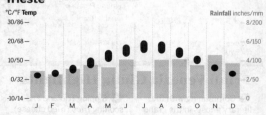

Feb Discover the uncrowded slopes of the Carnic and Giulie Alps.

Jun Feast on prosciutto at San Daniele's Aria di Festa.

Oct Watch sails fill the horizon at Trieste's Barcolana Regatta.

History

The semiautonomous region of Friuli Venezia Giulia came into being as recently as 1954; its new capital, Trieste, had already traded national allegiances five times since the beginning of the century. Such is the region's history, a rollicking, often blood-stained one of boom, bust and conquest that began with the Romans in Aquileia, saw Cividale rise to prominence under the Lombards, and witnessed the Venetians do their splendid thing in Pordenone and Udine. It was Austria, however, that established the most lasting foothold, with Trieste as its main seaport. While the region today is a picture of quiet prosperity, much of the 20th century was another story. War, poverty, political uncertainty and a devastating earthquake saw Friulians become the north's largest migrant population, most bound for Australia and Argentina.

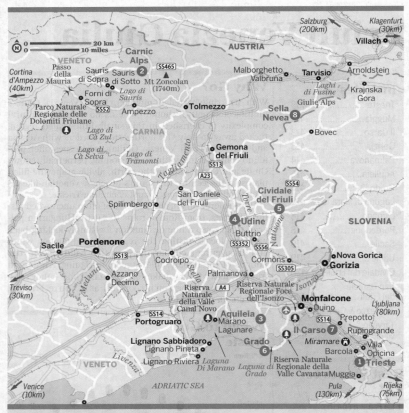

Friuli Venezia Giulia Highlights

1 Communing with the literary ghosts in the grand cafes of **Trieste** (p405).

2 Retreating to the wilds of the **Carnic Alps** (p426).

3 Picturing a 4th-century-AD Roman port as you wander **Aquileia** (p415).

4 Sipping Friulano and scoffing *frico* (fried cheese) in one of the rowdy bars of **Udine** (p419).

5 Marvelling at an 8th-century Lombard chapel in **Cividale del Friuli** (p425).

6 Strolling the lively old town of sun-drenched beach resort **Grado** (p416).

7 Tasting your way through the rustic vineyards of the Colli Orientali and the **Carso** (p413).

8 Skiing across borders at **Sella Nevea** (p428).

ℹ Getting There & Around

Most of the region's major destinations can be reached by train or road from Venice in around two hours. **Friuli Venezia Giulia airport** (No-Borders; www.aeroporto.fvg.it; Via Aquileia 46, Ronchi Dei Legionari), aka Ronchi dei Legionari or Trieste No-Borders, is 33km northwest of Trieste, near Monfalcone, with daily flights from Rome, London, Munich and Frankfurt, and less-frequent services from Belgrade and Tirana. The Austrian cities of Salzburg and Graz are around four hours' drive from Udine.

Trieste

POP 205,500

Trieste, as travel writer Jan Morris once opined, 'offers no unforgettable landmark, no universally familiar melody, no unmistakable cuisine', yet it's a city that enchants many, its 'prickly grace' inspiring a cultlike roll-call of writers, travellers, exiles and misfits. Devotees come to think of its glistening belle époque cafes, dark congenial bars and even its maddening bora wind as their own; its lack of intensive tourism can make this often feel like it's true.

Tumbling down to the Adriatic from a karstic plateau and almost entirely surrounded by Slovenia, the city is physically isolated from the rest of the Italian peninsula. Its historical singularity is also no accident. From as long ago as the 1300s, Trieste has faced east, becoming a free port under Austrian rule. The city blossomed under the 18th- and 19th-century Habsburgs; Vienna's seaside salon was also a fluid borderland where Italian, Slavic, Jewish, Germanic and even Greek culture intermingled.

◉ Sights

Most of Trieste's sights are within walking distance of the city's centre, the vast Piazza dell'Unità d'Italia, or can be accessed by Trieste's efficient bus network.

★**Castello di Miramare**   HISTORIC BUILDING
(☑ 0412 77 04 70; www.castello-miramare.it; adult/reduced €4/2; ☺ 9am-7pm summer, to 4pm winter) Sitting on a rocky outcrop 7km from the centre, Castello di Miramare is Trieste's elegiac bookend, the fanciful neo-Gothic home of the hapless Archduke Maximilian of Austria.

Maximilian came to Trieste in the 1850s as the commander-in-chief of Austria's imperial navy, an ambitious young aristocrat known for his liberal ideas. After chancing upon Miramare's site while sailing, he de-

ℹ FRIULI VENEZIA GIULIA TOURISM ONLINE

Tourist offices throughout the region fall under the regional FVG tourist organisation and share the same website (www.turismofvg.it). The offices are helpful and stock excellent maps and information for the entire region.

cided to build a home there. In 1864, while work was still in progress, he was talked into taking up the obsolete crown of Mexico, but after Benito Juárez reestablished republican rule in 1867, Maximilian was shot by a firing squad. His wife, Princess Charlotte of Belgium, was so stricken with grief that she spent the rest of her life believing Maximilian was still alive, and only briefly returned to live at Miramare.

The house has remained essentially as she left it, a reflection of Maximilian's eccentric wanderlust along with the various obsessions of the imperial age: a bedroom is modelled to look like a frigate's cabin, there's ornate orientalist salons and a red silk-lined throne room. Upstairs, a suite of rooms used by the Anglophile military hero Duke Amadeo of Aosta in the 1930s is intact, furnished in the Italian Rationalist style. Amadeo proved as ill-fated as Maximilian: appointed viceroy of Ethiopia in 1937, he was to die five years later in a British POW camp in Kenya.

Maximilian was a keen botanist and the castle is set in 22 hectares of **gardens** (☺ 8am-7pm summer, to sunset winter), which burst with the colour and scent of rare and exotic trees.

Piazza dell'Unità d'Italia   PIAZZA
This vast public domain – said to be the biggest square opening onto a waterfront in Italy – is an elegant triumph of Austro-Hungarian town planning and contemporary civil pride. Pristine but peopled, it's not only a good place for a drink or a chat, but it's also perfect for a quiet moment staring out at ships on the horizon.

Borgo Teresiano   NEIGHBOURHOOD
Much of the graceful city-centre area north of Corso Italia dates to the 18th-century reign of Empress Maria Theresa, including the photogenic **Canal Grande**. Reflecting centuries of religious tolerance, it's here you'll also find the mosaic-laden 1868 Serbian Orthodox

Trieste

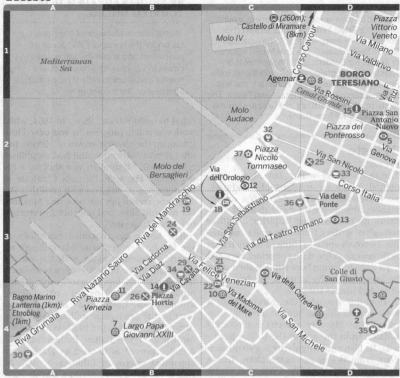

Chiesa di Santo Spiridione (Via F Filzi) juxtaposed with the neoclassical 1842 Catholic **Chiesa di Sant'Antonio Taumaturgo** (Via Della Zonta). On the Via Roma bridge stands a life-sized **statue of James Joyce** (Piazza Hortis is home to a similar bronze of **Italo Svevo**).

Castello di San Giusto   MUSEUM
(☑ 040 30 93 62; Piazza della Cattedrale 3; adult/reduced €6/3; ⏱ 9am-7pm summer, to 1pm winter) Once a Roman fort, this sturdy 15th-century castle was begun by Frederick of Habsburg and finished off by blow-in Venetians. The city museum is housed here, with temporary exhibitions and a well-stocked armoury. Wander around the walls for magnificent views.

Basilica di San Giusto   CHURCH
(⏱ 8am-5pm) Completed in 1400, this Ravennan-Byzantine hybrid is the synthesis of two earlier palaeo-Christian basilicas. The interior contains 13th-century frescoes and wonderfully preserved 12th- and 13th-century mosaics, including one of St Justus, the town's patron saint.

Synagogue   SYNAGOGUE
(☑ 040 672 67 36; www.triestebraica.it; Via San Francesco d'Assisi 19; admission €3.50; ⏱ guided tours 10am, 11am & noon Sun) This imposing and richly decorated neoclassical synagogue, built in 1912, is testament to the strength of Trieste's Jewish community. Heavily damaged during WWII, it has been meticulously restored and remains one of the most important synagogues in Italy.

Arco di Riccardo   ROMAN SITE
(Via del Trionfo) The Arco di Riccardo is an early Roman remnant, one of the old town gateways, dating from 33 BC, and looks over a pretty residental square. The gate is named for the English King Richard, who was supposed to have passed through en route from the Crusades.

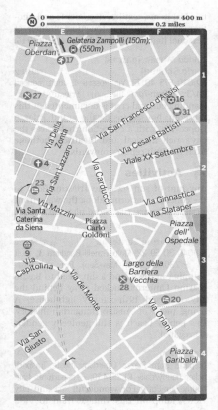

N
0 —————————— 400 m
0 —————————— 0.2 miles

Trieste

Roman Theatre ROMAN SITE

(Via del Teatro Romano) Behind Piazza dell'Unità d'Italia rise remains of the Roman theatre, which was built between the 1st and 2nd centuries AD. Concerts are held here occasionally during summer.

Museo Revoltella MUSEUM

(📞 040 675 43 50; www.museorevoltella.it; Via Diaz 27; adult/reduced €7/5; ⊙ 10am-7pm Wed-Mon) This city museum was founded in 1872 and now spills into two neighbouring buildings. Baron Revoltella's original mid-19th-century house throbs with conspicuous consumption; his cup runneth over with chandeliers, ornate gilded plasterwork and flamboyant silk wallpaper. The modern Palazzo Brunner has an interesting collection of 19th- and 20th-century works by Triestine artists, including some arresting early-20th-century portraiture and busts. There's also a pretty rooftop cafe and good bookshop.

> **ⓘ FVG CARD**
>
> This discount card (48 hour/72 hour/7 days €15/20/29) provides free admission to all civic museums; free transport in Udine, Lignano and on the Udine–Cividale del Friuli train and free audio tours plus numerous discounts in the region's shops, spas, beaches and parks. The cards are available from all FVG tourist offices, some hotels and online.

Civico Museo Sartorio MUSEUM
(✆040 30 14 79; Largo Papa Giovanni XXIII 1; adult/child €6/3; ◎9am-6pm Tue-Sun) Another significant city villa, stuffed with art, ceramics and jewellery, and featuring beautiful ceiling frescoes – some dating to the late 18th century – and a basement Roman mosaic. Don't miss the room of superb **Tiepolo drawings**, virtuosic and intimate in turns, or the **Triptych of Santa Chiara**, an exquisitely detailed, extremely intimate wooden altarpiece from the 14th century.

Civico Museo di Storia ed Arte ed Orto Lapidario MUSEUM
(History & Art Museum & Stone Garden; ✆040 31 05 00; Piazza della Cattedrale 1; adult/reduced €5/3; ◎9am-7pm Tue-Sun summer, to 1pm winter) This creaky old museum houses Roman antiquities unearthed in and around Trieste and Aquileia, including the impressive iron horde of the Necropolis of Reka from the Slovenian border. The **Orto Lapidario** (Stone Garden) has a pot-luck assembly of weather-resistant stone finds scattered among flowers and fruit trees.

Museo Joyce & Svevo MUSEUM
(✆040 359 36 06; 2nd fl, Via Madonna del Mare 13; ◎9am-1pm Mon-Sat & 3-7pm Thu) FREE Joyce would enjoy the irony: his museum really belongs to friend and fellow literary great, Italo Svevo, housing a significant collection of the Triestini's first editions, photos and other memorabilia. Joyce is dealt with ephemerally, with a wall map of his haunts and homes and a Bloomsday bash in June (Svevo's birthday is also celebrated, on 19 December).

Museo della Comunità Ebraica Carlo e Vera Wagner MUSEUM
(✆040 63 38 19; Via del Monte 5; adult/reduced €5/3; ◎10am-1pm Mon, Wed, Fri & Sun, 4-7pm Tue & Thu) A small, highly prized collection of liturgical items, textiles, documents and photographs, including a touching number of personal items stolen by Nazi troops in 1945.

Civico Museo Teatrale Carlo Schmidl MUSEUM
(✆040 675 40 72; Via Rossini 4; adult/reduced €4/3; ◎9am-7pm Tue-Sun) Trieste's long-standing cultural cred is documented at this museum, housed inside the grand Palazzo Gopcevich, with a collection that traces the city's rich musical and theatrical heritage from the 18th century onwards.

🏃 Activities

Any hint of sun sees the Triestini flock to the concrete platforms along the waterfront **Viale Miramare** (it's more pleasant than it sounds).

Bagno Marino Lanterna SWIMMING
(✆040 30 59 22; Molo Fratelli Bandiera 3; adult €1; ◎7.30am-7.30pm May-Sep) For sun-worshipping in town, and a dip, head to Bagno Marino Lanterna, tucked away behind the city's disused 19th-century lighthouse. A living piece of Austro-Hungarian history, this pebbly beach is still genteelly gender-segregated.

No 2 Tram TRAM
(departs from Piazza Oberdan; Trieste Trasporti ticket hourly/daily €1.25/4.10; ◎departures half-hourly 7am-8pm) For wonderful sea and city views, jump on this vintage tram to **Villa Opicina**. For most of the 5km journey it's a regular tram, but a funicular section tackles the steep gradient as it heads up into the Carso. It's a short but significant trip; Villa Opicina was once almost entirely Slovenian-speaking and today retains a decidedly un-Italian feel.

🛏 Sleeping

Trieste's mid- to high-end places often slash rates on weekends and can be astonishingly good value, especially compared with other Italian cities.

Residenzale 6a BOUTIQUE HOTEL €
(✆0406 72 67 15; www.residenzale6a.it; Via Santa Caterina 7; s/d €65/85; ☼🖂) Upstairs in an imposing Borgo Teresiano building, this small, cosy hotel mixes traditional furnishings with bright, modern bathrooms. Poetically, each of the elegant rooms is named and decorated for one of Italo Svevo's women characters. There's a large lounge and leafy internal courtyard for relaxing with a cup of tea.

Residence del Mare
APARTMENT €

(☑ 040 30 73 46; www.residencedelmare.it; Via della Madonna del Mare 4; apt 1/2 persons €85/100; ❄️🛜) If you're not after high design or pots of atmosphere, these apartments are large, very well equipped and brilliantly located. Upper floors have city views and staff are helpful.

⭐ L'Albero Nascosto
BOUTIQUE HOTEL €€

(☑ 040 30 01 88; www.alberonascosto.it; Via Felice Venezian 18; s/d €85/150; ❄️🛜🅿️) A friendly little hotel hidden smack in the middle of the old town, Nascosto exemplifies Trieste's discreet, no-fuss style. Rooms are generously sized and decorated with a vintage piece or two; all except the single have a small kitchen. Breakfasts are similarly simple but thoughtful, with local cheese, top-quality preserves and Illy coffee on tap.

Hotel Savoia Excelsior Palace
LUXURY HOTEL €€

(☑ 040 7 79 41; http://savoiaexcelsiorpalace.starhotels.com; Riva del Mandracchio 4; d €170; ❄️🛜) This glamorous 'newcomer' to Trieste's hotel scene, a classic but contemporary (and ever so slightly camp) refit of the great-boned Habsburg-era Grand Hotel, is giving the city's famed Duchi a run for its money. Grand it still is, with over 100 light-filled luxurious rooms, first-rate public areas, sea views and reasonable prices.

Hotel Victoria
HOTEL €€

(☑ 040 36 24 15; www.hotelvictoriatrieste.com; Via Oriani 2; d €130; ❄️🛜🅿️) This is a far-from-bland business-oriented place: there's a crisp Upper East Side aesthetic in the rooms, a guest-only sauna and Turkish bath, and a reading room. James Joyce was once a resident and there are small homages to him throughout the hotel, including a dedicated suite and contemporary art works.

Hotel Miramare
HOTEL €€

(☑ 040 224 70 85; www.hotelmiramaretrieste.it; Viale Miramare 325/1; d €150; 🅿️❄️🛜) Beautiful sea views from all rooms, simple beachy design and a well-priced but stylish – love the Cassina leather chairs – restaurant and summery bar.

Grand Hotel Duchi d'Aosta
LUXURY HOTEL €€€

(☑ 040 760 00 11; www.grandhotelduchidaosta.com; Piazza dell'Unità d'Italia 2; r €140-259; ❄️🛜) There's been a hotel of sorts on this prime site since Roman times, and the Duchi remains Trieste's grand dame. Public spaces are hushed and intimate, and the rooms are opulently traditional – the way repeat visitors like them. The bathrooms might be a tad frumpy for some five-star tastes, but the moody basement pool is a good trade-off.

Hotel Vis a Vis
HOTEL

(☑ 040 760 00 11; www.hotelvisavis.net; Piazza dello Squero Vecchio 1; s/d €160/175) Vis a Vis is the Duchi's slickly modern offshoot, with smallish but luxurious, all-mod-con rooms. A great choice if your tastes tend towards the contemporary, but you'd like in on the Duchi facilities.

✗ Eating

Trieste's long years as one of the Austro-Hungarian empire's busiest ports, along with its Slavic hinterland, are nowhere clearer than in the kitchen. Seafood is fantastic,

WORTH A TRIP

RISIERA DI SAN SABBA

This former rice-husking plant became a concentration camp in 1943 and has been a **national monument and museum** (☑ 040 82 62 02; Via Palatucci 5; admission free; ⊙ 9am-7pm) since the 1960s.

The site commemorates the 5000 people who perished here and the many thousands more that passed through on the way to Nazi forced labour and death camps. These included a great many of the city's Jewish population along with Triestine and Slovenian Resistance fighters.

Although the death cells remain, most of the camp's horrific wartime structures were destroyed by the retreating German forces in 1945. The monument solemnly traces their outlines in metal and stone, their absence creating areas of reflection. A collection of prisoners' photographs, letters and other artefacts are deeply personal and vividly alive.

Take bus 8 from the train station, or bus 10 from the Riva, a 20 minute trip; from the last bus stop walk past the stadium, turning left into Via Palatucci.

THE DUBLINER

Think you're escaping and run into yourself. Longest way round is the shortest way home.
James Joyce, Ulysses

Stifled by the gloom and obligations of Dublin, James Joyce escaped to Trieste in 1905 with a contract to teach English at the local Berlitz language school. Along with lover (and soon wife) Nora Barnacle, the precocious but still unpublished 22-year-old arrived in a city that epitomised the twilight years of the Austro-Hungarian empire.

Trieste was a booming, brilliantly cosmopolitan place, with a polyglot creative class and no shortage of dissolute aristocrats. The gregarious Irishman wasted no time immersing himself in this fertile scene and quickly picked up the floral Triestini dialect. In between his teaching commitments, failed business ventures, family life and all-night benders, he slowly set about drafting the text of his first two ground-breaking novels, *Dubliners* and *Portrait of the Artist as a Young Man*. Perennially poor, he spent the bulk of his writing hours in the city's fin de siècle cafes, Trieste life all about him.

The Joyces remained in the city until 1915, when the outbreak of WWI forced them to relocate to neutral Zurich. Joyce returned after the war, but he was unimpressed by the brash new order and quickly made tracks for Paris. *Ulysses* may have been given form in the City of Light, but its genesis was undoubtedly in the multilingual melting pot that was pre-WWI Trieste.

with dishes often reminiscent of Venice, but Trieste's most characteristic culinary experience is to be had in its still-thriving swag of buffets. Triestine bakeries are a scented, sweet delight: grab a *putizza* (a nut-filled brioche) to have with an excellent Illy coffee.

★**SaluMare** SEAFOOD €
(www.salumare.it; Via Cavana 13a; meals €15; ⊙11.30am-2.30pm & 6-10pm Tue-Sat) This bright, buzzing reinvention of the Triestine buffet features fish and seafood. Order at the bar from a menu of small dishes: white polenta and *baccalá mantecato* (salt-cod purée), prawn ceviche, smoked eel and green apple *tartines*. Wash it down with a well-chosen Friulian or Veneto white. There are plenty of reasons to linger, starting with the huge library of cookbooks and restaurant guides, a welcoming communal table and a daily delivery of international newspapers.

Buffet da Siora Rosa BUFFET €
(☑040 30 14 60; Piazza Hortis 3; meals €24; ⊙8am-9.30pm Tue-Sat) Opened before WWII by Mrs Rosa Caltaruzza (a portrait of whom still graces the wall), the family-run Siora Rosa is still one of the most traditional of Trieste's buffets, set in a wonderfully retro room. Sample sausages, sauerkraut and other Germanic and Hungarian offerings, or opt for the dumplinglike gnocchi or seafood stews with fried polenta.

Buffet Da Pepi BUFFET €
(Via Cassa di Risparmio 3; meals €15; ⊙8.30am-8pm Mon-Sat) The counter here is a site of porcine carnage: legs, necks, bellies, tongues and testicles, all awaiting a slap of relish from the huge ceramic jars and a grate of *kren* (horseradish). Hot, takeaway brisket or pork rolls (€3) are great for lunch.

Buffet Rudy BUFFET €
(Via Valdirivo 32; meals €20; ⊙10am-midnight Mon-Sat) Rudy has been concocting traditional boiled meats, cold cuts and beer since, oh, 1897. Come for the pork joints, served up with the house sauerkraut or just drinks and snacks at the bar (this being the beer-iest of all the buffets).

Pirona PASTRIES & CAKES €
(Largo Barriera Vecchia 12; ⊙7.30am-8pm Tue-Sat) This jewel-box pastry shop and cafe was one of Joyce's favourites. Its nutty, spicy, boozy Triestine speciality cakes, *putizza, presnitz* and *pinza,* are particularly good.

Gelateria Zampolli GELATO €
(Via Carlo Ghega 10; ⊙9.30am-midnight Thu-Tue) Be prepared for the crowds if you want to sample the city's best gelato: the Sachertorte flavour is a must, and its mousse-style range can't be beaten.

Al Bagotto SEAFOOD €€€
(☑040 30 17 71; www.albagatto.it; Via Cadorna 7; meals/degustation €50/60; ⊙7.30pm-midnight Mon-Sat) This old-timer, with its dark, brood-

ing dining room, could be stuffy, but it's far from it, with young, engaging staff and bold flavours on the plate. The seafood *degustazione* – something involving squid ink and *fritto misto* (fried seafood) will invariably play a part – is daunting but delicious. The 'seasonal creative' menu is just that, or you can try ordering like the suited regulars: the freshest of fish by the *etto* (100g), weighed and filleted at the table.

Drinking & Nightlife

Trieste's historic cafes conjure times past, but remain a thriving, and deeply satisfying, part of daily city life (the Triestini drink twice as much coffee as the national average). Cafes, bars and buffets blur, as does what constitutes *aperitivo* (predinner drinks with snacks). Evenings out are a refined, relaxed mix of young and old and early-evening drinks often stretch well into the night with the help of hearty buffet snacks. Via San Nicolo's bars cater to a smart after-work set, while the old town's cluster of bars have a more boho bent. In summer there are come-and-go outdoor places along the Viale Miramare.

Chocolat
CAFE
(Via Cavana 15b; ⊙7.30am-8pm Tue-Sat) This lovely cafe and chocolate shop makes everything in-house, including the hot chocolate slowly simmering in a great pot behind the counter and, in summer, gelato. Happily there's no surcharge for sitting at the big communal table outside on the square.

Caffè Torinese
CAFE
(Corso Italia 2; ⊙7am-9pm Tue-Sun) The smallest and, dare we say, friendliest of the historic bunch, this is an exquisite room that's just as nice for an evening wine as a morning *capo un' b* (macchiato in a glass).

Osteria da Marino
WINE BAR
(Via della Ponte 5; ⊙from noon Mon-Fri, from 6pm Sat & Sun) They know their wine at this bottle-and barrel-lined place. If you can't make it to the Carso wine region, get the owner to ply you with indigenous grape varieties (their Vitovska selection is encyclopedic). Or just settle in with a Franciacorte sparkling or a Tuscan red and wait for the little meatballs to appear.

Grip Wunderbar
BAR
(Via San Giusto 22; ⊙7pm-2am Tue-Thu, to 4am Fri & Sat) Booths, beer on tap and vinyl! Yes, Trieste goes indie at this great little corner bar beneath Castello di San Giusto.

Buffet Al Spaceto
BUFFET
(Via Belpoggio 3a; snacks €1.80-3; ⊙8am-10pm Mon-Fri, to 3pm Sat) An eccentric and convivial grab bag of locals gather here for glasses of local wine and a few rounds of whatever is on offer in the snack counter.

Caffè San Marco
CAFE
(Via Battisti 18; ⊙8am-9pm Tue-Sat) Opening just before WWI, this melancholy giant is spectacularly decorated with theatrical mask paintings, dark chocolate-coloured walls and miles of marble tables. Service can be surly.

Caffè Tommaseo
BAR
(☑040 36 26 66; www.caffetommaseo.com; Riva III Novembre; ⊙8am-12.30am) Virtually unchanged since its 1830 opening, the richly moulded ceilings, primrose yellow walls and Viennese mirrors here couldn't be any more evocative. Take coffee at the bar or sit down for a schnitzel (meals €22) and a chance to linger among the ghosts.

Entertainment

Teatro Verdi
OPERA
(☑040 672 21 11; www.teatroverdi-trieste.com; Riva III Novembre 1) Trieste's opera house is a little bit Scala and a little bit Fenice (thanks to a pair of duelling architects), but wears the mix well. Don't miss a chance to see a performance here; the Triestini are passionate opera lovers and make a great audience.

BUFFET, TRIESTE-STYLE

You'll be sure to eat well, in fact extremely well, at a Triestine buffet, but banish any thought of all-you-can-eat meal deals. These rowdy bar-restaurants are yet another legacy of the city's Austro-Hungarian past; if Trieste's bakeries conjure up Vienna, its buffets are Budapest all over. Usually all-day, and night, affairs, small snacks – cod or zucchini fritters, topped toasts and *panini* – are available from early morning and gobbled over lunch or at *aperitivo* (predinner drinks) time. But, hey, who's here for zucchini? Beef brisket may be a stalwart, but pork – baked, boiled, cured, stuffed into a sausage or fried – is the star attraction. Fresh grated *kren* (horseradish), *capuzi* (sauerkraut) and *patate in tecia* (mashed potatoes) are traditional accompaniments.

COFFEE, TRIESTE-STYLE

This coffee capital has its own, often confounding, terminology. For an espresso ask for *un nero*, for a cappuccino, order a caffe latte, for a macchiato order a *capo* – a cappuccino – and, for either in a glass, specify '*un b*' – the 'b' short for *bicchiere*, a glass.

Tours

Walking Tours   WALKING TOUR
(€7/free with FVG card; ⊙10.30am daily Apr-Sep, Sat & Sun Oct, Sat Nov-Mar) Book through the tourist office.

❶ Information

Hospital (☑0403 99 11 11; Piazza dell'Ospedale 2)
Police station (☑0403 66 111; Via Genova 6)
Tourist office (☑0403 47 83 12; turismofvg. it; Via dell'Orologio 1; ⊙9am-6pm Mon-Sat, to 1pm Sun)

❶ Getting There & Away

AIR

Friuli Venezia Giulia airport (p405; aka Ronchi dei Legionari or Trieste No-Borders) has direct daily flights to and from Rome, London, Munich and Frankfurt, and less-frequent services for Belgrade and Tirana. Venice's Marco Polo airport is around 1½ hours away by car or you can catch the train to Mestre (two to three hours) and then bus it from there.

BOAT

From mid-June to late September motor-boat services run to and from Grado, Lignano and points along the Istrian coast in Slovenia and Croatia; check with the tourist office for the current operator.

Agemar (☑040 36 37 37; Nuova Stazione Marittima – Molo IV; deck seat 1 way winter/summer €65/80) sells tickets for the twice-weekly car ferry to and from Durres in Albania.

BUS

National and international services operate from the **bus station** (☑040 42 50 20; www. autostazionetrieste.it; Via Fabio Severo 24). These include services to destinations in Slovenia and Croatia, including Zagreb (€22.50, five hours, daily Tuesday to Saturday) and Dubrovnik (€79, 15 hours, twice weekly).

APT (Azienda Provinciale Trasporti Gorizia; ☑800 955957; www.aptgorizia.it) Bus 51 runs to the airport approximately every 30 minutes

between 4.30am and 10.35pm from Trieste bus station (€4, one hour).

Florentia Bus (☑040 42 50 20; www.florentiabus.it) Operates bus services to Ljubljana (€14.50, 2¾ hours, daily), Belgrade (€55, 10 hours, two days a week) and Sofia in Bulgaria (€55, 16½ hours, daily).

TRAIN

Train station (Piazza della Libertà 8) Serves Gorizia (€3.80, 50 minutes, hourly), Udine (€6.70, one to 1½ hours, at least hourly), Venice (€9.20 to €13.50, two hours, at least hourly) and Rome (€70, 6½ to 7½ hours; most require a change at Mestre).

❶ Getting Around

BOAT

Trieste Trasporti (☑800 016675; www.triestetrasporti.it) Shuttle boats depart from the stazione marittima to Muggia year-round (one way/return €4/7, 30 minutes, six to 10 times daily). Check for other seasonal services with the tourist office.

BUS

Trieste Trasporti (☑800 016675; www.triestetrasporti.it) Bus 30 connects the train station with Via Roma and the waterfront; bus 24 runs from the station to Castello di San Giusto; bus 36 links Trieste bus station with Miramare. One-hour tickets cost €1.25, all-day €4.15.

TAXI

Radio Taxi Trieste (☑040 30 77 30; www.radiotaxitrieste.it) Operates 24hours; from the train station to the centre will cost around €7.

There's a €3 flag fall and €2 surcharge between 10pm and 6am, €2 surcharge on public holidays.

Muggia

POP 13,400

The fishing village of Muggia, 5km south of Trieste, is the only Italian settlement on the historic Istrian peninsula. Slovenia is just 4km south and Croatia (the peninsula's main occupant) a score more. With its 14th-century castle and semi-ruined walls, the port has a Venetian feel and its steep hills make for lovely views back towards Trieste.

Locals gather over jugs of wine and groaning platters of deer or boar salami at **Pane, Vine e San Daniele** (Piazza Marconi 5; ⊙8am-2pm & 8pm-2am Mon-Sat) on the main square behind the port, or there are a number of same-ish seafood restaurants along the waterfront. Ferries shuttle between Muggia and Trieste.

Il Carso

If Trieste is known for its cultural idiosyncrasy, its hinterland is also fittingly distinct. Dramatically shoehorned between Slovenia and the Adriatic, the Carso (Karst in German, Kras in Slovenian) is a windswept calcareous tableland riddled with caves and sinkholes. This wild landscape has long inspired myths and legend, not to mention those of a romantic inclination, while its geology has lent its name – karst – to geologically similar terrain around the world. It's a compelling place to visit in any season but is particularly pretty in spring, when the grey-green hills are speckled with blossom, or in autumn, when the vines and *ruje* (smoke trees) turn crimson and rust.

◎ Sights

Grotta Gigante   CAVE
(☑040 32 73 12; www.grottagigante.it; adult/reduced €11/9; ⊙50min guided tours hourly 10am-6pm daily summer, 10am-4pm Tue-Sat winter) The area's big-ticket attraction is near Villa Opicina, 5km northeast of Trieste. At 120m high, 280m long and 65m wide, it's one of the largest and most spectacular caves that's accessible on the continent. It's easily reached from Trieste on bus 42, or by tram 2 and bus 42 in the other direction.

Casa Carsica   MUSEUM
(☑040 32 71 24; Rupingrande 31; ⊙10-11.30am & 3-5pm Sun Apr-Oct) **FREE** This house museum in Rupingrande re-creates life in the premodern Slovenian-speaking Carso. It also organises the plateau's most important folk festival, Nozze Carsiche (Kraška ohcet; Karstic Wedding), held every two years for four days at the end of August in a 16th-century fortress in Monrupino.

Castello di Duino   CASTLE
(☑040 20 81 20; www.castellodiduino.it; adult/reduced €8/5; ⊙9.30am-5.30pm Wed-Mon Apr-Sep, reduced access & hours Mar & Oct-Nov) Fourteen kilometres northwest along the coast from Miramare, this 14th- and 15th-century bastion picturesquely marches down the cliff, surrounded by a verdant garden. The Czech poet Rainer Maria Rilke was a guest here from 1911, a melancholy and windswept winter stay which produced the *Duino Elegies*. To get here, take bus 41 from Trieste's Piazza Oberdan.

Gorizia

POP 36,000 / ELEV 86M

Considering its serene modern incarnation, you'd never guess the turmoil of Gorizia's past. An oft-shifting border zone throughout much of its history and the scene of some of the most bitter fighting of WWI's eastern front, it was most recently an Iron Curtain checkpoint. The town's name is unmistakably Slovenian in origin and before the outbreak of WWI it was not uncommon to hear conversations in several different languages – German, Slovenian, Friulian, Italian, Venetian and Yiddish – in the main square.

Gorizia's appeal today lies in its aristocratic ambience, its unique Friulian-Slovenian cooking and its easy access to surrounding countryside, famed for its wine and rustic restaurants.

POP-UP WINE SHOPS

Osmize predate the trendy retail pop-up phenomena by a few centuries, care of an 18th-century Austrian law that gave Carso farmers the right to sell surplus from their barns or cellars once a year (the term *osmiza* comes from the Slovenian word for eight, the number of days of the original licence). It's mainly vineyards that hold *osmiza* today, and farm cheeses and cured meats are always on offer too. While the Carso is known for its gutsy, innovative winemakers, *osmize* traditions still hold sway. Don't try asking for a list: finding an *osmiza* is part of the fun. Look first, along Carso roads, for the red arrows. Then look up, to gates or lintels bearing a *frasca* – a leafy branch hung ceremoniously upside down announcing that the *osmiza* is open for business. Don't forgo the chance to try the Carso's native wines: the complex, often cloudy, sometimes fierce, white Vitovska; or Terrano, aka Teran, a berry-scented red. Winemakers Zidarich (☑040 20 12 23; www.zidarich.it; Prepotto 23) and Skerk (☑040 20 01 56; www.skerk.com; Prepotto 20) do, in fact, announce *osmiza* dates, usually in November and April, on their websites, and cellar visits can be arranged at other times.

⊙ Sights

Borgo Castello
CASTLE

(☑ 0481 53 51 46; Borgo Castello 36; adult/reduced €3.50/2.50; ⊙ 10am-7pm Tue-Sun) Gorizia's main sight is its castle, perched atop a knoll-like hill. It has some convincing re-creations and a fine wood-panelled great hall. Beneath the main fortress huddle two oddly paired museums. The tragic, gory history of the WWI Italian-Austrian front is explored at the Museo della Grande Guerra including a to-scale re-creation of a trench. Then there's fashion: 19th- and early-20th-century finery at the Museo della Moda e delle Arti Applicate. The price covers entry to Borgo Castello, the Museo della Grande Guerra and the Museo della Moda e delle Arti Applicate

Piazza Transalpina
HISTORIC SITE

One for cold war kids. The Slovenian border – a mere formality since December 2007 – bisects the edge of Gorizia, and you can celebrate Schengen with a bit of border hopscotch at this piazza's centre, while contemplating the now crumbling fences, border posts and watchtowers.

Palazzo Coronini Cronberg
PALACE

(☑ 0481 53 34 85; www.coronini.it; Viale XX Settembre 14; adult/reduced €5/3; ⊙ 10am-1pm & 2-7pm Tue-Sun) This 16th-century residence is jammed with antiquities and is surrounded by lush gardens, which are free to visit on their own.

Chiesa di Sant'Ignazio
CHURCH

(Piazza della Vittoria; ⊙ 8am-noon & 3-7pm) Constructed from 1654 to 1724, the onion-shaped domes of this high-baroque church watch over Gorizia's old town square.

🛏 Sleeping & Eating

Cafes and bars can be found on Corso Italia and Via Terza Armata, while the old-town streets below the castle and around the covered food market (Via Verdi 30) are the best places to find casual restaurants.

★ Palazzo Lantieri
B&B €€

(☑ 0481 53 32 84; www.palazzo-lantieri.com; Piazza Sant'Antonio 6; s/d €80/140; P 🛜 ♿) This palazzo-stay offers light, spacious rooms in the main house or self-catering apartments in former farm buildings, all overlooking a glorious Persian-styled garden. Goethe, Kant and Empress Maria Theresa were repeat guests back in the day, and antiques fill both public and private spaces, but the charming Lantieri family are far from stuck in the past. Their contemporary art commissions mean there's a Michelangelo Pistoletto on the ceiling and a Jannis Kounellis in the attic. Nonguests can arrange guided tours.

Grand Hotel Entourage
HOTEL €€

(☑ 0481 55 02 35; www.entouragegorizia.com; Piazza Sant'Antonio 2; s/d €80/120; P ❄ ♿ @) Well-mannered traditional hotel that's every inch the Mitteleuropean, with sunny yellow walls, Biedermeier-style furniture and oak parquet floors. Tip: superior rooms have up-to-date mosaic-tiled bathrooms.

Majda
GORIZIAN €

(☑ 0481 3 08 71; Via Duca D'Aosta 71; meals €25; ⊙ noon-3pm & 7.30-11pm Mon-Sat) With a courtyard bar, friendly staff and enthusiastic decor, Majda is a happy place to sample local specialities such as ravioli with beetroot and local herbs or Slovenian-style with potato; wild boar on polenta; and interesting sides like steamed wild dandelion.

Pasticeria Centrale
PASTRIES & CAKES €

(Via Garibaldi 4a; ⊙ 7.30am-7.30pm) No visit to Gorizia would be complete without tasting the town's signature pastry, *gubana,* a fat snail of shortcrust filled with nuts, sultanas and spices.

ℹ Information

Tourist office (☑ 0481 53 57 64; Corso Italia 9; ⊙ 9am-6pm Mon-Sat, to 1pm Sun)

ℹ Getting There & Away

The train station (Piazzale Martiri Libertà d'Italia), 2km southwest of the centre, has regular connections to and from Udine (€3.80, 30 minutes, at least hourly) and Trieste (€3.90, 50 minutes, hourly). APT (☑ 800 955957; www.aptgorizia.it) runs buses from the train station across to Slovenia's Nova Gorica bus station (€1.15, 25 minutes).

Palmanova
POP 5340

Shaped like a nine-pointed star – although you'd need an aeroplane to check – Palmanova is a defensively designed town-within-a-fortress built by the Venetians in 1593. Once common throughout Europe, these military monoliths were known as 'star forts' or *trace italienne.* So impregnable were the town's defences that Napoleon used and extended them in the late 1700s, as did the Austrians

RUSTIC TABLES

Friulian food is essentially rural food. Its bold flavours and earthy ingredients make the most of the seasons and of traditional *miseria* (poverty) techniques, even when it's taken way upmarket. These much-lauded country restaurants are all within an hour's drive of Udine, either in the Colli Orientali or south towards the coast.

★ **La Frasca** (☏ 0432 67 51 50; Viale Grado 10, Pavia di Udine; meals €35; ⊙ noon-3pm & 7-10pm Thu-Tue) The *frasca* tradition is similar to that of the *osmize*, a rustic place serving *salumi* (cured meats) and wine. Walter Scarbolo's relaxed roadside dining room has retained the *frasca* experience, and his fans gather for his artisan cured meats, menus that highlight a single seasonal crop and, naturally, Scarbolo wines.

★ **La Subida** (☏ 0481 6 05 31; www.lasubida.it; Via Subida, Cormons; meals €50; ⊙ lunch & dinner Sat & Sun, dinner Mon, Thu, Fri) A famous family-run inn, with border-crossing dishes and ingredients – rabbit, boar, flowers and berries – that bring the landscape to the plate in a very modern way. Stay over in one of their stunning forest houses and wake to birdsong and rustling leaves.

Terre e Vini (☏ 0481 6 00 28; www.terraevini.it; Via XXIV Maggio, Brazzano di Cormons; meals €52; ⊙ dinner Tue-Sat, lunch Tue-Sun) The Felluga family are Friulian wine royalty and their 19th-century *osteria* (casual eatery presided over by a host) looks out over the plantings. Feast on tripe on Thursdays, salt cod on Fridays and goose stew or herbed frittata any day of the week.

Elliott (☏ 0432 75 13 83; www.elliotenoteca.com; Via Orsaria 50, Buttrio; meals €32; ⊙ 10am-3pm & 5pm-midnight) Eat well on Friulian bounty at alfresco wooden tables looking out across the Collio to snowcapped mountains and Slovenia. There are 12 B&B rooms upstairs with private terraces and more of that view.

Orsone at Bastianich (p425) Nestled among the vines, this intimate inn and dining room uses local produce and traditional dishes but there's a definite new world sensibility at work (the bar menu goes even further, with a roll call of New York-Italian favourites).

during WWI. To this day the Italian army maintains a garrison here.

◉ Sights

From hexagonal Piazza Grande, at the star's centre, six roads radiate through the old town to the defensive walls. An inviting grassy path connects the bastions and three main porte (gates): Udine, Cividale and Aquileia.

Civico Museo Storico　　　MUSEUM
(☏ 0432 91 91 06; Borgo Udine 4; adult/reduced €2/1.50; ⊙ 9.30am-12.30pm Tue-Sun summer, or by arrangement) Head along Borgo Udine to uncover local history and weaponry from the Venetian and Napoleonic eras in the Civico Museo Storico, inside **Palazzo Trevisan**. The museum also acts as a **tourist office** (☏ 0432 92 48 15; ⊙ 9.30am-12.30pm & 3.30-6.30pm Mon, Tue & Thu-Sat) and has information on secret-tunnel tours that wind beneath the city walls.

Museo Storico Militare　　　MUSEUM
(☏ 0432 92 81 75; Piazza Grande 21; ⊙ 9am-noon daily & 4-6pm Mon-Sat) **FREE** The Museo Storico Militare is inside Porta Cividale. The military museum traces the history of troops stationed in Palmanova from 1593 to WWII.

❶ Getting There & Away

Regular buses link Palmanova with Udine (€3.15, 30 minutes) and Aquileia (€2.65, 40 minutes), leaving from Via Rota, just inside the walls.

Aquileia

POP 3500

Aquileia, off the beaten track? It certainly wasn't 2000 years ago. Colonised in 181 BC, Aquileia was once one of the largest and richest cities of the Roman Empire, at times second only to Rome, with a population of at least 100,000 at its peak. After the city was levelled by Attila's Huns in AD 452, its inhabitants fled south and west where they founded Grado and then Venice. A smaller town rose in Aquileia's place in the early Middle Ages with the construction of the present basilica; it too went onto greater significance, becoming the largest Christian diocese in Europe. Conferred with a

Unesco World Heritage listing in 1998, this charmingly rural town and living museum still, rather thrillingly, guards one of the most complete, unexcavated Roman sites in Europe.

Sights

★ Basilica CHURCH

(Piazza Capitolo; crypts adult/reduced €3/2.50, bell tower €2; ⊙9am-6pm Mon-Sat, from 11.30am Sun, bell tower summer only) The entire floor of the Latin cross-shaped basilica, rebuilt after an earthquake in 1348, is covered with one of the largest and most spectacular Roman-era mosaics in the world. The 760-sq-metre floor of the basilica's 4th-century predecessor is protected by glass walkways, allowing visitors to wander above the long-hidden tilework, which includes astonishingly vivid episodes from the story of Jonah and the whale, the Good Shepherd, exacting depictions of various lagoon wildlife, and portraits of, presumably, its wealthy Roman patrons and their quotidian business interests.

Treasures also fill the basilica's two crypts. The 9th-century Cripta degli Affreschi (Crypt of Frescoes) is adorned with faded 12th-century frescoes depicting the trials and tribulations of saints, while the Cripta degli Scavi (Excavations Crypt) reveals more mosaic floors in varying states of preservation. Some images were destroyed or badly damaged by the erection of the basilica's 73m-high bell tower, built in 1030 with stones from the Roman amphitheatre.

Roman Ruins ROMAN SITE

Scattered remnants of the Roman town include extensive ruins of the Porto Fluviale (River Port; Via Sacra; ⊙8.30am-1hr before sunset), the old port, which once linked the settlement to the sea. It's also possible to wander among the partially restored remains of houses, roads and the standing columns of the ancient Forum on Via Giulia Augusta.

Guided tours of the extraordinary Roman sights are organised by the tourist office (☑0431 91 94 91; ⊙9am-7pm summer, 9am-1pm & 2-6pm winter), otherwise, wander at will.

Museo Archeologico Nazionale MUSEUM

(☑0431 9 10 16; www.museoarcheo-aquileia.it; Via Roma 1; adult/reduced €4/2; ⊙8.30am-7.30pm Tue-Sun) There is a daunting number of statues, pottery, glassware and jewellery – all locally excavated – displayed in this museum, representing one of northern Italy's most important collections of Roman-era treasures.

Museo Paleocristiano MUSEUM

(☑0431 9 11 31; Piazza Pirano; ⊙8.30am-1.45pm Tue-Sun) FREE This museum, part of the Museo Archeologico Nazionale, houses early-Christian-era mosaics and funerary monuments gathered from the surrounding ruins.

Sleeping

Camping Aquileia CAMPGROUND €

(☑043 19 10 42; www.campingaquileia.it; Via Gemina 10; camping 2 people, car & tent €28, bungalows €56) This well-maintained campground is set beside pretty fields; its comfortable new bungalows look towards the Basilica and old Roman port.

Ostello Domus Augusta HOSTEL €

(☑0431 9 10 24; www.ostelloaquileia.it; Via Roma 25; s/d €28/46; ⓟ⌨) A spotless if rather institutional hostel with two- to six-bed rooms and private bathrooms down the hall. Friendly, relaxed staff are helpful and happy to dole out maps and timetables.

Drinking

Taberna Marciani Aquileia WINE BAR

(www.tabernamarciani.com; Via Roma 10) The bearded and slightly dishevelled crew holding up the bar at this gently 2nd-century-AD-themed place might look, and act, like they are in an a touring indie band, but they're more likely to be Austrian archaeologists on a dig. Popular for plates of local meats and cheese (€4), and good wines by the glass, not to mention late opening hours.

Grado

POP 8600

Another Friulian surprise, the tasteful beach resort of Grado, 14km south of Aquileia, spreads along a narrow island backed by lagoons and is linked to the mainland by a causeway. Behind the less-than-spectacular beaches you'll find a mazelike medieval centre, criss-crossed by narrow *calli* (lanes) and dominated by the Romanesque Basilica di Sant'Eufemia (Campo dei Parriarchi) and the nearby remains of a 4th- to 5th-century church mosaic (Piazza Biagio Marin). Belle époque mansions, beach huts and thermal baths line the cheerful seafront (the greyish local sand is considered curative and used in treatments). Grado comes alive from May to September, but is also prime *passeggiata* (evening stroll) territory on any sunny Sunday.

Small *casoni* (reed huts) used by fishers dot the tiny lagoon islands. In summer some can be visited by boat. Many of the islands are, however, protected nature reserves and off limits. The tourist office (☑0431 87 71 11; Viale Dante Alighieri 66; ☺9am-7pm) has the details.

On the first Sunday in July, a votive procession sails to the Santuario di Barbana (☑0431 8 04 53; www.santuariodibarbana.it), an 8th-century church on a lagoon island. Fishers have done this since 1237 when the Madonna of Barbana was claimed to have miraculously saved the town from the plague. Boats link the sanctuary with Grado; contact Motoscafisti Gradesi (☑0431 8 01 15; www.motoscafistigradesi.it; Riva Scaramuzza; ☺daily summer, Sun only winter) for specific departures and prices.

🛏 Sleeping & Eating

The town has a huge number of hotels and holiday rentals, though rooms can be scarce in summer and only bookable on a weekly basis. The old town's streets are known for their boisterous wine bars, casual *fritterias* and upmarket seafood restaurants.

Albergo Alla Spiaggia   HOTEL €€
(☑0431 8 48 41; www.albergoallaspiaggia.it; Via Mazzini 2; s/d €77-140; ☺Apr-Oct; P❄@) The Spiaggia sports a South Beach look, set in a lovely prewar modernist building, with a fresh maritime-toned fit out. It's in a great position, wedged between pedestrian zone, historic centre and beach.

Trattoria de Toni   SEAFOOD €€
(☑0431 8 01 04; Piazza Duca d'Aosta 37; meals €37; ☺noon-3pm & 6.30-10pm Thu-Tue) This place is undeniably old school, and charmingly so, matching genial service with the best local seafood. Sample Grado's signature *boreto*, a lagoon fish stew served with white polenta, or stick with the brimming seafood pasta dishes and superfresh whole grilled fish by the gram, filleted at the table.

Max'in Botega de Mar   SEAFOOD
(Piazza Duca d'Aosta 7; ☺ 11am-3pm & 6-11pm Wed-Mon) Snack on a *tartine* from its extensive menu of seafood-themed toasts (€1 to €3 each) while downing a few lemon-infused white-wine spritzers at one of its pavement tables. Still hungry? There are fish *polpettone* (meatballs) and large *crudo* plates as well. Doesn't allow bookings, so arrive early.

L'Osteria da Sandra   WINE BAR
(Campo San Niceta 16; ☺10am-11pm Tue-Sun) Cute hole-in-the-wall bar that attracts a local crew for an early-evening spritzer or two on an old-town corner. Has an excellent chilled white selection available for purchase if you're considering a picnic.

❶ Getting There & Away

Regular **SAF** (☑0432 60 81 11, 800 915303; www.saf.ud.it) buses link Aquileia with Grado (€1.50, 10 minutes) and Palmanova (€3.15, 45 minutes, up to eight daily), other buses run between Grado and Udine (€4.50, 1¼ hours, 12 daily) via Aquileia. Trains to Venice and Trieste run to the Cervignano-Aquileia-Grado station, in Cervignano, around 15km away.

Around Grado

Beyond Grado's perpetual holiday bustle lie two picturesque nature reserves; a scant 15-minute drive will take you into a watery landscape of marsh and reeds, rich in local fauna and with intriguing examples of traditional coastal life.

◉ Sights

Riserva Naturale Regionale della Valle Cavanata   NATURE RESERVE
(☑0431 8 82 72; www.vallecavanata.it; ☺9am-12.30pm Mon, Wed & Fri, 10am-6pm Sat & Sun) This reserve protects a 1920s fish-farming area and extraordinary birdlife in the east of the lagoon. More than 230 bird species have been observed, including the greylag goose and many wading birds.

Riserva Naturale Regionale Foce dell'Isonzo   NATURE RESERVE
(☑0432 99 81 33; www.parks.it/riserva.foce. isonzo; Isola della Cona; adult/reduced €5/3.50; ☺9am-5pm Fri-Wed) The final stretch of the Isonzo river's journey into the Adriatic flows through this 23.5-sq-km nature reserve where visitors can birdwatch, horse ride, cycle or walk around salt marshes and mudflats. The visitors centre also has a cafe.

Laguna di Marano

At the head of the Adriatic, sandwiched between the beach resorts of Grado and Lignano, Italy succumbs to nature – in particular birdlife – in the Laguna di Marano.

Marano Lagunare, a Roman fishing port that was later fortified, is the only settlement on the lagoon shore. Beyond the workaday docks and medieval streets, peace and quiet is ensured by two nature reserves – the 13.77-sq-km **Riserva Naturale della Foci dello Stella**, protecting the marshy mouth of the Stella river and reached by boat, and the **Riserva Naturale della Valle Canal Novo**, a 121-hectare reserve in a former fishing valley. The **visitor centre** (☑0431 6 75 51; www.riservenaturali.maranolagunare.com; Via delle Valli 2; park admission adult/reduced €2.50/1.50; ☺9am-6pm Tue-Sun), in a characteristic reed hut, is shared by the two reserves.

Lignano

Modern Lignano is one of northern Italy's premier beach destinations, with sweeping stretches of sand set against a backdrop of dark pines in **Lignano Pineta** and **Lignano Riviera**, and theme parks and multistorey car parks in brash, but never boring, **Lignano Sabbiadoro**.

Three camping grounds, including **Pino Mare** (☑0431 42 44 24; www.campingpinomare. it; Lungomare Riva 15; camping 2 people, car & tent €60), a tree-shaded cabin village at the mouth of the Tagliamento river, supplement the 100-plus hotels.

The **tourist office** (☑0431 42 21 69; Via dei Pini 53, Lignano Pineta; ☺9am-2pm summer) can help with holiday rentals. Lignano Sabbiadoro is linked by bus to Udine (€6.50, two hours, many daily).

Pordenone

POP 51,300

Pordenone may not make it on to many travel hot lists, but that's not to say it's not the kind of place – youthful, lively – you wouldn't mind calling home. Pedestrianised Corso Vittorio Emanuele II draws an elegant curve between Piazza Cavour and the *duomo* (cathedral). Lined with an almost unbroken chain of covered *portici* (porches), the historic streetscape buzzes with smart shops and busy cafes.

◉ Sights

Duomo di San Marco   CATHEDRAL
(Piazza San Marco; ☺7.30am-noon & 3-7pm) The bare Romanesque-Gothic facade of the Duomo di San Marco betrays signs of frequent changes down the centuries. Inside, among the frescoes and other artworks, is the *Madonna della misericordia,* by the Renaissance master Il Pordenone (1484–1539).

Palazzo del Comune   TOWN HALL
In defiance of the other-worldly, the Palazzo del Comune (Town Hall) stands facing away from the *duomo*. The 13th-century brick structure has three Gothic arches and some extravagant Renaissance additions.

Museo Civico d'Arte   MUSEUM
(☑0434 39 29 35; www.comune.pordenone.it/museoarte; Corso Vittorio Emanuele II 51; adult/reduced €3/1; ☺3.30-7.30pm Tue-Sun, plus 10am-1pm Sun) Located in Palazzo Ricchieri's richly decorated upper rooms is the city's modest Museo d'Arte. Its collection of Friulian and Veneto artists ranges from the 15th to the 18th centuries. The building is in itself a treasure, with timber ceilings and remains of 14th-century frescoes suddenly appearing throughout.

✗ Eating & Drinking

La Vecia Osteria del Moro   REGIONAL €€
(☑0434 2 86 58; www.laveciaosteriadelmoro.it; Via Castello 2; meals €35; ☺noon-2pm & 7-10pm Mon-Sat) La Vecia Osteria del Moro, just off the Corso near the Comune, is a vaulted den offering snacks, grills and local specialities like Venetian-style *baccalá* (cod) and snails.

Al Campanile   WINE BAR
(☑0434 52 06 28; Vicolo del Campanile 1/C; ☺noon-11pm, Tue-Sun) The streetside barrels here make an atmospheric spot for a glass or two.

🛏 Sleeping

Civico 22   B&B €
(☑335 67 9 13 30; www.bbcivico22.it; Via San Quirino 22; s/d €45/80; ❇🏠) You might have come to Friuli for rustic inns, but for a city pit stop, this unashamedly contemporary B&B is a great choice. Three bright, white design-led rooms are housed in an assertive show of contemporary architectural taste, in a quiet street.

ℹ Information

Tourist office (☑0434 52 03 81; Piazza XX Settembre 11; ☺9am-1pm daily & 2.30-6.30pm Mon-Fri)

ℹ Getting There & Away

Pordenone is on the Venice–Udine train line. Frequent services run to and from Udine (€3.80, 30 to 40 minutes) and Mestre (€4.95, 1¼ hours). **ATAP** (☑800 101040; www.atap.pn.it) Runs buses to the surrounding towns.

Sacile

POP 20,200

Sacile, the self-styled Giardino della Serenissima (Garden of Serenity), is formed by two islands standing amid the willow-lined Livenza river and a network of canals. Sacile indeed took much of its early architectural inspiration from the Most Serene Republic of Venice, which is reflected in the typically Venetian townhouses and palazzo that, despite various earthquakes and WWII bombings, still line the tranquil little waterways. Of the many, the impressively frescoed Pa lazzo Ragazzoni-Flangini-Billia is worth a peek.

The annual August Sagra dei Osei (bird festival) has been held since 1274 and is one of the oldest festivals in Italy. Look out for exhibitions, a market and a (bird) song contest.

Friendly La Piola (☎0434 78 18 93; www. lapiolasacile.it; Piazza del Popolo 9; meals €28; ☺noon-2.30pm & 7-10pm Tue-Sat, noon-3pm Sun) has windows and a terrace backing on to the canal. Its menu of Serenissima-style seafood is delivered with a fresh eye, and the wine selection is impressive. If a riverside stroll calls for gelato, Il Gelatone (Viale Pietro Zancanaro 1; ☺ 10am-10pm Tue-Sun) can help you out.

Sacile is on the main train line between Venice (€4.60, one hour) and Udine (€5.50, 45 minutes).

Udine

POP 98,400 / ELEV 114M

While reluctantly ceding its premier status to Trieste in the 1950s, this confident, wealthy provincial city remains the spiritual and gastronomic capital of Friuli. Udine gives little away in its sprawling semirural suburbs, but encased inside the peripheral ring road lies an infinitely grander medieval centre: a dramatic melange of Venetian arches, Grecian statues and Roman columns. The old town is pristine, but lively. Bars here are not just for posing – kicking on is the norm.

◎ Sights

Piazza della Libertà   PIAZZA
A shimmering Renaissance epiphany materialising from the surrounding maze of medieval streets, Piazza della Libertà is dubbed the most beautiful Venetian square on the mainland. The arched Palazzo del Comune (Town Hall), also known as the Loggia del

Lionello after its goldsmithing architect, Nicolò Lionello, is another clear Venetian keepsake, as is the Loggia di San Giovanni opposite, its clock tower modelled on the one gracing Venice's Piazza San Marco. The Arco Bollani (Bollani Arch), next to the Loggia di San Giovanni, an Andrea Palladio work from 1556, leads up to the castle used by the Venetian governors.

★Museum of Modern and
Contemporary Art   ART GALLERY
(Casa Cavazzini; ☎0432 41 47 72; Via Cavour 14; adult/reduced €5/2.50; ☺10.30am-5pm Sun, Mon, Wed & Thu, to 7.30pm Fri & Sat) Udine's newest museum brings together a number of bequests, creating a substantial collection of 20th-century Italian artists, including De Chirico, Morandi, Campigli and Mušič. There's also a surprise horde of notable American work, including a Willem de Kooning, Sol LeWitt and Carl Andre, all donated by the artists after the 1976 Friulian earthquake. The gallery itself is a beautiful cultural asset, its bold reconstruction designed by the late Gae Aulenti. Discover intriguing remnants of the 16th-century building's previous lives: spectacular, previously unknown 14th-century frescoes that were uncovered during construction, and the Cavazzini family's 1930s Rationalist apartment, where you can peek at the old-style gym rings in the bathroom and a formal dining room's intensely hued murals.

Cathedral   CATHEDRAL
(Piazza Duomo) The chapels of Udine's 13th-century Romanesque-Gothic cathedral house the Museo del Duomo (☎0432 50 68 30; ☺9am-noon & 4-6pm Tue-Sat, 4-6pm Sun) FREE, with 13th- to 17th-century frescoes in the Cappella di San Nicolò. Across the street, the cathedral's 17th-century Oratorio della Purità (Piazza del Duomo; guided tours only) FREE was originally a theatre; its Tiepolos are certainly dramatic, including the ceiling painting *The Assumption* and eight biblical scenes in exquisite chiaroscuro by his son, Giandomenico, on the walls.

Castello   MUSEUM
Rebuilt in the mid-16th century after an earthquake in 1511, Udine's castle affords rare views of the city and snowy peaks beyond. It houses the Galleria d'Arte Antica (☎0432 27 15 91; adult/reduced €5/2.50; ☺10.30am-5pm Tue-Sun, to 7pm summer), with a handful of works by Caravaggio (a portrait

Udine

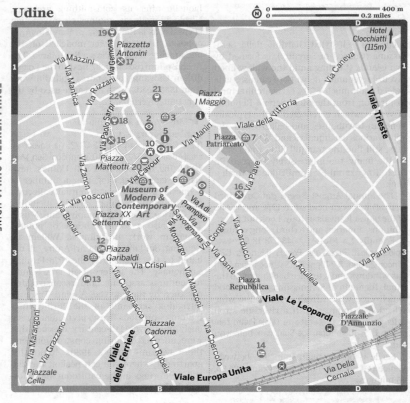

Udine

◎ **Top Sights**
- 1 Museum of Modern and Contemporary Art B2

◎ **Sights**
- 2 Arco Bollani B2
- Cappella di San Nicolò .... (see 6)
- 3 Castello B2
- 4 Cathedral B2
- Galleria d'Arte Antica .... (see 3)
- 5 Loggia di San Giovanni B2
- 6 Museo del Duomo B2
- 7 Museo Diocesano and Tiepolo Galleries C2
- 8 Museo Etnografico del Friuli A3
- 9 Oratorio della Purità B2
- 10 Palazzo del Comune B2
- 11 Piazza della Libertà B2

🛏 **Sleeping**
- 12 Albergo Vecchio Tram A3
- 13 Hotel Allegria A3
- 14 Stop & Sleep C4

🍴 **Eating**
- 15 Antica Maddalena B2
- 16 Aquila Nera C2
- 17 Trattoria ai Frati B1

🍷 **Drinking & Nightlife**
- 18 Al Cappello B2
- 19 Caffè Caucigh B1
- 20 Caffè Contarena B2
- 21 Casa della Contadinanza B1
- 22 Osteria delle Mortadele B1

of St Francis in room 7) and Tiepolo (several works in room 10). The bulk of the collection is dedicated to lesser-known Friulian painters and religious sculpture.

Museo Diocesano and Tiepolo Galleries
ART GALLERY

(www.musdioc-tiepolo.it; Piazza Patriarcato 1; adult/reduced €7/5; ⊙10am-1pm & 3-6pm Wed-Sun) The drawcards here are the two rooms featuring early frescoes by Giambattista Tiepolo, including the wonderfully over-the-top *Expulsion of the Rebellious Angels* (1726) at the apex of a grand staircase.

Museo Etnografico del Friuli
MUSEUM

(☑0432 27 19 20; Via Grazzano 1; adult/reduced €5/2.50; ⊙10.30am-5pm Tue-Sun, to 7pm summer) A small but engaging museum of daily life, with various exhibitions devoted to the Friulian hearth, unusual spiritual practices, folk medicine and dress. The building itself features intricate 19th-century woodwork, with carved Friulian forest scenes, and its own little canal gurgling by the entrance.

🛏 Sleeping

Central Udine has a number of small, smart midrange hotels, but only one notable budget place. If you're driving, consider a B&B or farm stay in the surrounding suburbs or countryside. The tourist office has online listings.

★ Stop & Sleep
B&B €

(www.stopsleepudine.com; s/d €35/55; ❄🤶) Don't be put off by the unprepossessing locale. This is a rare budget find and you'll be greeted by the caring, knowledgable owner. The B&B occupies a bright top-floor apartment and and has colourful, cutely decorated rooms, mosaic-tiled bathrooms, a full kitchen with DIY breakfast supplies and self-catering facilities. One room is en suite, while the other four rooms share two (spotless) bathrooms.

Albergo Vechhio Tram
HOTEL €€

(☑0432 50 71 64; www.hotelvecchiotram.com; Via Brenari 28; s/d €80/130; ❄🤶) This is a small, friendly business-oriented place in a corner townhouse. Rooms are streamlined and contemporary, though the larger ones retain the mansard lines and rafters of the original townhouse. There's a bijou bar and courtyard.

Hotel Clocchiatti Next
DESIGN HOTEL €€

(☑0432 50 50 47; www.hotelclocchiatti.it; Via Cividale 29; r villa/Next €95/140; P❄🤶🏊) Two properties, one location: older-style (cheaper) rooms are in the original villa, while the contemporary steel-and-glass 'Next' rooms line up around a pool and outdoor bar in the garden. Fresh cakes, Mariage Frères teas and attentive service make breakfast special. It's a pleasant walk from the centre, with easy access out of the city if you're driving.

Hotel Allegria
BOUTIQUE HOTEL €€

(☑0432 20 11 16; www.hotelallegria.it; Via Grazzano 18; s/d €95/135; P❄@) 🐾 This hotel occupies a historic townhouse opposite one of Udine's loveliest little churches. The rooms are large and what might be described as Udinese-organic in style, with lightwood beams, parquetry floors and shuttered windows. Quirk factor points: the hotel has a *bocciofila* (bowling area) on-site.

🍴 Eating

Udine's flavours are as intriguing as the city itself. Look out for country-style cheeses – smoked ricotta and Montasio – game, San Daniele prosciutto (ham) and delicious gnocchi and dumplings. Open-air cafes and restaurants are dotted around Piazza Matteotti and the surrounding pedestrian streets. Via Paolo Sarpi and its surrounding streets are lined with lively bars.

Antica Maddalena
FRIULIAN €

(☑0432 50 05 44; Via Pellicceria 4; meals €24; ⊙noon-3pm & 6-10pm Tue-Sat, 6-10pm Mon) This low-key restaurant, spread over two floors, is known for its quality produce. This is a great place to try *frico* – it's served both ways, *morbido*, a cheese and potato omelette, and *croccante*, its snackier crispy-fried form. *Aperitivo* time, Venetian-style seafood *stuzzicini* (snacks, usually in the form of toasts with various toppings) can be devoured at a laneway table.

Trattoria ai Frati
FRIULIAN €€

(☑0432 50 69 26; Piazzetta Antonini 5; meals €25-30; ⊙Mon-Sat) A popular old-style eatery on a cobbled cul-de-sac where you can expect such local specialities as *frico*, pumpkin gnocchi with smoked ricotta, or, in season, white asparagus and fish stew. It's loved by locals for its whopper steaks and its raucous front bar.

Coffee Culture

From Trapani to Tarvisio, every day begins with coffee. A quick cup from a stove-top Moka pot might be the first, but the second (third, fourth and fifth) will inevitably be from a neighbourhood bar. Italians consider these visits a moment to pause, but rarely linger. It's a stand-up sniff, swirl and gulp, a *buon proseguimento* to the barista, and on your way.

Origins

Coffee first turned up in mid-16th-century Venice, then a few years later in Trieste, care of the Viennese. While basic espresso technology made an appearance in the early 19th century, it wasn't until 1948 that Gaggia launched the first commercial machines. These reliably delivered full-bodied espresso shots with

the characteristic aromatic *crema*: Italy was hooked. The machines, in fact the whole espresso ritual, spoke of a hopeful modernity as Italy reimagined itself as an urban, industrial postwar nation.

Today's Cup

Italy's superior coffee-making technology took seed around the world, carried by postwar immigrants, then fashion. Global coffee culture today may embrace single origin beans, lighter roasts, latte art and new brewing technologies, but in Italy tradition holds sway. Italians still overwhelmingly favour Arabica and Robusta blends with a dense *crema*, higher caffeine jolt and, crucially, a price point everyone can afford. Roasts remain dark and often bitter – espresso is routinely sweetened – but Italian baristas use far

1. Caffè Sant'Eustachio, Rome (p139)
2. Espresso coffee being made
3. Waiter delivering coffee, Perugia

less coffee per shot and expert blends keep things smooth. Takeaway cups remain rare and clutching one while walking is seen as an American folly, a misunderstanding of coffee's dual purpose – contemplation and social belonging.

Bean Hunting

Finding your ultimate Italian espresso is trial and error, albeit enjoyable and inexpensive. Best-of lists will only get you so far: Rome's famed Caffè Sant'Eustachio, Florence's Gilli and Naples' Caffè Gambrinus will almost certainly get it right, but so too will many small town bars. Take note of *torrefazione* (bean roasters): global giants like Trieste's Illy and Turin's Lavazza are reliable, but do seek out regional favourites, such as Verona's Giamaica, Parma's Lady, Turin's Coffee Lab and Pascucci from Le Marche.

BARISTA BASICS

➡ **Caffè, espresso** Short shot of black coffee.

➡ **Ristretto** Short espresso.

➡ **Lungo** Long espresso.

➡ **Americano** Espresso with added hot water.

➡ **Macchiato** Espresso 'stained' with a little milk.

➡ **Cappuccino** Espresso with steamed milk.

➡ **Cappuccino scuro** Strong (dark) cappuccino.

➡ **Marochino** Small cappuccino with cocoa.

➡ **Latte macchiato** Dash of coffee in steamed milk.

➡ **Deca** Decaf.

➡ **Corretto** Spiked espresso, usually with grappa.

Aquila Nera
FRIULIAN €€

(📞 0432 21 645; www.aquilanera.biz; Via Piave 2/A; meals €28; ⏱ 10am-3pm & 6-11.30pm Mon-Sat) A bright, casual dining room with a terrace over the canal, the kitchen here offers no surprises with a best-of-Friuli line-up, all cooked with care. Seafood is on the menu and its extensive *taglieri* list – proscuitto, cheese, vegetable platters – can be a deliciously authentic meal substitute.

Drinking & Nightlife

The Udinese have a reputation for being fond of a drink or three, and with such stellar wines produced in their backyard, who can blame them? Wine bars here are unpretentious though serious about their wares, with blackboards full of local drops. *Stuzzichini* are plentiful at most bars and, if not complimentary, can be had for pocket change.

Osteria delle Mortadele
WINE BAR

(Riva Bartolini 8; ⏱ Mon-Sat) Yes, there's a popular restaurant out back, but it's the spill-onto-the-road front bar that will hold your interest. A rock-and-roll soundtrack, excellent wine by the glass and great company make this a one-drink-or-many destination.

Caffè Caucigh
BAR

(www.caucigh.com; Via Gemona 36) This ornate dark-wooded bar is a perfect Udinese compass point – it feels far more like Prague than points south. Regulars take glasses of red to the pavement for a chat with passing strangers. A calendar of jazz acts – Friuli's finest and some international surprises – play from 10pm on Friday nights.

Caffè Contarena
CAFE

(Via Cavour 11; ⏱ closed Sun) Beneath the arcades of Palazzo d'Aronco, Contarena's soaring domed ceilings glitter with gold leaf and other Liberty fancy. Designed by a master of the genre and one-time local, Raimondo d'Aronco, it's a glamorous espresso stop or late cocktail venue.

Al Cappello
WINE BAR

(Via Paolo Sarpi 5; ⏱ closed Sun night) Follow the locals' lead and order what may be Italy's most reasonably priced spritzer (€1.50) through the window. *Stuzzichini* here are generous enough to constitute dinner.

WINE-TASTING TIPS

Friulians are proud, hard-working, tight-knit people – they often describe themselves as cold but I disagree. They love to socialise, especially with visitors. Friuli isn't touristy, so getting attention from the outside world is a pleasure. Prepare to stop and chat and have a glass of wine or an espresso.

World-Class Whites

There's no other place in the world where the combination of soil, climate and the interplay between sea and mountain comes together to create whites like these. Local grape Friulano is fresh and aromatic. The sauvignon blancs are special too, and don't overlook the outstanding white blends (*uvaggi*). Reds to try: Refosco, merlot and the interesting Schioppettino.

Tasting Tips

Look for wines from Ronchi di Cialla, Moschioni, Venica & Venica and Vie di Romans. And Bastianich, of course!

Stomach Liners

Frico! It's a melted Montasio cheese pancake made with potatoes and, sometimes, bacon and onions...*awesome*.

Night Out

Udine is a great little city and deserves respect. There's a fantastic old bar called Caffè Caucigh: go for wine, coffee or live jazz. Or head to the countryside, to upscale La Frasca for *salumi* (cured meats) and proscuitto.

Wayne Young: communications and marketing (and former cellar-hand), Bastianich Wines

Casa della Contadinanza BAR, CAFE
(☑0432 50 96 96; Via Daniele Manin; ⊙9.30am-6pm Tue-Sun) At Udine's only *aperitivo*-with-a-view option, you also get history in spades and grass to loll on.

ⓘ Information

Hospital (☑0432 55 21; Piazza Santa Maria della Misericordia 15) About 2km north of the centre.

Tourist office (☑0432 29 59 72; Piazza I Maggio 7; ⊙9am-7pm Mon-Sat, to 1pm Sun)

ⓘ Getting There & Away

SAF (p417) operates buses to and from Trieste (€7, 1¼ hours, hourly), Aquileia (€3, one to 1¼ hours, up to eight daily), Lignano Sabbiadoro (€5, 1½ hours, eight to 11 daily) and Grado (€4.50, 1¼ hours, 12 daily).

APT (p412) buses link Udine and Friuli Venezia Giulia airport (€3.55, one hour, hourly).

Bus Station (☑0432 50 69 41; Viale Europa Unita 31)

Train Station (Viale Europa Unita) From Udine's train station services run to Trieste (€8, one hour), Venice (€11, two hours, several daily) Gorizia (€3.80, 30 minutes, hourly) and Salzburg (€19, four hours).

Cividale del Friuli

POP 11,600 / ELEV 138M

Cividale del Friuli, 15km east of Udine, may be a small town these days but in terms of Friulian history and identity it remains hugely significant. Founded by Julius Caesar in 50 BC as Forum de Lulii (ultimately condensed into 'Friuli'), the settlement reached its apex under the Lombards (who first arrived in AD 568) and by the 8th century had usurped Roman Aquileia. Cividale is hauntingly picturesque and rambling around its dark stone streets makes for a rewarding morning. Even better, stay to enjoy its hearty table and cracking bars.

◉ Sights

Tempietto Longobardo CHAPEL
(Oratorio di Santa Maria in Valle; ☑0432 70 08 67; www.tempiettolongobardo.it; Borgo Brossano; combined ticket incl Museo Cristiano adult/reduced €6/4; ⊙10am-1pm & 3-7pm Mon-Fri, to 5pm winter, 10am-6pm Sat & Sun) Cividale's most important sight is this stunning complex that houses the only surviving example of Lombard architecture and artwork in Europe. Its ethereal stuccowork and later dark wooden stalls are both unusual and extremely moving; some elements date as far back as the 8th century.

Ponte del Diavolo BRIDGE
Splitting the town in two is the symbolic Devil's Bridge that crosses the emerald-green Natisone river. The 22m-high bridge was first constructed in the 15th century with its central arch supported by a huge rock said to have been thrown into the river by the devil. It was rebuilt post-WWI, after it was blown up by retreating Italian troops.

Cathedral CATHEDRAL
(Piazza del Duomo) This 16th-century cathedral houses the Museo Cristiano (☑0432 73 04 03; adult/reduced €4/3; ⊙10am-1pm & 3-6pm Wed-Sun). Its 8th-century stone Altar of Ratchis is a stunning early-Christian relic. Sharp-etched carvings, including a be-quiffed Jesus with one piercing stare, dramatically pop against the smooth white background.

✗ Eating & Drinking

Antico Leon d'Oro FRIULIAN €
(☑0432 73 11 00; Borgo di Ponte 24; meals €22) Eat in the courtyard of this friendly, festive place, just over the Ponte del Diavolo, and, if you're in luck, watch a polenta cook stirring the pot. Dishes here couldn't be more regional: sublime d'Osvaldo *proscuitto crudo* (cured ham), seasonal pasta enlivened with asparagus and *sclupit* (a mountain herb), a Friulian tasting plate of *frico*, salami and herbed frittata, and roast deer.

Al Monastero FRIULIAN €€
(☑0432 70 08 08; www.almonastero.com; Via Ristori 9; meals €26; ⊙noon-2.30pm Tue-Sun & 7pm-9pm Tue-Sat) Feast on *cjalcions* (dumplings), duck with carrot pudding and *gubana* with plum brandy at this posh, undeniably touristy but well-regarded restaurant.

Central Caffè del Corso CAFE
(Corso Mazzini 38) *The* place on the square for an expertly made spritzer or coffee.

Bastianich WINE CELLAR
(☑0432 70 09 43; www.bastianich.com; Via Darnazzacco 44/2, Gagliano) Joe Bastiniach is a certified celebrity in the US, but his Italian vineyards, a few minutes' drive from Cividale, remain all about the wine and gracious Friulian hospitality. Pull up a stool at the new tasting room and sniff and swirl your way through drops made from the

DON'T MISS

CIVIDALE CERAMICS

Working with ancient Roman and Middle Eastern techniques, local ceramic artist Stefania Zurchi creates sculptures, reliefs and beautifully decorated utilitarian objects. Her palette evokes the Friulian landscape: moody indigos and olives cut through with the flash of bright oxide yellow and dusty pinks. Her 'girl' figures representing the seasons are highly sought after, as are her touching Madonna-and-child reliefs. The work can be found at her central Cividale del Friuli shop, **Tirare** (Via Ristori 12; ☉ 9.30am-12.30pm & 4-7pm Mon-Sat).

surrounding plantings and the Bastiniach holdings in nearby Buttrio. Savour the complex, wildflower and honey-tinged Vespa Bianco, a 'superwhite' blended from sauvignon, chardonnay and a dash of Picolit: Friuli in a bottle. Email ahead to visit.

ⓘ Information

Cividale Tourist Website (www.cividale.com) Look to the 'lodging and eating' section of the city's website for a comprehensive listing of *agriturismo* (farmstay accommodation) and farm restaurants.

Tourist office (☑ 0432 71 04 60; Piazza Paolo Diacono 10; ☉ 10am-1pm & 3-5pm) Has information on walks around the medieval core.

ⓘ Getting There & Away

Ferrovie Udine Cividale (☑ 0432 58 18 44; www.ferrovieudinecividale.it) Private (and cute) trains connect Cividale with Udine (€2, 20 minutes), at least hourly.

San Daniele del Friuli

POP 8200

Hilltop San Daniele sits in an undulating landscape that comes as a relief after the Venetian plains, with the Carnic Alps jutting up suddenly on the horizon. While ham is undoubtedly the town's raison d'être, it's also got a general gastronomic bent, with many good *alimentari* (grocery stores), and other culinary industries springing up such as sustainably farmed local trout.

⊙ Sights & Activities

Frescoes are another of San Daniele's fortes and you'll find some colourful examples etched by Pellegrino da San Daniele, aka Martino da Urbino (1467–1547), in the small Romanesque **Chiesa di San Antonio Abate** (Via Garibaldi). Next to the church, the **Biblioteca Guarneriana** (☑ 0432 95 79 30; www.guarneriana.it; Via Roma 1; guided tours €3; ☉ Wed-Sat, by appointment only) is one of Italy's oldest and most venerated libraries. Founded in 1466,

it contains 12,000 antique books, including a priceless manuscript of Dante's Inferno.

If you want to get out into the countryside, three cycling itineraries, each 22km, take you past pristine lakes and through the castle-dotted hills around the village; ask at the **tourist office** (☑ 0432 94 07 65; Via Roma 3; ☉ 9.30am-noon Mon-Fri, 4-6pm Tue, Wed & Fri, 10.30am-12.30pm & 4-6pm Sat & Sun).

✕ Eating & Drinking

Bottega di Prosciutto   DELI
(www.bottegadelprosciutto.com; Via Umberto I; ☉ 9am-1pm & 3-7pm, closed Mon & Wed afternoon) Buy all the ham your heart and stomach desire at Bottega di Prosciutto, as well as browsing the regional cheeses and wines and an excellent selection of pan-Italian produce.

Osteria di Tancredi   REGIONAL CUISINE **€€**
(☑ 0432 94 15 94; www.osteriaditancredi.it; Via Sabotino 10; plates €8, meals €25-30; ☉ noon-10pm Thu-Tue) Serves up the Friulian classics: *cjalcions*, *frico* and apple gnocchi.

Enoteca la Trappola   WINE BAR
(☑ 0432 94 20 90; Via Cairoli 2; plates €8) Head to dark and moody Trappola for crowd-pleasing platters of prosciutto or trout and well-priced wine by the glass.

ⓘ Getting There & Away

Regular buses run to San Daniele from Udine (€4.50, 45 minutes), 25km to the southeast.

North of Udine

Hit the hard north of Italy's most north-easterly region and you'll find yourself surrounded by the Carnic and Giulie Alps, the latter named after Julius Caesar. The former stretches as far west as the Dolomites and far north as the border with Austria. Meanwhile, the loftier Giulie's rugged, frigid peaks are shared with Slovenia – the Triglavski Narodni Park lies just across the border. Both areas offer excellent hiking terrain and deliver some of the loneliest, most scenic trails in Italy. As the area stands at the meeting point of three different cultures, multilingual skills can come in handy. Hikers should get ready to swap their congenial *salve* (Italian) for a *grüss gott* (German) or *dober dan* (Slovenian).

Tolmezzo & Carnia

The region known as Carnia is intrinsically Friulian (the language is widely spoken here) and named after its original Celtic inhabitants – the Carnics. Geographically, it contains the western and central parts of the Carnic Alps and presents wild and beautiful walking country flecked with curious villages.

Tolmezzo

POP 10,700 / ELEV 323M

Stunningly sited Tolmezzo is the region's capital and gateway. The **Museo Carnico delle Arti e Tradizioni Popolari** (☑0433 4 32 33; www.carniamusei.org; Via della Vittoria 2; adult/reduced €5/3; ☺9am-1pm & 3-6pm Tue-Sun) has a rich display on mountain life and folklore. Pleasant rooms at **Albergo Roma** (☑0433 46 80 31; www.albergoromatolmezzo.it; Piazza XX Settembre 14; s/d €80/100; **P**✳@) overlook the main piazza or one of the town's many hills. An interesting detour, 6km northeast of the town, is **Illegio**, a 4th-century hill village with a still-operating 16th-century mill and dairy. Tolmezzo's **tourist office** (☑0433 4 48 98; Piazza XX Settembre 9, Tolmezzo; ☺9am-1pm daily

& 2.30-6.30pm Mon-Sat) is helpful for information on surrounding hiking trails and *agriturismi*.

SAF buses run to Udine approximately every hour (€3.90, 50 minutes) from Via Carnia Libera.

Sauris di Sotto & Sauris di Sopra

To the northwest, a minor, and insanely twisted, road passes the plunging Lumiei Gorge to emerge at the cobalt-blue **Lago di Sauris**, an artificial lake 4km east of Sauris di Sotto. Another 4km on (up eight switchbacks and through a few dripping rock tunnels) is the breathtakingly pretty Sauris di Sopra. This twin hamlet (in German, Zahre) is an island of dark timber houses and German-speakers, known for its fine hams, sausages and locally brewed beer. There are lots of good walking trails, much fresh air and silence.

Part of the larger *alberghi diffusi* movement in the Carnic region – a number of rooms and apartments scattered throughout the historic centre – the **Albergo Diffuso Sauris** (www.albergodiffusosauris.com; apt €100-200) offers various apartments spread over refurbished village houses, all constructed in the unusual vernacular style with deep verandas screened with horizontal slats. Inside they are extremely cosy and well-equipped: live a little Carnic fantasy life, sampling Zahre beer, catching up with the village gossip and stocking up on supplies at **Speck Stube** (Via Sauris di Sopra 44, Sauris di Sopra; ☺8am-9.30pm), then head 'home' to prepare dinner and light a fire.

HAMMING IT UP

There are two world-revered prosciuttos manufactured in Italy: the lean, deliciously nutty (and more famous) ham from Parma, and the dark, exquisitely sweet Prosciutto di San Daniele. It might come as a surprise to find that the latter – Friuli Venezia Giulia's greatest culinary gift to the world – comes from a village of only 8000 people, where it is salted and cured in 27 *prosciuttifici* (ham-curing plants) safeguarded by EU regulations.

Standards are strict. San Daniele's prosciutto is made only from the thighs of pigs raised in a small number of northern Italian regions. Salt is the only method of preservation allowed – no freezing, chemicals or other preservatives can be used. The X factor is, of course, terroir, the land itself. Some *prosciuttifici* claim it's the cool, resinous Alpine air meeting the Adriatic's humid, brackish breezes that define their product, others argue that it's about San Daniele's fast-draining soil: such effective ventilation makes for perfect curing conditions.

In August the town holds the **Aria di Festa**, a four-day annual ham festival when *prosciuttifici* do mass open-house tours and tastings, musicians entertain and everyone tucks in. San Daniele's tourist office has a list of *prosciuttifici* that welcome visitors year-round; call ahead to book.

CROSS-BORDER SKIING

Multiday passes (one/three/six days from €35/95/168) enable you to ski Italy, Slovenia and Austria on the slopes of Sella Nevea-Kanin, Tarvisio, Zoncolan, Bovec and Arnoldstein. Both day and multiday passes can also be used at the Friulian resorts of Piancavallo and Forni di Sopra. The Monte Canin ski lift is free to FVG Card holders, and they receive discounts on multiday passes and equipment hire. **Promotur** (☑ 0428 65 39 15; www.promotur.org) sells passes at each of the resorts.

Forni di Sopra

Close to the border with Veneto, Forni di Sopra is a popular ski resort that receives heavy winter snow and offers sledging, skating and ice-climbing as well as downhill skiing. Forni is equally revered for its carpet of summer wildflowers and herbs; the latter utilised in the local cuisine and the central theme of the annual spring **Festa delle Erbe di Primavera**. There are numerous hotels in the town, most of them family-friendly places. The **tourist office** (☑ 0433 88 67 67; Via Cadore 1; ⊙ 9am-1pm & 2-6pm) has information on activities and lifts.

Regular SAF buses from Tolmezzo head to Ampezzo (€3.15, 35 minutes) and Forni de Sopra (€4.50, 1½ hours).

Tarvisio & the Giulie Alps

POP 5000 / ELEV 754M

The Giulie Alps are dramatic limestone monoliths rather like their more famous Dolomite cousins. Though there's been some recent development of the region, including a cross-border ski lift, the area is still relatively pristine and retains a wildness often lacking in the west.

Tarvisio

Tarvisio (Tarvis) is 7km short of the Austrian border and 11km from Slovenia. Down to earth and prettily wedged into the Val Canale between the Giulie and eastern Carnic Alps, it's a good base for both winter and summer activities.

Tarvisio is famous for its historic Saturday **market**, which has long attracted day trippers from Austria and Slovenia. It has a definite border-town buzz.

Activities

The coldest, snowiest pocket in the whole Alpine region, is increasingly touted for its uncrowded skiing. The main ski centres are at Tarvisio – with a good open 4km run that promises breathtaking views and 60km of cross-country tracks – and at Sella Nevea just to the south. The **Sella Nevea** (www.sellane-vea.net) resort is linked to increasingly glamorous **Bovec** in Slovenia, making for around 30km of slopes, with a number of satisfying red runs and good freeride and backcountry skiing. In summer the hiking, caving, canoeing and windsurfing are all good.

Sleeping

Casa Oberrichter BOUTIQUE HOTEL €
(☑ 3482 713157; www.casaoberrichter.com; Via Superiore 4, Malborghetto; d €95) Located in a village 12km to the west, Casa Oberrichter is a special place with interiors that take the Friulian-folk aesthetic to a new level, beautiful dining rooms and a calendar of events and exhibitions.

Hotel Edelhof HOTEL €€
(☑ 0428 4 00 81; www.hoteledelhof.com; Via Armando Diaz 13; s/d €75/120; 🅿 🛜) Situated right by the lifts with large, airy rooms with handpainted wooden furniture and a spa.

Information

Tourist office (☑ 0428 21 35; Via Roma 14; ⊙ 9am-1pm & 2-7pm)

Getting There & Away

Trains connect Tarvisio with Udine (€9, 1½ hours, up to seven daily).

Laghi di Fusine

The Laghi di Fusine (Fusine Lakes) lie close to the Slovenian border and are popular with hikers in summer and cross-country skiers in winter. The two lakes – Lago Superiore and Lago Inferiore – are ringed by paths and surrounded by the **Parco Naturale di Fusine**. For more-adventurous walkers, there's an 11km hike up to **Rifugio Zacchi** (www.rifugiozacchi.it; Località Conca delle Ponze; dm €27; ⊙ mid-Jun–mid-Sep). In summer buses run up four times a day from Tarvisio (€1.50, 15 minutes).

Emilia-Romagna & San Marino

Best Places to Eat

➡ Osteria dell'Orsa (p439)

➡ Trattoria del Tribunale (p452)

➡ Trattoria Aldina (p445)

➡ Trattoria dal Biassanot (p439)

Best Places to Stay

➡ Hotel Metropolitan (p438)

➡ Hotel Centrale Byron (p463)

➡ Hotel Button (p452)

➡ Grand Hotel (p467)

Why Go?

The secret's in the mud. The roots of Emilia-Romagna's supersonic economy lie not in the mechanics of its famous Ferraris, but in its exceptionally fertile soil. Since antiquity, the verdant plains of the region's Po river valley have sown enough agricultural riches to feed a nation and finance an unending production line of lavish products: luxury cars, regal *palazzi* (mansions), fine Romanesque churches, prosperous towns, a sturdy industrial infrastructure, a gigantic operatic legacy (Verdi and Pavarotti, no less) and food. Ah yes, did anyone mention the food?

You can eat like a Roman emperor here, and, if you have any appetite left, dip your toe tentatively into the places that time-poor Rome-o-philes serially miss. There's Bolshie Bologna with its *ragù* (meat and tomato sauce) and porticoes, posh Parma with its opera and cheese, Modena and its balsamic vinegar, the wealthy micronation of San Marino, and Ravenna with its mosaics. Come to Emilia-Romagna *ragazzi* (guys). Just don't forget the mud that made it.

When to Go
Bologna

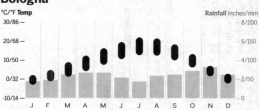

Mar–Apr Enjoy mild temperatures on the Po plains and fewer crowds on Rimini's beaches.

Jun–Aug Summer festivals galore in Bologna, Modena, Ravenna and Rimini.

Sep Ideal hiking conditions in Parco Nazionale dell'Appennino Tosco-Emiliano.

Emilia-Romagna & San Marino Highlights

1 Taking a very long, very slow and very delicious lunch in that well-known bastion of good taste, **Parma** (p452).

2 Reawakening your enthusiasm for dark Italian churches amid the lucid mosaics of the **Basilica di San Vitale** (p460) in Ravenna.

3 Discovering the personal history behind the fast cars at Modena's **Museo Casa Enzo Ferrari** (p443).

4 Hiring a bike and circumnavigating the muscular medieval walls of Renaissance **Ferrara** (p455).

5 Leaving the flat lands behind and taking a bus out to the **Pietra di Bismantova** (p449) for a day of hiking.

6 Following the undergraduates and discovering cheap bars and restaurants in Bologna's **university quarter** (p440).

7 Swapping high culture for high decibels at Rimini's famous **clubs** (p467).

EMILIA-ROMAGNA

Bologna

POP 380,000

Fusing haughty elegance with down-to-earth grit in one beautifully colonnaded medieval grid, Bologna is a city of two intriguing halves. On one side is a hard-working, hi-tech city located in the super-rich Po valley where suave opera-goers waltz out of regal theatres and reconvene in some of the nation's finest restaurants and trattorias. On the other is a Bolshie, politically edgy city that hosts the world's oldest university and is famous for its graffiti-embellished piazzas filled with mildly inebriated students swapping gothic fashion tips. No small wonder Bologna has earned so many historical monikers. La Grassa (the fat one) celebrates a rich food legacy (*ragù* or bolognese sauce was first concocted here). La Dotta (the learned one) doffs a cap to the city university founded in 1088. La Rossa (the red one) alludes to the ubiquity of the terracotta medieval buildings adorned with kilometres of porticoes, as well as the city's longstanding penchant for left-wing politics. All three names still ring true. Bologna is the kind of city where you can be discussing Chomsky with a leftie newspaper-seller one minute, and be eating like an erstwhile Italian king in a fine restaurant the next.

◉ Sights

◉ Piazza Maggiore & Around

Flanked by the world's fifth-largest basilica and a series of impressive Renaissance *palazzi*, all roads lead to pivotal Piazza Maggiore.

Fontana del Nettuno　　　FOUNTAIN
(Neptune's Fountain; Piazza del Nettuno) Adjacent to Piazza Maggiore, Piazza del Nettuno owes its name to this explicit bronze statue sculpted by Giambologna in 1566. Beneath the muscled sea god, four cherubs represent the winds, and four buxom sirens, water spouting from every nipple, symbolise the four known continents of the pre-Oceania world.

★ Museo della Storia di Bologna　　　MUSEUM
(☑ 051 1993 6370; Via Castiglione 8; admission €10; ☉ 10am-7pm Tue-Sun) Walk in a historical neophyte and walk out an A-grade honours student in Bologna's golden past. This mag-

nificent new interactive museum skillfully encased in the regal Palazzo Pepoli is – in a word – an 'education'.

Using a 3D film, a mock-up of an old Roman canal, and supermodern presentations of ancient relics, the innovative displays start in a futuristic open-plan lobby and progress through 34 chronologically themed rooms that make Bologna's 2500-year history at once engaging and epic. There are many hidden nuggets (who knew Charles V was crowned Holy Roman Emperor in the city?). The only glaring omission is much talk of Mussolini, who was born 'down the road' in Forli.

Palazzo Comunale　　　ART GALLERY
(Piazza Maggiore; ☉ art galleries 9am-6.30pm Tue-Fri, 10am-6.30pm Sat & Sun) **FREE** The palace that forms the western flank of Piazza Maggiore has been home to Bologna city council since 1336. A salad of architectural styles, it owes much of its current look to makeovers in the 15th and 16th centuries.

The statue of Pope Gregory XIII, the Bolognese prelate responsible for the Gregorian calendar, was placed above the main portal in 1580, while inside, Donato Bramante's 16th-century staircase was designed to allow horse-drawn carriages to ride directly up to the 1st floor.

On the 2nd floor you'll find the *palazzo's* **Collezioni Comunali d'Arte** (☑ 051 20 36 29; Palazzo Comunale; adult/reduced €5/3; ☉ 9am-6.30pm Tue-Fri, 10am-6.30pm Sat & Sun) with its interesting collection of 13th- to 19th-century paintings, sculpture and furniture.

Outside the *palazzo*, three large panels bear photos of hundreds of partisans killed in the resistance to German occupation, many on this very spot.

Palazzo Fava　　　GALLERY
(☑ 051 1993 6305; www.genusbononiae.it; Via Manzoni 2; admission €10; ☉ 10am-7pm Tue-Sun) This astounding museum is an exposition space encased in a Renaissance mansion given over primarily to temporary art. The biggest draw, however, is the heavily frescoed rooms on the 1st floor painted in bright naturalistic style by the precocious young Carraccis (two brothers and a cousin) in the 1580s.

There's a lovely cafe on-site.

Palazzo del Re Enzo　　　PALACE
(Piazza del Nettuno) This 13th-century palace is named after King Enzo, the illegitimate son of Holy Roman Emperor Frederick II, who was held here by papal forces between

Bologna

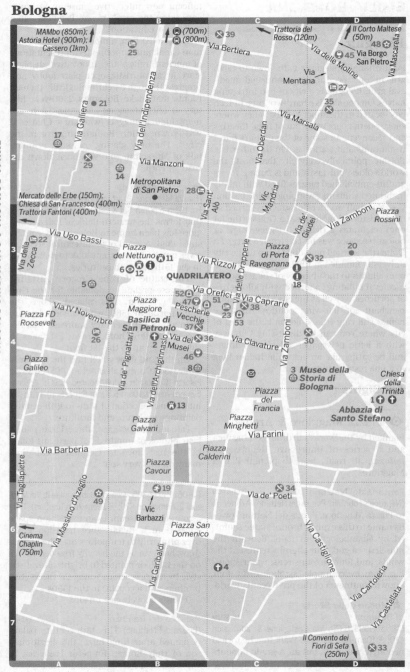

MAMbo (850m);
Astoria Hotel (900m);
Cassero (1km)

(700m)
(800m)

Trattoria del
Rosso (120m)

Il Corto Maltese
(50m)

48

39

Via Bertiera

45 Via delle Moline

Via Borgo
San Pietro

Via Mascarella

25

Via dell'Indipendenza

Via
Mentana

27

21

Via Marsala

35

17

Via Galliera

Via Manzoni

Via Oberdan

14

Metropolitana
di San Pietro

28

Via Sant'
Alò

Vic
Mandria

Via Zamboni

Piazza
Rossini

29

Mercato delle Erbe (150m);
Chiesa di San Francesco (400m);
Trattoria Fantoni (400m)

Via Ugo Bassi

22

Via della Zecca

Piazza
del Nettuno

11

Via Rizzoli

Via delle Drapperie

Via de' Giudei

Piazza
di Porta
Ravegnana

20

6 12

7

32

QUADRILATERO

18

5

10

Via IV Novembre

Piazza FD
Roosevelt

Piazza
Maggiore

Via Orefici

52

47 51

Pescherie
Vecchie

23

Via Caprarie

38

30

26

Basilica di
San Petronio

Via dei
Musei

2

37

36

53

Via Clavature

Via Zamboni

Piazza
Galileo

46

8

Via de' Pignattari

Via de' Archiginnasio

Piazza
del Francia

Museo della
Storia di
Bologna

3

Chiesa
della
Trinità

Piazza
Galileo

13

1

Abbazia di
Santo Stefano

Piazza
Galvani

Piazza
Minghetti

Via Farini

Via Barberia

Via Tagliapietre

Piazza
Calderini

Piazza
Cavour

Piazza
San
Domenico

19

Vic
Barbazzi

Via de' Poeti

34

Cinema
Chaplin
(750m)

Via Massimo d'Azeglio

49

Via Garibaldi

4

Via Castiglione

Via Cartoleria

Via Castellata

Il Convento dei
Fiori di Seta
(250m)

33

1249 and 1272. Dating to the same period, the neighbouring **Palazzo del Podestà** (Piazza Maggiore 1) was the original residence of Bologna's chief magistrate.

Beneath the *palazzo*, there's a **whispering gallery** where two perpendicular passages intersect. Stand diagonally opposite someone and whisper: the acoustics are amazing. Both *palazzi* are off limits to the public unless there's a temporary exhibition on (check with the tourist office found in the same square).

★**Basilica di San Petronio**   CHURCH
(Piazza Maggiore; ⊙8am-1pm & 3-6pm) The world's fifth-largest church, measuring 132m by 66m by 47m, hides some interesting oddities. Firstly, though construction started in 1390, the church wasn't consecrated (officially blessed) until 1954. Secondly, it has been the target of two thwarted terrorist attacks, in 2002 and 2006. Thirdly, the church exhibits an unusual scientific intrusion into a religious setting: inside, a huge sundial stretches 67.7m down the eastern aisle. Designed in 1656 by Gian Cassini and Domenico Guglielmi, the sundial was instrumental in discovering the anomalies of the Julian calendar and led to the creation of the leap year.

Lastly, take a look at the incomplete front facade and you'll quickly deduce that the church was never finished. Originally it was intended to be larger than St Peter's in Rome, but in 1561, some 169 years after building had started, Pope Pius IV blocked construction by commissioning a new university on the basilica's eastern flank. If you walk along Via dell'Archiginnasio you can see semiconstructed apses poking out oddly.

Quadrilatero   HISTORIC QUARTER
To the east of Piazza Maggiore, the grid of streets around Via Clavature (Street of Locksmiths) sits on what was once Roman Bologna. Known as the Quadrilatero, this compact district is less shabby than the adjoining university quarter, with the emphasis on old-style delis selling the region's world-famous produce.

⊙ **South & West of Piazza Maggiore**

Museo Civico Archeologico   MUSEUM
(Via dell'Archiginnasio 2; adult/reduced €5/3; ⊙9am-3pm Tue-Fri, 10am-6.30pm Sat & Sun) Impressive in its breadth of coverage, this museum displays well-documented Egyptian

Bologna

and Roman artefacts along with one of Italy's best Etruscan collections.

Palazzo dell'Archiginnasio PALACE, MUSEUM
(Piazza Galvani 1) **FREE** The result of Pope Pius IV's project to curtail the Basilica di San Petronio, this palace was the seat of the city university from 1563 to 1805. Today it houses Bologna's 700,000-volume **Biblioteca Comunale** (Municipal Library; ⊙9am-6.45pm Mon-Fri, to 1.45pm Sat) and the fascinating 17th-century **Teatro Anatomico** (⊙9am-6.45pm Mon-Fri, to 1.45pm Sat), where public body dissections were held under the sinister gaze of an Inquisition priest, ready to intervene if proceedings became too spiritually compromising.

Rather than a museum, the large room is a preserved anatomical theatre where trainee surgeons once studied. Cedar-wood tiered seats surround a central marble-topped table, while a sculptured Apollo looks down

from the ceiling. The canopy above the lecturer's chair is supported by two skinless figures carved into the wood.

Basilica di San Domenico CHURCH
(Piazza San Domenico 13; ⊙9.30am-12.30pm & 3.30-6.30pm Mon-Fri, to 5.30pm Sat & Sun) Part of Italy's attraction and myth is its hallowed ground. Every chapel in every church tells a slightly different story. Luring you towards this basilica built in 1238 is the legend of San Domenico, founder of the Dominican order, who died in 1221.

His remains lie in an elaborate sarcophagus in the **Cappella di San Domenico**, which was designed by Nicola Pisano and later added to by a host of artists. Other famous ghosts present in the church include Michelangelo, who carved the angel on the right of the altar when he was only 19, and Mozart, who spent a month at the city's music academy and occasionally played the church's organ.

San Colombano – Collezione Tagliavini
MUSEUM

(☑ 051 1993 6366; www.genusbononiae.it; Via Parigi 5; admission €10; ☺ 10am-1pm & 3-7pm Tue-Sun) A beautifully – repeat *beautifully* – restored church with original frescoes and a medieval crypt rediscovered in 2007, the San Colombano hosts a wonderful collection of over 80 musical instruments amassed by the octogenarian organist, Luigi Tagliavini. Many of the assembled harpsichords, pianos and oboes date from the 1500s and, even more surprisingly, are still in full working order.

Listen out for regular free concerts.

Chiesa di San Francesco
CHURCH

(Piazza San Francesco; ☺ 6.30am-noon & 3-7pm) Think Gothic. This dark, mysterious church was one of the first in Italy to be built in the French Gothic style. Inside check out the tomb of Pope Alexander V and the remarkable 14th-century marble altarpiece depicting sundry saints and scenes from the life of St Francis.

☉ University Quarter

Bolshie graffiti, communist newspaper-sellers and the whiff of last night's beer (and urine) characterise the scruffy but strangely contagious streets of the university quarter, the site of Bologna's former Jewish ghetto.

Le Due Torri
TOWER

(Piazza di Porta Ravegnana) Standing sentinel over Piazza di Porta Ravegnana, Bologna's two leaning towers are the city's main symbol. The taller of the two, the 97.6m-high **Torre degli Asinelli** (admission €3; ☺ 9am-6pm, to 5pm Oct-May) is open to the public, although it's not advisable for vertigo-sufferers or owners of arthritic knees (there are 498 steps up a semiexposed wooden staircase).

Superstitious students also boycott it: local lore says if you climb the tower you'll never graduate. Built by the Asinelli family between 1109 and 1119, today the tower leans 1.3m off vertical. The neighbouring 48m **Torre Garisenda** is sensibly out of bounds given its drunken 3.2m tilt.

★ Abbazia di Santo Stefano
CHURCH

(www.abbaziasantostefano.it; Via Santo Stefano 24; ☺ 10am-12.30pm & 3.30-6.45pm) Not *just* another church, the Santo Stefano is a rather unique (and atmospheric) medieval religious complex. Originally there were seven churches – hence the basilica's nickname Sette Chiese – but only four remain.

Entry is via the 11th-century **Chiesa del Crocefisso**, which houses the bones of San Petronio and leads through to the **Chiesa del Santo Sepolcro**. This austere octagonal structure probably started life as a baptistery. Next door, the **Cortile di Pilato** is named after the central basin in which Pontius Pilate is said to have washed his hands after condemning Christ to death. In

EMILIA-ROMAGNA & SAN MARINO BOLOGNA

BOLOGNA'S SECOND RENAISSANCE

It's not easy giving a 3000-year-old city a second Renaissance, especially when the first one was so spectacular, but with the help of some rehabilitated churches, an innovative new history museum and molto investment from a local bank foundation, Bologna has had a damned good stab at it. The project to protect and beef up the city's historic heritage was first hatched in 2003 and has, to date, added eight new locations to the city's already impressive stash of cultural treasures. Called Genus Bononiae: Museums in the City, the project was completed in January 2012 with the opening of the **Museo della Storia di Bologna** (p431). This museum takes you on a striking modern voyage through the city's past courtesy of ingenious architect Mario Bellini. The Genus Bononiae's three main sights – the aforementioned history museum, **Palazzo Fava** (p431) and **San Colombano – Collezione Tagliavini** – are covered by a joint ticket costing €10. Other venues include San**ta Maria della Vita** (Via Clavature 8-10; ☺ 10am-noon & 3-7pm Tue-Sun) FREE, a sanctuary-cum-sculpture museum, the **San Giorgio Poggiale** (Via Nazario Sauro 20/2; ☺ 9am-1pm Mon, Wed-Fri, to 5pm Tue) FREE library, which contains a vast collection of historic books, and the **Chiesa di Santa Cristina** (Piazzetta Morandi 2), a church now used as a classical concert hall. Open sporadically for expos is the renaissance **Casa Saraceni** (Via Farini 15). You can also visit the church at the old **San Michele in Bosco monastery** (Piazzale di San Michele in Bosco; ☺ 9am-noon & 4-6pm).

DON'T MISS

THE CHURCH ON THE HILL

About 3.5km southwest of the city centre, the hilltop **Basilica Santuario della Madonna di San Luca** (Via di San Luca 36; ⏱7am-12.30pm & 2.30-7pm Apr-Sep, to 6pm Mar, to 5pm Oct-Feb) occupies a powerful and appropriately celestial position overlooking the teeming red-hued city below. The church houses a representation of the Virgin Mary, supposedly painted by St Luke and transported from the Middle East to Bologna in the 12th century. The 18th-century sanctuary is connected to the city walls by the world's longest portico, held aloft by 666 arches, beginning at Piazza di Porta Saragozza. Take bus 20 from the city centre to Villa Spada, from where you can continue by minibus to the sanctuary. Alternatively, continue one more stop on bus 20 to the Meloncello arch and walk the remaining 2km under the arches.

fact, it's an 8th-century Lombard artefact. Beyond the courtyard, the **Chiesa della Trinità** connects to a modest cloister and a small **museum**. The fourth church, the **Santi Vitale e Agricola**, is the city's oldest. Incorporating recycled Roman masonry and carvings, the bulk of the building dates from the 11th century. The considerably older tombs of two saints in the side aisles once served as altars.

Oratorio di Santa Cecilia　　　CHURCH
(Via Zamboni 15; ⏱10am-1pm & 2-6pm) This is one of Bologna's unsung gems. Inside, the magnificent 16th-century frescoes by Lorenzo Costa depicting the life and Technicolor death of St Cecilia and her husband Valeriano are in remarkably good nick, their colours vibrant and their imagery bold and unabashed. The Oratorio hosts regular free chamber-music recitals. Check the board outside for upcoming events.

University Museums　　　MUSEUM
FREE The world's oldest university has a slew of museums that make a break from the ecclesiastical art/dark-church alternatives. Some of them are free. Most are in the **Palazzo Poggi** (www.museopalazzopoggi.unibo.it; Via Zamboni 33; admission €3; ⏱10am-1pm & 2-4pm Tue-Fri, 10.30am-1.30pm & 2.30-5.30pm Sat & Sun), where you can peruse waxwork uteri in the **Obstetrics Museum** and giant tortoiseshells in the **Museum of Natural Sciences**.

There's free entry to see the stuffed exhibits over at the **Museo di Zoologia** and the **Museo di Antropologia** on nearby Via Selma 3.

Pinacoteca Nazionale　　　ART GALLERY
(Via delle Belle Arti 56; admission €4; ⏱9am-1.30pm Tue-Wed, 9am-7pm Thu, 2-7pm Fri-Sun) The city's main art gallery has a powerful collection of works by Bolognese artists

from the 14th century onwards, including a number of important canvases by the late-16th-century Carracci cousins Ludovico, Agostino and Annibale.

Among the founding fathers of Italian baroque art, the Carraccis were deeply influenced by the Counter-Reformation sweeping through Italy in the latter half of the 16th century. Much of their work is religious and their imagery is often highly charged and emotional, designed to appeal to the piety of the viewing public. Works to look out for include Ludovico's *Madonna Bargellini*, the *Comunione di San Girolamo* (Communion of St Jerome) by Agostino and the *Madonna di San Ludovico* by Annibale. Elsewhere in the gallery you'll find several works by Giotto, as well as Raphael's *Estasi di Santa Cecilia* (Ecstasy of St Cecilia). El Greco and Titian are also represented, but by comparatively little-known works.

⊙ North of Piazza Maggiore

MAMbo　　　ART GALLERY
(Museo d'Arte Moderna di Bologna; www.mambo-bologna.org; Via Don Minzoni 14; adult/reduced €6/4; ⏱noon-6pm Tue, Wed & Fri, to 8pm Thu, Sat & Sun) Avant-gardes, atheists and people who've had their fill of dark religious art can seek solace in one of Bologna's newer museums (opened 2007) housed in a cavernous former municipal bakery. Its permanent and rotating exhibits showcase the work of up-and-coming Italian artists. Entrance to the permanent collection is free on Wednesday.

🏃 Activities

Hammam Bleu　　　SPA
(☎051 58 01 62; www.hammam.it; Vicolo Barbazzi 4; ⏱noon-10pm Mon-Fri, 11am-7pm Sat & Sun) If the tranquillity of all those churches hasn't

calmed you down, try this Turkish bath in the historic centre. Prices start at €50 for a half-hour rub-down or €40 for just the spa facilities (steam room, sauna, jacuzzi).

Courses

La Vecchia Scuola Bolognese COOKING
(☎051 649 15 76; www.lavecchiascuola.com; Via Galliera 11) It stands to reason: Bologna is also a good place to learn to cook and this is one of several schools that offer courses for English speakers. Prices range from €80 for a single four-hour course to €210 for three days.

☞ Tours

Various outfits offer guided, two-hour walking tours in English (€13). Groups assemble outside the main tourist office on Piazza Maggiore (no booking required).

La Chiocciola WALKING TOUR
(☎051 22 09 64; www.bolognawelcome.com/guida-turistica; Via San Vitale 22) Authorised guiding group that offers walking tours of the city.

City Red Bus BUS TOUR
(www.cityredbus.com) Runs an hour-long, hop-on, hop-off bus tour of the city departing from the train station several times daily. Tickets (€12) can be bought on board.

Festivals & Events

Bologna has an eclectic events calendar, mainly centred on music. Performances – or in rock-and-roll parlance, 'gigs' – range from street raves to jazz concerts, ballet performances and religious processions. Summer is generally the best time.

Bologna Estate ARTS
(www.bolognaestate.it) A three-month (mid-June to mid-September) program of concerts, film projections, dance performances and much more. Held in open-air venues throughout the city, many events are free. Tourist offices have details.

Sleeping

Accommodation in Bologna is geared to the business market, with a glut of midrange to top-end hotels in the convention zone to the north of the city. If possible, avoid the busy spring and autumn trade-fair seasons when prices skyrocket, hotels get heavily booked and advance reservations are essential. Outside of fair season, some hotels offer dis-counts of up to 50% and attractive weekend rates.

Hotel University Bologna HOTEL €
(☎051 22 97 13; www.hoteluniversitybologna.com; Via Mentana 7; s/d €61/75; ❋@🛜) Remember student digs? Well, heave a sigh of relief, they were nothing like this. It's good to see that the world's oldest university town can still muster up a hotel that's not a million miles beyond the price range of its large undergraduate population. The HU Bologna is billed as a three-star hotel, but it's recently renovated and punches well above its weight.

Astoria Hotel HOTEL, APARTMENT €
(☎051 52 14 10; www.astoria.bo.it; Via Fratelli Rosselli 14; 1-/2-/3-person apt €60/70/88; 🛜) Bypass the rather lacklustre hotel rooms and ask for one of the spacious apartments sprinkled in convenient locations between the station and the city centre.

Albergo delle Drapperie HOTEL €
(☎051 22 39 55; www.albergodrapperie.com; Via delle Drapperie 5; s/d €70/85; ❋🛜) Right in the heart of the atmospheric Quadrilatero district, the Drapperie is one of those 'hidden' hotels encased in the upper floors of a larger building. Buzz in at ground level and climb the stairs to discover 21 attractive rooms with wood-beamed ceilings, the occasional brick arch and colourful ceiling frescoes. Breakfast is €5 extra.

Albergo Rossini HOTEL €
(☎051 23 77 16; www.albergorossini.com; Via dei Bibiena 11; s/d €62/72; ⊙closed mid-Jul–mid-Aug; ❋) The approach isn't promising: a short walk off Piazza Verdi along an alley that tipsy drinkers use as an alfresco pee-spot. But, once inside, the journeyman Rossini is warm, friendly and eager to please. Try to bag a room on the top floor, where strategically placed skylights let the sun pour in.

Ostello Due Torri-San Sisto HOSTEL €
(☎051 50 18 10; www.ostellodibologna.com; Via Viadagola 5 & 14; dm €18, s/d €26/46, without bathroom €23/42; 🅿@🛜) Some 6km north of the centre, Bologna's two HI hostels, barely 100m apart, are modern, functional and cheap. Take bus 93 (Monday to Saturday, until 8.20pm) from Via Irnerio, bus 301 (Sunday) from the bus station, or bus 21B (evenings, hourly from 8.40pm to 12.40am) opposite the train station.

Albergo Centrale
HOTEL €

(☑ 051 22 51 14; www.albergocentralebologna.it; Via della Zecca 2; s/d €63/82, without bathroom €49/72; ✱) Offering comfort and a central location, the large old-fashioned rooms at Albergo Centrale come with parquet floors, modern furniture and an ample buffet breakfast.

Hotel Orologio
DESIGN HOTEL €€

(☑ 051 745 74 11; www.bolognarthotels.it; Via IV Novembre 10; r from €140; P ✱ @ 🛜) One of four upmarket hotels run by Bologna Art Hotels, this refined pile just off Piazza Maggiore seduces guests with its slick service, smart rooms furnished in elegant gold, blue and burgundy, swirling grey-and-white marble bathrooms, complimentary chocs and an unbeatable downtown location.

★ Hotel Metropolitan
BOUTIQUE HOTEL €€€

(☑ 051 22 93 93; www.hotelmetropolitan.com; Via dell'Orso 6; r from €140; ✱ @ 🛜) Providing another lesson in Italian interior design, the Met doesn't miss a trick. It mixes functionality with handsome modern furnishings and finishes everything off with an all-pervading Thai-Buddhist theme, presumably to inject a bit of peace and tranquillity into its frenetic city-centre location. It works.

Prendiparte B&B
B&B €€€

(☑ 051 58 90 23; www.prendiparte.it; Via Sant'Alò 7; r from €350) You will never – repeat, *never* – stay anywhere else like this. Forget the B&B tag: you don't just get a room here, you get an entire 900-year-old tower (Bologna's second tallest). The living area (bedroom, kitchen and lounge) is spread over three floors and there are nine more levels to explore, with a 17th-century prison halfway up and outstanding views from the terrace up top.

Find a millionaire to shack up with and pretend you're an errant medieval prince(ss) for the night.

Il Convento dei Fiori di Seta
BOUTIQUE HOTEL €€€

(☑ 051 27 20 39; www.silkflowersnunnery.com; Via Orfeo 34; r €140-420, ste €250-520; ✱ 🛜) Before you get to Bologna's budget options, you have to gawp at all the pricey places, including this chic boutique hotel housed in a 14th-century convent. Religious-inspired frescoes sit alongside Mapplethorpe-style flower photos and snazzy modern light fixtures; beds come with linen sheets and bathrooms feature cool mosaic tiles.

✖ Eating

Gastronomic tip number one: learn the local lingo and ask for *tagliatelle al ragù*. Call-

---

SPAGHETTI BOLOGNESE

If you came to Emilia-Romagna in search of authentic spaghetti bolognese you're out of luck. The name is a misnomer. Spaghetti bolognese is about as Bolognese as roast beef and Yorkshire pudding and Bologna's fiercely traditional trattorias never list it. Instead, the city prides itself on a vastly superior meat-based sauce called *ragù*, consisting of slow-cooked minced beef simmered with pancetta, onions and carrots, and enlivened with liberal dashes of milk and wine.

So why the misleading moniker? Modern legend suggests that *ragù* may have acted as spaghetti bolognese's original inspiration when British and American servicemen passing through Emilia in WWII fell in love with the dish. Returning home after the war, they subsequently asked their immigrant Italian chefs to rustle up something similar. Details clearly got lost in translation. The 'spag bol' eaten in contemporary London and New York is fundamentally different to Bologna's centuries-old *ragù*. First there's the sauce. Spaghetti bolognese is heavy on tomatoes while *ragù* is all about the meat. Then there's the pasta. Spag bol is served with dry durum-wheat spaghetti from Naples taken straight from a packet. *Ragù* is spread over fresh egg-based *tagliatelle* (ribbon pasta) allowing the rich meat sauce to stick to the thick al dente strands.

Ever keen to safeguard their meat sauce from mediocrity, Bologna's chamber of commerce registered an official *ragù* recipe in 1982, although, ironically, it's still nigh on impossible to find two Bologna *ragù* that taste the same. The concoction made at Osteria dell'Orsa is popularly considered to be the Verdi of its field.

ing the city's signature meat sauce 'spag bol' is like calling champagne 'fizzy wine'. Two meals into your Bologna stay and you'll start to understand why the city's known as La Grassa. Food is second only to Catholicism here.

The university district northeast of Via Rizzoli harbours hundreds of restaurants, trattorias, takeaways and cafes catering to hard-up students and gourmet diners alike. If you're cooking your own, head to the historic delis in the Quadrilatero.

★ **Osteria dell'Orsa**   ITALIAN €
(📞 051 23 15 76; www.osteriadellorsa.com; Via Mentana 1; meals €22-25; ⊙ noon-midnight) If you were to make a list of the great wonders of Italy, hidden amid Venice's canals and Rome's Colosseum would be cheap, pretension-free *osterie* (casual eateries presided over by a host) such as Osteria dell'Orsa, where the food is serially sublime and the prices are giveaway cheap. So what if the waiter's wearing an AC Milan shirt and the wine is served in a water glass?

Nothing can equal the deliciousness of your al dente pumpkin *cappellacci* (a type of ravioli) doused in butter and sage.

Trattoria del Rosso   TRATTORIA €
(📞 051 23 67 30; www.trattoriadelrosso.com; Via A Righi 30; mains €7.50-10; ⊙ noon-11pm) You don't have to pay big euros to eat well in Bologna. Doubters should step inside the Rosso, where unfancy decor and quick service attract plenty of hard-up single diners enjoying pop-by lunches. They say that the trattoria is the oldest in the city, further proof that ancient formulas work best.

Colazione da Bianco   BREAKFAST €
(📞 051 588 44 25; Via Santa Stefano 1; snacks €5-10; ⊙ 7.30am-9pm Wed-Mon) An ideal place for breakfast or an afternoon '*pausa*', La Colazione oozes elegance like only the Italians can with theatrical curtains, opulent chandeliers and creamy croissants. Plenty of table space encourages lingering. Oops, there goes a second slice of cake.

Tamburini   BUFFET, DELI €
(www.tamburini.com; Via Caprarie 1; meals €10-20; ⊙ 8.30am-8pm Mon-Sat, 10am-6.30pm Sun) Fast food done fresh and imaginatively is no oxymoron at Tamburini, a traditional delicatessen full of swinging hams and pungent cheeses that also runs a popular grab-a-tray buffet. Fill up on alluringly decorated cheese and meat boards, colourful salad bowls and

a choice of three to four daily pasta dishes. Prepare for queues.

Gelateria Gianni   GELATO €
(www.gelateriagianni.com; Via San Vitale 2; ⊙ noon-10pm) Edging Italy's most ubiquitous ice cream chain, Grom, into third place is this ice-cream temple where generous dollops of flavours such as white chocolate and cherry have brought a sweet ending to many an undergraduate date night.

La Sorbetteria Castiglione   GELATO €
(www.lasorbetteria.it; Via Castiglione 44; ⊙ 8.30am-midnight Tue-Sat, 9am-11.30pm Sun) Everyone has a wondrous Italian ice-cream story and more than a few (including one of a recent *New York Times* reviewer) were made in this temple to gelati. It's a bit peripheral to the centre but worthy of the walk.

Trattoria Fantoni   TRATTORIA €
(Via del Pratello 11a; meals €15; ⊙ noon-2.15pm & 8-10pm Tue-Sat, noon-2.15pm Mon) A much-loved eatery dishing up classic Italian food at welcome prices. The atmosphere's jovial and the decor is an agreeable clash of clutter and modern art.

P122@s   PIZZERIA €
(Via dei Musei 2-4; pizzas €6-9; ⊙ 12:30-3:30pm & 7:30pm-1am) Purists don't go to Bologna for the pizzas, but if you need to spiritually visit southern Italy, drop by this trendy spot with wood-fired pies set under the porticoes near Piazza Maggiore.

★ **Trattoria dal Biassanot**   TRATTORIA €€
(📞 051 23 06 44; www.dalbiassanot.it; Via Piella 16a; meals from €25; ⊙ noon-2.30pm & 7-10.30pm Tue-Sat, noon-2.30pm Sun) The waiters in bow ties suggest an underlying grandiosity, but the Biassanot is about as down to earth as its earthy menu, which lists such rustic throwbacks as wild boar, goat, and veal with balsamic vinegar and mushrooms. Get in early: the check-clothed tables get busy. The pear *torta* (cake) and hot custard dessert round off proceedings very nicely.

Buca Manzoni   EMILIAN €€
(📞 051 27 13 07; www.bucamanzoni.it; Via Manzoni 6g; meals €25-30; ⊙ 12.30-3.30pm & 7-11pm Wed-Sat & Mon, 12.30-4pm Sun) 'We only serve proper Bolognese food here, none of that spaghetti stuff', announces your loquacious but humorous waiter. You'd better believe him. At Buca Manzoni the menu is printed in Bolognese dialect, the lasagne comes *verde*

(green), and those long stringy bits of pasta are called *tagliatelle* and are nothing – dare you ask – like spag bol.

Drogheria della Rosa
TRATTORIA €€

(☑ 051 22 25 29; www.drogheriadellarosa.it; Via Cartoleria 10; meals €35-40; ⊘ noon-3pm & 7.30-11.45pm) With its wooden shelves and apothecary jars, it's not difficult to picture this place as the pharmacy it once was. Nowadays it's a charming, high-end trattoria, run by a congenial owner who seems to find time to get round to every table and explain the day's short, sweet menu.

Expect superbly prepared versions of Bolognese classics such as tortellini or steak with balsamic vinegar.

Osteria de' Poeti
RISTORANTE €€

(www.osteriadepoeti.com; Via de' Poeti 1b; mains €12; ⊘ 7.30pm-3am Tue-Sat, 12.30-2.30pm Sun) In the wine cellar of a 14th-century *palazzo*, this historic eatery is an atmospheric place to enjoy hearty local fare. Take a table by the impressive stone fireplace and order from a selection of staples such as *taglioline con fiori di zucca, zucchini e prosciutto di Parma* (pasta with pumpkin flowers, zucchini and Parma ham). Evenings feature frequent live music.

Self-Catering

Stock up on victuals at the Mercato delle Erbe (Via U Bassi 27; ⊘ 7am-1.15pm Mon-Sat, 5-7.30pm Mon-Wed & Fri), Bologna's main covered market. Alternatively, the Quadrilatero area east of Piazza Maggiore harbours a daily produce market (Via Clavature; ⊘ 7am-1pm Mon-Sat, 4.15-7.30pm Mon-Wed, Fri & Sat) and some of the city's best-known delis.

Drinking & Nightlife

Hit the graffiti-strewn streets of the university district after sunset and the electrifying energy is enough to make a jaded 40-year-old feel 20 again. Clamorous bars spill out into the street, groups of earnest drinkers sit down in circles on the hard pavement, and talented musicians jam old Thelonius Monk numbers. Piazza Verdi is the nexus for thirsty students; for a more upmarket, dressier scene head to the Quadrilatero.

★ Le Stanze
WINE BAR

(www.lestanzecafe.com; Via Borgo San Pietro 1; ⊘ 11am-3am Mon-Sat) If La Scuderia reeks of undergraduate days you'd rather forget, hit the more chic Le Stanze, a former chapel where each of the four interior rooms has its own design concept. The *aperitivo* (pre-dinner drinks with snacks) buffet is top-notch here, with paellas, pastas and chicken drumsticks to accompany your wine or cocktail.

La Scuderia
BAR, CAFE

(www.lascuderia.bo.it; Piazza Verdi 2; ⊘ 8am-2.30am; ☎) On Piazza Verdi, the shabby-chic Scuderia envelops the whole square on a good night. This being Bologna, the clientele is made up of a socialist republic of pavement loungers, hairy goths, down-but-not-quite-out students, and the odd stray opera-goer swept up in the nostalgia of their undergraduate days.

The bar occupies the Bentivoglio family's former stables and features towering columns, vaulted ceilings and arty photos.

English Empire
BAR

(Via Zamboni 24a; ⊘ 7pm-3am) Despite the fact that Bologna never was part of any English Empire, this pungent pub does a roaring

BOLOGNA ON THE CHEAP

Bologna is a student city, which means cheap deals are rife if you know where to look. For the most economical meals, eat in the University Cafeteria (Via Zamboni 33; ⊘ lunch & dinner Mon-Fri) for as little as €8 for three courses (and you don't have to be a student). Afterwards, consider hitting Il Corto Maltese (Via Borgo San Pietro 9/2a; ⊘ 9pm-3am) for two-for-one cocktails and live DJs. For caffeine infusions, La Scuderia slams down cappuccinos for less than a euro. Aperitifs are lined up on the bar at 6.30pm-ish and are free if you buy a drink. Nearby in ITIT, you can linger for an hour or two guilt-free nursing the same coffee and using the free wi-fi.

Bologna's eclectic university museums (p436) are all free to visit, as are most of its churches (including the Basilica). Furthermore, free classical concerts are held regularly in the Oratorio di Santa Cecilia (p436) and the Chiesa di Santa Cristina (p435).

trade in both Guinness and Bass (on tap), spilling its patrons halfway up the colonnaded sidewalks. Early-morning joggers glide past the remnants.

Osteria del Sole
BAR

(www.osteriadelsole.it; Vicolo Ranocchi 1d; ☺10.30am-9.30pm Mon-Sat) Welcome to a rather pleasant form of chaos! The sign outside this ancient Quadrilatero dive bar tells you all you need to know – '*vino*' (wine). It's as simple as that.

Bring in your own food, find some elbow room amid a cacophony of smashed students, mildly inebriated grandpas and the odd misplaced Anglo tourist, and fight your way to the bar for a sloppily poured glass of chianti, Sangiovese or Lambrusco. It's a spot-on formula that's been working since – no word of a lie – 1465.

ITIT
CAFE

(Largo dei Respighi 2; ☺8am-8pm; 🛜) A new trend in coffee consumption? This new student-quarter cafe is a haven of wi-fi geeks, hungover revellers and lunch-breakers choosing prepacked sandwiches. It offers coffee in takeaway cups, double shots, low-fat milk and numerous other 'Americanisms'.

Modo Infoshop
BAR

(www.modoinfoshop.com; Via Mascarella 24; ☺10am-1pm & 4pm-midnight Mon-Fri, 6pm-midnight Sat & Sun) If Bologna is a city of two halves, then Modo Infoshop is definitely in the 'red' student half. An indie bookshop with an affiliated cafe-bar next door, this is where postgrads sit down to write up their theses in a room decorated with *antifascismo* banners and enlivened with David Bowie on repeat.

There's cheap beer, good wine, modest appies and tempting chocolate brownies to enjoy. Conversations start getting interesting around 8pm.

Nu-Lounge Bar
BAR

(Via dei Musei 6f; ☺8.30pm-2:30am) A swish bar in the Quadrilatero quarter, Nu-Lounge's well-groomed Italian crowd quaffs *aperitivi* while checking their reflections in the large glass windows of the porticoed terrace.

Bravo Caffè
BAR

(Via Mascarella 1; ☺8pm-late) Across from Cantina Bentivoglio, Bravo is a sexy wine bar with red walls, black furniture and soft, subtle lighting. It also features regular live jazz and a full food menu.

☆ Entertainment

Bologna, courtesy of its large student population, knows how to rock – but it also knows how to clap politely at the opera. The most comprehensive listings guide is *Bologna Spettacolo* (€1.50, in Italian), available at newsstands.

Cantina Bentivoglio
JAZZ

(www.cantinabentivoglio.it; Via Mascarella 4b; ☺8pm-2am) Bologna's top jazz joint, the Bentivoglio is a jack of all trades. Part wine bar (choose from over 500 labels), part restaurant (the daily *prix-fixe* menu costs €28) and part jazz club (there's live music nightly), this much-loved institution oozes cosy charm with its ancient brick floors, arched ceilings and shelves full of wine bottles.

Cassero
CLUB

(www.cassero.it; Via Don Minzoni 18; ☺8:30pm-late) Wednesday and Saturday are the big nights at this legendary gay-and-lesbian (but not exclusively) club, home of Italy's Arcigay organisation.

Villa Serena
LIVE MUSIC

(www.villaserena.bo.it; Via della Barca 1; ☺9.30pm-3am Fri & Sat) Three floors of film screenings and music, live and canned, plus a garden for outdoor chilling.

Cinema Chaplin
CINEMA

(www.cinemachaplin.it; Piazza di Porta Saragozza 5; admission €5) Screens films in English every Monday from September through May.

Teatro Comunale
THEATRE

(www.tcbo.it; Largo Respighi 1) Wagner's works were heard for the first time in Italy in Bologna's main opera and classical-music venue.

🔒 Shopping

If you came for the food, head for the Quadrilatero, a haven of family-run delis and speciality food shops. Leaders in the field are Paolo Atti (Via delle Drapperie 6; ☺7.30am-1.30pm & 4-7.15pm Mon-Sat) and La Baita (Via Pescheria Vecchie 3; ☺8am-8pm, closed Sun Jun-Aug).

Librerie Coop
BOOKS

(Via Orefici 19; ☺9am-midnight Mon-Sat, to 8pm Sun) A dream for hungry bookworms (or erudite gourmands), this three-level bookshop is a joint project with ethical Turin supermarket chain, Eataly. There are two eating options and thousands of books inside.

FERRARI & OTHER CAR FANTASIES

Fiats might be functional, but to appreciate the true beauty of Italian workmanship you must visit the small triangle of land between Modena and Bologna sometimes called 'Motor Valley' where they construct the world's finest luxury cars, namely Ferraris and Lamborghinis. The metaphoric haj for all petrolheads is to the **Galleria Ferrari** (www.galleria.ferrari.com; Via Ferrari 43; adult/reduced €13/9; ☺9.30am-7pm May-Sep, to 6pm Oct-Apr) in Maranello; they come here to obsess over the world's largest collection of Ferraris, including Formula 1 exhibits, a trajectory of the cars' mechanical evolution and a revolving feature of 40 of the landmark models. A second Ferrari museum, the Museo Casa Enzo Ferrari has recently opened in Modena with a shuttle bus linking the two.

More treats are available at the **Lamborghini Museum** (☎051 681 76 11; www.lamborghini.com; Via Modena 12; adult/reduced €13/10; ☺10am-12.30pm & 1.30-5pm), situated 20km east of Modena in the village of Sant'Agata Bolognese. Here you get the chance to visit the company factory where Lamborghinis are custom-made. Factory tours must be prebooked and cost €40 – small change compared to the gold-on-wheels you'll be looking at. Bus 576 runs from Bologna bus station to Sant'Agata Bolognese.

❶ Information

Ospedale Maggiore (☎051 647 81 11; Largo Nigrisoli 2) West of the city centre; take bus 19 from Via Bassi.

Post Office (Piazza Minghetti 4)

Tourist Office (www.bolognaturismo.info; Piazza Maggiore 1e; ☺9am-7pm) Also offices at the airport and in the train station.

❶ Getting There & Away

AIR

Bologna's **Guglielmo Marconi airport** (☎051 647 96 15; www.bologna-airport.it) is 8km northwest of the city. It's served by over two dozen airlines including easyJet (daily flights to Gatwick) and Ryanair (daily flights to Stansted).

BUS

Intercity buses leave from the **main bus station** (www.autostazionebo.it) off Piazza XX Settembre, just southeast of the train station. However, for nearly all destinations, the train's better option.

CAR & MOTORCYCLE

Bologna is linked to Milan, Florence and Rome by the A1 Autostrada del Sole. The A13 heads directly to Ferrara, Padua and Venice, and the A14 to Rimini and Ravenna. Bologna is also on the SS9 (Via Emilia), which connects Milan to the Adriatic coast. The SS64 goes to Ferrara.

Major car-hire companies are represented at Guglielmo Marconi airport and outside the train station. City offices include **Budget** (Via G Amendola 12f) and **Hertz** (Via G Amendola 16a).

TRAIN

Bologna is a major transport junction for northern Italy. The high-speed train to Florence (€24) takes only 37 minutes. Rome (€56, two hours 20 minutes) and Milan (regional €16, 2¼ hours; Eurostar €40, one hour) also offer quick links.

Frequent trains from Bologna serve cities throughout Emilia-Romagna.

❶ Getting Around

TO/FROM THE AIRPORT

Aerobus shuttles (www.atc.bo.it) depart from the main train station for Guglielmo Marconi airport every 15 to 30 minutes between 5.30am and 11.10pm. The 20-minute journey costs €5 (tickets can be bought on board).

BICYCLE

You can hire a bike at **Autorimessa Pincio** (Via dell'Indipendenza 71z; per 12/24hr €13/18; ☺7am-midnight Mon-Sat), located near the bus station.

CAR & MOTORCYCLE

Much of the city centre is off limits to vehicles. If you're staying downtown, your hotel can provide a ticket (€7 per day) that entitles you to enter the Zona a Traffico Limitato (ZTL), park in designated spaces and make unlimited trips on city buses for 24 hours.

PUBLIC TRANSPORT

Bologna has an efficient bus system, run by **ATC** (www.atc.bo.it). It has information booths at the main train station, the bus station and on Via Marconi. Buses 25 and 30 are among several that connect the train station with the city centre.

West of Bologna

Modena

POP 186,000

If Italy were a meal, Modena would be the main course. Here, on the flat plains of the slow-flowing Po, lies one of the nation's great gastronomic centres, the creative force behind *real* balsamic vinegar, giant tortellini stuffed with tantalising fillings, sparkling Lambrusco wine and backstreets crammed with some of the best restaurants no one's ever heard of. For those with bleached taste buds, the city has another equally lauded legacy: cars. The famous Ferrari museum is situated in the nearby village of Maranello. Modena is also notable for its haunting Romanesque cathedral and as the birthplace of the late Italian opera singer Pavarotti.

◉ Sights

★ **Cathedral** CATHEDRAL
(Corso Duomo; ⊘7am-12.30pm & 3.30-7pm) Modena's celebrated cathedral combines the austerity of the Dark Ages with throwback traditions from the Romans in a style known in Europe as Romanesque. The church stands out among Emilia-Romagna's many other ecclesial relics for its remarkable architectural purity. It is, by popular consensus, the finest Romanesque church in Italy, and in 1997 was listed as a Unesco World Heritage Site.

While not as large or spectacular as other Italian churches, the cathedral – dedicated to the city's patron saint, St Geminianus – has a number of striking features. The dark interior is dominated by the huge Gothic rose window (actually a 13th-century addition) that shoots rays of light down the grand central apse. To the sides, a series of vivid bas-reliefs depicting scenes from Genesis are the work of the 12th-century sculptor Wiligelmo. Interior highlights include an elaborate rood screen decorated by Anselmo da Campione and, in the crypt, Guido Mazzoni's *Madonna della pappa*, a group of five painted terracotta figures.

Opposite the entrance to the cathedral, the Musei del Duomo (Via Lanfranco 6; adult/child €3/2; ⊘9.30am-12.30pm & 3.30-6.30pm Tue-Sun) has more of Wiligelmo's stonework.

Inseparable from the cathedral is the early-13th-century Torre Ghirlandina (Corso Duomo; admission €2; ⊘9:30am-12:30pm & 3-7pm Sat-Sun Apr-Sep), an 87m tower topped with a Gothic spire that was named after Seville's famous 'Giralda' in the early 16th century by exiled Spanish Jews. Facing it across Piazza Grande is the elegant facade of the Palazzo Comunale.

Museo Casa Enzo Ferrari MUSEUM
(www.museocasaenzoferrari.it; Via Paolo Ferrari 85; adult/reduced €13/11; ⊘9.30am-7pm) While Maranello's Ferrari museum focuses on supersonic cars, this new place, inaugurated in 2012 and a five-minute walk from Modena train station, celebrates the man himself – Signor Enzo Ferrari. The memorabilia is cleverly juxtaposed in two separate buildings.

The traditional house where Enzo was born in 1898 relates his life story (with multilingual audio commentaries and film footage), and a slick curvaceous modern

---

DON'T LEAVE TOWN WITHOUT TRYING...

Every Emilia-Romagna city has its gastronomic secrets, weird and wonderful local recipes that'll you'd be unlikely to find on the menu of your local Italian restaurant back home. Don't leave these towns without trying....

➡ **Piacenza** Anolini in brodo – pasta pockets filled with meat, Parmesan and breadcrumbs swimming in a rich brothlike soup.

➡ **Parma** Trippa alla Parmigiano – slow-cooked tripe in a tomato sauce enlivened with Parmesan.

➡ **Modena** Cotechino di Modena – pork sausage stuffed with seasoned mince and paired with lentils and mashed potatoes.

➡ **Bologna** Tagliatelle al ragu – thick meat-heavy sauce served with wide-cut egg-based noodles.

➡ **Ferarra** Cappellaci di zucca – raviolilike pasta stuffed with squash and nutmeg, and doused in butter and sage.

➡ **Ravenna** Piadina – thick unleavened bread stuffed with rocket, tomato and local soft *squaquarone* cheese.

➡ **Rimini** Brodetto – a hearty fish soup served over lightly toasted bread.

Modena

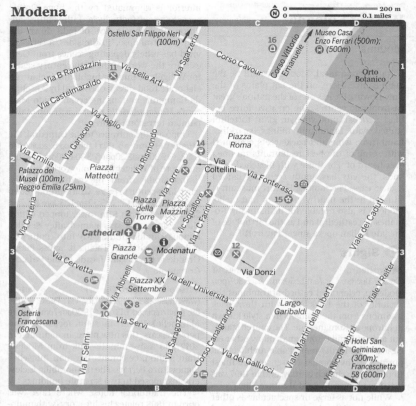

Modena

◎ Top Sights

building acts as a gigantic car showroom painted in bright 'Modena yellow'. Here you'll find the ticket office, a cafe and plenty of Ferraris and Maseratis to gawp at. A shuttle bus (one way €6) connects to the Maranello museum six times daily.

Palazzo dei Musei MUSEUM
(Piazzale Sant'Agostino 337) Modena's main museums and galleries are all conveniently housed in the Palazzo dei Musei on the western fringes of the historic centre.

The most interesting, the Galleria Estense (admission €4; ⊙8.30am-7.30pm Tue-Sun) features the Este family's collection of northern Italian paintings from late medieval times to the 18th century. There are also some fine Flemish works and a canvas or two by Velázquez, Correggio and El Greco. Downstairs, the Biblioteca Estense (admission free; ⊙9am-1pm Mon-Sat) holds one of Italy's most valuable collections of books, letters and manuscripts, including the celebrated *Bibbia di Borso d'Este*, a masterpiece of medieval illustration.

A combined ticket (€4) gives entry to the Museo Archeologico Etnologico (⊙9am-noon Tue-Fri, 10am-7pm Sat & Sun) and the Museo Civico d'Arte (⊙9am-noon Tue-Fri, 10am-1pm & 3-6pm Sat & Sun). The former has some well-displayed local finds from Palaeolithic to medieval eras, as well as exhibits from Africa, Asia, Peru and New Guinea. Most interesting among the Museo Civico d'Arte's eclectic collection are the sections devoted to traditional paper-making, textiles and musical instruments.

Museo della Figurina   MUSEUM
(Corso Canalgrande 103; ⊙10.30am-1pm & 4-7.30pm Wed-Fri, 10.30am-7.30pm Sat & Sun) FREE A nostalgic journey back in time for any kid that ever owned a *Panini* football sticker collection, this geeky museum is tucked away upstairs in the Palazzo Santa Margherita. It displays that precious Paolo Rossi sticker that cruelly eluded you in 1982, along with numerous other card collections, calendars and scrapbooks.

✪ Festivals & Events

Modena Terra di Motori   CAR
(www.modenaterradimotori.com) Between late March and early May, vintage cars and snazzy Ferraris take to Modena's historic streets in this annual car fest.

🛏 Sleeping

Hotel San Geminiano   HOTEL €
(☎059 21 03 03; www.hotelsangeminiano.it; Viale Moreali 41; s/d €60/80; P ⊚) Geminiano's slightly off-centre location and dark, unspectacular rooms are saved by steady-Eddie service and a salt-of-the-earth restaurant next door, which serves shockingly economical pizzas (€4.50), and pesto sauce that tastes like it's been dug straight out of the Emiliano soil.

Ostello San Filippo Neri   HOSTEL €
(☎059 23 45 98; www.ostellomodena.it; Via Santa Orsola 48-52; dm/s/d €18.50/25/40; @ ⊡) Modena's businesslike HI hostel has 80 beds in single-sex dorms and family units. Pluses include disabled access, capacious lockers, uncrowded rooms (maximum three beds per dorm) and a bike-storage area. Drawbacks are the 10am to 2pm lockout and no breakfast (though you can bring takeaway food into the hostel's dining area).

Hotel Cervetta 5   HOTEL €€
(☎059 23 84 47; www.hotelcervetta5.com; Via Cervetta 5; s/d/tr €80/120/155; ❋⊚) Cervetta is about as posh as Modena gets without pampering to the convention crowd. A location adjacent to intimate Piazza Grande is complemented by quasi-boutique facilities, clean, modern bathrooms and the latest in TV technology. Fruity breakfasts and wi-fi are included; garage parking (€12) isn't.

Canalgrande Hotel   HOTEL €€
(☎059 21 71 60; www.canalgrandehotel.it; Corso Canalgrande 6; s/d €90/120; ❋@⊚) A venerable Modenese institution, the Canalgrande exudes old-school elegance with its acres of marble, gilt-framed paintings, sparkling chandeliers and a spacious terrace overlooking the garden out back. Parking costs €12.

🍴 Eating

Modena would easily make a top-10 list of best Italian culinary towns. The beauty lies not just in the food, but in the way it is unpretentiously presented in nondescript restaurants up blind alleys or hidden inside office blocks, often without signage.

★ Trattoria Aldina   TRATTORIA €
(Via Albinelli 40; meals €17; ⊙lunch Mon-Sat, dinner Fri & Sat) Forget the Michelin stars for a second. Cloistered upstairs in a utilitarian apartment block, Aldina is a precious secret guarded loyally by local shoppers from the adjacent produce market. The lunch-only menu is spearheaded by the kind of homemade grub that only an Italian nonna raised on hand-made pasta can concoct. There's no written menu; take what's in the pot and revel in the people-watching potential.

Trattoria Ermes   TRATTORIA €
(Via Ganaceto 89; meals €20; ⊙lunch Mon-Sat) Here's yet another fabulous, affordable little lunch spot, tucked into a single wood-panelled room at the northern edge of downtown Modena. An older couple runs

the place – she cooks, he juggles plates and orders while keeping up a nonstop stream of banter with the customers. The menu changes daily depending on what's fresh at the market.

Trattoria Il Fantino TRATTORIA €

(☑059 22 36 46; www.gustamodena.it/ilfantino; Via Donzi 7; meals €15; ⊘7-10.30pm Tue-Sat) More homemade Modenese miracles forged in a hole-in-the-wall-sized dining room that can't have changed much since the Risorgimento (reunification period). Arrive early and squeeze into one of 45 narrow pews.

Ristorante da Danilo TRADITIONAL ITALIAN €€

(Via Coltellini 29-31; meals €25-30; ⊘noon-3pm & 7pm-midnight Mon-Sat) Speedy waiters glide around balancing bread baskets, wine bottles and pasta dishes in this deliciously traditional dining room where first dates mingle with animated families and office groups on a birthday jaunt.

What would pass as outstanding in any other country passes as normal in Danilo: antipasti of salami, pecorino and fig marmalade; *secondos* (second courses) of *bollito misto* (mixed boiled meats) and a vegetarian *risotto al radicchio trevigiano* (with red chicory).

Hosteria Giusti GASTRONOMIC €€€

(☑059 22 25 33; www.hosteriagiusti.it; Vicolo Squallore 46; meals €70; ⊘12.30-2pm Tue-Sat) With only four tables, a narrow back-alley location, no real signage and a 90-minute daily opening window, this perplexingly unassuming *osteria* isn't really setting itself up for legendary status. But tentative whispers turn to exuberant shouts when regional specialities like *cotechino fritto con zabaglione al lambrusco* (fried Modena sausage with wine-flavoured egg custard) arrive at your table.

The plaudits are growing, including from hard-to-impress Italian-American 'Iron Chef' Mario Batelli, who lists it as one of his favourite hang-outs in Italy.

Osteria Francescana GASTRONOMIC €€€

(☑059 21 01 18; www.osteriafrancescana.it; Via Stella 22; tasting menu €110; ⊘lunch & dinner Mon-Fri, dinner Sat, closed Jan & Aug) Claiming the number-three spot on San Pellegrino's influential 'World's 50 Best Restaurants' list is a *big* deal, especially when your business is based, not in Paris or New York, but...Modena. Owner Massimo Bottura is now onto his third Michelin star (earned in 2011), a rare honour for this small 11-table restaurant

where the food is the art, the decor is secondary and tasting menus top out at €110.

For a cheaper option, try Bottura's equally diminutive bistro **Franceschetta 58** (☑059 309 10 08; www.franceschetta58.it; Via Vignolese 58; courses €8.50; ⊘dinner Mon-Sat), encased in an old car showroom in Modena's suburbs.

Self-Catering

Modena's fresh-produce **market** (⊘6.30am-2.30pm Mon-Sat yr-round, 4.30-7pm Sat Oct-May) has its main entrance on Via Albinelli.

Drinking & Nightlife

A youthful bar-hopping crowd congregates along Via dei Gallucci. There's also a cluster of bars along Via Emilia near the cathedral.

Compagnia del Taglio BAR

(www.compagniadeltaglio.it; Via Taglio 12; ⊘10am-3pm & 4.30pm-2am Mon-Fri, 5pm-2am Sat, 5pm-midnight Sun) Boisterous bar with little room but a lot of people.

Cafe-Ristorante Concerto CAFE, BAR

(www.cafeconcertomodena.com; Piazza Grande 26; ⊘8am-3am) This Piazza Grande establishment manages a delicate juxtaposition between trendy (ubercontemporary decor) and old (cobbled central-square location) without appearing out of place. Inside any 19-hour window it wears three hats: all-day cafe, pricey restaurant and evening bar-club.

The latter is its best incarnation, primarily because of the free bar snacks (minimum consumption €5), chilled Lambrusco and footloose party atmosphere so often lacking in Italy's Renaissance cities.

☆ Entertainment

During July and August, outdoor concerts and ballet are staged on Piazza Grande.

Teatro Comunale Luciano Pavarotti THEATRE

(www.teatrocomunalemodena.it; Corso Canalgrande 85) It will come as no surprise that the birthplace of Pavarotti has a decent opera house. The Comunale opened in 1841 and has 900 seats and 112 boxes. Following the death of the city's exalted native son in September 2007, it was renamed in his honour.

Shopping

Enoteca Ducale FOOD, WINE

(Corso Vittorio Emanuele II 15; ⊘9am-7pm Tue-Sun) Do your friends back home a favour by loading up on balsamic-vinegar presents here – aged anywhere from three to 100 years (tasting is allowed). They'll never buy the supermarket stuff again!

ℹ️ Information

Modenatur (www.modenatur.it; Via Scudari 8; ⊙2.30-6.30pm Mon, 9am-1pm & 2.30-6.30pm Tue-Sat) A private agency that organises tours to balsamic-vinegar producers and *parmigiano reggiano* (Parmesan) dairies.

Post office (Via Emilia 86)

Tourist office (☑059 203 26 60; http://turismo.comune.modena.it; Piazza Grande 14; ⊙3-6pm Mon, 9am-1pm & 3-6pm Tue-Sat, 9.30am-12.30pm Sun) Provides city maps and the useful *Welcome to Modena* brochure.

ℹ️ Getting There & Around

The bus station is on Via Molza, northwest of the centre. **ATCM** (www.atcm.mo.it) buses connect Modena with most towns in the region.

By car, take the A1 Autostrada del Sole if coming from Rome or Milan, or the A22 from Mantua and Verona.

The train station is north of the historic centre, fronting Piazza Dante. Destinations include Bologna (€3.60, 30 minutes, half-hourly), Parma (€5, 30 minutes, half-hourly) and Milan (regional €14.65, two hours, hourly/express €27.50, 1¾ hours, every two hours).

ATCM's bus 7 links the train station with the bus station and city centre.

Reggio Emilia

POP 170,000

Often written off as an emergency pit stop on the Via Emilia, Reggio Emilia states its case as birthplace of the Italian flag – the famous red, white and green tricolour – and a convenient base for sorties south into the region's best natural attraction, the Parco Nazionale dell'Appennino Tosco-Emiliano. Those savvy enough to get out of their train/car/bus will find a city of attractive squares, grand public buildings and a leafy park. In 2010 Reggio Emilia was named Italy's most cycle-friendly city.

Known also as Reggio nell'Emilia, the town started life in the 2nd century BC as a Roman colony along the Via Emilia. Much of Reggio was built by the Este family during the 400 years it controlled the town, beginning in 1406.

👁️ Sights

Reggio's pedestrianised city centre is an agreeable place to wander or cycle. The main

sights are centred on Piazza Prampolini and adjacent Piazza San Prospero.

Duomo CATHEDRAL
(Piazza Prampolini; ⊙8am-noon & 4-7pm) Reggio's 13th-century cathedral was first built in the Romanesque style but was given a comprehensive makeover 300 years later. Nowadays, virtually all that remains of the original is the upper half of the facade and, inside, the crypt.

Museo del Tricolore MUSEUM
(Piazza Prampolini; ⊙9am-noon Tue-Fri, 10am-1pm & 3-7pm Sat & Sun) FREE A small exhibition that attempts to cover a large subject, this proud memorial to the Italian tricolour flag is in the main square. Next door in the 14th-century **Palazzo del Comune** is where the flag was actually conceived.

At a meeting in the multitiered **Sala del Tricolore** in 1797, Napoleon's short-lived Cispadane Republic was proclaimed and the green, white and red tricolour was adopted for the first time.

Basilica della Beata Vergine della Ghiara CHURCH
(Corso Garibaldi) Reggio's most important church is associated with a miracle involving a boy called Marchino who couldn't hear or speak. After he witnessed an apparition of the Virgin Mary in front of the *Blessed Virgin of Ghiara* painting (by G Bianchi) in 1569, Marchino found his voice and was able to hear.

The church was built in 1597 as a sanctuary to honour this miracle and the Virgin has been faithfully reproduced in a chapel inside. Architecturally the church is classic baroque with notable paintings and frescoes by the top Emiliano artists of the period.

Musei Civici MUSEUM
(www.musei.re.it; ⊙9am-noon Tue-Fri, 10am-1pm & 4-7pm Sat & Sun) FREE Reggio Emilia has five city museums, collectively called the Musei Civici, but the best artefacts are located inside the **Palazzo San Francesco** (Via Spallanzani; ⊙9am-noon & 9-11pm Tue-Sat, 9-11pm Sun). Thematic collections here include Roman archaeological finds (look out for the mosaics), 18th-century art, natural-history exhibits and a precis of the town's history.

Galleria Parmeggiani ART GALLERY
(Corso Cairoli 1; ⊙9am-noon Tue-Fri, 10am-1pm & 4-7pm Sat & Sun) FREE The town's main art gallery hails some worthwhile Italian, Flemish

EMILIA-ROMAGNA & SAN MARINO WEST OF BOLOGNA

and Spanish paintings, as well as a heterogeneous collection of costumes, arms, jewellery and cutlery.

🛏 Sleeping

Ostello Basilica della Ghiara HOSTEL €
(📞 0522 45 23 23; Via Guasco 6; dm €18, d €50, without bathroom €44) There's no shortage of space at Reggio's memorable HI hostel, housed in a former convent. The two- to six-bed guest rooms line vast, echoing corridors, and in summer breakfast is served under the porticoes in the internal garden.

Albergo Morandi HOTEL €
(📞 0522 45 43 97; www.albergomorandi.com; Via Emilia San Pietro 64; s/d €65/100; 🅿 ❄ 🛜) Halfway between the train station and historic centre, the Morandi features spruce rooms with big beds, gleaming bathrooms and satellite TV. There's free parking, and the service is unfailingly courteous.

Hotel Posta HOTEL €€
(📞 0522 43 29 44; www.hotelposta.re.it; Piazza del Monte 2; s/d/tr €80/120/150; ❄ @ 🛜) Elegant inside and out, the grand four-star Posta is housed in the 13th-century Palazzo del Capitano del Popolo, one-time residence of Reggio's governor. Rooms are individually decorated, with plenty of heavy floral fabrics, gilt-framed mirrors and antique furniture. Parking costs €12. Just around the corner, you'll find the hotel's less expensive, 16-room annexe, **Albergo Reggio** (📞 0522 45 15 33; www.albergoreggio.it; Via San Giuseppe 7; s/d €75/105).

🍴 Eating

Reggio's central squares host a **produce market** (Piazza Prampolini; ⊘ 7am-1pm Tue & Fri). Typical local snacks include *erbazzone* (herb pie with cheese or bacon) and *gnocco fritto* (fried salted dough). Parmesan is also produced locally.

Ristorante da Penna TRADITIONAL ITALIAN €
(Via dell'Aquila 6a; meals €20-25; ⊘ Tue-Sat) With its colourful, funky decor, jazzy soundtrack and tasty homemade food, this bright eatery is a bit different from your classic wood-and-wine-bottle trattoria. The fixed-price lunch menus (€6 to €12) are exceptionally good value.

La Bottega dei Briganti OSTERIA €€
(📞 522 43 66 43; www.bottegadeibriganti.it; Via San Carlo 14b; meals €25-35; ⊘ lunch & dinner Tue-Sun) Duck under the porticoes to this cosy *oste-ria* with its conspiratorial atmosphere and small leafy courtyard. The food is excellent, particularly the pasta and risottos.

☆ Entertainment

Teatro Municipale Valli THEATRE
(www.iteatri.re.it; Piazza Martiri VII Luglio) Reggio's splendid neoclassical theatre – recognised as one of the finest in Italy – stages a full season of dance, opera and theatre. It's named after local-born actor Romolo Valli, who starred alongside Burt Lancaster in *The Leopard* (1963).

ℹ Information

Tourist office (www.municipio.re.it/turismo; Via Farini 1a; ⊘ 8.30am-1pm & 2.30-6pm Mon-Sat, 9am-noon Sun)

ℹ Getting There & Around

Bus operator **ACT** (www.actre.it) serves the city and region from its brand-new bus station, just behind Reggio's train station. Destinations include Carpi (€3.50, one hour, 10 daily) and Castelnovo ne' Monti (€4.30, 1¼ hours, seven to 14 daily).

Reggio is on the Via Emilia (SS9) and A1 autostrada. The SS63 is a tortuous but scenic route that takes you southwest across the Parma Apennines to La Spezia on the Ligurian coast.

The train station is east of the town centre. Frequent trains serve all stops on the Milan–Bologna line, including Milan (regional/express €12.25/25.50, 1½ to 2½ hours, hourly), Parma (€2.80, 15 minutes, half-hourly), Modena (€2.80, 15 minutes, half-hourly) and Bologna (€5.60, 45 minutes, half-hourly).

Parma

POP 187,000

If reincarnation ever becomes an option, pray you come back as a Parmesan. Where else do you get to cycle to work through traffic-light free, cobbled streets in uncrinkled Prada, lunch on fresh-from-the-attic prosciutto and aged *parmigiano reggiano* cheese, quaff full-bodied Sangiovese wine in regal art-nouveau cafes, and spend sultry summer evenings listening to classical music in architecturally dramatic opera houses? From its position as one of Italy's most prosperous cities, Parma has every right to feel smug. More metropolitan than Modena, yet less clamorous than Bologna, this is the city that gave the world Lamborghinis, a composer called Verdi and enough ham and cheese to start a deli chain. Stopping here isn't an option, it's a duty.

◉ Sights

★ Duomo
CATHEDRAL

(Piazza del Duomo; ⊘ 9am-12.30pm & 3-7pm) Another daring Romanesque beauty? Well, yes and no. Consecrated in 1106, Parma cathedral's facade is classic Lombard-Romanesque, but inside, the gilded pulpit and ornate lampholders scream baroque. Take note: there are some genuine treasures here.

Up in the dome, Antonio da Correggio's *Assunzione della Vergine* (Assumption of the Virgin) is a kaleidoscopic swirl of cherubims and whirling angels, while down in the southern transept, Benedetto Antelami's *Deposizione* (Descent from the Cross; 1178) relief is considered a masterpiece of its type.

★ Battistero
BAPTISTERY

(Piazza del Duomo; adult/reduced €6/4; ⊘ 9am-12.30pm & 3-6.45pm) Overshadowing even the cathedral, the octagonal pink-marble baptistery on the south side of the piazza is one of the most important such structures in Italy. Its architecture is a hybrid of Romanesque and Gothic, and its construction started in 1196 on the cusp of the two great architectural eras.

Architect and sculptor Benedetto Antelami oversaw the project and it contains his best work, including a celebrated set of figures representing the months, seasons and signs of the zodiac. The baptistery wasn't completed until 1307 thanks to several interruptions, most notably when the supply of pink Verona marble ran out.

EMILIA-ROMAGNA & SAN MARINO WEST OF BOLOGNA

WORTH A TRIP

PARCO NAZIONALE DELL'APPENNINO TOSCO-EMILIANO

In the late 1980s Italy had half a dozen national parks. Today it has 24. One of the newest additions is **Parco Nazionale dell'Appennino Tosco-Emiliano** (www.appenninoreggiano.it), a 260-sq-km parcel of land that straddles the border between Tuscany and Emilia-Romagna. Running along the spine of the Apennine mountains, the park is notable for its hiking potential, extensive beech forests and small population of wolves.

Of its many majestic peaks, the highest is 2121m **Monte Cusna**, easily scalable from the village of Civago, near the Tuscan border, on a path (*sentiero* No 605) that passes the region's best mountain hut, the **Rifugio Cesare Battisti** (☎ 0522 89 74 97; www.rifugio-battisti.it). The *rifugio* sits alongside one of Italy's great long-distance walking trails: the three-week, 375km-long **Grande Escursione Appenninica (GEA)**, which bisects the park in five stages from Passo della Forbici (near the Rifugio Cesare Battisti) up to its termination point just outside the park's northwest corner in Montelungo. Sections of the GEA can be done as day walks. *Trekking in the Apennines* by Gillian Price (published by Cicerone) provides an excellent detailed guide of the whole route.

One of the best gateways to the park is the village of **Castelnovo ne' Monti**, about 40km south of Reggio Emilia along the winding SS63 on a delightfully scenic ACT bus route. The large village has an ultrahelpful **tourist office** (www.reappennino.com; Via Roma 15b; ⊘ 9am-1pm & 3-6pm Mon-Sat) that stocks bags of free information and sells cheap maps of the region for hikers, cyclists and equestrians.

If you've arrived by bus, you can walk 3km from the village centre up to one of the national park's defining landmarks, the surreal **Pietra di Bismantova** (1047m), a stark limestone outcrop visible for kilometres around that's popular with climbers and weekend walkers. In its shadow lies the **Rifugio della Pietra**, open for food and drinks in summer, and the tiny **Eremo di Bismantova** monastery, which dates from 1400. From here various paths fan out to the rock's summit (25 minutes). You can also circumnavigate the rock on the lovely 5km **Anella delle Pietra** or even tackle it on a difficult *via ferrata* (trail with permanent cables and ladders) with the proper equipment.

Castelnovo ne' Monti offers a variety of overnight accommodation, including **Albergo Residence Tre Re** (☎ 0522 61 13 73; www.residencetrere.it; Via Roma 17; studio/2-bed apt €65/80). Satiate your posthike appetite at **Trattoria da Geremia** (☎ 0522 81 11 94; Via Franceschini 10; meals €20-25; ⊘ noon-2.30pm Fri-Wed, 7.30-10.30pm Fri-Tue).

Getting to the park on public transport is possible by bus with **ACT** (www.actre.it) from Reggio Emilia or **TEP** (www.tep.pr.it) from Parma. Several buses run every day.

Parma

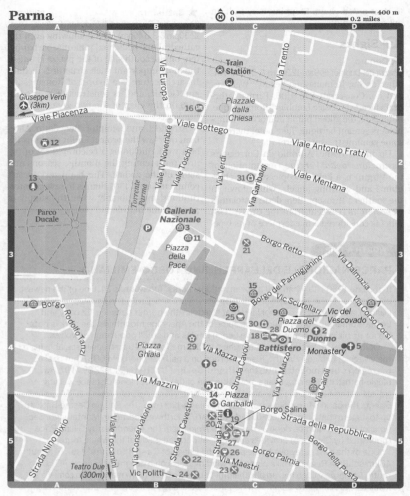

Pinacoteca Stuard
MUSEUM

(Borgo del Parmigianino 2; adult/reduced €4/2; ⊗9am-6.30pm Wed-Mon) Giuseppe Stuard was a 19th-century Parmese art collector who amassed 500 years worth of epoch-defining art linking the Tuscan masters of the 1300s to the *novecento* romantics. In 2002 the collection was moved into a wing of this 10th-century Benedictine monastery dedicated to St Paul, where it has been artfully laid out over 24 rooms on the site of an old Roman villa.

Museo Bocchi
MUSEUM

(☏0521 22 82 89; www.museobocchi.it; Via Cairoli; ⊗Tue-Sun 10.30am-1pm) Don't underestimate

Amedeo Bocchi, a 20th-century Parma-born artist whose painting owes a debt to the symbolism of Gustav Klimt. This museum spreads his stirring work over six rooms. Most compelling are the impressionistic studies of his beloved daughter Bianca who died tragically in 1934 aged 26.

Museo Diocesano
MUSEUM

(Vicolo del Vescovado 3a; admission €4; ⊗9am-12.30pm & 3-6.30pm) On the other side of the square to the Duomo, in the cellars of the former bishop's palace, this museum displays statuary. Highlights include a finely

Parma

sculpted Solomon and Sheba, and a 5th-century early-Christian mosaic, which was discovered under Piazza del Duomo.

A combined ticket (€6) allows entry into the baptistery and Museo Diocesano.

Chiesa di San Giovanni
Evangelista   CHURCH
(Piazzale San Giovanni; ☺ 8.30-11.45am & 3-5.30pm, monastery 9-11.45am & 3-5pm Mon-Wed, Fri & Sat) This abbey church rises directly behind the Duomo and is attached to a monastery. Its 16th-century facade is mannerist (the less harmonious, rational style that followed the High Renaissance) and is noted for its magnificent frescoed dome, the work of Correggio. The dome was highly influential for its time and inspired many later works.

The adjoining monastery is known as much for the oils and unguents that its monks produce as for its Renaissance cloisters. Upstairs, a library is adorned with huge old maps that hang from the walls of a musty reading room.

Palazzo della Pilotta   MUSEUM
(Piazza della Pilotta) Looming over Piazza della Pace's manicured lawns and modern fountains, this monumental palace is hard to miss. Supposedly named after the Spanish ball game of *pelota* that was once played within its walls, it was originally built for the Farnese family between 1583 and 1622. Heav-

ily bombed in WWII, it has since been largely rebuilt and today houses several museums.

The most important of these, the Galleria Nazionale (adult/reduced incl Teatro Farnese €6/3; ☺ 8.30am-1.30pm Tue-Sun), displays Parma's main art collection. Alongside works by local artists Correggio and Parmigianino, you'll find paintings by Fra Angelico, El Greco and a piece attributed to da Vinci. Before you get to the gallery, you'll pass through the Teatro Farnese (☑ 23 33 09; Piazzale della Pilotta 15; adult/child €2.00/free; ☺ 8:30am-2pm Tue-Sun), a copy of Andrea Palladio's Teatro Olimpico in Vicenza. Constructed entirely out of wood, it was almost completely rebuilt after being bombed in WWII.

For a change of period, the Museo Archeologico Nazionale (☑ 0521 23 37 18; admission €4; ☺ 9am-5pm Tue-Fri, 12.30-7.30pm Sat & Sun) exhibits Roman artefacts discovered around Parma and Etruscan finds from the Po valley.

Piazza Garibaldi   PIAZZA
On the site of the ancient Roman forum, Piazza Garibaldi is Parma's cobbled hub bisected by the city's main east–west artery, Via Mazzini, and its continuation, Strada della Repubblica. On the square's north side, the facade of the 17th-century Palazzo del

Governatore, these days municipal offices, sports a giant sundial, added in 1829.

Behind the palace in the **Chiesa di Santa Maria della Steccata** (Piazza Steccata 9; ☺9am-noon & 3-6pm), you'll find some of Parmigianino's most extraordinary work, notably the stunning, if rather faded, frescoes on the arches above the altar. Many members of the ruling Farnese and Bourbon families lie buried here.

Parco Ducale   PARK
(☺6am-midnight Apr-Oct, 7am-8pm Nov-Mar) Stretching along the west bank of the Parma river, these formal gardens seem like Parma personified – refined, peaceful and with barely a blade of grass out of place. They were laid out in 1560 around the Farnese family's **Palazzo Ducale**, which now serves as headquarters of the provincial *carabinieri* (military police).

Casa Natale di Toscanini   MUSEUM
(www.museotoscanini.it; Borgo R Tanzi 13; admission €2; ☺9am-1pm Tue, 9am-1pm & 2-6pm Wed-Sat, 2-6pm Sun) At the Parco Ducale's southeast corner, the birthplace of Italy's greatest modern conductor, Arturo Toscanini (1867–1957) retraces his life and travels through relics and records. Of interest are his collaborations with acclaimed Italian tenor Aureliano Pertile.

La Casa del Suono   MUSEUM
(Piazzale Salvo D'Acquisto; admission €2; ☺9am-6pm Thu-Sat, 2-6pm Sun) Oh no, not another church, you groan, until you realise that this one (the 17th-century Chiesa di Santa Elisabetta) has been converted into a funky modern museum that focuses on the history of music technology. Review the 'ancient' 1970s tape recorders, ponder over jazz-age gramophones and stop to listen under a high-tech 'sonic chandelier'.

🛏 Sleeping

★ Hotel Button   HOTEL €
(☑0521 20 80 39; www.hotelbutton.it; Borgo Salina 7; s/d €75/100; ❋@☎) The Button grows on you. Once you realise that, rather like Parma, it's not trying to win you over as a euro-brandishing tourist, you'll fall hopelessly for its simple charms: the fresh breakfast croissants, the made-to-order cappuccinos, the spacious rooms, and the quiet sense of order and cleanliness. The location's just about perfect too.

Century Hotel   HOTEL €€
(☑0521 03 98 00; www.centuryhotel.it; Piazzale dalla Chiesa 5a; s/d/ste €80/120/200; ❋@☎) Hotels next to train stations are often scruffy little abodes designed for economically minded fly-by-nighters, but the trussed-up Century, still smarting from a modern makeover, offers slick four-star fixtures and amenities at three-star prices.

Palazzo dalla Rosa Prati   BOUTIQUE HOTEL €€€
(☑0521 38 64 29; www.palazzodallarosaprati. co.uk; Piazza del Duomo 7; s/d €150/300; ❋☎) Kick back like Marie Antoinette in regal digs right next to Parma cathedral. Choose one of seven historic suites all renovated to be appropriately posh and palatial.

🍴 Eating

Parma specialities need no introduction to anyone familiar with the food of planet Earth. Both *prosciutto di Parma* (Parma ham) and *parmigiano reggiano* make excellent antipasto plates accompanied by a good Sangiovese red. Nab one of the following perches and dig in.

★ Trattoria del Tribunale   TRATTORIA €
(www.trattoriadeltribunale.it; Vicolo Politti 5; meals €22; ☺noon-11pm Sun-Fri, 5-11pm Sat) Walk through a gauntlet of ham slicers and waiters gouging lumps out of giant *parmigiano reggiano* cheeses in a pungent entrance vestibule, and you've arrived at one of about 25 contenders for Parma's best restaurant. Start with an elaborate plate of Parma ham, proceed to the *tortelli di Erbette* (pasta stuffed with spinach in butter and Parmesan), and finish, if you dare, with *trippa alla parmigiana* (tripe in Parmesan and breadcrumbs). Pure Parma!

La Duchessa   PIZZERIA, EMILIAN €
(☑0521 23 59 62; www.laduchessaparma.com; Piazza Garibaldi; pizzas from €5; ☺noon-3.30pm & 7pm-midnight Tue-Sun) For atmosphere alone, this Piazza Garibaldi pit stop beloved by famished postperformance opera stars is well worth contemplating. It's primarily a pizzeria, but the extensive menu conjures up other tricks such as tortelli stuffed with sweet *zucca* (pumpkin). Athletic waiters rush up and down the stairs amid the din of crashing cutlery and operatic voices.

Gallo d'Oro   TRADITIONAL ITALIAN €€
(☑0521 20 88 46; www.gallodororistorante.it; Borgo Salina 3; meals €25; ☺noon-2.30pm & 7-11pm Mon-Sat, noon-2.30pm Sun) Young *caminieri* (wait-

ers) operate meat slicers, slide dexterously between tables and plonk down plates of raw horse meat, ravioli and veal done all ways (all of them good) in the inauspiciously named 'golden chicken'. Magazine covers adorn the walls and the whole place emits the smooth, agreeable energy of a small bistro.

Osteria del Gesso
EMILIAN €€

(📞 0521 23 05 05; www.osteriadelgesso.it; Via Maestri 11; meals €30-35; ⊗ noon-3pm & 7.30-11pm Mon-Fri) A familiar Italian story: family-run restaurant, great local food, charming romantic interior, laid-back (OK, slow) service and bags of atmosphere and tradition. Like most Parma restaurants, Gesso doesn't play up to tourists, it just performs naturally for people who love fantastic simple food.

Osteria dei Mascalzoni
OSTERIA €€

(www.osteriadeimascalzoniparma.it; Vicolo delle Cinque Piaghe 1; meals €25-35; ⊗ 12.30-3pm & 7.30-10.30pm Mon-Fri, 7.30-10.30pm Sat) Cosy inside and out, this restaurant features a beamed dining room and outdoor tables that take over the adjacent alleyway on summer evenings. The menu emphasises grilled meat, plus an excellent selection of Parma's famous cheeses and pork products, including *culatello* and *fiocchetto*.

La Greppia
GASTRONOMIC €€€

(📞 0521 23 36 86; Via Garibaldi 39a; meals from €45; ⊗ lunch & dinner Wed-Sun) A legend in its own lunchtime (and dinnertime, come to that), La Greppia is hallowed ground for the kind of Emilia-Romagna gourmands who know their *ragù* from their bolognese. Sticking tradition and modernity in the same blender, it comes up with Parmesan mousse, pear poached in wine and plenty more surprises. Service is impeccable.

Drinking & Nightlife

Enoteca Fontana
BAR

(📞 0521 28 60 37; Strada Farini 24a; glasses of wine from €1.20, sandwiches from €2.80; ⊗ noon-8pm Tue-Sat) A loud, elbow-in-the-ribs type of wine bar (it gets busy!) with some tables in a room out back where you can sup wine and munch grilled *panini* while making a local friend or three.

T-Cafe
CAFE, BAR

(Strada Duomo 7; ⊗ 8am-8pm Mon-Wed, to 3pm Thu & Sun, to 9pm Fri & Sat) An ultramodern cafe in historic digs next to the Batisttero. Here you can collapse into round futuristic sofas or perch on Ikea-style chairs for wine,

coffee and some light Mediterranean snacks to fuel your next spate of church-visiting.

Cavour Gran Caffè
CAFE

(Strada Cavour 30b; ⊗ 7am-8pm) Echoes of Turin are evident in the finely frescoed interior of this classic Parmesan cafe. You'll pay extra for that cappuccino, of course.

Le Malve
BAR

(Via Farini 12a; ⊗ 11am-midnight Mon-Sat) A cool young scene kicks off nightly in Via Farini with cocktails and beer on outside tables at Malve. Revellers make regular forays inside to load up on free bar aperitifs.

Entertainment

There are few better places in Italy to see live opera, concerts and theatre. The season runs from October to April and in summer there are outdoor-music programs.

Teatro Regio
THEATRE

(www.teatroregioparma.org; Via Garibaldi 16a) Offers a particularly rich program of music and opera, even by exacting Italian standards.

Teatro Due
THEATRE

(www.teatrodue.org; Via Salnitrara 10) Presents the city's top drama.

Shopping

Libreria Fiaccadori
BOOKS

(Strada Duomo 8a; ⊗ 9am-7.30pm Mon-Sat, 10am-1pm & 3.30-7.30pm Sun) Good old-fashioned bookshop with ladders to reach the high shelves and plenty of titles in English.

Salumeria Garibaldi
FOOD

(Via Garibaldi 42; ⊗ 8am-8pm Mon-Sat) Tempting new visitors cruelly just steps from the train station is this bountiful delicatessen with dangling sausages, shelves of Lambrusco wines, slabs of Parma ham and wheel upon wheel of *parmigiano reggiano*.

🛈 Information

Police station (📞 0521 21 94; Borgo della Posta 16a)

Post office (Via Melloni)

Tourist office (Piazza Garibaldi; ⊗ 9am-1pm & 3-7pm Mon, 9am-7pm Tue-Sat, 9am-1pm Sun)

🛈 Getting There & Away

Parma's **Giuseppe Verdi Airport** (www.parma-airport.it) is a mere 2.5km from the city centre and has thrice-weekly flights to London Stansted with Ryanair. Bus 6 links to the train station.

From Piazzale dalla Chiesa in front of Parma's train station, **TEP** (www.tep.pr.it) operates buses throughout the region.

Parma is on the A1 connecting Bologna and Milan, and just east of the A15, which runs to La Spezia. Via Emilia (SS9) passes right through town.

There are frequent trains to Milan (regional/express €10.45/23, 1¼ to 1¾ hours, hourly), Bologna (€6.80, one hour, half-hourly), Modena (€5, 30 minutes, half-hourly) and Piacenza (€5, 40 minutes, half-hourly).

ℹ Getting Around

Traffic is banned from the historic centre, so leave your car at the underground car park on Viale Toschi and grab a bike, available for hire next door at **Parma Punto Bici** (www.parmapuntobici.pr.it; Viale Toschi 2a; bicycles per hour/day €0.70/10, electric bikes €0.90/20; ⊙9am-1pm & 3-7pm Mon-Sat, 10am-1pm & 2.30-7.30pm Sun).

Busseto & Verdi Country

During the 'golden age of opera' in the second half of the 19th century, only Wagner came close to emulating Giuseppe Verdi, Italy's operatic genius who was born in the tiny village of Roncole Verdi in 1813. You can tour his gigantic legacy starting in the town of Busseto, 35km northwest of Parma, a pleasant place imbued with history and endowed with some good cafes and restaurants. There are enough sights for a decent musical day out.

◉ Sights

★Museo Nazionale
Giuseppe Verdi   MUSEUM
(www.museogiuseppeverdi.it; Via Provesi 35; adult/reduced €9/7; ⊙10am-6.30pm Tue-Sun) His name may translate as plain old 'Joe Green' in English, but there was nothing remotely ordinary about Giuseppe Verdi. Still fresh after two centuries, his music is implanted into most people's subconscious without them even realising it. Take a trip through the rooms of this fine country mansion-turned-museum and you'll undoubtedly recognise numerous stanzas from classic operas such as *Il Trovatore* and *Aida*.

The museum, on the outskirts of the small town of Busseto, cleverly maps out the story of Verdi's life through paintings, music and audio guides (included in the price).

Teatro Verdi   THEATRE
(Piazza Verdi; adult/reduced €4/3; ⊙9.30am-1pm & 3-6.30pm Tue-Sun) A stately theatre on Busseto's aptly named Piazza Verdi was built in 1868, although Verdi himself initially poohpoohed the idea. It opened with a performance of his masterpiece *Rigoletto*.

Casa Natale di Giuseppe Verdi   MUSEUM
(adult/child €4/3; ⊙9.30am-12.30pm & 2.30-6.30pm Tue-Sun) The humble cottage where Giuseppe Verdi was born in 1813 is now a small museum. It's in the hamlet of Roncole Verdi, 5km southeast of Busseto.

Casa Barezzi   MUSEUM
(Via Roma 119; adult/child €4/3; ⊙10am-12.30pm & 3-6.30pm Tue-Sun) Another museum in the centre of Busseto is encased in the home of the composer's patron and the site of Verdi's first concert. It's lovingly curated and filled with Verdi memorabilia including papers, furnishings and valuable recordings.

Villa Verdi   MUSEUM
(www.villaverdi.org; Via Verdi 22; adult/reduced €8/6.50; ⊙9-11.45am & 2.30-6.45pm Tue-Sun, closed Dec & Jan) Verdi's villa, where he composed many of his major works, is in Sant'Agata di Villanova sull'Arda, 5km northwest of Busseto. Verdi lived and worked here from 1851 onwards. Guided visits through the furnishings and musical instruments should be booked in advance online.

ℹ Information

A combined ticket for the Casa Natale di Giuseppe Verdi, Casa Barezzi and Villa Verdi costs €8.50. For more information, contact Busseto's **tourist office** (www.bussetolive.com; Piazza Verdi 10; ⊙9.30am-1pm & 3-6.30pm Tue-Sun).

ℹ Getting There & Away

TEP (www.tep.pr.it) buses from Parma run to Busseto six times daily, or you can catch a train from Parma to Busseto (€3.60, 45 minutes), changing in Fidenza.

Piacenza

POP 100,300

Named 'pleasant place' (Placentia) by the Romans, Piacenza soon proved itself to be an important strategic location as well. Just short of the regional border with Lombardy, the contemporary city is day-trip fodder, though there are some decent hotels if you've been priced out of Parma. Its picturesque centre reveals a beautiful Gothic town hall and a couple of august churches.

◉ Sights

Piazza dei Cavalli
PIAZZA

Dominated by **Palazzo Gotico**, the impressive 13th-century town hall, Piacenza's main square is named after its two martial bronze horses. The two baroque statues, cast by the Tuscan sculptor Francesco Mochi between 1612 and 1625, depict the Farnese dukes Alessandro and Ranuccio.

Duomo
CATHEDRAL

(Piazza del Duomo 33; ☉ 7am-noon & 4-7pm) An ultradark church even by Italian standards, Piacenza's cold, dungeonlike cathedral is classic Romanesque. If you can strain your eyes hard enough, you'll make out the two-dozen pillars that hold up the roof and the heavenly frescoes by Morazzone and Guercino that adorn it.

One of a trio of classic Romanesque cathedrals in Emilia, it rose (like Parma's) from the ruins of the devastating 1117 earthquake.

Palazzo Farnese
MUSEUM

(www.musei.piacenza.it; Piazza Citadella; combined admission €6; ☉ 9am-1pm Tue-Thu, 9am-1pm & 3-6pm Fri-Sun) On the northern edge of the *centro storico* (historic centre), this vast palace was started in 1558 but never fully completed. It now houses the **Pinacoteca**, an art gallery, along with minor museums of archaeology, carriages, Italian unification and ceramics.

Ricci Oddi Galleria d'Arte Moderna
ART GALLERY

(☎ 0523 32 07 42; www.riccioddi.it; Via San Siro 13; admission €5; ☉ 9.30am-12.30pm Tue-Thu, 9.30am-12.30pm & 3-6pm Fri-Sun) Guidebooks covering Piacenza will lead you to the striking Palazzo Farnese, but the city's hidden secret is this modern art collection amassed by local aficionado, Ricci Oddi, in the early 20th century.

The man clearly had taste. Well-lit and cleverly laid out over a purpose-built gallery, the collection catalogues various artistic schools (Emilian, Lombard) and stylistic movements (symbolism, *novecento*) from the 1830s to the 1930s. Jumping out at you are Boldini's *Retrato di Signora* and Bocchi's light-filled *La Colazione del Mattino*.

🛏 Sleeping & Eating

Ostello Don Zermani
HOSTEL €

(☎ 0523 71 23 19; www.ostellodipiacenza.it; Via Zoni 38-40; dm/s/d €19/26/48; 🅿) In a quiet residential area 20 minutes' walk southwest of the city centre, this well-run private hostel offers bright, spotless rooms. Laundry facilities are available, and the building has access for guests with disabilities. Take bus 1, 16 or 17 from the train station.

Antica Trattoria Dell'Angelo
TRATTORIA €

(Via Tibini 14; meals €20-25; ☉ noon-2pm & 7.30-10pm Thu-Tue) With its beamed ceiling, wood-fired heater and red-checked tablecloths, this laid-back trattoria is as traditional as they come. The food is hearty, homemade fare – think spinach-and-ricotta *tortelloni*, roast meat and fizzy local red wine. Weekday lunch specials are a steal, with pasta/main courses costing €4/5.

❶ Information

Tourist office (www.comune.piacenza.it/english; Piazza dei Cavalli 7; ☉ 9am-1pm & 3-6pm Tue-Sat, 9.30am-12.30pm Sun & Mon) Handily placed in central Piazza dei Cavalli.

❶ Getting There & Around

Piacenza's bus station is located on Piazza Citadella; however, the train is a more convenient way to reach most destinations. There are frequent trains to/from Milan (regular/Eurostar €6.45/14, one hour, hourly), Parma (€5, 40 minutes, half-hourly) and Bologna (regular/Eurostar €10.40/22.50, 1½ hours, hourly).

Piacenza is just off the A1 linking Milan and Bologna and the A21 joining Brescia and Turin. Via Emilia (SS9) also runs past on its way to Rimini and the Adriatic Sea.

Bus 2 (€1) runs between the train station and Piazza dei Cavalli.

East of Bologna

Ferrara

POP 135,000

A heavyweight Renaissance art city peppered with colossal palaces and still ringed by its intact medieval walls, Ferrara jumps out at you like an absconded Casanova (he once stayed here) on the route between Bologna and Venice. But, like any city situated in close proximity to *La Serenissima*, it is serially overlooked. As a result, Venice avoiders will find Ferrara's bike-friendly streets

Ferrara

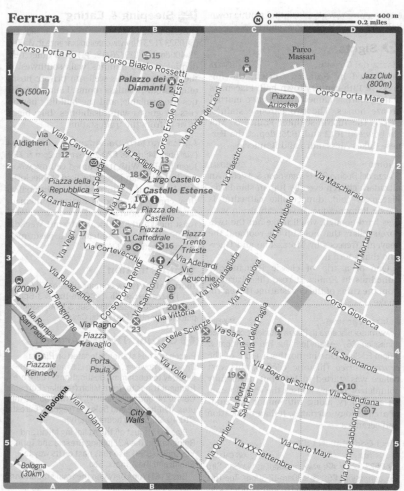

and frozen-in-time *palazzi* relatively unexplored and deliciously tranquil.

Historically Ferrara was once the domain of the powerful Este clan, rivals to Florence's Medici in power and prestige, who endowed the city with its signature building – a huge castle complete with moat positioned slapbang in the city centre. Ferrara suffered damage from bombing raids during WWII, but its historical core remains intact. Of particular interest is the former Jewish ghetto, the region's largest and oldest, which prevailed from 1627 until 1859.

◉ Sights

Renaissance palaces reborn as museums are Ferrara's tour de force. Also check out the intricate old town with its one-time Jewish ghetto. An entry card valid for seven of Ferrara's museums costs €11.50, is valid for 15 days and can be bought from the tourist office. Most museums are closed on Monday.

★ Castello Estense CASTLE

(Viale Cavour; adult/reduced €8/6.50, tower extra €1; ⊙9.30am-5.30pm) Complete with moat and drawbridge, Ferrara's towering castle was commissioned by Nicolò II d'Este in

Ferrara

EMILIA-ROMAGNA & SAN MARINO EAST OF BOLOGNA

1385. Initially it was intended to protect him and his family from the town's irate citizenry, who were up in arms over tax increases, but in the late 15th century it became the family's permanent residence.

Although sections are now used as government offices, a few rooms, including the royal suites, are open for viewing. Highlights are the **Sala dei Giganti** (Giants' Room) and **Salone dei Giochi** (Games Salon), the **Cappella di Renée de France** and the claustrophobic **dungeon**. It was here in 1425 that Duke Nicolò III d'Este had his young second wife, Parisina Malatesta, and his son, Ugo, beheaded after discovering they were lovers, providing the inspiration for Robert Browning's *My Last Duchess*.

Linked to the castle by an elevated passageway, the 13th-century crenellated **Palazzo Municipale** (admission free; ◎ 9am-2pm Mon-Fri) was the Este family home until they moved next door to the castle in the late 15th century. Nowadays, it's largely occupied by administrative offices but you can wander around its twin courtyards.

Duomo   CATHEDRAL
(Piazza Cattedrale; ◎ 7.30am-noon & 3-6.30pm Mon-Sat, 7.30am-12.30pm & 3.30-7.30pm Sun) The outstanding feature of the pink-and-white 12th-century cathedral is its three-tiered marble facade, combining Romanesque and Gothic styles on the lower and upper tiers respectively. Much of the upper level is a graphic representation of *The Last Judgment*, and heaven and hell (notice the four figures clambering out of their coffins).

Astride a pair of handsome lions at the base of the front facade squats an oddly secular duo, mouths agape at the effort of holding up the pillars situated on either side of the main doorway.

On the other side of nearby Piazza Trento Trieste, the **Museo della Cattedrale** (Via San Romano; adult/reduced €6/3; ◎ 9am-1pm & 3-6pm Tue-Sun) houses various artefacts from the cathedral, including a serene Madonna by Jacopo della Quercia, a couple of vigorous Cosimo Tura canvases, and some witty bas-reliefs illustrating the months of the year.

★ **Palazzo dei Diamanti**   PALACE, MUSEUM
(Corso Ercole I d'Este 21) Named after the spiky diamond-shaped ashlar stones on its facade, the 'diamond palace' was built for Sigismondo d'Este late in the 15th century.

The mystery behind the history of Italian art can be partially uncovered in the **Pinacoteca Nazionale** (www.pinacotecaferrara.it; adult/reduced €2/1; ◎ 9am-2pm Tue-Sun, to 7pm Thu), housed in the palace. Here you can contemplate the erstwhile genius of the so-called 16th- to 17th-century 'Ferrara school', spearheaded by artists better known by their odd nicknames, such as Guercino (the squinter) and El Maestro degli Occhi Spalancati (master of the wide-open eyes). Free guides enhance the experience.

**Museo del Risorgimento
e della Resistenza**   MUSEUM
(Corso Ercole I d'Este 19; adult/reduced €4/2; ◎ 9am-1pm & 3-6pm Tue-Sun) Next door to Pinacoteca Nazionale, this small museum

exhibits documents, proclamations and posters from the Italian unification movement and WWII, as well as numerous uniforms, guns and hand grenades.

Casa Romei
PALACE, MUSEUM

(Via Savonarola 30; adult/reduced €3/1.50; ☺8.30am-7.30pm Tue-Sun) This palace was once owned by Giovanni Romei, a top administrator to the Este clan – and his importance shows in the architecture. The austere brick exterior hides a peaceful inner patio (once part of an adjacent monastery). On the 1st floor is a 16th-century apartment preserved in its original state. There's plenty more art and frescoes dotted around.

Palazzo Schifanoia
PALACE, MUSEUM

(Via Scandiana 23; adult/reduced €6/3; ☺9am-6pm Tue-Sun) Ferrara's most famous frescoes are in the Este's 14th-century pleasure palace built in 1385. The museum is bitingly ordinary at first, but hold out until the Salone dei Mesi (Room of the Months), where frescoes executed by Francesco del Cossa in 1470 depict the months, seasons and signs of the zodiac.

Some are badly faded, but they are unusually unreligious in tone and the only ones of their type in Italy.

Museo Lapidario
MUSEUM

(Via Camposabbionario; ☺9am-6pm Tue-Sun) Your ticket to Schifanoia also gives entry to this nearby museum, which has a small, undocumented collection of Roman and Etruscan stele, tombs and inscriptions.

Palazzo Massari
PALACE, MUSEUM

(Corso Porta Mare 9) This is another early Renaissance palace, but this time the art inside is punchier and more modern. The best of the building's museums is the Museo Giovanni Boldini (adult/reduced incl Museo dell'Ottocento €6/3; ☺9am-1pm & 3-6pm Tue-Sun), dedicated solely to the works of Ferrara-born Giovanni Boldini, the so-called 'Master of Swish' (check out the brush technique). His portraits of women from Victorian rigidity to 1920s chic are amazing.

The entrance fee also gets you into the Museo dell'Ottocento (adult/reduced incl Museo Giovanni Boldini €6/3; ☺9am-1pm & 3-6pm Tue-Sun) with its 19th-century art and a pleasant sculpture garden. You must pay extra for the Museo d'Arte Moderna e Contemporanea Filippo de Pisis (adult/reduced €4/2; ☺9am-1pm & 3-6pm Tue-Sun), half of which is devoted to the said modern Ferraranese painter famous for his cityscapes and still-life works.

The palazzo and its museums were temporarily closed for restoration at time of writing, but should have reopened by the time you read this.

Festivals & Events

Il Palio
HORSE RACING

(www.paliodiferrara.it) On the last Sunday of May each year, the eight *contrade* (districts) of Ferrara compete in a horse race that momentarily turns Piazza Ariostea into medieval bedlam. Claimed to be the oldest race of its kind in Italy, the first official competition was held in 1279.

Sleeping

Hotel Astra
HOTEL €

(☐0532 20 60 88; www.astrahotel.info; Viale Cavour 55; s/d €59/85; ❄@) An old dame in need of a bit of Botox, Astra can still cut it with the budget-minded thanks to spacious rooms, equally ample bathrooms, voluminous (for Italy) breakfasts, and plenty of downstairs seating space where the antediluvian furniture is doing its best to look antiquelike. The *centro storico* is within strolling distance and the station is close enough to drag your suitcase.

Student's Hostel Estense
HOSTEL €

(☐0532 20 11 58; www.ostelloferrara.it; Corso Biagio Rossetti 24; dm/s/d/tr incl breakfast €16/35/40/48; ☎) ✦ Ferrara's hostel has classic hostel rooms plus extras like geothermal hot water, a bar, a back patio and fantastic amenities for cyclists (bike pumps, a maintenance area and a bike-storage zone).

★ Albergo Annunziata
HOTEL €€

(☐0532 20 11 11; www.annunziata.it; Piazza della Repubblica 5; r from €120; P❄@☎) In a place so clean even the apples on reception look valuable, you're rarely going to be disappointed. Romantics can be forgiven for having visions of Casanova (he once stayed here) in the sharp modernist rooms with their mosaic bathrooms and white dressing gowns. Downstairs, an exquisite breakfast buffet can be enjoyed while the kids run riot with the complementary table football.

Hotel Ferrara
HOTEL €€

(☐0532 20 50 48; www.hotelferrara.com; Largo Castello 36; s/d/apt €80/110/160; ❄@☎) Slick modern furnishings in the ancient centre a mere arrow-shot from the castle, the Ferrara is what design gurus would call 'contemporary' – ie accented colours, minimalist lines, up-to-the-minute electronics, and lots of glass and shiny surfaces. But any pretensions are cancelled out by genuine good service and value-for-money rates. The hotel also has 10 apartment suites from €160.

Hotel de Prati HOTEL €€
(☎0532 24 19 05; www.hoteldeprati.com; Via Padiglioni 5; s €49-85, d €85-110, ste €110-150; ❄) Smarter than the average three-star hotel, de Prati charms with its central location, antique furniture and friendly owner. Wrought-iron bedsteads reign upstairs while downstairs public rooms are enlivened by contemporary art.

✗ Eating

Like all Emilian cities Ferrara has its gastronomic nuances. Don't leave town without trying *cappellacci di zucca*, a hat-shaped pasta pouch filled with pumpkin and herbs, and brushed with sage and butter. Delicious! *Salama da sugo* is a stewed pork sausage, while *pasticcio di maccheroni* is an oven-baked macaroni pie topped with Parmesan. Even Ferrarese bread is distinctive, shaped into a crunchy twisted knot.

Self-caterers can fill up at the covered market (Via Vegri; ☉7am-1.30pm Mon-Sat).

Pizzeria-Ristorante Este Bar PIZZERIA €
(☎0532 24 03 23; www.pizzeriaestebar.com; Via delle Scienze 15; meals €20; ☉lunch & dinner Tue-Sun) No fanfare. No trumpets. Just a decent, family-run *ristorante* in business since 1975 that's still adhering to a well-worn and successful formula of great pizzas, formidable fish dishes and simple but effective Emilian pasta specialities.

Il Sorpasso TRATTORIA €
(www.trattoriailsorpasso.it; Via Sarceno 120; meals €20-25; ☉noon-2.30pm & 7.30-11.30pm Wed-Fri, Sun & Mon, 7.30-11.30pm Sat) Funky yellow signage beckons you into this laid-back trattoria, which tries out creative interpretations of traditional Emilian dishes. Pride of place is the lasagne: al dente layers of red, green and black pasta underlaid with moist chunks of pork. Assorted cookbooks and kids' games shorten the wait.

★ Osteria del Ghetto OSTERIA €€
(☎0532 76 49 36; www.osteriadelghetto.it; Via Vittoria 26; meals €25-30; ☉noon-2.30pm & 7.30-10.30pm Tue-Sun) Yet another understated jewel amid the winding streets of Ferrara's

FERRARA'S CITY WALLS

Only Lucca in Tuscany can claim a more complete set of walls than Ferrara, though with a total circumference of 9km, Ferrara's are longer. Adorned with a well-marked set of paths, unbroken on the northern and eastern sections, the walls make an idyllic walking or cycling loop.

old Jewish ghetto, this *osteria* leads you through a nondescript downstairs bar up to a bright upstairs dining room embellished with striking modern murals. The excellent menu mixes Ferrara staples like *cappellacci di zucca* with a less predictable fish menu.

Al Brindisi OSTERIA €€
(www.albrindisi.net; Via Adelardi 11; meals €25-30; ☉11am-midnight Tue-Sun) The oldest *osteria* in the world (according to Guinness), this scruffy-meets-stylish wine bar was already an established drinking den in 1435. Titian drank here, while the soon-to-be Pope John Paul II dropped by 550 years later. Succinct pasta dishes are well supplemented by wine drawn from racks that are thick with a healthy coating of Ferrara dust.

Trattoria de Noemi TRATTORIA €€
(☎0532 76 90 70; www.trattoriadanoemi.it; Via Ragno 31; meals €25-35; ☉lunch & dinner Wed-Mon) All of Ferrara's classic dishes are delivered *con molto amore* (with much love) here. Arrive early (yes, it's busy) to get the city's best *cappellacci di zucca*, grilled meats and macaroni pie. Enough said!

Osteria Quattro Angeli TRADITIONAL ITALIAN €€
(www.osteriaquattroangeli.it; Piazza della Repubblica; meals €25; ☉8am-1am Tue-Sun) Relax beneath fat, sausage-shaped salamis opposite the castle and demolish enormous portions of Ferrarese classics supplemented by complementary cuts of the local cured meat. Come 6pm, the tented section out front becomes a busy street bar, upping the noise levels and heightening the atmosphere.

Il Don Giovanni GASTRONOMIC €€€
(☎0532 24 33 63; www.ildongiovanni.com; Corso Ercole I d'Este 1; meals €45-75; ☉8-11pm Tue-Sun) Open only for dinner, this highly acclaimed eatery specialises in fresh-caught fish from the Adriatic, vegetables harvested from the restaurant's own garden, eight varieties of

bread baked daily and a wine list featuring more than 600 Italian and international labels. The menu is an imaginative feast of unconventional concoctions; guinea-fowl-stuffed pasta and roast eel stand out.

☆ Entertainment

Jazz Club CLUB, LIVE MUSIC
(www.jazzclubferrara.com; Via Rampari di Belfiore 167; admission €15-25; ☺7.30pm-late) Enjoy the sounds of bebop and jazz-funk in a tower built into Ferrara's old city walls. Concerts start at 9.30pm. Monday and Wednesday nights are free.

ℹ Information

Police station (☏0532 29 43 11; Corso Ercole I d'Este 26)

Post office (Viale Cavour 27)

Tourist office (☏0532 20 93 70; www.ferrarainfo.com; ☺9am-1pm & 2-6pm Mon-Sat, 9.30am-1pm & 2-5pm Sun) In Castello Estense's courtyard.

ℹ Getting There & Around

ACFT (www.acft.it) buses operate within the city and to surrounding towns such as Comacchio (€4.10, one hour, 11 daily), as well as to the Adriatic beaches. Long-distance buses originate at the bus station on Via Rampari San Paolo, then swing by the train station on their way out of town. The train is the better option for Bologna (€4.40, 30 to 50 minutes, half-hourly) and Ravenna (€6.20, 1¼ hours, 14 daily).

Most traffic is banned from the city centre. Overnight parking (€3 per 24 hours) is available at a large car park off Via Darsena (just outside the *centro storico*).

Get in the saddle and join the hundreds of other pedallers in one of Italy's most cycle-friendly cities. Many places, such as **Romanelli** (Via Aldighieri 28a; ☺9.30am-12.30pm & 3.15-7pm), rent bikes (per day €7 to €10).

Ravenna

POP 160,000

Stray a few blocks from its diminutive train station and Ravenna feels immediately different, even by multilayered Italian standards. Historically it fills a little-known void between the fall of the Roman Empire and the advent of the High Middle Ages, an era when the Ravennese were enjoying a protracted golden age while the rest of the Italian peninsula flailed in the wake of Barbarian invasions. Between 402 and 476 Ravenna was briefly capital of the Western Roman Empire and a fertile art studio for skilled Byzantine craftsmen, who left their blindingly colourful mosaics all over the terracotta-bricked Christian churches.

No matter how impervious you might have become to zealous religious art, Ravenna's brilliant 4th- to 6th-century gold, emerald and sapphire masterpieces will leave you struggling for adjectives. A suitably impressed Dante once described them as a 'symphony of colour' and spent the last few years of his life admiring them. Romantic toff Lord Byron added further weight to Ravenna's literary credentials when he spent a couple of years here before decamping to Greece. In 1996 the mosaics were listed as Unesco World Heritage Sites.

⊙ Sights

Ravenna's essential business is its eight Unesco World Heritage Sites, most of which lie scattered around the town (with one situated 5km outside). Five of them must be visited on the same ticket (€11.50), on sale at the **tourist office** (Via Argentario; ☺9am-5.15pm). One is free. The other two can be paid for separately. The website www.ravennamosaici.it gives more information.

★**Basilica di San Vitale** CHURCH
(Via Fiandrini, entrance on Via San Vitale; ☺9am-7pm Apr-Sep, to 5.30pm Mar & Oct, 9.30am-5pm Nov-Feb) Sometimes, after weeks of trolling around dark Italian churches, you can lose your sense of wonder. Not here! The lucid mosaics that adorn the altar of this ancient church consecrated in 547 by Archbishop Massimiano invoke a sharp intake of breath in most visitors. Gaze in wonder at the rich greens, brilliant golds and deep blues bathed in shafts of soft yellow sunlight.

The mosaics on the side and end walls represent scenes from the Old Testament: to the left, Abraham prepares to sacrifice Isaac in the presence of three angels, while the one on the right portrays the death of Abel and the offering of Melchizedek. Inside the chancel, two magnificent mosaics depict the Byzantine emperor Justinian with San Massimiano and a particularly solemn and expressive Empress Theodora, who was his consort.

Mausoleo di Galla Placidia MAUSOLEUM
(Via Fiandrini; ☺9am-7pm Apr-Sep, to 5.30pm Mar & Oct, 9.30am-5pm Nov-Feb) In the same complex as Basilica di San Vitale, the small but equally incandescent Mausoleo di Galla

Ravenna

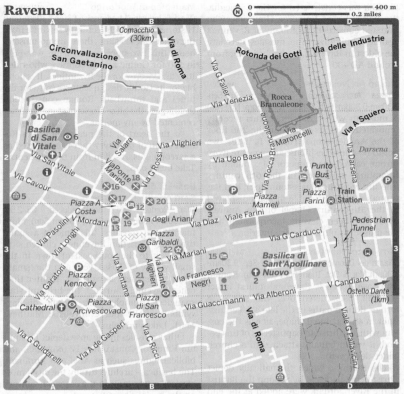

Ravenna

Placidia was constructed for Galla Placidia, the half-sister of Emperor Honorius, who initiated construction of many of Ravenna's grandest buildings. The mosaics here are the oldest in Ravenna, probably dating from around AD 430.

Museo Arcivescovile
MUSEUM

(Piazza Arcivescovado; ⊙ 9am-7pm Apr-Sep, 9.30am-5.30pm Oct & Mar, 10am-5pm Nov-Feb) A museum with a difference, this recently renovated religious gem is on the 2nd floor of the Archiepiscopal Palace. It hides two not-to-be-missed exhibits: an exquisite ivory throne carved for Emperor Maximilian by Byzantium craftsmen in the 6th century (the surviving detail is astounding); and Ravenna's most improbable mosaics displayed in the 5th-century chapel of San Andrea, which has been cleverly incorporated into the museum's plush modern interior.

Battistero Neoniano
BAPTISTERY

(Piazza del Duomo; ⊙ 9am-7pm Apr-Sep, 9.30am-5.30pm Mar & Oct, 10am-5pm Nov-Feb) Roman ruins aside, this is Ravenna's oldest intact building, constructed over the site of a former Roman baths in the late 4th century. Built in an octagonal shape, as was the custom with all Christian baptisteries of this period, it was originally attached to a church (since destroyed).

The mosaics, which thematically depict Christ being baptised by St John the Baptist in the River Jordan, were added at the end of the 5th century.

★ Basilica di Sant'Apollinare Nuovo
CHURCH

(Via di Roma; ⊙ 9am-7pm Apr-Sep, 9.30am-5.30pm Mar & Oct, 10am-5pm Nov-Feb) An old legend states that Pope Gregory the Great once ordered the Apollinare's mosaics to be blackened as they were distracting worshippers from prayer. A millennium and a half later, the dazzling Christian handiwork is still having the same effect. It's almost impossible to take your eyes off the 26 white-robed martyrs heading towards Christ with his Apostles on the right (south) wall.

On the opposite side, an equally expressive procession of virgins bears similar offerings for the Madonna. The basilica dates originally from the 560s and its architectural fusion of Christian east and west can be seen in its marble porticoes and distinctive conical bell tower.

Mausoleo di Teodorico
MAUSOLEUM

(Via delle Industrie 14; admission €3; ⊙ 8.30am-7pm) Historically and architecturally separate from the other Unesco sites (there are no mosaics here), this two-storey mausoleum was built in 520 for Gothic king Teodorico, who ruled Italy as a viceroy for the Byzantines. It is notable for its Gothic design features (rare for the time) and throwback Roman construction techniques: the huge blocks of stone were not cemented by any mortar.

At the heart of the mausoleum is a Roman basin of porphyry that was recycled as a sarcophagus. It's 2km from the city centre. Take bus 2 or 5.

Basilica di Sant'Apollinare in Classe
CHURCH

(Via Romea Sud; adult/reduced €5/2.50; ⊙ 8.30am-7.30pm Mon-Sat, 1-7.30pm Sun) More magnificent mosaics, this time in a signature early-Christian Ravennese church situated 5km to the southeast of town in the small village of Classe. Fear not: the (small) effort to get here is worth it. Lighter than other Ravenna churches, the brilliant star-spangled triumphal-arch mosaic displays symbols of the four evangelists: Matthew, Mark, Luke and John.

Other mosaics in the apse depict Byzantium Emperor Constantine IV (652–685) and biblical figures such as Abel and Abraham. The basilica – architecturally the city's most 'perfect' – was built in the early 6th century on the burial site of Ravenna's patron saint, who converted the city to Christianity in the 2nd century. To get there take bus 4 to Classe or take the train one stop in the direction of Rimini.

Battistero degli Ariani
BAPTISTERY

(Via degli Ariani; ⊙ 8.30am-7.30pm Apr-Sep, to 4.30pm Oct-Mar) FREE Aside from its breathtaking dome mosaic depicting the baptism of Christ, the Ariani's main quirk is that it's the only Unesco site you can enter for free. But the gratis entry is no reflection of the quality of the artistry inside, a vivid display of Christ being baptised encircled by the 12 Apostles.

The Ariani's mosaics were completed over a period of years beginning in the 5th century. You can clearly detect slight variations in colour on some of the green stones.

Museo d'Arte della Città di Ravenna
GALLERY

(www.museocitta.ra.it; Via di Roma 13; adult/reduced €9/7; ⊙ 9am-6pm Tue-Thu, to 9pm Fri, to

7pm Sat & Sun) Arranged in a converted 15th-century monastery abutting a public garden, here you'll find Ravenna's permanent art collection backed up by regular temporary expos. The top floor is dedicated to some rather fetching modern mosaics first brought together in the 1950s.

Domus dei Tappeti di Pietra MUSEUM
(Via B Gianbattista; adult/reduced €4/3; ☉10am-5pm Tue-Fri, to 6pm Sat & Sun) More mosaics, but noticeably different ones, these 6th-century floor mosaics from a 14-room late-Roman palace were only unearthed in 1993–94. Now fully restored, they show considerable artistic merit, and are decorated with geometric and floral designs.

Tomba di Dante MAUSOLEUM
(Via D Alighieri 9; ☉9.30am-6.30pm) FREE A son of Florence, Italy's Sommo Poeta (supreme poet), Dante Alighieri, was expelled from the city of his birth in 1302 for political reasons and spent many years 'on the run'. He finally sought refuge in Ravenna, where he died in 1321. As a perpetual act of penance, Florence still supplies the oil for the lamp that burns continually in his tomb.

Courses

Gruppo Mosaicisti ARTS
(www.gruppomosaicisti.com; Via Fiandrini; beginner courses €550) Runs mosaic courses catering to everyone from beginners to artists.

Mosaic Art School ARTS
(www.mosaicschool.com; Via Francesco Negri 14; 1-week course €660-760) Runs mosaic courses catering to everyone from beginners to artists.

Festivals & Events

Ravenna hosts one of Italy's top classical-music events, and jazz fans are well served by a jazz festival every May.

Ravenna Festival MUSIC
(www.ravennafestival.org) Renowned Italian conductor Riccardo Muti has close ties with Ravenna and is intimately involved each year with this festival. Concerts are staged from June to late July at venues all over town, including the **Teatro Alighieri** (www.teatroalighieri.org; Via Mariani 2). Ticket prices start at around €15.

Sleeping

Hotel Ravenna HOTEL €
(☑0544 21 22 04; www.hotelravenna.ra.it; Via Maroncelli 12; s €45-55, d €60-90; P ❋ 🛜) A stone's throw from the train station, Hotel Ravenna is a safe bet. The bland rooms feature fading beige and gold decor and unexceptional furniture, but they're large and comfortable enough. Parking is free; wi-fi costs €4 per hour.

Ostello Galletti Abbiosi HOSTEL €
(☑0544 3 13 13; www.galletti.ra.it; Via Roma 140; r €84-94; P ❋ @ 🛜) Corralled in a monumental 18th-century town house, this place is more hotel than hostel. With high-ceilinged, spacious rooms, a small gym, a courtyard and even its own small chapel, it's an excellent deal.

★**Hotel Centrale Byron** HOTEL €€
(☑0544 21 22 25; www.hotelbyron.com; Via IV Novembre 14; s €55-65, d €90-110; ❋ @ 🛜) Locations don't get much better than this, especially in the car-free, wonderfully ingratiating streets of central Ravenna. It's no lie to say you could lob a football from the window of your clean, modern Centrale Byron room into pivotal (and beautiful) Piazza del Popolo. Regularly updated and improved, Byron keeps ahead of the game. So what if the great poet never stayed here?

Albergo Cappello BOUTIQUE HOTEL €€
(☑0544 21 98 13; www.albergocappello.it; Via IV Novembre 41; r from €110; P ❋ @ 🛜) Colour-themed rooms are called 'suites' at this finely coiffed hotel where Murano glass chandeliers, original 15th-century frescoes and coffered ceilings are set against modern fixtures and flat-screen TVs. The ample breakfast features pastries from Ravenna's finest *pasticceria* (pastry shop). There's also an excellent restaurant and wine bar attached.

Eating

Self-caterers and sandwich-fillers can load up at the city's **covered market** (Piazza Andrea Costa; ☉9am-5pm Mon-Sat).

La Gardela TRATTORIA €
(☑0544 21 71 47; Via Ponte Marino 3; mains €8-16, fixed-price menu €15/25; ☉noon-2.30pm & 7-10pm Fri-Wed) Economical prices and formidable home cooking mean La Gardela can be crowded, but in a pleasant, gregarious way. Professional waiters glide by with

EMILIA-ROMAGNA & SAN MARINO EAST OF BOLOGNA

plates full of Italian classics: think thin-crust pizza, *ragù*, fried fish. Lap it up.

Babaleus
PIZZERIA €

(www.ristorantebabaleus.com; V Gabbiani 7; pizzas from €4, meals €20-25; ⊗noon-2.30pm & 7pm-midnight Thu-Tue) Remember the days before TV chefs went viral, when hard-working cooks in white hats used to sit down with their diners and sip glasses of wine between courses? True to the tradition, cheap and cheerful Babaleus still ensures its fresh-from-the-oven pizza is brought to your table by congenial kitchen helpers in well-used pinnies armed with plenty of banter.

La Piadina del Melarancio
FAST FOOD €

(⊋0544 21 20 71; Via IV Novembre 31; piadinas €3-5; ⊗11.30am-8.30pm) You'll notice marked differences between Emilian and Romagnan food, with the latter best known for its local spin on the grilled *panini*, the *piadina* (a stuffed flatbread). To taste one of Ravenna's *piadinas* (which are thicker than those in Rimini), duck into this simple city-centre spot where you place your order at the front counter and wait in a back room until they call out your number.

They're hot and fresh and best served stuffed with tomato sauce and sausage.

★ Osteria La Mariola
MODERN ITALIAN €€

(⊋0544 20 14 45; Via P Costa 1; meals €35-40; ⊗noon-2.30pm & 8-11.30pm) Trying to fancy up Italian food is a precarious profession in a country where tradition and simplicity rule. All the more reason to offer kudos to La Mariola, where food is more artistic than the usual homespun fare, and wine can be ordered by the *quartino* (quarter-litre measure). Housed in the 16th-century Palazzo Grossi, its three trendy, purple-accented rooms divide into a wine bar, restaurant and *enoteca* (wine bar).

Drinking & Nightlife

★ Ca' de Vèn
BAR

(www.cadeven.it; Via Corrado Ricci 24; meals €25-35; ⊗Tue-Sun) Old men with canine companions mix with wine snobs swapping oenological tips in this atmospheric wine bar-cum-restaurant beautified with floor-to-ceiling shelves stuffed with bottles, books and other curiosities. Use it for its excellent *aperitivi* and, when the frescoed ceiling starts to spin, you can either stay put

or make tracks for your main course elsewhere.

ⓘ Information

Post office (Piazza Garibaldi 1)
Tourist office (Via Salara 8-12; ⊗8.30am-7pm Mon-Sat, 10am-6pm Sun)

ⓘ Getting There & Around

ATM (www.atm.ra.it) local buses depart from Piazza Farini. Intercity buses for Ferrara and towns along the coast leave from the bus station on the east side of the railroad tracks (reached by a pedestrian underpass). **Punto Bus** (Piazza Fanini; ⊗6.30am-7.30pm Mon-Sat, from 7.30am Sun), on the piazza, is ATM's information and ticketing office.

Ravenna is on a branch (A14 *dir*) of the main east-coast A14 autostrada. The SS16 (Via Adriatica) heads south to Rimini and on down the coast. The main car parks are east of the train station and north of the Basilica di San Vitale.

Trains connect with Bologna (€6.80, 1¼ hours, hourly), Ferrara (€6.20, 1¼ hours, 14 daily), Rimini (€4.40, one hour, hourly) and the south coast.

In town, cycling is popular. The main (Via Salara) branch of the tourist office offers a free bike-hire service for visitors. Register by presenting a photo ID, then simply grab a yellow bike from one of the cycle stalls outside and return it to the same rack within normal business hours.

Just outside Ravenna's train station, **Cooperativa Sociale la Formica** (Piazza Farini; bikes per hour/day €1.10/8.50; ⊗7am-7pm Mon-Fri) also rents out bikes.

Rimini
POP 146,000

Roman relics, jam-packed beaches, hedonistic nightclubs and the memory (and memories) of film director and native son Federico Fellini make sometimes awkward bedfellows in seaside Rimini. Although there's been a settlement here for over 2000 years, Rimini's coast was just sand dunes until 1843, when the first bathing establishments took root next to the ebbing Adriatic. The beach huts gradually morphed into a megaresort that was sequestered by a huge nightclub scene in the 1990s. Despite some interesting history, Fellini-esque movie memorabilia and a decent food culture, 95% of Rimini's visitors come for its long, boisterous, sometimes tacky beachfront.

Once a thriving Latin colony known as Ariminum, Rimini changed hands like a well-worn library book in the Middle Ages when periods of Byzantine, Lombard and Papal rule culminated in the roguish reign of Sigis-

Rimini

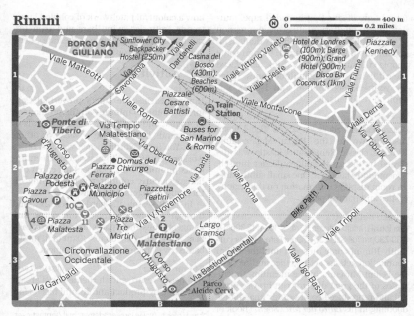

mondo Malatesta in the 15th century. But the worst was to come. Rimini got whacked more than any other Italian city during WWII, when bombing raids were followed by the brutal 'Battle of Rimini', during which an estimated 1.5 million rounds of Allied ammunition were fired on the German-occupied city.

◉ Sights

Piazza Cavour is Rimini's main square, containing the city's finest *palazzi*, including the 16th-century **Palazzo del Municipio**, reconstructed after being razed during WWII, and the 14th-century Gothic **Palazzo del Podestà**. The palaces aren't open to the public, but provide an attractive backdrop to the modern-day toings and froings in the square.

★ Tempio Malatestiano   CHURCH
(Via IV Novembre 35; ⊘ 8.30am-12.30pm & 3.30-7pm Mon-Sat, 9am-1pm & 3.30-7pm Sun) Rimini's cathedral is the result of a medieval love story with a rather ambiguous ending. Built originally in Gothic style in the 1200s and dedicated to St Francis, it was transformed in the 15th century into a kind of Renaissance Taj Mahal for the tomb of Isotta degli Atti, the beloved mistress of roguish ruling clansman Sigismondo Malatesta.

Rimini

Sigismondo, known disparagingly as the 'Wolf of Rimini', gave Leon Battista Alberti, a Florentine architect with grandiose Roman ideas, the job of redesigning the church in 1450, but it was a task he never finished. Sigismondo, thanks to his aggressive military campaigns, had fallen out with the pope, Pius II (himself no angel), who burned his effigy in Rome and condemned him to hell for a litany of sins that included rape, murder, incest, adultery and severe oppression of the people. With his credibility dented, Sigismondo's popularity waned, though some people still superstitiously think he defaced the cathedral with pagan undertones. Judge for yourself. Sigismondo and Isotta's sarcophagi reside inside.

Castel Sismondo
MUSEUM

(Piazza Malatesta; admission €2; ☉ 8.30am-1.30pm) Also known as the Rocca Malatestiana, Rimini's classic Renaissance castle was designed by the great military leader himself, Sigismondo Malatesta. One small subterranean room displays information on the region's castles and natural parks.

Museo della Città
MUSEUM

(Via Tonini 1; adult/reduced €6/4; ☉ 10am-12.30pm & 4.30-7.30pm Tue-Sat, 4.30-7.30pm Sun) This is currently Rimini's only museum until the Fellini Foundation gets its act together and reopens the Fellini Museum. In the meantime, aficionados of the great director can browse original and reproduced copies of his imaginative doodling in his *Libro dei Miei Sogni* (Book of My Dreams). Otherwise, this rambling museum is best known for its Roman section.

Spread over several rooms with excellent bilingual (Italian/English) signage are finds from two nearby Roman villas, including splendid mosaics, a rare and exquisite representation of fish rendered in coloured glass, and the world's largest collection of Roman surgical instruments.

★ Ponte di Tiberio
LANDMARK

The start of the arterial Roman road, the Via Emilia, no less, the majestic five-arched Tiberius' Bridge dates from AD 21. It still links the city centre to the old fishing quarter of Borgo San Giuliano and rests on its original foundations consisting of an ingenious construction of wooden stilts.

Arco di Augusto
LANDMARK

(Corso d'Augusto) This great Roman ruin was commissioned by Emperor Augustus in 27 BC and stands 17m high on modern-day Corso d'Augusto. It was once the end point of the ancient Via Flaminia that linked Rimini with Rome. Buildings that had grown up around the arch were demolished in 1935 to improve its stature.

Borgo San Giuliano
NEIGHBOURHOOD

Just over the Ponte di Tiberio, Rimini's old fishing quarter has been freshened up and is now a colourful patchwork of cobbled lanes, trendy trattorias, wine bars and trim terraced houses (read: prime real estate). Look out for the numerous murals.

Activities

Beaches
BEACH

Rimini beaches are Italy's proverbial California. Spend 10 minutes on the promenade in August and you'll realise that all kinds of new trends kick off here – wacky or otherwise. You'll see Nordic beach-walkers, office workers getting a reiki massage, gym enthusiasts pumping iron, clubbers in search of a hangover cure, computer geeks surfing on their sun loungers, and more.

In peak season it's hard to see the sand through all the assembled umbrellas, sun loungers, amusement parks and crowded beach bars. Suffice it to say there's 40km of it, mostly backed by clamorous hotel development.

Theme Parks
AMUSEMENT PARK

In a beach resort, garish theme parks are an inevitable by-product and Rimini has its fair share. The truly committed can buy a **Fantasticket** (www.larivieradeiparchi.it/fantasticket. php) granting reduced-price admission to multiple parks. The tourist office can provide a full list. Major ones include **Fiabilandia** (www.fiabilandia.it; Via Cardano 15; adult/child €23/16; 🏨), which focuses on fun for kids, and **Aquafàn** (www.aquafan.it; Via Ascoli Piceno 6; adult/child €28/20; ☉ 10am-6.30pm Jun–mid-Sep), a huge water park in Riccione (take bus 42 or 45 from Riccione station).

☆☆ Festivals & Events

Gradisca
CARNIVAL

On 21 June Rimini marks the beginning of summer with dancing, fireworks and eating – it's estimated that revellers consume some two tonnes of grilled sardines and 12,000L of sangiovese wine in one night.

🛏 Sleeping

Ironically for a city with more than 1200 hotels, finding accommodation can be tricky. In July and August places can be booked solid and prices are sky-high, especially as many proprietors insist on full board. In winter a lot of places simply shut up shop.

Hotel Villa Lalla
HOTEL €

(☎ 0541 5 51 55; www.villalalla.com; Viale V Veneto 22; s/d €48/96; P ❋ @) One of the better hotels in the leafy residential district between

RIMINI'S CLUBBING SCENE

Some come to Rimini in search of Roman relics. Others prefer to seek out its lavish modern nightclubs. Rimini first garnered a reputation for megahip nightclubbing in the 1990s when an electric after-dark scene took off in the hills of **Misano Monte** and **Riccone** several kilometres to the south of the city centre. Far from being a tacky rerun of Torremolinos or Magaluf, Rimini's new clubs quickly established themselves as modish, fashionable affairs that appealed to a broader age demographic than the 18 to 30 dives of yore. That's not to say they were boring.

Byblos (www.byblosclub.com; Via Pozzo Castello 24, Misano Monte), a converted villa complex with swimming pool, restaurant and highly acclaimed DJs feels more like a hedonistic Beverley Hills house party than a club. It fills up nightly with ridiculously beautiful people. **Baia Imperiale** (www.baiaimperiale.net; Via Panoramica 195; ⏰10pm-4am) drips with marble staircases, pools, and assorted obelisks and statues of Roman emperors. Even the stone-cold sober agree that it's one of the most beautiful discos in the world. **Cocoricò** (www.cocorico.it; Viale Chieti 44; ⏰11pm-5.30am) convenes under a glass pyramid where 2000 clammy strangers quickly become friends to the sounds of techno, house and underground. **Disco Bar Coconuts** (www.coconuts.it; Lungomare C Tintori 5; ⏰11.30pm-4am) on Rimini's waterfront exudes a summer-beach-party atmosphere, with palm trees sprouting from the wooden deck and a 'flower power' VW convertible parked out the front.

Part of the fabric of the Rimini club scene is the **Blue Line** (www.bluelinebus.com; tickets €4; ⏰10pm-6am), a fleet of multicoloured disco buses (complete with DJs and coffee bars) that ferry clubbers from Piazzale Kennedy in the city centre to and from the various nightclubs to the south.

the beach and the train station. Its smart white rooms are fresh and cool and, in winter, its rates are a snip. From mid-June to mid-September when the restaurant's open, it's a good idea to invest in half board or full board (a mere €8 extra per meal). Bikes are free for guests.

Sunflower City Backpacker Hostel　　　　　　　　　　HOSTEL €
(☑0541 2 51 80; www.sunflowerhostel.com; Viale Dardanelli 102; dm €18-27, s €26-49, d €46-79; @☏) Run by three ex-backpackers, the chilled-out Sunflower welcomes travellers with laundry and cooking facilities, spacious lockers, retro Austin Powers–style wallpaper, pool tables, a bar and free bike hire. There's another **branch** (☑0541 37 34 32; Viale Siracusa 25; ⏰Mar-Oct) near the beach.

Hotel de Londres　　　　　　　　　　HOTEL €€
(☑0541 5 01 14; www.hoteldelondres.it; Viale Amerigo Vespucci 24; s/d €115/139; P☏) Well-appointed little place near the beach with enough thoughful extras to usurp the competition. Making a stopover worthwhile are the rooftop spa, the small gymnasiun, the flower terrace and the free bikes.

★ **Grand Hotel**　　　　　　LUXURY HOTEL €€€
(☑0541 5 60 00; www.grandhotelrimini.com; Parco Federico Fellini; s €110-315, d €155-400; P✳@

☏✉) Rimini's only five-star hotel is as much a monument as a place to stay. Despite a 1920 fire and serious damage incurred during WWII, it has remained true to its 1908 roots with rooms clad in authentic 18th-century Venetian antiques. Beloved by Fellini, the hotel has lured many other celebs with its pool, private beach and elegant communal areas.

✗ Eating

Rimini's cuisine is anchored by the *piadina* and *pesce azzurro* (oily fish), especially sardines and anchovies. The favourite tipple is Sangiovese wine.

Casina del Bosco　　　　　　　　SNACKS €
(Via Beccadelli 15; piadine €4-7; ⏰noon-late) It's very simple (isn't all good food?). It's called a *piadina* – a toasted half-moon of unleavened bread with a savoury filling – and it's Romagna's retort to the wrap. You can get them in many places, but they're rarely as consistent or wide-ranging as they are at this fast and efficient alfresco joint overlooking Parco Federico Fellini near the beach.

Gelateria Pellicano　　　　　　　GELATO €
(www.gelateriapellicano.com; Via S Mentana 10; ⏰7.30am-7.30pm Mon-Sat) This Rimini-based, five-store chain makes some seriously good

Like...? Try...

Like Florence? Try Bologna

Climb the 498 steps of medieval Torre degli Asinelli and the city unfurls before you like a map. There were once more than 100 such towers here, but only some 20 remain. Massimo Medica, director of Bologna's Musei Civici d'Arte Antica, explains. 'In the Middle Ages Bologna was an important city. Its university was comparable to Paris's. There wasn't the space to have a castle, so every tower belonged to a powerful family – the height showed the extent of their power. When a family was defeated, their tower would be cut.'

In the central square, Piazza Maggiore, locals and tourists recline as if at the beach. They're probably considering Bologna's other great achievement, its food. This is the home of yolky pasta: fine ribbons of tagliatelle entwined with *ragù* (meat sauce), *tortellini in brodo* (pork pasta parcels in a thin soup), and the artisanal ice cream of 1950s parlour La Sorbetteria Castiglione.

Like the Dolomites? Try Monti Sibillini

'On a clear day you can see Croatia from here,' says affable Maurizio Fusari, zoologist and trekking guide in the Monti Sibillini, gesturing out at the views that stretch off into the Adriatic. In this weathered mountain range, split between Umbria and Le Marche, the predominant sounds are birdsong and the swirl of the breeze, yet the wild hills are appealingly approachable. 'It's possible to reach even the tallest without Alpine equipment. These are mountains for everyone.'

Walks range from gentle afternoon strolls through mountain valleys to night-

1. Promontorio del Gargano (p714), Puglia
2. Bologna (p431)
3. Horses in front of the village of Castelluccio, Piano Grande (p620)

time hikes to watch the sunrise, or a nine-day trek on the Grande Anello trail (75 miles). En route, look out for wildlife. Maurizio reels off a list: 'Wild boar, roe deer, wolves, golden eagles, peregrine falcons. Oh, and one bear. He has come here from Abruzzo. It seems he's looking for a mate.'

Like the Amalfi Coast?
Try the Gargano Promontory

The Gargano, the sea-thrusting spur of the Italian boot, was once an island. Knowing this makes sense of the place. It feels a region apart, with a skirt of sea so blue it makes you blink. The land is a tumultuous mix: bleached sea cliffs, dense dark-green scrub, wild orchids, pine forests and silver beaches, protected as a national park.

Vieste and Peschici are the main coastal towns, bunched-up clusters of narrow lanes and heavy limestone houses. Their pale buildings seem to grow out of the sea cliffs, with fierce-blue views in every direction. In high summer, it seems that everyone in Italy is here, but June and September are the Gargano's finest months, when the carnival-like crowds are gone, but not everything is closed.

ice cream. Try the *pinoli* (pine nut), with toasted whole nuts on top.

Brodo di Giuggiole TRADITIONAL ITALIAN €€
(www.brododigiuggiole.info; Via Soardi 11; meals €35; ⏰11.30am-11.30pm Fri-Wed; 🛜) Tucked down an alley off Piazza Tre Martiri, this intimate spot is great for an elegant night out, with its wood-panelled dining room, lantern-lit terrace and an ever-changing menu featuring some of the freshest, best-prepared fish in town. Reservations are recommended, especially on live-jazz Tuesdays.

Tonino Il Lurido SEAFOOD €€€
(www.ristoranteillurido.com; Via Ortaggi 7; meals €45; ⏰noon-2.30pm & 7.30-10.30pm Wed-Mon) When Fellini said it was 'easier to be faithful to a restaurant than a woman', he might have been talking about this place. The great film director's (allegedly) favourite eating establishment in Rimini has been in operation since 1949. Can it still cut it? Sample the small, tasty portions of fresh fish and decide.

🍷 Drinking & Nightlife

Most Italian drinking trends begin life in Rimini – or so the locals claim – from street bars to free aperitifs. The action spins on two hubs: the old *pescaria* (fish market) through the brick triple archway off Piazza Cavour, and the seafront around Marino Centro.

Caffè Cavour CAFE
(Piazza Cavour 12; ⏰7am-midnight) Early risers bump into the remnants of last night's dance marathons in this swish cafe on Rimini's main square. Mornings are for cappuccinos, evenings for *aperitivi*, the plush leather seats inside for anytime.

Rock Island BAR
(www.rockislandrimini.net; Piazzale Boscovich; ⏰7pm-midnight Fri-Wed plus lunch Sun; 🛜) Perched on stilts over the Adriatic on the pier next to the marina, Rock Island is the place for beer, sunset cocktails, live rock music and bikers with beards.

Barge IRISH PUB
(Lungomare C Tintori 13; ⏰closed Mon winter) A magnet for modish 20-somethings, this seafront pub offers an irresistible combo: draught Guinness, regular DJs and frequent live music.

Il Vecchio e Il Mare BAR
(Via Pisacane 10; ⏰5pm-1am) In the historic fish market, this rustic place recently underwent a name change and upped the ante at its appy buffet at the same time. Pay a €5 minimum cover and the food table is yours. Piano music adds to the ambience between 7pm and 9pm.

❶ Information

Hospital (📞0541 70 51 11; Viale L Settembrini 2) Located 1.2km southeast of the centre.

Police station (📞0541 35 31 11; Corso d'Augusto 192)

Post office (Via Gambalunga 40)

Tourist office (www.riminiturismo.it) Parco Federico Fellini (Parco Federico Fellino 3; ⏰8.30am-7pm Mon-Sat, to 2pm Sun); Train Station (Piazzale Cesare Battisti, Train Station; ⏰8.30am-7pm Mon-Sat, to 1.30pm Sun)

❶ Getting There & Away

Darwin Airlines offers direct flights from Rome to Rimini's Federico Fellini airport, 8km south of the city centre. Air Berlin links with several German cities.

There are regular buses from Rimini's train station to San Marino (return €9, 45 minutes, 11 daily).

By car, you have a choice of the A14 (south into Le Marche or northwest towards Bologna and Milan) or the toll-free but very busy SS16.

Hourly trains run down the coast to the ferry ports of Ancona (regional/Eurostar €5.70/15, one to 1¼ hours) and Bari (€48.50/62.50, five to six hours). Up the line, they serve Ravenna (€4.40, one hour, hourly) and Bologna (regional/Eurostar €9.20/20, one to 1½ hours, half-hourly).

❶ Getting Around

TRAMServizi (www.tramservizi.it) buses operate throughout the city. Local bus 9 runs between Rimini's train station and the airport (€1, 25 minutes). For Riccione (€1.50, 30 minutes), catch local bus 11 from the train station or along the *lungomare* (seafront promenade); it leaves every eight to 15 minutes between 6am and 2am.

You can hire bikes and scooters from various kiosks on Piazzale Kennedy. Free bikes are also available from Rimini's municipal offices at Corso d'Augusto 158.

SAN MARINO

Of the world's 193 independent countries, San Marino is the fifth smallest and – arguably – the most curious. How it exists at all is something of an enigma. A sole survivor of Italy's once powerful city-state network, this landlocked micronation clung on long after the more powerful kingdoms of Genoa and Venice folded. And still it clings, secure in its status as the world's oldest surviving sovereign state and its oldest republic (since AD 301). San Marino also enjoys the lowest unemployment rate in Europe and one of the planet's highest GDPs.

Measuring 61 sq km, the country is larger than many outsiders imagine, being made up of nine municipalities each hosting its own settlement. The largest 'town' is Dogana (on the bus route from Italy), a place 99.9% of the two million annual visitors skip on their way through to the Città di San Marino, the medieval settlement on the slopes of 750m-high Monte Titano that was added to the Unesco World Heritage list in 2008.

Though San Marino is old and commands some astounding views, it retains a curious lack of intimacy and (for want of a better word) soul.

Sights & Activities

Citta di San Marino's highlights are its spectacular views, its Unesco-listed streets, and a stash of rather bizarre museums dedicated to vampires, torture, wax dummies and strange facts. Ever popular is the half-hourly changing of the guard (☉May-Sep) in Piazza della Libertà.

Castello della Cesta   CASTLE
(admission €4.50; ☉8am-8pm mid-Jun–mid-Sep, 9am-5pm mid-Sep–mid-Jun) Dominating the skyline and offering superb views towards Rimini and the coast, the Cesta dates from the 13th century and sits atop 750m Monte Titano. Today you can walk its ramparts and peep into a small museum devoted to medieval armaments.

The admission price also includes entry to the Castello della Guaita (Salita alla Roca; admission €4.50; ☉8am-8pm mid-Jun–mid-Sep, 9am-5pm mid-Sep–mid-Jun), the older of San Marino's castles, dating from the 11th century. It was still being used as a prison until as recently as 1975.

Museo delle Curiosità   MUSEUM
(www.museodellecuriosita.sm; Salità alla Rocca 26; adult/reduced €7/4; ☉10am-6pm) If you're overtly curious or just a little bored, you can brush up on your Trivial Pursuit skills at this shrine to throwaway facts.

Museo di Stato   MUSEUM
(www.museidistato.sm; Piazza Titano 1; ☉8am-8pm mid-Jun–mid-Sep, 9am-5pm mid-Sep–mid-Jun) FREE San Marino's best museum by far is

the well-laid-out if disjointed state museum displaying art, history, furniture and culture.

Sleeping & Eating

Albergo Diamond   PENSION €
(☎0549 99 10 03; Contrada del Collegio 50; r €50) Few of the two million annual visitors stay overnight in San Marino, but if they checked out the Diamond's giveaway prices they might be tempted. Cute, modest rooms look like something your grandma put together and there's a large, busy restaurant below.

Hotel Titano   HOTEL €€
(☎0549 99 10 07; www.hoteltitano.com; Contrada del Collegio 31; r with/without view €115/88; P @ ☎) The Titano is San Marino's best all-rounder, with a tearoom, fine-view restaurant (La Terrazza) and enough mod cons to justify a three-star rating.

Caffè Titano   INTERNATIONAL €
(Pizzetta del Titano 4; ☉8am-8pm) In the eponymous square and not directly connected to its namesake hotel, the Titano appears to be San Marino's sleekest inexpensive option. Seating is in cool booths, there's a bit of local action and the plates of sliced beef, rocket and *parmigiano* are delicious.

Shopping

Azienda Filatelica-Numismatica   SOUVENIRS
(www.aasfn.sm; Piazza Garibaldi 5; ☉8.15am-6pm Mon & Thu, to 2.15pm Tue, Wed & Fri) Collectors can pick up rare San Marino stamps and coins at this small shop.

Information

Post office (Viale A Onofri 87) Vital for sending those 'proof-you've-been-there' postcards.
Tourist office (www.visitsanmarino.com; Contrada del Collegio 40; ☉10am-5pm) You can get your passport stamped with a San Marino visa for a rip-off €5 here.

Getting There & Away

Buses run to/from Rimini (return €9, 45 minutes, 11 daily), arriving at Piazzale Calcigni. The SS72 leads up from Rimini.

Leave your car at one of the numerous car parks and walk up to the *centro storico*. Alternatively, park at car park 11 and take the **funivia** (cable car; return €4.50; ☉7.50am-sunset Sep-Jun, to 1am Jul & Aug).

Florence & Tuscany

Best Places to Eat

➡ Il Santo Bevitore (p501)

➡ iO Osteria Personale (p501)

➡ Filippo (p521)

➡ Enoteca I Terzi (p535)

Best Places to Stay

➡ Antica Torre di Via de' Tornabuoni 1 (p495)

➡ Academy Hostel (p495)

➡ Villa Sassolini (p543)

➡ La Bandita (p553)

Why Go?

Laden with grand-slam sights and experiences, Tuscany (Toscana in Italian) offers the perfect introduction to Italy's famed *dolce vita*. It truly does have it all: extraordinary art and architecture, magnificent landscapes, vibrant festivals and a seasonally driven cuisine that is emulated the world over. There are few places in the world where food, fashion, art and nature intermingle so effortlessly and to such magnificent effect.

This part of Italy has been value-adding since Etruscan times, so there's plenty to see and do. You can explore a World Heritage site in the morning, visit a vineyard in the afternoon and bunk down in a palatial villa or atmospheric *agriturismo* at night. Renaissance paintings and Gothic cathedrals? Check. Spectacular trekking and sensational Slow Food? Yep. Hills laden with vines and ancient olive groves? More than you can possibly imagine.

When to Go
Florence

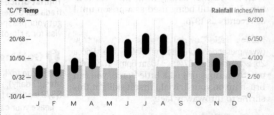

May–Jun Wildflower-adorned landscapes beg outdoor action, be it walking, cycling or horse riding.	**Jul** Not as madbusy as August (avoid) and there are plenty of music festivals.	**Sep–Nov** Grapes and olives are harvested, and forests yield truffles and porcini mushrooms.

Off the Beaten Track

Though many of Tuscany's monuments and towns are crowded year-round, even in top-drawer destinations it is still possible to follow a less-trodden road. In Florence, enjoy extraordinary art in lesser-known museums such as the Palazzo Medici-Riccardi (p486), Museo Marino Marini (p485) and Museo di Orsanmichele (p481). In Pisa save the Leaning Tower for sunset, after the coachloads have departed, and spend the day meandering along the Arno River (p509). In Siena, relax in the tranquil setting of the Orto de' Pecci (p527) or head to the oft-ignored Pinacoteca (p533), with its outstanding collection of Sienese art.

ITINERARIES

Four days
Base yourself in Florence for three nights: spend one day visiting the Uffizi Gallery, another wandering through the San Marco, Santa Maria Novella and San Lorenzo neighbourhoods, and the third crossing the Arno to explore the artisan's neighbourhood of Oltrarno. On your last day, explore outside the city. Fiesole, Siena and San Gimignano are easily accessed by bus, and Lucca, Pisa and Arezzo by train.

One week
Three days in Florence, two in Siena and a final couple of days exploring the countryside will give you a true appreciation of Tuscany's charms. If you have a car, a two-day drive around Chianti or through the Val d'Orcia and Val di Chiana will reap manifold rewards; if using public transport, day trips to Pisa, Lucca, San Gimignano or Arezzo are easily achieved.

10 days
This option caters to most interests. After spending three days in Florence, move on to Lucca for one night, pop into Pisa to visit the Piazza dei Miracoli the next morning, and then make your way to Pietrasanta or Volterra. Spend two nights in your choice of these lesser-known but alluring towns before heading to a beach on Elba or to the Chianti wine region for two days. End your trip with two nights in gloriously Gothic Siena.

Top Five Wine Tastings

➜ Vernaccia (p546) in San Gimignano

➜ Brunello (p551) in Montalcino

➜ Chianti in...you guessed it (p538)

➜ Vino Nobile (p554) in Montepulciano

➜ Vin Santo (p538) accompanied by *cantuccini* (crunchy, almond-studded biscuits)

TASTE SENSATIONS

Tuscan cuisine is justly famous. Nosh on delicacies including white truffles from San Miniato, Chianina beef (best sampled in a *bistecca alla fiorentina*), *cinghiale* (local wild boar), porcini mushrooms and chewy *ricciarelli* (almond biscuits).

Blogs to Excite

➜ www.arttrav.com

➜ www.freyasflorence. com/blog

➜ http://tuscantraveler.com

Advance Planning

➜ Book tickets/ accommodation for Siena's Palio one year in advance!

➜ Buy tickets for Pisa's Leaning Tower and Florence's Galleria degli Uffizi and Galleria dell'Accademia between 12 and 20 days before your visit.

➜ Tuscany's key music festivals – Maggio Musicale Fiorentino in Florence (April to June) Settimana Musicale Senese (July) and Estate Musicale Chigiana in Siena (July and August) – require advance ticket purchase.

Resources

➜ **Firenze Turismo** (www. firenzeturismo.it)

➜ **Terre di Siena** (www. terresiena.it)

➜ **Turismo in Toscana** (www.turismo.intoscana.it)

FLORENCE & TUSCANY

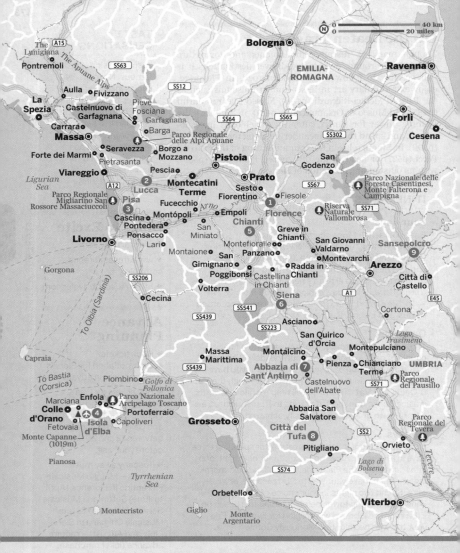

Florence & Tuscany Highlights

1 Discovering Renaissance treasures in Florence's **Uffizi Gallery** (p477).

2 Pedalling and picnicing atop the Renaissance-era city wall in **Lucca** (p515).

3 Scaling Pisa's iconic **Leaning Tower** (p510) at sunset.

4 Setting sail for the classic Mediterranean island of **Elba** (p524).

5 Vineyard-hopping through the world-famous region of **Chianti** (p538).

6 Gorging on Gothic architecture and almond biscuits in **Siena** (p527).

7 Listening to Gregorian chants in the **Abbazia di Sant'Antimo** (p552).

8 Exploring the fascinating Etruscan heritage of the **Città del Tufa** (p557).

9 Admiring Piero della Francesca's paintings in his birthplace, **Sansepolcro** (p562).

FLORENCE

POP 357,300

Return time and again and you still won't see it all. Though surprisingly small, Florence (Firenze) is packed with attractions, laden with history and famous for its robust cuisine and genteel charm. Towers and palaces evoke a thousand tales of its medieval past; designer boutiques and artisan workshops stud its streets; and there's a buzzing cafe, restaurant and bar scene. Cradle of the Renaissance and home of Machiavelli, Michelangelo and the Medici, this is a magnetic, romantic and – above all – memorable city.

History

Controversy continues over who founded Florence. The most commonly accepted story tells us that Emperor Julius Caesar founded Florentia around 59 BC, but archaeological evidence suggests the presence of an earlier village founded by the Etruscans of Fiesole around 200 BC.

In the 12th century Florence became a free *comune* (town council), ruled by 12 *priori* (consuls) assisted by the Consiglio di Cento (Council of One Hundred), drawn mainly from the merchant class. Agitation among different factions led to the appointment of a foreign governing *podestà* (magistrate) in 1207.

The first conflicts between two of the factions, the pro-papal Guelphs (Guelfi) and the pro-imperial Ghibellines (Ghibellini), started in the mid-13th century, with power passing between the two groups for almost a century.

A plague in 1348 halved the city's population and in 1378 the government was rocked by a revolt by the city's *ciompi* (wool carders), who sought a greater voice in the *comune*'s decision-making processes. Though initially successful, the major and minor guilds soon closed ranks to re-establish the old order, with members of the Medici family, bankers to the pope, taking a major role in the city's government.

In 1434, Cosimo il Vecchio (the Elder, also known simply as Cosimo de' Medici, 1389–1464) became Florence's de facto ruler. His eye for talent saw a constellation of artists such as Alberti, Brunelleschi, Lorenzo Ghiberti, Donatello, Fra' Angelico and Fra' Filippo Lippi flourish.

The rule of Lorenzo il Magnifico (1469–92), Cosimo's grandson, ushered in the most glorious period of Florentine civilisation and of the Italian Renaissance. His court fostered a flowering of art, music and poetry, turning Florence into Italy's cultural capital. Not long before Lorenzo's death, the Medici bank failed and the family was driven out of Florence. The city fell under the control of Savonarola, a Dominican monk who led a puritanical republic, burning the city's wealth on his 'bonfire of vanities'. His lure proved to be short-lived, and after falling from favour he was tried as a heretic and executed in 1498.

After the Spanish defeated Florence in 1512, Emperor Charles V married his daughter to Lorenzo's great-grandson Alessandro de' Medici, whom he made duke of Florence in 1530. Seven years later Cosimo I, one of the last truly capable Medici rulers, took charge, becoming grand duke of Tuscany after Siena fell to Florence in 1569.

In 1737 the grand duchy of Tuscany passed to the French House of Lorraine, which retained control, apart from a brief interruption under Napoleon, until it was incorporated into the Kingdom of Italy in 1860. Florence briefly became the national capital but Rome assumed the mantle permanently in 1870.

The city was severely damaged during WWII and was ravaged by floods in 1966. In 1993 the Mafia exploded a massive car bomb, destroying part of the Uffizi Gallery. A much-anticipated renovation and expansion of the gallery is currently underway.

> ## ℹ MUSEUM PASSES
>
> The **Firenze Card** (www.firenzecard. it; €72) is valid for 72 hours and covers admission to 72 museums, villas and gardens in Florence as well as unlimited use of public transport. Buy it online (and collect upon arrival in Florence) or in Florence at tourist offices, the ticketing desks of the Uffizi (Entrance 2), Palazzo Pitti, Palazzo Vecchio, Museo del Bargello, Cappella Brancacci, Basilica e Chiostri Monumentali di Santa Maria Novella and Giardini Bardini. If you're an EU citizen your card also covers under-18s travelling with you.
>
> A **combined ticket** to the *duomo*'s dome, campanile, crypt, the Battistero di San Giovanni and the Museo dell'Opera di Santa Maria del Fiore costs €10.

Florence

Map showing Florence with labels: Via Benedetto Marcello, Stazione Porta al Prato, Viale Fratelli Rosselli, Viale Spartaco Lavagnini, Viale Giacomo Matteotti, Viale dei Mille, Stazione Campo di Marte, See San Lorenzo & San Marco Map (p487), Stazione di Santa Maria Novella, See The Duomo & Santa Maria Novella Map (p478), Lungarno Amerigo Vespucci, Lungarno Guicciardini, Via Viencenzo Giberti, See Santa Croce Map (p489), Lungarno delle Grazie, Lungarno del Tempio, Arno, Lungarno Francesco Ferrucci, Viale Francesco Petrarca, See Oltrarno & Boboli Map (p490)

◉ Sights

Florence's major sights lie in the geographic, historic and cultural heart of the city – the tight grid of streets between Piazza del Duomo and Piazza della Signoria.

◉ Piazza del Duomo

★ Duomo   CATHEDRAL
(Cattedrale di Santa Maria del Fiore or St Mary of the Flower; Map p478; www.operaduomo.firenze. it; Piazza del Duomo; Duomo free admission, combined ticket to dome, baptistry, campanile, crypt and museum adult/child under 14 €10/free; ⊙ 10am-5pm Mon-Wed & Fri, to 4pm Thu, to 4.45pm Sat, 1.30-4.45pm Sun; dome 8.30am-6.20pm Mon-Fri, to 5pm Sat; crypt 10am-5pm Mon-Fri, to 4pm Thu, to 4.45pm Sat; campanile 8.30am-6.50pm) The city's most iconic landmark is among Italy's 'Big Three' (with Pisa's Leaning Tower and Rome's Colosseum). Its red-tiled dome, graceful *campanile* (bell tower) and breathtaking pink, white and green marble facade have the wow factor in spades.

Begun in 1296 to a design by Sienese architect Arnolfo di Cambio, the *duomo*'s construction took almost 150 years. Its neo-Gothic facade was designed in the 19th century by architect Emilio de Fabris to replace the original, which was torn down in the 16th century.

After the visual wham-bam of the facade and dome, the sparse decoration of the cathedral's vast interior, 155m long and 90m wide, comes as a surprise – most of its artistic treasures have been removed over centuries according to the vagaries of ecclesiastical fashion, and many are now on show in the Museo dell'Opera di Santa Maria del Fiore.

Scaling the 463 steep stone steps to the famous dome, built between 1420 and 1436 to a design by Filippo Brunelleschi, is highly recommended but should be avoided by those who are unfit or claustrophobic. As you climb, snapshots of Florence can be spied through small windows. The final leg – a straight somewhat hazardous flight up the curve of the inner dome – rewards with an unforgettable 360-degree panorama of one of Europe's most beautiful cities.

Equally physical is the 414-step climb up the 85m-high campanile, which was designed by Giotto.

Battistero di San Giovanni   BAPTISTRY
(Map p478; Piazza di San Giovanni; combined ticket to dome, baptistry, campanile, crypt and museum adult/child under 14 €10/free; ⊙ 11.15am-6.30pm Mon-Sat, 8.30am-1.30pm Sun & 1st Sat of month)

Lorenzo Ghiberti designed the famous gilded bronze bas-reliefs that originally adorned the eastern doors of Florence's octagonal 11th-century Romanesque baptistry (what you see now are copies, with the originals on show in the Museo dell'Opera di Santa Maria del Fiore). Dante counts among the many famous Florentines who were dunked in its baptismal font. Buy tickets from the office opposite the northern doors at Via de' Cerretani 7.

Grande Museo del Duomo   MUSEUM
(Cathedral Museum; Map p478; www.operaduomo.firenze.it; Piazza del Duomo 9; combined ticket to dome, baptistry, campanile, crypt and museum adult/child under 14 €10/free; ⊙9am-6.50pm Mon-Sat, 9am-1.05pm Sun) Surprisingly overlooked by the crowds, this impressive museum – currently being massively reorganised and enlarged – safeguards sacred and liturgical treasures that once adorned the *duomo, battistero* and *campanile*. Make a beeline for the glass-topped courtyard with its awe-inspiring showpiece encased in glass, Ghiberti's original 15th-century masterpiece, the *Porta del Paradiso* (Gate of Paradise) designed for the eastern entrance of the *battistero*. Afterwards, search out Michelangelo's *Pietà*, intended for his own tomb.

⊙ Piazza della Signoria & Around

Crammed with Renaissance sculptures and presided over by the magnificent Palazzo Vecchio, this photogenic piazza has been the hub of local life for centuries. Florentines flock here to take a *passeggiata* (evening stroll), breaking for a coffee, hot chocolate or an *aperitivo* at the city's most famous cafe, Caffè Rivoire (p502).

It was here that preacher-leader Savonarola set light to the city's art – books, paintings, musical instruments, mirrors, fine clothes and so on – on his famous bonfire of vanities in 1497. A year later the Dominican monk was burnt as a heretic on the same spot, marked by a bronze plaque in front of Ammannati's monumental but ugly **Fontana di Nettuno** (Neptune Fountain; Map p478). Other sculptures in the piazza include Giambologna's equestrian statue of **Cosimo I** (Map p478) and the much-photographed copy of Michelangelo's *David* that has guarded the western entrance to the Palazzo Vecchio

since 1910 (the original stood here until 1873 but is now in the Galleria dell'Accademia).

At the southern end of the piazza is the 14th-century **Loggia dei Lanzi** (Map p478) **FREE**, an open-air museum where works such as Giambologna's *Rape of the Sabine Women* (c 1583), Benvenuto Cellini's bronze *Perseus* (1554) and Agnolo Gaddi's *Seven Virtues* (1384–89) are displayed. The *loggia* owes its name to the Lanzichenecchi (Swiss bodyguards) of Cosimo I, who were stationed here.

★Palazzo Vecchio   MUSEUM
(Map p478; ☑055 276 82 24; www.musefirenze.it; Piazza della Signoria; museum adult/reduced/child €10/8/free, tower €6.50, guided tours €2; ⊙museum 9am-midnight Fri-Wed, 9am-2pm Thu summer, 9am-7pm Fri-Wed, 9am-2pm Thu winter; tower 9am-8.30pm Fri-Wed, 9am-1.30pm Thu summer, 10am-4.30pm Fri-Wed, 10am-1.30pm Thu winter) Florence's 'Old Palace' was designed by Arnolfo di Cambio between 1298 and 1314 for the *signoria* (highest level of city government). Highlights include the view from the top of the *palazzo*'s 94m-high **Torre d'Arnolfo**, and the decoration of the **Salone dei Cinquecento**, a huge room created within the original building in the 1490s for the Consiglio dei Cinquecento (Council of 500) that ruled Florence during the late 15th century. It's home to Michelangelo's sculpture *Genio della Vittoria* (Genius of Victory).

In 1540 Cosimo I made the palace his ducal residence and centre of government, commissioning Vasari to renovate and decorate the interior. Not too long after the renovation, he and his wife Eleonora di Toledo decided that the newly renovated apartments were too uncomfortable for their large family to live in year-round, and he purchased Palazzo Pitti as a summer residence. After the death of Eleonora and their sons Giovanni and Garzia from malaria in 1562, Cosimo moved the rest of his family to Palazzo Pitti permanently. At this time, the building became known as Palazzo Vecchio. It remains the seat of the city's power, home to the mayor's office and the municipal council. The best way to discover this den of political drama and intrigue is by thematic guided tour (book ahead).

★Galleria degli Uffizi   MUSEUM
(Uffizi Gallery; Map p478; www.uffizi.firenze.it; Piazzale degli Uffizi 6; adult/reduced €6.50/3.25, incl temporary exhibition €11/5.50; ⊙8.15am-6.05pm Tue-Sun) Housed inside the Palazzo degli

The Duomo & Santa Maria Novella

Piazza della Stazione
Via de' Panzani
7

Via Valfonda
Via Sant'Antonino
Piazza dell'Unità Italiana
Via del Melarancio

Via Faenza
Via del Canto de' Nelli
Piazza San Lorenzo
Via dell'Ariento
68
10
6
Piazza Madonna degli Aldobrandini
9

Via del Giglio
Via de' Panzani
Via dell'Alloro
Via de' Conti
Via F. Zanetti

Piazza di Santa Maria Novella
29
Via de' Banchi
Via de' Rondinelli
Piazza di Santa Maria Maggiore
Via de' Cerretani
30
53
Piazza del Cavallari
Piazza dell'Olio

Via della Scala
Via de' Fossi
Via del Trabbio
Piazza degli Antinori
Via degli Antinori
Via degli Agli
Via de' Vecchietti
Via dei Pecori
Via de' Brunelleschi
Via Roma

Via Palazzuolo
Piazza degli Ottaviani
Via del Sole
Via delle Belle Donne
Via de' Giaconini
Via de' Corsi
Via dei Pescioni
Via del Campidoglio
50
54

Via de' Fossi
Via del Moro
Piazza San Pancrazio
63
Via della Spada
17
45
57
33
20
Via degli Strozzi
Piazza della Repubblica

Via del Parchetti
40
43
65
Via della Vigna Nuova
19
56
Via degli Strozzi
Piazza Strozzi
Via de' Sassetti
Via Anselmi

Piazza de' Rucellai
67
Via del Purgatorio
Via dell'Inferno
Via de' Tornabuoni
31
62
23
Via de' Lamberti
Via Calimala

Via Parioncino
Via del Parione
44
Piazza de' Davanzati
Via Pellicceria

Lungarno Corsini
11 Piazza Santa Trinita
Via Porta Rossa
59
Via Porta Rossa
28 Il Porcellino
69
Via del Panico

26
25
Via del Fiordaliso
Via delle Terme

Piazza del Limbo
66
32
Borgo SS Apostoli
Via di Capaccio
Via Por Santa Maria

Lungarno Guicciardini
Ponte Santa Trinita
Lungarno degli Acciaiuoli
Vic dell'Oro
58
Piazza del Pesce
Via de' Girolami

Via di Santo Spirito
Piazza de' Frescobaldi
Arno
Piazza de' Santo Stefano

SANTO SPIRITO
Via Maggio
Palazzo Frescobaldi
Borgo San Jacopo
21

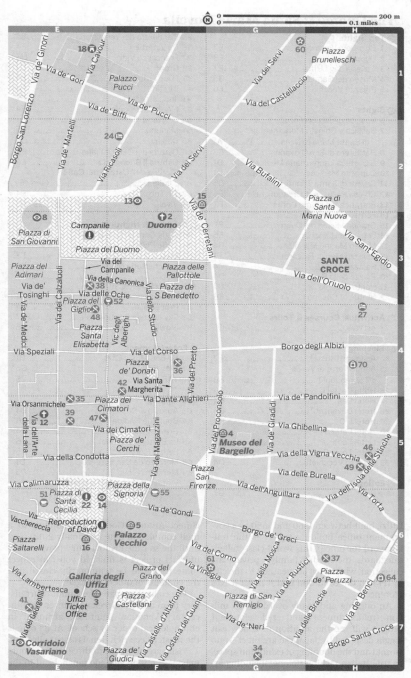

The Duomo & Santa Maria Novella

Uffizi, built between 1560 and 1580 as a government office building (*uffizi* is the Italian word for office), this world-class gallery safeguards the Medici family's private art collection, which was bequeathed to the city in 1743 on the condition that it never leaves Florence.

An ongoing and vastly overdue €65 million refurbishment and redevelopment project will see the addition of a new exit loggia designed by Japanese architect Arato Isozaki and the doubling of exhibition space. In true Italian fashion no one, including architect Antonio Godoli, will commit to a final completion date (originally 2013), and until the so-called Nuovi Uffizi (www.nuovi-uffizi.it) project is finished you can expect some rooms to be temporarily closed and the contents of others changed.

The collection spans the gamut of art history from ancient Greek sculptures to 18th-century Venetian paintings, arranged in chronological order by school. At its core is the masterpiece-rich Renaissance collection.

Visits are best kept to three or four hours max. When it all gets too much, head to the rooftop cafe (aka the terraced hanging garden where the Medici clan listened to music performances on the square below) for fresh air and fabulous views.

To the left of the staircase, room 2 highlights 13th-century art and is designed like a medieval chapel to reflect its fabulous contents: three large altarpieces by Tuscan masters Duccio di Buoninsegna, Cimabue and Giotto. These clearly reflect the transition from the Gothic to the nascent Renaissance style.

Room 3 moves into the 14th century, with a strong showing of Sienese works. The highlight is Simone Martini's shimmering *Annunciation* (1333), painted with Lippo Memmi and setting the Madonna in a sea of gold. Also of note is the *Madonna with Child and Saints* triptych (1340), by Pietro Lorenzetti.

Masters in 14th-century Florence paid as much attention to detail as their Sienese counterparts, as works in room 4 demonstrate: savour the realism of *San Reminio Pietà* (1360–65), by gifted Giotto pupil Giottino.

A concern for perspective was a hallmark of the early-15th-century Florentine school (room 7) that pioneered the Renaissance. A panel from Paolo Uccello's striking *Battle of San Romano* triptych (the other two are in the Louvre and London's National Gallery) shows the artist's efforts to create perspective with amusing effect as he directs the lances, horses and soldiers to a central disappearing point. The painting celebrates a Florentine victory over Siena in 1432.

In room 8, highlights include Piero della Francesca's famous profile portraits of the crooked-nosed, red-robed Duke and Duchess of Urbino (1472–75). Also in this room are works by Carmelite monk Fra' Filippo Lippi; search out his self-portrait as a podgy friar in *Coronation of the Virgin* (1439–47) and don't miss his later *Madonna and Child with Two Angels* (1460–65), an exquisite work that clearly influenced his pupil Sandro Botticelli.

The spectacular Sala del Botticelli, numbered 10 to 14 but in fact one large hall, is one of the Uffizi's most popular rooms. Of the 15 works by the Renaissance master, *Birth of Venus* (c 1485), *La Primavera* (Spring; c 1482), *Annunciation* (1489–90), *Adoration of the Magi* (1475) and *The Madonna of the Magnificat* (1483) are the best known.

Room 15 displays two early Florentine works by Leonardo da Vinci: an incomplete *Adoration of the Magi* (1481–82), drawn in red earth pigment; and his *Annunciation* (c 1475–80).

The naturalism inherent in the work of the Venetian school can be admired in room 28, where 11 Titians are displayed. Masterpieces include the sensual nude *Venus of Urbino* (1538), the seductive *Flora* (1515) and the striking portrait of *Eleonora Gonzaga, Duchess of Urbino* (1536–37).

In room 35, Michelangelo dazzles with the Doni Tondo, a depiction of the Holy Family that steals the High Renaissance show. The composition is unusual – Joseph holding an exuberant Jesus on his muscled mother's shoulder as she twists round to gaze at him – and the colours are as vibrant as when they were first applied in 1506–08.

Downstairs, the Sala di Caravaggio showcases three works by the phenomenally talented but criminally inclined painter.

Chiesa e Museo di Orsanmichele

CHURCH, MUSEUM

(Map p478; Via dell'Arte della Lana; ⊙ church 10am-5pm, museum 10am-5pm Mon) **FREE** This unusual church was created in the 14th century when the arcades of a grain market dating back to 1290 were walled in and two storeys were added. Its interior features a splendid Gothic tabernacle by Andrea Orcagna.

The building's exterior is exquisitely decorated with niches and tabernacles bearing statues representing the patron saints of Florence's many guilds. These were commissioned in the 15th and 16th centuries after the *signoria* ordered the city's guilds to finance the church's decoration, and they represent the work of some of the greatest Renaissance artists. These days, copies adorn the building's exterior – the originals are beautifully displayed in the church's little-known museum two floors above the church, which is open only on Mondays.

★ Museo del Bargello

ART MUSEUM

(Map p478; www.polomuseale.firenze.it; Via del Proconsolo 4; adult/reduced €4/2, temporary exhibitions €6/3; ⊙ 8.15am-4.20pm Tue-Sun & 1st & 3rd Mon of month, to 2pm winter) It was behind the stark exterior of Palazzo del Bargello, Florence's earliest public building, that the *podestà* meted out justice from the late 13th century until 1502. Today the building safeguards Italy's most comprehensive collection of Tuscan Renaissance sculpture.

The Uffizi

JOURNEY INTO THE RENAISSANCE

Navigating the Uffizi's main art collection, chronologically arranged in 45 rooms on one floor, is straightforward; knowing which of the 1500-odd masterpieces to view before gallery fatigue strikes is not. Swap coat and bag (travel light) for floor plan and audioguide on the ground floor, then meet 16th-century Tuscany head-on with a walk up the *palazzo's* magnificent bust-lined staircase (skip the lift – the Uffizi is as much about masterly architecture as art).

Allow four hours for this journey into the High Renaissance. At the top of the staircase, 2nd floor, show your ticket, turn left and pause to admire the full length of the first corridor sweeping south towards the Arno river. Then duck left into room 2 to witness first steps in Tuscan art – shimmering altarpieces by **Giotto 1** et al. Journey through medieval art to room 8 and **Piero della Francesca's 2** impossibly famous portrait, then break in the corridor with playful **ceiling art 3**. After Renaissance heavyweights **Botticelli 4** and **da Vinci 5**, meander past the Tribuna (potential detour) and enjoy the daylight streaming in through the vast windows and panorama of the **riverside second corridor 6**. Lap up soul-stirring views of the Arno, crossed by Ponte Vecchio and its echo of four bridges drifting towards the Apuane Alps on the horizon. Then saunter into the third corridor, pausing between rooms 25 and 34 to ponder the entrance to the enigmatic Vasari Corridor. End on a high with High Renaissance maestros **Michelangelo 7** and **Raphael 8**.

Portraits of the Duke & Duchess of Urbino
Room 8
Revel in realism's voyage with these uncompromising, warts-and-all portraits (1472–75) by Piero della Francesca. No larger than A3 size, they originally slotted into a portable, hinged frame that folded like a book.

The Ognissanti Madonna
Room 2
Draw breath at the shy blush and curvaceous breast of Giotto's humanised Virgin (*Maestà*; 1310) – so feminine compared with those of Duccio and Cimabue painted just 25 years before.

Start of Vasari Corridor (linking the Palazzo Vecchio with the Uffizi and Palazzo Pitti)

Entrance to 2nd Floor Gallery

Palazzo Vecchio

Piazza della Signoria

Grotesque Ceiling Frescoes
First Corridor
Take time to study the make-believe monsters and most unexpected of burlesques (spot the arrow-shooting satyr outside room 15) waltzing across this eastern corridor's fabulous frescoed ceiling (1581).

IMAGE REPRODUCED WITH THE PERMISSION OF MINISTERO PER I BENI E LE ATTIVITÀ CULTURALI

ALINARI ARCHIVES, FLORENCE ©

PIERO DELLA FRANCESCA/GETTY IMAGES ©

The Genius of Botticelli
Room 10–14

The miniature form of *The Discovery of the Body of Holofernes* (c 1470) makes Botticelli's early Renaissance masterpiece all the more impressive. Don't miss the artist watching you in *Adoration of the Magi* (1475), left of the exit.

View of the Arno

Indulge in intoxicating city views from this short glassed-in corridor – an architectural masterpiece. Near the top of the hill, spot one of 73 outer towers built to defend Florence and its 15 city gates below.

Second Corridor

Tribuna

First Corridor

6

Arno River

5

4

7

8

2

3

1

Tribuna

No room in the Uffizi is so tiny or so exquisite. It was created in 1851 as a 'treasure chest' for Grand Duke Francesco and in the days of the Grand Tour, the Medici Venus here was a tour highlight.

Entrance to Vasari Corridor

Third Corridor

Doni Tondo
Room 35

The creator of *David*, Michelangelo, was essentially a sculptor and no painting expresses this better than *Doni Tondo* (1506–08). Mary's muscular arms against a backdrop of curvaceous nudes are practically 3D in their shapeliness.

Annunciation
Room 15

Admire the exquisite portrayal of the Tuscan landscape in this painting (c 1472), one of few by Leonardo da Vinci to remain in Florence.

❶ CUT THE QUEUE: PRE-BOOKED TICKETS

In July, August and other busy periods such as Easter, long queues are a fact of life at Florence's key museums – if you haven't pre-booked your ticket you could well end up standing in line for four hours or so.

For a fee of €3 per ticket (€4 for the Uffizi and Galleria dell'Accademia), tickets to nine *musei statali* (state museums) including the Uffizi, Galleria dell'Accademia (where *David* lives), Palazzo Pitti, Museo del Bargello and the Cappelle Medicee can be reserved. In reality, the only museums where pre-booking is recommended are the Uffizi and Accademia – to organise your ticket, call **Firenze Musei** (Florence Museums; ✆ 055 29 48 83; www.firenzemusei.it; ☺ telephone booking line 8.30am-6.30pm Mon-Fri, to 12.30pm Sat) or visit its website, or go to the ticketing desk at the rear of Chiesa di Orsanmichele or at every state museum in the city except the Accademia (including the Uffizi, Bargello, Pitti Palace and Museo di San Marco).

At the Uffizi, signs point pre-booked-ticket holders to the building opposite the gallery where tickets can be collected; once you've got the ticket you go to Door 1 of the museum (for pre-booked tickets only) and queue again to enter the gallery. It's annoying, but you'll still save hours of queuing time overall.

Many hotels in Florence also pre-book museum tickets for guests.

Crowds clamour to see *David* in the Galleria dell'Accademia but few rush to see his creator's early works, many of which are displayed in the Bargello's downstairs **Sala di Michelangelo**. The artist was just 21 when a cardinal commissioned him to create the drunken grape-adorned *Bacchus* (1496–97). Other Michelangelo works to look out for here include the marble bust of Brutus (c 1539–40), the David/Apollo from 1530–32 and the large, uncompleted roundel of the *Madonna and Child with the Infant St John* (1503–05), aka the Tondo Pitti.

On the 1st floor, to the right of the staircase, is the **Sala di Donatello** where two versions of David, a favourite subject for sculptors, are displayed. Donatello fashioned his slender, youthful dressed image in marble in 1408 and his fabled bronze between 1440 and 1450. The latter is extraordinary – the more so when you consider it was the first freestanding naked statue to be sculpted since classical times.

The 2nd floor moves into the 16th century with a superb collection of terracotta pieces by the prolific della Robbia family.

Museo Galileo
SCIENCE MUSEUM

(Map p490; ✆ 055 26 53 11; www.museogalileo.it; Piazza dei Giudici 1; adult/reduced/family €9/5.50/22; ☺ 9.30am-5.30pm Wed-Mon, 9.30am-12.30pm Tue) On the river next to the Uffizi in 12th-century Palazzo Castellani (look for the sundial telling the time on the pavement outside) is this state-of-the-art science museum, named after the great Pisa-born scientist who was invited by the Medici court to Florence in 1610.

A visit will unravel a mesmerising curiosity box of astronomical and mathematical treasures (think telescopes, beautiful painted globes, barometers, watches, clocks and so on) collected by Cosimo I and other Medicis from 1562 and, later, by the Lorraine dynasty. Allow plenty of time for the interactive area where various hands-on exhibits allow visitors to discover first-hand how and why some of the historic instruments displayed in the museum actually work.

◉ Around Piazza della Repubblica

Piazza della Repubblica
PIAZZA

(Map p478) The site of a Roman forum and heart of medieval Florence, this busy civic space was created in the 1880s as part of a controversial plan of 'civic improvements' involving the demolition of the old market, Jewish ghetto and slums, and the relocation of nearly 6000 residents. These days it's best known for its concentration of historic cafes.

Palazzo Strozzi
ART GALLERY

(Map p478; www.palazzostrozzi.org; Via de' Tornabuoni; variable admission prices; ☺ 10am-8pm Tue-Sun, to 11pm Thu) This 15th-century *palazzo* is one of Florence's most impressive Renaissance mansions. It was built for wealthy merchant Filippo Strozzi, one of the Medicis' major political and commercial rivals, and now hosts some of the city's most exciting art exhibitions. The contemporary art in its basement Strozzini gallery (free admission after 6pm Thu) and imposing internal courtyard are equally alluring.

There's always a buzz about this place, with young Florentines congregating in the courtyard Renaissance Café (p502) (run by Florentine designer Roberto Cavalli, no less) – one of the best spots in the city to pick up free wi-fi.

Museo Marino Marini ART GALLERY
(Map p478; Piazza San Pancrazio 1; adult/reduced €4/2; ☉10am-5pm Wed-Sat & Mon) Deconsecrated in the 19th century, the Chiesa di San Pancrazio is home to this small art museum displaying sculptures, portraits and drawings by the Pistoia-born sculptor Marino Marini (1901–80). But what really stuns is the superbly restored **Cappella Rucellai** and the tiny scale copy of Christ's Holy Sepulchre in Jerusalem – a Renaissance gem by Leon Battista Alberti – that it contains.

⊙ Santa Maria Novella

Basilica e Chiostri Monumentali di Santa Maria Novella CHURCH, CLOISTERS
(Map p478; www.chiesasantamarianovella.it; Piazza di Santa Maria Novella 18; adult/reduced €5/3; ☉9am-5.30pm Mon-Thu, 11am-5.30pm Fri, 9am-5pm Sat, 1-5pm Sun) This monumental complex, fronted by the green-and-white marble facade of the 13th- to 15th-century **Basilica di Santa Maria di Novella**, includes romantic church cloisters and a stunning frescoed chapel. The basilica itself is a treasure chest of artistic masterpieces, climaxing with a series of frescoes by Domenico Ghirlandaio. Allow at least a couple of hours to take it all in.

As you enter the basilica, look straight ahead to see Masaccio's superb fresco *Trinity* (1424–25), one of the first artworks to use the then newly discovered techniques of perspective and proportion. Close by, hanging in the central nave, is a luminous painted *Crucifix* by Giotto (c 1290).

The first chapel to the right of the altar, the **Cappella di Filippo Strozzi**, features spirited late-15th-century frescoes by Filippino Lippi (son of Fra' Filippo Lippi) depicting the lives of St John the Evangelist and St Philip the Apostle.

Behind the main altar itself are the highlights of the interior – Domenico Ghirlandaio's series of frescoes in the **Cappella Maggiore**. Relating the life of the Virgin Mary, these vibrant frescoes were painted between 1485 and 1490 and are notable for their depiction of Florentine life during the Renaissance. They feature portraits of Ghirlandaio's contemporaries and members of the Tornabuoni family, who commissioned them.

To the far left of the altar, up a short flight of stairs, is the **Cappella Strozzi di Mantova**, covered in wonderful 14th-century frescoes by Niccolò di Tommaso and Nardo di Cione. The fine altarpiece (1354–57) here was painted by the latter's brother Andrea, better known as Andrea Orcagna.

From the church, walk through a side door into the serenely beautiful **Chiostro Verde** (Green Cloister; 1332–62), part of the vast monastical complex occupied by Dominican friars who arrived in Florence in 1219 and settled in Santa Maria Novella two years later. On its north side is the spectacular **Cappellone degli Spagnoli** (Spanish Chapel), originally the friars' chapter house and given its current name in 1566 when it was used by the Spanish colony in Florence. The tiny chapel is covered in extraordinary frescoes (c 1365–67) by Andrea di Bonaiuto.

There are two entrances to the Santa Maria Novella complex: the main entrance to the basilica or through the tourist office opposite the train station on Via de' Partzani. Firenze Card holders are obliged to use the latter.

Chiesa di Santa Trìnita CHURCH
(Map p478; Piazza Santa Trìnita; ☉8am-noon & 4-5.45pm Mon-Sat, 8-10.45am & 4-7pm Sun) **FREE** Built in Gothic style and later given a Mannerist facade, this 14th-century church shelters some of the city's finest frescoes, including Lorenzo Monaco's *Annunciation* (1422) in the **Cappella Salimbenes/Bartholini** and eye-catching frescoes by Ghirlandaio depicting the life of St Francis of Assisi in the **Cappella Sassetti**, to the right of the altar. The latter were painted between 1483 and 1485, and feature portraits of illustrious Florentines of the time.

⊙ San Lorenzo

Basilica di San Lorenzo CHURCH
(Map p478; Piazza San Lorenzo; admission €4.50, with Biblioteca Medicea Laurenziana €7; ☉10am-5.30pm Mon-Sat, plus 1.30-5pm Sun Mar-Oct) In 1425 Cosimo the Elder, who lived nearby,

commissioned Brunelleschi to rebuild the original 4th-century basilica on this site. The new building would become the Medici parish church and mausoleum.

Considered one of the most harmonious examples of Renaissance architecture, the basilica has never been finished. Michelangelo was commissioned to design the facade in 1518 but his design in white Carrara marble was never executed, hence the building's rough unfinished appearance.

In the austere interior, columns of pietra serena (soft grey stone) crowned with Corinthian capitals separate the nave from the two aisles. Donatello, who was still sculpting the two bronze pulpits (1460–67) adorned with panels of the Crucifixion when he died, is buried in the chapel featuring Fra' Filippo Lippi's *Annunciation* (c 1450). Left of the altar is the Sagrestia Vecchia (Old Sacristy), designed by Brunelleschi and decorated in the main by Donatello.

Biblioteca Medicea Laurenziana   LIBRARY
(Medici Library; Map p478; www.bml.firenze.sbn.it; Piazza San Lorenzo 9; admission €3, incl basilica €7; ⊙ 9.30am-1.30pm Mon-Fri) Beyond the basilica ticket office lie peaceful cloisters framing a pretty garden with buxom orange trees. Stairs lead up to the loggia and the Biblioteca Laurenziana Medicea, commissioned by Giulio de' Medici (Pope Clement VII) in 1524 to house the extensive Medici library. The extraordinary staircase in the vestibule, intended as a 'dark prelude' to the magnificent *Sala di Lettura* (Reading Room), was designed by Michelangelo.

Cappelle Medicee   MAUSOLEUM
(Map p478; ☑ 055 294 883; www.polomuseale. firenze.it; Piazza Madonna degli Aldobrandini; adult/ reduced €6/3; ⊙ 8.15am-1.20pm, closed 2nd & 4th Sun & 1st, 3rd & 5th Mon of month) Nowhere is the Medici conceit expressed so explicitly as in their mausoleum, the Medician Chapels. Sumptuously adorned with granite, marble, semiprecious stones and some of Michelangelo's most beautiful sculptures, it is the burial place of 49 members of the dynasty.

Francesco I lies in the grandiose Cappella dei Principi (Princes' Chapel) alongside Ferdinando I and II and Cosimo I, II and III. Lorenzo il Magnifico is buried in the stark but graceful Sagrestia Nuova (New Sacristy), Michelangelo's first architectural work and a showcase for three of his most haunting sculptures: *Dawn and Dusk* on the sar-

cophagus of Lorenzo, Duke of Urbino; *Night and Day* on the sarcophagus of Lorenzo's son Giuliano; and *Madonna and Child,* on Lorenzo's tomb.

Palazzo Medici-Riccardi   PALACE
(Map p478; ☑ 055 276 03 40; www.palazzo-medici. it; Via Cavour 3; adult/reduced €7/4; ⊙ 9am-6.30pm Thu-Tue summer, to 5.30pm winter) Cosimo the Elder entrusted Michelozzo with the design of the family's townhouse in 1444. The result was this palace, a blueprint that influenced the construction of Florentine family residences such as Palazzo Pitti and Palazzo Strozzi for years to come. Inside, the upstairs Cappella dei Magi houses one of the supreme achievements of Renaissance painting and is an absolute must-see for art lovers.

The tiny chapel is covered in a series of wonderfully detailed and recently restored frescoes (c 1459–63) by Benozzo Gozzoli, a pupil of Fra' Angelico. His ostensible theme of Procession of the Magi to Bethlehem is but a slender pretext for portraying members of the Medici clan in their best light; try to spy Lorenzo il Magnifico and Cosimo the Elder in the crowd. Only 10 visitors are allowed in at a time; in high season reserve in advance at the palace ticket desk.

Mercato Centrale   MARKET
(Central Market; Map p487; Piazza del Mercato Centrale; ⊙ 7am-2pm Mon-Fri, to 5pm Sat) Housed in a 19th-century iron-and-glass structure, Florence's oldest and largest food market is noisy, smelly and full of wonderful fresh produce to cook and eat. For a snack while you're here, follow the stream of stallholders making their way to Da Nerbone (p499).

⊙ San Marco

★ **Galleria dell'Accademia**   ART GALLERY
(Map p487; www.polomuseale.firenze.it; Via Ricasoli 60; adult/reduced €6.50/3.25; ⊙ 8.15am-6.50pm Tue-Sun) A lengthy queue usually marks the door to this gallery, which was built to house one of the Renaissance's greatest masterpieces, Michelangelo's *David*. Fortunately, the world's best-known statue is well worth the wait.

Carved from a single block of marble, the statue of the nude warrior assumed its pedestal in front of Palazzo Vecchio on Piazza della Signoria in 1504, providing Florentines with a powerful emblem of their city's power, liberty and civic pride.

San Lorenzo & San Marco

San Lorenzo & San Marco

Michelangelo was also the master behind the unfinished *San Matteo* (St Matthew; 1504–08) and four *Prigioni* ('Prisoners' or 'Slaves'; 1521–30), also displayed in the gallery. Adjacent rooms contain paintings by Andrea Orcagna, Taddeo Gaddi, Domenico Ghirlandaio, Filippino Lippi and Sandro Botticelli.

★ **Museo di San Marco**   MUSEUM
(Map p487; www.polomuseale.firenze.it; Piazza San Marco 1; adult/reduced €4/2; ◷8.15am-1.20pm Mon-Fri, 8.15am-4.20pm Sat & Sun, closed 1st, 3rd & 5th Sun & 2nd & 4th Mon of month) At the heart of Florence's university area sits the Domenican Chiesa di San Marco and its adjoining 15th-century monastery where both gifted painter Fra' Angelico (c 1395–1455) and the sharp-tongued Savonarola piously served God. Today the monastery, which showcases the work of Fra' Angelico, is one of Florence's most spiritually uplifting museums.

Enter via Michelozzo's Cloister of Saint Antoninus (1440). Turn immediately right to enter the Sala dell'Ospizio (Pilgrims' Hospital) where Fra' Angelico's attention to perspective and the realistic portrayal of nature comes to life in a number of major paintings, including the *Deposition of Christ* (1432).

Giovanni Antonio Sogliani's fresco *The Miraculous Supper of St Domenic* (1536) dominates the former monks' refectory in the cloister; and Fra' Angelico's huge *Crucifixion and Saints* fresco (1441–42) decorates the former chapterhouse.

The museum's highlights are on the 1st floor. At the top of the stairs, Fra' Angelico's most famous work, *Annunciation* (c 1440), commands all eyes. Further on, the 44 monastic cells reveal snippets of many more fine religious reliefs by the Tuscan-born friar, who decorated the cells between 1440 and 1441 with deeply devotional frescoes to guide the meditation of his fellow friars. Among several masterpieces is the magnificent *Adoration of the Magi* in the cell used by Cosimo the Elder as a meditation retreat (Nos 38 to 39).

Contrasting with the pure beauty of these frescoes are the plain rooms that Savonarola called home from 1489. These house a portrait and a few personal items.

Piazza della Santissima Annunziata
PIAZZA

(Map p487) Giambologna's equestrian statue of Grand Duke Ferdinando I de' Medici commands the scene from the centre of this majestic square, dominated by the facades of **Chiesa della Santissima Annunziata** (Map p487) (1250) and the **Ospedale degli Innocenti** (Hospital of the Innocents; Map p487; Piazza della SS Annunziata 12), Europe's first orphanage (founded 1421).

Look up to admire the hospital's classically influenced portico, designed by Brunelleschi and famously decorated with terracotta medallions of babies in swaddling clothes by Andrea della Robbia (1435–1525). At the north end of the portico, the false door surrounded by railings was once a revolving door where unwanted children were left. You can pay €1 to visit its lovely courtyard (open 10am to 3.30pm Monday to Saturday, and to 1.30pm Sunday), but the interior is closed until April 2015 for major restoration works; it will reopen as a Museum of Childhood.

⊙ Santa Croce

Basilica di Santa Croce
CHURCH

(Map p489; www.santacroceopera.it; Piazza di Santa Croce; adult/reduced €6/4, family ticket €12; ⊙9.30am-5pm Mon-Sat, 2-5pm Sun) When Lucy Honeychurch, the hero of EM Forster's *A Room with a View*, is stranded in Santa Croce without a Baedeker, she looks around and wonders why the basilica is thought to be such an important building. After all, doesn't it look just like a barn? On entering, many visitors to this massive Franciscan church share the same sentiment – the austere interior is indeed a shock after the magnificent neo-gothic facade enlivened by varying shades of coloured marble.

Although most visitors come to see the tombs of famous Florentines buried here –

including Michelangelo, Galileo, Ghiberti and Machiavelli – it's the frescoes by Giotto and his school in the chapels to the right of the altar that are the real highlights. Some of these are much better preserved than others; Giotto's murals in the Cappella Peruzzi are in particularly poor condition.

From the transept chapels a doorway designed by Michelozzo leads into a corridor, off which is the **Sagrestia**, an enchanting 14th-century room dominated on the left by Taddeo Gaddi's fresco of the Crucifixion. There are also a few relics of St Francis on show, including his cowl and belt. Through the next room, the church bookshop, you can access the **Scuola del Cuoio**, a leather school where you can see bags being fashioned and buy the finished products.

The second of Santa Croce's two serene cloisters was designed by Brunelleschi just before his death in 1446. His unfinished **Cappella de' Pazzi** at the end of the first cloister is notable for its harmonious lines and restrained terracotta medallions of the Apostles by Luca della Robbia, and is a masterpiece of Renaissance architecture.

Located off the first cloister, the **Museo dell'Opera di Santa Croce** (admission incl basilica adult/concession €5/3) features a Crucifixion by Cimabue, restored to the best degree possible after flood damage in 1966, when more than 4m of water inundated the Santa Croce area. Other highlights include a wonderful terracotta bust of St Francis receiving the stigmata by the della Robbia workshop; and frescoes by Taddeo Gaddi, including *The Last Supper* (1333).

⊙ The Oltrarno

Literally 'beyond the Arno', the atmospheric Oltrarno takes in all of Florence south of the river.

Ponte Vecchio
BRIDGE

(Map p478; ⊡B) Florence's iconic bridge has twinkled with the glittering wares of jewellers ever since the 16th century, when Ferdinando I de' Medici ordered them here to replace the often malodorous presence of the town butchers, who had an unfortunate tendency to toss unwanted leftovers into the river.

The first documentation of a stone bridge here, at the narrowest crossing point along the entire length of the river, dates from 972. The Arno looks placid enough, but when it gets mean, it gets very mean. Floods in 1177

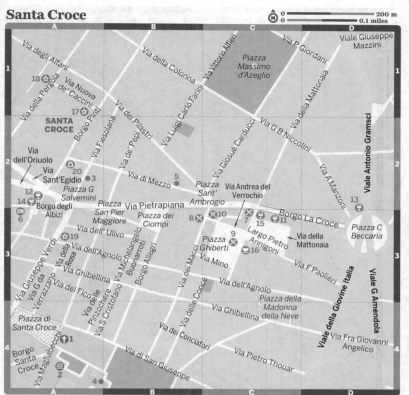

Santa Croce

N 0 ——— 200 m
0 ——— 0.1 miles

Santa Croce

◎ **Sights**
1 Basilica di Santa Croce A4
2 Museo dell'Opera di Santa Croce A4

➕ **Activities, Courses & Tours**
3 Florence by Bike A2
4 Scuola del Cuoio A4
5 Scuola di Arte Culinaria Cordon
   Bleu B2

🛏 **Sleeping**
6 Hotel Orchidea A3

🍴 **Eating**
7 Il Giova C3
8 Il Pizzaiuolo B3
   Il Teatro del Sale .... (see 8)
9 Mercato di Sant'Ambrogio C3
   Pollini .... (see 10)

10 Trattoria Cibrèo C3

🍷 **Drinking & Nightlife**
11 Drogheria C3
12 Eby's Bar A2
13 Kitsch D2
14 Lion's Fountain A2
15 Monkey Bar C3
16 Nano Caffè C3

🎭 **Entertainment**
17 Jazz Club A1
18 Teatro della Pergola A1
19 Twice Club A3

🛍 **Shopping**
20 Mrs Macis A2

Oltrarno & Boboli

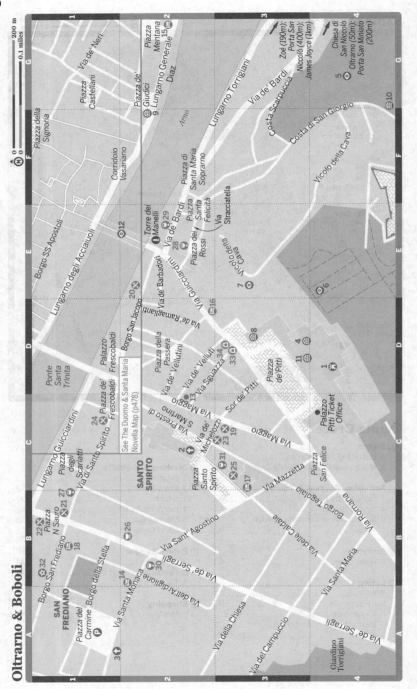

FLORENCE & TUSCANY FLORENCE

Oltrarno & Boboli

and 1333 destroyed the bridge, and in 1966 it came close to being destroyed again. The bridge as it now stands dates from 1345 and was the only one saved from destruction at the hands of the retreating Germans in 1944. What you see above the shops on the eastern side is the infamous **Corridoio Vasariano** (☎055 29 48 83; ⊙by guided tour) built rather oddly around – rather than straight through – the medieval **Torre dei Mannelli** at the bridge's southern end.

Palazzo Pitti   MUSEUM
(Map p490; www.polomuseale.firenze.it; Piazza dei Pitti; Ticket 1 adult/EU 18-25/EU child & senior €8.50/4.25/free, Ticket 2 €7/3.50/free, Ticket 3 €11.50/5.75/free; ⊙8.15am-6.05pm Tue-Sun) This vast palace was begun in 1458 for the Pitti family, rivals of the Medici. Cosimo I and Eleonora di Toledo acquired it in 1549 and it remained the official residence of Florence's rulers until 1919, when the Savoys gave it to the state.

The ground-floor **Museo degli Argenti** (Silver Museum; ⊙8.15am-6.05pm summer, shorter hours outside summer, closed 1st & last Mon of month) hosts temporary exhibitions in its elaborately frescoed audience chambers.

Raphaels and Rubens vie for centre stage in the enviable collection of 16th- to 18th-century art amassed by the Medici and Lorraine dukes in the 1st-floor **Galleria Palati-**

na (⊙8.15am-6.50pm Tue-Sun summer, shorter hrs winter). Highlights include Filippo Lippi's *Madonna and Child with Stories from the Life of St Anne* (aka the Tondo Bartolini; 1452–53) and Botticelli's *Madonna with Child and a Young Saint John the Baptist* (c 1490–95) in the Sala di Prometeo; Raphael's *Madonna of the Window* (1513–14) in the Sala di Ulisse; and Caravaggio's *Sleeping Cupid* (1608) in the Sala dell'Educazione di Giove.

Don't miss the Sala di Saturno, full of magnificent works by Raphael. The sentimental favourite, Tiberio Titi's charming

---

ℹ PALAZZO PITTI TICKETING

Ticketing for the palace complex and surrounding gardens is complicated. All three tickets are available from the office to the right of the palace entrance.

Ticket 1 Access to the Galleria Palatina, Appartamenti Reali and Galleria d'Arte Moderna.

Ticket 2 Access to the Galleria del Costume, Museo degli Argenti, Giardino di Boboli, Giardino Bardini and Museo delle Porcellane.

Ticket 3 Access to all sights; valid for three days.

portrait of the young Prince Leopoldo de' Medici, hangs in the Sala di Apollo and the Sala di Venere shines with Titian's *Portrait of a Lady* (c 1536).

Past the Sala di Venere are the **Appartamenti Reali** (Royal Apartments; ⊙8.15am-6.50pm Tue-Sun Feb-Dec), a series of rooms presented as they were c 1880–91, when they were occupied by members of the House of Savoy. The style and division of tasks assigned to each room is reminiscent of Spanish royal palaces, all heavily bedecked with drapes, silk and chandeliers.

Forget about Marini, Mertz or Clemente – the collection of the 2nd-floor **Galleria d'Arte Moderna** (Gallery of Modern Art; ⊙8.15am-6.50pm Tue-Sun summer, shorter hrs winter) is dominated by late-19th-century works by artists of the Florentine Macchiaioli school (the local equivalent of Impressionism).

Few visitors visit the **Galleria del Costume** (Costume Gallery; ⊙8.15am-6.05pm summer, shorter hours outside summer, closed 1st & last Mon of month), thus missing its fascinating, if somewhat macabre, display of the semi-decomposed burial clothes of Cosimo I, his wife Eleonora di Toledo and their son Don Garzia.

Giardino di Boboli   GARDENS

(Boboli Gardens; Map p490; Piazza Pitti; adult/reduced/child €7/3.50/free; ⊙8.15am-7.30pm summer, shorter hrs winter) The expansive gardens of the Pitti Palace were laid out in the mid-16th century to a design by architect Niccolò Pericoli, and are a prime example of a formal Tuscan garden. At the upper, southern limit, beyond the box-hedged rose garden and Museo delle Porcellane, there are fantastic views over the Florentine countryside.

The garden is blessed with plenty of statues and hidden paths. Other features include a rather neglected **Cypress Alley**, the walled **Giardino del Cavaliere** (Knights' Garden), and the **Isoletto**, a gorgeous ornamental pool.

By the garden exit, hundreds of seashells decorate the facade of **Grotta del Buontalenti** (⊙11am, 1pm, 3pm, 4pm & 5pm), a fanciful grotto by Giambologna. Peer inside to see a fleshy Venere (Venus) rising from the waves. The wall to the left of the grotto is the outer facade of the final leg of the Corridoio Vasariano (p491) linking the palace with the Uffizi.

Giardino Bardini   GARDENS

(Map p490; www.bardinipeyron.it; entrances at Via de' Bardi 1r & Costa di San Giorgio 2; adult/EU reduced €10/free, entry also included in Palazzo Pitti combined ticket 2 or 3; ⊙8.15am-7.30pm summer, shorter hrs winter) This tranquil retreat was named after art collector Stefano Bardini (1836–1922), who bought the villa in 1913 and restored its medieval garden. Smaller and more manicured than the Boboli, it has all the features of a quintessential Tuscan garden but is blessedly free of the crowds that can be found in its neighbour. Inside the villa, the **Museo Roberto Capucci** (www.bardinipeyron.it; Giardini Bardini; adult/reduced €8/6; ⊙10am-9pm Wed-Sun Apr-Oct) hosts a collection of Capucci-designed haute couture and temporary exhibitions.

A springtime stroll past the artificial grottos, orangery, marble statues and fountains is idyllic. Beds of azaleas, peonies and wisteria bloom in April and May, irises in June. The romantic **summer cafe** (open 10am to 6pm April to September) is set in a stone loggia overlooking the Florentine skyline and is a wonderful spot for a *panino* lunch, ice cream or afternoon tea.

Piazzale Michelangelo   VIEWPOINT

Turn your back on the bevy of ticky-tacky souvenir stalls flogging *David* statues and boxer shorts and take in the spectacular city panorama from this vast square, pierced by one of Florence's two *David* copies (sunset here is particularly dramatic). It's a 10-minute uphill walk along the serpentine road, paths and steps that scale the hillside from the Arno and Piazza Giuseppe Poggi; from Piazza San Niccolò walk uphill and bear left up the long flight of steps signposted Viale Michelangelo. Or take bus 13.

Basilica di San Miniato al Monte   CHURCH

(www.sanminiatoalmonte.it; Via Monte alle Croce; ⊙8am-7pm May-Oct, 8am-noon & 3-6pm Nov-Apr) Five minutes further uphill from Piazzale Michelangelo is this wonderful Romanesque church, dedicated to St Minius, an early-Christian martyr in Florence who is said to have flown to this spot after his death down in the town (or, if you want to believe an alternative version, walked up the hill head tucked underneath his arm).

The church dates to the early 11th century, although its typical Tuscan multicoloured marble facade was tacked on a couple of centuries later. Inside, 13th- to 15th-century frescoes adorn the south wall and intricate inlaid marble designs line the nave, leading to a fine Romanesque crypt. The sacristy in the southeast corner features frescoes by Spinello Arentino depicting the life of St Benedict. Slap-bang in the middle of the nave is the bijou **Cappella del Crocefisso**, to which Michelozzo, Agnolo Gaddi and Luca della Robbia all contributed.

Cappella Brancacci CHAPEL
(Map p490; ☑ 055 276 82 24; www.musefirenze.it; Piazza del Carmine 14; adult/reduced €6/4.50; ☺10am-4.30pm Wed-Sat & Mon, 1-4.30pm Sun) In the 18th century fire all but destroyed 13th-century **Basilica di Santa Maria del Carmine**, but the magnificent frescoes in its chapel, to the right of the church entrance, were miraculously spared. Visits are by guided tour (20 minutes, every 20 minutes), and advance reservations are recommended in season given that only 30 people at a time are allowed in.

This chapel is a treasure of paintings by Masolino da Panicale, Masaccio and Filippino Lippi. Masaccio's fresco cycle illustrating the life of St Peter is considered among his greatest works, representing a definitive break with Gothic art and a plunge into new worlds of expression in the early stages of the Renaissance. The *Expulsion of Adam and Eve from Paradise* and *The Tribute Money*, both on the left side of the chapel, are the highlights.

Basilica di Santo Spirito CHURCH
(Map p490; Piazza Santo Spirito; ☺8.30am-12.30pm & 4-5.30pm Thu-Tue) **FREE** The facade of this Brunelleschi church on Florence's most shabby-chic piazza is particularly striking in summer, when it forms an atmospheric backdrop to open-air concerts and a buzzing social scene. Inside, artworks include Domenico di Zanobi's *Madonna of the Relief* (1485) in the Cappella Velutti, in which the Madonna wards off a little red devil with a club, and Filippino Lippi's poorly lit *Madonna with Child and Saints* (1493–94) in the Cappella Nerli in the right transept.

Don't miss the door next to Capella Segni in the left aisle, which leads to the **sacristy**. Inside, you'll find a poignant wooden crucifix attributed by some experts to Michelangelo.

Courses

Scuola di Arte Culinaria Cordon Bleu COOKING
(Map p489; ☑ 055 234 54 68; www.cordonbleu-it.com; Via di Mezzo 55r) Serious cooking school for amateurs and professionals, with heaps of short-term, long-term and one-off courses.

Scuola del Cuoio LEATHER WORKING
(Map p489; ☑ 055 24 45 34; www.scuoladelcuoio.com; Via San Giuseppe 5r) Leather-working courses in a leather school created by Franciscan friars after WWII.

In Tavola COOKING
(Map p490; ☑ 055 21 76 72; www.intavola.org; Via dei Velluti 18r) Take your pick from dozens of carefully crafted courses for beginners and professionals: pizza and gelato, pasta making, easy Tuscan dinners etc.

Tours

City Sightseeing Firenze BUS TOUR
(Map p487; ☑ 055 29 04 51; www.firenze.city-sightseeing.it; Piazza della Stazione 1; adult 1/2/3 days €20/25/30) Explore Florence by red open-top bus, hopping on and off at 15 bus stops around the city. Tickets, sold by the driver, are valid for 24 hours.

★500 Touring Club VINTAGE CAR TOUR
(☑ 346 826 23 24; www.500touringclub.com; Via Gherardo Silvani 149a) Hook up with Florence's 500 Touring Club for a guided tour in a vintage motor – with you behind the wheel! Every car has a name in the fleet of vintage Fiat 500s from the 1960s (Giacomo is the playboy, Olivia the kind rebel and so on). Motoring tours are guided – hop in your car and follow the leader – and themed.

Families love the picnic trip, couples the wine-tasting. March to November tours need to be booked well in advance.

ArtViva WALKING TOUR
(Map p478; ☑ 055 264 50 33; www.italy.artviva.com; Via de' Sassetti 1; per person from €25) Marketed as the 'Original & Best', these excellent one- to three-hour city walks (from €25) are led by historians or art-history graduates; tours include the Uffizi, the Original David tour and an Evening Walk/Murder Mystery Tour. ArtViva also runs trips further afield to Chianti (wine tasting) and a Renaissance villa outside Florence (includes lunch and a swim).

Freya's Florence Tours
WALKING TOUR

(☑349 074 89 07; www.freyasflorence.com; per hr €70) Australian-born, Florence-based private tour guide; admission fees not included in guiding fee.

Faith Willinger - Lessons & Tours
CULINARY TOUR

(www.faithwillinger.com) Food-lovers' walking tour, cooking classes, market stroll and much more, by American-born, Florence-based food writer Faith Willinger.

Accidental Tourist
WINE, CULINARY TOUR

(☑055 69 93 76; www.accidentaltourist.com) Become an Accidental Tourist (membership €10), then sign up for a wine tour (€60), cooking class (€70), gourmet picnic (€35) and so on; tours happen in and around Florence.

✱ Festivals & Events

Festa di Anna Maria Medici
HISTORICAL

Florence's Feast of Anna Maria Medici marks the death in 1743 of the last Medici with a costumed parade from Palazzo Vecchio to Anna Maria's tomb in the Cappelle Medicee; 18 February.

Scoppio del Carro
LIGHT SHOW

A cart of fireworks is exploded in front of the cathedral at 11am on Easter Sunday – get there at least two hours early to grab a good position.

Maggio Musicale Fiorentino
ARTS

(www.maggiofiorentino.com) This arts festival – Italy's oldest – held in Florence's Teatro del Maggio Musicale Fiorentino stages world-class performances of theatre, classical music, jazz and dance; April to June.

Festa di San Giovanni
MIDSUMMER

Florence celebrates its patron saint, John, with a *calcio storico* (traditional football) match on Piazza di Santa Croce and fireworks over Piazzale Michelangelo; 24 June.

Festival Firenze Classica
MUSIC

(www.orcafi.it) July sees Florence's highly regarded Orchestra da Camera Toscana performing classical music in the atmospheric settings of the Oratorio di San Michele a Castello and Palazzo Strozzi.

🛏 Sleeping

🛏 Around Piazza del Duomo & Piazza della Signoria

★ Hotel Scoti
HISTORIC HOTEL €

(Map p478; ☑055 29 21 28; www.hotelscoti.com; Via de' Tornabuoni 7; s/d/tr/q €80/125/150/175; 🖻 📶) Wedged between Prada and McQueen, this is a splendid mix of old-fashioned charm and value for money. Run with smiling aplomb by Australian Doreen and Italian Carmello, the hotel is enthroned in a 16th-century *palazzo* on Florence's smartest shopping strip. The 16 rooms are clean and comfortable, but the star is the frescoed lounge dating from 1780. Breakfast €5.

Hotel Cestelli
BOUTIQUE HOTEL €

(Map p478; ☑055 21 42 13; www.hotelcestelli.com; Borgo SS Apostoli 25; d €100-115, s/d with shared bathroom €60/80, extra bed €25; ⊙closed 4 wks Jan-Feb, 3 wks Aug) A stiletto hop and skip from the Arno and fashionable Via de' Tornabuoni, this eight-room hotel in a 12th-century *palazzo* is a gem. Its large, quiet rooms ooze understated style – think washbasin with silk screen and vintage art. Before stepping out, quiz the couple, Italian photographer Alessio and gracious Japanese Asumi, on new eating, drinking and shopping openings.

Hotel Torre Guelfa
HISTORIC HOTEL €€

(Map p478; ☑055 239 63 38; www.hoteltorreguelfa.com; Borgo SS Apostoli 8; d/tr/q €200/250/300; 🌢 @ 🖻) Keen to kip in a Real McCoy Florentine *palazzo* without breaking the bank? If so, this 31-room hotel with a fortress-style facade is the answer. Scale its 13th-century, 50m-tall tower – Florence's tallest privately owned *torre* – for a sundowner overlooking Florence and you'll be blown away. Rates are practically halved in low season.

Hotel Davanzati
HOTEL €€

(Map p478; ☑055 28 66 66; www.hoteldavanzati.it; Via Porta Rossa 5; s/d/q €132/199/342; 🌢 @ 🖻 📶) Twenty-odd steps lead up to this swish hotel snug against Palazzo Davanzati. A beguiling labyrinth of enchanting rooms, unexpected frescoes and modern comforts, it has bags of charisma – and that includes Florentine debonair Tommaso and father Fabrizio, who run the show (Grandpa Marcello surveys proceedings). Laptops are in every room and iPads are in reception.

Hotel Perseo

HOTEL €€

(Map p478; ☑055 21 25 04; www.hotelperseo.it; Via de' Cerretani 1; s €125, d €147-165, tr €166-195, q €205-230; ❄@🞔🌐) This perfect family choice offers 20 large rooms, down-to-earth decor and friendly host couple New Zealander Louise and Italian Giacinto. Top-floor rooms smooch with the rooftops and gorgeous views of the *duomo*. Should you have trouble tracking down (black) no 1 on the street, look for red no 23. Low-season rates drop by more than 50%.

★ Antica Torre di Via de' Tornabuoni 1

BOUTIQUE HOTEL €€€

(Map p478; ☑055 21 92 48; www.tornabuoni1.com; Via de' Tournabuoni 1; d from €325; ⊗reception 7am-10pm; 🌐🞔) Footsteps from the Arno, inside the beautiful 14th-century Palazzo Gianfigliazzi, languishes this raved-about hotel. Its 20 rooms are stylish, spacious and contemporary. But what completely steals the show is the stunning rooftop breakfast terrace – easily the best in the city.

Palazzo Vecchietti

LUXURY HOTEL €€€

(Map p478; ☑055 230 28 02; www.palazzovecchietti.com; Via degli Strozzi 4; d from €285; ❄@🌐) This *residenza d'epoca* with 14 hopelessly romantic rooms in a 15th-century *palazzo* is a buzzword for hotel chic. Tapestries, bookshelves and artworks adorn stone walls, and colour schemes mix traditional hues with bolder blues, reds and violets. Three rooms have a terrace to breakfast between rooftops.

🛏 Santa Maria Novella

Hotel L'O

LUXURY HOTEL €€€

(Map p478; ☑055 27 73 80; www.hotelorologioflorence.com; Piazza di Santa Maria Novella 24; d from €315; 🅿❄@🌐) The type of seductive address where James Bond would feel right at home, this super-stylish hotel oozes panache. Designed as a showcase for the (very wealthy) owner's (exceedingly expensive) luxury wristwatch collection, L'O (the hip take on its full name, Hotel L'Orologio) has four stars, rooms named after watches, and clocks pretty much everywhere. Don't be late...

🛏 San Lorenzo & San Marco

★ Academy Hostel

HOSTEL €

(Map p478; ☑055 239 86 65; www.academyhostel.eu; Via Ricasoli 9; dm €32-34, d with shared bathroom €76, s/d €42/86; ❄🞔@🌐) That cheap accommodation shouldn't compromise on comfort is the much-appreciated philosophy of this modern 10-room hostel occupying the 1st floor of Baron Ricasoli's 17th-century *palazzo*. The reception area was once a theatre and 'dorms' sport a maximum of four or six beds, high moulded ceilings, brightly coloured lockers and chic flower-adorned screens. No credit cards for payments under €150. Breakfast included.

Ostello Archi Rossi

HOSTEL €

(Map p487; ☑055 29 08 04; www.hostelarchirossi.com; Via Faenza 94r; dm €28-32, s/d €62/90; ⊗closed 2 wks Dec; 🞔@🌐) Guests' paintings and artwork brighten up the walls at this private hostel near Santa Maria Novella train station. Bright white dorms have up to 12 beds (those across the garden are quieter), and there are washing machines, frozen meal dispensers and microwaves for guests. No curfew (knock to enter after 2am). Free two-hour walking tours for guests, daily at 10am.

Hotel Morandi alla Crocetta

BOUTIQUE HOTEL €€

(Map p487; ☑055 234 47 47; www.hotelmorandi.it; Via Laura 50; s €70-120, d €100-170, tr €130-210, q €150-250; 🅿❄🌐) This medieval convent-turned-hotel away from the madding crowd in San Marco is a stunner. Rooms are refined, tasteful and full of authentic period furnishings and paintings. A couple of rooms have handkerchief-sized gardens to laze in, but the pièce de résistance is frescoed room no 29, the former chapel.

Antica Dimora Johlea

B&B €€

(Map p487; ☑055 463 32 92; www.johanna.it; Via San Gallo 80; s €50-160, d €70-220; ❄@🌐) This well-established and highly regarded place is just one of five beautifully decorated and well-equipped B&Bs set in historic residences scattered on or around Via San Gallo. It has a terrace with wonderful views, and offers a delicious breakfast and all-day tea, coffee (Nespresso) and cake.

Hotel Azzi

HOTEL €€

(Locanda degli Artisti; Map p487; ☑055 21 38 06; www.hotelazzi.com; Via Faenza 56/88r; d €105-115, tr/q €130/150; ❄🞔) A five-minute walk from the central market and train station only adds to the convenience of this well-maintained hotel. Its old-world style coupled with a lounge, library full of books, terrace and jacuzzi makes it particularly popular among older travellers. The hotel also has cheaper hotel rooms and self-contained apartments in nearby annexes.

🛏 Santa Croce

★ Hotel Dalí
HOTEL €

(Map p478; ☑ 055 234 07 06; www.hoteldali.com; Via dell'Oriuolo 17; d/tr €85/110, apt from €95, with shared bathroom s/d €40/70; P@🛜🚗) This overwhelmingly friendly hotel is the passion and unrelenting love of world-travellers-turned-parents Marco and Samanta ('running the hotel is like travelling without moving'). Ten spacious, home-like rooms are equipped with a kettle, coffee and tea; there is a shared microwave guests can use; and bathrooms are modern.

The icing on the cake is a trio of gorgeous self-contained apartments – one with *duomo* view – sleeping two, four or six. No breakfast, but free parking in the leafy inner courtyard compensates. Low season rates drop by 30%.

Hotel Orchidea
HOTEL €

(Map p489; ☑ 055 248 03 46; www.hotelorchidea-florence.it; Borgo degli Albizi 11; s/d/tr/q with shared bathroom €60/75/100/120) This old-fashioned *pensione* in the mansion where the Donati family roosted in the 13th century (Dante's wife, Gemma, was allegedly born in the tower) is charm personified. Its seven rooms with sink share bathrooms that are simple, but their outlook is five-star. Rooms 5, 6 and 7 have huge windows overlooking a gorgeous garden and no 4 spills out onto an old stone terrace. No breakfast, but there are free tea- and coffee-making facilities.

Hotel Balestri
HISTORIC HOTEL €€

(Map p490; ☑ 055 21 47 43; www.hotel-balestri.it; Piazza Mentana 7; d €100-160, tr €140-165; 🌀@🛜) Dating to 1888, this hotel on the banks of the Arno remains the only riverside place to stay in downtown Florence. As part of the chic, quality-guaranteed Whythebest Florence hotel group (they're the guys behind Hotel L'O, Villa Cora and other chic pads), Balestri is comfortably contemporary while retaining a distinct old-world charm.

Villa Landucci
B&B €€

(☑ 055 66 05 95; www.villalanducci.it; Via Luca Landucci 7; d €100-120; P🛜🚗) Five elegant and refreshingly spacious rooms are named after Tuscan wines at this gourmet-themed B&B, a short walk away from Santa Croce. The best in the house, 'Bolgheri' and 'Chianti', open to the wonderful flower-adorned back garden with a play area that kids will love.

Hosts Debora and Matteo are founts of knowledge when it comes to dining well, and they can organise wine-tasting and food tours for guests. Breakfast is predominantly organic and the free parking is a rarity in the city.

🛏 The Oltrarno

Hostel Santa Monaca
HOSTEL €

(Map p490; ☑ 055 26 83 38; www.ostellosanta-monaca.com; Via Santa Monaca 6; dm €18-22, d/q per person €25.50/22; ⊙ reception 6am-2am; @🛜) This 112-bed hostel set in an 1880s convent opened in 1966 to give shelter to flood victims and is warmly recommended. It has a great little terrace, the size of a pocket handkerchief, and guests can rent bicycles to pedal around town (€2/10 per hour/day).

Facilities include a well-equipped kitchen, washing machine (charge applies), free safe deposits, free wi-fi and two computers to surf. Girls-only or mixed dorms sleep four to 22 and are closed for cleaning between 10am and 2pm. Curfew 2am.

★ Palazzo Guadagni Hotel
HOTEL €€

(Map p490; ☑ 055 265 83 76; www.palazzo-guadagni.com; Piazza Santo Spirito 9; s €100-140, d €140-180, extra bed €35; 🌀🛜🚗) Plump above Florence's liveliest summertime square is this legendary hotel with its impossibly romantic loggia (immortalised by Zefferelli in *Tea with Mussolini*). Florentines Laura and Ferdinando are the creative duo behind the transformation of this Renaissance palace into a brilliant-value hotel, with 15 spacious rooms tastefully mixing old and new.

Hotel La Scaletta
HOTEL €€

(Map p490; ☑ 055 28 30 28; www.hotellascaletta.it; Via Guicciardini 13; s €94-119, d €110-154) An austere air wafts through this maze of a hotel, hidden in a 15th-century *palazzo* near Palazzo Pitti. But rooms – the priciest ones peeping down on the Boboli gardens – are spacious, and the view from the roof terrace is nothing short of fabulous.

Palazzo Magnani Feroni
LUXURY HOTEL €€€

(Map p490; ☑ 055 239 95 44; www.florencepalace.com; Borgo San Frediano 5; d from €379; P🌀@🛜🚗) This extraordinary old *palazzo* is the stuff of dreams. The 12 elegant suites, which occupy four floors, with the family's private residence wedged in-between, are vast, featuring authentic period furnishings, rich fabrics and Bulgari toiletries. The 360-degree city view from the rooftop is unforgettable.

 Eating

Quality ingredients and simple execution are the hallmarks of Florentine cuisine, climaxing with the fabulous *bistecca alla fiorentina,* a huge slab of prime T-bone steak rubbed with olive oil, seared on the char grill, garnished with salt and pepper and served *al sangue* (bloody).

Other typical dishes include *crostini* (toast topped with chicken-liver pâté or other toppings), *ribollita* (a thick vegetable, bread and bean soup), *pappa al pomodoro* (bread and tomato soup) and *trippa alla fiorentina* (tripe cooked in a rich tomato sauce).

✖ Around Piazza del Duomo & Piazza della Signoria

★ **Osteria Il Buongustai** OSTERIA **€**
(Map p478; Via dei Cerchi 15r; meals €15; ⊘11.30am-3.30pm Mon-Sat) Run with breathtaking speed and grace by Laura and Lucia, this place heaves at lunchtime with locals who work nearby and with savvy students who flock here to fill up on tasty Tuscan homecooking at a snip of other restaurant prices. The place is brilliantly no-frills – expect to share a table and pay in cash; no credit cards.

★ **Mariano** SANDWICHES **€**
(Map p478; Via del Parione 19r; ⊘8am-3pm & 5-7.30pm Mon-Fri, 8am-3pm Sat) Our favourite for its simplicity, around since 1973. Sunrise to sunset this brick-vaulted, 13th-century cellar gently buzzes with Florentines propped at the counter sipping coffee, or wine, or eating salads and *panini.*

'**Ino** SANDWICHES **€**
(Map p478; Via dei Georgofili 3r-7r; panini €8, tasting platter €12; ⊘11am-8pm Mon-Sat, noon-5pm Sun) Artisan ingredients sourced locally and mixed creatively by passionate gourmet Alessandro Frassica provide the secret behind this stylish gourmet sandwich bar near the Uffizi. Create your own combo, pick from dozens of house specials or go for a tasting platter (salami, cheese, pecorini).

I Due Fratellini SANDWICHES **€**
(Map p478; www.iduefratellini.com; Via dei Cimatori 38r; panini €3; ⊘9am-8pm Mon-Sat, closed Fri & Sat 2nd half of Jun & all Aug) This hole in the wall has been in business since 1875. Wash *panini* down with a beaker of wine and leave the empty on the wooden shelf outside.

TOP FOUR GELATERIE

Florentines take gelato seriously and there's healthy rivalry among local *gelaterie artigianale* (makers of handmade gelato), who strive to create the city's creamiest, most flavourful and freshest ice cream. Flavours are seasonal and a cone or tub costs €2/3/4/5 per small/medium/large/maxi.

➡ **Vivoli** (Map p478; Via dell'Isola delle Stinche 7; tub €2-10; ⊘7.30am-midnight Tue-Sat, 9am-midnight Sun summer, to 9pm winter) Indoor seating and the additional inducement of coffee, tea and cakes make this ice-cream shop stand out. Pay at the cash desk then trade the receipt for ice. No cones, only tubs.

➡ **Grom** (Map p478; www.grom.it; cnr Via del Campanile & Via delle Oche; ⊘10.30am-midnight Apr-Sep, to 11pm Oct-Mar) Rain, hail or shine, queues halfway down the street are a constant at this sweet address; flavours are all delectable and many ingredients are organic. Rather tasty hot chocolate and milkshakes, too.

➡ **La Carraia** (Map p490; Piazza Nazario Sauro 25r; ⊘9am-11pm summer, to 10pm winter) Take one look at the constant queue out the door of this bright green-and-citrus shop with its exciting flavours and you know you're at a real Florentine favourite. Ricotta and pear, anyone?

➡ **Carabé** (Map p487; www.gelatocarabe.com; Via Ricasoli 60r; ⊘10am-midnight, closed mid-Dec–mid-Jan) Sicilian gelato, *granita* (sorbet) and *brioche* (ice-cream sandwich); handy while waiting in line to see *David.*

TIP-TOP PIZZERIAS

Expect to pay between €4.50 and €10 for a pizza at this trio of recommended addresses:

➜ **Gustapizza** (Map p490; Via Maggio 46r; pizza €4.50-8; ⏰ 11.30am-3pm & 7-11pm Tue-Sun) This unpretentious pizzeria close to Piazza Santa Spirito gives new meaning to the word 'packed'. Arrive early to grab a bar stool at a wooden-barrel table and pick from eight pizza types.

➜ **Pizzeria del' Osteria del Caffè Italiano** (Map p478; www.osteriacaffeitaliano.com; Via dell'Isola delle Stinche 11-13r; pizza €8; ⏰ 7.30-11pm) Simplicity is the buzzword at this pocket-sized pizzeria that makes just three pizza types: margherita, napoli and marinara. No credit cards.

➜ **Il Pizzaiuolo** (Map p489; ☎ 055 24 11 71; Via dei Macci 113r; pizzas €5-10, pastas €6.50-12; ⏰ lunch & dinner Mon-Sat, closed Aug) Young Florentines flock to the Pizza Maker to nosh Neapolitan thick-crust pizzas hot from the wood-fired oven. Bookings are essential for dinner.

Cantinetta dei Verrazzano BAKERY €
(Map p478; Via dei Tavolini 18-20; focaccia €2.50-3; ⏰ noon-9pm Mon-Sat, 10am-4.30pm Sun) A *forno* (baker's oven) and *cantinetta* (small cellar) make a heavenly match. Sit at a marble-topped table, admire prized vintages displayed behind glass wall cabinets and sip a glass of wine (€4 to €10) produced on the Verrazzano estate in Chianti. The focaccia topped with caramelised radicchio is a must, as is a mixed cold-meat platter (ignore the bristly boar legs strung in the open kitchen).

Tic Toc BURGERS €
(Map p478; Via dell' Oche 15r; burgers €10, club sandwiches €7; ⏰ 11am-11pm Mon-Sat) This new kid on the block is worth a pit stop. There's a US diner vibe, all-day service and the culinary lure of burgers made from the finest handcut beef, chicken or vegetables accompanied by homemade salsa, bacon and fries.

★**Obikà** CHEESE €€
(Map p478; ☎ 055 277 35 26; www.obika.it; Via de' Tornabuoni 16; 2/3/5 mozzarella €13/20/30, pizza €10-13.50; ⏰ noon-4pm & 6.30-11.30pm Mon-Fri, noon-11pm Sat & Sun) Given its exclusive location in Palazzo Tornabuoni, this designer address is naturally übertrendy. Taste different mozzarella cheeses with basil, organic veg or sundried tomatoes in the cathedral-like interior or snuggle beneath heaters on sofa seating in the elegant, star-topped courtyard. The €9 *aperitivi* comprising a drink and twinset of tasting platters (mozzarella and prosciutto) is copious, as is Sunday brunch.

✗ Santa Maria Novella

L'Osteria di Giovanni TUSCAN €€
(Map p478; ☎ 055 28 48 97; www.osteriadigiovanni.it; Via del Moro 22; meals €35; ⏰ dinner Mon-Fri, lunch & dinner Sat & Sun) It's not the decor that stands out at this friendly neighbourhood eatery. It's the cuisine, which is Tuscan and creative. Think chickpea soup with octopus or pear-and-ricotta-stuffed *tortelli* (a type of ravioli) bathed in a leek and almond cream. Throw in the complimentary glass of *prosecco* and plate of *coccoli* (traditional Florentine salted fritters) as *aperitivo* and you'll return time and again.

Il Latini TRATTORIA €€
(Map p478; ☎ 055 21 09 16; www.illatini.com; Via dei Palchetti 6r; meals €35; ⏰ lunch & dinner Tue-Sun) A veteran guidebook favourite built around melt-in-your-mouth *crostini*, Tuscan meats, pasta and roasted meats served at shared tables. There are two dinner sittings (7.30pm and 9pm), with service ranging from charming to not so charming. Bookings mandatory.

✗ San Lorenzo & San Marco

★**Trattoria Mario** TUSCAN €
(Map p487; www.trattoriamario.com; Via Rosina 2; meals €20; ⏰ noon-3.30pm Mon-Sat, closed 3 wks Aug) Arrive by noon to ensure a stool around a shared table at this noisy, busy, brilliant trattoria – a legend that retains its soul (and allure with locals) despite being in every

guidebook. Charming Fabio, whose grandfather opened the place in 1953, is front of house while big brother Romeo and nephew Francesco cook with speed in the kitchen.

Monday and Thursday are tripe days, Friday is fish and Saturday sees local Florentines flock here for a brilliantly blue *bistecca alla fiorentina* (€35 per kilo). No advance reservations, no credit cards.

Da Nerbone
MARKET STALL €

(Map p487; Mercato Centrale, Piazza del Mercato Centrale; ☺7am-2pm Mon-Sat) Forge your way past cheese, meat and sausage stalls in Florence's Mercato Centrale to join the lunchtime queue at Nerbone, in the biz since 1872. Go local and order *trippa alla fiorentina* (tripe and tomato stew) or follow the crowd with a feisty *panini con bollito* (a hefty boiled-beef bun, dunked in the meat's juices before serving). Eat standing up or fight for a table.

La Forchetta Rotta
TUSCAN €

(☑ 055 384 19 98; Via San Zanobi 126r; lunch/dinner €7.50/25; ☺lunch & dinner Mon-Sat) The restaurant arm of the dynamic duo behind Santa Croce's Monkey Bar, this place is staggeringly good value and tasty to boot. Its kitchen caters predominantly to workers from surrounding offices and the result is superb: the pick of three or four homespun *primi*, *secondi* and *contorni* (side dishes) for €7.50. The nibble banquet for *aperitivo*, laid out from 7pm, is equally generous.

Clubhouse
AMERICAN, PIZZERIA €

(Map p487; ☑ 055 21 14 27; www.theclubhouse.it; Via de' Ginori 6r; pizza €6-12, meals €20; ☺noon-midnight) This cavernous American bar, pizzeria and restaurant is close to the Accademia and makes for the perfect dining–drinking hybrid any time of day (including Sunday brunch). Design buffs will appreciate its faintly industrial vibe and foodies will love its pizza-making courses. Gluten-free menu, and €7 cocktail *aperitivo* from 6pm.

Antica Trattoria da Tito
TRATTORIA €€

(☑ 055 47 24 75; www.trattoriadatito.it; Via San Gallo 112r; meals €30; ☺lunch & dinner Mon-Sat) The 'No well-done meat here' sign strung in the window says it all: the best of Tuscan culinary tradition is the only thing this iconic trattoria serves. In business since 1913, Da Tito does everything right – tasty Tuscan dishes such as onion soup and wild boar pasta are served with friendly gusto and

hearty goodwill to a local crowd. Don't be shy about entering.

La Cucina del Garga
TUSCAN €€

(Map p487; ☑ 055 47 52 86; www.garga.it; Via San Zanobi 33r; meals €30) A contemporary reincarnation of the original Garga – one of Florence's great culinary legends – this newbie kitchen opened by New York chef Alessandro Gargani sports boldly painted walls crammed with modern art. It cooks up Garga classics including *tagliatelle de magnifico* (pasta ribbons with mint and citrus zest in a creamy brandy sauce), the signature dish of Alessandro's father, Giuliano 'Garga' Gargani. Reservations are essential at weekends.

✕ Santa Croce

Mercato di Sant'Ambrogio
MARKET €

(Map p489; Piazza Ghiberti; ☺7am-2pm Mon-Sat) Outdoor food market with an intimate, local flavour.

Il Giova
TRATTORIA €

(Map p489; ☑ 055 248 06 39; www.ilgiova.com; Borgo La Croce 73r; meals €25; ☺lunch & dinner Mon-Sat) Pocket-sized and packed, this cheery trattoria is everything a traditional Florentine eating place should be. Dig into century-old dishes including *zuppa della nonna* (grandma's soup), *risotto del giorno* (risotto of the day) *or mafalde al ragù* (long-ribboned pasta with meat sauce) and pride yourself on finding a place to dine with locals.

Brac
VEGETARIAN €

(Map p478; ☑ 055 094 48 77; www.libreriabrac.net; Via dei Vagellai 18r; meals €20; ☺noon-midnight, closed 2 wks mid-Aug; ✍) This hipster cafebookshop – a hybrid dining-stroke-*aperitivi* address – cooks up inventive, home-style and strictly vegetarian and vegan cuisine. Its decor is recycled vintage and the vibe is artsy. Reserve in advance at weekends. It can be tricky to find – there is no sign outside, just an inconspicuous doorway a block back from the river with a jumble of books in the window.

★ Il Teatro del Sale
TUSCAN €€

(Map p489; ☑ 055 200 14 92; www.teatrodelsale.com; Via dei Macci 111r; breakfast/lunch/dinner €7/20/30; ☺9-11am, 12.30-2.15pm & 7-11pm Tue-Sat, closed Aug) Florentine chef Fabio Picchi is one of Florence's living treasures, and he steals the Sant'Ambrogio show with this eccentric, good-value members-only club (everyone welcome, annual membership €7) inside an old theatre. He cooks up breakfast, lunch and dinner, culminating at 9.30pm in a live performance of drama, music or comedy arranged by his wife, artistic director and comic actor Maria Cassi.

Dinners are hectic: grab a chair, serve yourself water, wine and antipasti and wait for the chef to yell out what's about to be served before queuing at the glass hatch for your *primo* (first course) and *secondo* (second course). Dessert and coffee are laid out buffet-style just prior to the performance.

Trattoria Cibrèo   TRATTORIA €€
(Map p489; www.edizioniteatrodelsalecibreofirenze. it; Via dei Macci 122r; meals €30; ⊘lunch & dinner Tue-Sat, closed Aug) Dine here and you'll instantly understand why a queue gathers outside before it opens. Once in, revel in top-notch Tuscan cuisine served in small-ish portions. No advance reservations, no credit cards, no coffee, and arrive early to snag a table.

Francesco Vini   TUSCAN €€
(Map p478; ☏ 055 21 87 37; www.francescovini. com; Piazza de' Peruzzi 8r, Borgo de' Greci 7r; meals €40; ⊘9am-midnight Mon-Sat) Built on top of Roman ruins, this wine specialist has two entrances – one with pavement terrace on people-busy Borgo de' Greci and a second, lovelier one on a hidden, quintessentially Florentine square. Winter dining is between bottle-lined wall and red brick and in summer everything spills outside.

Osteria del Caffè Italiano   TUSCAN €€€
(Map p478; ☏ 055 28 93 68; www.osteriacaffeitaliano.com; Via dell'Isola delle Stinche 11-13r; meals €45; ⊘lunch & dinner Tue-Sun) The menu at this Florence dining veteran is packed with classics like *mozzarella di bufala* with Parma ham, ravioli stuffed with ricotta and *cavolo nero* (black cabbage), and the city's famous *bistecca alla fiorentina* (per kilo €60). End with the devilish profiteroles, with hot chocolate sauce ladled at the table from an old-fashioned copper pot.

✕ The Oltrarno

★**Tamerò**   PASTA BAR €
(Map p490; ☏ 055 28 25 96; www.tamero.it; Piazza Santa Spirito 11r; meals €20; ⊘lunch & dinner Tue-Sun) Admire pasta cooks at work in the open kitchen while you wait for a table alongside members of the party-loving crowd that flocks here to fill up on imaginative, fresh pasta dishes (€7.50 to €10), giant salads (€7.50) and copious cheese/salami platters (€9). Weekend DJs spin sets from 10pm.

La Casalinga   TRATTORIA €
(Map p490; www.trattorialacasalinga.it; ☏ 055 21 86 24; Via de' Michelozzi 9r; meals €25; ⊘lunch & dinner Mon-Sat) Family run and locally loved, this busy, unpretentious place is one of Florence's cheapest trattorias. Don't be surprised if Paolo, the patriarch figure who conducts the mad-busy show from behind the bar, relegates you behind locals in the queue: it's a fact of life, eventually rewarded with hearty Tuscan dishes cooked to exacting perfection.

Il Ristoro   TUSCAN €
(Map p490; http://ilristorodeiperditempo.it; ☏ 055 264 55 69; Borgo San Jacopo 48r; meals €20; ⊘noon-4pm Mon, noon-10pm Tue-Sun) A disarmingly simple address not to be missed, this two-room restaurant with deli counter is a great budget choice – its two-course €15 lunch deal is a steal. Pick from classics like *pappa al pomodoro* or a plate of cold cuts,

---

TRIPE: FAST-FOOD FAVOURITE

When Florentines fancy a fast munch on the move, they flit by a *trippaio* – a cart on wheels or mobile stand – for a tripe *panino* (sandwich). Think cow's stomach chopped up, boiled, sliced, seasoned and bunged between bread.

One of those great bastions of good old-fashioned Florentine tradition, *trippai* still going strong include the cart on the southwest corner of Mercato Nuovo (p505), **L'Antico Trippaio** (Map p478; Piazza dei Cimatori), **Pollini** (Map p489; Piazza Sant'Ambrogio), and hole-in-the-wall **Da Vinattieri** (Map p478; Via Santa Margherita 4; ⊘10am-7.30pm Mon-Fri, to 8pm Sat & Sun). Pay up to €4.50 for a *panino* with tripe doused in *salsa verde* (pea-green sauce of smashed parsley, garlic, capers and anchovies) or garnished with salt, pepper and ground chilli. Alternatively, opt for a bowl (€5.50 to €7) of *lampredotto* (cow's fourth stomach chopped and simmered for hours).

and swoon at views of the Arno swirling beneath your feet.

⭐ **Il Santo Bevitore** MODERN TUSCAN €€
(Map p490; ☑055 21 12 64; www.ilsantobevitore.com; Via di Santo Spirito 64-66r; meals €35; ⏱lunch & dinner Sep-Jul) Reserve or arrive dot-on 7.30pm to snag the last table at this raved-about address, an ode to stylish dining where gastronomes dine by candlelight in a vaulted, whitewashed, bottle-lined interior. The menu is a creative reinvention of seasonal classics, different for lunch and dinner.

Olio & Convivium TUSCAN €€
(Map p490; ☑055 265 81 98; Via di Santo Spirito 4; meals €35; ⏱lunch & dinner Tue-Sat, lunch Mon) A key location on any gastronomy agenda: your tastebuds will tingle at the sight of the legs of ham, conserved truffles, wheels of cheese, artisan bread and other delectable delicatessen products sold in its shop. Dine out the back.

Da Ruggero TUSCAN €€
(☑055 22 05 42; Via Senese 89r; meals €25; ⏱lunch & dinner Thu-Mon, closed mid-Jul–mid-Aug) A 10-minute stroll through the Boboli Gardens (or along the street from Porta Romana) uncovers this trattoria, run by the gracious Corsi family since 1981 and much loved for its pure, unadulterated Florentine tradition. Cuisine is simple, hearty and utterly delicious.

⭐ **iO Osteria Personale** MODERN TUSCAN €€€
(☑055 933 13 41; www.io-osteriapersonale.it; Borgo San Frediano 167r; meals €45; ⏱dinner Mon-Sat) Persuade everyone at your table to order the tasting menu to avoid the torture of picking just one dish, because everything at this fabulously contemporary and creative 'osteria' is to die for. Chef Nicolo' Baretti uses seasonal products, natural ingredients and traditional flavours to sensational effect. Dinner from 8pm.

🍷 Drinking & Nightlife

Florence's drinking scene is split between *enoteche* (wine bars that invariably make great eating addresses too), trendy bars with lavish *aperitivo* buffets, and cafes that often double as lunch venues.

Many bars offer *aperitivi* (predinner drinks from around 7pm to 10pm) and/or late-night cocktails (around midnight, before clubbing), two trends embraced with gusto by Florentines.

To savour the best of Florentine clubs, don't arrive before midnight – dance floors generally fill by 2am. In June to September everything grinds to a halt when most clubs shut. Admission, variable depending on the night, is usually more expensive for males than females and is sometimes free if you arrive early (between 9.30pm and 11pm).

🍷 Around Piazza del Duomo & Piazza della Signoria

La Terrazza BAR
(Map p478; www.continentale.it; Vicolo dell' Oro 6r; ⏱2.30-11.30pm Apr-Sep) This rooftop bar with wooden decking terrace is accessible from the 5th floor of the chic, Ferragamo-owned Hotel Continentale. Its *aperitivo* buffet is a modest affair, but no one cares – the fabulous, drop-dead-gorgeous panorama of one of Europe's most beautiful cities is the major draw. Dress the part or feel out of place.

Coquinarius WINE BAR
(Map p478; www.coquinarius.com; Via delle Oche 11r; crostini & carpacci €4; ⏱noon-10.30pm) With its old stone vaults, scrubbed wooden tables and refreshingly modern air, this *enoteca* run by the dynamic and charismatic Igor is spacious and stylish. The wine list features bags of Tuscan greats and unknowns, and a substantial *crostini* (toast with various toppings) and *carpacci* (cold sliced meats) menu ensures you won't leave hungry.

Slowly LOUNGE BAR
(Map p478; www.slowlycafe.com; Via Porta Rossa 63r; ⏱9pm-3am Mon-Sat, closed Aug) Sleek and sometimes snooty, this lounge bar with a candle flickering on every table is known for its glam interior, Florentine Lotharios and lavish fruit-garnished cocktails – €10 including buffet during the bewitching *aperitivo* 'hour' (6.30pm to 10pm).

Procacci CAFE
(Map p478; www.procacci1885.it; Via de' Tornabuoni 64r; ⏱10am-8pm Mon-Sat) The last remaining bastion of genteel old Florence on Via de' Tornabuoni, this tiny cafe was born in 1885 as a delicatessen serving truffles in its repertoire of tasty morsels. Bite-sized *panini tartufati* (truffle pâté rolls) remain the

FLORENCE & TUSCANY FLORENCE

TOP CAFES

Good cafes are a dime a dozen in Florence. Prime squares to sit and people-watch from a pavement terrace are Piazza della Repubblica, Piazza Santo Spirito and Piazza della Signoria. Note that a coffee taken sitting down at a table is up to four times pricier than one drunk standing up at a bar (a cappuccino costs around €1.40/5.50 standing up/sitting down).

Caffè Rivoire (Map p478; Piazza della Signoria 4; ☺ Tue-Sun) The golden oldie to refuel at inside or out after an Uffizi visit, this pricey little number with unbeatable people-watching terrace has been serving coffee, cocktails and delectable hot chocolate since 1872.

Gilli (Map p478; www.gilli.it; Piazza della Repubblica 39r; ☺ Wed-Mon) The most famous of historic cafes on the city's old Roman forum, Gilli has been serving utterly delectable cakes, chocolates and fruit tartlets to die for since 1733 (it moved to this square in 1910 and sports a beautifully preserved art nouveau interior).

Caffè Concerto Paszkowski (Map p478; www.paszkowski.com; Piazza della Repubblica 31-35r; ☺ Tue-Sun) Born as a brewery overlooking the city's fish market in 1846, this Florentine institution with heated terrace and elegant, piano-clad interior lured a literary set a century on. Today it pulls the whole gambit of punters, mobile-touting Florentine youths, suit-clad businessmen and well-dressed old women sipping tea.

Cuculia (Map p490; www.cuculia.it; Via dei Serragli 11; ☺ 10am-midnight Tue-Fri, 10am-1am Sat) This hybrid bookshop-cafe is a wonderfully serene spot in which to while away a few hours in the company of classical music and shelves loaded with books. The vibe is very much old-world refinement and the tiny candlelit nook out back is perfect for a romantic moment over a cocktail. Food too.

Gucci Museo Caffè (Map p478; Piazza della Signoria 10; meals €25; ☺ 10am-11pm; 🛜) Everything from the crockery to G-shaped sugar 'cubes' is emblazoned with the Gucci monogram at this recently opened cafe next to Palazzo Vecchio. Over-zealous branding aside, this smart laid-back cafe is one of the city's hippest place to hang over coffee, lunch, aperitivo, newspapers, design books or in-house iPads. A huge table hooked up with plugs makes it a laptop-user favourite.

Le Renaissance Café (Map p478; Piazza Strozzi; ☺ 9am-8pm Fri-Wed, 9am-11pm Thu) A high vaulted ceiling, sleek black Panton chairs and exquisitely low drink prices seduce a mixed crowd at this artsy hangout in Palazzo Strozzi, plumb on Florence's most designer-chic street. The chocolate-swirled cappuccino (€1.40 sitting down) is among the best in town.

thing to order, best accompanied by a glass of *prosecco*.

Fiaschetteria Nuvoli　　　WINE BAR
(Map p478; Piazza dell'Olio 15r; ☺ 7am-9pm Mon-Sat) Pull up a stool on the street and chat with a regular over a glass of *vino della casa* (house wine) at this old-fashioned *fiaschetteria*, a street away from the *duomo*.

YAB　　　NIGHTCLUB
(Map p478; www.yab.it; Via de' Sassetti 5r; ☺ 9pm-4am Oct-May) It's crucial to pick your night according to your age and tastes at Florence's busiest disco club. Thursdays is the evening the over-30s hit the dance floor – otherwise, the set is predominantly student.

🍷 Santa Maria Novella

Sei Divino　　　WINE BAR
(Borgo Ognissanti 42r; ☺ 10am-2am) This stylish wine bar tucked beneath a red-brick vaulted ceiling is privy to one of Florence's most happening *aperitivo* scenes. From the pale aqua-coloured Vespa parked inside to the music, occasional exhibition and summertime pavement action, Sei Divino is a vintage that is eternally good. *Aperitivi* 'hour' kicks in from 5pm to 10pm.

Space Club　　　NIGHTCLUB
(www.spaceclubfirenze.com; Via Palazzuolo 37r; admission €16 incl one drink; ☺ 10pm-4am) Sheer size alone at this vast club in Santa Maria Novella impresses – the moment you walk in and join the mixed student–

international crowd you'll know you are in for a good night of dancing, drinking and video-karaoke in the bar. Put drinks on an electronic card 'tab' and pay at the end of the night (but risk forking out €50 if you lose the card).

Santa Croce

Drogheria
LOUNGE BAR

(Map p489; www.drogheriafirenze.it; Largo Annigoni 22; ⊙10am-3am) A large vintage-chic space with dark wood furnishings and soft leaf-green chairs that are perfect for lounging in for hours on end. Come spring, the action moves outside onto the terrace, plumb on the huge piazza behind Sant'Abrogio market. The kitchen cooks up various bar-style dishes including burgers – beef, veggie, tofu or felafel.

Nano Caffè
CAFE, BAR

(Map p489; www.nanocaffe.info; Largo Annigoni, Piazza Ghiberti; ⊙9am-3am) This L-shape bar behind Sant'Ambrogio market is loved by Florentines for its al fresco terrace, aka a fantastic twinset of large cream parasols shading an eclectic collection of colourfully painted chairs, stools and benches covered in sackcloth. All ages and types hang out in warm weather.

Monkey Bar
PUB

(Map p489; Via della Mattonaia 20r; ⊙6pm-2am) Duck behind Sant' Abrogio market to find this busy pub, packed most nights with a mix of Florentine and foreign students downing shots and sipping cocktails. Italian double-act Lorenzo and Freddy are the duo behind the place.

Lion's Fountain
IRISH PUB

(Map p489; www.thelionsfountain.com; Borgo degli Albizi 34r; ⊙10am-2am) If you have the urge to hear more English than Italian – or to hear local bands play – this is the place. Plump on a pretty pedestrian square, Florence's busiest Irish pub buzzes in summer when the beer-loving crowd spills across most of the square.

Eby's Bar
LATIN BAR

(Map p489; Via dell'Oriulolo 5r; ⊙10am-3am Mon-Sat) A lively student crowd packs out this young, fun, colourful address with wooden-benches tucked outside in a covered alleyway. The kitchen is Mexican.

Kitsch
BAR

(Map p489; www.kitschfirenze.com; Viale A Gramsci 5; ⊙6.30pm-2.30am; 🐱) This hipster American-styled bar is known among cent-conscious Florentines for its lavish spread at *aperitivi* time – €8.50 for drink and sufficient nibbles to not need dinner. It sports a dark-red theatrical interior and a bright 20s-to-early-30s crowd out for a good time. DJ sets set the place rocking after dark.

Blob Club
NIGHTCLUB

(Map p478; Via Vinegia 21r; ⊙11pm-3am Mon-Wed, to 5am Thu-Sat) No surprise that Florence's trendiest club of the moment is in its hippest part of town. Small and edgy, Blob lures an international crowd with its music theme nights – loads of '60s, hip hop, alternative rock, all sounds in fact. No entrance fee, but first-timers need to buy a membership card (€20).

Twice Club
NIGHTCLUB

(Map p489; www.twiceclub.com; Via Giuseppe Verdi 57r; ⊙9pm-4am) There's no admission cost but you need to look good to get past the bouncers on the door at this Santa Croce club. Once in, Twice is a relaxed club with stylish decor and a hip cocktail-quaffing crowd. Music is mainstream dance. Happy hour is 9pm to 11pm; don't expect action on the dance floor until well past midnight.

The Oltrano

★ Il Santino
WINE BAR

(Map p490; Via Santo Spirito 34; glass of wine & crostini €6.50-8; ⊙10am-10pm) Just a few doors down from one of Florence's best gourmet addresses, Il Santo Bevitore, is this pocket-sized wine bar run by the same crew. Inside, squat modern stools contrast with old brick walls but the real action is outside, from around 9pm, when the wine-loving crowd spills onto the street.

★ Volume
BAR

(Map p490; www.volumefirenze.com; Piazza Santo Spirito 3r; ⊙9am-1.30am) Fabulous armchairs, lots of recycled and upcycled vintage furniture, books to read and a juke box give this hybrid cafe-bar-gallery in an old hat-making workshop real appeal. Watch for various music, art and DJ events and happenings.

Vivanda
WINE BAR

(Map p490; www.vivandafirenze.it; Via Santa Monaca 7r; meals €25; ⊙lunch & dinner) A first for gourmet Florence, the focus of this bright modern *enoteca* is organic wine. Locally sourced products ensure a delightful lunch, or you can reserve in advance for an early-evening tasting of four different organic wines perfectly paired with ash-aged pecorino, bufala ricotta cheese, cinta Senese salami and so forth (€25).

★ **Le Volpi e l'Uva** WINE BAR
(Map p490; www.levolpieluva.com; Piazza dei Rossi 1; crostini €6.50, cheese/meat platters €8-10; ⏲ 11am-9pm Mon-Sat) The city's best *enoteca con degustazione* bar none: this intimate address with marble-topped bar crowning two oak ageing wine barrels chalks up an impressive list of wines by the glass. To attain true bliss, indulge in *crostini* (€6.50) topped with honeyed speck perhaps or *lardo*, or a platter of boutique Tuscan cheeses.

Flò LOUNGE BAR
(www.flofirenze.com; Piazzale Michelangelo 84; ⏲ 7.30pm-late summer) Without a doubt the hottest and hippest place to be seen in the city on hot sultry summer nights is this ab fab seasonal lounge bar, which pops up each May or June on Piazzale Michelangelo. Different themed lounge areas include a dance floor and a VIP area (where you have no chance of reserving a table unless you're in the Florentine in-crowd, alas).

Open Bar LOUNGE BAR
(Map p490; www.goldenviewopenbar.com; Via de' Bardi 58; ⏲ 7.30am-1.30am) A prime location near Ponte Vecchio ensures that it is touristy, but this place is worth a pit stop nonetheless – preferably at *aperitivo* hour when chic Florentines sip cocktails, slurp oysters and enjoy the 'golden view' of the Arno swirling below their feet.

Zoé BAR
(Via dei Renai 13r; ⏲ 8am-3am) Bright white and shiny, this savvy bar knows exactly what its hip punters want – a relaxed, faintly industrial space to hang out at all hours (well, almost). Be it breakfast, lunch, cocktails or after-dinner party, Zoé is your woman. Come springtime's warmth, the scene spills out onto a wooden decking street terrace in front.

James Joyce PUB
(☎ 055 658 08 56; Lungarno Benvenuto Cellini 1r; ⏲ 6pm-2am Sun-Thu, to 3am Fri & Sat) Neither as Irish nor as literary as the name suggests, this veteran pub with beer garden attracts a gregarious student and post-grad crowd thanks to its fabulous and large riverside terrace, Guinness on tap, table football and requisite U2 soundtrack.

☆ **Entertainment**

Hanging out on warm summer nights on cafe and bar terraces aside, Florence enjoys a vibrant entertainment scene thanks in part to its substantial student population.

La Cité LIVE MUSIC
(Map p490; www.lacitelibreria.info; Borgo San Frediano 20r; ⏲ 3pm-1am Mon-Thu, 5pm-2am Fri & Sat; 🖥) By day this cafe-bookshop is a hip cappuccino stop with an eclectic choice of vintage seating to flop down on. From 10pm, the intimate bookshelf-lined space morphs into a vibrant live-music den: think swing, fusion, jam-session jazz... The staircase next to the bar hooks up with mezzanine seating up top.

Jazz Club JAZZ
(Map p489; www.jazzclubfirenze.com; Via Nuovo de' Caccini 3; ⏲ 10pm-2am Tue-Sat, closed Jul & Aug) Catch salsa, blues, Dixieland and world music as well as jazz at Florence's top jazz venue.

Be Bop Music Club LIVE MUSIC
(Map p478; Via dei Servi 76r; ⏲ 8pm-2am) Inspired by the swinging '60s, this beloved retro venue features everything from Led Zeppelin and Beatles cover bands to swing jazz and 1970s funk.

Teatro del Maggio Musicale Fiorentino OPERA, BALLET
(☎ 055 28 72 22; www.maggiofiorentino.com; Corso Italia 16) The curtain rises on opera, classical concerts and ballet at this lovely theatre, host to the summertime Maggio Musicale Fiorentina.

Teatro della Pergola THEATRE
(Map p489; ☎ 055 2 26 41; www.teatrodellapergola. com; Via della Pergola 18) Beautiful city theatre with stunning entrance; host to classical concerts October to April.

🛍 **Shopping**

Tacky mass-produced souvenirs (boxer shorts emblazoned with David's packet) and cheap poor-quality leathergoods are everywhere, not least at the city's two main markets: **Mercato de San Lorenzo** (Map p478; Piazza San Lorenzo; ⏲ 9am-7pm Mon-Sat) and

Mercato Nuovo (Map p478; Loggia Mercato Nuovo; ⊗8.30am-7pm Mon-Sat).

But serious shoppers keen to delve into a city synonymous with craft since medieval times will discover plenty of top-quality ateliers, studios and boutiques. Leather goods, jewellery, hand-embroidered linens, designer fashion, perfume, marbled paper, wine and gourmet foods are among the distinctively Florentine treats to take home.

★ Mrs Macis   FASHION
(Map p489; www.mrsmacis.it; Borgo Pinti 38r; ⊗4-7.30pm Mon, 10.30am-1pm & 4-7.30pm Tue-Sat) Workshop and showroom of the talented Carla Macis, this eye-catching boutique – dollhouse-like in design – specialises in very feminine 1950s, '60s and '70s clothes and jewellery made from new and recycled fabrics. Every piece is unique and fabulous.

★ Casini Firenze   FASHION
(Map p490; www.casinifirenze.it; Piazza Pitti 30-31r; ⊗10am-7pm Mon-Sat, 11am-6pm Sun) One of Florence's oldest and most reputable fashion houses, this lovely boutique across from Palazzo Pitti keeps its edge thanks to American-Florentine designer and stylist (she does personal wardrobe consultations) Jennifer Tattanelli.

★ Letizia Fiorini   PUPPETS
(Map p478; Via del Parione 60r; ⊗10am-7pm Tue-Sat) This charming shop is a one-woman affair – Letizia Fiorini sits at the counter and makes her distinctive puppets by hand in-between assisting customers. You'll find Pulchinella (Punch), Arlecchino the clown, beautiful servant girl Colombina, Doctor Peste (complete with plague mask), cheeky

Brighella, swashbuckling Il Capitano and many other characters from traditional Italian puppetry.

★ Giulio Giannini e Figlio   STATIONERY
(Map p490; www.giuliogiannini.it; Piazza Pitti 37r; ⊗10am-7pm Mon-Sat, 11am-6.30pm Sun) Easy to miss, this quaint old shopfront has watched Palazzo Pitti turn pink with the evening sun since 1856. One of Florence's oldest artisan families, the Gianninis – bookbinders by trade – make and sell marbled paper, beautifully bound books, stationery and so on. Don't miss the workshop upstairs.

Boutique Nadine   VINTAGE
(Map p478; www.boutiquenadine.com; Via de' Benci 32r; ⊗2.30-7.30pm Mon, 10.30am-8pm Tue-Sat, noon-7pm Sun) There is no more elegant and quaint address to shop for vintage clothing, jewellery, homewares and other pretty little trinkets. From the wooden floor and antique display cabinets to the period changing cabin, Nadine's attention to detail is impeccable.

Officina Profumo-Farmaceutica
di Santa Maria Novella   PERFUMERY
(www.santamarianovella.com.br; Via della Scala 16; ⊗9.30am-7.30pm) In business since 1612, this perfumery-pharmacy began life when the Dominican friars of Santa Maria Novella began to concoct cures and sweet-smelling unguents using medicinal herbs cultivated in the monastery garden. The shop today sells a wide range of fragrances, remedies, teas and skin-care products. A real treasure, it has touchscreen catalogues and a state-of-the-art payment system yet still manages to ooze vintage charm.

FLORENCE & TUSCANY FLORENCE

DESIGNER OUTLET STORES

Keen to replenish your wardrobe with a few designer pieces but don't want to break the bank? Then head for Florence's out-of-town outlet malls, where you can pick up previous-season designer clothing for 30% to 50% less.

Barberino Designer Outlet (www.mcarthurglen.it; Via Meucci, Barberino di Mugello; ⊗10am-8pm Mon-Fri, to 9pm Sat & Sun) Polo Ralph Lauren, D&G, Prada, Class Roberto Cavalli, Missoni, Furla, Benetton and Bruno Magli are just a few of the 100 labels with shops here. Outlet shuttle buses (adult/reduced return €15/8, 35 inutes) depart from Piazza della Stazione in Florence at 10am and 2.30pm daily, returning from the outlet, 40km north in Barberino di Mugello, at 1.30pm and 6pm.

The Mall (www.themall.it; Via Europa 8, Leccio; ⊗10am-7pm) Gucci, Ferragamo, Burberry, Ermenegildo Zegna, Yves Saint Laurent, Tod's, Fendi, Giorgio Armani, Marni, Valentino and others are represented in this mall, 30km from Florence. Buses (€5, seven daily) depart from the SITA bus station between 8.50 and 1pm and return between 2pm and 6.30pm. By car, take the Incisa exit off the northbound A1 and follow signs for Leccio.

Aprosio & Co ACCESSORIES, JEWELLERY
(Map p478; www.aprosio.it; Via della Spada 38; ☺10.30am-1.30pm & 2.30-5.30pm Mon-Sat) Ornella Aprosio fashions teeny tiny glass and crystal beads into dazzling pieces of jewellery, hair accessories, animal-shaped brooches, handbags, even glass-flecked cashmere. It is all quite magical.

Grevi HATS
(Map p478; www.grevi.com; Via della Spada 11-13r; ☺10am-2pm & 3-8pm Mon-Sat) It was a hat made by Siena milliner Grevi that actor Cher wore in the film *Tea with Mussolini;* ditto Maggie Smith in *My House in Umbria.* So if you want to shop like a star, this hopelessly romantic boutique is the address. Hats range in price from €30 to unaffordable.

**Vintage di
Antonini Alessandra** FASHION
(Map p478; Piazza Piero Calamandrei; ☺3.30-7.30pm Mon, 10.30am-1.15pm & 3.30-7.30pm Tue-Sat) For Real McCoy haute-couture pieces – Chanel handbags, strappy 1970s Dior sandals and so on – look no further than this stylish boutique off Via delle Seggiole.

La Bottega dell'Olio OLIVE OIL
(Map p478; Piazza del Limbo 2r; ☺10am-1pm & 2-6.30pm Tue-Sat) This bijou boutique takes great care with its displays of olive oils, olive oil soaps, platters made from olive wood and skincare products made with olive oil (the Lepo range is particularly good).

❶ Information

EMERGENCY

Police station (Questura; ☏055 4 97 71; http://questure.poliziadistato.it; Via Zara 2; ☺24hr)
Tourist police (Polizia Assistenza Turistica; ☏055 20 39 11; Via Pietrapiana 50r; ☺8.30am-6.30pm Mon-Fri, to 1pm Sat) English-speaking service for filing reports of thefts etc.

MEDICAL SERVICES

24-Hour Pharmacy (Stazione di Santa Maria Novella)
Dr Stephen Kerr: Medical Service (☏335 836 16 82, 055 28 80 55; www.dr-kerr.com; 4th fl, Piazza Mercato Nuovo 1; ☺3-5pm Mon-Fri (or by appt) Resident British doctor.

TOURIST INFORMATION

Tourist office (☏055 31 58 74; Via del Termine, Airport; ☺9am-7pm Mon-Sat, to 4pm Sun)
Tourist office (Map p478; ☏055 21 22 45; Piazza della Stazione 4; ☺9am-7pm Mon-Sat, to 4pm Sun)

Tourist Office (Map p487; ☏055 29 08 33, 055 29 08 32; www.firenzeturismo.it; Via Cavour 1r; ☺8.30am-6.30pm Mon-Sat)

USEFUL WEBSITES

Firenze Spettacolo (www.firenzespettacolo.it)
The Florentine (www.theflorentine.net)

❶ Getting There & Away

AIR

Florence Airport (www.aeroporto.firenze.it) Also known as Amerigo Vespucci or Peretola airport, 5km northwest of the city centre; domestic and a handful of European flights.
Pisa Airport (www.pisa-airport.com) Tuscany's main international airport (named after Galileo Galilei) is near Pisa, but is well linked with Florence by public transport.

BUS

Services from the **SITA bus station** (www.sitabus.it; Via Santa Caterina da Siena 17r; ☺information office 8.30am-12.30pm & 3-6pm Mon-Fri, 8.30am-12.30pm Sat), just west of Piazza della Stazione, go to the following towns:
Assisi, Umbria €12.50, 2½ hours, twice weekly
Greve in Chianti €3.30, one hour, hourly
Montepulciano €11.20, 1½ hours, three daily
Siena *Corso rapide* €7.80, 1¼ hours, at least hourly
San Gimignano €6.80, 1¼ to 2 hours, 14 daily, often via Poggibonsi
Volterra €8.35, two hours, four daily – usually with a change at Colle di Val d'Elsa

CAR & MOTORCYCLE

Florence is connected by the A1 northward to Bologna and Milan, and southward to Rome and Naples. The Autostrada del Mare (A11) links Florence with Pistoia, Lucca, Pisa and the coast, but most locals use the FI-PI-LI – a superstrada (dual carriageway, hence no tolls); look for blue signs saying FI-PI-LI (as in Firenze–Pisa–Livorno). Another dual carriageway, the S2, links Florence with Siena.

TRAIN

Florence's central train station is **Stazione di Santa Maria Novella** (Piazza della Stazione). The **left-luggage counter** (Deposito Bagagliamano; first 5hr €5, then €0.70 per hr six–12 hours and €0.30 per hour after that; ☺6am-11.50pm) is located on platform 16 and the *Assistenza Disabili* (Disabled Assistance) office is on platform 5. International train tickets are sold in the **ticketing hall** (☺6am-9pm). For domestic tickets, skip the queue and buy your tickets from the touch-screen automatic ticket-vending machines; machines have an English option and accept cash and credit cards.

FIESOLE DAY TRIPPER

Over the centuries, the cooler air, olive groves, Renaissance-styled villas and spectacular views from this hilltop village 9km northeast of Florence have seduced visitors including Boccaccio, Marcel Proust, Gertrude Stein and Frank Lloyd Wright.

Morning

Hop aboard a bus from Florence's Piazza San Marco and alight 30 minutes later on Fiesole's central square, Piazza Mino di Fiesole. Founded in the 7th century BC by the Etruscans, Fiesole was the most important city in northern Etruria and its Area Archeologica (www.museidifiesole.it; Via Portigiani 1; adult/reduced Fri-Sun €10/6, Mon-Thu €8/4, family €20; ⊙10am-7pm summer, shorter hrs rest of yr) a couple of doors down from the tourist office (☑055 596 13 23, 055 596 13 11; www.fiesoleforyou.it; Via Portigiani 3, Fiesole; ⊙10am-6.30pm summer, shorter hrs rest of yr) provides the perfect flashback to its fabulous past. Meander around the ruins of a small Etruscan temple, Roman baths and an archaeological museum with exhibits from the Bronze Age to the Roman period. Later, take a break on one of the stone steps of the 1st-century-BC Roman amphitheatre where musicians, actors and artists take to the stage in summer during Italy's oldest open-air festival, Estate Fiesolana (www.estatefiesolana.it). July's Vivere Jazz Festival (www.viverejazz.it) is the other hot date at this atmospheric theatre.

Afterwards, pop into the neighbouring Museo Bandini (www.museidifiesole.it; Via Dupré; adult/reduced €5/3 or free with Area Archeologica ticket; ⊙10am-7pm summer, shorter hrs rest of yr) to view early Tuscan Renaissance art, including fine medallions (c 1505–20) by Giovanni della Robbia and Taddeo Gaddi's luminous *Annunciation* (1340–45).

From the museum, a 300m walk along Via Giovanni Dupré brings you to the Fondazione Primo Conti (☑055 59 70 95; www.fondazioneprimoconti.org; Via Giovanni Dupré 18; admission €3, with archives €5; ⊙9am-2pm Mon-Fri) where the eponymous avant-garde 20th-century artist lived and worked. Inside hang more than 60 of his paintings, and the views from the garden are inspiring. Ring to enter.

Lunch

Meander back to Piazza Mino Fiesole, where cafe and restaurant terraces tempt on all sides. It also hosts an antiques market the first Sunday of each month. The pagoda-covered terrace of four-star hotel-restaurant Villa Aurora (☑055 5 93 63; www.villaurora.net; Piazza Mino Fiesole 39; meals €50; ⊙lunch & dinner, closed Mon winter), around since 1860, is the classic choice, not so much for the gourmet cuisine but for the spectacular panoramic view of Florence it cooks up. For a wholly rustic and typical Tuscan lunch built around locally produced salami and cheese, homemade pasta and Chianina T-bones eaten at a shared table, *enoteca*-cum-bistro Vinandro (☑055 5 91 21; www.vinandrofiesole.com; Piazza Mino da Fiesole 33; meals €20; ⊙lunch & dinner summer) is the best choice.

Afternoon

Stagger around Cattedrale di San Romolo (Piazza Mino di Fiesole; ⊙7.30am-noon & 3-5pm) FREE, the central square's centrepiece, which dates from the 11th century but was renovated in the 19th. A terracotta statue of San Romolo by Giovanni della Robbia guards the entrance inside.

Afterwards, from the far end of the square, make your way up steep walled Via San Francesco and be blown away by the beautiful panorama of Florence that unfolds from the terrace adjoining 15th-century Basilica di Sant'Alessandro. (If you're lucky, the church might be open and have a temporary exhibition inside.) Grassy-green afternoon-nap spots abound and the tourist office has brochures outlining several short trails (1km to 3.5km) fanning from here, should you prefer to carry on walking.

Getting There & Around

ATAF bus 7 (€1.20, 20 minutes, every 15 minutes) goes from Florence's Piazza San Marco uphill to Piazza Mino di Fiesole.

Florence is on the Rome–Milan line. Services include the following:

Lucca (€5.10, 1½ hours to 1¾ hours, half-hourly)

Pisa (€5.80, 45 minutes to one hour, half-hourly)

Pistoia (€3.10, 45 minutes to one hour, half-hourly)

Rome (€17.25, 1¾ hours to 4¼ hours)

Bologna (€10.50 to €25, one hour to 1¾ hours)

Milan (€29.50 to €53, 2¼ hours to 3½ hours)

Venice (€24 to €43, 2¾ hours to 4½ hours)

ℹ Getting Around

TO/FROM THE AIRPORT
Bus

A shuttle (single/return €6/8, 25 minutes) travels between Florence airport and the Stazione di Santa Maria Novella train station every 30 minutes between 6am and 11.30pm (5.30am to 11pm from city centre). **Terravision** (www.terravision.eu) runs daily services (one way €4.99, 1¼ hours, hourly) between the bus stop outside Florence's Stazione di Santa Maria Novella on Via Alamanni (under the station's digital clock) and Pisa's Galileo Galilei airport – buy tickets online, on board or from the Terravision desk inside the Deanna Bar. At Galileo Galilei airport, the Terravision ticket desk is in the arrival hall.

Taxi

A taxi between Florence airport and town costs a flat rate of €20, plus surcharges of €2 on Sunday and holidays, €3.30 between 10pm and 6am and €1 per bag. Exit the terminal building, bear right and you'll come to the taxi rank.

Train

Regular trains link Florence's Stazione di Santa Maria Novella with Pisa's Galileo Galilei airport (€7.80, 1½ hours, at least hourly from 4.30am to 10.25pm).

BICYCLE & SCOOTER

Milleunabici (www.bicifirenze.it; Piazza della Stazione; per hr/day €2/5; ⊗10am-7pm Mar-Oct) Violet coloured bikes to rent in front of Stazione di Santa Maria Novella; leave ID as a deposit.

Florence by Bike (Map p487; www.florence-bybike.com; Via San Zanobi 120r; ⊗9am-1pm & 3.30-7.30pm Mon-Sat) Top-notch bike shop, itinerary suggestions, bike tours and rental outlet (city bike/scooter per day €14.50/68).

CAR & MOTORCYCLE

There is a strict ZTL (*Zona a Traffico Limitato*; Limited Traffic Zone) in Florence's historic centre between 7.30am and 7.30pm Monday to Friday and 7.30am and 6pm Saturday for all nonresidents, monitored by cameras positioned at all entry points. The exclusion also applies on Wednesday, Friday and Saturday from 11pm to 4am mid-May to mid-September. Motorists staying in hotels within the zone are allowed to drop off luggage, but must tell reception their car registration number and the time they were in no-cars-land (there's a two-hour window) so that the hotel can organise a permit. If you transgress, the fine is around €150. For more information see www.comune.fi.it.

There is some free street parking around Piazzale Michelangelo, but none within the ZTL. Blue lines indicate paid street parking. Pricey (around €20 per day) underground parking can be found around Fortezza da Basso and in the Oltrarno beneath Piazzale di Porta Romana. Otherwise, search for a car park on www.firenzeparcheggi.it or ask if your hotel can arrange parking.

PUBLIC TRANSPORT

Buses, electric *bussini* (minibuses) and trams (all lines to be up and running by 2016) run by **ATAF** (☑199 104245, 800 424500; www.ataf.net) serve the city. Most buses start/terminate at the ATAF bus stops opposite the southeastern exit of Stazione di Santa Maria Novella.

Tickets valid for 90 minutes (no return journeys) cost €1.20 (€2 on board; drivers don't give change) and are sold at kiosks, tobacconists and the **ATAF ticket and information office** (Map p487; Piazza della Stazione; ⊗7.30am-7.30pm) adjoining the train station.

A travel pass valid for 1/3/7 days is €5/12/18. Upon boarding time-stamp your ticket (punch on board) or risk a fine.

TAXI

Taxis can't be hailed in the street. Pick one up at the train station or call ☑055 42 42 or ☑055 43 90.

NORTHWESTERN TUSCANY

Travel through this part of Tuscany and you will truly understand the term 'slow travel'. Lingering over a lunch of regional specialities swiftly becomes the norm, as does meandering through medieval hilltop villages, taking leisurely bike rides along coastal wine trails with spectacular scenery or hiking on an island where Napoleon was once exiled. Even the larger towns – including the university hub of Pisa and 'love at first sight' Lucca – have an air of tranquillity and tradition that begs the traveller to stay for a few days of cultural R&R.

Pisa

POP 85,500

Once a maritime power to rival Genoa and Venice, Pisa now draws its fame from an architectural project gone terribly wrong. But the world-famous Leaning Tower is just one of many noteworthy sights in this compact and compelling city. Education has fuelled the local economy since the 1400s, and students from across Italy still compete for places in its elite university and research schools. This endows the centre of town with a vibrant and affordable cafe and bar scene, and balances an enviable portfolio of well-maintained Romanesque buildings, Gothic churches and Renaissance piazzas with a lively street life dominated by locals rather than tourists.

History

Possibly of Greek origin, Pisa became an important naval base under Rome and remained a significant port for many centuries. The city's so-called golden days began late in the 9th century when it became an independent maritime republic and a rival of Genoa and Venice. The good times rolled on into the 12th and 13th centuries, by which time Pisa controlled Corsica, Sardinia and most of the mainland coast as far south as Civitavecchia. Most of the city's finest buildings date from this period, when the distinctive Pisan-Romanesque architectural style flourished.

Pisa's support for the Ghibellines during the tussles between the Holy Roman Emperor and the pope brought the city into conflict with its mostly Guelph Tuscan neighbours, including Siena, Lucca and Florence. The real blow came when Genoa's fleet defeated Pisa in devastating fashion at the Battle of Meloria in 1284. After the city fell to Florence in 1406, the Medici encouraged great artistic, literary and scientific endeavours and re-established Pisa's university. Galileo Galilei, the city's most famous son, later taught here.

◉ Sights

◉ Along the Arno

Pisa comes into its own along the Arno river banks. Splendid *palazzi,* painted a multitude of hues, line the southern *lungarno* (riverside embankment) from where Pisa's main shopping boulevard, Corso Italia, legs it south to the train station.

Pisa's medieval heart lies north of the water. From riverside **Piazza Cairoli** with its evening bevy of bars and *gelaterie,* meander along Via Cavour and get lost in the surrounding narrow lanes and alleys. A daily fresh-produce market fills **Piazza delle Vettovaglie**, ringed with 15th-century porticoes and popular *aperitivo* bar and cafe terraces. And marvel at graffiti on the facade of **Chiesa di San Michele in Borgo** (Borgo Stretto) that dates all the way back to a 15th-century election for the rector of a local school.

On the southern bank, the exquisite **Chiesa di Santa Maria della Spina** (Lungarno Gambacorti) is a showcase of the Pisan-Gothic architectural style Its interior is currently closed to the public.

Palazzo Blu   ART GALLERY
(www.palazzoblu.it; Lungarno Gambacorti 9; ◉10am-7pm Tue-Fri, to 8pm Sat & Sun) **FREE** Facing the river is this magnificently restored, 14th-century building that has a striking dusty-blue facade. Its over-the-top 19th-century interior decoration is the perfect backdrop for the Foundation CariPisa's art collection – predominantly Pisan works from the 14th to the 20th century, plus various temporary exhibitions (charges may apply for the latter).

Museo Nazionale di San Matteo   ART GALLERY
(Piazza San Matteo in Soarta; adult/reduced €5/2.50; ◉8.30am-7pm Tue-Sat, to 1.30pm Sun) This inspiring repository of medieval masterpieces sits in a 13th-century Benedictine convent on the Arno's northern waterfront boulevard. The collection of paintings from the Tuscan school (c 12th to 14th centuries) is notable, with works by Lippo Memmi, Taddeo Gaddi, Gentile da Fabriano and Ghirlandaio. Don't miss Masaccio's *St Paul,* Fra Angelico's *Madonna of Humility* and Simone Martini's *Polyptych of Saint Catherine.*

Equally engaging is the collection of 14th- and 15th-century Pisan sculptures, including pieces by Nicola and Giovanni Pisano, Andrea and Nino Pisano, Francesco di Valdambrino, Donatello, Michelozzo and Andrea della Robbia.

◉ Piazza dei Miracoli

No Tuscan sight is more immortalised in kitsch souvenirs than the iconic tower teetering on the edge of this gargantuan piazza, which is called both the **Campo dei Miracoli** (Field of Miracles) and **Piazza del Duomo** (Cathedral Sq). The piazza's expansive green lawns provide an urban carpet on which

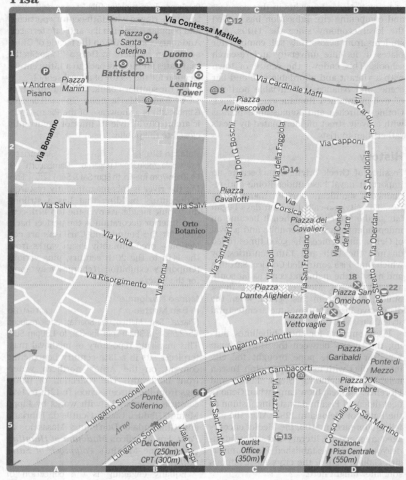

Europe's most extraordinary concentration of Romanesque buildings – in the form of the cathedral, baptistry and tower – are arranged. With two million visitors every year, crowds are the norm, many arriving by tour bus from Florence for a whirlwind visit.

★ **Leaning Tower**　　　　LANDMARK
(Torre Pendente; www.opapisa.it; Piazza dei Miracoli; incl admission to cathedral €18, combination ticket covering Battistero, Camposanto, Museo dell'Opera del Duomo and Museo delle Sinópie 1/2/3/4 sights €5/7/8/9 (reduced €3/4/5/6); ⏰ 8.30am-8pm summer, 10am-4.30pm winter) Yes, it's true: the Leaning Tower is nowhere near straight. Construction started in 1173 but stopped a decade later when the structure's first three tiers started tilting. In 1272 work started again, with artisans and masons attempting to bolster the foundations but failing miserably. Despite this, they kept going, compensating for the lean by gradually building straight up from the lower storeys.

The tower has tilted an extra 1mm each year. By 1993 it was 4.47m out of plumb, more than five degrees from the vertical. The most recent solution saw steel braces slung around the third storey that were then

Pisa

◎ **Top Sights**

FLORENCE & TUSCANY PISA

online or go straight to a ticket office when you arrive in Pisa to book a slot for later in the day. Visits last 30 minutes and involve a steep climb up 300-odd occasionally slippery steps. All bags, handbags included, must be deposited at the free left-luggage desk next to the central ticket office – cameras are about the only thing you can take up.

★ **Duomo**   CATHEDRAL
(Piazza dei Miracoli; admission free (with coupon from ticket office); ⊙ 10am-7.30pm summer, 10am-12.45pm & 2-4.30pm winter) **FREE** Pisa's cathedral was built with funds raised from spoils brought home after Pisans attacked an Arab fleet entering Palermo in 1063. Begun a year later, the cathedral, with its striking cladding of alternating bands of green and cream marble, became the blueprint floor for Romanesque churches throughout Tuscany. The elliptical dome, the first of its kind in Europe at the time, was added in 1380.

The cathedral was the largest in Europe when it was constructed; its breathtaking

joined to steel cables attached to neighbouring buildings. This held the tower in place as engineers began gingerly removing soil from below the northern foundations. After some 70 tonnes of earth had been extracted, the tower sank to its 18th-century level and, in the process, rectified the lean by 43.8cm. Experts believe that this will guarantee the tower's future for the next three centuries.

Access to the Leaning Tower is limited to 40 people at one time – children under eight are not allowed in/up and those aged eight to 12 years must hold an adult's hand. To avoid disappointment, book in advance

ℹ TOWER & COMBO TICKETS

Reserve and buy tickets for the Leaning Tower from one of two well-signposted ticket offices: the main ticket office behind the tower or the smaller office inside the Museo delle Sinópie (www.opapisa.it; Piazza dei Miracoli; ⊘ 8am-8pm summer (10am-5pm winter).

To guarantee your visit to the tower and to save the long queue in high season, buy tickets in advance online – tickets can be purchased up to 20 days in advance but no later than 12 days before visiting.

Ticket offices in Pisa also sell combination tickets covering admission to the Baptistry, Camposanto, Museo dell'Opera del Duomo and Museo delle Sinópie: a ticket covering 1/2/3/4 sights costs €5/7/8/9 (reduced €3/4/5/6). Admission to the cathedral is free, but you need to show a ticket – either for one of the other sights or a cathedral coupon distributed at ticket offices. Combination tickets covering four sights are valid for two days.

proportions were designed to demonstrate Pisa's domination of the Mediterranean. Its main facade – not completed until the 13th century – has four exquisite tiers of columns diminishing skywards, while the vast interior, 96m long and 28m high, is propped up by 68 hefty granite columns in classical style. The wooden ceiling decorated with 24-carat gold is a legacy from the period of Medici rule.

Before entering, study the three pairs of 16th-century **bronze doors** at the main entrance. Designed by the school of Giambologna to replace the wooden originals destroyed (along with most of the cathedral interior) by fire in 1596, the doors are quite spellbinding – hours can be spent deciphering the biblical scenes illustrating the immaculate conception of the Virgin and birth of Christ (central doors), the road to Calvary and crucifixion of Christ etc, and the Ministry of Christ. Kids can play spot the rhino.

Inside, don't miss the extraordinary early-14th-century octagonal **pulpit** in the north aisle. Sculpted from Carrara marble by Giovanni Pisano and featuring nude and heroic

figures, its depth of detail and heightening of feeling brought a new pictorial expressionism and life to Gothic sculpture. Pisano's work forms a striking contrast to the modern pulpit and altar by Italian sculptor Giuliano Vangi, controversially installed in 2001.

★ **Battistero** RELIGIOUS
(Baptistry; Piazza dei Miracoli; adult/reduced €5/3, combination ticket covering Battistero, Camposanto, Museo dell'Opera del Duomo and Museo delle Sinópie 1/2/3/4 sights €5/7/8/9 (reduced €3/4/5/6); ⊘ 8am-7.30pm summer, 10am-4.30pm winter) The unusual round baptistry has one dome piled on top of another, each roofed half in lead, half in tiles, and topped by a gilt bronze John the Baptist (1395). Construction began in 1152, but the building was remodelled and continued by Nicola and Giovanni Pisano more than a century later and was finally completed in the 14th century. The lower level of arcades is Pisan-Romanesque; the pinnacled upper section and dome are Gothic.

Inside, the hexagonal marble **pulpit** (1259–60) by Nicola Pisano is the highlight. Pisan scientist Galileo Galilei (who, so the story goes, came up with the laws of the pendulum by watching a lamp in Pisa's cathedral swing), was baptised in the octagonal font (1246).

Don't leave without climbing to the **Upper Gallery** to listen to the custodian demonstrate the double dome's remarkable acoustics and echo effects, which occurs every half-hour on the hour/half-hour.

Camposanto CEMETERY
(Piazza dei Miracoli; adult/reduced €5/3, combination ticket covering Battistero, Camposanto, Museo dell'Opera del Duomo and Museo delle Sinópie 1/2/3/4 sights €5/7/8/9 (reduced €3/4/5/6); ⊘ 8am-7.30pm summer, 10am-4.30pm winter) Soil shipped from Calvary during the Crusades is said to lie within the white walls of this hauntingly beautiful final resting place for many prominent Pisans. During WWII, Allied artillery destroyed many of the cloisters' frescoes, but a couple were salvaged and are now displayed in the **Sala Affreschi** (Frescoes Room).

Most notable is the *Triumph of Death* (1336–41), a remarkable illustration of Hell attributed to 14th-century painter Buonamico Buffalmacco. Fortunately, the mirrors apparently once stuck next to the graphic, no-holds-barred images of the damned being roasted alive on spits have since been removed – meaning a marginally less uncomfortable time for visitors who would have once seen their own faces peering out of the cruel wall painting. Buffalmacco's *Last Judgement & Hell* (1336–41), in the same room, is equally brutal.

Museo delle Sinópie   MUSEUM

(Piazza dei Miracoli; adult/reduced €5/3, combination ticket covering Battistero, Camposanto, Museo dell'Opera del Duomo and Museo delle Sinópie 1/2/3/4 sights €5/7/8/9 (reduced €3/4/5/6); ☺8am-7.30pm summer, 10am-4.30pm winter) This museum safeguards several *sinópie* (preliminary sketches) drawn by artists in red earth pigment on the walls of the Camposanto in the 14th and 15th centuries. The museum makes for a compelling study in fresco painting, with short films and scale models filling in the gaps.

Museo dell'Opera del Duomo   MUSEUM

(Piazza dei Miracoli; adult/reduced €5/3, combination ticket covering Battistero, Camposanto, Museo dell'Opera del Duomo and Museo delle Sinópie 1/2/3/4 sights €5/7/8/9 (reduced €3/4/5/6); ☺8am-8pm summer, 10am-5pm winter) A repository for works of art once displayed in the cathedral and baptistry, this museum's highlights include Giovanni Pisano's ivory carving of the *Madonna and Child* (1299), which was made for the cathedral's high altar, as well as his mid-13th-century *Madonna del colloquio*, originally from a gate of the *duomo*. Don't miss the tranquil cloister garden with great views of the Leaning Tower.

⚜️ Festivals & Events

Luminaria   LIGHT SHOW

The night before Pisa's patron saint's day is magical: thousands upon thousands of candles and blazing torches light up the river and riverbanks while fireworks bedazzle the night sky; 16 June.

Regata Storica di San Ranieri   SPORT

The Arno comes to life with a rowing regatta to commemorate the city's patron saint; 17 June.

Gioco del Ponte   CULTURE

During Gioco del Ponte (Game of the Bridge) two teams in medieval costume battle it out over the Ponte di Mezzo; last Sunday in June.

Palio delle Quattro Antiche Repubbliche Marinare   REGATTA

(Regatta of the Four Ancient Maritime Republics) In this regatta, the four historical maritime rivals – Pisa, Venice, Amalfi and Genoa – meet yearly in June for a procession of boats and a dramatic race; it will be in Pisa in 2017.

🛏️ Sleeping

Hostel Pisa Tower   HOSTEL €

(☑ 329 7017387, 05 0520 2454; www.hostelpisatower.it; Via Piave 4; dm €18-22, apt €49-69; @ 🛜) This extremely friendly place near Piazza dei Miracoli occupies a suburban villa with a garden. Rooms are cheerful, clean and comfortable but lack bathroom facilities (only two showers and two toilets for 22 beds) and there's no communal kitchen. The apartment sleeps two or three, and comes with small kitchen and private car park. There's free wi-fi but internet access costs €4/hr.

Royal Victoria Hotel   HOTEL €€

(☑ 05 094 01 11; www.royalvictoria.it; Lungarno Pacinotti 12; d €110-170, tr €130-170, q €170, s/d with shared bathroom €70/80; ❄️ 🛜 🚗) This doyen of Pisan hotels, run with pride by the Piegaja family since 1837, offers old-world luxury accompanied by warm, attentive service. The word on the street says rooms vary, but those we saw were the perfect shabby-chic mix of Grand Tour antique – love the parquet floors and flashes of exposed stone – and modern-day comfort. Garage parking/bike hire is €20/15 per day, wi-fi is €2.50 per hour, breakfast is €5.

Hotel Bologna   HOTEL €€

(☑ 05 050 21 20; www.hotelbologna.pisa.it; Via Mazzini 57; d €134-198, tr €188-278, q €194-298; ❄️ @ 🛜 🚗) Well away from the Piazza dei Miracoli mayhem (but an easy 1km walk or bike ride), this four-star choice on the south side of the Arno is a 68-room oasis of peace and tranquillity. Its rooms have wooden floors and high ceilings, and some are nicely frescoed. Those for four make it a practical, if pricey, family choice. Courtyard parking/bike hire costs €10/12 per day.

Hotel Relais dell'Orologio   HOTEL €€€

(☑ 05 083 03 61; www.hotelrelaisorologio.com; Via della Faggiola 12-14; s/d from €120/195; ❄️ 🛜) Something of a honeymoon venue, Pisa's dreamy five-star hotel occupies a tastefully restored 14th-century fortified tower house in a quiet street. Some rooms have original frescoes and the flowery patio restaurant makes a welcome retreat from the crowds. Book through its website to bag the cheapest deal.

Eating

Being a university town, Pisa has a good range of eating places, especially around Borgo Stretto and south of the river in the trendy San Martino quarter.

Il Montino
PIZZERIA €

(Vicolo del Monte 1; pizzas €3-6.50; ⊙10.30am-3pm & 5-10pm Mon-Sat) There is nothing flash or fancy about this Pisan institution. Take away or order at the bar then grab a table, inside or out, and munch on house specialities like *cecina* (chickpea pizza) and *castagnacci* (chestnut cake) washed down with a *spuma* (sweet, nonalcoholic drink). Or go for a *foccacine* (flat roll) filled with salami, pancetta or *porchetta* (suckling pig).

It's hidden in a back alley – the quickest way to find the place is to head west along Via Ulisse Dini from the northern end of Borgo Stretto (opposite the Lo Sfizio cafe at Borgo Stretto 54) to Piazza San Felice where it is easy to spot, on your left, a telling blue neon 'Pizzeria' sign.

Il Crudo
SANDWICHES €

(www.ilcrudopisa.it; Piazza Cairoli 7; panini €4.50-6; ⊙11am-3.30pm & 5pm-1am Mon-Thu, to 2am Fri, 11am-2am Sat, 11am-1am Sun) Grab a well-filled *panino* to munch on the move or enjoy one al fresco with a glass of wine at this pocket-sized *panineria* and *vineria* (wine bar). Find it by the river on one of Pisa's prettiest squares.

Osteria Bernardo
MODERN TUSCAN €€

(☑05 057 52 16; www.osteriabernardo.it; Piazza San Paolo all'Orto 1; meals €30; ⊙lunch & dinner Tue-Sun) This small *osteria* on one of Pisa's loveliest squares is the perfect fusion of easy dining and gourmet excellence. Its menu is small – just four or five dishes to choose from for each course – and its cuisine is creative.

Osteria del Porton Rosso
OSTERIA €€

(☑05 058 05 66; www.portonrosso.com; Vicolo del Porton Rosso 11; meals €25; ⊙lunch & dinner Mon-Sat) Don't be put off by the rather dank alley leading to this busy *osteria* (casual eatery) a block north of the river. Inside, you'll encounter friendly staff and excellent regional cuisine from the land and the nearby sea. Pisan specialities such as fresh ravioli with salted cod and chickpeas happily coexist with Tuscan classics such as grilled fillet steak, and the €10 lunchtime deal is unbeatable value.

biOsteria 050
ORGANIC €€

(☑05 054 31 06; Via San Francesco 36; meals €20-30; ⊙lunch Mon-Sun, dinner Tue-Sun; ☑)
 Everything that Marco and Raffaele at Zero Cinquante (Zero Fifty) cook is strictly seasonal, local and organic, products being sourced from farms within a 50km radius of Pisa. Try pasta, risotto, meat dishes or one of the excellent-value daily lunch specials. Ample choice for vegetarians and coeliacs, too.

Drinking & Nightlife

Most of the student drinking action is in and around Piazza delle Vettovaglie and the university on cafe-ringed Piazza Dante Alighieri.

Sottobosco
CAFE

(www.sottoboscocafe.it; Piazza San Paolo all'Orto; ⊙10am-midnight Tue-Fri, noon-1am Sat, 7pm-midnight Sun) A creative cafe with a few books for sale and vintage-themed decor, Sottobosco is a lovely spot for a coffee, light lunch or drink. At dusk, jazz bands play or DJs spin tunes.

Bazeel
BAR

(www.bazeel.it; Lungarno Pacinotti 1; ⊙5pm-2am) A generous *aperitivo* spread, live music or a DJ, and a great little terrace out front ensure Bazeel is always busy. Check its Twitter feed for what's on.

Salza
CAFE

(Borgo Stretto 44; ⊙8am-8.30pm summer, shorter hrs Tue-Sun winter) This old-fashioned cake shop has been tempting Pisans off Borgo Stretto and into sugar-induced wickedness since 1898. It's an equally lovely spot for a cocktail – anytime.

⊕ Information

Tourist office (☑05 091 03 50; www.pisaunicaterra.it; Piazza Vittorio Emanuele II, 16; ⊙9am-6pm)

⊕ Getting There & Away

AIR

Galileo Galilei Airport (www.pisa-airport.com) Tuscany's main international airport, 2km south of town, has flights to most major European cities.

BUS

Pisan company **CPT** (www.cpt.pisa.it; Piazza Sant'Antonio) runs buses to/from Volterra

(€6.10, two hours, up to 10 daily) and Livorno (€2.75, 55 minutes, half-hourly to hourly).

CAR

Pisa is close to the A11 and A12. The SCG FI-PI-LI (SS67) is a toll-free alternative for Florence and Livorno, while the north–south SS1, the Via Aurelia, connects the city with La Spezia and Rome.

TRAIN

There is a handy **left luggage office** (Deposito Bagagli; 1st 12hr €4, subsequent 12hr €2; ⊘ 6am-9pm) at **Pisa Centrale** (Piazza della Stazione) train station – not to be confused with north-of-town Pisa San Rossore station. Regional train services to/from Pisa Centrale include:
Florence €7, 1¼ tours, frequent
Livorno €2.50, 15 minutes, frequent
Lucca €3.30, 30 minutes, every 30 minutes
Viareggio €3.30, 15 minutes, every 20 minutes

ℹ Getting Around

TO/FROM THE AIRPORT
Bus

The LAM Rossa (red) bus line (€1.10, 10 minutes, every 10 to 20 minutes) passes through the city centre and the train station en route to/from the airport. Buy tickets from the blue ticket machine, next to the bus stops to the right of the train station exit.

Taxi

A taxi between the airport and city centre costs around €10. To book, call **Radio Taxi Pisa** (⌑ 05 054 16 00; www.cotapi.it).

Train

Services run to/from Pisa Centrale (€2.50, five minutes, at least 30 per day); purchase and validate your ticket before boarding.

BICYCLE

Many hotels rent bikes. Otherwise, stands at the northern end of Via Santa Maria and other streets off Piazza dei Miracoli rent four-wheel rickshaws for up to three/six people (€10/15 per hour) and regular bicycles (€3 per hour).

CAR & MOTORCYCLE

Parking costs up to €2 per hour, but you must be careful that the car park you choose is not in the city's ZTL. There's a free car park outside the zone on Lungarno Guadalongo near the Fortezza di San Gallo on the south side of the Arno.

HORSE & CARRIAGE

From Easter to October, horse-drawn carriages sit in front of the Museo dell'Opera del Duomo on Piazza dei Miracoli, waiting to take tourists for a ride. Count on €40 for a 20-minute tour of town.

Lucca

POP 86,884

This beautiful old city elicits love at first sight with its rich history, handsome churches and excellent restaurants. Hidden behind imposing Renaissance walls, it is an essential stopover on any Tuscan tour and a perfect base for exploring the Apuane Alps and the Garfagnana.

Founded by the Etruscans, Lucca became a Roman colony in 180 BC and a free *comune* (self-governing city) during the 12th century, when it enjoyed a period of prosperity based on the silk trade. In 1314 it briefly fell under the control of Pisa but under the leadership of local adventurer Castruccio Castracani degli Antelminelli, the city regained its freedom and remained an independent republic for almost 500 years.

Napoleon ended all this in 1805, when he created the principality of Lucca and placed his sister Elisa in control. Twelve years later the city became a Bourbon duchy, before being incorporated into the Kingdom of Italy. It miraculously escaped being bombed during WWII, so the fabric of the historic centre has remained unchanged for centuries.

◉ Sights

Threading its way through the medieval heart of the old city, cobbled Via Fillungo is full of sleek, modern boutiques housed in great old buildings – cast your eyes above the street-level bustle to appreciate ancient awnings and architectural details.

East of Via Fillungo is one of Tuscany's loveliest piazzas, oval, cafe-studded Piazza Anfiteatro, so called after the amphitheatre that was located here in Roman times. Look closely to spot remnants of the amphitheatre's brick arches and masonry on the exterior walls of the medieval houses ringing the piazza.

Palazzo Pfanner   PALACE
(www.palazzopfanner.it; Via degli Asili 33; palace or garden adult/reduced €4.50/4, both €6/5; ⊘ 10am-6pm summer) Fire the romantic in you with a stroll around this beautiful 17th-century palace where parts of *Portrait of a Lady* (1996) starring Nicole Kidman and John Malkovich were shot. Its baroque-styled garden – the only one of substance within the city walls – is irresistible with its ornamental pond, belle époque lemon house and 18th-century statues

FLORENCE & TUSCANY LUCCA

Lucca

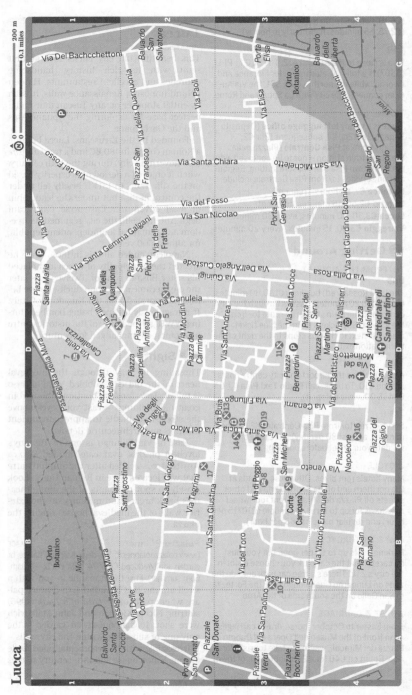

200 m
0.1 miles

Via Del Bachcchettoni

Baluardo San Salvatore

Porta Elisa

Baluardo della Libertà

Via del Bacchettoni

Baluardo San Regolo

Via Paoli

Via Elisa

Orto Botanico

Moat

Piazza San Francesco

Via della Quarquonia

Via Santa Chiara

Via San Michetto

Via del Fosso

Via del Fosso

Via San Nicolao

Porta San Gervasio

Via Rosi

Piazza Santa Maria

Via Santa Gemma Galgani

Via della Fratta

Piazza San Pietro

Via Dell'Angelo Custode

Via del Giardino Botanico

Passeggiata della Mura

Via della Cavallerizza

Via della Quarquonia

Via Fillungo

Via Canuleia

Piazza Anfiteatro

Via Mordini

Via Sant'Andrea

Via Guinigi

Via Santa Croce

Via Della Rosa

Cattedrale di San Martino

Piazza Scarpellini

Piazza San Frediano

Piazza del Carmine

Via dei Servi

Piazza Antelminelli

Piazza San Martino

Via Vallisneri

Via Battisti

Via degli Angeli

Via Fillungo

Via del Moro

Via Buia

Via Cenami

Piazza Bernardini

Via del Molinetto

Piazza San Giovanni

Piazza San Michele

Via Santa Lucia

Piazza del Giglio

Via del Battistero

Via di Poggio

Piazza San Michele

Piazza Napoleone

Piazza Veneto

Via San Giorgio

Via Tegrimi

Corte Campana

Piazza Sant'Agostino

Via Santa Giustina

Via del Toro

Via Vittorio Emanuele II

Piazza San Romano

Orto Botanico

Moat

Passeggiata della Mura

Via Delle Conce

Via Galli Tassi

Baluardo Santa Croce

Porta San Donato

Piazzale San Donato

Via San Paolino

Piazzale Verdi

Piazzale Boccherini

Lucca

of Greek gods posing between potted lemon trees.

Afterwards, climb the grand outdoor staircase to the frescoed and furnished *piano nobile* (main reception room), home to Felix Pfanner, an Austrian émigré who first brought beer to Italy – and brewed it in the mansion's cellars from 1846 until 1929. In summer, chamber-music concerts are often held here.

City Wall
CITY WALLS

Lucca's monumental *mura* (wall) was built around the old city in the 16th and 17th centuries and remains in almost perfect condition due to the long periods of peace the city has enjoyed. It's 12m high and 4km long; the ramparts are crowned with a tree-lined footpath that looks down on the *centro storico* and out towards the Apuane Alps.

This path is the favourite Lucchesi location for a *passeggiata*, be it on foot, bicycle or inline skate. Children's playgrounds, swings and picnic tables beneath shady plane trees add a buzz of activity to Baluardo San Regolo, Baluardo San Salvatore and Baluardo Santa Croce – three of the 11 bastions studding the way – and older kids kick balls around on the vast green lawns of Baluardo San Donato.

★ Cattedrale di San Martino
CATHEDRAL

(Piazza San Martino; sacristy adult/reduced €3/2, with cathedral museum & Chiesa dei SS Giovanni e Reparata €7/5; ⏱ 7am-6pm summer, to 5pm winter; sacristy 9.30am-4.45pm Mon-Fri, 9.30am-6.45pm Sat, 11.30am-5pm Sun) Lucca's predominantly Romanesque cathedral dates to the start of the 11th century. Its stunning facade was constructed in the prevailing Lucca-Pisan style and was designed to accommodate the pre-existing *campanile*. The reliefs over the

left doorway of the portico are believed to be by Nicola Pisano.

The cathedral interior was rebuilt in the 14th and 15th centuries with a Gothic flourish. The **Volto Santo** (literally 'Holy Countenance') is not to be missed. Legend has it this simply fashioned image of a dark-skinned, life-sized Christ on a wooden crucifix was carved by Nicodemus, who witnessed the crucifixion. In fact, the sculpture has recently been dated to the 13th century. A major object of pilgrimage, it is carried in procession through the streets on 13 September each year at dusk during the Luminaria di Santa Croce, a solemn torchlit procession marking its miraculous arrival in Lucca.

The cathedral's many other works of art include a magnificent *Last Supper* by Tintoretto above the third altar of the south aisle and Domenico Ghirlandaio's 1479 *Madonna Enthroned with Saints*. This impressive work by Michelangelo's master is currently located in the **sacristy**. Opposite lies the exquisite, gleaming marble memorial to Ilaria del Carretto carved by Jacopo della Quercia in 1407. The young second wife of the 15th-century lord of Lucca, Paolo Guinigi, Ilaria died in childbirth aged only 24. At her feet lies her faithful dog.

Chiesa e Battistero dei SS Giovanni e Reparata
CHURCH

(Piazza San Giovanni; adult/reduced €4/3, with cathedral museum & sacristy €7/5; ⏱ 10am-6pm summer, to 5pm Sat & Sun winter) The 12th-century interior of this deconsecrated church is a hauntingly atmospheric setting for summertime **opera recitals**; buy tickets in advance inside the church. In the north transept, the Gothic **baptistry** crowns an archaeological area comprising five building levels going back to the Roman period. End with a hike up the red-brick campanile – what a view!

Chiesa di San Michele in Foro CHURCH
(Piazza San Michele; ⊙ 7.40am-noon & 3-6pm summer, 9am-noon & 3-5pm winter) One of Lucca's many architecturally significant churches, this lovely Romanesque edifice marks the spot where the city's Roman forum once stood. The present building with its exquisite wedding-cake facade was constructed on the site of its 8th-century precursor over a period of nearly 300 years, beginning in the 11th century.

Crowning the structure is a figure of the archangel Michael slaying a dragon. Inside, don't miss Filippino Lippi's 1479 painting of *SS Helen, Jerome, Sebastian and Roch* (complete with plague sore) in the south transept.

☆ Festivals & Events

Summer Festival MUSIC
(www.summer-festival.com) Top international artists perform in a variety of musical genres at this July fest.

Puccini Festival MUSIC
(www.puccinifestival.it; Torre del Lago) Hosted by the nearby village of Torre del Lago in July and August, this festival has been going for more than 50 years.

⊨ Sleeping

Tourist offices have accommodation lists and, if you visit in person, can make reservations for you (free of charge); pay 10% of the room price as an on-the-spot deposit and the remainder at the hotel.

★ Piccolo Hotel Puccini HOTEL €
(⧉ 05 835 54 21; www.hotelpuccini.com; Via di Poggio 9; s/d €73/98; ❀ �☎) Snug around the corner from the great man himself (or at least a bronze statue) and the house where he was born is this well-run small hotel. Decor is old-fashioned, and its 14 rooms have high ceilings, modern bathrooms and vintage ceiling fans. A simple breakfast costs €3.50 and rates are around 30% lower in the depths of winter.

Ostello San Frediano HOSTEL €
(⧉ 05 8346 9957; www.ostellolucca.it; Via della Cavallerizza 12; dm/s/d/tr/q €22/45/65/80/105; ⊙ mid-Feb–Dec; ☎) Hostellers won't get closer to the action than this staggeringly historic

building slap-bang in the centre of walled Lucca. Top notch in comfort and service, this Hostelling International–affiliated hostel with 141 beds in voluminous rooms is serviced with a bar and grandiose dining room (breakfast €3, lunch or dinner €11). Non-HI members can join on the spot for €2 per year.

★ Locanda Vigna Ilaria B&B €€
(⧉ 05 833 32 09; www.locandavignailaria.it; Via della Pieve Santo Stefano 967c, St Alessio; d/q €110/120; ℗) Those on a Tuscan road trip will be instantly smitten with this lovely stone house 4km north of Lucca (leave the car in the free car park, then meander along green lanes, past vast villas bathed in olive groves). The *locanda* (inn) has five rooms, varying in size and each funished with a mix of old, new and upcycled. Its downstairs restaurant, open in the evening, is a gastronomic fish-driven treat (meals €45, menus €30 to €79).

2italia APARTMENT €€
(⧉ 392 9960271; www.2italia.com; Via della Anfiteatro 74; apt for 2 adults & up to 4 children €190; ☎ ♿) Five family-friendly self-contained apartments overlooking Piazza Anfiteatro, with a communal kids' playroom in the attic. Available on a nightly basis (minimum two nights), 2italia is the brainchild of well-travelled parents-of-three Kristin (English) and Kaare (Norwegian). Spacious apartments sleep up to six, have fully equipped kitchen and washing machine, and come with sheets and towels.

Alla Corte degli Angeli BOUTIQUE HOTEL €€
(⧉ 05 8346 9204; www.allacortedegliangeli.com; Via degli Angeli 23; s/d €120/190; ❀ @ ☎) Occupying three floors of a 15th-century townhouse, this four-star boutique hotel has just 10 rooms and a lovely beamed lounge. Beautifully frescoed rooms are named after flowers: lovers in the hugely romantic Rosa room can lie beneath a pergola and swallow-filled sky, while guests in Orchidea have their own private shower-sauna. Breakfast costs €10.

✕ Eating

Da Felice PIZZERIA €
(www.pizzeriadafelice.com; Via Buia 12; focaccias €1-3, pizza slices €1.30; ⊙ 10am-8.30pm Mon-Sat) This buzzing local, which has sat behind Piazza San Michele since 1960, is easy to spot – come noon look for the crowd packed around two tiny tables inside, spilling out

A WALLTOP PICNIC

When in Lucca, picnicking atop its city walls – on grass or at a wooden picnic table – is as lovely (and typical) a Lucchesi lunch as any.

Buy fresh-from-the-oven pizza and focaccia with a choice of fillings and toppings from fabulous 'n' famed bakery **Forno Amedeo Giusti** (Via Santa Lucia 20; pizzas & filled focaccias per kg €9-16; ⊙7am-1pm & 4-7.30pm Mon-Sat, 4-7.30pm Sun), then nip across the street for a bottle of Lucchesi wine and Garfagnese *biscotti al farro* (spelt biscuits) at **Antica Bodega di Prospero** (Via Santa Lucia 13; ⊙9am-1pm & 4-7.30pm); look for the old-fashioned shop window fabulously stuffed with sacks of beans, lentils and other local pulses.

Complete the perfect picnic with a slice of *buccellato*, a traditional sweet bread loaf with sultanas and aniseed seeds, baked by **Taddeucci** (www.taddeucci.com; Piazza San Michele 34; buccellato per 300/600/900g loaf €4.50/9/13.50; ⊙8.30am-7.45pm, closed Thu winter) since 1881. Or tantalise your tastebuds with truffles and other heavenly chocolate creations from **Caniparoli** (www.caniparolicioccolateria.it; Via San Paolino 96; ⊙9.30am-1pm & 3.30-9.30pm), the best *cioccolateria* (chocolate maker) in town.

the door or squatting on one of two street-side benches. *Cecina* and *castagnacci* are the raison d'être.

Trattoria da Leo
TRATTORIA €
(☑05 8349 2236; Via Tegrimi 1; meals €25; ⊙lunch & dinner Mon-Sat) A veteran everyone knows and loves, Leo is famed around town for its friendly ambience and cheap food – which ranges from plain Jane acceptable to grand-ma delicious. Get here early in summer to snag one of 10 checked-cloth-draped tables crammed beneath parasols on the narrow street outside. No credit cards.

Cantine Bernardini
TUSCAN €€
(☑05 8349 4336; www.cantinebernardini.com; Via del Suffragio 7; meals €40; ⊙lunch & dinner Tue-Sun) This maze of a hybrid *osteria-enoteca*, hidden in the red-brick vaulted cellars of 16th-century Palazzo Bernardini, has got the balance just right. Seasonal Tuscan dishes tempt, and the wine list is exceptional. Extra kudos for the kids' menu and Friday-evening DJs and live music.

Canuleia
TUSCAN €€
(☑05 8346 7470; Via Canuleia 14; meals €35; ⊙lunch & dinner Tue-Sun) What makes this dining location stand out from the crowd is its secret walled garden out the back – the perfect spot to escape the tourist hordes and listen to birds tweet over partridge risotto, artichoke and prawn spaghetti or a tradi-tional *peposa* (beef and pepper stew).

Osteria Baralla
OSTERIA €€
(☑05 8344 0240; www.osteriabaralla.it; Via An-fiteatro 5; meals €30; ⊙lunch & dinner Mon-Sat)

This traditional *osteria* dating to 1860 is in every guidebook, and for good reason. Feast on local specialities beneath huge red-brick vaults. Thursday is *bolito misto* (mixed boiled meat) day; Saturday celebrates roast pork.

★Ristorante Giglio
TUSCAN €€€
(☑05 8349 4058; www.ristorantegiglio.com; Piazza del Giglio 2; meals €40, 2-person tasting menu €70; ⊙lunch & dinner Thu-Mon, dinner Wed) Don't let the tacky plastic-covered pavement terrace on Lucca's largest pedestrian city square de-ter. Inside, Giglio is stunning. Dine at white-clothed tables, sip a complimentary glass of *prosecco*, watch the fire crackle in the ornate marble fireplace and know you're dining in the finest restaurant in town. Cuisine is tra-ditional Tuscan with a modern twist.

Buca di Sant'Antonio
TUSCAN €€€
(☑05 835 58 81; www.bucadisantantonio.com; Via della Cervia 3; meals €50; ⊙lunch & dinner Tue-Sat, lunch Sun) Gosh, what a fabulous collection of copper pots strung from the wood-beamed ceiling! This atmosphere-laden restaurant has wooed romantic diners since 1782 and is still going strong. The Tuscan cuisine does not quite live up to the exceptional wine list, but it remains a favourite nonetheless.

❶ Information

Tourist office (☑05 8358 3150; www.comune. lucca.it; Piazzale Verdi; ⊙9am-7pm summer, to 5.30pm winter) Free hotel reservations; bicycle hire and a left-luggage service.

❶ Getting There & Away

BUS

From the bus stops around Piazzale Verdi, **Vaibus** (www.vaibus.it) runs services throughout the region, including to Pisa airport (€3.20, 45 minutes to one hour, 30 daily) and Castelnuovo di Garfagnana (€4.20, 1½ hours, eight daily)

CAR & MOTORCYCLE

The A11 runs westwards to Pisa and Viareggio and eastwards to Florence. To access the Garfagnana, take the SS12 and continue on the SS445.

The easiest parking option is Parcheggio Carducci, just outside Porta Sant'Anna. Within the walls, most car parks are for residents only, indicated by yellow lines. Blue lines indicate where anyone, including tourists, can park (€1.50 to €2 per hour). If you are staying within the city walls, contact your hotel ahead of your arrival and enquire about the possibility of getting a temporary resident permit during your stay.

TRAIN

The station is south of the city walls: take the path across the moat and through the tunnel under Baluardo San Colombano.

Florence €7, 1¼ to 1¾ hours, hourly
Pisa €3.30, 30 minutes, every half hour
Viareggio €3.30, 25 minutes, hourly

❶ Getting Around

Rent a bicycle (€3/15 per hour/day; ID required) from the Piazzale Verdi tourist office or from the following places:

Cicli Bizzarri (☑ 05 8349 6682; www.ciclibizzarri.net; Piazza Santa Maria 32; per day €15; ◷ 9am-7pm summer)

Biciclette Poli (☑ 05 8349 3787; www.biciclettepoli.com; Piazza Santa Maria 42; per day €15; ◷ 9am-7pm summer)

Viareggio

Italy's beach-loving hoi polloi pack out the coastal strip known as the Versilian Riviera, which legs it north from this major town to the regional border with Liguria.

Frolicking on the long sandy beach and lapping up the seafront's gorgeous line-up of 1920s art nouveau facades aside, the main reason to visit Viareggio is for its flamboyant, four-week Mardi Gras Carnevale (www.viareggio.ilcarnevale.com) in February, which is second only to Venice for party spirit.

Pietrasanta

POP 24,900

Often overlooked by Tuscan travellers, this refined art town – an easy day trip by train from Pisa (€3.30, 25 minutes) – is an unexpected and charming surprise. Its bijou historic heart, originally walled, is car-free and loaded with tiny art galleries, workshops and fashion boutiques – perfect for a day's amble broken only by lunch.

Founded in 1255 by Guiscardo da Pietrasanta, *podestà* of Lucca, Pietrasanta was seen as a prize by Genoa, Lucca, Pisa and Florence, all of whom jostled for possession of its marble quarries and bronze foundries. Florence predictably won and Leo X (Giovanni de' Medici) took control in 1513, putting the town's famous quarries at the disposal of Michelangelo, who came here in 1518 to source marble for the facade of Florence's San Lorenzo. The artistic inclination of Pietrasanta dates from this time, and today it is the home of many artists, including internationally lauded Colombian-born sculptor Fernando Botero, whose work can be seen here.

◉ Sights

From Pietrasanta train station (Piazza della Stazione) head straight across Piazza Carducci to the old city gate and onto central square Piazza del Duomo, where the attractive Duomo di San Martino (1256), with its red-brick and 36m-tall bell tower, awaits. Neighbouring 13th-century Chiesa di Sant'Agostino (Piazza del Duomo; ◷ hrs vary) was deconsecrated and is now a wonderfully evocative venue for art exhibitions. Next, dip into Pietrasanta's art heritage with dozens of moulds of famous sculptures cast or carved in Pietrasanta, at the Museo dei Bozzetti (☑ 05 8479 5500; www.museodeibozzetti.it; Via Sant'Agostino 1; ◷ 2-7pm Tue-Sat, 4-7pm Sun) FREE inside the convent adjoining the church.

Cross to the other side of the square and meander along Via Giuseppe Mazzini, the town's main shopping strip bookended by contemporary street sculptures. Tucked between boutiques at No 103 is the superb Chiesa della Misericordia, frescoed with the *Gate of Paradise* and *Gate of Hell* by Botero (the artist portrays himself in hell).

🛏 Sleeping

⭐ **Albergo Pietrasanta**　　BOUTIQUE HOTEL €€€
(☑ 05 8479 3726; www.albergopietrasanta.com; Via Garibaldi 35; s €132-231, d €213-277; P ✳ @ 🛜)
Should you find yourself totally smitten with Pietrasanta and unable to leave, this chic 17th-century *palazzo* – a perfect fusion of old and new – is among Tuscany's loveliest boutique town hotels.

🍴 Eating & Drinking

⭐ **Filippo**　　MODERN TUSCAN €€
(☑ 05 847 00 10; http://ristorantefilippo.com; Via Stagio Stagi 22; meals €30; ⊙ lunch & dinner, closed Mon winter) 🖊 This exceptional foodie address never disappoints. Cuisine is seasonal and as creative as the interior design. Its salads in particular are superb, as are its unusual pasta *primi*. Arrive before 1pm to ensure a table; reserve in advance to dine after dusk.

⭐ **L'Enoteca Marcucci**　　WINE BAR
(☑ 05 8479 1962; www.enotecamarcucci.it; Via Garibaldi 40; ⊙ 10am-1pm & 5pm-1am Tue-Sun) Taste fine Tuscan wine, perched on bar stools at high wooden tables or beneath big parasols on the street outside. Whichever you pick, the distinctly funky, artsy spirit of Pietrasanta's best-loved *enoteca* enthrals.

Livorno

POP 156,800

Tuscany's second-largest city is a quintessential port town. Though first impressions are unlikely to be kind, this is a 'real' city that really does grow on you. Its seafood is the best on the Tyrrhenian coast, its historic quarter threaded with Venetian-style canals is shabby-chic, and pebbly beaches stretch south from the town's belle époque seafront. Be it a short stay between ferries or a day trip from Florence or Pisa, Livorno (Leghorn in English) is understated and agreeable.

◉ Sights & Activities

⭐ **Terrazza Mascagni**　　PROMENADE
(Viale Italia) No trip to Livorno is complete without a stroll along (and photo shoot of) this dazzling 'work of art' – an elegant 1920s terrace with stone balustrades that sweeps gracefully along the seafront in a dramatic chessboard flurry of black and white checks. Wedged between the terrace

and Livorno's naval academy a little further south is the elegant soft apricot facade of **Bagni Pancaldi**, old-fashioned baths where you can swim, rent pedalos and canoes, hang out in coloured canvas cabins and frolic in the sun.

⭐ **Piccola Venezia**　　HISTORIC QUARTER
The area known as Piccola Venezia or 'Little Venice' is crossed with small canals built during the 17th century using Venetian methods of reclaiming land from the sea. **Fortezza Nuova** (New Fort; ⊙ 24hr) **FREE**, built for the Medici court in the late 16th century, is the quarter's main attraction although little of it remains. Canals link it with the **Fortezza Vecchia** (Old Fort; ⊙ 24hr) **FREE**, constructed 60 years earlier on the waterfront.

End your exploration of the quarter on gorgeous **Piazza dei Domenicani**, across the bridge at the northern end of Via Borra. **Chiesa di Santa Catarina**, with its ancient, thick stone walls, stands sentry on the western side of the square as it did for the Medicis four centuries ago. Stroll down the causeway by the bridge to **La Bodeguita** (Scala Rosciano 9; ⊙ 9pm-1am Mon-Sat), a red-brick cellar bar with sun-drenched wooden-decking terrace floating on the canal.

Museo Civico Giovanni Fattori　　ART GALLERY
(Via San Jacopo in Acquaviva 65; adult/reduced €4/2; ⊙ 10am-1pm & 4-7pm Tue-Sun) Set in a pretty park, this museum features works by the 19th-century Italian Impressionist Macchiaioli school led by Livorno-born Giovanni Fattori. The group, inspired by the Parisian Barbizon school, flouted stringent academic art conventions and worked directly from nature, emphasising immediacy and freshness through patches, or 'stains' *(macchia),* of colour.

🛏 Sleeping

⭐ **Hotel al Teatro**　　BOUTIQUE HOTEL €
(☑ 05 8689 8705; www.hotelalteatro.it; Via Mayer 42; s/d €85/110; P ✳ @ 🛜) One of Tuscany's loveliest urban hotels, this bijou eight-room address with marble staircase, antique furniture, tapestries and individually designed rooms is irresistible. But the real stunner is the gravel garden out back where guests can lounge on green wicker furniture beneath a

Livorno

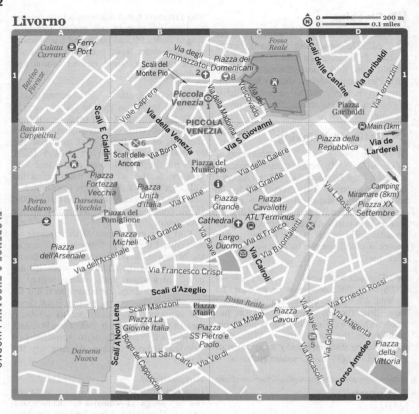

N 0 ———— 200 m
0 ———— 0.1 miles

Livorno

◎ Top Sights
1 Piccola Venezia	B1

◎ Sights
2 Chiesa di Santa Catarina	B1
3 Fortezza Nuova	C1
4 Fortezza Vecchia	A2

⊜ Sleeping
5 Hotel al Teatro	D4

⊗ Eating
6 L'Ancora	B2
7 Mercato Centrale	D3

◉ Drinking & Nightlife
8 La Bodeguita	C1

breathtakingly beautiful, 350-year-old magnolia tree.

Camping Miramare CAMPGROUND €
(☎ 05 8658 0402; www.campingmiramare.it; Via del Littorale 220; camping 2 people, car & tent €40-80; ⊛ ⊞) Be it a tent pitched beneath trees or the deluxe version with wooden terrace and sun-loungers on the sandy beach, this site – open year-round thanks to its village of mobile homes, maxi caravans and bungalows – has it all. Rates out of high season drop by at least 50%. Find the site 8km south of town in Antignano.

Grand Hotel Palazzo LUXURY HOTEL €€
(☎ 05 8626 0836; www.grandhotelpalazzo.com; Viale Italia 195; d €140-180; P ⊛ @ ⊚ ⊛) This shimmering ship of a 19th-century palace on the seafront, with 123 perfectly thought-

out rooms and glistening sea views, is belle époque Livorno relived. Dip into the rooftop infinity pool and, afterwards, gorge poolside on a sunset aperitif and panoramic sea view. It's 3km south of the city centre.

Eating

Sampling traditional *cacciucco*, a remarkable mixed seafood stew, is reason enough to visit Livorno.

Mercato Centrale   MARKET €
(Via Buontalenti; ☉6am-2pm Mon-Sat) Livorno's magnificent late-19th-century neoclassical food market miraculously survived Allied WWII bombing. Arresting both gastronomically and architecturally, the market is a gargantuan maze of tasty food stalls bursting with local produce, including the most astonishing fish and seafood.

★ Surfer Joe's Diner   AMERICAN €
(☑05 8680 9211; www.surferjoe.it/diner; Terrazza Mascagni; meals €15-30; ☉noon-1am Tue-Sun) What a burst of dynamism this zesty surf bar on the seafront adds to Livorno's drinking 'n' dining scene! Burgers, onion rings, pancakes and smoothies are on the menu, the 'look' is 1950s diner and surf music dominates the soundtrack. A huge terrace licked by the sea breeze and shaded by bamboo huts is the icing on the cake. Families flock here during the day but after dark, a younger crowd arrives for DJ and jam sessions, concerts and various other happenings.

Cantina Nardi   TUSCAN €
(☑05 8680 8006; Via Cambini 6-8; meals €20; ☉lunch & dinner Mon-Sat) In business since 1965, the Nardis know a thing or three about cooking up hearty, wholly affordable Tuscan fare in the company of friendly knowledgeable staff and fabulous wine. As much *enoteca* (wine bar) as Slow Food–hailed restaurant, the bistro organises wine tastings and pre-dinner *aperitivi*. Dine between bottled-filled shelves inside, on the patio or on the street terrace.

★ L'Ancora   SEAFOOD €€
(☑05 8688 1401; www.ristoranteancoralivorno. com; Scali delle Ancora 10; meals €35; ☉lunch & dinner summer, Wed-Mon winter) Gorgeous! Its canal-side terrace is the white-hot ticket in good weather, though settling for a table in the elegantly simple, 17th-century, barrel-ceilinged, brick boat house is hardly a hardship. You can get *cacciucco* here, but the *carbonara di mare* (seafood and pasta in white sauce) is the family's pride and joy.

ℹ️ Information

Tourist office (☑05 8689 4236; www.costadeglietruschi.it; Via Pieroni 18; ☉8am-5.30pm summer, shorter hrs winter)

ℹ️ Getting There & Away

BOAT

Regular ferries for Sardinia and Corsica depart from Calata Carrara, beside the Stazione Marittima; and ferries to Capraia (via Gorgona) use the smaller Porto Mediceo near Piazza dell'Arsenale. Boats to Spain and Sicliy, plus some Sardinia services, use Porto Nuovo, 3km north along Via Salvatore Orlando.

Ferry companies running these services include the following:

Corsica Ferries (www.corsica-ferries.it) Two to seven services per week to Bastia, Corsica (from €36, four hours) and Golfo Aranci, Sardinia (from €45, six to hours).

Grimaldi Lines (www.grimaldi-ferries.com) Weekly sailings to Barcelona (€35 to €85, 21 hours) and Tangiers, Morocco (€80 to €240, 58 hours).

Moby (www.moby.it) Boats to Bastia, Corsica (from €28, four hours) and Olbia, Sardinia (€46 to €97, six to 10½ hours).

Toremar (www.toremar.it) Services year-round to Capraia (€20, 2¾hr).

CAR

The A12 runs past the city and the SS1 connects Livorno with Rome. There are several car parks near the waterfront.

TRAIN

From the **main train station** (Piazza Dante) walk westwards (straight ahead) along Viale Carducci, Via de Larderel, then Via Grande into central Piazza Grande, Livorno's main square. Trains are less frequent at Stazione Marittima, the station for the ports.

Florence €9, 1½ hours, 16 daily
Pisa €2.50, 15 minutes, frequent
Rome €21.65 to €33, three to four hours, 12 daily

ℹ️ Getting Around

ATL Terminus (www.atl.livorno.it; Largo Duomo 2) Bus 1 runs from the central train station to Porto Mediceo (€1.20, on board €1.70), via Piazza Grande. To reach Stazione Marittima, take bus 1 to Piazza Grande then bus 5 from Via Cogorano, just off Piazza Grande.

Isola d'Elba

Napoleon would think twice about fleeing Isola d'Elba (the island of Elba) were he exiled here today. Substantially more congested now than when he arrived in 1814 (he engineered an escape in less than a year), the island is nonetheless an ever-glorious setting of rocky-beach-laced coves, vineyards, blue waters, thoroughly fabulous hairpin-bend motoring and mind-bending views crowned by the peak of Monte Capanne. Predictably, given the rugged terrain, hiking and biking are big.

Elba is the largest and most heavily populated island in the Parco Nazionale Arcipelago Toscano, Europe's largest marine protected area. More than a million visitors a year take the one-hour ferry cruise here, and in the island's main town and port Portoferraio in August it feels decidedly like

everyone's turned up the same weekend. Avoid coming then!

But in springtime and early summer, or autumn for grape and olive harvests, you'll find plenty of tranquil nooks on this stunningly picturesque, 28km-long, 19km-wide island.

 Activities

A dizzying network of walking and mountain-biking trails blanket Elba. Many start at Portoferraio, but some of the best, far-flung trailheads kick off elsewhere on the island.

Marciana to Chiessi A 12km hike starting high in Marciana, then heading downhill past ancient churches, sea vistas and granite boulders for about six hours to the seaside in Chiessi.

The Great Elba Crossing A three-to-four day, 60km east–west island crossing, including Monte Capanne, Elba's highest point,

---

LOCAL KNOWLEDGE

TOP ELBA BEACH SPOTS

It pays to know your *spiagge* (beaches), given that the ones along Elba's 147km of coastline embrace every shade of sand, pebble and rock. The quietest, most select beaches are tucked in rocky coves and involve a steep clamber down from the street. Parking is invariably roadside and scant.

Enfola

It's not so much the grey pebbles as the outdoor action that lures the crowds here, in the shape of pedalos to rent, a beachside diving school and a family-friendly 2.5km-long circular hiking trail around the green cape. The Parco Nazionale dell'Arcipelago Toscano visitors centre (Tuscan Archipelago National Park; ☑ 05 6591 9411; www.islepark. it; Enfola) is also here. Just 6km west of Portoferraio.

Sansone & Sorgenta

This twinset of cliff-ensnared white-shingle and pebble beaches stands out for its turquoise, crystal-clear waters just made for snorkelling. By car from Portoferraio, follow the SP27 to Enfola. Parking can be challenging.

Morcone, Pareti & Innamorata

Find this trio of charming sandy-pebble coves framed by sweet-smelling pine and eucalyptus trees some 3km south of Capoliveri, on the southeastern part of the island. Rent a kayak and paddle out to sea from Innamorata, the wildest of the three; or fine dine and stay overnight on Pereti beach at Hotel Stella Maris (☑ 05 6596 8425; www.albergostellamaris.com; Pareti; half-board per person d €70-110; ℗ ✳), one of the few island hotels to be found plump on the sand.

Colle d'Orano & Fetovaia

The standout highlight of these two gorgeous swaths of golden sand on Elba's western coast is the dramatic drive – not to be missed – along the SP25 that links the two. Legend has it that Napoleon frequented Colle d'Orano to sit and swoon over his native Corsica visible across the water. Heavenly scented maquis (herbal scrubland) covers the promontory protecting sandy Fetovaia, where nudists flop on nearby granite rocks known as Le Piscine.

and overnighting on the coast as camping is not allowed on the paths. The highlight is the final 19km leg from Poggio to Pomonte, passing the Sanctuary of Madonna del Monte and the Masso dell'Aquila rock formation.

Colle Reciso to San Martino A 15km (round-trip), medium-difficulty mountain-bike trail that peaks at about 280m. The trail continues past San Martino, and descends into Marmi, but save some breath for the return trip, as circling back to Portoferraio from Marmi on the main road is neither pleasant nor particularly safe in high season.

❶ Getting There & Away

Elba is a one-hour ferry crossing from Piombino on the mainland to Portoferraio (at least hourly, passenger/car and driver €10/50); in season a handful of boats sail from Piombino to the smaller Elban ports of Cavo and Rio Marina.

Elba's airstrip, **Aeroporto Isola d'Elba** (www.elbaisland-airport.it), is 2km north of Marina di Campo in La Pila.

❶ Getting Around

Car is the easiest way to get around the island, except in traffic-clogged August when you really won't get very far at all. The southwest coast proffers the most dramatic and scenic motoring – traffic aside, count on one hour to motor the 35km from Procchio to Cavoli.

In Portoferraio, rent a mountain bike, scooter or bike from **Twn Rent** (www.twn-rent.it; Viale Elba 32); or take an ATL bus from the bus station, almost opposite the Toremar jetty.

Portoferraio

POP 11,600

Known to the Romans as Fabricia and later Ferraia (since it was a port for iron exports), this small harbour was acquired by Cosimo I de' Medici in the mid-16th century, when the fortifications took shape.

It can be a hectic place in high season, but wandering the streets and steps of the historic centre, indulging in the exceptional eating options and bargaining for sardines with fisherfolk at the old port more than makes up for the squeeze.

◉ Sights & Activities

Old Town   HISTORIC QUARTER
From the ferry terminal, it's less than a kilometre along the foreshore to the Old Town, a spiderweb of narrow streets and alleys that stagger uphill from the old harbour and waterfront to Portoferraio's defining twinset of forts, **Forte Falcone** and the salmon-pink **Forte Stella**.

From central square Piazza Cavour head uphill along Via Giuseppe Garibaldi to the foot of the monumental **Scalinata Medici**, a fabulous mirage of 140 wonky stone steps cascading up through every sun-lit shade of amber to the dark, dimly lit 17th-century **Chiesa della Misericordia** (Via della Misericordia). Inside is Napoleon's death mask. Continue to the top of the staircase to reach the forts and Napoleonic villa.

Museo Nazionale della Residenza Napoleoniche HOUSE MUSEUM
(Piazzale Napoleone; ⊘9am-7pm Mon & Wed-Sat, to 1pm Sun) Up on the bastions, between the two forts, is Villa dei Mulini (also known as Palazzo dei Mulini), home to Napoleon during his stint as emperor of this small isle. With its Empire-style furnishings, splendid library, fig-tree-studded Italianate gardens and unbeatable sea view, the emperor certainly didn't want for creature comforts during his brief Elban exile – contrast his Elba lifestyle with the simplicity of his camp bed and travelling trunk when he was on the campaign trail. The museum was closed for renovation at the time of writing.

🛏 Sleeping

Half-board is usually the only option in August and many hotels close between November and Easter. The best places to stay are a short drive from the town centre.

Villa Ombrosa   HOTEL €
(☑05 6591 4363; www.villaombrosa.it; Via Alcide de Gasperi 3; d from €95; ℗🔊📶) One of the few Portoferraio hotels in town (and also open year-round), three-star Ombrosa looks out to sea and the pinprick islet of Lo Scoglietto. The decor is a jumble of styles, but summer rates include a lounger and umbrella on a strip of Spiaggia delle Ghiaie (Ghiaie Beach) across the street, and rooms with a sea view tout pocket-sized balconies.

Rosselba Le Palme   CAMPGROUND €
(☑05 6593 3101; www.rosselbalepalme.it; Ottone; adult/tent/car €12/14.50/5.40; ⊘mid-Apr–Sep; ℗🔊♨📶) Set around a botanic garden backed by Mediterranean forest, few campsites are as leafy or large. The beach is a 400m walk between trees, and accommodation ranges from simple pitches to cute wooden chalets, 'glamping' tents with running water and bathtubs on legs, and apartments in a

typical Tuscan villa. Find it 9km east of Portoferraio, near Ottone.

Eating

★ **Il Castagnacciao** PIZZERIA €

(Via del Mercato Vecchio 5; pizza €4.50-7; ☺9am-2.30pm & 4.30-11pm Thu-Tue) Hidden in an alley near Piazza Cavour, this iconic address with bench seating at wooden tables is no-frills pizza bliss. Watch your thin-crust, rectangular pizza go in and out of the wood-fired oven, and save space for dessert – *castagnaccio* (chestnut 'cake') baked in the same oven.

Osteria Libertaria TUSCAN €€

(☑ 05 6591 4978; Calata Giacomo Matteotti 12; meals €30; ☺lunch & dinner summer) Across from the fishing boats, this waterfront *osteria* cooks up a tasty fish-driven cuisine. Simple dishes such as fried calamari or *tonno in crosta di pistacchi* (pistachio-encrusted tuna fillet) are fresher than fresh and cooked to perfection every time. Dine at one of two tile-topped tables on the traffic-noisy street outside or on the back-alley terrace. No coffee.

ⓘ Information

Tourist office (☑ 05 6591 4671; www.isoleditoscana.it; Viale Elba 4; ☺9am-7pm Mon-Sat, 10am-1pm & 3-6pm Sun summer, 9am-5pm Mon-Thu, 9am-1pm Fri winter) The helpful staff here have a particularly abundant supply of information on walking and biking paths on the island. Find the office near the ferry port, around the corner from waterfront Calata Italia 33.

Around Portoferraio

★ **Tenuta La Chiusa** (☑ 05 6593 3046; www.tenutalachiusa.it; Magazzini 93; d €65-120, up to 5 people €110-185, per wk d €450-850, up to 5 people per wk €750-1300; ℗🐾), Elba's oldest winemaking estate is 8km east of Portoferraio along the SP26 and SP28. Plumb on the seashore, it has a 17th-century farmhouse, an 18th-century villa, almost 8 hectares of vineyards tumbling towards the sea, olive groves, palm trees and 10 apartments to rent – some on the beach in former peasant-worker cottages. The self-contained accommodation (minimum two nights September to July, five nights in August) has a simple charm; guests can buy olive oil and wine at reception; and, should you not fancy cooking, harbourside Hotel e Ristorante Mare is a wonderful two-minute stroll away along the pebbly seashore in the tiny harbour of Magazzini. The estate also organises wine tasting in its cellar.

Marciana

POP 2190

From Portoferraio cruise 20km west along the coast to Marciana Marina, from where it's another 9km inland to the island's highest (375m) and oldest village. Park at the entrance to Marciana and follow Via delle Fonti and its continuation, Via delle Coste, out of the village to the **Santuario della Madonna del Monte** (627m) – a 40-minute uphill hike through scented parasol pine and chestnut forest. Fourteen Stations of the Cross pave the old mule track up to the pilgrimage site, and the coastal panorama that unfolds as you get higher is remarkable. Play I Spy Corsica.

Back down in Marciana village, lunch à la Slow Food at **Osteria del Noce** (☑ 05 6590 1285; Via della Madonna 27; meals €25; ☺lunch & dinner), a simple family-run place that cooks up a mean spaghetti laced with Granseolo Elbano (a large crab typical to Elba). End your typical Elban feast with a wander around the village, past arches, flowerboxes and petite balconies to drop-offs revealing views of Marciana Marina and neighbouring **Poggio** below.

Monte Capanne

If you only have time for just one road trip from Portoferraio, it has to be this. Some 750m south of Marciana on the road to Poggio, the **Cabinovia Monte Capanne** (Cableway; ☑ 05 6590 1020; single/return €12/18; ☺10am-1pm & 2.20-5pm summer) whisks walkers in open, barred cabins – akin to canary-yellow parrot cages – up the mountain to the summit of Elba's highest point, Monte Capanne (1019m). Alight 20 minutes later and hike a little further around the peak to savour an astonishing 360-degree panorama of the entire island, surrounding Tuscan archipelago, Etruscan Coast and Corsica.

CENTRAL TUSCANY

When people imagine classic Tuscan countryside, they usually conjure up images of central Tuscany. However there's more to this popular region than gently rolling hills, sun-kissed vineyards and artistically planted avenues of cypress trees. Truth be told, the real gems are the historic towns and cities, most of which are medieval and Renaissance time capsules magically transported to the modern day.

Siena

POP 52,800

The rivalry between historic adversaries Siena and Florence continues to this day, and participation isn't limited to the locals – most travellers tend to develop a strong preference for one over the other. These allegiances often boil down to aesthetic preference: while Florence saw its greatest flourishing during the Renaissance, Siena's enduring artistic glories are largely Gothic.

Sadly, the city has recently been seriously affected by the financial mismanagement of the Banca Monte di Paschi di Siena – the world's oldest bank which was, until recently, a source of immense local pride, employment and arts patronage.

History

Legend tells us that Siena was founded by the son of Remus, and the symbol of the wolf feeding the twins Romulus and Remus is as ubiquitous in Siena as it is in Rome. In reality the city was probably of Etruscan origin, although it didn't begin to grow into a proper town until the 1st century BC, when the Romans established a military colony here called Sena Julia.

In the 12th century, Siena's wealth, size and power grew along with its involvement in commerce and trade. Its rivalry with neighbouring Florence grew proportionately, leading to numerous wars during the first half of the 13th century between Guelph Florence and Ghibelline Siena. Eventually, Siena was forced to ally with its rival in 1270.

In the ensuing century the city was ruled by the Consiglio dei Nove (Council of Nine, a bourgeois group constantly bickering with the aristocracy) and enjoyed its greatest prosperity.

A plague outbreak in 1348 killed two-thirds of Siena's 100,000 inhabitants and led to a period of decline that culminated in the city being handed over to Cosimo I de' Medici, who barred the inhabitants from operating banks and thus severely curtailed its power.

This centuries-long economic downturn in the wake of the Medici takeover was a blessing in disguise, as lack of funds meant that it was subject to very little redevelopment or new construction. This has led to the historic centre's listing on Unesco's World Heritage list as the living embodiment of a medieval city.

◎ Sights

★ Piazza del Campo   PIAZZA

This sloping piazza, popularly known as Il Campo, has been Siena's civic and social centre since being staked out by the Consiglio dei Nove in the mid-12th century. It was built on the site of a former Roman marketplace, and its pie-piece paving design is divided into nine sectors to represent the number of members of the council.

In 1346 water first bubbled forth from the Fonte Gaia (Happy Fountain; Piazza del Campo) in the upper part of the square. These days, the fountain's panels are reproductions; the severely weathered originals, sculpted by Jacopo della Quercia in the early 15th century, are on display in the Complesso Museale Santa Maria della Scala.

At the lowest point of the square stands the spare, elegant Palazzo Comunale (Palazzo Pubblico), purpose-built in the late 13th century as the piazza's centrepiece and now home to the Museo Civico. One of the most graceful Gothic buildings in Italy, it has an ingeniously designed concave facade that mirrors the opposing convex curve formed by the piazza.

Entry to the *palazzo*'s ground-floor central courtyard is free. From it soars the graceful Torre del Mangia (admission €8;

OFF THE BEATEN TRACK

ORTO DE' PECCI

Head behind the Palazzo Comunale and down the hill past Piazza del Mercato and the city's historic, now decommissioned communal laundry to discover this urban oasis (www.ortodepecci. it; ⊙24hr) FREE. Kids love visiting the geese, goats, ducks and donkeys that live here, and locals can often be found hiding from the tourist masses in its green spaces (perfect for picnics or an afternoon snooze). There's a cooperative organic farm that grows fruit and vegetables and supplies the on-site restaurant (⊙12.30-2.30pm & 7.30-10pm Tue-Sat, 12.30-2.30pm Sun Mar-Oct, 12.30-2.30pm & 7.30-10pm Fri & Sat, 12.30-2.30pm Sun Nov-Feb) with produce, a medieval garden and an experimental vineyard which Siena University's agriculture department has planted with clones of medieval vines. On summer evenings, concerts are sometimes held here, too.

Siena

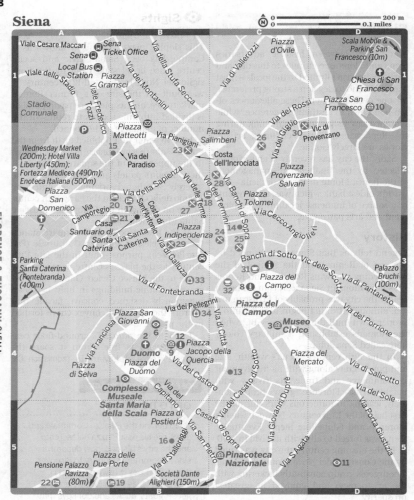

0 — 200 m
0 — 0.1 miles

Viale Cesare Maccari — Sena — Sena Ticket Office
Sena — Local Bus Station — Piazza Gramsci
Viale dello Stadio — Viale Frederico Tozzi — La Lizza
Stadio Comunale
Via della Stufa Secca
Via dei Montanini
Via di Vallerozzi
Piazza d'Ovile
Scala Mobile & Parking San Francesco (10m)
Chiesa di San Francesco
Piazza San Francesco — 10
Piazza Matteotti — 15 — Via Pianigiani — Via del Paradiso — 23
Piazza Salimbeni — 26 — Via dei Rossi — Via del Giglio — 30 — Vic di Provenzano
Costa dell'Incrociata
Wednesday Market (200m); Hotel Villa Liberty (450m); Fortezza Medicea (490m); Enoteca Italiana (500m)
Piazza San Domenico — 7 — Via Camporegio — 20 — 17 — 21 — Casa Santuario di Santa Caterina — Via Santa Caterina
Via della Sapienza — Costa di Sant'Antonio — Via delle Terme — 28 — 18 — 27 — Via Banchi di Sopra
Piazza Provenzano Salvani
Piazza Tolomei — Via Cecco Angiolieri
Piazza Indipendenza — 24 — 14 — 25
Via di Galluzza — 29
Banchi di Sotto — 31 — i — Vic delle Scotte — Via di Pantaneto
Palazzo Bruchi (100m)
Parking Santa Caterina (Fontebranda) (400m)
Via di Fontebranda — 33 — 32 — 8 — 4 — Piazza del Campo
Via dei Pellegrini — 34
Piazza San Giovanni — 2 — 6 — 12 — 9 — Piazza Jacopo della Quercia
Duomo — Piazza del Duomo
Via Francosa — Via di Città — 3 — Museo Civico
Piazza del Mercato — Via del Porrione
Via di Salicotto
Piazza di Selva
1 — Complesso Museale Santa Maria della Scala
Via del Capitano — Via del Castoro — 13 — Via del Casato di Sotto — Via di Città
Piazza di Postierla — Casato di Sopra — Via San Pietro — Via Giovanni Dupré
Via del Sole
Via Porta Giustizia
Pensione Palazzo Ravizza (80m)
Piazza delle Due Porte — 16 — Via di Stalloreggi — 5 — Pinacoteca Nazionale — Via S Agata
22 — 19 — Società Dante Alighieri (150m)
11

10am-6.15pm Mar–mid-Oct, to 3.15pm mid-Oct–Feb), 102m high and with 500-odd steps. The views from the top are magnificent, but if you want to see them you should expect to wait in high season, as only 30 people are allowed up at any time.

★ **Museo Civico**   MUSEUM
(www.comune.siena.it; Palazzo Comunale, Il Campo; adult/EU reduced €8/4.50; ⊙10am-6.15pm mid-Mar–Oct, to 5.15pm Nov–mid-Mar) The city's most famous museum occupies rooms richly frescoed by artists of the Sienese school. These are unusual in that they were com-

missioned by the governing body of the city, rather than by the Church, and many depict secular subjects instead of the favoured religious themes of the time.

Purchase your ticket at the office to the right of the entrance then head upstairs past the gift shop to the Sala del Risorgimento, with its impressive late-19th-century frescoes serialising key events in the Risorgimento (unification of Italy). Next is the Sala di Balia (Rooms of Authority). The 15 scenes depicted in frescoes around the walls recount episodes in the life of Pope Alexander III (the Sienese Rolando Bandinelli), includ-

Siena

FLORENCE & TUSCANY SIENA

ing his clashes with the Holy Roman Emperor Frederick Barbarossa. Straight ahead is the **Sala del Concistoro** (Hall of the Council of Clergymen), dominated by the allegorical ceiling frescoes of the Mannerist Domenico Beccafumi; and through a vestibule to the left are the Anticappella (Chapel entrance hall) and Cappella (Chapel). The **Anticappella** features frescoes painted in 1415 by Taddeo di Bartolo. These include figures representing the virtues needed for the proper exercise of power (Justice, Magnanimity, Strength, Prudence, Religion), as well as depictions of some of the leading Republican lights of ancient Rome. The **Cappella** contains a fine Holy Family and St Leonard by Il Sodoma. Next to the Anticappella is the **Vestibolo** (Vestibule), whose star attraction is a bronze wolf, the symbol of the city.

The best is saved for last, though. From the vestibule, you emerge into the **Sala del Mappamondo** (Hall of the World Map), home to the museum's highlight: Simone Martini's powerful and striking **Maestà** (Virgin Mary in Majesty). Completed in 1315, it features the Madonna beneath a canopy surrounded by saints and angels and is Martini's first known work. On the other side

of the room is another work attributed to Martini, his oft-reproduced fresco (1328–30) of Guidoriccio da Fogliano, a captain of the Sienese army.

The next room, the **Sala dei Nove** (or Hall of the Nine), is where the Council of Nine was based. It is decorated with Ambrogio Lorenzetti's fresco cycle known as the *Allegories of Good and Bad Government* (c 1338–40). The central allegory portrays scenes with personifications of Justice, Wisdom, Virtue and Peace, all unusually (at the time) depicted as women, rendered along with scenes of criminal punishment and rewards for righteousness. Set perpendicular from it are the frescoes *Allegory of Good Government* and *Allegory of Bad Government*, which feature intensely contrasting scenes set in the recognisable environs of Siena. The good depicts a sunlit, idyllic, serene city, with joyous citizens and a countryside filled with crops; the bad city is filled with vices, crime and disease. These frescoes are often described as the most important secular paintings of the Renaissance, and shouldn't be missed.

530

1. Duomo (p476), Florence
The city's most iconic landscape took almost 150 years to complete.

2. Lucca (p515)
At almost every turn there is a pavement terrace to dine alfresco.

3. Siena (p527)
Classic Tuscan countryside: gently rolling hills, sun-kissed vineyards and avenues of cypress trees.

4. Tuscan treats
Tuscany is a paradise for foodies, especially sweet tooths.

★ **Duomo** CHURCH

(www.operaduomo.siena.it; Piazza del Duomo; Mar-Oct €4, Nov-Feb free; ⊙ 10.30am-6.30pm Mon-Sat, 1.30-5.30pm Sun Mar-Oct, to 5pm Nov-Feb) Construction of the *duomo* started in 1215 and work continued well into the 14th century. The magnificent facade of white, green and red polychrome marble was designed by Giovanni Pisano (the statues of philosophers and prophets are copies; you'll find the originals in the Museo dell'Opera).

The interior is truly stunning. Walls and pillars continue the black-and-white-stripe theme of the exterior, while the vaults are painted blue with gold stars. The inlaid-marble floor, decorated with 56 panels by about 40 artists and executed over the course of 200 years (14th to 16th centuries), depicts historical and biblical subjects. Unfortunately, about half of the panels are obscured by unsightly, protective covering, and are revealed only from 21 August through to 27 October each year (admission is €6 during this period).

Other drawcards include the exquisitely crafted marble and porphyry pulpit carved by Nicola Pisano, assisted by Arnolfo di Cambio, who later designed the *duomo* in Florence. Intricately carved with vigorous, realistic crowd scenes, it's one of the masterpieces of Gothic sculpture.

Through a door from the north aisle is the enchanting Libreria Piccolomini, built to house the books of Enea Silvio Piccolomini, better known as Pius II. The walls of the small hall are decorated with vividly coloured narrative frescoes painted between 1502 and 1507 by Bernardino Pinturicchio and depicting events in Piccolomini's life.

Museo dell'Opera del Duomo MUSEUM

(Piazza del Duomo; admission €7; ⊙ 10.30am-6.30pm Mon-Sat, 1.30-5.30pm Sun Mar-Oct, to 5pm Nov-Feb) The collection here showcases artworks that formerly adorned the cathedral, including the 12 statues of prophets and philosophers by Giovanni Pisano that decorated the facade. Their creator designed them to be viewed from ground level, which is why they look so distorted as they crane uncomfortably forward.

The museum's highlight is Duccio di Buoninsegna's striking *Maestà* (1311), which was painted on both sides as a screen for the *duomo*'s high altar. The main painting portrays the Virgin surrounded by angels, saints and prominent Sienese citizens of the period; the rear panels (sadly incomplete) portray scenes from the Passion of Christ.

Battistero di San Giovanni BAPTISTRY

(Piazza San Giovanni; admission €4; ⊙ 10.30am-6.30pm Mon-Sat, 1.30-5.30pm Sun Mar-Oct, to 5pm Nov-Feb) Behind the *duomo* and down a steep flight of steps is the Baptistry, which is richly decorated with frescoes. At its centre is a hexagonal marble font by Jacopo della Quercia decorated with bronze panels depicting the life of St John the Baptist by artists including Lorenzo Ghiberti *(Baptism of Christ* and *St John in Prison)* and Donatello *(The Head of John the Baptist Being Presented to Herod).*

Cripta CRYPT

(Piazza San Giovanni; admission incl audioguide €6; ⊙ 10.30am-6.30pm Mon-Sat, 1.30-5.30pm Sun Mar-Oct, to 5pm Nov-Feb) This crypt below the cathedral's pulpit was rediscovered and restored in 1999 after having been filled to the roof with debris in the 1300s. The walls are completely covered with *pintura a secco* (dry painting) dating back to the 1200s.

Panorama del Facciatone TOWER

(⊙ 10.30am-6.30pm Mon-Sat, 1.30-5.30pm Sun Mar-Oct) For a great panoramic view, haul yourself up the 131-step, narrow corkscrew stairway to this panorama at the top of the facade of the never-finished Duomo Nuovo (New Cathedral). Entrance is included in the Museo dell'Opera ticket.

★ **Complesso Museale Santa Maria della Scala** CULTURAL BUILDING

(www.santamariadellascala.com; Piazza del Duomo 1; adult/reduced/child under 11 €6/3.50/free; ⊙ 10.30am-4pm, to 6.30pm in high season) This former hospital, parts of which date from the 13th century, was built as a hospice for pilgrims travelling the Via Francigena, a route from Canterbury to Rome. Located opposite the *duomo,* its highlight is the Pellegrinaio (Pilgrim's Hall), with vivid 15th-century frescoes by Lorenzo Vecchietta, Priamo della Quercia and Domenico di Bartolo lauding the good works of the hospital and its patrons.

The building now functions as a cultural centre and houses three museums – the Archaeological Museum, Art Museum for Children and Center of Contemporary Art (SMS Contemporanea) – as well as a variety of historic halls, chapels and temporary exhibition spaces. Don't miss the atmospheric Archaeological Museum housed in the basement tunnels and the medieval *fienile* (hayloft) on level three, which houses Jacopo della Quercia's original Fonte Gaia sculptures.

★ **Pinacoteca Nazionale** ART GALLERY
(Via San Pietro 29; adult/reduced €4/2; ⊙10am-5.45pm Tue-Sat, 9am-12.45pm Sun & Mon) Occupying the once grand but now sadly dishevelled 14th-century Palazzo Buonsignori, this labyrinthine gallery displays an extraordinary collection of Gothic masterpieces from the Sienese school. The highlights are all on the 2nd floor.

The collection demonstrates the gulf cleaved between artistic life in Siena and Florence in the 15th century. While the Renaissance flourished 70km to the north, Siena's masters and their patrons remained firmly rooted in the Byzantine and Gothic precepts that had stood them in such good stead from the early 13th century. Religious images and episodes predominate, typically pasted lavishly with gold and generally lacking any of the advances in painting (eg, perspective, emotion or movement) that artists in Florence were exploring. That's not to say that the works here are second-rate – many are among the most beautiful and important creations of their time.

There are too many knock-'em-dead canvasses on the 2nd floor to list here, but you should be sure not to miss Duccio's *Madonna and Child* (Room 2), *Madonna with Child and Four Saints* (Room 4) and *Santa Maria Maddalena* (Room 5); Simone Martini's *Madonna della Misericordia* and *Madonna with Child* (both in Room 4); *Madonna and Child* and *Blessed Agostino* altarpiece (both in Room 6); Lippo Memmi's *Adoration of the Magi* (Room 6); Ambrogio Lorenzetti's luminous *Annunciation* and *Madonna with Child* (both in Room 8); Pietro Lorenzetti's *Madonna Enthroned with Saint Nicholas and the Prophet Elia* and *Crucifixion* (both in Room 8); and Taddeo di Bartolo's *The Annunciation of the Virgin Mary* (Room 11).

Note that the gallery occasionally rearranges its exhibits; we have cited the room numbers that applied when we last visited.

Chiesa di San Domenico CHURCH
(Piazza San Domenico; ⊙9am-12.30pm & 3-7pm) St Catherine was welcomed into the Dominican fold within this imposing church, and its **Cappella di Santa Caterina** is adorned with frescoes by Il Sodoma depicting events in her life. Catherine died in Rome, where most of her body is preserved, but her head was returned to Siena (it's in a 15th-century tabernacle above the altar in the *cappella*).

Oratorio di San Bernardino ART GALLERY
(www.operaduomo.siena.it; Piazza San Francesco 9; adult/reduced €3/2.50; ⊙1.30-6.30pm Mar–Oct) Nestled in the shadow of the huge Gothic church of San Francesco is this 15th-century oratory, which is dedicated to St Bernardino and decorated with Mannerist frescoes by Il Sodoma, Beccafumi and Pacchia. Upstairs, the small **Museo Diocesano di Arte Sacra** has some lovely paintings, including a *Madonna del Latte* (Nursing Madonna, c 1340) by Ambrogio Lorenzetti.

Note that admission to the oratory is included in the OPA SI Pass.

---

❶ SIENA MUSEUM PASSES

If you are planning to visit the major monuments, be sure to purchase one or more of the money-saving combined passes on offer.

OPA SI Pass is valid for three days and gives entrance to the Duomo, Libreria Piccolomini, Museo dell'Opera, Battistero di San Giovanni, Cripta and Oratorio di San Bernardino. It costs €12 between March and October, €8 between November and February.

SIA Summer gives entrance to the Museo Civico, Complesso Museale Santa Maria della Scala, Museo dell'Opera, Battistero di San Giovanni, Oratorio di San Bernardino and Chiesa di San Agostino. It costs €17 and is valid for seven days between 15 March and 31 October.

SIA Winter gives entrance to the Museo Civico, Complesso Museale Santa Maria della Scala, Museo dell'Opera and Battistero di San Giovanni. It costs €14 and is valid for seven days during the period 1 November to 14 March.

Two additional combination tickets are available: the **Museo Civico and Torre del Mangia** (€13) and the **Museo Civico and Complesso Museale Santa Maria della Scala** (€11, valid for two days).

The OPA SI Pass can be booked in advance at www.operaduomo.siena.it; other passes and tickets are purchased directly at the museums.

Courses

Accademia Musicale Chigiana MUSIC
(☑ 0577 2 20 91; www.chigiana.it; Via di Città 89) Offers competitive-entry classical-music masterclasses and workshops every summer.

Fondazione Siena Jazz MUSIC
(☑ 0577 27 14 01; www.sienajazz.it; Fortezza Medicea 1) One of Europe's foremost institutions of its type, offering courses and workshops for experienced jazz musicians.

Scuola Leonardo da Vinci LANGUAGE
(☑ 0577 24 90 97; www.scuolaleonardo.com; Via del Paradiso 16) Italian-language school with supplementary cultural programs.

Società Dante Alighieri LANGUAGE
(☑ 0577 4 95 33; www.dantealighieri.com; Via Tommaso Pendola 37) Language and cultural courses southwest of the city centre.

Tuscan Wine School WINE TASTING
(☑ 333 7229716; www.tuscanwineschool.com; Via Stalloreggi 26) Daily two-hour wine-tasting classes introducing Italian and Tuscan wines (€40).

Università per Stranieri LANGUAGE
(University for Foreigners; ☑ 0577 24 01 00; www.unistrasi.it; Piazza Carlo Rosselli 27-28) Offers various courses in Italian language and culture. You'll find it near the train station.

Tours

Centro Guide Turistiche Siena e Provincia (☑ 0577 4 32 73; info@guidesiena.it; Galleria Odeon, Via Banchi di Sopra 31; ⊙ 10am-1pm & 3-5pm Mon-Fri), an association of accredited professional tour guides, operates four recommended tours between Easter and October: a one-hour tour of the **Duomo** (11am, noon and 4pm daily; €5 plus entrance fee); a 90-minute **Classical Siena Walking Tour** (11am Monday to Saturday; €20 including *duomo* entrance fee); and a 90-minute **Secret Siena Walk** (11am Sunday; €20 including Complesso Museale Santa Maria della Scala entrance fee). The Duomo tour departs from the OPA SI ticket office next door, and the walking tours depart from outside the tourist office in the Campo; all are in English and Italian. Bookings are advisable. Children under the age of 11 are free.

Festivals & Events

The Accademia Musicale Chigiana presents three highly regarded series of concerts featuring classical musicians from around the world: **Micat in Vertice** from November to April, **Settimana Musicale Senese** in July, and **Estate Musicale Chigiana** between July and August. Venues include the Teatro dei Rinnovati in the Campo, Teatro dei Rozzi in Piazza Indipendenza, Chiesa di Sant'Agostino and Palazzo Chigi-Saraconi in Via di Città.

Sleeping

★ **Hotel Alma Domus** HOTEL €
(☑ 0577 4 41 77; www.hotelalmadomus.it; Via Camporegio 37; s €40-48, d without view €60-75, d with view €65-85, q €95-125; ❈ @ ☛) Owned by the Catholic diocese and still home to six Dominican nuns, this convent now operates as a budget hotel. And though its prices are low, the standard of its recently renovated 4th-floor rooms is anything but. Most have new bathrooms and beds, air-con and views over the narrow green Fontebranda valley across to the *duomo*.

Families are welcome, and will be charmed by the particularly lovely room 12, which sleeps four and has a balcony. Note that there's a 1am curfew.

Antica Residenza Cicogna B&B €
(☑ 0577 28 56 13; www.anticaresidenzacicogna.it; Via dei Terme 67; s €65-90, d €85-110, ste €120-150; ❈ @ ☛) Charming host Elisa supervised the restoration of this 13th-century building and will happily recount its history (it's been owned by her family for generations). The seven rooms are clean and well maintained, with comfortable beds, painted ceilings and tiled floors. There's also a tiny lounge where you can relax over complimentary Vin Santo and *cantucci* (hard, sweet almond biscuits).

Bed and Breakfast Alle Due Porte B&B €
(☑ 0577 28 76 70; www.sienatur.it; Via Stalloreggi 51; s €65, d €75-85; ❈ ☛) Taking its name from the nearby city gate, this well-located B&B has loads of character and a real 'home away from home' feel. Run by an elderly couple, it offers three rooms (two with air-con) and a small breakfast room on the 1st floor of a rebuilt 12th-century tower house.

Albergo Bernini PENSION €
(☑ 0577 28 90 47; www.albergobernini.com; Via della Sapienza 15; d with/without bathroom €85/65; ☛) Pros: this is a welcoming, family-run hotel with 10 neat rooms and a gorgeous terrace

sporting views across to the *duomo* and Chiesa di San Domenico. Cons: uncomfortable beds and the fact that only two rooms – the single and triple – have air-con. Breakfast costs €3 to €7.50, rates are negotiable in winter and payment is cash only.

★**Pensione Palazzo Ravizza** BOUTIQUE HOTEL €€
(☑ 0577 28 04 62; www.palazzoravizza.it; Pian dei Mantellini 34; loft r €80-150, d €100-220, ste €180-320; P ⊛ @ ☎) Occupying a Renaissance-era *palazzo* located in a quiet but convenient corner of the city, this extremely friendly hotel offers standard rooms with frescoed ceilings, huge beds and small but well-equipped bathrooms. Suites are even more impressive, with views over the delightful rear garden. The free on-site parking is a major draw and low-season rates are a huge bargain.

Hotel Athena HOTEL €
(☑ 0577 28 63 13; www.hotelathena.com; Via Paolo Mascagni 55; s €55-140, superior d €65-180, deluxe d €90-280; ☹ closed Feb; P ⊛ @ ☎) Hotel management schools looking for an exemplar of a well-run business could easily cite the Athena. Operated by the Bianciardi family for the past four decades, it's clean, comfortable, meticulously maintained and friendly. The deluxe countryside rooms are knockouts (well worth the price) and the summertime terrace bar and restaurant is the stuff of which lasting holiday memories are made.

Standard rooms on the lower floors are nowhere near as attractive as the superior and deluxe versions upstairs, but they are considerably cheaper – check the website for deals. On-site parking is free and easy to access.

Hotel Villa Liberty HOTEL €€
(☑ 0577 4 49 66; www.villaliberty.it; Viale Vittorio Veneto 11; s €62-167, d €102-294, ste €122-368; ⊛ ☎) Located in a tree-lined boulevard opposite the Fortezza Medicea, this Liberty-style villa has been converted into a 17-room hotel and is one of the city's best midrange choices. Though the Campo is only a 15-minute walk away, the area is less touristy than the historic centre and there is free (but highly contested) parking right outside the hotel. Rooms are light and modern, with comfortable beds and small but perfectly adequate bathrooms.

★**Campo Regio Relais** BOUTIQUE HOTEL €€€
(☑ 0577 22 20 73; www.camporegio.com; Via della Sapienza 25; s €150-300, d €190-300, ste €250-600; ⊛ @ ☎) Siena's most charming hotel has only six rooms, all of which are individually decorated and luxuriously equipped. Breakfast is served in the sumptuously decorated lounge or on the terrace, which has a sensational view of the *duomo* and Torre del Mangia.

✗ Eating & Drinking

Morbidi DELI €
(www.morbidi.com; Via Banchi di Sopra 75; ☹ 9am-8pm Mon-Sat, lunch buffet 12.30-2.30pm) Local gastronomes shop here as the range of cheese, cured meats and imported delicacies is the best in Siena. Also notable is the downstairs lunch buffet, which offers fantastic value. For a mere €12, you can graze on platters of *antipasti*, salads, pastas and a dessert of the day. Bottled water is supplied, wine and coffee cost extra.

Consorzio Agrario di Siena DELI €
(Via Pianigiani 13; ☹ 8am-7.30pm Mon-Sat) Operating since 1901, this farmer's co-op is a rich emporium of food and wine, much of which has been locally produced. There's a small bar area where you can purchase and eat a slab of freshly cooked pizza (€12 to €14.30 per kg).

Grom GELATO €
(www.grom.it; Via Banchi di Sopra 11-13; gelato €2.50-5.50; ☹ 11am-midnight Sun-Thu, to 12.30am Fri & Sat Apr-Sep, 11am-11pm Sun-Thu, to midnight Fri & Sat Oct-Mar) Delectable gelato with flavours that change with the season; many of the ingredients are organic or Slow Food–accredited.

Kopa Kabana GELATO €
(www.gelateriakopakabana.it; Via dei Rossi 52-55; gelati €1.80-4.30; ☹ noon-8pm mid-Feb–mid-Nov, later hrs in warm weather) Come here for fresh gelato made by self-proclaimed ice-cream master Fabio (we're pleased to concur).

★**Enoteca I Terzi** MODERN TUSCAN €€€
(☑ 0577 4 43 29; www.enotecaiterzi.it; Via dei Termini 7; meals €35, antipasto plate €9; ☹ 11am-1am Mon-Sat) Close to the Campo but off the well-beaten tourist trail, this classy modern *enoteca* (wine bar) is a favourite with sophisticated locals, who linger over working lunches, *aperitivi* sessions and casual dinners featuring top-notch *salumi* (cured

FLORENCE & TUSCANY SIENA

IL PALIO

Dating from the Middle Ages, this spectacular annual event stages a series of colourful pageants and a wild horse race on 2 July and 16 August. Ten of Siena's 17 *contrade* (town districts) compete for the coveted *palio* (silk banner). Each *contrada* has its own traditions, symbol and colours plus its own church and *palio* museum.

From about 5pm, representatives from each *contrada* parade around the Campo in historical costume, all bearing their individual banners.

The race is held at 7.45pm in July and 7pm in August. For scarcely one exhilarating minute, the 10 horses and their bareback riders tear three times around a temporary dirt racetrack at a speed and violence that makes spectators' hair stand on end.

Join the crowds in the centre of the Campo at least four hours before the start if you want a place on the rails, but be aware that once there you won't be able to leave until the race has finished. Alternatively, the cafes in the Campo sell places on their terraces; these cost between €350 and €400 per ticket, and can be booked through the tourist office up to one year in advance.

Note that during the Palio, hotels raise their rates between 10% and 50% and enforce a minimum-stay requirement.

---

meats), delicate handmade pasta, flavoursome risotto and succulent grilled meats. The wine list is fantastic, and includes an excellent choice by the glass.

Ristorante Grotta Santa Caterina da Bagoga
TUSCAN €€

(☑ 0577 28 22 08; www.bagoga.it; Via della Galluzza 26; meals €28; ⊕ 12.30-2.30pm & 7.30-10.30pm Tue-Sat, 12.30-2.30pm Sun) Pierino Fagnani ('Bagogga'), one of Siena's most famous Palio jockeys, swapped his saddle for an apron in 1973 and has been operating this much-loved restaurant near the Casa Santuario di Santa Caterina ever since. Traditional Tuscan palate pleasers feature on the menu, and are perhaps best appreciated in the four-course 'tipico' (€35) or 'degustazione' (€50 with wine) menus.

La Compagnia dei Vinattieri
WINE BAR €€

(☑ 0577 23 65 68; www.vinattieri.net; Via delle Terme 79; antipasto platter €7-9, meals €35; ⊕ noon-10pm, closed late Feb–late Mar) Duck down the stairs to enjoy a quick glass of wine and a meat or cheese platter in this cellar, or settle in for a leisurely meal accompanied by your choice from an impressive wine list. It's popular with locals and tourists alike; you'll need to try your luck for a drink, and book in advance for a meal.

Tre Cristi
SEAFOOD €€€

(☑ 0577 28 06 08; www.trecristi.com; Vicolo di Provenzano 1; 3-course tasting menus €35-45, 5-course menus €65; ⊕ 12.30-3pm & 7.30-10.30pm Mon-Sat) Seafood restaurants are thin on the ground in this meat-obsessed region, so the long existence of Tre Cristi (it's been around since 1830) should be heartily celebrated. The menu is as elegant as the decor, and added touches such as a complimentary glass of *prosecco* (dry sparkling wine) at the start of the meal add to the experience.

Enoteca Italiana
WINE BAR

(www.enoteca-italiana.it; Fortezza Medicea; ⊕ noon-1am Mon-Sat Apr-Sep, to midnight Oct-Mar) The former munitions cellar and dungeon of this Medici fortress has been artfully transformed into a classy *enoteca* that carries more than 1500 Italian labels. You can take a bottle with you, ship a case home or enjoy a glass or two in the attractive courtyard or atmospheric vaulted interior of the wine bar. There's usually food available, too.

Caffè Fiorella
CAFE

(www.torrefazionefiorella.it; Via di Città 13; ⊕ 7am-8pm Mon-Sat) Squeeze into this tiny space behind the Campo to enjoy Siena's best coffee. In summer, the coffee *granita* with a dollop of cream is a wonderful indulgence.

Bar Il Palio
CAFE

(Piazza del Campo 47; ⊕ 8am-midnight) The best coffee on the Campo; drink it standing at the bar or suffer the financial consequences.

Shopping

Panificio Il Magnifico
FOOD

(www.ilmagnifico.siena.it; Via dei Pellegrini 27; ⊕ 7.30am-7.30pm Mon-Sat) Lorenzo Rossi is Siena's best baker, and his *panforte, ricciarelli* (sugar-dusted chewy almond biscuits) and *cavallucci* (almond biscuits made with Tuscan millefiori honey) are a weekly purchase for most local households. Try them at his bakery and shop behind the Duomo, and you'll understand why.

Il Pellicano CERAMICS
(☑ 0577 24 79 14; www.siena-ilpellicano.it; Via Diacceto 17a; ⊙ 10.30am-7pm Easter-Oct, 10.30am-7pm Mon-Sat Nov-Easter) Elisabetta Ricci has been making traditional hand-painted Sienese ceramics for more than 30 years. She shapes, fires and paints her ceramic creations – often using Renaissance-era styles or typical *contrade* designs – at her atelier near Parking Santa Caterina and sells them at this shop near the Duomo. Elisabetta also conducts lessons in traditional ceramic techniques; contact her for details.

Wednesday Market MARKET
(⊙ 7.30am-1pm) Spreading around Fortezza Medicea and towards the Stadio Comunale, this is one of Tuscany's largest markets and is great for foodstuffs and cheap clothing. An antiques market is also held here on the third Sunday of each month.

ℹ Information

Hospital (☑ 0577 58 51 11; Viale Bracci) Just north of Siena at Le Scotte.
Police station (☑ 0577 20 11 11; Via del Castoro 6)
Tourist office (☑ 0577 28 05 51; www.terresiena.it; Piazza del Campo 56; ⊙ 9.30am-6.30pm Easter-Sep, 9.30am-5.30pm Mon-Fri, to 12.30pm Sun Oct-Easter) Reserves accommodation, sells a map of Siena (€1), organises car and scooter hire, and sells train tickets (commission applies).

ℹ Getting There & Away

BUS

Siena Mobilità (☑ 800 570530; www.sienamobilita.it), part of the Tiemme network, runs services between Siena and other parts of Tuscany. It has a **ticket office** (⊙ 6.30am-7.30pm Mon-Fri, 7am-7.30pm Sat & Sun) underneath the main bus station in Piazza Gramsci; there's also a left-luggage office here (per 24 hours €5.50).

Frequent *Corse Rapide* (Express) buses race up to Florence (€7.80, 1¼ hours); they are a better option than the standard *Corse Ordinarie* services, which stop in Poggibonsi and Colle di Val d'Elsa en route. Other regional destinations include the following:

Arezzo €6.60, 1½ hours, eight daily

San Gimignano €6, one to 1½ hours, 10 daily either direct or changing in Poggibonsi
Montalcino €3.65, 1½ hours, six daily
Poggibonsi €4.35, 50 minutes, every 40 minutes
Montepulciano €5.15, 1¾ hours
Colle di Val d'Elsa €3.40, 30 minutes, hourly, with connections to Volterra (€2.75)

Services to Montalcino, Montepulciano and Pienza depart from outside the train station.

Sena (☑ 861 199 19 00; www.sena.it) buses run to/from Rome Tibertina (€23, 3½ hours, six daily), Fiumicino Airport (€23, 3¾ hours, two daily), Turin (€36, 8¼ hours, one daily), Milan (€36, 4¼ hours, two daily), Venice (€29, 5½ hours, one daily) and Perugia (€12, 1½ hours, one daily). Its **ticket office** (⊙ 8.30am-7.45pm Mon-Sat) is also underneath the bus station in Piazza Gramsci.

CAR & MOTORCYCLE

For Florence, take the RA3 (Siena–Florence superstrada) or the more attractive SR222.

TRAIN

Siena isn't on a major train line so buses are generally a better alternative. You'll need to change at Chiusi for Rome and at Empoli for Florence.

ℹ Getting Around

TO/FROM THE AIRPORT

A Siena Mobilità bus travels between Pisa airport and Siena (one way/return €14/26, two hours), leaving Siena at 7.10am and Pisa at 1pm. Tickets should be purchased at least one day in advance from the bus station or online.

BUS

Siena Mobilità operates city bus services (€1.10 per 90 minutes). Buses 8 and 9 run between the train station and Piazza Gramsci.

CAR & MOTORCYCLE

There's a ZTL in the historical centre, although visitors can drop off luggage at their hotel, then get out (don't forget to have reception report your licence number or risk receiving a hefty fine).

Large, conveniently located car parks are at the Stadio Comunale and around the Fortezza Medicea, both just north of Piazza San Domenico. Some free street parking (look for white lines) is available in Viale Vittorio Veneto, on the southern edge of the Fortezza Medicea, but it is hotly contested. The paid car parks at San Francesco and Santa Caterina (aka Fontebranda) each have a *scala mobile* (escalator) to take you up into the centre.

All paid car parks charge €1.70 per hour. For more information on parking, go to www.sienaparcheggi.com (in Italian).

FLORENCE & TUSCANY SIENA

Chianti

The ancient vineyards in this postcard-perfect part of Tuscany produce the grapes used in Chianti Classico, a Sangiovese-dominated drop sold under the Gallo Nero (Black Cockerel/Rooster) trademark.

Split between the provinces of Florence (Chianti Fiorentino) and Siena (Chianti Sienese), Chianti is usually accessed via the SR222 (Via Chiantigiana) and is criss-crossed by a picturesque network of *strade provinciale* (provincial roads) and *strade secondaria* (secondary roads), some of which are unsealed. You'll pass immaculately maintained vineyards and olive groves, honey-coloured stone farmhouses, graceful Romanesque *pieve* (rural churches), handsome Renaissance villas and imposing castles built by Florentine and Sienese warlords during the Middle Ages.

For information about the Consorzio Vino Chianti Classico (the high-profile consortium of local producers), go to www.chianticlassico.com/en.

Greve in Chianti

POP 13,888

Located 26km south of Florence, Greve is the main town in the Chianti Fiorentino. As well as being the hub of the local wine industry, it is home to the enthusiastic and entrepreneurial Falorni family, who operate the town's two main tourist attractions.

Greve's annual wine fair is held in the first or second week of September – make sure that you book accommodation well in advance if you plan to visit at this time.

◉ Sights & Activities

Museo del Vino   MUSEUM
(Museum of Wine; www.museovino.it; Piazza Nino Tirinnanzi 10; ⊘hrs vary) Opened in 2010, this privately established and operated museum is a labour of love by Lorenzo and Stefano Falorni, who have spent over 40 years documenting the history of the local wine industry and adding to their father's collection of artefacts and materials associated with it. An audioguide provides a fascinating narrative, as does an interview-based audiovisual presentation.

At the time of research, the museum was welcoming visitors by appointment only. Email for an update.

Le Cantine di
Greve in Chianti   WINE TASTING
(www.lecantine.it; Galleria delle Cantine 2; ⊘10am-7pm) Another Falorni family enterprise, this vast commercial *enoteca* stocks more than 1200 varieties of wine. To indulge in some of the 140 different wines available for tasting (including Chianti, Super Tuscans, top DOCs and DOCGs, Vin Santo and grappa), buy a prepaid wine card costing €10 to €25 from the central bar, stick it into one of the many taps and out will trickle your tipple of choice. Any unused credit will be refunded when you return the card. It's fabulous fun, though somewhat distressing for designated drivers. To find the *cantine,* look for the supermarket on the main road – it's down a staircase opposite the supermarket entrance.

CYCLING CHIANTI

Exploring Chianti by bicycle is a highlight for many travellers. The tourist office in Greve in Chianti publishes a brochure listing walking and cycling routes in the Greve area, and you can rent bicycles from **Ramuzzi** (☑055 85 30 37; www.ramuzzi.com; Via Italo Stecchi 23; touring bike/125cc scooter per day €20/55; ⊘9am-1pm & 3-7pm Mon-Fri, 9am-1pm Sat) in the town.

A number of companies offer guided cycling tours leaving from Florence:

Florence by Bike (Map p489; ☑055 48 89 92; www.florencebybike.it; Via San Zanobi 120r) Day tour of northern Chianti, including lunch and wine tasting (€76; March to October).

I Bike Italy (☑342 935 23 95; www.ibikeitaly.com) Offers a day tour including lunch at a winery (€83; mid-March to October). A shuttle takes you from Florence to the starting point in Chianti. Students receive a 10% discount.

I Bike Tuscany (p51) Year-round one-day tours (€120 to €150) for riders of every skill level. The company transports you from your Florence hotel to Chianti by minibus, where you join the tour. Both hybrid and electric bikes are available, as is a support vehicle. Also offers one-day Florence to Siena tours (€145).

ℹ Information

Tourist office (☑ 055 854 62 99; Piazza Matteotti 11; ☺10am-7pm) Can help with accommodation and tour bookings, *cantine* visits and bus tickets.

ℹ Getting There & Around

BUS

SITA buses travel between Greve and Florence (€3.30, one hour, hourly).

CAR & MOTORCYCLE

Chianti's roads can be frighteningly narrow and frustratingly difficult to navigate – to cut down on driving stress, be sure to purchase a copy of *Le strade del Gallo Nero* (€2.50), a useful map of the wine-producing zone that shows both major and secondary roads and also includes a comprehensive list of wine estates. It's available at newsstands in the region.

Greve is located on the Via Chiantigiana. There is free parking in the two-level, open-air car park on Piazza della Resistenza, on the opposite side of the main road to Piazza Matteotti. On Fridays, don't park overnight in the paid spaces in Piazza Matteotti – your car will be towed to make room for Saturday market stalls.

Around Greve in Chianti

⭐**Antinori nel Chianti Classico**   WINERY
(www.antinorichianticlassico.it; Via Cassia per Siena 133, Località Bargino; tour & tasting €20, bookings essential; ☺11am-6pm Mon-Sat, till 2pm Sun) Visiting this cellar complex is a James Bond–esque experience. Show a print-out of your reservation at the gated, guarded entrance and then approach the sculptural main building, which is built into the hillside. Inside, your one-hour guided tour (English and Italian) finishes with a tasting of three Antinori wines in an all-glass tasting room suspended above barrels in the cellar (wow!).

There is a state-of-the-art bar where you can taste 16 different wines (€4 to €9 per tasting); have a 'guided tasting' of three different wines with the sommelier (€9 or €12); or simply drink a glass of wine (ranging from €7 for a glass of Marchese Antinori 2009 to €35 for a glass of Solaia 2009). Afterwards, be sure to enjoy lunch in the Rinuccio 1180 (p543) restaurant.

Bargino is a scenic 20km drive northwest of Greve via the SS222, SP3 and SS2.

Badia a Passignano   WINERY
(www.osteriadipassignano.com)This 11th-century abbey located 6km west of Montefioralle is surrounded by vines and olive trees. The main building is closed for a restoration that doesn't look as if it will be completed for many years, but the vineyards and historic cellars can be visited on a variety of guided tours. The most popular is the four-hour 'Antinori at Badia a Passignano' tour (€150; Monday to Saturday at 11.15am and 6.15pm), which includes a visit to the vineyard and cellars followed by lunch or dinner in the estate's restaurant accompanied by four Antinori wines.

Bookings for tours are essential. It's also possible to taste and purchase wines and olive oil at La Bottega, the estate's wine shop. You don't need to make a reservation for this.

Castello di Verrazzano   WINERY
(☑ 055 85 42 43; www.verrazzano.com; Via Citille, Greti) The castle at this wine estate 3km north of Greve was once home to Giovanni da Verrazzano (1485–1528), who explored the North American coast and is commemorated in New York by the Verrazano Narrows bridge (the good captain lost a 'z' from his name somewhere in the mid-Atlantic). Today, the castle presides over a 220-hectare historic wine estate.

There are a number of guided tours on offer, each of which incorporate a short visit to the historic wine cellar and gardens, and tastings of the estate's wines (including its flagship Chianti Classico). Check the website for details.

Castellina in Chianti

POP 2873

Established by the Etruscans and fortified by the Florentines in the 15th century as a defensive outpost against the Sienese, Castellina in Chianti is now a major centre of the wine industry, as the huge cylindrical silos brimming with Chianti Classico attest. To taste some of the local product, head to **Antica Fattoria la Castellina** (Via Ferruccio 26), the town's best-known wine shop.

From the southern car park, follow Via Ferruccio or the panoramic path next to the town's eastern defensive walls to access the atmospheric **Via delle Volte**, an arched medieval passageway that was originally used for ancient sacred rites and later enclosed with a roof and incorporated into the Florentine defensive structure.

Etruscan archaeological finds from the local area are on display at the **Museo**

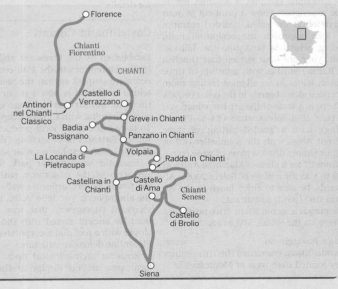

Florence

Chianti
Fiorentino

CHIANTI

Castello di
Verrazzano

Antinori
nel Chianti
Classico

Greve in Chianti

Badia a
Passignano

Panzano in Chianti

Volpaia

La Locanda di
Pietracupa

Radda in Chianti

Castellina in
Chianti

Castello
di Ama

Chianti
Senese

Castello
di Brolio

Siena

 4 DAYS Wine Tour of Chianti

Tuscany has more than its fair share of highlights, but few can match the glorious indulgence of a leisurely drive through Chianti. On offer is an intoxicating blend of scenery, acclaimed restaurants and ruby-red wine.

From Florence, take the superstrada towards Siena, exit at Bargino and follow the signs to **Antinori nel Chianti Classico** (p539), a recently opened and utterly magnificent estate with an architecturally innovative winery building. Take a tour, prime your palate with a wine tasting and enjoy lunch in the estate's **Rinuccio 1180** (p543) restaurant. Head southeast along the SS2, SP3 and SS222 (Via Chiantigiana) towards Greve in Chianti. Stop at historic **Castello di Verrazzano** (p539) for a tasting and tour en route.

The next day, make your way to Greve to visit its **Museo del Vino** (p538) and then test your new-found knowledge over a self-directed tasting in the nearby **Le Cantine di Greve in Chianti** (p538). For lunch, eat a Tuscan-style burger at **Dario DOC** (p544) in Panzano in Chianti or linger over lunch at **La Locanda di Pietracupa** (p543). Your destination in the afternoon should be **Badia a Passignano** (p539), an 11th-century, still-functioning Vallombrosian abbey surrounded by an Antinori wine estate. Enjoy a tasting in the *enoteca* and consider staying for an early pizza dinner at **L'Antica Scuderia** (p544) opposite the abbey, where you'll be able to watch the sun set over the vineyards.

On day three, pop into the pretty hilltop hamlet of Volpaia near Radda in Chianti and take a tour of the **Castello di Volpaia** (p542) cellars before relaxing over lunch at **Bar Ucci** (p542) or heading to the Michelin-starred **Ristorante Albergaccio** (p544) in Castellina in Chianti.

On the final day, head towards Siena. Along the way, take a guided tour of the **Castello di Brolio** (p542), ancestral home of the aristocratic Ricasoli family. Their wine estate is the oldest in Italy, so be sure to sample some Baron Ricasoli Chianti Classico at the cantina or over lunch in its *osteria*. Afterwards, investigate award-winning wines and contemporary art at **Castello di Ama** (p542).

Top: Badia a Passignano (p539), Greve in Chianti
Bottom: Wine barrels in a Chianti cellar

Archeologico del Chianti Senese (www.museoarcheologicochianti.it; Piazza del Comune 18; adult/reduced €5/3; ☻10am-6pm daily Apr-May & Sep-Oct, 11am-7pm Jun-Aug, 10am-5pm Sat & Sun Nov-Mar), located in the town's medieval *rocca* (fortress). Room 4 showcases artefacts found in the 7th-century-BC Etruscan tombs of Montecalvario (Ipogeo Etrusco di Monte Calvario; ☻24hr) FREE, which is located on the northern edge of town off the SR222.

❶ Information

Tourist office (☏0577 74 13 92; ufficioturistico@comune.castelina.si.it; Via Ferruccio 40; ☻10am-noon & 3-6pm Tue, Thu, Sat & Sun mid-Mar–May, 10am-1pm & 3-7pm Jun-Oct, 3-6pm Sat & Sun Nov, 10am-noon Fri & 10am-noon & 3-6pm Sat & Sun Dec–mid-Jan) The privately run office can help with maps, tours, accommodation and information.

❶ Getting There & Around

BUS
Siena Mobilità (www.sienamobilita.it) buses travel between Castellina and Siena (€3.40, 35 minutes, 10 daily).

CAR & MOTORCYCLE
The most convenient car park is at the southern edge of town off Via IV Novembre (€1/5 per hour/day).

Radda in Chianti
POP 1688

Shields and escutcheons add a dash of drama to the facade of 16th-century Palazzo del Podestà on the main square in this important wine centre 11km east of Castellina in Chianti. The tourist office (☏0577 73 84 94; proradda@chiantinet.it; Piazza Castello 2; ☻10am-1pm & 3-7pm Easter-Sep, 10.30am-12.30pm & 3.30-6.30pm Oct-Easter) can book accommodation and tours for this pocket of Chianti, and supply information about walks in the area.

Around Radda in Chianti

◉ Sights & Activities

Castello di Brolio   CASTLE
(☏0577 73 02 80; www.ricasoli.it; self-guided tour of garden, chapel & crypt €5, guided tour of museum, chapel & crypt €8; ☻10am-5.30pm mid-Mar–Nov, guided tours every 30 minutes 10am-1pm & 2.30-5.30pm Tue-Sun) The ancestral estate of the aristocratic Ricasoli family dates from the 11th century and is the oldest winery in

Italy. Currently home to the 32nd baron, it opens its formal garden, panoramic terrace and museum to day trippers.

Occupying three rooms in the tower, the small but fascinating museum is dedicated to documenting the fascinating life of Baron Bettino Ricasoli (1809–80), the second prime minster of the Republic of Italy and a true polymath (scientist, farmer, winemaker, statesman, businessman). A leading figure in the Risorgimento, his greatest claim to fame (in our view, at least) is that he invented the formula for Chianti Classico that is enshrined in current DOC regulations.

The estate produces wine and olive oil, and the huge terrace commands a spectacular view of the vineyards and olive groves. Near the estate carpark is the Osteria del Castello (☏0577 73 02 90; four-course tasting menu with wines €50; ☻noon-2.30pm & 7.30-9.30pm Fri-Wed late-Mar–Oct) and just outside the estate's entrance gates, on the SP484, is a modern cantina (☻9am-7pm Mon-Fri & 11am-7pm Sat & Sun Mar-Dec, 9am-6pm Mon-Fri Jan & Feb) where you can taste the estate's well-regarded Chianti Classico.

Castello di Ama   WINERY
(☏0577 74 60 31; http://arte.castellodiama.com; guided tours €15, with wine & oil tasting €35; ☻year round, by appt) This highly regarded estate produces a range of wines including the internationally renowned 'L'Apparita' Merlot, the 'Haiku' Sangiovese/Cabernet Franc/Merlot blend and a delicious 'Vigneto Bellavista' Chianti Classico. In recent years it has also developed a sculpture park showcasing 13 site-specific artworks by artists including Louise Bourgeois, Chen Zhen, Anish Kapoor, Kendell Geers and Daniel Buren. Guided tours of the cellar, villa and sculpture park are in English, French, Italian or German. You'll find the estate 11km southwest of Gaiole, near Lecchi in Chianti.

Castello di Volpaia   WINERY
(☏0577 73 80 66; www.volpaia.it; Località Volpaia) Wines, olive oils, vinegars and honey have been produced for centuries at this estate based in the medieval hill-top hamlet of Volpaia (the estate's name is misleading, as there's no actual castle here). Book ahead to enjoy a tour of the cellars, or pop into its *enoteca*, which is inside the main tower.

While here, consider enjoying a snack at Bar Ucci (www.bar-ucci.it; crostoni €4.50-6, antipasti plates €8, salads €4-8; ☻8am-9pm Tue-Sun) or a more formal meal at Ristorante La

Bottega (☑0577 73 80 01; www.labottegadivol-paia.it; meals €25; ☺noon-2.30pm & 7.30-10pm Wed-Mon Easter-Jan), a pretty restaurant serving *cucina contadina* (food from the farmers' kitchen). Both are operated by members of the local Barucci family, and are located on the main square of the hamlet. The restaurant's outdoor terrace (which has lovely views) is next to the Baruccis' productive kitchen garden.

🛏 Sleeping

Ostello del Chianti   HOSTEL €
(☑055 805 02 65; www.ostellodelchianti.it; Via Roma 137, Tavarnelle Val di Pesa; dm €14-16, q with private/shared bathroom €70/76; ☺reception 8.30-11am & 4pm-midnight, hostel closed Nov–mid-Mar; P@🛜) This is one of Italy's oldest hostels and though it occupies an ugly building in the less-than-scenic town of Tavarnelle Val di Pesa, the friendly staff and bargain prices compensate. Dorms max out at six beds and bike hire can be arranged for €8 per day. Breakfast costs €2. Florence is easily accessed by SITA bus (€3.30, one hour).

Fattoria di Rignana   AGRITURISMO €€
(☑055 85 20 65; www.rignana.it; Rignana; d with/without bathroom in fattoria €90/100, d villa €110-130; P@🛜🏊) This old farmstead and noble villa 3.8km from Badia a Passignano has everything you'll need for the perfect Chianti experience – an historic setting, glorious views, a large swimming pool and walking access to a decent local eatery. Two accommodation options are on offer: elegant rooms in the 17th-century villa and more rustic rooms in the adjoining *fattoria* (farmhouse).

Villa Il Poggiale   BOUTIQUE HOTEL €€
(☑055 82 83 11; www.villailpoggiale.it; Via Empolese 69, San Casciano Val di Pesa; d €80-250, ste €120-350; ☺closed mid-Jan–mid-Feb; P@🛜🏊) Accommodation in Chianti is often prohibitively expensive, but this Renaissance-era villa in an elevated location looking toward the Val d'Elsa (Il Poggiale means 'Top of the Hill') bucks the trend. It offers a labyrinthine arrangement of 24 spacious and individually decorated rooms and suites, some with four-poster beds and frescoed ceilings. Guests enjoy the complimentary afternoon tea that is served in the gracious reception salon, and appreciate the buffet dinner after a big day of sightseeing in the region.

Villa I Barronci   HOTEL €€
(☑055 82 05 98; www.villaibarronci.com; Via Sorripa 10, San Casciano Val di Pesa; s €85-150, d €115-230; P❄@🛜🏊🚹) Located on the northwestern edge of Chianti between Florence and Pisa, this extremely comfortable modern country hotel offers exemplary service and amenities. You can relax in the bar and restaurant, rejuvenate in the spa, laze by the pool or head off for easy day trips to Volterra, San Gimignano and Siena.

★**Villa Sassolini**   BOUTIQUE HOTEL €€€
(☑055 970 22 46; www.villasassolini.it; Largo Moncioni, Località Moncioni; d €198-355, ste €324-443, dinner €50; ☺closed Nov–mid-Mar; ❄🛜🏊) It would be almost impossible to top the romantic credentials of this gorgeous hotel perched high in dense forest on the border of Chianti and the Valdarno. Luxe rooms, an intimate restaurant (dinner €50) and a spectacular pool terrace are three of many elements contributing to an utterly irresistible package.

🍴 Eating & Drinking

Rinuccio 1180   MODERN TUSCAN €€
(☑055 235 97 20; www.antinorichianticlassico.it; Via Cassia per Siena 133, Bargino; meals €32, tasting platters €9-12; ☺noon-4pm) Imagine lunching inside a glass box on a terrace with intoxicating panoramic views of pea-green vines and rolling hills. This is what the latest starlet of the Chianti dining scene – the restaurant at the new Antinori cellar in Bargino – is about. Cuisine is Tuscan, modern, seasonal and sassy. Advance reservations are essential.

La Locanda di Pietracupa   GASTRONOMIC €€
(☑055 807 24 00; www.locandapietracupa.com; Via Madonna di Pietracupa 31, San Donato in Poggio; meals €40; ☺closed Tue; 🛜) The prices at this restaurant near the late-Renaissance sanctuary of the Madonna di Pietracupa are remarkably reasonable considering the quality of the modern Tuscan cuisine on offer. You can enjoy a long lunch on the outdoor terrace, or book one of the four B&B rooms (single/double €70/80) and settle in for an indulgent dinner in the elegant dining room.

Osteria Mangiando Mangiando   TUSCAN €€
(☑055 854 63 72; www.mangiandomangiando.it; Piazza Matteotti 80, Greve in Chianti; meals €36; ☺noon-2.30pm & 7-10pm Feb-Dec) It may be the much-lauded recipient of a coveted

Slow Food snail of excellence, but this unpretentious place on Greve's main piazza has a friendly and casual vibe, a cheerful but simple decor, and a menu balancing Tuscan standards and some light and flavoursome options (especially soups) that differ from the usual Tuscan fare.

L'Antica Macelleria Cecchini
TRADITIONAL ITALIAN €€

(www.dariocecchini.com; Via XX Luglio 11; ⊗9am-4pm) The small town of Panzano in Chianti southwest of Greve in Chianti is known throughout Italy for the *macellerìa* (butcher shop) owned and run by extrovert butcher Dario Cecchini. This Tuscan celebrity has carved out a niche for himself as a poetry-spouting guardian of the *bistecca* (steak) and other Tuscan meaty treats, and he operates three eateries here as well as the *macellerìa*: Officina della Bistecca (☑055 85 21 76; set menu €50; ⊗from 8pm Tue, Fri & Sat, from 1pm Sun), with a simple set menu built around the famous *bistecca;* Solociccia (☑055 85 27 27; set menu €30; ⊗from 7pm & 9pm Thu, Fri & Sat, from 1pm Sun), where guests share a communal table to sample meat dishes other than *bistecca;* and Dario DOC (burger €10-15, light menu €20; ⊗noon-3pm Mon-Sat), his casual lunchtime-only eatery. Book ahead for the Officina and Solociccia.

L'Antica Scuderia
TUSCAN €€

(☑055 807 16 23; www.ristorolanticascuderia.com; Via di Passignano 17, Badia a Passignano; meals €44, pizzas €7-15; ⊗12.30-2.30pm & 7.30-10.30pm Wed-Mon) If you fancy the idea of lunching on a garden terrace overlooking one of the Antinori vineyards, this casual eatery may well fit the bill. Lunch features antipasti, pastas and traditional grilled meats, while dinner sees plenty of pizza-oven action. Kids love the playground set, and adults love that it's at the opposite end of the garden.

Ristorante Albergaccio
GASTRONOMIC €€€

(☑0577 74 10 42; www.albergacciocast.com; Via Fiorentina 63, Castellina in Chianti; 3-course kids menu €27, 4-course menu €58, 5-course menu €68; ⊗lunch & dinner Mon-Sat, closed parts of Dec-Mar) One kilometre outside Castellina in Chianti on the road to San Donato in Poggio, this upmarket restaurant in a restored farmhouse showcases what it describes as 'the territory on the table', making full use of local, seasonal and organic produce.

Val d'Elsa

A convenient base for visiting the rest of Tuscany, this valley stretching from Chianti to the Maremma can be relied upon to tick many of the boxes on your Tuscan 'must-do' list, with plenty of opportunities to enjoy food, wine, museums and scenery.

San Gimignano

POP 7638

As you crest the hill coming from the east, the 15 towers of this walled hill town look like a medieval Manhattan. Originally an Etruscan village, the town was named after the bishop of Modena, San Gimignano, who is said to have saved the city from Attila the Hun. It became a *comune* in 1199 and was very prosperous due in part to its location on the Via Francigena – building a tower taller than those built by one's neighbour (there were originally 72) became a popular way for the town's prominent families to flaunt their power and wealth. In 1348 plague wiped out much of the population and weakened the local economy, leading to the town's submission to Florence in 1353. Today, it's possible to believe that not even the plague could deter the swarms of summer day trippers, who are lured by the town's palpable sense of history, intact medieval streetscapes and enchanting rural setting.

◎ Sights & Activities

The two most important sights in town are the Collegiata and the Museo Civico. You can purchase individual tickets, or take advantage of two money-saving combined entry tickets. The first (adult/child €7.50/5.50) gives admission to the Museo Civico, the Archaeological Museum complex and the Ornithological museum. The second (adult/child €5.50/2.50) gets you into the Collegiata and the Museo d'Arte Sacra.

★ Collegiata
CHURCH

(Duomo Collegiata o Basilica di Santa Maria Assunta; Piazza del Duomo; adult/child €3.50/1.50; ⊗10am-7.10pm Mon-Fri, to 5.10pm Sat, 12.30-7.10pm Sun Apr-Oct, shorter hrs rest of year, closed 2nd half Nov & Jan) San Gimignano's Romanesque cathedral is named after the college of priests who originally managed it. Parts of the building date to the second half of the 11th century, but its remarkably vivid frescoes, which resemble a vast medieval comic strip, date from the 14th century.

Entry is via the side stairs and through a loggia that was originally covered and functioned as the baptistry. After entering the main space, face the altar and look to your left (north). On the wall are scenes from Genesis and the Old Testament by Bartolo di Fredi, dating from around 1367. The top row runs from the creation of the world through to the forbidden fruit scene. This in turn leads to the next level and fresco, the expulsion of Adam and Eve from the Garden of Eden, which has sustained some war damage. Further scenes include Cain killing Abel, and the stories of Noah's ark and Joseph's coat. The last level continues with the tale of Moses leading the Jews out of Egypt, and the story of Job.

On the right (south) wall are scenes from the New Testament by the workshop of Simone Martini (probably led by Lippo Memmi, Martini's brother-in-law), which were completed in 1336. Again, the frescoes are spread over three levels, starting in the six lunettes at the top. Commencing with the Annunciation, the panels proceed through episodes such as the Epiphany, the presentation of Christ in the temple and the massacre of the innocents on Herod's orders. The subsequent panels on the lower levels summarise the life and death of Christ, the Resurrection and so on. Again, some have sustained damage, but most are in good condition.

On the inside wall of the front facade, extending onto adjoining walls, is Taddeo di Bartolo's striking depiction of the Last Judgment – on the upper-left side is a fresco depicting *Paradiso* (Heaven) and on the upper-right *Inferno* (Hell). The fresco of San Sebastian under them is by Benozzo Gozzoli.

Off the south aisle, near the main altar, is the Cappella di Santa Fina, a Renaissance chapel adorned with naive and touching frescoes by Domenico Ghirlandaio depicting events in the life of one of the town's patron saints.

★ Museo Civico   MUSEUM
(Piazza del Duomo 2; adult/reduced €5/4; ⊙9.30am-7pm Apr-Sep, 11am-5.30pm Oct-Mar) The 12th-century Palazzo Civico has always been the centre of local government; its Sala di Dante is where the great poet addressed the town's council in 1299, urging it to support the Guelph cause, and its pinacoteca has a charming collection of paintings from the Sienese and Florentine schools of the 12th to 15th centuries.

The Sala di Dante (also known as the Sala del Consiglio) is home to Lippo Memmi's early-14th-century *Maestà*, which portrays the enthroned Virgin and Child surrounded by angels, saints and local dignitaries – the kneeling noble in red-and-black stripes was the *podestà* (chief magistrate) of the time. Other frescoes in the room portray jousts, hunting scenes, castles and other medieval goings-on.

On the floor above the Sala di Dante is the small but charming *pinacoteca*. Highlights of its collection are two large *Annunciation* panels (1482) by Filippino Lippi, *Madonna of Humility Worshipped by Two Saints* (1466) and *Madonna and Child with Saints* (1466) by Benozzo Gozzoli and an altarpiece by Taddeo di Bartolo (1401) illustrating the life of St Gimignano.

In the Camera del Podestà, at the top of the stairs, is a meticulously restored cycle of frescos by Memmo di Filippuccio illustrating a moral history – the rewards of marriage are shown in the scenes of the husband and wife naked in the bath and in bed.

While here, be sure to climb the 154 steps of the *palazzo*'s Torre Grossa for a spectacular view over the town and surrounding countryside.

Chiesa di Sant'Agostino   CHURCH
(Piazza Sant'Agostino; ⊙9am-noon & 3-7pm mid-Mar–Oct, to 6pm Nov-Dec, 4-6pm Mon, 10am-noon & 3-6pm Tue-Sun Jan–mid-Mar) This late-13th-century church at the northern end of town is best known for Benozzo Gozzoli's charming fresco cycle illustrating the life of St

San Gimignano

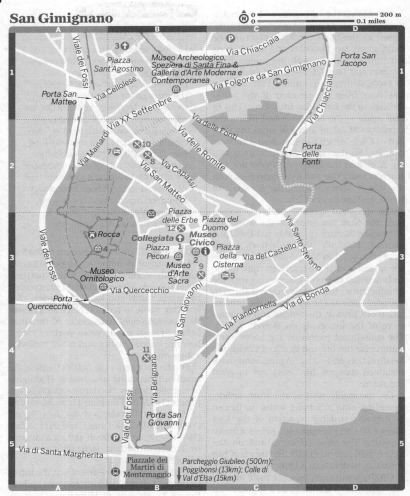

△ N 0 ———————— 200 m
0 ———————— 0.1 miles

Augustine. You'll find it behind the altar and will need €0.50 to illuminate it.

Gozzoli also painted the highly unusual fresco of San Sebastian on the north wall, which shows the fully clothed saint protecting the citizens of San Gimignano, helped by a bare-breasted Virgin Mary and semi-robed Jesus (it alludes to the saint's supposed intervention to protect citizens during the 1464 plague).

Museo del Vino MUSEUM, WINE TASTING
(Wine Museum; museodelvino@sangimignano.com; Parco della Rocca; ⏰11.30am-6.30pm Apr-Oct)

FREE This operation housed in an unmarked gallery next to the *rocca* (fortress) celebrates Vernaccia, San Gimignano's famous white wine. It comprises a small exhibition on the history of the varietal (Italian language only) and an *enoteca* where you can purchase a glass of Vernaccia to enjoy on the terrace, which has a panoramic view.

☞ Tours

The tourist office takes advance bookings for a range of guided English-language tours. These include a **Vernaccia di San Gimignano Vineyard Visit** (€20; ⏰5-7pm Tue & Thu

San Gimignano

Apr–Oct) that includes tastings of local foods and wines. Also on offer are **nature walks** (€15 to €22) through the hills surrounding San Gimignano, along a 6km stretch of the Via Francigena, and through Riserva Naturale di Castelvecchio, southwest of town.

✯ Festivals & Events

San Gimignano Estate   ARTS
(www.sangimignano.com) Includes performances of opera in Piazza del Duomo, films in the *rocca,* concerts, theatre and dance. Held between June and September.

Ferie delle Messi   CULTURAL
Held in June (usually the third weekend), this pageant evokes the town's medieval past through re-enacted battles, archery contests and plays.

Festival Barocco di San Gimignano   MUSIC
A season of baroque music concerts in September and early October.

🛏 Sleeping

★ **Al Pozzo dei Desideri**   B&B €
(📞370 310 25 38, 0577 90 71 99; www.alpozzodeidesideri.it; Piazza della Cisterna 32; d €75-110, tr €95-120, q €115-160; ❀ 🛜) Three rooms with a view (two over the Tuscan countryside and one over the town's main piazza) are on offer in this recently opened B&B. All have charming decor, stylish modern bathrooms, a fridge and tea- and coffee-making facilities. No breakfast, but there's a good cafe close by.

Foresteria Monastero di San Girolamo   HOSTEL €
(📞0577 94 05 73; www.monasterosangirolamo.it; Via Folgore da San Gimignano 26-32; s/tw/tr €37.50/75/112.50) This is an excellent budget choice. Run by friendly Benedictine Vallumbrusian nuns, it has basic but comfortable rooms sleeping two to five people; all have attached bathrooms. Parking and kitchen use are available for a small fee. Book in advance at www.monasterystays.com, as it's usually full.

If you don't have a reservation, arrive between 9am and 12.30pm or between 3.30pm and 5.45pm and ring the monastery bell (not the Foresteria one, which is never answered).

Hotel L'Antico Pozzo   BOUTIQUE HOTEL €€
(📞0577 94 20 14; www.anticopozzo.com; Via San Matteo 87; s €80-95, d €90-135, superior d €169-180; ⊙closed 1st 2 wks Nov & Jan; ❀ @ 🛜) Named after the old, softly illuminated *pozzo* (well) just off its lobby, this hotel occupies a 15th-century *palazzo* on busy Via San Matteo. Most rooms feature high ceilings, simple but elegant decor and good-sized if dated bathrooms; we suggest avoiding the cheaper top-floor rooms. There's a handsome breakfast room and a pretty rear courtyard.

🍴 Eating & Drinking

San Gimignano is known for its *zafferano* (saffron). You can purchase meat, vegetables, fish and takeaway food at the **Thursday morning market** (Piazza delle Erbe) in and around Piazzas Cisterna, Duomo and Erbe.

Dal Bertelli   SANDWICHES €
(Via Capassi 30; panini €3-5, glasses of wine €1.50; ⊙1-7pm Mar-early Jan) The Bertelli family has lived in San Gimignano since 1779, and its current patriarch is fiercely proud of both his heritage and his sandwiches. Sig Brunello Bertelli sources his salami, cheese, bread and wine from local artisan producers and sells his generously sized offerings from an atmospheric space as far away as possible from what he calls the town's 'tourist grand bazaar'. Fabulous.

Gelateria Dondoli   GELATO €
(www.gelateriadipiazza.com; Piazza della Cisterna 4; gelati €2-3; ⊙8.30am-11pm Mar–mid-Nov) Master gelato-maker Sergio Dondoli uses only the choicest ingredients to create his creamy and icy delights. Get into the local swing of things with a *crema di santa fina* (saffron cream) gelato or a Vernaccia sorbet.

★ **Ristorante La Mandragola**　TUSCAN €€
(📞 0577 94 03 77; www.locandalamandragola.it; Via Berignano 58; meals €37, set menus €14-25, kids menu €10; ⏰ noon-2.30pm & 7.30-9.30pm, closed Thu Nov-early Mar) Locals wouldn't dream of eating at the tourist restaurants on Via San Giovanni, but they love La Mandragola. Built into the city walls, it's big enough to seat regulars, day-tripping Italians and foreign tour groups and still have space for the rest of us. Great food (especially the pasta), an excellent house Vernaccia and friendly staff contribute to the winning formula.

Perucà　TUSCAN €€
(📞 0577 94 31 36; www.peruca.eu; Via Capassi 16; meals €30; ⏰ 12.30-2pm Tue-Sun mid-Feb–early Dec, open Mon Apr-Sep) The female owner is as knowledgeable about regional food and wine as she is enthusiastic, and the food is excellent. Try the house speciality of *fagottini del contadino* (ravioli with *pecorino*, pears and saffron cream) with a glass of Fattoria San Donato's Vernaccia – it's a match made in heaven.

ℹ Information

The extremely helpful **tourist office** (📞 0577 94 00 08; www.sangimignano.com; Piazza del Duomo 1; ⏰ 10am-1pm & 3-7pm Mar-Oct, 10am-1pm & 2-6pm Nov-Feb) organises tours, supplies maps and can book accommodation.

Free wi-fi is available in and around Piazza del Duomo.

ℹ Getting There & Away

BUS

The **bus station** is next to the Carabinieri (police station) at Porta San Giovanni. Buy bus tickets at the tourist office. Buses run to/from Florence (€6.80, 1¼ to 2 hours, 14 daily) but often require a change at Poggibonsi. Buses also run to/from Siena (€6, one to 1½ hours, 10 daily Monday to Saturday). For Volterra you need to go to Colle di Val d'Elsa (€3.40, 35 minutes, four daily Monday to Saturday) and and take a connecting bus (€2.75, 50 minutes, four daily).

CAR & MOTORCYCLE

From Florence and Siena, take the Siena–Florence superstrada, then the SR2 and finally the SP1 from Poggibonsi. From Volterra, take the SR68 east and follow the turn-off signs north to San Gimignano on the SP47.

Parking is expensive here. The cheapest option (per hour/24 hours €1.50/6) is at Parcheggio Giubileo on the southern edge of town; the most convenient is at Parcheggio Montemaggio

next to Porta San Giovanni (per hour/24 hours €2/20).

TRAIN

The closest train station is located at Poggibonsi (by bus €2.50, about 30 minutes, frequent).

Volterra

POP 10,675

Volterra's well-preserved medieval ramparts give the windswept town a proud, forbidding air that author Stephenie Meyer deemed ideal for the discriminating tastes of the planet's principal vampire coven in her wildly popular book series *Twilight*. Fortunately, the reality is considerably more welcoming, as any wander through the winding cobbled streets attests.

◉ Sights

Though it's a relatively small town, Volterra has a lavish array of museums, churches and archaeological sites. If you plan on visiting a number of these, it's worth purchasing a *biglietto cumulativo*, which gives admission to the Museo Etrusco Guarnacci, the Pinacoteca Comunale and the Ecomuseo dell'Alabastro (adult €10, student and child €6, family €20).

★ **Museo Etrusco Guarnacci**　MUSEUM
(Via Don Minzoni 15; adult/student €8/6; ⏰ 9am-7pm mid-Mar–Oct, 10am-4.30pm Nov–mid-Mar) One of Italy's most impressive collections of Etruscan artefacts is exhibited here. These were unearthed locally and include a vast collection of some 600 funerary urns carved mainly from alabaster and tufa and displayed according to subject and period. The best examples (those dating from later periods) are on the 2nd and 3rd floors.

Highlights include the Urn of the Sposi, a strikingly realistic terracotta rendering of an elderly couple; a crested helmet excavated from the Tomba del Guernero at nearby Poggio alle Croci; and the *L'Ombra della Sera* (Shadow of the Evening), an elongated bronze nude figurine that bears a striking resemblance to the work of the Italian sculptor Alberto Giacometti.

Cattedrale di Santa Maria Assunta　CATHEDRAL
(Duomo di Volterra; Piazza San Giovanni; ⏰ 8am-12.30pm & 3-6pm Sat-Thu, 4-6pm Fri) Built in the 12th and 13th centuries, the *duomo's* interior was remodelled in the 16th century and features a handsome coffered ceiling. The

Volterra

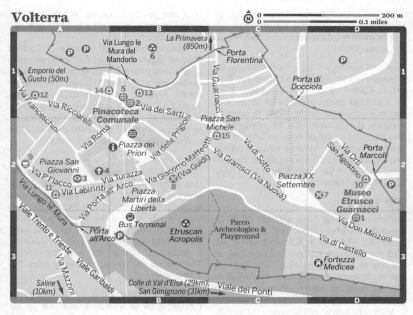

N 0 ——————— 200 m
0 ——————— 0.1 miles

FLORENCE & TUSCANY VAL D'ELSA

Volterra

◎ Top Sights
1 Museo Etrusco Guarnacci	D3
2 Pinacoteca Comunale	B1

◎ Sights
3 Baptistry	A2
4 Cattedrale di Santa Maria Assunta	A2
5 Ecomuseo dell'Alabastro	B1
6 Roman Theatre	B1

⊗ Eating
7 La Carabaccia	D2

8 L'Incontro	B2

◎ Drinking & Nightlife
9 Caffè dei Fornelli	A2

◎ Shopping
10 Alab'Arte	D2
11 Alessandro Marzetti	A2
12 Emporio del Gusto	A1
13 Fabula Etrusca	B1
14 Opus Artis	A1
15 Paolo Sabatini	C2

Chapel of Our Lady of Sorrows on the left as you enter from Piazza San Giovanni has two sculptures by Andrea della Robbia and a small fresco of the *Procession of the Magi* by Benozzo Gozzoli.

In front of the *duomo*, a 13th-century **baptistry** (Piazza San Giovanni) features a small marble font (1502) by Andrea Sansovino.

★ **Pinacoteca Comunale**   ART GALLERY
(Via dei Sarti 1; adult/student €8/6; ⊙9am-7pm mid-Mar–early Nov, 10am-4.30pm early Nov–mid-Mar) Occupying the Palazzo Minucci Solaini, this modest collection of local, Sienese and Florentine art includes Taddeo di Bartolo's

lovely *Madonna Enthroned with Child* (1411) and Rosso Fiorentino's strikingly modern representation of the *Deposition from the Cross* (1521).

Ecomuseo dell'Alabastro   MUSEUM
(Via dei Sarti 1; admission incl in Pinacoteca entrance ticket; ⊙9.30am-7pm mid-Mar–Oct, 10.30am-4.30pm Nov–mid-Mar) As befits a town that has hewn the precious rock from nearby quarries since Etruscan times, Volterra is the proud possessor of an alabaster museum. On the ground floor are contemporary creations while on the two upper floors are choice

examples from Etruscan times onwards as well as a re-created artisan's workshop.

The museum shares the same building as the *pinacoteca*.

Roman Theatre
ARCHAEOLOGICAL SITE

(admission €3.50; ⊘10.30am-5.30pm mid-Mar–Oct, to 4.30pm Sat & Sun Nov–mid-Mar) Used as a rubbish dump in medieval times, this site was excavated in the 1950s to reveal a complex dating from the 1st century BC. Two stairways and 19 rows of seating are easily identifiable. Truth be told, an admission ticket isn't really necessary, as there's a great view over the theatre from Via Lungo Le Mura del Mandorlo.

Tours

Volterra Walking Tour
(☑0588 08 62 01; www.volterrawalkingtour.com; per person (min three) €10; ⊘6pm Apr-Jul & Sep-Oct) offers just that – a one-hour English-language tour of the city by foot. Operated by licensed tour guides, it leaves from Piazza Martiri della Libertà. Bookings aren't necessary and payment is cash only.

Volterra's tourist office runs a 90-minute **Volterra by Night** (www.volterratur.it/en/volterra-by-night; adult/child €10/free; ⊘9.30pm Sat mid-Jun–mid-Sep) walking tour in English and Italian. Advance bookings are essential.

Festivals & Events

Volterra AD 1398
CULTURAL

(www.volterra1398.it; day pass €9) On the third and fourth Sundays of August, the citizens of Volterra roll back the calendar some 600 years, take to the streets in period costume and celebrate all the fun of a medieval fair.

Volterragusto
FOOD

(www.volterragusto.com) Events in mid-March, late October and early November showcase local produce, including cheese, white truffles, olive oil and chocolate.

🛏 Sleeping

★ Podere San Lorenzo
AGRITURISMO €

(☑0588 3 90 80; www.agriturismo-volterra.it; Via Allori 80; B&B d €100, 2-/3-/4-bed apt without breakfast €100-130; 🔊🗷🏠) This model of slow tourism is located on an olive farm 3.4km outside Volterra. The two rooms and five self-contained apartments (two with private terraces) are relatively basic, but the surrounds are bucolic, there's an alluring mountain spring–fed biological swimming pool and gourmet dinners (per person €30 including wine) are served in a 12th-century Franciscan chapel.

Walking, biking and hands-on, seasonal olive-oil production (October to November) opportunities are available, as are cooking classes given by chef Mariana (per person €100). Arriving on the SS68 from Siena, Florence and San Gimignano, you'll pass a sculpture of the red circle at the entrance to town and should then turn right into the narrow lane after the car sale yard.

★ La Primavera
B&B €

(☑0588 8 72 95; www.affittacamere-laprimavera.com; Via Porta Diana 15; s/d/tr €50/75/100; ⊘mid-Mar–mid-Nov; 🅿🗷) Silvia Pineschi's simply splendid home-style B&B is located just outside the city walls, a five-minute walk from Piazza dei Priori. It offers four good-sized rooms with soothing pastel colour schemes, a communal lounge and a pretty garden. The free on-site parking is a huge asset. No credit cards.

Chiosco delle Monache
HOSTEL €

(☑0588 8 66 13; www.ostellovolterra.it; Via del Teatro 4, Località San Girolamo; dm €16-20, B&B s €48-53, B&B d €62-69; ⊘mid-Mar–Oct; 🅿🗷) Opened in 2009 after a major renovation, this excellent private hostel occupies a 13th-century monastery complete with a frescoed refectory where breakfast is served. Airy rooms overlook the cloisters and have good beds and bathrooms; dorms sleep up to six. Breakfast for those in dorms costs €6.

The hostel is located outside town, near the hospital, but the historic centre is only a 30-minute (albeit steep) walk away and local buses from Piazza Martiri della Libertà stop right outside the entrance (€1). Reception is open 8am to noon and 5pm to 11pm, but often stays open for the full day in high summer.

Eating & Drinking

La Carabaccia
TUSCAN €

(☑0588 8 62 39; www.lacarabacciavolterra.it; Piazza XX Settembre 4-5; meals €20; ⊘noon-2.30pm & 7.30-9.30pm, closed Mon Oct-Easter; 🗷) Sisters Sara, Lalla and Patrizia have put their heart and soul into this fantastic trattoria, which is the city's best lunch option. Named after a humble Tuscan vegetable soup, it has a small menu that changes daily according to what local producers are offering, and always has vegetarian options. Sit in the rustic interior or on the front terrace.

L'Incontro
CAFE €
(Via G Matteotti 18; sandwiches €2.50-3.50; ⊙6.30am-1am Thu-Tue) L'Incontro's rear *salone* is a great spot to grab a quick antipasto plate or *panino* for lunch, and its front bar area is always crowded with locals enjoying a coffee or *aperitivo*. The house-baked biscuits are noteworthy – try the chewy and nutty *brutti mai buoni* ('ugly but good') or its alabaster-coloured version, *ossi di morto* (bones of the dead).

Caffè dei Fornelli
CAFE, BAR
(www.caffedeifornelli.it; Piazza dei Fornelli 3-4; ⊙9am-late, closed Thu in winter) The city's bohemian set congregates here, drawn by genial host Carlo Bigazzi, cheap house wine (€1.50 per glass), live jazz, poetry readings and exhibitions. Though the cafe's interior is pleasant, the most sought-after tables are on the streetside terrace.

🛍 Shopping

For information about artisans in Volterra, see www.arteinbottegavolterra.it.

Emporio del Gusto
FOOD
(Via San Lino 2; ⊙9.30am-1pm & 4.30-8pm Mon-Fri) This food co-op is sponsored by the *comune* and sells produce from around the region. It stocks olive-oil products (including toiletries), fresh milk and yoghurt, cheese, vegetables, locally grown saffron, truffles, pasta, bread and wine.

Fabula Etrusca
JEWELLERY
(www.fabulaetrusca.it; Via Lungo Le Mura del Mandorlo 10; ⊙10am-7pm Easter-Christmas) Distinctive pieces in 18-carat gold – many based on Etruscan designs – are handmade in this workshop on the city's northern walls.

Alabaster Workshops
ARTISANAL
Volterra is known as the city of alabaster, and has a number of shops specialising in hand-carved alabaster items; many of these shops double as ateliers where the artisans work. Among the best are **Opus Artis** (www.opusartis.com; Piazza Minucci 1), **Paolo Sabatini** (www.paolosabatini.com; Via G Matteotti 56), and the atelier of sculptor **Alessandro Marzetti** (www.alessandromarzetti.it; Via dei Labirinti). To watch alabaster being carved, head to **Alab'Arte** (Via Orti San Agostino 28; ⊙9.30am-12.30pm & 3-7pm Mon-Sat).

ⓘ Information

The extremely efficient **tourist office** (☑0588 8 72 57; www.volterratur.it; Piazza dei Priori 19-20; ⊙9.30am-1pm & 2-6pm) provides free maps, offers a free hotel-booking service and rents out an audioguide tour (€5) of the town.

ⓘ Getting There & Around

BUS
The **bus station** is in Piazza Martiri della Libertà. **CPT** (☑800 570530; www.cpt.pisa.it) buses connect the town with Pisa (€6.10, two hours, up to 10 daily).

You'll need to go to Colle di Val d'Elsa (€2.75, 50 minutes, four daily) to catch connecting bus services to San Gimignano (€3.40, 35 minutes, four daily) and Siena (€3.40, two hours, four daily). For Florence, you'll need only one ticket (€8.35, two hours, three to four daily) but you'll usually have to change buses at Colle di Val d'Elsa. Note that all bus services are greatly reduced on Sundays.

CAR & MOTORCYCLE
Volterra is accessed via the SR68, which runs between Cecina on the coast and Colle di Val d'Elsa, just off the Siena–Florence superstrada.

A ZTL applies in the historic centre. The most convenient car park is beneath Piazza Martiri della Libertà (per hour/day €1.50/11), but there are other car parks around the circumference – P5, P6 and P8 are free. Don't park in P5 overnight on Friday, as the city's weekly produce market is held there on Saturday morning.

Val d'Orcia & Val di Chiana

These two valleys are showcases of classic Tuscan scenery. In fact, the landscape of the Val d'Orcia is so magnificent that it is protected as a Unesco World Heritage Site. Added enticement is provided by the local food and wine on offer, which is among the best in Italy.

Montalcino
POP 5155
This medieval hill town is known throughout the world for its coveted wine, Brunello. In February each year, the new vintage is celebrated at **Benvenuto Brunello**, a weekend of tastings and award presentations organised by the Consorzio del Vino Brunello di Montalcino (www.consorziobrunellodimontalcino.it), the association of local producers.

◉ Sights

The main activity in town is visiting *enoteche*. For non-alcoholic diversion, consider popping into the modest **Museo Civico e Diocesano d'Arte Sacra** (☑ 0577 84 60 14; Via Ricasoli 31; adult/child €4.50/3; ☺10am-1pm & 2-5.50pm Tue-Sun), just off Piazza Sant'Agostino. It has a fine collection of painted wooden sculptures by the Sienese school.

Within the 14th-century **fortezza** (Piazzale Fortezza; courtyard free, ramparts adult/child €4/2; ☺9am-8pm Apr-Oct, 10am-6pm Nov-Mar) is an *enoteca* where you can sample and buy local wines (tasting of 2/3/5 Brunellos €9/13/19) and also climb up to the fort's ramparts.

A combined ticket giving full access to the museum and fortezza costs €6.

⌂ Sleeping

Hotel Vecchia Oliviera BOUTIQUE HOTEL €€
(☑ 0577 84 60 28; www.vecchiaoliviera.com; Via Landi 1; s €70-85, d €120-190, ste €200-240; ☺closed Dec–mid-Feb; P❉ 🛜 🛀) Just beside the Porta Cerbaia, this former olive mill has been tastefully restored and converted into a stylish small hotel. Each of the 11 rooms is individually decorated; the superior ones come with view and jacuzzi. The garden terrace has stunning views, and the pool is in an attractive garden setting.

Hotel Il Giglio HOTEL €€
(☑ 0577 84 81 67; www.gigliohotel.com; Via Soccorso Saloni 5; s €95, d €135-145, annex s/d €60/95,

apt €100-150; P 🛜) The comfortable wrought-iron beds here are each gilded with a painted *giglio* (lily), and all doubles in the main building have a panoramic view. Room 1 has a private terrace, and the small single is very attractive.

✕ Eating & Drinking

★ **Osticcio** WINE BAR €€
(www.osticcio.it; Via Matteotti 23; antipasto plates €13-24, meals €37; ☺noon-4pm & 7-11pm Fri-Wed, noon-7pm Thu mid-Feb–mid-Jan) A huge selection of Brunello and its more modest – but still very palatable – sibling Rosso di Montalcino joins dozens of bottles of wine from around the world at this excellent *enoteca*. After browsing the selection of wines downstairs, claim a table in the upstairs dining room for a glass of wine with an antipasto plate or pasta.

Fiaschetteria Italiana 1888 CAFE
(Piazza del Popolo 6; ☺7.30am-midnight, closed Thu Oct-Easter) We doff our hats to this atmosphere-laden *enoteca*/cafe on the main piazza, which has been serving coffee and glasses of Brunello to locals since 1888 and has managed to retain both its decor and charm for the duration.

ℹ Information

Tourist office (☑ 0577 84 93 31; www.pro-locomontalcino.com; Costa del Municipio 1; ☺10am-1pm & 2-5.50pm)

WORTH A TRIP

ABBAZIA DI SANT'ANTIMO

This beautiful Romanesque **church** (www.antimo.it; Castelnuovo dell'Abate; ☺10.30am-12.30pm & 3-6.30pm Mon-Sat, 9.15-10.45am & 3-6pm Sun) **FREE** lies in an isolated valley just below the village of Castelnuovo dell'Abate, 10.5km from Montalcino. It's best visited in the morning, when the sun, streaming through the east windows, creates an almost surreal atmosphere. At night, too, it's impressive, lit up like a beacon.

Tradition tells us that Charlemagne founded the original monastery here in 781 AD. The exterior, built in pale travertine stone, is simple except for the stone carvings, which include various fantastical animals. Inside, study the capitals of the columns lining the nave, especially the one representing Daniel in the lion's den (second on the right as you enter).

Monks perform Gregorian chants in the abbey during daily services – check times on the website.

Three to four buses per day (€1.50, 15 minutes, Monday to Saturday only) connect Montalcino with the village of Castelnuovo dell'Abate.

It's a two-to-three-hour walk from Montalcino to the abbey. The route starts next to the police station near the main roundabout in town. Many visitors choose to walk there and return by bus – check the timetable with the tourist office.

❶ Getting There & Away

BUS
Regular Siena Mobilità buses (€4.90, 1½ hours, six daily Monday to Saturday) run to/from Siena.

CAR & MOTORCYCLE
From Siena, take the SR2 (Via Cassia) and exit onto the SP14 at Lama. There's plenty of parking around the *fortezza* (€1.50 per hour 8am to 8pm).

Around Montalcino

Poggio Antico   WINERY
(🖉0577 84 80 44; www.poggioantico.com; ⏺cantina 10am-6pm, restaurant 12.30-2.30pm & 7.30-9.30pm Tue-Sun Apr-Oct, 12.30-2.30pm Tue-Sun Nov-Dec & Feb) Located 4.5km outside Montalcino on the road to Grosseto, Poggio Antico makes award-winning wines (try its Brunello Altero or Riserva), conducts free cellar tours in Italian, English and German, offers tastings (approx €25 depending on wines) and has an on-site restaurant (tasting menus without wine €40 to €50). Tours must be booked in advance.

★ Il Leccio   TUSCAN €€
(🖉0577 84 41 75; www.illeccio.net; Costa Castellare 1/3, Sant'Angelo in Colle; meals €40; ⏺12.30-2.30pm & 7.30-9.30pm Thu-Tue) Sometimes, simple dishes are the hardest to perfect. And perfection is the only term to use when discussing this trattoria in Brunello's heartland. Watching the chef make his way between stove and kitchen garden to gather produce for each order puts a whole new spin on the word 'fresh', and both the results and the house Brunello are spectacular.

Pienza

POP 2134

If the road to Montepulciano didn't pass right through town, Pienza might still be the sleepy hamlet it was before Enea Silvio Piccolomini (later Pius II) decided to rebuild it in magnificent Renaissance style. And, frankly, that could have been a very good thing. Summer weekends here are horrendous, with tourists outnumbering locals by a ratio of around 50:1. Come midweek if at all possible.

Unesco added Pienza's historic centre to its World Heritage list in 1996, citing the revolutionary vision of urban space realised in Piazza Pio II and the buildings around it.

◉ Sights

Piazza Pio II   PIAZZA
Stand in this magnificent square and spin 360 degrees. You have just taken in Pienza's major monuments. Gems of the Renaissance constructed in a mere three years (between 1459 and 1462), they are arranged according to the urban design of Bernardo Rossellino, who applied the principles of Renaissance town planning devised by his mentor, Leon Battista Alberti.

The *duomo* is the focal point of the piazza. Next to it (to the right as you face the *duomo*) is **Palazzo Piccolomini** (www.palazzopiccolominipienza.it; 30-min guided tours adult/reduced €7/5; ⏺10am-6pm Tue-Sun mid-Mar–mid-Oct, to 4pm mid-Oct–mid-Mar), built as Pius II's residence. This has a fine courtyard, a three-level loggia and apartments filled with an assortment of period furnishings, minor art and the like. Guided tours of the 1st floor are conducted every 30 minutes, but you can peek into the courtyard for free.

To the left as you face the *duomo* is **Palazzo Vescovile**, modified and enlarged in 1492 by Roderigo Borgia, the future Pope Alexander VI. It and the adjoining **Palazzo Borgia e Jouffrey** are now home to the **Museo Diocesano** (🖉0578 74 99 05; Corso Rossellino 30; adult/reduced €4.50/3; ⏺10am-1pm & 2-5pm Wed-Mon mid-Mar–Oct, 10am-4pm Sat & Sun Nov–mid-Mar), as well as the tourist office (enter via the courtyard onto Corso Rossellino). Tucked in behind Palazzo Vescovile, next to the *duomo*, is the **Casa dei Canonici** (House of the Church Canons).

🛏 Sleeping & Eating

★ La Bandita
Townhouse   BOUTIQUE HOTEL €€€
(🖉0578 74 90 05; www.labanditatownhouse.com; Corso Rossellino 111; r €195-495, ste €275-695; ⏸❄@🛜🐾) Conceived to give travellers a glimpse into Tuscan village life, this recently opened hotel is Pienza's best sleeping option. Occupying a remodelled Renaissance-era convent, it offers 12 luxurious rooms and suites with minimalist decor, as well as a communal library/lounge. The same owners run the idyllic La Bandita (🖉333 4046704; www.la-bandita.com; d €195-500; ⏺Mar-Dec; ⏸❄@🛜🏊🐾) rural retreat, 14km southeast of the town.

Pummarò   PIZZERIA €

(Via del Giglio 4; slice €2.20, pizza €5.50-9; ⊙ to
11pm Tue-Sun; 🐾) Look for bicycles painted
red, white and green parked in a laneway
off Via Rossellino and you'll find this teensy
pizzeria, which is a great place to source a
cheap and quick snack. Try the *pizza pummarò* (with cherry tomatoes, *mozzarella di
bufala* and basil).

Townhouse Caffè   MODERN TUSCAN €€

(📋 0578 74 90 05; www.labanditatownhouse.com;
Via Rossellino 111, enter from Via San Andrea; breakfast €10, light lunch €15, dinner €30; ⊙ 7-11pm Mon
& Tue, 8am-11pm Wed-Sun,) After visiting Piazza Pio II, consider spending an hour or two
lingering over a light lunch, coffee or glass
of wine in this cafe's medieval walled garden. The menu relies heavily on local organic produce for its inspiration (fancy a burger
made with Chianina beef and topped with
melted fresh pecorino and mint mayon-
naise?) and there's a well-considered wine
list.

ℹ Getting There & Away

BUS

Two Siena Mobilità buses run between Siena and
Pienza (€5.50, 70 minutes) and nine travel to/
from Montepulciano (€2.50). The bus stops are
just off Piazza Dante Alighieri. Buy tickets at one
of the nearby bars.

CAR & MOTORCYCLE

The public car park near the centre charges
€1.50 per hour and fills quickly. Be warned that
local traffic officers are quick to fine cars that
overstay their ticket.

Montepulciano

POP 14,188

Exploring this reclaimed narrow ridge of
volcanic rock will push your quadriceps to
their failure point. When this happens, self-
medicate with a generous pour of the highly
reputed Vino Nobile while drinking in the
spectacular views over the Val di Chiana and
Val d'Orcia.

👁 Sights

Montepulciano's streets harbour a wealth of
palazzi, other fine buildings and churches.

The main street, called in stages Via
di Gracciano nel Corso, Via di Voltaia del
Corso and Via dell'Opio nel Corso ('the
Corso'), climbs uphill from Porta dal
Prato, near the car park on Piazza Don

Minzoni. Halfway along its length are
Michelozzo's **Chiesa di Sant'Agostino**
(Piazza Michelozzo; ⊙ 9am-noon & 3-6pm)
and the **Torre di Pulcinella**, a medieval tower house topped by the hunched figure of Pulcinella (Punch of Punch and Judy
fame), who strikes the hours on the town
clock.

After passing historic **Caffè Poliziano**,
which has been operating since 1868, the
Corso eventually does a dog-leg at Via del
Teatro, continuing uphill past **Cantine
Contucci** (www.contucci.it; Via del Teatro 1;
fee for tastings; ⊙ 9.30am-12.30pm & 2.30-6pm
Mon-Fri, from 9.30am Sat & Sun) **FREE**, housed
underneath the handsome *palazzo* of the
same name. You can visit the historic cellars and taste local tipples here. Palazzo
Contucci fronts onto **Piazza Grande**, the
town's highest point. Also here are the
14th-century **Palazzo Comunale** (panoramic terrace €2) and the late-16th-century
duomo (Piazza Grande), with its unfinished
facade. Behind the high altar is Taddeo
di Bartolo's lovely *Assumption* triptych
(1401).

From Piazza Grande, Via Ricci runs
downhill past **Palazzo Ricci** (www.palaz-
zoricci.com; Via Ricci 9-11); its lovely main
salon hosts occasional concerts during the
year (see the website for details). From the
palazzo's courtyard, stairs lead down to
another historic wine cellar, **Cantina del
Redi** (Via Ricci; fee for tastings; ⊙ 10.30am-7pm
mid-Mar–early-Jan, Sat & Sun only early-Jan–mid-
Mar) **FREE**. Via Ricci continues past the **Museo Civico** (www.museociviomontepulciano.it;
Via Ricci 10; adult/reduced €5/3; ⊙ 10am-1pm &
3-6pm Tue-Sun Mar-July & Sep-Oct, 10am-7pm Tue-
Sun Aug, 10am-1pm & 3-6pm Sat & Sun Nov-Feb),
home to an eclectic collection of art works
and artefacts, and terminates in Piazza San
Francesco, where you can admire a panoramic view of the Val di Chiana.

🍵 Courses & Tours

The office of the **Strada del Vino Nobile di
Montepulciano** (www.stradavinonobile.it) organises a range of tours and courses, including cooking courses (€60 to €180), vineyard
tours (€18 to €48), Slow Food tours (€100 to
€155), wine-tasting lessons (€37) and walking tours in the vineyards culminating in
a wine tasting (€45 to €60). You can make
bookings at its information office in Piazza
Grande.

⭐ Festivals & Events

Musica di Stelle ARTS
(Music of the Stars; www.fondazionecantiere.it)
Performances of opera, theatre and classical
and contemporary music are staged in venues throughout the town.

Bravio delle Botti CULTURAL
(www.braviodellebotti.com) Members of the
city's eight *contrade* race to push 80kg wine
barrels uphill in this race held on the last
Sunday in August.

Festival of Chamber Music MUSIC
(www.palazzoricci.com) Held at Palazzo Ricci in
late August and September.

🛌 Sleeping

Camere Bellavista HOTEL €
(☑ 347 8232314; www.camerebellavista.it; Via Ricci
25; s €65-70, d €75; ℙ ☎) Nearly all of the 10
high-ceilinged double rooms at this excellent budget hotel have fantastic views; room
6 also has a private terrace (€100). No one
lives here so phone ahead in order to be met
and given a key (if you've missed this stage,
there's a phone in the lobby from where you
can call). No breakfast.

⭐ **Locanda San Francesco** B&B €€
(☑ 349 6721302; www.locandasanfrancesco.it; Piazza San Francesco 5; r €150-240; ☺ closed mid-Jan;
ℙ ✳ @ ☎) Four handsome rooms with magnificent views and lovely bathrooms await at
this luxury B&B. Host Cinzia Caporali runs
both it and the attached E Lucevan Le Stelle
wine bar with friendly efficiency.

⭐ **Fattoria San Martino** AGRITURISMO €€
(☑ 0578 71 74 63; www.fattoriasanmartino.it; Via
di Martiena 3; r €140-180; ☺ closed Dec-Easter;
ℙ ☎ ✼ ♨) ✿ Dutch-born Karin and Italian
Antonio met when working in Milan's high-velocity fashion industry, but eventually decided that organic farming was more to their
liking than haute couture. The homespun-chic rooms in this rebuilt 12th-century farmhouse and purpose-built annexe are sure to
please, as will the all-vegetarian meals (dinner €35 plus wine), pretty garden, biological
filtered pool and emphasis on sustainability.

🍴 Eating & Drinking

Osteria Acquacheta OSTERIA €
(☑ 0578 71 70 86; www.acquacheta.eu; Via del
Teatro 22; meals €20; ☺ 12.15-4pm & 7.30-10.30pm
Wed-Mon) Hugely popular with locals and
tourists alike, this bustling place special-

ises in *bistecca alla fiorentina* (chargrilled
T-bone steak), which comes to the table
in huge, lightly seared and exceptionally
flavoursome slabs. Lunch sittings are at
12.15pm and 2.15pm; dinner at 7.30pm and
9.15pm – book ahead.

⭐ **La Grotta** TRADITIONAL ITALIAN €€€
(☑ 0578 75 74 79; www.lagrottamontepulciano.it;
Via San Biagio 15; meals €44, 6-course tasting menu
€48; ☺ 12.30-2.30pm & 7.30-10pm Thu-Tue, closed
mid-Jan–mid-Mar) Facing the High Renaissance
Tempio di San Biagio on the road to Chiusi,
La Grotta has elegant dining rooms and a
gorgeous courtyard garden that's perfect for
summer dining. The food is traditional with
a modern twist or two, and service is exemplary. A hint: don't skip dessert.

ℹ Information

Tourist office (☑ 0578 75 73 41; www.pro-locomontepulciano.it; Piazza Don Minzoni 1;
☺ 9.30am-12.30pm & 3-7pm Mon-Sat, 9am-1pm Sun Easter-Sep, 9.30am-12.30pm & 3-6pm
Mon-Sat, 9.30am-12.30pm Sun Oct-Easter) Reserves accommodation, offers internet access
(€3.50 per hour), supplies maps of the town,
rents mountain bikes (per hour/day €2.50/15)
and sells bus and train tickets (commission
applies for train tickets).

ℹ Getting There & Around

BUS
The bus station is next to Car Park No 5. Siena
Mobilità runs four buses daily between Siena
and Montepulciano (€6.60, one hour) stopping
at Pienza (€2.50) en route. There are three
services per day to/from Florence (€11.20, 90
minutes).

Regular buses connect with Chiusi-Chianciano
Terme (€3.40, 40 minutes), from where you can
catch a train to Florence (€12.50, two hours,
frequent) via Arezzo (€6.40, 50 minutes).

CAR & MOTORCYCLE
Coming from Florence, take the Valdichiana exit
off the A1 (direction Bettolle-Sinalunga) and then
follow the signs; from Siena, take the Siena–Bettolle–Perugia autostrada.

A 24-hour ZTL applies in the historic centre
between May and September; in October and
April it applies from 8am to 8pm, and from
November to March it applies from 8am to
5pm. Your hotel can usually supply a permit.
The most convenient car park is at Piazza Don
Minzoni (€1.30 per hour April to October, free
November to March), from where minibuses
(€1) weave their way up the hill to Piazza
Grande.

SOUTHERN TUSCANY

With its landscape of dramatic coastlines, mysterious Etruscan sites and medieval hill-top villages, this little-visited pocket of the region offers contrasts galore.

Massa Marittima

POP 8820

Drawcards at this tranquil hill town include an eccentric yet endearing jumble of museums, an extremely handsome central piazza and largely intact medieval streets that are blessedly bereft of tour groups.

Briefly under Pisan domination, Massa Marittima became an independent *comune* in 1225 but was swallowed up by Siena a century later. The 1348 plague, followed by the decline of the town's lucrative mining industry 50 years later, reduced it to the brink of extinction. It was brought back to life by the draining of surrounding marshes (formerly a malarial risk) and the re-establishment of mining in the 18th century.

Massa's big event is the **Ballestro del Girifalco**, a medieval crossbow competition held twice yearly: on the first Sunday after 20 May and on a Sunday in either July or August (usually the second Sunday in August).

◉ Sights

The *città vecchia* (old town) is dominated by the impressive bulk of the **duomo** (◉8am-noon & 3-5pm), which presides over photogenic **Piazza Garibaldi** (aka Piazza Duomo). Cleverly set asymmetrically to the square to better show off its splendour, it dates from 1260 and is dedicated to St Cerbonius, Massa's patron saint, who is always depicted surrounded with a flock of geese; carved panels on the facade depict scenes from his life. Inside, don't miss the freestanding *Maestà* (Madonna and Child enthroned in majesty; 1316) attributed by some experts to Duccio di Buoninsegna.

The *duomo* was once home to a splendid *Maestà* by Ambrogio Lorenzetti, now the central exhibit in the diminutive **Museo di Arte Sacra** (Museum of Sacred Art; www.museiartesacra.net; Corso Diaz 36; adult/child €5/3; ◉10am-1pm & 3-6pm Tue-Sun summer, 11am-1pm & 3-5pm Tue-Sun winter) in the *città nuova* (new town).

Next to the *duomo,* the Palazzo del Podestà houses Massa's musty **Museo Archeologico** (Piazza Garibaldi 1; adult/child €3/2; ◉10am-12.30pm & 3.30-7pm Tue-Sun summer, 10am-12.30pm & 3-5pm Tue-Sun winter), whose only truly noteworthy exhibit is *La Stele del Vado all'Arancio,* a simple but compelling stone stela (funeral or commemorative marker) dating from the 3rd millennium BC.

Downhill from Piazza Garibaldi, opposite the main car park, is a 13th-century building that was once used to store wheat. Under its loggia is a disused public drinking fountain topped by an extraordinary fresco of the *Albero della Fecondità* (Fertility Tree). Look closely to see what type of fruit the tree bears!

A cumulative ticket (adult/reduced €15/10) gives access to all of Massa's museums.

⌷ Sleeping

Residenza d'Epoca Palazzo Malfatti   APARTMENT €

(☑05 6690 4181; www.palazzomalfattiresidenzadepoca.com; Via Moncini 10; d €60-115, tr €90-165, q €120-230, 5-bed €150-290; 🛜) These seven apartments in an 13th-century *palazzo* overlooking Piazza Garibaldi are an attractive option for self-catering guests wanting to stay for a while (rates drop for stays of more than two nights). The building's conversion hasn't been handled as cleverly as it could have been, but the strangely arranged spaces are comfortable and reasonably well equipped, with good bathrooms.

✕ Eating & Drinking

★ **La Tana del Brillo Parlante**   TUSCAN €€

(☑05 6690 1274; Vicolo del Ciambellano 4; meals €32; ◉noon-2.30pm & 7.30-10pm Thu-Tue Dec-Oct) Satisfying the Slow Food checklist to the letter, this self-described 'smallest *osteria* in Italy' seats a mere 10 people (in summer another six can squeeze into tiny alley tables) and serves deliciously authentic Maremmese dishes. If you intend to dine here in summer or on the weekend, reserve well in advance. No credit cards.

L'Osteria da Tronca   TUSCAN €€

(☑05 6690 1991; Vicolo Porte 5; meals €28; ◉7.30-10.30pm Thu-Tue Mar-Jul & Sep–mid-Dec, 7.30-10pm Aug) Squeezed into a side street (it's behind Hotel Il Sole), this stone-walled restaurant specialises in the rustic dishes of the Maremma. Specialities include *acquacotta* (a hearty vegetable soup with bread and egg), *tortelli alla maremma* (pasta parcels filled with ricotta and a type of spinach) and *coniglio in porchetta* (roasted stuffed rabbit).

ℹ Information

The **tourist office** (📞 05 6690 2756; www.altamaremmaturismo.it; Via Todini 3-5; ⊙ 9.30am-1pm & 2-6.30pm Tue-Sun) is down a side street beneath the Museo Archeologico.

ℹ Getting There & Away

BUS

The bus station is at Piazza del Risorgimento, 800m down the hill from Piazza Garibaldi. There is one bus daily to Grosseto (€3.70, one hour) and two to Siena (€5.30, two hours) at 7.05am and 4.40pm. To get to Volterra you'll need to change at Monterotondo Marittimo. **Massa Veternensis** (Piazza Garibaldi 18) sells both bus and train tickets.

CAR & MOTORCYCLE

There's a convenient car park (€1 per hour during the day, free at night) close to Piazza Garibaldi; head up the hill and you'll find it on your left.

There's also a free car park at Piazzetta di Borgo further down the hill.

TRAIN

The nearest train station is in Follonica, 22km southwest of Massa, and is served by a regular shuttle bus (€2.60, 25 minutes, 10 daily).

Città del Tufa

The picturesque towns of Pitigliano, Sovana and Sorano form a triangle enclosing a dramatic landscape where local buildings have been constructed from the volcanic porous rock called tufa since Etruscan times. This inland area is called the Città del Tufa (City of the Tufa) or, less commonly, the Paese del Tufa (Land of the Tufa).

Pitigliano

POP 3840

This spectacularly sited town is surrounded by gorges on three sides, constituting a

---

WORTH A TRIP

PARCO REGIONALE DELLA MAREMMA

This spectacular **regional park** (www.parco-maremma.it; adult/reduced €10/5, mountain bike hire per day €15) incorporates the Uccellina mountain range, a 600-hectare pine forest, marshy plains and a 20km stretch of unspoiled coastline. The main **visitor centre** (📞 05 6440 7098; Via del Bersagliere 7-9; ⊙ 8.30am-6pm mid-Jun–mid-Sep, to 5pm mid-Sep–mid-Nov, to 2pm mid-Nov–mid-Jun) is in Alberese, on the park's northern edge.

Park access is limited to 13 signed walking trails, varying in length from 2.5km to 13km; the most popular is A2 ('Le Torri'), a 5.8km walk to the beach. The entry fee (paid at the visitor centres) varies according to whether a park-operated bus transports you from the visitor centre to your chosen route. From 15 June to 15 September the park can only be visited on a guided tour due to possible bushfire threat.

As well as the walking trails, there are four guided mountain-bike tours (€10 to €15 plus bike hire, two to six hours) and a guided 2½-hour canoe tour (adult/child €16/10); book these at the visitor centres. A number of private operators offer horse and pony treks through the park – contact **Il Gelsomino** (📞 347 7746476; www.ilgelsomino.com; Via Strada del Barbicato 4, Alberese) or **Circolo Ippico Uccellina** (📞 334 9797181; www.circoloippicouccellina.it; Località Collecchio 38, Magliano in Toscana); both offer accommodation and horse-riding treks and lessons.

Parts of the regional park are farmed as they have been for centuries, mainly to graze the famous Maremma breed of cattle. The huge **Agienza Regionale Agricola di Alberese** (📞 05 6440 7180; www.alberese.com; Via della Spergolaia) farm operation produces beef, wine, olive oil and its own organic pasta and is a regional headquarters for the Slow Food organisation. It offers visitors a **farm experience** (📞 05 6440 7100; €25; ⊙ 10am-1pm Thu Jul & Aug, other times by reservation) including an introduction to the work of the Maremma's famed *butteri* (traditional cowboys) and tastings of farm produce.

The farm offers accommodation in the 15th-century **Villa Fattoria Granducale** (📞 05 6440 7100; www.alberese.com/fattoria-granducale; B&B d & tr €90-100, self-contained apt €75-125; both 2-night min) and also rents out simple apartments in surrounding farm buildings; check the website for details.

natural bastion completed to the east by a constructed fortress. Within the Old Town, twisting stairways disappear around corners, cobbled alleys bend tantalisingly out of sight beneath graceful arches and quaint stone houses are crammed next to each other in higgledy-piggledy fashion.

Originally built by the Etruscans, who left a rich legacy of tombs and *vie cave* (sunken roads) that remain to this day, Pitigliano came under Roman rule before becoming a fiefdom of the wealthy Aldobrandeschi and Orsini families; the Orsinis, who were from Rome, enlarged the fortress, reinforced the defensive walls and built an imposing aqueduct. Their rule came to an end in 1608 when the town was absorbed into the grand duchy of Tuscany under Cosimo I de' Medici.

There's a fine walk from Pitigliano to Sovana (8km) that incorporates parts of the *vie cave*. For a description and map, go to www.trekking.it and download the pdf in the Maremma section.

The major event of the year is the **Torciata di San Giuseppe**, a torchlit procession on 19 March. This wends its way down the Via Cava di San Giuseppe before culminating in a huge bonfire in Piazza Garibaldi.

Sights

La Piccola Gerusalemme MUSEUM
(Little Jerusalem; ☎05 6461 4230; www.lapiccolagerusalemme.it; Vicolo Manin 30; adult/reduced €4/3; ⏲10am-1.30pm & 2.30-6.30pm Sun-Fri summer, 10am-12.30pm & 3-5.30pm Sun-Fri winter) Head down Via Zuccarelli and turn left at a sign indicating 'La Piccola Gerusalemme' (Little Jerusalem) to visit this fascinating time capsule of Pitogliano's rich but sadly near-exinct Jewish culture. It incorporates a tiny, richly adorned synagogue (established in 1598 and one of only five in Tuscany), ritual bath, kosher butcher, bakery, wine cellar and dyeing workshops.

Museo Civico Archeologico di Pitigliano MUSEUM
(Piazza della Fortezza; adult/child €3/2; ⏲10am-5pm Mon, Thu & Fri, to 6pm Sat & Sun Jun-Aug, 10am-5pm Sat & Sun Easter-May) Accessed via a stone staircase opposite the entrance to Palazzo Orsini, this small but well-run museum has a rich display of finds from local Etruscan sites. Highlights include some huge intact *bucchero* (black earthenware pottery) urns dating from the 6th century BC and a collection of charming pinkish-cream-clay oil containers in the form of small deer.

Sleeping & Eating

★**Le Camere del Ceccottino** PENSION €€
(☎05 6461 4273; www.ceccottino.com; Via Roma 159; r €80-150; ❄📶) Owned and operated by the extremely helpful Chiara and Alessandro, who live on-site and also run a nearby *osteria* and *enoteca* of the same name, this *pensione* boasts an excellent location near the *duomo* and four immaculately maintained and well-equipped rooms. Opt for the superior or prestige room if possible, as the standard versions are slightly cramped. No breakfast.

La Rocca WINE BAR €
(Piazza della Repubblica 92; panino €3.50, meals €24; ⏲10am-11pm Tue-Sun) Generous pourings of local wine and *prodotti tipici* (typical local products), including rustic pastas, antipasti platters and *panini* stuffed with pecorino cheese and cured meats, are on offer at this cavernous wine bar, cafe and restaurant.

★**Il Tufo Allegro** TRADITIONAL ITALIAN €€
(☎05 6461 6192; www.iltufoallegro.com; Vicolo della Costituzione 5; meals €35; ⏲noon-1.30pm Thu-Mon & 7.30-9.30pm Wed-Mon Mar-Dec) The aromas emanating from the kitchen door off Via Zuccarelli should be enough to draw you down the stairs and into the cosy dining rooms, which are carved out of tufa. Chef Domenico Pichini offers two menus – one traditional and one modern – and all of his creations rely heavily on local produce for inspiration. It's near Piccola Gerusalemme.

Information

Tourist office (☎05 6461 7111; www.comune.pitigliano.gr.it; Piazza Garibaldi 12; ⏲10am-12.20pm & 3.30-6pm Tue-Sat summer, 10am-12.30pm & 2.30-5pm Fri & Sat, 10am-12.30pm Sun winter)
Just inside the old city's main gate.

Getting There & Away

BUS

Rama Mobilità (☎199 848787; www.ramamobilita.it) buses travel between Via Santa Chiara, just off Piazza Petruccioli, and Grosseto four times daily (€5.80, two hours). There's also one daily service to Siena (€8.50, three hours), four services to Sorano (€1.35, 20 minutes) and one service to Sovana (€1.35, 10 minutes). Buses don't usually operate on Sundays. Buy tickets at Bar Guastini in Piazza Petruccioli.

CAR & MOTORCYCLE

There are plenty of free car parks around town; look for white lines. Alternatively, the car park near Piazza Petruccioli charges €0.50 per hour from 8am to 1pm and from 3pm to 8pm.

Around Pitigliano

Tuscany's most significant Etruscan tombs are found within the **Parco Archeologico 'Città del Tufa'** (Necropoli di Sovana; www.levie-cave.it; €5; ⏰10am-7pm summer, to 5pm Sat & Sun Nov & Mar) 9km northeast of Pitigliano, near the postcard-pretty town of Sorano. Interpretative panels in Italian and English impart interesting information about the site.

There are four tombs in total. The **Tomba dei Demoni Alati** (Tomb of the Winged Demons) was discovered in 2004 and features a headless recumbent figure in terracotta. The carving of a sea demon with huge wings that was the original centrepiece of the tomb is now protected in a roofed enclosure nearby. The **Tomba Ildebranda**, named after Gregory VII, still preserves traces of its carved columns and stairs and is the park's headline exhibit. The **Tomba del Tifone** (Tomb of the Typhoon) is about 300m down a trail running alongside a rank of tomb facades cut from the rock face. Two arresting lengths of *via cave* (one known as 'Cavone' and the other 'Poggio Prisca') are nearby.

On the opposite side of the site is the **Tomba della Sirena** and another *via cava* ('San Sebastiano'), which was closed due to safety concerns at the time of research.

Sant'Egle　　　　　　　　　AGRITURISMO €€
(☎34 8888 4810; www.santegle.it; Case Sparse Sant'Egle 18; d €110, ste €160; 🅿🐾🖤) 🌿 Atmospheric rooms, a pretty garden setting and a strong commitment to sustainability make Sant'Egle a great choice. Occupying a meticulously restored 17th-century customs house on an organic farm between Sorano and Pitigliano, it offers attractive rooms and a restaurant serving dinners featuring home-grown fruit and vegetables, hand-made pasta and bread and free-range meats (€30). Mountain bikes are available for guests' use.

EASTERN TUSCANY

The eastern edge of Tuscany is beloved of local and international film directors, who have immortalised its landscape, medieval hilltop towns and laid-back locals in a range of visually splendid films. Despite this, the region is strangely bereft of foreign tourists and so offers uncrowded trails to those visitors who decide to devote a week or so to exploring them.

Arezzo

POP 98,018

Arezzo may not be a Tuscan centrefold, but those parts of its historic centre that survived merciless WWII bombings are as compelling as any destination in the region. The setting for much of Roberto Benigni's Oscar-winning film *La vita è bella* (Life Is Beautiful), it's well worth a visit.

Once an important Etruscan town, Arezzo was later absorbed into the Roman Empire. A free republic as early as the 10th century, it supported the Ghibelline cause in the violent battles between pope and emperor and was eventually subjugated by Florence in 1384.

Today, the city is known for its churches, museums and shopping – Arentini (residents of Arezzo) flock to the huge antiques fair held in Piazza Grande on the first weekend of every month, and love nothing more than combining the *passeggiata* with a spot of upmarket retail therapy on Corso Italia.

👁 Sights

A combined ticket (€12) gives entry to the Cappella Bacci, Museo Archeologico Nazionale and Casa di Vasari.

⭐**Cappella Bacci**　　　　　　　　CHURCH
(☎0575 35 27 27; www.pierodellafrancesca.it; Piazza San Francesco; adult/reduced €8/5; ⏰9am-6.30pm Mon-Fri, to 5.30pm Sat & 1-5.30pm Sun May-Aug; 9am-5.30pm Mon-Fri, to 5pm Sat & 1-5pm Sun Sep-Apr) Gracing the apse of the 14th-century **Basilica di San Francesco** is the Capella Bacci, a chapel housing one of the greatest works of Italian art, Piero della Francesca's fresco cycle of the *Legend of the True Cross*. Painted between 1452 and 1466, it relates in 10 episodes the story of the cross on which Christ was crucified.

This medieval legend is as entertaining as it is inconceivable. The illustrations begin in

Arezzo

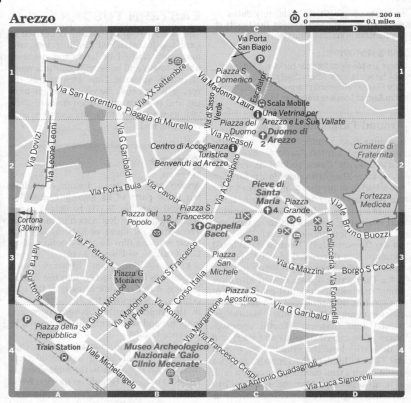

FLORENCE & TUSCANY AREZZO

the top right-hand corner and follow the story of the tree that Seth plants on the grave of his father, Adam, and from which the True Cross is made.

Rarely will you get a better sense of medieval frescoes as strip cartoons, telling a tale with vigour and sheer beauty. Art buffs will be struck by Piero's innovations with light, perspective and geometric perfection; and film buffs will be reminded of the famous scene where an airborne Juliette Binoche views the frescoes by the light of a flare in Anthony Minghella's 1996 adaptation of Michael Ondaatje's novel *The English Patient*.

Only 25 people are allowed into the chapel every half-hour (maximum 30-minute visit), so advance booking is recommended. The ticket office is down the stairs at the basilica's entrance.

★ **Pieve di Santa Maria** CHURCH
(Corso Italia 7; ☺ 8.30am-12.30pm & 3-7pm May-Sep, to noon & 3-6pm Oct-Apr) This 12th-century church (Arezzo's oldest) has a magnificent Romanesque arcaded facade adorned with dozens of carved columns, each uniquely decorated. Above the central doorway are 13th-century carved reliefs known as the *Cyclo dei Mesi*, which represent the months of the year. January's figure has two faces: one looks back on the previous year and the other looks forward.

Inside, the undoubted highlight is Pietro Lorenzetti's polyptych, *Madonna and Saints* (1320–24), located beneath the semi-dome of the apse.

Piazza Grande PIAZZA
This lopsided and steeply sloping piazza is located behind the *pieve* and is overlooked at its upper end by the porticos of the **Palazzo delle Logge Vasariane**, completed in 1573. The church-like **Palazzo della Fraternità dei Laici** in the northwest corner was started in 1375 in the Gothic style and finished after the onset of the Renaissance.

★ **Duomo di Arezzo** CATHEDRAL
(Cattedrale di SS Donato e Pietro; Piazza del Duomo; ☺ 7am-12.30pm & 3-6.30pm) Though construction started in the 13th century, Arezzo's *duomo* wasn't completed until well into the 15th century. In the northeast corner, to the left of the intricately carved main altar, is an exquisite fresco of *Mary Magdalene* (c 1459) by Piero della Francesca. Also notable are five splendid glazed terracottas by Andrea della Robbia and his studio.

★ **Museo Archeologico Nazionale 'Gaio Cilnio Mecenate'** MUSEUM
(Via Margaritone 10; adult/reduced/child €6/3/free; ☺ 8.30am-7.30pm early-Mar–mid-Jan, to 2pm mid-Jan–early-Mar) Overlooking the remains of a Roman amphitheatre that once seated up to 10,000 spectators, this museum in a 14th-century convent building has a sizeable collection of Etruscan and Roman artefacts, the highlight of which is the *Cratere di Euphronios,* a large 6th-century-BC Etruscan vase decorated with vivid scenes showing Hercules in battle. It's in room 6, upstairs.

Casa Vasari MUSEUM
(Via XX Settembre 55; adult/reduced €4/2; ☺ 9am-7pm Mon & Wed-Sat, to 1pm Sun) This small house was built and sumptuously decorated by the Arezzo-born painter, architect and art historian Giorgio Vasari (1511–74). Ring the bell to be granted entrance.

☞ **Tours**

Two-hour guided English-language **walking tours** (✆ 0575 40 33 19, 334 3340608; www.centroguidearezzo.it; adult/child €10/free) are conducted every Thursday from 11am between May and October. Bookings are essential.

★☆ **Festivals & Events**

Fiera Antiquaria di Arezzo ANTIQUES
(Arezzo Antique Fair; www.arezzofieraantiquaria.org) Tuscany's most famous antiques fair is held on the first Sunday and preceding Saturday of every month.

Giostra del Saracino CULTURAL
(Joust of the Saracino; www.giostradelsaracino.arezzo.it; Piazza Grande) This medieval jousting competition is held in Piazza Grande on the third Saturday of June and first Sunday of September each year. It's the highlight of the year for the city's four *quartieri* (quarters), each of which puts forward a team of 'knights'.

🛏 **Sleeping**

Palazzo dei Bostoli B&B €
(✆ 334 1490558; www.palazzobostoli.it; 2nd fl, Via G Mazzini 1; s/d/tr €50/70/90; ❋ 🗑) This old-fashioned place offers five simple but comfortable rooms in a 13th-century *palazzo* close to Piazza Grande. The breakfast – a coffee and *cornetto* (croissant) – is served at Bar Stefano in nearby Corso Italia.

La Corte Del Re B&B €€
(✆ 0575 40 16 03; www.lacortedelre.com; Via Borgunto 5; s €80-100, d €90-120; ❋ 🗑) Owner Franca has a bubbly personality and is remarkably helpful (she even picks guests up from the railway station). Located centimetres from Piazza Grande, her B&B has nine simple rooms; some have kitchenettes and views of the square, and most suffer from a lack of noise insulation. Breakfast is brought to each room at a pre-agreed time.

★ **Villa Fontelunga** BOUTIQUE HOTEL €€
(✆ 0575 66 04 10; www.fontelunga.com; Via Cunicchio 5, Foiano della Chiana; d/tw €160-350, ste €210-395; ☺ closed Nov–early-Mar; 🅿 ❋ @ 🗑 ❄ 🛗) Gorgeous is the only word to use when describing this 19th-century villa 30 minutes southwest of Arezzo. Restored, decorated and run by three charming friends (one an architect, one a landscape designer

and one a former international banker), it perfectly balances traditional Tuscan elegance with jet-set pizzazz. Two-night minimum stay.

✕ Eating & Drinking

★ LAB Pasticceria
PATISSERIE €

(www.pasticcerialab.com; Corso Italia 40; coffee & cake €3.50; ⊙10am-1.30pm & 4.30-8.30pm Wed-Sun) There are no mad scientists working in this glass-fronted lab, just a team of pastry chefs who delight Arentini with their exquisite sweet creations. Enter through the covered courtyard off Corso Italia and you'll discover a super-stylish cafe with indoor and outdoor seating, friendly staff and glass display cases filled with cakes, pastries, biscuits and *grissini* (breadsticks).

La Bottega di Gnicche
SANDWICHES €

(www.bottegadignicche.com; Piazza Grande 4; panini €3-5; ⊙11am-8pm Thu-Tue) There's a delectable array of artisan meats and cheeses to choose from when you order a *panini imbottiti* (roll filled with meat and cheese) at this wonderful *alimentari* (grocery store) on Arezzo's main piazza. Eat on the tiny front terrace, or perch on a stool inside.

La Torre di Gnicche
WINE BAR €

(www.latorredignicche.it; Piaggia San Martino 8; soup €7, meat & cheese platters €11; ⊙noon-3pm & 6pm-1am Thu-Tue, closed 2 wks in Jan) This cosy bottle-lined room just off Piazza Grande offers a huge choice of Tuscan wine (by glass and bottle), platters of cheese and meat, and rustic tummy-fillers including *pappa al pomodoro* (a thick bread and tomato soup served in summer) and *ribollita* (a 'reboiled' bean, vegetable, cabbage and bread soup served in winter).

★ Trattoria del Leone
MODERN TUSCAN €€

(☑0575 35 79 27; Scalinata Camillo Berneri 2; meals €28; ⊙noon-2.30pm Tue-Sun & 7.30-10pm Tue-Sat, closed Aug) A perfect example of the trattoria model that is trending in Tuscany today, del Leone is found in a slightly obscure location on some stairs leading down into Piazza del Popolo and has a clever, design-driven interior. The food is delicious – small-ish portions of beautifully prepared modern riffs on Tuscan classics, with home-made pasta, *bruschette* and salads featuring.

❶ Information

Centro di Accoglienza Turistica Benvenuti ad Arezzo (☑0575 40 19 45; www.benvenutiadarezzo.it; Palazzo Comunale, Via Ricasoli;

⊙10am-1pm & 2-7pm Mon-Fri, 10am-1pm Sat & Sun Jun-Sep, to 4pm Oct-May) The region's main tourist office is located opposite the *duomo*. There's another branch with similar hours in Piazza della Repubblica next to the train station.

Una Vetrina per Arezzo e Le Sue Vallate (☑0575 182 27 70; ⊙9am-7pm) A private tourist office located on the *scala mobile* leading up to Piazza del Duomo. Offers toilet facilities (€0.50) and maps (€0.50). It operates another branch (10.30am to 5.30pm Saturday and Sunday) in Piazza Grande.

❶ Getting There & Away

BUS

Siena Mobilità services depart Piazza della Repubblica for Siena (€6.60, 1½ hours, seven daily) and Etruria Mobilità buses for Sansepolcro (€4.10, one hour, frequent on weekdays, fewer services on weekends) and Cortona (€3.50, one hour, frequent).

CAR & MOTORCYCLE

To drive here from Florence, take the A1; the SS73 heads west to Siena. There is car parking (some spaces free, some €0.70/5 per hour/day) at Via Pietri, from where a *scala mobile* takes you up to Piazza del Duomo. Parking at the train station costs €1.50 per hour.

TRAIN

Arezzo is on the Florence–Rome train line, and there are frequent services to Florence (Regionale €7.80, 1½ hours) and Rome (Intercity €19 to €25, two hours). There are also hourly regional services to Cortona (€3.30, 20 minutes).

Sansepolcro

POP 16,077

Sansepolcro was the birthplace of the 15th-century artist Piero della Francesca, and its splendid Museo Civico is home to three of his masterpieces. Other important artworks are on display in the town's churches – look for Perugino's *Ascension* in the **Cattedrale di San Giovanni Evangelista** (Duomo di Sansepolcro; Via Giacomo Matteotti 4; ⊙8.30am-12.30pm & 3-7pm mid-Jun–mid-Sep, to 6pm mid-Sep–mid-Jun), Luca Signorelli's processional banner in the **Chiesa di Sant'Antonio Abate** (cnr Via San Antonio & Via del Campaccio; ⊙8.30am-1pm & 3-6pm), Rosso Fiorentino's *Deposition of Christ* in the **Chiesa di San Lorenzo** (cnr Via di San Croce & Via Lucca Pacioli) and Raffaellino del Colle's *Madonna delle Grazie* in the **Chiesa di Santa Maria delle Grazie** (Piazza Beato Ranieri; ⊙8.30am-1pm & 3-6pm).

Art isn't the only reason to come here, though. The historical centre ('Il Borgo') is full of handsome Renaissance churches and *palazzi*, and there are a number of good restaurants to choose from.

On the second Sunday of September, the town hosts the **Palio della Ballestra**, a crossbow tournament between local archers and rivals from the nearby Umbrian town of Gubbio. Contestants and the crowd dress in medieval costumes, and a great time is had by all.

◉ Sights

★ Museo Civico   MUSEUM
(www.museocivicosansepolcro.it; Via Niccolò Aggiunti 65; adult/reduced/child €8/5/3; ⊙ 9.30am-1.30pm & 2.30-7pm mid-Jun–mid-Sep, 9.30am-1pm & 2.30-6pm mid-Sep–mid-Jun) The town's flagship museum is home to a small but topnotch collection of artworks, the highlights of which are three Piero della Francesca masterpieces: *Resurrection* (1458–74), the *Madonna della Misericordia* polyptych (1445–56) and *Saint Julian* (1455–58). Piero's authorship of a fourth work, *Saint Louis of Toulouse* (1460), is disputed by some art historians – see what you think.

In the main exhibition room, look out for two works by the studio of Andrea della Robbia: a polychrome terracotta called *The Nativity and Adoration of the Shepherds* (1485) and a gorgeous tondo (circular sculpture) known as the *Virgin and Child with Manetti Coat of Arms* (1503).

⌂ Sleeping

★ Relais Palazzo Magi   B&B €
(☑ 0575 74 04 77; www.hotelmagisansepolcro.it; Via XX Settembre 160-162; s €65-80, d €90-100, ste €120-200; ❋ 🕲) Comfort and charm are perfectly aligned at Sansepolcro's best sleeping option. Located in a 15th-century *palazzo* in the heart of the historic centre, it offers sixteen comfortable rooms (some with frescoed walls), a billiard room and a comfortable TV lounge. In the low season, reception is only open during the day and guests are provided with keys for evening access.

Foresteria Ostello Santa Maria dei Servi   HOSTEL €
(☑ 339 6246194, 0575 74 23 47; www.santamariadeiservi.it; Piazza Andrea Dotti 2; dm €20; ⊙ May-Oct; @🕲) Attached to the 14th-century church of the same name, this former monastery offers accommodation in five small

dorms (two with bathroom) between May and October.

✕ Eating & Drinking

★ Ristorante Da Ventura   TRADITIONAL ITALIAN €€
(☑ 0575 74 25 60; www.albergodaventura.it; Via Niccolò Aggiunti 30; meals €32; ⊙ noon-2.30pm Tue-Sun, 7.30-10pm Tue-Sat) Beware the trollies at this fabulous local eatery! Heavily laden with the huge joints of roasted meat that the place is famous for (roast pork, beef stewed in Chianti Classico and roasted veal shank), these zoom around the old-fashioned dining room pushed by waiters intent on piling diners' plates high.

Vegetarians have no need to fear – the *uova con tartufo marzolino fresco* (omelette topped with shaved black truffles) is delectable, as are the generous plates of home-made pasta served with truffles or fresh porcini mushrooms, the *antipasti* spread and the tasty vegetable *cortorni* (side dishes).

Enoteca Guidi   WINE BAR
(☑ 0575 74 19 07; www.locandaguidi.it; Via Luca Pacioli 44-46; ⊙ 11am-midnight Thu-Sat, Mon & Tue, 6-11pm Sun) Owner Saverio presides over the teensy *enoteca*, but also keeps a close eye on the rear dining space, where simple meals are served. Enjoy a local artisan beer (Saverio recommends 'La Tipografica') or a glass of *vino* (everything from local drops to fashionable super-Tuscans).

Torrefazione Alessandrini   CAFE
(Via Luca Pacioli 31; ⊙ 7.45am-1pm & 4.30-8pm Mon-Sat Jun-Sep, 7.45am-1pm & 4-7.30 Mon-Sat Oct-May) The interior of the town's best-loved cafe has hardly changed over the decades. We love the fact that staff close the doors for three hours so that they can go home for lunch with their families, and that a bag of the aromatic house blend – roasted on site – is an essential weekly purchase for most locals.

ⓘ Information

Ufficio Turistico Valtiberina Toscana
(☑ 0575 74 05 36; info@valtiberinaintoscana.it; Via Giacomo Matteotti 8; ⊙ 9.30am-1pm & 2.30-6.30pm daily Apr-Oct, 10am-1pm daily & 3-5pm Fri-Sun Nov-Mar; @🕲) You'll find the extremely helpful tourist office opposite the Cattedrale di San Giovanni Evangelista. Free public internet and wi-fi access are available.

❶ Getting There & Away

BUS

Etruria Mobilità (www.etruriamobilita.it) buses link Sansepolcro with Arezzo (€4.10, one hour, frequent on weekdays, fewer on weekends).
Sulga (www.sulga.it) operates a service to Rome and Fiumicino Airport (€18.50, 3½ to 4¼ hours), leaving at 7am every day except Sunday. All buses leave from the bus station off Via G Marconi, near the Porta Fiorentina; purchase tickets at the Bar Autostazione.

CAR & MOTORCYCLE

A ZTL applies within the city walls; you'll find free parking just outside.

TRAIN

Umbria Mobilità (www.umbriamobilita.it) operates a Ferroviaria e Interscambio FS (train) service between Sansepolcro and Perugia (€4.60, two hours, seven daily Monday to Saturday, three on Sunday).

Cortona

POP 22,487

Rooms with a view are the rule rather than the exception in this spectacularly sited hilltop town. In the late 14th century Fra' Angelico lived and worked here, and fellow artists Luca Signorelli and Pietro da Cortona were both born within the walls – all are represented in the Museo Diocesano's collection. More recently, the town featured in *Under the Tuscan Sun,* the soap-in-the-sun book and subsequent film recounting author Frances Mayes' experience in restoring a villa and forging a new life here.

◉ Sights

Brooding over lopsided Piazza della Repubblica is the **Palazzo Comunale**, built in the 13th century. To the northwest is attractive **Piazza Signorelli** and, on its west side, the 13th-century **Palazzo Casali**, whose rather plain facade was added in the 17th century.

A combined ticket (adult/child €13/9) gives entry to the Museo Diocesano and the Museo dell'Accademia Etrusca.

★ Museo Diocesano   MUSEUM
(Piazza del Duomo 1; adult/child €5/3, audioguide €3; ◷10am-7pm Tue-Sun Apr-Oct, to 5pm Tue-Sun Nov-Mar) Little is left of the original Romanesque character of Cortona's *duomo,* which is situated northwest of Piazza Signorelli and has been rebuilt several times in a less-than-felicitous fashion. Fortunately, its won-

derful artworks have been saved and are on display in this museum, which occupies the former church of the Gesù on the opposite side of the piazza.

Room 1 features a remarkable Roman sarcophagus decorated with a frenzied battle scene between Dionysus and the Amazons, but the museum's real treasures are in room 3. These include a moving *Crucifixion* (1320) by Pietro Lorenzetti and two beautiful works by Fra' Angelico: *Annunciation* (1436) and *Madonna with Child and Saints* (1436–37).

★ Museo dell'Accademia
Etrusca   MUSEUM
(MAEC; www.cortonamaec.org; Piazza Signorelli 9; adult/child 6-12yr €10/7; ◷10am-7pm daily Apr-Oct, to 5pm Tue-Sun Nov-Mar) Occupying Palazzo Casali, this fascinating museum displays substantial local Etruscan and Roman finds, Renaissance globes, 18th-century decorative arts and contemporary paintings. The Etruscan collection is the highlight, particularly those objects excavated from the tombs at Sodo, just outside town.

Fortezza Medicea   LANDMARK
(adult/child €3/1.50; ◷10am-1pm & 3-6pm Sat & Sun May & Jun, 10am-1pm & 4-7pm Jul-Sep) There's a stupendous view over the Val di Chiana to Lake Trasimeno in Umbria from the remains of this Medici fortress, which stands atop the highest point in town. For the less fit, a **belvedere** at the eastern end of Via Nazionale, down in the centre of town, also has a panoramic view.

☞ Tours

English-language **walking tours** (✆334 3340608, 0575 40 33 19; www.centroguidearezzo. it; adult/reduced €10/free) are conducted every Monday from 11am to 1pm between May and October. The ticket includes entrance to Museo dell'Accademia Etrusca. Bookings essential.

⚜ Festivals & Events

Giostra dell'Archidado   CULTURAL
(www.giostraarchidado.com) A full week of medieval merriment in May or June (the date varies to coincide with Ascension Day) culminates in a crossbow competition.

Festival of Sacred Music   MUSIC
(www.cortonacristiana.it) Held in late June and early July each year.

Cortona Mix Festival ARTS
(www.mixfestival.it) Arts festival held in late July and early August each year.

Cortonantiquaria ANTIQUES
(www.cortonantiquaria.it) Cortona's well-known antiques market sets up in the beautiful 18th-century halls of Palazzo Vagnotti in late August and early September each year.

🛏 Sleeping

★ Casa Chilenne B&B €
(✆0575 60 33 20; www.casachilenne.com; Via Nazionale 65; s €80-85, d €88-110; ❄ @ 🛜 🍴) Run by American-born Jeanette and her Cortonese husband, Luciano, this wonderfully welcoming B&B has it all – great hosts, a central location, comfortable rooms, a lavish breakfast spread and keen prices. Each of the five rooms has a satellite TV, but there's also a communal lounge with TV, small terrace and cooking corner.

Villa Marsili HOTEL €€
(✆0575 60 52 52; www.villamarsili.net; Viale C Battisti 13; s €90-110, d €99-250, ste €240-340; ❄ @ 🛜 🍴) Service is the hallmark at this attractive villa nestled against the city walls. Guests rave about the helpful staff, lavish breakfast buffet and early-evening *aperitivo*, which is served in the garden. Consider booking one of the suites, which have jacuzzis and wonderful views across the Val di Chiana to Lake Trasimeno

🍴 Eating & Drinking

Taverna Pane e Vino WINE BAR €
(www.pane-vino.it; Piazza Signorelli 27; meals €6-11; ⊙noon-11pm Tue-Sun Easter-Jan, 5-11pm Tue-Sat & noon-11pm Sun Feb & Mar) Serving more than 900 wines, this casual place is a perfect spot for a light lunch (bruschetta €4, meat and cheese platters €6 to €11, pasta €6.50 to €9), afternoon drink or rustic dinner. Claim a table in the front courtyard or vaulted interior, settle back over a glass or two of wine and relax with the local bon vivants.

La Bucaccia TUSCAN €€
(✆0575 60 60 39; www.labucaccia.it; Via Ghibellina 17; meals €35; ⊙noon-2.30pm & 7.30-10pm Tue-Sun) Set in a medieval stable that was incorporated into a Renaissance *palazzo,* this is an atmospheric and enjoyable dinner venue, but is a bit dark at lunchtime. The set menu (€29) of four courses, one glass of wine and water offers extremely good value.

ℹ Information

Tourist office (✆0575 63 72 23; infocortona@ apt.arezzo.it; Palazzo Comunale; ⊙9am-1pm & 3-6pm Mon-Sat, 9am-1pm Sun late-Apr–Sep, 9am-1pm & 3-6pm Mon-Fri, 9am-1pm Sat Oct–late-Apr) This friendly office has maps, brochures and timetables. It also sells bus and train tickets and can book accommodation.

ℹ Getting There & Around

BUS
Etruria Mobilità buses connect the town with Arezzo (€3.50, one hour, frequent).

CAR & MOTORCYCLE
The city is on the north–south SS71 that runs to Arezzo. It's also close to the Siena–Bettolle–Perugia autostrada, which connects to the A1. There are paid car parks around the circumference of the city walls and a free car park at Parcheggio San Spirito Santo that is connected to the historical centre by a *scala mobile* (escalator). A ZTL applies inside the walls.

TRAIN
The nearest train station is located about 6km away at Camucia, and can be accessed via a local bus (€1.30, 15 minutes, hourly). Destinations include Arezzo (€3.30, 25 minutes, hourly), Florence (€9.80, 1¾ hours, hourly), Rome (€11.15, 2¼ hours, eight daily), Perugia (€4.25, 55 minutes, six daily) and Orvieto (€7, 55 minutes, seven daily).

Note that Camucia station has no ticket office, only machines. If you need assistance purchasing or booking tickets, you'll need to go to the station at Terontola, south of Camucia, instead.

Umbria & Le Marche

Includes ➡

Best Places to Eat

➡ La Taverna (p575)

➡ DivinPeccato (p580)

➡ Osteria dei Priori (p587)

➡ Tempio del Gusto (p597)

Best Places to Stay

➡ B&B San Fiorenzo (p574)

➡ Casale della Staffa (p580)

➡ Palazzo Seneca (p599)

➡ Acanto Country House (p609)

➡ Misia Resort (p603)

Why Go?

For years Italophiles have waxed lyrical about Tuscany's natural, artistic and culinary wonders, without so much as a passing nod to neighbours: Umbria and Le Marche. How they have missed out! This phenomenally beautiful yet unsung region is Italy in microcosm: olive groves, vineyards, sun-ripened wheat fields stippled with wildflowers and hills plumed with cypress trees roll gently west to the snow-dusted Apennines and east to the glittering Adriatic. In between, castle-topped medieval hill towns wait, glowing like warm honey in the fading light of sundown.

Then there are the region's artistic attributes, as the birthplace of Renaissance masters Raphael and Perugino, and sprightly composer Rossini; while St Francis of Assisi, St Benedict and St Valentine make the spiritual pilgrimage here a profound one. So next time you glance at the map and your eyes alight on old-favourite Tuscany, why not press on south? You won't regret it.

When to Go
Perugia

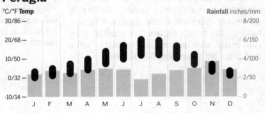

Feb Celebrate all things truffle at Norcia's Mostra Mercato del Tartufo Nero.

May Hit Le Marche's beaches, as wildflowers bloom on the Piano Grande.

Jun & Jul Get lost in music at the Spoleto Festival and Perugia's Umbria Jazz.

UMBRIA

Italy's green heart, Umbria is a land unto itself, the only Italian region that borders neither the sea nor another country. Removed from outside influences, it has kept alive many of Italy's old-world traditions. You'll see grandmothers in aprons making pasta by hand and front doors that haven't been locked in a century.

Separated from Le Marche by the jagged spine of the Monti Sibillini, it contrasts wild, in-your-face beauty with the gentle fall and rise of overlapping hills and wildflower-flecked meadows. The Etruscans, Romans and medieval feuding families have left their indelible imprint on its pretty hill towns, where history seems to creep up on you on every corner – from the Gothic wonder of Orvieto to Assisi's saintly calling.

Foodies are in their element here, with the rich earthiness of the *tartufo* (truffle), fine cured meats from Norcia and full-bodied local wines finding their way onto menus.

History

Umbria is named in honour of its first inhabitants, the Umbri tribe who settled east of the Tiber around 1000 BC, establishing the towns of Spoleto, Gubbio and Assisi. They jockeyed for regional supremacy with the Etruscans to the west of the river – the founders of Perugia and Orvieto – until the 3rd century BC, when the Romans came marching through, conquering them both.

Following the collapse of the Western Roman Empire, the region spent much of the Middle Ages being fought over by Holy Roman Empire advocates (Ghibellines) and supporters of the Pope (Guelphs). Intriguingly, it was during this turbulent period that peace-loving St Francis came to prominence in Assisi.

Eventually the region became one of the Papal States, though this was not to its long-term benefit. Indeed, historians like to say that time stopped in Umbria in 1540 when the pope imposed a salt tax. The resulting war brought Umbrian culture to a standstill, which is partly why the medieval hearts of Umbrian towns are so well preserved.

Perugia has a strong artistic tradition. In the 15th century it was home to fresco painters Bernardino Pinturicchio and his master Pietro Vannucci (known as Perugino), who would later teach Raphael. Its cultural tradition continues to this day in the form of the University of Perugia and the famous Università per Stranieri (University for Foreigners), which teaches Italian, art and culture to thousands of students from around the world.

🛈 Getting Around

While having your own wheels certainly makes it easier to reach those off-the-radar hill towns and rural corners of Umbria, it is possible to get to many places by public transport with a little pre-planning.

Buses head from Perugia to most towns in the area; check at the tourist office or the bus station for exact details. **Trenitalia** (Ferrovie dello Stato; ☑ 892021; www.trenitalia.com) sparsely criss-crosses Umbria, but the regional **Umbria Mobilità** (☑ 075 963 70 01; www.umbriamobilita.it) fills in the blanks.

Perugia

POP 162,100

Lifted by a hill above a valley patterned with fields, where the Tiber River runs swift and clear, Perugia is Umbria's petite and immediately likeable capital. Its *centro storico* (historic centre) rises in a helter-skelter of cobbled alleys, arched stairways and piazzas framed by magnificent *palazzi* (mansions). History seeps through every shadowy corner of these streets and an aimless wander through them can feel like time travel.

Back in the 21st century, Perugia is a party-loving, pleasure-seeking university city, with students pepping up the nightlife and filling cafe terraces. The hopping summer event line-up counts one of Europe's best jazz festivals. Together with its spiritual sister,

---

USEFUL WEBSITES ON UMBRIA

Bella Umbria (www.bellaumbria.net) Accommodation and restaurant listings for Umbria. Search for festivals and events by location or date.

Regione Umbria (www.regioneumbria. eu) The official Umbrian tourist website.

Sistema Museo (www.sistemamuseo. it) Get the inside scoop on Umbria's museums and upcoming events.

Umbria Online (www.umbriaonline. com) Find information on accommodation, events and itineraries across Umbria.

Umbria & Le Marche Highlights

1 Making the spiritual pilgrimage in the footsteps of a peace-seeking saint to Assisi's **Basilica di San Francesco** (p583).

2 Gazing at endless acres of spring wildflowers or trek up the snow-capped peaks of **Monti Sibillini** (p619).

3 Spelunking your way through a forest of stalactites at **Grotte di Frasassi** (p615), Europe's largest cave.

4 Swimming, chilling and eating just-caught shellfish by the Adriatic in coastal **Parco del Conero** (p609).

5 Savouring towering views on a rickety ride up Monte Ingino aboard Gubbio's **Funivia Colle Eletto** (p591).

6 Cashing in your golden ticket for a tour of the **Casa del Cioccolato Perugina** (p572).

7 Slipping into the relaxed groove of lake life: swimming, cycling and sipping locally grown wines at **Lago Trasimeno** (p578).

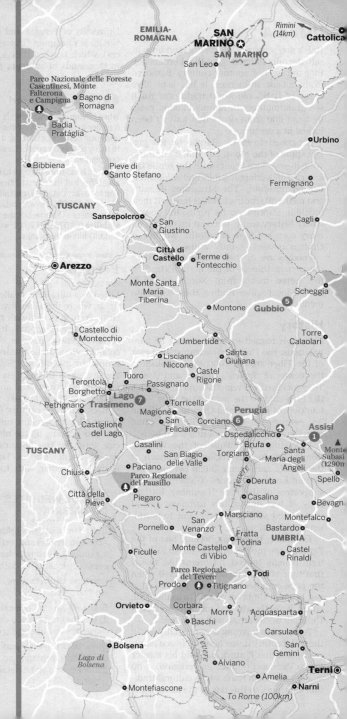

Perugia

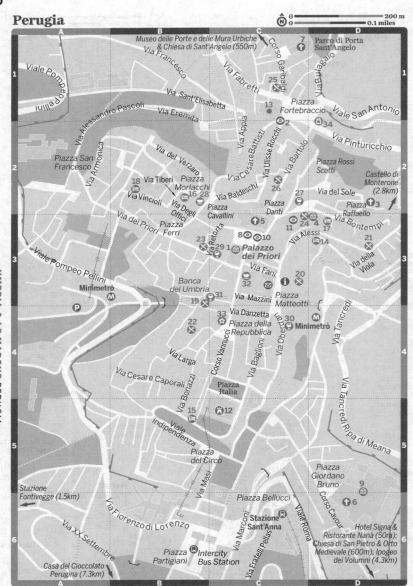

Assisi, Perugia is a candidate for European Capital of Culture 2019. Watch this space.

◉ Sights

In Perugia all roads seem to lead to **Piazza IV Novembre**, once the meeting point for the ancient Etruscan and Roman civilisations. In the medieval period, it was the political centre of Perugia. Now people from all walks of life gather here to chat, slurp gelato and watch street entertainers or the odd budding opera singer.

Perugia

★**Palazzo dei Priori**   MUSEUM
Rising proudly above the main piazza, this palace, constructed between the 13th and 14th centuries, is architecturally striking with its tripartite windows, Gothic portal and fortress-like crenelations. It was formerly the headquarters of the city's magistrature.

Today it harbours some of the city's finest museums, including Umbria's foremost art gallery, the stunning **Galleria Nazionale dell'Umbria** (www.gallerianazionaleumbria.it; Corso Vannucci 19; adult/reduced €8/4; ⊙ 8.30am-7.30pm Tue-Sun). Entered via Corso Vannucci, it's an art historian's dream, with 30 rooms of works featuring everything from Byzantine art to the Renaissance creations of homegrown heroes Pinturicchio and Perugino.

Perugia's piggy bank in medieval times, the extravagantly adorned **Nobile Collegio del Cambio** (Exchange Hall; Corso Vannucci 25; admission €4.50, combined ticket with Nobile Collegio della Mercanzia €5.50; ⊙ 9am-12.30pm & 2.30-5.30pm Mon-Sat, 9am-1pm Sun) has three rooms: the Sala dei Legisti (Legist Chamber), with 17th-century wooden stalls carved by Giampiero Zuccari; the Sala dell'Udienza (Audience Chamber), with outstanding Renaissance

frescoes by Perugino; and the Chapel of San Giovanni Battista, painted by a student of Perugino's, Giannicola di Paolo. Nearby sits the **Nobile Collegio della Mercanzia** (Merchant's Hall; Corso Vannucci 15; admission €1.50, combined ticket with Nobile Collegio del Cambio €5.50; ⊙ 9am-1pm & 2.30-5.30pm Tue-Sat, 9am-1pm Sun), showcasing a 14th-century audience chamber with exquisite wood panelling.

The **Sala dei Notari** (Notaries' Hall; Piazza IV Novembre; admission free; ⊙ 9am-1pm & 3-7pm daily) was built from 1293 to 1297 and is where the nobility met. The arches supporting the vaults are Romanesque, covered with frescoes depicting biblical scenes and

---

ⓘ **PERUGIA CITTÀ MUSEO CARD**

Planning on ticking off several sights? Invest in a **Perugia Città Museo Card** (www.perugiacittamuseo.it; adult/reduced €10/6), which provides admission to five museums of your choice. It's available at all the participating sights and the tourist office.

TOP FIVE UMBRIAN DELICACIES

Once something of a culinary backwater, much of the world is now playing catch up with Umbria's Slow Food commitment in a region where three-hour dinners, organic and locavore dining have long been part of daily life. Eat like an Umbrian by sampling these dishes on your travels:

Cinghiale Richly gamey but tender, wild boar is often served over pasta or stewed in sauce.

Tartufi Umbrian black truffles (preferably the stronger *nero* variety) give menus earthy edge, especially in the autumn harvest months.

Lenticchie These small, thin lentils from Castelluccio are at their best in a thick soup topped with bruschetta and virgin olive oil.

Piccione Umbrians readily order pigeon, often from the highest-end restaurants. The delicate poultry was a mainstay for townsfolk under siege in the Middle Ages.

Farro Emmer wheat still graces tables today. Classic *zuppa di farro* is rich, nutty and distinctly Umbrian , perfect for a warm lunch on a cold, misty day in the hills.

Aesop's fables. To reach the hall, walk up the steps from Piazza IV Novembre.

Cattedrale di San Lorenzo CATHEDRAL
(Piazza IV Novembre; ⊙7.30am-noon & 4-6.30pm) Although a church has been here since the 900s, the version you see at the northern end of Piazza IV Novembre was begun in 1345 from designs created by Fra Bevignate. Building of the cathedral continued until 1587, although the main facade was never completed. Inside you'll find dramatic late Gothic architecture, an altarpiece by Signorelli and sculptures by Duccio.

The steps in front of the facade are where seemingly all of Perugia congregates; they overlook the piazza's centrepiece: the delicate pink-and-white marble Fontana Maggiore (Great Fountain; Piazza IV Novembre). Another of Fra Bevignate's designs, the fountain was completed in 1278 by famous sculptors Nicola and Giovanni Pisano. Bas-relief statues grace the polygonal basin, representing scenes from the Old Testament, the founding of Rome, the seven 'liberal arts', the signs of the zodiac, and a griffin and lion. The griffin is the symbol of Perugia and the lion that of the Guelphs, the Middle Ages faction that favoured rule by the papacy over rule by the Holy Roman Empire.

Museo Archeologico
Nazionale dell'Umbria MUSEUM
(Piazza Giordano Bruno 10; adult/reduced €4/2; ⊙8.30am-7.30pm Tue-Sun, 10am-7.30pm Mon) The convent adjoining the Chiesa di San Domenico is home to a superior collection of Etruscan and prehistoric artefacts – carved funerary urns, coins and Bronze Age statuary – dating as far back as the 16th century BC. The *Cippo Perugino* (Perugian Memorial Stone) has the longest Etruscan-language engraving ever found, offering a rare window into this obscure culture.

Casa del Cioccolato Perugina MUSEUM
(☑075 527 67 96; www.perugina.it; Van San Sisto 207, Loc San Sisto; adult/reduced €5/4; ⊙9am-noon & 2-4pm Mon-Fri ; ⓖ) To visit the Wonka-esque world of Perugian chocolate, call ahead to latch onto a 1¼-hour guided tour (in Italian or English, times vary). After visiting the museum, you'll wend your way through an enclosed sky bridge, watching as the white-outfitted Oompa Loompas – er, factory workers – go about their chocolate-creating business.

Check the website for the calendar of three- to four-hour chocolate-making workshops. Held at 10am and 3.30pm on Saturdays, they cost between €55 and €65. Drive through the gates of the humorously nondescript factory entrance marked Nestlé, or take the bus to San Sisto.

Chiesa di San Pietro CHURCH
(Borgo XX Giugno 74; ⊙8am-noon & 3-6pm) South of the town centre, past the Porta di San Pietro, this 10th-century church's interior is an incredible mix of gilt and marble, and contains a *Pietà* (a painting of the dead Christ supported by the Madonna) by Perugino. For a glimpse into gardens past, take a stroll or picnic at the serene Orto Medievale

(Borgo XX Giugno 74; admission free; ⊘8am-5pm Mon-Fri) gardens, behind the church.

During the medieval period, monasteries often created gardens reminiscent of the Garden of Eden and biblical stories, with plants that symbolised myths and sacred stories. Numbered locations through this garden include the Cosmic Tree, symbolising the forefather of all trees; the Tree of Light and Knowledge; and the Tree of Good and Evil.

Rocca Paolina   FORT, GARDEN

(Piazza Italia) FREE At the southern end of Corso Vannucci is the tiny Giardini Carducci, with expansive views across the city's spires to the countryside and cypress-cloaked hills beyond. The gardens stand atop a once-massive 16th-century fortress, now known as the Rocca Paolina. Built by Pope Paolo III Farnese in the 1540s, it wiped out entire sections of a formerly wealthy neighbourhood.

Now used as the throughway for the *scale mobili* (escalators), its nooks and crannies are venues for art exhibits and the last weekend of the month sees Perugia's antiques market held here.

Casa Museo di Palazzo Sorbello   MUSEUM

(www.casamuseosorbello.org; Piazza Piccinino 9; adult/reduced €5/3; ⊘guided tours 11am-2pm) A few steps from the Piazza IV Novembre, this exquisite 17th-century mansion, once owned by the noble Sorbello family, has recently been restored to its frescoed, gilt-clad, chandelier-lit 18th-century prime. Guided tours (in Italian) let you admire the family's almost ludicrously opulent collection of art, porcelain, embroidery and manuscripts.

Capella di San Severo   CHURCH

(Piazza Raffaello; adult/reduced €3/2; ⊘10am-1.30pm & 2.30-6pm, closed Mon winter) Walking for a couple of minutes northeast from Piazza IV Novembre brings you to this rather bland, boxy-looking church. Your efforts will be rewarded, however, once you step inside and find the chapel decorated with Raphael's lush *Trinity with Saints* (thought by many to be his first fresco), painted during the artist's residence in Perugia (1505–08).

Ipogeo dei Volumni   HISTORIC SITE

(Via Assisana 53, Località Ponte San Giovanni; adult/reduced €3/1.50; ⊘9am-1pm & 3.30-6.30pm) About 5km southeast of the city, the Ipogeo dei Volumni is a 2nd-century BC underground Etruscan burial site, holding the funerary urns of the Volumni, a local noble family. The surrounding grounds are a massive expanse of partially unearthed burial chambers, with several buildings housing the artefacts that haven't been stolen over the years.

Take a train from Piazza Italia to Ponte San Giovanni and walk west from there. By car, take the Bonanzano exit heading south on the E45.

Pozzo Etrusco   HISTORIC SITE

(Etruscan Well; Piazza Danti 18; adult/reduced €3/2; ⊘10am-1.30pm & 2.30-6pm Tue-Sun summer, 11am-1.30pm & 2.30-5pm winter) Just north of Piazza IV Novembre, you can venture down into a 37m-deep well. Dating from the 3rd century BC, it was the main water reservoir of the Etruscan town, and, more recently, a source of water during WWII bombing raids.

Chiesa di San Domenico   CHURCH

(Piazza Giordano Bruno; ⊘7am-noon & 4-7pm) Erected in the early 14th century, Umbria's largest church is an imposing vision, with a 17th-century interior lit by immense stained-glass windows. The church's pride and joy is the Gothic tomb of Pope Benedict XI, who died after eating poisoned figs in 1304.

Arco Etrusco   HISTORIC SITE

(Etruscan Arch) At the end of Via Ulisse Rocchi, facing Piazza Fortebraccio and the Università per Stranieri, are the ancient city's Etruscan gates dating from the 3rd century BC. The upper part is Roman and bears the inscription 'Augusta Perusia'.

Chiesa di Sant'Agostino   CHURCH

(Piazza Lupattelli; ⊘10am-1pm & 5.30-7pm Mon-Sat, 8am-12.30pm Sun) North of the Università per Stranieri, along Corso Garibaldi, this formerly magnificent church still boasts a beautiful 16th-century choir by sculptor Baccio d'Agnolo. However, small signs forlornly mark the places where artworks once hung before they were carried off to France by Napoléon's troops.

Chiesa di Sant'Angelo   CHURCH

(Via Sant'Angelo; ⊘9am-5pm daily) Further north along Corso Garibaldi, Via del Tempio branches off to one of Italy's oldest churches, the Romanesque Chiesa di Sant'Angelo, parts of which date back to the 5th century. It stands on the foundations of an even older Roman temple.

DON'T MISS

ALL THAT JAZZ

Ever since making its debut in 1973, Perugia's swinging 10-day July festival, **Umbria Jazz** (☏ 075 573 24 32; www. umbriajazz.com), has put the city firmly on the world jazz map, with such headline acts as BB King, Van Morrison, James Brown, Sting, Chet Baker and, more recently, Herbie Hancock and Diana Krall. The **Arena Santa Giuliana** hosts most performances, but events are also held at other venues, including the Teatro Morlacchi and Galleria Nazionale dell'Umbria. Tickets go for anything between €15 and €120. See the website for the full line-up.

Museo delle Porte e delle Mura Urbiche
MUSEUM

(Museum of the City Walls and Gates; Porta Sant'Angelo; adult/reduced €3/2; ⏲10.30am-1.30pm & 3-6pm Tue-Sun) Next door to the Chiesa di Sant'Angelo, in the 14th-century Porta Sant'Angelo, the city's largest medieval gateway, this museum whisks you through the history of the city's defences. Even more engrossing are the sweeping views of Perugia from this vantage point.

Courses

Università per Stranieri
LANGUAGE

(☏075 5 74 61; www.unistrapg.it; Piazza Fortebraccio 4) This is Italy's foremost academic institution for foreigners, offering courses in language, literature, history, art, music, opera and architecture. One-, three- and six-month language courses start at €400 a month; intensive courses in summer cost €600 a month.

Festivals & Events

Check www.bellaumbria.net or www.regioneumbria.eu for details on Perugia's gazillions of festivals, concerts, summer outdoor film screenings and *sagre* (traditional festivals).

Eurochocolate
FOOD

(www.eurochocolate.com) Perugia celebrates the cocoa bean over nine days in mid-October. More than a million chocolate lovers flock here for choc-crazy exhibitions, cookery classes, giant chocolate sculptures and – the real reason everyone is here – to hoover up the free samples. Book accommodation well in advance if you're planning on visiting this one.

Sleeping

Hotel Signa
HOTEL €

(☏ 075 572 41 80; www.hotelsigna.it; Via del Grillo 9; s €40-58, d €65-80, tr €80-90, q €98-120; ❉ 🐾 🛜 📶) Slip down an alley off Corso Cavour to reach Signa, one of Perugia's best budget picks. The petite rooms are simple yet bright and well kept; many have balconies with cracking views of the city and countryside. There's a kettle for making a cuppa and free wi-fi. Breakfast costs an extra €7. The owner, Mario, hands out maps and tips freely.

Hotel Morlacchi
HOTEL €

(☏075 572 03 19; www.hotelmorlacchi.it; Via Tiberi 2; s €46-66, d €72-92, tr €95-115; 🛜 📶) In a great old-town location near the Università per Stranieri, this friendly, family-run hotel occupies a 17th-century townhouse. The spotlessly clean rooms are furnished with simple but comfortable antique furnishings, and a few even have fireplaces.

Primavera Minihotel
GUESTHOUSE €

(☏075 572 16 57; www.primaveraminihotel.it; Via Vincioli 8; s €45-65, d €65-90, tr €95-105; ❉ @ 🛜 📶) This central hotel run by a dedicated English- and French-speaking mother-daughter team is tucked in a quiet corner. Magnificent views complement the bright rooms, decorated with period furnishings and characterful features like exposed stone, beams and wood floors. Breakfast costs €5 to €8 extra.

Ostello di Perugia
HOSTEL €

(☏075 572 28 80; www.ostello.perugia.it; Via Bontempi 13; dm €17; @ 🛜) Perugia's hostel is rather charming inside, with 16th-century frescoed ceilings, tidy four- to six-person dorms kept immaculately clean, a library and big country views from the terrace. There's a lock-out between 11am and 3.30pm.

★ B&B San Fiorenzo
B&B €€

(☏393 3869987; www.sanfiorenzo.com; Via Alessi 45; r €70-120; 🛜 📶) Buried in Perugia's medieval maze of a centre is this charming 15th-century *palazzo*, where Luigi and Monica make you welcome in one of three unique rooms. A Florentine architect has carefully incorporated mod cons and marble bathrooms into spacious quarters with brick vaulting, lime-washed walls and antique furnishings, including an apartment with an 11th-century well shower and a 13th-century tower room.

Breakfast is a handsome spread, with homemade cakes, fresh fruit and decent cappuccino. Incidentally, the church of the same name that sits opposite once harboured Raphael's *Ansidei Madonna* altarpiece, now in London's National Gallery.

Castello di Monterone   CASTLE HOTEL €€

(☑ 075 572 42 14; www.castellomonterone.com; Strada Montevile 3; s €100-160, d €160-250; P ✳ @ ☰) Ever fancied spending the night in a medieval castle? This is the real McCoy, with all the turreted, ivy-clad, vaulted trappings you would imagine. The individually designed rooms have been finished to great effect, with exposed stone, wooden furniture, handmade wrought-iron beds and antiques. A pool with sweeping views over the rolling countryside and a first-rate restaurant add to its appeal.

The hotel is situated 3km southeast of the centre; see the website for exact directions.

Hotel Brufani Palace   LUXURY HOTEL €€€

(☑ 075 573 25 41; www.brufanipalace.com; Piazza Italia 12; s €115-175, d €125-220, ste €263-530; P ✳ @ ☞ ☰) From its hilltop perch, this five-star hotel has captivating views of the valley below and hills beyond. The hotel itself matches this initial impression with frescoed public rooms, impeccably decorated bedrooms with marble bathrooms, a garden terrace for summer dining, and helpful trilingual staff. Swim over Etruscan ruins in the subterranean fitness centre. There's access for disabled guests.

✗ Eating

Perugia has a staggering number of places to eat. The first days the mercury rises above 15°C or so (usually in March), dozens of open-air locales spring up along and around Corso Vannucci.

Pizzeria Mediterranea   PIZZERIA €

(☑ 075 572 13 22; Piazza Piccinino 11/12; pizzas €5-12; ☺ daily) Perugians know to come here for the best pizza in town. A spaceship-sized wood-fired brick oven heats up pizzas, from the simplest *margherita* to the 12-topping 'his and hers'. It gets busy enough to queue on Saturday nights.

Ristorante Nanà   TRADITIONAL ITALIAN €

(☑ 075 573 35 71; www.ristorantenana.it; Corso Cavour 202; meals €25-35; ☺ Mon-Sat) Straw bonnet lamps cast a quirkily rustic light on this family-run, 15-table restaurant. Simply furnished with a small menu, the food is hearty

and done in refined *nuovo* style – try the pigeon with capers.

Al Mangiar Bene   ORGANIC, PIZZERIA €

(☑ 075 573 10 47; www.almangiarbene.com; Via della Luna 21; pizzas €5-8.50, meals €25-30; ☺ Mon-Sat) This subterranean restaurant at the end of a narrow alley sources nearly all its ingredients locally from organic suppliers, from the flour used in its pasta to the tender cuts of beef, thinly sliced and served with rocket or truffle. Pizza and calzone are baked in a hearth-like brick oven. Even the beer and wines are organic.

Ristorante dal Mi'Cocco   UMBRIAN €

(☑ 075 573 25 11; Corso Garibaldi 12; set meals €13; ☺ Tue-Sun) Don't ask for a menu because there isn't one. Diners get a set menu of a starter, main course, side dish and dessert. You may receive asparagus risotto in May or *tagliatelle* with peas and ham in November. Extremely popular with students, it's best to call ahead.

Covered Market   MARKET €

(Piazza Matteotti; ☺ 7am-1.30pm Mon-Fri, 7.30am-1.30pm & 4.30-7.30pm Sat) Found below a rather desultory craft and tourist-tat market, you can buy fresh produce, bread, cheese and meat here. Head through the arched doorway to the immediate right of the tourist office.

★ La Taverna   ITALIAN €€

(☑ 075 572 41 28; www.ristorantelataverna.com; Via delle Streghe 8; meals €30-40; ☺ lunch & dinner daily) Way up there on the Perugia dining wish list, La Taverna consistently wins the praise of local foodies. Chef Claudio cooks market-fresh produce with flair and precision, while waiters treat you like one of the *famiglia*.

Brick vaults and candlelit tables create an intimate backdrop for season-rooted dishes, from homemade pasta with black truffles to herb-crusted lamb, all paired with superb wines.

Osteria a Priori   OSTERIA €€

(☑ 075 572 70 98; www.osteriaapriori.it; Via dei Priori 39; meals €20-€30; ☺ Wed-Mon) Above a wine shop and deli, where you can buy Umbrian wines, extra virgin olive oil and artisanal ales, this *osteria* (casual tavern or eatery presided over by a host) is a wonderful surprise. Careful local sourcing and brilliantly fresh ingredients shine through in dishes such as meltingly tender lamb with black truffle. Weekday lunch is a snip at €9.

Wine Bartolo Hosteria
OSTERIA €€

(🖉075 571 60 27; Via Bartolo 30; meals €25-35; ⊘dinner Thu-Tue) Descend a staircase into a hobbit-like burrow where walls of wine bottles surround a handful of cosy tables underneath a low brick ceiling. The food is winningly fresh and inspired by the seasons, along the lines of *taglierini* with Norcia black truffles and Chianina beef stewed with sangiovese.

Il Gufo
UMBRIAN €€

(🖉075 573 41 26; Via della Viola 18; meals €29; ⊘8pm-1am Tue-Sat) The owner-chef gathers ingredients from local markets and cooks up whatever is fresh and in season. Go for robustly seasoned dishes such as wild boar with fennel or pappardelle with rabbit *ragù*.

Drinking & Nightlife

Much of Perugia's nightlife parades outside the cathedral and around Fontana Maggiore, where local and foreign students gather to chat, flirt and play guitars and drums. Grab a gelato and go for a people-watching *passeggiata* (evening stroll) to watch the street theatre unfold.

As day fades into dusk at *aperitivo* hour in summer, locals spill out onto pavement terraces and patios with far-reaching views across the surrounding valley and hills.

Sandri
CAFE, PATISSERIE

(Corso Vannucci 32; ⊘8am-8pm Tue-Sun) Going strong since 1860, this delicately frescoed, chandelier-lit cafe lures locals to its marble counter like moths to a sugar-coated flame. Besides delectable chocolate cake, it does a fine line in pastries, espresso and candied fruit. Staff wrap all take-home purchases in beautiful red paper with a ribbon bow.

Bottega del Vino
WINE BAR

(Via del Sole 1; ⊘7pm-1am Mon-Sat) A fire or candles burn romantically on the terrace, while inside live jazz and hundreds of bottles of wine lining the walls add to the romance of the setting. You can taste dozens of Umbrian wines, which you can purchase with the help of sommelier-like experts.

Il Sole
BAR

(Via delle Rupe 1; ⊘Tue-Sun) Better for drinking than dining, Il Sole is all about the engrossing view over town, country and wooded hill

from its terrace. It's a beautiful spot for a sundowner.

Caffè Morlacchi
CAFE

(Piazza Morlacchi 6/8; ⊘8am-1am Mon-Sat, 4-10pm Sun; 🖘) Students, professors and all-comers flock to this vibrantly coloured, blissfully relaxed hangout for coffee by day and cocktails to the backbeat of DJ tunes by night.

Lunabar Ferrari
BAR

(Via Scura 1/6; ⊘8am-1.30am) This lounge bar spins together frescoed plaster walls and luxuriant rugs with modern art and crazy chandeliers. Go for the cocktails, DJ sets and decent snack selection.

Gold
WINE BAR

(Via dei Priori 7; ⊘6pm-1am) This lounge bar-cum-restaurant is maybe trying a bit too hard to be classy with its endless 'gold' and 'luxury' theming. Still, it attracts a fun crowd and has plenty of wine choices. Happy hour is from 6pm.

Entertainment

When the student population grows, some of the clubs on the outskirts of town run a bus to Palazzo Gallenga, starting around 11pm. Students hand out flyers on Corso Vannucci, so check with them or ask at the steps. Most clubs get going around midnight, so it's worth remembering that the *scale mobili* stop running at 2am.

Cinema Teatro del Pavone
CINEMA

(🖉075 572 81 53; www.teatrodelpavone.it; Corso Vannucci 67) Dating back to 1717, the grand theatre plays host to not only films but also musical performances and special events.

Shopping

Via Oberdan, the main boulevard Corso Vannucci and the steep Via Sant'Ercolano, wedged between the high townhouses of the *centro storico*, are dotted with boutiques, music shops, bookstores and jewellers.

Augusta Perusia Cioccolato e Gelateria
CHOCOLATE

(www.cioccolatoaugustaperusia.it; Via Pinturicchio 2; ⊘10.30am-8pm; 🖘) Giordano worked for Perugina for 25 years. In 2000, he opened his own shop, creating delectable morsels from the old tradition, including *baci* (hazelnut 'kisses' covered in chocolate) from the original Perugian recipe.

❶ Information

Banks line Corso Vannucci. All have ATMs.

InfoUmbria (☑ 075 3 26 39; www.umbriabest. com; Via della Pallotta 5; ⊗9am-1pm & 2.30-6.30pm Mon-Fri, 9am-1pm Sat) Also known as InfoTourist, it offers information on all of Umbria and is a fantastic resource for *agriturismi* (farm stay accommodation).

Ospedale Perugia (☑075 57 81)

Post office (Piazza Matteotti 1; ⊗8.20am-7.05pm Mon-Fri, 8am-12.35pm Sat)

Tourist office (☑075 573 64 58; http://turismo.comune.perugia.it; Piazza Matteotti 18; ⊗9am-7pm) Housed in the 14th-century Loggia dei Lanari, Perugia's main tourist office has stacks of info on the city, maps and up-to-date bus and train timetables.

❶ Getting There & Away

AIR

Aeroporto Sant'Egidio (PEG; ☑ 075 59 21 41; www.airport.umbria.it; Via dell'Aeroporto, Sant'Egidio), 13km east of the city, is small and easy to navigate, with five weekly **Ryanair** (www. ryanair.com) flights to London Stansted.

BUS

Umbria Mobilità (p567) operates all intercity buses, which leave from Piazza Partigiani in the city's south (take the *scale mobili* through the Rocca Paolina from Piazza Italia). Services go to the following destinations:

TO	FARE (€)	DURATION	FREQUENCY
Assisi	4	45min	9 daily
Castiglione del Lago	6	1hr	9 daily
Deruta	3.50	30min	13 daily
Florence	10	2hr	1 daily
Gubbio	5.50	1¼hr	10 daily
Todi	6.50	1¼hr	9 daily
Torgiano	3	30min	9 daily

CAR & MOTORCYCLE

From Rome, leave the A1 at the Orte exit and follow the signs for Terni. Once there, take the SS3bis/E45 for Perugia. From the north, exit the A1 at Valdichiana and take dual-carriageway SS75 for Perugia. The SS75 to the east connects the city with Assisi.

Rental companies have offices at the airport and train station.

TRAIN

In the southwest of town, Perugia's main **train station** (☑ 075 963 78 91; Piazza Vittorio Veneto) has trains running to the following destinations:

TO	FARE (€)	DURATION	FREQUENCY
Arezzo	7-12	1hr	every 2 hours
Assisi	2.50	20min	hourly
Florence	13.50-19	2hr	every 2 hours
Orvieto	7-14.50	1¾-3hr	10 daily
Rome	11-23	2¼-3½hr	17 daily
Spello	3	30min	hourly
Spoleto	5-9	1hr	hourly
Terni	6-12.50	1½hr	hourly

❶ Getting Around

If you're not carrying too much luggage, the simplest way of getting from Perugia's intercity bus station to the town centre is by hopping aboard the *scale mobili* linking Piazza Partigiani with Piazza Italia. There are also *scale mobili* from the car park at the Piazzale della Cuppa outside the city walls up to the Via dei Priori.

TO/FROM THE AIRPORT

Umbria Mobilità (p567) runs a frequent bus service from the airport to Perugia (€3, 30 minutes) and Assisi (€3, 20 minutes); you'll need the exact change. Tickets are a third cheaper if you buy them from the airport bar.

Alternatively, a shuttle bus (€8) leaves from Piazza Italia for the airport about two hours before each flight, stopping at the train station. From the airport, buses leave once everyone is on board.

A taxi costs approximately €30.

BUS

It's a steep 1.5km climb from Perugia's train station, so a bus is highly recommended (and essential for those with luggage). The bus takes you to Piazza Italia. Tickets cost €1.50 from the train-station kiosk or €2 on board. Validate your ticket on board to avoid a fine. A 10-ticket pass costs €12.90.

CAR & MOTORCYCLE

Perugia is humorously difficult to navigate and most of the city centre is only open to residential or commercial traffic. Perugia has several fee-charging car parks (€0.80 to €1.60 per hour, 24 hours a day). Piazza Partigiani and the Mercato Coperto are the most central and convenient. There's also a free car park at Piazza Cupa.

MINIMETRÒ

These single-car people-movers traverse between the train station and Pincetto (just off Piazza Matteotti) every minute. A €1.50 ticket works for the bus and Minimetrò. From the train station facing the tracks, head right up a long platform.

578

GOING TO ROME?

Blue-and-white **Sulga** (☏ 075 500 96 41; www.sulga.it) buses link the bus station on Piazza Partigiani with Terminal 3 at Rome's Fiumicino (FCO) airport (€22, 3¼hr); they depart at 6.30am, 8am and 9am daily from Monday to Saturday. The same buses also run to Rome's Tiburtina train station (€17, 2½hr, five daily). Several buses stop in Deruta and Todi. Check the website for details.

TAXI

Available from 6am to 2am (24 hours from July to September); call ☏ 075 500 48 88 to arrange pick-up. A ride from the city centre to the main train station will cost about €10 to €15. Tack on €1 for each suitcase.

Torgiano

POP 6510

Vineyards and olive groves sweep up to this medieval walled town on a hilltop perch overlooking the confluence of the Chiascio and Tiber rivers. Torgiano has an irresistible draw for gastronomes, and is renowned for its thick, green, extra-virgin olive oil and spicy, peppery red wines, such as Rubesco Rosso DOC, produced with 70% sangiovese grapes.

Torgiano has a twinset of one-of-a-kind museums. First up is the **Museo del Vino** (Wine Museum; www.lungarotti.it/fondazione/muvit; Corso Vittorio Emanuele 31; adult/reduced incl Museo dell'Olivo e dell'Olio €7/4; ⊙10am-6pm daily summer, to 5pm & closed Mon winter), which takes a thematic romp through viticulture in a 20-room, 17th-century mansion. Greek, Etruscan and Roman ceramics, jugs and vessels, glassware and various wine-making

implements race you from the Bronze Age to the present, covering topics such as wine as medicine and its role in mythology. Showcasing mills, presses and crafts, the **Museo dell'Olivo e dell'Olio** (www.lungarotti.it/fondazione/moo; Via Garibaldi 10; adult/reduced incl Museo del Vino €7/4; ⊙10am-6pm daily summer, to 5pm & closed Mon winter) is an ode to olive oil and its symbolic, medicinal and dietary uses. Audioguides are included in the ticket price.

🛏 Sleeping & Eating

Al Grappolo d'Oro   HOTEL €€
(☏ 075 98 22 53; www.algrappolodoro.net; Via Principe Umberto 24; s €55, d €95-110; P ❄ 🛜 🛋) The view across vineyards from the tree-rimmed pool is soothingly beautiful at this bijou hotel in the centre of town. Smartly furnished 19th-century rooms are bright, serene and kept spotlessly clean. There's free bike hire if you fancy peddling off into the countryside. Breakfast is included.

Ristorante Siro   TRADITIONAL ITALIAN €€
(☏ 075 98 20 10; Via Giordano Bruno 16; meals €25) Overflowing with regulars, this convivial, picture-plastered restaurant is big on old-school charm. The mixed antipasti starter for two would feed a small family. Loosen a belt notch, next, for gnocchi cooked in Rubesco wine sauce, and mains such as wild boar stew and butter-soft steaks.

ℹ Getting There & Away

Umbria Mobilità (p567) *extraurbano* buses head to Perugia (€3, 30 minutes, nine daily).

Lago Trasimeno

A splash of inky blue on the hilly landscape, Lago Trasimeno is where Umbria spills over into Tuscany. Italy's fourth-largest lake is a prime spot if you want to tiptoe off the well-

---

DON'T MISS

TASTING OLIVE & GRAPE

The Lungarottis, who operate most of the wineries around here, are the closest thing Umbria has to a ruling noble family these days. At their wine estate, **Cantine Giorgio Lungarotti** (☏ 075 988 66 49; http://lungarotti.it; Viale Giorgio Lungarotti 2; ⊙9am-12.30pm & 3-6pm Mon-Fri, 9am-12.30pm & 3-6pm Sat), you can take a spin of their cellars and taste the fruits of their labours. A basic €12 tasting gets you three wines: a full-bodied Rubino red; a citrusy, straw-coloured Torre di Giano white; and Grifone, a fresh, floral rosé. For the more expensive tastings (€18 to €25), they'll crack open some of their best bottles. All tastings are accompanied by Umbrian bread and extra-virgin olive oil. Stock up on Lungarotti wine, olive oil, balsamic vinegar and brandy in the *enoteca* (wine bar).

POT LUCK IN DERUTA

If Torgiano is a two-note town, then **Deruta**, a few kilometres to the south, has just the one: majolica ceramics. The blue and yellow metallic-oxide glazing technique imported from Majorca in the 15th century has been the mainstay of the local industry ever since.

For the best-quality stuff, eschew factory mass productions, which are cheaper and lower quality, in favour of the real deal at smaller workshops rooted in centuries-old tradition.

At **Maioliche Nulli** (☑ 075 97 23 84; www.maiolichenulli.com; Via Tiberina 142; ⊙ daily), Rolando Nulli creates each item by hand, while his brother Goffredo finishes them with intricate paintings, specialising in classic medieval designs. If they're not busy and you ask nicely in Italian, they might even bring you downstairs and teach you to throw a bowl on the wheel.

Get a taste for the genuine article and trace the history of pottery in Deruta from the 14th century to the 20th century at the **Museo Regionale della Ceramica** (Largo San Francesco; adult/reduced €5/4; ⊙ 10.30am-1pm & 3-6pm Wed-Sun), housed in the former Franciscan convent.

L'Antico Forziere (☑ 075 972 43 14; www.anticoforziere.it; Via della Rocca 2; s/d €75/100, incl half board €113/138, meals €30-40; ⊙ restaurant Tue-Sun; P ✱ ✲), a 17th-century farmhouse turned stylishly rustic *agriturismo*, resides in the dozy hamlet of **Casalina**, just south of Deruta. Here twin-brother celebrity chefs Stefano and Andrea Rodella wow foodies with their culinary high-wire theatrics. Their inventive menu brims with season-inspired, artistically assembled showstoppers like chive-flavoured beer risotto with brie and 30-month-aged parmesan and smoked guinea fowl with gorgonzola mousse – all washed down with excellent wines.

Buses connect the town with Perugia (€3.50, 30 minutes, 13 daily).

trodden trail for a spell and slip into the languid rhythm of lake life. Around this 128 sq km lake, silver-green olive groves, vines, woods of oak and cypress and sunflower fields frame castle-topped medieval towns, such as Castiglione del Lago and Passignano, which are draped along its shores like a daisy chain. A gentle and unhurried ambiance hangs over the lake's trio of islands – Maggiore, Minore and Polvese – all wonderfully relaxing escapes.

Hannibal destroyed the Roman army here in 217 BC, and the lake's numerous fortifications attest to its strategic position and turbulent past.

⊙ Sights & Activities

Dotted with nature reserves and criss-crossed with well-signposted trails, Lago Trasimeno begs outdoor escapades. For the inside scoop on activities from hiking and cycling to sailing and wine tasting, visit www.lagotrasimeno.co.uk.

Ask at any of the tourist offices around the lake or in Perugia for a booklet of walking and horse-riding tracks. Horse-riding centres include **La Rosa Canina** (☑ 075 835 06 60; www.larosacanina.com; Via dei Mandorli 23, Panicale), to the south of the lake.

One of the best places to base yourself is **Castiglione del Lago**, which has a fine beach where you can lounge, swim, windsurf, or hire a pedalo or kayak, as well as a sprinkling of cultural attractions. A covered passageway connects **Palazzo della Corgna** (Piazza Gramsci; adult/reduced €3/2 incl Rocca del Leone; ⊙ 10am-1pm & 4-7.30pm summer, 9.30am-4.30pm Sat & Sun winter), a 16th-century ducal palace housing frescoes by Giovanni Antonio Pandolfi and Salvio Savini, with the 13th-century **Rocca del Leone** fortress a stellar example of medieval military architecture.

The lake's main inhabited island – **Isola Maggiore**, near Passignano – was reputedly a favourite with St Francis. The hilltop **Chiesa di San Michele Arcangelo** contains a crucifixion painted by Bartolomeo Caporali dating from around 1460. You can also visit the mostly uninhabited island and environmental lab at **Isola Polvese** on a day trip with Fattoria Il Poggio.

🛏 Sleeping

⭐ **Fattoria Il Poggio**   HOSTEL €
(☑ 075 965 95 50; www.fattoriaisolapolvese.com; Isola Polvese; dm €18, d €40-56, apt €80, meals €12-14; ⊙ Mar-Oct, reception closed 3-7pm; @ 🛜 ♿)

It's an HI youth hostel but you'd never know it. Nestled in gardens on the tranquil islet of Isola Polvese, this eco-minded farmstead has bright, spick-and-span rooms and gorgeous lake views. If you don't mind catching a ferry back by 7pm, you'll be rewarded handsomely with a family-style meal prepared with organic produce and homegrown herbs.

The people that run the place are lovely – whether you want to go canoeing or fishing, learn about macrobiotic cooking or sign up for a reiki or yoga course, just say the word.

La Casa sul Lago HOSTEL €
(☑ 075 840 00 42; www.lacasasullago.com; Via del Lavoro 25, Torricella di Magione; dm €18, r per person €25-30, meals €15; ℗ @ 🛜 🚮 🎦) This is one of central Italy's top-rated hostels. The private rooms could be in a three-star hotel, and guests have access to every amenity known to hostelkind: bicycles and wi-fi (both free!), games, home-cooked meals, an outdoor pool and a garden with hammocks strung between the trees for whiling away a lazy afternoon – all within 50m of the lake.

Il Torrione B&B €
(☑ 075 95 32 36; www.iltorrionetrasimeno.com; Via delle Mura 4, Castiglione del Lago; s €50, d/apt €70-80) Romance abounds at this artistically minded tranquil retreat. Each room is decorated with artworks painted by the owner, and a private flower-filled garden overlooks the lake, complete with chaises longues

---

THROUGH THE GRAPEVINE

One look at the olive groves draped across the hillsides and the vineyards that slide down to the lake shores gives Trasimeno's gastronomic game away. Vines and olives thrive in the local microclimate, and locals are justifiably proud of their top-quality DOC red and white wines, as well as their goldgreen DOP olive oils. The **Strada del Vino Colli del Trasimeno** (☑ 075 84 74 11; www.stradadelvinotrasimeno. it) is made for slow touring, taking in cantine (wineries) and cellars offering tastings, farms and agriturismi where you can sleep off the overindulgence. Visit the website for the lowdown on five mapped wine-related itineraries, or pick up a brochure at the tourist office in Castiglione del Lago.

---

from which to watch the sunset and a 16th-century tower. Rent the tower room (up a flight of pirate-ship stairs) for an intimate private apartment. Breakfast included.

La Torre HOTEL €
(☑ 075 95 16 66; www.latorretrasimeno.com; Via Vittoria Emanuele 50, Castiglione del Lago; s €40-70, d €45-100; ❄ 🐾 🛜) Housed in a lovingly renovated, whitewashed *palazzo* in Castiglione's historic centre, La Torre extends a warm, family-run welcome. The spotless, old-style rooms are decorated in florals and a chalk box of pastels. Breakfast is delicious but costs €6 extra.

Camping Badiaccia CAMPGROUND €
(☑ 075 965 90 97; www.badiaccia.com; Via Pratovecchio 1, Badiaccia; camping 2 people, car & tent €24; ℗ @ 🛜 🚮 🎦) Right on the lakefront, this tree-shaded campground is kid heaven, with a playground, pizzeria, tennis courts, a private beach, two pools, mini golf and loads of activities to keep the *bambini* (and their parents) amused. Kayaks, bikes and pedalos are available for hire.

★ **Casale della Staffa** AGRITURISMO €€
(☑ 075 847 26 02; www.casaledellastaffa.com; Case Sparse 7, Magione; s/d/tr/q €100/120/145/170; 🐾 🚮) Ah, what a restful view! The vista reaches over vine, olive grove and hill from the poolside of this *agriturismo,* a beautifully converted 15th-century farmstead, situated 8km south of Magione. Beams, wrought-iron bedsteads and hand-woven fabrics add a dash of elegant rusticity to the large rooms. Breakfast is a fine spread, with homemade jams and pastries.

The kindly owners will willingly pack you up a picnic or arrange for you to go cycling or horse riding. Let them know in advance and they can also organise everything from painting and ceramics workshops to cookery classes.

🍴 Eating

Specialities of the Trasimeno area include *fagiolina* (little white beans), carp in *porchetta* (cooked in a wood oven with garlic, fennel and herbs) and *tegamaccio,* a kind of soupy stew of the best varieties of local fish, cooked in olive oil, white wine and herbs.

DivinPeccato TRATTORIA €€
(☑ 075 968 01 18; www.ristorantedivinpeccato.com; Via Trasimeno 95, Panicarola; menus €30-35; ☺ Thu-Tue) Chef Nicola works culinary magic at this wonderful trattoria, well worth the 10km

trek south of Castiglione del Lago. Homemade bread is an appetising lead to a menu fizzing with seasonal oomph – think duck breast in strawberry sauce, wild boar and ravioli in porcini sauce. Sommelier Mirko pairs the food with fine Umbrian wines drawn from the cellar. Perfection.

Ristorante Monna Lisa UMBRIAN €€
(☑075 95 10 71; www.ristorantemonnalisa.com; Via del Forte 2, Castiglione del Lago; meals €30-35; ☺daily summer, Thu-Tue winter) You can imagine Mona Lisa giving a wry smile of approval to the food served at this intimate, art-strewn restaurant in the heart of town. You, too, will be smiling about specialities like *fagiolina*, carpaccio of wild boar on rocket, and rich stews prepared with Trasimeno lake fish. The spaghetti vongole deserves a gold star, too.

La Cantina UMBRIAN €€
(☑075 965 24 32; Via Vittoria Emanuele 91, Castiglione del Lago; meals €20-30; ☺Tue-Sun) Sunset is primetime lake viewing from the flowery terrace of this old-town restaurant, housed in a converted 17th-century olive mill. A fire warms the brick-vaulted interior in the cooler months. It does terrific wood-oven pizza for pocket-money prices, as well as local fare like trout with *fagiolina*.

❶ Information

Tourist office (☑075 965 24 84; info@iat. castiglione-del-lago-pg.it; Piazza Mazzini 10; ☺8.30am-1pm & 3.30-7pm Mon-Sat, 9am-1pm Sun) Advises on *agriturismi* and activities like cycling and water sports, and has an impressive collection of maps.

❶ Getting There & Around

BICYCLE
You can hire bikes at most campgrounds or at **Cicli Valentini** (☑075 95 16 63; www.ciclivalentini.it; Via Firenze 68b; per half-/full day €8/10; ☺9am-8pm Mon-Sat).

BUS
Umbria Mobilità (p567) buses link Perugia with Passignano (€4, one hour, 10 daily) and Castiglione del Lago (€6, one hour, nine daily).

CAR & MOTORCYCLE
Two major highways skirt the lake: the SS71, which heads from Chiusi to Arezzo on the west side (in Tuscany); and SS75bis, which crosses the north end of the lake, heading from the A1 in Tuscany to Perugia.

FERRY
Umbria Mobilità (p567) ferry services run from late March to late September. Hourly ferries head from San Feliciano to Isola Polvese (€5.60 return, 10 minutes), Tuoro to Isola Maggiore (€5.60 return, 10 minutes), Castiglione del Lago to Isola Maggiore (€7.50 return, 30 minutes) and Passignano to Isola Maggiore (€6.80 return, 25 minutes). Ferries stop running around 7pm.

TRAIN
Services run roughly hourly from Perugia to Passignano (€3, 35 minutes) and Castiglione del Lago (€4.40 to €10.50, 50 minutes), and twice daily to Torricella (€2.40, 25 minutes).

Todi
POP 16,900

A collage of soft-stone houses, *palazzi* and belfries pasted to a hillside, Todi looks freshly minted for a fairy-tale. Wandering its steeply climbing backstreets is like playing a game of medieval snakes and ladders. The pace of life inches along, keeping time with the wildflowers and vines that seasonally bloom and ripen in the valley below.

Like rings around a tree, Todi's history can be read in layers: the interior walls show Todi's Etruscan and even Umbrian influence, the middle walls are an enduring example of Roman know-how, and the 'new' medieval walls boast of Todi's economic stability and prominence during the Middle Ages.

◉ Sights

Just try to walk through the **Piazza del Popolo** without feeling compelled to sit on the medieval building steps and write a postcard home. The 13th-century **Palazzo del Capitano** links to the Palazzo del Popolo to create what is now the **Museo Pinacoteca e Museo della Città di Todi** (Piazza del Popolo; admission €3.10; ☺10am-1.30pm & 3-6pm summer, 10.30am-1pm & 2.30-5pm Tue-Sun winter) holding a fine (if hardly overwhelming) collection of paintings, and a rather more successful archaeological section – lots of old coins and ceramics.

The **cathedral** (☑075 894 30 41; Piazza del Popolo; ☺8.30am-1pm & 3.30-6.30pm), at the northwestern end of the square, has a magnificent rose window. You can skip it, however, to visit two of Umbria's most impressive churches. The lofty **Tempio di San Fortunato** (Piazza Umberto 1; ☺10am-1pm & 2.30-7pm summer, 10am-1pm & 2.30-5pm Wed-Mon winter) has frescoes by Masolino da Panicale and holds the tomb of Beato Jacopone, Todi's beloved patron saint. Inside, make it a point to climb the Campanile di San Fortunato (adult/reduced €1.50/1; ☉ 10am-1pm & 3-6.30pm summer, 10.30am-1pm & 2.30-5pm winter, closed Mon), where views of the hills and castles surrounding Todi await.

The postcard you've just written from the Piazza del Popolo? Most likely it's of Todi's famed church, the late-Renaissance masterpiece Chiesa di Santa Maria della Consolazione (Via della Consolazione; ☉ 9.30am-12.30pm & 2.30-6.30pm summer, 9.30am-12.30pm & 2.30-5pm Wed-Mon winter). Inside, architecture fans can admire its geometrically perfect Greek cross design.

☆ Festivals & Events

Todi Arte Festival   CULTURAL
(www.todiartefestival.com) Held for 10 days each September, this is a mixture of classical and jazz concerts, theatre, ballet and cinema.

🛏 Sleeping

San Lorenzo Tre   B&B €
(☑ 075 894 45 55; www.sanlorenzo3.it; Via San Lorenzo 3; s €55-95, d €75-110, ste €85-150; @) Five generations of the same family have lived at this 17th-century abode. Awaiting guests are rooms full of character, with polished brick floors, delicately painted beams and carefully chosen antiques. There's no TV, but books to browse, in keeping with the blissfully laid-back vibe. Breakfasts are home-cooked and the garden terrace has magical views.

Fonte Cesia   BOUTIQUE HOTEL €€
(☑ 075 894 37 37; www.fontecesia.it; Via Lorenzo Leonj 3; s €80-120, d €90-219, ste €180-219; P ❄ @) Just south of the main square, this renovated 17th-century *palazzo* has great old-world charm. The rooms are a bit small,

but come with elegant antique touches, and some have views of the surrounding hills. The suites step up the romance – one has a jacuzzi tub, another a canopy bed.

Todi Castle   HISTORIC HOTEL €€€
(☑ 074 495 20 04; www.todicastle.com; Vocabolo Capecchio; villa per week €1250-4950, castle per week €3250-7300; P ☎ ❄ 🐾) Here's your chance to live in an honest-to-goodness castle, or in one of three beautiful (and more affordable) villas. With private pools, medieval ruins, a deer park and staff waiting on you hand and foot (including arranging babysitting and farm visits for the kids), you'll feel positively royal.

🍴 Eating

Bar Pianegiani   GELATO €
(Corso Cavour 40; ☉ 6am-midnight Tue-Sun) Around 50 years of tradition has created the world's most perfect gelato. Try the black cherry (*spagnola*) or hazelnut (*nocciola*).

Antica Hosteria de la Valle   OSTERIA €€
(☑ 075 894 48 48; Via Ciuffelli; meals €25-40; ☉ Tue-Sun) Art vies with food for top billing at this most creative of restaurants. John and his wife, Eleanor, make you incredibly welcome and their seasonally inspired menus are a delight. Truffles find their way onto plenty of dishes (try them with *tagliolini*) of tender filet of beef. There are only a handful of tables and it's popular, so book ahead.

Pizzeria Ristorante Cavour   PIZZERIA €€
(☑ 075 894 37 30; Coro Cavour 21; meals €20-30; ☉ Tue-Sun) If it's a fine day, bypass the brick-vaulted interior and head straight outside to the terrace for towering views. Try the thin-crust pizza or house specialities like fettuccine with goose *ragù* (meat and tomato sauce).

WORTH A TRIP

NARNI – THE MAGICAL HEART OF ITALY

Like Greenwich or the North Pole, Narni is a place best known for where it is, almost slap-bang at the geographical centre of Italy. You can walk to a stone marking the exact spot just outside the town. But Narni has a lot more going for it than merely being the answer to a trivia question. It boasts one of the finest medieval town centres in Umbria, with a collection of churches, piazzas, *palazzi* and fortresses that are quite magical – and fittingly so given that CS Lewis used the Roman name for the town (plucked at random from an ancient atlas) for his own fictional magical kingdom: Narnia.

The town lies 21km south of Todi, just east of the A1 autostrada (from the south take the Magliano Sabina exit; from the north the Orte exit) and is well served by buses from Terni (€3, 30 minutes) and Orvieto (€6.50, 1½ hours).

❶ Information

Post office (Piazza Garibaldi 4; ⊘8.20am-1.35pm Mon-Fri, 8.20am-12.35pm Sat)

Tourist office (📋075 895 62 27; Piazza del Popolo 38; ⊘9.30am-1pm & 3-6pm Mon-Sat, 10am-1pm Sun)

❶ Getting There & Away

Umbria Mobilità (p567) operates buses between Todi and Perugia (€6.50, 1¼ hours, nine daily).

By car, Todi is easily reached on the SS3bis-E45, which runs between Perugia and Terni, or take the Orvieto turn-off from A1 (the Milan–Rome–Naples route).

Trains run to Perugia (€5.10, 50 minutes, 18 daily). Although the train station is 3km away, city bus C (€1.50, eight minutes) coincides with arriving trains, and every other hour on Sunday.

Assisi

POP 27,400

As if cupped in celestial hands, with the plains spreading picturesquely below and Monte Subasio rearing steep and wooded above, the mere sight of Assisi in the rosy glow of dusk is enough to send pilgrims' souls spiralling to heaven. It is at this hour, when the pitter-patter of daytripper footsteps have faded and the town is shrouded in saintly silence, that the true spirit of St Francis of Assisi, born here in 1181, can be felt most keenly.

◉ Sights

★**Basilica di San Francesco** CHURCH
(Piazza di San Francesco; ⊘upper church 8.30am-6.45pm summer, to 6pm winter, lower church 6am-6.45pm summer, to 6pm winter) **FREE** Visible for miles around, the Basilica di San Francesco is the jewel in the spiritual and architectural crown of Assisi's Unesco World Heritage ensemble. For almost six centuries, its twinset of churches have been a beacon to knee-crawling, blister-footed pilgrims, brown-robed friars, Italian art lovers and saintly sightseers.

The half-light and architectural restraint of the Romanesque lower church best embodies the ascetic, introspective spirit of Franciscan life, while the brighter upper church is a Gothic wonder, containing an elaborate tableau of frescoes. Divine works by Sienese and Florentine masters like Giotto, Cimabue, Pietro Lorenzetti and Simone Martini represent an artistic weather-vane for stylistic developments across the ages.

The basilica has its own **information office** (📋075 819 00 84; ⊘9.15am-noon & 2.15-5.30pm Mon-Sat), opposite the entrance to the lower church. Here you can schedule an hour-long tour in English or Italian, led by a resident Franciscan friar. Guided tours are from 9am to 5pm Monday to Saturday; a donation of €5 to €10 per person is suggested.

Rocca Maggiore FORT
(Via della Rocca; adult/reduced €5/3.50; ⊘10am-sunset) Dominating the city is the massive 14th-century Rocca Maggiore, an oft-expanded, pillaged and rebuilt hill-fortress offering 360-degree views of Perugia to the north and the surrounding valleys below. Walk up winding staircases and claustrophobic passageways to reach the archer slots that served Assisians as they went medieval on Perugia.

Basilica di Santa Chiara CHURCH
(Piazza Santa Chiara; ⊘6.30am-noon & 2-7pm summer, to 6pm winter) Built in the 13th century in a Romanesque style, with steep ramparts and a striking white and pink facade, the basilica was raised in honour of St Clare, a spiritual contemporary of St Francis and founder of the Sorelle Povere di Santa Chiara (Order of the Poor Ladies), now known as the Poor Clares. She is buried in the church's crypt. The Byzantine cross that is said to have spoken to St Francis is also housed here.

Basilica di Santa Maria degli Angeli CHURCH
(Santa Maria degli Angeli; ⊘6.15am-12.30pm & 2.30-7.30pm) That enormous domed church you can see as you approach Assisi along the Tiber Valley is the 16th-century Basilica di Santa Maria degli Angeli, the seventh largest church in the world, some 4km west and several hundred metres further down the hill from old Assisi.

Built between 1565 and 1685, its vast ornate confines house the tiny, humble **Porziuncola Chapel**, where St Francis first took refuge having found his vocation and given up his worldly goods, and which is generally regarded as the place where the Franciscan movement started. St Francis died at the site of the **Cappella del Transito** on 3 October 1226.

Eremo delle Carceri RELIGIOUS
(www.eremocarceri.it; ⊘6.30am-7pm summer, to 6pm winter) **FREE** In around 1205 St Francis chose these caves above Assisi as his hermit-

UMBRIA & LE MARCHE ASSISI

Assisi

0 200 m
0 0.1 miles

Basilica di
San Francesco

8 1

Piazza Superiore
di San Francesco

Basilica
di San Francesco
Information Office

Via San Giacomo

14

17

Via D'Stella

V Frate Elia

Piazza
Unità
d'Italia

Porta San
Pietro

Intercity
Bus Station

Alla Madonna
del Piatto (8km)

Via Frate Elia

Via Giorgetti

Via Fontebella

Via San Francesco

Via Metastasio

Via San Croce

Via Brizi

Via San Paolo

Via Aluigi

Via Capobove

Via Giotto

Via S Maria delle Rose

Piazzetta
Garibaldi 15

Via B da Quintavalle

Via Antonio Crisofani

Via del Fosso Cupo

Via Borgo San Pietro

Viale Vittorio Emanuele

Via S. Apollinare

Chiesa di San
Damiano (1.5km)

Ostello della Pace (2.5km);
Basilica di Santa Maria
degli Angeli (4km)

Viale G Marconi

Via della Rocca

Via del Colle

6

Piazza del
Comune

7

Via Macelli Vecchi

18

3

Via Sant'Antonio

Piazza
Vescovado

Via Sant'Agnese

Via Acro
dei Priori 20

12

Via San Rufino
19 16

Via S Gabriele dell'Addolorata

Corso Mazzini
9

Piazza San
Rufino

4

Via Porta Perlici

Via Porta Mojano

Via Porta S Chiara

Piazza Santa
Chiara

Via S Chiara

2

Piazza S
Chiara

13

Via Galeazzo Alessi

10

Viale Umberto I

APM Bus
Station

Piazza
Matteotti

11

Via Eremo delle Carceri

Vicolo Bovi

Via Villamena

Eremo
delle Carceri
(3.5km)

P

5

APM (250m)

APM

(4km)

Assisi

age where he could retire to contemplate spiritual matters and be at one with nature. The *carceri* (isolated places, or 'prisons') along Monte Subasio's forested slopes are as peaceful today as in St Francis' time, albeit now surrounded by various religious buildings.

Take a contemplative walk or picnic under the oaks. It's a 4km drive (or walk) east of Assisi, and a dozen nearby hiking trails are well signposted.

Chiesa di San Damiano   CHURCH
(Via San Damiano; ⊘ 10am-noon & 2-6pm summer, to 4.30pm winter) It's a 1.5km olive tree-lined stroll to the church where St Francis first heard the voice of God and where he wrote his *Canticle of the Creatures*. The serene surroundings are popular with pilgrims.

Foro Romano   HISTORIC SITE
(Roman Forum; Via Portica; adult/reduced €4/2.50, with Rocca Maggiore €8/5; ⊘ 10am-1pm & 2.30-6pm summer, to 5pm winter) On Piazza del Comune, just round the corner from the tourist office, is the entrance to the town's partially excavated Roman Forum, while on

the piazza's northern side is the well-preserved facade of a 1st-century Roman temple, the **Tempio di Minerva** (Temple of Minerva; admission free; ⊘ 7.30am-noon & 2-7pm Mon-Sat, 8.30am-noon & 2-7pm Sun) hiding a rather uninspiring 17th-century church.

Duomo di San Rufino   CHURCH
(Piazza San Rufino; ⊘ 8am-1pm & 2-7pm summer, to 6pm winter) The 13th-century Romanesque church, remodelled by Galeazzo Alessi in the 16th century, contains the fountain where St Francis and St Clare were baptised. The facade is festooned with grotesque figures and fantastic animals.

Chiesa Nuova   CHURCH
(Piazza Chiesa Nuova; ⊘ 6.30am-noon & 2.30-6pm summer, to 5pm winter) Just southeast of the Piazza del Comune, this domed church is a peaceful place for contemplation. It was built by King Philip III of Spain in the 1600s on the spot reputed to be the house of St Francis' family. A bronze statue of the saint's parents stands outside.

Activities

To really feel the spirituality of Assisi, do as St Francis did and make the pilgrimage into the surrounding wooded hills. Many make the trek to **Eremo delle Carceri** or **Santuario di San Damiano** on foot. The tourist office has several maps, including a route that follows in St Francis' footsteps to Gubbio (18km). A popular spot for hikers is nearby **Monte Subasio**. Local bookshops sell walking and mountain-biking guides and maps for the area.

Bicycle rentals are available at **Angelucci Andrea Cicli Riparazione Noleggio** (☑075 804 25 50; www.angeluccicicli.it; Via Risorgimento 54a; bike rental per hr/day €5/20) in Santa Maria degli Angeli.

Festivals & Events

The **Festa di San Francesco** falls on 3 and 4 October and is the main religious event in the city. **Settimana Santa** (Easter Week) is celebrated with processions and performances.

Festa di Calendimaggio   CULTURE
(www.calendimaggiodiassisi.com) This festival takes a joyous leap into spring with flamboyant costumed parades, jousting and other medieval fun. It starts the first Thursday after 1 May.

CHURCH TOUR

Basilica di San Francesco

➡ **Length**: 1½ hours

➡ **See** p583

Entering the Romanesque **lower church**, immediately to your left is the **Cappella di San Martino**, bearing the imprint of Sienese genius Simone Martini, whose 10-piece fresco cycle (1313–1318) spells out the life and deeds of St Martin of Tours. Pietro Lorenzetti's frescoes depicting **The Passion of Christ** (1320) dance across the walls of the left transept, while Cimabue's **Madonna Enthroned with Child, St Francis and Four Angels** (1289) will hold you captive in the right transept. The vault above the high altar showcases the quadriptych allegorical marvel of the **Quattro Vele** (1315–20), an ode to St Francis' virtues of poverty, chastity and obedience, alongside a fresco showing the saint's apotheosis. Descend to the crypt to the **Tomb of St Francis**. Hidden for almost 600 years, it was discovered in 1818 following a 52-day dig, and painstakingly restored in 2011.

Steps lead from the courtyard to the **upper church**, the brighter twin of the two, lit by a cosmatesque rose window. In the **nave** draw your gaze heavenwards to cross-rib vaults shimmering with tiny stars like a midnight sky. The walls are a giant canvas for one of the world's greatest works of art: the 28 fresco cycle **Life of St Francis** (1297–1300), widely attributed to Florentine master Giotto, though this is still a bone of contention for art historians. Contemplate emotive works such as the *Renunciation of Worldly Goods*, *Miracle of the Spring* and *Death and Ascension of St Francis*. Painted in the spirit of artistic devotion, they are a fascinating window on the life of the poverty-preaching saint. Above them, frescoes depicting scenes from the **Old and New Testament** unfold, from the *Creation of the World* through to the *Three Marys at the Sepulchre*. Decay and oxidation have reduced Cimabue's frescoes (1280) in the apse and transepts to ghostly silhouettes, rendering them all the more enigmatic; **The Crucifixion** shows St Francis kneeling below the cross.

🛏 Sleeping

Keep in mind that in peak periods such as Easter, August and September, and during the Festa di San Francesco, you will need to book accommodation well in advance. The tourist office has a list of private rooms, religious institutions (of which there are 17), flats and *agriturismi* in and around Assisi.

St Anthony's Guesthouse B&B €
(☎ 075 81 25 42; atoneassisi@tiscali.it; Via Galeazzo Alessi 10; s/d/tr €45/65/85; ⊙ Mar–mid-Nov; [P]) Look for the iron statue of St Francis feeding the birds and you've found your Assisian oasis – a peaceful convent run by sweet sisters. Rooms are spartan but welcoming and six have balconies with breathtaking views. Olive tree-shaded gardens and an 800-year-old breakfast room make this a heavenly choice. There is a two-night minimum stay and an 11pm curfew.

Ostello della Pace HOSTEL €
(☎ 075 81 67 67; www.assisihostel.com; Via Valecchie 177; dm €17, d €44; ⊙ 1 Mar-8 Nov & 27 Dec-6 Jan; [P] [@]) Snug below the city walls and housed in a beautifully converted 17th-century farmhouse, this hostel is a charmer. The dorms and handful of private rooms are kept spick and span and the well-tended gardens have magical views of Assisi, crowned by the dome of its famous basilica. Find it just off the road coming in from Santa Maria degli Angeli.

Hotel Ideale B&B €
(☎ 075 81 35 70; www.hotelideale.it; Piazza Matteotti 1; s/d €50/85; [P] [✳] [🛜]) Ideal indeed, this welcoming family-run B&B sits plumb on Piazza Matteotti. Romeo the cat has the run of the shop. Many of the bright, simple rooms open onto balconies with uplifting views of the Rocca Maggiore. Breakfast is done properly, with fresh pastries, fruit and frothy cappuccino, and is served in the garden when the weather's fine.

★ Alla Madonna del Piatto AGRITURISMO €€
(☎ 075 819 90 50; www.incampagna.com; Via Petrata 37; d €85-105; ⊙ Mar-Nov; [P] [🐾]) Waking up to views of meadows and olive groves sweeping up to Assisi is bound to put a spring in your step at this quiet *agriturismo*, less than

15 minutes' drive from the basilica. Each of the six rooms has been designed with care, love and character, with wrought-iron beds, antique furnishings and intricate handmade fabrics.

If you can tear yourself away from the vine-draped terrace, hook onto one of the intimate cooking classes, which Letizia runs (in Italian or English) twice a week. Start the day in local markets and finish it off with a feast of your own creation. Six-hour classes cost €120 per person. There's a minimum two-night stay.

Hotel Alexander   B&B €€
(☑075 81 61 90; www.hotelalexanderassisi.it; Piazza Chiesa Nuova 6; s €60-80, d €80-140; ❄🛜) Right by the Chiesa Nuova, Hotel Alexander has just a few rooms. Try to get the one on the top floor, which is huge and has great countryside views. It can get a bit noisy at times, owing both to the location and the sparse, modern decor (wooden floors, no rugs), which provides a nice contrast to the carefully preserved antiquity all around.

Nun Assisi   LUXURY HOTEL €€€
(☑075 815 51 50; www.nunassisi.com; Via Eremo delle Carceri 1a; s €230-280, d €280-330, ste €320-550; 🅿@❄🛜) This former convent has been reborn as a super-stylish boutique hotel, with a clean, modern aesthetic. Stone arches and beams provide original flair in pared-down rooms with virginal white walls and flat-screen TVS. The restaurant (meals €30 to €40) puts a contemporary spin on seasonal Umbrian fare, and the gorgeous subterranean spa is set within 1st-century Roman ruins.

Residenza D'Epoca San Crispino   HISTORIC HOTEL €€€
(☑075 815 51 24; www.assisibenessere.it; Via Sant'Agnese 11; ste €150-330; @📶) Big on medieval charm, this 14th-century mansion has soul-stirring views of Assisi from its gardens. Each of the generously sized suites is different, but all have oodles of character, with original vaulting and eye-catching features such as fireplaces, four-poster beds and antique trappings. It's a short stroll to the Basilica di Santa Chiara. Breakfast is included.

✕ Eating & Drinking

Pizzeria da Andrea   PIZZERIA €
(Via San Ruffino 26; pizza slice €1.20; ⏱8.30am-8.30pm) The go-to place on the square for perfectly thin, crisp *pizza al taglio* (by the slice) and *torta al testo* (filled Umbrian flat bread) for a fistful of change.

Trattoria Pallotta   UMBRIAN €€
(☑075 81 26 49; www.pallottaassisi.it; Vicolo della Volta Pinta; set menus €18-27; ⏱lunch & dinner Wed-Mon; ✏) Head through the Volta Pinta off Piazza del Comune – being careful not to bump into someone as you gaze at the 16th-century frescoes above you – into this gorgeous setting of vaulted brick walls and wood-beamed ceilings. They cook all the Umbrian classics here: rabbit, homemade *strangozzi* (wheat noodles) and pigeon.

Osteria dei Priori   UMBRIAN €€
(☑075 81 21 49; Via Giotto 4; meals €25-35; ⏱Tue-Sun) Sabrina believes wholeheartedly in sourcing the best local ingredients at this wonderfully cosy *osteria*, where tables draped in white linen are gathered under brick vaults. Presuming you've booked ahead, you're in for quite a treat: Umbrian specialities like Norcina (pasta in a creamy mushroom-sausage sauce) and rich wild boar stew are brilliantly fresh, full of flavour and beautifully presented.

La Locanda del Podestà   UMBRIAN €€
(☑075 81 65 53; www.locandadelpodesta.it; Via San Giacomo 6; meals €20-30; ⏱daily) This inviting cubbyhole of a restaurant is big on old-world charm, with low arches and stone walls. Distinctly Umbrian dishes such as *torta al testo*

ALL SAINTS

As saintly performances go, Umbria has a star-studded cast. Besides being the much-venerated birthplace of St Francis, the region has given rise to two other greats: St Benedict and the Casanova of the saint world, St Valentine. St Benedict, founder of the Benedictine rule and western monasticism, was born in 480 AD in Norcia. St Valentine, meanwhile, was a bishop from Terni, allegedly martyred on 14 February 273 AD. His remains are entombed in the Basilica di San Valentino, now a much-loved wedding venue and the scene of a great feast on St Valentine's Day. Want to impress someone special? You could draw back your cupid bow and bring them here for a romantic weekend – it sure beats a bunch of petrol station roses. For inspiration, visit www.sanvalentinoterni.it.

The Saint of Assisi

That someone could found a successful movement based on peace, love, compassion, charity and humility in any age is remarkable; that Francis Bernardone was able to do it in war-torn 13th-century Umbria was nothing short of a miracle. But then again, in his early years Francis was very much a man of the times – and anything but saintly.

Not-So-Humble Beginnings

Born in Assisi in 1181, the son of a wealthy cloth merchant and a French noblewoman, Francis was a worldly chap: he studied Latin, spoke passable French, had a burning fascination with troubadours and spent his youth carousing. In 1202 Francis joined a military expedition to Perugia and was taken prisoner for nearly a year until his father paid ransom. Following a spate of ill health, he enlisted in the army of the Count of Brienne and was Puglia-bound in 1205 until a holy vision sparked his spiritual awakening.

Life & Death

Much to the shock horror and ridicule of his rich, pleasure-seeking friends, Francis decided to renounce all his possessions in order to live a humble, 'primitive' life in imitation of Christ, preaching and helping the poor. He travelled widely around Italy and beyond, performing miracles such as curing the sick, communicating with animals, spending hermit-like months praying in a cave, and founding monasteries. Before long, his wise words and goodly deeds had attracted a faithful crowd of followers.

St Francis asked his followers to bury him in Assisi on a hill known as Colle

d'Inferno (Hell Hill), where people were executed at the gallows until the 13th century, so as to be in keeping with Jesus, who had died on the cross among criminals and outcasts.

Saintly Spots

Today various places claim links with St Francis, including Greccio in Lazio where he supposedly created the first (live) nativity scene in 1223; Bevagna in Umbria where he is said to have preached to the birds; and La Verna in Tuscany where he received the stigmata shortly before his death at the age of 44. He was canonised just two years later, after which the business of 'selling' St Francis began in earnest. Modern Assisi, with its glorious churches and thriving souvenir industry, seems an almost wilfully ironic comment on Francis' ascetic and spiritual values.

TOP ST FRANCIS SITES

➡ **Assisi** (p583) His home town and the site of his birth and death, his hermitage, his chapel, the first Franciscan monastery and the giant basilica containing his tomb.

➡ **Gubbio** (p591) Where the saint supposedly brokered a deal between the townsfolk and a man-eating wolf – he tamed the wolf with the promise that it would be fed daily.

➡ **Rome** Francis was given permission by Pope Innocent III to found the Franciscan order at the Basilica di San Giovanni in Laterano (p97).

1. Basilica di San Francesco, Assisi
2. Basilica di San Giovanni, Rome
3. Interior of the Basilica di San Francesco, Assisi

with prosciutto and truffle-laced *strangozzi* are expertly matched by regional wines. Friendly service adds to the familiar vibe.

Ristorante Metastasio ITALIAN €€

(☑ 075 81 65 25; Via Metastasio 9; meals €20-30; ⊘ Thu-Tue) Sunset makes the terrace of this restaurant a magnet – the valley below Assisi spreading picturesquely before you. The food is good, too, particularly spot-on pasta dishes such as pappardelle with porcini and wild boar.

Bibenda Assisi WINE BAR

(www.bibendaassisi.it; Via Nepis 9; ☎) Everyone has been singing the praises of this rustic-chic wine bar recently. Here you can taste regional *vini* with tasting plates of local *salumi e formaggi* (cold meats and cheeses). Nila will talk you through the wine list.

Gran Caffè CAFE

(Corso Mazzini 16; ⊘8am-11pm) Head here for fabulous gelato, pastries, cakes and coffee. The *tè freddo alla pesca* (iced tea with peach) is refreshing on a hot day.

❶ Information

Post office (Porta San Pietro; ⊘8.20am-1.45pm Mon-Fri, to 12.45pm Sat)

Tourist office (☑ 075 813 86 80; www.assisi.regioneumbria.eu; Piazza del Comune 22; ⊘8am-2pm & 3-6pm Mon-Sat, 10am-1pm & 2-5pm Sun summer, 9am-1pm Sun winter) Stop by here for maps, leaflets and info on accommodation.

❶ Getting There & Around

BUS

Umbria Mobilità (p567) run buses run to Perugia (€4, 45 minutes, nine daily) and Gubbio (€6.50, 70 minutes, 11 daily) from Piazza Matteotti. **Sulga** (☑ 075 500 96 41; www.sulga.it) buses leave from Porta San Pietro for Florence (€12, 2½ hours, one daily at 7am) and Rome's Stazione Tiburtina (€18.50, 3¼ hours, three daily).

CAR & MOTORCYCLE

From Perugia take the SS75, exit at Ospedalicchio and follow the signs. In town, daytime parking is all but banned. The nearest car park to the old town is on Piazza Giovanni Paolo II; parking costs €1 per hour.

TAXI

For a cab, call ☑ 075 81 31 00.

TRAIN

Assisi is on the Foligno–Terontola train line with regular services to Perugia (€2.50, 20 minutes, hourly). You can change at Terontola for Florence (€14.50 to €21, two to three hours, 11 daily) and at Foligno for Rome (€10 to €22, two to three hours, 14 daily). Assisi's train station is 4km west in Santa Maria degli Angeli; shuttle bus C (€1, 13 minutes) runs between the train station and Piazza Matteotti every 30 minutes. Buy tickets from the station *tabaccaio* or in town.

Spello
POP 8620

Sometimes it seems like it's just not possible for the next Umbrian town to be prettier than the last. And then you visit Spello: a higgledy-piggledy ensemble of honey-coloured houses spilling down a hillside, guarded by three stout Roman gates and chess-piece towers.

Come summer, the green-fingered locals try to outdo each other with their billowing hanging baskets and flowerpots, filling the streets with a riot of colour and scent.

◉ Sights

A leisurely stroll is the best way to click into Spello's easygoing groove. Begin at **Porta Consolare**, which dates from Roman times, then head towards Piazza Matteotti, the heart of Spello, where the impressive 12th-century **Chiesa di Santa Maria Maggiore** (Piazza Matteotti; ⊘8.30am-12.30pm & 3-7pm Mar-Oct, to 6pm Nov-Feb) houses the town's real treat. In its **Cappella Baglioni**, Pinturicchio's beautiful frescoes of the life of Christ are in the right-hand corner as you enter. Even the floor, dating from 1566, is a masterpiece. Stay in the same piazza for the gloomier **Chiesa di Sant'Andrea** (Piazza Matteotti; ⊘8am-7pm), where you can admire Pinturicchio's *Madonna with Child and Saints*.

To see the view of all views, head up past the **Arco Romano** to the **Chiesa di San Severino**. The active Capuchin monastery is closed to the public but its Romanesque facade is so stunning you'll have trouble deciding whether you'd like to gaze at its architecture or the bucolic countryside view below.

✦ Festivals & Events

Corpus Domini RELIGIOUS

The people of Spello celebrate this feast in June (the Sunday 60 days after Easter) by skilfully decorating the main street with fresh flowers in colourful designs. Come on the Saturday evening before the Sunday procession to see the floral fantasies being laid out (from about 8.30pm). The Corpus procession begins at 11am on Sunday.

🛏 Sleeping

Agriturismo il Bastione   AGRITURISMO €

(☑ 320 6761004; www.bastione.it; Via Fontemonte 3; d €75-90, incl half-board €125-140; @ 🖶) What a delight this medieval farmstead is! On the slopes of 1290m Monte Subasio and surrounded by olive trees, the *agriturismo* has stirring views over patchwork plains and hills. The rooms and suites have a cosily rustic flavour, with wrought-iron beds, beams and stone walls. Dinner, served in the barrel-vaulted restaurant, is a feast of homegrown produce.

You could easily hole up here for a day or two to cycle (mountain bikes are available), ride horses, or hike through the Monte Subasio nature park to Assisi, around 6km distant.

La Residenza dei Cappuccini   B&B €

(☑ 331 4358591; www.residenzadeicappuccini.it; Via Cappuccini 5; d €50-65; 🖥) Up the steep, winding lane lies this little gem of a B&B, which plays up the historic charm with its atrium of exposed stone and beams. All rooms come with kitchenettes and a DIY breakfast basket. Loveliest of all is Saio, with its own fireplace. If you fancy a hack in the hills, the owners can arrange for you to go horse riding.

Palazzo Bocci   HISTORIC HOTEL €€

(☑ 0742 30 10 21; www.palazzobocci.com; Via Cavour 17; s/d/ste €100/160/230; 🅿 ❄ 🖥 🖶) Within the walls of this 17th-century *palazzo*'s lavishly frescoed salon, you get a real sense of Spello's history. Quarters are understated yet elegant, with tiled floors and beams or ceiling murals. There's a garden terrace with soothingly lovely country views and a restaurant ensconced in a 14th-century mill, which makes the most of Umbrian produce such as Norcia truffles.

🍴 Eating & Drinking

Osteria del Buchetto   OSTERIA €€

(☑ 0742 30 30 52; Via Cappuccini 19; meals €25-30; ⊙ Tue-Sun) Right at the top of town near the Roman arch, you eat at a raised platform with romantic views of the valley towards Assisi. The food is proudly local, and lingering positively encouraged. Perhaps start with the *strangozzi* with truffles (or, if in season, asparagus), and move on to the specialty – expertly grilled steaks.

Enoteca Properzio   WINE BAR

(☑ 074 230 1521; www.enotecaproperzio.com; Palazzo dei Canonici, Piazza Matteotti 8; ⊙ 9am-11pm summer, 9am-8pm winter) At the most charming *enoteca* in town, for €30 you can try a half-dozen Umbrian wines while snacking on cheese, prosciutto and bruschetta.

ℹ Information

Tourist office (Pro Loco; ☑ 074 230 1009; www.prospello.it; Piazza Matteotti 3; ⊙ 9.30am-12.30pm & 3.30-6pm) Has town maps, a list of accommodation options and walking maps, including an 8km walk across the hills to Assisi.

ℹ Getting There & Away

CAR & MOTORCYCLE

Spello is on the SS75 between Perugia and Foligno.

TRAIN

There are services at least hourly to Perugia (€3, 30 minutes) and Assisi (€1.70, 10 minutes). The station is often unstaffed, so buy your tickets at either the self-service ticket machine. It's a 10-minute walk into town.

Gubbio

POP 32,400

While most of Umbria feels soft and rounded by the millennia, Gubbio is angular, sober, imposing and medieval through and through. Perched on the steep slopes of Monte Ingino, the Gothic buildings wend their way up the hill towards Umbria's closest thing to a theme-park ride, its open-air *funivia*.

👁 Sights

★ Funivia Colle Eletto   LOOKOUT

Although the **Basilica di Sant'Ubaldo**, perched high up on Monte Ingino, is a perfectly lovely church, the real adventure is reaching it on the **funivia** (adult/reduced €5/4; ⊙ 9am-8pm daily summer, 10am-5pm Thu-Tue winter; 🖶), as exhilarating as any roller-coaster. The word *funivia* suggests an enclosed cable car, but it's actually a ski lift of sorts, whisking visitors up the mountain in precarious-looking metal baskets.

In order to board you have to stand on a red dot and then get thrown into a basket by the operator as it whizzes past – health and safety be damned. Once the giddiness has worn off, you can watch Gubbio, which

Gubbio

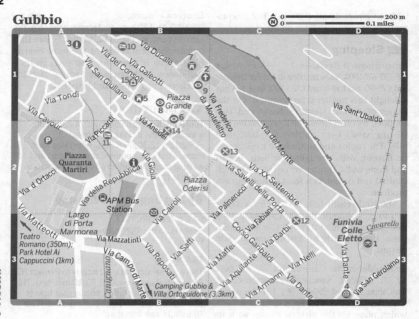

Map scale: 0 — 200 m / 0 — 0.1 miles

Gubbio

◉ Top Sights

◉ Sights

🛏 Sleeping

✴ Eating

🛍 Shopping

moments before had seemed so impossibly hilly, gradually transform into a flat little toy town far below. The entire valley spreads picturesquely before you from the top.

The basilica, which can't help but come as a bit of an anticlimax after the approach, displays the body of St Ubaldo, the 12th-century bishop of Gubbio, in a glass coffin above the altar. It also has a small museum dedicated to the Corsa dei Ceri where you can see the massive statues carried through the streets during the town's most popular festival, the Corsa dei Ceri. There's a cafe on top of the hill by the *funivia* entrance, but the nicest way to spend the day is to bring a picnic and have a wander.

Piazza Grande   PIAZZA

Gubbio's medieval showpiece is Piazza Grande, where the Corsa dei Ceri event takes place. The piazza is dominated by the 14th-century **Palazzo dei Consoli**, attributed to Gattapone – its crenelated facade and tower can be seen from all over the town. The building houses the **Museo Civico** (Piazza Grande; adult/reduced €5/2.50; ⏰10am-1pm & 3-6pm summer, 10am-1pm & 2.30-5.30pm winter), which displays the famous Eugubian Tablets, discovered in 1444. Dating from between 300 and 100 BC, these seven bronze tablets are the best existing example of the ancient Umbrian script. Upstairs is a picture gallery featuring works from the Gubbian school, while downstairs – and accessed round the back – is a small archaeological museum. Across the square is the **Palazzo del Podestà**, built along similar lines to its grander counterpart, and now the active town hall.

Via Federico da Montefeltro STREET
(cathedral donations welcome; ☉10am-5pm, cathedral 10am-5pm) Walk up Via Ducale to the Via Federico da Montefeltro where you'll encounter a triumvirate of ancientness, beginning at the 13th-century pink **cathedral** (Via Federico da Montefeltro; donations welcome; ☉10am-5pm), with a fine 12th-century stained-glass window and a fresco attributed to Bernardino Pinturicchio. Opposite, the 15th-century **Palazzo Ducale** (adult/reduced €5/2.50; ☉8.30am-7.30pm) was built by the Duke of Montefeltro's family as a scaled-down version of their grand *palazzo* in Urbino. Next door is the **Museo Diocesano** (adult/reduced €5/2.50; ☉10.30am-6pm Tue-Sun), an art gallery tracing 2000 years of ecclesiastical history.

Museo della Maiolica a Lustro MUSEUM
(Via Dante 24; admission €2.50; ☉10.30am-1pm & 3.30-7pm) Just below the Funivia Colle Eletto, this museum is dedicated to the *a lustro* ceramic style, which has its origins in 11th-century Muslim Spain. Up in the tower, on the 2nd floor, ceramics from prehistoric times share space with medieval and Renaissance pieces.

Fontana dei Pazzi MONUMENT
In front of the 14th-century **Palazzo del Bargello**, the city's police station and prison in medieval times, stands the Fontana dei Pazzi (Fountain of the Lunatics), so-named because of a belief that you'll go mad if you run around it three times. On summer weekends, the number of visitors carrying out this ritual does indeed pose questions about the collective sanity!

Teatro Romano HISTORIC SITE
(Roman Theatre; ☉8.30am-7.30pm Apr-Sep, 8am-1.30pm Oct-Mar) FREE Southwest of Piazza Quaranta Martiri, off Viale del Teatro Romano, are the overgrown remains of a 1st-century Roman theatre.

 Festivals & Events

Corsa dei Ceri CULTURE
(www.ceri.it) The 'Candles Race' is a centuries-old event held each year on 15 May to commemorate the city's patron saint, Sant'Ubaldo. It starts at 5.30am and involves three teams, each carrying a *cero* (massive wooden pillars weighing about 400kg, each bearing a statue of a 'rival' saint) and racing through the city's streets. This is one of Italy's liveliest festivals and has put Gubbio on the map.

Palio della Balestra CULTURE
On the last Sunday in May, Gubbio gets out its medieval crossbows for its annual archery competition with regional rival Sansepolcro. The festival carries over all year in tourist shops alive with rather scary-looking crossbow paraphernalia.

Sleeping

Camping Gubbio & Villa Ortoguidone CAMPGROUND €
(☎075 927 20 37; www.gubbiocamping.com; Loc Ortoguidone, Cipoletto 49; camping 2 people, car & tent €29; ☉Easter-Sep; ☒) This campground is a sure-fire family-pleaser, with terrific facilities including a tennis court, jacuzzi, pool, playground and snack bar. From the SS298, follow the signs for 3km to 'Agriclub Villa Ortoguidone'.

Residenza di Via Piccardi HISTORIC HOTEL €
(☎075 927 61 08; www.residenzadiviapiccardi.it; Via Piccardi 12; s/d €40/60) Step through the arched gate into the romantic garden of this period residence. Share an amorous breakfast for two in the garden or cook up a simple dinner in the mini-apartment's kitchenette. Family-owned, the medieval stone building has cosy rooms decorated in cheery florals, with all the basic comforts.

Relais Ducale HOTEL €€
(☎075 922 01 57; www.relaisducale.com; Via Galeotti 19; s €75-105, d €85-175; @) You'll need to be in shape, as this hotel is a stiff walk up the

 CENT SAVER

The tourist office sells the good-value Gubbio Turisticard (€7), which gives you a return ride on the funivia, an audioguide and entry to the Museo della Maiolica a Lustro, plus discounts on all other key sights.

UMBRIA & LE MARCHE GUBBIO

DON'T MISS

OH CHRISTMAS TREE!

Listed by the *Guinness Book of Records* in 1991 and flicked on by Pope Benedict XVI from the Vatican in 2011 and Italian president Giorgio Napolitano in 2012, Gubbio's shimmering, 650m-high whopper of a Christmas tree is officially the world's biggest. Spreading up the slopes of Monte Ingino and topped by a shooting star, its 3000 photovoltaic-powered lights are visible from miles afar and draw visitors to the medieval town in their thousands between 7 December (Immaculate Conception) and 6 January (Epiphany). For details of this year's light fantastic event, visit www.alberodigubbio.com.

hill and two flights of steps, but it's worth it. Set in a converted annex of the Ducale Palace, its rooms are utterly charming, with polished wood floors and antique furnishings; one even has a barrel-vaulted stone ceiling. The flowery terrace overlooks Piazza della Signoria.

Park Hotel
Ai Cappuccini   BOUTIQUE HOTEL €€€
(✆ 075 92 34; www.parkhotelaicappuccini.it; Via Tifernate; s €140-190, d €160-240, meals €35-45; P❄❅⛱❄) Silence still hangs like a monk's habit over this stunningly converted 17th-century monastery, which skillfully intertwines history with contemporary comfort. Rooms are classically elegant, with fine fabrics and lots of polished wood. Its own art gallery, an excellent restaurant serving Mediterranean cuisine, an indoor pool and spa, and beautiful gardens all make this one of the top places to stay in town.

✗ Eating

For a quick pastry or pizza, try the snack bars on Corso Garibaldi and Via dei Consoli.

Picchio Verde   TRADITIONAL ITALIAN €
(✆ 075 927 66 49; www.ristorantepicchioverde.com; Via Savelli della Porta 65; meals €15-25; ☺ daily) Huddled away in the old town, the 'green woodpecker' attracts a faithful local following for its cosy vaulted interior, authentic food and modest prices. Homemade pasta (try the *mezzelune* stuffed with braised hare) segues smoothly into mains of meat grilled to perfection over an open fire. The

two-course lunch including wine, water and coffee is a snip at €15.

Ristorante Ulisse e Letizia   UMBRIAN €€
(✆ 075 922 19 70; Via Mastro Giorgio 2; meals €25-35; ☺ Tue-Sun) Dine below wood beams in this atmospheric, stone-walled restaurant, occupying a restored ceramics workshop. The vibe is warm and familiar, and most of the food (including the olive oil and pasta) is either made in-house or (in the case of the mushrooms and truffles) sourced locally.

Taverna del Lupo   UMBRIAN €€€
(✆ 075 927 43 68; www.tavernadellupo.it; Via Ansidei 21; meals €35-45; ☺ Tue-Sun) Soft light casts flattering shadows across the barrel-vaulted interior of Gubbio's most sophisticated restaurant, serving Umbrian cuisine with a pinch of creativity and a dash of medieval charm. It's a class act, with tables draped in white linen and polished service. Flavours ring true in specialities like ravioli in asparagus-porcini sauce and tender capon with truffles, expertly matched with wines.

🛍 Shopping

Leo Grilli Arte   ARTISANAL
(Via dei Consoli 78) In the Middle Ages, ceramics were one of Gubbio's main industries, and there are some fabulous contemporary samples for sale in this crumbly 15th-mansion.

ℹ Information

Post office (✆ 075 927 39 25; Via Cairoli 11; ☺ 8am-6.30pm Mon-Fri, 9am-12.30pm Sat)
Tourist office (✆ 075 922 06 93; www.comune.gubbio.pg.it; Via della Reppublica 15; ☺ 8.30am-1.45pm & 3.30-6.30pm Mon-Fri, 9am-1pm & 3-6.30pm Sat & Sun) Sells the Gubbio Turisticard and lends out multilingual audioguides (€3).

ℹ Getting There & Around

Gubbio has no train station but Umbria Mobilità (p567) buses run to Perugia (€5.50, 1¼ hours, 10 daily) from Piazza Quaranta Martiri.

By car, take the SS298 from Perugia or the SS76 from Ancona, and follow the signs.

Spoleto

POP 39,300

Presided over by a formidable medieval fortress and backed by the broad-shouldered Apennines, their summits iced with snow in winter, Spoleto is visually stunning. The hill town is also something of a historical picnic:

the Romans left their mark in the form of grand arches and an amphitheatre; the Lombards made it the capital of their duchy in 570, building it high and mighty and leaving it with a parting gift of a Romanesque cathedral in the early 13th century.

Today, the town has winged its way into the limelight with its mammoth Festival dei Due Mondi, a 17-day summer feast of opera, dance, music and art.

◉ Sights

Rocca Albornoziana   FORT, MUSEUM
(Piazza Campello; adult/reduced €7.50/6.50; ⊗9.30am-7.30pm summer, to 6.30pm winter) Rising high and mighty on a hilltop above Spoleto, the Rocca, a glowering 14th-century former papal fortress, is now a fast, scenic escalator ride from Via della Ponzianina. The fortress contains the Museo Nazionale del Ducato, which traces the history of the Spoleto Duchy through a series of Roman, Byzantine, Carolingian and Lombard artefacts, from 5th-century sarcophagi to Byzantine jewellery.

Museo Archeologico   MUSEUM
(Via S Agata; adult/reduced €4/2; ⊗8.30am-7.30pm) Down in the centre of town, the prime draw is the town's archaeological museum, located on the western edge of Piazza della Libertà. It holds a well-displayed collection of Roman and Etruscan bits and bobs from the area, spread over four floors.

You can step outside to view the mostly intact 1st-century Teatro Romano (Roman amphitheatre), which often hosts live performances during the summer; check with the museum or the tourist office.

Museo Carandente   MUSEUM
(www.palazzocollicola.it; Piazza Collicola; adult/reduced €4/3; ⊗10.30am-1pm & 3.30-7pm Wed-Sun) Formerly the Galleria d'Arte Moderna, the town's premier collection of modern art has been renamed after its late former director and noted art critic, Giovanni Carandente, and significantly revamped. The collection is dominated by works of late-20th-century Italian artists, including the sculptor Leonardo Leoncillo.

Casa Romana   HISTORIC BUILDING
(Roman House; Via di Visiale; adult/reduced €3/2; ⊗11am-7pm Wed-Mon summer, to 5pm winter) This excavated Roman house isn't exactly Pompeii, but it gives visitors a peek into what a typical home of the area would have looked like in the 1st century BC. Just to the south, near the Piazza Fontana, stand the remains of the Arco di Druso e Germanico (Arch of Drusus and Germanicus, named for the sons of Emperor Tiberius), which once marked the entrance to the Roman forum.

Duomo di Spoleto   CATHEDRAL
(Piazza Duomo; ⊗8.30am-12.30pm & 3.30-7pm summer, to 6pm winter) A flight of steps sweeps down to Spoleto's pretty pale-stone cathedral, originally built in 11th century, using huge blocks of salvaged stones from Roman buildings for its slender bell tower. A 17th-century remodelling saw a striking Renaissance porch added. The rainbow swirl of mosaic frescoes in the domed apse was executed by Filippo Lippi and his assistants.

Lippi died before completing the work and Lorenzo de Medici travelled to Spoleto from Florence and ordered Lippi's son, Filippino, to build a mausoleum for the artist. This now stands in the right transept of the cathedral.

Museo del Tessile e del Costume   MUSEUM
(Museum of Textiles and Costumes; Via delle Terme; adult/reduced €3/2.50; ⊗3-7pm Sat & Sun) Housed in the Palazzo Rosari-Spada, just around the corner from the revamped modern art museum, this museum holds a collection of antique noble finery from the 15th to the 20th century donated from the wardrobes of the some of the area's leading families.

Chiesa di San Pietro   CHURCH
(Località San Pietro; ⊗9am-6.30pm summer, 9am-noon & 3.30-5pm winter) An hour-long stroll can be made along the Via del Ponte to the Ponte delle Torri, which was erected in the 14th century on the foundations of a Roman aqueduct. Cross the bridge and follow the lower path, Strada di Monteluco, to reach the church where the 13th-century facade is liberally bedecked with sculpted animals.

◉ Giro dei Condotti

As impressive as the Rocca is, its ramparts are the irresistible draw for photographers, keen walkers and anyone who appreciates a jaw-dropping view. Many people literally draw breath the first time they glimpse the medieval Ponte delle Torri, a 10-arch bridge that leaps spectacularly across a steeply wooded gorge – a scene beautifully captured by Turner in his 1840 oil painting. To maximise the incredible vista, slip on a

Spoleto

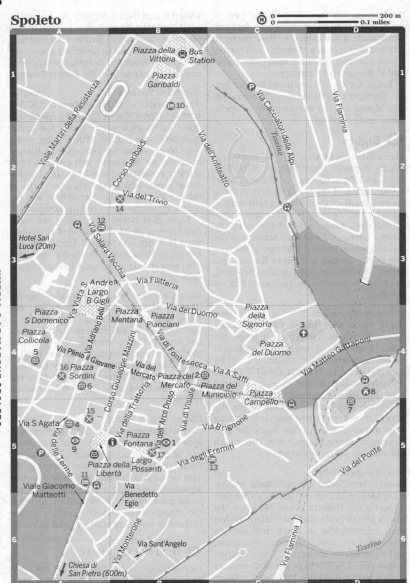

Piazza della Vittoria

Bus Station

Piazza Garibaldi

Piazza della Resistenza

Via Cacciatori delle Alpi

Via Flaminia

Via dell'Anfiteatro

Tessino

Viale Martiri della Resistenza

Corso Garibaldi

Via del Trivio

Hotel San Luca (20m)

Via Salara Vecchia

Via Filitteria

Via S Andrea

Largo B Gigli

Piazza S Domenico

Piazza Collicola

Via Viata S Adriano Belli

Piazza Mentana

Piazza Pianciani

Via del Duomo

Piazza della Signoria

Piazza della Signoria

Piazza del Duomo

Via Plinio il Giovane

Corso Giuseppe Mazzini

Via del Mercato

Via di Fontesecca

Piazza del Mercato

Via A Saffi

Piazza del Municipio

Piazza Sordini

Piazza Campello

Via Matteo Gattaponi

Via S Agata

Via delle Terme

Via della Trattoria

Via dell'Arco Druso

Via di Visiale

Via Brignone

Piazza Fontana

Via degli Eremiti

Piazza della Libertà

Largo Possenti

Via del Ponte

Viale Giacomo Matteotti

Via Benedetto Egio

Via Monterone

Via Sant'Angelo

Via Flaminia

Tessino

Chiesa di San Pietro (600m)

pair of comfy shoes to walk the 6km **Giro dei Condotti**, which takes you along sun-dappled woodland trails to a lookout with a classic postcard view of the bridge, valley and fortress-crowned hilltop.

✦ Festivals & Events

Spoleto Festival ARTS
(www.festivaldispoleto.it; ⊘ late Jun–mid-Jul) The Italian-American composer Gian Carlo Menotti conceived the Festival dei Due Mondi (Festival of Two Worlds) in 1958.

UMBRIA & LE MARCHE SPOLETO

Spoleto

Now simply known as the Spoleto Festival, it has given the town a worldwide reputation. Events at the 17-day festival range from opera and theatre performances to ballet and art exhibitions. For details and tickets, visit the website.

🛏 Sleeping

Stop by the tourist office for info on *affitta-camere* (rooms for rent), hostels, campsites and *agriturismi* in the surrounding area. Prices rocket during the festival and drop considerably during low season; good deals can often be snapped up at the following places by prebooking online.

Much of the pedestrianised old town is off-limits to traffic – hotels generally give you a free pass to park outside the medieval walls.

L'Aura B&B €
(074 34 46 43; Piazza Torre dell'Olio 5; s €40-50, d €60-70; P@) You'll feel as snug as an Italian bug at this cute B&B on the top floor of a 200-year-old *palazzo*. Claudia makes you welcome and gives excellent tips on Spoleto. It's a tidy, homey place, with bright, wood-beamed rooms and a terrace overlooking rooftops to the hills beyond. There's no lift, so be prepared to schlep your bags up the stairs.

Hotel dei Duchi HOTEL €€
(074 34 45 41; www.hoteldeiduchi.com; Viale Giacomo Matteotti 4; s €75-85, d €90-200; P❄@🛜) Next to a tidy park just outside the old town, this is a purpose build rather than a renovation. So although the rooms are spacious, contemporary and well kept, they aren't exactly oozing old-world charm. Its elevated position gives it fine views of the countryside and, slightly closer to home, the Roman theatre from the terrace.

Cavaliere Palace HISTORIC HOTEL €€
(074 322 03 50; www.hotelcavaliere.eu; Corso Garibaldi 49; s €70, d €80-115, tr €110-150; ❄🛜) Housed in a 17th-century *palazzo*, this hotel affords a slice of affordable luxury. The interior is charming, with classically elegant rooms gathered around an inner courtyard and a secluded garden. Best of all is the breakfast room, where you can nibble pastries and sip a perfectly frothy cappuccino surrounded by original frescoes.

Hotel San Luca BOUTIQUE HOTEL €€
(074 322 33 99; www.hotelsanluca.com; Via Interna delle Mura 21; ☺s €110-240, d €210-300; ❄@🛜) Once a convent and now a heavenly boutique hotel, the San Luca has polished service and refined interiors to rival any of the five-stars in Umbria, yet the atmosphere is relaxed enough to cater to cyclists and walkers. Pastel tones and antique furnishings inside complement the 17th-century manicured garden. The homemade cakes are the stars of the breakfast buffet.

Palazzo Leti GUESTHOUSE €€€
(074 322 49 30; www.palazzoleti.com; Via degli Eremiti 10; s €110-200, d €130-250; P❄@🛜) In the southeast part of town facing the hills, this beautifully converted 13th-century noble palace exudes romance and charm down to the last detail, from the delicate breakfast china to the historical oak and wrought-iron furnishings. With the view and perfect silence, you'll feel like you're staying in the country, but you're a three-minute walk from the centre of Spoleto.

🍴 Eating

★ **Tempio del Gusto** MODERN ITALIAN €€
(074 34 71 12; www.iltempiodelgusto.com; Via Arco di Druso 11; meals €25-40; ☺Fri-Wed) Intimate, inventive and unmissable, Tempio del Gusto is fine dining without the Michelin-starred price tag. The food here speaks volumes about a chef who believes in sourcing,

HUNTERS AND GATHERERS

Gastronomically speaking, Norcia is a town of hunters and gatherers. As the country's cured-meat capital, its shops brim with delectable pork and wild boar prosciutto, salami and sausages. In fact, the word 'Norcineria' has become synonymous with 'butcher' throughout Italy.

Pigs aren't the only animals that like to snuffle around in the undergrowth of the surrounding oak woods, however. The area is also one of the region's largest producers of the elusive *tartufo nero*, unearthed by dogs led by a *cavatore*, or truffle hunter. Should you wish to embark on your own tuber treasure hunt, Palazzo Seneca offers **truffle-hunting** packages, or ask the tourist office to put you in touch with local guides heading out in search of culinary gold.

If you're here on the last weekend in February or the first weekend in March, you're in for a treat at the **Mostra Mercato del Tartufo Nero** (www.neronorcia.it) festival, where thousands turn out to taste and buy wonderful truffles and *salumi* direct from the producers.

cooking and presenting with real pride and purpose. Eros Patrizi is the whiz behind the stove. Freshly made pasta, a trio of smoked fish, herb-crusted pork – every dish strikes perfect balance.

Osteria del Trivio
OSTERIA €€

(☎074 34 43 49; Via del Trivio 16; meals €25-30; ☽Wed-Mon, closed Jan) Strings of garlic and dried peppers and old black-and-white family photos grace the walls of this most homey of restaurants run by a husband-and-wife team. This is a great place to try the *strangozzi alla spoletina* (local pasta in a tangy tomato sauce), and the stuffed artichokes are legendary.

San Lorenzo
MODERN ITALIAN €€

(☎074 322 18 47; www.ristorantesanlorenzo.com; Piazza Sordini 6, Hotel Clitunno; meals €25-35; ☽daily) Next to an eponymous medieval chapel, this restaurant is sheer class, with its elegant interior of candlelight and crisp linen, silky smooth service and clean, refined Mediterranean flavours. Winningly fresh ingredients shine through in everything from *strangozzi* in tangy tomato-chilli sauce to filet of Argentine beef elevated with the zestiness of Sorrento lemons. There are wonderful wines to match.

Ristorante Apollinaire
UMBRIAN €€

(☎074 322 32 56; www.ristoranteapollinaire.it; Via S Agata 14; meals €25-35; ☽Wed-Sun) Flair and creativity meet Umbrian tradition at Apollinaire, where the chef brings nous and an artistic eye for detail to winningly fresh produce. On the menu you might find seasonal showstoppers like pork tenderloin in *pecorino* (sheep's milk cheese) sauce with wine-poached pears and rabbit in black

olive sauce. You are constantly enveloped in low wood-beamed ceilings and candlelight flickering against brick.

ℹ Information

Post office (Viale Giacomo Matteotti 2; ☽8.20am-7.05pm Mon-Fri, to 12.35pm Sat)

Tourist office (☎074 321 86 20; www.visitspoleto.it; Piazza della Libertà 7; ☽9am-1.30pm & 2.30-6.15pm Mon-Sat, 9am-1pm & 3-5pm Sun)

ℹ Getting There & Around

Umbria Mobilità (p567) buses run frequently to Norcia (€6, 50 minutes, seven daily).

Trains from the main station connect with Rome (€8 to €12.30, 1½ hours, hourly), Perugia (€4.80, one hour, nine daily) and Assisi (€3.25, 40 minutes, hourly). From the train station, about 1km from the centre, take city bus A, B or C for €1 to the Piazza dell Libertà (make sure the bus reads 'Centro').

By car, the city lies on the E45 and is an easy connection via the SS209 to the Valnerina.

Norcia & the Valnerina

After the thigh-challenging hill towns of western and northern Umbria, the flatter, less elevated prospects of Norcia can come as a relief. You'll still need to do something to work up an appetite, however. The merest mention of Norcia sends Italian gastronomes into raptures about the earthy delights of its *tartufo nero* (black truffle) and the prized *salumi* from its acorn-fed pigs, both of which feature prolifically on restaurant menus and in shop windows.

Crisp mountain air, picture-book medieval looks and the town's spiritual claim to fame as the birthplace of St Benedict are other reasons for lingering here. Norcia's other great draw is its proximity to the rugged, exhilarating wilderness of Monti Sibillini (p619). Almost as scenic is Norcia's own valley, the steep-sided Valnerina valley, brushed with wildflowers in summer, which is best explored on a meandering drive along the SS209.

◉ Sights

Often devastated by earthquakes – the last major rumble was in 1979 – Norcia's petite, walled centre is a joy to explore on foot. Its medieval buildings have been seriously patched up over the years, but the town has preserved its charm. On the centrepiece Piazza San Benedetto, a statue of Norcia's famous son, St Benedict, with hand outstretched in blessing, stands proud. The saint and his twin sister, St Scholastica, were born here to a well-to-do family in 480 AD, apparently in the Roman crypt of the 13th-century Basilica di San Benedetto (Piazza San Benedetto; ⊙9am-6pm). The church's pale, delicate facade gives way to a calm, contemplative interior, where monks often shuffle past bearing prayer books or on their way to Gregorian chant at 7.45pm. Filippo Napoletano's early 17th-century frescoes depict scenes from the life of the saint.

Next to the church is the 14th-century Palazzo Comunale, with a striking portico and belfry, while opposite lies the Castellina, a 16th-century papal fortress.

🛌 Sleeping & Eating

Hotel Grotta Azzura   HOTEL €€
(✆074 381 65 13; www.hotelgrottaazzurra.com; Via Alfieri 12; s €76-115, d €113-135; ❋) This 18th-century palazzo with suits of armour in the reception offers fabulous deals during the week and in winter. Cross-vaulted rooms are stately if a bit dark, complete with carved ceilings and recently upgraded bathrooms. Its restaurant is a tad touristy, but the food is excellent, making best use of the local truffles and other seasonal produce.

★Palazzo Seneca   HISTORIC HOTEL €€€
(✆074 381 74 34; www.palazzoseneca.com; Via Cesare Battisti 12; s €105-155, d €130-245, ste €300-700; ℗❋☎) Sometimes you truly feel like you live in a palace, even just for a night or two. Perhaps it's as you play chess in an leather chair in front of the fireplace or maybe it's with a soothing Thai massage in the subterranean spa. In family hands since

1850, Palazzo Seneca gives guests a tantalising glimpse of the high life.

Four-poster beds and marble bathrooms meld seamlessly with ancient stone walls and oak floors, and the accompanying Ristorante Vespasia is a gourmet delight. See the website of special themed packages, covering everything from cookery classes to truffle hunting.

Trattoria dal Francese   TRATTORIA €€
(✆074 381 62 90; Via Riguardati 16; meals €30; ⊙Sat-Thu) Maybe it's its presence in many of the Italian 'best restaurant' guides that keeps this trattoria permanently packed (and often turning away custom when other places are struggling for trade) or perhaps it's the quality of the food, which is a cut above even for this renowned foodie town. It's in Norcia, so expect a menu packed with piggy products (salami, ham, sausages), truffles and cheese.

Ristorante Vespasia   UMBRIAN €€€
(✆074 381 74 34; www.palazzoseneca.com; Via Cesare Battisti 10; meals €55-110; ⊙daily) Set in a 16th-century palazzo, the elegantly simple furnishings complement the understated gourmet cuisine. Try excellent homemade pasta with truffles or porcini mushrooms, or locally grown saffron to accompany risotto and local pork. Herbs come from its own garden. In warmer months, dine in the garden to jazz or blues.

ℹ Information

Casa del Parco (✆074 382 81 73; www.sibillini.net; Piazza San Benedetto; ⊙9.30am-12.30pm & 3.30-6.30pm) Has tourist information about the area, including Monti Sibillini.

ℹ Getting There & Around

Buses run to and from Spoleto (€6, 50 minutes, seven daily) and Perugia (€8.50, two hours, one daily).

By car, from Spoleto, take the SS209 to the SS396. The closest train station is in Spoleto.

Orvieto

POP 21,100

Sitting astride a volcanic plug of rock above fields streaked with vines, olive and cypress trees, Orvieto is visually stunning from the first. Like the love child of Rome and Florence and nestled midway between the two cities, history hangs over the cobbled lanes, medieval piazzas and churches of this

Orvieto

200 m
0.1 miles

Piazza Cahen

Funicular Station

Bus Station

Via Roma

Via Belisario

Corso Cavour

Via San Stefano

Via Montemarte

Via Porcari

Via Sollana

Via Postierla

Piazza Angelo da Orvieto

Piazza Marconi

Parco delle Grotte

Via da Orvieto

13

Via Cavallotti

Corso Cavour

Via Nebbia

5

20

1

4

12

Piazza XXIX Marzo

Piazza del Popolo

Fracassini Piazza

15

21

11

6 7

Piazza Duomo

Via degli Orti

Via di Loreto

Viale G Carducci

Via Gualtieri

Via del Duomo

9

Via Lorenzo Maitani

Piazza di Febei

17

8

Via della Misericordia

Via Luca Signorelli

Via Angelico

10

Via Saracinelli

Piazza Clementini

18

Via Pecorelli

Piazza della Repubblica

3

Via dell'Olmo

Via Magalotti

Via Garibaldi

16

Piazza San Giovenale

2

Via Malabranca

Via della Cava

Via Ripa Serancia

14

19

Locanda Palazzone (4.7km); Misia Resort (5.3km)

Orvieto

cinematically beautiful city. And few cathedrals in Italy can hold a candle to its wedding cake of a Gothic cathedral, which frequently elicits gasps of wonder with its layers of exquisite detail.

◉ Sights

Cattedrale di Orvieto CATHEDRAL
(☎076 334 11 67; www.opsm.it; Piazza Duomo; admission €3; ◷9.30am-7pm Mon-Sat, 1-6.30pm Sun summer, 9.30am-1pm & 2.30-5pm Mon-Sat, 2.30-5.30pm Sun winter) Nothing can prepare you for the visual feast that is Orvieto's Gothic cathedral, begun in 1290. The black-and-white marble banding of the main body of the church is overshadowed by the rainbow frescoes, jewel-like mosaics, bas-reliefs and delicate braids of flowers and vine – as intricate as embroidery – adorning the facade. Bathed gold at dusk, it is a soul-stirring sight to behold.

The building took 30 years to plan and three centuries to complete. It was started by Fra Bevignate and later additions were made by Sienese master Lorenzo Maitani, Andrea Pisano (of Florence Cathedral fame) and his son Nino Pisano, Andrea Orcagna and Michele Sanicheli.

Inside, Luca Signorelli's fresco cycle *The Last Judgement* shimmers with life. Look for it to the right of the altar in the **Cappella di San Brizio**. Signorelli began work on the series in 1499, and Michelangelo is said to have taken inspiration from it. Indeed, to some, Michelangelo's masterpiece runs a close second to Signorelli's work. The **Cappella del Corporale** houses a 13th-century altar cloth stained with blood that miraculously poured from the communion

bread of a priest who doubted the transubstantiation.

Next to the cathedral is the **Museo dell'Opera del Duomo** (Museale dell'Opera del Duomo di Orvieto; ☎076 334 24 77; www.museomodo.it; Piazza Duomo 26; €4, includes Palazzi Papali & Chiesa S Agostino; ◷9.30am-7pm summer, 10am-5pm Wed-Mon winter), which houses a clutter of religious relics from the cathedral, as well as Etruscan antiquities and works by artists such as Simone Martini and the three Pisanos: Andrea, Nino and Giovanni.

Orvieto Underground HISTORIC SITE
(www.orvietounderground.it; Piazza Duomo 24; adult/reduced €6/5; ◷tours 11am, 12.15pm, 4pm & 5.15pm daily) The coolest place in Orvieto (literally), this series of 440 caves has been used for millennia by locals for various purposes, including as WWII bomb shelters, refrigerators, wells and, during many a pesky Roman or barbarian siege, as dovecotes to trap the usual one-course dinner: pigeon (still seen on local restaurant menus as *palombo*).

The 45-minute tours (with English-speaking guides) leave from in front of the tourist office.

Museo Claudio Faina e Civico MUSEUM
(www.museofaina.it; Piazza Duomo 29; adult/reduced €4.50/3; ◷9.30am-6pm summer, 10am-5pm Tue-Sun winter) Stage your own archaeological dig at this fantastic museum opposite the cathedral. It houses one of Italy's foremost collection of Etruscan artefacts, including plenty of stone sarcophagi and terracotta pieces, as well as some significant Greek ceramic works.

MAKING THE MOST OF YOUR EURO

The **Carta Unica Orvieto** (www.cartaunica.it; adult/reduced €18/15) permits entry to the town's nine main attractions (including the Cappella di San Brizio in the cathedral, Museo Claudio Faina e Civico, Orvieto Underground, Torre del Moro and Museo dell'Opera del Duomo) and a round trip on the funicular and city buses. It can be purchased at many of the attractions, the tourist office, the Piazza Cahen tourist office and the railway station.

Torre del Moro   HISTORIC BUILDING
(Moor's Tower; Corso Cavour 87; adult/reduced €2.80/2; ⊙10am-8pm summer, 10.30am-1pm & 2.30-5pm winter) From the Piazza Duomo, head northwest along Via del Duomo to Corso Cavour and the 13th-century Torre del Moro. Climb all 250 steps for sweeping views of the city.

Chiesa di San Giovenale   CHURCH
(Piazza San Giovenale; ⊙8am-12.30pm & 3.30-6pm) At the western end of town is this stout little church, constructed in the year 1000. Its Romanesque-Gothic art and frescoes from the later medieval Orvieto school are an astounding contrast. Just to the north, you can enjoy towering views of the countryside from the town walls.

Museo Archeologico Nazionale   MUSEUM
(Piazza Duomo, Palazzo Papale; adult/reduced €3/1.50; ⊙8.30am-7.30pm) Ensconced in the medieval Palazzo Papale, the archaeological museum holds plenty of interesting artefacts, some over 2500 years old. Etruscan ceramics, necropolis relics, bronzes and frescoed chamber tombs are among the items on display.

Chiesa di Sant'Andrea   CHURCH
(Piazza della Repubblica; ⊙8.30am-12.30pm & 3.30-7.30pm) This 12th-century church, with its curious decagonal bell tower, presides over the Piazza della Repubblica, once Orvieto's Roman Forum and now lined with cafes. It lies at the heart of what remains of the medieval city.

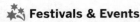

Festivals & Events

Palombella   RELIGIOUS
(⊙Pentecost Sun) For traditionalists, this rite has celebrated the Holy Spirit and good luck since 1404. For animal rights activists, the main event celebrates nothing more than scaring the living crap out of a bewildered dove. Take one dove, cage it, surround the cage with a wheel of exploding fireworks, and hurtle the cage 300m down a wire towards the cathedral steps. If the dove lives (it usually does), the couple most recently married in the cathedral becomes its caretakers.

Umbria Jazz Winter   MUSIC
(www.umbriajazz.com; ⊙late Dec-early Jan) This celebration of cool musical styles jazzes up the dull patches of winter, with a great feast and party on New Year's Eve.

Sleeping

It's always a good idea to book ahead in summer, on weekends, or if you're planning to come over New Year, when the Umbria Jazz Winter festival is in full swing.

B&B Michelangeli   B&B €
(☑076 339 38 62; www.bbmichelangeli.com; Via Saracinelli 22; s €60-100, d €70-160; ℗) Francesca is your kindly host at this sweet B&B in Orvieto's historical heart, just a two-minute toddle from the Duomo. What to expect? A bright, spacious apartment, scattered with homely trinkets and with a well-stocked kitchen where you can knock up a speedy pasta dish should you so wish. We love the beautiful wood carvings and wrought-iron beds.

B&B La Magnolia   B&B €
(☑349 4620733, 076 334 28 08; www.bblamagnolia.it; Via del Duomo 29; d €60-90; ❄) Tucked down a sidestreet north of the Duomo (the sign is easily missed), this light-filled Renaissance residence has delightful rooms and apartments, an English-speaking owner, a large shared kitchen and a balcony overlooking the rooftops. Serena can tell you all about Orvieto – whatever you want to know, just ask.

Villa Mercede   B&B €
(☑076 334 17 66; www.villamercede.it; Via Soliana 2; s/d/tr €50/70/90; ℗) Heavenly close to the *duomo*, with 23 rooms there's space for a gaggle of pilgrims. The building dates back to the 1500s, so the requisite frescoes adorn several rooms. High ceilings, a quiet garden

and free parking seal the deal. Vacate rooms each morning by 9.30am or you'll earn the housekeepers' wrath.

⭐**Misia Resort** BOUTIQUE HOTEL €€
(📞 076 334 23 36; Località Rocca Ripesena 51/52; s €80, d €130-160; ❄️📶♿) You won't regret going the extra mile to this boutique hotel on the rocks, with fabulous views of Orvieto from its hilltop hamlet perch. This stunning country house conversion has been designed with the utmost taste. The light, spacious rooms in soft, earthy tones come with retro-cool touches – a chesterfield sofa here, a distressed wood beam there.

They say that a hotel is only as good as its host, and Giorgio (together with his sidekick canine, Rocco) is as good as they get, welcoming you with a glass of wine and whipping up delicious breakfasts. Misia sits 6km west of Orvieto.

Hotel Duomo HOTEL €€
(📞 076 334 18 87; www.orvietohotelduomo.com; Vicolo di Maurizio 7; s €70-90, d €100-130, ste €120-160; 🅿️📶♿) Orvieto's captivating *duomo* is almost close enough to touch at Hotel Duomo, where the church bells will most likely be your wake-up call. This Liberty-style *palazzo*, where Orvieto-born artist Livio Orazio Valentini has left his bold, abstract imprint on the refined, neutral-hued rooms (all have marble bathrooms), has service both discreet and polite.

✖️ Eating

Pasqualetti GELATO €
(Piazza Duomo 14; 3-scoop cone €3) This gelateria serves mouth-watering gelato, plus there are plenty of tables on the piazza for you to gaze at the magnificence of the cathedral while you gobble.

Trattoria del Moro Aronne TRATTORIA €
(📞 076 334 27 63; www.trattoriadelmoro.info; Via San Leonardo 7; meals €20-30; ⊘ Wed-Mon) This sweet, simple living room of a trattoria has a convivial feel, authentic food and respectable prices. There's just a handful of tables – if you manage to snag one, you're in for a treat. Specialities like *scafata di fave fresche* (fava bean stew) and *nidi di rondine*, cheese-topped pasta nests, are a match made in heaven with Umbrian wines.

Trattoria dell'Orso TRATTORIA €€
(📞 076 334 16 42; Via della Misericordia 18; meals €25-35; ⊘ Wed-Sun) As the owner of Orvieto's oldest restaurant, Gabriele sees no need for such modern fancies as written menus, instead reeling off the day's dishes at you as you walk in the door. Go with his recommendations – perhaps the *zuppa di farro* (spelt soup) followed by fettuccine with porcini – as he knows what he's talking about. Be prepared to take your time.

Ristorante Zeppelin UMBRIAN €€
(📞 076 334 14 47; www.ristorantezeppelin.it; Via Garibaldi 28; meals €30-35; ⊘ Mon-Sat, lunch Sun; 🍴♿) This natty place has a cool 1920s atmosphere, jazz on the stereo and a long wooden bar where Ingrid Bergman would have felt right at home. Cheery waiters bring creative Umbrian food to the table, including such local delights as homemade *umbrichelli* pasta (spaghetti's Umbrian sister) and wild boar stewed in black olive, cherry tomato and cocoa sauce.

A TASTE OF ORVIETO

If you're keen to slip on an apron and get behind the stove, Orvieto's the place. At Ristorante Zeppelin, English-speaking chef Lorenzo Polegri whips up an Umbrian feast at his one-day cookery classes, where you'll learn to prepare specialities such as wild boar ragout and hand-rolled *umbricelli* pasta. He also prepares a five-course menu as the culinary climax of truffle hunts, and runs market mornings and tours of local *pecorino*, olive oil and wine producers. Prices range from €50 to €120 per person and full details are given on the website.

Decugnano dei Barbi (📞 076 330 82 55; www.decugnanodeibarbi.com; Località Fossatello 50) estate, perched above vineyards 18km east of Orvieto, offers unique tastings and four-hour cookery classes. The winery can trace its viticultural lineage back 800 years and the lovely master sommelier Anna Rita will guide you through its cellars and talk you through a tasting of its minerally whites and full-bodied Orvieto Classico reds. Or sign up in advance to assemble a four-course meal together with Rosanna, paired (naturally) with homegrown wines and served in the atmospheric surrounds of a converted chapel.

DON'T MISS

ORVIETO'S WINE COUNTRY

Now famed for its white DOC vintages, Orvieto's wine-growing potential was first spotted by the Etruscans more than 2000 years ago. They were attracted not just by the ideal soil and climate, but also by the soft tufa rock that underpins much of the landscape from which deep cool cellars could be (and indeed still are) cut to allow the grapes to ferment. From the Middle Ages onwards, Orvieto became known across Italy and beyond for its super-sweet gold-coloured wines. Today these have largely given way to drier vintages, such as Orvieto and Orvieto Classico.

If you want to see (and more importantly taste) what the fuss is about, head to Orvieto's **Enoteca Regionale dell'Umbria** (☑ 076 334 18 18; www.ilpalazzodelgusto.it; Via Ripa Serancia 16; ⊙ 11am-1pm & 5-7pm Mon-Fri summer, 11am-1pm & 3-5pm winter) in the Palazzo del Gusto where you can sample a huge range of wines for between €8 and €30.

To really immerse yourself in the world of viticulture, spend a night or two at the **Locanda Palazzone** (☑ 076 339 36 14; www.locandapalazzone.com; Località Rocca Ripesena; d €185-320, q €280-390), a highly respected winery a few kilometres outside Orvieto that also rents out rather stylish suites in a restored medieval farmhouse.

Le Grotte del Funaro UMBRIAN €€
(☑ 076 334 32 76; www.grottedelfunaro.it; Via Ripa Serancia 41; pizza €5-7.50, meals €25-35; ⊙ daily) What could be more romantic – well, at least in a *Snow White* fairy-tale kind of way – than dining in a proper underground grotto? But this restaurant has more going for it than novelty factor alone. Alfredo and Sandra make a cracking kitchen duo, preparing wood-oven pizzas alongside Umbrian dishes like truffle-ricotta-filled ravioli and braised Chianina beef.

I Sette Consoli MODERN ITALIAN €€€
(☑ 076 334 39 11; www.isetteconsoli.it; Piazza Sant'Angelo 1a; meals €40, 6-course degustation menu €42; ⊙ 12.30-3pm & 7.30-10pm Thu-Tue) This restaurant walks the culinary high wire in Orvieto, with inventive, artfully presented dishes, from pasta so light it floats off the fork to beautifully cooked guinea fowl stuffed with chestnuts. In good weather, try to get a seat in the garden, with the *duomo* in view. Dress for dinner and reserve ahead.

Drinking

Vinosus WINE BAR
(Piazza Duomo 15; ⊙ Tue-Sun) In photo-op range of the cathedral's northwest wall is this wine bar and eatery. Try the cheese platter with local honey and pears for an elegant addition to wine. Open until the wee hours.

☆ Entertainment

Teatro Mancinelli THEATRE
(☑ 076 334 04 93; www.teatromancinelli.com; Corso Cavour 122; adult/reduced €2/1, tickets €15-60; ⊙ box office 10am-1pm & 4-6pm Tue-Sat)

The theatre plays host to Umbria Jazz in winter but offers everything from ballet and opera to folk music and Pink Floyd tributes throughout the year. If you're not able to catch a performance, it's worth a visit to see the allegorical frescoes and tufa walls.

 Information

Farmacia del Moro (☑ 076 334 41 00; Corso Cavour 89; ⊙ 9am-1pm & 4.30-7.30pm Mon-Sat) Posts 24-hour pharmacy information.

Police Station (☑ 076 33 92 11; Piazza Cahen)

Post Office (Via Largo M Ravelli; ⊙ 8.20am-7.05pm Mon-Fri, to 12.35pm Sat)

Tourist Office (☑ 076 334 17 72; info@iat.orvieto.tr.it; Piazza Duomo 24; ⊙ 8.15am-1.50pm & 4-7pm Mon-Fri, 10am-1pm & 3-6pm Sat & Sun) In summer, you can buy funicular, bus and Carta Unica Orvieto tickets here.

 Getting There & Away

BUS

Buses depart from the station on Piazza Cahen, stopping at the train station, and include services to Todi (€5, two hours, one daily) and Terni (€7, two hours, twice daily).

TRAIN

Connections include Rome (€7.50 to €16, 1¼ hours, hourly), Florence (€15 to €21, 1½ to 2½ hours, hourly) and Perugia (€7.10 to €14.40, 1½ hours, every two hours).

CAR & MOTORCYCLE

Orvieto is on the Rome–Florence A1, while the SS71 heads north to Lago Trasimeno. There's plenty of metered parking on Piazza Cahen and in designated areas outside the city walls, including Campo della Fiera.

ⓘ Getting Around

A century-old **funicular** (€1 each way; ⊙ every 10min 7.05am-8.25pm Mon-Fri, every 15min 8.15am-8pm Sat & Sun) creaks up the wooded hill from the train station west of the centre to Piazza Cahen. The fare includes a bus ride from Piazza Cahen to Piazza Duomo.

Bus 1 runs up to the old town from the train station (€1), ATC bus A connects Piazza Cahen with Piazza Duomo and bus B runs to Piazza della Repubblica.

LE MARCHE

From the white-pebble, cliff-backed bays along the Adriatic to sloped hill towns and the high-rise mountain ranges of Monti Sibillini, Le Marche is one of Italy's little-known treasures.

It's inland where Le Marche really shines. Urbino, Raphael's hometown, presents a smorgasbord of Renaissance art and history up and down its vertical streets. Pale but lovely Ascoli Piceno has beauty and history in bounds. Equally walkable is Macerata, with a famous open-air opera theatre and festival. Covering its western reaches, and bleeding over into neighbouring Umbria, is the wild and wonderful Parco Nazionale dei Monti Sibillini.

History

The first well-known settlers of Le Marche were the Piceni tribe, whose 3000-year-old artefacts can be seen in the Museo Archeologico in Ascoli Piceno. The Romans invaded the region early in the 3rd century BC, and dominated it for almost 700 years. After they fell, Le Marche was sacked by the Goths, Vandals, Ostrogoths and, finally, the Lombards.

In the 8th century AD, Pope Stephen II decided to call upon foreigners to oust the ungodly Lombards. The first to lead the charge of the Frankish army was Pepin the Short, but it was his rather tall son Charlemagne who finally took back control from the Lombards for good. On Christmas Day in 800, Pope Leo III crowned him Emperor of the Holy Roman Empire.

After Charlemagne's death, Le Marche entered into centuries of war, anarchy and general Dark Ages mayhem. In central Italy, two factions developed: the Guelphs (who backed papal rule) and the Ghibellines (who supported the emperor). The Guelph faction eventually won out and Le Marche became part of the Papal States. It stayed that way until Italian unification in 1861.

ⓘ Getting There & Around

Drivers have two options on the coastline: the A14 autostrada (main highway) or the SS16 *strada statale* (state highway). Inland roads are either secondary or tertiary and much slower. Regular trains ply the coast on the Bologna–Lecce line and spurs head to Macerata and Ascoli Piceno.

Ancona

POP 102,500

Often brushed aside as being just another of Italy's bolshie, gritty port towns, Ancona is no beauty at first glance from the ferry, it's true. But there's more to Ancona than meets the superficial eye, and to simply bypass it is to miss much. In the old town, crowned by the *duomo*, you can peel back layers of history of the city founded by Greek settlers from Syracuse around 387 BC, admiring Roman ruins, the rich stash of its archaeological museum and its Renaissance *palazzi*, which glow softly in the evening light. Linger long enough in its hilltop parks overlooking the Adriatic and lively boulevards and cafe-rimmed piazzas and you'll see a more likeable side to Le Marche's seafront capital, promise.

◉ Sights

★Museo Archeologico
Nazionale delle Marche   MUSEUM
(Via Ferretti 6; adult/reduced €4/2; ⊙8.30am-7.30pm Tue-Sun) Housed in the beautiful 16th-century **Palazzo Ferretti**, where the ceilings are covered with original frescoes and bas-reliefs, this museum presents a fascinating romp through time, from the Palaeolithic period to the Middle Ages. Although not as well curated as it could be (English information is sorely lacking), persevere, as this museum holds real treasures.

Among them are Neolithic flint daggers, richly embellished Attic vases, Etruscan votive bronzes, Celtic gold (the torques are stunning) and a pristine copy of the famous bronzes of Pergola (50–30 BC). Keep an eye out, too, for the Venus of Frasassi, a statuette of a buxom dame, 8.7cm tall, carved from stalactite 28,000 years ago.

Ancona

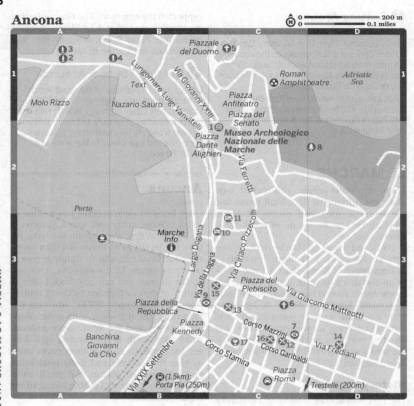

N 0 — 200 m
0 — 0.1 miles

Chiesa di San Domenico CHURCH
(Piazza del Plebiscito; ⊙10am-noon & 4-8pm)
Flanked by cafes, the elegant Piazza del
Plebiscito has been Ancona's meeting spot
since medieval times. It's dominated by
this baroque church, containing the superb
Crucifixion by Titian and *Annunciation*
by Guercino. That gigantic statue in front
is Pope Clement XII, who was honoured by
the town for giving it free port status. The
nearby fountain is from the 19th century.

Cattedrale di San Ciriaco CATHEDRAL
(Piazzale del Duomo; ⊙8am-noon & 3-7pm summer,
to 6pm winter) A stiff but scenic climb up from
the old town, Ancona's perkily domed cathedral commands sweeping views of the city
and port from its hilltop perch. Guarded by
two marble lions, the cathedral sits grandly
atop the site of an ancient pagan temple and
is an architectural potpourri of Byzantine,
Romanesque and Gothic features.

Wandering downhill from here along
Piazza Anfiteatro, you will glimpse the remains of the city's **Roman amphitheatre**,
believed to have been built during the reign
of Emperor Augustus.

Parco del Cardeto PARK
(www.parcodelcardeto.it; ⊙8.30am-8.30pm summer, 8am-5.30pm winter) The din of central
Ancona fades to a distant hum from this
park straddling the hill behind the city,
with broad views across the rooftops of the
old town to the port and Adriatic. The pine
shade and sea breezes up here are refreshing in summer. Fortifications, a 19th-century
lighthouse and a Napoléonic-era cemetery
can be found in its grounds.

Fontana del Calamo FOUNTAIN
(Corso Mazzini) Head along Corso Mazzini,
where you will see the 16th-century Fontana
del Calamo, 13 masked spouts supposedly

Ancona

representing effigies of those who had been beheaded.

Ancona's Arches   MONUMENT
North of Piazza Dante Alighieri, at the far end of the port, is the **Arco di Traiano** (Trajan's Arch), erected in 115 BC by Apollodorus of Damascus in honour of the Roman Emperor Trajan. Luigi Vanvitelli's grand **Arco Clementino** (Clementine's Arch), inspired by Apollodorus' arch and dedicated to Pope Clement XII, is further on, near Molo Rizzo.

Head south along the coastal road and, after about 750m, you'll come across the enormous **Mole Vanvitelliana**, designed by Luigi Vanvitelli in 1732 for Pope Clementine. Just past the pentagonal building, on Via XXIX Settembre, is the baroque Porta Pia, built as a monumental entrance to the town in the late 18th century at the request of Pope Pius VI.

Teatro delle Muse   THEATRE
(🏛 071 5 25 25; www.teatrodellemuse.org; Via della Loggia) On Piazza della Republica, this ornate theatre was built in 1826 and has a neoclassical facade that melds with Greek friezes portraying Apollo and the Muses.

🛏 Sleeping

There are several cheap, bare-bones hotels near the station; it's a grimy area but busy enough to be safe during the day. If you want something a little fancier, you'll have to head into town.

Trestelle   B&B €
(📞 345 4562337; www.bbtrestelle.it; Via San Martino 10; s/d €40/70; ❄) This welcoming B&B is right in the thick of things, a three-minute amble from Piazza Roma. Rooms are simple yet modern and immaculately kept, with tiled floors and the odd burst of colour.

Grand Hotel Passetto   HOTEL €€
(📞 071 3 13 07; www.hotelpassetto.it; Via Thaon de Revel 1; s €90-130, d €140-190, ste €195-215; P❄@🛜🏊) Near Ancona's white-shingle beach, a 20-minute walk east of the centre, this hotel has a genteel atmosphere, a relaxing pool area and incredible sea views. The light rooms are done out with parquet floors and crisp white linen; the best have four-poster beds and the suite has its own jacuzzi. Substantial discounts are offered on weekends and around holidays.

Residence Vanvitelli   APARTMENT €€
(📞 071 20 60 23; www.residencevanvitelli.it; Piazza Saffi; studio per night/week €65/375, 1-rm apt €80/475, 2-rm apt €95/575; P@) In a tiny piazza a few minutes' walk from the ferry terminal and Ancona's key sights are these comfortable, quiet digs. The apartments are nothing flash, but they are central and well kept and come with kitchenettes for preparing a coffee or snack.

Grand Hotel Palace   HOTEL €€
(📞 071 20 18 13; www.hotelancona.it; Lungomare Vanvitelli 24; s €85-110, d €100-170; P❄🛜) 'Grand' is a bit of an overstatement, but this early 19th-century *palazzo* still has the occasional antique and opulent flourish. The high-ceilinged rooms are classically decorated in muted tones, thought some could do with a spruce up. It's well placed for the ferries, which you can watch come and go over a generous breakfast spread in the top-floor room.

🍴 Eating

Corso Garibaldi and Corso Mazzini are packed with restaurants, gelatarie and by-the-slice pizza places, some of which can be fiercely packed at lunchtime (aim to arrive early).

Pizzeria Bontà Delle Marche
PIZZERIA €

(☑ 071 5 57 76; Via Benincasa 7; pizza slice around €1.50; ⏰ 10.30am-2.45pm & 4.30-10.30pm Mon-Sat, 4.30-11pm Sun; ☑) For good, honest sub-€5 grub, you can't beat this jam-packed pizzeria, where the pizzas fly bubbling hot out of the oven quicker than you can say *delizioso!* And they are the real deal: thin, crisp, with chewable elasticity and oodles of flavour. They're served *al taglio* (by the slice) or whole to take away.

Bontà Delle Marche
DELI €

(☑ 071 5 39 85; http://bontadellemarche.it; Corso Mazzini 96; lunch €10; ⏰ 9am-8pm Mon-Wed, 9am-11pm Thur-Sat, 10am-3pm & 6-11pm Sun) Run by the same folk as the Pizzeria Bontà Delle Marche, this terrific deli is the go-to place for a speedy pasta, salad or antipasti lunch, as well as a tempting array of local olive oil, wine, *salumi* and cheese.

Mercato delle Erbe
MARKET €

(Piazza dell'Erbe; ⏰ 7.30am-1pm & 5-8pm Mon-Sat) Going strong since 1926, this market hall does a brisk trade in fresh produce, pastries and bread, cheese, *salumi* and other picnic goodies.

Osteria del Pozzo
OSTERIA €€

(☑ 071 207 39 96; Via Bonda 2; meals €25-35; ⏰ Mon-Sat) Unless you've booked ahead, you'll be lucky to grab one of the cheek-by-jowl tables at this inviting *osteria,* which overflows with regulars. They are here for the spot-on seafood: generous helpings of pasta with shellfish, beautifully cooked sea bass and the like, all washed down with in-expensive house wine.

Enopolis
TRADITIONAL ITALIAN €€

(☑ 071 207 15 05; www.enopolis.it; Corso Mazzini 7; meals €35-45; ⏰ Wed-Mon) A visit to this restaurant and enoteca is worth it simply for the tour of the labyrinthine cellars of the 18th-century Palazzo Jona. You can sit among contemporary art or next to an ancient well as you sample fresh fish (the main event) along with recommended wines for each course.

🍷 Drinking

Piazza del Plebiscito is one of the most relaxed spots for an al fresco drink, with tables set up on the pretty square.

Liberty Cocktail Lounge
BAR

(Via Traffico 7-10; ⏰ 11.30am-2am Thu-Tue) Hidden on a back alley and identified only by a discreet sign, this art deco-inspired cafe is an atmospheric spot to kick off a night with a cocktail (€8). Tiffany glass lamps and a bohemian crowd will make you want to paint the scene and sell it as a framed poster.

ℹ️ Information

Farmacia Centrale (☑ 071 20 27 46; Corso Mazzini 1)

Marche Info (☑ 071 35 89 91; www.comune. ancona.it; Via della Loggia 50; ⏰ 9am-1pm & 3-8pm Mon-Sat summer, 9am-1pm Mon-Sat, plus 3-5pm Tue-Sat winter) Within the ferry terminal, this is the tourist office for Ancona Le Marche province. Stop by for leaflets, maps, itineraries and more.

Police station (☑ 071 2 28 81; Via Giovanni Gervasoni 19) South of the city centre.

Post office (Largo XXIV Maggio; ⏰ 8.30am-7pm Mon-Fri, 8.30am-12.30pm Sat)

ℹ️ Getting There & Away

AIR

Falconara Airport (☑ 071 2 82 71; www. ancona-airport.com) Situated 19km west of Ancona, **Falconara Airport** is small and easy to navigate. Major airlines that fly into Ancona include Lufthansa, Alitalia and Ryanair; the latter operates daily flights to London Stansted.

BUS

Most buses leave from Piazza Cavour, inland from the port (it's a five-minute walk east of the seafront along Corso Giuseppe Garibaldi), except for a few going to Falconara and Portonovo, which originate at the train station.

TO	FARE (€)	DURATION	FREQUENCY
Falconara Airport	1.80	45min	hourly
Jesi	2.60	45min	hourly
Macerata	3.75	1½hr	12 daily
Numana	2.10	45min	hourly
Portonovo	2.20	30min	9 daily Jun-Aug
Recanati	2.85	1¼hr	hourly
Senigallia	2.40	1hr	hourly

CAR & MOTORCYCLE

Ancona is on the A14, linking Bologna with Bari. The SS16 coastal road runs parallel to the autostrada and is pleasant, toll-free alternative if you're not looking to get anywhere fast. The SS76 connects Ancona with Perugia and Rome.

There's plenty of parking, which gets steadily more expensive the closer to the centre you get (€1.20 to €2.70 per hour). At the multistorey Parcheggio Degli Archi near the train station it's just €2 to park all day.

You'll find all the major car hire companies at the airport, including **Europcar** (☑ 071 916 22 40; www.europcar.it), **Maggiore** (☑ 071 918 88 05), **Avis** (☑ 071 5 22 22; www.avis.com) and **Hertz** (☑ 071 207 37 98; www.hertz.com).

FERRY

Ferries operate to Greece, Croatia, Albania and Turkey. See p947.

TRAIN

Ancona is on the Bologna–Lecce line. Check whether you're taking a Eurostar service, as there can be a substantial supplement.

TO	FARE (€)	DURATION	FREQUENCY
Bari	42-55	4hr	hourly
Bologna	14-40	2-3hr	every 30min
Florence	21-56	3hr	hourly
Milan	29-71	3-4hr	hourly
Pesaro	9-12	25-35min	every 2hr
Rome	16-35	3-4hr	every 2hr

ℹ Getting Around

TO/FROM THE AIRPORT

There is a frequent train service between Castelferreti station, opposite the terminal, and Ancona (15 to 25 minutes, €1.50). Alternatively, Conero bus J runs roughly hourly from the train station to the airport (from 6.50am to 8.30pm Monday to Saturday); bus C runs four times a day on Sunday and public holidays. The trip costs €1.80 and takes 35 to 45 minutes. From the airport to Ancona, line J runs until 11.30pm. The airport **taxi consortium** (☑ 334 1548899) can take you to central Ancona (€38) and Portonovo (€57).

BUS

About six **Conero Bus** (www.conerobus.it) services, including bus 1/3, 1/4 and 1/5, connect the main train station with the centre (Piazza Cavour), while bus 12 connects the main station with the ferry port (€1.20); look for the bus stop with the big signpost displaying Centro and Porto.

TAXI

Call ☑ 071 4 33 21 at the train station or ☑ 071 20 28 95 in the town centre.

Parco del Conero

Only minutes from Ancona but a world unto itself, Parco del Conero is stunning, with limestone cliffs razoring above the cobalt blue Adriatic and crescent-shaped, white pebble bays backed by fragrant woods of pine, oak, beech, broom and oleander trees. Walking trails thread through the 60 sq km park, which is a conservation area. Remarkably still off the radar for many travellers, the park retains a peaceful, unspoilt air found nowhere else along Le Marche's coastline. Its highest peak is 572m Monte Conero, which takes a spectacular nosedive into the sea. The vineyards that taper down its slopes produce the excellent, full-bodied Rosso Conero red wine.

Parco del Conero encompasses the cliff-backed seaside resorts of Portonovo, Sirolo and Numana, all of which make fine bases for exploring. Boat trips from Portonovo and Sirolo are the best way to cove hop.

🛏 Sleeping

Camping Internazionale CAMPGROUND €
(☑ 071 933 08 84; www.campinginternazionale.com; Via San Michele 10, Sirolo; camping 2 people, car & tent €30-52; ☻mid-May–mid-Sep; @ 🛜 🛜 ♿) Shaded in the trees just a few metres from the scenic beaches below Sirolo, this full-service campsite is replete with a swimming pool, pizzeria, bar, grocery store and children's club with plenty of activities to keep the little ones amused. Free walking tours of the park are offered in summer.

★ **Acanto Country House** GUESTHOUSE €€
(☑ 071 933 11 95; www.acantocountryhouse.com; Via Ancarano 18, Sirolo; s €65-70, d €110-130, tr €135-150; P ✳ 🛜 🛜) Set back from Sirolo's beaches and surrounded by cornfields, meadows and olive groves, this converted farmhouse is a gorgeous country escape, taking in the full sweep of the coast. Named after flowers like peony and rose, rooms have been designed with the utmost attention to detail, with gleaming wood floors, exposed stone and embroidered bedspreads.

There's an outdoor pool and jacuzzi for a relaxing bubble, and the owners are more than happy to oblige whether you want to hire a bike or make use of the barbecue area.

WORTH A TRIP

THE FLYING HOUSE OF LORETO

Straddling a hilltop and visible from afar, Loreto is absorbed entirely by its bauble-domed **Basilica della Santa Casa** (Piazza della Madonna; ⊙6.15am-7.45pm summer, to 7.15pm winter). While the original basilica started in 1468 was Gothic, Renaissance additions have made today's basilica an architectural masterpiece, with its riot of gold-leafed halos, impressive frescoes and religious triptychs. Inside stands the elaborate marble **Santa Casa di Loreto**, or the Holy House shrine, where pilgrims flock to glimpse a jewel-encrusted black statue of the Virgin and pray in the candlelit twilight. The chapel is allegedly where Jesus was raised as a child. Legend has it a host of angels winged the chapel over from Nazareth in 1294 after the Crusaders were expelled from Palestine.

If you fancy staying the night in the calm, pretty old town, 18th-century townhouse **B&B Antica Maison** (🖉366 1754341; www.anticamaison.net; Via Francesco Asdrubali 24 ; s/d €55/65; 🖥) brims with charming features like beams and four-poster beds. Fausta and Livio extend a very warm welcome. Foodie pilgrims won't want to miss out on the grilled meats prepared with a gourmet twist at Michelin-starred **Ristorante Andreina** (🖉071 97 01 24; www.ristoranteandreina.it; Via Buffolareccia 14; menus €25-60; ⊙Thu-Mon).

Loreto can be easily reached by train from Ancona (€2.20, 15 minutes, hourly).

Hotel Fortino Napoleonico   LUXURY HOTEL €€€
(🖉071 80 14 50; www.hotelfortino.it; Via Poggio 166, Portonovo; s €130-150, d €180-250; ❄@🖥🏊) One of Le Marche's most stunning beachfront hotels, this former Napoléonic fort begs for a romantic tryst. Its stone-built walls, antique furnishings and plush sitting rooms might lure you inside from the ocean-fronted terrace, and the gilded restaurant (open daily, meals €50) specialising in fresh fish might make you linger even longer.

✗ Eating

Il Clandestino   SEAFOOD €€
(🖉071 80 14 22; www.morenocedroni.it; Via Portonovo, Portonovo; meals €35-45; ⊙daily) Right on the water's edge, the cool-blue Clandestino is a kind of gourmet beach bar, with a lovely sea-facing terrace and a menu highly recommended by Italy's food critics. There's no formality here: after a swim you can drop in for a taste of its Mediterranean sushi, tapas or some fresh fish.

La Torre   SEAFOOD €€
(🖉071 933 07 47; www.latorrenumana.it; Via la Torre 1, Numana; meals €30-40; ⊙Wed-Mon, closed Sun dinner) Floor-to-ceiling glass walls maximise on the wraparound sea views from this sleek, industrial-chic restaurant, with bare wood floors, crisp white tablecloths and exposed silver pipework. Go for brilliantly fresh sushi, antipasti and artistically presented mains, mostly – surprise, surprise – with a seafood slant. It's hugely popular with the locals.

Il Molo   SEAFOOD €€
(🖉071 80 10 40; www.ilmolo.it; Spiaggia di Portonovo, Portonovo; meals €30; ⊙daily Jun-Aug, Wed-Mon Apr-May & Oct) Whatever splashes around in the sea around Monte Conero lands on the menu at Il Molo, generously supplied by the local fishermen who show up here each morning with their fresh catches. Expect various inventive combinations of pasta and shellfish.

ℹ Information

Tourist office (🖉071 933 18 79; www.parcodelconero.com; Via Peschiera 30, Sirolo; ⊙9am-1pm & 4-7pm mid-Jun–mid-Sep, 9am-1pm Mon-Sat mid-Sep–Dec, closed Jan & Feb) For information on the park or to arrange guided tours.

ℹ Getting There & Away

Buses from Ancona run sporadically throughout the year, peaking in July and August, but the area is much easier to explore with your own set of wheels.

Urbino

POP 15,500

Raphael's Renaissance 'hood, the vibrant university town of Urbino is often the first stop on a trip to Le Marche and understandably so. The patriarch of the Montefeltro family, Duca Federico da Montefeltro, created the hippest art scene of the 15th century here, gathering the great artists, architects and scholars of his day to create a sort of think tank. The town's splendour was made official by Unesco, which deemed the entire city centre a World Heritage Site.

◎ Sights

Palazzo Ducale
PALACE, MUSEUM
(www.palazzoducaleurbino.it; adult/reduced €5/2.50; ⊙8.30am-7.15pm Tue-Sun, to 2pm Mon) A microcosm of Renaissance architecture, art and history, the Palazzo Ducale contains the **Galleria Nazionale delle Marche**, **Museo Archeologico** and **Museo della Ceramica**. The museum triptych is housed within Federico da Montefeltro's palace. The duke enlisted the foremost artists and architects of the age to create this whimsically turreted Renaissance masterpiece.

A monumental staircase, one of Italy's first, leads to the *piano nobile* (literally 'noble floor') and the Ducal Apartments. Piero della Francesca was one of the artists employed by the duke, and his work, *The Flagellation*, adorns the duke's library. The collection also includes a large number of drawings by Federico Barocci, as well as stunning Renaissance works by Raphael, Titian and Signorelli.

From Corso Garibaldi you get the best view of the complex, with its unusual Facciata dei Torricini, a three-storey loggia in the form of a triumphal arch, flanked by circular towers.

Cattedrale di Urbino
CHURCH
(⊙7.30am-1pm & 2-7pm) Rebuilt in the early 19th century in neoclassical style, the interior of Urbino's *duomo* commands much greater interest than its austere facade. Particularly memorable is Federico Barocci's *Last Supper*. The basilica's **Museo Diocesano Albani** (www.museodiocesanourbino.it; admission €3; ⊙9.30am-1pm & 2.30-6.30pm Wed-Mon) contains religious artefacts, vestments and more paintings, including Andrea da Bologna's *Madonna del Latte* (Madonna Breastfeeding).

Casa Natale di Raffaello
HOUSE MUSEUM
(Via Raffaello 57; adult/reduced €3.50/2.50; ⊙9am-1pm & 3-7pm Mon-Fri, 10am-1pm Sat & Sun summer, 9am-2pm Mon-Fri winter) North of the Piazza della Repubblica you'll find the 15th-century house where Raphael was born in 1483 and spent his first 16 years. On the 1st floor is possibly one of Raphael's first frescoes, a Madonna with child. The museum takes a touching look at Raphael's family life.

Above all it homes in on the influence of his father, Giovanni Santi, who was a court painter and taught his talented young son all he knew.

Museo della Città
MUSEUM
(Via Valerio 1; adult/reduced €1/0.50; ⊙9.30am-1.30pm Mon & Wed-Fri, 10am-6pm Sat & Sun) South of the piazza, the museum in the Renaissance Palazzo Odasi has displays on Urbino's history, including a scale model of the city (useful for finding your bearings) and various archaic signs. It centres on a lovely arcaded inner courtyard.

Oratorio di San Giovanni
CHURCH
(Via Barocci 31; admission €2.50; ⊙10am-12.30pm & 3-5.30pm Mon-Sat, 10am-12.30pm Sun) The 14th-century oratorio features brightly coloured frescoes by Lorenzo and Giacomo Salimbeni.

✴ Festivals & Events

The city swings into summer at **Urbino Jazz Festival** in June, with performances held all over town, followed by the **International Festival of Ancient Music** in July and the **Festa dell'Aquilone**, a kite festival, on the first weekend in September.

Festa dell'Duca
CULTURE
(⊙3rd Sun Aug) The city time travels back to the Middle Ages, with medieval fun hitting the streets in the shape of a costumed procession and the re-enactment of a tournament on horseback.

🛏 Sleeping

B&B Albornoz
B&B €
(☑347 2987897; www.bbalbornoz.com; Via dei Maceri 23; s €50, d €70-80) Wedged in a quiet old-town corner, this B&B has boutique flavour. A spiral staircase links three studios full of designer touches, with murals, funky lighting and bold artworks, from the monochromatic 'You and Me' to the floral, lilac-kissed romance of 'Osaka'. All come with kitchenettes and espresso machines. The friendly owners will squeeze in an extra bed for €20.

★ Locanda della Valle Nuova
AGRITURISMO €€
(☑0722 33 03 03; www.vallenuova.it; La Cappella 14, Sagrata di Fermignano; s/d €81/112, half-board €30 per person; ⊙Jun-Nov; 🅿@🛜🌊) 🥬 What a delight this organic farm is, with bright, immaculate rooms and lovely views across wooded hills to the mountains beyond. Whether you want to rustle up an Italian feast with a cookery class, go horse riding

Urbino

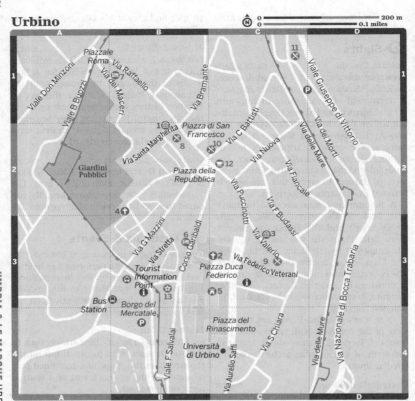

or learn basket-weaving, Giulia obliges. She is also terrific cook and dinners are a feast of homegrown goodies.

The farm is 16km south of Urbino (follow signs to Fermignanom, then Sagrata), but the English-speaking owners will assist you with transport and visiting the local towns. Minimum stay is three nights.

Urbino Resort   AGRITURISMO, SPA HOTEL **€€**
(www.tenutasantigiacomoefilippo.it; Via San Giacomo in Foglia 7, Pantiere; s €108-132, d €120-175, ste €180-240, meals €30-40; P❊🛜🏊🐾) 🐾
And relax... You can't help but unwind the minute you check into this gorgeous country abode, surrounded by vineyards and gardens fragrant with flowers and herbs. Spread across six stylishly converted stone farm buildings, the wood-floored rooms are individually designed – some are decorated in soothing pastels with Laura Ashley fabrics, others are slick and contemporary.

An infinity pool overlooking the hills, a spa offering treatments from massage to shiatsu, a horse-riding school and a lakefront restaurant that uses organic, farm-fresh produce in its creative cuisine, will make you want to linger here more than a night or two. The resort sits 13km north of Urbino.

Albergo Italia   HOTEL **€€**
(☏0722 27 01; www.albergo-italia-urbino.it; Corso Garibaldi 32; s €50-70, d €80-120; ❊🛜) Set behind the Palazzo Ducale, the Italia could not be better positioned. Modern and well designed, the shuttered townhouse is restfully quiet and staff are genuinely friendly. In warmer months, take breakfast on the balcony.

🍴 Eating & Drinking

Don't miss Italy's only homicidal pasta – *strozzapreti* (priest stranglers) – available in most restaurants. One legend has it that

Urbino

the shredded pasta was designed to choke priests who would eat for nothing at local restaurants, so if you happen to wear the collar – be careful.

La Trattoria del Leone   TRATTORIA €
(✆0722 32 98 94; www.latrattoriadelleone.it; Via Cesare Battisti 5; meals €20-25; ⊙dinner Mon-Sat, lunch Sat & Sun) This homely, rustic basement trattoria raids Le Marche's larder for the best regional produce. *Olive all'ascolana* (stuffed olives fried in breadcrumbs) whets appetites for dishes such as ravioli with the local Casciotta d'Urbino cheese, and baked rabbit with olives, bacon and sausages, with true depth of flavour. Save an inch for the excellent chocolate cake.

La Balestra   ITALIAN €
(✆0722 29 42; Via Valerio 16; meals €20-25; ⊙lunch & dinner daily) Urbino's literati and university students congregate below a historical vaulted brick ceiling or outside at the convivial decking area. Try specialities like the famous *strozzapreti* and pappardelle with wild boar, or fill up on pizza baked in a wood-fired oven.

★**Antica Osteria de la Stella**   OSTERIA €€
(✆0722 32 02 28; www.anticaosteriadalastella.com; Via Santa Margherita 1; meals €25-40; ⊙lunch & din-

ner Tue-Sun) Duck down a quiet side street to this rustically elegant, beamed 15th-century inn once patronised by the likes of Piero della Francesca. Legendary in these parts, Osteria de la Stella puts its own inventive twist on seasonal food. Every dish strikes perfect balance, be it cocoa ravioli or venison with wild berries and polenta.

The owners take genuine pride in sourcing and everything is homemade, from the bread served with syrup-thick balsamic vinegar to the dreamily light pasta and *petits fours*.

Osteria L'Angolo Divino   OSTERIA €€
(✆0722 32 75 59; www.angolodivino.com; Via Sant'Andrea 14; meals €30; ⊙daily) This subterranean *osteria* oozes atmosphere. Arched brick alcoves overflow with wine bottles, which are available for tastings. On the menu are simple but perfectly flavoured pasta specialities, including gnocchi with truffle and better-than-it-sounds *pasta nel sacco* (pasta in a sack, or fresh pasta coated with eggs and breadcrumbs).

Caffè Centrale   CAFE
(Piazza della Repubblica; ⊙6.30am-2am) Popular with Urbino's students, this is the best of the piazza cafes. Its outdoor tables get a relaxing dose of afternoon sun. Pastries, sandwiches and gelato are served any time of day, and *aperitivi* accompany late-afternoon drinks.

☆ Entertainment

Teatro Sanzio   THEATRE
(✆0722 22 81; Corso Garibaldi) This grand old 19th-century theatre hosts plays and concerts, particularly from July to September. Pick up a brochure at the tourist office.

❶ Information

Tourist information point (✆0722 26 31; Piazza Mercatale; ⊙9am-6pm Mon-Sat) At the entrance of the lift into town.
Tourist office (✆0722 26 13; Via Puccinotti 3; ⊙9am-1pm Mon-Sat, 3-6pm Tue-Fri) Pick up a free map and the miniguide *Urbino City of Art* for €5.

❶ Getting There & Around

BUS
Adriabus (✆0722 37 67 38, 0800 66 43 32; www.adriabus.eu) runs an hourly service daily between Urbino and Pesaro (€3.20, 48 minutes), from where you can pick up a train for Bologna.

CAR

Most vehicles are banned from the walled city. There are car parks outside the city gates, including the main one at Borgo del Mercatale. Parking costs €1.20 per hour.

TAXI

Call ☑ 0722 25 50; shuttle buses operate from Piazza della Repubblica and Piazza Mercatale.

TRAIN

There is no train service to Urbino (pick up trains in Pesaro, about 35km away).

Pesaro

POP 94,600

Look beyond the concrete high-rise hotels and the crowds of bronzed holidaymakers jostling for towel space on the beach in August, and you'll find a lot to like about Pesaro.

The town's setting is perfect, with beaches of fine golden sand fringing the Adriatic, a backdrop of undulating hills, and a pretty old town centred on the cafe-rimmed Piazza del Popolo, where the Renaissance Palazzo Ducale stands proud. The composer Rossini was so fond of his home town that he left it all of his possessions when he died (be sure to check out Casa Rossini while you're here).

⊙ Sights & Activities

In 1792 famous composer Rossini was born in a typical Pesaro townhouse that is now the Casa Rossini (Via Rossini 34; adult/reduced €4/2, incl entry to Musei Civici €7/3; ⊙ 10am-1pm & 4-7.30pm Tue-Sun, closed Wed afternoon). His mother was a singer, his father a horn player and the young lad was composing when he was knee-high to a grasshopper. Prints, personal items and portraits provide an insight into the life of the virtuoso and his operas, such as the jaunty *Barber of Seville*.

Opened in the 1860s just after Italian reunification, the town's original art gallery is now the Musei Civici (www.museicivicipesaro.it; Piazza Toschi Mosca 29; adult/reduced €4/2, incl entry to Casa Rossini €7/3; ⊙ 10am-1pm & 4-7.30pm Tue-Sun, closed Wed afternoon), which also showcases Pesaro's 700-year-old pottery tradition with one of Italy's best collections of majolica ceramics.

Pesaro has four major beach areas – the Blue Flag–awarded Levante, Ponente, Baia Flaminia and the free beach. Levante and Ponente are the jam-packed hotel-fronted beaches, so for more elbow room head to the free beach *(spiaggia libera)* to the south of the city, under Monte Ardizio.

✦ Festivals & Events

Rossini Opera Festival · MUSIC

(☑ 0721 380 02 94; www.rossinioperafestival.it; Via Rossini 24; ⊙ box office 10am-noon & 4-6.30pm during festival) This two-week festival in August is a love letter to Rossini. Operas and concerts are staged at the Teatro Rossini and Adriatic Arena. Tickets are €20 to €150, with big student and last-minute discounts.

🛏 Sleeping & Eating

Most hotels close from October to Easter. Though many places are uninspiring 1960s concrete blocks, you can find some charmers. For a room, contact the Associazione Pesarese di Albergatori (☑ 0721 6 79 59; www.apahotel.it; Piazzale della Libertà 10) or try the tourist office.

Marinella · CAMPGROUND €

(☑ 0721 5 57 95; www.campingmarinella.it; SS16 km244; camping 2 people, car & tent €24-39.50; ⊙ Easter- Sep; 🛜🏠) Drift off in your seaside tent to the sound of waves. A pizzeria is on site, as well as a minimarket, beach volleyball and lots of child-friendly activities.

Hotel Clipper · HOTEL €€

(☑ 0721 3 09 15; www.hotelclipper.it; Viale Guglielmo Marconi 53; s €55-105, d €85-120, tr €105-145; [P]❄🛜🏠) In the capable hands of the friendly Gasparini family, Clipper is literally steps from the beach and a five-minute stroll from the centre. The bright and breezy rooms are well kept and have balconies; it's worth shelling out an extra €5 per night for a sea view. Rates include bike rental and beach towels.

L'Angolo di Mario · SEAFOOD, PIZZERIA €€

(☑ 0721 6 58 50; http://angolodimario.it; Via Nazario Sauro; pizza €2.50-10, meals €20-30; ⊙ daily) L'Angolo di Mario couples sea views with contemporary decor, pleasant service and great food. Bag a table on the terrace to gaze out across the Adriatic as you dig into heaped plates of mussels and clams or seafood pasta, before mains of grilled fish or beef. They also do a mean pizza.

☆ Entertainment

Teatro Rossini · THEATRE

(☑ 0721 3 24 82; www.enteconcerti.it; Via Rossini) This theatre was renamed in the composer's honour, and its grand ceiling and ornate box seats make it a breathtaking spot to catch a concert, especially during the Rossini Opera Festival.

ℹ Information

Pesaro Urbino Tourism (www.turismo.
pesarourbino.it) Has excellent information in
English, with maps, hotels and sights.
Tourist office (☑ 0721 6 93 41; www.comune.
pesaro.ps.it; Piazzale della Libertà 11; ◷ 9am-
1pm Mon-Sat, plus 3-6pm Tue & Fri)

ℹ Getting There & Around

BUS

The main bus station is on Piazza Matteotti, with
regular buses to Ancona (€3.10, 1¼ hours, four
daily). **Adriabus** (☑ 0722 37 67 38, 0800 66
43 32; www.adriabus.eu) operates a twice daily
service to Rome (€38, 4¾ hours) and hourly
buses to Urbino (€3.20, 48 minutes).

TRAIN

Pesaro is on the Bologna–Lecce train line and
you can reach Rome (€18 to €45, 3½ to 5¾
hours, nine daily) by changing trains at Falconara
Marittima, just before Ancona. There are at least
hourly services to Ancona (€3.65 to €12, 30 to
50 minutes), Rimini (€3.60 to €11, 19 to 33 minutes) and Bologna (€10.40 to €21.50, 1¼ to two
hours). The train station is on the western edge
of town, about 2km from the beach.

Grotte di Frasassi

In September 1971 a team of climbers stumbled across a hole in the hill country around
Genga. On closer inspection, this 'hole'
turned out to be one of the biggest cave
systems in Europe, the **Grotte di Frasassi**
(☑ 0732 9 00 90, 0732 9 00 80; www.frasassi.com;
adult/reduced €15.50/13.50; ◷ 10am-5pm), now
Le Marche's unmissable geological marvel.

The fast-flowing River Sentino has
gouged out this karst wonderland, which
can be admired on a 70-minute tour through
its warren of chambers and tunnels. Tours
in English depart at roughly 11am, 12.30pm,
2.30pm and 4pm daily. Wear comfortable
shoes and bring a sweater even in summer.

On a tour you'll take in the cave's rock
stars. First up is the **Ancona Abyss**, a cavernous 200m-high, 180m-long chamber,
which would comfortably accommodate
Milan Cathedral. Highlights here include
Niagara, a petrified cascade of pure calcite
and a crystallised lake. In the so-called **Gran
Canyon**, look out for parallel stalactites resembling pipe organs and waxy stalagmites
that rise up like melted candles.

To reach the caves from Ancona, take the
SS76 off the A14 and look for the Genga-
Sassoferrato exit. The car park, 1.5km east

ℹ EXTREME CAVING

If the Grotte di Frasassi tour leaves you
hungry for more of a challenge, sign
up for a **Speleo Avventura**. This will
up the adventure ante considerably
as you pass across 30m chasms and
crawl on your hands and knees along
narrow passages and tunnels. There
are two versions: blue (easy-ish), which
lasts two hours and costs €35, and red
(hard, as you'll be going right into the
cave's bowels), which lasts three hours
and costs €45. Book at least a week in
advance and happy spelunking.

of the cave entrance at San Vittore Terme,
is where you buy your tickets and catch the
shuttle bus to the caves. The closest train
station, Genga San Vittore Terme, is also
next to the car park and ticket office.

Macerata

POP 42,000

Macerata combines charming hill-town
scenery with the verve of student life – its
university is one of Europe's oldest, dating
to 1290. Its old town, a jumble of cobbled
streets and honey-coloured *palazzi*, springs
to life for the month-long opera festival.

◉ Sights & Activities

One of Europe's most stunning outdoor theatres is the neoclassical **Arena Sferisterio**
(☑ 0733 23 07 35; www.sferisterio.it; Piazza Mazzini 10; adult/reduced €3/2, incl guided tour €5/4;
◷ 10am-4pm Mon, 9am-1pm & 3-7pm Tue-Sun,
guided tours noon & 5pm), a grand colonnaded
affair resembling an ancient Roman arena,
built between 1820 and 1829. Its acoustics
are second to none. From mid-July to mid-
August it's the backdrop for the **Macerata
Opera Festival**, one of Italy's foremost musical events, attracting the cream of the operatic world.

The historic centre Renaissance is presided over by the **Loggia dei Mercanti** on
Piazza della Libertà. Built in 1505 for Cardinal Alessandro Farnese, the soon-to-be
Pope Paul III, the arcaded building housed
travelling merchants selling their wares.
Across the square is the **Teatro Lauro Rossi**
(☑ 0733 23 35 08; Piazza della Libertà), an elegant
theatre built in 1774 for the nobility, which
now allows well-dressed riff-raff to attend.

Macerata's museums cluster in the **Musei Civici di Palazzo Buonaccorsi** (☑0733 25 63 61; www.maceratamusei.it; Via Don Minzoni 24; adult/reduced €3/2; ⊙10am-6pm Tue-Sun) On the ground floor is the **Museo delle Carozza**, housing an extensive collection of 18th- to 20th-century coaches (partly closed for renovation at the time of writing). Stepping up to the 1st floor brings you to the city's **Arte Antica** collection, with works dating from the 13th to the 19th centuries, while the 2nd floor is dedicated to **Arte Moderna** (modern art), with several rooms given over to Macerata-born painter Ivo Pannaggi, a driving force behind Italian futurism in the 1920s and '30s.

🛏 Sleeping

Albergo Arena HOTEL €
(☑0733 23 09 31; www.albergoarena.com; Vicolo Sferisterio 16; s €45-65, d €65-95; 🅿❄@🛜) Bang in the heart of the old town, this shuttered stone house offers modest, spotlessly kept rooms. It's a welcoming base for exploring the historic centre.

Hotel Arcadia HOTEL €
(☑0733 23 59 61; www.harcadia.it/dove.htm; Via Matteo Ricci 134; s €40-65, d €65-95; 🅿❄🛜) On a quiet lane not far from the cathedral, the Arcadia gives three-star comfort at wallet-friendly prices. Thanks to a recent makeover, the pick of the rooms sport a contemporary look, with warm hues, parquet floors and flat-screen TVs.

★**Le Case** AGRITURISMO €€
(☑0733 23 18 97; www.ristorantelecase.it; Via Mozzavinci 16/17; s €105-110, d €140-150, ste €230, meals €40-90; ❄🛜❄🍴) 🌿 A cypress-lined drive sweeps up to this country manor and organic farm, nestled in glorious isolation 9km west of Macerata. The pale-hued, wood-floored rooms combine an air of discreet luxury with original trappings such as beams, flagstone floors and antique furnishings. A spa area and an indoor pool overlooking rolling hills, two gourmet restaurants, including Michelin-starred L'Enoteca, and farmyard animals to please the kids all make this an outstanding pick. Homemade jams, breads and tarts make their way onto the breakfast table. Staff will happily squeeze in a cot or an extra bed if you ask.

To reach Le Case, head north of Macerata to Villa Potenza, then follow the signs near the chapel for Le Case; full directions are given on the website.

🍴 Eating & Drinking

Osteria dei Fiori OSTERIA €
(☑0733 26 01 42; www.osteriadeifiori.it; Via Lauro Rossi 61; meals €25-30; ⊙Mon-Sat; 🍴🍴) This *osteria* has a homely, low-key vibe and al fresco seating in summer. The cuisine is season-focused, but the creative menu might include, say, spaghetti with spring chicory and hazelnuts, followed by roasted rabbit with fennel, and coffee-aniseed ice cream. Kids and vegetarians are well catered for.

Da Secondo TRATTORIA €€
(☑0733 26 09 12; Via Pescheria Vecchia 26/28; meals €30-40; ⊙Tue-Sun) Trace the town's history through both photos covering the walls and the regional ingredients in your meal: *pecorino, tartufo* and osso buco with porcini mushrooms. In summer dine on the romantic outdoor terrace. Its famed warm chocolate *torta* (cake) caps off a perfect meal.

★**L'Enoteca** GASTRONOMIC €€€
(☑0733 23 18 97; www.enotecalecase.it; Via Mozzavinci 16/17; meals €40-55, tasting menus €40-90; ⊙dinner Tue-Sat) Worth the trek to the countryside, Le Case's Michelin-starred restaurant has enough gourmet panache to keep foodies coming from afar. Beams and exposed stone create a rustically elegant scene. Meat reared on the organic farm, foraged herbs and flowers and garden veg all go into Michele Biagiola's menus created with love, precision and a razor-sharp eye for detail.

Choose a wine from the 1700-bottle list to pair with such show-stoppers as apple cake with sticky pork ribs and ginger gelato or tortelli stuffed with guinea fowl.

Caffè Venanzetti CAFE
(Via Gramsci 21/23, Galleria Scipione; ⊙7am-11pm) High ceilings and an old-world wood-mirror decor make this cafe a visual treat to go with delectable pastries and a fine cappuccino.

ℹ Information

Post office (Via Gramsci 44; ⊙8.20am-7.05pm Mon-Fri, 8.20am-12.35pm Sat)

Tourist office (☑0733 23 48 07; www.turismo.provinciamc.it; Piazza della Libertà 12; ⊙9am-1pm & 3-6pm Mon-Sat, to 1pm Sun) Pick up info on Macerata and its surrounds and book tours here.

❶ Getting There & Around

BUS
Services head to Rome (€23, four hours, six daily) and Citanova Marche (€2.25, one hour, hourly). Timetables for local buses are available at the bus terminal.

CAR & MOTORCYCLE
The SS77 connects the city with the A14 to the east and roads for Rome in the west. There is paid parking (from 8am to 8pm) skirting the city walls and free parking at the Giardini Diaz, where the buses arrive.

TRAIN
From the **train station** (☎ 0733 24 03 54; Piazza XXV Aprile 8/10) there are good connections to Ancona (€4.70, 1¼ hours, hourly) and Rome (€15.40 to €32, four to five hours, eight daily). To reach Ascoli Piceno (€6.30, 2¼ to three hours, 10 daily), change trains in San Benedetto del Tronto and Civitanova Marche. Bus 6 links the station with the Piazza della Libertà in the city centre.

Ascoli Piceno

POP 49,900

With a continuous history dating from the Sabine tribe in the 9th century, Ascoli is like the long-lost cousin of ancient Rome and a small *Marchigiani* village, heavy on the history and food. Weary legs will appreciate its lack of hills and all travellers will enjoy its historical riches, excellent pinacoteca, one of Italy's unsung perfect piazzas and the veal-stuffed fried olives treat *(olive all'ascolana)*.

◉ Sights

Chiesa di San Francesco   CHURCH
(Piazza del Popolo; ☺ 7am-12.30pm & 3.30-8pm) This beautiful church was started back in 1262 as homage to a visit from St Francis himself. In the left nave is a 15th-century wooden cross that miraculously made it through a 1535 fire at the Palazzo dei Capitani, and has since reputedly spilled blood twice. Virtually annexed to the church is **Loggia dei Mercanti**, built in the 16th century by the powerful guild of wool merchants to hide their rough-and-tumble artisan shops.

The church stands on the imposing Piazza del Popolo, which since Roman times has been Ascoli's *salotto* (sitting room). The square is flanked on the west by the 13th-century Palazzo dei Capitani del Popolo. The statue of Pope Paul III above the main entrance was erected in recognition of his efforts to bring peace to the town.

Pinacoteca   MUSEUM
(www.ascolimusei.it; Piazza Arringo; adult/reduced €8/5; ☺ 10am-7pm Tue-Sun summer, 10.30am-5pm winter) Gathered around a tree-shaded courtyard, the second-largest art gallery in Le Marche sits inside the 17th-century **Palazzo Comunale**. It boasts an outstanding display of art, sculpture and religious artefacts; there are 400 works in total, including paintings by Van Dyck, Titian and Rembrandt, and a stunning embroidered 13th-century papal cape worn by Ascoli-born Pope Nicholas IV.

Your ticket also gives you entry to two small collections in Ascoli's old quarter: the **Galleria d'Arte Contemporanea** and the **Museo dell'Arte Ceramica** (☎ 0736 29 82 13; Piazza San Tommaso), which has displays on the major Italian pottery towns, including Deruta, Faenza and Genoa.

**Duomo della Città
di Ascoli Piceno**   CATHEDRAL
(Piazza Arringo; ☺ 7am-6pm) Topped by a pair of mismatched towers, Ascoli's *duomo* was built in the 16th century over a medieval building and dedicated to St Emidio, patron saint of the city. In the **Cappella del Sacramento** is the *Polittico*, a polyptych executed in 1473 by Carlo Crivelli. The **crypt of Sant Emidio** has a notable set of mosaics.

Next to the cathedral and something of a traffic barrier today, the **battistero** (baptistry) has remained unchanged since it was constructed in the 11th century.

Vecchio Quartiere   HISTORIC QUARTER
The town's Old Quarter stretches from Corso Mazzini (the main thoroughfare of the Roman-era settlement) to the Castellano river. Its main street is the picturesque Via delle Torri, which eventually becomes Via Solestà; it's a perfect spot to wander round.

On Via delle Donne (Street of Women) is the 14th-century **Chiesa di San Pietro Martire** (Piazza Ventidio Basso; ☺ 7.30am-12.30pm & 3.30-7pm), dedicated to the saint who founded the Dominican community at Ascoli. The chunky Gothic structure houses the **Reliquario della Santa Spina**, containing what is claimed to be a thorn from Christ's crown.

Torre degli Ercolani   HISTORIC BUILDING
The 40m-high tower located on Via dei Soderini, west of the Chiesa di San Pietro Martire, is the tallest of the town's medieval towers. **Palazzetto Longobardo**, a 12th-century Lombard-Romanesque defensive position and now the Ostello dei Longobardi

youth hostel, abuts the tower. Just to the north is the well-preserved **Ponte Romano**, a single-arched Roman bridge.

Museo Archeologico MUSEUM
(Piazza Arringo; adult/reduced €2/1; ⊙ 8.30am-7.30pm Tue-Sun) Ascoli's archaeological museum holds a small collection of tribal artefacts from Piceni and other European people dating back to the first centuries AD.

✨ Festivals & Events

Fritto Misto all'Italiana FOOD
(www.frittomistoallitaliana.it; ⊙ late Apr) This four-day festival of fried food aims to 'debunk the prejudice that it's unhealthy'. After a few hours spent grazing stalls packed with heavy-duty treats – *cannoli* from Sicily, *panzerotti* from Puglia and, of course, fried stuffed Ascoli olives – your body may not agree, although your taste buds will have had a blast.

Quintana CULTURE
(www.quintanadiascoli.it; ⊙ 2nd Sat Jul & 1st Sun Aug) This is one of Italy's most famous medieval festivals, and with good reason. Expect thousands of locals dressed in typical medieval garb: knights in armour, flag-throwers and ladies in flamboyant velvet robes. Processions and flag-waving contests take place throughout July and August, but the big draw is the Quintana joust, when the town's six *sestieri* (quarters) face off.

🛏 Sleeping

For a town of such modest proportions, Ascoli Piceno has an extraordinary number of charming hotels, many of which offer early booking discounts. The tourist office has lists of apartments, *agriturismi* and B&Bs.

★Hotel Palazzo dei Mercanti HISTORIC HOTEL €€
(☑ 0736 25 60 44; www.palazzodeimercanti.it; Corso Trento e Trieste 35; r €80-190; P 🕸) This 16th-century *palazzo* was once part of the Sant'Egido convent. Today you'll count your blessings in rooms with soothing pastel tones, hand-crafted furniture and nice touches like bathrobes (handy for the spa's whirlpool, sauna and hammam). The *palazzo* successfully blends original stone-vaulted interiors with a contemporary aesthetic.

Palazzo Guiderocchi BOUTIQUE HOTEL €€
(☑ 0736 25 97 10; www.palazzoguiderocchi.com; Via Cesare Battisti 3; s €60-140, d €70-170; P 🕸 @ 🕸)

Not many places offer the history, atmosphere and comfort of this 16th-century *palazzo*. Beautifully gathered around an inner courtyard, it retains the romance of vaulted ceilings on the 1st floor, low wood-beamed ceilings on the 2nd, and frescoes and several original doors throughout. During slow months, palatial rooms can be an absolute steal.

Albergo Piceno BOUTIQUE HOTEL €€
(☑ 0736 25 30 17; www.albergopiceno.it; Via Minucia 10; s € 60-75, d €90-115; 🕸 @) Just round the corner from the *duomo* on a narrow street, this is a great boutique place in a converted 17th-century *palazzo* with large rooms decorated in a bright modern style (but with the odd bit of rustic stone poking out here and there to give it character). It offers a generous breakfast plus a gym to help you work it off.

🍴 Eating & Drinking

Degusteria 25 Doc & Dop ITALIAN €
(☑ 0736 31 33 24; Via Panichi 3; meals €15; ⊙ Tue-Sun) Strings of garlic and chilli hang from the ceiling of this convivial deli-*enoteca*, where the locals squeeze in or spill out onto the terrace for wine and tasting plates of regional *salumi*, cheese and, of course, *olive all'ascolana*. They also rustle up decent day specials for pocket-money prices (€6).

★Il Desco MEDITERRANEAN €€
(☑ 0736 25 07 57; www.ildescoristorante.it; Via Vidacilio 10; meals €30-40; ⊙ closed Mon and dinner Sat) Funky chandeliers, high vaults and white distressed wood create a country-chic backdrop at this gorgeously styled *palazzo*. When the weather warms, diners spill out into the garden courtyard, lit by tealights. A clever use of herbs elevates seafood-focused specialities, from homemade pasta with prawns and zingy lemon to filet of sea bass with zucchini and almonds. It's all delicious.

Rua dei Notari TRADITIONAL ITALIAN €€
(☑ 0736 25 83 93; www.ruadeinotari.it; Via Cesare Battisti 3; meals €30-35; ⊙ dinner Wed-Sat & Mon, lunch & dinner Sun) Nestling in the vaulted 16th-century Palazzo Guiderocchi, this refined restaurant is one of the top tables in town. Artfully presented specialities play up seasonal, regional flavours: a pappardelle with porcini and winter truffles might prelude a prefectly layered *millefeuille* of veal and aubergine. The five-course degustation menu is a respectable €30.

Caffè Meletti
CAFE

(Piazza del Popolo 20; ⊙7.30am-11pm Tue-Sun) From the elegant shade of the portico you can sip a coffee or a glass of the famous homemade *anisette* with *olive all'ascolana* as you gaze onto the piazza. The cafe, founded in 1904, was once a popular haunt of Ernest Hemingway and Jean-Paul Sartre.

ⓘ Information

Police station (☑0736 35 51 11; Viale della Repubblica 8)

Post office (Via Crispi 2; ⊙8.20am-7.05pm Mon-Fri, 8.20am-12.35pm Sat)

Tourist office (☑0736 29 82 04; turismo@ comune.ascolipiceno.it; Piazza Arringo 7; ⊙9am-6.30pm Mon-Fri, 9am-1pm & 3-6.30pm Sat, 10am-6pm Sun)

ⓘ Getting There & Away

BUS

Services leave from Piazzale della Stazione, in front of the train station in the new part of town, east of the Castellano river. **Start** (☑0736 33 80 28; www.startspa.it) runs buses to Rome (€14.50, three hours, eight daily) and Civitanova Marche (€4.95, two hours, 12 daily).

TRAIN

Connections to Ancona (€6.95, two hours, 14 daily) often involve a change in Porto d'Ascoli. Trains to Macerata require one or two changes (€6.30, 2¼ hours, 10 daily). The station is a 15-minute walk east of the centre.

Monti Sibillini

Straddling the Le Marche–Umbria border in rugged splendour, the **Parco Nazionale dei Monti Sibillini** is always extraordinary, whether visited in winter, when its peaks are dusted with snow, or in summer, when its meadows are carpeted with wildflowers. The 70,000-hectare national park covers some of the most dramatic landscapes in central Italy, with glacier-carved valleys, beautifully preserved hilltop hamlets, quiet beech forests where deer roam and mountains, 10 of which tower above 2000m.

The park is a magnet to anyone seeking outdoor adventure or a brush with wildlife, with an expansive network of walking trails criss-crossing the area. *Rifugi* (mountain huts) welcome hikers every few kilometres with hearty meals and warm beds; most open summer only and details are available at all local tourist offices.

There's a terrifically scenic driving loop around the mountains, which visitors can easily reach from Norcia (in Umbria) or Ascoli Piceno, Macerata or Ancona. From the southwest, start in Norcia, heading to Castelluccio. Follow signs to Montemonaco, Montefortino and Amandola. Just past **Montefortino**, take the road marked for Madonna dell'Ambro, which will take you to the **Gola dell'Infernaccio**, Monti Sibillini's waterfall masterpiece. Backtrack to Montefortino and continue on the circle.

Although not technically in the Monti Sibillini national park, the largest and prettiest town is **Sarnano**, on the SS78, which leads to **Sasso Tetto**, the main ski area in Monti Sibillini. From here, the road drops down to Lago Fiastra. To continue on an equally stunning drive, circle around to the SS209 through the Valnerina in Umbria.

🏃 Activities

Perched like an eyrie on a 1452m hilltop and ringed by the mighty summits of the Appenines, **Castelluccio** is a lone ranger of a village, with just 150 inhabitants admiring its jaw-dropping backdrop on a daily basis. Technically in Umbria, although only just, it makes a terrific base for hiking in the park. It's famous for its *lenticchie* (small, sweet lentils), and *pecorino* and ricotta cheeses, but it's the location that brings in visitors. The Casa del Parco (p599) in Norcia has information on walking and other activities, including paragliding, mountain biking and horse-riding, in the surrounding area.

🛏 Sleeping & Eating

Taverna di Castelluccio
GUESTHOUSE €

(☑0743 82 11 58; www.tavernacastelluccio.it; Via Dietro la Torre 8; s €45-60, d €65-100, tr €82.50-120, incl half-board €63-78, €100-136, €135-174; 🛜) One of Castelluccio's few hotels, this abode has bright, pleasantly simple rooms, some with gorgeous Piano Grande views. It's worth forking out the extra for half-board, as the food (thick lentil soup, homemade pasta, grilled lamb and the like) is superb.

La Quercia della Memoria
AGRITURISMO €

(☑0733 69 44 31; www.querciadellamemoria.it; Contrada Vellato, San Ginesio; r per person €35-40, meals €30; 🅿🛜) 🌿 Follow the pandas to this one-in-a-million find. It's about 15 minutes off the Monti Sibillini route, but is so worth the drive, with its refurbished stone houses, where dozens of sustainable touches include

PIANO GRANDE

What sounds like a finely tuned instrument is in fact a lyrical landscape. Tucked in the far-eastern corner of Umbria, between Castellucio and Norcia, the Piano Grande is a 1270m-high plain flanked by the bare-backed peaks of the Appenines. When the snow melts, it gives way to a springtime eruption of wildflowers more beautiful than any Monet painting; its canvas streaked red, gold, violet and white with poppies, cornflowers, wild tulips, daisies, crocuses and narcissi. It's a florist's heaven, a hay-fever sufferer's hell and an endless source of camera-clicking fascination for walkers, who flock here for serendipitous strolls through the meadows.

radiant floor heating made from wine bottles. There's an organic restaurant and kids will adore the *asineria* (donkey farm).

Casa Sibillini B&B €
(☑ 0736 85 90 44; www.casasibillini.com; Via dei Tiratori 11, Montefortino; s/d/apt incl breakfast €40/60/80; 🛜🅿️) This English-owned B&B is a gracious home with appreciated touches: an indoor brick oven, a comfortable living-room area filled with books, and a home-cooked breakfast each morning. The owners can help you plan your day or trip around the mountain.

Hotel Paradiso HOTEL €
(☑ 0737 84 74 68; www.sibillinihotels.it; Piazza Umberto I, Amandola; s €40, d €65-100; 🅿️) It's not easy to find but this hilltop retreat is worth the trek for the view alone. With 40 spick-and-span rooms (most with balconies), a restaurant serving Umbrian home cooking (breakfast €5, lunch or dinner €20), tennis courts and a romantic arched walkway, this is a cracking base for a mountain holiday.

La Citadella AGRITURISMO €
(☑ 0736 85 63 61; www.cittadelladeisibillini.it; Loc Citadella, Montemonaco; s €55-65, d €80-100, meals €15; 🐾🅿️) At this serene *agriturismo* just north of the village of Montemonaco, goat bells are likely to be your wake-up call. Rooms are pretty simple, but with a great restaurant serving homegrown fare, a swimming pool and easy access to the Monti Sibillini walks you probably won't spend much time in them. Minimum stay two nights.

ℹ️ Information

The official park website (www.sibillini.net) has a wealth of information on where to say, what to do and how to get around. There are also 11 'Casa del Parco' visitor information centres, including at Norcia (p599) and **Amandola** (☑ 0736 84 85 98; Chiostro di San Francesco, Largo Leopardi 4; ⏰ 10am-12.30pm & 3.30-6.30pm).

ℹ️ Getting There & Away

Monti Sibillini is best reached by bus from Ascoli Piceno or Macerata. The services are busiest when school is in session, so can be spotty for tourists. Check with tourist offices in Ascoli or Macerata, or with the bus companies: **Contram** (☑ 0733 23 09 06; www.contram.it) in Macerata and **Start** (☑ 0736 33 80 28; www.startspa.it) in Ascoli Piceno.

The nearest train stations are in Ascoli Piceno to the south and Tolentino to the north.

Sarnano

Spilling photogenically down a hillside, its medieval heart a maze of narrow cobbled lanes, Sarnano looks every inch the Italian hill-town prototype, particularly when its red-brick facades glow warmly in the late-afternoon sun. It is a charming, hospitable base for exploring the Monti Sibillini range.

The tranquil flower-filled garden at **Albergo La Villa** (☑ 0733 65 72 18; www.hrlavilla.com; Viale della Rimembranza 46; s/d €36/€56; 🅿️) is reason enough to stay, but the total silence, five-minute walk into town, price, adjoining restaurant with local treats (rabbit, truffles, lamb etc) and children's playground make it an all-round winner.

On the Sassotetto road lies the sparklingly modern **Hotel Eden** (☑ 0733 65 71 23; www.hoteledensarnano.it; Via de Gasperi 26; s €50-65, d €90-120, all incl breakfast; 🅿️🍽️@🛜🏊) serving weary skiers, view seekers and spa aficionados. The bright, wood-floored rooms make a comfortable base for enjoying the cosseted warmth of the next-door Novidra spa.

Right in the centre of town, **Le Clarisse** (☑ 345 4959389; www.osterialeclarisse.it; Via Mazzini 240; meals €15-38; ⏰ daily) is a classic *osteria*, serving whatever is fresh and seasonal, with an emphasis on regional truffles, in a warm brick-walled, candlelit interior.

The **Sarnano tourist office** (☑ 0733 65 71 44; Largo Ricciardi 1; ⏰ 9am-1pm Mon-Sat, plus 3-6pm Tue-Thu) has information on walking, climbing and accommodation in the park.

Abruzzo & Molise

Best Places to Eat

➡ Locanda Sotto gli Archi (p625)

➡ Hosteria dell'Arco (p626)

➡ Ristorante Clemente (p626)

➡ Ristorante da Paolino (p628)

Best Places to Stay

➡ Sextantio (p625)

➡ Locanda Alfieri (p636)

➡ Le Torri Hotel (p628)

Why Go?

A stunning mountain region little known to foreign visitors, Abruzzo is an area of unspoiled natural beauty and back-country charm. Only an hour from Rome, it feels like a world apart with its great Apennine peaks, still, silent valleys and pretty hilltop towns. To the south, Molise offers more of the same, albeit on a smaller, less dramatic scale.

The landscape is extraordinary. In the region's three national parks, thick forests and flowering meadows give way to high barren plains and snowcapped granite peaks, and wolves and bears roam free in the vast beech woods. A mecca for outdoor enthusiasts, it offers wonderful hiking, skiing and mountain biking, while the coast boasts beautiful sandy beaches.

Across this verdant landscape, there's a string of cultural gems to discover. Pescocostanzo's baroque centre and Sulmona's historic *palazzi* (mansions) testify to past glories, while isolation has ensured the survival of age-old customs such as Cocullo's bizarre snake charmers' procession.

When to Go
L'Aquila

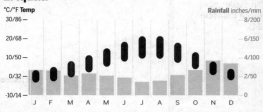

May Cocullo's unique snake festival involves a statue, procession and writhing nest of snakes.

Jul Sulmona's square fills with prancing horses and jousting during this medieval tournament.

May, Jun & Sep Wildflowers, pleasant summer sun – perfect conditions for hiking.

Abruzzo & Molise Highlights

1 Breathing in the pure mountain air of **Pescocostanzo** (p627), one of Abruzzo's hidden jewels.

2 Spending a night in the village of **Civitella Alfedena** (p630), where bears, wolves and lynx inhabit the surrounding mountains.

3 Driving or hiking the high windswept plateau of **Campo Imperatore** (p624), Italy's 'Little Tibet'.

4 Feeling the call of the wild as you climb the **Corno Grande** (p624), summit of the Gran Sasso and the Apennines' highest peak.

5 Travelling back in time as you walk through the ancient Roman town of **Saepinum** (p635).

6 Driving through the breathtaking **Gole di Sagittario** (p628) between Sulmona and Scanno.

7 Marvelling at the many imposing hilltop castles, such as **Rocca Calascio** (p624).

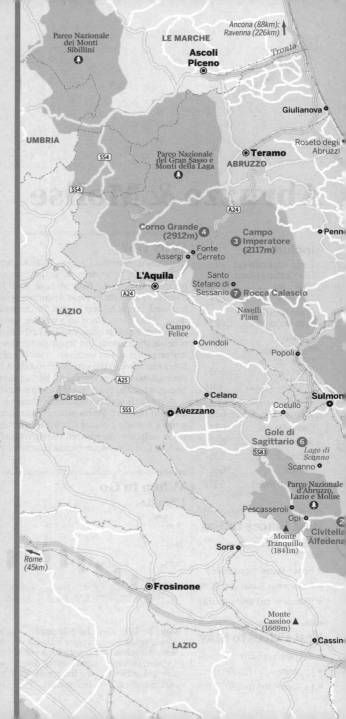

ABRUZZO

Best known for its dramatic mountain scenery, Abruzzo's landscape is surprisingly diverse. A vast plain extends east of Avezzano, the coastline is flat and sandy, and there are ancient forests in the Parco Nazionale d'Abruzzo, Lazio e Molise.

Many towns retain a medieval look, while the numerous hilltop castles and isolated, sometimes abandoned, *borghi* (medieval towns) exude a sinister charm, lending credence to Abruzzo's fame as an ancient centre of magic, and the land of a thousand castles.

Parco Nazionale del Gran Sasso e Monti della Laga

About 20km northeast of L'Aquila, the Gran Sasso massif is the centrepiece of the Parco Nazionale del Gran Sasso e Monti della Laga, one of Italy's largest national parks. The park's predominant feature is its jagged rocky landscape through which Europe's southernmost glacier, the Calderone, cuts its course. It's also a haven for wildlife, home to an estimated 40 wolves, 350 chamois and six pairs of royal eagles. Hiking trails criss-cross the park and atmospheric castles and medieval hill towns crown the foothills.

Rocca Calascio, 6km west of Santo Stefano di Sessanio, is one such imposing castle dominating the skyline above the Navelli Plain. There's not much to see inside, but the views are stupendous, and from a distance the castle makes an impressive photograph.

Fonte Cerreto is the main gateway to the Gran Sasso and **Campo Imperatore** (2117m), a high windswept plateau 27km long and known as Italy's 'Little Tibet'. A **funivia** (cable car; ☑ 0862 60 61 43; €15 Mon-Fri, €17 Sat & Sun; ⊙ 8am-5pm Mon-Sat, to 6pm Sun, closed May) runs up to the Campo from Fonte Cerreto. Up top, there's hiking in summer and skiing in winter. For more information contact the **park office** (☑ 0862 6 05 21; www.gransassolagapark.it; Via del Convento 1; ⊙ 10.30am-1pm Mon-Fri & 4-6pm Tue & Thu) in Assergi.

One of the most popular trekking routes is the surprisingly straightforward climb up **Corno Grande** – at 2912m, it's the Apennines' highest peak. The 9km *via normale* (normal route) starts in the main parking area at Campo Imperatore and heads to the summit. The trail should be clear of snow from early June to late September/early October. If attempting the ascent, or any other serious route, be sure to arm yourself with the CAI 1:25,000 map *Gran Sasso d'Italia* (€10).

The park has a network of *rifugi* (mountain huts) for walkers. Otherwise, you can bed down at a modest campground in Fonte Cerreto, **Camping Funivia del Gran Sasso** (☑ 0862 60 61 63; Fonte Cerreto; camping per person/tent/car €27; ⊙ mid-May–mid-Sep). At the top of the cable-car lift, the **Hotel Campo Imperatore** (☑ 0862 40 00 00; www.hotelcampoimperatore.it; Campo Imperatore; half-board from €60; ☎ ☜), where Mussolini was briefly imprisoned in 1943, also has a **hostel** (dm per person €30, incl dinner €45) that offers basic year-round digs.

Fonte Cerreto is just off the A24 motorway (clearly signposted). It's best to have your own transport to navigate the park.

Sulmona

POP 25,200

Sulmona lies in a picturesque location, nestled in a valley with the Morrone massif as a backdrop. A lively and prosperous provincial town with an atmospheric medieval core, it makes a convenient base from which to explore southern Abruzzo.

Despite its medieval appearance, Sulmona's origins pre-date the Romans (the poet Ovid was born here in 43 BC). In the Middle Ages it became an important commercial centre, but much of Sulmona's modern wealth is based on the production of *confetti* – the insanely colourful sugar almonds presented to guests at Italian weddings – and jewellery.

◎ Sights

Most sights are on or near the main street, Corso Ovidio, which runs southeast from the Villa Comunale park to Piazza Garibaldi, Sulmona's main square. It's a five-minute stroll and the *corso* (boulevard) is closed to traffic outside business hours. About halfway down is Piazza XX Settembre, with its **statue of Ovid** – a popular meeting point.

Piazza Garibaldi   PIAZZA

The large town square is home to Sulmona's extensive Wednesday and Saturday morning market: you'll find fresh fish, veg, fruit and flowers as well as the ubiquitous *porchetta* van, selling pork in a roll. Along Corso Ovidio is a striking series of arches, all

SANTO STEFANO DI SESSANIO

Known as Sextantio in Roman times, this atmospheric hilltop village has a commanding position overlooking two valleys. Although the 2009 earthquake that struck L'Aquila damaged a number of buildings in Santo Stefano, including the iconic 18m-high watchtower (which completely collapsed), a stroll through the *centro storico* (historic centre) reveals why the village is regarded as one of Gran Sasso's most picturesque, and why it made the list as a *borghi più belli d'Italia* (one of the most beautiful towns in Italy).

The town flourished in the 16th century under the rule of the Medici family, and the Medici coat of arms can still be seen on the entrance portal to the main piazza. Subsequently left behind by history, Santo Stefano was untouched by development, making it a perfect place for radical eco-restorer Daniele Kihlgren to carry out his work. He invested in the town, on an agreement with the authorities that no unsympathetic and ugly development would mar his vision.

The result is Sextantio (☑ 0862 89 91 12; www.sextantio.it; Via Principe Umberto; r €150-450; ☎), an enchanting *albergo diffuso* (diffused hotel), which has a number of rooms and apartments scattered throughout the *centro storico*. Rooms capture the authenticity of the past with handmade blankets and rustic furniture made in the village, yet remain refined thanks to modern conveniences such as underfloor heating, mood lighting and divinely deep bathtubs.

In Sextantio's restaurant, Locanda Sotto gli Archi (meals €50; ☺ dinner daily, lunch Sat & Sun), tables adorned with soft candlelight evoke a medieval mood for a fixed menu of traditional Abruzzese dishes.

Taking the SS17, Santo Stefano di Sessanio is 27km from L'Aquila, but a more scenic route takes you through Fonte Cerreto on the main 17bis road and across the grand plateau of Campo Imperatore before turning south to Santo Stefano (about 50km).

that remains of a 13th-century aqueduct. In the centre of the piazza, the Renaissance Fontana del Vecchio (Fountain of the Old One) is said by some to depict Solimo, the founder of Sulmona. To the northeast, the 14th-century Chiesa di San Filippo Neri boasts an impressive Gothic portal.

Also in the square is the Polo Museale Santa Chiara (☑ 0864 21 29 62; admission €3; ☺ 9am-1pm & 3.30-7.30pm Tue-Sun), a small museum with an eclectic collection of religious and contemporary art including a fascinating *presepe* (nativity scene) depicting 19th-century Sulmona.

Palazzo dell'Annunziata   PALACE
(Corso Ovidio) The most impressive of the *palazzi*, founded in 1320 but rebuilt many times over, sits above a 1st-century-BC Roman *domus* (villa). The building has a harmonious blend of Gothic and Renaissance architecture. Inside, the Museo Archeologico in situ (☺ 9am-1pm Wed, Fri & Sat, 3.30-7.30pm Tue & Thu) FREE showcases relics and remains of the Roman domus. The Museo Civico, also found here, has a small collection of Roman mosaics and Renaissance sculptures.

Porta Napoli   LANDMARK
(Piazza Vittorio Veneto) This monumental 14th-century town gate has an unusual rusticated masonry finish.

Museo dell'Arte Confettiera   MUSEUM
(☑ 0864 21 00 47; www.pelino.it; Via Stazione Introdacqua 55; ☺ 9am-12.30pm & 3.30-6.30pm Mon-Sat) FREE The museum is housed in the Fabbrica Confetti Pelino, Sulmona's most famous manufacturer of *confetti*. The reconstructed 16th-century laboratory looks more like an old-time science lab than a sweet-making plant. It's about 1km from Porta Napoli, at the southern end of Corso Ovidio.

🎊 Festivals & Events

Madonna che Scappa in Piazza   RELIGIOUS
In this unique Easter Sunday ritual, a mourning, black-clad Virgin Mary races across the square when she sees her newly resurrected son – well, the statue bearers do the running – while the Madonna's mourning cloak disappears and a flock of white doves fly into the air.

Giostra Cavalleresca di Sulmona   CULTURE
(www.giostrasulmona.it) On the last weekend in July, local horse riders gallop around

WORTH A TRIP

SNAKES IN COCULLO

A one-horse hamlet in the hills west of Sulmona, Cocullo is the unlikely setting for one of Italy's weirdest festivals. The **Processione dei Serpari** (Snake Charmers' Procession) is the highlight of celebrations to honour San Domenico, Cocullo's patron saint and protector against snake bites. Events kick off at noon on the first Thursday of May when villagers gather in the main square to adorn a statue of St Dominic with jewellery, banknotes and dozens of writhing snakes. Once dressed, the saint is paraded through the streets by a team of fearless *serpari*. Local lore holds that if the snakes twist around the saint's head it's good news for the year ahead; if they crawl up the arms, the omens are bad.

Despite the religious element of the festivities, its origins are said to be pagan. Before the arrival of Christianity, locals worshipped a goddess called Angizia, who supposedly had powers to cure snake bites. As Christianity spread, the ancient deities were substituted by Christian saints and San Domenico inherited Angizia's mantle.

The serpents used for the festival are harmless *cervoni* and *saettoni*. They are caught in the surrounding countryside in late March and released back into the hills once the festivities are over.

Cocullo is accessible by a daily bus from Sulmona (€1.80, 30 minutes), although on festival day extra services are laid on – ask at Sulmona tourist office for details.

Piazza Garibaldi in this medieval tournament. A week later, the competition is opened up to riders from across Europe in the **Giostra Cavalleresca d'Europa**.

🛏 Sleeping

★ **B&B Il Marchese del Grillo**   B&B €
(☎ 0327 3570889; www.bebilmarchesedelgrillo.it; Via Corfinio 62; d/tr €90/110; P ☜) A wonderful old-town B&B, combining terracotta floor tiles, rugged stone walls and great home comforts including huge wooden beds. The welcome is particularly warm, and the breakfast, with fruit, homemade salami and pastries, is superb.

Albergo Ristorante Stella   HOTEL €
(☎ 0864 5 26 53; www.hasr.it; Via Panfilo Mazara 18; s €40-50, d €70-80; ✳ @) A bright little three-star place in the *centro storico* (historic centre), the Stella offers 10 airy, modern rooms and a smart, ground-floor restaurant-wine bar (€15 to €25). Discounts of around 20% are available for stays of more than one night.

🍴 Eating & Drinking

★ **Hosteria dell'Arco**   TRADITIONAL ITALIAN €
(☎ 0864 21 05 53; Via M D'Eramo 20; meals €20-25; ☺ closed Mon evening & Sun) Superb food, lovely, rustic surroundings, laid-back atmosphere and friendly service. First up is the fabulous antipasto buffet, prepared from scratch every night, follow this with, say, delicious grilled lamb and scrumptious homemade desserts.

★ **Ristorante Clemente**   TRADITIONAL ITALIAN €€
(☎ 0864 21 06 79; Vico Quercia 5; meals €25; ☺ Fri-Wed) Photos of family members on the wall remind you that this is a proud, family-run restaurant. The menu is based on the cornerstones of Abruzzese cooking, using seasonal products to produce delicious meals.

La Cantina di Biffi   TRADITIONAL ITALIAN €€
(☎ 0864 3 20 25; www.cantinadibiffi.it; Via Barbato 1; meals €25; ☺ closed Sun evening & Mon) Just off Corso Ovidio, this is a charming and atmospheric bistro-wine bar. Exposed-stone walls and the arched, vaulted ceiling set the stage for excellent homemade food and local wine (served by the glass from €4).

Gran Caffè dell'Annunziata   CAFE
(☎ 0864 21 11 21; Piazza SS Annunziata 2; ☺ 9am-1pm daily, 4-8pm Mon-Sat) Grab an outdoor table and sip something cool as you watch the evening parade on the piazza at Corso Ovidio.

ⓘ Information

Tourist Office (☎ 0864 5 32 76; www.abruzzo-turismo.it; Corso Ovidio 208; ☺ 9am-1pm daily & 4-7pm Mon-Sat, mid-May–mid-Sep, 9am-1pm Mon-Sat, 3-6pm Mon, Wed & Fri mid-Sep–mid-May)

❶ Getting There & Away

BUS

Agenzia Fai (☑ 0864 3 33 49; Via Circonvallazione Orientale 3; ☉ 9am-1pm & 4-7.30pm Mon-Sat) Buses leave from a confusing array of points, including Villa Comunale, the hospital, train station, and beneath Ponte Capograssi. Find out which stop you need when you get your ticket here, near Porta Napoli.

ARPA (☑ 800 762 622; www.arpaonline. it) Buses go to and from L'Aquila (€12.60, 1½ hours, nine daily).

SATAM (☑ 0871 34 49 76; www.gruppolapanoramica.it/satam/) Runs services to Pescara (€7, one hour, four daily) and other nearby towns, plus four daily services to Naples (€18, 2½ hours).

TRAIN

Trains link with L'Aquila (€4.50, one hour, 10 daily), Pescara (€4.50, 1¼ hours, 16 daily) and Rome (€15.60, three to 4½ hours, 10 daily). The train station is 2km northwest of the historic centre; the half-hourly bus A runs between the two.

Parco Nazionale della Majella

More than half of Parco Nazionale della Majella's 750 sq km is at an altitude of over 2000m. Wolves roam in the woods and 500km of paths and cycling trails criss-cross the area. Monte Amaro (2793m), the Apennines' second-highest peak, lies in a dramatic landscape of ominous mountains and empty valleys.

From Sulmona the two easiest access points are **Campo di Giove** (elevation 1064m), a small skiing village 18 tortuous kilometres to the southeast, and the lovely town of Pescocostanzo, 33km south of Sulmona along the SS17.

Pescocostanzo

ELEV 1400M

Set amid verdant highland plains, Pescocostanzo is a real gem, a weatherbeaten hilltop town whose historical core has changed little in more than 500 years. Much of the cobbled centre dates from the 16th and 17th centuries when it was an important town on the 'Via degli Abruzzi', the main road linking Naples and Florence.

◉ Sights & Activities

Of particular note is the **Collegiata di Santa Maria del Colle**, an atmospheric church that combines a superb Romanesque portal with a lavish baroque interior. Nearby, **Piazza del Municipio** is flanked by a number of impressive *palazzi*, including **Palazzo Comunale**, with its distinctive clock tower, and **Palazzo Fanzago**, designed by the great baroque architect Cosimo Fanzago in 1624; look out for the carved wooden dragons under the roof.

L'AQUILA: AFTER THE SHOCK WAVE

Destruction from the devastating 6.3 magnitude earthquake that struck northern Abruzzo in 2009 was severe: 309 people died in the regional capital L'Aquila; the city centre, famed for its university, elegant squares and historic *palazzi* (mansions), was partially destroyed; and 65,000 residents were evacuated to camps on the edge of the city. In one of his all-time crass gaffes, then prime minister Silvio Berlusconi instructed residents to enjoy their 'camping weekend'.

Controversy continued in 2012 when six scientists and an official were convicted of multiple counts of manslaughter for failing to warn residents of the quake risk. And in 2013 three builders and a technician were also found guilty of manslaughter charges for neglecting to properly maintain a student residence in which eight people died.

Several years on from the quake, L'Aquila's *centro storico* (historic centre) resembles a giant construction site. Nearly two-thirds of the displaced residents have returned to their homes, and the rest are housed in temporary antiseismic residences on the edge of town. Efforts are focusing on restoring historic buildings, and an attempt to imbue the centre with new life by opening bars and restaurants. But, with Italy in deep recession, progress in L'Aquila is frustratingly slow for the inhabitants, and there is little to draw in casual visitors.

Abruzzo and neighbouring Molise are particularly vulnerable to earthquakes as they sit on a major fault line that follows the Apennines from Sicily up to Genoa.

TOP FIVE HILLTOP TOWNS IN ABRUZZO

In Abruzzo's mountainous terrain, the hills are crowned with ruined castles and medieval villages. Wander through these pretty and atmospheric hilltop towns:

➡ **Pescocostanzo (p627)**
➡ **Scanno**
➡ **Vasto (p634)**
➡ **Chieti (p633)**
➡ **Sulmona (p624)** OK, it's not exactly hilltop, but Ovid's birthplace makes an attractive base for exploring the Parco Nazionale della Majella.

History apart, Pescocostanzo also offers skiing on **Monte Calvario** and summer hiking in the **Bosco di Sant'Antonio**.

🛏 Sleeping & Eating

★ **Albergo La Rua**　　　　HOTEL €
(☑ 0864 64 00 83; www.larua.it; Via Rua Mozza 1; d €70-100; 🌐) Hikers should head straight for this charming little hotel in the historic centre. The look is country cosy with low wood-beamed ceilings and a stone fireplace, and the superfriendly owners are a mine of local knowledge on the town's distinctive domestic architecture, fine jewellery and dialect.

★ **Le Torri Hotel**　　　　HOTEL €€
(☑ 0864 64 20 40; www.letorrihotel.it; Via del Vallone 4; d €100-160; ❄ @) This stylish and enticing hotel, in a *palazzo* once owned by a baron, has large, comfortable rooms with wooden floors, antique furnishings and inviting white bedspreads.

★ **Ristorante da Paolino**　　　　TRADITIONAL ITALIAN €€
(☑ 0864 64 00 80; www.ristorantedapaolino.com; Strada Vulpes 34; meals €30) A bustling and popular little inn-restaurant in the heart of the village near Palazzo Fanzago: be sure to book ahead. Pasta dishes make full use of local seasonal ingredients such as truffles and chestnuts, and you can follow up with rabbit, veal or beef – and a creamy pudding.

Il Gallo di Pietra　　　　TRADITIONAL ITALIAN €€
(☑ 0864 64 20 40; www.ilgallodipietra.it; Via del Vallone 4; meals €35; ⊙ lunch & dinner) Attached to Le Torri Hotel; you can dine alfresco in the garden or beside the fire in the cosy indoor restaurant. The menu features the enticing flavours of Abruzzese and Neapolitan cuisine.

ℹ Information

Tourist Office (☑ 0864 64 14 40; Vico delle Carceri; ⊙ 9am-1pm & 3-6pm Mon-Fri Sep-Jun, 9am-1pm & 4-7pm daily Jul & Aug) Off the central Piazza del Municipio. Also see the Parco Nazionale della Majella's comprehensive website (www.parcomajella.it).

ℹ Getting There & Away

Buses run from Sulmona to Pescocostanzo (€4, one hour, three daily) via Castel di Sangro, and to Campo di Giove (€2.30, 45 minutes, three daily).

Scanno

POP 1990

A tangle of steep alleyways and sturdy, greystone houses, Scanno is a dramatic and atmospheric medieval *borgo,* known for its finely worked filigree gold jewellery. For centuries a centre of wool production, it is one of the few places in Italy where you can still see women wearing traditional dress – especially during the week-long **costume festival** (www.costumediscanno.org) held at the end of April. The somewhat sombre but imposing costumes were famously photographed by Cartier Bresson in 1951. They comprise a full black skirt and bodice with puffed sleeves, a headdress of braided fabric topped with an angular cap, and filigree jewellery including star-shaped charms, given as betrothal gifts by shepherds before they departed on the long *transhumanza* (sheep migration).

Be sure to take the exhilarating drive up to Scanno from Sulmona through the rocky **Gole di Sagittario**, a WWF reserve and gorge, and past tranquil Lago di Scanno. Here there's a scattering of bars and cafes, and you can hire boats in summer.

🛏 Sleeping & Eating

★ **Il Palazzo**　　　　B&B €
(☑ 0864 74 78 60; www.ilpalazzobb.it; Via Ciorla 25; €60-90; P 🌐) This elegant and gently welcoming B&B spans seven rooms on the 2nd floor of an old *palazzo* in the *centro storico.* The rooms are stylishly decorated with antique furnishings, and breakfast is served under a frescoed ceiling.

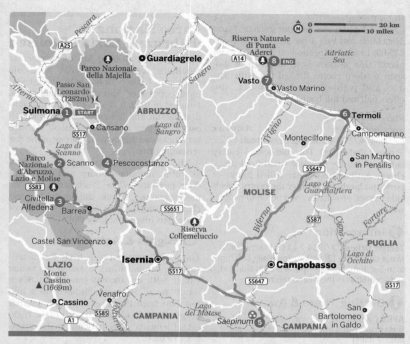

🏃 Driving Tour
Cut to the Heart

START SULMONA
END RISERVA NATURALE DI PUNTA ADERCI
LENGTH 245KM TO 310KM; ONE WEEK

An oasis in the mountainous terrain of southern Abruzzo, ① **Sulmona** (p624) is the place to start. With its attractive historic centre, welcoming vibe and great trattorias, it's the archetypal Italian town. Check out the market stalls on Piazza Garibaldi and join the locals on their *passeggiata* (evening stroll) along Corso Ovidio. After a night in Sulmona, push on southward to hilltop ② **Scanno** (p628). It's a slow, scenic ride that takes you through the breathtaking Gole di Sagittario, a rocky gorge that squeezes the road like a natural vice, and up past the beautiful Lago di Scanno. Scanno's dramatic appearance has made it something of a tourist attraction, but visit out of summer and you'll find it a tranquil spot.

From Scanno, the next leg takes you into the national parks. From Lago di Barrea you

can head deep into the magnificent Parco Nazionale d'Abruzzo, Lazio e Molise, the most popular of Abruzzo's three national parks and set up camp in ③ **Civitella Alfedena** (p630). Or you can head north and take the long way round to pretty ④ **Pescocostanzo** (p627) in the Parco Nazionale della Majella. Either way, spend a couple of days exploring the surrounding mountains. Once you've recharged your batteries, continue on past Isernia to the well-preserved Roman ruins at ⑤ **Saepinum** (p635).

After the mountains, it's time to hit the coast and top up your tan at ⑥ **Termoli** (p636), or further up the road at ⑦ **Vasto** (p634), both popular Adriatic resorts. From Termoli, the Isole Tremiti are just a day trip away. But if the crowds get too much (and they might in summer), go north to the Spiaggia di Punta Penna, a lovely beach in the ⑧ **Riserva Naturale di Punta Aderci** (p634).

Hotel Belvedere HOTEL €

(☑0864 7 43 14; www.belvederescanno.it; Piazza Santa Maria della Valle 3; per person incl breakfast €35-60) In a good location on Scanno's main piazza, this pleasant hotel offers spick-and-span modern rooms decked out with parquet and polished wood trimmings. Also offers half and full board.

Pizzeria Trattoria
Vecchio Mulino TRATTORIA €

(☑0864 74 72 19; Via Silla 50; pizzas/meals €7/25; ☺closed Wed winter) This old-school eatery is a good bet for a classic wood-fired pizza, cheesy antipasti and char-grilled hunks of pork and lamb. In summer the pretty streetside terrace provides a good perch to people-watch.

❶ Information

Tourist Office (☑0864 7 43 17; Piazza Santa Maria della Valle 12; ☺9am-1pm daily & 4-7pm Mon-Sat Jun-Sep, 9am-1pm & 3-6pm Mon-Sat Oct–mid-May) In the village centre.

❶ Getting There & Away

APRA (☑800 762 622; www.arpaonline.it) Buses run to and from Sulmona (€3.20, one hour, 7 daily)

Parco Nazionale d'Abruzzo, Lazio e Molise

Encompassing 1100 sq km of spectacular mountain scenery, the Parco Nazionale d'Abruzzo, Lazio e Molise is the oldest and most popular of Abruzzo's national parks, founded in 1922. It is also an important natural habitat and home to the native Marsican brown bear and Apennine wolf. If you're very lucky you might also spot one of the few remaining lynx.

The park offers superb hiking as well as skiing, mountain biking and other outdoor pursuits. While Pescasseroli has the most amenities, it lacks the remote feel and charm of tiny Civitella Alfedena, the base of numerous hikes, and lofty Opi.

◉ Sights & Activities

The park's main centre is lively Pescasseroli (elevation 1167m), a rather sprawling village with an ancient core about 80km southwest of Sulmona. Situated on a hilltop 6km from Pescasseroli is Opi, another *borghi più belli d'Italia*. It's one of the highest settlements in the park and makes an attractive base.

WALKING & WILDLIFE

With about 150 well-marked routes, signalled by white and red marks daubed on trees and rocks, the Parco Nazionale d'Abruzzo, Lazio e Molise is a mecca for hikers. Trails range from easy family jaunts to multiday hikes over rocky peaks and exposed highlands. The best time to go is between June and September, although access to some of the busier routes around Pescasseroli is often limited in July and August. To book entry to trails contact the Centro di Visita in Pescasseroli or the Centro Lupo in Civitella Alfedena.

Don't set off without the official hiking map (€12) available at all local tourist offices. Note that the time estimates given are one way only.

Two of the area's most popular hikes are the climbs up Monte Amaro (2793m; Route F1) and Monte Tranquillo (1841m; Route C3). The Monte Amaro route, a 2¼-hour hike, starts from a car park 7km southeast of Pescasseroli (follow the SS83 for about 2km beyond Opi) and rises steeply up to the peaks where you're rewarded with stupendous views over the Valle del Sangro. There's quite a good chance of spotting a chamois on this walk.

The Monte Tranquillo route takes about 2½ hours from a starting point 1km south of Pescasseroli (follow signs for the Hotel Iris and Centro Ippico Vallecupa). If you still have your breath at the top, you can continue northwards along the Rocca Ridge before descending down to Pescasseroli from the north. This beautiful but challenging 19.5km circuit takes six or seven hours.

You may be lucky enough to spot an Apennine wolf or a Marsiscan brown bear on your hike: this might sound like a scary prospect, but the animals are extremely shy, the only possible threat being from a female bear protecting her cubs. Lynx, chamois, roe deer, wild boar, golden eagles and peregrine hawks also inhabit the park, and fauna includes the rare lady's slipper orchid.

The little **Centro Visita del Camoscio** (Opi; ☉ 10am-1pm & 3-7pm Sat & Sun, daily July & Aug), a wildlife sanctuary, studies the Apennine chamois, with a viewpoint from which you can see the animals roaming.

On the park's eastern edge and about 17km from Opi is the picturesque **Lago di Barrea** with the venerable and handsome town of **Barrea** positioned on a rocky spur above the lake.

At nearby **Civitella Alfedena**, a seductive hamlet reached via a bridge across the lake, you can study the local flora and fauna at the **Centro Lupo** (Wolf Centre; ☑ 0864 89 01 41; admission €3; ☉ 10am-2pm & 2.30-5.30pm), which has an impressive amount of information (in Italian only) on the wolf and its role in myth and literature, as well as an extensive photo gallery that will help you identify everything from rare orchids to chamois. Try to spot the two wolves who regularly trot through their large enclosure at the free **Area Faunistica del Lupo** behind the museum. To see a rare lynx follow the signs to the **Area Faunistica delle Lince**.

Hiking opportunities abound, whether you want to go it alone or with an organised group. There are numerous outfits offering guided excursions, including **Ecotur** (☑ 0863 91 27 60; www.ecotur.org; Via Piave 9, Pescasseroli), which organises treks, bike rides and various other excursions.

Between May and October, the **Centro Ippico Vallecupa** (☑ 0863 91 04 44; www.agriturismomaneggiovallecupa.it; Via della Difesa, Pescaseroli; rides 1hr/full day €20/80) offers guided horse rides in the park.

🛏 Sleeping & Eating

⭐ **Albergo Antico Borga La Torre**   HOTEL €
(☑ 0864 89 01 21; www.albergolatorre.com; Via Castello 3, Civitella Alfedena; s €30-40, d €45-60; P @) Housed in an atmospheric 18th-century *palazzo* in Civitella Alfedena's medieval centre, this attractive and spotless hotel is popular with hikers. It also runs a small restaurant serving hot, fortifying food, after which the owner might treat you to his homemade and eye-wateringly strong *digestivo*.

B&B La Sosta   B&B €
(☑ 0863 91 60 57; Via Marsicana 17, Opi; per person €25; P) This delightful B&B on the main road below Opi is run with passionate care by a hospitable elderly couple. There are six very clean, smart rooms, a sunny terrace, and excellent access to the nearby mountains. The breakfasts are quite special too,

with cakes and lashings of homemade jam. Excellent value.

Campeggio Wolf   CAMPGROUND €
(☑ 0864 89 03 60; Via Sotto i Cerri, Civitella Alfedena; camping €13-16.50; ☉ May-Sep) This campground is a fairly simple affair but has free hot showers.

Il Duca degli Abruzzi   RESTAURANT €€
(☑ 0863 91 10 75; www.pescasseroli.net/ducadegliabruzzi/; Piazza Duca degli Abruzzi, Pescaseroli; meals €25) This handsome hotel-restaurant is located on a quiet square in the *centro storico*. Everything is homemade: try the truffle pasta or potato gnocchi, and follow up with baked cod or grilled pork, washed down with Montepulciano d 'Abruzzo.

ℹ Information

Centro di Visita (☑ 0863 911 32 21; Viale Colli d'Oro; ☉ 9am-7.30pm Apr-Aug, 10am-5.30pm Sep-Mar) Located in Pescaseroli. There is information available here and also a small museum and a clinic for sick animals: you might see bears here.

ℹ Getting There & Away

Pescasseroli, Civitella Alfedena and other villages in the national park are linked by daily buses to Avezzano (€5, 1½ hours), from where you can change for L'Aquila, Pescara and Rome; and to Castel di Sangro (€3.90, 1¼ hours) for connections to Sulmona and Naples.

Pescara

POP 123,100

Abruzzo's largest city is a heavily developed seaside resort with one of the largest marinas on the Adriatic. The city was heavily bombed during WWII and much of the city centre was reduced to rubble. It's a lively place with an animated seafront, especially in summer, but unless you're coming for the 16km of sandy beaches there's no great reason to hang around. One sight not to miss is the Museo delle Genti d'Abruzzo, which has plenty that will appeal to kids too.

◉ Sights

Pescara's main attraction is its long stretch of beachfront, and the shopping precinct around pedestrianised Corso Umberto. From Piazzale della Repubblica, the beach is a short walk down Corso Umberto. There are also a few sights worth a quick look.

TAKE TO THE PISTES

Abruzzo and Molise might lack the glamour of the northern Alps, but skiing is enthusiastically followed and there are resorts across the regions (bank on about €35 for a daily ski pass).

➡ **Campitello Matese** In Molise's Monti del Matese, Campitello offers 40km of pistes, including 15km for cross-country skiers.

➡ **Campo di Giove** At the foot of the Parco Nazionale della Majella, this resort offers Abruzzo's highest skiing, at 2350m.

➡ **Campo Felice** A small resort 40km south of L'Aquila with 40km of pistes (30km downhill, 10km cross-country).

➡ **Campo Imperatore** Twenty-two kilometres of mainly downhill pistes and more than 60km of cross-country trails in the Parco Nazionale del Gran Sasso e Monti della Laga.

➡ **Ovindoli** Abruzzo's biggest ski resort, with 30km of downhill pistes and 50km of cross-country trails.

➡ **Pescasseroli** A popular outpost deep in the Parco Nazionale d'Abruzzo with 30km of downhill slopes.

➡ **Pescocostanzo** Good for ski hiking as well as downhill skiing, it's celebrated for its medieval architecture.

➡ **Rivisondoli-Roccaraso** Near Pescocostanzo, this is one of the best equipped, with 28 ski lifts, two cable cars and more than 100km of ski slopes.

Museo delle Genti d'Abruzzo MUSEUM
(☑ 085 451 00 26; www.gentidabruzzo.it; Via delle Caserme 24; adult/reduced €6/3, half-price Sun; ⊙ 9am-1.30pm Mon-Sat, 5-8pm Sun Sep-Jun, to midnight Fri & Sat Jul & Aug) Located on a quiet road parallel to the river on the opposite bank from the centre, this wonderful museum illustrates Abruzzo peasant culture. The information is mainly in Italian, but the objects speak eloquently for themselves: there are shepherds' capes, carnival masks, outlandish silver saddle pommels and even a conical stone hut. The section on Scanno costume and jewellery is outstanding – altogether this amounts to a moving exploration of a lost way of life.

Museo Casa Natale Gabriele D'Annunzio MUSEUM
(☑ 0865 6 03 91; Corso Manthonè 116; admission €2; ⊙ 9am-1.30pm) Birthplace of controversial fascist poet Gabriele D'Annunzio.

Museo d'Arte Moderna Vittoria Colonna ART GALLERY
(☑ 085 428 37 59; Via Gramsci 26; adult/reduced €6/4; ⊙ 9.30am-1.30pm & 4-8pm) Near the seafront, one block back from the beach, the gallery boasts a Picasso and Miró among its small collection of modern art.

 Tours

Absolutely Abruzzo Tours TOUR
(☑ 0699 197460; www.absolutelyabruzzo.com; day tours from €250; ⊙ May-Oct) Australian-Italian Luciana leads private small-group tours from one day to a week-long (including cooking courses and cultural and hiking tours) and offers specialised heritage services to retrace your ancestral family village. Bookings essential.

Festivals

Pescara Jazz MUSIC
(www.pescarajazz.com) This international jazz festival is held in mid-July at the Teatro D'Annunzio. In the past it has featured big name stars including Keith Jarrett, Herbie Hancock and Stan Getz.

Sleeping & Eating

B&B Villa del Pavone B&B €
(☑ 085 421 17 70; www.villadelpavone.it; Via Pizzoferrato 30; d €70-80; ℗ ❋ ☎) Over the tracks on a quiet residential street about 300m behind the train station, you'll find a home away from home. A model of old-fashioned pride, it's laden with gleaming antiques and chichi knick-knacks. Outside, the lush garden is presided over by a resident peacock.

Hotel Alba
HOTEL €

(☑085 38 91 45; www.hotelalba.pescara.it; Via Michelangelo Forti 14; s €50-80, d €75-120, tr €135-150; [P][❄][@]) A glitzy three-star place, the Alba provides comfort and a central location. Rooms vary but the best sport polished wood, firm beds and plenty of sunlight. Rates are lowest at weekends and garage parking costs €10.

Caffè Letterario
CAFE €

(☑085 6 42 43; Via delle Caserme 62; lunch €7-12; ☺9am-6pm Sun-Wed, to 3am Thu-Sat) With its huge floor-to-ceiling windows and exposed-brick walls, this is a popular lunchtime spot. The menu is chalked up on a daily board, but typically comprises a few mains and several vegetable side dishes. There's live music Thursday to Saturday nights.

Ristorante Marechiaro da Bruno
SEAFOOD €€

(☑085 421 38 49; www.ristorantemarechiaro.eu; Lungomare Matteotti 70; pizzas €6.50-9, meals €30; ☺Thu-Tue) With a prime position on the seafront, the speciality is bound to be seafood – in all shapes and sizes. It's a lively place, smarter than its neighbours, with suited waiters and white linen, and there's an impressive array of pizzas at night.

❶ Information

Tourist Office You can find a tourist information centre at the Piazzale della Repubblica (☑085 422 54 62; www.proloco.pescara. it; Piazzale della Repubblica; ☺9am-1pm & 3-6pm Oct-May, 9am-1pm & 4-7pm Jun-Sep) or another office at the Airport (☑085 432 21 20; Airport).

❶ Getting There & Away

AIR
Pescara Airport (☑899 130 310; www.abruzzoairport.com) Pescara airport is 3km out of town and easily reached by bus 38 (€1.10, 20 minutes, every 15 minutes) from in front of the train station. Ryanair and Air One are among the airlines flying to Pescara.

BOAT
Agenzia Sanmar (☑0854 451 08 73; www. sanmar.it; Stazione Marittima Banchina Sud) Contact Agenzia Sanmar at the port for ferry information and tickets.

SNAV (☑071 207 61 16; www.snav.it) Throughout August, a daily SNAV jetfoil runs to the Croatian island of Hvar and on to Split (Spalato in Italian). One-way tickets for the 5¾-hour journey cost €120 per person and per car.

BUS
ARPA (☑800 762 622; www.arpaonline.it) Buses leave from Piazzale della Repubblica for L'Aquila (€8, two hours, 10 daily), Sulmona (€6, one hour, 11 daily), Naples (€26, 4½ hours, four daily), Rome (€17, 2¾ hours, 11 daily) and towns throughout Abruzzo and Molise.

TRAIN
Direct trains run to Ancona (from €8.15, 1¼ to two hours, 20 daily), Bari (from €19, three hours, 16 daily), Rome (from €11.90, four hours, six daily) and Sulmona (€4.50, 1¼ hours, 16 daily).

Chieti
POP 54,300

Overlooking the Aterno valley, Chieti is a hilltop town with roots dating back to pre-Roman times when, as capital of the Marrucini tribe, it was known as Teate Marrucinorum. Later, in the 4th century BC, it was conquered by the Romans and incorporated into the Roman Republic. These days the main reason to stop by is to the visit the town's two fascinating archaeology museums.

★Museo Archeologico Nazionale dell'Abruzzo (☑0871 40 43 92; www.archeoabruzzo.beniculturali.it; Villa Frigerj; adult/reduced €4/2; ☺9am-7.30pm Tue-Sun) is housed in a neoclassical villa in the Villa Comunale park. Displays include a comprehensive collection of local finds, with the star event the 6th-century-BC *Warrior of Capestrano,* considered the most important pre-Roman find in central Italy. Mystery surrounds the identity of the warrior, but there are some who think it to be Numa Pompilo, the second king of Rome and successor to Romulus. The museum also showcases 5th-century-BC funerary steles, an impressive coin collection, and some colossal statues – including that of a seated Hercules – dating from the 1st century BC.

Nearby is the **Complesso Archeologico la Civitella** (☑0871 6 31 37; www.lacivitella.it; Via Pianell; adult/reduced €4/2; ☺9am-7.30pm Tue-Sun), a modern museum built round a Roman amphitheatre. Exhibits chart the history of Chieti and include weapons and pottery dating back to the Iron Age.

About 3km downhill from the historic centre, **Agriturismo Il Quadrifoglio** (☑0871 63 4 00; www.agriturismoilquadrifoglio.com; Strada Licini 22; s/d €40/50; [P]) is a picturesque farmhouse with rustic rooms, panoramic views and a lovely, overflowing garden. Meals are

€15 to €20. To get here follow signs to Colle Marcone.

Chieti's helpful **tourist office** (☑ 0871 63 40; Via Spaventa 47; ☺ 8am-1pm & 4-7pm Mon-Sat Jul-Sep, 8am-1pm Mon-Sat & 3-6pm Tue, Thu & Fri Oct-Jun) can provide information and accommodation lists for the town and surrounding area.

Regular buses (€2.20, 20 minutes) link Chieti with Pescara.

Vasto

POP 39,800

On Abruzzo's southern coast, the hilltop town of Vasto has an atmospheric medieval quarter and superb sea views. Much of the *centro storico* dates from the 15th century, a golden period in which the city was known as 'the Athens of the Abruzzi'; it is also distinguished as the birthplace of the poet Gabriele Rossetti.

Two kilometres downhill is the blowzy resort of **Vasto Marina**, a strip of hotels, restaurants and camp grounds fronting a long sandy beach. About 5km further north along the coast is the beautiful **Spiaggia di Punta Penna** and the **Riserva Naturale di Punta Aderci** (www.puntaderci.it), a 285-hectare area of uncontaminated rocky coastline, ideal for long beach walks, swimming and diving.

◉ Sights & Activities

In summer the action is on the beach at Vasto Marina. Up in the old town, interest centres on the small historic centre, with the landmark **Castello Caldoresco** located on Piazza Rossetti.

Cattedrale di San Giuseppe   CATHEDRAL
(☑ 0873 36 71 93; Piazza Pudente; ☺ 8.30am-noon & 4.30-7pm) The facade is a lovely low-key example of Romanesque architecture; the rest of the building was destroyed in 1566 when the city was sacked by the Turks, and later rebuilt.

Museo Civico Archaeologica   MUSEUM
(☑ 0873 36 77 73; Piazza Pudente; admission €1.50; ☺ 9.30am-12.30pm & 4.30-7.30pm Tue-Sun) The Renaissance **Palazzo d'Avalos** houses this museum, with its eclectic collection of ancient bronzes, glasswork and paintings. Three other museums are also within the Palazzo d'Avalos – the **Pinacoteca Comunale** (admission €3.50), the **Galleria d'Arte Moderna** (admission free) and the **Museo**

del **Costume** (admission €1.50). A combined ticket to see all museums costs €5.

🛏 Sleeping & Eating

Locanda dei Baroni   HOTEL €€
(☑ 0873 37 07 37; www.locandadeibaroni.it; San Francesco d'Assisi 68/70; s €60-75, d €80-140; ☎) An attractive hotel in a historic *palazzo* on the eastern edge of the old town, with terracotta floors and four-poster beds. You can relax on the roof terrace, and there's an elegant brick-vaulted restaurant.

Sunrise   RESTAURANT €
(☑ 0873 6 93 41; Loggia Amblingh 51; mains €6.50-8.50; ☺ Wed-Mon; ⊞) A friendly, slightly brash little place with swoon-worthy Adriatic views and delicious home cooking, including sumptuous risottos. To get here, follow the *passeggiata* (evening stroll) sign to the right of the Museo Civico.

ⓘ Information

Tourist Office (☑ 0873 36 73 12; Piazza del Popolo 18; ☺ 9am-1pm daily & 4-7pm Mon-Sat Jul-mid-Sep, 9am-1pm Mon-Fri & 3-6pm Tue, Thu & Fri mid-Sep–Jun) In the *centro storico*.

ⓘ Getting There & Away

The train station (Vasto-San Salvo) is about 2km south of Vasto Marina. Trains run frequently to Pescara (€4.50, one hour) and Termoli (from €2.40, 15 minutes). From the station take bus 1 or 4 for Vasto Marina and the town centre.

MOLISE

One of Italy's forgotten regions, Molise is one of the few parts of the country where you can still get off the beaten track. And while it lacks the grandeur of its northern neighbour, the lack of a slick tourist infrastructure and the raw, unspoiled countryside ensure a gritty authenticity that's often missing in more celebrated areas.

To get the best out of Molise, you really need your own transport.

Campobasso

POP 51,000

Molise's regional capital and main transport hub is a sprawling, uninspiring city with little to recommend it. However, if you do find yourself passing through, the pocket-sized *centro storico* is worth a quick look.

Although rarely open, the Romanesque churches of **San Bartolomeo** (Salita San Bartolomeo) and **San Giorgio** (Viale della Rimembranza) are fine examples of their genre. Further up the hill, at the top of a steep tree-lined avenue, sits **Castello Monforte** (☑ 0874 6 32 99; ☺ 9am-1pm & 3.30-6.30pm Tue-Sun) **FREE**. Ceramics found in the castle are now on show at the small **Museo Samnitico** (Samnite Museum; ☑ 0874 41 22 65; Via Chiarizia 12; ☺ 9am-5.30pm) **FREE**, along with artefacts from local archaeological sites.

For a spot of lunch, **Trattoria La Grotta di Zi Concetta** (☑ 0874 31 13 78; Via Larino 9; meals €25; ☺ lunch & dinner Mon-Fri) is an old-school trattoria serving delicious homemade pasta and superb meat dishes.

The **tourist office** (☑ 0874 41 56 62; Piazza della Vittoria 14; ☺ 8.30am-1.30pm Mon-Fri, 3-5.30pm Mon & Wed) can provide further information on the city and surrounding province.

Unless you're coming from Isernia, Campobasso is best reached by bus. Services link with Termoli (€3.50, 1¼ hours, 10 daily), Naples (€9.80, 2¾ hours, four daily on weekdays), and Rome (€12.10, three hours, five daily). Up to 14 daily trains run to/from Isernia (€3, one hour).

Around Campobasso

Looming over Campobasso and the Saepinum ruins are the **Monti del Matese** (Matese Mountains). **Campitello Matese** (elevation 1430m) is a popular ski resort with facilities for winter and summer sports. Outside of the ski season and summer holiday period, the resort pretty much shuts up.

Between December and March, **Autolinee Micone** (☑ 0874 78 01 20) runs three daily buses from Campobasso up to Campitello Matese (one hour).

Saepinum

A hidden Molise treasure, the **Roman ruins** of Saepinum are among the best preserved and least visited in the country. Unlike Pompeii and Ostia Antica, which were both major ports, Saepinum was a small provincial town of no great importance. It was originally established by the Samnites but the Romans conquered it in 293 BC, paving the way for an economic boom in the 1st and 2nd centuries AD. Some 700 years later, it was sacked by Arab invaders. The walled

town retains three of its four original gates and its two main roads, the *cardus maximus* and the *decamanus*. Highlights include the forum, basilica and theatre, near to which the **Museo Archeologico Vittoriano** (admission €2; ☺ 9.30am-1pm & 3-6.30pm Tue-Sun) displays artefacts unearthed on the site.

It's not easy to reach Saepinum by public transport, but the bus from Campobasso to Sepinio (€1.20, six daily weekdays) generally stops near the site at Altilia, although it's best to ask the driver.

Isernia

POP 22,000

Surrounded by remote, sparsely populated hills, Isernia doesn't make a huge impression. Earthquakes and a massive WWII bombing raid spared little of its original *centro storico* and the modern centre is a drab, workaday place. The one reason to stop over is to visit the site of one of Europe's oldest human settlements, a 700,000-year-old village unearthed by road workers in 1978. Excavations are ongoing, although you can visit by calling the **site office** (☑ 0865 41 35 26; Contrada Ramiera Vecchia 1).

If you don't make it to the site, the dusty **Museo Santa Maria delle Monache** (☑ 0865 41 05 00; Corso Marcelli 48; admission €2; ☺ 8.30am-7pm) houses many of its finds, including piles of elephant and rhino bones, fossils and stone tools.

If you want to stay the night, **Hotel Sayonara** (☑ 0865 5 09 92; www.sayonara.is.it; Via G Berta 131; s/d €55/85; ❋) is the most centrally located hotel. It's an anonymous business-style set-up, but rooms are comfortable and there's a convenient restaurant.

Isernia's **tourist office** (☑ 0865 39 92; 6th fl, Via Farinacci 9, Palazzo della Regione; ☺ 8am-2pm Mon-Sat) can provide accommodation lists but little more in the way of practical help.

From the bus terminus next to the train station on Piazza della Repubblica, **Azienda di Trasporti Molisana** (www.atm-molise.it) runs buses to Campobasso (€3.50, 50 minutes, five daily) and Termoli (€8.80, 1¾ hours, three daily). Get tickets from Bar Ragno d'Oro on the square.

Trains connect Isernia with Sulmona (€7.10, three to four hours, two daily), Campobasso (€2.80, one hour, 14 daily), Naples (€6, two hours, five daily) and Rome (€10.70, two hours, six daily).

Around Isernia

While Isernia itself is a let-down, the surrounding hills are peppered with sights rich in history, from an ancient Samnite theatre/temple to a 9th-century fresco cycle.

◉ Sights

Abbazia di San Vincenzo al Volturno
CHURCH

(☑0865 95 52 46; ☉by appointment) A 30km drive northwest of Isernia, near Castel San Vincenzo, the Abbazia di San Vincenzo al Volturno is famous for its cycle of 9th-century frescoes by Epifano (824–842). The abbey, one of the foremost monastic and cultural centres in 9th-century Europe, is now home to a community of Benedictine nuns.

Marinelli Pontificia Fonderia di Campane
MUSEUM

(☑0865 7 82 35; www.campanemarinelli.com; Via D'Onofrio 14; adult/reduced €5/3.50; ☉guided tours 11am, noon, 4pm & 6pm Mon-Sat, 11am Sun Aug, noon & 4pm Mon-Sat, noon Sun Sep-Jul) Agnone is an ancient hilltop town famous for its bell making. For more than 1000 years, local artisans have been producing church bells for some of Italy's most famous churches, including St Peter's Basilica in Rome. Learn all about bell-making at this museum. For further information and details of accommodation in the area, ask at the helpful tourist office (☑0865 7 72 49; www.prolocoagnone.com; Corso Vittorio Emanuele 78; ☉9.30am-12.30pm & 3.30-6pm).

Riserva Collemeluccio
PARK

(☉9.30am-7pm Jun-Sep, to 5.30pm Apr-May, to 4.30pm Oct-Mar) The 350-hectare Riserva Collemeluccio is a prime picnic venue. It also offers good walking, with several trails leading off from the roadside visitors centre.

Samnite Theatre-Temple Complex
ARCHAEOLOGICAL SITE

(☑0865 7 61 29; adult/reduced €2/1; ☉10am-6pm) About 30km northeast of Isernia outside Pietrabbondante, the remains of a 2nd-century-BC Samnite theatre-temple complex reward a visit, as much as anything for its panoramic setting high above the rolling green countryside.

ⓘ Getting There & Away

From Isernia, **SATI** (☑0874 60 52 20) buses serve Pietrabbondante (€1.60, 35 minutes, two daily) and Agnone (€2.10, one hour, nine daily).

Buy tickets on the bus. There's also a service between Isernia and Castel San Vincenzo (€1.30, 45 minutes, two daily), a 1km walk from the Abbazia di San Vincenzo al Volturno.

Termoli
POP 32,600

Despite its touristy trattorias and brassy bars, Molise's top beach resort retains a winning, low-key charm. At the eastern end of the seafront, the pretty *borgo antico* (old town) juts out to sea atop a natural pier, dividing the sandy beach from Termoli's small harbour. From the port, year-round ferries sail for the Isole Tremiti.

The town's most famous landmark, Frederick II's 13th-century Castello Svevo (☑0875 71 23 54; ☉on request) guards entry to the tiny *borgo* – a tangle of narrow streets, pastel-coloured houses and souvenir shops. From the castle, follow the road up and you come to Piazza Duomo and Termoli's majestic 12th-century cathedral (☑0875 70 80 25). A masterpiece of Puglian-Romanesque architecture, the cream-coloured facade features a striking round-arched central portal.

🛏 Sleeping

★ Locanda Alfieri
ALBERGO DIFFUSO €

(☑0875 70 81 13; www.locandalfieri.com; Via Duomo 39; s incl breakfast €40-55, d incl breakfast €75-110; ❄🛜) A 'diffused hotel' with rooms scattered throughout the *centro storico*, this is a great base from which to explore Termoli, the Isole Tremiti and Molise. Room styles vary from 'creative' traditional to modern-chic (some with ubercool showers with mood lighting).

Coppola Villaggio Camping Azzurra
CAMPGROUND €

(☑0875 5 24 04; www.camping.it/molise/azzurra; SS16 km538; camping €17-27, 4-person bungalow €60-120; ☉mid-May–Sep; Ⓟ) Termoli's only campground is a modern, beachfront affair 2km outside town on the SS16 coastal road. As well as shady tent pitches and bungalows, on-site facilities include a minimarket and restaurant.

★ Residenza Sveva
ALBERGO DIFFUSO €€

(☑0875 70 68 03; www.residenzasveva.com; Piazza Duomo 11; s €50-80, d €89-180; ❄🛜) This elegant *centro storico* 'diffused hotel' has its reception on Piazza Duomo, near the cathedral, but the 21 rooms are squeezed into several *palazzi* in the *borgo*. The style is summery with plenty of gleaming blue tiles and traditional embroidery. There's also an excellent elegant seafood restaurant (open Wednesday to Sunday) on site.

Eating

La Sacrestia   TRADITIONAL ITALIAN €
(☑ 0875 70 56 03; Via Ruffini 48-50; pizzas €7-8, meals €25; ☺ daily summer, Wed-Mon winter) This is one of the better restaurants in the lively area between Corso Nazionale and Via Fratelli Brigida. Sit streetside or in the brick vaulted interior and chow down on knock-out pizza or fresh-off-the-boat seafood.

Ristorante Da Nicolino   SEAFOOD €€
(☑ 0875 70 68 04; Via Roma 3; meals €35; ☺ Fri-Wed) Well regarded by locals, this discreet restaurant near the entrance to the old town serves the best seafood in town. Highly recommended is the *brodetto di pesce* (fish soup).

❶ Information

Tourist Office (☑ 0875 70 39 13; www.termoli.net; 1st fl, Piazza Bega 42; ☺ 8am-2pm Mon-Fri & 3-6pm Mon & Wed-Fri) Helpful but hard to find, it's tucked away in a dodgy-looking car park behind a small shopping gallery, 100m east of the train station.

❶ Getting There & Away

BOAT

Termoli is the only port with year-round ferries to the Isole Tremiti. **Tirrenia Navigazione** (☑ 0875 70 53 43; www.tirrenia.it; tickets €16-20) runs a year-round ferry and **Navigazione Libera del Golfo** (☑ 0875 70 48 59; www.navlib.it; €36.50 round trip; ☺ Apr-Sep) operates a quicker hydrofoil. Buy tickets at the port.

BUS

Termoli's bus station is beside Via Martiri della Resistenza. Various companies have services to/from Campobasso (€3.50, 1¼ hours, 10 daily), Isernia (€7.20, 1¾ hours, three daily), Pescara (€6.40, 1¼ hours, four daily), Naples (€14.20, 3½ hours, four daily) and Rome (€15.50, four hours, frequent).

TRAIN

Direct trains serve Bologna (from €41, four to 5½ hours, 10 daily), Lecce (from €29, 3½ to 4½ hours, 10 daily) and stations along the Adriatic coast.

Albanian Towns

Several villages to the south of Termoli form an Albanian enclave that dates back to the 15th century. These include **Campomarino**, **Portocannone**, **San Martino in Pensilis** and **Ururi**. Although the inhabitants shrugged off their Orthodox religion in the 18th century, they still use a version of Albanian that's incomprehensible to outsiders. However, it's for their riotous and partisan **carressi** (chariot races) that the villages are best known. Each year San Martino in Pensilis (30 April), Ururi (3 May) and Portocannone (the Monday after Whit Sunday, seven weeks after Easter) stage a no-holds-barred chariot race. The chariots (more like carts) are pulled by bulls and hurtle around a traditional course, urged on by villagers on horseback. Bear in mind that, dramatic as these festivals are, they're in no way geared to tourists.

Getting to these villages is quite a trial without your own transport, but **ATM** (☑ 0874 64 744; www.atm-molise.it) runs daily buses to all four from the bus station at Termoli.

Naples & Campania

Why Go?

Campania could be a multi-Academy Award winner, swooping everything from Best Cinematography to Best Original Screenplay. Strewn with three millennia worth of temples, castles and palaces, it heaves with legend – Icarus plunged to his death in the Campi Flegrei, sirens lured sailors off Sorrento, and Wagner put quill to paper in lofty Ravello. Campania's cast includes some of Europe's most fabled destinations, from haunting Pompeii and Herculaneum to Medchic Capri and Positano. At its heart thumps bad-boy Naples, a love-it-or-loathe-it sprawl of operatic *palazzi* (mansions) and churches, mouth-watering markets, and art-crammed museums. Home to Italy's top coffee and pizza, it's also one of the country's gastronomic superstars. Beyond its pounding streets lies a wonderland of lush bay islands, faded fishing villages and wild mountains. Seductive, vivacious and often contradictory: welcome to Italy at its nail-biting best.

Best Places to Eat

➡ L'Ebbrezza di Noè (p657)

➡ Il Focolare (p671)

➡ Da Gelsomina (p668)

➡ Viva Lo Re (p675)

Best Places to Stay

➡ La Minerva (p668)

➡ Hotel Piazza Bellini (p655)

➡ Hotel Luna Convento (p692)

➡ Casale Giancesare (p699)

When to Go
Naples

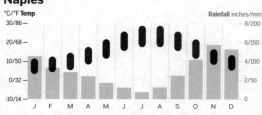

Easter Follow the faithful at Sorrento and Procida's mystical Easter processions.

May Naples celebrates culture with its event-packed Maggio dei Monumenti festival.

Sep Hit the coast for warm, languid days without the August crowds.

The Subterranean City

Mysterious shrines, secret passageways, forgotten burial crypts: it might sound like the set of an Indiana Jones film, but it's actually what lurks beneath Naples' loud and greasy streets. Subterranean Naples is one of the world's most thrilling urban wonderlands; a silent, mostly undiscovered sprawl of cathedral-like cisterns, pin-thin conduits, catacombs and ancient ruins.

Speleologists (cave specialists) estimate that about 60% of Neapolitans live and work above this network, known in Italian as the *sottosuolo* (underground). Since the end of WWII, some 700 cavities have been discovered, from original Greek-era grottoes to palaeo-Christian burial chambers and royal Bourbon escape routes. According to the experts, this is simply a prelude, with another 2 million sq metres of troglodytic treats to unfurl.

Naples' dedicated caving geeks are quick to tell you that their underworld is one of the largest and oldest on earth. Sure, Paris might claim a catacomb or two, but its subterranean offerings don't come close to this giant's 2500-year history.

And what a history it is. Naples' most famous saint, San Gennaro, was interred in the Catacomba di San Gennaro in the 5th century. A century later, in 536, Belisario and his troops caught Naples by surprise by storming the city through the city's ancient tunnels. According to legend, Alfonso of Aragon used the same trick in 1442, undermining the city walls by using an underground passageway leading into a tailor's shop and straight into town. Even the city's dreaded Camorra has got in on the act. In 1992 the notorious Stolder clan was busted for running a subterranean drug lab, with escape routes heading straight to the clan boss' pad.

CAMPANIA'S NATURAL WONDERS

➡ **Grotta Azzurra** (p666) Nature outdazzles Disney in this magical coastal cave.

➡ **Sentiero degli Dei** (p687) Experience the Amalfi Coast from a heavenly elevation.

➡ **Parco Nazionale del Cilento e Vallo di Diano** (p702) A wild and rugged playground begging to be hiked.

➡ **Mt Vesuvius** (p675) Peer into the crater of a panoramic time bomb.

➡ **Capri Hiking Trails** (p667) Explore the island's bucolic side.

Don't Miss

Naples' Cappella Sansevero (p642) is home to the astounding *Cristo velato* (Veiled Christ), its marble veil so translucent it baffles to this day.

HOLD THE PRAWNS

Order a pizza marinara in Naples and you'll get a simple affair of tomato, garlic and olive oil. And the seafood? There is none. The pizza was named after fishers, who took it out to sea for lunch.

Best Places to Say 'Ti Amo'

➡ Villa Cimbrone (p694)
➡ Palazzo Petrucci (p657)
➡ Monte Solaro (p666)
➡ Teatro San Carlo (p652)
➡ La Conchiglia (p673)

Naples' Top Museums

➡ **Museo Archeologico Nazionale** (p643) A trove of ancient art and erotica.

➡ **Museo di Capodimonte** (p653) From Caravaggio to Warhol.

➡ **Novecento a Napoli** (p651) A stylish ode to Naples' 20th-century art scene.

Resources

➡ **Turismo Regione Campania** (www.incampania.it) Up-to-date events, as well as articles and itineraries.

➡ **Napoli Unplugged** (www.napoliunplugged.com) Smart, updated website covering sights, events, news and practicalities.

➡ **Italy Traveller** (www.italytraveller.com) Boutique hotel listings, themed itineraries and travel ideas.

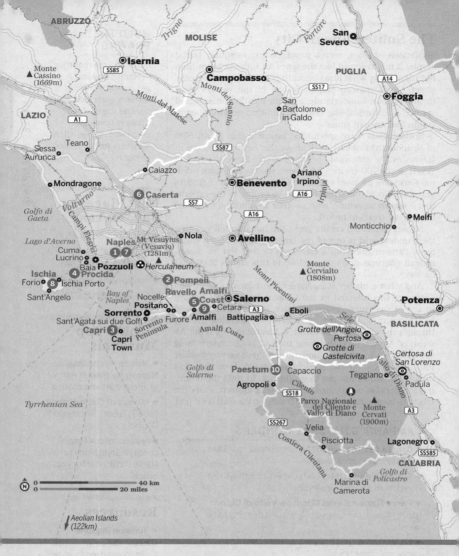

Naples & Campania Highlights

① Exploring Naples' labyrinthine underworld on a **Tunnel Borbonico** (p654) tour.

② Channelling the ancients on the ill-fated streets of **Pompeii** (p676).

③ Being bewitched by Capri's ethereal **Grotta Azzurra** (p666).

④ Lunching by lapping waves on pastel-hued **Procida** (p672).

⑤ Treating your senses to a concert at Ravello's dreamy **Villa Rufolo** (p693).

⑥ Pretending you're royalty at Caserta's **Palazzo Reale** (p663).

⑦ Re-evaluating artistic ingenuity in Naples' **Cappella Sansevero** (p642).

⑧ Indulging in a little thermal therapy on **Ischia** (p670).

⑨ Walking with the gods on the **Amalfi Coast** (p687).

⑩ Admiring Hellenic ingenuity at the World Heritage–listed temples of **Paestum** (p698).

NAPLES

POP 970,400

Italy's most misunderstood city is also one of its most intriguing – an exhilarating mess of bombastic baroque churches, cocky baristas and electrifying street life. Contradiction is the catchphrase here; a place where anarchy and pollution sidle up beside glorious churches, tranquil cloisters and story-book seaside castles. Naples' *centro storico* (historic centre) is a Unesco World Heritage Site, its museums lay claim to some of Europe's finest archaeology and art, and its gilded royal palaces make Rome look positively provincial. But what about the pickpockets? The Camorra? Certainly, Naples has its fair share of problems, yet the city is far safer than many imagine, its streets packed with some of Italy's warmest, kindest denizens. Expect to be caught in mafia gunfire and you'll be sorely disappointed. Expect a city packed with history, humanity and flavour and you'll be thoroughly satisfied.

History

According to legend, traders from Rhodes established the city on the island of Megaris (where Castel dell'Ovo now stands) in about 680 BC. Originally called Parthenope, in honour of the siren whose body had ear-lier washed up there (she drowned herself after failing to seduce Ulysses), it was eventually incorporated into a new city, Neapolis, founded by Greeks from Cumae (Cuma) in 474 BC. However, within 150 years it was in Roman hands, becoming something of a VIP resort favoured by emperors Pompey, Caesar and Tiberius.

After the fall of the Roman Empire, Naples became a duchy, originally under the Byzantines and later as an independent dukedom, until it was captured in 1139 by the Normans and absorbed into the Kingdom of the Two Sicilies. The Normans, in turn, were replaced by the German Swabians, whose charismatic leader Frederick II injected the city with new institutions, including its university.

The Swabian period came to a violent end with the victory of Charles I of Anjou at the 1266 battle of Benevento. The Angevins did much for Naples, promoting art and culture, building Castel Nuovo and enlarging the port, but they were unable to stop the Spanish Aragons taking the city in 1442. However, Naples continued to prosper. Alfonso I of Aragon, in particular, introduced new laws and encouraged the arts and sciences.

In 1503 Naples was absorbed by Spain, which sent viceroys to rule as virtual dictators. Despite Spain's heavy-handed rule,

Naples

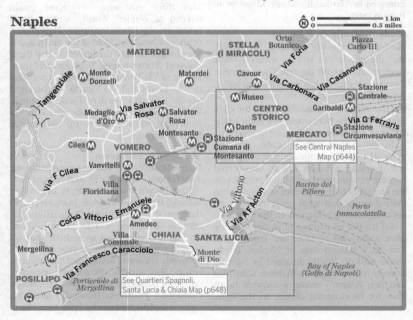

NAPLES IN...

Two Days

Start with a burst of colour in the cloister of the **Basilica di Santa Chiara** (p643), meditate on a Caravaggio masterpiece at **Pio Monte della Misericordia** (p646), and get dizzy under Lanfranco's dome fresco at the *duomo* (p646). After lunch, head underground on a **Napoli Sotterranea** (p654) tour, lose your breath over the astounding *Cristo velato* (Veiled Christ) in the **Cappella Sansevero** (p642), and kick back in bohemian Piazza Bellini. Next morning, explore ancient treasures at the **Museo Archeologico Nazionale** (p643), then head up to the **Certosa e Museo di San Martino** (p650) for extraordinary baroque interiors, Neapolitan art, and a sweeping panorama. Cap the night on the fashionable, bar-packed streets of **Chiaia** (p658).

Four Days

Spend the morning of day three cheek-to-crater with **Mt Vesuvius** (p675), then ponder its bone-chilling fury at **Herculaneum** (p674) or **Pompeii** (p676). Alternatively, spend the day at Caserta's mammoth, art-crammed **Palazzo Reale** (p663). On day four, grab some picnic provisions at the **Mercato di Porta Nolana** (p647) and devour them in the ground of **Palazzo Reale di Capodimonte** (p653). Nourished, eye up the bounty of artistic masterpieces inside, then spend a romantic evening shouting 'encore' at the luscious **Teatro San Carlo** (p652).

Naples flourished artistically and acquired much of its splendour. Indeed, it continued to bloom when the Spanish Bourbons reestablished Naples as the capital of the Kingdom of the Two Sicilies in 1734. Aside from a Napoleonic interlude under Joachim Murat (1806–15), the Bourbons remained until unseated by Garibaldi and the Kingdom of Italy in 1860.

Modern Struggles & Hopes

Naples was heavily bombed in WWII, and the effects can still be seen on many monuments around the city. Since the war, Campania's capital has continued to suffer. Endemic corruption and the reemergence of the Camorra have plagued much of the city's postwar resurrection, reaching a nadir in the 1980s after a severe earthquake in 1980.

In 2011, the city's sporadic garbage-disposal crisis flared up again, leading frustrated residents to set fire to uncollected rubbish in the streets. In March 2013 it was the city's much-loved science museum, Città della Scienza, that went up in flames – an act of arson widely blamed on the Camorra.

Yet it's not all doom and gloom in a city often known for its trials and tribulations. The 2013 inauguration of Naples' Toledo metro station – partly designed by internationally renowned artists William Kentridge and Bob Wilson – made worldwide headlines for its stunning design. In the same year, the city welcomed the world as host of the Universal Forum of Cultures.

Sights

Centro Storico

The three east–west *decumani* (main streets) of Naples' World Heritage–listed *centro storico* follow the original street plan of ancient Neapolis. Most of the major sights are grouped around the busiest two of these classical thoroughfares: 'Spaccanapoli' (consisting of Via Benedetto Croce, Via San Biagio dei Librai and Via Vicaria Vecchia) and Via dei Tribunali. North of Via dei Tribunali, Via della Sapienza, Via Anticaglia and Via Santissimi Apostoli make up the quieter third *decumanus*.

★ **Cappella Sansevero**   CHAPEL
(Map p644; ☑ 081 551 84 70; www.museosansevero. it; Via Francesco de Sanctis 19; adult/reduced €7/5; ☉10am-5.40pm Mon & Wed-Sat, to 1.10pm Sun; Ⓜ Dante) It's in this Masonic-inspired chapel that you'll find Giuseppe Sanmartino's incredible sculpture, *Cristo velato* (Veiled Christ), its marble veil so realistic that it's tempting to try to lift it and view Christ underneath. It's one of several artistic wonders, which also include Francesco Queirolo's sculpture *Disinganno* (Disillusion), Antonio Corradini's *Pudicizia* (Modesty) and riotously colourful frescoes by Francesco Maria

Russo, the latter untouched since their creation in 1749.

Downstairs, two meticulously preserved human arterial systems are a testament to the insatiable curiosity and geniality of alchemist Prince Raimondo di Sangro (1710–71), the man who commissioned the chapel's 18th-century makeover. According to Italian philosopher Benedetto Croce (1866–1952), di Sangro held a Faustian fascination for the *centro storico*'s masses, who accused him of everything from replicating the miracle of San Gennaro's blood to making furniture with the skin and bones of seven cardinals.

★ Basilica di Santa Chiara
BASILICA, CLOISTER

(Map p644; ☑ 081 797 12 31; www.monasterodis-antachiara.eu; Via Benedetto Croce; cloisters adult/reduced €6/4.50; ⊘ basilica 7.30am-1pm & 4.30-8pm, cloisters 9.30am-5pm Mon-Sat, 10am-2pm Sun; ⓜ Dante) Vast, Gothic and cleverly deceptive, this mighty basilica is actually a 20th-century re-creation of Gagliardo Primario's 14th-century Angevin original, severely damaged by Allied bombing in August 1943. The pièce de résistance, however, is the basilica's adjoining majolica cloister.

Colourful 17th-century, Franciscan-themed frescoes adorn the 14th-century porticoes, while uplifting 18th-century ceramic tiles idealise country living in the cloister garden. Adjacent to the cloister, a small museum displays objects from the original 14th-century church, elaborate ecclesiastical props, as well as the excavated ruins of a 1st-century spa complex; look out for the remarkably well-preserved *laconicum* (sauna).

★ Museo Archeologico Nazionale
MUSEUM

(Map p644; ☑ 081 44 01 66; www.coopculture.it; Piazza Museo Nazionale 19; admission €8; ⊘ 9am-7.30pm Wed-Mon; ⓜ Museo, Piazza Cavour) Head here for one of the world's finest collections of Graeco-Roman artefacts. Originally a cavalry barracks and later the seat of the city's university, the museum was established by the Bourbon king Charles VII in the late 18th century to house the rich collection of antiquities he had inherited from his mother, Elisabetta Farnese, as well as treasures looted from Pompeii and Herculaneum.

Before tackling the collection, consider investing in a copy of the *National Archaeological Museum of Naples*, published by Electa, or, if you want to concentrate on the highlights, audio guides are available in English. It's also worth calling ahead to ensure that the galleries you want to see are open, as staff shortages often mean that sections of the museum close for part of the day.

While the basement houses the Borgia collection of Egyptian relics and epigraphs, the ground-floor Farnese collection of colossal Greek and Roman sculptures includes the *Toro Farnese* (Farnese Bull) in Room XVI and the muscle-bound *Ercole* (Hercules) in Room XI. Sculpted in the early 3rd century AD and noted in the writings of Pliny, the *Toro Farnese*, probably a Roman copy of a Greek original, depicts the humiliating death of Dirce, Queen of Thebes. Carved from a single colossal block of marble, the sculpture was discovered in 1545 near the Baths of Caracalla in Rome and was restored by Michelangelo, before eventually being shipped to Naples in 1787. *Ercole* was discovered in the same Roman excavations, albeit without his legs. When they turned up at a later dig, the Bourbons had them fitted.

If you're short on time, take in both these masterpieces before heading straight to the mezzanine floor, home to an exquisite collection of mosaics, mostly from Pompeii. Of the series taken from the Casa del Fauno, it is *La battaglia di Alessandro contro Dario* (The Battle of Alexander against Darius) in Room LXI that stands out. The best-known

---

ⓘ **BEFORE YOU EXPLORE**

If you're planning to blitz the sights, the Campania artecard (☑ 800 600601, 0639 96 76 50; www.campaniaartecard.it) is an excellent investment. A cumulative ticket that covers museum admission and transport, it comes in various forms. The Naples and Campi Flegrei three-day ticket (adult/reduced 18-25 yrs €16/10) gives free admission to three participating sites, a 50% discount on others and free transport in Naples and the Campi Flegrei. Other options range from €12 to €30 and cover sites as far afield as Pompeii and Paestum. The tickets can be bought at the Stazione Centrale (Central Station) tourist office, participating museums and archaeological sites, online, or through the call centre.

Central Naples

0 — 500 m
0 — 0.25 miles

Corso Novara

Intercity Bus Station
Stazione Centrale
SITA Sud & CTS Bus Stop
Garibaldi M

ANM Bus Information Kiosk

ANM Bus Station

Via Firenze

Piazza Principe Umberto

21

Piazza Garibaldi

Via Duchesca

Via Carbonara

Via Maricini

12

Via G Pica

Via S Cosmo Fuori Porta Nolana

Stazione Circumvesuviana

Via E Cosenz

Vico S Giovanni

Via Amerigo Vespucci

Via Nolana Porta Nolana

Via Sopramuro

Corso G Garibaldi

Via C Carmignano

Via D Carmine

Piazza G Pepe

Chiesa di Santa Maria del Carmine

Via della Marinella

Via Ranieri

Via Lavinaio

Via A de Pace

Via G Savarese

Piazza del Mercato

Masaniello Santa Maria del Carmine

Via Nuova Marina

Via dell'Annunziata

Vico Barre

Via Duca di San Donato

Via S Eligio

MERCATO

SITA Sud Bus Stop (180m)

Via P Colletta

Via S Nicola dei Caserti

Corso Umberto I

Piazza del Nicola Amore M

Via Duomo

Via C Muzy

Via del Tribunali

Vico della Pace

Via della Zite

Vico Zuroli

Via Vicaria Vecchia

Via d'Alagno

Via dei Cimbri

Piazza Nicola Amore

Duomo (under construction) M

Via Scialoia

Corso Umberto I

Piazzetta Orefici

MADRE (50m)

Via Santissimi Apostoli

19

Vicolo Sedil Capuano

8

13   11

CENTRO STORICO

7

6   15

Via San Gregorio Armeno

Via San Biagio dei Librai

Vico S Severino

Vico S Nicola al Nilo

Via B Capasso

Via G Paladino

See Quartieri Spagnoli, Santa Lucia & Chiaia Map (p648)

Via Duomo

28

Vico Giganti

Via d'Anticaglia

16   31

22   24

Via San Paolo

Vico Donnaromita

Via Mezzocannone

Cerasiello B&B (350m)

Via S Gaudioso

Via Atri

Via F del Guidice

Via del Sole

Cappella Sansevero

2 Piazza San Domenico Maggiore

5   23

10

Vico San Geronimo

18

Largo Giusso

See Sedile di Porto

25

Via S Pisanelli

29   32

Vico San 30

Basilica di Santa Chiara

Via Santa Chiara

Via Domenicana

Piazza Luigi Miraglia

27

Piazza San Domenico Maggiore

Santa Chiara

1

Via San Sebastiano

26

Piazza Bellini

Via Santa Maria di Costantinopoli

17   20

4

Via B Benedetto Croce

9

Piazza del Gesù Nuovo

Via S Anna dei Lombardi

Via Brogcia

Museo Archeologico Nazionale

Museo M

3

Piazza Museo Nazionale

Catacomba di Gennaro (1km);
Palazzo Reale di Capodimonte (2km)

Via Tommasi

Via Bellini

Dante M

Piazza Dante

Via Enrico Pessina

Via Port'Alba

Via D Lioy

Piazza Carità

Via Pignasecca

Via Toledo

Via G Brombeis

Central Naples

depiction of Alexander the Great, the 20-sq-metre mosaic was probably made by Alexandrian craftsmen working in Italy around the end of the 2nd century BC.

Beyond the mosaics, the **Gabinetto Segreto** (Secret Chamber) contains a small but much-studied collection of ancient erotica. Guarding the entrance is a marble statue of a lascivious-looking Pan draped over a very coy Daphne. Pan is then caught in the act, this time with a nanny goat, in the collection's most famous piece – a small and surprisingly sophisticated statue taken from the Villa dei Papiri in Herculaneum. There is also a series of nine paintings depicting erotic positions – a menu of sorts for brothel clients.

Originally the royal library, the enormous **Sala Meridiana** (Great Hall of the Sundial) on the 1st floor is home to the Farnese Atlante, a statue of Atlas carrying a globe on his shoulders, as well as various paintings from the Farnese collection. Look up and you'll find Pietro Bardellino's riotously colourful 1781 fresco depicting the Triumph of Ferdinand IV of Bourbon and Marie Caroline of Austria.

The rest of the 1st floor is largely devoted to fascinating discoveries from Pompeii, Herculaneum, Boscoreale, Stabiae and Cuma. Among them are vivid wall **frescoes** from the Villa of Agrippa Postumus and the Casa di Meleagro, as well as ceramics, glassware, engraved coppers and Greek funerary vases.

**Complesso Monumentale
di San Lorenzo Maggiore** BASILICA
(Map p644; ☑ 081 211 08 60; www.sanlorenzomaggiorenapoli.it; Via dei Tribunali 316; church admission free, excavations & museum adult/reduced €9/7; ◷ 9.30am-5.30pm Mon-Sat, to 1.30pm Sun; ☐ C55 to Via Duomo) A masterpiece of French Gothic architecture, this late-13th-century basilica features the 14th-century, mosaic-covered tomb of Catherine of Austria, as well as splashes of frescoes by Giotto-collaborator Giovanni Barile in the ambulatory. According to legend, it was here that Boccaccio first fell for Mary of Anjou, the inspiration for his character Fiammetta, while the poet Petrarch called the adjoining convent home in 1345.

Beneath the complex are some remarkable *scavi* (excavations) of the original Graeco-Roman city, including the ruins of ancient bakeries, wineries and communal laundries. At the far end of the subterranean *cardo* (road) stands a *cryptoporticus* (covered market) with seven barrel-vaulted rooms.

THE ART OF THE NEAPOLITAN PRESEPE

Christmas nativity cribs may not be exclusive to Naples, but none match the artistic brilliance of the *presepe napoletano* (Neapolitan nativity crib). What sets the local version apart is its incredible attention to detail, from the lifelike miniature *prosciutti* (hams) in the tavern to the lavishly costumed *pastori* (crib figurines or sculptures) adoring the newborn Christ.

For the nobility and bourgeoisie of 18th-century Naples, the *presepe* provided a convenient marriage of faith and ego, becoming as much a symbol of wealth and good taste as a meditation on the Christmas miracle. The finest sculptors were commissioned and the finest fabrics used. Even the royals got involved: Charles III of Bourbon consulted the esteemed *presepe* expert, Dominican monk Padre Rocco, on the creation of his 5000-*pastore* spectacular, still on show at the Palazzo Reale (p652). Yet even this pales in comparison to the upsized Cuciniello crib on display at the Certosa e Museo di San Martino, considered the world's greatest.

Centuries on, the legacy continues. The craft's epicentre is the *centro storico* (historic centre) street of **Via San Gregorio Armeno** (Map p644), its clutter of shops and workshops selling everything from doting donkeys to kitsch celebrity caricatures. Serious connoisseurs, however, will point you towards the very few workshops that completely handcraft their *pastori* the old-fashioned way. Among the latter are **Ars Neapolitana** (Map p644; ✆ 392 537 71 16; Via dei Tribunali 303; ⊙10am-6.30pm Mon-Fri, to 3pm Sat, also open 10am-6.30pm Sat & Sun late Oct-early Jan; ☐C55 to Via Duomo) and **La Scarabattola** (Map p644; ✆ 081 29 17 35; www.lascarabattola.it; Via dei Tribunali 50; ⊙10am-2pm & 3.30-7.30pm Mon-Sat; ☐C55 to Via Duomo), both in the *centro storico*.

The religious complex is also home to the **Museo dell'Opera di San Lorenzo Maggiore** and its booty of local archaeological finds, including Graeco-Roman sarcophagi, ceramics and crockery from the digs below.

Pio Monte della Misericordia
CHURCH, MUSEUM

(Map p644; ✆081 44 69 44; www.piomontedellamisericordia.it; Via dei Tribunali 253; admission €6; ⊙9am-2pm Thu-Tue; ☐C55 to Via Duomo) Caravaggio's masterpiece *Le sette opere di Misericordia* (The Seven Acts of Mercy) is considered by many to be the single most important painting in Naples. And it's in this small, octagonal 17th-century church that you'll see it.

The 1st-floor museum is home to the *Declaratoria del 14 Ottobre 1607*, an original church document acknowledging payment of 400 ducats to Caravaggio for the masterpiece. The collection also includes a small, satisfying collection of Renaissance, baroque and 19th-century art, including works by Francesco de Mura and Giuseppe de Ribera.

Duomo
CATHEDRAL

(Map p644; ✆081 44 90 97; www.duomodinapoli.com/it/main.htm; Via Duomo; baptistry admission €1.50; ⊙cathedral & baptistry 8am-12.30pm & 4.30-7pm Mon-Sat, 8am-1.30pm & 5-7.30pm Sun; ☐C55 to Via Duomo) Whether you go for Giovanni Lanfranco's fresco in the Cappella di San Gennaro (Chapel of St Janarius), the 4th-century mosaics in the baptistry, or the thrice-annual miracle of San Gennaro, don't miss Naples' spiritual centrepiece. Sitting on the site of an ancient temple to Neptune, the cathedral was initiated by Charles I of Anjou in 1272, consecrated in 1315 and largely destroyed in a 1456 earthquake. Copious alterations over the subsequent centuries have created a melange of styles and influences.

While the neo-Gothic facade was only added in the late 19th century, the high sections of the nave and the transept are the work of baroque overachiever Luca Giordano. Off the left aisle, the 17th-century **Cappella di San Gennaro** (Chapel of St Januarius, also known as the Chapel of the Treasury) was designed by Giovanni Cola di Franco and completed in 1637. The most celebrated artists of the period worked on the chapel – Giuseppe de Ribera painted the gripping canvas *St Gennaro Escaping the Furnace Unscathed* and Giovanni Lanfranco created the dizzying dome fresco. Hidden away in a strongbox behind the altar is a 14th-century silver bust in which sit the skull of San Gennaro and the two phials that hold his miraculously liquefying blood.

Below the high altar is the **Cappella Carafa**, a Renaissance chapel built to house yet more of the saint's remains.

Off the north aisle sits one of Naples' oldest basilicas, dating to the 4th century. Incorporated into the main cathedral, the Basilica di Santa Restituta was subject to an almost complete makeover after the earthquake of 1688. From it you can access Western Europe's oldest baptistry, pimped with glittering 4th-century mosaics. At the time of writing, the *duomo*'s subterranean archaeological zone – featuring the remains of Greek and Roman buildings and roads – was closed indefinitely.

If you're intrigued by Naples' cultish love affair with San Gennaro, consider popping into the Duomo's adjacent Museo del Tesoro di San Gennaro (Map p644; ☑ 081 29 49 80; www.museosangennaro.com; Via Duomo 149; adult/reduced €7/5; ⊙9am-5pm Fri-Tue, to 3pm Thu; ⬜C55 to Via Duomo); its glittering collection of precious ex-voto gifts includes bronze busts, silver ampullae, sumptuous paintings and a gilded 18th-century sedan chair used to shelter the saint's bust on rainy procession days.

★ MADRE   ART GALLERY

(Museo d'Arte Contemporanea Donnaregina; ☑ 081 1931 3016; www.coopculture.it; Via Settembrini 79; admission €7, Mon free; ⊙10am-7.30pm Mon & Wed-Sat, to 8pm Sun; Ⓜ Piazza Cavour) Seek refuge from the ancient at Naples' impressive contemporary-art museum. While the 1st floor is dedicated to specially commissioned installations (among them Rebecca Horn's eerie *Spirits* and Francesco Clemente's erotically charged Neapolitan fresco *Ave Ovo*), the 2nd floor's 'Historical Collection' of modern painting, photography, sculpture and installations includes blockbuster names like Damien Hirst, Cindy Sherman and Olafur Eliasson.

The museum also hosts top-notch temporary exhibitions spanning local to international artists.

Chiesa del Gesù Nuovo   CHURCH

(Map p644; ☑ 081 551 86 13; Piazza del Gesù Nuovo; ⊙7am-1pm & 4.15-8pm Mon-Sat, 7am-1.45pm Sun; Ⓜ Dante) In a case of architectural recycling, this 16th-century church actually sports the 15th-century, Giuseppe Valeriani–designed facade of Palazzo Sanseverino, converted to create the church. Inside, it's a baroque affair, with greats like Francesco Solimena, Luca Giordano and Cosimo Fanzago transforming the barrel-vaulted interior into the frescoed wonder that you see today. Puncturing the Piazza del Gesù Nuovo is Giuseppe Genuino's lavish Guglia dell'Immacolata (Map p644), an 18th-century obelisk.

Mercato di Porta Nolana   MARKET

(Map p644; Porta Nolana; ⊙8am-6pm Mon-Sat, to 2pm Sun; ⬜R2 to Corso Umberto I) Bellies rumble at this evocative street market, one of the city's best. The market's namesake is medieval city gate Porta Nolana, which stands at the head of Via Sopramuro. Its two cylindrical towers, optimistically named Faith and Hope, support an arch decorated with a bas-relief of Ferdinand I of Aragon on horseback.

The *mercato* itself is an intoxicating place, where bellowing fishmongers and *frutti vendoli* (greengrocers) mix it with fragrant delis, bakeries and a growing number of ethnic food shops.

Chiesa e Chiostro di San Gregorio Armeno   CHURCH, CLOISTER

(Map p644; ☑ 081 420 63 85; Via San Gregorio Armeno 44; ⊙9am-noon Mon-Fri, to 1pm Sat & Sun; ⬜C55 to Via Duomo) Overstatement knows no bounds at this richly ornamented 16th-century monastic complex, its church featuring lavish wood and papier-mâché choir stalls, a sumptuous altar by Dionisio Lazzari, and Luca Giordano's masterpiece fresco *The Embarkation, Journey and Arrival of the Armenia Nuns with the Relics of St Gregory*.

Accessible by a gate on Vicolo Giuseppe Maffei is the complex's superb cloister. Here you'll find Matteo Bottigliero's whimsical baroque fountain and (at the southern end of the cloister) the convent's old bakery.

From a door at the southeast corner of the cloister you can access the beautiful *coro delle monache* (nuns' choir stall) that looks down on the church. The sneaky windows lining the oval cupola above belong to a second choir stall.

Chiesa di San Domenico Maggiore   CHURCH

(Map p644; ☑ 081 45 91 88; Piazza San Domenico Maggiore 8a; ⊙8.30am-noon & 4-7pm Mon-Sat, 9am-1pm & 4.30pm Sun; Ⓜ Dante) Completed in 1324 on the orders of Charles I of Anjou, this was the royal church of the Angevins. Of the few 14th-century remnants surviving the church's countless makeovers, the frescoes by Pietro Cavallini in the Cappella Brancaccio take the cake. The sacristy is equally noteworthy, featuring a beautiful ceiling fresco by Francesco Solimena and 45 coffins of Aragon princes and other nobles.

In the Cappellone del Crocifisso, the 13th-century *Crocifisso tra La Vergine e San Giovanni* is said to have spoken to St Thomas Aquinas, asking: *'Bene scripsisti*

Quartieri Spagnoli, Santa Lucia & Chiaia

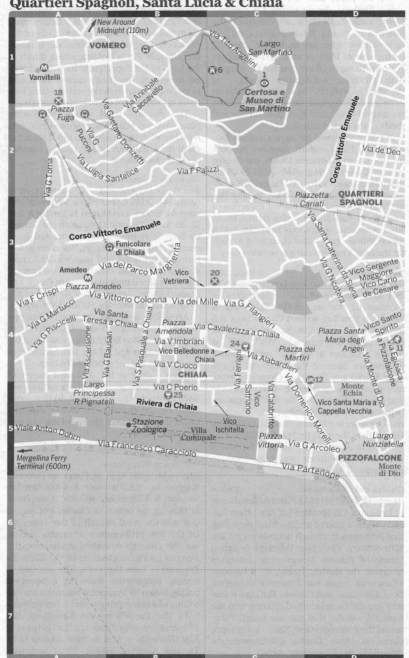

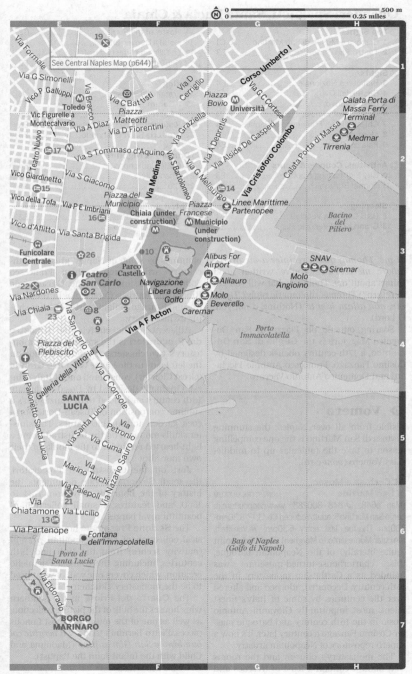

Quartieri Spagnoli, Santa Lucia & Chiaia

di me, Thoma; quam recipies a me pro tu labore mercedem?' (You've written good things about me, Thomas, what will you get in return?) Thomas' diplomatic reply? *'Domine, non aliam nisi te'* (Nothing if not you, O Lord).

Soaring outside on Piazza di San Domenico Maggiore is the **Guglia di San Domenico**, a 17th-century obelisk designed by Cosimo Fanzago, Francesco Antonio Picchiatti and Domenico Antonio Vaccaro.

⊙ Vomero

Visible from all over Naples, the stunning Certosa di San Martino is the one compelling reason to take the funicular up to middleclass Vomero (*vom*-e-ro).

★ **Certosa e Museo di San Martino**   MONASTERY, MUSEUM
(Map p648; ☑848 800288; www.coopculture.it; Largo San Martino 5; adult/reduced €6/3; ⊙8.30am-7.30pm Thu-Tue, last entry 6.30pm; Ⓜ Vanvitelli, funicular Montesanto to Morghen) The high point (quite literally) of the Neapolitan baroque, this charterhouse-turned-museum was founded as a Carthusian monastery in the 14th century. Decorated, adorned and altered over the centuries by some of Italy's finest talent, most importantly Giovanni Antonio Dosio in the 16th century and baroque master Cosimo Fanzago a century later, it's now a superb repository of Neapolitan artistry.

The monastery's **church** and the rooms that flank it contain a feast of frescoes and paintings by some of Naples' greatest 17th-century artists, among them Francesco Solimena, Massimo Stanzione, Giuseppe de Ribera and Battista Caracciolo. In the nave, Cosimo Fanzago's inlaid marble-work is simply extraordinary.

Adjacent to the church, the **Chiostro dei Procuratori** is the smaller of the monastery's two cloisters. A grand corridor on the left leads to the larger **Chiostro Grande** (Great Cloister), considered one of Italy's finest. Originally designed by Dosio in the late 16th century and added to by Fanzago, it's a sublime composition of Tuscan-Doric porticoes, garden and marble statues. The sinister skulls mounted on the balustrade were a light-hearted reminder to the monks of their own mortality.

Just off the Chiostro dei Procuratori, the small **Sezione Navale** documents the history of the Bourbon navy from 1734 to 1860, and features a small collection of beautiful royal barges.

The **Sezione Presepiale** houses a whimsical collection of rare Neapolitan *presepi* (nativity scenes) from the 18th and 19th centuries, including the colossal Cuciniello creation, which covers one wall of what used to be the monastery's kitchen.

The **Quarto del Priore** in the southern wing houses the bulk of the picture collection, as well as one of the museum's most famous pieces, Pietro Bernini's tender *La vergine col bambino e San Giovannino* (Madonna and Child with the Infant John the Baptist).

A pictorial history of Naples is told in the section **Immagini e Memorie di Napoli** (Images and Memories of Naples). Here you'll find portraits of historic characters; antique maps, including a 35-panel copper map of 18th-century Naples in Room 45; and rooms dedicated to major historical events such as the Revolt of the Masaniello (Room 36) and the plague (Room 37). Room 32 boasts the beautiful Tavola Strozzi (Strozzi Table); its fabled depiction of 15th-century maritime Naples is one of the city's most celebrated historical records.

Castel Sant'Elmo   CASTLE, MUSEUM
(Map p648; ☑ 081 558 77 08; www.coopculture.it; Via Tito Angelini 22; adult/reduced €5/2.50; ☺ castle 8.30am-7.30pm Wed-Mon, last entry 6.30pm; Ⓜ Vanvitelli, funicular Montesanto to Morghen) Commanding spectacular city and bay views, this star-shaped castle was originally a church dedicated to St Erasmus. Some 400 years later, in 1349, Robert of Anjou turned it into a castle before Spanish viceroy Don Pedro de Toledo had it further fortified in 1538. Used as a military prison until the 1970s, it's now home to the satisfying **Novecento a Napoli** (☑ 081 558 77 08; ☺ 9am-6pm

NAPLES & CAMPANIA NAPLES

OFF THE BEATEN TRACK

CAMPI FLEGREI

Stretching west of Posillipo Hill to the Tyrrhenian Sea, the Campi Flegrei (Phlegraean – or 'Fiery' – Fields) is home to some of Campania's most remarkable – and overlooked – Graeco-Roman ruins. Gateway to the area is the port town of Pozzuoli. Established by the Greeks around 530 BC, its most famous resident is the **Anfiteatro Flavio** (☑ 081 526 60 07; Via Terracciano 75; admission €4, incl entry to Parco Archeologico di Baia, Museo Archeologico dei Campi Flegrei & Scavi Archeologici di Cuma; ☺ varies, usually every hour from 9am-1pm Wed-Mon), Italy's third-largest ancient Roman amphitheatre.

A further 6km west, Baia was once a glamorous Roman holiday resort frequented by sun-seeking emperors. Fragments of this opulence linger among the 1st-century ruins of the **Parco Archeologico di Baia** (☑ 081 868 75 92; Via Sella di Baia; Sat & Sun adult/reduced €4/2, incl entry to Anfiteatro Flavio, Museo Archeologico dei Campi Flegrei & Scavi Archeologici di Cuma, Tue-Fri free; ☺ 9am-1hr before sunset Tue-Sun; ☒ EAV BUS to Baia or ☒ Cumana to Fusaro, then walk 900m), its mosaics, stuccoed *balneum* (bathroom) and imposing Tempio di Mercurio once part of a sprawling palace and spa complex. While the ruins are free on weekdays, weekend visitors need to purchase their tickets at the equally fascinating **Museo Archeologico dei Campi Flegrei** (Archaeological Museum of the Campi Flegrei; ☑ 081 523 37 97; http://museoarcheologicocampiflegrei.campaniabeniculturali.it; Via Castello 39; Sat & Sun €4, admission incl entry to Anfiteatro Flavio, Parco Archeoligico di Baia & Scavi Archeologici di Cuma, Tue-Fri free; ☺ varies, usually 9am-2.30pm Tue-Sun, last entry 1pm; ☒ EAV BUS to Baia), a further 2km south along the coast.

Yet another 2km south, in the sleepy town of Bacoli, lurks the magical **Piscina Mirabilis** (Marvellous Pool; ☑ 333 6853278; Via Piscina Mirabilis; donation appreciated; ☺ varies; ☒ EAV BUS to Bacoli then ☒ Cumana to Fusaro), the world's largest Roman cistern. You'll need to call the custodian to access the site, but it's well worth the effort. Bathed in an eerie light and featuring 48 soaring pillars and a barrel-vaulted ceiling, the so-called 'Marvellous Pool' is more 'subterranean cathedral' than 'giant water tank'. While entrance is free, show your manners by offering the custodian a €2 or €3 tip.

Both the Ferrovia Cumana and the Naples metro (line 2) serve Pozzuoli, and the town is also connected to Ischia and Procida by frequent car and passenger ferries. To reach Baia, take the Ferrovia Cumana train to Fusaro station, walk 150m north, turning right into Via Carlo Vanvitelli (which eventually becomes Via Bellavista). The ruins are 750m to the east. To reach Bacoli, catch a Bacoli-bound EAV Bus from Fusaro.

Unfortunately, the Campi Flegrei's second-rate infrastructure and unreliable public transport, plus the fickle opening times of its sites make pretrip planning a good idea. Contact the **tourist office** (☑ 081 526 66 39; www.infocampiflegrei.it; Largo Matteotti 1a; ☺ 9am-3pm Mon-Fri; Ⓜ Pozzuoli, ☒ Cumana to Pozzuoli) in Pozzuoli for updated information on the area's sights and opening times, or consider exploring the area with popular local tour outfit Yellow Sudmarine (p680).

Wed-Mon, entry on the hour, every hour), an art museum dedicated to 20th-century southern Italian art.

⊙ Santa Lucia & Chiaia

★ **Teatro San Carlo** THEATRE
(Map p648; ☎ 081 797 24 68; www.teatrosancarlo.it; Via San Carlo 98; guided tour adult/reduced €6/3; ⊙ guided tours every hour from 10.30am-4.30pm Mon-Sat, to 12.30pm Sun, morning tours only Jan & Feb; ☐ R2 to Via San Carlo) Even if you're not an opera fan, a guided tour of Italy's biggest and oldest opera house is worth an 'encore'. While the original 1737 theatre burnt down in 1816, Antonio Niccolini's 19th-century reconstruction is an extraordinary architectural gem, lavished with six gilded levels of boxes and a living testament to Naples' former status as Europe's music capital. Tickets for the guided tour are available at the theatre box office.

The adjoining Palazzo Reale is also home to the theatre's fascinating museum, **Memus** (Museum & Historical Archive of the Teatro San Carlo; Map p648; http://memus.squarespace.com; Piazza del Plebiscito, Palazzo Reale; adult/reduced incl Palazzo Reale €10/5; ⊙ 10am-5pm Mon, Tue,

Thu & Fri, to 7pm Sat & Sun; ☐ R2 to Piazza Trieste e Trento), and its collection of costumes, set designs and multimedia music features.

Standing opposite the theatre is the **Galleria Umberto I**, a breathtaking 19th-century arcade.

Palazzo Reale PALACE, MUSEUM
(Royal Palace; ☎ 081 40 04 54; www.coopculture.it; Piazza del Plebiscito; adult/reduced €4/3; ⊙ 9am-7pm Thu-Tue; ☐ R2 to Via San Carlo) Envisaged as a 16th-century monument to Spanish glory (Naples was under Spanish rule at the time), the magnificent Palazzo Reale is home to the **Museo del Palazzo Reale**, a rich and eclectic collection of baroque and neoclassical furnishings, porcelain, tapestries, statues and paintings, spread across the palace's royal apartments.

Among the many highlights is the restored Teatrino di Corte, a lavish private theatre created by Ferdinando Fuga in 1768 to celebrate the marriage of Ferdinand IV and Marie Caroline of Austria. The Cappella Reale (Royal Chapel) houses a colossal 18th-century *presepe* (nativity scene) the *pastori* (crib figurines or sculptures) of which were crafted by

---

LOCAL KNOWLEDGE

NEAPOLITAN NUANCES

Local historian, architect and author Andrea Maglio says to keep an eye out for these easily missed musts.

Tunnel Borbonico

In this subterranean tunnel (p654) you can still see dusty old vehicles, graffiti and toilets from when it was used as a WWII air-raid shelter. It's a wonderful place to see Naples' stratified history.

Rival Obelisks

The impressive *guglie* (obelisks) that dot Spaccanapoli exemplify the collision of religion and politics in Naples. When a deputation of noblemen devout to San Gennaro erected the **Guglia di San Gennaro** (Map p644; Piazza Riario Sforza; ☐ C55 to Via Duomo), the competing Dominicans quickly commissioned the **Guglia di San Domenico** (Map p644; Piazza San Domenico Maggiore), arguing that Naples' true patron saint was San Domenico. The bickering beckoned the mediation of the pope, who declared both saints patrons of the city.

Sacred Profanity

Naples is famous for blurring the boundary between the sacred and the profane. The Guglia di San Gennaro is built around an ancient Roman obelisk found under the city, while the Cimitero delle Fontanelle (p654) was home to a very cultish brand of Catholicism. In the paintings of Jusepe de Ribera, such as his *St Jerome and the Angel of Judgement* in the Palazzo Reale di Capodimonte the holy protagonists were often inspired by the city's poor. The result was a very human representation of the divine, reflecting the familiarity and irreverence that Neapolitans have always felt towards their much-loved saints.

a series of celebrated Neapolitan artists including Giuseppe Sanmartino, creator of the *Cristo velato* (Veiled Christ) inside the Cappella Sansevero (p642).

Designed by Domenico Fontana and completed two long centuries later in 1841, the palace also houses the **Biblioteca Nazionale** (National Library; Map p648; ☑ 081 781 92 31; www.bnnonline.it; Piazza del Plebiscito, Palazzo Reale; admission free; ☺ 8.30am-7.15pm Mon-Fri, to 1.15pm Sat, papyri exhibition closes 1pm; ☐ R2 to Piazza Trieste e Trento), which includes at least 2000 papyri discovered at Herculaneum and fragments of a 5th-century Coptic Bible. Entry to the library requires photo ID.

Facing the palace on Piazza del Plebiscito, the 19th-century **Chiesa di San Francesco di Paola** (Map p648; ☑ 081 74 51 33; Piazza del Plebiscito; ☺ 8.30am-noon & 4-7pm; ☐ R2 to Via San Carlo) was inspired by Rome's ancient Pantheon.

Castel Nuovo   CASTLE, MUSEUM
(Map p648; ☑ 081 795 58 77; Piazza Municipio; admission €6; ☺ 9am-7pm Mon-Sat, last entry 6pm; ☐ R2 to Piazza Municipio) Dubbed the Maschio Angioino (Angevin Keep), this strapping castle was built in the late 13th century as part of Charles I of Anjou's ambitious urban expansion program. Christened the Castrum Novum (New Castle) to distinguish it from the older Castel dell'Ovo and Castel Capuano, the original structure's only survivor is the Cappella Palatina. The rest is the result of Aragonese renovations two centuries later, as well as a meticulous restoration effort prior to WWII.

The two-storey Renaissance triumphal arch at the entrance – the Torre della Guardia – commemorates the victorious entry of Alfonso I of Aragon into Naples in 1443, while the stark stone **Sala dei Baroni** (Hall of the Barons) is named after the barons slaughtered here in 1486 for plotting against King Ferdinand I of Aragon. Its striking ribbed vault fuses ancient Roman and Spanish late-Gothic influences.

Only fragments of Giotto's frescoes remain in the **Cappella Palatina**, on the splays of the Gothic windows. To the left of the chapel, the glass-floored **Sala dell'Armeria** (Armoury Hall) reveals Roman ruins discovered during restoration works on the Sala dei Baroni.

All this forms part of the **Museo Civico**, spread across several halls on three floors. The 14th- and 15th-century frescoes and sculptures are of the most interest, as is

Guglielmo Monaco's 15th-century bronze door, complete with embedded cannonball.

Castel dell'Ovo   CASTLE
(Map p648; ☑ 081 795 45 93; Borgo Marinaro; ☺ 9am-7.30pm Mon-Sat, to 2pm Sun; ☐ 154 to Via Santa Lucia) **FREE** Built by the Normans in the 12th century, Naples' oldest castle owes its name (Castle of the Egg) to Virgil. The Roman scribe reputedly buried an egg on the site where the castle now stands, warning that when the egg breaks, the castle (and Naples) will fall. Thankfully, both are still in one piece, and walking up to the castle's ramparts will reward you with a breathtaking panorama... and a steady string of lip-locked couples.

☉ Capodimonte & La Sanità

★ **Palazzo Reale di Capodimonte**   PALACE, MUSEUM, PARK
(☑ 081 749 91 11; www.coopculture.it; Parco di Capodimonte; museum adult/reduced €7.50/3.75, park admission free; ☺ museum 8.30am-7.30pm Thu-Tue, last entry 1hr before closing, park 7am-8pm daily; ☐ 2M or 178) On the northern edge of the city, this colossal palace took more than a century to build. It was originally intended as a hunting lodge for Charles VII of Bourbon, but as construction got under way in 1738, the plans kept on getting grander and grander. By its completion in 1759, Naples had a new palazzo. It's now home to the exceptional **Museo Nazionale di Capodimonte**.

It's spread over three floors and 160 rooms, you'll never see the whole art museum in one day. For most people, though, a full morning or afternoon is sufficient for an abridged best-of tour, and forking out €5 for the insightful audio guide is a worthy investment. Unfortunately, funding cutbacks have seen entire sections of the museum occasionally close for part of the day, so consider calling ahead if you're set on seeing a particular work.

On the 1st floor you'll find works by Bellini, Botticelli, Caravaggio, Masaccio and Titian. While the highlights are many, look out for Masaccio's *Crocifissione* (Crucifixion) and Parmigianino's *Antea*.

Upstairs, the 2nd-floor galleries display work by Neapolitan artists from the 13th to the 19th centuries, plus some spectacular 16th-century Belgian tapestries. The piece that many come to Capodimonte to see, Car-

CATACOMBA DI SAN GENNARO

An evocative other-world of tombs, corridors and broad vestibules, the **Catacomba di San Gennaro** (☑ 081 744 37 14; www.catacombedinapoli.it; Via Tondo di Capodimonte 13; adult/reduced €8/5; ☉ 1hr tours every hour 10am-5pm Mon-Sat, to 1pm Sun) is Naples' oldest and most sacred catacomb. Not only home to 2nd-century Christian frescoes and 5th-century mosaics, it harbours the oldest known image of San Gennaro as the protector of Naples. Indeed, it was the interment of the saint's body here in the 5th century that turned this city of the dead into a Christian pilgrimage site.

Tours of the catacomb are run by the **Cooperativa Sociale Onlus 'La Paranza'** (☑ 081 744 37 14; www.catacombedinapoli.it; Via Tondo di Capodimonte 13; ☉ info point 10am-5pm; ☐ R4 to Via Capodimonte), the ticket office of which is to the left of the **Chiesa di Madre di Buon Consiglio** (☑ 081 741 00 06; Via Tondo di Capodimonte 13; ☉ 8am-12.30pm & 5-7pm Mon-Sat, 9am-1pm & 5-7pm Sun), a snack-sized replica of St Peter's in Rome completed in 1960. The co-operative also runs a fascinating walking tour called Il Miglio Sacro (The Holy Mile), which explores the neighbouring Sanità district. See its website for details.

avaggio's *Flagellazione* (Flagellation; 1607-10), hangs in reverential solitude in Room 78, at the end of a long corridor.

If you have any energy left, the small gallery of modern art on the 3rd floor is worth a quick look, if for nothing else than Andy Warhol's poptastic *Mt Vesuvius*.

Once you've finished in the museum, the **Parco di Capodimonte** – the palace's 130-hectare park – provides a much-needed breath of fresh air.

★**Cimitero delle Fontanelle** CEMETERY
(☑ 081 744 37 14; Piazza Fontanelle alla Sanità 154; ☉ 10am-5pm; ☐ C51 to Via Fontanelle) Currently holding an estimated eight million human bones, the ghoulish Fontanelle Cemetery was first used during the plague of 1656, before becoming the city's main burial site during the cholera epidemic of 1837. At the end of the 19th century it became a cult spot for the worship of the dead, which saw locals adopting skulls and praying for their souls.

It was hoped that once a soul was released from purgatory, it would bestow blessings in gratitude.

While you can visit the the cemetery independently, the lack of information makes joining a guided tour such as those organised by the Cooperativa Sociale Onlus 'La Paranza' much more rewarding. Avoid guides offering tours at the entrance.

☞ Tours

★**Tunnel Borbonico** WALKING TOUR
(Map p648; ☑ 366 2484151, 081 764 58 08; www.tunnelborbonico.info; Vico del Grottone 4; 75min standard tour adult/reduced €10/5; ☉ standard tour 10am, noon, 3.30pm & 5.30pm Fri-Sun; ☐ R2 to Via San Carlo) Traverse five centuries of history along Naples' engrossing Bourbon Tunnel. Conceived by Ferdinand II in 1853 to link the Palazzo Reale to the barracks and the sea, the never-completed escape route is part of the 17th-century Carmignano Aqueduct system, itself incorporating 16th-century cisterns. An air-raid shelter and military hospital during WWII, this underground labyrinth rekindles the past with wartime artefacts.

Beyond the standard tour are an Adventure Tour (80 minutes,; adult/reduced €15/10) and an adults-only Speleo Tour (2½ hours; €40), both of which require pre-booking.

There is a second Tunnel Borbonico entrance, through the **Parcheggio Morelli** (Via Domenico Morelli 40) parking complex in Chiaia.

Napoli Sotterranea WALKING TOUR
(Underground Naples; Map p644; ☑ 081 29 69 44; www.napolisotterranea.org; Piazza San Gaetano 68; tours €9; ☉ English tours 10am, noon, 2pm, 4pm & 6pm; ☐ C55 to Via Duomo) This evocative 80-minute tour leads you 40m below street level to explore the historic centre's ancient labyrinth of aqueducts, passages and cisterns.

The passages were originally hewn by the Greeks to extract tufa stone used in construction and to channel water from Mt Vesuvius. Extended by the Romans, the network of conduits and cisterns was more recently used as an air-raid shelter in WWII.

Kayak Napoli
BOAT TOUR

(☑ 331 9874271; www.kayaknapoli.com; three-hour tour €20) This popular kayaking tour along the Neapolitan coastline will have you gliding past ancient ruins, neoclassical villas and into grottoes. Tours cater to both rookie and experienced paddlers and depart from Villa Volpicelli on Via Ferdinando Russo, in the Posillipo district.

City Sightseeing Napoli
BUS TOUR

(Map p648; ☑ 081 551 72 79; www.napoli.city-sightseeing.it; adult/reduced €22/11) City Sightseeing Napoli operates a hop-on, hop-off bus service with four routes across the city. All depart from Piazza Municipio–Largo Castello, and tickets are available on board. Tour commentaries are provided in eight languages, including English.

⚡ Festivals & Events

Festa di San Gennaro
RELIGIOUS

(☉ Sat before 1st Sun May, 19 Sep, 16 Dec) The faithful flock to the *duomo* to witness the miraculous liquefaction of San Gennaro's blood on the Saturday before the first Sunday in May. Repeat performances take place on 19 September and 16 December.

Maggio dei Monumenti
CULTURE

(☉ May) A month-long cultural feast, with a bounty of concerts, performances, exhibitions, guided tours and other events across the city; takes place throughout May.

Napoli Teatro Festival
THEATRE

(www.napoliteatrofestival.it) Three weeks of local and international theatre and performance art, staged in conventional and unconventional venues across the city; June. A shorter, six-day edition takes place in September.

🛏 Sleeping

Spanning funky B&Bs and cheery hostels to old-school seafront luxury piles, slumber options in Naples are varied, plentiful and relatively cheap. For maximum atmosphere, consider the *centro storico*, where you'll have many of the city's sights on your doorstep.

🛏 Centro Storico & Port Area

Cerasiello B&B
B&B €

(☑ 338 9264453, 081 033 09 77; www.cerasiello.it; Via Supportico Lopez 20; s €40-60, d €55-80, tr €70-95, q €85-110; 🅿 ❄ 🛜; Ⓜ Piazza Cavour, Museo) This gorgeous B&B has four rooms with private bathroom, an enchanting communal terrace and decor melding Neapolitan art with North African furnishings. The stylish communal kitchen offers fabulous views of the Certosa di San Martino, a view shared by all rooms (or their bathroom) except room Fuoco (Fire), which looks out at a church cupola. Bring €0.10 for the lift.

DiLetto a Napoli
B&B €

(Map p644; ☑ 338 9264453, 081 033 09 77; www.dilettoanapoli.it; Vicolo Sedil Capuano 16; s €35-55, d €50-75, tr €65-90, q €80-105; 🅿 ❄ 🛜; Ⓜ Piazza Cavour) In a 15th-century *palazzo*, this savvy B&B features four rooms with vintage *cotto* floor tiles, organza curtains, local artisan lamps and handmade furniture designed by its architect owners. Bathrooms are equally stylish, while the urbane communal lounge comes with a kitchenette and dining table for convivial noshing and lounging.

★ Hotel Piazza Bellini
BOUTIQUE HOTEL €€

(Map p644; ☑ 081 45 17 32; www.hotelpiazzabellini.com; Via Santa Maria di Costantinopoli 101; s €70-140, d €80-165; ❄ @ 🛜; Ⓜ Dante) This funky art hotel inhabits a 16th-century *palazzo*, its white spaces spiked with original maiolica tiles and the work of emerging artists. Rooms offer pared-back cool, with designer fittings, chic bathrooms and mirror frames drawn straight on the wall. Rooms on the 5th and 6th floors feature panoramic terraces.

Costantinopoli 104
BOUTIQUE HOTEL €€

(Map p644; ☑ 081 557 10 35; www.costantinopoli104.it; Via Santa Maria di Costantinopoli 104; s €140-170, d €160-280, ste €200-250; ❄ @ 🛜 ♒; Ⓜ Dante) Chic and tranquil, Costantinopoli 104 is set in a neoclassical villa in the city's bohemian heartland. Although showing a bit of wear in places, rooms remain elegantly understated, comfortable and spotlessly clean – those on the 1st floor open onto a sun terrace, while ground-floor rooms face the small, palm-fringed pool.

Decumani Hotel de Charme
BOUTIQUE HOTEL €€

(Map p644; ☑ 081 551 81 88; www.decumani.it; Via San Giovanni Maggiore Pignatelli 15; s €99-124, d €99-164; ❄ @ 🛜; 🚌 R2 to Via Mezzocannone) Slumber in the former *palazzo* of Cardinal Sisto Riario Sforza, the last bishop of the Bourbon Kingdom. The simple, stylish rooms feature high ceilings, parquet floors,

19th-century furniture and modern bathrooms with roomy showers and rustic wooden benchtops. Deluxe rooms boast a jacuzzi.

🛏 Toledo & Quartieri Spagnoli

Sui Tetti di Napoli
B&B €

(Map p648; ☑338 9264453, 081 033 09 77; www.suitettidinapoli.net; Vico Figuerelle a Montecalvario 6; s €35-65, d €45-80, tr €60-95, q €80-115; ❄️ 🐕; Ⓜ Toledo) This well-priced B&B is more like four compact apartments atop a thigh-toning stairwell. While two apartments share a terrace, the rooftop mini-apartment boasts its own, complete with mesmerising views. All include a kitchenette (the cheapest two share a kitchen), bright, simple furnishings and a homey vibe.

★ La Ciliegina Lifestyle Hotel
BOUTIQUE HOTEL €€

(Map p648; ☑081 1971 8800; www.cilieginahotel.it; Via PE Imbriani 30; d €170-230, junior ste €260-300; ❄️ @ 🐕; 🚌 R2 to Piazza del Municipio) All 13 spacious, minimalist rooms at this chic, fashionista favourite include top-of-the-range Hästens beds, flat-screen TV and marble-clad bathrooms with water-jet jacuzzi showers (one junior suite has a jacuzzi tub). Breakfast in bed, or on the rooftop terrace, which comes complete with sunbeds, hot tub and a view of Vesuvius.

Hotel Il Convento
HOTEL €€

(Map p648; ☑081 40 39 77; www.hotelilconvento.com; Via Speranzella 137a; s €45-90, d €55-150, tr €65-140; ❄️ 🐕; 🚌 R2 to Via San Carlo) A soothing blend of antique Tuscan furniture, erudite bookshelves and candlelit stairs, this cosy hotel sits snugly in the atmospheric Quartieri Spagnoli. The elegant rooms combine creamy tones and dark woods with patches of 16th-century brickwork. For €80 to €180 you get a room with a private roof garden.

🛏 Santa Lucia & Chiaia

Hostel of the Sun
HOSTEL €

(Map p648; ☑081 420 63 93; www.hostelnapoli.com; Via G Melisurgo 15; dm €16-18, s €30-35, d €60-70; ❄️ @ 🐕; 🚌 R2 to Via Depretis) HOTS is an ultrafriendly hostel near the ferry terminal. Located on the 7th floor (have €0.05 for the lift), it's a bright, sociable place with multicoloured dorms, a cute in-house bar,

and a few floors down a series of hotel-standard private rooms, seven with private bathroom.

B&B Cappella Vecchia
B&B €

(Map p648; ☑081 240 51 17; www.cappellavecchia11.it; Vico Santa Maria a Cappella Vecchia 11; s €60-65, d €80-90; ❄️ @ 🐕; 🚌 C24 to Piazza dei Martiri) Run by a superhelpful young couple, this B&B is a first-rate choice. Six simple, comfy rooms feature funky bathrooms and different Neapolitan themes. There's a spacious communal area for breakfast, and free internet available 24/7. Check the website for monthly packages.

Grand Hotel Vesuvio
LUXURY HOTEL €€€

(Map p648; ☑081 764 00 44; www.vesuvio.it; Via Partenope 45; s €199-500, d €215-520; ❄️ @ 🐕; 🚌 154 to Via Santa Lucia) Known for bedding legends (past guests include Rita Hayworth and Humphrey Bogart), this five-star heavyweight is a decadent wonderland of dripping chandeliers, period antiques and opulent rooms. Count your lucky stars while drinking a martini at the rooftop restaurant.

🍴 Eating

Pizza and pasta are the staples of Neapolitan cuisine. Pizza was created here and nowhere will you eat it better. Seafood is another local speciality and you'll find mussels and clams served in many dishes.

Neapolitan street food is equally brilliant. *Misto di frittura* – zucchini flowers, deep-fried potato and aubergine – makes for a great snack, especially if eaten from paper outside a tiny streetside stall.

It's always sensible to book a table if dining at a restaurant on a Friday or Saturday night. Also note that many eateries close for two to four weeks in August, so check before heading out.

🍴 Centro Storico

★ Pizzeria Gino Sorbillo
PIZZERIA €

(Map p644; ☑081 44 66 43; www.accademiadellapizza.it; Via dei Tribunali 32; pizzas €3-7.30; ⊗ noon-3.30pm & 7-11.30pm Mon-Sat; Ⓜ Dante) Gino Sorbillo is king of the pizza pack. Head in for gigantic, wood-fired perfection, best followed by a velvety *semifreddo*; the chocolate and *torroncino* (almond nougat) combo is divine. Head in super early or expect to queue.

Trattoria Mangia e Bevi CAMPANIAN €
(Map p644; ☑ 081 552 95 46; Via Sedile di Porto 92; meals €7; ⏱ 12.30-3.30pm Mon-Fri; Ⓜ Università) Everyone from pierced students to bespectacled *professori* squeeze around the lively, communal tables for brilliant home cooking at rock-bottom prices. Scan the daily-changing menu (in Italian), jot down your choices and brace for gems like juicy *salsiccia* (pork sausage) and *peperoncino*-spiked *friarielli* (local broccoli).

Attanasio BAKERY €
(Map p644; ☑ 081 28 56 75; Vico Ferrovia 1-4; snacks from €1.10; ⏱ 6.30am-8pm Tue-Sun; Ⓜ Garibaldi) This retro pastry peddler makes one mighty *sfogliatella* (sweetened ricotta pastry), not to mention creamy *cannolli siciliani* (pastry shells stuffed with sweet ricotta) and runny, rummy *babà* (rum-soaked yeast cake). Savoury fiends shouldn't pass up the hearty *pasticcino rustico* (savoury bread), stuffed with *provola* (provolone) cheese, ricotta and salami.

La Campagnola CAMPANIAN €€
(Map p644; ☑ 081 45 90 34; www.campagnolatribunali.com; Via dei Tribunali 47; meals €18; ⏱ 12.30-4pm & 7-11.30pm Wed-Mon; Ⓜ Dante) Boisterous and affable, this Neapolitan stalwart serves up soul-coaxing classics. Daily specials may include a killer *genovese* (pasta with a slow-cooked lamb, tomato and onion *ragù*) or a decadent *penne alla siciliana* (pasta with fried aubergine, *fior di latte* cheese, tomato and basil).

Palazzo Petrucci MODERN ITALIAN €€€
(Map p644; ☑ 081 552 40 68; www.palazzopetrucci.it; Piazza San Domenico Maggiore 4; meals €50; ⏱ 1-2.30pm & 7.30-10.30pm Tue-Sat, dinner only Mon, lunch only Sun; Ⓜ Dante) Progressive Petrucci thrills with new-school creations like chickpea soup with prawns and concentrated coffee, or succulent lamb with dried apricots, *pecorino* (sheep's milk cheese) and mint. Polished service and a fine-dining air make it a perfect spot to celebrate something special.

✗ Toledo, Quartieri Spagnoli & Vomero

Friggitoria Vomero SNACKS €
(Map p648; ☑ 081 578 31 30; Via Cimarosa 44; snacks from €0.20; ⏱ 9.30am-2.30pm & 5-9.30pm Mon-Fri, to 11pm Sat; 🚠 Centrale to Fuga) Crunch blissfully at this spartan Vomero snack bar, famed for finger-licking *fritture* (fried snacks) like *frittatine di maccheroni* (fried pasta and egg) and *supplì di riso* (rice balls). Located opposite the funicular, it's a handy pit stop before legging it to the Certosa di San Martino.

Il Garum ITALIAN €€
(Map p648; ☑ 081 542 32 28; Piazza Monteoliveto 2a; meals €35; ⏱ noon-3.30pm & 7-11.30pm ; Ⓜ Toledo) One of the very few restaurants open on Sunday nights, softly lit Il Garum serves up delicately flavoured, revamped classics. Stand-out dishes include an exquisite grilled calamari stuffed with seasonal vegetables and cheese. Just leave room for desserts like *torta di ricotta e pera* (ricotta and pear cake), all made on-site.

Trattoria San Ferdinando CAMPANIAN €€
(Map p648; ☑ 081 42 19 64; Via Nardones 117; meals €30; ⏱ 12.30-3.30pm Mon-Sat, 7-11.30pm Tue-Fri; 🚌 R2 to Piazza Trieste e Trento) Hung with theatre memorabilia, San Ferdinando pulls in well-spoken theatre types and intellectuals. Ask for a rundown of the day's antipasti and choose your favourites for an *antipasto misto* (mixed antipasto). The homemade desserts make for a satisfying dénouement.

✗ Santa Lucia & Chiaia

★**L'Ebbrezza di Noè** CAMPANIAN €€
(Map p648; ☑ 081 40 01 04; www.lebbrezzadinoe.com; Vico Vetriera 9; meals €30; ⏱ 8.30pm-midnight Tue-Sun; Ⓜ Piazza Amedeo) A wine shop by day, 'Noah's Drunkenness' transforms into a culinary hot spot by night. Slip inside for vino and conversation at the bar, or settle into one of the intimate, bottle-lined dining rooms for beautiful, creative dishes dictated by the morning's market finds. Adding X-factor are over 2000 wines, artfully selected by sommelier owner Luca Di Leva.

★**Ristorantino dell'Avvocato** CAMPANIAN €€
(Map p648; ☑ 081 032 00 47; www.ilristorantinodellavvocato.it; Via Santa Lucia 115-117; meals €37, degustation menus €35-40; ⏱ noon-3pm & 7.30-11pm, lunch only Mon & Sun; 🐾; 🚌 154 to Via Santa Lucia) This elegant nosh spot is home to affable chef and owner Raffaele Cardillo, whose passion for Campania's culinary heritage merges with a knack for subtle, refreshing twists – think gnocchi with fresh mussels, clams, crumbed pistachio, lemon, ginger and garlic.

The degustation menus are good value, as is the simpler three-course lunch menu (€15), available Monday to Friday.

✗ La Sanità

Pizzeria Starita
PIZZA €

(☑ 081 557 46 82; Via Materdei 28; pizzas €3.50-13; ⏱ noon-3.30pm & 7.30pm-midnight Mon-Sat, dinner only Sun; Ⓜ Materdei) The giant fork and ladle hanging on the wall at this cultish pizzeria were used by Sophia Loren in *L'Oro di Napoli*, and the kitchen made the *pizze fritte* sold by the actress in the film. While the 60-plus pizza varieties include a tasty *fiorilli e zucchini* (zucchini, zucchini flowers and *provola*), our allegiance remains to its classic marinara.

Cantina del Gallo
CAMPANIAN €

(www.cantinadelgallo.com; Via Alessandro Telesino 21; pizzas €4-8, meals €15; ⏱ 11am-4pm & 7pm-midnight Mon-Sat, 12.30-4pm Sun; ⏰; ☐ C51 to Via Fontanelle) Catholic kitsch and a bucket of feet-warming hot coals under the table. No, you're not at nonna's house, just at one of Naples' best-kept foodie secrets. Tuck into rarer specialities like *calzoncini* (wood-fired pizza dough with various fillings) or *A'Cafona*, a spicy, garlicky wood-fired pizza. The staff are sweet but speak little English.

🍷 Drinking & Nightlife

The city's student and alternative drinking scene is around the piazzas and alleyways of the *centro storico*. For a chicer vibe, hit the cobbled lanes of upmarket Chiaia. While some bars operate from 8am, most open from around 5.30pm and close around 2am.

Clubs usually open at 10.30pm or 11pm but don't fill up until after midnight. Many close in summer (July to September), some transferring to out-of-town beach locations. Admission charges vary, but expect to pay between €5 and €30, which may or may not include a drink.

Caffè Gambrinus
CAFE

(Map p648; ☑ 081 41 75 82; www.grancaffegambrinus.com; Via Chiaia 12; ⏱ 7am-1am Sun-Thu, to 2am Fri, to 3am Sat; ☐ R2 to Via San Carlo) Grand, chandeliered Gambrinus is Naples' oldest and most venerable cafe. Oscar Wilde knocked back a few here and Mussolini had some of the rooms shut down to keep out left-wing intellectuals. Sure, the prices may be steeper, but the coffee is superlative, the *aperitivo* (pre-dinner drinks with snacks)

and nibbles are decent and sipping a *spritz* (a type of cocktail made with *prosecco*) on Piazza Triesto e Trento is a moment worth savouring.

Intra Moenia
CAFE

(Map p644; ☑ 081 29 07 20; Piazza Bellini 70; ⏱ 10am-2am; ⏰; Ⓜ Dante) This free-thinking cafe-bookshop-publishing house on Piazza Bellini is a good spot for chilling out. Browse limited-edition books on Neapolitan culture, pick up a vintage-style postcard, or simply sip a *prosecco* and act the intellectual. The house wine costs €4 a glass and there's a range of salads, snacks and classic Neapolitan grub for peckish bohemians.

Clu
BAR, RESTAURANT

(Map p648; www.clunapoli.com; Via Carlo Poerio 47; ⏱ 8am-1am Mon-Sun Sep-May, to 5pm Jun; ☐ 128 to Riviera di Chiaia) Uberfashionable Clu is a huge hit with Chiaia's *aperitivo* crowd. Order a cumin-seed-infused Spice Vesper martini and snack on fab, free nibbles like oven-baked rice and pasta dishes, and ricotta and spinach pie. Sure there's a restaurant out the back (meals €25), but with so much free grub, why bother?

Chandelier
BAR

(Map p648; ☑ 081 41 45 76; Vico Belledonne a Chiaia 34; ⏱ 6pm-late; ☐ C25 to Piazza dei Martiri) A sleek, sexy combo of tinted glass, lipstick-red neon and ambient tunes, Chandelier draws a smart, after-work crowd with its crafty libations and fabulous *aperitivo* spread. Order a negroni *sbagliato* (the negroni's much smoother sibling) and schmooze over mini bruschettas, focaccias and pasta dishes – all free with your well-mixed drink.

⭐ Entertainment

Options run the gamut from nail-biting football games to world-class opera. For cultural listings check www.incampania.it; for the latest club news check out the free minimag *Zero* (www.zero.eu, in Italian), available from many bars.

From May until September, al fresco concerts are common throughout the city. Tourist offices have details.

You can buy tickets for most cultural events at the box office inside **Feltrinelli** (☑ 081 764 21 11; Piazza dei Martiri; ⏱ 4.30-8pm Mon-Sat).

Teatro San Carlo
OPERA, BALLET

(Map p648; ☑ 081 797 23 31; www.teatrosancarlo.it; Via San Carlo 98; ⏱ box office 10am-7pm Mon-Sat, to 3.30pm Sun; ☐ R2 to Via San Carlo) One of Italy's premier opera venues, the theatre stages a year-round program of opera, ballet and concerts, though tickets can be fiendishly difficult to come by.

Galleria 19   CLUB

(Map p644; www.galleria19.it; Via San Sebastiano 19; ⊗11pm-5am Tue-Sun; ⓜDante) Set in a long, cavernous cellar scattered with chesterfields and industrial lamps, this cool and edgy club draws a uni crowd early in the week and 20/30-somethings with its Friday live-music sets and Saturday electronica sessions. It's also home to one of the city's best mixologists, Gianluca Morziello, famed for his Cucumber Slumber.

New Around Midnight   LIVE MUSIC

(☑331 2326093; www.newaroundmidnight.it; Via Bonito 32a; admission €15; ⊗7.30pm-2am Thu-Sun mid-Sep–Jun; ⓜVanvitelli, funicular Montesanto to Morghen) This hybrid jazz club and eatery features mostly homegrown acts, with the occasional blues band putting in a performance. Check the website for upcoming gigs.

Football

Naples' football team, Napoli, is the third-most supported in the country after Juventus and Milan, and watching it play at the Stadio San Paolo (Piazzale Vincenzo Tecchio; ⓜNapoli Campi Flegrei) is a highly charged rush. The season runs from late August to late May, with seats costing between €20 and €100. Book tickets at Azzurro Service (☑081 593 40 01; www.azzurroservice.net; Via Francesco Galeota 19; ⊗9am-1pm & 3.30-7pm Mon-Fri, also Sat & Sun match days; ⓜNapoli Campi Flegrei), Box Office (Map p648; ☑081 551 91 88; www.boxofficenapoli.it; Galleria Umberto I 17; ⊗9.30am-8pm Mon-Fri, 9.30am-1.30pm & 4.30-8pm Sat; ⛆R2 to Piazza Trieste e Trento), as well as from some tobacconists, and don't forget your photo ID. On match days, tickets are also available at the stadium itself.

🛍 Shopping

Vico San Domenico Maggiore   ARTISANAL

Connecting Via dei Tribunali and Piazza San Domenico Maggiore, this skinny street is home to a fistful of artisan studios. Pop into tiny Bottega 21 (Map p644; bottega21@ live.it; Vico San Domenico Maggiore 21; ⊗10.30am-1.30pm & 3-8pm Mon-Sat) for beautiful, handmade leather goods, from boho-chic handbags and satchels to jewellery, belts and butter-soft notebook covers.

Laboratorio Galleria Pensatoio (Map p644; ☑339 1175276; Vico San Domenico Maggiore 2; ⊗11am-2pm & 5-8pm Fri & Sat, also open by prior appointment) is the studio of husband-and-wife art duo Sergio and Teresa Cervo. While Sergio is best known for his organic, industrial-style metal sculptures and furniture, Teresa cleverly recycles old materials into anything from funky lampshades to wire sculptures of Neapolitan espresso cups. Next door, heavenly scented Kiphy (Map p644; ☑393 8703280; www.kiphy.it; Vico San Domenico Maggiore 3; ⊗10.30am-2pm & 3-8pm Tue-Sat, open Mon & closed Sat & Sun Jun & Jul, closed Aug; ⓜDante) peddles pure, handmade slabs of soap, as well as freshly made shampoos, creams and oils using organic, fair-trade ingredients.

ⓘ Information

I Naples (www.inaples.it) Naples' official tourist board site.

In Campania (www.incampania.com) Campania's official tourist website.

Loreto-Mare Hospital (Ospedale Loreto-Mare; ☑081 20 10 33; Via Amerigo Vespucci 26)

Napoli Unplugged (www.napoliunplugged.com) Smart, up-to-date website covering sights, events, news and practicalities.

Pharmacy (Stazione Centrale; ⊗7am-10pm Mon-Sat, 8am-9pm Sun)

Police station (☑081 794 11 11; Via Medina 75) For emergencies or to report a stolen car, call ☑113.

Post office (Piazza Matteotti; ⊗8am-6.30pm Mon-Sat)

Tourist offices For information and a map of the city visit one of these branches: Piazza del Gesù Nuovo 7 (Map p644; Piazza del Gesù Nuovo 7; ⊗9.30am-1.30pm & 2.30-6.30pm Mon-Sat, 9am-1.30pm Sun); Stazione Centrale (Map p644; Stazione Centrale; ⊗9am-6pm); Via San Carlo 9 (Map p648; Via San Carlo 9; ⊗9.30am-1.30pm & 2.30-6.30pm Mon-Sat, 9am-1.30pm Sun; ⛆R2 to Piazza Trieste e Trento)

ⓘ Getting There & Away

AIR

Capodichino airport (NAP; ☑081 789 61 11; www.gesac.it), 7km northeast of the city centre, is southern Italy's main airport, linking Naples with most Italian and several major European cities. Budget carrier easyJet has several connections to/from Naples, including London (Gatwick and Stansted), Paris (Orly) and Berlin (Schönefeld).

BOAT

Naples, the bay islands and the Amalfi Coast are served by a comprehensive ferry network.

HYDROFOILS & HIGH-SPEED FERRIES

DESTINATION (FROM NAPLES – MOLO BEVERELLO)	FERRY COMPANY	PRICE (€)	DURATION (MINS)	DAILY FREQUENCY (HIGH SEASON)
Capri	Caremar / Navigazione Libera del Golfo / SNAV	16.30 / 20.50 / 20.10	50	4 / 9 / 24
Ischia (Casamicciola Terme & Forio)	Caremar / Alilauro / SNAV	16.40 / 17.60 / 18.60	50-65	6 / 10 / 8
Procida	Caremar / SNAV	13.20 / 15.90	40	8 / 4
Sorrento	Alilauro / Navigazione Libera del Golfo	12 / 12.30	35-40	6

There are several ferry and hydrofoil terminals in central Naples.

Molo Beverello (Map p648), right in front of Castel Nuovo, services fast ferries and hydrofoils for Capri, Sorrento, Ischia (both Ischia Porto and Forio) and Procida. Some hydrofoils for Capri, Ischia and Procida also leave from Mergellina, 5km further west.

Molo Angioino (Map p648), right beside Molo Beverello, services slow ferries for Sicily, the Aeolian Islands and Sardinia.

Calata Porta di Massa (Map p648), beside Molo Angioino, services slow ferries to Ischia, Procida and Capri.

Ferry services are pared back considerably in the winter, and adverse sea conditions may affect sailing schedules.

The tables list hydrofoil and ferry destinations from Naples. The fares, unless otherwise stated, are for a one-way, high-season, deck-class single.

Tickets for shorter journeys can be bought at the ticket booths on Molo Beverello, Calata Porta di Massa or at Mergellina. For longer journeys try the offices of the ferry companies or a travel agent.

The following is a list of hydrofoil and ferry companies:

Alilauro (Map p648; ☑ 081 497 22 01; www.alilauro.it)

Caremar (Map p648; ☑ 081 551 38 82; www.caremar.it)

Medmar (Map p648; ☑ 081 333 44 11; www.medmargroup.it)

Navigazione Libera del Golfo (NLG; Map p648; ☑ 081 552 07 63; www.navlib.it)

Siremar (Map p648; ☑ 081 497 2999; www.siremar.it)

SNAV (Map p648; ☑ 081 428 55 55; www.snav.it)

Tirrenia (Map p648; ☑ 892123; www.tirrenia.it)

BUS

Most national and international buses leave from Corso Meridionale, on the north side of Stazione Centrale.

On Piazza Garibaldi, **Biglietteria Vecchione** (☑ 081 563 03 20; Piazza Garibaldi; ☺ 6:30am-7.30pm Mon-Sat) displays timetables and sells tickets for most regional and inter-city buses. It also sells Unico Napoli bus and metro tickets.

Regional bus services are operated by numerous companies, the most useful of which is SITA Sud (p685). Connections from Naples include the following:

Amalfi €4.10, two hours, three daily Monday to Saturday

Salerno €4.10, 75 minutes, every 15 to 60 minutes Monday to Saturday

You can buy SITA Sud tickets and catch buses either from Porto Immacolatella, near Molo Angioino, or from outside Stazione Centrale. Tickets are also available from bars and tobacconists displaying the Unico Campania sign.

ATC (☑ 0823 96 90 57; www.atcbus.it) runs from Naples to:

Assisi 5¼ hours, twice daily

Perugia 4½ hours, twice daily

Miccolis (☑ 081 563 03 20; www.miccolis-spa.it) connects Naples to:

Brindisi €31, five hours, three daily

Lecce €34, 5½ to 6 hours, three daily

Taranto €23, four hours, three daily

Marino (☑ 080 311 23 35; www.marinobus.it) runs from Naples to:

Bari €17, three to 3¾ hours, three to five daily

Matera €20, four to 4½ hours, two daily

CAR & MOTORCYCLE

Naples is on the Autostrada del Sole, the A1 (north to Rome and Milan) and the A3 (south to Salerno and Reggio di Calabria). The A30 skirts Naples to the northeast, while the A16 heads across the Apennines to Bari.

On approaching the city, the motorways meet the Tangenziale di Napoli, a major ring road around the city. The ring road hugs the city's northern fringe, meeting the A1 for Rome in the east and continuing westwards towards the Campi Flegrei and Pozzuoli.

TRAIN

Naples is southern Italy's main rail hub. Most national trains arrive at or depart from **Stazione Centrale** (☑ 081 554 31 88; Piazza Garibaldi) or underneath the main station, from Stazione Garibaldi. Some services also stop at Mergellina station.

State-owned Trenitalia (p952) runs most inter-city train services, including up to 42 trains daily to Rome. Travel times and prices vary. Options to/from Rome include the following:

Frecciarossa High Velocity; 2nd class one-way €43, 70 minutes

IC InterCity; 2nd class one way €24.50, two hours

Regionale Regional; one way €11.20, 2¾ hours

Privately owned **Italo** (☑ 060708; www.ita-lotreno.it) runs high-velocity trains between Stazione Centrale in Naples and numerous major Italian cities, including Rome (2nd class one way €43, 70 minutes). Note that Italo trains from Naples to Rome stop at Roma-Tiburtina station and not at the main Roma-Termini station.

Tickets for high-velocity trains can work out much cheaper if booked even a few days in advance.

Circumvesuviana (p685) trains connect Naples to Sorrento (€4.10, 68 minutes, around 30 daily). Stops along the way include Ercolano (€2.20, 19 minutes) and Pompeii (€2.90, 38 minutes). Trains leave from **Stazione Circumvesuviana** (☑ 800 211388; www.eavcampania.it; Corso Garibaldi), adjacent to Stazione Centrale (follow the signs from the main concourse).

Ferrovia Cumana (☑ 800 211388; www.eav-campania.it) trains leave from Stazione Cumana di Montesanto on Piazza Montesanto, 500m southwest of Piazza Dante, running to Pozzuoli (€1.30, 22 minutes, every 20 minutes) and other Campi Flegrei towns beyond.

Ferrovia Circumflegrea, also based at Stazione Cumana di Montesanto, runs services to other Campi Flegrei towns, most of little interest to travellers.

❶ Getting Around

TO/FROM THE AIRPORT

By public transport you can catch the **Alibus** (☑ 800 639525; www.unicocampania.it) airport shuttle (€3, 45 minutes, every 20 to 30 minutes) to/from Molo Beverello or Piazza Garibaldi. Tickets are available on board.

Official taxi fares to the airport are as follows: €23 from a seafront hotel or from the Mergellina hydrofoil terminal; €19 from Piazza del Municipio; and €15.50 from Stazione Centrale.

BUS

In Naples, buses are operated by the city transport company **ANM** (☑ 800 639525; www.anm.it). There's no central bus station, but most buses pass through Piazza Garibaldi, the city's chaotic transport hub. To locate your bus stop you'll probably need to ask at the information kiosk in the centre of the square.

CAR & MOTORCYCLE

Vehicle theft and anarchic traffic make driving in Naples a bad option.

Officially much of the city centre is closed to nonresident traffic for much of the day. Daily restrictions are in place in the *centro storico*, in the area around Piazza del Municipio and Via Toledo, and in the Chiaia district. Hours vary but are typically from 7am to 6pm, possibly later.

FERRIES

DESTINATION (FROM NAPLES – CALATA PORTA DI MASSA & MOLO ANGIOINO)	COMPANY	PRICE (€)	DURATION	FREQUENCY (HIGH SEASON)
Aeolian Islands	Siremar / SNAV (summer only)	from 50 / from 65	9¾ / 4½ hr	2 weekly / 1 daily
Cagliari (Sardinia)	Tirrenia	from 49	16¼ hr	2 weekly
Capri	Caremar	12.70	80 min	3 daily
Ischia (Ischia Porto)	Caremar / Medmar	12.20 / 11.30	90 / 75 min	5 / 6 daily
Milazzo (Sicily)	Siremar	from 57	10½ hr	2 weekly
Palermo (Sicily)	SNAV / Tirrenia	from 57 / from 49	10¼-11¾ hr	1 to 2 / 1 daily
Procida	Caremar	12.20	65 min	5 daily

ℹ TICKETS PLEASE

Tickets for public transport in Naples and the surrounding Campania region are managed by **Unico Campania** (www.unicocampania.it) and sold at stations, ANM booths and tobacconists. There are various tickets, depending on where you plan to travel. The following is a rundown of the various tickets on offer:

➜ **Unico Napoli** (90 minutes €1.30; daily €3.70 weekdays; €3.10 weekends) Unlimited travel by bus, tram, funicular, metro, Ferrovia Cumana or Circumflegrea.

➜ **Unico 3T** (3 days €20) Unlimited travel throughout Campania, including the Alibus, EAV buses to Mt Vesuvius and transport on the islands of Ischia and Procida.

➜ **Unico Ischia** (90 minutes €1.90; 1/2/3 days €6/10/13) Unlimited bus travel on Ischia.

➜ **Unico Capri** (60 minutes €2.70; 24 hours €8.60) Unlimited bus travel on Capri. The 60-minute ticket also allows a single trip on the funicular connecting Marina Grande to Capri Town; the daily ticket allows for two funicular trips.

➜ **Unico Costiera** (45 minutes €2.50; 90 minutes €3.80; 1/3 days €7.60/18) A money-saver if you plan on much travelling by SITA Sud or EAV bus and/or Circumvesuviana train in the Bay of Naples and Amalfi Coast area. The one- and three-day tickets also cover the City Sightseeing tourist bus between Amalfi and Ravello, and Amalfi and Maiori, which runs from April to October.

East of the city centre, there's a 24-hour car park at Via Brin (€1.30 for the first four hours, €7.20 for 24 hours).

If renting a car, expect to pay around €60 per day for an economy car or a scooter. The major car-hire firms are all represented in Naples.

Avis (☑ 081 28 40 41; www.avisautonoleggio.it; Corso Novara 5) Also at Capodichino airport.

Hertz (☑ 081 20 28 60; www.hertz.it; Corso Arnaldo Lucci 171) Also at Via Marina Varco Pisacane (beside the ferry terminal), at Capodichino airport and in Mergellina.

Maggiore (☑ 081 28 78 58; www.maggiore.it; Stazione Centrale) Also at Capodichino airport.

Rent Sprint (☑ 081 764 34 52; www.rentsprint.it; Via Santa Lucia 32) Scooter hire only.

FUNICULAR

Unico Napoli tickets are valid on the funiculars. Three of Naples' four funicular railways connect the centre with Vomero (the fourth, Funicolare di Mergellina, connects the waterfront at Via Mergellina with Via Manzoni).

Funicolare Centrale Ascends from Via Toledo to Piazza Fuga.

Funicolare di Chiaia From Via del Parco Margherita to Via Domenico Cimarosa.

Funicolare di Montesanto From Piazza Montesanto to Via Raffaele Morghen.

METRO

Naples' **Metropolitana** (☑ 800 568866; www.metro.na.it) metro system is covered by Unico Napoli tickets.

Line 1 Runs north from Università (Piazza Bovio), stopping at Toledo, Piazza Dante, Museo (for Piazza Cavour and Line 2), Materdei,

Salvator Rosa, Cilea, Piazza Vanvitelli, Piazza Medaglie D'Oro and seven stops beyond. The expected 2014 completion of the Line 1 extension will see trains run to Garibaldi (Stazione Centrale), with the opening of an additional station in Piazza Municipio (between Università and Toledo stations).

Line 2 Runs from Gianturco, just east of Stazione Centrale, with stops at Piazza Garibaldi (for Stazione Centrale), Piazza Cavour, Montesanto, Piazza Amedeo, Mergellina, Piazza Leopardi, Campi Flegrei, Cavalleggeri d'Aosta, Bagnoli and Pozzuoli.

TAXI

Official taxis are white and have meters; always ensure the meter is running. There are taxi stands at most of the city's main piazzas or you can call one of the following taxi cooperatives:

Consortaxi (☑ 081 22 22)

Consorzio Taxi Napoli (☑ 081 88 88; www.consorziotaxinapoli.it)

Radio Taxi La Partenope (☑ 081 01 01; www.radiotaxilapartenope.it)

The minimum taxi fare is €4.50, of which €3 is the starting fare. The minimum charge increases to €5.50 between 10pm and 7am, on Sundays and on holidays. There is also a baffling range of additional charges, including €1 for a radio taxi call and €0.50 per piece of luggage in the boot.

Official flat rates do exist on some routes, including to/from the airport, Stazione Centrale and the ferry ports. Where available, flat-rate fares must be requested at the beginning of your trip.

From Stazione Centrale, fixed-fare routes include Mergellina (€13.50), seafront hotels (€11.50) and Molo Beverello (€10.50).

See the taxi company websites for a comprehensive list of fares.

Capri

◪ 13,400

A stark mass of limestone rock rising sheerly through impossibly blue water, Capri (pronounced *ca*-pri) is the perfect microcosm of Mediterranean appeal – a smooth cocktail of vogueish piazzas and cool cafes, Roman ruins, rugged seascapes and holidaying VIPs. While it's also a popular day-trip destination, consider staying a couple of nights to explore beyond Capri Town and its uphill rival Anacapri. It's here, in Capri's hinterland, that the island really seduces with its overgrown vegetable plots, sun-bleached stucco and indescribably beautiful walking trails.

⊙ Capri Town & Around

Whitewashed buildings, labyrinthine laneways, and luxe boutiques and cafes: Capri Town personifies upmarket Mediterranean chic.

Piazza Umberto I   PIAZZA

The heart of Capri Town, this 'flaunt-it-baby' *piazzetta* (little square) seems tailor-made for people-watching and feeling fabulous. While kicking back at the cafes and bars may be expensive, it's an essential Capri experience, especially in the evening, when the main activity in these parts is to style up and scan the candy crowd.

Just off the square, the 17th-century **Chiesa di Santo Stefano** (Piazza Umberto I; ⊗ 8am-8pm) is known for its well-preserved

---

WORTH A TRIP

PALAZZO REALE DI CASERTA

The one compelling reason to stop at the otherwise nondescript town of Caserta, 30km north of Naples, is to gasp at its colossal, World Heritage-listed **Palazzo Reale** (Map p648; ☑ 0823 44 80 84; www.reggiadicaserta.beniculturali.it; Viale Douhet 22; adult/reduced €12/6; ⊗ palace 8.30am-7pm Wed-Mon, park 8.30am-2hr before sunset Mon-Wed, Giardino Inglese 8.30am-3hr before sunset Mon-Wed). With film credits including *Mission Impossible III* and the interior shots of Queen Amidala's royal residence in *Star Wars: Episode 1 – The Phantom Menace* and *Star Wars: Episode 2 – Attack of the Clones*, this former royal pad is one of the greatest – and last – achievements of Italian baroque architecture.

Known to Italians as the Reggia di Caserta, the *palazzo* (mansions) began life in 1752 after King Charles VII of Bourbon ordered a palace to rival Versailles. Neapolitan Luigi Vanvitelli was commissioned for the job and built a palace bigger than its French rival. With its 1200 rooms, 1790 windows, 34 staircases and a 250m-long facade, it was reputedly the largest building in 18th-century Europe.

Vanvitelli's immense staircase leads up to the royal apartments, richly decorated with tapestries, furniture, crystal and art. The recently restored back rooms of the Throne Room house an extraordinary collection of historic wooden models of the palace, along with architectural drawings and early sketches of the building by Luigi Vanvitelli and his son, Carlo.

The apartments are also home to the Mostra Terrea Motus, an underrated collection of international modern art commissioned after the region's devastating earthquake in 1980.

To clear your head afterwards, explore the elegant landscaped park, which stretches for some 3km to a waterfall and fountain of Diana. Within the park is the famous Giardino Inglese (English Garden), a romantic oasis of intricate pathways, exotic flora, pools and cascades. Bicycle hire (€4) is available on the grounds.

If you're feeling peckish, ditch the uninspiring on-site cafeteria for contemporary cafe **Martucci** (☑ 0823 32 08 03; Via Roma 9, Caserta; pastries from €0.80, salads from €4; ⊗ 5am-10.30pm), located 250m east of the palace. The counters here heave with freshly made *panini* (sandwiches), salads, vegetable dishes, baked savouries, pastries and substantial cooked-to-order meals.

Regular trains connect Naples to Caserta (€3.50, 35 to 50 minutes) from Monday to Saturday. Services are reduced and inconvenient on Sunday. Caserta train station is located opposite the palace grounds. If you're driving, follow signs for the Reggia.

Capri

Enlargement

0 — 100 m
0 — 0.05 miles

0 — 1 km
0 — 0.5 miles

Tyrrhenian Sea

Punta del Capo

Salto di Tiberio 7

Punta dell'Arcera

Tyrrhenian Sea

Via Grotta Azzurra

5

Grotta Azzurra

Bagno di Tiberio

Gulf of Naples (Golfo di Napoli)

9 f
23
10

Via Marina Grande

Marina di Caterola

Via Tiberio

Arco Naturale

Monte Tiboro (261m)

Punta Massullo

Pizzolungo

Scoglio del Monacone

Porto di Tragara

Punta di Tragara

Via Camerelle
Via Tuoro
Via Tragara

14
24
15
26
2
13
4

See Enlargement

CAPRI TOWN

Via Roma

Isole Faraglioni

La Fontelina

Gulf of Salerno (Golfo di Salerno)

Scoglio dell'Unghia Marina

Via Marina Piccola

Bagni di Gioia

Scoglio delle Sirene

Torre Saracena

Punta di Mulo

Punta Ventroso

Tyrrhenian Sea

Seggiovia (Funicular)
Via Seggiovia del Monte Solaro
Via Provinciale Anacapri

ANACAPRI

Piazza Vittoria
Via Giuseppe Orlandi
Via La Fabbrica
Piazza Diaz
11
12
27
8
1
21
Piazzetta Cimitero
Via de Tommaso

17

16

Via Tuoro Via Pagliaro

Monte Cappello (514m)

Monte Santa Maria (495m)

Santa Maria a Cetrella

Monte Solaro (589m)

Via Migliera

Via Nuove del Faro

Migliera (304m)

20

Sentiero dei Fortini

Cala del Rio

Cala del Tombosiello

Lido del Faro

Punta Carena

Punta del Tuono

Cala Marmolata

Enlargement detail:

Piazza Umberto I
Via M Serafina
Via Vittorio Emanuele III
Via Le Botteghe
Via Longano

19
25
18
22
3
6
f
Piazzetta Cerio

Capri

◎ Top Sights

◎ Sights

◎ Activities, Courses & Tours

◎ Sleeping

◎ Eating

◎ Entertainment

◎ Shopping

marble floor (taken from Villa Jovis). Opposite the church, the **Museo Cerio** (☎081 837 66 81; Piazzetta Cerio 5; adult/reduced €2.50/1; ☺10am-1pm Tue-Sat) harbours a library of books and journals (mostly in Italian), and a collection of locally found fossils.

Villa Jovis   RUIN
(Jupiter's Villa; ☎081 837 06 86; Via Amaiuri; adult/reduced €2/1; ☺11am-3pm, closed Tue 1st-15th of month, closed Sun rest of month) A comfortable 2km walk along Via Tiberio, Villa Jovis was the largest and most sumptuous of the island's 12 Roman villas. It was also Tiberius' main Capri residence. Although reduced to ruins, wandering around will give you a good idea of the scale on which Tiberius liked to live.

The vast pleasure complex famously pandered to the emperor's lustful desires, and included imperial quarters and extensive bathing areas set in dense gardens and woodland. His private rooms were on the northern and eastern sides of the complex.

The stairway behind the villa leads to the 330m-high **Salto di Tiberio** (Tiberius' Leap), a sheer cliff from where, as the story goes, Tiberius had out-of-favour subjects hurled into the sea. True or not, the breathtaking views are real enough; if you suffer from vertigo, tread carefully.

A short walk from the villa, down Via Tiberio and Via Matermània, is the **Arco Naturale** – a huge, photogenic rock arch formed by the pounding sea.

Certosa di San Giacomo   MONASTERY
(☎081 837 62 18; Viale Certosa 40; ☺9am-2pm Tue-Sun) **FREE** Generally considered the finest surviving example of Caprese architecture, this picturesque monastery now houses a school, library, temporary exhibition space and a museum with some evocative 17th-century paintings. While the chapel has some soothing 17th-century frescoes, it's the two cloisters that have a real sense of faded glory (the smaller dates to the 14th century, the larger to the 16th century).

To reach here take Via Vittorio Emanuele, to the east of Piazza Umberto I, which meanders down to the monastery.

Giardini di Augusto   GARDEN
(Gardens of Augustus; admission €1; ☺9am-1hr before sunset) Get away from the Capri crowds by heading southwest from the Certosa di San Giacomo monastery where, at the end of Via G Matteotti, you'll come across the unexpected green oasis of the colourful Giardini di Augusto, founded by the Emperor Augustus. You should spend a few minutes contemplating the breathtaking view from here: gaze ahead to the **Isole Faraglioni**, the three dramatic limestone pinnacles that rise vertically out of the sea.

◎ Anacapri & Around

Delve beyond the Villa San Michele di Axel Munthe and the souvenir stores and you'll discover that Capri Town's more subdued sibling is, at heart, the laid-back rural village that it's always been.

⭐ **Seggiovia del Monte Solaro**   VIEW POINT
(☎ 081 837 14 28; single/return €7.50/10; ⊙ 9.30am-4.30pm summer, to 3.30pm winter) Hop onto this *seggiovia* (chairlift) and head up to the summit of **Monte Solaro** (589m), Capri's highest point. The views from the top are utterly unforgettable – on a clear day, you can see the entire Bay of Naples, the Amalfi Coast and the islands of Ischia and Procida.

Villa San Michele
di Axel Munthe   MUSEUM, GARDEN
(☎ 081 837 14 01; www.villasanmichele.eu; Via Axel Munthe 34; admission €7; ⊙ 9am-6pm summer, reduced hours rest of year) A short walk from Anacapri's Piazza Vittoria awaits the former home of self-aggrandising Swedish doctor Axel Munthe. Other than the collection of Roman sculpture, the villa's winning feature is the beautifully preserved gardens and their inspiring views. Between late June and early August, the gardens play host to classical concerts – check the Axel Munthe Foundation website for program details and reservation information.

Beyond the villa, Via Axel Munthe continues to the 800-step stairway leading down to Capri Town.

🏃 Activities

Beaches   BEACH
Come summer, it's hard to resist Capri's turquoise waters. Top swimming spots include **La Fontelina** (☎ 081 837 08 45; www.fontelina-capri.com), reached along Via Tragara. Access to the private beach will set you back €20 but it's right beside Capri's craggy Faraglioni stacks and is one of the few beaches with direct sunlight until late in the day.

On the west coast, **Lido del Faro** (☎ 081 837 17 98; www.lidofaro.com) at Punta Carena is another good option; €20 will get you access to the private beach, complete with swimming pool and a pricey but fabulous restaurant. For a free dip, opt for the neighbouring public beach, and grab a decent bite at snack bar Da Antonio. To get here from Anacapri, catch the bus to Faro (every 20 minutes, April to October) and follow the steps down to the beach.

Sercomar   DIVING
(☎ 081 837 87 81; www.capriseaservice.com; Via Colombo 64, Marina Grande; ⊙ Apr-Oct; ♿) Marina Grande is the hub of Capri's thriving watersports business and this outfit is a solid choice for diving fans. Dives start from €100 for a single dive (maximum of three people)

DON'T MISS

GROTTA AZZURRA

Glowing in an ethereal blue light, the bewitching **Grotta Azzurra** (Blue Grotto; grotto admission €12.50, return boat trip €13.50; ⊙ 9am-1hr before sunset) is Capri's most famous single attraction.

Long known to local fishers, the legendary sea cave was rediscovered by two Germans – writer Augustus Kopisch and painter Ernst Fries – in 1826. Subsequent research, however, revealed that Emperor Tiberius had built a quay in the cave around AD 30, complete with a nymphaeum. Remarkably, you can still see the carved Roman landing stage towards the rear of the grotto.

Measuring 54m by 30m and rising to a height of 15m, the grotto is said to have sunk by up to 20m in prehistoric times, blocking every opening except the 1.3m-high entrance. And this is the key to the magical blue light. Sunlight enters through a small underwater aperture and is refracted through the water; this, combined with the reflection of the light off the white sandy sea floor, produces the vivid blue effect to which the cave owes its name.

The easiest way to visit it is to take a boat tour from Marina Grande. A return trip will cost €26, comprising a return motorboat to the cave, the rowing boat into the cave itself and admission fee; allow a good hour.

The grotto is closed if the sea is too choppy, and swimming in the cave is forbidden, although you can swim outside the entrance – get a bus to Grotta Azzurra, take the stairs down to the right and dive off the small concrete platform. When visiting, keep in mind that the singing 'captains' are included in the price, so don't feel any obligation if they push for a tip.

SOOTHING ISLAND HIKES

Away from the yachts, bikini crowds and glossy boutiques, Capri offers some seriously soul-lifting hikes. Favourite routes include from Arco Naturale to the Belvedere di Tragara (1.2km, 1¼ hours), best tackled in this very direction to avoid a final climb up to Arco Naturale. Another popular route is from Anacapri to Monte Solaro (2km, two hours), the island's highest point. If you don't fancy an upward trek, take the *seggiovia* (chairlift) up and walk down.

Running along the island's oft-overlooked western coast, the Sentiero dei Fortini (Path of the Small Forts; 5.2km, three hours), which connects Punta dell'Arcera near the Grotta Azzurra to Punta Carena, promises more bucolic bliss. For the best effect, start at Punta dell'Arcera so you can end your hike with sunset drinks at Punta Carena. Capri's tourist offices can provide information and maps of the island's various trails.

to €150 for an individual dive. A four-session beginner's course will set you back €350.

Banana Sport BOATING
(☑ 081 837 51 88; Marina Grande; 2hours/day rental €120/220; ☉ May-Oct) Located on the Marina Grande waterfront, Banana Sport hires out five-person motorised dinghies, allowing you to explore the island's more secluded coves and grottoes.

🛏 Sleeping

Capri's accommodation is top-heavy, with plenty of four- and five-star hotels and fewer budget options. This said, the recent financial downturn has seen many hotels lower their prices in the past couple of years, making the island a little less prohibitive than it used to be. Prices are often cheaper Monday to Thursday and, as a general rule, the further you go from Capri Town, the less you'll pay. Camping is forbidden.

Always book ahead. Hotel space is at a premium during the summer, and many places close in winter, typically between November and March.

Capri Suite GUESTHOUSE €€
(☑ 349 5252881, 335 5280647; www.caprisuite.it; Via Finestrale 9, Anacapri; standard ste €140-190, superior ste €190-260; ❄ 🛜) This striking two-suite guesthouse occupies part of a 17th-century convent in central Anacapri. While low-slung lamps and huge arched windows define the kitchen, traces of frescoes contrast sharply against resin floors, blown-up contemporary photography and designer furniture in the living room. The superior suite comes with chromotherapy soaking tub, right at the foot of your bed.

Villa Eva HOTEL €€
(☑ 081 837 15 49; www.villaeva.com; Via La Fabbrica 8, Anacapri; d €100-140, tr €150-180, apt per person €55-65; ☉ Easter-Oct; 🛜) Villa Eva is a top 'budget' option, complete with small swimming pool and lush, palm-fringed gardens. Whether it's a stained-glass window or a vintage fireplace, each room is distinct; some come with sea-view terraces. The four- and six-person apartments are ideal for families or groups of friends.

Free wi-fi is available in the pool area. Air-conditioning is optional and charged separately.

Casa Mariantonia BOUTIQUE HOTEL €€
(☑ 081 837 29 23; www.casamariantonia.com; Via Guiseppe Orlandi 80, Anacapri; r €100-260; P ❄ 🛜🛜) This fabulous boutique retreat counts Jean-Paul Sartre and Alberto Moravia among its past guests, which may well give you something to muse upon while you're lounging by the fabulous pool. Rooms deliver restrained elegance in soothing hues, and there are private terraces with gorgeous garden views.

Hotel Villa Sarah HOTEL €€
(☑ 081 837 78 17; www.villasarah.it; Via Tiberio 3, Capri Town; s €90-160, d €135-235; ☉ Easter-Oct; ❄ 🛜) On the road up to Villa Jovis – a 10-minute walk from the centre of Capri Town – Villa Sarah retains a rustic appeal that so many of the island's hotels have long lost. Surrounded by its own fruit-producing gardens and with a small pool, it has 20 airy rooms, all decorated in classical local style with ceramic tiles and old-fashioned furniture. The healthy breakfast includes organic produce.

Hotel La Tosca
PENSION €€

(☑ 081 837 09 89; www.latoscahotel.com; Via Dalmazio Birago 5, Capri Town; s €50-100, d €75-160; ☉ Apr-Oct; ❈ 🛜) Away from the glitz of the town centre, this one-star charmer is hidden down a quiet back lane overlooking the Certosa di San Giacomo and the mountains. Rooms are airy and comfortable, with whitewashed walls, striped fabrics and large bathrooms. Several have private terraces, complete with deck chairs and rattan furniture.

★ La Minerva
BOUTIQUE HOTEL €€€

(☑ 081 837 70 67; www.laminervacapri.com; Via Occhio Marino 8, Capri Town; superior d €170-410, deluxe d €230-520; ☉ mid-Mar–early Nov; ❈ 🛜 🏊) This stylish, family-run hotel is highly coveted (book five to six months ahead). All 16 rooms deliver crisp, white-on-white luxury, from silk drapes, plush sofas and 100% linen sheets to heavenly mattresses and your choice of pillows. Deluxe rooms feature jacuzzis and larger terraces. Then there's the gorgeous pool, surrounded by lush greenery and dreamy sea views.

Orsa Maggiore
BOUTIQUE HOTEL €€€

(☑ 081 837 33 51; www.orsamaggiore-capri.com; Via Tuoro 30, Anacapri; d €160-340; ☉ mid-Apr–mid-Oct; ❈ @ 🛜 🏊) If sunset-gazing from a mosaic-lined infinity pool strikes a chord, this airy boutique hotel has your name written all over its whitewashed walls. Umbrian stone floors, wisteria-laced terraces and lush grounds set a suitably chic scene, the hotel's 14 rooms featuring large terraces with chaise longes for sun-kissed R&R.

A small, private spa area (60 minutes, €60 per couple) comes with sauna, Turkish bath, jacuzzi and chromotherapy shower.

🍴 Eating

Traditional food in traditional trattorias is what you'll find on Capri. The island's culinary gift to the world is *insalata caprese,* a salad of fresh tomato, basil and mozzarella bathed in olive oil. Also look out for *caprese* cheese, a cross between mozzarella and ricotta, and *ravioli caprese,* ravioli stuffed with ricotta and herbs.

Many restaurants, like the hotels, close over winter.

Capri Pasta
TAKEAWAY €

(Via Parrocco R Canale 12, Capri Town; mains €8; ☉ closed Mon) Locals come here for a cheap, tasty takeaway lunch. The just-cooked soul food might include *parmigiana di melanzana* (aubergine parmigiana) and *friarelle* (local broccoli). The house ravioli are legendary and offered fresh or ready-to-eat in dishes like *ravioli fritti* (fried ravioli) stuffed with Caciotta cheese and marjoram.

Salumeria da Aldo
DELI €

(Via Cristoforo Colombo 26, Marina Grande; panini from €3.50) Ignore the restaurant touts and head straight to this honest portside deli, where bespectacled Aldo will make you his legendary *panino alla Caprese* (crusty bread stuffed with silky mozzarella and tomatoes from his own garden). Grab a bottle of Falanghina and you're set for a day at the beach.

★ Da Gelsomina
CAMPANIAN €€

(☑ 081 837 14 99; www.dagelsomina.com; Via Migliera 72, Anacapri; meals €38; ☉ lunch & dinner Mon-Sun May-Sep, reduced hours rest of year; 🛜) Sublime home-grown produce and wine; sea and vineyard views; a swimming pool for a postprandial dip – it's no wonder you're advised to book three days ahead in the summer. Da Gelsomina ditches culinary clichés for turf classics like *coniglio alla cacciatore* (rabbit with lightly spiced tomato, sage and rosemary) and not-to-be-missed *ravioli caprese,* filled with Cacciotta cheese.

The property also offers five pleasant rooms (doubles €120 to €160) with terraces and sea views. From Anacapri, Da Gelsomina is a 20-minute walk along sleepy Via Migliera. Alternatively, call ahead for a free pick-up from Anacapri.

Pulalli
WINE BAR €€

(☑ 081 837 41 08; Piazza Umberto I 4, Capri Town; meals €25; ☉ lunch & dinner Wed-Mon Easter-Oct, dinner Tue Aug) Climb the clock-tower steps to the right of Capri Town's tourist office and your reward is a laid-back local hang-out, where fabulous vino meets a discerning selection of cheeses, *salumi* (charcuterie) and more substantial fare like spaghetti with zucchini flowers. Try for a seat on the terrace or, if you're feeling lucky, the coveted table on its own petite balcony.

Buca di Bacco
CAMPANIAN, PIZZERIA €€

(☑ 081 837 07 23; Via Longano 35, Capri Town; pizzas €6.50-12.50, meals €40; ☉ noon-3pm & 7-11pm) A famous hang-out for artists early last century, this hidden Capri Town treasure is now better known for its solid local cooking, bubbling pizzas and amiable staff. The seafood is especially good, as is the window table with dreamy sea views.

Le Arcate
CAMPANIAN, PIZZERIA **€€**

(☑081 837 35 88; Via de Tommaso 24, Anacapri; pizzas €7-11, meals €30; ☺noon-3pm & 7pm-midnight) An unpretentious place with hanging baskets of ivy, sunny yellow tablecloths and well-aged terracotta tiles, Le Arcate specialises in delicious *primi* (first courses) and pizzas. A real show-stopper is the *seppie con verdure all'aceto balsamico* (cuttlefish with vegetables in a balsamic reduction).

 Drinking & Nightlife

The main evening activity is styling up and hanging out, ideally on Capri Town's Piazzetta. There are few nightclubs to speak of and just a few upmarket taverns. Most places open around 10pm (don't expect a crowd until midnight), charging anywhere between €30 and €40 for admission. Many close between November and Easter.

Taverna Anema e Core
CLUB

(☑081 837 64 61; Via Sella Orta 39e, Capri Town; ☺11.30pm-late daily Jul & Aug, closed Mon & Wed Easter-Jun, Sep & Oct) In Capri Town, this nightlife institution is a hit with permatanned VIPs and holidaying celebs. Dress sharp – you never know who you might stumble across.

Il Celeste
CLUB

(☑081 837 73 08; www.celestecapri.it; Via Camerelle 63, Capri Town; ☺11.45pm-4am Fri-Sun) A huge hit with the 18-to-25 crowd, Il Celeste channels retro Capri chic with its chintzy chandeliers, candelabras and champagne chesterfields. Dress to impress and groove to house and mainstream dance.

Shopping

If you're not in the market for a new Rolex or Prada bag, look out for ceramic work, lemon-scented perfume and *limoncello* (lemon liqueur). For perfume don't miss **Carthusia I Profumi di Capri** (☑081 837 53 35; www.carthusia.it; Via F Serena 28, Capri Town; ☺9am-6pm); for *limoncello* head up to Anacapri and **Limoncello di Capri** (☑081 837 29 27; Via Capodimonte 27; ☺9am-7.30pm).

If you *are* in the market for a new Rolex or Prada bag, head to Via Vittorio Emanuele and Via Camerelle.

Information

Tourist office (Marina Grande; ☺9.15am-1pm & 3-6.15pm Mon-Sat, 9am-3pm Sun Apr-Sep) Each tourist office can provide a free map of the island with town plans of Capri and Anacapri, and a more detailed one for €1. For hotel listings and other useful information, ask for a free copy of *Capri è*. Branches at Capri Town (☑081 837 06 86; www.capritourism. com; Piazza Umberto I; ☺8.30am-8.30pm) and Anacapri. (☑081 837 15 24; Via G Orlando 59; ☺9am-3pm Mon-Sat Apr-Sep).

Capri Island (www.capri.net) Includes listings, itineraries and ferry schedules.

Capri Tourism (www.capritourism.com) Official website of Capri's tourist office.

Farmacia Internazionale (Via Roma 45)

Hospital (☑081 838 12 05; Via Provinciale Anacapri 5)

Police station (☑081 837 42 11; Via Roma 68)

Post office (Via Roma 50; ☺8am-6.30pm Mon-Fri, 8am-12.30pm Sat) Also a branch in Anacapri (Viale de Tommaso 8).

Getting There & Away

See Naples and Sorrento for details of ferries and hydrofoils to the island.

In summer hydrofoils connect with Positano (€17.40 to 19.30, 30 to 40 minutes) and Ischia (€18, one hour).

Note that some companies require you to pay a small supplement for luggage, typically around €2.

Getting Around

BUS

Sippic (☑081 837 04 20; Via Roma, Bus Station, Capri Town; €1.80) runs regular buses between Capri Town and Marina Grande, Anacapri and Marina Piccola. It also operates buses from Marina Grande to Anacapri and from Marina Piccola to Anacapri.

Staiano Autotrasporti (☑081 837 24 22; Via Tommaso, Bus Station, Anacapri; €1.80) buses serve the Grotta Azzurra and Faro of Punta Carena.

SCOOTER

Ciro dei Motorini (☑081 837 80 18; www. capriscooter.com; Via Marina Grande 55, Marina Grande; 3/24 hrs €40/65) For scooter hire at Marina Grande, stop here.

FUNICULAR

Funicular (€1.80; ☺6.30am-12.30am) connects Marina Grande to Capri Town. Like the buses, single tickets cost €1.80.

TAXI

From Marina Grande, a *taxi* (☑in Anacapri 081 837 11 75, in Capri Town 081 837 05 43) costs around €20 to Capri and €25 to Anacapri; from Capri to Anacapri costs about €16.

Ischia

POP 61,100

Sprawling over 46 sq km, Ischia is the biggest and busiest island in the bay. It's a lush concoction of sprawling spa towns, mud-wrapped Germans and ancient booty. Also famous for its thermal waters, it has some fine beaches and spectacular scenery.

Most visitors stay on the touristy north coast, but go inland and you'll find a rural landscape of chestnut forests, dusty farms and earthy hillside towns.

◉ Sights

★**Castello Aragonese** CASTLE
(Castle D'Aragona; ☑ 081 99 28 34; Rocca del Castello, Ischia Ponte; adult/reduced €10/6; ⊘ 9am-90min before sunset) Ischia's imposing castle sits on a rocky islet just off Ischia Ponte. A sprawling complex dating largely to the 1400s, when King Alfonso of Aragon gave an older Angevin fortress a makeover, its attractions include an offbeat torture and armoury museum, local art exhibitions, historic church buildings and a macabre burial chamber. And did we mention the breathtaking coastal panoramas?

★**La Mortella** GARDEN
(☑ 081 98 62 20; www.lamortella.it; Via F Calese 39, Forio; adult/reduced €12/7; ⊘ 9am-7pm Tue, Thu, Sat & Sun Apr-early Nov) Over 1000 rare and exotic plants flourish in this veritable Garden of Eden on Ischia's west coast. Designed by Russell Page and inspired by the Moorish gardens of Granada's Alhambra in Spain, the gardens were established by the late British composer Sir William Walton and his Argentinian wife, Susana, who made La Mortella their home in 1949. Classical-music concerts are staged on the premises; check the website.

🏃 Activities

Beaches BEACH
Unlike Capri, Ischia has some great beaches. From chic Sant'Angelo on the south coast, water taxis reach the sandy **Spiaggia dei Maronti** (one way €5) and the intimate cove of **Il Sorgeto** (one way €7; ⊘ Apr-Oct), with its steamy thermal spring. Sorgeto can also be reached on foot down a poorly signposted path from the village of Panza.

Giardini Poseidon SPA
(Poseidon Gardens; ☑ 081 908 71 11; www.giardini poseidonterme.com; Via Mazzella, Spiaggia di Citara; day pass €32; ⊘ 9am-7pm summer) No, you haven't died and gone to heaven. You're just south of Forio, at this sprawling spa nirvana. Spoil yourself rotten from a wide choice of treatments and facilities, including massages, saunas, jacuzzis and terraced pools spilling down the volcanic cliffside. Waiting at the bottom is your own private beach.

Monte Epomeo WALKING TRAIL
Lace up those hiking boots and set out on a roughly 2.5km, 50-minute uphill walk from the village of Fontana, which will bring you to the top of **Monte Epomeo** (788m). Formed by an underwater eruption, it delivers superlative views of the Bay of Naples.

The little church near the summit is the 15th-century **Cappella di San Nicola di Bari**, which features a pretty maiolica floor.

Ischia Diving DIVING
(☑ 081 98 18 52; www.ischiadiving.net; Via Iasolino 106, Ischia Porto; single dive €60) This well-established diving outfit offers some attractively priced dive packages, like five dives (including equipment) for €225.

🛏 Sleeping

Most hotels close in winter and prices normally drop considerably among those that stay open.

Camping Mirage CAMPGROUND €
(☑ 081 99 05 51; www.campingmirage.it; Via Maronti 37, Spiaggia dei Maronti, Barano d'Ischia; camping 2 people, car & tent €34.50-41.50; P 🐾) On one of Ischia's best beaches within walking distance of Sant'Angelo, this shady camping ground offers 50 places, showers, laundry facilities, a bar and a restaurant serving great seafood pasta.

Albergo Macrì HOTEL €
(☑ 081 99 26 03; Via Iasolino 78a, Ischia Porto; s €45-65, d €84-110; P ❄) Down a blind alley near the main port, this place is run by a smiley lady and has a friendly, low-key vibe. While the pine and bamboo furnishings won't snag any design awards, rooms are clean, bright and comfy. All 1st-floor rooms have terraces and the small downstairs bar serves a mean espresso.

Albergo il Monastero HOTEL €€
(☑ 081 99 24 35; www.albergoilmonastero.it; Castello Aragonese, Rocca del Castello; s €85, d €120-

IL FOCOLARE: A SLOW FOOD WONDER

Tucked away in the hills above Casamicciola Terme is one restaurant verified foodies cannot afford to miss – **Il Focolare** (☑ 081 90 29 44; Via Creajo al Crocefisso, Barano d'Ischia; meals €30; ⏱ 12.30-2.45pm Fri-Sun, 7.30-11.45pm, closed Wed Nov-May).

Forget *spaghetti alle vongole* (spaghetti with clams) – this proud Slow Food stalwart celebrates all things turf. Indeed, it's one of the best spots to savour the island's legendary *coniglio all'Ischitana* (a claypot-cooked local rabbit with garlic, onion, tomatoes, wild thyme and white wine), a dish that needs to be booked two days in advance.

If you haven't pre-ordered the rabbit, don't fret – the daily menu brims with beautiful, seasonal dishes, from *tagliatelle al ragù di cinghiale* (ribbon-shaped pasta with wild boar ragout) to a sublime *antipasto misto*, where you might get anything from *rotolino di zucchini* (fried, bread-crumbed zucchini filled with buffalo mozzarella) to *terrina di parmigiano tartufata con i funghi* (think porcini-mushroom crème brûlée).

To get here, catch bus 16 from Piazza Marina in Casamicciola Terme and ask the driver to let you off at the restaurant (it's the last stop). During the summer high season, the last bus back to town departs at around 12.50am.

170; ⏱ Easter-Oct; ✤) The former monks' cells retain a certain appealing sobriety, with dark-wood furniture, vintage terracotta tiles and no TV (the views are sufficiently prime time). Elsewhere there's a sense of space and style, with vaulted ceilings, plush sofas, a sprinkle of antiques and bold contemporary art by the late owner and artist Gabriele Mattera. The hotel restaurant has an excellent reputation.

Hotel Semiramis　　　　　HOTEL €€
(☑ 081 90 75 11; www.hotelsemiramisischia.it; Spiaggia di Citara, Forio; d €118-156; ⏱ late Apr-Oct; P ✤ � 🛜 ⩼) A few minutes' walk from the Poseidon spa complex, this bright hotel, run by friendly Giovanni and his German wife, channels the tropics with its central pool surrounded by lofty palms. Rooms are large and beautifully tiled in traditional yellow-and-turquoise style. The garden is a lush, glorious oasis of fig trees, vineyards and distant sea views.

✖ Eating

Seafood aside, Ischia is famed for its rabbit, which is bred on inland farms. Another local speciality is *rucolino* – a green liquoriceflavoured liqueur made from *rucola* (rocket) leaves.

Montecorvo　　　　　ITALIAN €€
(☑ 081 99 80 29; www.montecorvo.it; Via Montecorvo 33, Forio; meals €30; ⏱ 12.30-3.30pm & 7.30pm-1am) While the cave-set dining room and junglelike terrace are memorable enough, it's owner Giovanni's imaginative home cooking that steals the show. The antipasti see some inspired pairings, whether it's prawns with orange, or oven-baked sardines with mozzarella. Perfect pasta dishes include a zesty *linguine al limone* (linguine with lemon), while the grilled meats are sublimely succulent.

★Cantine di Pietratorcia　　　CAMPANIAN €€
(☑ 081 90 82 06; www.pietratorcia.it; Via Provinciale Panza 267, Forio; meals €30; ⏱ lunch & dinner Mon-Thu, till late Fri-Sun) Set among tumbling vines and rosemary bushes, this family-run winery is a foodie's nirvana. Tour the 18th-century stone cellars, sip a local drop and graze on rare cheese, including offerings from the Cilento's revered father-and-son team Antonio and Angelo Madaio.

The owners breed their own rabbits in traditional *fosse* (pits), and serve up an extraordinary *coniglio all'ischitana* (Ischia-style rabbit with local herbs) if requested in advance. Lunch bookings are obligatory, and it's advisable to book their degustation dinners too. The winery is closed for lunch from mid-June to mid-September, and closed entirely from mid-November to the end of March.

Ristorante da Ciccio　　　CAMPANIAN €€
(☑ 081 99 16 86; Via Luigi Mazzella 32, Ischia Ponte; meals €25; ⏱ noon-3.30pm & 7.30-11.30pm, closed Tue Dec-Feb) Solid seafood and charming host Carlo make this atmospheric place a winner. Highlights include *tubattone* pasta with mussels and *pecorino* cheese, a zesty mussel soup topped with fried bread and *peperoncino* (chilli), and a delicious chocolate and almond cake. Tables spill out onto the pavement in the summer, from where there's a gorgeous castle view.

ℹ Information

Ischia online (www.ischiaonline.it) Good all-round website including sights, restaurants and hotels.

Tourist office (www.infoischiaprocida.it; Via Sogliuzzo 72; ⊙9am-2pm & 3-8pm Mon-Sat, plus 9am-1pm Sun Jul-Sep)

ℹ Getting There & Away

Regular hydrofoils and ferries run to/from Naples. You can also catch hydrofoils direct to Capri (€18) and Procida (€8.20).

ℹ Getting Around

The island's main bus station is in Ischia Porto. There are two principal lines: the Circo Sinistra CS; Left Circle), which circles the island anticlockwise, and the (Circo Destra CD; Right Circle), which travels clockwise. These buses pass through each town and depart every 30 minutes. Buses pass near all hotels and campsites. A single ticket, valid for 90 minutes, costs €1.90; a daily, multiuse ticket is €6; and a two-day ticket is €10. Taxis and microtaxis (scooter-engined three-wheelers) are also available.

Help the island avoid congestion and pollution by not bringing your car. If you want to hire one (or a scooter), there are plenty of rental firms, including **Fratelli del Franco** (☑ 081 99 13 34; www.noleggiodelfranco.it; Via A de Luca 127), which hires out cars (from €30 per day), scooters (around €30) and mountain bikes (around €10 per day). You can't take a rented vehicle off the island.

Procida

POP 10,200

Dig out your paintbox: the Bay of Naples' smallest island (and its best-kept secret) is a soulful blend of hidden lemon groves, weathered fishing folk and pastel-hued houses. August aside – when beach-bound mainlanders flock to its shores – its narrow sun-bleached streets are the domain of the locals.

◉ Sights & Activities

The best way to explore the island – a mere 4 sq km – is on foot or by bike. However, the island's narrow roads can be clogged with cars – one of its few drawbacks.

From panoramic Piazza dei Martiri, the village of Corricella tumbles down to its marina in a riot of pinks, yellows and whites. Further south, a steep flight of steps leads down to Chiaia beach, one of the island's most beautiful.

All pink, white and blue, little Marina di Chiaiolella has a yacht-stocked marina, old-school eateries and a languid disposition. Nearby, the Lido is a popular beach.

Abbazia di San Michele Arcangelo CHURCH, MUSEUM
(☑ 334 8514028, 334 8514252; associazionemillennium@virgilio.it; Via Terra Murata 89, Terra Murata; donation appreciated; ⊙9.45am-12.45pm & 3.30-6pm) This former Benedictine abbey was built in the 11th century and remodelled between the 17th and 19th centuries. While the main church is open to all, it's worth joining one of the regular guided tours to gain access to the pretty barrel-vaulted library and Secret Chapel.

The latter is home to some curious 18th-century coffins, one complete with arm holes for convenient kissing of the deceased's hands. English-language tours should be requested a couple of days in advance.

Procida Diving Centre DIVING
(☑ 081 896 83 85; www.vacanzeaprocida.it; Via Cristoforo Colombo 6, Marina di Chiaiolella; ⊙Jun-Sep; 🅿) Conveniently located right on the marina, this outfit runs diving courses and hires out equipment. Prices range from €45 for a single dive to €130 for a snorkelling course, with more advanced open-water diving and rescue courses also on offer.

Blue Dream Yacht Charter Boating BOATING
(☑ 339 5720874, 081 896 05 79; www.bluedream-charter.com; Via Vittorio Emanuele 14, Marina Grande) If you have grand 'champagne on the deck' aspirations, you can always charter a yacht from here (from €1500 per week). Sleeps six.

🎉 Festivals & Events

Procession of the Misteri RELIGIOUS
Procida's famous Good Friday procession sees a wooden statue of Christ and the Madonna Addolorata, along with life-sized tableaux of plaster and papier-mâché illustrating events leading to Christ's crucifixion, carted across the island.

🛏 Sleeping

★**Hotel La Vigna** BOUTIQUE HOTEL €€
(☑ 081 896 04 69; www.albergolavigna.it; Via Principessa Margherita 46; s €75-150, d €90-180, ste €140-230; ❄◉◌) Enjoying a cliffside lo-

cation 1km east of the main port, this 18th-century villa is a delight. Five of the spacious, simply furnished rooms offer direct access to the hotel's soothing garden. Superior rooms (€110 to €200) feature family-friendly mezzanines, while the main perk of the suite is the bedside jacuzzi; perfect for romancing couples.

Casa Sul Mare HOTEL €€
(✆081 896 87 99; www.lacasasulmare.it; Salita Castello 13; r €99-170; ✴🏠) Overlooking the obscenely picturesque Marina Corricella, friendly Casa Sul Mare offers rooms with exquisite tiled floors and wrought-iron bedsteads. During summer there's a boat service to the nearest beaches.

Casa Giovanni da Procida B&B €€
(✆081 896 03 58; www.casagiovannidaprocida. it; Via Giovanni da Procida 3; d €80-130, €100-145; P✴🏠) This chic converted farmhouse B&B features split-level minimalist rooms with low-rise beds and contemporary furniture. Bathrooms are small but slick, with huge showerheads and the occasional vaulted ceiling.

Eating

La Conchiglia SEAFOOD €€
(✆081 896 76 02; www.laconchigliaristorante.com; Via Pizzaco 10, Solchiaro; meals €25; ☉1-3.30pm & 8-9.30pm summer) With lapping turquoise water below and pastel Marina Corricella glowing in the distance, this beachside gem is a top spot to savour a superb *spaghetti alla povera* (spaghetti with *peperoncino*, green capsicum, cherry tomatoes and anchovies). To get here, take the steep steps down from Via Pizzaco or call the restaurant and book a boat from Corricella.

Caracalè SEAFOOD €€
(✆081 896 91 92; Via Marina Corricella 6, Marina Corricella; meals €28; ☉12.30-3.30pm & 7-11pm, closed Tue Mar-Jun & Sep–mid-Nov) Slap bang on Marina Corricella's cinematic waterfront, Caracalè peddles superb seafood dishes like spaghetti with calamari and artichokes, and succulent grilled swordfish. Menus change twice daily, depending on the morning and afternoon catch.

ⓘ Information

Procida Holidays (✆081 896 95 94; www. isoladiprocida.it; Via Roma 117; ☉9am-1pm & 4-8pm Mon-Sat Apr-Oct, closed Sat afternoon Nov-Mar) Can organise accommodation (single/

double from €90/120) and also has a free map of the island.

ⓘ Getting There & Around

Procida is linked by boat and hydrofoil to Ischia (€8.20), Pozzuoli (€8.20) and Naples.

There is a limited bus service (€1), with four lines radiating out from Marina Grande. Bus L1 connects the port and Marina di Chiaiolella.

Contact **Sprint** (✆339 8659600, 081 896 94 35; www.sprintprocida.com; Via Roma 28; scooters per day €25-30; ☉8am-1pm & 4-8pm Mon-Sat, 10am-1pm Sun) for scooter and electric-bike hire.

Taxis can be hired for two to three hours for about €35, depending on your bargaining prowess.

SOUTH OF NAPLES

Ercolano & Herculaneum

Ercolano is an uninspiring Neapolitan suburb that's home to one of Italy's best-preserved ancient sites – Herculaneum. A superbly conserved Roman fishing town, Herculaneum is smaller and less daunting than Pompeii, allowing you to visit without that nagging itch that you're bound to miss something.

History

In contrast to modern Ercolano, classical Herculaneum was a peaceful fishing and port town of about 4000 inhabitants, and something of a resort for wealthy Romans and Campanians.

Herculaneum's fate paralleled that of nearby Pompeii. Destroyed by an earthquake in AD 63, it was completely submerged in the AD 79 eruption of Mt Vesuvius. However, as it was much closer to the volcano than Pompeii, it drowned in a 16m-thick sea of mud rather than in the lapilli (burning pumice stone) and ash that rained down on Pompeii. This essentially fossilised the town, ensuring that even delicate items, like furniture and clothing, were remarkably well preserved when uncovered.

The town was rediscovered in 1709, and amateur excavations were carried out intermittently until 1874, with many finds being carted off to Naples to decorate the houses of its well-to-do inhabitants or to end up in museums. Serious archaeological work began again in 1927 and continues to this day, although with much of the ancient site buried beneath modern Ercolano, it's slow going.

◉ Sights

★ Ruins of Herculaneum

RUIN

(☏ 081 732 43 38; www.pompeiisites.org; Corso Resina 6, Ercolano; adult/reduced €11/5.50, combined ticket incl Pompeii €20/10; ☻ 8.30am-7.30pm summer, to 5pm winter, last entry 90min before closing; ⊠ Circumvesuviana to Ercolano-Scavi) Unfairly upstaged by Pompeii's ancient offerings, the Ruins of Herculaneum have a wealth of archaeological finds. Indeed, this superbly conserved Roman fishing town of 4000 inhabitants is smaller and easier to navigate than Pompeii, and can be explored with a map and audio guide (€6.50, €10 for two). Archaeological work began again in 1927 and continues to this day.

From the site's main gateway on Corso Resina, head down the wide boulevard, where you'll find the ticket office on the left. Pick up a free map and guide booklet here, then follow the boulevard right to the actual entrance into the ruins themselves.

With Vesuvius erupting above them, thousands of people tried to escape by boat but were suffocated by the volcano's poisonous gases. Indeed, what appears to be a moat around the town is in fact the ancient shoreline. It was here in 1980 that archaeologists discovered some 300 skeletons, the remains of a crowd that had fled to the beach only to be overcome by the terrible heat of clouds surging down from Vesuvius.

CASA D'ARGO & CASA DELLO SCHELETRO

As you begin your exploration northeast along Cardo III you'll stumble across Casa d'Argo (Argus House). This noble pad would originally have opened onto Cardo II (as yet unearthed). Onto its porticoed, palm-treed garden open a *triclinium* (dining room) and other residential rooms. Across the street sits the Casa dello Scheletro (House of the Skeleton), a modestly sized house boasting five styles of mosaic flooring, including a design of white arrows at the entrance to guide the most disorientated of guests. In the internal courtyard, don't miss the skylight, complete with the remnants of an ancient security grill. Of the house's mythically themed wall mosaics, only the faded ones are originals; the others now reside in the Museo Archeologico Nazionale (p643).

TERME MASCHILI

Just across the Decumano Inferiore (one of ancient Herculaneum's main streets), the Terme Maschili (Male Baths) were the men's section of the Terme del Foro (Forum Baths). Note the ancient latrine to the left of the entrance before you step into the *apodyterium* (changing room), complete with bench for waiting patrons and a nifty wall shelf for sandal and toga storage. While those after a bracing soak would pop into the *frigidarium* (cold bath) to the left, the less stoic headed straight into the *tepadarium* (tepid bath) to the right. The sunken mosaic floor here is testament to the seismic activity preceding Mt Vesuvius' catastrophic eruption. Beyond this room lies the *caldarium* (hot bath), as well as an exercise area.

DECUMANO MASSIMO

At the end of Cardo III, turn right into the Decumano Massimo. This ancient high street is lined with shops; fragments of advertisements still adorn the walls, such as that to the right of the Casa del Salone Nero. This ancient consumer information listed everything from from the weight of goods to their price.

Further east along Decumano Massimo, a crucifix found in an upstairs room of the Casa del Bicentenario (Bicentenary House) provides possible evidence of a Christian presence in pre-Vesuvius Herculaneum.

CASA DI NETTUNO E ANFITRITE

Turning into Cardo IV from Decumano Massimo, you'll soon hit the Casa di Nettuno e Anfitrite (House of Neptune and Amfitrite), an aristocratic pad taking its name from the extraordinary mosaic in the *nymphaeum* (fountain and bath). The warm colours in which the sea god and his nymph bride are depicted hint at how lavish the original interior must once have been.

A quick walk further southwest along Cardo IV leads you to the women's section of the Terme del Foro, the Terme Femminili. Though smaller than its male equivalent, it boasts finer floor mosaics – note the beautifully executed naked figure of Triton in the *apodyterium* (changing room).

CASA DEL TRAMEZZO DI LEGNO

Across the Decumano Inferiore is the Casa del Tramezzo di Legno (House of the Wooden Partition), which unusually features two atria. It's likely that the atria belonged to two separate houses merged together in the 1st century AD. Predictably, the most famous relic here is a wonderfully well-preserved wooden screen, separating the atrium from the *tablinum*, where the owner talked business with his clients. The second room off the left side of the atrium features the remains of an ancient bed.

CASA DELL'ATRIO A MOSAICO

Further southwest on Cardo IV, ancient mansion Casa dell'Atrio a Mosaico (House of the Mosaic Atrium) harbours extensive floor mosaics, although time and nature have left the floor buckled and uneven. Particularly noteworthy is the black-and-white chessboard mosaic in the atrium.

Backtrack up Cardo IV and turn right at Decumano Inferiore. Here you'll find the Casa del Gran Portale (House of the Large Portal), named after the elegant brick Corinthian columns that flank its main entrance. Step inside to admire some well-preserved wall paintings.

CASA DEI CERVI

Accessible from Cardo V, the Casa dei Cervi (House of the Stags) is an imposing example of a Roman noble family's house which, before the volcanic mudslide, boasted a seafront address. Constructed around a central courtyard, the two-storey villa contains murals and some beautiful still-life paintings. Waiting for you in the courtyard is a diminutive pair of marble deer assailed by dogs, and an engaging statue of a drunken, peeing Hercules.

TERME SUBURBANE

Marking the site's southernmost tip is the 1st-century-AD Terme Suburbane (Suburban Baths), one of the best-preserved bath complexes in existence, with deep pools, stucco friezes and bas-reliefs looking down upon marble seats and floors. This is also one of the best places to observe the soaring volcanic deposits that literally smothered the ancient coastline.

MAV   MUSEUM
(Museo Archeologico Virtuale; ☑ 081 1980 6511; www.museomav.com; Via IV Novembre 44; adult/reduced €7.50/6, optional 3D documentary €4; ⊙ 9am-4.30pm Tue-Fri, to 5.30pm Sat & Sun; ⊠ Circumvesuviana to Ercolano-Scavi) Using high-tech holograms and computer-generated footage, this 'virtual archaeological museum' brings ruins like Pompeii's forum and Capri's Villa Jovis back to virtual life. Especially fun for kids, it's on the main street linking Ercolano-Scavi train station to the Ruins of Herculaneum.

✗ Eating

★ Viva Lo Re   CAMPANIAN €€
(☑ 081 739 02 07; www.vivalore.it; Corso Resina 261, Ercolano; meals €27; ⊙ noon-4pm & 8.30-late Tue-Sat, lunch Sun; ⊠ Circumvesuviana to Ercolano-Scavi) Stylish Viva Lo Re (Long Live the King) mixes vintage prints and bookshelves with superb wines, gracious service and some of Campania's finest revamped dishes. Start with the artful antipasto – 'tastings' might include *polpettina di baccalà* (salted cod patty) or *crocchetta di taleggio con porcino* (Taleggio and porcini croquette). End with the *tris*, a decadent trio of desserts.

❶ Information

Tourist office (☑ 081 788 12 74; Via IV Novembre 82; ⊙ 8am-6pm Mon-Sat) You'll pass this office on your right as you walk from the train station to the excavations.

❶ Getting There & Away

The best way to get to Ercolano is by Circumvesuviana train (get off at Ercolano-Scavi station and walk 500m downhill to the ruins – follow the signs for the *scavi* down the main street, Via IV Novembre. Trains run regularly to/from Naples (€2.20), Pompeii (€1.60) and Sorrento (€2.20).

By car take the A3 from Naples, exit at Ercolano Portico and follow the signs to car parks near the site's entrance.

Mt Vesuvius

Towering (at 1281m) darkly over Naples and its environs, Mt Vesuvius (Vesuvio, 1281m), is the only active volcano on the European mainland. Since it exploded into history in AD 79, burying Pompeii and Herculaneum and pushing the coastline out several kilometres, it has erupted more than 30 times. The most devastating of these was in 1631, the most recent in 1944.

Another full-scale eruption would be catastrophic. Some 600,000 people live within 7km of the crater and, despite incentives to relocate, few are willing to go.

Established in 1995, **Parco Nazionale del Vesuvio** (☑ 081 239 5653; adult/reduced €10/8; ⊙ 9am-7pm Jul & Aug, to 5pm Apr-Jun & Sep, to 4pm Mar & Oct, to 3pm Nov-Feb, ticket office closes 1hr before the crater) attracts some 400,000 visitors annually. From a car park at the summit, an 860m path leads up to the volcano's **crater** (admission incl tour €8; ⊙ 9am-6pm Jul & Aug, to 5pm Apr-Jun & Sep, to 4pm Mar & Oct, to 3pm Nov-Feb). It's not a strenuous walk, but it's more comfortable in trainers than in sandals or flip-flops.

You'd also do well to take sunglasses – useful against swirling ash – and a sweater, as it can be chilly up top, even in summer.

Shuttle-bus operator **Vesuvio Express** (☑081 739 36 66; www.vesuvioexpress.it; Piazzale Stazione Circumvesuviana, Ercolano) runs services from Ercolano to Mt Vesuvius, departing from Piazza Stazione Circumvesuviana, right outside Ercolano-Scavi train station. Buses depart every 40 minutes from 9.30am to 4pm daily, with a journey time of 20 minutes each way. Return tickets (which include entry to the volcano summit) are €18.

From Pompeii, **Busvia del Vesuvio** (☑340 9352616; www.busviadelvesuvio.com; Via Villa dei Misteri, Pompeii) runs a shuttle service from outside Pompeii-Villa dei Misteri train station (hourly from 9am to 3pm) to its bus terminal in nearby Boscoreale. From here, it's a 25-minute journey up the national park on a 4WD-style bus. Return tickets (including entry to the volcano summit) cost €22.

If you're keen to explore the national park **Naples Trips & Tours** (☑349 7155270; www.naplestripsandtours.com) runs a daily horse-riding tour of the park (weather permitting) for €50 and running between three to four hours. It includes transfers to/from Naples or Ercolano-Scavi train station.

If travelling by car, exit the A3 at Ercolano Portico and follow signs for the Parco Nazionale del Vesuvio. Note that when weather conditions are bad the summit path is shut and bus departures are suspended.

Pompeii

POP 25,500

A stark reminder of the malign forces that lie deep inside Vesuvius, Pompeii (Pompei in Italian) is Europe's most compelling archaeological site. Each year about 2.5 million people pour in to wander the ghostly shell of what was once a thriving commercial centre.

Its appeal goes beyond tourism, though. From an archaeological point of view, it's priceless. Much of the value lies in the fact that it wasn't simply blown away by Vesuvius: rather it was buried under a layer of lapilli, as Pliny the Younger describes in his celebrated account of the eruption. The result is a remarkably well-preserved slice of ancient life, where visitors can walk down Roman streets and snoop around millennia-old abodes and businesses (including a brothel).

History

The eruption of Vesuvius wasn't the first disaster to strike the Roman port of Pompeii. In AD 63 a massive earthquake hit the city, causing widespread damage and the evacuation of much of the 20,000-strong population. Many had not returned when Vesuvius blew its top on 24 August AD 79, burying the city under a layer of lapilli and killing some 2000 men, women and children.

The origins of Pompeii are uncertain, but it seems likely that it was founded in the 7th century BC by the Campanian Oscans. Over the next seven centuries the city fell to the ancient Greeks and the Samnites before becoming a Roman colony in 80 BC. After its tragic demise, Pompeii receded from the public eye until 1594, when the architect Domenico Fontana stumbled across the ruins while digging a canal. However, short of recording the find, he took no further action. Exploration proper began in 1748 under the Bourbon king Charles VII and continued into the 19th century. In the early days many of the more spectacular mosaics were siphoned off to decorate Charles' palace in Portici; thankfully, though, most were subsequently moved up to Naples, where they now sit in the Museo Archeologico Nazionale (p643).

◎ Sights

★**Ruins of Pompeii**   RUIN
(☑081 857 53 47; www.pompeiisites.org; entrances at Porta Marina & Piazza Anfiteatro; adult/reduced €11/5.50, combined ticket incl Herculaneum €20/10; ☉8.30am-7.30pm summer, to 5pm winter, last entry 90min before closing) Of Pompeii's original 66 hectares, 44 have now been excavated. Of course that doesn't mean you'll have unhindered access to every inch of the Unesco-listed site – expect to come across areas cordoned off for no apparent reason, a noticeable lack of clear signs and the odd stray dog. Audio guides are a sensible investment.

At the time of writing, the Casa dei Vettii was closed for restoration. The Terme Suburbane, just outside the city walls, can be visited on weekends subject to prior booking at www.arethusa.net. It's here that you'll find the erotic frescoes that scandalised the Vatican when they were revealed in 2001. The saucy panels decorate the changing rooms of what was once a private baths complex.

Old Pompeii

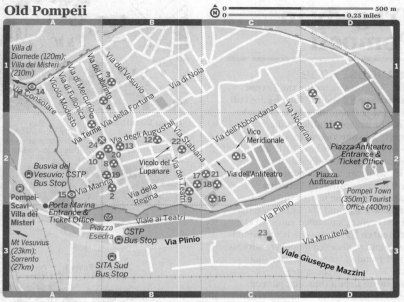

Old Pompeii

PORTA MARINA

The site's main entrance is at **Porta Marina**, the most impressive of the seven gates that punctuated the ancient town walls. A busy passageway now as it was then, it originally connected the town with the nearby harbour, hence the gateway's name. Immediately on the right as you enter the gate is the 1st-century-BC Tempio di Venere (Temple of Venus), formerly one of the town's most opulent temples.

THE FORUM

Continuing northeast along Via Marina you'll hit the grassy **foro** (forum). Flanked by limestone columns, this was the ancient city's main piazza and the buildings surrounding it are testament to its role as the city's hub of civic, commercial, political and religious activity.

At its southwestern end sit the remains of the **basilica**, the 2nd-century-BC seat of the city's law courts and exchange. Their semicircular apses would later influence the design of early Christian churches. Opposite the ba-

Tragedy in Pompeii

24 AUGUST AD 79

8am Buildings including the **Terme Suburbane** 1 and the **foro** 2 are still undergoing repair after an earthquake in AD 63 caused significant damage to the city. Despite violent earth tremors overnight, residents have little idea of the catastrophe that lies ahead.

Midday Peckish locals pour into the **Thermopolium di Vetutius Placidus** 3 . The lustful slip into the **Lupanare** 4 , and gladiators practise for the evening's planned games at the **anfiteatro** 5 . A massive boom heralds the eruption. Shocked onlookers witness a dark cloud of volcanic matter shoot some 14km above the crater.

3pm–5pm Lapilli (burning pumice stone) rains down on Pompeii. Terrified locals begin to flee; others take shelter. Within two hours, the plume is 25km high and the sky has darkened. Roofs collapse under the weight of the debris, burying those inside.

25 AUGUST AD 79

Midnight Mudflows bury the town of Herculaneum. Lapilli and ash continue to rain down on Pompeii, bursting through buildings and suffocating those taking refuge within.

4am–8am Ash and gas avalanches hit Herculaneum. Subsequent surges smother Pompeii, killing all remaining residents, including those in the **Orto dei Fuggiaschi** 6 . The volcanic 'blanket' will safeguard frescoed treasures like the **Casa del Menandro** 7 and **Villa dei Misteri** 8 for almost two millennia.

Terme Suburbane
The *laconicum* (sauna), *caldarium* (hot bath) and large, heated swimming pool weren't the only sources of heat here; scan the walls of this suburban bathhouse for some of the city's raunchiest frescoes.

Villa di Diomede

Casa dei Vettii

Casa del Poeta Tragico

Porta Ercolano

Casa del Fauno

Basilica

Tempio di Apollo

Porta Marina

Terme del Foro

Macellum

Teatro Grande

Quadriportico dei Teatri

Porta di Stabia

Teatro Piccolo

Foro
An ancient Times Square of sorts, the forum sits at the intersection of Pompeii's main streets and was closed to traffic in the 1st century AD. The plinths on the southern edge featured statues of the imperial family.

TOP TIPS

» Visit in the afternoon
» Allow three hours
» Wear comfortable shoes and a hat
» Bring drinking water
» Don't use flash photography

Villa dei Misteri

Home to the world-famous *Dionysiac Frieze* fresco. Other highlights at this villa include *trompe l'oeil* wall decorations in the *cubiculum* (bedroom) and Egyptian-themed artwork in the *tablinum* (reception).

Lupanare

The prostitutes at this brothel were often slaves of Greek or Asian origin. Mattresses once covered the stone beds and the names engraved in the walls are possibly those of the workers and their clients.

Thermopolium di Vetutius Placidus

The counter at this ancient snack bar once held urns filled with hot food. The *lararium* (household shrine) on the back wall depicts Dionysus (the god of wine) and Mercury (the god of profit and commerce).

Eyewitness Account

Pliny the Younger (AD 61–c 112) gives a gripping, first-hand account of the catastrophe in his letters to Tacitus (AD 56–117).

Porta del Vesuvio

Porta di Nola

Casa della Venere in Conchiglia

Porta di Sarno

3

7

6

Grande Palestra

5

Tempio di Iside

Casa del Menandro

This dwelling most likely belonged to the family of Poppaea Sabina, Nero's second wife. A room to the left of the atrium features Trojan War paintings and a polychrome mosaic of pygmies rowing down the Nile.

Orto dei Fuggiaschi

The Garden of the Fugitives showcases the plaster moulds of 13 locals seeking refuge during Vesuvius' eruption – the largest number of victims found in any one area. The huddled bodies make for a moving scene.

Anfiteatro

Magistrates, local senators and the games' sponsors and organisers enjoyed front-row seating at this veteran amphitheatre, home to gladiatorial battles and the odd riot. The parapet circling the stadium featured paintings of combat, victory celebrations and hunting scenes.

silica, the **Tempio di Apollo** (Temple of Apollo) is the oldest and most important of Pompeii's religious buildings. Most of what you see today, including the striking columned portico, dates to the 2nd century BC, although fragments remain of an earlier version dating to the 6th century BC.

At the forum's northern end is the **Tempio di Giove** (Temple of Jupiter), which has one of two flanking triumphal arches remaining, and the **Granai del Foro** (Forum Granary), now used to store hundreds of amphorae and a number of body casts that were made in the late 19th century by pouring plaster into the hollows left by disintegrated bodies. The **macellum** nearby was once the city's main meat and fish market.

LUPANARE

From the market head northeast along Via degli Augustali to Vicolo del Lupanare. Halfway down this narrow alley is the **Lupanare**, the city's only dedicated brothel. A tiny two-storey building with five rooms on each floor, its collection of raunchy frescoes was a menu of sorts for its randy clientele.

TEATRO GRANDE

Heading back south, Vicolo del Lupanare becomes Via dei Teatri. At the end you'll find the verdant **Foro Triangolare**, which would originally have overlooked the sea and the River Sarno. The main attraction here was, and still is, the 2nd-century-BC Teatro Grande, a 5000-seat theatre carved into the lava mass on which Pompeii was originally built. Behind the stage, the porticoed **Quadriportico dei Teatri** was initially used for the audience to stroll between acts, and later as a barracks for gladiators. Next door, the **Teatro Piccolo** (also known as the Odeion) was once an indoor theatre renowned for its acoustics, while the pre-Roman **Tempio di Iside** (Temple of Isis) was a popular place of cult worship.

CASA DEL MENANDRO

Just to the east, Via dell'Anfiteatro (which becomes Vico Meridionale) is where you'll find Casa del Menandro. One of Pompeii's grander homes, its drawcards include an elegant peristyle (colonnaded garden) and a striking mosaic floor in the *caldarium*.

TERME STABIANE & CASA DELLA VENERE IN CONCHIGLIA

As it shoots eastward, Via Marina becomes Via dell'Abbondanza (Street of Abundance). Lined with ancient shops, this was the city's main thoroughfare and where you'll find the **Terme Stabiane**, a typical 2nd-century-BC bath complex. Entering from the vestibule, bathers would stop off in the vaulted *apodyterium* before passing through to the *tepidarium* and *caldarium*. Particularly impressive is the stuccoed vault in the men's changing room, complete with whimsical images of *putti* (winged babies) and nymphs.

Towards the northeastern end of Via dell'Abbondanza, **Casa della Venere in Conchiglia** (House of the Venus Marina) has recovered well from the WWII bomb that damaged it in 1943. Although unexceptional from the outside, it houses a gorgeous peristyle that looks onto a small, manicured garden. And it's here in the garden that you'll find the striking Venus fresco after which the house is named.

ANFITEATRO

Just southeast of the Casa della Venere in Conchiglia, gladiatorial battles thrilled up to 20,000 spectators at the grassy **anfiteatro**

ⓘ TOURS

You'll almost certainly be approached by a guide outside the *scavi* (excavations) ticket office. Authorised guides wear identification tags and you can expect to pay between €100 and €120 for a two-hour tour, whether you're alone or in a group. Reputable tour operators include **Yellow Sudmarine** (☑ 329 1010328, 334 1047036; www.yellowsudmarine.com) and **Torres Travel** (☑ 081 856 78 02; www.torrestravel.it), both of which offer tours of the ruins, as well as excursions to other regional highlights, including Naples, Capri and the Amalfi Coast.

Yellow Sudmarine also runs cheaper walking tours of Pompeii. Costing €12 per person (excluding entry to the ruins), these two-hour guided walks depart at 11am every Saturday to Thursday (at 3pm on Fridays) from outside the Pompei Scavi-Villa dei Misteri Circumvesuviana train station. Tours should be booked a day ahead, either by email or phone.

(amphitheatre). Built in 70 BC, it's the oldest known Roman amphitheatre in existence. Over the way, lithe ancients kept fit at the Grande Palestra, an athletics field with an impressive portico dating to the Augustan period. At its centre lie the remains of a swimming pool.

CASA DEL FAUNO

From the Grande Palestra, backtrack along Via dell'Abbondanza and turn right into Via Stabiana to view some of Pompeii's grandest houses. Turn left into Via della Fortuna and then right down Via del Labirinto to get to Vicolo del Mercurio and the entrance to Casa del Fauno (House of the Faun; Via Stabiana), Pompeii's largest private house. Covering an entire *insula* (city block) and boasting two atria at its front end (humbler homes had one), it is named after the delicate bronze statue in the *impluvium* (rainwater pool). It was here that early excavators found Pompeii's greatest mosaics, most of which are now in Naples' Museo Archeologico Nazionale (p643). Valuable on-site remainders include a beautiful, geometrically patterned marble floor.

A couple of blocks away, the Casa del Poeta Tragico (House of the Tragic Poet) features one of the world's first 'Beware of the Dog' (*Cave Canem*) warnings. To the north, the currently closed Casa dei Vettii on Via di Mercurio is home to a famous depiction of Priapus whose oversized phallus balances on a pair of scales...much to the anxiety of many a male observer.

VILLA DEI MISTERI

From the Casa del Fauna, follow the road west and turn right into Via Consolare, which takes you out of the town through Porta Ercolano. Continue past Villa di Diomede and you'll come to the 90-room Villa dei Misteri, one of the most complete structures left standing in Pompeii. The Dionysiac frieze, the most important fresco still on site, spans the walls of the large dining room. One of the largest paintings from the ancient world, it depicts the initiation of a bride-to-be into the cult of Dionysus, the Greek god of wine. A farm for much of its life, the villa's own vino-making area is still visible at the northern end.

🛏 Sleeping & Eating

There's really no need to stay overnight in Pompeii. The ruins are best visited on a day trip from Naples, Sorrento or Salerno, and once the excavations close for the day, the area around the site becomes decidedly seedy. Most of the restaurants near the ruins are characterless affairs set up for feeding busloads of tourists. Wander down to the modern town and it's a little better, with a few decent restaurants serving excellent local food.

If you'd rather eat at the ruins, the on-site cafeteria (Via di Mercurio) peddles the standard choice of *panini*, pizza slices, salads, hot meals and gelato. You'll find it near the Tempio di Giove.

★ President   CAMPANIAN €€
(☑ 081 850 72 45; www.ristorantepresident.it; Piazza Schettini 12; meals €35; ⊙ 11.40am-3.30pm & 7pm-midnight Tue-Sun, closed Jan; ⓡ FS to Pompei, ⓡ Circumvesuviana to Pompei Scavi-Villa dei Misteri) With its dripping chandeliers and gracious service, the President feels like a private dining room in an Audrey Hepburn film. Conducting the charm is owner Paolo Gramaglia, whose passion for local produce sparkles in creations like aubergine *millefoglie* (flaky puff pastry) with Cetara anchovies, mozzarella *filante* (melted mozzarella) and grated *tarallo* (savoury almond biscuit). Treat yourself with a degustation menu (€30 to €50).

ℹ Information

Police station (☑ 081 856 35 11; Piazza Porta Marina Inferiore)

Pompeii sites (www.pompeiisites.org) Background and practicalities for Pompeii, Herculaneum and other archaeological must-sees.

Post office (Piazza Esedra)

Tourist office (☑ 081 850 72 55; www.pompeiturismo.it; Via Sacra 1; ⊙ 8am-3.30pm Mon-Fri, to 1pm Sat)

ℹ Getting There & Away

Circumvesuviana trains run from Pompei Scavi-Villa dei Misteri station to Naples (€2.90, 35 minutes) and Sorrento (€2.20, 30 minutes).

CSTP (☑ 800 016659; www.cstp.it) bus 4 runs to/from Salerno (€2.20, 90 minutes).

Shuttle buses to Vesuvius depart from outside the Pompei-Scavi-Villa dei Misteri train station.

To get here by car, take the A3 from Naples. Use the Pompeii exit and follow signs to Pompeii Scavi. Car parks (approximately €5 per hour) are clearly marked and vigorously touted.

Sorrento

POP 16,500

On paper, cliff-straddling Sorrento is a place to avoid – a package-holiday centre with few must-see sights, no beach to speak of and a glut of brassy English-style pubs. In reality, it's a strangely appealing place, its laid-back southern Italian charm resisting all attempts to swamp it in graceless development.

Dating to Greek times and known to Romans as Surrentum, it's ideally situated for exploring the surrounding area: to the west, the best of the peninsula's unspoiled countryside and, beyond that, the Amalfi Coast; to the north, Pompeii and the archaeological sites; offshore, the fabled island of Capri.

According to Greek legend, it was in Sorrento's waters that the mythical sirens once lived. Sailors of antiquity were powerless to resist the beautiful song of these charming maidens-cum-monsters, who would lure them and their ships to their doom. Homer's Ulysses escaped by having his oarsmen plug their ears with wax and by strapping himself to his ship's mast as he sailed past.

Sights

Spearing off from Piazza Tasso, Corso Italia (closed to traffic from 7pm to 1am daily during the summer, as well as from 10am to 1pm on Sundays and public holidays) cuts through the *centro storico*, whose narrow streets throng with tourists on summer evenings. An attractive area, it's thick with loud souvenir stores, cafes, churches and restaurants.

Chiesa di San Francesco CHURCH
(Via San Francesco; ⊙8am-1pm & 2-8pm) The real attraction here is not the church but the beautiful medieval cloister. A harmonious marriage of architectural styles – two sides are lined with 14th-century crossed arches, the other two with round arches supported by octagonal pillars – it is often used to host exhibitions and summer concerts.

Museo Correale MUSEUM
(☑081 878 18 46; www.museocorreale.it; Via Correale 50; admission €7; ⊙9.30am-6.30pm Tue-Sat, to 1.30pm Sun summer, reduced hours winter) Located to the east of the city centre, this museum is well worth a visit. In addition to a rich assortment of 17th- to 19th-century Neapolitan art and crafts, you'll find Japanese, Chinese and European ceramics, clocks and furniture, as well as Greek and Roman artefacts.

Museo Bottega della Tarsia Lignea MUSEUM
(☑081 877 19 42; www.museomuta.it; Via San Nicola 28; adult/reduced €8/5; ⊙10am-6.30pm summer, to 5pm winter) Since the 18th century, Sorrento has been famous for its *intarsio* furniture, made with elaborately designed inlaid wood. Some wonderful examples can be found in this museum, housed in an 18th-century palace complete with beautiful frescoes. There's also an interesting collection of paintings, prints and photographs depicting the town and surrounding area in the 19th century.

Duomo CATHEDRAL
(Corso Italia; ⊙8am-12.30pm & 4.30-8.30pm) To get a feel for Sorrento's history, stroll down Via Pietà from Piazza Tasso and past two medieval palaces en route to the cathedral with its striking exterior fresco, triple-tiered bell tower, four classical columns and elegant maiolica clock. Take note of the striking marble bishop's throne (1573) and the beautiful wooden choir stalls decorated in the local *intarsio* style.

Activities

Bagni Regina Giovanna BEACH
(Pollio Felix) Sorrento famously lacks a proper beach, so consider splashing around at Bagni Regina Giovanna, a rocky beach about 2km west of town. Set among the ruins of the Roman Villa Pollio Felix, the water is clean and clear. While you can walk here (follow Via Capo), you'll save your swimming strength by catching the SITA Sud bus or the EAV Bus (Linea A) headed for Massa Lubrense.

Sic Sic BOATING
(☑081 807 22 83; www.nauticasicsic.com; Marina Piccola; ⊙May-Oct) To seek out the best beaches, rent a boat from this outfit. There's a variety of options, starting at around €50 per hour or €150 per day. It also organises boat excursions.

Tours

City Sightseeing Sorrento BUS TOUR
(☑081 877 47 07; www.sorrento.city-sightseeing. it; adult/reduced €12/6; ⊙Apr-Oct) A hop-on, hop-off bus tour of Sorrento and the surrounding area. Daily departures are at 9.30am, 11.30am, 1.30pm and 3.30pm from Piazza De Curtis (Circumvesuviana station). English-language commentaries are

Sorrento

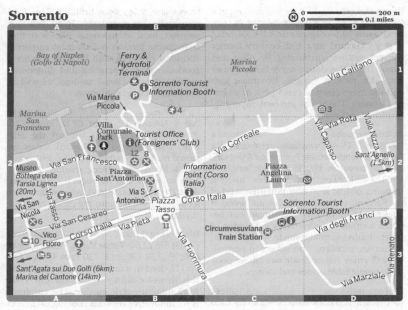

provided, and tickets, available on board, are valid for six hours.

🎊 Festivals & Events

Sant'Antonino   RELIGIOUS
(⊙14 Feb) The city's patron saint, Sant' Antonino, is remembered annually with processions and huge markets. The saint is credited with having saved Sorrento during WWII when Salerno and Naples were heavily bombed.

Settimana Santa   RELIGIOUS
(Holy Week) Sorrento's Settimana Santa Easter processions are famous throughout Italy. There are two main processions: one at midnight on the Thursday preceding Good Friday, the second on Good Friday.

🛏 Sleeping

Most accommodation is in the town centre or clustered along Via Capo, the coastal road west of the centre. Be sure to book early for the summer season.

Casa Astarita   B&B €
(☏081 877 49 06; www.casastarita.com; Corso Italia 67, Sorrento; d €90-120, tr €110-140; ❄ @ 🛜) All six rooms at this pretty B&B combine original structural elements, like niches and

Sorrento

vaulted ceilings, with the modern comforts of flat-screen TV, fridge and excellent water pressure. Brightly painted doors, tasteful art and antiques complete the eclectic look. Rooms surround a central parlour, where breakfast is served at a large rustic table.

Seven Hostel

HOSTEL €

(☑081 878 67 58; www.sevenhostel.com; Via Lommella Grande 99, Sant'Agnello; dm/s/d €30/75/80; ✳@⊛) Located in a 19th-century former convent setting surrounded by olive and lemon trees, this design-savvy hostel comes with chic rooftop terraces, live-music gigs and the more down-to-earth perk of an onsite laundry. The rooms are contemporarily furnished and spacious.

Nube d'Argento

CAMPGROUND €

(☑081 878 13 44; www.nubedargento.com; Via Capo 21, Sorrento; camping 2 people, car & tent €35, 2-person bungalows €60-85, 4-person bungalows €90-120; ⊙Mar-Dec; ⊛⊛⊛) This inviting camping ground is an easy 1km drive west of the Sorrento city centre. Pitches and wooden chalet-style bungalows are spread out beneath a canopy of olive trees – a source of much-needed summer shade – and the facilities are excellent. Youngsters in particular will enjoy the open-air swimming pool, table-tennis table, slides and swings.

La Tonnarella

LUXURY HOTEL €€

(☑081 878 11 53; www.latonnarella.it; Via Capo 31; d €112-140, ste €240-350; ⊙Apr-Oct & Christmas; P✳@⊛) La Tonnarella is a dazzling canvas of blue-and-yellow maiolica tiles, antiques, chandeliers and statues. Rooms, most of which have their own balcony or small terrace, continue the sumptuous classical theme with traditional furniture and discreet mod cons. The hotel also has its own private beach, accessible by lift, and a highly regarded terrace restaurant.

Hotel Cristina

HOTEL €€

(☑081 878 35 62; www.hotelcristinasorrento.it; Via Privata Rubinacci 6, Sant'Agnello; s €120, d €120-200, tr €230; ⊙Mar-Oct; ✳⊛⊛) Located high above Sant'Agnello, this hotel has superb views, particularly from the swimming pool. The spacious rooms have sea-view balconies and combine inlaid wooden furniture with contemporary flourishes, like Philippe Starck chairs. There's an in-house restaurant and a free shuttle bus to/from Sorrento's Circumvesuviana train station.

✗ Eating

A local speciality to look out for is *gnocchi alla sorrentina* (gnocchi baked in tomato sauce with mozzarella).

Inn Bufalito

CAMPANIAN €€

(☑081 365 69 75; www.innbufalito.it; Vico Fuoro 21; meals €25; ⊙noon-midnight summer, reduced hours winter; ⊛⊘) ⊘ A brilliant Slow Food mozzarella bar-restaurant. Head here for moreish local concoctions like Sorrento-style cheese fondue, buffalo-meat carpaccio and local *salsiccia* with broccoli. There's a good choice of vegetarian and gluten-free options, regular cheese tastings, as well as the occasional art exhibition.

La Basilica

ITALIAN, PIZZERIA

(Via S Antonino 12; pizzas €6-12, meals €40; ⊙noon-midnight) Elegant without the attitude, barrel-vaulted La Basilica serves regional nosh with subtle yet confident twists (think house-made black *scialatielli* pasta with calamari and *pomodorini* or a decadent dark chocolate and whisky tart). For a cheaper feed, dig into the excellent wood-fired pizzas.

Ristorante il Buco

CAMPANIAN €€€

(☑081 878 23 54; Rampa Marina Piccola 5; meals €60; ⊙12.30-2.30pm & 7.30-11pm Thu-Tue Feb-Dec) Housed in a monks' former wine cellar, this dress-for-dinner restaurant offers far from monastic-style cuisine. The emphasis is on innovative regional cooking, so expect modern combos like mozzarella and lemon-stuffed ravioli, or zesty risotto with smoked *provola* cheese, green apple and prawns. Reservations recommended.

Drinking & Nightlife

From wood-panelled wine bars to cocktail-centric cafes, you'll find no shortage of drinking dens in Sorrento.

Cafè Latino

CAFE, BAR

(☑081 878 37 18; Vico Fuoro 4a; ⊙10am-1am summer) Think locked-eyes-over-cocktails time. This is the place to impress your partner with cocktails (from €7) on the terrace, surrounded by orange and lemon trees. Sip a Mary Pickford (rum, pineapple, *grenadino* and maraschino) or a glass of chilled white wine. If you can't drag yourselves away, you can also eat here (meals around €30).

Bollicine

WINE BAR

(☑081 878 46 16; Via Accademia 9; ⊙7.30pm-2am) The wine list at this unpretentious wine bar with a dark, woody interior includes all the big Italian names and a selection of interesting local labels. If you can't decide what to go for, the amiable bar staff will advise you. There's also a small menu of *panini*, bruschette and one or two pasta dishes.

Fauno Bar

CAFE

(📞 081 878 11 35; Piazza Tasso; ⊗ 7-2am midnight mid-Mar–mid-Jan) On Piazza Tasso, this elegant cafe covers half the square and offers the best people-watching in town. It serves stiff drinks at stiff prices – cocktails start at €7. Snacks, sandwiches, salads and pizzas are also available (from €6).

☆ Entertainment

Teatro Tasso

THEATRE

(📞 081 807 55 25; www.teatrotasso.com; Piazza Sant'Antonino; admission €25; ⊗ 9.30pm summer) The southern Italian equivalent of a London old-world music hall, Teatro Tasso is home to the *Sorrento Musical*, a sentimental 75-minute revue of Neapolitan classics such as 'O Sole Mio' and 'Trona a Sorrent'.

❶ Information

Hospital (📞 081 533 11 11; Corso Italia 1)
Police station (📞 081 807 31 11; Via Capasso 11)
Post office (Corso Italia 210)
Sorrento Tour (www.sorrentotour.it) Extensive website with tourist and transport information on Sorrento and environs.

Tourist information For maps and useful information, head to one of Sorrento's tourist information kiosks, located outside the Circumvesuviana train station (Piazza de Curtis, Circumvesuviana station; ⊗ 10am-1pm & 3-7pm summer, to 5pm winter), in town at Corso Italia (⊗ 9am-1pm & 3-10pm) and the Foreigners' Club (Via Luigi De Maio 35; ⊗ 8.30am-4.15pm Mon-Fri), and at the ferry port (Marina Piccola; ⊗ 9am-5pm summer, closed winter).

❶ Getting There & Away

BOAT

Sorrento is the main jumping-off point for Capri and also has good ferry connections to Naples, Ischia and Amalfi coastal towns.

Caremar (p660) Runs ferries to Capri (€13.20, 25 minutes, four daily).

Alilauro (📞 081 497 22 22; www.alilauro.it) runs up to five daily hydrofoils between Naples and Sorrento (€12.30, 40 minutes).

Linee Marittime Partenopee (p690) runs hydrofoils from Sorrento to Capri from April to November (€18.30, 20 minutes, 17 daily).

All ferries and hydrofoils depart from the port at Marina Piccola, where you buy your tickets.

BUS

Curreri (📞 081 801 54 20; www.curreriviaggi.it) runs six daily services to Sorrento from Naples' Capodichino airport, departing from outside the arrivals hall and arriving in Piazza Tasso.

Buy tickets (€10) for the 75-minute journey on the bus.

SITA Sud (📞 089 40 51 45; www.sitasudtrasporti.it) buses serve the Amalfi Coast and Sant'Agata sui Due Golfi. Buses depart from outside the Circumvesuviana train station. Buy tickets at the station bar or from shops bearing the blue SITA sign.

TRAIN

Circumvesuviana (📞 800 211388; www.eavcampania.it) trains run every 30 minutes between Sorrento and Naples (€4.10), via Pompeii (€2.20) and Ercolano (€2.20).

❶ Getting Around

Local bus Line B runs from Piazza Sant'Antonino to the port at Marina Piccola (€1.30).

Jolly Service & Rent (📞 081 877 34 50; www.jollyrent.eu; Via degli Aranci 180) has Smart cars from €60 a day and 50cc scooters from €27.

For a **taxi**, call 📞 081 878 22 04.

West of Sorrento

The countryside west of Sorrento is the very essence of southern Italy. Tortuous roads wind their way through hills covered in olive trees and lemon groves, passing through sleepy villages and tiny fishing ports. There are magnificent views at every turn, the best being from Sant'Agata sui Due Golfi and the high points overlooking Punta Campanella, the westernmost point of the Sorrentine Peninsula.

Sant'Agata sui Due Golfi

Perched high in the hills above Sorrento, sleepy Sant'Agata sui due Golfi commands spectacular views of the Bay of Naples on one side and the Bay of Salerno on the other (hence its name, Saint Agatha on the Two Gulfs). The best viewpoint is the **Convento del Deserto** (📞 081 878 01 99; Via Deserto; ⊗ gardens 8am-7pm, panoramic lookout 10am-noon & 5-7pm summer, 10am-noon & 3-5pm winter), a Carmelite convent 1.5km uphill from the village centre.

Agriturismo Le Tore (📞 081 808 06 37; www.letore.com; Via Pontone 43; s €50-80, d €90-120, dinner €25-35; ⊗ Easter-early Nov; 🅿 @ 🛜 🐾) is a wonderful organic farm with eight barn-like rooms and an apartment that sleeps six (€600 to €1100 per week). A short drive, or a long walk, from the village, the setting is lovely, a rustic farmhouse hidden among fruit trees and olive groves. Request the especially charming Terrazzo room, which comes with a large terrace. Conveniently, the owners also offer a shuttle-bus pick-up from Naples' Capodichino airport or Stazione Centrale, costing around €25 per person one way.

From Sorrento, there's a pretty 3km (approximately one hour) trail up to Sant'Agata. Hourly SITA Sud buses leave from the Circumvesuviana train station.

Marina del Cantone

From Sorrento, follow the coastal road round to **Termini**. Stop a moment to admire the views before continuing on to **Nerano**, from where a beautiful hiking trail leads down to the stunning **Bay of Ieranto**, one of the coast's top swimming spots, and the tranquil, unassuming village of **Marina del Cantone**.

◉ Sights & Activities

A popular diving destination, the protected waters here are part of an 11-sq-km marine reserve called the **Punta Campanella**, its underwater grottoes lush with flora and fauna.

Nettuno Diving   DIVING
(☏ 081 808 10 51; www.sorrentodiving.com; Via Vespucci 39; ⊕) Be under the sea with this PADI-certified outfit, which runs various underwater activities. Options include snorkelling excursions, beginner courses and cave dives. Adult rates start at €25 for a day-long outing to the Bay of Ieranto.

🍴 Sleeping & Eating

**Villaggio Residence
Nettuno**   CAMPGROUND, APARTMENTS €
(☏ 081 808 10 51; www.villaggionettuno.it; Via A Vespucci 39; camping 2 people, tent & car per person €15-35, bungalows €35-85, apt €60-250; ⊙ Mar-early Nov; 🅿 ❄ @ 🛜 ⛱) Set among olive groves at the village entrance, Marina's camping ground offers an array of accommodation options, including campsites, mobile homes, and (best of all) apartments in a 16th-century tower for two to five people. It's a friendly, environmentally sound place with excellent facilities and a comprehensive activities list.

Lo Scoglio   ITALIAN €€€
(☏ 081 808 10 26; Marina del Cantone; meals €60; ⊙ 12.30-5pm & 7.30-11pm) The only one of the marina's restaurants directly accessible

from the sea, Lo Scoglio is a darling of peckish celebrities and VIPs. While meat dishes are available, you'd be sorry to miss the superb seafood. Highlights include a €30 antipasto of raw seafood and *spaghetti al riccio* (spaghetti with sea urchins).

ℹ Getting There & Around

SITA Sud (p685) runs regular bus services between Sorrento and Marina del Cantone (on timetables as Nerano Cantone; €2.50, one hour).

AMALFI COAST

Stretching about 50km along the southern side of the Sorrentine Peninsula, the Amalfi Coast (Costiera Amalfitana) is one of Europe's most breathtaking. Cliffs terraced with scented lemon groves sheer down into sparkling seas; sherbet-hued villas cling precariously to unforgiving slopes while sea and sky merge in one vast blue horizon.

Yet its stunning topography has not always been a blessing. For centuries after the passing of Amalfi's glory days as a maritime superpower (from the 9th to the 12th centuries), the area was poor and its isolated villages were regular victims of foreign incursions, earthquakes and landslides. But it was this very isolation that first drew visitors in the early 1900s, paving the way for the advent of tourism in the latter half of the century. Today the Amalfi Coast is one of Italy's premier tourist destinations, a favourite of cashed-up jet-setters and love-struck couples.

The best time to visit is in spring or early autumn. In summer the coast's single road (SS163) gets very busy and prices are inflated; in winter much of the coast simply shuts down.

ℹ Getting There & Away

BOAT

Boat services to the Amalfi Coast towns are generally limited to the period between April and October.

Alicost (☏ 089 87 14 83; www.alicost.it; Salita Sopramuro 2, Amalfi) operates one daily ferry from Salerno to Amalfi (€7), Positano (€11) and Capri (€20.70) from mid-April to October. On Mondays, Wednesdays, Fridays and Sundays, it also runs two daily hydrofoils between Sorrento and Positano (€15.80) and Amalfi (€16.80).

WALK THE COAST

Rising steeply from the coast, the densely wooded Lattari mountains provide some stunning walking opportunities. An extraordinary network of paths traverses the craggy, precipitous peaks, climbing to remote farmhouses through wild and beautiful valleys. It's tough going, though – long ascents up seemingly endless flights of steps are almost unavoidable.

Probably the best-known walk, the 12km Sentiero degli Dei (Path of the Gods; 5½ to six hours) follows the steep, often rocky paths linking Positano to Praiano. It's a spectacular trail passing through some of the area's least developed country-side. The route is marked by red-and-white stripes daubed on rocks and trees, although some of these have become worn in places and might be difficult to make out. Pick up a map of the walk at local tourist offices, included in a series of three excellent booklets containing the area's most popular hikes, including the equally famed, and lyrically named, Via degli Incanti (Trail of Charms) from Amalfi to Positano.

To the west, the tip of the Sorrentine Peninsula is another hiking hot spot. Some 110km of paths criss-cross the area, linking the spectacular coastline with the rural hinterland. These range from tough all-day treks – such as the 14.1km Alta Via dei Monti Lattari from the Fontanelle hills near Positano down to the Punta Campanella – to shorter walks suitable for the family. Tourist offices throughout the area can provide maps detailing the colour-coded routes. With the exception of the Alta Via dei Monti Lattari (marked in red and white), long routes are shown in red on the map; coast-to-coast trails in blue; paths connecting villages in green; and circular routes in yellow.

If you're intent on trying one of the more demanding routes in the region, invest in a detailed map such as *Monti Lattari, Penisola Sorrentina, Costiera Amalfitana: Carta dei Sentieri* (€9) at 1:30,000 scale by Club Alpino Italiano (CAI). If you prefer a guided hike, there are a number of reliable local guides, including Zia Lucy (www.zialucy.it).

TraVelMar (p693) connects Salerno with Amalfi (€8, six daily) and Positano (€12, six daily) from April to October.

BUS

SITA Sud (p685) operates a frequent, year-round service along the SS163 between Sorrento and Salerno (€3.40), via Amalfi.

CAR & MOTORCYCLE

If driving from the north, exit the A3 autostrada at Vietri sul Mare and follow the SS163 along the coast. From the south leave the A3 at Salerno and head for Vietri sul Mare and the SS163.

TRAIN

From Naples you can take either the Circumvesuviana to Sorrento or a Trenitalia train to Salerno, then continue along the Amalfi Coast, eastwards or westwards, by SITA Sud bus.

Positano

POP 3860

The pearl in the pack, Positano is the coast's most photogenic and expensive town. Its steeply stacked houses are a medley of peach-es, pinks and terracottas, and its near-vertical streets (many of which are, in fact, staircases) are lined with voguish shop displays, jewellery stalls, elegant hotels and smart restaurants. Look closely, though, and you'll find reassuring signs of everyday reality – crumbling stucco, streaked paintwork and even, on occasion, a faint whiff of drains.

An early visitor, John Steinbeck wrote in May 1953 in *Harper's Bazaar*: 'Positano bites deep. It is a dream place that isn't quite real when you are there and becomes beckoningly real after you have gone.' More than 60 years on, his words still ring true.

◎ Sights

Chiesa di Santa Maria Assunta   CHURCH
(Piazza Flavio Gioia; ⊙8am-noon & 4-9pm) This church is the most famous and – let's face it – only major sight in Positano. Inside, it's a delightfully classical affair, its pillars topped with gilded Ionic capitals and winged cherubs peeking from above every arch. Above the main altar is a 13th-century Byzantine Black Madonna and Child.

Positano

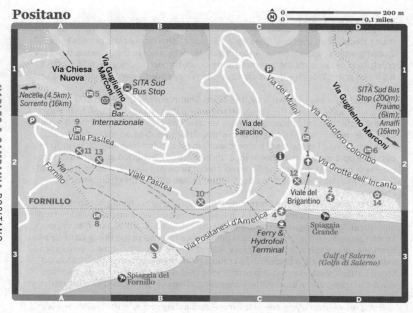

Positano

⊙ Sights
1 Chiesa di Santa Maria Assunta	C2

⊕ Activities, Courses & Tours
2 Blue Star	D2
3 Centro Sub Costiera Amalfitana	B3
4 L'Uomo e il Mare	C3

⊜ Sleeping
5 Hostel Brikette	A1
6 Hotel California	D2
7 Hotel Palazzo Murat	C2
8 Pensione Maria Luisa	A3
9 Villa Gabrisa	A2

⊗ Eating
10 Da Vincenzo	B2
11 Il Saraceno d'Oro	A2
12 La Brezza	C2
13 Next2	A2

⊕ Entertainment
14 Music on the Rocks	D2

🏃 Activities

Although Spiaggia Grande is no one's dream beach, with greyish sand covered by legions of brightly coloured umbrellas, the water's clean and the setting is striking. Hiring a chair and umbrella in the fenced-off areas costs around €20 per person per day, but the crowded public areas are free.

Blue Star BOATING
(☑ 089 81 18 88; www.bluestarpositano.it; Spiaggia Grande; ⊙ 8.30am-9pm summer) Operating out of a kiosk on Spiaggia Grande, Blue Star hires out small motorboats for €70 per hour (€250 for four hours). It also organises excursions to Capri and the Grotta dello Smeraldo (€55).

L'Uomo e il Mare BOATING
(☑ 089 81 16 13; www.gennaroesalvatore.it; ⊙ 9am-8pm summer) This Italian-English couple offer a range of tours, including Capri and Amalfi day trips (from €55), out of a kiosk near the ferry terminal.

🛏 Sleeping

Most hotels are three-star rated and above and prices are universally high. Cheaper accommodation is more limited and must usually be booked well in advance for summer. Ask at the tourist office about rooms or apartments in private houses.

Hostel Brikette HOSTEL €
(☑ 089 87 58 57; www.hostel-positano.com; Via Marconi 358; dm €20-26, premium dm €25-40, d

€55-100, apt €60-130; ☉ late Mar-Nov; ✳ @ ☎) A short walk from the Chiesa Nuova (Bar Internazionale) bus stop, this bright and cheerful hostel offers the cheapest accommodation in town. There are various options: five- to 10-person dorms (single sex and mixed), premium dorms (with private bathroom and panoramic terrace), double rooms and apartments for two to eight people. Extra services include laundry (€10), left-luggage facilities and cheap, delicious home-cooked meals.

Conveniently, the hostel also offers a 'daily hostelling' option, which allows day trippers use of the hostel's facilities (including showers, wi-fi and left-luggage service) for €10.

Pensione Maria Luisa
PENSION €

(☑ 089 87 50 23; www.pensionemarialuisa.com; Via Fornillo 42; r €70-85; ☉ Mar-Oct; @ ☎) A solid budget choice, Maria Luisa is run by the lovely Carlo, a wonderfully helpful, larger-than-life character. Rooms and bathrooms feature shiny blue tiles and fittings; those with private terraces are well worth the extra €10 for the bay view. Most rooms have fridges and the sunny communal area is another major plus. Breakfast costs an additional €5.

Hotel California
HOTEL €€

(☑ 089 87 53 82; www.hotelcaliforniapositano.com; Via Cristoforo Colombo 141; d €160-185; P ✳ ☎) While you won't spot the Eagles at this Hotel California, you will find yourself slumbering in a magnificent, pastel-hued 18th-century palace. The rooms in the older part of the house are magnificent, with original friezes adorning the ceilings. The new rooms are spacious and luxuriously decorated, and breakfast is served on a leafy front terrace.

★ Hotel Palazzo Murat
LUXURY HOTEL €€€

(☑ 089 87 51 77; www.palazzomurat.it; Via dei Mulini 23; r €175-260; ☉ May–mid-Jan; ✳ @ ☎) Hidden behind an ancient wall from the surge of tourists who pass this pedestrian thoroughfare daily, the Palazzo Murat is a magnificent hotel. Housed within the 18th-century *palazzo* that the one-time King of Naples used as his summer residence, the lush gardens contain banana trees, bottlebrush, Japanese maple and pine trees. Rooms, five in the original part of the building (more expensive), 25 in the newer section, are decorated with sumptuous antiques, original oil paintings and plenty of glossy marble.

Villa Gabrisa
BOUTIQUE HOTEL €€€

(☑ 089 81 14 98; www.villagabrisa.it; Via Pasitea 223; d €220; ✳ ☎) Tastefully restored, this historical building dates to the 18th century. Rooms exude classic Italian style with painted Tuscan furniture, wrought-iron beds, Murano glass chandeliers, and maiolica and terracotta tiles. While all rooms have fridge and sea-view terrace, some come with bubblelicious jacuzzi. Extras include SKY TV access and on-site restaurant serving regional grub.

✖ Eating

Most restaurants, bars and trattorias, many of which are unashamedly touristy, close over winter, making a brief reappearance for Christmas and New Year.

La Brezza
CAFE, BAR €

(☑ 089 87 58 11; Via Regina Giovanna 2; snacks around €6; ☉ 9am-1am; ☎) With free wi-fi, web-connected computers (€5 for 30 minutes), and a terrace with beach views, this contemporary, buzzing hangout is the best frontline place for a *panino* or snack. There are regular art exhibitions and a daily 'happy hour' (from 6pm to 8pm), with drinks accompanied by complimentary light eats. Fresh juices and smoothies keep the virtuous hydrated.

★ Next2
CAMPANIAN €€

(☑ 089 812 35 16; www.next2.it; Viale Pasitea 242; meals €40; ☉ 6.30-11.30pm) Sleek and refreshingly contemporary, this wine bar-restaurant hybrid gives regional cooking satisfying makeovers. Whenever possible, local and organic ingredients are put to impressive use in creations such as fried ravioli with ricotta and mozzarella on fresh tomatoes, or *parmigiana di pesce bandiera*, a surf variation on the classic aubergine dish. Desserts are wickedly creamy and the alfresco terrace is summertime perfection.

Da Vincenzo
CAMPANIAN €€

(☑ 089 87 51 28; Viale Pasitea 172-178; meals €40; ☉ noon-2.30pm & 6-11pm Wed-Mon, 6.30-11pm Tue) Superbly prepared dishes are served here by the third generation of restaurateurs. The emphasis is on fish dishes, which range from the adventurous, like skewers of grilled octopus tentacles with deep-fried artichokes, to seasonal pasta dishes. Enjoy twanging Neapolitan guitarists during the summer months and make room for co-owner Marcella's legendary desserts, considered the best in town. Reservations recommended.

Il Saraceno d'Oro
ITALIAN €€

(Viale Pasitea 254; pizzas €6-10, meals €35; ☉ 12.30-3pm & 6.30-11pm daily in summer) A busy, bustling place, the Saracen's blend of

NOCELLE

A world apart from self-conscious Positano, the tiny, left-alone mountain village of No-celle (450m) affords some of the most spectacular views on the entire coast. A stop on the Sentieri degli Dei hiking route, it's a sleepy, silent place where not much ever happens, much to the delight of its very few residents.

If you can't pull yourself away, consider checking in at **Villa della Quercia** (☑089 812 34 97; www.villadellaquercia.com; Via Nocelle 5; r €70-75; ⊗Apr-Oct; 🛜), a former monastery with heavenly views. If peckish, tuck into delicious, regional dishes at **Trattoria Santa Croce** (Via Nocelle 19; ⊗Apr-Oct), a reliable low-key nosh spot in the main part of the village.

The easiest way to get here is by local bus from Positano (€1.30, 30 minutes, 17 daily). If you're driving, follow the signs from Positano.

cheery service, uncomplicated food and reasonable prices continues to please the punters. The pizza and pasta choices are good, and the *contorni* (side dishes) excellent (the grilled-vegetable antipasto makes a good choice for vegetarians). The legendary profiteroles in chocolate sauce make for a pleasing epilogue, as does the complimentary end-of-meal glass of *limoncello*.

☆ Entertainment

Generally speaking, Positano's nightlife is genteel, sophisticated and safe.

Music on the Rocks CLUB
(☑089 87 58 74; www.musicontherocks.it; Via Grotte dell'Incanto 51; admission €10-30; ⊗summer) This is one of the town's few genuine nightspots and one of the best clubs on the coast. Music on the Rocks is dramatically carved into the tower at the eastern end of Spiaggia Grande. Join the flirty, eye-candy crowd and some of the region's top DJs for mainstream house and reliable disco.

ℹ Information

Positano (www.positano.com) A slick website with hotel and restaurant listings, itineraries and transport information.
Post office (Via Marconi 318)
Tourist office (☑089 87 50 67; Via del Saracino 4; ⊗8.30am-7pm Mon-Sat, to 2pm Sun Easter-Oct, 9am-4.30pm Mon-Sat Nov-Easter)

ℹ Getting There & Away

BOAT

Positano has excellent ferry connections to the coastal towns and Capri from April to October.

Alicost (p686) operates one daily service to Amalfi (€7), Salerno (€11) and Capri (€17.40). On Monday, Wednesday, Friday and Sunday, it also sails once to Sorrento (€15.80).

TraVelMar (p693) runs six daily ferries to Amalfi (€8) and Salerno (€12).

Linee Marittime Partenopee (Map p648; ☑081 704 19 11; www.consorziolmp.it) runs four daily hydrofoils and four daily ferries to Capri (€18.90).

BUS

SITA Sud (p685) runs frequent buses to/from Amalfi (€2.50, 40 to 50 minutes) and Sorrento (€2.50, one hour). Buses drop you off at one of two main bus stops: coming from Sorrento and the west, opposite Bar Internazionale; arriving from Amalfi and the east, at the top of Via Colombo. When departing, buy bus tickets at Bar Internazionale or, if headed eastwards, from the tobacconist at the bottom of Via Colombo.

ℹ Getting Around

Getting around Positano is largely a matter of walking. If your knees can handle them, there are dozens of narrow alleys and stairways that make walking relatively easy and joyously traffic-free. Otherwise, an orange bus follows the lower ring road every half-hour, passing along Viale Pasitea, Via Colombo and Via Marconi. Buy your ticket on board (€1.60) or at a *tabaccaio* (tobacconist's shop; €1.30). It passes by both SITA Sud bus stops.

Praiano & Furore

An ancient fishing village, Praiano has one of the coast's most popular beaches, Marina di Praia. From the SS163 (next to the Hotel Continental), take the steep path that leads down the side of the cliffs to a tiny inlet with a small stretch of coarse sand and deep-blue water.

The **Centro Sub Costiera Amalfitana** (☑089 81 21 48; www.centrosub.it; Via Marina di

Praia; dives from €80; [icon]) runs beginner to expert dives exploring the area's coral, marine life and grottoes.

Stunningly set on a cliffside overlooking Marina di Praia, **Hotel Onda Verde** ([icon]089 87 41 43; www.hotelondaverde.com; Via Terramare 3, Praiano; r €110-230; [icons]Apr-Nov; [icons]) is a sound slumber party, its 25 rooms a smart, soothing combo of satin bedheads, Florentine-style furniture, and deckchair-pimped terraces. The hotel restaurant also comes highly recommended, and breakfast and parking are included in the price.

A few kilometres further on, Marina di Furore sits at the bottom of what's known as the fjord of Furore, a giant cleft that cuts through the Lattari mountains. The main village, however, stands 300m above, in the upper Vallone del Furore. A one-horse place that sees few tourists, it breathes a distinctly rural air despite the colourful murals and unlikely modern sculpture.

To get to upper Furore by car follow the SS163 and then the SS366 signposted to Agerola; from Positano, it's 15km. Otherwise, regular SITA Sud buses depart from the bus terminus in Amalfi (€2.50, 25 minutes, at least five daily).

Amalfi

POP 5160

Believe it or not, pretty little Amalfi, with its sun-filled piazzas and small beach, was once a maritime superpower with a population of more than 70,000. For one thing, it's not a big place – you can easily walk from one end to the other in about 20 minutes. For another, there are very few historical buildings of note. The explanation is chilling – most of the old city, and its populace, simply slid into the sea during an earthquake in 1343.

Just around the headland, neighbouring Atrani is a picturesque tangle of whitewashed alleys and arches centred on a lively, lived-in piazza and popular beach.

◉ Sights

Cattedrale di Sant'Andrea   CATHEDRAL
([icon]089 87 10 59; Piazza del Duomo; [icon]7.30am-7.30pm) A melange of architectural styles, Amalfi's iconic cathedral makes a striking impression from the top of its sweeping flight of stairs. Between 10am and 5pm (from 12.15pm on Sundays), entrance to the cathedral is through the adjacent Chiostro

del Paradiso, where you have to pay an entrance fee of €3. It's well worth it.

The cathedral dates in part from the early 10th century and its distinctive striped facade has been rebuilt twice, most recently at the end of the 19th century. While the two-toned masonry and 13th-century bell tower are largely Sicilian Arabic-Norman, the interior is predominately baroque. The lavish **crypt** is home to the reliquary of St Andrew the Apostle. The fresco facing the crypt's altar is by Neapolitan baroque maestro Aniello Falcone.

The pint-sized **Chiostro del Paradiso** was built in 1266 to house the tombs of Amalfi's prominent citizens. From here you enter the **Basilica del Crucifisso** (closed January and February), the town's original 9th-century cathedral, itself built on the remains of an earlier palaeo-Christian temple. It's home to a small but fascinating collection of ecclesial treasures.

Museo della Carta   MUSEUM
([icon]089 830 45 61; www.museodellacarta.it; Via delle Cartiere 23; admission €4; [icon]10am-6.30pm) Amalfi's paper museum is housed in a 13th-century paper mill (the oldest in Europe). It lovingly preserves the original paper presses, which are still in full working order, as you'll see during the 15-minute guided tour (three-day advance booking requested for English tour) which explains the original cotton-based paper production and the later wood-pulp manufacturing.

Clued up, you may well be inspired to pick up some of the stationery sold in the gift shop, alongside calligraphy sets and paper pressed with flowers.

Museo Arsenale Amalfi   MUSEUM
([icon]089 87 11 70; Largo Cesareo Console 3; admission €2; [icon]10am-1.30pm & 3.30-7pm) Amalfi's other museum of note is home to the *Tavole Amalfitane,* an ancient manuscript draft of Amalfi's maritime code, and other historical documents. Harking back to Amalfi's days as a great maritime republic, the museum is housed in the cavernous Arsenale, once the town's main shipbuilding depot.

✹ Activities

For all its seafaring history, Amalfi's main beach is not a particularly appealing swimming spot. If you're intent on a dip, think about hiring a boat. You'll find a number of operators along Lungomare dei Cavalieri, charging about €50 for a couple of hours.

Grotta dello Smeraldo
GROTTO

(Emerald Grotto; admission €5; ☺9am-4pm summer, to 3pm winter) Four kilometres west of Amalfi, Conca dei Marini is home to one of the coast's most popular sights. Named after the eerie emerald colour that emanates from the water, the Grotta dello Smeraldo is well worth a visit. Stalactites hang down from the 24m-high ceiling, while stalagmites grow up to 10m tall. Each year, on 24 December and 6 January, skin divers from all over Italy make their traditional pilgrimage to the ceramic *presepe* (nativity scene) submerged beneath the water.

SITA Sud buses regularly pass the car park above the cave entrance (from where you take a lift or stairs down to the rowing boats). Alternatively, Coop Sant'Andrea (p693) runs hourly boats from Amalfi (€15 return) between 9.30am and 3.30pm, March to November. Allow 1½ hours for the return trip.

🎉 Festivals & Events

Every 24 December and 6 January, divers from all over Italy make a pilgrimage to the ceramic *presepe* (nativity scene) submerged in the Grotta dello Smeraldo.

The **Regatta of the Four Ancient Maritime Republics**, which rotates between Amalfi, Venice, Pisa and Genoa, is held on the first Sunday in June. Amalfi's turn comes round again in 2017.

🛏 Sleeping

A'Scalinatella Hostel
HOSTEL €

(☎089 87 14 92; www.hostelscalinatella.com; Piazza Umberto I; dm €20-25, s €35-50, d €70-90, all incl breakfast) This bare-bones operation, just round the headland in Atrani, has dorms, rooms and apartments scattered across the village. There is also a laundry available (€7). Doors are locked at 2am.

Hotel Lidomare
HOTEL €€

(☎089 87 13 32; www.lidomare.it; Largo Duchi Piccolomini 9; s/d €50/120; ❄@) Family run, this gracious hotel oozes character. Rooms are spacious, with appealingly haphazard decor, vintage tiles and fine antiques. Some rooms have jacuzzi bath-tubs, others have sea views and a balcony, some have both. Breakfast is laid out on top of a grand piano. Highly recommended.

Hotel Centrale
HOTEL €€

(☎089 87 26 08; www.amalfihotelcentrale.it; Largo Piccolomini 1; s €60-120, d €70-140, tr €90-170, q €100-180; P❄@@) For the money, this is one of the best-value hotels in Amalfi. The entrance is on a tiny little piazza in the *centro storico* but many rooms actually overlook Piazza del Duomo (rooms 21 to 24 are good choices). The bright-green-and-blue tilework gives the place a vibrant fresh look and the views from the rooftop terrace are magnificent.

★ Hotel Luna Convento
HOTEL €€€

(☎089 87 10 02; www.lunahotel.it; Via Pantaleone Comite 33; s €230-290, d €250-300; P❄@@) This former convent founded by St Francis in 1222 has been a hotel for some 170 years. Rooms in the original building are former monks' cells, but there's nothing pokey about the bright tiles, balconies and seamless sea views. The newer wing is equally beguiling, with religious frescoes over the bed (to stop any misbehaving). The cloistered courtyard is magnificent.

🍽 Eating

Pasticceria Pansa
PASTRIES & CAKES €

(Piazza Duomo 40; pastries from €1.50; ☺7.30am-1am summer, to 10.30pm winter) Compromising waistlines since 1830, this vintage pastry peddler is a must for gluttons. Must-tries include the *scorzetta d'arancia* (chocolate-dipped candied orange peels), *torta setteveli* (a multilayered chocolate and hazelnut cake) and the *limoncello*-laced local *delizia al limone*.

Le Arcate
CAMPANIAN €€

(☎089 87 13 67; www.learcate.net; Largo Orlando Buonocore, Atrani; pizzas from €6, meals €25; ☺12.30-3pm & 7.30-11.30pm Tue-Sun, open Mon Jul&Aug) On a sunny day, it's hard to beat the dreamy location – at the far eastern point of the harbour overlooking the beach – with Atrani's ancient rooftops and church tower behind you. Huge white parasols shade the sprawl of tables, while the dining room is a stone-walled natural cave. Tuck into bubbling pizzas or more substatial dishes like risotto with seafood and grilled swordfish; the food is good, but it's a step down from the setting.

Trattoria Il Mulino
ITALIAN €€

(Via delle Cartiere 36; pizzas €6-11, meals €29; ☺noon-midnight) A TV-in-the-corner, kids-running-between-the-tables sort of place, this is about as authentic a trattoria-pizzeria as you'll find in Amalfi. There are no culinary acrobatics, just hearty, honest pasta and simple grilled meat, fish and seafood.

The *calamari alla griglia* (grilled calamari) is simple, succulent perfection. You'll find it near the Museo della Carta.

Ristorante La Caravella
CAMPANIAN €€€

(☑ 089 87 10 29; www.ristorantelacaravella.it; Via Matteo Camera 12; tasting menus €50-120; ⊘ noon-2.30pm & 7.30-11pm Wed-Mon) The regional food here has recently earned the restaurant a Michelin star with dishes that offer nouvelle zap, like black ravioli with cuttlefish ink, scampi and ricotta, or that are unabashedly simple, like the catch of the day served grilled on lemon leaves. Wine aficionados are likely to find something to try on the 15,000-label list. Reservations essential.

❶ Information

Post office (Corso delle Repubbliche Marinare 31) Next door to the tourist office.

Tourist office (www.amalfitouristoffice.it; Corso delle Repubbliche Marinare; ⊘ 9am-1pm & 2-6pm Mon-Sat, 9am-1pm Sun, closed Sun Apr, May & Sep, closed Sat & Sun Oct-Mar) Good for bus and ferry timetables.

❶ Getting There & Away

BOAT

Between April and October there are daily sailings to/from Amalfi.

Alicost (p686) operates one daily service to Amalfi (€7), Salerno (€11) and Capri (€19). On Monday, Wednesday, Friday and Sunday, it also sails once to Sorrento (€16.80).

TraVelMar (☑ 089 87 29 50; www.travelmar. it) runs ferries to Positano (€8, seven daily) and Salerno (€8, six daily).

Linee Marittime Partenopee (p690) runs three daily hydrofoils and four daily ferries to Capri (€21/20.50).

Coop Sant'Andrea (☑ 089 87 29 50; www. coopsantandrea.com; Lungomare dei Cavalieri 1) connects Amalfi to Salerno (€8, six daily) and Positano (€8, seven daily).

BUS

SITA Sud (p685) runs at least 17 daily services from Piazza Flavio Gioia to Sorrento (€3.80, 100 minutes) via Positano (€2.50, 50 minutes). It runs at least 24 daily services to Ravello (€2.50, 25 minutes) and at least nine services to Salerno (€2.50, 1¼ hours).

There are two early-morning connections to Naples (€4.10, two hours), with no services on Sunday, so you're better off catching a bus to Sorrento and then the Circumvesuviana train to Naples.

Buy tickets and check schedules at **Bar Il Giardino delle Palme** (Piazza Flavio Gioia), opposite the bus stop.

Ravello
POP 2460

Sitting high in the hills above Amalfi, refined Ravello is a polished town almost entirely dedicated to tourism. Boasting impeccable bohemian credentials – Wagner, DH Lawrence and Virginia Woolf all lounged here – it's today known for its ravishing gardens and stupendous views, the best in the world according to former resident Gore Vidal.

Most people visit on a day trip from Amalfi – a nerve-tingling 7km drive up the Valle del Dragone – although to best enjoy Ravello's romantic otherworldly atmosphere you'll need to stay overnight.

◉ Sights & Activities

★ Villa Rufolo
GARDEN

(☑ 089 85 76 21; Piazza Duomo; adult/reduced €5/3; ⊘ 9am-sunset) To the south of Ravello's cathedral, a 14th-century tower marks the entrance to this villa, famed for its beautiful cascading gardens. Created by a Scotsman, Scott Neville Reid, in 1853, they are truly magnificent, commanding celestial panoramic views packed with exotic colours, artistically crumbling towers and luxurious blooms.

The villa itself was built in the 13th century for the wealthy Rufolo dynasty and housed several popes, as well as King Robert of Anjou. On seeing the gardens on 26 May 1880, Wagner said he had finally found the enchanted garden of Klingsor (the setting for the second act of the opera *Parsifal*). Today the gardens are used to stage concerts during the town's celebrated festival.

Cathedral
CATHEDRAL

(Piazza Duomo; museum admission €3; ⊘ 8.30am-noon & 5.30-8.30pm) Forming the eastern flank of Piazza Duomo, Ravello's cathedral was originally built in 1086 but has since undergone various makeovers. The facade is 16th century, even if the central bronze door, one of only about two dozen in the country, is an 1179 original; the interior is a late-20th-century interpretation of what the original must once have looked like.

Of particular interest is the striking pulpit, supported by six twisting columns set on marble lions and decorated with flamboyant mosaics of peacocks, birds and dancing lions. Note also how the floor is tilted towards the square – a deliberate measure to enhance the perspective effect. To the left of the central nave is the entrance to the cathedral museum and its modest collection of religious artefacts. In the afternoon, entrance to the church is through the side-street Viale Richard Wagner, costing €3 (including museum admission).

Villa Cimbrone GARDEN
(📞 089 85 80 72; Via Santa Chiara 26; adult/reduced €6/3; ⏱ 9am-sunset) If Villa Rufolo's gardens leave you longing for more, the 12th-century Villa Cimbrone has you covered; we're talking vast views from delightfully ramshackle gardens. The best viewpoint is the Belvedere of Infinity, an awe-inspiring terrace lined with classical-inspired statues and busts. You'll find it some 600m south of Piazza Duomo.

⭐ Festivals & Events

⭐ **Ravello Festival** ARTS
(📞 089 85 83 60; www.ravellofestival.com; ⏱ Jun–mid-Sep) Come summer, the Ravello Festival turns much of the town centre into a stage. Events range from orchestral concerts and chamber music to ballet performances; film screenings and exhibitions are held in atmospheric outdoor venues, most notably the famous overhanging terrace in the Villa Rufolo gardens.

You don't have to come in high summer to catch a concert, however. The town's program of chamber-music concerts runs from April to October. Tickets, bookable by phone or online, start at €25 (plus a €2 booking fee). For further information, contact the **Ravello Concert Society** (www.ravelloarts.org).

🛏 Sleeping

Agriturismo Monte Brusara AGRITURISMO €
(📞 089 85 74 67; www.montebrusara.com; Via Monte Brusara 32; s/d €45/90) An authentic working farm, this mountainside *agriturismo* (farm stay accommodation) is located a tough half-hour walk of about 1.5km from Ravello's centre (call ahead and the owners can arrange to pick you up). It is especially suited to families: children can feed the pony while you sit back and admire the views – or for those who simply want to escape the crowds. The three rooms are comfy but basic and the food is fabulous.

Hotel Villa Amore PENSION €€
(📞 089 85 71 35; www.villaamore.it; Via dei Fusco 5; s/d incl breakfast €80/120; ⏱ May-Oct; @) A welcoming family-run *pensione*, this is the best budget choice in town, with modest, homey rooms and sparkling bathrooms. All rooms have their own balcony and some have bath-tubs. The on-site restaurant (meals around €25) is a further plus.

Hotel Caruso LUXURY HOTEL €€€
(📞 089 85 88 01; www.hotelcaruso.com; Piazza San Giovanni del Toro 2; s €575-720, d €757-976 all incl breakfast; ⏱ Apr-Nov; P ❄ 🛜 ☀) There can be no better place to swim than the Caruso's sensational infinity pool. Seemingly set on the edge of a precipice, its blue waters merge with sea and sky to magical effect. Inside, the sublimely restored 11th-century *palazzo* is no less impressive, with Moorish arches doubling as window frames, 15th-century vaulted ceilings and high-class ceramics. Rooms are suitably mod-conned.

🍴 Eating

Cumpà Cosimo CAMPANIAN €€
(📞 089 85 71 56; Via Roma 44-46; pizzas €7-12, meals €40; ⏱ 12.30-3pm & 7.30pm-midnight) Netta Bottone's rustic cooking is so good that even US celebrity Rosie O'Donnell tried to get her on her show. Netta didn't make it to Hollywood but she stills rules the roost at this historic trattoria. Order the *piatto misto* (mixed plate), which may include Ravello's trademark *crespolini* (cheese and prosciutto-stuffed crepes). Evening options include pizza.

Da Salvatore CAMPANIAN €€
(📞 089 85 72 27; www.salvatoreravello.com; Via della Republicca 2; meals €28; ⏱ noon-3pm & 7.30-10pm Tue-Sun) Located just before the bus stop and the Albergo Ristorante Garden, Da Salvatore has nothing special by way of decor, but the view more than compensates. Count your lucky stars over creative dishes like tender squid on a bed of pureed chickpeas with spicy *peperoncino*. In the evening, options include top-notch wood-fired pizzas.

ℹ Information

Tourist office (📞 089 85 70 96; www.ravellotime.it; Via Roma 18bis; ⏱ 9am-8pm) Has information on the town and a handy map with walking trails.

ℹ Getting There & Away

SITA Sud operates at least 24 buses daily from the eastern side of Piazza Flavio Gioia in Amalfi (€2.50, 25 minutes). By car, turn north about 2km east of Amalfi. Vehicles are not permitted in Ravello's town centre, but there's plenty of space in supervised car parks on the perimeter.

South of Amalfi

From Amalfi to Salerno

The 26km drive to Salerno, though less exciting than the 16km stretch westwards to Positano, is exhilarating and dotted with a series of small towns, each with their own character and each worth a brief look.

Three and a half kilometres east of Amalfi, or a steep 1km-long walk down from Ravello, **Minori** is a small, workaday town, popular with holidaying Italians. If you're a sweet tooth, make a pit stop at Minori's famous pastry shop, **Sal De Riso** (089 85 36 18; www.salderiso.it; Piazza Cantilena 1, Minori; gelati €2, focaccias €3.70, pastries €4; 7.30am-late summer, reduced hours winter), owned by one of Italy's most revered pastry chefs, Salvatore De Riso. The place also peddles decent focaccia and gelato.

Further along, **Maiori** is the coast's biggest resort, a brassy place full of large seafront hotels, restaurants and beach clubs.

Just beyond **Erchie** and its beautiful beach, **Cetara** is a picturesque tumbledown fishing village with a reputation as a gastronomic highlight. Tuna and anchovies are the local specialities, appearing in various guises at **Al Convento** (089 26 10 39; www.alconvento.net; Piazza San Francesco 16, Cetara; meals €25; 12.30-3pm & 7-11pm summer, closed Wed winter), a sterling seafood restaurant near the small harbour.

Shortly before Salerno, the road passes through **Vietri sul Mare**, the ceramics capital of Campania. Pop into **Ceramica Artistica Solimene** (089 21 02 43; www.solimene.com; Via Madonna degli Angeli 7, Vietri sul Mare; 9am-7pm Mon-Fri, 10am-1pm & 4-7pm Sat), a vast factory outlet with an extraordinary glass-and-ceramic facade.

Salerno

POP 132,700

Upstaged by the glut of postcard-pretty towns along the Amalfi Coast, Campania's second-largest city is actually a pleasant surprise. A decade of civic determination has turned this major port and transport hub into one of southern Italy's most liveable cities, and its small but buzzing *centro storico* is a vibrant mix of medieval churches, tasty trattorias and good-spirited, bar-hopping locals.

Originally an Etruscan and later a Roman colony, Salerno flourished with the arrival of the Normans in the 11th century. Robert Guiscard made it the capital of his dukedom in 1076 and, under his patronage, the Scuola Medica Salernitana was renowned as one of medieval Europe's greatest medical institutes. More recently, it was left in tatters by the heavy fighting that followed the 1943 landings of the American 5th Army, just south of the city.

Sights

★ **Duomo** CATHEDRAL
(Piazza Alfano; 9.30am-6pm Mon-Sat, 4-6pm Sun) You can't miss the looming presence of Salerno's impressive cathedral, widely considered to be the most beautiful medieval church in Italy. Built by the Normans in the 11th century and later aesthetically remodelled in the 18th century, it sustained severe damage in the 1980 earthquake. It is dedicated to San Matteo (St Matthew), whose remains were reputedly brought to the city in 954 and now lie beneath the main altar in the exquisite vaulted crypt.

Take special note of the magnificent main entrance, the 12th-century **Porta dei Leoni**, named after the marble lions at the foot of the stairway. It leads through to a beautiful harmonious courtyard, surrounded by graceful arches, overlooked by a 12th-century bell tower.

While the huge bronze doors (similarly guarded by lions) were cast in Constantinople in the 11th century, the three-aisled interior is largely baroque, with only a few traces of the original church. These include parts of the transept and choir floor and the two raised pulpits in front of the choir stalls. Extraordinarily detailed and colourful 13th-century mosaics lace the church.

In the right-hand apse, don't miss the **Cappella delle Crociate** (Chapel of the Crusades), containing stunning frescoes and more marvellous mosaics. The chapel was so named because crusaders' weapons were blessed here. Under the altar lies the tomb of 11th-century pope Gregory VII.

Museo Virtuale della Scuola Medica Salernitana MUSEUM
(089 257 61 26; Via Mercanti 74; adult/reduced €3/1; 9am-1pm Mon-Sat;) Slap bang in Salerno's historic centre, this engaging museum deploys 3D and touch-screen technology to explore the teachings and wince-inducing procedures of Salerno's once-famous, now-defunct medical institute. Established around the 9th century,

Salerno

500 m
0.25 miles

Via Dalmazia

Via Torrione

Lungomare Guglielmo Marconi

A3 (Southbound);
Paestum (36km)

Piazza
Vittorio
Veneto

Via Torrione

4

Via Nizza

SITA Sud
Buses to
Naples

Corso Garibaldi

Piazza
Giuseppe
Mazzini

CSTP

Piazza della
Concordia

Via Volpe

Corso Vittorio Emanuele II

Via Diaz

Porto Turistico
Ferry & Hydrofoil
Terminal

Piazza
XXIV
Maggio

Via Cilento

Lungomare Trieste

Via San Benedetto

Tourist
Infopoint

Via Vella

Piazza Alfano

Via S Michele

6

3

Via Iannelli

1 Duomo

Piazza
Matteotti

Via Roma

Via Mercanti

2

8

Tourist
Office

Via del Canali

5

7

Vico della
Neve

Piazza
Sedile del
Campo

Gulf of Salerno
(Golfo di Salerno)

Piazza
Amendola

Amalfi (26km);
Positano (42km)

Porto Commerciale
Ferry & Hydrofoil
Terminal

Molo
Manfredi

Salerno

the school was the most important centre of medical knowledge in medieval Europe, reaching the height of its prestige in the 11th century. It was closed in the early 19th century.

Museo Pinacoteca Provinciale   MUSEUM
(☏089 258 30 73; Via Mercanti 63; ⊙9am-7.45pm Tue-Sun) FREE Art enthusiasts should seek out the Museo Pinacoteca Provinciale, located deep in the heart of the historic quarter. Spread throughout six galleries, this museum houses an interesting art collection dating from the Renaissance right up to the first half of the 20th century.

Among the works are some fine canvases by local boy Andrea Sabatini da Salerno, who was notably influenced by Leonardo da Vinci.

Castello di Arechi   CASTLE
(☏089 296 40 15; www.ilcastellodiarechi.it; Via Benedetto Croce; adult/reduced €3/1.50; ⊙9am-7pm Tue-Sat, to 6.30pm Sun summer, to 5pm Tue-Sun winter) Bus 19 from Piazza XXIV Maggio heads to Salerno's most famous landmark, the forbidding Castello di Arechi, dramatically positioned 263m above the city. Originally a Byzantine fort, it was built by the Lombard duke of Benevento, Arechi II, in the 8th century and subsequently modified by the Normans and Aragonese, most recently in the 16th century. The views of the Gulf of Salerno and Salerno's rooftops are spectacular; you can also visit a permanent collection of ceramics, arms and coins.

⌂ Sleeping

Ostello Ave Gratia Plena   HOSTEL **€**
(☏089 23 47 76; www.ostellodisalerno.it; Via dei Canali; dm/s/d €16/45/52; @🛜) Housed in a

16th-century convent, Salerno's HI hostel is right in the heart of the *centro storico*. Inside there's a charming central courtyard and a range of bright rooms, from dorms to doubles with private bathroom. The 2am curfew is only for the dorms. The hostel offers bike rental (€2 for the first hour, then €1 per subsequent hour, or €10 per day).

Hotel Plaza   HOTEL **€**
(☏089 22 44 77; www.plazasalerno.it; Piazza Vittorio Veneto 42; s/d €65/100; ❊@🛜) A two-minute chug from the train station, the Plaza is convenient, comfortable and fairly charmless (especially the dowdy public areas), but it's not an unfriendly place and the good-sized rooms, with their brown carpet and gleaming bathrooms, are actually pretty good value for money. Those around the back have terraces overlooking the city and, beyond, the mountains.

✖ Eating

Head to Via Roma and Via Mercanti in the lively medieval centre, where you'll find everything from traditional, family-run trattorias and gelaterie to wine bars, pubs and restaurants.

Cicirinella   CAMPANIAN **€€**
(☏089 22 65 61; Via Genovesi 28; meals €25; ⊙8pm-midnight daily, plus 1-3pm Sat & Sun) Where weary horses once snoozed, gastronomes now toast, savour and swoon at what is one of Salerno's top eating spots. A handsome combo of white linen, stone walls, and bottled-lined shelves, its open kitchen has a soft spot for seasonal produce and twists on traditional recipes. Highlights include a beautifully presented *antipasto misto* and a sublimely buttery entrecôte. Book ahead Friday and Saturday.

La Cucina di Edoardo   CAMPANIAN **€€**
(☏089 296 26 67; Vico della Neve 14; meals €30; ⊙12.30-3pm & 7.30-11pm) Snugly tucked away in a *centro storico* side street, Edoardo's Kitchen is one of those scrumptious finds any local *buongustaio* (foodie) will direct you to. The focus is on regional dishes with subtle creative touches – think pistachio-crumbed tuna escalope on a bed of artichoke. Leave room for the *tortino al cioccolato* (chocolate tartlet) and book ahead on weekends.

Pasticceria Pantaleone   PASTRIES & CAKES **€**
(Via Mercanti 75; pastries from €1.50; ⊙8am-2pm & 4.30-8.30pm, morning only Tue & Sun) Where

better to commit dietary sins than in a deconsecrated church? It's now home to Salerno's finest pastry shop, best known for inventing the *scazzetta*, a pastry of *pan di spagna* sponge, fresh berries and Chantilly cream, soaked in Strega liqueur and finished with a strawberry glacé. Wash down the guilt with a glass of the house liqueur, Elisir, made with aromatic herbs and orange.

ℹ Information

Post office (Corso Garibaldi 203)

Tourist office (☑ 089 23 14 32; Lungomare Trieste 7; ☺ 9am-1pm & 3-7pm Mon-Sat) Main tourist office by the seafront.

Tourist infopoint (☑ 089 662 951; Corso Vittorio Emanuele II 193; ☺ 9am-1pm & 5-8pm Mon-Fri, 9am-1pm Sat) Inside the Galleria Capitol Cinema shopping centre, has brochures, bus and ferry timetables and accommodation information.

ℹ Getting There & Away

BOAT

Between April and October there are daily sailings to/from Salerno.

Alicost (p686) operates one daily service to Amalfi (€7), Positano (€11) and Capri (€20.70).

Linee Marittime Partenopee (p690) runs one daily hydrofoil and three daily ferries to Capri (€23/22.20).

TraVelMar (p693) runs six daily ferries to Amalfi (€8) and Positano (€12).

Departures are from the Porto Turistico, 200m down the pier from Piazza della Concordia. You can buy tickets from the booths by the embarkation point.

Departures for Capri leave from Molo Manfredi at the Porto Commerciale.

BUS

SITA Sud (p685) buses for Amalfi (€2.50, 1¼ hours, at least hourly) depart from **Piazza Vittorio Veneto**, beside the train station, stopping en route at Vietri sul Mare, Cetara, Maiori and Minori. Tickets are available inside the train station.

CSTP (☑ 089 48 70 01; www.cstp.it) bus 50 runs from Piazza Vittorio Veneto to Pompeii (€2.20, 70 minutes, 17 daily). For Paestum (€3.40, one hour, hourly) take bus 34 from Piazza della Concordia.

CAR & MOTORCYCLE

Salerno is on the A3 between Naples and Reggio di Calabria, which is toll-free from Salerno southwards.

TRAIN

Salerno is a major stop on southbound routes to Calabria and the Ionian and Adriatic coasts. From the station in Piazza Vittorio Veneto there are regular trains to Naples (IC; €8.50, 35 minutes), Rome (Frecciarossa; €39, two hours) and Reggio di Calabria (IC; €41, 4½ hours).

ℹ Getting Around

Walking is the most sensible option; from the train station it's a 1.2km walk along Corso Vittorio Emanuele II to the historic centre.

If you want to hire a car there's a **Europcar** (☑ 089 258 07 75; www.europcar.com; Via Clemente Mauro 18) agency not far from the train station.

Paestum

Paestum's Unesco-listed temples are among the best-preserved monuments of Magna Graecia, the Greek colony that once covered much of southern Italy. An easy day trip from Salerno or Agropoli, they are one of the region's most iconic sights and absolutely unmissable.

Paestum, or Poseidonia as the city was originally called (in honour of Poseidon, the Greek god of the sea), was founded in the 6th century BC by Greek settlers and fell under Roman control in 273 BC. It became an important trading port and remained so until the fall of the Roman Empire, when periodic outbreaks of malaria and savage Saracen raids led its weakened citizens to abandon the town.

Its temples were rediscovered in the late 18th century by road builders – who proceeded to plough their way right through the ruins.

The **tourist office** (☑ 0828 81 10 16; www.infopaestum.it; Via Magna Grecia 887, Paestum; ☺ 9am-1pm & 3-5pm Mon-Sun) has information on the area and the Costiera Cilentana.

◉ Sights

Ruins of Paestum   RUIN

(☑ 0828 72 26 54; adult/reduced, incl museum €10/5; ☺ 8.45am-2hrs before sunset) Tickets to the ruins are sold at the main entry point, near the tourist office, or from the museum, where you can also hire an audio guide (€5).

The first temple you encounter from the main entrance is the 6th-century-BC **Tempio di Cerere** (Temple of Ceres). Originally dedicated to Athena, it served as a Christian church in medieval times.

As you head south, you can pick out the basic outline of the large rectangular forum, the heart of the ancient city. Among the partially standing buildings are the vast domestic housing area and, further south, the amphitheatre; both provide evocative glimpses of daily life here in Roman times.

The **Tempio di Nettuno** (Temple of Neptune), dating from about 450 BC, is the largest and best preserved of the three temples at Paestum; only parts of its inside walls and roof are missing. Almost next door, the so-called **basilica** (in fact, a temple to the goddess Hera) is Paestum's oldest surviving monument. Dating from the middle of the 6th century BC, it's a magnificent sight, with nine columns across and 18 along the sides. Ask someone to take your photo next to a column here, it's a good way to appreciate the scale.

Just east of the site, the **museum** (☏ 0828 81 10 23; ☺ 8.30am-7.30pm, last entry 6.45pm, closed 1st & 3rd Mon of month) houses a collection of fascinating, if weathered, *metopes* (bas-relief friezes). This collection includes 33 of the original 36 *metopes* from the **Tempio di Argiva Hera** (Temple of Argive Hera), situated 9km north of Paestum, of which virtually nothing else remains. The star exhibit is the 5th-century-BC fresco *Tomba del Truffatore* (Tomb of the Diver), thought to represent the passage from life to death with its depiction of a diver in midair (don't try this at home).

🛏 Sleeping & Eating

★ **Casale Giancesare** B&B €
(☏ 333 1897737, 0828 72 80 61; www.casale-giancesare.it; Via Giancesare 8; s €45-90, d €65-120, apt per wk €600-1300; [P][❄][@][📶][⛱]) A 19th-century former farmhouse, this chic, charming, stone-clad B&B is run by the Voza family, who will happily ply you with their homemade wine, *limoncello* and fabulous food. Located 2.5km from Paestum (complimentary pick-up available from Paestum train station), the place is surrounded by vineyards and olive and mulberry trees. There are stunning views, especially from the swimming pool.

Beware of road signs advertising another bed and breakfast, called Residenza Giancesare.

Nonna Scepa CAMPANIAN €€
(☏ 0828 85 10 64; Via Laura 53; meals €35; ☺ noon-3pm & 7.30-11pm, closed Thu winter; [♿]) There are various restaurants at the site;

however, most serve mediocre food at inflated prices. Instead, seek out the superbly prepared, robust dishes at Nonna Scepa, a family-friendly restaurant that's rapidly gaining a reputation throughout the region for excellence. Dishes are firmly seasonal and, during the summer, concentrate on fresh seafood like the refreshingly simple grilled fish with lemon.

Other popular choices include risotto with zucchini and artichokes, and spaghetti with lobster.

❶ Getting There & Away

The best way to get to Paestum by public transport is to take **CSTP** (☏ 089 48 70 01; www.cstp.it) bus 34 from Piazza della Concordia in Salerno (€3.40, one hour, hourly), or, if approaching from the south, the same bus from Agropoli (€1.30, 15 minutes, hourly).

If you're driving you could take the A3 from Salerno and exit for the SS18 at Battipaglia. Better, and altogether more pleasant, is the Litoranea, the minor road that hugs the coast. From the A3 take the earlier exit for Pontecagnano and follow the signs for Agropoli and Paestum.

COSTIERA CILENTANA

Southeast of the Gulf of Salerno, the coastal plains begin to give way to wilder, jagged cliffs and unspoilt scenery, a taste of what lies further on in the stark hills of Basilicata and the wooded peaks of Calabria. Inland, dark mountains loom over the remote highlands of the Parco Nazionale del Cilento e Vallo di Diano, one of Campania's best-kept secrets.

Several destinations on the Cilento coast are served by the main rail route from Naples to Reggio di Calabria. Check **Trenitalia** (www.trenitalia.it) for fares and times.

By car take the SS18, which connects Agropoli with Velia via the inland route, or the SS267, which hugs the coast.

Agropoli
POP 20,600

The main town on the southern stretch of the coast, Agropoli makes a good base for Paestum and the beaches to the northwest. Popular with holidaying Italians, it's an otherwise tranquil place with a ramshackle medieval core on a promontory overlooking the sea.

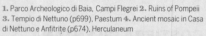

1. Parco Archeologico di Baia, Campi Flegrei 2. Ruins of Pompeii
3. Tempio di Nettuno (p699), Paestum 4. Ancient mosaic in Casa
di Nettuno e Anfitrite (p674), Herculaneum

NEIL SETCHFIELD / GETTY IMAGES ©

Historical Riches

Few Italian regions can match Campania's historical legacy. Colonised by the ancient Greeks and loved by the Romans, it's a sun-drenched repository of A-list antiquities, from World Heritage wonders to lesser-known archaeological gems.

Paestum

Great Greek temples never go out of vogue and those at Paestum (p698) are among the greatest outside Greece itself. With the oldest structures stretching back to the 6th century BC, this place makes Rome's Colosseum feel positively modern.

Herculaneum

A bite-sized Pompeii, Herculaneum (p673) is even better preserved than its nearby rival. This is the place to delve into the details, from once-upon-a-time shop advertisements and furniture, to quirky mosaics and even an ancient security device.

Pompeii

Short of stepping into the Tardis, Pompeii (p676) is your best bet for a little time travel. Snap-locked in ash for centuries, its excavated streetscapes offer a tangible, 3D encounter with the ancients and their daily lives.

Subterranean Naples

Eerie aqueducts, mysterious burial crypts and ancient streetscapes: beneath Naples' hyperactive streets lies a wonderland of Graeco-Roman ruins. For a taste, head below the Complesso Monumentale di San Lorenzo Maggiore (p645) or follow the leader on a Napoli Sotterranea (p654) tour.

Campi Flegrei

The Phlegraean Fields simmer with ancient clues. Roam where emperors bathed at the Parco Archeologico di Baia (p651), sneak into a Roman engineering marvel at the Piscina Mirabilis, or spare a thought for doomed martyrs at the Anfiteatro Flavio.

The tourist office (📞0974 82 74 14; Piazza della Repubblica 3; ⊙10am-1pm & 4-8pm Mon-Sun) can provide you with a city map.

🛏 Sleeping & Eating

Anna
B&B, APARTMENTS €

(📞0974 82 37 63; www.bbanna.it; Via S Marco 28-30, Agropoli; s €35-50, d €50-120; P☀) Across from Agropoli's sweeping sandy beach, Anna offers bright, spacious rooms with smart striped fabrics and balconies; request a sea view. Sunbeds and bicycles come free, and Anna's downstairs restaurant (pizzas from €3, meals €22) serves gluten-free grub. The friendly owners also offer two simple four-person apartments (€80 to €150) 300m away, both with modern kitchenette and small patio.

Ostello La Lanterna
HOSTEL €

(📞0974 83 83 64; lanterna@cilento.it; Via Lanterna 8; dm €13-16, s €17-20, d €32-45, tr €45-54; ⊙mid-Mar–Oct) Agropoli's friendly Ostello La Lanterna has dorms, doubles and four-bed family rooms, as well as a garden and optional evening meals (€10). The beach is a two-minute walk away.

Il Vecchio Saracino
SEAFOOD €€

(📞0974 82 64 15; www.vecchiosaracino.it; Via Granatelle 18, Agropoli; meals €25; ⊙8.30pm-midnight daily, also 1-4pm Sun; 📶) Raise your fork to good-value, whisker-licking seafood at this local institution. Dishes sing with flavour, whether it's the beautifully textured shrimp and artichoke gratin with homemade artichoke conserve, the *paccheri* (large, tube-shaped pasta) with clams and monkfish, or the soul-coaxing Cilento fish soup. Many ingredients and products are proudly homemade, from the salted anchovies to a string of smooth liqueurs.

Parco Nazionale del Cilento e Vallo di Diano

Stretching from the coast up to Campania's highest peak, Monte Cervati (1900m), and beyond to the regional border with Basilicata, the Parco Nazionale del Cilento e Vallo di Diano is Italy's second-largest national park. A little-explored area of barren heights and empty valleys, it's the perfect antidote to the holiday mayhem on the coast.

For further information stop by the **tourist office** (p698) in Paestum.

👁 Sights & Activities

★ Grotte di Castelcivita
CAVE

(📞0828 77 23 97; www.grottedicastelcivita.com; Piazzale N Zonzi, Castelcivita; adult/reduced €10/8; ⊙standard tours 10.30am, noon, 1.30pm, 3pm Mar-Oct, also 4.30pm & 6pm Apr-Sep, 4hr tours 10am Sat Jun-Oct; P♿) Located about 20km northeast of Paestum, the Grotte di Castelcivita complex is where Spartacus is said to have taken refuge following his slave rebellion in 71 BC. The standard one-hour tour winds through a route surrounded by extraordinary stalagmites and stalactites, and a mesmerising play of colours, caused by algae, calcium and iron tinting the naturally sculpted rock shapes.

The longer four-hour tours (€25) take place between June and October, when the water deep within the cave complex has dried up. Hard hats and a certain level of fitness and mobility are required. Visits should be booked a day in advance.

To get here by car take the SS18 from Paestum towards Salerno and follow the signs.

Grotte dell'Angelo
CAVE

(📞0975 39 70 37; www.grottedellangelo.sa.it; Pertosa; guided visits adult/reduced €13/10; ⊙9am-7pm Apr & May, 10am-7pm Jun-Aug, 10am-6pm Sep, reduced hours rest of year; P♿) At the park's eastern edge, this cave system is younger than the Grotta di Castelcivita, dating back a mere 35 million years to the Neolithic period. Used by the Greeks and Romans as places of worship, the caves burrow through the mountains for 2500m, with long underground passages and lofty grottoes filled with a mouthful of stalagmites and stalactites.

By car, take the A3 southbound from Salerno, exit at Petina and follow the SS19 for 9km.

Certosa di San Lorenzo
MONASTERY

(📞0975 77 74 45; Padula; adult/reduced €4/2; ⊙9am-7pm Wed-Mon) One of southern Europe's largest monasteries, the Certosa di San Lorenzo covers 250,000 sq metres. Begun in the 14th century and modified over time, it was abandoned in the 19th century, then suffered further degradation as a children's holiday home and later a concentration camp. Numerologists can swoon at the following: 320 rooms and halls, 2500m of corridors, galleries and hallways, 300 columns, 500 doors, 550 windows, 13 courtyards, 100 fireplaces, 52 stairways and 41 fountains – it's *huge*.

As you will unlikely have time to see everything here, be sure to visit the highlights, including the vast central courtyard, the magnificent wood-panelled library, sumptuously frescoed chapels and the kitchen with its grandiose fireplace, vibrant maiolica tiles and famous tale: apparently this is where the legendary 1000-egg omelette was made in 1534 for Charles V. Unfortunately, the historic frying pan is not on view – just how big was it, one wonders?

Within the monastery you can also peruse the modest collection of ancient artefacts at the **Museo Archeologico Provinciale della Lucania Occidentale** (☑0975 7 71 17; ☉8am-1.15pm & 2-3pm Tue-Sat, 9am-1pm Sun) `FREE`.

For guided hiking opportunities, contact **Gruppo Escursionistico Trekking** (☑0975 7 25 86; www.getvallodidiano.it; Via Provinciale 29, Silla di Sassano) or **Associazione Trekking Cilento** (☑0974 84 33 45; www.trekkingcilento.it; Via Cannetiello 6, Agropoli).

🛏 Sleeping & Eating

★ **Agriturismo i Moresani**   AGRITURISMO €
(☑0974 90 20 86; www.imoresani.com; Località Moresani; s €45-55, d €90-110; ☉Mar-Oct; ❊ 🐾 ☲)
Surrounded by rolling hills splashed with vines, pastures and olive trees, this family-run farm puts its homemade *caprino* goat's cheese, wine, olive oil and preserves to good use at its on-site restaurant. Sleep off the feast in one of the warm, rustic rooms on offer, or sign up for the regular horse-riding, cooking and painting courses on offer.

Fattoria Alvaneta   CAMPANIAN €
(☑0975 7 71 39; www.fattoriaalvaneta.it; Contrada Pantagnoni, Padula; meals €20; ☉1pm-3pm & 7.30-10.30pm Wed-Mon, also open Tue Aug, closed first week Jul) Farm-to-table feasting awaits at this wonderful hillside *agriturismo*, complete with sweeping views of the Vallo di Diano. Earthy flavours dominate the menu, the farm's home-reared boar, veal and pork shining through in options like *pasta fresca* (fresh egg pasta) with *cinghiale* (boar) and porcini mushrooms.

The creative *antipasto misto* delivers treats like anchovy-laced *zeppole* (fried pizza dough) or *parmigiana di scarola* (escarole parmigiana), a clever adaptation of the classic aubergine version. Young, affable owner Francesco is passionate about the Cilento, and offers on-site accommodation (single/double/triple €35/50/65) and organised tours of the area. If driving from the Certosa, head northeast along Viale Certosa (towards the town centre), turn right into Strada Provinciale 180 and follow the signs for Fattoria Alvaneta.

❶ Getting There & Away

To get the best out of the park and the surrounding region, you will need a car. There is a car-hire company (p698) in Salerno.

Public transport in the area is lacking and frustratingly inconvenient. For a reliable taxi service in the Agropoli area, call **Gennaro Di Giovanni** (☑338 8743105) or **Raffaello Perez** (☑333 1324422).

NAPLES & CAMPANIA PARCO NAZIONALE DEL CILENTO E VALLO DI DIANO

Puglia, Basilicata & Calabria

Why Go?

Southern Italy is the land of the *mezzogiorno* – the midday sun – which sums up the Mediterranean climate and the languid pace of life. From the heel to the toe of Italy's boot, the landscape reflects the individuality of its people. Basilicata is a crush of mountains and rolling hills with a dazzling stretch of coastline. Calabria is Italy's wildest area with fine beaches and a mountainous landscape with peaks frequently crowned by ruined castles. Puglia is the sophisticate of the south with charming seaside villages along its 800km of coastline, lush flat farmlands, thick forests and olive groves.

The south's violent history of successive invasions and economic hardship has forged a fiercely proud people and influenced its distinctive culture and cuisine. A hotter, edgier place than the urbane north of Italy, this is an area that still feels like it has secret places to explore, although you will need your own wheels (and some Italian) if you plan to seriously sidestep from the beaten track.

Best Places to Eat

➜ Cucina Casareccia (p730)
➜ La Locanda di Federico (p709)
➜ Il Frantoio (p722)
➜ Taverna Al Cantinone (p716)

Best Places to Stay

➜ Sotto le Cummerse (p723)
➜ Palazzo Rollo (p729)
➜ Locanda delle Donne Monache (p749)
➜ Le Monacelle (p745)
➜ Donnaciccina (p763)

When to Go
Bari

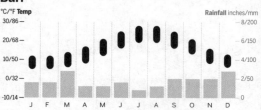

Apr–Jun Spring wildflowers are blooming: a perfect time for hiking in the mountains.

Jul & Aug Summer is beach weather and the best party time for festivals and events.

Sep & Oct No crowds, mild weather and wild mushrooms galore.

PUGLIA

Puglia is comprised of sun-bleached landscapes, silver olive groves, picturesque seascapes, and memorable hilltop and coastal towns. It is a lush, largely flat farming region, skirted by a long coast that alternates between glittering limestone precipices and long sandy beaches. The heel of Italy juts into the Adriatic and Ionian Seas and the waters of both are stunningly beautiful, veering between translucent emerald green and dusky powder blue. Its extensive coastline bears the marks of many conquering invaders: the Normans, the Spanish, the Turks, the Swabians and the Greeks. Yet, despite its diverse influences, Puglia has its own distinct and authentic identity.

In a land where the cuisine is all-important, Puglia's *cucina povera* (peasant cooking) is legendary. Olive oil, grapes, tomatoes, eggplants, artichokes, peppers, salami, mushrooms, olives and fresh seafood strain its table. Although boasting some of Italy's best food and wines, in some places it's rare to hear a foreign voice. But in July and August Puglia becomes a huge party, with *sagre* (festivals, usually involving food), concerts and events, and thousands of Italian tourists heading down here for their annual break.

History

At times Puglia feels and looks Greek – and for good reason. This tangible legacy dates from when the Greeks founded a string of settlements along the Ionian coast in the 8th century BC. A form of Greek dialect (Griko) is still spoken in some towns southeast of Lecce. Historically, the major city was Taras (Taranto), settled by Spartan exiles who dominated until they were defeated by the Romans in 272 BC.

The long coastline made the region vulnerable to conquest. The Normans left their fine Romanesque churches, the Swabians their fortifications and the Spanish their flamboyant baroque buildings. No one, however, knows exactly the origins of the extraordinary 16th-century conical-roofed stone houses, the *trulli,* unique to Puglia.

Apart from invaders and pirates, malaria was long the greatest scourge of the south, forcing many towns to build away from the coast and into the hills. After Mussolini's seizure of power in 1922, the south became the frontline in his 'Battle for Wheat'. This initiative was aimed at making Italy self-sufficient when it came to food, following the sanctions imposed on the country after its conquest of Ethiopia. Puglia is now covered in wheat fields, olive groves and fruit arbours.

PUGLIA, BASILICATA & CALABRIA HISTORY

PUGLIA ON YOUR PLATE

Puglia is home to Italy's most uncorrupted, brawniest, least known vernacular cuisine. It has evolved from *cucina povera* – literally 'cooking of the poor' or peasant cooking: think of pasta made without eggs and dishes prepared with wild greens gathered from the fields.

Most of Italy's fish is caught off the Puglian coast, 80% of Europe's pasta is produced here and 80% of Italy's olive oil originates in Puglia and Calabria. Tomatoes, broccoli, chicory, fennel, figs, melons, cherries and grapes are all plentiful in season and taste better than anywhere else. Almonds, grown near Ruvo di Puglia, are packed into many traditional cakes and pastries, which used to be eaten only by the privileged.

Like their Greek forebears, the Puglians eat *agnello* (lamb) and *capretto* (kid). *Cavallo* (horse) has only recently galloped to the table while *trippa* (tripe) is another mainstay. Meat is usually roasted or grilled with aromatic herbs or served in tomato-based sauces.

Raw fish (such as anchovies or baby squid) are marinated in olive oil and lemon juice. *Cozze* (mussels) are prepared in multitudinous ways, with garlic and breadcrumbs, or as *riso cozze patata*, baked with rice and potatoes – every area has its variations on this dish.

Bread and pasta are close to the Puglian heart, with per-capita consumption at least double that of the USA. You'll find *orecchiette* (small ear-shaped pasta, often accompanied by a small rod-shaped variety, called *strascinati* or *cavatelli*), served with broccoli or *ragù* (meat sauce), generally topped by the pungent local cheese *ricotta forte*.

Previously known for quantity rather than quality, Puglian wines are now developing apace. The best are produced in Salento (the Salice Salentino is one of the finest reds), in the *trulli* area around Locorotondo (famous for its white wine), around Cisternino (home of the fashionable heavy red Primitivo) and in the plains around Foggia and Lucera.

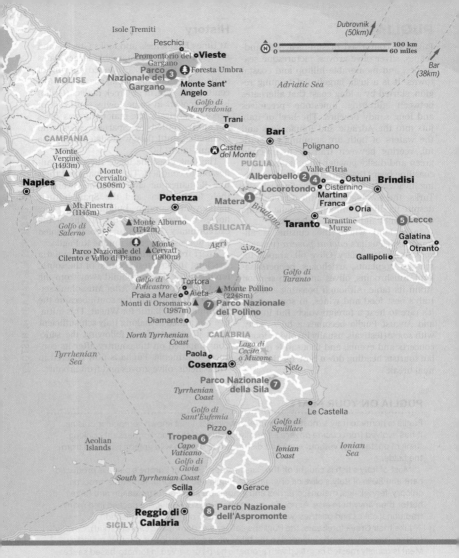

Puglia, Basilicata & Calabria Highlights

① Marvelling at otherworldly *sassi* (cave dwellings) and ancient history of **Matera** (p740).

② Dipping into the Disney-style scenario of conical *trulli* dwellings in **Alberobello** (p721).

③ Hiking in shady forests and swimming in aqua-blue seas in the **Parco Nazionale del Gargano** (p715).

④ Strolling through the old centre of **Locorotondo** (p723), one of Puglia's prettiest towns.

⑤ Wondering at ornate baroque facades in **Lecce** (p726).

⑥ Discovering Calabria's picturesque seaside at **Tropea** (p763).

⑦ Vanishing into the vast hills of the **Parco Nazionale della Sila** (p753) or the **Parco Nazionale del Pollino** (p755).

⑧ Driving or trekking into the wilds of the mysterious **Parco Nazionale dell'Aspromonte** (p759).

Bari

POP 320,200

Once regarded as the Bronx of southern Italy, Bari's reputation has gradually improved and the city, Puglia's capital and one of the south's most prosperous, deserves more than a cursory glance. Spruced up and rejuvenated, Bari Vecchia, the historic old town, is an interesting and atmospheric warren of streets. In the evenings the piazzas buzz with trendy restaurants and bars, but there are still parts of the old town that carry a gritty undertone.

ⓘ Dangers & Annoyances

Petty crime can be a problem, so take all of the usual precautions: don't leave anything in your car; don't display money or valuables; and watch out for bag-snatchers on scooters. Be careful in Bari Vecchia's dark streets at night.

⊙ Sights

Most sights are in or near atmospheric Bari Vecchia, a medieval labyrinth of tight alleyways and graceful piazzas. It fills a small peninsula between the new port to the west and the old port to the southeast, cramming in 40 churches and more than 120 shrines.

Castello Svevo   CASTLE

(Swabian Castle; ☑ 083 184 00 09; Piazza Federico II di Svevia; admission adult/reduced €2/1; ⊙ 8.30am-7.30pm Thu-Tue) The Normans originally built over the ruins of a Roman fort, then Frederick II built over the Norman castle, incorporating it into his design – the two towers of the Norman structure still stand. The bastions, with corner towers overhanging the moat, were added in the 16th century during Spanish rule, when the castle was a magnificent residence.

Basilica di San Nicola   BASILICA

(www.basilicasannicola.it; Piazza San Nicola; ⊙ 7am-1pm & 4-7pm Mon-Sat, 7am-1pm & 4-9pm Sun) One of the south's first Norman churches, the basilica is a splendid example of Puglian-Romanesque style, built to house the relics of St Nicholas (better known as Father Christmas), which were stolen from Turkey in 1087 by local fishing folk. His remains are said to emanate a miraculous manna liquid with special powers. For this reason – and because he is also the patron saint of prisoners and children – the basilica remains an important place of pilgrimage. The interior is huge and simple with a decorative 17th-century wood-

en ceiling. The magnificent 13th-century ciborium over the altar is Puglia's oldest. The shrine in the crypt, lit by hanging lamps, is beautiful.

Cathedral   CATHEDRAL

(Piazza dell'Odegitria; ⊙ 8am-12.30pm & 4-7.30pm Mon-Fri, 8am-12.30pm & 5-8.30pm Sat & Sun) Built over the original Byzantine church, the 11th-century Romanesque cathedral retains its basilica plan – the plain walls punctuated with deep arcades – and the eastern window is a tangle of plant and animal motifs. Recent **excavations** (€1; ⊙ 12.30-4pm Sun-Wed, Apr-Oct) have revealed an ancient Christian basilica with a substantial floor mosaic featuring octopus, fish and plant motifs.

Piazza Mercantile   PIAZZA

This beautiful piazza is fronted by the Sedile, the headquarters of Bari's Council of Nobles. In the square's northeast corner is the **Colonna della Giustizia** (Column of Justice; Piazza Mercantile), where debtors were once tied and whipped.

⁂ Festivals

Festa di San Nicola   RELIGIOUS

(⊙ 7-9 May) The Festival of St Nicholas is Bari's biggest annual shindig, celebrating the 11th-century arrival of St Nicholas' relics from Turkey. On the first evening a procession leaves Castello Svevo for the Basilica di San Nicola. The next day there's a deafening fly-past and a fleet of boats carries the statue of St Nicholas along the coast. The evening – and the next – ends with a massive fireworks

---

TOP FIVE HISTORIC CENTRES IN PUGLIA

Locorotondo A blinding white backdrop decked with blood-red geraniums (p723).

Ostuni Narrow streets circle ever upwards to a stunning 15th-century cathedral (p725).

Vieste Whitewashed buildings, intriguing lanes and the sea lapping round the edges (p715).

Martina Franca A wonderfully picturesque townscape of baroque and rococo buildings (p724).

Lecce Fanciful mansions and churches cut from glowing golden sandstone (p726).

Puglia

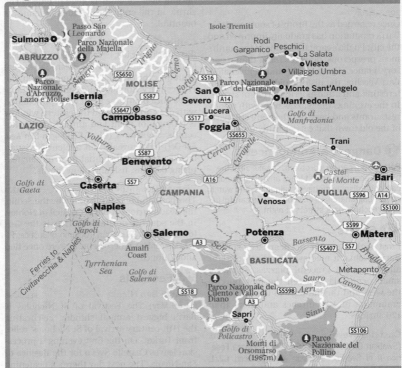

display. It's a jolly, crowded family affair, attended by many Russian visitors who come to view the relics.

🛏 Sleeping

Most hotel accommodation here tends to be bland and overpriced, aimed at business clientele: B&Bs are generally a better option.

Santa Maria del Buon Consiglio B&B $
(📞 0388 1063436; www.santamariadelbuonconsiglio.com; Via Forno Santa Scolastica 1-3; s €35-70, d €60-100, tr €85-90; ❄ 🛜) A graciously hosted B&B in the heart of old Bari near the port. Rooms have rough-cast stone walls and four-poster beds with drapes.

B&B Casa Pimpolini B&B $
(📞 080 521 99 38; www.casapimpolini.com; Via Calefati 249; s €45-60, d €70-80; ❄ @) This lovely B&B in the new town is within easy walking distance to shops, restaurants and Bari Vecchia. The rooms are warm and welcoming, and the homemade breakfast is a treat. Great value.

Villa Romanazzi Carducci HOTEL $$$
(📞 080 542 74 00; www.villaromanazzi.com; Via Capruzzi 326; d €79; 🛜) The one hotel in Bari daring to show some flare, the Villa Romanazzi is housed in the pastel pink, 19th-century Villa Rachele. Rooms are a mixture of old and new, although the decor in the villa rooms is more characterful. Add to this an enormous fitness centre, pool and huge verdant park and this is probably Bari's best hotel.

🍴 Eating & Drinking

⭐ **Terranima** PUGLIAN $
(📞 080 521 97 25; www.terranima.com; Via Putignani 215; meals €8-15; ⏰ 7-11pm Mon-Sat, lunch Sun) Peep through the lace curtains into the cool interior of this rustic trattoria where worn flagstone floors and period furnishings

0 ——— 100 km
0 ——— 60 miles

Adriatic Sea

Polignano a
SS16 Mare

Grotte di Castellana
Castellana Grotte
Valle d'Itria
Alberobello Cisternino SS379
Martina Ostuni
Riserva Franca Locorotondo Brindisi
Naturale
Regionale Orientata
Oria SS7
Taranto Lecce
Tarantine Murge

Reserva Galatina Otranto
Marina
Porto Cesareo
Golfo di Gallipoli
Taranto Santa
Maria di
Ionian Leuca
Sea

breakfast, lunch and *aperitivi* (predinner drinks with snacks).

★ **La Locanda di Federico** PUGLIAN $$
(☑080 522 77 05; www.lalocandadifederico.com; Piazza Mercantile 63-64; meals €30; ☺lunch & dinner) With domed ceilings, archways and medieval-style artwork on the walls, this restaurant oozes atmosphere. The menu is typical Puglian, the food delicious and the price reasonable. *Orecchiette con le cime di rape* ('little ears' pasta with turnip tops) is highly recommended.

Barcollo BAR
(☑080 521 38 89; Piazza Mercantile 69/70; cocktails €7; ☺8am-3am) Sit outside on the twinkling square sipping a cocktail and nibbling work-of-art hors d'oeuvres. Incongruously, you'll be gazing at the 'column of justice', to which debtors were once tied and lashed.

🛍 Shopping

Designer shops and the main Italian chains line Via Sparano da Bari, while delis and gourmet food shops are located throughout the city.

Il Salumaio FOOD
(☑080 521 93 45; www.ilsalumaio.it; Via Piccinni 168; ☺8.30am-2pm & 5.30-9.30pm Mon-Sat) Breathe in the delicious scents of fine regional produce at this venerable delicatessen.

Enoteca Vinarius de Pasquale WINE
(☑080 521 31 92; Via Marchese di Montrone 87; ☺8am-2pm & 4-8.30pm Mon-Sat) Stock up on Puglian wines such as Primitivo di Manduria at this gorgeous old shop, founded in 1911.

ℹ Information

From Piazza Aldo Moro, in front of the main train station, streets heading north will take you to Corso Vittorio Emanuele II, which separates the old and new parts of the city.

CTS (☑080 521 88 73; Via Garruba 65-67) Good for student travel and discount flights.
Hospital (☑080 559 11 11; Piazza Cesare)
Morfimare Travel Agency (☑080 578 98 26, booking office 080 578 98 11; www.morfimare. it; Corso de Tullio 36-40) Ferry bookings.
Police Station (☑080 529 11 11; Via Murat 4)
Post Office (Piazza Umberto I 33/8)
Tourist Office (☑080 990 93 41; www. viaggiareinpuglia.it; 1st fl, Piazza Moro 33a; ☺8.30am-1pm & 3-6pm Mon-Fri, 10am-1pm Sat) There is also an information kiosk (☺9am-

make you feel like you're dining in someone's front room. The menu features earthy offerings like *capocollo* (thin slices of lard), potatoes and *cardoncelli* mushrooms, and *sporcamusi* (lemon custard in filo pastry).

Paglionico Vini e Cucina OSTERIA $
(☑338 212 03 91; Strada Vallisa 23; meals €10; ☺lunch & dinner) Run by the same family for more than a century, this boisterous *osteria* (casual eatery) chalks up its daily specials of well-prepared and filling Puglian dishes. Grab a seat in the brick-flanked tunnel of a dining room and wait (and wait) to be served by the impressively indefatigable waiter.

Caffè Borghese CAFE $
(☑080 524 21 56; Corso Vittorio Emanuele II 22; dishes €6-10; ☺8am-2am Tue-Sun) You'll experience genuine hospitality and friendly service in this small cafe. Its understated charm and simple dishes will have you returning for

Bari

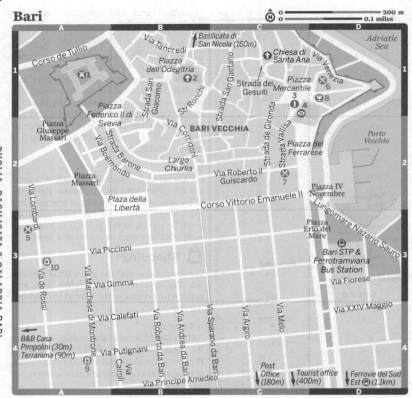

7pm May-Sep) in front of the train station in Piazza Aldo Moro.

ⓘ Getting There & Away

AIR

Bari's Palese **airport** (www.aeroportidipuglia.it) is served by a host of international and budget airlines, including British Airways, Alitalia and Ryanair.

Pugliairbus (http://pugliairbus.aeroportidipuglia.it) connects the airports of Bari, Brindisi, Taranto and Foggia. It also has a service from Bari airport to Matera (€5, 1¼ hours, three daily), and to Vieste (€20, 3½ hours, four daily May to September).

BOAT

Ferries run from Bari to Albania, Croatia, Greece and Montenegro. All boat companies have offices at the ferry terminal, accessible on bus 20 from the main train station. Fares vary considerably among companies and it's easier to book with a travel agent such as Morfimare (p709).

The main companies and their routes are as follows:

Jadrolinija (www.jadrolinija.hr)

Montenegro Lines (☑382 3031 1164; www.montenegrolines.net) To Bar in Montenegro; Cephalonia, Corfu, Igoumenitsa in Greece; and Durrës in Albania.

Superfast (☑080 528 28 28; www.superfast.com) To Corfu, Igoumenitsa and Patras in Greece. Depart at 7pm or 8pm depending on the route.

Ventouris Ferries (☑for Albania 080 521 27 56, for Greece 080 521 76 99; www.ventouris.gr) Regular ferries to Corfu and Igoumenitsa (Greece) and daily ferries to Durrës (Albania).

BUS

Intercity buses leave from three main locations. From Via Caruzzi, south of the main train station, **SITA** (☑080 579 01 11; www.sitabus.it) covers local destinations. **Ferrovie Appulo-Lucane** (☑080 572 52 29; http://ferrovieappulolucane.it) buses serving Matera (€4.50, 1¼ hours, six daily) also depart from here, as do

Bari

⊙ Sights
1 Castello Svevo	A1
2 Cathedral	B1
3 Colonna della Giustizia	C1
4 Piazza Mercantile	C1

⊗ Eating
5 Caffè Borghese	A3
6 La Locanda di Federico	D1
7 Paglionico Vini e Cucina	C2

⊜ Drinking & Nightlife
8 Barcollo	D1

⊟ Shopping
9 Enoteca Vinarius de Pasquale	A4
10 Il Salumaio	A3

Marozzi (☑ 080 556 24 46; www.marozzivt. it) buses for Rome (from €33.50, eight hours, eight daily – note that the overnight bus departs from Piazza Moro) and other long-distance destinations.

Buses operated by **Ferrovie del Sud-Est** (FSE; ☑ 080 546 21 11; www.fseonline.it) leave from Largo Ciaia, south of Piazza Aldo Moro and service the following locations:

Alberobello (€3.90, 1¼ hours, hourly) Continues to **Locorotondo** (€5, 1 hour 35 minutes) and **Martina Franca** (€5, 1 hour 50 minutes)

Grotte di Castellana (€2.60, one hour, five daily)

Taranto (€7.50, 1¾ to 2¼ hours, frequent)

TRAIN
A web of train lines spreads out from Bari. Note that there are fewer services on the weekend.

From the **main train station** (☑ 080 524 43 86) trains go to Puglia and beyond:

Brindisi (from €14, one hour, hourly)

Foggia (from €19, one hour, hourly)

Milan (from €77.50, about eight hours, every four hours)

Rome (from €50, four hours, every four hours)

Ferrovie Appulo-Lucane serves two main destinations:

Matera (€4.50, 1½ hours, 12 daily)

Potenza (€9.50, four hours, four daily)

FSE trains leave from the station in Via Oberdan – cross under the train tracks south of Piazza Luigi di Savoia and head east along Via Capruzzi for about 500m. They serve the following towns:

Alberobello €4.50, 1½ hours, hourly

Martina Franca €5, two hours, hourly

Taranto from €7.50, 2½ hours, nine daily

❶ Getting Around

Central Bari is compact – a 15-minute walk will take you from Piazza Aldo Moro to the old town. For the ferry terminal take bus 20 from Piazza Moro (€1.50).

Street parking is migraine-inducing. There's a large parking area (€1) south of the main port entrance; otherwise, there's a large multistorey car park between the main train station and the FSE station. Another car park is on Via Zuppetta opposite Hotel Adria.

TO/FROM THE AIRPORT
For the airport, take the **Tempesta shuttle bus** (€4, 30 minutes, hourly) from the main train station, with pick-ups at Piazza Garibaldi and the corner of Via Andrea da Bari and Via Calefati. Alternatively, normal city bus 16 covers the same route and a trip is much cheaper (€1), though marginally slower (40 minutes). A taxi trip from the airport to town costs around €24.

Around Bari

The Terra di Bari, or 'land of Bari', surrounding the capital is rich in olive groves and orchards, and the region has an impressive architectural history with some magnificent cathedrals, an extensive network of castles along its coastline, charming seaside towns like Trani and Polignano a Mare, and the mysterious inland Castel del Monte.

Trani
POP 53,900

Known as the 'Pearl of Puglia', beautiful Trani has a sophisticated feel, particularly in summer when well-heeled visitors pack the array of marinaside bars. The marina is the place

---

❶ TRAVELLING EAST

Puglia is the main jumping-off point for onward travel to Greece, Croatia and Albania. The two main ports are Bari and Brindisi, from where you catch ferries to Vlore in Albania, Bar in Montenegro, and Cephalonia, Corfu, Igoumenitsa and Patras in Greece. Fares from Bari to Greece are generally more expensive than those from Brindisi. Taxes are usually from €9 per person and €12 per car. High season is generally the months of July and August, with reduced services in low season. Tariffs can be up to one-third cheaper in low season.

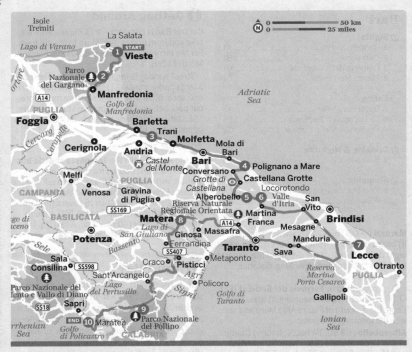

🏃 Driving Tour
Italy's Authentic South

START VIESTE
END MARATEA
LENGTH 650KM TO 700KM; ONE WEEK

Consider a gentle start in lovely, laid-back **1 Vieste** (p715) with its white sandy beaches and medieval backstreets, but set aside half a day to hike or bike in the lush green forests of the **2 Parco Nazionale del Gargano** (p715). Follow the coastal road past dramatic cliffs, salt lakes and flat farming land to **3 Trani** (p711) with its impressive seafront cathedral and picturesque port. The next day, dip into pretty **4 Polignano a Mare** (p714), which has a dramatic location above the pounding surf, before heading to **5 Alberobello** (p721), home to a dense neighbourhood of extraordinary cone-shaped stone homes called *trulli*; consider an overnight *trulli* stay.

Stroll around one of the most picturesque *centro storicos* (historic centres) in southern Italy at **6 Locorotondo** (p723). Hit the road and cruise on to lively baroque **7 Lecce**

(p726), where you can easily chalk up a full day exploring the sights, the shops and the flamboyantly fronted *palazzi* (mansions) and churches, including the Basilica di Santa Croce.

Day five will be one to remember. Nothing can prepare you for Basilicata's **8 Matera** (p740) where the *sassi* (former cave dwellings) are a dramatic reminder of the town's poverty-stricken past. After days of pasta, *fave* beans and *cornetti* (Italian croissants), it's high time you laced up those hiking boots and checked out the trails and activities on offer in the spectacular **9 Parco Nazionale del Pollino** (p755). Finally, wind up the trip and soothe those aching muscles with a dip in the sea at postcard-pretty **10 Maratea** (p748) with its surrounding seaside resorts, medieval village and cosmopolitan harbour offset by a thickly forested and mountainous interior.

to promenade and watch the white yachts and fishing boats in the harbour, while the historic centre, with its medieval churches, glossy limestone streets and faded yet charming *palazzi* (mansions) is an enchanting area to explore. But it's the cathedral, pale against the deep-blue sea, that is the town's most arresting sight.

◉ Sights

Cathedral
CATHEDRAL

(Piazza del Duomo; ☉ 9am-12.30pm & 3-6.30pm) The dramatic seafront cathedral is dedicated to St Nicholas the Pilgrim, famous for being foolish. The Greek Christian wandered through Puglia, crying '*Kyrie eleison*' (Greek for 'Lord, have mercy'). First thought to be a simpleton, he was revered after his death (aged 19) after several miracles attributed to him occurred.

Construction of the cathedral started in 1097 on the site of a Byzantine church and completed in the 13th century. The magnificent original bronze doors (now displayed inside) were cast by Barisano da Trani, an accomplished 12th-century artisan.

The interior of the cathedral reflects typical Norman simplicity and is lined by colonnades. Near the main altar are the remains of a 12th-century floor mosaic, stylistically similar to that in Otranto. Below the church is the crypt, a forest of ancient columns where the bones of St Nicholas are kept beneath the altar. You can also visit the **campanile** (bell tower; admission €3).

Castle
CASTLE

(☎ 0883 50 66 03; www.castelloditrani.benicultural.it; Piazza Manfredi 16; admission €3; ☉ 8.30am-7.30pm) Two hundred metres north of the cathedral is Trani's other major landmark, the vast, almost modernist Swabian castle built by Frederick II in 1233. Charles V later strengthened the fortifications; it was used as a prison from 1844 to 1974.

Ognissanti Church
CHURCH

(Via Ognissanti; ☉ hours vary) Built by the Knights Templar in the 12th century, this church is where Norman knights swore allegiance to Bohemond I of Antioch, their leader, before setting off on the First Crusade.

Scolanova Church
CHURCH

(☎ 0883 48 17 99; Via Scolanova 23; ☉ hours vary) This church was one of four former synagogues in the ancient Jewish quarter, all of which were converted to churches in the

14th century. Inside is a beautiful Byzantine painting of Madonna dei Martiri.

⊨ Sleeping

★ Albergo Lucy
HOTEL $

(☎ 0883 48 10 22; www.albergolucy.com; Piazza Plebiscito 11; d/tr/q from €65/85/105; ❋ ☎) Located in a restored 17th-century *palazzo* overlooking a leafy square and close to the shimmering port, this family-run place oozes charm. Bike hire and guided tours available. Great value: it doesn't serve breakfast, but there are plenty of cafes a short stroll away.

B&B Centro Storico Trani
B&B $

(☎ 0883 50 61 76; www.bbtrani.it; Via Leopardi 28; s €35-50, d €50-70, tr €70-80, q €85-100, quint €100-125) This simple, old-fashioned B&B inhabits an old backstreet monastery and is run by an elderly couple. It's basic, but the rooms are large and 'Mama' makes a mean *crostata* (jam tart).

Hotel Regia
HOTEL $$

(☎ 0883 58 44 44; www.hotelregia.it; Piazza del Duomo 2; s €120-130, d €130-150; ❋ ☎) A lone building facing the cathedral, the understated grandeur of 18th-century Palazzo Filisio houses this charming hotel. Rooms are sober and stylish.

✗ Eating

★ Corteinfiore
SEAFOOD $$

(☎ 0883 50 84 02; www.corteinfiore.it; Via Ognissanti 18; meals €30; ☉ Tue-Sun) Romantic, urbane, refined. The wooden decking, buttercup-yellow tablecloths and marquee-conservatory setting are refreshing. The wines are excellent and the cooking delicious. It also has modern and attractive rooms (from €100) decked out in pale colours.

La Darsena
SEAFOOD $$

(☎ 0883 48 73 33; Via Statuti Marittimi 98; meals €30; ☉ Tue-Sun) Renowned for its seafood, swish La Darsena is housed in a waterfront *palazzo*. Outside tables overlook the port while inside photos of old Puglia cover the walls beneath a huge wrought-iron dragon chandelier.

ℹ Information

From the train station, Via Cavour leads through Piazza della Repubblica to Piazza Plebiscito and the public gardens. Turn left for the harbour and cathedral.

Tourist Office (☑ 0883 58 88 30; www.trani-web.it; 1st fl, Palazzo Palmieri, Piazza Trieste 10; ☻ 8.30am-1.30pm Mon, Wed & Fri, 8:30am-1:30pm & 3.30-5.30pm Tue & Thu) Located 200m south of the cathedral.

❶ Getting There & Away

STP (☑ 0883 49 18 00; www.stpspa.it) has frequent bus services to Bari (€3.90, 45 minutes). Services depart from **Bar Stazione** (Piazza XX Settembre 23), which also has timetables and tickets.

Trani is on the main train line between Bari (€4.40, 40 to 60 minutes, frequent) and Foggia (€9.50, one hour, frequent).

Castel del Monte

You'll see Castel del Monte (☑ 0883 56 99 97; www.casteldelmonte.beniculturali.it; adult/reduced €5/2.50; ☻ 9am-6pm Oct-Feb, 10.15am-7.45pm Mar-Sep), an unearthly geometric shape on a hilltop, from miles away. Mysterious and perfectly octagonal, it's one of southern Italy's most talked-about landmarks and a Unesco World Heritage Site.

No one knows why Frederick II built it – there's no nearby town or strategic crossroads. It was not built to defend anything, as it has no moat or drawbridge, no arrow slits and no trapdoors for pouring boiling oil on invaders.

Some theories claim that, according to mid-13th-century beliefs in geometric symbolism, the octagon represented the union of the circle and square, of God-perfection (the infinite) and human-perfection (the finite). The castle was therefore nothing less than a celebration of the relationship between humanity and God.

The castle has eight octagonal towers. Its interconnecting rooms have decorative marble columns and fireplaces, and the doorways and windows are framed in corallite stone. Many of the towers have washing rooms with what are thought to be Europe's first flush loos – Frederick II, like the Arab world he admired, set great store by cleanliness.

It's difficult to reach here by public transport. By car, it's about 35km from Trani.

Polignano a Mare

Dip into this spectacularly positioned small town if you can. Located around 34km south of Bari on the S16 coastal road, Polignano a Mare is built on the edge of a craggy ravine pockmarked with caves. The town is thought to be one of the most important ancient settlements in Puglia and was later inhabited by successive invaders ranging from the Huns to the Normans.

◉ Sights & Activities

On Sunday the *logge* (balconies) are crowded with day trippers from Bari who come here to view the crashing waves, visit the caves and crowd out the *cornetterias* (shops specialising in Italian croissants) in the atmospheric *centro storico*. There are several baroque churches, an imposing Norman monastery and the medieval Porta Grande, which was the only access to the historic centre until the 18th century. You can still see the holes that activated the heavy drawbridge and the openings from where boiling oil was poured onto any unwelcome visitors to town.

Several operators organise boat trips to the grottoes, including Dorino (☑ 329 6465 904), costing around €20 per person.

🛏 Sleeping & Eating

B&B Santo Stefano   B&B $
(www.santostefano.info; Vico Santo Stefano 9-13; d €69-99; ☎) Six attractive rooms located in an ancient tower in the old part of Polignano, complete with tufa walls, antique furniture and bright bathrooms.

Antiche Mura   PUGLIAN $$
(☑ 080 424 24 76; www.ristoranteantichemura.it; Via Roma 11; meals €20-35) This delightful little restaurant features a vaulted cavelike interior with lanterns and bells adorning the walls. Unsurprisingly, fish is a speciality, with sea bass, octopus and lobster on the menu.

❶ Getting There & Away

Although there is a twice-daily bus service from Bari, your own car is the best way to reach Polignano.

Promontorio del Gargano

The coast surrounding the promontory seems permanently bathed in a pink-hued, pearly light, providing a painterly contrast to the sea, which softens from intense to powder blue as the evening draws in. It's one of Italy's most beautiful areas, encompassing white limestone cliffs, fairy-tale grottoes, sparkling sea, ancient forests, rare orchids and tangled, fragrant maquis. Once connected to what is now Dalmatia (in Croatia), the 'spur' of the Italian boot has more in common with the land mass across the sea than with the rest of Italy. Creeping urbanisation was halted in 1991 by the creation of the **Parco Nazionale del Gargano**. Aside from its magnificent national park, the Gargano is home to pilgrimage sites and the lovely seaside towns of Vieste and Peschici.

Along the coast you'll spot strange cat's-cradle wood-and-rope arrangements, unique to the area. These are *trabucchi*, ancient fishing traps (possibly Phoenician in origin) from which fishing folk cast their nets, 'walk the plank' and haul in their catch.

Vieste

POP 13,900

Vieste is an attractive whitewashed town jutting off the Gargano's easternmost promontory into the Adriatic Sea. It's the Gargano capital and sits above the area's most spectacular beach, a gleaming wide strip backed by sheer white cliffs and overshadowed by the towering rock monolith, **Scoglio di Pizzomunno**. It's packed in summer and ghostly quiet in winter.

◉ Sights

Vieste is primarily a beach resort, though the steep alleys of the old town make for an atmospheric wander. The **castle** built by Frederick II is occupied by the military and closed to the public.

Chianca Amara   HISTORIC SITE
(Bitter Stone; Via Cimaglia) Vieste's most gruesome sight is this stone where thousands were beheaded when Turks sacked Vieste in the 16th century.

Museo Malacologico   MUSEUM
(☑ 0884 70 76 88; Via Pola 8; ⊙ 9.30am-12.30pm & 4-8pm, to 10pm Apr-Oct) **FREE** This impressive shell museum has four rooms of fossils and molluscs, some enormous and all beautifully patterned and coloured.

Cathedral   CATHEDRAL
(Via Duomo) Built by the Normans on the ruins of a Vesta temple, the cathedral is in Puglian-Romanesque style with a fanciful tower that resembles a cardinal's hat. It was rebuilt in 1800.

La Salata   HISTORIC SITE
(adult/child €4/free; ⊙ 5.30pm & 6.30pm Mon, Wed & Fri Jun; 5.30pm & 6.30pm Mon-Fri Jul & Aug; 4pm & 4.45pm Mon, Wed & Fri Sep; on request Oct-May) This palaeo-Christian graveyard dating from the 4th to 6th centuries AD is 9km out of town. Inside the cave, tier upon tier of narrow tombs are cut into the rock wall; others form shallow niches in the cave floor. Guided tours are essential. Book with **Agenzia Sinergie** (☑ 338 840 62 15; www.agenziasinergie.com), which can also arrange customised tours of the Gargano.

PUGLIA, BASILICATA & CALABRIA PROMONTORIO DEL GARGANO

CAMPING IN STYLE

If your experience of camping is the scout version of flapping tents, freezing nights and eating cold baked beans out of a tin, you will be delighted at the five-star quality of the typical campsites in this southern region of Italy. They are also prolific, particularly in and around the national parks. In the Gargano region alone there are an astonishing 100 campsites, compared to the relatively modest number of *pensioni* and hotels. If you don't fancy sleeping under canvas (or need a plug for those heated rollers) then consider a bungalow rental.

Virtually all these camping *villaggios* (villages) include well-furnished and equipped bungalows. This means you can really economise on eating out, as well as having the advantages of the campsite facilities, which often include tennis courts, a swimming pool, a children's playground and small supermarket. Bungalows (normally only available for week-long rentals) start from around €200/500 (low/high season) for a two-person bungalow or mobile-home rental. Traditional under-canvas campers can expect to pay a daily rate of approximately €15/25 (winter/summer), which includes camping for two people, tent and car parking space.

Check the following websites for more information and camping listings: www.camping.it; www.camping-italy.net and www.caravanandcampsites.eu.

Activities

Superb sandy beaches surround the town: in the south are Spiaggia del Castello, Cala San Felice and Cala Sanguinaria; due north, head for the area known as La Salata. Diving is popular around the promontory's rocky coastline, which is filled with marine grottoes.

From May to September fast boats zoom to the Isole Tremiti (p720).

Boat hire and tours can be arranged at the port.

Centro Ormeggi e Sub BOATING
(☑0884 70 79 83) Offers diving courses and rents out sailing boats and motorboats.

☞ Tours

Agenzia Sol GUIDED TOUR
(☑0884 70 15 58; www.solvieste.it; Via Trepiccioni 5; ⊙9.20am-1.15pm & 5-9pm winter, to midnight summer) Organises hiking, cycling and 4WD tours in the Foresta Umbra; boat tours around the Gargano; and gastronomic tours and small group tours into Puglia. It also sells bus tickets and ferry tickets for the Isole Tremiti.

Leonarda Motobarche BOAT TOUR
(☑0884 70 13 17; www.motobarcheleonarda.it; per person €13; ⊙Apr-Sep) Boat tours of marine caves.

⌖ Sleeping

★B&B Rocca sul Mare B&B $
(☑0884 70 27 19; www.roccasulmare.it; Via Mafrolla 32; per person €25-70; ☎) In a former convent in the old quarter, this popular and reasonably priced place has charm, with large, comfortable high-ceilinged rooms. There's a vast rooftop terrace with panoramic views and a suite with a steam bath. Simple but tasty meals (€18 for four courses) and bike hire are available; staff also arrange fishing trips and will cook up your catch in the evening. You can arrange to be collected from Bari airport.

Campeggio Capo Vieste CAMPGROUND $
(☑0884 70 63 26; www.capovieste.it; Km8; camping 2 people, car & tent €33, 1-bedroom bungalow €77-164; ⊙Mar-Oct; ☎) This tree-shaded camping ground is right by a sandy beach at La Salata, around 8km from Vieste and accessible by bus. Activities include tennis and a sailing school.

Hotel Seggio HOTEL $$
(☑0884 70 81 23; www.hotelseggio.it; Via Veste 7; d €80-150; ⊙Apr-Oct; 🅿🌀@🛜🏊) A buttercoloured *palazzo* in the town's historic centre with steps that spiral down to a pool and sunbathing terrace with a backdrop of the sea. The rooms are modern and plain but it's family run.

✗ Eating

★Osteria Al Duomo OSTERIA $
(☑0884 70 82 43; www.osterialduomo.it; Via Alessandro III 23; meals €25; ⊙lunch & dinner Mar-Nov) Tucked away in a picturesque narrow alley in the heart of the old town, this welcoming *osteria* has a cosy cave interior and outdoor seating under a shady arbour. Homemade pastas with seafood sauces feature prominently.

★Taverna Al Cantinone TRADITIONAL ITALIAN $$
(☑0884 70 77 53; Via Mafrolla 26; meals €25-30; ⊙lunch & dinner Wed-Mon) Run by a charming Italian-Spanish couple who have a passion for cooking; the food is exceptional and exquisitely presented. The menu changes with the seasons.

Enoteca Vesta TRADITIONAL ITALIAN $$
(☑0884 70 64 11; www.enotecavesta.it; Via Duomo 14; meals €30-35) You can savour a magnificent selection of Puglian wines to accompany innovative seafood dishes in this restaurant, which is housed in a cool vaulted cave.

❶ Information

Post Office (Via Vittorio Veneto)
Tourist Office (☑0884 70 88 06; Piazza Kennedy; ⊙8am-8pm Jun-Sep, 8am-1.30pm Mon-Fri & 4-7pm Tue-Thu Oct-May)

❶ Getting There & Around

BOAT
Vieste's port is to the north of the town, about a five-minute walk from the tourist office. In summer several companies, including **Navigazione Libera del Golfo** (☑0884 70 74 89; www. navlib.it), head to the Isole Tremiti. Tickets can be bought portside and there are several daily boats (€14.50 to €20, 1½ hours).

Several companies also offer tours of the caves that pock the Gargano coast – a threehour tour costs around €13.

BUS
From Piazzale Manzoni, where intercity buses terminate, a 10-minute walk east along Viale

LUCERA

Lovely Lucera has one of Puglia's most impressive castles and a handsome old town centre with mellow sand-coloured brick- and stonework, and chic shops lining wide, shiny stone streets. Founded by the Romans in the 4th century BC, it was abandoned by the 13th century. Following excommunication by Pope Gregory IX, Frederick II decided to bolster his support base in Puglia by importing 20,000 Sicilian Arabs, simultaneously diminishing the headache Arab bandits were causing him in Sicily. It was an extraordinary move by the Christian monarch, even more so because Frederick allowed Lucera's new Muslim inhabitants the freedom to build mosques and practise their religion a mere 290km from Rome. History, however, was less kind; when the town was taken by the rabidly Christian Angevins in 1269, every Muslim who failed to convert was slaughtered.

Frederick II's enormous **castle** (◷9am-2pm year-round & 3-7pm Apr-Sep) **FREE**, shows just what a big fish Lucera once was in the Puglian pond. Built in 1233, it's 14km northwest of the town on a rocky hillock surrounded by a perfect 1km pentagonal wall, guarded by 24 towers.

On the site of Lucera's Great Mosque, Puglia's only Gothic **cathedral** (◷8am-noon & 4-7pm May-Sep, 8am-noon & 5-8pm Oct-Apr) was built in 1301 by Charles II of Anjou. The altar was once the castle banqueting table.

Dominated by a huge rose window, the contemporaneous Gothic **Chiesa di San Francesco** (◷8am-noon & 4-7pm) incorporates recycled materials from Lucera's 1st-century-BC **Roman amphitheatre** (◷9am-2pm & 3.15-6.45pm Tue-Sun Apr-Sep) **FREE**. The amphitheatre was built for gladiatorial combat and accommodated up to 18,000 people.

The **tourist office** (☎0881 52 27 62; ◷9am-2pm & 3-8pm Tue-Sun Apr-Sep, 9am-2pm Oct-Mar) is near the cathedral.

Ferrovie del Gargano trains run to Lucera from Foggia (€1.50, 20 minutes, three daily) which is on the east coast train line between Bari and Pescara.

XXIV Maggio, which becomes Corso Fazzini, brings you into the old town and the Marina Piccola's attractive promenade. In summer buses terminate at Via Verdi.

SITA (☎0881 35 20 11; www.sitabus.it) buses run between Vieste and Foggia (€6.50, 2¾ hours, four daily) via Manfredonia. There are also services to Monte Sant'Angelo (€5) via Manfredonia but **Ferrovie del Gargano** (☎0881 58 72 11; www.ferroviedelgargano.com) buses have a direct daily service to Monte Sant'Angelo (€6, two hours) and frequent services to Peschici (€1.70, 35 minutes).

From May to September, **Pugliairbus** (☎080 580 03 58; pugliairbus.aeroportidipuglia.it) runs a service to the Gargano, including Vieste, from Bari airport (€20, 3½ hours, four daily).

Monte Sant'Angelo

POP 13,300 / ELEV 796M

One of Europe's most important pilgrimage sites, this isolated mountaintop has an extraordinary atmosphere. Pilgrims have been coming here for centuries – and so have the hustlers, pushing everything from religious kitsch to parking spaces.

The object of devotion is the Santuario di San Michele. Here, in AD 490, St Michael the Archangel is said to have appeared in a grotto to the bishop of Siponto. He left behind his scarlet cloak and instructions not to consecrate the site as he had already done so.

During the Middle Ages, the sanctuary marked the end of the Route of the Angel, which began in Mont St-Michel (in Normandy) and passed through Rome. In 999 the Holy Roman Emperor Otto III made a pilgrimage to the sanctuary to pray that prophecies about the end of the world in the year 1000 would not be fulfilled. His prayers were answered, the world staggered on and the sanctuary's fame grew.

◉ Sights

The town's serpentine alleys and jumbled houses are perfect for a little aimless ambling. Look out for the different shaped *cappelletti* (chimney stacks) on top of the neat whitewashed houses.

PADRE PIO: SAINT OF THE GARGANO

Pilgrims flock to San Giovanni Rotondo, home to Padre Pio, a humble and pious Capuchin priest 'blessed' with the stigmata and a legendary ability to heal the sick. Pio (1887–1968) was canonised in 2002 and immortalised in the vast numbers of prefabricated statues to be found throughout the Gargano. There's even a statue of Pio beneath the waters off the Isole Tremiti.

The ailing Capuchin priest arrived in San Giovanni Rotondo, then a tiny isolated medieval village, in 1916. As Pio's fame grew, the town too underwent a miraculous transformation. These days, it's a mass of functional hotels and restaurants catering to eight million pilgrims a year. It's all overlooked by the palatial Home for the Relief of Suffering, one of Italy's premier hospitals (established by Pio in 1947).

The Convent of the Minor Capuchin Friars (☑ 0882 41 71; www.conventosantuariopadrepio.it; Piazza Santa Maria delle Grazie) includes Padre Pio's cell (⊙ 7am-7pm summer, 7.30am-6.30pm winter), a simple room containing mementoes such as his blood-stained socks. The old church, where he used to say Mass, dates from the 16th century. The spectacular new church, designed by Genovese Renzo Piano (who also designed Paris' Pompidou Centre), resembles a huge futuristic seashell, with an interior of bony vaulting. Padre Pio's body now lies in the geometric perfection of the semicircular crypt.

SITA buses run daily to San Giovanni Rotondo from Monte Sant'Angelo (€2, 50 minutes) and Vieste (€6, 2½ hours).

Santuario di San Michele
GROTTO

(Via Reale Basilica; ⊙ 7.30am-7.30pm Jul-Sep, 7.30am-12.30pm & 2.30-7pm Apr-Jun & Oct, 7.30am-12.30pm & 2-5pm Nov-Mar) FREE Look for the 17th-century pilgrims' graffiti as you descend the steps. St Michael is said to have left a footprint in stone inside the grotto, so it became customary for pilgrims to carve outlines of their feet and hands. Etched Byzantine bronze and silver doors, cast in Constantinople in 1076, open into the grotto itself. Inside, a 16th-century statue of the archangel covers the site of St Michael's footprint.

Tomba di Rotari
HISTORIC SITE

(admission €1; ⊙ 10am-1pm & 3-7pm Apr-Oct) A short flight of stairs opposite the Santuario di San Michele leads not to a tomb but to a 12th-century baptistry with a deep sunken basin for total immersion. You enter the baptistry through the facade of the Chiesa di San Pietro with its intricate rose window squirming with serpents – all that remains of the church, destroyed in a 19th-century earthquake. The Romanesque portal of the adjacent 11th-century Chiesa di Santa Maria Maggiore has some fine bas-reliefs.

Castle
HISTORIC SITE

(Largo Roberto Giuscardo 2; admission €2; ⊙ 9.30am-1pm & 2.30-7pm) At the highest point is this rugged bijou, a Norman castle

with Swabian and Aragonese additions as well as panoramic views.

🛏 Sleeping & Eating

Hotel Michael
HOTEL $

(☑ 0884 56 55 19; www.hotelmichael.com; Via Basilica 86; s €50-60, d €70-80; 🖢) A small hotel with shuttered windows, located on the main street, across from the Santuario di San Michele, this traditional place has spacious rooms with extremely pink bedspreads. Ask for a room with a view.

Casa li Jalantuúmene
TRATTORIA $$

(☑ 0884 56 54 84; www.li-jalantuumene.it; Piazza de Galganis 5; meals €40; ⊙ lunch Wed-Mon Feb-Dec; 🖢) This renowned restaurant has an entertaining and eccentric chef, Gegè Mangano, and serves excellent fare. It's intimate, there's a select wine list and, in summer, tables spill into the piazza. It has four suites (€130), decorated in traditional Puglian style.

ℹ Getting There & Away

Ferrovie del Gargano has a direct service from Vieste (€5.90, two hours, five daily). Buy your tickets from Bar Esperia next to Santuario di San Michele.

SITA (☑ 0881 35 20 11; www.sitabus.it) buses run from Foggia (€4.60, 1¾ hours, four daily) and Vieste via Manfredonia.

Peschici

POP 4400

Perched above a turquoise sea and tempting beach, Peschici clings to the hilly, wooded coastline. It's a pretty resort area with a tight-knit old walled town of Arabesque whitewashed houses. The small town gets crammed in summer, so book in advance. Boats zip across to the Isole Tremiti (p720) in high season.

🛏 Sleeping & Eating

Locanda al Castello   B&B **$**
(☑ 0884 96 40 38; www.peschicialcastello.it; Via Castello 29; s €35-70, d €70-120; [P][✻][🖻]) Staying here is like entering a large, welcoming family home. It's by the cliffs with fantastic views. Enjoy hearty home cooking in the restaurant (meals €18).

Baia San Nicola   CAMPGROUND **$**
(☑ 0884 96 42 31; www.baiasannicola.it; camping €22-37, 2-person bungalow per week €320-620; ☺ mid-May–mid-Oct) The best campground in the area, 2km south of Peschici towards Vieste, Baia San Nicola is on a pine-shaded beach, offering camping, bungalows, apartments and myriad amenities.

★ Il Trabucco da Mimi   SEAFOOD **$$**
(☑ 0884 96 25 56; Localita Punta San Nicola; meals €30-40; ☺ lunch & dinner Easter-Oct) For the ultimate in fresh fish you can't beat eating in a *trabucco* (the traditional wooden fishing platforms lining the coast). Watch the process in operation – you can even help out – and dine on the catch. The decor is simple and rustic and you'll pay for the experience – but it's worth it.

Porto di Basso   SEAFOOD **$$**
(☑ 0884 91 53 64; www.portodibasso.it; Via Colombo 38; meals €30-40; ☺ Fri-Wed) Superb views of the ocean drop away from the floor-length windows beside the intimate alcove tables in this elegant clifftop restaurant. The menu of fresh local seafood changes daily. Close to the restaurant, two extremely stylish suites with fantastic sea views offer *albergo diffuso*–style accommodation (€110 to €120).

ℹ Information

Tourist Office (☑ 0884 91 53 62; Via Magenta 3; ☺ 8am-2pm & 5-9pm Mon-Sat summer, 8am-2pm Mon-Fri & 9am-noon & 4-7pm Sat in winter)

ℹ Getting There & Away

The bus terminal is beside the sportsground, uphill from the main street, Corso Garibaldi.

Ferrovie del Gargano (p717) buses run frequent daily services between Peschici and Vieste (€1.70, 35 minutes).

From April to September, ferry companies including **MS&G Societá di Navigazione** (☑ 0884 96 27 32; www.msgnavigazioni. it; Corso Umberto I 20) and **Navigare SRL** (☑ 0884 96 42 34; Corso Garibaldi 30) serve the Isole Tremiti (adult €25 to €30, child €16 to €21, one to 1½ hours).

Foresta Umbra

The 'Forest of Shadows' is the Gargano's enchanted interior – thickets of tall, epic trees interspersed with picnic spots bathed in dappled light. It's the last remnant of Puglia's ancient forests: Aleppo pines, oaks, yews and beech trees shade the mountainous terrain. More than 65 different types of orchid have been discovered here; the wildlife includes roe deer, wild boar, foxes, badgers and the increasingly rare wild cat.

◉ Sights & Activities

Walkers and mountain bikers will find plenty of well-marked trails within the forest's 5790 sq km.

The small visitor centre in the middle of the forest houses a **museum and nature centre** (www.ecogargano.it; admission €1.20; ☺ 9am-7pm mid-Apr–mid-Oct) with fossils, photographs, and stuffed animals and birds. Half-day guided hikes (per person €10), bike hire (per hour/day €5/25), and walking maps (€2.50) are available.

ALBERGO DIFFUSO

Albergo diffuso doesn't necessarily have a direct translation in English, but the term refers to the Italian hospitality concept that emerged in the 1980s. Designed as a means to revive historic centres in small towns and villages, the concept allows neighbouring apartments and houses to be rented to guests through a centralised hotel-style reception. The aim is to respect the integrity of ancient buildings, so that guest accommodation blends harmoniously into the surrounding streetscape.

Specialist tour operators organise hiking, biking and 4WD excursions in the park. These include Agenzia Sol (p716) and **Explora Gargano** (☑0884 70 22 37; www.exploragargano.it; Via Santa Maria di Merino 62; hiking & mountain biking half-day from €70, quad tours & jeep safari per day from €50) in Vieste and **Soc Cooperative Ecogargano** (☑0884 56 54 44; www.ecogargano.it) in Monte Sant'Angelo.

🛏 Sleeping

La Chiusa delle More   B&B $$$

(☑330 54 37 66; www.lachiusadellemore.it; B&B per person €200-240; ☺May-Sep; P❋❀🛜🏊) La Chiusa delle More offers an escape from the cramped coast. An attractive stone-built *agriturismo* (farm stay), only 1.5km from Peschici, it's set in a huge olive grove, and you can dine on home-grown produce, borrow mountain bikes and enjoy panoramic views from your poolside lounger. Note there is a three-night minimum stay.

Isole Tremiti

POP 500

This beautiful archipelago of three islands, 36km offshore, is a picturesque sight of raggedy cliffs, sandy coves and thick pine woods, surrounded by the glittering dark-blue sea.

Unfortunately the islands are no secret, and in July and August some 100,000 holidaymakers descend on the archipelago. At this time it's noisy, loud and hot. If you want to savour the islands' tranquillity, visit during the shoulder season. In the low season most tourist facilities close down and the few permanent residents resume their quiet and isolated lives.

The islands' main facilities are on San Domino, the largest and lushest island, which was formerly used to grow crops. It's ringed by alternating sandy beaches and limestone cliffs, while the inland is covered in thick maquis flecked with rosemary and foxglove. The centre harbours a nondescript small town with several hotels.

Easily defended, small San Nicola island is the traditional administrative centre – a castlelike cluster of medieval buildings rises up from the rocks. The third island, Capraia, is uninhabited.

Most boats arrive at San Domino. Small boats regularly make the brief crossing to San Nicola (€6 return) in high season –

from October to March a single boat makes the trip after meeting the boat from the mainland.

◉ Sights & Activities

San Domino   ISLAND

Head to San Domino for walks, grottoes and coves. It has a pristine, marvellous coastline and the islands' only sandy beach, Cala delle Arene. Alongside the beach is the small cove Grotta dell'Arene, with calm, clear waters for swimming.

You can also take a boat trip (€12 to €15 from the port) around the island to explore the grottoes: the largest, **Grotta del Bue Marino**, is 70m long. A tour around all three islands costs €15 to €17. Diving in the translucent sea is another option with **Tremiti Diving Center** (☑337 64 89 17; www.tremiti-divingcenter.com; Via Federico 2). There's an undemanding, but enchanting, walking track around the island, starting at the far end of the village.

San Nicola   ISLAND

Medieval buildings thrust out of San Nicola's rocky shores, the same pale-sand colour as the barren cliffs. In 1010, Benedictine monks founded the **Abbazia e Chiesa di Santa Maria** here; for the next 700 years the islands were ruled by a series of abbots who accumulated great wealth.

Although the church retains a weather-worn Renaissance portal and a fine 11th-century floor mosaic, its other treasures have been stolen or destroyed throughout its troubled history. The only exceptions are a painted wooden Byzantine crucifix brought to the island in AD 747 and a black Madonna, probably transported here from Constantinople in the Middle Ages.

Capraia   ISLAND

The third of the Isole Tremiti, Capraia, (named after the wild caper plant) is uninhabited. Birdlife is plentiful, with impressive flocks of seagulls. There's no organised transport, but trips can be negotiated with local fishing folk.

🛏 Sleeping & Eating

In summer you'll need to book well ahead and many hotels insist on full board. Camping is forbidden.

La Casa di Gino   B&B $$

(☑0882 46 34 10; www.hotel-gabbiano.com; Piazza Belvedere; r €180; ❋) A tranquil accommodation choice on San Nicola, away from the frenzy of San Domino, this B&B run by the Hotel Gabbiano has stylish white-on-white rooms.

Hotel Gabbiano HOTEL $$
(☑ 0882 46 34 10; www.hotel-gabbiano.com; Piazza Belvedere; s incl breakfast €45-105, d incl breakfast €120-128; ❉ ❧) An established icon on the island and run for more than 30 years by a Neapolitan family, this smart hotel has pastel-coloured rooms with balconies overlooking San Nicola and the sea. It also has a seafood restaurant.

Architiello SEAFOOD $$
(☑ 0882 46 30 54; meals €25; ☉ Apr-Oct) A class act with a seaview terrace, this specialises in – what else? – fresh fish.

❶ Getting There & Away

Boats for the Isole Tremiti depart from several points on the Italian mainland: Manfredonia, Vieste and Peschici in summer, and Termoli in nearby Molise year-round.

Valle d'Itria

Between the Ionian and Adriatic coasts rises the great limestone plateau of the Murgia (473m). It has a strange karst geology: the landscape is riddled with holes and ravines through which small streams and rivers gurgle, creating what is, in effect, a giant sponge. At the heart of the Murgia lies the idyllic Valle d'Itria. Here you will begin to spot curious circular stone-built houses dotting the countryside, their roofs tapering up to a stubby and endearing point. These are *trulli*, Puglia's unique rural architecture. It's unclear why the architecture developed in this way; one popular story says that it was so the dry-stone constructions could be quickly dismantled, to avoid payment of building taxes.

The rolling green valley is criss-crossed by dry-stone walls, vineyards, almond and olive groves, and winding country lanes. This is the part of Puglia most visited by foreign tourists and is the best served for hotels and luxury *masserias* (working farms) or manor farms. Around here are also many of Puglia's self-catering villas; to find them, try websites such as www.tuscanynow.com, www.ownersdirect.co.uk, www.holidayhomesinitaly.co.uk and www.trulliland.com.

Grotte di Castellana

Don't miss these spectacular limestone caves (☑ 080 499 82 11/21; www.grottedicastellana.it; Piazzale Anelli; admission €15; ☉ 9am-6pm), 40km southeast of Bari and Italy's longest natural subterranean network. The interlinked galleries, first discovered in 1938, contain an incredible range of underground landscapes, with extraordinary stalactite and stalagmite formations – look out for the jellyfish, the bacon and the stocking. The highlight is the Grotta Bianca (White Grotto), an eerie white alabaster cavern hung with stiletto-thin stalactites.

There are two tours in English: a 1km, 50-minute tour that doesn't include the Grotta Bianca (€10, on the half-hour) and a 3km, two-hour tour (€15, on the hour) that does include it. The temperature inside the cave averages 18°C so take a light jacket. Visit, too, the **Museo Speleologico Franco Anelli** (☑ 080 499 82 30; ☉ 9.30am-1pm & 3.30-6.30pm mid-Mar–Oct, 10am-1pm Nov–mid-Mar) **FREE** or the **Osservatorio Astronomico Sirio** (☑ 080 499 82 13; admission €4), with its telescope and solar filters allowing for maximum solar-system visibility. Guided visits only with advance notification.

The grotto can be reached by rail from Bari on the FSE Bari–Taranto train line but not all trains stop at Grotte di Castellana. However, all services stop at Castellana Grotte (€2.90, 50 minutes, roughly hourly), 2km before the grotto, from where you can catch a local bus (€1.10) to the caves.

Alberobello

POP 11,000

Unesco World Heritage Site Alberobello resembles an urban sprawl – for gnomes. The Zona dei Trulli on the western hill of town is a dense mass of 1500 beehive-shaped houses, white-tipped as if dusted by snow. These dry-stone buildings are made from local limestone; none are older than the 14th century. Inhabitants do not wear pointy hats, but they do sell anything a visitor might want, from miniature *trulli* to woollen shawls.

The town is named after the primitive oak forest Arboris Belli (beautiful trees) that once covered this area. It's an amazing area, but also something of a tourist trap – from May to October busloads of tourists pile int

MASSERIAS: LUXURY ON THE FARM

Masserias are unique to southern Italy. Modelled on the classical Roman villa, these fortified farmhouses – equipped with oil mills, cellars, chapels, storehouses and accommodation for workers and livestock – were built to function as self-sufficient communities. These days, they still produce the bulk of Italy's olive oil, but many have been converted into luxurious hotels, *agriturismi* (farm stay accommodation), holiday apartments or restaurants. Staying in a *masseria* is a unique experience, especially when you can dine on home-grown produce.

The following masserias are recommended:

★ **Il Frantoio** (☑ 0831 33 02 76; www.trecolline.it; SS16, Km 874; d €140-260, apt €320-350; P @) Stay in a charming, whitewashed farmhouse, where the owners still live and work, producing high-quality organic olive oil. (Or else book yourself in for one of the marathon eight-course lunches; the food is superb.) Armando takes guests for a tour of the farm each evening in his 1949 Fiat. Il Frantoio lies 5km outside Ostuni along the SS16 in the direction of Fasano. You'll see the sign on your left-hand side when you reach the Km 874 sign.

Masseria Torre Coccaro (☑ 080 482 93 10; www.masseriatorrecoccaro.com; Contrada Coccaro 8; d €284-1365; ❄ @ 🛜 🏊) For pure luxury, stay in this superchic yet countrified *masseria*. There's a glorious spa set in a cave, a beach-style swimming pool, cooking courses on offer and a restaurant (meals €90) dishing up home-grown produce.

Masseria Maizza (www.masseriatorremaizza.com; d €290-548, ste €422-1522; ❄ @ 🛜 🏊) This farmhouse is located next door to Masseria Torre Coccaro and run by the same people, so you know luxury is assured. The two *masserias* share a balmy beach club (about 4km away) and a neighbouring golf course.

Borgo San Marco (☑ 080 439 57 57; www.borgosanmarco.it; Contrada Sant'Angelo 33; s €130-140, d €160-230; P ❄ 🛜 🏊) Once a *borgo* (medieval town), this *masseria* has 16 rooms, a spa in the orchard and is traditional with a bohemian edge. Nearby are some frescoed rock churches. It's 8km from Ostuni; to get here take the SS379 in the direction of Bari, exiting at the sign that says SC San Marco–Zona Industriale Sud Fasano, then follow the signs. Note that there's a one-week minimum stay in August.

trullo homes, drink in *trullo* bars and shop in *trullo* shops.

If you park in Lago Martellotta, follow the steps up to the Piazza del Popolo where Belvedere Trulli offers fabulous views over the whole higgledy-piggledy picture.

◉ Sights

Rione Monti   HISTORIC QUARTER
Within the old town quarter of Rione Monti more than 1000 trulli cascade down the hillside, most of which are now souvenir shops. The area is surprisingly quiet and atmospheric in the late evening, once the gaudy stalls have been stashed away.

Rione Aia Piccola   HISTORIC QUARTER
To the east, on the other side of Via Indipendenza, is Rione Aia Piccola. This neighbourhood is much less commercialised, with 400 *trulli*, many still used as fam-

ily dwellings. You can climb up for a rooftop view at many shops, although most do have a strategically located basket for a donation.

Trullo Sovrano   HISTORIC QUARTER
(☑ 080 432 60 30; Piazza Sacramento; admission €1.50; ⊙10am-6pm) In the modern part of town, the 18th-century Trullo Sovrano is the only two-floor *trullo*, built by a wealthy priest's family. It's a small museum giving something of the atmosphere of *trullo* life, with sweet, rounded rooms that include a re-created bakery, bedroom and kitchen. The souvenir shop here has a wealth of literature on the town and surrounding area, plus Alberobello recipe books.

🛏 Sleeping

It's a unique experience to stay in your own *trullo*, though some people might find Alberobello too touristy to use as a base.

Trullidea   TRULLI $$
(☑080 432 38 60; www.trullidea.it; Via Monte San
Gabriele 1; 2-person trullo €99-150; ☎) A series
of 15 renovated *trulli* in Alberobello's Trulli
Zone, these are quaint, cosy and atmospher-
ic. They're available on a self-catering, B&B,
or half- or full-board basis.

Fascino Antico   TRULLI $$
(☑080 432 50 89; www.fascinoantico.eu; 1 bed
€49-89, 2 bed €59-119, 3 bed €69-139, 4 bed €89-
149; ☒) This lovely *trulli* complex sits just
half a kilometre from Alberobello on the
SS172 to Locorotondo. Set in a pretty landscaped garden, the rooms are light and
comfortable with terracotta tiled floors and
kitchenettes. A number of rooms also have
bunks and cater for families.

Camping dei Trulli   CAMPGROUND $
(☑080 432 36 99; www.campingdeitrulli.com; Via
Castellana Grotte; camping 2 people, car & tent
€26.50, bungalows per person €25-40, trulli €30-
60; P@☒) This campsite is 1.5km out of
town and has some nice tent sites. It has a
restaurant, a market, two swimming pools,
tennis courts and bicycle hire and you can
also rent *trulli* off the grounds.

🍴 Eating

Trattoria Amatulli   TRATTORIA $
(☑080 432 29 79; Via Garibaldi 13; meals €16;
☺Tue-Sun) Excellent trattoria with a cheer-
ily cluttered interior papered with photos
of smiley diners, plus superb down-to-earth
dishes like *orecchiette scure con cacioricot-
ta pomodoro e rucola* ('little ears' pasta with
cheese, tomato and rucola). Wash it down
with the surprisingly drinkable house wine,
costing the lordly sum of €4 a litre.

La Cantina   TRADITIONAL ITALIAN $
(☑080 432 34 73; www.ilristorantelacantina.it; cnr
Corso Vittorio Emanuele & Vico Lippolis; meals €25;
☺Wed-Mon) Although tourists have discovered this place, located to the side of a little Doric temple, it has maintained the high
standards established back in 1958. There
are just seven tables (book ahead), and it
serves delicious meals made with fresh seasonal produce.

Il Poeta Contadino   TRADITIONAL ITALIAN $$$
(☑080 432 19 17; www.ilpoetacontadino.it; Via
Indipendenza 21; meals €65; ☺Tue-Sun Feb-Dec)
Located just outside the main throng, the
dining room here has a medieval banquet-
ing feel with its sumptuous decor and chan-
deliers. Dine on a poetic menu that includes

the signature dish, fava bean purée with *ca-
vatelli* (rod-shaped pasta) and seafood.

ℹ️ Information

Tourist Office (☑080 432 51 71; Via Garibaldi;
☺8am-1pm Mon, Wed & Fri, plus 3-6pm Tue &
Thu) Just off the main square. In the Zona dei
Trulli there is another tourist information office
(☑080 432 28 22; www.prolocoalberobello.it;
Monte Nero 1; ☺9am-7.30pm).

ℹ️ Getting There & Away

Alberobello is easily accessible from Bari
(€4.50, 1½ hours, hourly) on the FSE Bari–
Taranto train line. From the station, walk straight
ahead along Via Mazzini, which becomes Via
Garibaldi, to reach Piazza del Popolo.

Locorotondo
POP 14,200

Locorotondo has an extraordinarily beauti-
ful and whisper-quiet pedestrianised *centro
storico,* where everything is shimmering
white aside from the blood-red geraniums
that tumble from the window boxes. Situ-
ated on a hilltop on the Murge Plateau, it's a
borghi più belli d'Italia (www.borghitalia.it)
– that is, it's rated as one of the most beau-
tiful towns in Italy. The streets are paved
with smooth ivory-coloured stones, with the
church of Santa Maria della Graecia as
their sunbaked centrepiece.

From Villa Comunale, a public garden,
you can enjoy panoramic views of the sur-
rounding valley. You enter the historic quar-
ter directly across from here.

Not only is this deepest *trulli* country, but
it's also the liquid heart of the Puglian wine
region. Sample some of the local spumante
at Cantina del Locorotondo (☑080 431 16
44; www.locorotondodoc.com; Via Madonna della
Catena 99; ☺9am-1pm & 3-7pm).

🛏️ Sleeping

★ Truddhi   TRULLI $
(☑080 443 13 26; www.trulliresidence.it; Contrada
da Trito 292; d €65-80, apt €100-150, per week from
€450-741; P☒) This charming cluster of 10
self-catering *trulli* in the hamlet of Trito
near Locorotondo is surrounded by olive
groves and vineyards. It's a tranquil place
and you can take cooking courses (per day
€80) with Mino, a lecturer in gastronomy.

★ Sotto le Cummerse   APARTMENT $$
(☑080 431 32 98; www.sottolecummerse.it; Via Vit-
torio Veneto 138; apt incl breakfast €82-298; ✳☒)

As this is an *albergo diffuso* (difused hotel), you can stay in tastefully furnished apartments scattered throughout the *centro storico*. The apartments are traditional buildings that have been beautifully restored and furnished. Excellent value and a great base for exploring the region.

Eating

★ **Quanto Basta** PIZZERIA $
(☑ 080 431 28 55; Via Morelli 12; pizzas €6-7; ☺ dinner Tue-Sun) With its wooden tables, soft lighting and stone floors this old-town pizzeria is cosy and welcoming. The pizzas are delicious and the beer list extensive.

La Taverna del Duca TRATTORIA $$
(☑ 080 431 30 07; Via Papadotero 3; meals €35; ☺ lunch & dinner, closed Sun night winter) In a narrow side street off Piazza Vittorio Emanuele, this well-regarded trattoria serves local classics such as *orecchiette* with various vegetable sidekicks.

❶ Information

Tourist Office (☑ 080 431 30 99; www.prolocolocorotondo.it; Piazza Vittorio Emanuele 27; ☺ 10am-1pm & 3-6pm Mon-Fri, 10am-1pm Sat) Offers free internet access.

❶ Getting There & Away

Locorotondo is easily accessible via frequent trains from Bari (€5.20, 1½ to two hours) on the FSE Bari–Taranto train line.

Cisternino

POP 12,000

An appealing, whitewashed hilltop town, slow-paced Cisternino has a charming *centro storico* beyond its bland modern outskirts; with its kasbahlike knot of streets, it has been designated as one of the country's *borghi più belli* (most beautiful towns). Beside its 13th-century **Chiesa Matrice** and **Torre Civica** there's a pretty communal garden with rural views. If you take Via Basilioni next to the tower you can amble along an elegant route right to the central piazza, Vittorio Emanuele.

Just outside the historic centre, the **tourist office** (☑ 080 444 66 61; www.prolococisternino.it; Via San Quirico 18; ☺ 10.15am-12.15pm & 4.30-7.30pm Mon-Sat) is not always open but can advise on B&Bs in the historic centre.

Cisternino has a grand tradition of *fornello pronto* (ready-to-go roast or grilled meat)

and in numerous butchers' shops and trattorias you can select a cut of meat, which is then promptly cooked on the spot. Try it under the whitewashed arches at no-frills but hugely popular **Rosticceria L'Antico Borgo** (☑ 080 444 64 00; www.rosticceria-lanticoborgo.it; Via Tarantini 9; roast meat €18-28).

Cisternino is accessible by regular trains from Bari (€6, 45 minutes).

Martina Franca

POP 49,800

The old quarter of this town is a picturesque scene of winding alleys, blinding white houses and blood-red geraniums. There are graceful baroque and rococo buildings here too, plus airy piazzas and curlicue ironwork balconies that almost touch above the narrow streets. This town is the highest in the Murgia, and was founded in the 10th century by refugees fleeing the Arab invasion of Taranto. It only started to flourish in the 14th century when Philip of Anjou granted tax exemptions (*franchigie*, hence Franca); the town became so wealthy that a castle and defensive walls complete with 24 solid bastions were built.

◉ Sights & Activities

The beauty of Martina Franca encourages wandering around the *centro storico*'s narrow lanes and alleyways.

Passing under the baroque **Arco di Sant'Antonio** at the western end of pedestrianised Piazza XX Settembre, you emerge into Piazza Roma, dominated by the imposing, austere 17th-century **Palazzo Ducale**, built over an ancient castle and now used as municipal offices.

From Piazza Roma, follow the fine Corso Vittorio Emanuele, with baroque town houses, to reach Piazza Plebiscito, the centre's baroque heart. The piazza is overlooked by the 18th-century **Basilica di San Martino**, its centrepiece city patron, St Martin, swinging a sword and sharing his cloak with a beggar.

Walkers can ask for the *Carta dei Sentieri del Bosco delle Pianelle* (free) from the tourist office, which maps out 10 walks in the nearby **Bosco delle Pianelle** (around 10km west of town). This lush woodland is part of the larger 12-sq-km **Riserva Naturale Regionale Orientata** – populated with lofty trees, wild orchids, and a rich and varied bird life with kestrels, owls, buzzards, hoopoe and sparrow hawks.

Festivals & Events

Festival della Valle d'Itria MUSIC
Festival della Valle d'Itria is an annual music festival (late July to early August) featuring international performances of opera, classical and jazz. For information, contact the **Centro Artistico Musicale Paolo Grassi** (☎080 480 51 00; www.festivaldellavalleditria.it; ⊙10am-1pm Mon-Fri) in the Palazzo Ducale.

Sleeping

B&B San Martino B&B $
(☎080 48 56 01; http://xoomer.virgilio.it/bed-and-breakfast-sanmartino; Via Abate Fighera 32; d €40-120; ❄) A stylish B&B in a historic palace with rooms overlooking gracious Piazza XX Settembre. The apartments have exposed stone walls, shiny parquet floors, wrought-iron beds and small kitchenettes.

Villaggio In APARTMENT $$
(☎080 480 59 11; www.villaggioincasesparse.it; Via Arco Grassi 8; apt per night €75-170, apt per week €335-1030; ❄) These charming arched apartments are located in original *centro storico* homes. The rooms are large, painted in pastel colours and decorated with antiques and country frills. A variety of apartments are on offer, sleeping from two to six people.

Eating

Il Ritrovo degli Amici TRADITIONAL ITALIAN $$
(☎080 483 92 49; www.ilritrovodegliamici.it; Corso Messapia 8; meals €35; ⊙lunch & dinner Tue-Sat, lunch Sun Mar-Jan) This excellent restaurant with stone walls and vaulting, in a street off Corso Italia, has a convivial atmosphere oiled by the region's spumante. Dishes are traditional, with salamis and sausages as the specialities.

Ciacco PUGLIAN $$
(☎080 480 04 72; Via Conte Ugolino; meals €30; ⊙lunch & dinner Tue-Sun) Dive into the historic centre to find Ciacco, a traditional restaurant with white-clad tables and a cosy fireplace, serving up Puglian cuisine in a modern key. It's tucked down a narrow pedestrian lane a couple of streets in from the Chiesa del Carmine.

La Piazzetta Garibaldi OSTERIA $$
(☎080 430 49 00; Piazza Garibaldi; meals €20-30; ⊙lunch & dinner Thu-Tue) A highly recommended green-shuttered *osteria* in the *centro storico*. Delicious aromas entice you into the cavelike interior and the *cucina tipica* menu doesn't disappoint. Worthy of a long lunch.

Information

Tourist Office (☎080 480 57 02; Piazza Roma 37; ⊙9am-1pm Mon-Fri, 4.30-7pm Tue & Thu, 9am-12.30pm Sat) The tourist office is within Palazzo Ducale (part of the Bibliotece Comunal).

Getting There & Around

The FSE train station is downhill from the historic centre. Go right along Viale della Stazione, continuing along Via Alessandro Fighera to Corso Italia; continue to the left along Corso Italia to Piazza XX Settembre. **FSE** (☎080 546 21 11) trains run to/from the following destinations:

Bari (€5.20, two hours, hourly)
Lecce (€7.10, two hours, five daily)
Taranto (€2.30, 40 minutes, frequent)

FSE buses run to Alberobello (€1.50, 30 minutes, five per day, Monday to Saturday).

Ostuni

POP 32,500

Ostuni shines like a pearly white tiara, extending across three hills with the magnificent gem of a cathedral as its sparkling centrepiece. It's the end of the *trulli* region and the beginning of the hot, dry Salento. Chic, with some excellent restaurants, stylish bars and swish yet intimate places to stay, it's packed in summer.

Sights

Ostuni is surrounded by olive groves, so this is the place to buy some of the region's DOC 'Collina di Brindisi' olive oil – either delicate, medium or strong – direct from producers.

Cathedral CATHEDRAL
(Via Cattedrale; admission €1; ⊙9am-1pm & 3-7pm) Ostuni's dramatic 15th-century cathedral has an unusual Gothic-Romanesque facade with a frilly rose window and an inverted gable.

Museo di Cività Preclassiche della Murgia MUSEUM
(☎0831 33 63 83; Via Cattedrale 15; ⊙10am-1pm Tue-Fri, 10am-1pm & 4-7pm Sat & Sun) FREE Located in the Convento delle Monacelle, the museum's most famous exhibit is the 25,000-year-old star of the show: Delia. She was pregnant at the time of her death and her well-preserved skeleton was found in a local cave. Many of the finds here come from the Palaeolithic burial ground, now the **Parco Archeologico e Naturale di Arignano** (☎0831 30 39 73), which can be visited by appointment.

🏃 Activities

The surrounding countryside is perfect for cycling.

Ciclovagando CYCLING
(☑330 985255; www.ciclovagando.com; half/full day €30/40) Organises guided tours. Each tour covers approximately 20km and departs daily from various towns in the district, including Ostuni and Brindisi. For an extra €15 you can sample typical Apulian foods on the tour.

🎉 Festivals & Events

La Cavalcata RELIGIOUS
Ostuni's annual feast day is held on 26 August, when processions of horsemen dressed in glittering red-and-white uniforms (resembling Indian grooms on their way to be wed) follow the statue of Sant'Oronzo around town.

🛏 Sleeping

Le Sole Blu B&B $
(☑0831 30 38 56; www.webalice.it/solebluostuni; Corso Vittorio Emanuele II 16; s €30-40, d €60-80) Located in the 18th-century (rather than medieval) part of town, Le Sole Blu only has one room available: it's large and has a separate entrance, but the bathroom is tiny. However, the two self-catering apartments nearby are excellent value.

★ La Terra HOTEL $$
(☑0831 33 66 51; www.laterrahotel.it; Via Petrarolo; d €130-170; P ❄ 🗢) This former 13th-century palace offers atmospheric and stylish accommodation with original niches, dark-wood beams and furniture, and contrasting light stonework and whitewash. The result is a cool contemporary look. The bar is as cavernous as they come – it's tunnelled out of a cave.

🍴 Eating

Osteria Piazzetta Cattedrale OSTERIA $$
(☑0831 33 50 26; www.piazzettacattedrale.it; Via Arcidiacono Trinchera 7; meals €25-30; ☺ Wed-Mon; 🍴) Just beyond the arch opposite Ostuni's cathedral is this tiny little hostelry serving up magical food in an atmospheric setting. The menu includes plenty of vegetarian options.

Osteria del Tempo Perso OSTERIA $$
(☑0831 30 33 20; www.osteriadeltempoperso.com; Gaetano Tanzarella Vitale 47; meals €30; ☺ Tue-Sun) A sophisticated rustic restaurant in a cavelike former bakery, this laid-back place serves great Puglian food, specialising in roasted meats. To get here, face the cathedral's south wall and turn right through the archway into Largo Giuseppe Spennati, then follow the signs to the restaurant.

Porta Nova MODERN ITALIAN $$
(☑0831 33 89 83; www.ristoranteportanova.com; Via G Petrarolo 38; meals €45) This restaurant has a wonderful location on the old city wall. Revel in the rolling views from the terrace or relax in the elegant interior while you feast on top-notch local cuisine, with fish and seafood the speciality.

ℹ Information

Tourist Office (☑0831 30 12 68; Corso Mazzini 8; ☺9am-1pm & 5-9pm Mon-Fri, 5.30-8.30pm Sat & Sun) Located off Piazza della Libertà; can organise guided visits of the town in summer and bike rental.

ℹ Getting There & Around

STP buses run to Brindisi (€2.30, 50 minutes, six daily) and to Martina Franca (€2.30, 45 minutes, three daily), leaving from Piazza Italia in the newer part of Ostuni.

Trains run frequently to Brindisi (€4, 25 minutes) and Bari (€9, 50 minutes). A half-hourly local bus covers the 2.5km between the station and town.

Lecce

POP 95,000

Historic Lecce is a beautiful baroque town; it's a glorious architectural confection of palaces and churches intricately sculpted from the soft local sandstone. It is a city full of surprises: one minute you are perusing sleek designer fashions from Milan, the next you are faced with a church – dizzyingly decorated with asparagus column tops, decorative dodos and cavorting gremlins. Swooning 18th-century traveller Thomas Ashe thought it 'the most beautiful city in Italy', but the less-impressed Marchese Grimaldi said the facade of Santa Croce made him think a lunatic was having a nightmare.

Either way, it's a lively, graceful but relaxed university town packed with upmarket boutiques, antique shops, restaurants and bars. Both the Adriatic and Ionian Seas are within easy access and it's a great base from which to explore the Salento.

Lecce

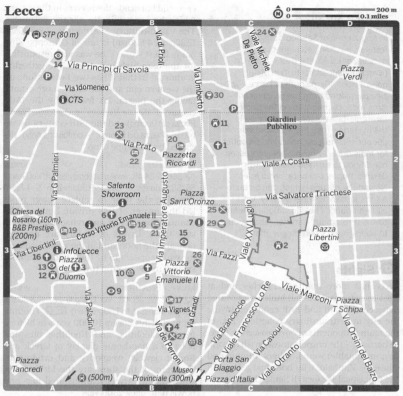

Lecce

◎ Sights

1 Basilica di Santa Croce	C2
2 Castello di Carlo V	C3
3 Cathedral	A3
4 Chiesa di San Matteo	B4
5 Chiesa di Santa Chiara	B3
6 Chiesa di Sant'Irene	B3
7 Colonna di Sant'Oronzo	B3
8 Museo Faggiano	B4
9 Museo Teatro Romano	B3
10 MUST	B3
11 Palazzo del Governo	C2
12 Palazzo Vescovile	A3
13 Piazza del Duomo	A3
14 Porta Napoli	A1
15 Roman Amphitheatre	B3
16 Seminario	A3

⌂ Sleeping

17 Azzuretta B&B	B4

Centro Storico B&B	(see 17)
18 Palazzo Belli B&B	B3
19 Palazzo Rollo	A3
20 Patria Palace Hotel	B2
21 Risorgimento Resort	B3
22 Suite 68	B2

⊗ Eating

23 Alle due Corti	B2
24 Cucina Casareccia	C1
25 Gelateria Natale	C3
26 Mamma Lupa	B3
27 Trattoria di Nonna Tetti	B4

⊖ Drinking & Nightlife

28 All'Ombra del Barocco	B3
29 Caffè Alvino	C3
30 Shui 13 Wine Bar	C1

SPIDER MUSIC

In August one of Salento's biggest festivals is a frenzied night of *pizzica* dancing at **La Notte della Taranta** (www.lanottedellataranta.it) in Melpignano, about 30km south of Lecce. *Pizzica* developed from the ritual *tarantismi,* a dance meant to rid the body of tarantula-bite poison. It's more likely the hysterical dancing was symbolic of a deeper societal psychosis and an outlet for individuals living in bleak, repressed conditions to express their pent-up desires, hopes and unresolved grief. Nowadays, *pizzica* (which can be quite a sensual dance) means 'party', with all-night dances held in various Salento towns throughout summer, leading up to Melpignano's humdinger affair.

⊙ Sights

Lecce has more than 40 churches and at least as many *palazzi,* all built or renovated between the 17th and 18th centuries, giving the city an extraordinary cohesion. Two of the main proponents of *barocco leccese* (Lecce baroque – the craziest, most lavish decoration imaginable) are brothers Antonio and Giuseppe Zimbalo, who both had a hand in the fantastical Basilica di Santa Croce.

Basilica di Santa Croce   CHURCH
(☑ 0832 24 19 57; www.basilicasantacroce.eu; Via Umberto I; ⊙ 9am-noon & 5-8pm) It seems that hallucinating stonemasons have been at work on the basilica. Sheep, dodos, cherubs and beasties writhe across the facade, a swirling magnificent allegorical feast. Throughout the 16th and 17th centuries, a team of artists under Giuseppe Zimbalo laboured to work the building up to this pitch. Look for Zimbalo's profile on the facade.

The interior is more conventionally Renaissance and deserves a look, once you've finished gazing outside. Zimbalo also left his mark in the former Convento dei Celestini, just north of the basilica, which is now the **Palazzo del Governo**, the local government headquarters.

Piazza del Duomo   PIAZZA
A baroque feast, Piazza del Duomo is the city's focal point and a sudden open space amid the surrounding enclosed lanes. During times of invasion the inhabitants of Lecce would barricade themselves in the square, which has conveniently narrow entrances. The 12th-century **cathedral** (⊙ 8.30am-12.30pm & 4-6.30pm) is one of Giuseppe Zimbalo's finest works – he was also responsible for the 68m-high bell tower. The cathedral is unusual in that it has two facades, one on the western end and the other, more ornate, facing the piazza. It's framed by the 15th-century **Palazzo Vescovile** (Episcopal Palace; Piazza del Duomo) and the 18th-century **Seminario** (Piazza del Duomo; ⊙ exhibitions only), designed by Giuseppe Cino.

Museo Faggiano   MUSEUM
(☑ 360 72 24 48; www.museofaggiano.it; Via Grandi 56/58; admission €3; ⊙ 9.30am-1pm & 4-8pm) Breaking the floor to replace sewer pipes led the owner of this private home to the chance discovery of an archaeological treasure trove. Layers of history are revealed beneath the floors and in the walls. Look out for what appears to be the Knights Templar symbol in the rooftop tower.

Museo Provinciale   MUSEUM
(☑ 0832 68 35 03; Via Gallipoli 28; ⊙ 8.30am-7.30pm Mon-Sat, to 1.30pm Sun) **FREE** The museum stylishly covers 10,000 years of history, from Palaeolithic and Neolithic bits and bobs to a handsome display of Greek and Roman jewels, weaponry and ornaments. The stars of the show are the Messapians, whose jaunty Mycenaean-inspired jugs and bowls date back 2500 years.

Roman Amphitheatre   HISTORIC SITE
(Piazza Sant'Oronzo; adult/reduced €2/1; ⊙ 10am-noon & 5-7pm May-Sep) Below the ground level of the piazza is this restored 2nd-century-AD amphitheatre, discovered in 1901 by construction workers. It was excavated in the 1930s to reveal a perfect horseshoe with seating for 15,000.

MUST   ART GALLERY
(www.mustlecce.it; Via degli Ammirati 11; admission €3; ⊙ 10am-1.30pm & 2.30-7.30pm) This beautiful conversion of the Monastery of Santa Chiara houses the work of local artists and has a great view of a Roman amphitheatre from the back window. There are plans to expand the remit to cover local history; at present the contemporary art is spread a bit thin.

Colonna di Sant'Oronzo   MONUMENT
(Piazza Sant'Oronzo) A statue of Lecce's patron saint perches precariously on a column in the piazza. The column, originally from

Brindisi, marked the end of the Via Appia – the Roman road that stretched from Rome to Brindisi.

Museo Teatro Romano   HISTORIC SITE
(☑0832 27 91 96; Via degli Ammirati; adult/reduced €3/2; ⊙9.30am-1.30pm & 5-7.30pm Mon-Fri, 9.30am-1.30pm Sat) Uncovered in the 1930s, this small Roman theatre has well-preserved russet-coloured Roman mosaics and frescoes.

Castello di Carlo V   CASTLE
(☑0832 24 65 17; ⊙9am-1pm & 5-9pm) `FREE`
This 16th-century castle was built around a 12th-century Norman tower to the orders of Charles V and consists of two concentric trapezoidal structures. It's been used as a prison, a court and military headquarters; now you can wander around the baronial spaces and visit the occasional art exhibition.

🎓 Courses

Awaiting Table   COOKING
(www.awaitingtable.com; day/week €195/1995) Silvestro Silvestori's splendid culinary and wine school provides day or weeklong courses with market shopping, tours, tastings, noteworthy lecturers – and lots of hands-on cooking. Book well in advance as courses fill up rapidly.

🛌 Sleeping

⭐**Palazzo Belli B&B**   B&B $
(☑380 7758456; www.palazzobelli.it; Corso Vittorio Emanuele II 33; s €50-60, d €70-80; 🛜) A wonderfully central, elegant and well priced op-

tion, located in a fine mansion building near the cathedral. Rooms have marbled floors and wrought-iron beds. Breakfast is served in the nearby All'Ombra del Barocco bar.

⭐**Palazzo Rollo**   APARTMENT $
(☑0832 30 71 52; www.palazzorollo.it; Corso Vittorio Emanuele II 14; s €50-60, d €70-90, ste €100-120, apt €70-90; 🅿❄@) Stay in a 17th-century palace – the Rollo family seat for more than 200 years. The three grand B&B suites (with kitchenettes) have high curved ceilings and chandeliers. Downstairs, contemporary-chic studios open onto an ivy-hung courtyard. The rooftop garden has wonderful views.

Azzurretta B&B   GUESTHOUSE $
(☑0832 24 22 11; www.hostelecce.com; Via Vignes 2; s €30-38, d €55-70; 🅿🛜) The friendly brother of the owner of Centro Storico B&B runs this artier version located within the same building; ask for the large double with a balcony, wooden floors and a vaulted ceiling. Massage is available in your room or on the roof terrace. You get a cafe voucher for breakfast. The brothers have a tiny studio flat, which is a little dark but a good option if you're self-catering on a budget.

Suite 68   BOUTIQUE HOTEL $
(☑0832 30 35 06; www.kalekora.it; Via Prato 7-9; s €70-80, d €80-120; ❄@🛜) Strong colours, abstract canvases and vividly patterned rugs in the large, bright rooms give this place a contemporary feel. It's simple and stylish. Bikes available.

LECCE'S NOTABLE CHURCHES

On Corso Vittorio Emanuele, the interior of 17th-century **Chiesa di Sant'Irene** contains a magnificent pair of mirror-image baroque altarpieces, facing each other across the transept. Other notable baroque churches include the following:

Chiesa di Santa Chiara (Piazza Vittorio Emanuele II; ⊙9.30-11.30am daily, plus 4.30-6.30pm Mon-Sat) A notable baroque church with every niche a swirl of twisting columns and ornate statuary.

Chiesa di San Matteo (Via dei Perroni 29; ⊙7.30-11am & 4-6pm) Located 200m to the south of Chiesa di Santa Chiara; and the last work of Giuseppe Zimbalo.

Chiesa del Rosario (Via Libertini) Instead of the intended dome roof, this church ended up with a quick-fix wooden one following Zimbalo's death before the building was completed.

Chiesa dei SS Nicolò e Cataldo (Via San Nicola; ⊙9am-noon Sep-Apr) The Chiesa dei SS Nicolò e Cataldo, near Porta Napoli, was built by the Normans in 1180. It got caught up in the city's baroque frenzy and was revamped in 1716 by the prolific Giuseppe Cino, who retained the Romanesque rose window and portal.

LECCE IN ONE DAY

Start the day with a cappuccino and *pasticciotto* (custard-filled pastry) at Caffè Alvino on Piazza Sant'Oronzo. All that sugar and froth should be good preparation for the fanciful Basilica di Santa Croce (p728), worth at least an hour of your time.

To get a sense of Lecce's history visit the fascinating Museo Faggiano (p728), then come back to the present with a spot of window-shopping and browsing through the entertaining mix of shops on Corso Vittorio Emanuele II. Be sure to stop for a campari and soda at one of the many bars in town before lunching on typical Puglian fare at firmly traditional Alle due Corti.

Walk off the pasta and beans by heading across town to the excellent Museo Provinciale (p728). Or, for more fancy facades, Lecce's baroque feast of *palazzi*-flanked streets (like Via Palmieri), churches and the cathedral (p728) will keep you happily wandering till dinner-time. Crown your day with a meal at Cucina Casareccia (p730), where you'll feel like one of the family. Stroll back to your hotel via the Basilica di Santa Croce, which is spectacularly lit up at night.

Centro Storico B&B
B&B $

(☑ 338 5881265; www.bedandbreakfast.lecce.it; Via Vignes 2b; s €35-40, d €70-100; P ※ ⑦) This friendly and efficient B&B located in a historic palace features big rooms, double-glazed windows and pleasantly old-fashioned decor. The huge rooftop terrace has sun loungers and views; you get a cafe voucher for breakfast, and it also has coffee-and-tea-making facilities.

B&B Prestige
B&B $

(☑ 349 7751290; www.bbprestige-lecce.it; Giuseppe Libertini 7; s €60-70, d €70-90, tr €100-110; P @ ⑦) On the corner of Via Santa Maria del Paradiso in the historic centre, the rooms in this lovely B&B are light, airy and beautifully finished. The communal sun-trap terrace has views over San Giovanni Battista church.

Risorgimento Resort
HOTEL $$

(☑ 0832 24 63 11; www.risorgimentoresort.it; Via Imperatore Augusto 19; d €145-165, ste €190-290; P ※ @ ⑦) A warm welcome awaits at this stylish five-star hotel in the centre of Lecce. The rooms are spacious and refined with high ceilings, modern furniture and contemporary details reflecting the colours of the Salento, and the bathrooms are enormous. There's a restaurant, wine bar and rooftop garden.

Patria Palace Hotel
HOTEL $$

(☑ 0832 24 51 11; www.patriapalacelecce.com; Piazzetta Riccardi 13; s €106-210, d €165-350; P ※ @ ⑦) This sumptuous hotel is traditionally Italian with large mirrors, darkwood furniture and wistful murals. The location is wonderful, the bar gloriously art deco with a magnificent carved ceiling, and the shady roof terrace has views over the Basilica di Santa Croce.

🍴 Eating

Gelateria Natale
GELATO $

(Via Trinchese 7a) Lecce's best ice-cream parlour also has an array of fabulous confectionery.

Mamma Lupa
OSTERIA $

(☑ 340 7832765; Via Acaja 12; meals €20-25; ☺ lunch Sun-Fri, dinner daily) Looking suitably rustic, this *osteria* serves proper peasant food – such as roast tomatoes, potatoes and artichokes, or horse meatballs – in snug surroundings with just a few tables and a stone-vaulted ceiling.

Trattoria di Nonna Tetti
TRATTORIA $

(☑ 0832 24 60 36; Piazzetta Regina Maria 28; mains €8-12; ☺ lunch & dinner) A warmly inviting restaurant, popular with all ages and budgets, this trattoria serves a wide choice of traditional dishes. Try the most emblematic Puglian dish here – braised wild chicory with a purée of boiled dried fava beans, along with *contorni* (side dishes) like *patate casarecce* (homemade thinly sliced fries).

★ Cucina Casareccia
TRATTORIA $$

(☑ 0832 24 51 78; Viale Costadura 19; mains €12; ☺ lunch Tue-Sun, dinner Tue-Sat) Ring the bell to gain entry into a place that feels like a private home, with its patterned cement floor tiles, desk piled high with papers, and charming owner Carmela Perrone. In fact, it's known locally as *le Zie* (the aunts). Here you'll taste the true *cucina povera*, including horse meat done in a *salsa piccante* (spicy sauce). Booking is a must.

Alle due Corti
PUGLIAN $$

(☑0832 24 22 23; www.alleduecorti.com; Via Prato 42; mains €12; ☺lunch & dinner daily, closed winter) For a taste of sunny Salento, check out this no-frills, fiercely traditional restaurant. The seasonal menu is classic Puglian, written in a dialect that even some Italians struggle with. Go for the real deal with a dish of *ciceri e tria* (crisply fried pasta with chickpeas).

 Drinking

Via Imperatore Augusto is full of bars, and on a summer's night it feels like one long party. Wander along to find somewhere to settle.

All'Ombra del Barocco
WINE BAR

(www.allombradelbarocco.it; Corte dei Cicala 9; ☺8am-1am) This cool restaurant/cafe/wine bar next door to the Liberrima bookshop has a range of teas, cocktails and *aperitivi*. It's open for breakfast and also hosts musical events; the modern cooking is well worth a try. Tables fill the little square outside, an ideal place from which to watch the *passeggiata* (evening stroll).

Caffè Alvino
CAFE

(Piazza Sant'Oronzo; ☺Wed-Mon) Treat yourself to great coffee and *pasticciotto* (custard-filled pastry) at this iconic chandeliered cafe in Lecce's main square: it has a sumptuous display of cakes.

Shui 13 Wine Bar
WINE BAR

(Via Umberto I 21; ☺10am-late summer, 10am-3pm & 6pm-midnight winter) A hip and atmospheric wine bar with candlelit outside tables and a range of Puglian wines.

ⓘ Information

The centre's twin main squares are Piazza Sant'Oronzo and Piazza del Duomo, linked by pedestrianised Corso Vittorio Emanuele II.

CTS (☑0832 30 18 62; Via Palmieri 89; ☺9am-1pm daily & 4-7.30pm Sun & Mon) Good for student travel.

Hospital (☑0832 66 11 11; Via San Cesario) About 2km south of the centre on the Gallipoli road.

InfoLecce (☑0832 52 18 77; www.infolecce.it; Piazza del Duomo 2; ☺9.30am-1.30pm & 3.30-7.30pm Mon-Sat, from 10am Sun) Independent and helpful tourist information office. Has guided tours and bike rental (per hour/day €3/15).

Police Station (☑0832 69 11 11; Viale Otranto 1)

Post Office (Piazza Libertini)

Puglia Blog (www.thepuglia.com) Voted in Italy as the most popular blog on Puglia, this informative site run by Fabio Ingrosso has articles on culture, history, food, wine, accommodation and travel in Puglia.

Salento Showroom (☑0832 179 03 57; www.salentotime.it; Via Revina Isabella 22; ☺9.30am-1.30pm & 3.30-7.30pm Mon-Sat, from 10am Sun) Independent tourist office that can provide help with accommodation and car hire. Has internet access (per hour €3).

Tourist Office (☑0832 24 80 92; www.viaggiare-inpuglia.it; Corso Vittorio Emanuele II 24; ☺9am-1pm & 4-7pm Mon-Thu, 9am-1pm Fri & Sat)

ⓘ Getting There & Away

BUS

The city bus terminal is located to the north of Porta Napoli.

STP (☑0832 35 91 42; www.stplecce.it) Runs buses to Brindisi (€6.30, 35 minutes, nine daily) and throughout Puglia from the **STP bus station** (☑800 43 03 46; Viale Porta D'Europa).

FSE (☑0832 66 81 11; www.fseonline.it) Runs buses to Gallipoli (€2.60, one hour, four daily) and Otranto (€2.60, 1½ hours, two daily), leaving from Largo Vittime del Terrorismo.

Pugliairbus (http://pugliairbus.aeroportidipuglia.it) Runs to Brindisi airport (€7, 40 minutes, nine daily). **SITA** also has buses to Brindisi airport (€6, 45 minutes, nine daily), leaving from Viale Porte d'Europa.

TRAIN

The train station is 1km southwest of Lecce's historic centre. It runs frequent services to the following destinations:

Bari (from €9, 1½ to two hours)

Bologna (from €82.50, 7½ to 9½ hours)

Brindisi (from €9, 30 minutes)

Naples (from €41, 5½ hours with transfer in Caserta)

Rome (from €66, 5½ to nine hours)

FSE trains head to Otranto, Gallipoli and Martina Franca; the ticket office is located on platform 1.

Brindisi

POP 89,800

Like all ports, Brindisi has its seamy side, but it's also surprisingly slow paced and balmy, particularly the palm-lined Corso Garibaldi linking the port to the train station and the promenade stretching along the interesting seafront.

The town was the end of the ancient Roman road Via Appia, down whose weary length trudged legionnaires and pilgrims, crusaders and traders, all heading to Greece and the Near East. These days little has

Brindisi

changed except that Brindisi's pilgrims are sun-seekers rather than soul-seekers.

◉ Sights

★ **Museo Archeologico Provinciale Ribezzo** MUSEUM
(☎0831 56 55 08; Piazza del Duomo 8; ◷9.30am-1.30pm Tue-Sat & 3.30-6.30pm Tue, Thu & Sat) **FREE** This superb museum covers several floors with well-documented exhibits (in English) including some 3000 bronze sculptures and fragments in Hellenistic Greek style. There are also terracotta figurines from the 7th century, underwater archaeological finds, and Roman statues and heads (not always together).

Chiesa di Santa Maria del Casale CHURCH
(☎0831 41 85 45; Via Ruggero de Simone; ◷8am-8pm) Located 4km north of town towards the airport, this church was built by Prince Philip of Taranto around 1300. The church mixes up Puglian Romanesque, Gothic and Byzantine styles, with a Byzantine banquet of interior frescoes. The immense *Last Judgement* on the entrance wall, full of blood and thunder, is the work of Rinaldo di Taranto.

Roman Column MONUMENT
(Via Colonne) The gleaming white column above a sweeping set of sun-whitened stairs leading to the waterfront promenade marks the imperial Via Appia terminus at Brindisi. Originally there were two, but one was presented to the town of Lecce back in 1666 as thanks to Sant'Oronzo for having relieved Brindisi of the plague.

Cathedral CATHEDRAL
(Piazza del Duomo; ◷8am-9pm Mon-Fri & Sun, to noon Sat) This 11th-century cathedral was substantially remodelled about 700 years later. You can see how it may have looked from the nearby **Porta dei Cavalieri Templari**, a fan-

Brindisi

ciful portico with pointy arches – all that remains of the Knights Templar's main church.

Tempio di San Giovanni al Sepolcro CHURCH
(Via San Giovanni) The Knights Templar's secondary church is a square brown bulk of Norman stone conforming to the circular plan the Templars so loved.

Monument to Italian Sailors MONUMENT
For a wonderful view of Brindisi's waterfront, take one of the regular boats (return €1.80) on Viale Regina Margherita across the harbour to the monument erected by Mussolini in 1933.

🛏 Sleeping

B&B Federico II APARTMENT $
(📞 0328 9277735; www.bbfederico2.it; Via Federico II di Svevia 27; s €35-40, d €60-70; 🛜) Positioned near the harbour, these are two simple but attractive apartments arranged around a palm-shaded courtyard. The stand-out factor is the great service, with a warm welcome and a thoughtfully stocked fridge.

Hotel Orientale HOTEL $$
(📞 0831 56 84 51; www.hotelorientale.it; Corso Garibaldi 40; s/d €75/130; P ✻ 🛜) This sleek, modern hotel overlooks the long palm-lined *corso*. Rooms are pleasant, the location is good and it has a small fitness centre, private car park and (rare) cooked breakfast option.

🍽 Eating

Trattoria Pantagruele TRATTORIA $$
(📞 0831 56 06 05; Via Salita di Ripalta 1; meals €30; ⊙ lunch & dinner Mon-Fri, dinner Sat) Named af-

ter French writer François Rabelais' satirical character, this charming trattoria three blocks from the waterfront serves up excellent fish and grilled meats.

Il Giardino PUGLIAN $$
(📞 0831 56 40 26; Via Tarantini 14-18; meals €30; ⊙ lunch & dinner Tue-Sat, lunch Sun) Established more than 40 years ago in a restored 15th-century *palazzo*, sophisticated Il Giardino serves refined seafood and meat dishes in a delightful garden setting.

ℹ Information

The new port is east of town, across the Seno di Levante at Costa Morena, in a bleak industrial wilderness.

The old port is about 1km from the train station along Corso Umberto I, which leads into Corso Garibaldi where there are numerous cafes, shops, ferry companies and travel agencies.

Ferries (www.ferries.gr) Details of ferry fares and timetables to Greek destinations.
Hospital (📞 0831 53 71 11) Southwest of the centre; take the SS7 for Mesagne.
Post Office (Piazza Vittoria)
Tourist Office (📞 0831 52 30 72; www.viaggiareinpuglia.it; Viale Regina Margherita 44; ⊙ 9am-1pm & 2-8pm Mon-Sat summer, 8.30am-2pm Mon-Sat & 3.30-7pm Mon-Fri winter) Has a wealth of information and brochures on the area. If you are interested in pedal power, pick up *Le Vie Verdi* map with eight bicycling routes in the Brindisi area, ranging from 6km to 30km.

ℹ Getting There & Away

AIR
From **Papola Casale** (BDS; www.aeroportidipuglia.it), Brindisi's small airport, there are domestic flights to Rome, Naples and Milan. Airlines include Alitalia, AirOne and easyJet. There are also direct flights from London Stansted with Ryanair.

Major and local car-rental firms are represented at the airport and there are regular SITA buses to Lecce (€6.50, 35 minutes, nine daily) and STP buses to central Brindisi (€1.60, 15 to 30 minutes, every 30 minutes).

Pugliairbus (http://pugliairbus.aeroportidipuglia.it) has services to Bari airport (€8, 1¾ hours) and Lecce (€7, 40 minutes).

BOAT
Ferries, all of which take vehicles, leave Brindisi for Greece and Albania.

Ferry companies have offices at Costa Morena (the newer port); the major ones also have offices in town.

Agoudimos Lines (www.ferries.gr/agoudimos) To Corfu, Igoumenitsa and Cephalonia in Greece; to Vlore in Albania.

Endeavour Lines (☑ 0831 57 38 00; www.endeavour-lines.com; Via Prov. Le per Lecce 27) To Igoumenitsa, Patras, Corfu and Cephalonia in Greece.

Red Star Ferries (☑ 0831 57 52 89; www.directferries.co.uk/red_star_ferries.htm) To Vlore in Albania.

BUS

STP (☑ 0831 54 92 45) buses go to Ostuni (€2.90, 50 minutes, six daily) and Lecce (€3.30, 45 minutes, two daily), as well as towns throughout the Salento. Most leave from Via Bastioni Carlo V, in front of the train station. Ferrovie del Sud-Est buses serving local towns also leave from the same place.

TRAIN

The train station has regular services to the following destinations:

Bari (from €14, one hour)

Lecce (from €9, 30 minutes)

Milan (from €99.50, 8½ to 11 hours)

Rome (from €66, five to seven hours)

Taranto (from €4.50, 1¼ hours)

❶ Getting Around

A free minibus connects the train station and old ferry terminal with Costa Morena. It departs two hours before boat departures. You'll need a valid ferry ticket.

To reach the airport take the STP-run Cotrap bus from Via Bastioni Carlo V.

Southern & Western Salento

The Penisola Salentina, better known simply as Salento, is hot, dry and remote, retaining a flavour of its Greek past. It stretches across Italy's heel from Brindisi to Taranto and down to Santa Maria di Leuca. Here the lush greenery of Valle d'Itria gives way to flat, ochre-coloured fields hazy with wildflowers in spring, and endless olive groves.

Oria

POP 15,400

The multicoloured dome of Oria's cathedral can be seen for miles around, surrounded by the narrow streets of this appealing medieval town. An intriguing, if ghoulish, sight is the cathedral's **Cripta delle Mummie** (Crypt of the Mummies), where 11 mummified corpses

of former monks are still preserved. Surmounting the town, the **Frederick II castle**, built in a triangular shape, has been carefully restored. It is privately owned.

Dating back to Frederick II's reign, **Il Torneo dei Rioni** is the annual battle between the town's quarters. It takes the form of a spectacular *palio* (horse race) and is held every mid-August.

★ **Borgo di Oria** (☑ 329 2307506; www.borgodioria.it; apt €50-100; ※) is a delightful *albergo diffuso* run by the charismatic and well-travelled Francesco Pipino. The self-catering apartments are large, comfortable and tastefully furnished. Reception is at Bar Kenya in Piazza Manfredi.

Waiters in medieval costume welcome you at **Alle Corte di Hyria** (☑ 329 6624507; Via Milizia 146; meals €20-25; ⊙ Thu-Tue), an atmospheric restaurant in a stone-walled cavern.

Oria is on the main Trenitalia line and there are frequent train services from both Brindisi and Taranto. You can also connect with Ostuni and change at Francavilla Fontana for Alberobello and Martina Franca.

Galatina

POP 27,300

With a charming historic centre, Galatina – 18km south of Lecce – is at the core of the Penisola Salentina's Greek past. It is almost the only place where the ritual *tarantismi* (Spider Music) is still practised. The tarantella folk dance evolved from this ritual, and each year on the feast day of St Peter and St Paul (29 June), it is performed at the (now deconsecrated) church.

◉ Sights

Basilica di Santa Caterina d'Alessandria　　　　CHURCH

(⊙ 8am-12.30pm & 4.30-6.45pm Apr-Sep, 8am-12.30pm & 3.45-5.45pm Oct-Mar) Most people come to Galatina to see the incredible 14th-century Basilica di Santa Caterina d'Alessandria. Its interior is a kaleidoscope of fresco. It was built by the Franciscans, whose patroness was Frenchwoman Marie d'Enghien de Brienne. Married to Raimondello Orsini del Balzo, the Salentine's wealthiest noble, she had plenty of cash to splash on interior decoration. The gruesome story goes that Raimondello (who is buried here) climbed Mt Sinai to visit relics of Santa Caterina (St Catherine). Kissing the dead saint's hand, he bit off a finger and brought it back as a holy relic.

The church is absolutely beautiful, with a pure-white altarpiece set against the frenzy of frescoes. It is not clear who the artists Marie employed really were; they could have been itinerant painters down from Le Marche and Emilia or southerners who'd absorbed the latest Renaissance innovations on trips north. Bring a torch.

🛏 Sleeping

Samadhi   AGRITURISMO
(📞 0836 60 02 84; www.agricolasamadhi.com; Via Stazione 116; per person from €40, per week from €390-995; 🅿 🛜 🌊) Soothe the soul further with a stay at Samadhi, located around 7km east of here in tiny Zollino. It's on a 10-hectare organic farm and the owners are multilingual. As well as ayurvedic treatments and yoga courses, there's a vegan restaurant offering organic meals. Check the website for upcoming retreats and courses.

ℹ Getting There & Away

FSE runs frequent trains between Lecce and Galatina (€1.90, 30 minutes), and Zollino (€1.30, 20 minutes).

Otranto
POP 5540

Otranto overlooks a pretty harbour on the turquoise Adriatic coast. In the historic centre, looming golden walls guard narrow car-free lanes, protecting countless little shops selling touristic odds and ends. In July and August it's one of Puglia's most vibrant towns.

Otranto was Italy's main port to the East for 1000 years and suffered a brutal history. There are fanciful tales that King Minos was here and St Peter is supposed to have celebrated the first Western Mass here.

A more definite historical event is the Sack of Otranto in 1480, when 18,000 Turks led by Ahmet Pasha besieged the town. The townsfolk were able to hold the Turks at bay for 15 days before capitulating. Eight hundred survivors were subsequently led up the nearby Minerva hill and beheaded for refusing to convert.

Today the only fright you'll get is the summer crush on Otranto's scenic beaches and in its narrow streets.

👁 Sights

★ Cathedral   CATHEDRAL
(📞 0836 80 27 20; Piazza Basilica; ⊙ 8am-noon daily, plus 3-7pm Apr-Sep, 3-5pm Oct-Mar) This ca-

thedral was built by the Normans in the 11th century, though it's been given a few facelifts since. On the floor is a vast 12th-century mosaic of a stupendous tree of life balanced on the back of two elephants. It was created by a young monk called Pantaleone (who had obviously never seen an elephant), whose vision of heaven and hell encompassed an amazing (con)fusion of the classics, religion and plain old superstition, including Adam and Eve, Diana the huntress, Hercules, King Arthur, Alexander the Great, and a menagerie of monkeys, snakes and sea monsters. Don't forget to look up; the cathedral also boasts a beautiful wooden coffered ceiling.

It's amazing that the cathedral survived at all, as the Turks stabled their horses here when they beheaded the martyrs of Otranto on a stone preserved in the altar of the chapel (to the right of the main altar). This **Cappella Mortiri** (Chapel of the Dead) is a ghoulishly fascinating sight, with the skulls and bones of the martyrs arranged in neat patterns in seven tall glass cases.

Castello Aragonese Otranto   CASTLE
(www.castelloaragoneseotranto.it; Piazza Castello; adult/child €2/free; ⊙ 10am-1pm & 3-5pm Oct-Mar, 10am-1pm & 3-7pm Apr-May, 10am-1pm & 3-10pm Jun & Sep, 10am-midnight Aug) This squat thick-walled fort, with the Charles V coat of arms above the entrance, has great views from the ramparts. There are some faded original murals and original cannonballs on display.

Chiesa di San Pietro   CHURCH
(Via San Pietro; ⊙ 10am-noon & 3-6pm) Vivid Byzantine frescoes decorate the interior of this church, which was being restored at the time of writing. Follow the signs from the castle: if it's closed, ask for the key at the cathedral.

DRAMATIC COASTLINE

For a scenic road trip, the drive south from Otranto to Castro takes you along a wild and beautiful coastline. The coast here is rocky and dramatic, with cliffs falling down into the sparkling, azure sea. When the wind is up you can see why it is largely treeless. Many of the towns here started life as Greek settlements, although there are few monuments to be seen. Further south, the resort town of Santa Maria di Leuca is the tip of Italy's stiletto and the dividing line between the Adriatic and Ionian Seas.

Activities

There are some great beaches north of Otranto, especially **Baia dei Turchi**, with its translucent blue water. South of Otranto a spectacular rocky coastline makes for an impressive drive down to Castro. To see what goes on underwater, **Scuba Diving Otranto** (☎0836 80 27 40; www.scubadiving.it; Via Francesco di Paola 43) offers day or night dives as well as introductory courses and diving courses.

Sleeping

★Balconcino d'Oriente B&B $

(☎0836 80 15 29; www.balconcinodoriente.com; Via San Francesco da Paola 71; d €60-120, tr €80-150; P ❄) This B&B has an African/Middle Eastern theme throughout with colourful bed linens, African prints, Moroccan lamps and orange colour washes on the walls. The downstairs restaurant serves traditional Italian meals (four courses €50).

★Palazzo Papaleo HOTEL $$

(☎0836 80 21 08; www.hotelpalazzopapaleo.com; Via Rondachi 1; r €120-490; P ❄ @ 🛜) Located next to the town cathedral, this sumptuous hotel was the first to earn the EU Eco-label in Puglia. Aside from its ecological convictions, the hotel has magnificent rooms with original frescoes, exquisitely carved antique furniture and walls washed in soft greys, ochres and yellows. Soak in the panoramic views while enjoying the rooftop spa. The staff are exceptionally friendly.

Palazzo de Mori B&B $$

(☎0836 80 10 88; www.palazzodemori.it; Bastione dei Pelasgi; r €120-150; ⏲Apr-Oct; ❄ @) In Otranto's historic centre, this charming B&B serves breakfast on the sun terrace overlooking the port. The rooms are decorated in soothing white-on-white.

Eating

La Bella Idrusa PIZZERIA $

(☎0836 80 14 75; Via Lungomare degli Eroi; pizzas €5; ⏲dinner Thu-Tue) You can't miss this pizzeria right by the huge Porta Terra in the historic centre. Despite the tourist-trap location, the food is well judged. And it's not just pizzas on offer: it also serves seafood standards.

Laltro Baffo SEAFOOD $$

(☎0836 80 16 36; www.laltrobaffo.com; Cenobio Basiliano 23; meals €30-35; ⏲Tue-Sun) This elegant modern restaurant near the castle – on a side street signed towards the cathedral – dishes up seafood with a contemporary twist. Try the *polipo alla pignata* (octopus stew).

Information

Tourist Office (☎0836 80 14 36; Piazza Castello; ⏲9am-1pm & 3-8pm Mon-Fri Jun-Sep, 9am-1pm Mon-Fri Oct-May) Faces the castle.

Getting There & Away

Otranto can be reached from Lecce by FSE train (€2.60, 1½ hours) or bus (€2.60, 1½ hours). **Marozzi** (☎0836 80 15 78; www.marozzivt.it) has daily bus services to Rome (€50, 10 hours, three daily). There are no trains on Sunday, so use the replacemement bus service.

For travel information and reservations, head to **Ellade Viaggi** (☎0836 80 15 78; www.ellade-viaggi.it; Via del Porto) at the port.

Gallipoli

POP 21,100

Though not as iconic as the Turkish town of the same name, this Gallipoli (meaning 'beautiful town' in Greek) fills an island in the Ionian Sea and is connected by a bridge to the mainland and modern city. It's a picturesque town surrounded by high walls, which were built to protect it against attacks from the sea. An important fishing centre, it feels like a working Italian town, unlike more seasonal coastal places. In the summer bars and restaurants make the most of the island's ramparts, looking out to sea.

Sights & Activities

Gallipoli has some fine beaches, including the **Baia Verde**, just south of town. Nature enthusiasts will want to take a day trip to **Parco Regionale Porto Selvaggio**, about 20km north – a protected area of wild coastline with walking trails amid the trees and diving off the rocky shore.

Cattedrale di Sant'Agata CATHEDRAL

(Via Antonietta de Pace; ⏲hours vary) In the centre, on the highest point of the island, is this 17th-century baroque cathedral, lined with paintings by local artists. Zimbalo, who imprinted Lecce with his crazy baroque styles, also worked on the facade.

Frantoio Ipogeo HISTORIC SITE

(☎338 1363063; Via Antonietta de Pace 87; ⏲10am-12.30pm & 4-6.30pm Jun-Sep, to midnight Jun & Jul) This is only one of some 35 olive presses buried in the tufa rock below the town. It's here that they pressed Gallipoli's olive oil, which was then stored in one of the 2000 cisterns carved beneath the old town.

Museo Civico
MUSEUM

(☑ 0833 26 42 24; Via Antonietta de Pace 108; adult €3; ☺ 9am-1pm & 4-9pm Mon-Fri, 10am-1pm Sat) Founded in 1878, the museum is a 19th-century time capsule featuring fish heads, ancient sculptures, a 3rd-century-BC sarcophagus and other weird stuff.

Farmacia Provenzana
HISTORIC BUILDING

(Via Antonietta de Pace; ☺ 8.30am-12.30pm & 4.30-8.30pm Sun-Fri) A beautifully decorated pharmacy dating from 1814.

🛏 Sleeping

La Casa del Mare
B&B $

(☑ 333 4745754; www.lacasadelmare.com; Piazza de Amicis 14; d €60-110; ✱ @ 🛜) This butter-coloured 16th-century building on a little square in the town centre is a great choice. Helpful and friendly Federico has also restored a flamboyant 18th-century *palazzo* nearby, **Palazzo Flora** (www.palazzoflora. com; Via d'Ospina 19; d €65-120, house €150-300), which sleeps four to six and has fantastic views, especially from the rooftop terrace. During the summer Federico cooks a sumptuous buffet feast for his guests every Friday night (per person €35).

Insula
B&B $

(☑ 366 3468357; www.bbinsulagallipoli.it; Via Antonietta de Pace 56; s €40-80, d €60-150; ☺ Apr-Oct; ✱ @) A magnificent 15th-century building houses this memorable B&B. The five rooms are all different but share the same princely atmosphere with exquisite antiques, vaulted high ceilings and cool pastel paintwork.

Relais Corte Palmieri
HOTEL $$

(☑ 0833 26 53 18; www.hotelpalazzodelcorso.it; Corte Palmieri 3; s €130-185, d €165-195; ✱ 🛜) This cream-coloured, well-kept hotel in the historic centre has elegant rooms accentuated by traditional painted furniture, wrought-iron bedheads and crisp red-and-white linen.

🍴 Eating

Caffè Duomo
CAFE $

(Via Antonietta de Pace 72; dessert €9) For good Gallipoli *spumone* (layered ice cream with candied fruit and nuts) and refreshing *granite* (ices made with coffee, fresh fruit or locally grown pistachios and almonds), head to Caffè Duomo.

La Puritate
TRATTORIA $$

(☑ 0833 26 42 05; Via S Elia 18; meals €40-45; ☺ Thu-Tue) A great place for fish in the old town with picture windows and sea views. Follow the excellent antipasti with delicious *primi* (first courses) such as seafood spaghetti, then see what's been caught that day – the swordfish is usually a good bet.

ℹ Information

Tourist Office (☑ 0833 26 25 29; Via Antonietta de Pace 86; ☺ 8am-9pm summer, 8am-1pm & 4-9pm Mon-Sat winter) Near the cathedral in the old town.

ℹ Getting There & Away

FSE buses and trains head to Lecce (€3.90, one hour, four daily).

Taranto
POP 193,100

According to legend, the city was founded by Taras, son of Poseidon, who arrived on the back of a dolphin (as you do). Less romantically, the city was actually founded in the 7th century BC by exiles from Sparta to become one of the wealthiest and most important colonies of Magna Graecia. The fun finished, however, in the 3rd century BC when the Romans marched in, changed its name to Tarentum and set off a two-millennium decline in fortunes. Its cultural heyday may be over but Taranto still remains an important naval base, second only to La Spezia.

Once a Roman citadel, the collapsing historic medieval centre is gritty and dirty but has a lovely seaside promenade. However, the mainland industrial centre, with Italy's largest steel plant, dominates the skyline.

⊙ Sights

Although Taranto's medieval town centre is rundown and has a gritty undertone, it's gradually being tastefully renovated. It is perched on the small island dividing the Mar Piccolo (Small Sea; an enclosed lagoon) and the Mar Grande (Big Sea). This peculiar geography means that blue sea and sky surround you wherever you go.

Museo Nazionale Archeologico
MUSEUM

(☑ 099 453 21 12; www.museotaranto.it; Via Cavour 10; adult/child €5/free; ☺ 8.30am-7.30pm) In the new town is one of Italy's most important archaeological museums, exploring ancient Taras. It houses, among other artefacts, the largest collection of Greek terracotta figures

Taranto

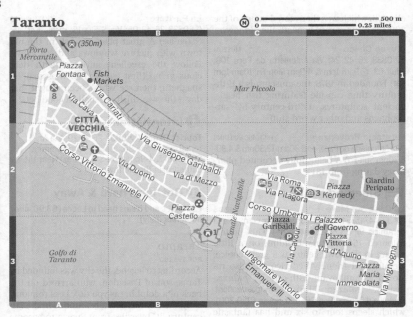

Taranto

⊙ Sights

1 Castello Aragonese	C3
2 Cathedral	A2
3 Museo Nazionale Archeologico	D2
4 Temple of Poseidon	B2

⊟ Sleeping

5 Europa Hotel	C2
6 Hotel Akropolis	A2

⊗ Eating

7 Trattoria al Gatto Rosso	C2
8 Trattoria L'Orologio	A1

in the world. Also on exhibit are fine collections of 1st-century-BC glassware, classic black-and-red Attic vases and stunning jewellery such as a 4th-century-BC bronze and terracotta crown.

Cathedral CATHEDRAL
(Via del Duomo) The 11th-century cathedral is one of Puglia's oldest Romanesque buildings and an extravagant treat. It's dedicated to San Cataldo, an Irish monk who lived and was buried here in the 7th century; the Capella di San Cataldo is a baroque riot of frescoes and polychrome marble inlay.

Castello Aragonese CASTLE
(☎099 775 34 38; www.castelloaragonesetaranto.it; Piazza Castello; ⊙by appointment 9am-noon Mon-Fri) Guarding the swing bridge that joins the old and new parts of town, this impressive 15th-century structure was once a prison and is currently occupied by the Italian navy. Opposite are the remaining columns of Taranto's ancient **Temple of Poseidon** (Piazza Castello).

✺ Festivals & Events

Le Feste di Pasqua RELIGIOUS
Taranto is famous for its Holy Week celebrations – the biggest in the region – when bearers in Ku Klux Klan–style robes carry icons around the town. There are three processions: the Perdoni, celebrating pilgrims; the Addolorata (lasting 12 hours but covering only 4km); and the Misteri (even slower at 14 hours to cover 2km).

⊨ Sleeping

Hotel Akropolis HOTEL $$
(☎099 470 41 10; www.hotelakropolis.it; Vico Seminario 3; s/d €105/145; ❀@⊛) A converted medieval *palazzo* in the crumbling old town, this luxurious hotel sits grandly beside the cathedral. There are 13 stylish cream-and-white rooms, original majolica-tiled floors

and tremendous views from the rooftop terrace. The downstairs bar and restaurant is enclosed in stone, wood and glass and has atmospheric curtained alcoves.

Europa Hotel HOTEL **$$**
(☑ 099 452 59 94; www.hoteleuropaonline.it; Via Roma 2; s €80-105, d €135-190; ❇ 🖭) On the seafront next to the swing bridge, this hotel has comfortable rooms (some with kitchenettes) overlooking the old town.

✖ Eating & Drinking

Trattoria L'Orologio TRATTORIA **$**
(☑ 099 460 87 36; Via Duca D'Aosta 27; meals €18-25; ⊙ lunch & dinner Mon-Fri, lunch Sat) This deeply traditional Tarantine trattoria is known for its seafood, which includes grilled mussels, octopus with lemon and olive oil, and fried prawns and squid.

Trattoria al Gatto Rosso TRATTORIA **$$**
(☑ 099 452 98 75; www.ristorantegattorosso.com; Via Cavour 2; meals €30-35; ⊙ Tue-Sun) A relaxed and unpretentious trattoria with a real touch of class – heavy tablecloths, deep wine glasses and the like. It is located in the new town and is very popular with discerning business types.

❶ Information

Taranto splits neatly into three. The old town is on a tiny island, lodged between the northwest port and train station and the new city to the southeast. Italy's largest steel plant occupies the city's entire western half. The grid-patterned new city contains the banks, most hotels and restaurants and the **tourist office** (☑ 099 453 23 97; Corso Umberto I 113; ⊙ 9am-1pm & 4.30-6.30pm Mon-Fri, 9am-noon Sat).

❶ Getting There & Around

BUS

Buses heading north and west depart from Porto Mercantile. FSE buses go to Bari (€6, 1¾ to 2¼ hours, frequent). Infrequent **SITA** (☑ 899 32 52 04; www.sitabus.it) buses leave for Matera (€5, 1¾ hours, one daily). STP and FSE buses go to Lecce (€6, two hours, four daily).

Marozzi (☑ 080 5799 0111; www.marozzivt. it) has express services serving Rome's Stazione Tiburtina (€43, six hours, three daily). **Autolinee Miccolis** (☑ 099 470 44 51; www.miccolis-spa. it) serves Naples (€23, four hours, three daily) via Potenza (€15, two hours).

The bus **ticket office** (⊙ 6am-1pm & 2-7pm) is at Porto Mercantile.

TRAIN

Trenitalia and FSE trains go to the following destinations:
Bari (€7.40, 2½ hours, frequent)
Brindisi (€5.10, 1¼ hours, frequent)
Rome (from €41, 6 to 7½ hours, five daily)
AMAT (☑ 099 452 67 32; www.amat.taranto. it) buses run between the train station and the new city.

BASILICATA

Basilicata has an other-worldly landscape of tremendous mountain ranges, dark forested valleys and villages so melded with the rockface that they seem to have grown there. Its isolated yet strategic location on routes linking ancient Rome to the eastern Byzantine empire has seen it successively invaded, pillaged, plundered, abandoned and neglected.

In the north the landscape is a fertile zone of gentle hills and deep valleys – once covered in thick forests, now cleared and cultivated with wheat, olives and grapes. The purple-hued mountains of the interior are impossibly grand and a wonderful destination for hikers and naturalists, particularly the soaring peaks of the Lucanian Apennines and the Parco Nazionale del Pollino.

On the coast, Maratea is one of Italy's most chic seaside resorts. However, Matera is Basilicata's star attraction, the famous *sassi* (former cave dwellings) of the cave city presiding over a rugged landscape of ravines and caves. Its ancient cave dwellings tell a tale of poverty, hardship and struggle; its history is best immortalised in writer Carlo Levi's superb book *Christ Stopped at Eboli* – a title suggesting Basilicata was beyond the hand of God, a place where pagan magic still existed and thrived.

Today, Basilicata is attracting a slow but steadily increasing trickle of tourists. For those wanting to experience a raw and unspoilt region of Italy, Basilicata's remote atmosphere and wild landscape will appeal.

History

Basilicata spans Italy's instep with slivers of coastline touching the Tyrrhenian and Ionian Seas. It was known to the Greeks and Romans as Lucania (a name still heard today) after the Lucani tribe who lived here as far back as the 5th century BC. The Greeks also prospered, settling along the coastline at Metapontum and Erakleia, but things

Basilicata

started to go wrong under the Romans, when Hannibal, the ferocious Carthaginian general, rampaged through the region.

In the 10th century the Byzantine emperor Basilikòs (976–1025) renamed the area, overthrowing the Saracens in Sicily and the south and reintroducing Christianity. The pattern of war and overthrow continued throughout the Middle Ages as the Normans, Hohenstaufens, Angevins and Bourbons constantly tussled over its strategic location, right up until the 19th century. As talk of the Italian unification began to gain ground, Bourbon-sponsored loyalists took to Basilicata's mountains to oppose political change. Ultimately, they became the much-feared bandits of local lore who make scary appearances in writings from the late 19th and early 20th centuries. In the 1930s Basilicata was used as a kind of open prison for political dissidents – most famously the painter, writer and doctor

Carlo Levi – sent into exile to remote villages by the fascists.

Matera

POP 60,500 / ELEV 405M

Approach Matera from virtually any direction and your first glimpse of its famous *sassi* is sure to stay in your memory forever. Haunting and beautiful, the *sassi* sprawl below the rim of a yawning ravine like a giant nativity scene. The old town is simply unique and warrants at least a day of exploration and aimless wandering. Although many buildings are crumbling and abandoned, others have been restored and transformed into cosy abodes, restaurants and swish cave-hotels. On the cliff top, the new town is a lively place, with its elegant churches, *palazzi* and especially the pedestrianised Piazza Vittorio Veneto.

History

Matera is said to be one of the world's oldest towns, dating back to the Palaeolithic Age and inhabited continuously for around 7000 years. The simple natural grottoes that dotted the gorge were adapted to become homes, and an ingenious system of canals regulated the flow of water and sewage. In the 8th century the caves became home to Benedictine and Basilian monks; the earliest cave paintings date from this period.

The prosperous town became the capital of Basilicata in 1663, a position it held until 1806 when the power moved to Potenza. In the decades that followed, an unsustainable increase in population led to the habitation of unsuitable grottoes – originally intended as animal stalls – even lacking running water. The dreadful conditions fostered a tough and independent spirit: in 1943, Matera became the first Italian city to rise up against German occupation.

By the 1950s more than half of Matera's population lived in the *sassi*, typical caves sheltering families with an average of six children. The infant mortality rate was 50%. In his poetic and moving memoir, *Christ Stopped at Eboli*, Carlo Levi describes how children would beg passers-by for quinine to stave off the deadly malaria. Such publicity finally galvanised the authorities into action and in the late 1950s about 15,000 inhabitants were forcibly relocated to new government housing schemes. In 1993 the *sassi* were declared a Unesco World Heritage Site, and the town is currently gearing up to be the European Capital of Culture in 2019. Ironically, the town's lack of development due to years of misery has transformed it into Basilicata's leading tourist attraction.

⊙ Sights & Activities

There are two *sasso* districts: the more restored, northwest-facing **Sasso Barisano** and the more impoverished, northeast-facing **Sasso Caveoso**. Both are extraordinary, riddled with serpentine alleyways and staircases, and dotted with frescoed *chiese rupestri* (cave churches) created between the 8th and 13th centuries. Today Matera contains some 3000 habitable caves.

The *sassi* are accessible from several points. There's an entrance off Piazza Vittorio Veneto, or take Via delle Beccherie to Piazza del Duomo and follow the tourist itinerary signs to enter either Barisano or Caveoso. Sasso Caveoso is also accessible from Via Ridola.

PUGLIA, BASILICATA & CALABRIA MATERA

WORTH A TRIP

POETIC VENOSA

About 70km north of Potenza, pretty Venosa used to be a thriving Roman colony, owing much of its prosperity to being a stop on the Appian Way. It was also the birthplace of the poet Horace in 65 BC. The main reason to come here is to see the remains of Basilicata's largest monastic complex.

Venosa's main square, Piazza Umberto I, is dominated by a 15th-century Aragonese castle with a small **Museo Archeologico** (📞 0972 3 60 95; Piazza Umberto I; admission €2.50; ⊗ 9am-8pm Wed-Mon, 2-8pm Tue) that houses finds from Roman Venusia and human bone fragments dating back 300,000 years.

Admission to the museum also gets you into the ruins of the **Roman settlement** (⊗ 9am-1hr before dusk Wed-Mon, 2pm-1hr before dusk Tue) and the graceful later ruins of **Abbazia della Santissima Trinità** (📞 0972 3 42 11). At the northeastern end of town, the *abbazia* (abbey) was erected above the Roman temple around 1046 by the Benedictines and predates the Norman invasions. Within the complex is a pair of churches, one unfinished. The earlier church contains the tomb of Robert Guiscard, a Norman crusader, and his fearsome half-brother Drogo. The other unfinished church was begun in the 11th century using materials from the neighbouring Roman amphitheatre. A little way south are some Jewish and Christian catacombs.

Hotel Orazio (📞 0972 3 11 35; www.hotelorazio.it; Vittorio Emanuele II 142; s €45-50, d/t €65/85) is a 17th-century palace complete with antique majolica tiles and marble floors, and is overseen by a pair of grandmotherly ladies.

Venosa can be reached by taking bus S658 north from Potenza and exiting at Barile onto the S93. Buses run Monday to Saturday from Potenza (€3.30, two hours, two daily).

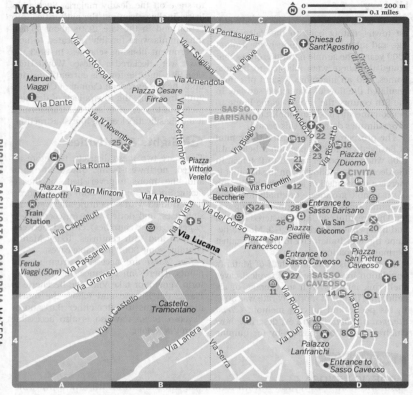

Matera

◉ Sights

1 Casa-Grotta di Vico Solitario..............D4
2 Cathedral D2
3 Chiesa di Madonna delle Virtù &
   Chiesa di San Nicola del Greci D2
4 Chiesa di San Pietro Caveoso D3
5 Chiesa di Santa Lucia alle Malve........B3
6 Chiesa di Santa Maria d'Idris.............D3
7 Chiesa San Pietro Barisano D2
8 La Raccolta delle Acque.....................D4
9 Museo della Scultura
   Contemporanea...........................D2
10 Museo Nazionale d'Arte Medievale
   e Moderna della Basilicata..............D4
11 Museo Nazionale Ridola C3
   Santa Maria di Costantinopoli........(see 2)

◉ Activities, Courses & Tours

12 Cooperativa Amici del Turista.............C2

⌂ Sleeping

13 Hotel in Pietra....................................D3

14 Il Vicinato...D3
15 La Dolce Vita B&B...............................D4
16 Le Monacelle......................................D2
17 Locanda di San Martino......................C2
18 Palazzo Viceconte..............................D2
19 Sassi Hotel...C2

◈ Eating

20 Baccanti...D3
21 La Talpa...C2
22 Le Botteghe..D2
23 Oi Marì...D2
24 Ristorante Il Cantuccio.......................C3
25 Trattoria Lucana.................................B2

◉ Drinking & Nightlife

26 L' Arturo Enogastronomia...................C3
27 Shibuya..C3

◉ Shopping

28 Geppetto..C3

For a great photograph, head out of town for about 3km on the Taranto-Laterza road and follow signs for the *chiese rupestri*. This takes you up on the Murgia Plateau to the **Belvedere** (Taranto-Laterza Rd), from where you have fantastic views of the plunging ravine and Matera.

◉ Sasso Barisano

Chiesa di Madonna delle Virtù & Chiesa di San Nicola del Greci   CHURCH
(Via Madonna delle Virtù; ⊙10am-7pm Sat & Sun) This monastic complex is one of the most important monuments in Matera and is composed of dozens of caves spread over two floors. **Chiesa Madonna delle Virtù** was built in the 10th or 11th century and restored in the 17th century. Above it, the simple **Chiesa di San Nicola del Greci** is rich in frescoes. The complex was used in 1213 by Benedictine monks of Palestinian origin.

Chiesa San Pietro Barisano   CHURCH
(Piazza San Pietro Barisano; adult/reduced €3/2, joint ticket with Chiesa di Santa Lucia alle Malve & Chiesa di Santa Maria d'Idris €6/4.50) Below the church is an ancient honeycomb of niches where corpses were placed for draining, while at the entrance level are 15th- and 16th-century frescoes. The empty frame of the altarpiece graphically illustrates the town's troubled recent history: the church was plundered when Matera was partially abandoned in the '60s and '70s.

◉ Sasso Caveoso

Chiesa di San Pietro Caveoso   CHURCH
(Piazza San Pietro Caveoso) The only church in the *sassi* not dug into the tufa rock, Chiesa di San Pietro Caveoso was originally built in 1300 and has a 17th-century Romanesque-baroque facade.

Chiesa di Santa Maria d'Idris   CHURCH
(Piazza San Pietro Caveoso; adult/reduced €3/2, joint ticket with Chiesa San Pietro Barisano & Chiesa di Santa Lucia alle Malve €6/4.50; ⊙10am-1pm & 2.30-7pm Tue-Oct, 10.30am-1.30pm Tue-Sun Nov-Mar) Dug into the Idris rock, this church has an unprepossessing facade, but the narrow corridor communicating with the recessed church of San Giovanni in Monterrone is richly decorated with 12th- to 17th-century frescoes.

Chiesa di Santa Lucia alle Malve   CHURCH
(Via la Vista; adult/reduced €3/2, joint ticket with Chiesa San Pietro Barisano & Chiesa di Santa Maria d'Idris €6/4.50; ⊙10am-1pm & 2.30-7pm Apr-Oct, 10.30am-1.30pm Tue-Sun Nov-Mar) Built in the 8th century to house a Benedictine convent, this church has a number of 12th-century frescoes including an unusual breastfeeding Madonna.

La Raccolta delle Acque   HISTORIC SITE
(☑340 6659107; www.laraccoltadelleacquemat-era.it; Via Bruno Buozzi 67; adult/child €2.50/1.50; ⊙9.30am-1pm & 2-7pm Apr-Oct, 9.30am-1pm Nov-Mar) Matera's fascinating water-storage system can be better understood when you visit this ancient complex of underground cisterns and canals, which was used to collect rainwater from roofs, streets and houses in the vicinity. The largest cistern is nearly 15m deep and 5m long.

Casa-Grotta di Vico Solitario   HISTORIC SITE
(admission €2) For a glimpse of life in old Matera visit this historic *sasso* off Via Bruno Buozzi. There's a bed in the middle, a loom, a room for manure and a section for a pig and a donkey. You also have access to a couple of neighbouring caves: in one, a black-and-white film depicts gritty prerestoration Matera.

Museo della Scultura Contemporanea   MUSEUM
(MUSMA; ☑366 9357768; www.musma.it; Via San Giacomo; adult/reduced €5/3.50; ⊙10am-2pm Tue-Sun & 4-8pm Sat & Sun Apr-Sep, 10am-2pm Tue-Sun Oct-Mar) Housed in Palazzo Pomarici, MUSMA is a fabulous contemporary

---

EXPLORING THE GORGE

In the picturesque landscape of the Murgia Plateau, the Matera Gravina cuts a rough gouge in the Earth, a 200m-deep canyon pockmarked with abandoned caves and villages. You can hike from the *sassi* (former cave dwellings) into the gorge (steps lead down from the parking place near the Monastero di Santa Lucia) and then up to the Belvedere in one to two hours, but a hike along the canyon rim gives you a better appreciation of the termitelike network of caves that gave birth to the *sassi*. Ferula Viaggi (p746) offers excellent guided hikes into the gorge, as well as a range of hiking and cycling tours throughout Basilicata and Puglia.

MATERA IN...

One Day

Zip out to the **Belvedere** (p743) for a photo-snap of the *sassi* (former cave dwellings) before any heat haze sets in. Back in the *sassi,* approach Sasso Barisano via Via Fiorentini and wind your way along to the monastic complex of **Madonna delle Virtù and San Nicola dei Greci** (p743) with its original frescoes. Then head for more frescoes in the rock churches of Sasso Caveoso, **Santa Maria d'Idris** (p743) and **Santa Lucia alle Malve** (p743). Wander through the *sassi,* imagining life in a cave, stopping to learn about Matera's fascinating system of underground cisterns at **La Raccolta delle Acque** (p743). Early evening, enjoy a *passeggiata* (evening stroll) in and around lively Piazza Vittorio Veneto, followed by dinner at classic **Ristorante Il Cantuccio** (p746).

Two Days

On day two, allow a couple of hours to visit the **Cripta del Peccato Originale**, with its magnificent frescoes. Then either spend the rest of the day hiking in the **gorge** or squeeze in a few museums in town, including the **Museo Nazionale d'Arte Medievale e Moderna della Basilicata**, which showcases Carlo Levi's bold panorama of village life, *Lucania '61*. In the heart of Sasso Caveoso the **Casa-Grotta di Vico Solitario** (p743) may sound a tad contrived but really *does* provide a vivid picture of former living conditions here – both the picturesque and rudimentary aspects. For contemporary sculptures, visit the cave-set **Museo della Scultura Contemporanea** (p743). Finish off with dinner and sunset vistas in a cave at stylish **Baccanti** (p746).

sculpture museum. The setting – deeply recessed caves and frescoed palace rooms – is extraordinary and the works themselves absorbing. You can also book a tour to visit the Cripta del Peccato Originale (Crypt of Original Sin), which is located 7km south of Matera and has well-preserved frescoes from the late 8th century. It's known as the Sistine Chapel of the cave churches and the frescoes depict dramatic Old Testament scenes.

⊙ The New Town

The focus of the town is Piazza Vittorio Veneto, an excellent, bustling meeting point for a *passeggiata* (evening stroll). It's surrounded by elegant churches and richly adorned *palazzi,* with their backs to the *sassi;* an attempt by the bourgeois to block out the shameful poverty the *sassi* once represented.

Museo Nazionale d'Arte Medievale e Moderna della Basilicata   MUSEUM
(⌨0835 31 42 35; Palazzo Lanfranchi; adult/reduced €2/1; ⊙9am-8pm Thu-Tue) The stars of the show are Levi's paintings, including the panoramic mural *Lucania '61* depicting peasant life in biblical Technicolor. There's also some centuries-old sacred art from the *sassi.*

Cathedral   CATHEDRAL
(Piazza del Duomo; ⊙closed for renovation) Set high up in town, the subdued, graceful exterior of the 13th-century Puglian-Romanesque cathedral makes the neobaroque excess within all the more of a surprise: ornate capitals, sumptuous chapels and tons of gilding. Pediments mounted on its altars came from the temples at Metaponto. Matera's patron saint, the Madonna della Bruna, is hidden within the older church, Santa Maria di Costantinopoli, which can be accessed from the cathedral if it's open.

Museo Nazionale Ridola   MUSEUM
(⌨0835 31 00 58; Via Ridola 24; adult/reduced €2.50/1.25; ⊙9am-8pm Tue-Sun, 2-8pm Mon) The impressive collection includes local Neolithic finds and some remarkable Greek pottery, such as the *Cratere Mascheroni,* a huge urn more than 1m high.

☞ Tours

There are plenty of official guides for the sassi – try www.sassiweb.it. Alternatively, contact the Cooperativa Amici del Turista (⌨0835 33 03 01; www.amicidelturista.it; Via Fiorentini 28-30) or English-speaking guide Amy Weideman (⌨339 2823618; aweideman@libero.it; half-day tour for 2 people €40).

For excellent and informative guided visits, Ferula Viaggi (p746) has tours of the *sas-*

si, classic tours, underground tours, tours that include tastings or cookery courses, longer trips to the Pollino or into Puglia, and also hiking and cycling tours. Hikes range from short walks to weeklong trips. For a detailed list of walks, see Ferula Viaggi's **Walk Basilicata** (www.walkbasilicata.it). Ferula Viaggi also runs **Bike Basilicata** (www.bike-basilicata.it), which rents bikes and helmets, and supplies a road book and map so you can head off on your own. Guided bike tours include a seven-night 500km odyssey across Puglia and Basilicata.

⚲ Festivals & Events

Sagra della Madonna della Bruna RELIGIOUS
(⊘2 Jul) The colourful Procession of Shepherds parades ornately decorated papier-mâché floats around town. The finale is the *assalto al carro,* when the crowd descends on the main cart and tears it to pieces.

Gezziamoci MUSIC
(☏0835 33 02 00; www.gezziamocimatera.on-yxjazzclub.it; ⊙Last week of Aug) This jazz festival in the *sassi* and surrounding Murgia park.

⌁ Sleeping

★**La Dolce Vita B&B** B&B $
(☏0835 31 03 24; www.ladolcevitamatera.it; Rione Malve 51; s €40-60, d €60-80; ☞) This delightful

ecofriendly B&B in Sasso Caveoso has self-contained apartments with solar panels and recycled rainwater for plumbing. They're cool, comfortable and homey. Vincenzo is passionate about Matera and is a mine of information on the *sassi.*

★**Le Monacelle** HOSTEL, HOTEL $
(☏0839 34 40 97; www.lemonacelle.it; Via Riscatto 9-10; dm/s/d €18/55/86; ❋☞) Near the *duomo* (cathedral), and incorporating the delightful small Chiesa di San Franceso d'Assisi chapel, this 16th-century building offers simple dorms and elegantly furnished rooms, as well as atmospheric cobbled terraces with stunning *sassi* views. It's warmly welcoming, and the gorge views from the breakfast terrace are a knockout.

Il Vicinato B&B $
(☏0835 31 26 72; www.ilvicinato.com; Piazzetta San Pietro Caveoso 7; s/d €60/70; ❋☞) This B&B enjoys a great, easy-to-find location. Rooms are decorated in clean modern lines, with views across to Idris rock and the Murgia Plateau. There's a room with a balcony and a small apartment, each with an independent entrance.

Sassi Hotel HOTEL $
(☏0835 33 10 09; www.hotelsassi.it; Via San Giovanni Vecchio 89; s/d €70/90, ste incl breakfast €110-160; ❋@) The first hotel in the *sassi*

PUGLIA, BASILICATA & CALABRIA MATERA

MATERA IN THE MOVIES

Matera's unique geography makes it wonderfully photogenic: Italian director, writer and intellectual Pier Paolo Pasolini filmed *Il Vangelo Secondo Matteo* (The Gospel According to St Matthew) here in 1964. Not a Christian himself, Pasolini set out on an exploration of the life of Christ using the words of the gospel itself. It is visually and conceptually hugely striking, infused with revolutionary spirit and featuring a cast of nonprofessional actors.

Forty years later, Mel Gibson came to town to make *The Passion of the Christ,* which follows in grueling detail the last 12 hours of Christ's life, from his arrest in the Garden of Gethsemane to his crucifixion at Golgotha; this was filmed at the Belvedere (p743). Mel's three-month stay in Matera was welcomed by the locals, many of whom were cast as extras; **Trattoria Lucana** (☏0835 33 61 17; Via Lucana 47; ⊙Mon-Sat) still serves its homage dish *Fettuccine alla Mel Gibson.*

Film fans might want to follow a visit to Matera with a stay in nearby Bernalda, the ancestral home of film maker Francis Ford Coppola. In what is clearly a labour of love, Coppola has restored a historic mansion in the town to create the upmarket **Palazzo Margherita** (☏0835 54 90 60; www.coppolaresorts.com/palazzomargherita; Corso Umberto 64; ste incl breakfast & cooking lessons from €360-€1800, 2-night minimum stay) hotel. The lovely salon upstairs doubles as a screening room where you can watch classic Italian movies from a library compiled by Coppola for guests. And if you're just passing through, have a coffee at the hotel's Cinecittà bar, hung with glamorous black-and-white images of Italian stars and directors. You'll have to ask locals to find the hotel as it has no sign: Coppola prefers it to blend in to this otherwise unstarry little town.

is set in an 18th-century rambling edifice in Sasso Barisano with some rooms in caves and some not. Singles are small but doubles are gracefully furnished. The balconies have superb views of the cathedral.

★ **Hotel in Pietra** BOUTIQUE HOTEL **$$**
(✆ 0835 34 40 40; www.hotelinpietra.it; Via San Giovanni Vecchio 22; s €70-150, d €85-160, ste €180-230; ❄ @ 🖤) The lobby is set in a former 13th-century chapel complete with soaring arches, while the eight rooms combine soft golden stone with the natural cave interior. Furnishings are Zen-style with low beds, and the bathrooms are super stylish and include vast sunken tubs.

Locanda di San Martino HOTEL **$$**
(✆ 0835 25 66 00; www.locandadisanmartino.it; Via Fiorentini 71; d €89-200; ❄ 🖤 ⏛) A sumptuous hotel where you can swim in a cave – in a subterranean underground swimming pool. The cave accommodation, complete with niches and rustic brick floors, is set around a warren of cobbled paths and courtyards.

Palazzo Viceconte HOTEL **$$**
(✆ 0835 33 06 99; www.palazzoviceconte.it; Via San Potito 7; d €95-140, ste €139-350; ❄ @) Rooms in this 15th-century *palazzo* near the cathedral have superb views of the *sassi* and gorge. The hotel is elegantly furnished and the rooftop terrace has panoramic views.

✗ Eating

Oi Marì PIZZERIA **$**
(✆ 0835 34 61 21; Via Fiorentini 66; pizzas from €6.50; ⏱ dinner daily, lunch Sat & Sun) In Sasso Barisano, this lofty and convivial cavern is styled as a Neapolitan pizzeria and has a great cheery atmosphere and excellent substantial pizzas to match, as well as *primi* of the day.

La Talpa TRADITIONAL ITALIAN **$**
(✆ 0835 33 50 86; Via Fiorentini 167; meals €15-20; ⏱ Wed-Mon) The cavernous dining rooms here are moodily lit and atmospheric. A popular spot for romancing couples.

★ **Ristorante Il Cantuccio** TRATTORIA **$$**
(✆ 0835 33 20 90; Via delle Becchiere 33; meals €25; ⏱ Tue-Sun) This quaint, homey trattoria near Piazza Vittorio Veneto is as welcoming as its chef and owner, Michael Lella. The menu is seasonal and the dishes traditional and delicious.

Le Botteghe TRATTORIA **$$**
(✆ 0835 34 40 72; Piazza San Pietro; mains €11.50-16; ⏱ lunch & dinner daily Apr-Sep, closed lunch Tue-Thu Oct-Mar) In Sasso Barisano, this is a classy but informal restaurant in arched whitewashed rooms. Try delicious local specialities like *fusilli mollica e crusco* (pasta and fried bread with local sweet peppers).

Baccanti TRADITIONAL ITALIAN **$$$**
(✆ 0835 33 37 04; www.baccantiristorante.com; Via Sant'Angelo 58-61; meals €50; ⏱ lunch & dinner Tue-Sat, lunch Sun) As classy as a cave can be. The design is simple glamour against the low arches of the cavern; the dishes are delicate and complex, using local ingredients. And the gorge views are sublime.

🍷 Drinking & Nightlife

L' Arturo Enogastronomia WINE BAR
(Piazza del Sedile 15) A chic little white-painted deli/wine bar towards the *duomo*. Staff will make you up an artisinal sandwich to go with your glass of local *vino*.

Shibuya BAR
(✆ 0835 33 74 09; Vico Purgatorio 12; ⏱ 9am-3am Tue-Sun) This cool little cafe and CD shop is also a bar and has regular DJs; make a beeline for the few outside tables at the top of an ancient alley.

🛍 Shopping

Geppetto CRAFT
(Piazza del Sedile 19; ⏱ 9.30am-1pm & 3.30-8pm) This craft shop stands out amongst the tawdrier outlets selling tufa lamps and tiles. Its speciality is the *cuccù*, a brightly painted ceramic whistle in the shape of a cockerel, which was once prized by Matera's children. The whistles were traditionally considered a symbol of good luck and fertility.

ℹ Information

The maps *Carta Turistica di Matera* and *Matera: Percorsi Turistici* (€1.50), available from various travel agencies, bookstores and hotels around town, describe a number of itineraries through the *sassi* and the gorge.

Basilicata Turistica (www.aptbasilicata.it) Official tourist website with useful information on history, culture, attractions and sights.

Ferula Viaggi (✆ 0835 33 65 72; www.ferula-viaggi.com; Via Cappelluti 34; ⏱ 9am-1.30pm & 3.30-7pm Mon-Sat) Excellent information centre and travel agency. Runs walking tours (www.walkbasilicata.it), cycling tours (www.

bikebasilicata.it), cooking courses and other great tours through Basilicata and Puglia.

Hospital (☎0835 25 31 11; Via Montescaglioso) About 1km southeast of the centre.

Internet Point (☎0835 34 41 66; Via San Biagio 9; per hour €3; ☺10am-1pm & 3.30-8.30pm)

Maruel Viaggi (☎0835 33 31 35; www.maruelviaggi.it; Via Dante; ☺9am-1.30pm & 4-8pm) Private travel agency and information centre with good information on buses. Can organise tours.

Parco Archeologico Storico Naturale delle Chiese Rupestri del Materano (☎0835 33 61 66; www.parcomurgia.it; Via Sette Dolori) For info on the Murgia park.

Police Station (☎0835 37 81; Via Gattini)

Post Office (Via Passerelli; ☺8am-6.30pm Mon-Fri, to 12.30pm Sat)

Sassiweb (www.sassiweb.it) Informative website on Matera.

ⓘ Getting There & Away

BUS

The **bus station** is north of Piazza Matteotti, near the train station.

Grassani (☎0835 72 14 43; www.grassani.it) Serves Potenza (€5.50, 1½ hours, four daily). Buy tickets on the bus.

Marino (www.marinobus.it) Runs two services daily to Naples (€12, four hours).

Marozzi (☎06 225 21 47; www.marozzivt.it) Runs three daily buses to Rome (€34, 6½ hours). A joint SITA and Marozzi service leaves daily for Siena, Florence and Pisa, via Potenza. Advance booking is essential.

Pugliairbus (☎080 580 03 58; http://pugliairbus.aeroportidipuglia.it) Operates a service to Bari airport (€5, 1½ hours, four daily).

SITA (☎0835 38 50 07; www.sitabus.it) Goes to Taranto (€5.50, two hours, six daily) and Metaponto (€2.90, one hour, up to five daily) and many small towns in the province. Buy tickets from newspaper kiosks on Piazza Matteotti.

TRAIN

Ferrovie Appulo-Lucane (FAL; ☎0835 33 28 61; http://ferrovieappulolucane.it) runs regular trains (€4.50, 1½ hours, 12 daily) and buses (€4.50, 1½ hours, six daily) to Bari. For Potenza, take a FAL bus to Ferrandina and connect with a Trenitalia train, or head to Altamura to link up with FAL's Bari–Potenza run.

Potenza

POP 68,600 / ELEV 819M

Basilicata's regional capital, Potenza, has been ravaged by earthquakes (the last in 1980) and as the highest town in the land, it broils in summer and shivers in winter. You may find yourself passing through as it's a major transport hub.

The centre straddles east to west across a high ridge. To the south lie the main Trenitalia and Ferrovie Appulo-Lucane train stations, connected to the centre by buses 1 and 10.

Potenza's few sights are in the old centre, at the top of the hill. To get there, take the elevators from Piazza Vittorio Emanuele II. The ecclesiastical highlight is the **cathedral**, erected in the 12th century and rebuilt in the 18th. The elegant Via Pretoria, flanked by a boutique or two, makes a pleasant traffic-free stroll, especially during the *passeggiata*.

In central Potenza, **Al Convento** (☎097 12 55 91; www.alconventopotenza.com; Largo San Michele Arcangelo 21; s/d €40/60; ❉ @) is a great accommodation choice housing a mix of polished antiques and design classics.

Grassani (☎0835 72 14 43) has buses to Matera (€5.50, 1½ hours, four daily). **SITA** (☎0971 50 68 11; www.sitabus.it) has daily buses to Melfi, Venosa and Maratea. Buses leave from Via Appia 185 and also stop near the Scalo Inferiore Trenitalia train station. **Liscio** (☎097 15 46 73; www.autolineeliscio.it) buses serve various cities including Rome (€24, 4½ hours, three daily).

There are regular train services from Potenza to Foggia (from €6, 2¼ hours), Salerno (from €6, two hours) and Taranto (from €8.50, two hours). For Bari (from €14, three to four hours, three daily), take the **Ferrovie Appulo-Lucane** (☎0971 41 15 61; ferrovieappulolucane.it) train at Potenza Superiore station.

Appennino Lucano

The Appenino Lucano (Lucanian Apennines) bite Basilicata in half like a row of jagged teeth. Sharply rearing up south of Potenza, they protect the lush Tyrrhenian coast and leave the Ionian shores gasping in the semiarid heat. Careering along its hair-raising roads through the broken spine of mountains can be arduous, but if you're looking for drama, the drive could be the highlight of your trip.

Aliano

The fascists exiled writer and political activist Carlo Levi to this isolated region in 1935.

PUGLIA, BASILICATA & CALABRIA POTENZA

He lived, and is buried, in the tiny hilltop town of Aliano. Remarkably little seems to have changed since he wrote his dazzling *Christ Stopped at Eboli*, which laid bare the boredom, poverty and hypocrisy of village life. The **Pinacoteca Carlo Levi** (☑0835 56 83 15; admission €3; ☉10am-1pm & 4-7.30pm summer, 10am-12.30pm & 3.30-6.30pm Thu-Tue winter) also houses the **Museo Storico di Carlo Levi**, featuring his papers, documents and paintings. Admission to the pinacoteca (art gallery) includes a tour of Levi's house and entry to the museum.

Aliano is accessible by SITA bus (€5.50) from Potenza.

Castelmezzano & Pietrapertosa

The two mountaintop villages of Castelmezzano (elevation 985m) and Pietrapertosa (elevation 1088m), ringed by the Lucanian Dolomites are spectacular. They are Basilicata's highest villages and are often swathed in cloud, making you wonder why anyone would build here – in territory best suited to goats.

Castelmezzano is surely one of Italy's most theatrical villages; the houses huddle along an impossibly narrow ledge that falls away in gorges to the Caperrino river. Pietrapertosa is even more amazing: the Saracen fortress at its pinnacle is difficult to spot as it is carved out of the mountain. You can now 'fly' between these two dramatic settlements courtesy of **Il Volo dell'Angelo** (The Angel Flight; ☑Pietrapertosa 0971 98 31 10, Castelmezzano 0971 98 60 42; www.volodellangelo. com; per person €35-40, couples €63-72), a heart-in-mouth ride where you are supended, belly down, in a cradle harness, and whizzed via cables across the gorge. The organisers factor in time to explore whichever town you land in before the return cable ride.

You can spend an eerie night in Pietrapertosa at a delightful B&B, **La Casa di Penelope e Cirene** (☑0971 98 30 13; Via Garibaldi 32; d from €70). Dine at the authentic Lucano restaurant **Al Becco della Civetta** (☑0971 98 62 49; www.beccodellacivetta. it; Vicolo I Maglietta 7; meals €25; ☉Wed-Mon) in Castelmezzano, which also offers traditionally furnished, simple whitewashed rooms (double €80).

You'll need your own vehicle to visit Castelmezzano and Pietrapertosa.

Basilicata's Western Coast

Resembling a mini-Amalfi, Basilicata's Tyrrhenian coast is short (about 20km) but sweet. Squeezed between Calabria and Campania's Cilento peninsula, it shares the same beguiling characteristics: hidden coves and pewter sandy beaches backed by majestic coastal cliffs. The SS18 threads a spectacular route along the mountains to the coast's star attraction, the charming seaside settlements of Maratea.

Maratea

POP 5220

Maratea is a charming, if confusing, place at first, being comprised of several distinct localities ranging from a medieval village to a stylish harbour. The setting is lush and dramatic, with a coastal road (narrower even than the infamous Amalfi Coast road!) that dips and winds past the cliffs and pocket-size beaches that line the sparkling Golfo di Policastro. Studded with elegant hotels, Maratea's attraction is no secret and you can expect tailback traffic and fully booked hotels in July and August. Conversely, many hotels and restaurants close from October to March.

◉ Sights & Activities

Your first port of call should be the pretty **Porto di Maratea**, a harbour where sleek yachts and bright-blue fishing boats bob in the water, overlooked by bars and restaurants. Then there's the enchanting 13th-century medieval *borgo* (small town) of **Maratea Inferiore**, with pint-sized piazzas, wriggling alleys and interlocking houses, which offers startling coastal views. Attractive little shops sell ceramics and artisan food.

It's all overlooked by a 21m-high, gleaming white statue of **Christ the Redeemer** – don't miss the roller-coaster road and stupendous views from the statue-mounted summit – below which lie the ruins of **Maratea Superiore**, all that remains of the original 8th-century-BC Greek colony. Another option is the waymarked woodland path, which leaves the village from just beyond the Cappelle dei Cappuccini and takes you to the statue in 45 minutes; where the path divides near the top, fork right.

The deep green hillsides that encircle this tumbling conurbation offer excellent walking trails and there are a number of easy day trips to the surrounding hamlets of **Acquafredda di Maratea** and **Fiumicello**, with its small sandy beach. The **tourist office** (☑0973 87 69 08; Piazza Gesù 40; ☉8am-2pm & 5-8pm Mon-Fri, 9am-1pm & 5-8pm Sat & Sun Jul & Aug, 8am-2pm Sep-Jun) is in Fiumicello.

Centro Sub Maratea (☑0973 87 00 13; www.marateaproloco.it/it/centro_sub_maratea; Via Santa Caterina 28) offers diving courses and boat tours that include visits to surrounding grottoes and coves.

A worthwhile day trip via car is to pretty **Rivello** (elevation 479m). Perched on a ridge and framed by the southern Apennines, it is a centre for arts and crafts and has long been known for its exquisite working of gold and copper. Rivello's interesting Byzantine history is evident in the tiny tiled cupolas and frescoes of its gorgeous churches.

🛏 Sleeping

B&B Nefer   B&B $
(☑0973 87 18 28; www.bbnefer.it; Via Cersuta; r €60-90; ☐☀@☎) This friendly B&B, set in the small hamlet of Cersuta 5km northwest of Maratea, has four rooms decorated in sea greens, blues and pinks. Rooms open onto a lush green lawn complete with deckchairs for contemplating the sea view. There's a simple outdoor kitchen area for guest use and a small rocky beach a short walk away.

★ Locanda delle Donne Monache   HOTEL $$
(☑0973 87 74 87; www.locandamonache.com; Via Mazzei 4; r €130-310; ☉Apr-Oct; ☐☀@☎☲) Overlooking the medieval *borgo,* this exclusive hotel is in a converted 18th-century convent with a suitably lofty setting. It's a hotchpotch of vaulted corridors, terraces and gardens fringed with bougainvillea and lemon trees. The rooms are elegantly decorated in pastel shades, while the Sacello restaurant prepares delicate dishes drawing on the regional flavours of Lucania.

Hotel Villa Cheta Elite   HOTEL $$
(☑0973 87 81 34; www.villacheta.it; Via Timpone 46; r €140-264; ☉Apr-Oct; ☐☀☎) A charming art nouveau villa at the entrance to the hamlet of Acquafredda, this hotel has a broad terrace with spectacular views, a fabulous restaurant and large rooms decorated with antiques.

🍴 Eating

La Caffetteria   CAFE $
(Piazza Buraglia; panini from €4; ☉7.30am-2am summer, to 10pm winter) The outdoor seating at this delightful cafe in Maratea's central piazza is ideal for dedicated people-watching, and it serves homemade snacks throughout the day.

Taverna Rovita   TRADITIONAL ITALIAN $$
(☑0973 87 65 88; www.tavernarovitamaratea.it; Via Rovita 13; meals €35; ☉Mar-Oct) This tavern is just off Maratea Inferiore's main piazza. Rovita is excellent value and specialises in hearty local fare, with Lucanian specialities involving stuffed peppers, game birds, local salami and fine seafood.

Lanterna Rossa   SEAFOOD $$
(☑0973 87 63 52; meals €40; ☉daily Jul & Aug, Wed-Mon Feb-Dec) Head for the terrace overlooking the port to dine on exquisite seafood. Highly recommended is the signature dish, *zuppa di pesce* (fish soup).

ℹ Getting There & Away

SITA (☑0971 50 68 11; www.sitabus.it) operates a comprehensive network of routes including a bus up the coast to Sapri in Campania (€1.80, 50 minutes, six daily). Local buses (€1.10) connect the coastal towns and Maratea train station with Maratea Inferiore, running frequently in summer. InterCity and regional trains on the Rome–Reggio line stop at Maratea train station, below the town.

CALABRIA

Tell a non-Calabrian Italian that you're going to Calabria and you will probably elicit some surprise, inevitably followed by stories of the 'ndrangheta – the Calabrian Mafia – notorious for smuggling and kidnapping wealthy northerners and keeping them hidden in the mountains.

But Calabria contains startling natural beauty and spectacular towns that seem to grow out of the craggy mountaintops. It has three national parks: the Pollino in the north, the Sila in the centre and the Aspromonte in the south. It's around 90% hills, but skirted by some 780km of Italy's finest coast (ignore the bits devoured by unappealing holiday camps). Bergamot grows here, and it's the only place in the world where the plants are of sufficient quality to produce the essential oil used in many perfumes and to flavour Earl Grey tea. As in Puglia, there

PUGLIA, BASILICATA & CALABRIA BASILICATA'S WESTERN COAST

are hundreds of music and food festivals here year-round, reaching a fever pitch in July and August.

Admittedly, you sometimes feel as if you have stepped into a 1970s postcard, as its towns, destroyed by repeated earthquakes, are often surrounded by brutal breeze-block suburbs. The region has suffered from the unhealthy combination of European and government subsidies (aimed to develop the south) and dark Mafia opportunism. Half-finished houses often mask well-furnished flats where families live happily, untroubled by invasive house taxes.

This is where to head for an adventure into the unknown.

History

Traces of Neanderthal, Palaeolithic and Neolithic life have been found in Calabria, but the region only became internationally important with the arrival of the Greeks in the 8th century BC. They founded a colony at what is now Reggio di Calabria. Remnants of this colonisation, which spread along the Ionian coast with Sibari and Crotone as the star settlements, are still visible. However, the fun didn't last for the Greeks and in 202 BC the cities of Magna Graecia all came under Roman control. The Romans did irreparable geological damage destroying the countryside's handsome forests. Navigable rivers became fearsome *fiumare* (torrents) dwindling to wide, dry, drought-stricken riverbeds in high summer.

Calabria's fortified hilltop communities weathered successive invasions by the Normans, Swabians, Aragonese and Bourbons, and remained largely undeveloped. Although the 18th-century Napoleonic incursion and the arrival of Garibaldi and Italian unification inspired hope for change, Calabria remained a disappointed, feudal region and, like the rest of the south, was racked by malaria.

A by-product of this tragic history was the growth of banditry and organised crime. Calabria's Mafia, known as the 'ndrangheta (from the Greek for heroism/virtue), inspires fear in the local community, but tourists are rarely the target of its aggression. For many, the only answer has been to get out and, for at least a century, Calabria has seen its young people emigrate in search of work.

Northern Tyrrhenian Coast

The good, the bad and the ugly line the region's western seashore.

The Autostrada del Sole (A3) is one of Italy's great coastal drives. It twists and turns through mountains, past huge swaths of dark-green forest and flashes of cerulean-blue sea. But the Italian penchant for cheap summer resorts has taken its toll here and certain stretches are blighted by shoddy hotels and soulless stacks of flats.

In the low season most places close. In summer many hotels are full, but you should have an easier time with the camping sites.

Praia a Mare

POP 6820

Praia a Mare lies just short of Basilicata, the start of a stretch of wide, pebbly beach that continues south for about 30km to Cirella and Diamante. This flat, leafy grid of a town sits on a wide pale-grey beach, looking out to an intriguing rocky chunk off the coast: the Isola di Dino.

Just off the seafront is the tourist office (☑ 0985 7 25 85; Via Amerigo Vespucci 6; ☺ 8am-1pm), which has information on the Isola di Dino sea caves. Alernatively, expect to pay around €5 for a guided tour from the old boys who operate off the beach.

Autolinee Preite (☑ 0984 41 30 01; www.autoservizipreite.it) operates buses to Cosenza (€5.50, two hours, 10 daily). SITA (☑ 0971 50 68 11; www.sitabus.it) goes north to Maratea and Potenza. Regular trains also pass through for Paola and Reggio di Calabria.

Aieta & Tortora

Precariously perched, otherworldly Aieta and Tortora must have been difficult to reach pre-asphalt. Rocco (☑ 0973 22 943; www.roccobus.it) buses serve both villages, 6km and 12km from Praia respectively. Aieta is higher than Tortora and the journey constitutes much of the reward. When you arrive, walk up to the 16th-century Palazzo Spinello at the end of the road and take a look into the ravine behind it – it's a stunning view.

Diamante

POP 5400

This fashionable seaside town, with its long promenade, is central to Calabria's famous *peperoncino* (chilli) the conversation-stalling spice that so characterises its cuisine. In early September a hugely popular **chilli-eating competition** takes place. Diamante is also famed for the bright murals that contemporary local and foreign artists have painted on the facades of the old buildings. For the best seafood restaurants head for the seafront at Spiaggia Piccola.

Autolinee Preite (✆ 0984 41 30 01; www.autoservizipreite.it) buses between Cosenza and Praia a Mare stop at Diamante.

Paola

POP 16,900

Paola is worth a stop to see its holy shrine. The large pilgrimage complex is above a sprawling small town where the dress of choice is a tracksuit and the main activity is hanging about on street corners. The 80km of coast south from here to Pizzo is mostly overdeveloped and ugly. Paola is the main train hub for Cosenza, about 25km inland.

Watched over by a crumbling castle, the **Santuario di San Francesco di Paola** (✆ 0982 58 25 18; ⊙ 6am-1pm & 2-6pm) FREE is a curious, empty cave with tremendous significance to the devout. The saint lived and died in Paola in the 15th century and the sanctuary that he and his followers carved out of the bare rock has attracted pilgrims for centuries. The cloister is surrounded by naïve wall paintings depicting the saint's truly incredible miracles. The original church contains an ornate reliquary of the saint. Also within the complex is a modern basilica, built to mark the second millennium. Black-clad monks hurry about.

There are several hotels near the station, but you'll be better off staying in towns further north along the coast.

Cosenza

POP 69,800 / ELEV 238M

Cosenza's medieval core is Calabria's best-preserved historic centre, the one piece of history that has managed to escape the earthquakes that have levelled almost everything else in the region. It rises above the confluence of the Crati and Busento rivers,

its narrow lanes winding ever upwards to the hilltop castle. Legend states that Alaric, a Visigoth king, was killed and buried at the confluence of the two rivers.

In the past Cosenza was a sophisticated and lively city, but nowadays there's a gritty feel to the old town with its dark, garbage-strewn streets and fading, once-elegant *palazzi*. It's the gateway to La Sila's mountains, home to Calabria's most important university and a major transport hub.

◉ Sights

In the new town, pedestrianised Corso Mazzini provides a pleasant respite from the chaotic traffic and incessant car honking. There are a number of sculptures lining the *corso,* including *Saint George and the Dragon* by Salvador Dalí.

In the old town, head up the winding, charmingly dilapidated Corso Telesio, which has a raw Neapolitan feel to it and is lined with ancient hung-with-washing tenements, antiquated shopfronts plus an instrument maker's and antiquated shoe mender's. The side alleys are a study in urban decay. At the top, the 12th-century **cathedral** (Piazza del Duomo; ⊙ 8am-noon & 3-7.30pm) was rebuilt in restrained baroque style in the 18th century. In a chapel off the north aisle is a copy of an exquisite 13th-century Byzantine Madonna.

From the cathedral, you can walk up Via del Seggio through a little medieval quarter before turning right to reach the 13th-century **Convento di San Francesco d'Assisi** (off Via del Seggio). Otherwise head along the *corso* to Piazza XV Marzo, an appealing square fronted by the Palazzo del Governo and the handsome neoclassical **Teatro Rendano** (Piazza XV Marzo).

From Piazza XV Marzo, follow Via Paradiso, then Via Antonio Siniscalchi for the route to the down-at-heel Norman **castle** (Piazza Frederico II), left in disarray by several earthquakes. It's closed for restoration, but the view merits the steep ascent.

⬟ Sleeping

★ **B&B Via dell'Astrologo** B&B $
(✆ 338 9205394; www.viadellastrologo.com; Via Rutilio Benincasa 16; s €35-40, d €55-80, extra bed €20; ☎) A gem in the historic centre, this small B&B is tastefully decorated with polished wooden floors, white bedspreads, and good-quality artwork. Brothers Mario and

Calabria

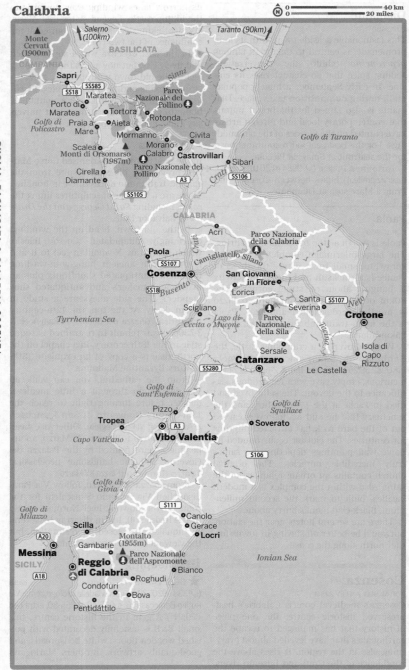

Marco are a mine of information on Cosenza and Calabria in general.

Ostello Re Alarico
HOSTEL $

(☑0984 79 25 70; www.ostellorealarico.com; Vico II Giuseppe Marini Serra 10; dm/s/d €16/30/50; 🛜) On the opposite side of the river from the *duomo*, this restored palazzo housing doubles and dorms is something of a challenge to find. But the decor is an appealing combination of old (check out the ancient oven) and new. There's a pretty garden, and the young owner is a great enthusiast for the region.

Royal Hotel
HOTEL $$

(☑0984 41 21 65; www.hotelroyalsas.it; Via Molinella 24; s/d/t €55/65/75; P ❄ @ 🛜) One of the few decent options in town, the Royal is a short stroll from Corso Mazzini. Rooms are impersonal but comfortable. Stay in the new section of the hotel.

✖ Eating

★ Gran Caffè Renzelli
CAFE $

(Corso Telesio 46) This venerable cafe behind the *duomo* has been run by the same family since 1803 when the founder arrived from Naples and began baking gooey cakes and desserts (cakes start at around €1.20). Sink your teeth into *torroncino torrefacto* (a confection of sugar, spices and hazelnuts) or *torta telesio* (made from almonds, cherries, apricot jam and lupins).

Ristorante Calabria Bella
CALABRIAN $

(☑0984 79 35 31; www.ristorantecalabriabella. it; Piazza del Duomo; meals €25; ⊙12.30-3pm & 7.15pm-midnight) Traditional Calabrian cuisine, such as *grigliata mista di carne* (mixed grilled meats), is regularly dished up in this cosy restaurant in the old town.

Per... Bacco!!
TRATTORIA $$

(☑0984 79 55 69; www.perbaccowinebar.it; Piazza dei Valdesi; meals €25) This smart yet informal restaurant has windows onto the square. Inside are exposed stone walls, vines and heavy beams. The reassuringly brief menu includes a generous and tasty antipasto (€8).

❶ Orientation

The main drag, Corso Mazzini, runs south from Piazza Bilotti (formerly known as Piazza Fera), near the bus station, and intersects Viale Trieste before meeting Piazza dei Bruzi. Head further south and cross the Busento river to reach the old town.

❶ Getting There & Around

AIR

Lamezia Terme airport (Sant'Eufemia Lamezia, SUF; ☑0968 41 43 33; www.sacal.it), 63km south of Cosenza, at the junction of the A3 and SS280 motorways, links the region with major Italian cities. The airport is served by Ryanair, easyJet and charters from northern Europe. A shuttle leaves the airport every 20 minutes for the airport train station where there are frequent trains to Cosenza (€4.60, one hour).

BUS

The main **bus station** (☑0984 41 31 24) is northeast of Piazza Bilotti. Services leave for Catanzaro (€4.80, 1¾ hours, eight daily) and towns throughout La Sila. **Autolinee Preite** (☑0984 41 30 01; www.autoservizipreite.it) has buses heading daily along the north Tyrrhenian coast; **Autolinee Romano** (☑0962 2 17 09; www.autolineeromano.com) serves Crotone as well as Rome and Milan.

TRAIN

Stazione Nuova (☑0984 2 70 59) is about 2km northeast of the centre. Regular trains go to Reggio di Calabria (from €12, three hours) and Rome (from €45, four to six hours), both usually with a change at Paola, and Naples (from €27, three to four hours), as well as most destinations around the Calabrian coast.

Amaco (☑0984 30 80 11; www.amaco.it) bus 27 links the centre and Stazione Nuova, the main train station.

Parco Nazionale della Sila

'La Sila' is a big landscape, where wooded hills create endless rolling views. It's dotted with small villages and cut through with looping roads that make driving a test of your digestion.

It's divided into three areas covering 130 sq km: the Sila Grande, with the highest mountains; the strongly Albanian Sila Greca (to the north); and the Sila Piccola (near Catanzaro), with vast forested hills.

The highest peaks, covered with tall Corsican pines, reach 2000m – high enough for thick snow in winter. This makes it a popular skiing destination. In summer the climate is coolly alpine, spring sees carpets of wildflowers and there's mushroom hunting in autumn. At its peak is the Bosco di Gallopani (Forest of Gallopani). There are several beautiful lakes, the largest of which is Lago di Cecita o Mucone near Camigliatello Silano. There is also plenty of wildlife here,

PARCO NAZIONALE DEL POLLINO

Italy's largest national park, the **Parco Nazionale del Pollino** (Pollino National Park; www.parcopollino.it), straddles Basilicata and Calabria and covers 1960 sq km. It acts like a rocky curtain separating the region from the rest of Italy and has the richest repository of flora and fauna in the south.

The park's most spectacular areas are **Monte Pollino** (2248m), **Monti di Orsomarso** (1987m) and the canyon of the **Gole del Raganello**. The mountains, often snowbound, are blanketed by forests of oak, alder, maple, beech, pine and fir. The park is most famous for its ancient *pino loricato* trees, which can only be found here and in the Balkans. The oldest specimens reach 40m in height.

The park has a varied landscape, from deep river canyons to alpine meadows, and is home to rare stocks of roe deer, wild cats, wolves, birds of prey (including the golden eagle and Egyptian vulture) and the endangered otters, *Lutra lutra*.

Good hiking maps are scarce. The *Carta Excursionistica del Pollino Lucano* (scale 1:50,000), produced by the Basilicata tourist board, is a useful driving map. The large-scale *Parco Nazionale del Pollino* map shows all the main routes and includes some useful information on the park, its flora and fauna and the park communities. Both maps are free and can be found in local tourist offices. You'll need your own vehicle to visit the Pollino.

Basilicata

In Basilicata the park's main centre is **Rotonda** (elevation 626m), which houses the official park office, **Ente Parco Nazionale del Pollino** (☑ 0973 66 93 11; Via delle Frecce Tricolori 6; ⊙ 8am-2pm Mon-Fri, plus 3-5.30pm Mon & Wed). Interesting villages to explore include the unique Albanian villages of **San Paolo Albanese** and **San Costantino Albanese**. These isolated and unspoilt communities fiercely maintain their mountain culture and the Greek liturgy is retained in the main churches. For local handicrafts visit **Terranova di Pollino** for wooden crafts, **Latronico** for alabaster, and **Sant'Arcangelo** for wrought iron.

Asklepios (☑ 347 2631462, 0973 66 92 90; www.asklepios.it; Contrada Barone 9; s/d €30/50) has basic accommodation but is the place to stay for walkers as it's run by an English-speaking guide Giuseppe Cosenza who can also arrange mountain-biking and rafting trips.

---

including the light-grey Apennine wolf, a protected species.

During August, **Sila in Festa** takes place, featuring traditional music. Autumn is mushroom season, when you'll be able to frequent mushroom festivals, including the **Sagra del Fungo** in Camigliatello Silano.

◉ Sights & Activities

La Sila's main town, **San Giovanni in Fiore** (1049m), is named after the founder of its beautiful medieval abbey. The town has an attractive old centre, once you've battled through the suffocating suburbs, and is famous for its Armenian-style hand-loomed carpets and tapestry. You can visit the studio and shop of **Domenico Caruso** (☑ 0984 99 27 24; www.scuolatappeti.it), but ring ahead.

A popular ski-resort town with 6km of slopes, **Camigliatello Silano** (1272m) looks much better under snow. A few lifts operate on Monte Curcio, about 3km to the south. Around 5.5km of slopes and a 1500m lift can

be found near **Lorica** (1370m), on gloriously pretty Lago Arvo – the best place to camp in summer.

Scigliano (620m), in Sila Piccola, is a small hilltop town and has a superb B&B. **Valli Cupe** (☑ 334 9174699, 333 8342866; www.vallicupe.it) runs hiking trips in the area around **Sersale** (739m) in the southeast, where there are myriad waterfalls and the dramatic Canyon Valli Cupe. Trips cost only €8 per person per day (Valli Cupe also runs horseriding tours). Specialising in botany, the guides (who speak Italian and French) also visit remote monasteries and churches. Stay in its rustic accommodation in the town.

🛏 Sleeping

★ **B&B Calabria**   B&B **$**
(☑ 349 8781894; www.bedandbreakfastcalabria.it; Via Roma 9, Frazione Diano; s/d/t/q €35/60/75/80; ⊙ Apr-Nov) In the mountains, this B&B has five comfortable rooms, all with separate entrances. Raffaele is a great source of infor-

Otherwise, the chalet-style **Picchio Nero** (☎0973 9 31 70; www.picchionero.com; Via Mulino 1; s/d incl breakfast €60/73; P) in Terranova di Pollino, with its Austrian-style wooden balconies and recommended restaurant, is a popular hotel for hikers; it's family-run, cosy and friendly, has a small garden and can help arrange excursions.

Two highly recommended restaurants include **Luna Rossa** (☎0973 9 32 54; Via Marconi 18; meals €35; ⊗Thu-Tue) in Terranova di Pollino, where creative local specialities are rustled up simply and with real flair in a rustic wood-panelled building providing breathtaking views, and **Da Peppe** (☎0973 66 12 51; Corso Garibaldi 13; meals €25-35; ⊗lunch & dinner Tue-Sun) in Rotonda, which uses wonderful local meat and woodland products such as truffles and mushrooms.

Calabria

Civita was founded by Albanian refugees in 1746. Other towns worth visiting are **Castrovillari**, with its well-preserved 15th-century Aragonese castle, and **Morano Calabro** – look up the beautiful MC Escher woodcut of this town. Naturalists should also check out the wildlife museum **Centro Il Nibbio** (☎0981 3 07 45; Vico Il Annunziata 11; admission €4; ⊗10am-1pm & 4-8pm summer, 10am-1pm & 3-6pm winter) in Morano, which explains the Pollino ecosystem.

White-water rafting down the spectacular Lao river is popular in the Calabrian Pollino. **Centro Lao Action Raft** (☎0985 2 14 76; www.laoraft.com; Via Lauro 10/12) in Scalea can arrange rafting trips as well as canyoning, trekking and mountain-biking trips. Ferula Viaggi in Matera runs mountain-bike excursions and treks into the Pollino. For guided trips in Calabria visit www.guidapollino.it.

The park has a number of *agriturismi* (farm stay accommodation). Tranquil **Agriturismo Colloreto** (☎347 3236914; www.colloreto.it; s/d €28/56), near Morano Calabro, is in a remote rural setting, gorgeous amid rolling hills. Rooms are comfortable and old-fashioned with polished wood and flagstone floors. Also in Calabria, **Locanda di Alia** (☎0981 4 63 70; www.alia.it; Via Letticelle 55; s/d €90/120; P❋▨) in Castrovillari offers bungalow-style accommodation in a lush green garden; it's famous for an outstanding restaurant, where you can sample delectable local recipes featuring peppers, pork, figs, anise and honey.

mation on the region and can recommend places to eat, visit and go hiking. Rooms have character and clean modern lines and there's a wonderful terrace overlooking endless forested vistas. Mountain bikes available.

Hotel Aquila & Edelweiss　　HOTEL **$**
(☎0984 57 80 44; www.hotelaquilaedelweiss.com; Viale Stazione 15, Camigliatello Silano; s €60-80, d €90-120; P❋@) This three-star hotel in Camigliatello Silano has a stark and anonymous exterior but it's in a good location and the rooms are cosy and comfortable.

Valli Cupe　　B&B **$**
(☎333 6988835; www.vallicupe.it; Sersale; per person from €20) Valli Cupe can arrange a stay in a charming rustic cottage in Sersale, complete with an open fireplace (good for roasting chestnuts) and a kitchen. All bookings via its website.

Camping del Lago Arvo　　CAMPGROUND **$**
(☎0984 53 70 60; www.campinglagoarvo.it; Lorica; camping 2 people, tent & car €10-14, bungalows €40-

60) Lorica's lakeside is a particularly great place to camp. Try this large comfortable spot, near the Calabrian National Park office.

Park Hotel 108　　HOTEL **$$**
(☎0521 64 81 08; www.hotelpark108.it; Via Nazionale 86, Lorica; r €90-130; P❈) Situated on the hilly banks of Lago Arvo, surrounded by dark-green pines, the rooms here are decorated in classic bland-hotel style – but who cares about decor with views like this!

🔒 Shopping

La Sila's forests yield wondrous wild mushrooms, both edible and poisonous. Sniff around the **Antica Salumeria Campanaro** (Piazza Misasi 5, Camigliatello Silano); it's a temple to all things fungoid, as well as an emporium of fine meats, cheeses, pickles and wines.

ℹ Information

Good-quality information in English is scarce. You can try the national park **visitors centre**

Surprises of the South

In the Mezzogiorno, the sun shines on a magical landscape: dramatic cliffs and sandy beaches fringed with turquoise seas; wild rocky mountains and gentle forested slopes; rolling green fields and flat plains. Sprinkled throughout are elegant *palazzi* (mansions), *masserias* (working farms), ancient cave-dwellings and gnome-like stone huts.

Promontorio del Gargano

Along with its charming seaside villages, sandy coves and crystalline blue waters, the Gargano (p715) is also home to the Parco Nazionale del Gargano. It's perfect for hikers, nature trippers and beach fiends alike.

Valle d'Itria

In a landscape of rolling green hills, vineyards, orchards and picture-pretty fields, conical stone huts called *trulli* sprout from the ground en masse in the Disneyesque towns of Alberobello (p721) and Locorotondo (p723).

Salento

In Salento, hot, dry plains covered in wildflowers and olive groves reach towards the gorgeous beaches and waters of the Ionian and Adriatic Seas. It's the unspoilt 'heel', with Lecce (p726) as its sophisticated capital.

Matera

The ancient cave city of Matera (p740) has been inhabited since Palaeolithic times. Explore the tangled alleyways, admire frescoes in rock churches, and sleep in millennia-old *sassi* (former cave dwellings).

Parco Nazionale dell'Aspromonte

In this wild park, narrow roads lead to hilltop villages such as semi-deserted Pentidàttilo (p759). Waterfalls, wide riverbeds, jagged cliffs and sandstone formations form the backdrop to a landscape made for hiking.

1. Promontorio del Gargano **2.** Conical *trulli* houses **3.** *Sassi* (former cave dwellings) in Matera **4.** Basilica di Santa Croce, Lecce, Salento

(☎ 0984 53 71 09) at Cupone, 10km from Camigliatello Silano, or the **Pro Loco tourist office** (☎ 0984 57 81 59; Via Roma; ⏱ 9.30am-12.30pm & 3.30-6.30pm Wed-Mon) in Camigliatello Silano. A useful internet resource is the official park website (www.parcosila.it). The people who run B&B Calabria in the park are extremely knowledgable and helpful.

For maps, you can use *Carta del Parco Nazionale della Sila* (€8), which has walking trails (in Italian). The *Sila for 4* is a miniguide in English that outlines a number of walking trails in the park. The booklet is available in tourist offices and from the privately run **New Sila Tourist Service Agency** (☎ 0984 57 81 25; Via Roma 16) – a good source of information on the park.

❶ Getting There & Away

You can reach Camigliatello Silano and San Giovanni in Fiore via regular Ferrovie della Calabria buses along the SS107, which links Cosenza and Crotone.

Ionian Coast

With its flat coastline and wide sandy beaches, the Ionian coast has some fascinating stops from Sibari to Santa Severina, with some of the best beaches on the coast around Soverato. However, the coast has borne the brunt of some ugly development and is mainly a long, uninterrupted string of resorts, thronged in the summer months and shut down from October to May.

It's worth taking a trip inland to visit Santa Severina, a spectacular mountain-top town, 26km northwest of Crotone. The town is dominated by a Norman castle and is home to a beautiful Byzantine church.

Le Castella

This town is named for its impressive 16th-century Aragonese castle (admission €3; ⏱ 9am-midnight summer, 9am-1pm & 3-6pm winter), a vast edifice linked to the mainland by a short causeway. The philosopher Pliny said that Hannibal constructed the first tower. Evidence shows it was begun in the 4th century BC, designed to protect Crotone in the wars against Pyrrhus.

Le Castella is south of a rare protected area (Capo Rizzuto) along this coast, rich not only in nature but also in Greek history. For further information on the park try www.riservamarinacaporizzuto.it.

With around 15 campsites near Isola di Capo Rizzuto to the north, this is the Ionian

---

MAGNA GRAECIA MUSEUMS OF THE IONIAN COAST

In stark contrast to the dramatic Tyrrhenian coast, the Ionian coast is a listless, flat affair dotted with large tourist resorts. However, the Greek ruins at **Metaponto** and **Policoro**, with their accompanying museums, bring alive the enormous influence of Magna Graecia in southern Italy.

Metaponto's Greek ruins are a rare site where archaeologists have managed to map the entire ancient urban plan. Settled by Greeks in the 8th and 7th centuries BC, Metapontum's most famous resident was Pythagoras, who founded a school here after being banished from Crotone (in Calabria) in the 6th century BC. After Pythagoras died, his house and school were incorporated into the Temple of Hera. The remains of the temple – 15 columns and sections of pavement – are Metaponto's most impressive sight. They're known as the **Tavole Palatine** (Palatine Tables; Parco Archeologico), since knights, or paladins, are said to have gathered here before heading to the Crusades. It's 3km north of town, just off the highway; to find it follow the slip road for Taranto onto the SS106.

In town, the **Museo Archeologico Nazionale** (☎ 0835 74 53 27; Via Aristea 21; admission €2.50; ⏱ 9am-8pm Tue-Sun, 2-8pm Mon) houses artefacts from Metapontum and other sites while in the **Parco Archeologico** FREE, 2km northeast of the train station, are the remains of a **Greek theatre** and the Doric **Tempio di Apollo Licio**.

In Policoro, 21km southwest of Matera, the **Museo della Siritide** (☎ 0835 97 21 54; Via Colombo 8; admission €2.50; ⏱ 9am-8pm Wed-Mon, 2-8pm Tue) has a fabulous display of artefacts from 7000 BC through to Lucanian ornaments, Greek mirrors and Roman spears and javelins.

SITA (p747) buses run from Matera to Metaponto (€2.90, one hour, up to five daily) and on to Policoro. Metaponto is on the Taranto–Reggio line; trains connect with Potenza, Salerno and occasionally Naples.

coast's prime camping area. Try **La Fattoria** (☎0962 79 11 65; Via del Faro; camping 2 people, car & tent €23, bungalows €60; ☺ Jun-Sep), 1.5km from the sea. Otherwise, **Da Annibale** (☎0962 79 50 04; Via Duomo 35; s/d €50/70; 🅿❄@🛜) is a pleasant hotel in town with a splendid fish **restaurant** (meals €30; ☺ lunch & dinner).

For expansive sea views dine at bright and airy **Ristorante Micomare** (☎0962 79 50 82; Via Vittoria 7; meals €20-25; ☺ lunch & dinner).

Gerace

POP 2830

A spectacular medieval hill town, Gerace is worth a detour for the views alone – on one side the Ionian Sea, on the other dark, interior mountains. About 10km inland from Locri on the SS111, it has Calabria's largest Romanesque **cathedral**. Dating from 1045, later alterations have not robbed it of its majesty.

For a taste of traditional Calabrian cooking, the modest and welcoming **Ristorante a Squella** (☎0964 35 60 86; Viale della Resistenza 8; meals €20) makes for a great lunchtime stop that serves reliably good dishes, specialising in seafood and pizzas. Afterwards you can wander down the road and admire the views.

Further inland is **Canolo**, a small village seemingly untouched by the 20th century. Buses connect Gerace with Locri and also Canolo with Siderno, both of which link to the main coastal railway line.

Parco Nazionale dell'Aspromonte

Most Italians think of the **Parco Nazionale dell'Aspromonte** (www.parcoaspromonte.gov.it) as a hiding place used by Calabrian kidnappers in the 1970s and '80s. It's still rumoured to contain 'ndrangheta strongholds, but as a tourist you're unlikely to encounter any murky business. The national park, Calabria's second largest, is startlingly dramatic, rising sharply inland from Reggio. Its highest peak, **Montalto** (1955m), is dominated by a huge bronze statue of Christ and offers sweeping views across to Sicily.

Subject to frequent mudslides and carved up by torrential rivers, the mountains are nonetheless awesomely beautiful. Underwater rivers keep the peaks covered in coniferous forests and ablaze with flowers in spring. It's wonderful walking country and the park has several colour-coded trails.

Extremes of weather and geography have resulted in some extraordinary villages, such as **Pentidàttilo** and **Roghudi**, clinging limpetlike to the craggy, rearing rocks and now all but deserted. It's worth the drive to explore these eagle-nest villages. Another mountain eyrie with a photogenic ruined castle is **Bova**, perched at 900m above sea level. The drive up the steep, dizzying road to Bova is not for the faint-hearted, but the views are stupendous.

Maps are scarce. Try the **national park office** (☎0965 74 30 60; www.parcoaspromonte.gov.it; Via Aurora; ☺9am-1pm Mon-Fri, 3-5pm Tue & Thu) in **Gambarie**, the Aspromonte's main town and the easiest approach to the park. The roads are good and many activities are organised from here – you can ski and it's also the place to hire a 4WD; ask around in the town.

It's also possible to approach from the south, but the roads aren't as good. The cooperative **Naturaliter** (☎347 3046799; www.naturaliterweb.it), based in Condofuri, is an excellent source of information, and can help arrange walking and donkey treks and place you in B&Bs throughout the region. **Cooperativa San Leo** (☎347 3046799) based in Bova, also provides guided tours and accommodation. In Reggio di Calabria, you can book treks and tours with **Misafumera** (☎0965 67 70 21; www.misafumera.it; Via Nazionale 306d; week-long treks €260-480).

Stay on a bergamot farm at **Azienda Agrituristica Il Bergamotto** (☎347 6012338; Via Amendolea; per person €25) where Ugo Sergi can also arrange excursions. Hiking trails pass nearby so it's a good hiking base. The rooms are simple but it's in a lovely rural location, the views are wonderful and the food is delicious.

To reach Gambarie, take ATAM city bus 127 from Reggio di Calabria (€1, 1½ hours, up to six daily). Most of the roads inland from Reggio eventually hit the SS183 road that runs north to the town.

Reggio di Calabria

POP 185,900

Reggio is the main launching point for ferries to Sicily, which sparkles temptingly across the Strait of Messina. It is also home to the spectacular Bronzi di Riace and has a long, impressive seafront promenade –

Reggio di Calabria

Reggio di Calabria

◎ Sights
1 Museo Nazionale della Magna
  Grecia...C2

🛏 Sleeping
2 B&B Casa Blanca.................................B4
3 Hotel Lido...C2

🍴 Eating
4 Cèsare...C2
5 La Cantina del Macellaio...................B4

🍸 Drinking & Nightlife
6 Caffe Matteotti...................................C2

packed during the *passeggiata*. Otherwise,
the city's grid system of dusty streets has the
slightly dissolute feel shared by most ports.

Beyond the seafront, the centre gives
way to urban sprawl. Ravaged by earthquakes, the most recent in 1908, this
once-proud ancient Greek city has plenty
of other woes. As a port and the largest
town close to the 'ndrangheta strongholds
of Aspromonte, organised crime is a major
problem, with the associated corrosive social effect.

On a lighter note, there are plenty of
festivals in Reggio – early August sees the
Festival dello Stretto (www.festivaldello-
stretto.it), featuring the traditional music of
the south.

◉ Sights

**Museo Nazionale della
Magna Grecia** MUSEUM
(📞0965 81 22 55; www.archeocalabria.benicul-
turali.it/; Piazza de Nava 26; adult/child €7/3;
⊙ museum closed at the time of writing) The museum's prides are the world's finest examples of ancient Greek sculpture: the **Bronzi
di Riace**, two extraordinary bronze statues

discovered on the seabed near Riace in 1972 by a snorkelling chemist from Rome. Larger than life, they depict the Greek obsession with the body: inscrutable, determined and fierce, their perfect form more godlike than human. The finest of the two has ivory eyes and silver teeth parted in a faint Mona Lisa smile. No one knows who they are – whether man or god – and even their provenance is a mystery. They date from around 450 BC; it's believed they're the work of two artists.

Aside from the bronzes, there are other magnificent ancient exhibits. Look for the 5th-century-BC bronze *Philosopher's Head*, the oldest-known Greek portrait in existence.

While the museum is undergoing extensive renovations, follow the brown 'laboratorio' signs to the Palazzo del Consiglio on Via Portanova where you can see the bronzes for free, albeit lying on their backs on trolleys. Ask to see the video (in English), which tells the gripping story of their discovery and restoration.

🛏 Sleeping

Finding a room should be easy, even in summer, since most visitors pass straight through en route to Sicily.

B&B Casa Blanca B&B $
(☑ 347 9459210; www.bbcasablanca.it; Via Arcovito 24; s €50-60, d €70-90; ❈ 🛜) A little gem in Reggio's heart, this 19th-century *palazzo* has spacious rooms gracefully furnished with romantic white-on-white decor. There's a self-serve breakfast nook, a small breakfast table in each room and two apartments available. Great choice.

Hotel Lido HOTEL
(☑ 0965 2 50 01; www.hotellido.rc.it; Via Tre Settembre 6; s/d €60/100; 🛜) A pleasant hotel with modern rooms washed in pastel colours with colourful artwork, Sky TV and the possibility of activities, including nearby windsurfing.

🍴 Eating & Drinking

La Cantina del Macellaio TRATTORIA $
(☑ 0965 2 39 32; www.lacantinadelmacellaio.com; Via Arcovito 26; meals €25; ⊙ dinner daily, lunch Sun) This popular trattoria, recommended by locals, dishes up typical Calabrian cuisine with an emphasis on meat dishes. The wine cellar is extensive and impressive.

Cèsare GELATERIA $
(Piazza Indipendenza; ⊙ 6am-1am) The most popular gelateria in town is in a green kiosk at the end of the *lungomare* (seafront).

Baylik SEAFOOD $$
(☑ 0965 4 86 24; Vico Leone 3; meals €30; ⊙ lunch daily, dinner Fri-Wed) Worth the slight trek, Baylik is friendly, and the calamari is so fresh your knife glides through it like butter; the spaghetti with clams is another winner.

Caffe Matteotti CAFE
(www.caffematteotti.it; Corso Vittorio Emanuele 39; ⊙ 7am-2am Tue-Sun) The stylish white tables and chairs on their terrace offer sea views with your *aperitivi*: it's a prime spot for people-watching.

ℹ Information

Walk northeast along Corso Garibaldi for the tourist office, shopping and other services. The *corso* has long been a de facto pedestrian zone during the ritual *passeggiata*.

Hospital (☑ 0965 39 71 11; Via Melacrino)

Police Station (☑ 0965 41 11 11; Corso Garibaldi 442)

Post Office (Via Miraglia 14)

Tourist Information Kiosk (Viale Genovese Zerbi; ⊙ 9am-noon & 4-7pm) There are also kiosks at both the Airport (☑ 0965 64 32 91) and the Stazione Centrale (☑ 0965 2 71 20).

ℹ Getting There & Away

AIR

Reggio's **airport** (REG; ☑ 0965 64 05 17; www.aeroportodellostretto.it) is at Ravagnese, about 5km south.

BOAT

Boats for Messina (Sicily) leave from the port (just north of Stazione Lido), where there are three adjacent ferry terminals. In high season there are up to 20 hydrofoils daily; in low season there are as few as two. Some boats continue to the Aeolian Islands.

Services are run by various companies, including **Meridiano** (☑ 0965 81 04 14; www.meridianolines.it). Prices for cars are €15 one way and for foot passengers €1.50 to €2.80. The crossing takes 20 minutes.

BUS

Most buses terminate at Piazza Garibaldi, in front of the Stazione Centrale. Several different companies operate to towns in Calabria and beyond. Regional trains are more convenient than bus services to Scilla and Tropea.

ATAM (☏ 800 43 33 10; www.atam-rc.it)
Serves the Aspromonte Massif, with bus 127 to
Gambarie (€1.10, 1½ hours, six daily).
Lirosi (☏ 0966 5 79 01) Serves Rome (€48,
eight hours, two daily).

CAR & MOTORCYCLE

The A3 ends at Reggio, via a series of long tunnels. If you are continuing south, the SS106 hugs
the coast round the 'toe', then heads north along
the Ionian Sea.

TRAIN

Trains stop at **Stazione Centrale** (☏ 0965 89 20 21), the main train station at the town's southern
edge, and less frequently at Stazione Lido, near
the museum. There are frequent trains to Milan
(from €140, 9½ to 11½ hours), Rome (from €70,
7½ hours) and Naples (from €55, 4½ to 5½
hours). Regional services run along the coast to
Scilla and Tropea, and also to Catanzaro and less
frequently to Cosenza and Bari.

ℹ Getting Around

Orange local buses run by ATAM cover most of
the city. For the port, take bus 13 or 125 from
Piazza Garibaldi outside Stazione Centrale. The
Porto–Aeroporto bus, bus 125, runs from the
port via Piazza Garibaldi to the airport and vice
versa (25 minutes, hourly). Buy your ticket at
ATAM offices, tobacconists or news stands.

Southern Tyrrhenian Coast

North of Reggio, along the coast-hugging
Autostrada del Sole (A3), the scenery rocks
and rolls to become increasingly beautiful
and dramatic, if you ignore the shoddy holiday camps and unattractive developments
that sometimes scar the land. Like the
northern part of the coast, it's mostly quiet
in winter and packed in summer.

Scilla

POP 5160

In Scilla, cream-, ochre- and earth-coloured
houses cling on for dear life to the jagged
promontory, ascending in jumbled ranks
to the hill's summit, which is crowned by
a castle and, just below, the dazzling white
confection of the Chiesa Arcipretale Maria
Immacolata. Lively in summer and serene
in low season, the town is split in two by the
tiny port. The fishing district of Scilla Chianalea, to the north, harbours small hotels
and restaurants off narrow lanes, lapped by
the sea. It can only be visited on foot.

Scilla's high point is a rock at the northern
end, said to be the lair of Scylla, the mythical six-headed sea monster who drowned
sailors as they tried to navigate the Strait
of Messina. Swimming and fishing off the
town's glorious white sandy beach is somewhat safer today. Head for Lido Paradiso
from where you can squint up at the castle
while sunbathing on the sand.

◎ Sights

Castello Ruffo   CASTLE
(☏ 0956 70 42 07; admission €1.50; ◷ 8.30am-
7.30pm) An imposing hilltop fortress, the
castle has at times been a lighthouse and a
monastery. It houses a *luntre,* the original
black boat used for swordfishing, and on
which the modern-day *passarelle* is based.

◎ Sleeping

Le Piccole Grotte   B&B $
(☏ 338 2096727; www.lepiccolegrotte.it; Via Grotte
10; d €90-120; ❋ ☜) In the picturesque Chianalea district, this B&B is housed in a 19th-
century fisher's house beside steps leading
to the crystal-clear sea. Rooms have small
balconies facing the cobbled alleyway or the
sea.

La Locandiera   B&B $
(☏ 0965 75 48 81; www.lalocandiera.org; Via Zagari
27; d €60-100; ❋ ☜) Run by the same people
who own Le Piccole Grotte, this B&B is
just as picturesque with large, comfortable
rooms and views over the sea.

✗ Eating & Drinking

Bleu de Toi   SEAFOOD $$
(☏ 0965 79 05 85; www.bleudetoi.it; Via Grotte 40;
meals €30-35; ◷ Wed-Mon) Soak up the Chianalea atmosphere at this little restaurant. It
has a terrace over the water and excellent
seafood dishes, including Scilla's renowned
swordfish.

Dali City Pub   BAR
(Via Porto) On the beach in Scilla town, this
popular bar has a Beatles tribute corner
(appropriately named The Cavern) and has
been going since 1972.

Capo Vaticano

There are spectacular views from this rocky
cape, with its beaches, ravines and limestone
sea cliffs. Birdwatchers' spirits should soar.
Around 7km south of Tropea, Capo Vaticano
has a lighthouse, built in 1885, which is close

to a short footpath from where you can see as far as the Aeolian Islands. Capo Vaticano beach is one of the balmiest along this coast.

Tropea

POP 6780

Tropea, a puzzle of lanes and piazzas, is famed for its captivating prettiness, dramatic position and sunsets the colour of amethyst. It sits on the Promontorio di Tropea, which stretches from Nicotera in the south to Pizzo in the north. The coast alternates between dramatic cliffs and icing-sugar-soft sandy beaches, all edged by translucent sea. Unsurprisingly, hundreds of Italian holidaymakers descend here in summer. If you hear English being spoken it is probably from Americans visiting relatives: enormous numbers left the region for America in the early 20th century.

Despite the mooted theory that Hercules founded the town, it seems this area has been settled as far back as Neolithic times. Tropea has been occupied by the Arabs, Normans, Swabians, Anjous and Aragonese, as well as being attacked by Turkish pirates. Perhaps they were after the town's famous red onions, so sweet they can be turned into marmalade.

◉ Sights

Cathedral

(⊙6.30-11.30am & 4-7pm) The beautiful Norman cathedral has two undetonated WWII bombs near the door: it's believed they didn't explode due to the protection of the town's patron saint, Our Lady of Romania. A Byzantine icon (1330) of the Madonna hangs above the altar – she is also credited with protecting the town from the earthquakes that have pumelled the region.

Santa Maria dell'Isola   CHURCH

The town overlooks Santa Maria dell'Isola, a medieval church with a Renaissance makeover, which sits on its own island, although centuries of silt have joined it to the mainland.

⌂ Sleeping

★ Donnaciccina   B&B **$$**

(☑0963 6 21 80; www.donnaciccina.com; Via Pelliccia 9; s €40-75, d €80-150; ❀@❀) Overlooking the main *corso,* this delightful B&B has retained a tangible sense of history with its carefully selected antiques, canopy beds and terracotta tiled floors. There's also a self-catering apartment perfectly positioned on the cliff overlooking the sea, and a chatty parrot in reception.

Residence il Barone   B&B **$$**

(☑0963 60 71 81; www.residenzailbarone.it; Largo Barone; €70-190; ❀@❀) This graceful *palazzo* has six suites decorated in masculine neutrals and tobacco browns, with dramatic modern paintings by the owner's brother adding pizazz to the walls. There's a computer in each suite and you can eat breakfast on the small roof terrace with views over the old city and out to sea.

✕ Eating

Al Pinturicchio   TRADITIONAL ITALIAN **$**

(☑0963 60 34 52; Via Dardona, cnr Largo Duomo; meals €16-22; ⊙dinner) Recommended by the locals, this restaurant in the old town has a romantic ambience, candlelit tables and a menu of imaginative dishes.

Osteria del Pescatore   SEAFOOD **$**

(☑0963 60 30 18; Via del Monte 7; meals €20-25; ⊙dinner Thu-Tue) Swordfish rates highly on the menu at this simple seafood place tucked away in the backstreets.

ℹ Information

CST Tropea (☑0963 6 11 78; www.csttropea.it; Largo San Michele 7; ⊙9am-1pm & 4-7.30pm Sep-Jun, to 10pm Jul & Aug) Helpful tourist office at the entrance to the old town. Can organize trekking, mountain biking, diving and cultural tours.

Tourist Office (☑0963 6 14 75; Piazza Ercole; ⊙9am-1pm & 4-8pm) In the old town centre.

ℹ Getting There & Away

Trains run to Pizzo (€1.95, 30 minutes, 12 daily), Scilla (€3.70, one hour 20 minutes, every 30 minutes) and Reggio (from €5, two hours, every 30 minutes). **SAV** (☑0963 611 29) buses connect with other towns on the coast.

Pizzo

POP 9240

Stacked high up on a sea cliff, pretty little Pizzo is the place to go for *tartufo,* a death-by-chocolate ice-cream ball, and to see an extraordinary rock-carved grotto church. It's a popular and cheerful tourist stop. Piazza della Repubblica is the epicentre, set high above the sea with great views. Settle here at one of the many gelateria terraces for an ice-cream fix.

Pizzo is located just off the major A3 autostrada; the nearest train station, Vibo Valentia-Pizzo, is located 4km south of town. A bus service connects you to Pizzo.

◉ Sights

Chiesa di Piedigrotta   CAVE
(admission €2.50; ⊘ 9am-1pm & 3-7.30pm) The Chiesa di Piedigrotta is an underground cave full of carved stone statues. It was carved into the tufa rock by Neapolitan shipwreck survivors in the 17th century. Other sculptors added to it and it was eventually turned into a church. Later statues include the less-godly figures of Fidel Castro and John F Kennedy. It's a bizarre, one-of-a-kind mixture of mysticism, mystery and kitsch. Buy tickets at the restaurant above the cave.

Chiesa Matrice di San Giorgio   CHURCH
(Via Marconi) In town, the 16th-century Chiesa Matrice di San Giorgio, with its dressed-up Madonnas, houses the tomb of Joachim Murat, brother of Napoleon and one-time king of Naples. Although he was the architect of enlightened reforms, the locals showed no great concern when Murat was imprisoned and executed here.

Castello Murat   CASTLE
(📞0963 53 25 23; adult/reduced €2.50/1.50; ⊘ 9am-1pm & 3pm-midnight Jun-Sep, 9am-1pm & 3-7pm Oct-May) At the neat little 15th-century Castello Murat, south of Piazza della Repubblica, you can see Murat's cell. His last days and death by firing squad are graphically illustrated by waxworks.

🛏 Sleeping & Eating

Armonia B&B   B&B $
(📞0963 53 33 37; www.casaarmonia.com; Via Armonia 9; s without bathroom €30-60, d without bathroom €40-75; @) Run by the charismatic Franco in his 18th-century family home, this B&B has a number of rooms.

Ristorante Pizzeria Don Diego   PIZZERIA $
(📞0963 06 01 07; www.ristorantedondiegopizzo. com; Via M Salomone 243; mains €20) Eat at Ristorante Pizzeria Don Diego, with its spectacular sea views and tasty pizzas.

Sicily

Best Places to Eat

➡ Trattoria Ai Cascinari (p779)
➡ Ti Vitti (p784)
➡ Fattoria delle Torri (p815)
➡ Il Liberty (p814)

Best Places to Stay

➡ Pensione Tranchina (p829)
➡ Villa Athena (p819)
➡ Hotel Signum (p790)
➡ Hotel Villa Belvedere (p796)

Why Go?

More of a sugar-spiked espresso than a milky cappuccino, Sicily rewards visitors with an intense, bittersweet experience. Overloaded with art treasures and natural beauty, under-supplied with infrastructure and continuously struggling against Mafia-driven corruption, Sicily's complexities sometimes seem unfathomable. To really appreciate this place, come with an open mind – and a healthy appetite. Despite the island's perplexing contradictions, one factor remains constant: the uncompromisingly high quality of the cuisine.

After 25 centuries of foreign domination, Sicilians are heirs to an impressive cultural legacy, from the refined architecture of Magna Graecia to the Byzantine splendour and Arab craftsmanship of the island's Norman cathedrals and palaces. This cultural richness is matched by a startlingly diverse landscape that includes bucolic farmland, smouldering volcanoes and kilometres of island-studded aquamarine coastline.

When to Go
Palermo

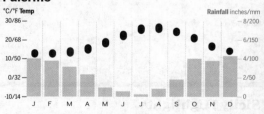

Easter Colourful religious processions and marzipan lambs in every bakery window.

May Wildflowers, dreamy coastal walking and Syracuse's festival of classic drama.

Sep Prime diving off Ustica and other seaside fun without summer prices.

Sicily Highlights

① Joining the ranks of opera-goers at elegant Teatro Massimo in **Palermo** (p769).

② Bargaining with the fish vendors at dawn, climbing Europe's most active volcano in the afternoon and enjoying Sicily's nightlife in **Catania** (p798).

③ Marvelling at the majesty of **Segesta** (p830), where a Doric temple sits in splendid isolation on a windswept hillside.

④ Watching international stars perform against the breathtaking backdrop of Mt Etna at the summer performing arts festivals in **Taormina** (p793).

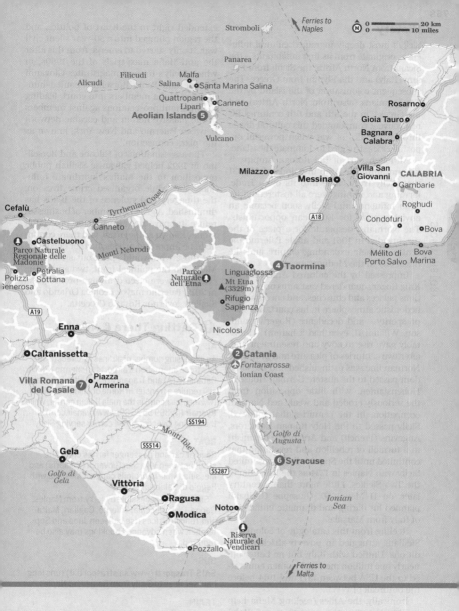

Ferries to Naples

Stromboli

Panarea

Filicudi
Alicudi
Malfa
Salina
Santa Marina Salina
Quattropani
Lipari
Canneto
Aeolian Islands 5
Vulcano

Rosarno
Gioia Tauro
Bagnara Calabra
Villa San Giovanni
CALABRIA
Gambarie
Roghudi
Condofuri
Bova
Mélito di Porto Salvo
Bova Marina

Messina

Milazzo

Cefalù

Tyrrhenian Coast

Canneto

Castelbuono
Parco Naturale Regionale delle Madonie
Petralia Sottana
Polizzi Generosa

Monti Nebrodi

Parco Naturale dell'Etna
Linguaglossa
Mt Etna (3329m)
4 **Taormina**
Rifugio Sapienza

Nicolosi

Enna

Caltanissetta

Villa Romana del Casale 7
Piazza Armerina

2 **Catania**
Fontanarossa
Ionian Coast

Monti Iblei

Golfo di Augusta

Gela
Golfo di Gela

SS194

SS514

SS287

6 **Syracuse**

Vittòria

Ragusa
Modica
Noto

Riserva Naturale di Vendicari

Ionian Sea

Pozzallo

Ferries to Malta

A18

A19

0   20 km
0   10 miles

5 Soaking up the sun, watching Stromboli's volcanic fireworks and hiking to your heart's content on the stunningly scenic **Aeolian Islands** (p785).

6 Wandering aimlessly in Ortygia's atmospheric alleys or among the citrus groves, caves and ruins of the vast archaeological park in **Syracuse** (p805).

7 Admiring prancing wild beasts and dancing bikini-clad gymnasts on the newly restored mosaic floors of **Villa Romana del Casale** (p824).

History

Sicily's most deeply ingrained cultural influences originate from its first inhabitants – the Sicani from North Africa, the Siculi from Latium (Italy) and the Elymni from Greece. The subsequent colonisation of the island by the Carthaginians (also from North Africa) and the Greeks, in the 8th and 6th centuries BC respectively, compounded this cultural divide through decades of war when powerful opposing cities struggled to dominate the island.

Although part of the Roman Empire, it was not until the Arab invasions of AD 831 that Sicily truly came into its own. Trade, farming and mining were all fostered under Arab influence and Sicily soon became an enviable prize for European opportunists. The Normans, desperate for a piece of the pie, invaded in 1061 and made Palermo the centre of their expanding empire and the finest city in the Mediterranean.

Impressed by the cultured Arab lifestyle, King Roger squandered vast sums on ostentatious palaces and churches, and encouraged a hedonistic atmosphere in his court. But such prosperity – and decadence (Roger's grandson, William II, even had a harem) – inevitably gave rise to envy and resentment and, after two centuries of pleasure and profit, the Norman line was extinguished and the kingdom passed to the austere German House of Hohenstaufen, with little opposition from the seriously eroded and weakened Norman occupation. In the centuries that followed, Sicily passed to the Holy Roman Emperors, Angevins (French) and Aragonese (Spanish) in a turmoil of rebellion and revolution that continued until the Spanish Bourbons united Sicily with Naples in 1734 as the Kingdom of the Two Sicilies. Little more than a century later, on 11 May 1860, Giuseppe Garibaldi planned his daring and dramatic unification of Italy from Marsala.

Reeling from this catalogue of colonisers, Sicilians struggled in poverty-stricken conditions. Unified with Italy, but no better off, nearly one million men and women emigrated to the USA between 1871 and 1914 before the outbreak of WWI.

Ironically, the Allies (seeking Mafia help in America for the reinvasion of Italy) helped in establishing the Mafia's stranglehold on Sicily. In the absence of suitable administrators, they invited the undesirable *mafioso* (Mafia boss) Don Calógero Vizzini to do the job. When Sicily became a semi-autonomous region in 1948, Mafia control extended right to the heart of politics, and the region plunged into a 50-year silent civil war. It only started to emerge from this after the anti-Mafia maxi-trials of the 1980s, in which Sicily's revered magistrates Giovanni Falcone and Paolo Borsellino hauled hundreds of Mafia members into court, leading to important prosecutions against members of the massive heroin and cocaine network between Palermo and New York, known as the 'pizza connection'.

The assassinations of Falcone and Borsellino in 1992 helped galvanise Sicilian public opposition to the Mafia's inordinate influence, and while organised crime lives on, the thuggery and violence of the 1980s has diminished. A growing number of businesses refuse to pay the extortionate protection money known as the *pizzo*, and there continue to be important arrests, further encouraging those who would speak out against the Mafia. On the political front, two anti-Mafia crusaders were elected to high-profile posts in 2012, Palermo mayor Leoluca Orlando and Sicilian governor Rosario Crocetta.

ⓘ Getting There & Away

AIR

An increasing number of airlines fly direct to Sicily's three international airports – Palermo (PMO), Catania (CTA) and Trapani (TPS) – although many still require a transfer in Rome or Milan. **Alitalia** (www.alitalia.com) is the main Italian carrier, while **Ryanair** (☑ 899 55 25 89; www.ryanair.com) is the leading low-cost airline carrier serving Sicily.

BOAT

Regular car and passenger ferries cross the strait between Villa San Giovanni (Calabria) and Messina, while hydrofoils connect Messina with Reggio di Calabria.

Sicily is also accessible by ferry from Naples, Genoa, Civitavecchia, Salerno, Cagliari, Malta and Tunisia. Prices rise between June and September, when advanced bookings may also be required.

BUS

SAIS Trasporti (www.saistrasporti.it) runs long-haul services to Sicily from Rome and Naples.

TRAIN

Direct trains run from Milan, Florence, Rome, Naples and Reggio di Calabria to Messina and on to Palermo, Catania and other provincial capitals – the trains are transported from the mainland by ferry from Villa San Giovanni.

For travellers originating in Rome and points south, InterCity trains cover the distance from mainland Italy to Sicily in the least possible time, without a change of train. If coming from Milan, Bologna or Florence, your fastest option is to take the ultra-high-speed Frecciarossa as far as Naples, then change to an InterCity train for the rest of the journey.

If saving money is your top priority, Espresso or InterCity night trains will still get you to Sicily relatively fast, and won't take such a big bite out of your budget.

ⓘ Getting Around

AIR
Regular domestic flights serve the offshore islands of Pantelleria and Lampedusa. Local carriers include Alitalia and Darwin Airline.

BUS
Bus services within Sicily are provided by a variety of companies. Buses are usually faster if your destination involves travel through the island's interior; trains tend to be cheaper (and sometimes faster) on the major coastal routes. In small towns and villages tickets are often sold in bars or on the bus.

CAR & MOTORCYCLE
Having your own vehicle is advantageous in the interior, where public transit is often slow and limited. Roads are generally good and autostradas connect most major cities. There's a cheap and worthwhile toll road running along the Ionian coast. Drive defensively; the Sicilians are some of Italy's most aggressive drivers, with a penchant for overtaking on blind corners, holding a mobile phone in one hand while gesticulating wildly with the other!

TRAIN
The coastal train service is very efficient. Services to towns in the interior tend be infrequent and slow, although if you have the time the routes can be very picturesque. InterCity trains are the fastest and most expensive, while the *regionale* is the slowest.

Sicily Ferry Crossings

ROUTE	COST € (HIGH SEASON ADULT FARE)	DURATION (HOURS)
Genoa-Palermo	90	20
Malta-Pozzallo	120	1¾
Naples-Catania	60	11
Naples-Palermo	52	11
Naples-Trapani	94	7
Reggio di Calabria-Messina	3.50	30min
Tunis-Palermo	62	10

PALERMO

POP 657,000

Palermo is a city of decay and of splendour and – provided you can handle its raw energy, deranged driving and chaos – has plenty of appeal. Unlike Florence or Rome, many of the city's treasures are hidden, rather than scrubbed up for endless streams of tourists.

At one time an Arab emirate and seat of a Norman kingdom, Palermo became Europe's grandest city in the 12th century, then underwent another round of aesthetic transformations during 500 years of Spanish rule. The resulting treasure trove of palaces, castles and churches is a unique architectural fusion of Byzantine, Arab, Norman, Renaissance and baroque gems.

While some of the crumbling *palazzi* (mansions) bombed in WWII are being restored, others remain dilapidated; turned into shabby apartments, the faded glory of their ornate facades is just visible behind strings of brightly coloured washing. The evocative history of the city remains very much part of the daily life of its inhabitants, and the dusty web of backstreet markets in the old quarter has a Middle Eastern feel.

The flip side is the modern city, a mere 15-minute stroll away, parts of which could be neatly jigsawed and slotted into Paris, with a grid system of wide avenues lined by seductive shops and handsome 19th-century apartments.

◉ Sights

Via Maqueda is the main street, running north from the train station, changing names to Via Ruggero Settimo as it passes the landmark Teatro Massimo, then finally widening into leafy Viale della Libertà north of Piazza Castelnuovo, the beginning of the city's modern district.

◉ Around the Quattro Canti

The busy intersection of Corso Vittorio Emanuele and Via Maqueda is known as the **Quattro Canti**. Forming the civic heart of Palermo, this crossroad divides the historic nucleus into four traditional quarters – Albergheria, Capo, Vucciria and La Kalsa.

La Martorana CHURCH
(Chiesa di Santa Maria dell'Ammiraglio; Piazza Bellini 3; donation requested; ⊘8.30am-1pm & 3.30-5.30pm Mon-Sat, 8.30am-1pm Sun) On the

Palermo

500 m
0.25 miles

Teatro della
Verdura (2km);
Mondello (9km); (3km)

Viale della Libertà

**NEW
CITY**

Via Archimede
Via Isidoro la Lumia
Via Via Gaetario
Via Puglisi
Via Torrearsa

Via XX Settembre
Via Nicolò Garzilli
Via E Parisi
Via XII Gennaio
Via Dante

Via Principe di Villafranca

Piazzetta
Mulino a
Vento

Buses to
Mondello

Piazza
Sturzo

Buses for
Airport

Piazza
Castelnuovo

Via Carducci

Via Sammartino

Piazza San
Francesco di
Paola

Via Goethe

Via Giovanni
Pacini

Via Volturno

Via Mura di S Vito

Via G Battista

Via Maqueda

Via Pignatelli Aragona

5 Teatro
Massimo

Via Ruggero Settimo

Central
Tourist Office

Via Mariano Stabile
Via Villaermosa
Via Riccardo Wagner

Via Emerico Amari

Via Principe di Belmonte

Via la Masa

Via Principe di Scordia

Via Roma

Via Cavour

Via Spinuzza

Via Bara all'Olivella

Piazza
Olivella

Via Valverde

Via dell'Orologo

Via Bandiera

Piazza San
Domenico

Piazza
Sant'Andrea

VUCCIRIA

Via G Meli

Via Fratelli Cianciolo

Via del Bambinai

Via Castello

Via Cassari

La Cala

Via della Cala

Piazzetta
Antonio
Pasqualino

*Golfo di
Palermo*

Molo Meridionale

Molo Vittorio Veneto

Molo Piave

Ustica
Lines

Grandi Navi
Veloci Ferries (50m)

Tirrenia

Siremar

Via del Mare

Grimaldi
Lines

Via Francesco Crispi

Via Sammuzzo

N

26

39 19

33

42

29

27 32

43

45

34

21

47
40

46
41

20

14

18

17

16

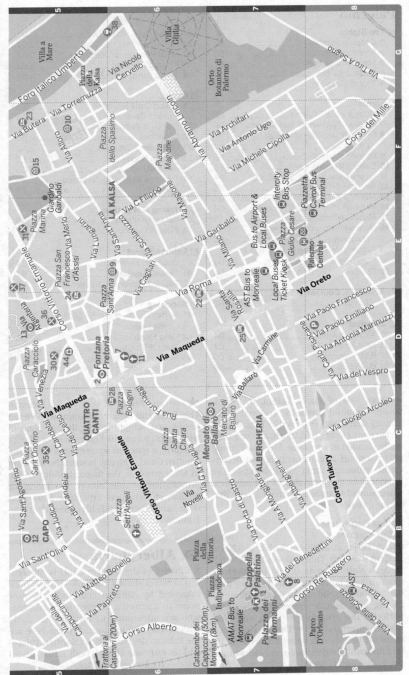

Palermo

southern side of Piazza Bellini, this luminously beautiful, recently restored 12th-century church was endowed by King Roger's Syrian emir, George of Antioch, and was originally planned as a mosque. Delicate Fatimid pillars support a domed cupola that depicts Christ enthroned amid his archangels. The interior is best appreciated in the morning, when sunlight illuminates magnificent Byzantine mosaics.

Chiesa Capitolare di San Cataldo
CHURCH

(Piazza Bellini 3; admission €2.50; ◷9.30am-12.30pm & 3-6pm) This 12th-century church in Arab-Norman style is one of Palermo's most striking buildings. With its dusky-pink bijoux domes, solid square shape, blind arcading and delicate tracery, it illustrates perfectly the synthesis of Arab and Norman architectural styles. The interior, while more austere, is still beautiful, with its inlaid floor and lovely stone-and-brickwork in the arches and domes.

★ Fontana Pretoria
FOUNTAIN

This huge and ornate fountain, with tiered basins and sculptures rippling in concentric circles, forms the centrepiece of **Piazza Pretoria**, a spacious square just south of the Quattro Canti. The city bought the fountain in 1573; however, the flagrant nudity of the provocative nymphs proved too much for Sicilian church-goers attending Mass next door, and they prudishly dubbed it the Fountain of Shame.

◎ Albergheria

Southwest of the Quattro Canti is Albergheria, a rather shabby, run-down district once inhabited by Norman court officials, now home to a growing number of immigrants who are attempting to revitalise its dusty backstreets. The top tourist draws here are the Palazzo dei Normanni (Norman Palace) and its exquisite chapel, both at the neighbourhood's far western edge.

★**Cappella Palatina** CHAPEL
(Palatine Chapel; adult €8.50, EU citizen 18-25yr €6.50, EU citizen 65+ €5, EU citizen under 18yr free; ☺8.15am-5pm Mon-Sat, 8.15-9.45am & 11.15am-12.15pm Sun) On the middle level of the Norman Palace's three-tiered loggia, this mosaic-clad jewel of a chapel, designed by Roger II in 1130, is Palermo's premier tourist attraction. Gleaming from a painstaking five-year restoration, its aesthetic harmony is further enhanced by the inlaid marble floors and wooden *muqarnas* ceiling, a masterpiece of Arabic-style honeycomb carving that reflects Norman Sicily's cultural complexity.

★**Palazzo dei Normanni** PALACE
(Palazzo Reale; Piazza Indipendenza 1; incl Cappella Palatina adult €8.50, youth 18-25yr €6.50, senior 65+ €5, child under 18yr free; ☺8.15am-5pm Fri, Sat & Mon, to 12.15pm Sun) On weekends, when Palermo's venerable Palazzo dei Normanni isn't being used by Sicily's parliament, visitors can take a self-guided tour of several upstairs rooms, including the gorgeous blue **Sala Pompeiana**, with its Venus & Eros frescoes, the **Sala dei Venti**, adorned with mosaics of geese, papyrus, lions, leopards and palms, and the **Sala di Ruggero II**, King Roger's mosaic-decorated bedroom.

Chiesa di San Giovanni degli Eremiti CHURCH
(☑091 651 50 19; Via dei Benedettini 16; adult/reduced €6/3; ☺9am-6:30pm Tue-Sat, 9am-1pm Sun & Mon) This remarkable, five-domed remnant of Arab-Norman architecture occupies a magical little hillside in the middle of an otherwise rather squalid neighborhood. Surrounded by a garden of citrus trees, palms, cactus and ruined walls, it's built atop a mosque that itself was superimposed on an earlier chapel. The peaceful Norman cloisters outside offer lovely views of the Palazzo Normanno.

★**Mercato di Ballarò** MARKET
Snaking for several city blocks east of Palazzo dei Normanni is Palermo's busiest street market, which throbs with activity well into the early evening. It's a fascinating mix of noises, smells and street life, and the cheapest place for everything from Chinese padded bras to fresh produce, fish, meat, olives and cheese – smile nicely and you may get a taste.

◉ **Capo**

Northwest of Quattro Canti is the Capo neighbourhood, another densely packed web of interconnected streets and blind alleys.

Cattedrale di Palermo CATHEDRAL
(www.cattedrale.palermo.it; Corso Vittorio Emanuele; Norman tombs & treasury adult/reduced €3/1.50; ☺8am-7pm) A feast of geometric patterns, ziggurat crenulations, majolica cupolas and blind arches, Palermo's cathedral is a prime example of the extraordinary Arab-Norman style unique to Sicily. The interior's most interesting features are the Norman tombs of Roger II and other Sicilian royalty, and the cathedral treasury, home to Constance of Aragon's fabulous gem-encrusted, gold-filigreed 13th-century crown.

Mercato del Capo MARKET
Capo's street market, running the length of Via Sant'Agostino, is a seething mass of colourful activity during the day, with vendors selling fruit, vegetables, meat, fish, cheese and household goods of every description.

Catacombe dei Cappuccini CATACOMB
(☑091 652 41 56; Piazza Cappuccini; adult €3, child under 8yr free; ☺9am-1pm & 3-6pm) These catacombs house the mummified bodies and skeletons of some 8000 Palermitans who died between the 17th and 19th centuries. Earthly power, gender, religion and professional status are still rigidly distinguished, with men and women occupying separate corridors, and a first-class section set aside for virgins. From Piazza Independenza, it's a 15-minute walk.

◉ **Vucciria**

Museo Archeologico Regionale MUSEUM
(☑091 611 68 05; www.regione.sicilia.it/beniculturali/salinas; Piazza Olivella 24; ☺8.30am-1.30pm & 3-6.30pm Tue-Fri, 8.30am-1.30pm Sat & Sun) Scheduled to reopen in late 2013 after comprehensive renovations, this splendid, wheelchair-accessible museum displays some of Sicily's most valuable Graeco-Roman artefacts. The museum's crown jewel is the series of decorative friezes from the temples at Selinunte; other treasures include the Hellenistic *Ariete di Bronzo di Siracusa* (Bronze Ram of Syracuse) and the world's largest collection of ancient anchors.

Oratories
CHAPEL

(Tesori della Loggia combined ticket adult/student/child under 6yr €5/4/free; ☺ Tesori della Loggia 9am-1pm Mon-Sat) Vucciria's greatest architectural treasures are its two baroque oratories: **Oratorio del Rosario di Santa Zita** (Via Valverde) and **Oratorio del Rosario di San Domenico** (Via dei Bambinai 2), covered top to bottom with the ornate stuccowork of Giacomo Serpotta (1652–1732). Known collectively as the **Tesori della Loggia**, they can be visited on a single ticket, together with a cluster of nearby churches.

Mercato della Vucciria
MARKET

(Piazza Caracciolo) The market here was once a notorious den of Mafia activity but is a muted affair today compared to the spirited Ballarò and Capo markets.

⊙ La Kalsa

Due to its proximity to the port, La Kalsa was subjected to carpet bombing during WWII, leaving it derelict and run down. Mother Teresa considered it akin to the shanty towns of Calcutta and established a mission here. Thankfully, this galvanised embarrassed authorities into action and the quarter is now undergoing extensive restoration.

Galleria Regionale della Sicilia
MUSEUM

(Palazzo Abatellis; ☑ 091 623 00 11; www.regione.sicilia.it/beniculturali/palazzoabatellis; Via Alloro 4; adult/EU 18-25yr/EU under 18yr & over 65yr €8/4/free; ☺ 9am-6pm Tue-Fri, to 1pm Sat & Sun) Housed in the stately 15th-century Palazzo Abatellis, this fine museum features works by Sicilian artists from the Middle Ages to the 18th century. Its greatest treasure is *Triunfo della Morte* (Triumph of Death), a magnificent fresco in which Death is represented as a demonic skeleton mounted on a wasted horse, brandishing a wicked-looking scythe while leaping over his hapless victims.

Galleria d'Arte Moderna
MUSEUM

(☑ 091 843 16 05; www.galleriadartemodernapalermo.it; Via Sant'Anna 21; adult €7, 19-25yr & over 60yr €5, under 19yr free; ☺ 9.30am-6.30pm Tue-Sun) This lovely, wheelchair-accessible museum is housed in a sleekly renovated 15th-century *palazzo* (mansion), which metamorphosed into a convent in the 17th century. Divided over three floors, the wide-ranging collection of 19th- and 20th-century Sicilian art is beautifully displayed. There's a regular program of modern-art exhibitions here, as well as an excellent bookshop and gift shop. English-language audioguides cost €4.

Museo dell'Inquisizione
MUSEUM

(Piazza Marina 61; adult/reduced €5/3; ☺ 10am-6pm) Housed in the basement of the 14th-century Palazzo Chiaromonte Steri, this recently opened museum offers a chilling but fascinating look at the legacy of the Inquisition in Palermo. The honeycomb of former cells has been painstakingly restored to reveal multiple layers of prisoners' graffiti and artwork (religious and otherwise). Excellent guided visits (in English upon request) are available.

Museo Internazionale delle Marionette
MUSEUM

(☑ 091 32 80 60; www.museomarionettepalermo.it; Piazzetta Antonio Pasqualino 5; adult/reduced €5/3; ☺ 9am-1pm & 2.30-6.30pm Mon-Sat year-round, plus 10am-1pm Sun Sep-May) This whimsical museum houses over 3500 marionettes, puppets, glove puppets and shadow figures from Palermo, Catania and Naples, as well as from further-flung places such as Japan, southeast Asia, Africa, China and India. From October to May, weekly puppet shows (adult/child €6/4) are staged on the museum's top floor in a beautifully decorated traditional theatre complete with a hand-cranked music machine.

⊙ New City

North of Piazza Giuseppe Verdi, Palermo elegantly slips into cosmopolitan mode. Here you'll find fabulous neoclassical and art nouveau buildings hailing from the last golden age of Sicilian architecture, along with late-19th-century mansion blocks lining the broad boulevard of Viale della Libertà.

★ Teatro Massimo
OPERA HOUSE

(☑ tour reservations 091 605 32 67; www.teatromassimo.it/servizi/visite.php; Piazza Giuseppe Verdi; guided tours adult/reduced €8/5; ☺ 9.30am-4.30pm Tue-Sun) Palermo's grand neoclassical opera house took over 20 years to complete and has become one of the city's iconic landmarks. The closing scene of *The Godfather: Part III*, with its visually stunning juxtaposition of high culture, crime, drama and death, was filmed here. Guided 25-minute tours are offered in English, Spanish, French and Italian daily except Monday.

Hammam
BATHHOUSE

(☑ 091 32 07 83; www.hammam.pa.it; Via Torrearsa 17d; admission €40; ⊘ women only 2-9pm Mon & Wed, 11am-9pm Fri, couples only 2-8pm Thu, men only 2-8pm Tue, 10am-8pm Sat) For a sybaritic experience, head to this luxurious marble-lined Moorish bathhouse, where you can indulge in a vigorous scrub-down, a steamy sauna and many different types of massages and therapies. There's a one-off charge (€10) for slippers and a hand glove.

★★ Festivals & Events

Festa di Santa Rosalia
RELIGIOUS

(U Fistinu) In mid-July, Palermo's biggest annual festival celebrates the patron saint of the city, Santa Rosalia, with fireworks, parades and four days of partying.

🛏 Sleeping

Most budget options can be found around Via Maqueda and Via Roma in the vicinity of the train station. Midrange and top-end hotels are concentrated further north. Parking usually costs an extra €10 to €15 per day.

B&B Amélie
B&B €

(☑ 091 33 59 20; www.bb-amelie.it; Via Prinicipe di Belmonte 94; s €40-60, d €60-80, tr €90-100; ❄ @ 🖰) On a pedestrianised New City street a stone's throw from Teatro Politeama, the affable, multilingual Angela has converted her grandmother's spacious 6th-floor flat into a cheery B&B. Rooms are colourfully decorated and the corner triple has a sunny terrace. Angela, a native Palermitan, generously shares her local knowledge and serves a tasty breakfast featuring homemade cakes and jams.

Palazzo Pantaleo
B&B €

(☑ 091 32 54 71; www.palazzopantaleo.it; Via Ruggero Settimo 74h; s/d/ste €80/100/140; P 🖰) Offering unbeatable comfort and a convenient location, Giuseppe Scaccianoce's cheerful B&B occupies the top floor of an old *palazzo* half a block from Piazza Politeama, hidden from the busy street in a quiet courtyard with free parking. The five rooms feature high ceilings, marble, tile or wooden floors, soundproofed windows and modern bathroom fixtures. There's also one spacious suite.

Butera 28
APARTMENT €

(☑ 333 3165432; www.butera28.it; Via Butera 28; apt per day €60-180, per week €380-1150; ❄ 🖰) Delightful owner, Nicoletta, rents 11 comfortable apartments in her elegant *palazzo* near Piazza della Kalsa. Units range in size from 30 to 180 sq m, most sleeping a family of four or more. Four apartments face the sea (number 9 is especially nice), most have laundry facilities, and all have well-equipped kitchens. Nicoletta also offers fabulous **cooking classes** (www.cookingwiththeduchess.com).

Hotel Orientale
HOTEL €

(☑ 091 616 57 27; www.albergoorientale.191.it; Via Maqueda 26; s €30, d €40-50, tr €50-60; ❄ 🖰) The grand marble stairway and arcaded courtyard of this *palazzo*, complete with rusty bicycles, stray cats and strung-up washing, is an evocative introduction to one of Palermo's most atmospherically faded budget hotels. Breakfast is served under the lovely frescoed ceiling in the library. Room 8 overlooks the tail end of the Ballaró market, close enough to hear vendors singing in the morning.

A Casa di Amici
HOSTEL €

(☑ 091 58 48 84; www.acasadiamici.com; Via Volturno 6; dm €19-23, d €65, without bathroom d €40; ❄ @ 🖰) In a renovated 19th-century *palazzo*, this artsy, hostel-type place behind Teatro Massimo has four colourful rooms sleeping two to four, with shared bathrooms and a guest kitchen. Two annexes, including one on Via Dante opened in 2013, offer additional rooms, including one family-friendly unit with private bath and terrace. Multilingual owner Claudia provides helpful maps, information displays, and advice.

B&B Panormus
B&B €

(☑ 091 617 58 26; www.bbpanormus.com; Via Roma 72; s €43-65, d €55-100; ❄ 🖰) A convenient location near the train station, coupled with attractive Liberty-style rooms, make this one of Palermo's most popular B&Bs. Each of the five impeccably clean units has its own private bathroom down the passageway.

Hotel Principe di Villafranca
BOUTIQUE HOTEL €€

(☑ 091 611 85 23; www.principedivillafranca.it; Via Turrisi Colonna 4; d €108-297; P ❄ @ 🖰) Furnished with fine linens and antiques, this sophisticated hotel is just west of Viale della Libertá in one of Palermo's most peaceful, exclusive neighbourhoods. Public spaces include a cosy sitting area with library, fireplace and displays of local designers' work; among the comfortable, high-ceilinged rooms, junior suite 105 stands out, decorated

Delightful Desserts

From citrus-scented pastries filled with ricotta, to ice cream served on a brioche, to the marzipan fruits piled in every confectioner's window, Sicily celebrates the joys of sugar morning, noon and night.

Multicultural Roots

People from the Arabs to the Aztecs have influenced Sicily's culture of sweets: the former introduced sugar cane; the latter's fiery hot chocolate so impressed the Spaniards that they brought it to the kingdom of Sicily. The land also supplied inspiration, from abundant citrus, almond and pistachio groves to Mt Etna's snowy slopes, legendary source of the first *granita*.

Sweet Sicilian Classics

The all-star list of Sicilian desserts starts with *cannoli*, crunchy pastry tubes filled with sweetened ricotta, garnished with chocolate, crumbled pistachios or a spike of candied citrus. Vying for the title of Sicily's most famous dessert is *cassata*, a coma-inducing concoction of sponge cake, cream, marzipan, chocolate and candied fruit. Feeling more adventurous? How about an *'mpanatigghiu*, a traditional Modican pastry stuffed with minced meat, almonds, chocolate and cinnamon?

A SUGAR-FUELLED ISLAND SPIN

➡ **Pasticceria Cappello** Renowned for its *setteveli*, a velvety seven-layer chocolate cake, made famous in Palermo.

➡ **Da Alfredo** Dreamy *granite* made with almonds and wild strawberries.

➡ **Ti Vitti** Divine *cannoli* featuring fresh-from-the-sheep ricotta from the Madonie Mountains.

➡ **Dolceria Bonajuto** Aztec-influenced chocolate with vanilla and hot peppers.

➡ **Gelati DiVini** Outlandish ice-cream flavours including Marsala wine, wild fennel and olive oil.

➡ **Maria Grammatico** Marzipan fruit, almond pastries and toasted-nut torrone.

1. Cakes 2. Traditional Sicilian sweets 3. *Cannoli* 4. Almond and coffee granita

with artwork loaned by Palermo's modern art museum.

Quintocanto Hotel & Spa HOTEL €€
(☎091 58 49 13; www.quintocantohotel.com; Corso Vittoria Emanuele 310; s €125-135, d €145-195, ste €254; ❄📶) Housed in a modernised 16th-century *palazzo*, Quintocanto woos visitors with its prime central city location and a wellness centre where guests enjoy free access to the sauna, Turkish bath and whirlpool tub (additional spa services including massages cost extra). Book ahead for rooms 319 and 420, which have terraces with superb views of San Giuseppe Teatini church next door.

Grand Hotel Piazza Borsa HOTEL €€
(☎091 32 00 75; www.piazzaborsa.com; Via dei Cartari 18; s €119-189, d €160-208, ste €350-790; P❄@📶) Opened in 2010 in Palermo's former stock exchange, this grand four-star encompasses three separate buildings housing 127 rooms. Nicest are the high-ceilinged suites with jaccuzi tubs and windows facing Piazza San Francesco.

Eating

Sicily's ancient cuisine is a mixture of spicy and sweet flavours, epitomised in the ubiquitous eggplant-based *caponata* and the Palermitan classic *bucatini con le sarde* (hollow tube-shaped noodles with sardines, wild fennel, raisins, pine nuts and breadcrumbs). Cakes, marzipan confections and pastries are all works of art – try the *cannoli* (tubes of pastry filled with sweetened ricotta).

Restaurants rarely start to fill up until 9.30pm. For cheap eats, visit Palermo's markets, wander the tangle of alleys east and south of Teatro Massimo, or spend a Saturday evening snacking with locals at the street food carts in Piazza Caracciolo in the Vucciria district.

Many places close on Sunday, especially in the evening.

★ **Ferro di Cavallo** TRATTORIA €
(☎091 33 18 35; Via Venezia 20; meals €13-17; ⏲lunch daily, dinner Wed-Sat) Tables line the pavement and religious portraits beam down upon the bustling mix of tourists and locals at this cheerful little trattoria near the Quattro Canti. Nothing costs more than €7 on the straightforward à la carte menu of Sicilian classics. If you have a sweet tooth save room for one of Palermo's very best *cannoli* (only €1.50).

DON'T MISS

PALERMO'S STREET FOOD

If you were taught that it was bad manners to eat in the street, you can break the rule in good company here. The mystery is simply how Palermo is not the obesity capital of Europe given just how much eating goes on! Palermitans are at it all the time: when they're shopping, commuting, discussing business, romancing...basically at any time of the day. What they're enjoying is the *buffitieri* – little hot snacks prepared at stalls and meant to be eaten on the spot.

Kick off the morning with *pane e panelle*, Palermo's famous chickpea fritter sandwich – great for vegetarians and a welcome change from a sweet custard-filled croissant. You might also want to go for some *crocchè* (potato croquettes, sometimes flavoured with fresh mint), *quaglie* (literally translated as quails, they're actually eggplants cut lengthwise and fanned out to resemble a bird's feathers, then fried) or *sfincione* (a spongy, oily pizza topped with onions and caciocavallo cheese). In summer, locals also enjoy a freshly baked brioche filled with ice cream or *granite* (crushed ice mixed with fresh fruit, almonds, pistachios or coffee).

From 4pm onwards the snacks become decidedly more carnivorous and you may just wish you hadn't read the following translations: how about some barbecued *stigghiola* (goat intestines filled with onions, cheese and parsley), for example? Or a couple of *pani ca meusa* (bread rolls stuffed with sauteed beef spleen). You'll be asked if you want your roll *schietta* (single) or *maritata* (married). If you choose *schietta*, the roll will only have ricotta in it before being dipped into boiling lard; choose *maritata* and you'll get the beef spleen as well.

You'll find street food stalls all over town, especially in Palermo's street markets.

Pizzeria Frida
PIZZERIA €

(www.fridapizzeria.it; Piazza Sant'Onofrio 37-38; pizzas €4.50-11; ⊙ 7pm-midnight, closed Tue) With pavement seating under umbrella awnings on a low-key Capo piazza, this local favorite makes pizzas in a variety of shapes, including *quadri* (square, picture frame-shaped pizzas) and *vulcanotti* (named after famous volcanoes and looking the part). Toppings include Sicilian specialties like tuna, capers, pistachios, mint, aubergines and ultra-fresh ricotta. Desserts (strawberry tiramisù, almond parfait) are also very tasty.

Zia Pina
TRATTORIA €

(Via Argenteria 67; meals €15-25; ⊙ noon-2.30pm) Tucked under a red-and-white-striped awning on a Vucciria backstreet, this highly informal eatery is run by venerable Aunt Pina and a bevy of her brothers. There's no fixed menu, but everything's dependably tasty. Grab a plate full of antipasti, choose your fish from the display up front, and pull up a plastic chair to one of the outdoor tables.

Francu U Vastiddaru
STREET FOOD €

(Corso Vittorio Emanuele 102; sandwiches €1.50-3.50; ⊙ 8am-late) Palermitan street food doesn't get any better or cheaper than the delicious panini hawked from this hole-in-the-wall sandwich stand just off Piazza Marina. Options range from the classic *panino triplo*, with *panelle* (chickpea fritters), *crocchè* (potato croquettes) and eggplant to the owner's trademark *panino vastiddaru* (with roast pork, salami, emmenthal cheese and spiced mushrooms).

I Cuochini
STREET FOOD €

(Via Ruggero Settimo 68; snacks from €0.70; ⊙ 8.30am-2.30pm Mon-Sat, plus 4.30-7.30pm Sat) Hidden inside a little courtyard off Via Ruggero Settimo, this long-standing Palermitan favourite specialises in low-cost snacks, including delicious *arancinette* (rice balls filled with meat sauce) and divine *panzerotti* (stuffed fried dough pockets). The latter come in countless delectable varieties: ricotta and mint, zucchini blossoms and cheese, mozzarella, cherry tomatoes and anchovies, just to name a few.

Pasticceria Cappello
PASTRIES & CAKES €

(www.pasticceriacappello.it; Via Nicoló Garzilli 10; ⊙ 7am-9.30pm Thu-Tue) Famous for the *setteveli* (seven-layer chocolate cake) that was invented here – and has long since been copied all over Palermo – this upscale bakery-cafe with its boudoir-style back room creates splendid pastries and desserts of all kinds. Not to be missed is the dreamy *delizia di pistacchio*, a granular pistachio cake topped with creamy icing and a chocolate medallion.

Antico Caffè Spinnato
CAFE €

(✆ 091 32 92 20; www.spinnato.it; Via Principe di Belmonte 107-15; ⊙ 7am-1am Sun-Fri, to 2am Sat) At this sophisticated cafe dating back to 1860, Palermitans throng the pavement tables daily to enjoy afternoon piano music, coffee, cocktails, ice cream, sumptuous cakes and snacks.

★ Trattoria Il Maestro del Brodo
TRATTORIA €€

(Via Pannieri 7; meals €19-30; ⊙ 12.30-3.30pm Tue-Sun, 8-11pm Fri & Sat) This no-frills, Slow Food–recommended eatery in the Vucciria offers delicious soups, an array of ultra-fresh seafood, and a sensational antipasto buffet (€8) featuring a dozen-plus homemade delicacies: *sarde a beccafico* (stuffed sardines), eggplant involtini, smoked fish, artichokes with parsley, sun-dried tomatoes, olives and more.

★ Trattoria Ai Cascinari
SICILIAN €€

(✆ 091 651 98 04; Via d'Ossuna 43/45; meals €20-28; ⊙ lunch Tue-Sun, dinner Wed-Sat) Friendly service, simple straw chairs and blue-and-white-checked tablecloths set the relaxed tone at this Slow Food–recommended neighbourhood trattoria, 1km north of the Cappella Palatina. Locals pack the labyrinth of back rooms, while waiters circulate non-stop with plates of scrumptious seasonal antipasti and divine main dishes. Save room for homemade ice cream and outstanding desserts from Palermo's beloved Pasticceria Cappello.

Piccolo Napoli
SEAFOOD €€

(✆ 091 32 04 31; Piazzetta Mulino a Vento 4; meals €25-34; ⊙ lunch Mon-Sat, dinner Tue-Sat) Known throughout Palermo for its fresh seafood, this bustling eatery is another hotspot for serious foodies. Nibble on toothsome sesame bread and plump olives while perusing the menu for a pasta dish that catches your fancy, then head to the seafood display (often still wriggling) to choose a second course. The genial owner greets his many regular customers by name.

🍷 Drinking & Nightlife

Palermo's liveliest clusters of bars can be found along Via Chiavettieri in the Vucciria neighbourhood (just northwest of Piazza Marina) and in the Champagneria district east of Teatro Massimo, centred on Piazza Olivella, Via Spinuzza, and Via Patania. Higher-end bars and dance venues are concentrated in the newer part of Palermo. In summer, many Palermitans decamp to Mondello by the sea.

★ Kursaal Kalhesa   BAR

(📞 091 616 21 11; www.kursaalkalhesa.it; Foro Italico Umberto I 21; ⏰ noon-3pm & 6pm-1.30am Tue-Sat, noon-1.30am Sun) This bar of choice for the city's avant garde occupies the remnants of a handsome early-19th-century palace next to the 16th-century town gate, Porta dei Greci. Recline on silk-covered divans beneath soaring vaulted ceilings and choose from an extensive list of cocktails and snacks while listening to live music or selections from the in-house DJ.

There's a roaring fire in winter, plus art exhibits, a good program of music and literary events and a bookstore with foreign newspapers. Meals (around €30) are served on the leafy patio upstairs.

Pizzo & Pizzo   WINE BAR

(📞 091 601 45 44; www.pizzoepizzo.com; Via XII Gennaio 1; ⏰ dinner Mon-Sat) Sure, this sophisticated wine bar is a great place for *aperitivi*, but the buzzing atmosphere and the tempting array of cheeses, cured meats and smoked fish might just convince you to stick around for dinner.

☆ Entertainment

The daily paper *Il Giornale di Sicilia* has a listing of what's on. The tourist office and information booths also have programs and listings. If you can read some Italian, www.balarm.it is another excellent resource.

Teatro Massimo   OPERA

(📞 091 605 35 80; www.teatromassimo.it; Piazza Giuseppe Verdi) Ernesto Basile's art nouveau masterpiece stages opera, ballet and music concerts. The theatre's program runs from September to June.

Cuticchio Mimmo   PUPPET THEATRE

(📞 091 32 34 00; www.figlidartecuticchio.com; Via Bara all'Olivella 95; ⏰ 6.30pm Sat & Sun Sep-Jul) This theatre is a charming low-tech choice for children (and adults), staging traditional shows with fabulous handcrafted puppets.

Cantieri Culturali alla Zisa   PERFORMING ARTS

(📞 091 652 49 42; Via Paolo Gili 4) West of the centre, this newly renovated industrial space has recently emerged as Palermo's trendiest contemporary and experimental arts venue, with frequent live performances and a brand new modern art gallery, ZAC (Zona Arti Contemporanee).

Teatro di Verdura   PERFORMING ARTS

(📞 091 765 19 63; Viale del Fante 70; ⏰ mid-Jun–Sep) A summer-only program of ballet and music in the lovely gardens of the Villa Castelnuovo, about 6km north of the city centre. There's a delightful open-air bar that opens during shows.

SICILIAN PUPPET THEATRE

Since the 18th century, the Opera dei Pupi (traditional Sicilian puppet theatre) has been enthralling adults and children alike. The shows are a mini theatrical performance with some puppets standing 1.5m high – a completely different breed from the glove puppet popular in the West. These characters are intricately carved from beech, olive or lemon wood with realistic-looking features; flexible joints ensure they have no problem swinging their swords or beheading dragons.

Effectively the soap operas of their day, Sicilian puppet shows expounded the deepest sentiments of life – unrequited love, treachery, thirst for justice and the anger and frustration of the oppressed. The swashbuckling tales centre on the legends of Charlemagne's heroic knights, Orlando and Rinaldo, with an extended cast including the fair Angelica, the treacherous Gano di Magonza and forbidding Saracen warriors. Good puppeteers are judged on the dramatic effect they can create – lots of stamping feet and a gripping running commentary – and on their speed and skill in directing the battle scenes.

Teatro Politeama Garibaldi
PERFORMING ARTS

(Piazza Ruggero Settimo) This grandiose theatre is a popular venue for opera, ballet and classical music, staging afternoon and evening concerts from October through to June. Designed by architect Giuseppe Damiani Almeyda between 1867 and 1874, it features a striking facade resembling a triumphal arch topped by a huge bronze chariot. It's home to Palermo's symphony orchestra, the **Orchestra Sinfonica Siciliana** (☑ 091 607 25 32; www.orchestrasinfonica-siciliana.it).

🛍 Shopping

Via Bara all'Olivella is good for arts and crafts. Check out the puppet workshop of the Cuticchio family, **Il Laboratorio Teatrale** (Via Bara all'Olivella 48-50; ☺ 10am-1pm & 4-7pm Tue-Sat).

For ceramics and pottery (albeit at higher prices than you'd find in Sicily's hinterland) stop by **Le Ceramiche di Caltagirone** (www.leceramichedicaltagirone.it; Via Cavour 114; ☺ 9am-1pm & 4-8pm Mon-Sat, 9am-1pm Sun) or **Casa Merlo** (www.casamerlo.it; Corso Vittorio Emanuele 231; ☺ 9am-1pm & 4-7.30pm Mon-Sat).

For edible souvenirs, visit **Gusti di Sicilia** (Via Emerico Amari 79; ☺ 8.30am-11pm Mon-Sat, 8.30am-2pm & 6-11pm Sun), an enticing gourmet food emporium, or **Bottega dei Sapori e dei Saperi della Legalità** (www.liberapalermo.org; Piazza Castelnuovo 13; ☺ 4-8pm Mon, 9.30am-1.30pm & 4-8pm Tue-Sat), a store that sells products grown on lands confiscated from the Mafia.

ℹ Information

EMERGENCY
Ambulance (☑ 091 666 55 28, 118)
Police (Questura; ☑ 091 21 01 11, 113; Piazza della Vittoria 8)

MEDICAL SERVICES
Ospedale Civico (☑ 091 666 11 11; www.ospedalecivicopa.org; Via Carmelo Lazzaro) Emergency facilities.

TOURIST INFORMATION
Central tourist office (☑ 091 58 51 72; informazionituristiche@provincia.palermo.it; Via Principe di Belmonte 42; ☺ 8.30am-2pm & 2.30-6pm Mon-Fri) Palermo's provincial tourist office offers maps and brochures as well as the helpful booklet *Un Ospite a Palermo* (www.unospiteapalermo.it), published bi-monthly and containing listings for museums, cultural centres, tour guides and transport companies.

City information booth (Piazza Bellini; 8.30am-1pm & 3-7pm Mon-Sat) The most dependable of Palermo's city-run information booths, next to the churches of San Cataldo and La Martorana. Other booths around the city – at the port, the train station, Piazza Castelnuovo and Piazza Marina – are only intermittently staffed and have unpredictable hours.

Falcone-Borsellino airport information office (☑ 091 59 16 98; in downstairs hall; ☺ 8.30am-7.30pm Mon-Fri, 8.30am-2.30pm Sat)

ℹ Getting There & Away

AIR
Falcone-Borsellino airport (PMO; ☑ 091 702 01 11; www.gesap.it) is at Punta Raisi, 31km west of Palermo.

Alitalia, easyJet, Ryanair and several other airlines operate between major European cities and Palermo. Falcone-Borsellino is also the hub airport for regular domestic flights to the islands of Pantelleria and Lampedusa.

BOAT
The ferry terminal is located just east of the corner of Via Francesco Crispi and Via Emerico Amari.

Grandi Navi Veloci (☑ 010 209 45 91, 091 58 74 04; www.gnv.it) Runs ferries from Palermo to Civitavecchia (from €73), Genoa (from €90), Naples (from €44) and Tunis (from €72).

Grimaldi Lines (☑ 081 49 64 44, 091 611 36 91; www.grimaldi-lines.com; Via del Mare) Ferries from Palermo to Salerno (from €65).

Siremar (☑ 091 749 31 11; www.siremar.it; Via Francesco Crispi 118) Ferries (€18.35, 2¼ hours) and summer-only hydrofoils (€23.55, 1½ hours) from Palermo to Ustica.

Tirrenia (☑ 091 976 07 73; www.tirrenia.it; Calata Marinai d'Italia) Ferries to Cagliari (from €51, Saturday only) and Naples (from €47).

Ustica Lines (☑ 092 387 38 13; www.usticalines.it) Year-round hydrofoils to Ustica (€22.95, 1½ hours). Summer-only hydrofoils to Lipari (€39.30, four hours) and the other Aeolian Islands.

BUS
Offices for all bus companies are located within a block or two of Palermo Centrale train station. The two main departure points are the brand-new **Piazzetta Cairoli bus terminal** (Piazzetta Cairoli), just south of the train station's eastern entrance, and the **intercity bus stop** on Via Paolo Balsamo, due east of the train station.

AST (Azienda Siciliana Trasporti; ☎091 680 00 32; www.aziendasicilianatrasporti.it; Via Rosario Gregorio 46) Services to southeastern destinations including Ragusa (€13.40, four hours, two to four daily).

Autoservizi Tarantola (☎092 43 10 20) Buses from Palermo to Segesta (one way/return €6.70/10.70, 80 minutes each way, two daily).

Cuffaro (☎091 616 15 10; www.cuffaro.info; Via Paolo Balsamo 13) Services to Agrigento (€8.70, two hours, three to eight daily).

SAIS Autolinee (☎091 616 60 28; www.sai-sautolinee.it; Piazza Cairoli) Buses to Messina (€15.80, 2¾ hours, three to five daily) and Catania (€14.90, 2½ hours, 10 to 14 daily).

SAIS Trasporti (☎091 617 11 41; www.saist-rasporti.it; Via Paolo Balsamo 20) Overnight service to Rome (€48, 12½ hours).

Salemi (☎092 398 11 20; www.autoservizisa-lemi.it) Several buses daily to Marsala (€9.20, 2½ hours), and Trapani's Birgi airport (€10.60, 1¾ to two hours).

Segesta (☎091 616 79 19; www.segesta.it; Piazza Cairoli) Services to Trapani (€9, two hours, at least 10 daily). Also sells Interbus tickets to Syracuse (€12, 3¼ hours, two to three daily).

CAR & MOTORCYCLE

Palermo is accessible on the A20-E90 toll road from Messina and the A19-E932 from Catania via Enna. Trapani and Marsala are also easily accessible from Palermo by motorway (A29), while Agrigento and Palermo are linked by the SS121, a good state road through the island's interior.

Most major auto hire companies are represented at the airport. You'll often save money by booking your rental online before leaving home. Given the city's chaotic traffic and expensive parking, and the excellent public transit from Palermo's airport, you're generally better off postponing rental car pickup until after you leave the city.

TRAIN

From Palermo Centrale station, just south of the centre at the foot of Via Roma, regular trains leave for Messina (from €11.80, 2¾ to 3½ hours, hourly), Agrigento (€8.30, two hours, eight to 10 daily) and Cefalù (from €5.15, one hour, hourly). There are also InterCity trains to Reggio di Calabria, Naples and Rome.

For Catania or Syracuse, you're generally better off taking the bus. There's only one direct train to Catania (€12.50, three hours, Monday to Friday early morning); all others require a time-consuming change at Messina.

ⓘ Getting Around

TO/FROM THE AIRPORT

Prestia e Comandè (☎091 58 63 51; www. prestiaecomande.it) runs a half-hourly bus service from the airport to the centre of town (one way/return €6.10/11), with stops outside Teatro Politeama Garibaldi (30 minutes) and Palermo Centrale train station (45 minutes). Buses are parked to the right as you exit the airport arrivals hall. Buy tickets on the bus. Return journeys to the airport run with similar frequency, picking up at the same points.

The Trinacria Express train (€5.80, 45 minutes to 1¼ hours) from the airport (Punta Raisi station) to Palermo takes longer and runs less frequently than the bus.

A taxi from the airport to downtown Palermo costs €45.

BUS

Palermo's orange, white and blue city buses, operated by **AMAT** (☎848 80 08 17; www.amat. pa.it), are frequent but often crowded and slow. The free map handed out at Palermo tourist offices details all the major bus lines; most stop at the train station. Tickets, valid for 90 minutes, cost €1.30 if pre-purchased from *tabacchi* (tobacconists) or AMAT booths, or €1.70 onboard the bus. A day pass costs €3.50.

Three small buses – Linea Gialla, Linea Verde and Linea Rossa (€0.52 for 24-hour ticket) – operate in the narrow streets of the *centro storico* (historic centre) and can be useful if you're moving between tourist sights.

CAR & MOTORCYCLE

Driving is frenetic in the city and best avoided. Use one of the staffed car parks around town (€12 to €20 per day) if your hotel lacks parking.

Around Palermo

Just outside Palermo's city limits, the beach town of Mondello and the dazzling cathedral of Monreale are both worthwhile day trips. Just offshore, Ustica makes a great overnight or weekend getaway.

Mondello's long, sandy beach became fashionable in the 19th century, when people came to the seaside in their carriages, prompting the construction of the huge art nouveau pier that still graces the waterfront. Most of the beaches near the pier are private (two sun lounges and an umbrella cost €10 to €20); however, there's a wide swath of public beach opposite the centre of town with all the prerequisite pedaloes and jet skis for hire. Given its easygoing seaside feel, Mondello is an excellent base for families. To get here, take bus 806 (€1.30, 30 minutes) from Piazza Sturzo in Palermo.

★**Cattedrale di Monreale** (☎091 640 44 03; Piazza del Duomo; admission to cathedral free, north transept €2, terrace €2; ⊘ 8.30am-12.45pm & 2.30-5pm Mon-Sat, 8-10am & 2.30-5pm Sun), 8km southwest of Palermo, is considered the finest example of Norman architecture in Sicily, incorporating Norman, Arab, Byzantine and classical elements. Inspired by a vision of the Virgin, it was built by William II in an effort to outdo his grandfather Roger II, who was responsible for the cathedral in Cefalù and the Cappella Palatina in Palermo. The interior, completed in 1184 and executed in shimmering mosaics, depicts 42 Old Testament stories. Outside the cathedral, the cloister (adult €6, EU citizen 18-25yr €3, under 18 & over 65yr free; ⊘ 9am-6.30pm Tue-Sat, 9am-1pm Sun & Mon) is a tranquil courtyard with a tangible oriental feel. Surrounding the perimeter, elegant Romanesque arches are supported by an exquisite array of slender columns alternately decorated with mosaics. To reach Monreale take AMAT bus 389 (€1.30, 35 minutes, half-hourly) from Piazza Indipendenza in Palermo or AST's Monreale bus (one way/return €1.80/2.80, 40 minutes, hourly) from in front of Palermo Centrale train station.

The 8.7-sq-km island of Ustica was declared Italy's first marine reserve in 1986. The surrounding waters are a playground of fish and coral, ideal for snorkelling, diving and underwater photography. To enjoy Ustica's wild coastline and dazzling grottoes without the crowds try visiting in June or September. There are numerous dive centres, hotels and restaurants on the island, as well as some nice hiking. To get here from Palermo, take the once-daily car ferry (€18.35, 2½ hours) operated by Siremar

(⊘ 091 844 90 02; www.siremar.it); or the faster hydrofoils (€23.55, 1½ hours) operated by both Siremar and Ustica Lines (⊘ 091 844 90 02; www.usticalines.it). For more details on Ustica, see Lonely Planet's *Sicily* guide.

TYRRHENIAN COAST

The coast between Palermo and Milazzo is studded with popular tourist resorts attracting a steady stream of holidaymakers, particularly between June and September. The best of these is Cefalù, a resort second only to Taormina in popularity. Just inland lie the two massive natural parks of the Madonie and Nebrodi mountains.

Cefalù
POP 14,300
This popular holiday resort wedged between a dramatic mountain peak and a sweeping stretch of sand has the lot: a great beach; a truly lovely historic centre with a grandiose cathedral; and winding medieval streets lined with restaurants and boutiques. Avoid the height of summer when prices soar, beaches are jam-packed and the charm of the place is tainted by bad-tempered drivers trying to find parking.

⊙ Sights

★ Duomo di Cefalù   CATHEDRAL
(⊘ 092 192 20 21; Piazza del Duomo; ⊘ 8am-7pm Apr-Sep, 8am-5pm Oct-Mar) Cefalù's cathedral is one of the jewels in Sicily's Arab-Norman

SICILY CEFALÙ

WORTH A TRIP

CEFALÙ'S BACKYARD PLAYGROUND

Due south of Cefalù, the 40,000-hectare Parco Naturale Regionale delle Madonie incorporates some of Sicily's highest peaks, including the imposing Pizzo Carbonara (1979m). The park's wild, wooded slopes are home to wolves, wildcats, eagles and the near-extinct ancient Nebrodi fir trees that have survived since the last ice age. Ideal for hiking, cycling and horse trekking, the park is also home to several handsome mountain towns, including Castelbuono, Petralia Soprana and Petralia Sottana.

The region's distinctive rural cuisine includes roasted lamb and goat, cheeses, grilled mushrooms and aromatic pasta with *sugo* (meat sauce). A great place to sample these specialities is Nangalarruni (⊘ 092 167 14 28; www.hostariananangalarruni.it; Via delle Confraternite 10; fixed menus €23-32; ⊘ 12.30-3pm & 7-10pm, closed Wed in winter) in Castelbuono.

For park information, contact the Ente Parco delle Madonie in Cefalù (p785) or Petralia Sottana (⊘ 092 168 40 11; Corso Paolo Agliata 16; ⊘ 8am-2pm & 3-7pm Mon-Fri, 3-7pm Sat, 10.30am-1pm & 4.30-7pm Sun).

Bus service to the park's main towns is limited; to fully appreciate the Madonie, you're better off hiring a car for a couple of days.

crown, only equalled in magnificence by the Cattedrale di Monreale and Palermo's Cappella Palatina. Filling the central apse, a towering figure of Christ All Powerful is the focal point of the elaborate Byzantine mosaics – Sicily's oldest and best preserved, predating those of Monreale by 20 or 30 years.

La Rocca VIEW POINT
(admission €3; ⏱ 9am-6.45pm May-Sep, 9am-4.45pm Oct-Apr) Looming over the town, this imposing craggy mass is the site where the Arabs built their citadel, occupying it until the Norman conquest forced them down to the port below. An enormous staircase, the **Salita Saraceno**, winds up through three tiers of city walls, a 30-minute climb. There are stunning views from the ruined 4th-century Tempio di Diana up top.

🏃 Activities

Cefalù's crescent-shaped beach, just west of the medieval centre, is lovely, but in the summer get here early to find a patch for your umbrella and towel. You can escape with a boat tour along the coast during the summer months with several agencies located along Corso Ruggero.

Scooter for Rent SCOOTER RENTAL
(☑ 092 142 04 96; www.scooterforrent.it; Via Vittorio Emanuele 57; per day/week 50cc Vespa €35/175, mountain bike €10/45) Rents out bicycles (€10 per day) and scooters (from €35 per day).

🛏 Sleeping

Cheap accommodation is generally scarce year-round. Bookings are essential.

B&B Casanova B&B €
(☑ 092 192 30 65; www.casanovabb.it; Via Porpora 3; s €40-70, d €55-100, q €80-140; ❊🏠) This B&B on the waterfront has rooms of varying size, from a cramped single with one minuscule window to the Ruggero room, a palatial space sleeping up to four, with a vaulted frescoed ceiling, decorative tile floors and French doors offering grand views of Cefalù's medieval centre. All guests share access to a small terrace overlooking the sea.

Hotel Kalura HOTEL €€
(☑ 092 142 13 54; www.hotel-kalura.com; Via Vincenzo Cavallaro 13; d €89-179; P❊@☎) East of town on a rocky outcrop, this German-run, family-oriented hotel has its own pebbly beach, restaurant and fabulous pool. Most rooms have sea views and the hotel arranges

loads of activities, including mountain biking, hiking, canoeing, pedaloes, diving and dance nights. It's a 20-minute walk into town.

La Plumeria HOTEL €€
(☑ 092 192 58 97; www.laplumeriahotel.it; Corso Ruggero 185; d €129-209; P❊🏠) Opened in 2010, this hotel's big selling point is its perfect location between the *duomo* and the waterfront, with free parking a few minutes away. Rooms are unexceptional, but clean and well appointed. Room 301 on the top floor is the sweetest of the lot, a cosy eyrie with checkerboard tile floors and a small terrace looking up to the *duomo*.

🍴 Eating & Drinking

There are dozens of restaurants, but the food can be surprisingly mundane and the ubiquitous tourist menus can quickly pall.

★ Ti Vitti SICILIAN €€
(www.ristorantetivitti.com; Via Umberto I 34; meals €30-40) At this up-and-coming eatery named after a Sicilian card game, talented young chef Vincenzo Collaro whips up divine pasta, fresh-from-the-market fish dishes and some of the best *cannoli* you'll find anywhere in Sicily. His insistence on using only the freshest ingredients means no swordfish out of season, and special, locally sourced treats such as basilisco mushrooms from the Monte Madonie.

La Botte SICILIAN €€
(☑ 092 142 43 15; www.labottecefalu.com; Via Veterani 20; meals €30-35; ⏱ 12.30-2.30pm & 7.30-10.30pm Tue-Sun) This small, family-run restaurant just off Corso Ruggero serves a good choice of antipasti, seasonally driven pasta dishes and seafood-dominated mains. The fixed menu of three fish courses plus a side dish offers good value.

La Galleria SICILIAN, CAFE €€
(☑ 092 142 02 11; www.lagalleriacefalu.it; Via Mandralisca 23; meals €25-40; ⏱ closed Thu year-round & Mon in winter) This is about as hip as Cefalù gets. Functioning as a restaurant, cafe, internet point, bookshop and occasional gallery space, La Galleria has an informal vibe, an internal garden and an innovative menu that mixes standard *primi* and *secondi* with a range of *piatti unici* (€12–15), each designed to be a meal in itself.

❶ Information

ATMs are concentrated along Corso Ruggero.

Ente Parco delle Madonie (☑ 092 192 33 27; www.parcodellemadonie.it; Corso Ruggero 116; ⊙ 8am-8pm daily May-Sep, 8am-6pm Mon-Sat Oct-Apr) Knowledgeable and friendly staff supply information about the Madonie regional park.

Hospital (☑ 092 192 01 11; Contrada Pietrapollastra) On the main road out of town in the direction of Palermo.

Police (Questura; ☑ 092 192 60 11; Via Roma 15)

Tourist office (☑ 092 142 10 50; strcefalu@ regione.sicilia.it; Corso Ruggero 77; ⊙ 9am-1pm & 3-7.30pm Mon-Sat) English-speaking staff, lots of leaflets and good maps.

❶ Getting There & Away

BOAT

SMIV (Società Marittima Italiana Veloce; www. smiv.it) runs daily boat trips between Cefalù and the Aeolian Islands, from May to September. Their 8am boat serves Lipari and Vulcano (one way/return €30/60), returning to Cefalù at 6.45pm. A second boat serves Panarea and Stromboli (one way/return €40/80), leaving at 11am and returning to Cefalù around 11.45pm. Rates include free pick up at any Cefalù hotel. Tickets are available at **Turismez Viaggi** (☑ 092 142 12 64; www.turismezviaggi. it; Corso Ruggero 83) next door to the tourist office.

TRAIN

The best way of getting to and from Cefalù is by rail. Hourly trains go to Palermo (from €5.15, 45 minutes to 1¼ hours) and virtually every other town on the coast.

AEOLIAN ISLANDS

The Aeolian Islands are a little piece of paradise. Stunning cobalt sea, splendid beaches, some of Italy's best hiking, and an awe-inspiring volcanic landscape are just part of the appeal. The islands also have a fascinating human and mythological history that goes back several millennia; the Aeolians figured prominently in Homer's *Odyssey,* and evidence of the distant past can be seen everywhere, most notably in Lipari's excellent archaeological museum.

The seven islands of Lipari, Vulcano, Salina, Panarea, Stromboli, Alicudi and Filicudi are part of a huge 200km volcanic ridge that runs between the smoking stack of Mt Etna and the threatening mass of Vesuvius above Naples. Collectively, the islands exhibit a unique range of volcanic characteristics, which earned them a place on Unesco's World Heritage list in 2000. The islands are mobbed with visitors in July and August but out of season things remain remarkably tranquil.

❶ Getting There & Away

Both **Ustica Lines** (www.usticalines.it) and **Siremar** (www.siremar.it) run hydrofoils year-round from Milazzo, the mainland city closest to the islands (see table, p786). Almost all boats stop first at Vulcano and Lipari. Most then continue onward to the ports of Santa Marina and/ or Rinella on Salina island. Beyond Salina, boats either branch off east to Panarea and Stromboli, or west to Filicudi and Alicudi. Frequency of service on all routes increases in the summer.

Both Siremar and **NGI Traghetti** (☑ 090 928 40 91; www.ngi-spa.it) also run car ferries from Milazzo to the islands; they're slightly cheaper, but slower and less regular than the hydrofoils.

Less frequent year-round services include Ustica Lines hydrofoils from Messina, and Siremar ferries from Naples. In summer only (late June to early September), Ustica Lines also offers a once-daily service from Palermo that makes stops on all seven islands. Boats are sometimes cancelled due to heavy seas.

❶ Getting Around

BOAT

Regular hydrofoil and ferry services operate between the islands. Ticket offices with posted timetables can be found close to the docks on all islands.

CAR & SCOOTER

You can take your car to Lipari, Vulcano or Salina by ferry, or garage it on the mainland from €12 per day. The islands are small, with narrow, winding roads. You'll often save money (and headaches) by hiring a scooter on site, or better yet, exploring the islands on foot.

Lipari

POP 11,200 / ELEV 602M

Lipari is the Aeolians' thriving hub, both geographically and functionally, with regular ferry and hydrofoil connections to all other islands. Lipari town, the largest urban centre in the archipelago, is home to the islands' only tourist office and most dependable banking services, along with enough restaurants, bars and year-round residents to offer a bit of cosmopolitan buzz. Meanwhile, the island's rugged shoreline offers excellent opportunities for hiking, boating and swimming.

Lipari has been inhabited for some 6000 years. The island was settled in the 4th millennium BC by Sicily's first known inhabitants, the Stentillenians, who developed a flourishing economy based on obsidian, a glassy volcanic rock. Commerce subsequently attracted the Greeks, who used the islands as ports on the east–west trade route, and pirates such as Barbarossa (or Redbeard), who sacked the city in 1544.

Lipari's two harbours, Marina Lunga (where ferries and hydrofoils dock) and Marina Corta (700m south, used by smaller boats) are linked by a bustling main street, Corso Vittorio Emanuele, flanked by shops, restaurants and bars. Overlooking the colourful snake of day trippers is Lipari's clifftop citadel, surrounded by 16th-century walls.

◉ Sights & Activities

★ Museo Archeologico Regionale Eoliano
MUSEUM

(☑ 090 988 01 74; www.regione.sicilia.it/beniculturali/museolipari; Castello di Lipari; adult/18-25yr/EU under 18yr & over 65yr €6/3/free; ⊙ 9am-1pm & 3-6pm Mon-Sat, 9am-1pm Sun) A must-see for lovers of Mediterranean history, Lipari's archaeological museum boasts one of Europe's finest collections of ancient finds. Especially worthwhile are the Sezione Preistorica, devoted to locally discovered artefacts from the Neolithic and Bronze Ages to the Graeco-Roman era, and the Sezione Classica, whose highlights include ancient shipwreck cargoes and the world's largest collection of Greek theatrical masks.

Other sections worth a quick look are the Sezione Epigrafica (Epigraphic Section), which has a small garden littered with engraved stones and a room of Greek and Roman tombs; and the Sezione Vulcanologica

(Vulcanology Section), which illustrates the Aeolians' volcanic geology.

★ Quattrocchi
VIEW POINT

Lipari's best views are from a celebrated view point known as Quattrocchi (Four Eyes), 3km west of town. Climb the main road towards Pianoconte and watch for a sensational coastal panorama unfolding to the south: great, grey cliffs plunge into the sea, while in the distance plumes of sinister smoke rise from the dark heights of neighbouring Vulcano.

★ Spiaggia Valle i Muria
BEACH

This dark, pebbly beach on the southwestern shore, lapped by clean waters and surrounded by dramatic cliffs, is one of Lipari's best swimming and sunbathing spots. The turnoff, about 3km west of Lipari Town, is easily reachable by car, scooter, or local bus; follow the road towards Pianoconte until you see signs. From here, it's a steep 15-minute downhill walk.

Come prepared for the day with water, sunscreen and a picnic lunch. In good weather, Lipari resident Barni serves food and drinks from his rustic cave-like bar on the beach, and also provides boat transfers to and from Marina Corta in Lipari (€5/10 one way/return), a half-hour voyage that offers unforgettable sunset views of Vulcano and the *faraglioni* (rock spires) along Lipari's western shore.

Eastern Beaches
BEACH

On Lipari's eastern shore, sunbathers and swimmers head for Canneto, a few kilometres north of Lipari town, to bask on the pebbly Spiaggia Bianca. Further north are the pumice mines of Pomiciazzo and Porticello, where there's another beach, Spiaggia della Papesca, dusted white by the fine pumice that gives the sea its limpid turquoise colour.

BOATS FROM MILAZZO TO THE AEOLIANS

DESTINATION	COST (€) HYDROFOIL/FERRY	DURATION HYDROFOIL/FERRY
Alicudi	28.70/20.40	3¼/6hr
Filicudi	23.25/17.55	2¾/5hr
Panarea	18.80/13.90	2¼/4½hr
Salina (Rinella)	17.55/13.15	2/3¾hr
Salina (Santa Marina)	19.05/14.65	1¾/3¼hr
Stromboli	21.95/16.75	2¾/6hr
Vulcano	16/12.30	45min/1½hr

Coastal Hikes
WALKING

Lipari's rugged northwestern coastline offers excellent walking opportunities. Most accessible is the pleasant hour-long stroll from Quattropani to Acquacalda along Lipari's north shore, which affords spectacular views of Salina and a distant Stromboli. Take the bus to Quattropani (€1.90), then simply proceed downhill on the main road 5km to Acquacalda, where you can catch the bus (€1.55) back to Lipari.

More strenuous, but equally rewarding in terms of scenery, is the three- to four-hour hike descending steeply from Pianoconte, down past the old Roman baths of Terme di San Calogero to the western shoreline, then skirting the clifftops along a flat stretch before climbing steeply back to the town of Quattropani.

Diving Center La Gorgonia
DIVING

(☎ 090 981 26 16; www.lagorgoniadiving.it; Salita San Giuseppe) This outfit offers courses, boat transport, equipment hire and general information about scuba diving and snorkelling around Lipari. See the website for a complete price list.

☞ Tours

Numerous agencies in town offer tours to the surrounding islands. Prices vary depending on the season, but typically are around €20 for a tour of Lipari and Vulcano, €45 to visit Filicudi and Alicudi, €45 for a day trip to Panarea and Stromboli, or €80 for a late afternoon trip to Stromboli including a guided hike up the mountain at sunset and a late night return to Lipari.

Da Massimo/Dolce Vita
BOAT TOUR

(☎ 090 981 30 86; www.damassimo.it; Via Maurolico 2) One of Lipari's best established agencies, well-positioned on a side street between Via Vittorio Emanuele and Via Garibaldi. Specialises in sunset hikes to the top of Stromboli, returning by boat to Lipari the same evening. They also hire boats and dinghies.

🛏 Sleeping

Lipari is the Aeolians' best-equipped base for island-hopping, with plenty of places to stay, eat and drink. Note that prices soar in summer; avoid August if possible.

★ Diana Brown
B&B €

(☎ 090 981 25 84; www.dianabrown.it; Vico Himera 3; s €30-90, d €40-100, tr €50-130; ❉ � 🛜) Tucked down a narrow alley, South African Diana's delightful rooms sport tiled floors, abundant hot water and welcome extras such as kettles, fridges, clothes-drying racks and satellite TV. Darker units downstairs are compensated for by built-in kitchenettes. There's a sunny breakfast terrace and solarium with deck chairs, plus book exchange and laundry service. Optional breakfast costs €5 extra per person.

Enzo Il Negro
GUESTHOUSE €

(☎ 090 981 31 63; www.enzoilnegro.com; Via Garibaldi 29; s €40-50, d €60-90; ❉ 🛜) This simple guesthouse near Marina Corta sports spacious, tiled, pine-furnished rooms with fridges. Two panoramic terraces overlook the rooftops, the harbour and the castle walls.

Casajanca
BOUTIQUE HOTEL €€

(☎ 090 988 02 22; www.casajanca.it; Via Marina Garibaldi 115, Canneto; d €80-200; ❉) A stone's throw from the beach at Canneto, this is a charming little hotel with 10 rooms, all decorated with polished antique furniture and impeccable taste. The dappled courtyard, a relaxing place to enjoy breakfast, boasts an inviting natural thermal pool. Pets are welcome, and transfers from Lipari's port are included in the price.

Hotel Giardino Sul Mare
HOTEL €€

(☎ 090 981 10 04; www.giardinosulmare.it; Via Maddalena 65; d €80-230; ⏱ Apr-Oct; ❉ ≋) This family-run hotel's top attraction is its superb seaside location, a few blocks south of Marina Corta. The pool terrace on the cliff edge is fabulous, but if you prefer to swim in the sea there's also direct access to a rocky platform below. Most rooms have terraces and high ceilings; they're a bit tired and bland otherwise.

🍴 Eating & Drinking

Fish abound in the waters of the archipelago and include tuna, mullet, cuttlefish and sole, all of which end up on local menus. Try *pasta all'eoliana,* a simple blend of the island's excellent capers with olives, olive oil, anchovies, tomatoes and basil.

Bars are concentrated along Corso Vittorio Emanuele and down by Marina Corta. In peak season everything stays open into the wee hours.

★ Le Macine
SICILIAN €€

(☎ 090 982 23 87; www.lemacine.org; Via Stradale 9, Pianoconte; meals €27-36; ⏱ 12.30-3pm &

7-10pm daily May-Sep, Sat & Sun Oct-Apr) This country restaurant in Pianoconte, 4.5km from Lipari Town, comes into its own in summer, when meals are served on the terrace. Seafood and fresh vegetables star in dishes such as swordfish cakes with artichokes, shrimp-filled ravioli or fish in *ghiotta* sauce (with olive oil, capers, tomatoes, garlic and basil). Reservations are advised, as is the free shuttle service.

Kasbah MODERN SICILIAN, PIZZERIA €€
(☑090 981 10 75; Vico Selinunte 41; pizzas €5-9, meals €28-33; ☺7-11pm Mar-Oct) Hidden down narrow Vico Selinunte is the new location of this perennial local favorite. Food runs from high-quality wood-fired pizzas to superb pastas, fish dishes and wild cards like stewed lamb with veggies or couscous-crusted anchovy fritters. The casual-chic dining room is all minimalist white decor juxtaposed against grey linen tablecloths and stone walls; out back there's a candlelit garden.

E Pulera MODERN SICILIAN €€€
(☑090 981 11 58; www.pulera.it; Via Isabella Conti; meals €35-50; ☺7.30-10pm May-Oct) With its serene garden setting, low lighting, artsy tile-topped tables and exquisite food, E Pulera makes an upscale but relaxed choice for a romantic dinner. Start with a carpaccio of tuna with blood oranges and capers, choose from a vast array of Aeolian and Sicilian meat and fish dishes, then finish with *cassata* or *biscotti* with sweet Malvasia wine.

🛍 Shopping

You simply can't leave these islands without a small pot of capers and a bottle of sweet Malvasia wine. You can get both, along with tuna, meats, cheeses and other picnic supplies at **La Formagella** (Via Vittorio Emanuele 250; ☺9am-1pm & 4-7pm) or **Fratelli Laise** (www.fratellilaise.com; Via Vittorio Emanuele 118; ☺9am-1pm & 4-7pm), both along Lipari's main pedestrian thoroughfare.

ℹ Information

Corso Vittorio Emanuele is lined with ATMs. The other islands have relatively few facilities, so it's best to sort out your finances here before moving on.

Ospedale Civile (☑090 988 51 11; Via Sant'Anna) Operates a first-aid service.

Police (☑090 981 13 33; Via Marconi)

Tourist office (☑090 988 00 95; Via Vittorio Emanuele 202; ☺9am-1pm & 4.30-7pm Mon,

Wed & Fri, 9am-1pm Tue & Thu) Lipari's office provides information covering all of the Aeolian Islands.

ℹ Getting There & Around

BOAT
The main port is Marina Lunga, where you'll find a joint **Siremar** (☑090 981 12 20; www.siremar.it) and **Ustica Lines** (☑090 981 24 48; www.usticalines.it) ticket office at the head of the hydrofoil jetty. Timetable information is displayed here and at the tourist office. Adjacent to the ticket offices is a left-luggage office.

Year-round ferries and hydrofoils serve Milazzo and all the other Aeolian islands; less frequent services include year-round hydrofoils to Messina and ferries to Naples, and summer-only hydrofoil service to Palermo. See the companies' websites for schedules and prices.

BUS
Autobus Guglielmo Urso (☑090 981 10 26; www.ursobus.com/orariursobus.pdf) runs frequent buses around the island (€1.55 to €1.90 depending on destination) from the bus stop opposite the Esso petrol station at Marina Lunga. One main route serves the island's eastern shore, from Canneto to Acquacalda, while the other serves the western highland settlements of Quattrocchi, Pianoconte and Quattropani. Multiride booklets (six/10/20 rides €7/10.50/20.50) will save you money if you're here for several days.

CAR, SCOOTER & BICYCLE
Several places around town rent bicycles (€10 per day), scooters (€15 to €40) and cars (€30 to €70), including **Da Luigi** (☑090 988 05 40; www.noleggiolipari.it; Marina Lunga) down at the ferry dock.

Vulcano

POP 720 / ELEV 500M

Vulcano is a memorable island, not least because of the vile smell of sulphurous gases. Once you escape the drab and dated tourist centre, Porto di Levante, there's a delightfully tranquil, unspoilt quality to the landscape. Beyond the well-marked trail to the looming Fossa di Vulcano, the landscape gives way to rural simplicity with vineyards, birdsong and a surprising amount of greenery. The island is worshipped by Italians for its therapeutic mud baths and hot springs, and its black beaches and weird steaming landscape make for an interesting day trip.

Boats dock at Porto di Levante. To the right, as you face the island, are the mud baths and the small Vulcanello peninsula, to the left is the volcano. Straight ahead is Porto di Ponente, 700m west, where you will find the Spiaggia Sabbia Nera (Black Sand Beach).

Activities

★ Fossa di Vulcano
WALKING

(admission €3) Vulcano's top attraction is the straightforward, hour-long trek up its 391m volcano (no guide required). Bring a hat, sunscreen and water and follow the signs south along Strada Provinciale, then climb the zigzag gravel track to the crater's edge (290m). From here, circle the rim to the summit for stunning views of the other Aeolians lined up to the north.

Laghetto di Fanghi
MUD BATHS

(admission €2, shower €1, towel €2.60; ⊙ 7am-11pm summer, 8.30am-5pm winter) Vulcano's harbourside pool of warm coffee-coloured sulphurous gloop has long been prized for its therapeutic qualities. If you don't mind smelling funny for a few days, dive on in, apply some mud to your body and face, wait for the clay mask to dry, rinse off, then head for the hot, bubbling springs in a small natural sea-water pool nearby.

Keep the acidic mud away from your eyes, and wear protective footwear – the springs can get scalding hot!

Beaches
BEACH

At Porto di Ponente, on the far side of the peninsula from the hydrofoil dock, the dramatic black **Spiaggia Sabbia Nera** curves around a pretty bay; it's one of the archipelago's few sandy beaches. A smaller, quieter black-sand beach, **Spiaggia dell'Asina**, can be found on the island's southern side near Gelso.

🛏 Sleeping & Eating

Unless you're here for the walking and the mud baths, Vulcano is not a great place for an extended stay; the town is pretty soulless, the hotels are expensive and the sulphurous fumes really do smell.

Casa Arcada
B&B, APARTMENT €

(☑ 347 649 76 33; www.casaarcada.it; Via Sotto Cratere; B&B per person €27-55, d apt per week €350-790; ❋) This sweet whitewashed complex offers bed and breakfast in five simple rooms with air-con and mini-fridges, along with weekly rental apartments. The communal upstairs terrace affords lovely views

up to the volcano and across the water to Lipari. It's conveniently located at the foot of the volcano, 20m back from the main road between the port and the crater path.

★ La Forgia Maurizio
SICILIAN, INDIAN €€

(☑ 339 137 91 07; Strada Provinciale 45, Porto di Levante; meals €30-40; ⊙ noon-3pm & 7-11pm) The owner of this devilishly good restaurant spent 20 winters in Goa, India; Eastern influences sneak into a menu of Sicilian specialities, all prepared and presented with flair. Don't miss the *liquore di kumquat e cardamom*, Maurizio's homemade answer to *limoncello*. The tasting menu is a good deal at €30 including wine and dessert.

❶ Getting There & Around

BOAT

Vulcano is an intermediate stop between Milazzo and Lipari; both Siremar and Ustica Lines run multiple vessels in both directions throughout the day.

Centro Nautico Baia di Levante (☑ 339 337 27 95; www.baialevante.it; ⊙ Apr-Oct), hire out boats from a shed on the beach to the left of the hydrofoil dock.

Sicily in Kayak (☑ 329 538 12 29; www.sicilyinkayak.com) offers kayaking tours of Vulcano and the neighbouring islands.

CAR, SCOOTER & BICYCLE

Sprint (☑ 090 985 22 08; Via Provinciale, Porto di Levante) rent out scooters (per day from €20), bicycles (from €5) and small cars (from €40) from their base well signposted near the hydrofoil dock. Friendly multilingual owners Luigi and Nidra offer tips for exploring the island and also rent out an apartment (€40–70 per night) in Vulcano's tranquil interior.

Salina

POP 2200 / ELEV 962M

In stark contrast to Vulcano's barren landscape, Salina's twin craters of Monte dei Porri and Monte Fossa delle Felci are lushly wooded, a result of the numerous freshwater springs on the island. Wildflowers, thick yellow gorse bushes and serried ranks of grapevines carpet the hillsides in vibrant colours and cool greens, while its high coastal cliffs plunge dramatically towards beaches. The famous Aeolian capers grow plentifully here, as do the grapes used for making Malvasia wine.

⊙ Sights & Activities

★ Monte Fossa delle Felci   HIKING

For jaw-dropping views, climb to the Aeolians' highest point, Monte Fossa delle Felci (962m). The two-hour ascent starts from the **Santuario della Madonna del Terzito**, an imposing 19th-century church at Valdichiesa, in the valley separating the island's two volcanoes. Up top, gorgeous perspectives unfold on the symmetrically arrayed volcanic cones of Monte dei Porri, Filicudi and a distant Alicudi.

★ Salus Per Aquam   SPA

(Wellness Center; ☎ 090 984 42 22; www.hotelsignum.it; Via Scalo 15, Malfa; admission €45, treatments extra; ⊙ Oct-Mar) Enjoy a revitalising hot-spring soak or a cleansing sweat in a traditional adobe-walled steam house at Hotel Signum's fabulous spa. The complex includes several stylish jacuzzi tubs on a pretty flagstoned patio, and blissful spaces where you can immerse your body in salt crystals, get a massage, or pamper yourself with natural essences of citrus, Malvasia and capers.

Wineries   WINERY

Outside Malfa there are numerous wineries where you can try the local Malvasia wine. Signposted off the main road, **Fenech** (☎ 090 984 40 41; www.fenech.it; Via Fratelli Mirabilo 41) is an acclaimed producer whose 2012 Malvasia won awards at five international competitions. Another important Malvasia is produced at the luxurious Capofaro resort on the 13-acre Tasca d'Almerita estate between Malfa and Santa Marina.

Pollara   TOWN

Famously featured in the 1994 film *Il Postino*, sleepy Pollara is sandwiched dramatically between the sea and an extinct volcanic crater on Salina's western edge. Landslide danger blocks pedestrian access to the gorgeous beach, but you can still descend the steep stone steps northwest of town and swim across, or simply admire the spectacular view, backed by volcanic cliffs.

🛏 Sleeping

The island remains relatively undisturbed by mass tourism, yet offers some of the Aeolians' finest hotels and restaurants. Accommodation can be found in Salina's three main towns: Santa Marina Salina on the east shore, Malfa on the north shore and Rinella on the south shore, as well as in Lingua, a village adjoining ancient salt ponds 2km south of Santa Marina.

Hotel Mamma Santina   BOUTIQUE HOTEL €€

(☎ 090 984 30 54; www.mammasantina.it; Via Sanità 40, Santa Marina Salina; d €110-250; ⊙ Apr-Oct; ❄ @ �� ⊠) A labour of love for its architect owner, this boutique hotel has inviting rooms decorated with pretty tiles in traditional Aeolian designs. Many of the sea-view terraces come equipped with hammocks, and on warm evenings the attached restaurant (meals €35–40) has outdoor seating overlooking the glowing blue pool and landscaped garden.

A Cannata   PENSION €€

(☎ 090 984 31 61; www.acannata.it; Via Umberto, Lingua; r per person incl breakfast €40-90, incl half-board €65-115; 🛜) Near Lingua's waterfront, this long-established family-run place offers three simple rooms above its superb Slow Food–acclaimed restaurant, but its best accommodations are in the cheerful orange and blue annexe down the street, completely remodelled in 2013. Here you'll find 25 spacious units gleaming with hand-painted tiles, many overlooking Lingua's picturesque salt lagoon. Half-board is optional year-round, but highly recommended.

★ Hotel Signum   BOUTIQUE HOTEL €€€

(☎ 090 984 42 22; www.hotelsignum.it; Via Scalo 15, Malfa; d €160-500; ❄ 🛜 ⊠) Hidden in Malfa's hillside lanes and sparkling with recent renovations is this alluring labyrinth of antique-clad rooms, peach-coloured stucco walls and vine-covered terraces with full-on views of Stromboli. The attached wellness centre, a stunning pool and one of the island's best-regarded restaurants make this the perfect place to unwind for a few days in utter comfort.

Capofaro   BOUTIQUE HOTEL €€€

(☎ 090 984 43 30; www.capofaro.it; Via Faro 3, Malfa; d €230-440, ste €370-640; ⊙ late Apr-early Oct; ❄ @ 🛜 ⊠) Immerse yourself in luxury at this five-star boutique resort halfway between Santa Marina and Malfa, surrounded by well-tended Malvasia vineyards and a picturesque lighthouse. The 20 rooms all have sharp white decor and terraces looking straight out to smoking Stromboli. Tennis courts, poolside massages, wine tasting, vineyard visits and occasional cooking courses complete this perfect vision of island chic.

Eating

★ Da Alfredo
SANDWICHES €

(Piazza Marina Garibaldi, Lingua; granite €2.60, sandwiches €8-12) Salina's most atmospheric option for an affordable snack, Alfredo's place is renowned all over Sicily for its *granite:* ices made with coffee, fresh fruit or locally grown pistachios and almonds. It's also worth a visit for its *pane cunzato* – open-faced sandwiches piled high with tuna, ricotta, eggplant, tomatoes, capers and olives; split one with a friend – they're huge!

Al Cappero
SICILIAN €

(☑ 090 984 39 68; www.alcappero.it; Pollara; meals €21-25; ☺ lunch Easter-May, lunch & dinner Jun-mid-Sep) This family-run place in Pollara with a sprawling outdoor terrace specialises in old-fashioned Sicilian home-cooking, including several vegetarian options. It also sells home-grown capers and rents out simple rooms down the street (€20 to €35 per person).

★ A Cannata
SICILIAN €€

(☑ 090 984 31 61; Via Umberto I 13, Lingua; meals €32; ☺ 12.30-2.30pm & 7.30-10pm) Delectable home-cooked seafood meals, accompanied by local vegetables, are served in a sun-filled seafront pavilion at this unassuming but exceptional restaurant, run by the same family for nearly four decades. Start with the house speciality, *maccheroni* with eggplant, pine nuts, mozzarella and ricotta, before moving onto a second course of *calamaretti* (baby squid) cooked with Salina's showpiece Malvasia wine.

★ Ristorante Villa Carla
SICILIAN €€

(☑ 090 980 90 13; Via S Lucia, Leni; meals €30-35; ☺ 7-10pm Jun-Aug, by arrangement rest of year) At their home in the hills above Rinella, Carla Rando and Carmelo Princiotta serve unforgettable meals featuring specialties such as homemade tagliatelle with pistachio and oranges, or fresh-caught fish grilled in a crust of parsley, basil, mint and citrus zest. Two outdoor terraces framed by roses and cactus offer pretty views across the water to the surrounding islands. Reservations required.

'nni Lausta
MODERN SICILIAN €€

(☑ 090 984 34 86; www.isolasalina.com; Via Risorgimento, Santa Marina Salina; meals €25-40; ☺ noon-11pm Easter-Oct) This stylish modern eatery with its cute lobster logo serves superb food based on fresh local ingredients, with 80% of the produce originating in the property's own garden. The downstairs bar is popular for *aperitivi* and late-night drinking. At lunchtime there's a fixed-price three-course menu including a glass of wine for €25, and takeaway gourmet sandwiches for €5.

❶ Information

Banco di Sicilia (Via Risorgimento) ATM on Santa Marina's main pedestrian street.

❶ Getting There & Around

BOAT
Hydrofoils and ferries serve Santa Marina Salina and Rinella from Lipari and the other islands. You'll find ticket offices in both ports.

BUS
CITIS (☑ 090 984 41 50; www.trasportisalina. it) runs buses every 90 minutes in low season (more frequently in summer) from Santa Marina Salina to Lingua and Malfa. In Malfa, make connections for Rinella, Pollara, Valdichiesa and Leni. Fares are €1.80 to €2.50 depending on destination. Timetables are posted at the ports and bus stops.

CAR, SCOOTER & BICYCLE
Above Santa Marina Salina's port, **Antonio Bongiorno** (☑ 090 984 34 09; www.rentbongiorno. it; Via Risorgimento 222, Santa Marina Salina) rents bikes (per day from €8), scooters (from €20) and cars (from €50). Several agencies in Rinella offer similar services – look for signs at the ferry dock.

Stromboli

POP 400 / ELEV 924M

Stromboli's perfect triangle of a volcano juts dramatically out of the sea. It's the only island whose smouldering cone is permanently active, attracting a steady stream of visitors like moths to its massive flame. Volcanic activity has scarred and blackened the northwest side of the island, while the eastern side is untamed, ruggedly green and dotted with low-rise whitewashed houses.

The youngest of the Aeolian volcanoes, Stromboli was formed a mere 40,000 years ago and its gases continue to send up an almost constant spray of liquid magma, a process defined by vulcanologists as *attività stromboliana* (Strombolian activity). The most recent major eruptions took place on 27 February 2007 when two new craters opened on the volcano's summit, producing two scalding lava flows down the mountain's western flank. Although seismic activity, including rock falls, continued for several days, fortunately no mass evacuation was deemed necessary. Previously, an eruption in April 2003 showered the village of Ginostra with rocks, and activity in December 2002 produced a tsunami, causing damage to Stromboli town, injuring six people and closing the island to visitors for a few months.

Boats arrive at Porto Scari-San Vincenzo, downhill from the town. Most accommodation, as well as the meeting point for guided hikes up the volcano, is a short walk up the Scalo Scari to Via Roma.

◉ Sights & Activities

★ Stromboli Crater   VOLCANO
For nature lovers, climbing Stromboli is one of Sicily's not-to-be-missed experiences. Since 2005 access has been strictly regulated: you can walk freely to 400m, but need a guide to continue any higher. Organised treks depart daily (between 3.30pm and 6pm, depending on season), timed to reach the summit (924m) at sunset and allowing 45 minutes to observe the crater's fireworks.

The climb itself takes 2½ to three hours, while the descent back to Piazza San Vincenzo is shorter (1½ to two hours). All told, it's a demanding five- to six-hour trek up to the top and back; you'll need to have proper walking shoes, a backpack that allows free movement of both arms, clothing for cold and wet weather, a change of T-shirt, a handkerchief to protect against dust (don't wear contact lenses), a torch/flashlight, one to two litres of water and some food. If you haven't got any of these, Totem Trekking (☑ 090 986 57 52; www.totemtrekkingstromboli. com; Piazza San Vincenzo 4; ☺ 9.30am-1pm & 3.30-7pm) hires out all the necessary equipment, including boots (€6), backpacks (€5), hiking poles (€4), torches (€3) and jackets (€5).

★ Sciara del Fuoco view point   VIEW POINT
(Trail of Fire) If you don't fancy climbing to the summit, you can go up to 400m for fabulous panoramas of the Sciara del Fuoco (the blackened laval scar that runs down the mountain's northern flank) and views of the crater's explosions from below. You're allowed to go to the Sciara on your own; bring a torch if you're walking at night.

The explosions usually occur every 20 minutes or so and are preceded by a loud belly-roar as gases force the magma into the air. After each eruption, you can watch as red-hot rocks tumble down the seemingly endless slope, creating visible splashes as they plop into the sea. For best viewing, come on a on a still night, when the livid red Sciara and exploding cone are dramatically visible.

Arriving here around sunset will allow you to hike one direction in daylight, then stop for pizza and more volcano-gawking at L'Osservatorio on the way back down. Making the trek just before dawn is also a memorable experience, as you'll likely have the whole mountain to yourself.

The trail starts in Piscità, 2km west of Stromboli's port. From here it's about 30 minutes to L'Osservatorio, and another half hour to the view point. Bring plenty of water – the climb gets steep towards the end.

Beaches   BEACH
Stromboli's black sandy beaches are the best in the Aeolian archipelago. The most accessible and popular swimming and sunbathing is at Ficogrande, a strip of rocks and black volcanic sand about a 10-minute walk northwest of the hydrofoil dock. Further-flung black pebble beaches worth exploring are at Piscità to the west and Forgia Vecchia, 300m south of the port.

La Sirenetta Diving   DIVING
(☑ 338 891 96 75, 347 596 14 99; www.lasirenettadiving.it; Via Marina 33; ☺ Jun–mid-Sep) Offers diving courses and accompanied dives.

☞ Tours

Magmatrek (☑ 090 986 57 68; www.magmatrek. it; Via Vittorio Emanuele) has experienced, multilingual vulcanological guides who lead regular treks (maximum group size 20) up to the crater every afternoon (per person €25 plus tax). It can also put together tailor-made treks for individual groups. Other agencies charging identical prices include Il Vulcano a Piedi (☑ 090 98 61 44; www.stromboliguide. it; Via Roma) and Stromboli Adventures (☑ 090 98 62 64; www.stromboliadventures.it; Via Vittorio Emanuele).

Società Navigazione Pippo (☑ 090 98 61 35; pipponav.stromboli@libero.it; Porto Scari) and Antonio Caccetta (☑ 090 98 60 23; Vico Salina 10) are among the numerous boat companies at Porto Scari offering three-hour daytime circuits of the island (€25) and 1½-hour sunset excursions to watch the Sciara del Fuoco from the sea (€20).

📖 Sleeping & Eating

Over a dozen places offer accommodation, including B&Bs, guesthouses and full-fledged hotels.

⭐ Casa del Sole   GUESTHOUSE €

(📱090 98 63 00; www.casadelsolestromboli.it; Via Cincotta; dm €25-30, s €30-50, d €60-100) This cheerful Aeolian-style guesthouse is only 100m from a sweet black-sand beach in Piscitá, the tranquil neighbourhood at the west end of town. Dorms, private doubles and a guest kitchen all surround a sunny patio, overhung with vines, fragrant with lemon blossoms, and decorated with the masks and stone carvings of sculptor-owner Tano Russo.

Call for free pickup (low season only) or take a taxi (€10) from the port 2km away.

Albergo Brasile   PENSION €

(📱090 98 60 08; www.strombolialbergobrasile.it; Via Soldato Cincotta; d €70-90, half-board per person €70-90; ⊙Easter-Oct; ❄) This laid-back budget option has cool, white rooms, a pretty entrance courtyard with lemon and olive trees and a multilingual paperback library for guests' reading pleasure. The roof terrace commands views of the sea one side and the volcano the other. Two larger rooms with air-con cost extra. Half-board is compulsory in July and August.

⭐ L'Osservatorio   PIZZERIA €

(📱090 98 63 60; pizzas €6.50-10.50; ⊙10.30am-late) Sure, you could eat a pizza in town, but come on – you're on Stromboli! Make the 45-minute uphill trek to this pizzeria and you'll be rewarded with exceptional volcano views from the newly expanded panoramic terrace, best after sundown.

La Bottega del Marano   GROCERY, DELI €

(Via Vittorio Emanuele; snacks from €2; ⊙8.30am-1pm & 4.30-7.30pm Mon-Sat) The perfect source for volcano-climbing provisions or a self-catering lunch, this reasonably priced neighbourhood grocery, five minutes west of the trekking agency offices, has a well-stocked deli case full of meats, cheeses, olives, artichokes and sun-dried tomatoes, plus shelves full of wine and awesomely tasty mini-focaccias (€2).

Ai Gechi   SEAFOOD €€

(📱090 98 62 13; Vico Salina 12, Porto Scari; meals €31-35; ⊙noon-3pm & 7-11pm Easter–mid-Oct) Follow the trail of painted lizards to this great hideaway, down an alley off Via Roma.

Flanked by a towering cactus, the shaded verandah of a whitewashed Aeolian house serves as the dining area, eclectically decorated with ship lamps and a whale skeleton discovered nearby by the owner. Gorgeous traditional seafood is served with a slightly modern twist, backed by an excellent local wine list.

ℹ Information

Bring enough cash for your stay on Stromboli. Many businesses don't accept credit cards, and the village's lone ATM on Via Roma is sometimes out of service. Internet access is limited and slow.

ℹ Getting There & Away

It takes four hours to reach the island from Lipari by ferry, or 1¼ to two hours by hydrofoil. There's also at least one direct hydrofoil daily from Milazzo (€21.95). Ticket offices for **Ustica Lines** (📱090 98 60 03; www.usticalines.it) and **Siremar** (📱090 98 60 16; www.siremar.it) are at the port.

IONIAN COAST

Magnificent, overdeveloped, crowded – and exquisitely beautiful – the Ionian coast is Sicily's most popular tourist destination and home to 20% of the island's population. Moneyed entrepreneurs have built their villas and hotels up and down the coastline, eager to bag a spot on Sicily's version of the Amalfi Coast. Above it all towers the muscular peak of Mt Etna (3329m), puffs of smoke billowing from its snow-covered cone.

Taormina

POP 11,100 / ELEV 204M

Spectacularly situated on a terrace of Monte Tauro, with views westwards to Mt Etna, Taormina is a beautiful small town, reminiscent of Capri or an Amalfi coastal resort. Over the centuries, Taormina has seduced an exhaustive line of writers and artists, aristocrats and royalty, and these days it's host to a summer arts festival that packs the town with international visitors.

Perched on its eyrie, Taormina is sophisticated, chic and comfortably cushioned by some serious wealth – very far removed from the banal economic realities of other Sicilian towns. But the charm is not manufactured. The capital of Byzantine Sicily in the 9th century, Taormina is an almost

Taormina

Scale:
0 — 200 m
0 — 0.1 miles

Via Rotabile per Castelmola

Via Leonardo da Vinci

Autostrada Messina-Catania

Castelmola (5km)

Via Fazzello

Post Office (50m); (3km)

Palazzo Duca di Santo Stefano

Via Pietro Rizzo

Piazza del Duomo

Palazzo Ciampoli

Corso Umberto I

Piazza San Domenico

Piazza Garibaldi

Via Paladini

Piazza Paladini

Torre dell'Orologio

Piazza IX Aprile

Via Circonvallazione

Salita del Gracchi

Via Don Bosco

Via Scesa Bastione

Via Roma

Via A Marziani

Corso Umberto I

Via Naumachie

Via Giardinazzo

Piazza Santa Caterina

Porta Messina

Via Timeo

Isoco Guest House (300m)

Via di Giovanni

Piazzetta Filea

Via Teatro Greco

Via Timoleone

Via Ginnasio

Parco Duchi di Cesarò (Villa Comunale)

Via Bagnoli Croce

Via Luigi Pirandello

Teatro Greco

Lido Mazzarò (500m); Isola Bella (1km); Nike Diving Centre (1km)

Interbus (200m); Lido Mazzarò (1.5km); (4km)

Taormina

perfectly preserved medieval town, and if you can tear yourself away from the shopping and sunbathing, it has a wealth of small but perfect tourist sites. Taormina is also a popular resort with gay men.

Be warned that in July and August the town and its surrounding beaches swarm with tourists.

◉ Sights

A short walk uphill from the bus station brings you to Corso Umberto I (abbreviated as Corso Umberto), a pedestrianised thoroughfare that traverses the length of the medieval town and connects its two historic town gates, Porta Messina and Porta Catania.

★ **Teatro Greco** AMPHITHEATRE
(📞 094 22 32 20; Via Teatro Greco; adult/reduced/ EU under 18yr & over 65yr €10/5/free; ⊘ 9am-1hr before sunset) Taormina's premier attraction is this horseshoe-shaped theatre, stunningly suspended between sea and sky, with its stage perfectly framing Mt Etna on the southern horizon. Built in the 3rd century BC, it's Sicily's second largest Greek theatre (after Syracuse). In summer it serves as the venue for international arts and film festivals. Visit early in the morning to avoid the crowds.

Corso Umberto STREET
One of Taormina's chief delights is wandering along its pedestrian-friendly medieval main avenue, lined with antique and jewellery shops, delis and designer boutiques. Midway down, pause to revel in the stunning panoramic views of Mt Etna and the seacoast from Piazza IX Aprile and pop your head into the charming rococo church, Chiesa San Giuseppe (Piazza IX Aprile; ⊘ 9am-7pm).

Continue west through the 12th-century clock tower, Torre dell'Orologio, into the Borgo Medievale, Taormina's oldest quarter. A few blocks further along is Piazza del Duomo, home to an ornate baroque fountain depicting a two-legged centaur with the bust of an angel, Taormina's town symbol. Here you'll find the 13th-century cathedral, a survivor of the Renaissance-style remodelling undertaken elsewhere in town by the 15th-century Spanish aristocracy. The Renaissance influence is better illustrated in various palaces along the Corso, including Palazzo Duca di Santo Stefano with its Norman-Gothic windows, Palazzo Corvaja (the tourist office) and Palazzo Ciampoli, now housing the Hotel El Jebel.

Villa Comunale PARK
(Parco Duchi di Cesarò; Via Bagnoli Croce; ⊘ 9am-midnight summer, 9am-sunset winter) To escape the crowds, wander down to these stunningly sited public gardens. Created by Englishwoman Florence Trevelyan, they're a lush paradise of tropical plants and delicate flowers. There's also a children's play area.

Castelmola HILLTOP VILLAGE
For eye-popping views of the coastline, head 5km up Via Leonardo da Vinci to this hilltop village crowned by a ruined castle. The walk will take you around an hour along a well-paved route. Alternatively, Interbus runs an hourly service (one way/return €1.80/2.80) up the hill.

🏃 Activities

Lido Mazzarò BEACH
Many visitors to Taormina come only for the beach scene. To reach Lido Mazzarò, directly beneath Taormina, take the cable car (Cable Car; one way/return €3/3.50; ⊘ 9am-8.15pm

OFFSHORE ISLANDS

Sicily is an island-lover's paradise, with more than a dozen offshore islands scattered in the seas surrounding the main island. Beyond the major Aeolian Islands of Lipari, Vulcano, Stromboli and Salina covered in this guide, you can detour to the smaller Aeolians: **Panarea**, **Filicudi** and **Alicudi**. Alternatively, cast off from Sicily's western coast to the slow-paced **Egadi Islands** or the remote, rugged volcanic island of **Pantelleria**. South of Agrigento, the sand-sprinkled **Pelagic Islands** of Lampedusa, Linosa and Lampione offer some fantastic beaches. **Ustica Lines** (www.usticalines.it) and **Siremar** (www.siremar.it) provide hydrofoil and/or ferry service to all of the islands listed above. For complete information about Ustica, the Egadi Islands and the lesser Aeolian islands, including where to sleep and eat, see Lonely Planet's *Sicily* guide.

Oct-Mar, 9am-1am Apr-Sep). This beach is well serviced with bars and restaurants; private operators charge a fee for umbrellas and deck chairs (discountable at some hotels).

Isola Bella　　　　　　　NATURE RESERVE
Southwest of the beach is the minuscule Isola Bella, set in a stunning cove with fishing boats. You can walk here in a few minutes but it's more fun to rent a small boat from Mazzarò and paddle round Capo Sant'Andrea.

Nike Diving Centre　　　　　　　DIVING
(✆ 339 196 15 59; www.diveniketaormina.com; single dive incl kite hire from €45) Opposite Isola Bella, this dive centre offers a wide range of courses for children and adults.

Gole dell'Alcantara　　SWIMMING, WALKING
(www.terralcantara.it/en; admission €8; ⏱ 8am-sunset) Perfect for cooling off on a hot summer day, this series of vertiginous lava gorges with swirling rapids is 20km west of town; take Interbus from Taormina (€5 return, 55 minutes).

✿ Festivals & Events

Taormina FilmFest　　　　　　　FILM
(www.taorminafilmfest.it) Hollywood big shots arrive in mid-June for a week of film screenings, premieres and press conferences at the Teatro Greco.

Taormina Arte　　　　PERFORMING ARTS
(www.taormina-arte.com) In July and August, this festival features opera, dance, theatre and music concerts from an impressive list of international names.

🛏 Sleeping

Taormina has plenty of luxurious accommodation although some less expensive places can be found. Many hotels offer discounted

parking (from €10) at Taormina's two public parking lots.

★ Isoco Guest House　　　　　　B&B €
(✆ 094 22 36 79; www.isoco.it; Via Salita Branco 2; s €65-120, d €85-120; ⏱ Mar-Nov; 🅿 ❄ @) Every room in this welcoming, gay-friendly B&B is dedicated to an artist – from Botticelli to the sculpted buttocks and pant-popping thighs on the walls of the Herb Ritts room. Inviting features include an excellent breakfast, a terrace and sundecks for lounging and an outdoor jacuzzi. German and English spoken.

B&B Le Sibille　　　　　　　B&B €
(✆ 349 726 28 62; www.lesibille.net; Corso Umberto 187a; d €60-110, apt per week without breakfast €400-620; ⏱ Apr-Oct; @ ❄) This B&B wins points for its prime location on Taormina's pedestrian thoroughfare, its rooftop breakfast terrace and its cheerful, artistically tiled self-catering apartments. Light sleepers beware: Corso Umberto can get noisy with holidaymakers!

Hostel Taormina　　　　　　　HOSTEL €
(✆ 349 102 61 61, 094 262 55 05; www.hosteltaormina.com; Via Circonvallazione 13; dm €17-23, d €58-80; ❄ @ ❄) The town's only hostel is open year-round and occupies a house with a roof terrace commanding panoramic sea views. It's small (only 23 beds in three dorms and one private room) and facilities are basic, but manager Francesco is a helpful and friendly guy, beds are comfortable and there's a communal kitchen. No breakfast.

★ Hotel Villa Belvedere　　　　HOTEL €€
(✆ 094 22 37 91; www.villabelvedere.it; Via Bagnoli Croce 79; s €70-190, d €80-280, ste €120-450; ⏱ Mar-late Nov; ❄ @ ❄ ❄) Built in 1902, the jaw-droppingly pretty Villa Belvedere was one of the original grand hotels, well-positioned with fabulous views and luxuriant

gardens, which are a particular highlight. There is also a swimming pool with a 100-year-old palm tree rising from a small island in the middle.

Hotel Villa Schuler
HOTEL €€

(☑094 22 34 81; www.hotelvillaschuler.com; Via Roma, Piazzetta Bastione; d €150-220; P ❋ @ ☎) Surrounded by shady terraced gardens and with views of Mt Etna, the rose-pink Villa Schuler has been run by the same family for over a century (longer than any other Taormina hotel) and preserves a homely atmosphere. A lovely breakfast is served on the panoramic terrace.

Casa Turchetti
B&B €€€

(☑094 262 50 13; www.casaturchetti.com; Salita dei Gracchi 18/20; d €200-250, jr ste €350; ❋ ☎) Every detail is perfect in this painstakingly restored former music school, recently converted to a luxurious B&B on a back alley just above Corso Umberto. Vintage furniture and fixtures, handcrafted woodwork, fine homespun sheets and modern bathrooms all contribute to the elegant feel; the spacious rooftop terrace is just icing on the cake.

✖ Eating

Eating out in Taormina goes hand in hand with posing. It's essential to make a reservation at the more exclusive choices. Be aware that Taormina's cafes charge extraordinarily high prices even for coffee.

Granduca
PIZZERIA €

(☑094 22 49 83; Corso Umberto 172; pizzas €7-11; ☺dinner) Forget the staid, typically pricey Taormina restaurant upstairs; the best reason to visit Granduca is for pizza on a summer evening, served on the vast downstairs terrace overlooking Mt Etna and the sea – an unbeatable combination of view, quality and price.

La Piazzetta
SICILIAN €€

(☑094 262 63 17; Via Paladini 5; meals €25; ☺closed Mon in winter) At this little eatery tucked into the corner of the very picturesque Piazzetta Paladini, enjoy classics such as *pasta alla Norma* (pasta with basil, eggplant, ricotta and tomato) and a variety of fresh fish, accompanied by good local reds and whites.

Tiramisù
PIZZERIA, SICILIAN €€

(☑094 22 48 03; Via Cappuccini 1; pizzas €7-14, meals €35; ☺Wed-Mon) This stylish place near Porta Messina makes fabulous meals, from *linguine cozze, menta e zucchine* (pasta with mussels, mint and zucchini) to old favourites like *scaloppine al limone e panna* (veal escalope in lemon cream sauce). When dessert rolls around, don't miss its trademark tiramisù, a perfect ending to any meal here.

Trattoria Da Nino
TRATTORIA €€

(☑094 22 12 65; Via Luigi Pirandello 37; meals €27-34; ☺lunch & dinner) Under the same family ownership for 50 years, Nino's place specialises in straightforward, reasonably priced Sicilian home cooking, including an excellent *caponata* plus fresh local fish served grilled, steamed, fried, stewed or rolled up in *involtini* (roulades).

La Giara
MODERN SICILIAN €€€

(☑094 22 33 60; Vico la Floresta 1; meals €60) A meal on La Giara's rooftop terrace is a Taormina classic. One of the best-looking restaurants in town, it's got a smooth art deco interior and a piano bar worthy of Bogart in *Casablanca* mood. The menu features modern dishes grounded in island tradition, such as risotto with wild herbs, and squid served in a Marsala reduction. Book ahead.

☕ Drinking & Nightlife

Shatulle
BAR

(Piazza Paladini 4; ☺Tue-Sun) One of the best and most popular bars on this intimate square just off Corso Umberto is this hip, gay-friendly spot with outdoor seating, an inviting vibe and a fine selection of cocktails (from €5.50). Piazza Paladini is a perennial favourite with Taormina's young, well-dressed night owls.

Bar Turrisi
BAR

(☺9am-2am) High above Taormina, in the hilltop community of Castelmola, this whimsical bar is built on four levels overlooking the church square. Its decor is an eclectic tangle of Sicilian influences, with everything from painted carts to a giant stone *minchia* (you'll need no translation once you see it). Sip a glass of almond wine and enjoy the view.

🛍 Shopping

Taormina is a window-shopper's paradise. The quality in most places is high but don't expect any bargains.

Carlo Mirella Panarello
CERAMICS

(Via Antonio Marziani) Sicily has a long tradition of producing ceramics and this is a good bet for original designs. The workshop is on Via A Marzani (ring the bell for admission), while around the corner on Corso Umberto I, the shop sells more traditional jewellery, bags and hats.

La Torinese
FOOD, WINE

(Corso Umberto 59) This is a fantastic place to stock up on local olive oil, capers, honey and wine. Smash-proof bubble wrapping helps to get everything home in one piece.

❶ Information

There are plenty of banks with ATMs along Corso Umberto.

Ospedale San Vincenzo (☑ 0942 57 92 97; Contrada Sirina) Downhill and 2km southwest of the centre. Call the same number for an ambulance.

Police station (☑ 094 261 02 01; Corso Umberto 219)

Tourist office (☑ 094 22 32 43; www.gate2taormina.com; Piazza Santa Caterina, off Corso Umberto I; ⊗ 8.30am-2.30pm & 3.30-7pm Mon-Fri year-round, 9am-1pm & 4-6.30pm Sat Apr-Oct) Has helpful multilingual staff and plenty of practical information.

❶ Getting There & Around

BUS

The bus is the easiest way to reach Taormina.

Interbus (☑ 094 262 53 01; Via Luigi Pirandello) services leave daily for Messina (€4.10, 55 minutes to 1¾ hours, 10 daily Monday to Saturday, two on Sunday) and Catania (€4.90, 1¼ hours, seven to 11 daily), the latter continuing to Catania's Fontanarossa airport (€7.90, 1½ hours).

CAR & SCOOTER

Taormina is on the A18 autostrada and the SS114 between Messina and Catania. Driving near the historic centre is a complete nightmare and Corso Umberto is closed to traffic. The most convenient places to leave your car are the **Porta Catania car park** (per 24hr €15), at the western end of Corso Umberto, or the Lumbi car park north of the centre, connected to Porta Messina (at Corso Umberto's eastern end) by a five-minute walk or a free yellow shuttle bus. Both car parks charge the same rates.

California (☑ 094 22 37 69; www.californiarentcar.com; Via Bagnoli Croce 86; Vespa per day/week €35/224, Fiat Panda €64/300) Rents out cars and scooters, just across from the Villa Comunale.

TRAIN

There are regular trains to and from Messina (€3.95 to €7.50, 40 to 75 minutes, hourly) and Catania (€3.95 to €7.50, 40 to 55 minutes, hourly), but the awkward location of Taormina's station (a steep 4km below town) is a strong disincentive. If you arrive this way, catch a taxi (€15) or an Interbus coach (€1.80, every 30 to 90 minutes) up to town.

Catania
POP 296,000

Catania is a true city of the volcano. Much of it is constructed from the lava that poured down the mountain and engulfed the city in the 1669 eruption in which nearly 12,000 people lost their lives. It is also lava-black in colour, as if a fine dusting of soot permanently covers its elegant buildings, most of which are the work of baroque master Giovanni Vaccarini. He almost single-handedly rebuilt the civic centre into an elegant, modern city of spacious boulevards and set-piece piazzas.

Today Catania is Sicily's second commercial city – a thriving, entrepreneurial centre with a large university and a cosmopolitan urban culture.

◉ Sights

Catania's sights are concentrated within a few blocks of Piazza del Duomo.

Piazza del Duomo
SQUARE

A Unesco World Heritage Site, Catania's central square revolves around its grand cathedral, fringed with baroque buildings constructed in the unique local style of contrasting lava and limestone. The piazza's centrepiece is the smiling **Fontana dell'Elefante** (Piazza del Duomo), crowned by a naive black-lava elephant dating from the Roman period and surmounted by an improbable Egyptian obelisk.

At the piazza's southwest corner, the **Fontana dell'Amenano** fountain marks the entrance to Catania's fish market and commemorates the Amenano River, which once ran above ground and on whose banks the Greeks first founded the city of Katáne.

Cattedrale di Sant'Agata
CATHEDRAL

(☑ 095 32 00 44; Piazza del Duomo; ⊗ 8am-noon & 4-7pm) Sporting an impressive marble facade with columns from Catania's Roman amphitheatre, this cathedral honours the city's patron, St Agata. The young virgin, whose remains lie sheltered in the cool, vaulted interior, famously resisted the advances of the nefarious Quintian (AD 250) and was horribly mutilated. Her jewel-drenched effigy is ecstatically venerated on 5 February in one of Sicily's largest festivals.

★ **La Pescheria** MARKET
(Via Pardo; ☉ 7am-2pm) The best show in Catania is this bustling fish market, where vendors raucously hawk their wares in Sicilian dialect, while decapitated swordfish cast sidelong glances at you across silvery heaps of sardines on ice.

Equally colourful is the adjoining **food market**, with carcasses of meat, skinned sheep's heads, strings of sausages, huge wheels of cheese and piles of luscious fruits and vegetables all rolled together in a few noisy, jam-packed alleyways.

★ **Graeco-Roman Theatre & Odeon** RUINS
(Via Vittorio Emanuele II 262; adult/reduced incl Casa Liberti €4/2; ☉ 9am-1pm & 2.30pm-1hr before sunset Tue-Sun) These twin theatres west of Piazza del Duomo constitute Catania's most impressive Graeco-Roman site. Set in a crumbling residential neighbourhood with laundry atmospherically flapping on the surrounding rooftops, the main theatre with its half-submerged stage is flanked by **Casa Liberti**, an elegantly restored 19th-century *palazzo* that now houses two millennia worth of artefacts discovered during the theatres' excavation. Directly adjacent are the ruins of the smaller Odeon theatre.

★ **Teatro Massimo Bellini** OPERA HOUSE
(☑ 095 730 61 11; www.teatromassimobellini.it; Via Perrotta 12; guided tours €2; ☉ tours 9.30am & 10.30am Tue, Thu & Sat) A few blocks northeast of the *duomo*, this sumptuous, gilt-encrusted opera house forms the centrepiece of Piazza Bellini. Both piazza and opera house were named after composer Vincenzo Bellini, the father of Catania's vibrant modern musical scene.

Museo Belliniano MUSEUM
(☑ 095 715 05 35; Piazza San Francesco 3; ☉ 9am-1pm Mon-Sat) FREE In 1801, renowned opera composer Vincenzo Bellini was born in this house on Piazza San Francesco, now converted into a museum. The collection comprises an interesting array of Bellini memorabilia, including original scores, photographs and the composer's death mask.

Museo Civico MUSEUM
(☑ 095 34 58 30; Piazza Federico II di Svevia; adult/reduced €6/4.80; ☉ 9am-1pm & 3-7pm Mon-Sat, 8.30am-1.30pm Sun) Housed in the grim looking 13th-century Castello Ursino, Catania's civic museum holds the noble Biscari family's collection of paintings, vases, sculpture, coins and other archaeological finds. This foreboding castle once guarded the city from atop a seafront cliff; however, the 1693 earthquake altered the landscape, leaving it completely landlocked.

Villa Bellini PARK
(☉ 8am-8pm) Escape the madding crowd and enjoy the fine views of Mt Etna from these lovely gardens along Via Etnea.

Roman Amphitheatre AMPHITHEATRE
The modest ruins of this Roman theatre, below street level in Piazza Stesicoro, are worth a quick look.

☆ Festivals & Events

Festa di Sant'Agata RELIGIOUS
In Catania's biggest religious festival (3 to 5 February), one million Catanians follow the Fercolo (a silver reliquary bust of Saint Agata) along the main street of the city accompanied by spectacular fireworks.

Carnevale di Acireale CARNIVAL
(www.carnevalediacireale.it) Nearby Acireale hosts Sicily's most flamboyant carnival for two weeks in February (sometimes spilling over into late January or early March). Streets in this baroque coastal resort come alive with gargantuan papier mâché puppets, flowery allegorical floats, confetti and fireworks.

⊨ Sleeping

Catania is served by a good range of reasonably priced accommodation, making it an excellent base for exploring the Ionian coast and Etna.

★ **B&B Crociferi** B&B €
(☑ 095 715 22 66; www.bbcrociferi.it; Via Crociferi 81; d €75-85, tr €100-110, 4-bed apt €120; ✳ ⓐ) Affording easy access to Catania's animated nightlife, this B&B in a beautifully decorated family home makes a wonderful base. Three spacious rooms (each with bathroom across the hall) and two glorious upstairs apartments come with high ceilings, antique tiles, frescoes and artistic accoutrements from the

Catania

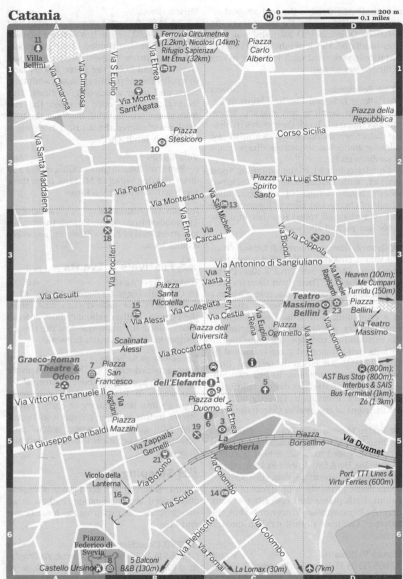

Ferrovia Circumetnea (1.2km); Nicolosi (14km); Rifugio Sapienza/ Mt Etna (32km)

Piazza Carlo Alberto

Villa Bellini

Via Cimarosa

Via Cimarosa

Via S Euplio

Via Etnea

Piazza della Repubblica

Via Monte Sant'Agata

Corso Sicilia

Via Santa Maddalena

Piazza Stesicoro

Piazza Spirito Santo

Via Luigi Sturzo

Via Penninello

Via Montesano

Via San Michele

Via Etnea

Via Carcaci

Via Coppola

Via Crocife022

Via Biondi

Via Antonino di Sangiuliano

Via Gesuiti

Piazza Santa Nicolella

Via Vasta

Via Mancini

Heaven (100m); Me Cumpari Turridu (150m)

Teatro Massimo Bellini

Piazza Bellini

Via Alessi

Via Collegiata

Via Cestia

Via Euplio Reina

Via Mazza

Via Teatro Massimo

Scalinata Alessi

Piazza dell' Università

Piazza Ogninello

Via Leonardi

Via Roccaforte

Graeco-Roman Theatre & Odeon

Piazza San Francesco

Fontana dell'Elefante

(800m); AST Bus Stop (800m); Interbus & SAIS Bus Terminal (1km); Zó (1.3km)

Via Vittorio Emanuele II

Via Gagliani

Piazza del Duomo

Via Etnea

Piazza Mazzini

Piazza Giuseppe Garibaldi

Via Zappalà-Gemelli

La Pescheria

Piazza Borsellino

Via Dusmet

Vicolo della Lanterna

Via Bozomo

Port, TTT Lines & Virtù Ferries (600m)

Via Colombo

Via Scuto

Via Colombo

Piazza Federico di Svevia

Castello Ursino

5 Balconi B&B (130m)

Via Plebiscito

Via Fornai

La Lomax (30m)

(7km)

---

owners' travels. Things fill up fast, so book ahead. English, German and French spoken.

Palazzu Stidda   APARTMENT €

(☎ 095 34 88 26; www.palazzu-stidda.com; Vicolo della Lanterna 5; d €70-100, q €120-140; 🛜 🏠)

These three delightful apartments in a *palazzo* on a peaceful dead-end alley perfectly blend comfort with whimsy; all are decorated with the owners' artwork, handmade furniture, family heirlooms and finds from local antiques markets. Perfect for fami-

Catania

lies, apartments 2 and 3 each come with a washing machine, kitchen, high chair and stroller. The smaller apartment 1 costs less. French and English spoken.

B&B Faro   B&B €
(☑ 349 457 88 56; www.bebfaro.it; Via San Michele 26; s/d/tr €50/80/100; ❄ @) A stylish B&B with five upstairs rooms incorporating polished wood floors, double-glazed windows, modern bathroom fixtures, antique tiles and bold colours. The two suites are especially nice, and during slower periods can be booked for the price of a double. Additional perks include free cable internet and bikes for guests' use. Visiting artists are invited to paint in the studio downstairs.

BAD   B&B €
(☑ 095 34 69 03; www.badcatania.com; Via Colombo 24; s €40-55, d €60-80, apt €70-120; ❄ 🛜) An uninhibitedly colourful, modern sense of style prevails at this trendy B&B. All rooms feature local artwork and TVs with DVD players. The two-level upstairs apartment with full kitchen and private terrace is a fab option for self-caterers, especially since the fish and vegetable markets are right around the corner. Staff are happy to suggest cultural goings-on about town.

5 Balconi B&B   B&B €
(☑ 095 723 45 34; www.5balconi.it; Via Plebiscito 133; s/d €35/50, with air-con €45/60; ❄ 🛜) You won't find a nicer low-end option than this lovingly remodelled antique *palazzo* in a workaday neighbourhood near Castello Ursino. The friendly owners offer three high-ceilinged rooms with a pair of shared

bathrooms, plus a breakfast featuring local organic bread and fresh fruit (delivered to your room upon request). Be advised that the street out front gets lots of traffic.

Il Principe   HOTEL €€
(☑ 095 250 03 45; www.ilprincipehotel.com; Via Alessi 24; d €109-189, ste €129-209; ❄ @ 🛜) This newly expanded boutique-style hotel in an 18th-century building features luxurious rooms and two-level suites on one of Catania's busiest nightlife streets (thank goodness for double glazing!). Perks include international cable TV and fluffy bathrobes to wear on your way to the Turkish steam bath. Some rooms have little natural light; check before booking. Special rates available online.

UNA Hotel Palace   HOTEL €€
(☑ 095 250 51 11; www.unahotels.it; Via Etnea 218; s €99-125, d €125-175, ste €201-329) This top-end hotel brings a bit of city slick to Catania. Part of an Italy-wide chain, it's got a gleaming white interior, polished service and good rooms. For icing on the cake, check out the views of Mt Etna from the rooftop garden bar, where cocktails and aperitifs are served at sunset. Prices drop significantly in the off-season.

🍴 Eating

Popular street snacks in Catania include *arancini* (fried rice balls filled with meat, cheese, tomatoes and/or peas) and *seltz* (fizzy water with fresh-squeezed lemon juice and natural fruit syrup). Don't leave town without trying *pasta alla Norma* (pasta with basil, eggplant and ricotta), a Catania original named after Bellini's opera *Norma*.

Trattoria di De Fiore
TRATTORIA €

(☑ 095 31 62 83; Via Coppola 24/26; meals €15-25; ☺ from 1pm Tue-Sun) This neighbourhood trattoria is presided over by septuagenarian chef Mamma Rosanna, who uses fresh, local ingredients to recreate her great-grandmother's recipes, including superb *pasta alla Norma* and *zeppoline di ricotta* (sweet ricotta fritters dusted with powdered sugar). Service can be excruciatingly slow and they don't always open promptly at 1pm, but food this good is worth the wait.

Locanda Cerami
PIZZERIA €

(☑ 095 224 67 82; www.locandacerami.com; Via Crociferi 69; pizza €5.50-11; ☺ 7.30-11pm) On the atmospheric Via Crociferi, this gorgeous pizzeria has an excellent setting – in the summer months, the tables are on the steps of one of the many baroque churches – and some of the most innovative pizzas you'll find anywhere on the island, plus an excellent wine list. Try the *principessa* pizza, with pistachio nuts and aromatic speck.

★ Me Cumpari Turridu
SICILIAN €€

(☑ 095 715 01 42; Via Ventimiglia 15; meals €35-40; ☺ Mon-Sat) Mixing tradition with modernity both in food and decor, this quirky little spot spoils meat eaters with a variety of barbecued meat, as well as fresh pasta dishes such as ricotta and marjoram ravioli in a pork sauce. Vegetarians can opt for the Ustica lentil stew, with broad beans and fennel; there's also a wealth of Sicilian cheeses on offer.

Le Tre Bocche
TRATTORIA €€

(☑ 095 53 87 38; Via Mario Sangiorgi 7; meals €35-45; ☺ Tue-Sun) This fantastic Slow Food–recommended trattoria takes pride in the freshest seafood and fish – so much so, they have a stand at the Pescheria market. Short pastas come with wonderful sauces such as *bottarga* (fish roe) and artichoke, spaghetti is soaked in sea urchins or squid ink, and risottos are mixed with zucchini and king prawns. It's about 800m due north of the train station.

Osteria Antica Marina
SEAFOOD €€

(☑ 095 34 81 97; Via Pardo 29; meals €35-45; ☺ Thu-Tue) This rustic but classy trattoria behind the fish market is *the* place to come for seafood. A variety of tasting menus showcases everything from swordfish to scampi,

cuttlefish to calamari. Decor-wise think solid wooden tables and rough stone walls. Reservations are essential.

Drinking & Nightlife

Not surprisingly for a busy university town, Catania has a reputation for its effervescent nightlife. Fun streets for bar-hopping include (from west to east) Via Alessi, Via Collegiata, Via Vasta, Via Mancini, Via Montesano, Piazza Spirito Santo and Via Teatro Massimo.

Heaven
BAR

(Via Teatro Massimo 39; ☺ 9pm-2am) Pedestrianised Via Teatro Massimo heaves late at night as crowds swill outside the many bars. One of the best-known addresses is Heaven, a trendy lounge bar sporting kooky black and white designs and a 12m-long LED-lit bar. Outside, where most people end up, there's seating on massive black leather sofas. DJs up the ante on Wednesday, Friday and Saturday nights.

Agorá Bar
BAR

(www.agorahostel.com; Piazza Currò 6; ☺ 6pm-late) This atmospheric bar occupies a neon-lit cave 18m below ground, complete with its own subterranean river. The Romans used it as a spa; nowadays a cosmopolitan crowd lingers over late-night drinks.

Energie Cafe
BAR, CAFE

(Via Monte Sant'Agata 10; ☺ noon-late) A favourite with Catania's stylish *aperitivo* crowd, this slick urban bar has kaleidoscopic 70s-inspired decor, streetside seating and laid-back jazz-infused tunes. On Sunday afternoons, its mellow 'Fashion Aperitif' happy hour features a rich buffet and live DJ set.

Entertainment

Pick up a copy of *Lapis,* a free bi-weekly program of music, theatre and art available throughout the city, or check the website www.lapisnet.it/catania.

Teatro Massimo Bellini
OPERA HOUSE

(☑ 095 730 61 11; www.teatromassimobellini.it; Via Perrotta 12; ☺ Nov-Jun) Catania's premier theatre is named after the city's most famous son, composer Vincenzo Bellini. Sporting the full red-and-gilt look, it stages a year-round season of opera and an eight-month program of classical music from November to June. Tickets start around €13.

Zò
CULTURAL CENTRE

(☑095 53 38 71; www.zoculture.it; Piazzale Asia 6) In the waterfront Le Ciminiere complex, Zò is dedicated to promoting contemporary art and performance. It hosts an eclectic programme of events that ranges from club nights, concerts and film screenings to art exhibitions, dance performances, installations and theatre workshops. Many events are free of charge.

La Lomax
CULTURAL CENTRE

(☑095 286 28 12; www.lalomax.it; Via Fornai 44) This multipurpose cultural centre hosts all sorts of events – club nights, folk-music festivals, modern art exhibitions and more. It's near Castello Urbino, hidden on a small street off Via Plebiscito.

ℹ Information

Banks with ATMs are concentrated around Piazza del Duomo and along Via Etnea.

Municipal tourist office (☑095 742 55 73; www.comune.catania.it; Via Vittorio Emanuele II 172; ⊙8.15am-7.15pm Mon-Fri, to 12.15pm Sat)

Ospedale Vittorio Emanuele (☑091 743 54 52; Via Plebiscito 628) Has a 24-hour emergency doctor.

Police station (☑095 736 71 11; Piazza Santa Nicolella)

ℹ Getting There & Away

AIR

Catania's airport, **Fontanarossa** (☑095 723 91 11; www.aeroporto.catania.it), is 7km southwest of the city centre. To get there, take the special Alibus 457 (€1, 30 minutes, half hourly from 5am to midnight) from outside the train station. **Etna Transporti/Interbus** (☑095 53 03 96; www.interbus.it) also runs a regular shuttle from the airport to Taormina (€7.90, 1½ hours, six to 11 daily). All the main car-hire companies are represented at the airport.

BOAT

The ferry terminal is located southwest of the train station along Via VI Aprile.

TTT Lines (☑095 34 85 86, 800 91 53 65; www.tttlines.it) runs nightly ferries from Catania to Naples (seat €38 to €60, cabin per person €52 to €165, 11 hours).

Virtu Ferries (☑095 53 57 11; www.virtuferries.com) runs direct ferries from Pozzallo (south of Catania) to Malta (1¾ hours) Friday through Wednesday from May through September; Thursday service is added from mid-July to August. Fares vary depending on length of stay in Malta (same-day return €80 to €132, open return €108 to €157 depending on season). Coach transfer between Catania and Pozzallo (€7 each way) adds 2½ hours to the journey.

BUS

All intercity buses terminate in the area just north of Catania's train station. AST buses leave from Piazza Giovanni XXIII; buy tickets at Bar Terminal on the west side of the square. Interbus/Etna and SAIS leave from a terminal one block further north, with their ticket offices diagonally across the street on Via d'Amico.

Interbus (☑095 53 03 96; www.interbus.it; Via d'Amico 187) runs buses to:

Piazza Armerina (€8.90, 1¾ hours, two to four daily)

Ragusa (€8.30, two hours, five to 12 daily)

Syracuse (€6, 1¼ to 1½ hours, hourly Monday to Friday, fewer on weekends)

Taormina (€4.90, 1¼ to 1¾ hours, eight to 17 daily)

SAIS Trasporti (☑095 53 61 68; www.saistrasporti.it; Via d'Amico 181) goes to:

Agrigento (€12.40, three hours, nine to 14 daily)

Rome (€49, 11 hours) Overnight service.

Its sister company **SAIS Autolinee** (www.saisautolinee.it) also runs services to:

Messina (€8.10, 1½ hours, hourly Monday to Saturday, 12 on Sunday)

Palermo (€14.90, 2¾ hours, hourly Monday to Saturday, 10 on Sunday)

AST (☑095 723 05 35; www.aziendasicilianatrasporti.it) runs to many smaller towns around Catania, inclusing Nicolosi (€2.50, 50 to 80 minutes, hourly) at the foot of Mt Etna.

CAR & MOTORCYCLE

Catania is easily reached from Messina on the A18 autostrada and from Palermo on the A19. From the autostrada, signs for the centre of Catania will bring you to Via Etnea.

TRAIN

From Catania Centrale station on Piazza Papa Giovanni XXIII there are frequent trains.

Agrigento (€10.40 to €14.50, 3¾ hours)

Messina (€7 to €10.50, 1¾ hours, hourly)

Palermo (€12.50 to to €15.30, three to 5¾ hours, one direct daily)

Syracuse (€6.35 to €9.50, 1¼ hours, nine daily) The private Ferrovia Circumetnea train circles Mt Etna, stopping at towns and villages on the volcano's slopes.

ℹ Getting Around

Several useful **AMT city buses** (☑095 751 96 11; www.amt.ct.it) terminate in front of the train station, including buses 1-4 and 4-7 (both running hourly from the station to Via Etnea) and Alibus 457 (station to airport every 30 minutes). A

90-minute ticket costs €1. From mid-June to mid-September, a special service (bus D-Est) runs from Piazza Raffaello Sanzio to the local beaches.

For drivers, some words of warning: there are complicated one-way systems around the city and the centre is pedestrianised, which means parking is scarce.

Catania's one-line metro currently has only six stops, all on the periphery of town. For tourists, it's mainly useful as a way to get from the central train station to the Circumetnea train that goes around Mt Etna. Tickets cost €1.

For a taxi, call **Radio Taxi Catania** (☑ 095 33 09 66).

Mt Etna

ELEV 3329M

Dominating the landscape of eastern Sicily and visible from the moon (if you happen to be there), Mt Etna is Europe's largest volcano and one of the world's most active. Eruptions occur frequently, both from the volcano's four summit craters and from its slopes, which are littered with fissures and old craters. The volcano's most devastating eruptions occurred in 1669 and lasted 122 days. Lava poured down Etna's southern slope, engulfing much of Catania and dramatically altering the landscape. More recently, in 2002, lava flows from Mt Etna caused an explosion in Sapienza, destroying two buildings and temporarily halting the cable-car service. Less destructive eruptions have continued to occur regularly over the past decade, with 2013 seeing several dramatic instances of lava fountaining – vertical jets of lava spewing from the mountain's southeast crater. Locals understandably keep a close eye on the smouldering peak.

The volcano is surrounded by the huge Parco dell'Etna, the largest unspoilt wilderness remaining in Sicily. The park encompasses a remarkable variety of environments, from the severe, almost surreal, summit to deserts of lava and alpine forests.

Sights & Activities

The southern approach to Mt Etna presents the easier ascent to the **craters**. The AST bus from Catania drops you off at **Rifugio Sapienza** (1923m) from where a **cable car** (☑ 095 91 41 41; www.funiviaetna.com; one way/return €14.50/27, incl bus & guide €51; ☉9am-4.30pm) runs up the mountain to 2500m. From the upper cable-car station it's a 3½- to four-hour return trip up the winding track to the authorised crater zone (2920m).

Make sure you leave enough time to get up *and* down before the last cable car leaves at 4.45pm. Or, you can pay the extra €24 for a guided 4WD tour to take you up from the cable car to the crater zone.

An alternative ascent is from **Piano Provenzano** (1800m) on Etna's northern flank. This area was severely damaged during the 2002 eruptions, as still evidenced by the bleached skeletons of the surrounding pine trees. To reach Piano Provenzano you'll need a car, as there's no public transport beyond Linguaglossa, 16km away.

☞ Tours

Several companies offer private excursions up the mountain.

Volcano Trek   WALKING TOUR
(☑ 333 209 66 04; www.volcanotrek.com) Run by expert geologists.

Gruppo Guide Alpine Etna Sud   WALKING TOUR
(☑ 095 791 47 55; www.etnaguide.com) The official guide service on Etna's southern flank, with an office just below Rifugio Sapienza.

Gruppo Guide Alpine
Etna Nord   WALKING TOUR
(☑ 095 777 45 02; www.guidetnanord.com) Offers similar service from Linguaglossa on Etna's northern flank.

STAR   DRIVING TOUR
(☑ 347 495 70 91; www.funiviaetna.com/star_etna_nord.html; €40) Between May and October, STAR runs 4WD excursions to the summit from Piano Provenzano.

🛏 Sleeping & Eating

There's plenty of B&B accommodation around Mt Etna, particularly in the small, pretty town of Nicolosi. Contact Nicolosi's tourist information office for a full list.

Agriturismo San Marco   AGRITURISMO €
(☑ 389 423 72 94; www.agriturismosanmarco.com; per person B&B/half-board/full board €35/53/68; ☀🐾) This delightful *agriturismo* – near Rovittello, on Etna's northern flank – is a bit off the beaten track, but the bucolic setting, rustic rooms and superb country cooking more than compensate. There's also a swimming pool and kids' play area complete with swing and slides. Call ahead for directions.

Rifugio Sapienza   MOUNTAIN CHALET €€
(☑ 095 91 53 21; www.rifugiosapienza.com; Piazzale Funivia; per person B&B/half-board/full board

€55/75/90) As close to the summit as you can get, this place adjacent to the cable car offers comfortable accommodation with a good restaurant.

ℹ️ Information

Catania's downtown tourist office provides information about Etna, as do several offices on the mountain itself.

Etna Sud Tourist Office (☑ 095 91 63 56; ⊙ 9am-4pm) Near the summit at Rifugio Sapienza.

Parco dell'Etna (☑ 095 82 11 11; www.parcoetna.ct.it; Via del Convento 45; ⊙ 9am-2pm & 4-7.30pm) In Nicolosi, on Etna's southern side.

Proloco Linguaglossa (☑ 095 64 30 94; www.prolocolinguaglossa.it; Piazza Annunziata 5; ⊙ 9am-1pm & 4-7pm Mon-Sat, 9am-noon Sun) In Linguaglossa, on Etna's northern side.

ℹ️ Getting There & Away

BUS

AST (☑ 095 723 05 35; www.aziendasicilianatrasporti.it) runs daily buses from Catania to Rifugio Sapienza (one way/return €3.40/5.60, one hour). Buses leave from the car park opposite Catania's train station at 8.15am, travelling via Nicolosi, and return at 4.30pm.

TRAIN

You can circle Etna on the private **Ferrovia Circumetnea** (FCE; ☑ 095 54 12 50; www.circumetnea.it; Via Caronda 352a) train line. Catch the metro from Catania's main train station to the FCE station at Via Caronda (metro stop Borgo) or take bus 429 or 432 going up Via Etnea and ask to be let off at the Borgo metro stop.

The train follows a 114km trail around the base of the volcano, providing fabulous views. It also passes through many of Etna's unique towns such as Adrano, Bronte and Randazzo. See the website for fares and timetables.

SYRACUSE & THE SOUTHEAST

Home to Sicily's most beautiful baroque towns and Magna Graecia's most magnificent ancient city, the southeast is one of Sicily's most compelling destinations. The classical charms of Syracuse are reason enough to visit, but once you leave the city behind you'll find an evocative checkerboard of river valleys and stone-walled citrus groves dotted with handsome towns. Shattered by a devastating earthquake in 1693, the towns of Noto, Ragusa and Modica are the superstars here, rebuilt in the ornate and much-lauded Sicilian baroque style that lends the region a cohesive aesthetic appeal. Writer Gesualdo Bufalino described the southeast as an 'island within an island' and, certainly, this pocket of Sicily has a remote, genteel air – a legacy of its glorious Greek heritage.

Syracuse

POP 124,000

A dense tapestry of overlapping cultures and civilisations, Syracuse is one of Sicily's most appealing cities. Settled by colonists from Corinth in 734 BC, this was considered to be the most beautiful city of the ancient world, rivalling Athens in power and prestige. Under the demagogue Dionysius the Elder, the city reached its zenith, attracting luminaries such as Livy, Plato, Aeschylus and Archimedes, and cultivating the sophisticated urban culture that was to see the birth of comic Greek theatre.

As the sun set on Ancient Greece, Syracuse became a Roman colony and was looted of its treasures. While modern-day Syracuse lacks the drama of Palermo and the energy of Catania, the ancient island neighbourhood of Ortygia continues to seduce visitors with its atmospheric squares, narrow alleyways and lovely waterfront, while the Parco Archaeologico della Neapolis, 2km across town, remains one of Sicily's great classical treasures.

👁 Sights

👁 Ortygia

⭐ **Duomo** CATHEDRAL
(Map p808; Piazza del Duomo; ⊙ 8am-7pm) Built on the skeleton of a 5th-century BC Greek temple whose Doric columns are still visible underneath, Syracuse's cathedral was converted into a church when the island was evangelised by St Paul. Its most striking feature is the columned facade (1728–53), added by Andrea Palma after the church was damaged in the 1693 earthquake.

The original temple, dedicated to Athena, was renowned throughout the Mediterranean, in part thanks to Cicero, who visited Ortygia in the 1st century BC. Its roof was crowned by a golden statue of Athena that served as a beacon to sailors at sea (nowadays replaced by a statue of the Virgin Mary). In the baptistry, look out for a 13th-century Norman font, adorned by seven bronze lions.

Syracuse

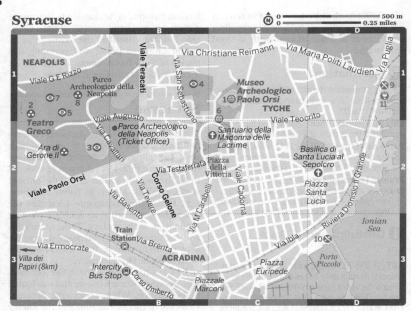

Syracuse

⊙ Top Sights

1 Museo Archeologico Paolo Orsi............C1
2 Teatro Greco A1

⊙ Sights

3 Anfiteatro Romano A2
4 Catacombe di San Giovanni.................B1
5 Latomia del Paradiso A1
6 Museo del Papiro C1

7 Orecchio di Dionisio...............................A1
8 Parco Archeologico della Neapolis.....A1

⊗ Eating

9 Jonico-a Rutta 'e Ciauli......................D1
10 Red Moon D3

⊖ Drinking & Nightlife

11 Bar Zen D1

★ **Fontana Aretusa** FOUNTAIN
(Map p808) At this ancient spring, fresh water still bubbles up as it did 2500 years ago
when this was Ortygia's main water supply.
According to legend, the goddess Artemis
transformed her beautiful handmaiden Aretusa into the spring to protect her from the
river god Alpheus. Now populated by ducks,
grey mullet and papyrus plants, it's a popular summer evening hangout.

**Galleria Regionale
di Palazzo Bellomo** ART GALLERY
(Map p808; ☎ 093 16 95 11; www.regione.sicilia.
it/beniculturali/palazzobellomo; Via Capodieci 16;
adult/reduced €8/4; ⊙ 9am-7pm Tue-Sat, 9am-1pm
Sun) Housed in a 13th-century Catalan-Gothic
palace, this art museum's eclectic collection

ranges from early Byzantine and Norman
stonework to 19th-century Caltagirone ceramics; in between, there's a good range of
medieval religious paintings and sculpture.

Castello Maniace CASTLE
(Map p808; adult/reduced €4/2; ⊙ 9am-6.30pm
Wed-Sat, 9am-1.30pm Tue & Sun) Guarding the
island's southern tip, Ortygia's 13th-century
castle is a lovely place to wander, gaze out
over the water and contemplate Syracuse's
past glories. It also hosts occasional rotating
exhibitions.

La Giudecca NEIGHBOURHOOD
Simply walking through Ortygia's tangled
maze of alleys is an atmospheric experience, especially down the narrow lanes of
Via Maestranza, the heart of the old guild

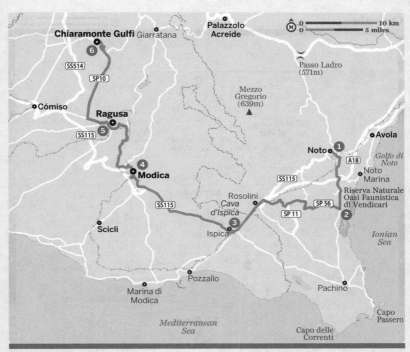

Driving Tour
Baroque Towns

DISTANCE 71KM
DURATION TWO DAYS

A land of remote rocky gorges, sweeping views and silent valleys, Sicily's southeastern corner is home to the 'baroque triangle', an area of Unesco-listed hilltop towns famous for their lavish baroque architecture. This tour takes in some of the finest baroque towns in Sicily, all within easy driving distance of each other.

Just over 35km south of Syracuse, **1 Noto** is home to what is arguably Sicily's most beautiful street – Corso Vittorio Emanuele, a pedestrianised boulevard lined with golden baroque *palazzi*. From Noto, head 12km south along the SP19 to the **2 Riserva Naturale Oasi Faunistica di Vendicari**, a coastal preserve whose trails, wetlands and beaches are prime territory for walking, birdwatching and swimming. Next, head 23km southwest along the SP56, SP11 and SS115 to **3 Ispica**, a hilltop town overlooking a huge canyon, the Cava d'Ispica,

riddled with prehistoric tombs. Continuing up the SS115 for a further 18km brings you to **4 Modica**, a bustling town set in a deep rocky gorge. There's excellent accommodation here and a wealth of great restaurants, so this makes a good place to overnight. The best of the baroque sights are up in Modica Alta, the high part of town, but make sure you have energy left for the *passeggiata* (evening stroll) on Corso Umberto I and dinner at Osteria dei Sapori Perduti.

Next morning, a short, winding, up-and-down drive through rock-littered hilltops leads to **5 Ragusa**, one of Sicily's nine provincial capitals. The town is divided in two – it's Ragusa Ibla that you want, a claustrophobic warren of grey stone houses and elegant *palazzi* that opens up onto Piazza Duomo, a superb example of 18th-century town planning. Although you can eat well in Ragusa, consider lunching in **6 Chiaramonte Gulfi**, a tranquil hilltop town some 20km to the north along the SP10, famous for its olive oil and delicious pork.

Ortygia

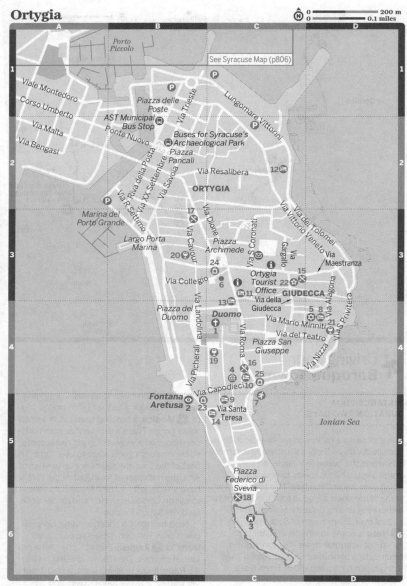

N ☉ 0 ————————————— 200 m
   0 ————————————— 0.1 miles

SICILY SYRACUSE

Porto Piccolo

See Syracuse Map (p806)

Viale Montedoro
Corso Umberto
Via Malta
Via Bengasi

Piazza delle Poste
AST Municipal Bus Stop
Ponte Nuovo
Via Trieste
Lungomare Vittorini

Buses for Syracuse's Archaeological Park
Piazza Pancali
Via Resalibera
12

ORTYGIA

Marina del Porto Grande
Largo Porta Marina

17
Via Dione
Via Cavour
Piazza Archimede
20
24
6
Via Collegio
Ortygia Tourist Office
13
11
Via della Giudecca
Piazza del Duomo
Duomo
1
19
Via Roma
Via Landolina
Via Picherali

Via S Coronati
Via dei Tolomei
Via Vittorio Veneto
Via Maestranza
Via Gargallo
15
22
GIUDECCA
5 8
21
Via Mario Minniti
Via del Teatro
Piazza San Giuseppe
Via Alagona
Via Privitera
Via S Nizza

Fontana Aretusa
2 23
Via Santa Teresa
14
16
4
25
10
9
7
Via Capodieci

Ionian Sea

Piazza Federico di Svevia
18
3

---

quarter, and the crumbling Jewish ghetto of **Via della Giudecca**.

At the hotel Alla Giudecca (p811) you can visit an ancient Jewish **miqwe** (ritual bath; Map p808; ☎ 093 12 22 55; Via Alagona 52; hourly tours €5; ☺11am & noon daily, 4pm, 5pm & 6pm Mon-Sat) some 20m below ground level. Blocked up in 1492 when the Jewish community was expelled from Ortygia, the baths were rediscovered during renovation work.

Ortygia

◉ Mainland Syracuse

**Parco Archeologico
della Neapolis**   ARCHAEOLOGICAL SITE
(Map p806; ☑ 093 16 50 68; Viale Paradiso; adult/
reduced €10/free-€5; ⊙ 9am-6pm Apr-Oct, 9am-
4pm Nov-Mar) For the classicist, Syracuse's
real attraction is this archaeological park,
with its pearly white, 5th-century BC **Teatro Greco** (Map p806; Parco Archeologico della
Neapolis), hewn out of the rock above the
city. This theatre saw the last tragedies of
Aeschylus (including *The Persians*), which
were first performed here in his presence.
In summer it is brought to life again with
an annual season of classical theatre.

Just beside the theatre is the mysterious **Latomia del Paradiso** (Map p806;
Parco Archeologico della Neapolis), a precipitous limestone quarry where stone for the
ancient city was extracted. Riddled with
catacombs and surrounded by citrus and
magnolia trees, this is also where the 7000
survivors of the war between Syracuse and
Athens in 413 BC were imprisoned. The **Orecchio di Dionisio** (Ear of Dionysius; Map
p806; Parco Archeologico della Neapolis, Latomia
del Paradiso), a grotto 23m by 3m deep, was
named by Caravaggio after the tyrant, who
is said to have used the almost perfect
acoustics of the quarry to eavesdrop on his
prisoners.

Nearer the park's entrance you'll find the
2nd-century AD **Anfiteatro Romano** (Map
p806), originally used for gladiatorial combats and horse races, and the 3rd-century
BC Ara di Gerone II, a monolithic sacrificial
altar to Heron II where up to 450 oxen could
be killed at one time.

To reach the park, take bus 1, 3 or 12 from
Ortygia's Piazza Pancali and get off at the
corner of Corso Gelone and Viale Teocrito.
Alternatively, the walk from Ortygia will
take about 30 minutes. If driving, you can
park along Viale Augusto (tickets available
at the nearby souvenir kiosks).

★**Museo Archeologico
Paolo Orsi**   MUSEUM
(Map p806; ☑ 093 146 40 22; Viale Teocrito; adult/
reduced €8/4; ⊙ 9am-6pm Tue-Sat, 9am-1pm Sun)
In the grounds of Villa Landolina, about
500m east of the archaeological park, the
wheelchair-accessible museum contains one
of Sicily's largest, best organised and most
interesting archaeological collections. Allow
plenty of time to get through the museum's
four distinct sectors; serious archaeology
buffs may even want to consider splitting
their visit into two days.

Museo del Papiro   MUSEUM
(Map p806; ☑ 093 16 16 16; www.museodelpapiro.
it; Viale Teocrito 66; ⊙ 9am-1pm Tue-Sun) **FREE**
This small museum includes papyrus documents and products, boats and an English-
language film about the history of papyrus.
The plant grows in abundance around the

Ciane River, near Syracuse, and was used to make paper in the 18th century.

Catacombe di San Giovanni
CATACOMB

(Map p806) A block north of the archaeological museum, this vast labyrinth of 10,000 underground tombs dates back to Roman times. A 30-minute guided tour ushers visitors through the catacombs as well as the atmospheric ruins of the Basilica di San Giovanni, Syracuse's earliest cathedral.

Activities

In midsummer, when Ortygia steams like a cauldron, people flock to the beaches south of town at **Arenella** (take bus 23 from Piazza della Posta) and **Fontane Bianche** (bus 21 or 22). There's also great sunbathing (for a fee) and diving off the rocks – but no sand – adjacent to Bar Zen (p812), 2km north of Ortygia.

Lido Maniace
BEACH

(Map p808; www.lidomaniace.it; 2 people €10) If you want something glam (though also a bit squashed) rent a pew on Syracuse's tiny Lido Maniace – a rocky platform of sun beds and shade where you can dip into the water. Otherwise, swim off one of the wooden platforms near the Giudecca.

Courses

Biblios Cafe
LANGUAGE

(Map p808; ☑ 093 12 14 91; www.biblios-cafe.it; Via del Consiglio Reginale 11) This well-loved cafe-cum-bookshop organises a whole range of cultural activities, including visits to local vineyards, art classes and language courses. The Italian lessons, which emphasise everyday conversational language, can be organised on an individual or group basis, from one hour to four weeks.

Festivals & Events

Ciclo di Rappresentazioni Classiche
PERFORMING ARTS

(Festival of Greek Theatre; www.indafondazione.org) Syracuse boasts the only school of classical Greek drama outside Athens, and in May and June it hosts live performances of Greek plays (in Italian) at the Teatro Greco, attracting Italy's finest performers. Tickets (€28 to €64) are available online, from the Via Cavour office in Ortygia or at the ticket booth outside the theatre.

Festa di Santa Lucia
RELIGIOUS

On 13 December a procession carrying the enormous silver statue of the city's patron saint wends its way from the cathedral to Piazza Santa Lucia, accompanied by fireworks.

Sleeping

Stay on Ortygia for atmosphere. Cheaper accommodation is located around the train station.

★ B&B dei Viaggiatori, Viandanti e Sognatori
B&B €

(Map p808; ☑ 093 12 47 81; www.bedandbreakfast-sicily.it; Via Roma 156, Ortygia; s €35-50, d €55-70, tr €75-80; ✳ ⑦) Decorated with verve and boasting a prime location in Ortygia, this B&B in an old *palazzo* at the end of Via Roma has a lovely bohemian feel, with books and pieces of antique furniture juxtaposed against bright walls. The sunny roof terrace with sweeping sea views makes a perfect breakfast spot. The owners also manage the nearby **B&B L'Acanto** (Map p808; ☑ 093 146 11 29; www.bebsicily.com; Via Roma 15; s €35-50, d €55-70, tr €75-85, q €100).

B&B Aretusa
APARTMENTS €

(Map p808; ☑ 093 148 34 84; www.aretusavacanze.com; Vicolo Zuccalà 1; d €59-90, tr €70-120, q €105-147; ℗ ✳ @ ⑦) This great budget option, elbowed into a tiny pedestrian street in a 17th-century building, has large rooms and apartments with kitchenettes, computers, wi-fi, satellite TV and small balconies from where you can shake hands with your neighbour across the way.

Palazzo del Sale
B&B €

(Map p808; ☑ 093 16 59 58; www.palazzodelsale.com; Via Santa Teresa 25, Ortygia; s €75-95, d €90-115, d with terrace €100-125; ✳ @ ⑦) The six rooms at this designer B&B are hot property in summer, so book ahead. All are well sized, with high ceilings and good beds. Coffee and tea are always available in the comfortable communal lounge. The owners also operate a second property right on the beach near Porto Piccolo (www.giuggiulena.it).

★ Hotel Gutkowski
HOTEL €€

(Map p808; ☑ 0931 46 58 61; www.guthotel.it; Lungomare Vittorini 26; s €60-80, d €75-130; ✳ @ ⑦) Book ahead for one of the sea-view rooms at this calmly stylish hotel on the Ortygia waterfront, at the edge of the Giudecca neighbourhood. Rooms are divided between two buildings, both with pretty tiled floors and a minimalist mix of vintage and industrial details. There's a nice sun terrace with sea views, and a cosy lounge area with fireplace.

Alla Giudecca HOTEL €€

(Map p808; ☑ 093 12 22 55; www.allagiudecca.it; Via Alagona 52; s €60-100, d €80-120; ❋ @ ❈) Located in the old Jewish quarter, this charming hotel boasts 23 suites with warm terracotta-tiled floors, exposed wood beams and lashings of heavy white linen. The communal areas are a warren of vaulted rooms full of museum-quality antiques and enormous tapestries, and feature cosy sofas gathered around huge fireplaces.

Villa dei Papiri AGRITURISMO €€

(☑ 093 172 13 21; www.villadeipapiri.it; Contrada Cozzo Pantano; d €50-132, 2-person ste €105-154, 4-person ste €140-208; P ❋ @ ❈) Immersed in an Eden of orange groves and papyrus reeds 8km outside Syracuse, this lovely *agriturismo* sits next to the Fonte Ciana spring immortalised in Ovid's *Metamorphosis*. Eight family suites are housed in a beautifully converted 19th-century farmhouse, with double rooms dotted around the lush grounds. Breakfast is served in a baronial stone-walled hall.

Hotel Roma HOTEL €€

(Map p808; ☑ 093 146 56 26; www.hotelroma-siracusa.it; Via Roma 66; s €75-105, d €105-149; P ❋ @ ❈) Within steps of Piazza del Duomo, this *palazzo* has rooms with parquet floors, oriental rugs, wood-beam ceilings and tasteful art work, plus free bike use, a gym and a sauna.

✗ Eating

Ortygia is the best place to eat. Its narrow lanes are chock-full of trattorias, restaurants, cafes and bars, and while some are obvious tourist traps, there are plenty of quality options in the mix. Most places specialise in seafood.

Sicilia in Tavola SICILIAN €

(Map p808; ☑ 392 461 08 89; Via Cavour 28; pasta €7-12; ❈ Tue-Sun) One of several popular eateries on Via Cavour, this snug hole-in-the-wall trattoria has built a strong local reputation on the back of its homemade pasta and fresh seafood. To taste for yourself try the prawn ravioli, which is served with small cherry tomatoes and chopped mint, or the delicious *fettuccine allo scoglio* (with seafood sauce).

Red Moon SEAFOOD €

(Map p806; ☑ 093 16 03 56; Riva Porto Lachio 36; meals €25; ❈ lunch & dinner Thu-Tue) Serving some of Syracuse's best seafood under its tented octagonal roof, this reasonably priced family-run place on the mainland makes a pleasant refuge from Ortygia's well-worn tourist track. Start with *spaghetti ai ricci* (spaghetti with sea urchin roe), move on to *fritto misto* (fried shrimp and squid) or grilled fish, then finish with a refreshing lemon sorbet.

★ Le Vin De L'Assassin Bistrot MEDITERRANEAN €€

(Map p808; ☑ 093 16 61 59; Via Roma 15; meals €30-45; ❈ dinner Tue-Sun, lunch Sun) At this stylish, high-ceilinged Ortygia eatery run by the Parisian-trained Saro, chalkboard offerings include French classics such as *quiche lorraine* and *croque monsieur*, Breton oysters, salads with impeccable vinaigrette dressing, a host of meat and fish mains, and a splendid *millefoglie* of eggplant and sweet red peppers. It's a perfect late-night stop for wine by the glass or homemade, over-the-top chocolatey desserts.

Taberna Sveva SICILIAN €€

(Map p808; ☑ 093 12 46 63; Piazza Federico di Svevia; meals €25-35; ❈ Thu-Tue) Away from the tourist maelstrom, the charming eatery is tucked away in a quiet corner of Ortygia. On warm summer evenings the outdoor terrace is the place to sit, with al fresco tables on a tranquil cobbled square in front of Syracuse's 13th-century castle. The food is traditional Sicilian; expect plenty of tuna and swordfish and some wonderful pastas.

Jonico-a Rutta 'e Ciauli SICILIAN €€

(Map p806; ☑ 093 16 55 40; Riviera Dionisio il Grande 194; pizza €4-7, meals €25-35; ❈ Wed-Mon Jun-Sep) It's a long and not particularly enticing hike to this seafront restaurant, but once you're there you'll appreciate the effort. Inside it's all exposed brickwork and rusty farm tools; outside on the terrace it's pure bliss, with the sun in your face, a cooling sea breeze and dreamy views. Not surprisingly, fish features heavily on the menu.

★ Don Camillo MODERN SICILIAN €€€

(Map p808; ☑ 093 16 71 33; www.ristorantedon-camillosiracusa.it; Via Maestranza 96; meals €55; ❈ lunch & dinner Mon-Sat) This elegant restaurant with top-notch service is full of classy surprises: 'black' king prawns in a thick almond cream soup, red snapper with fig and lemon, *tagliata di tonno* (grilled and sliced tuna) with a red pepper 'marmalade' and blood-orange ice cream for dessert. Slow Food recommended.

 Drinking & Nightlife

Syracuse is a vibrant university town, which means plenty of life on the streets after nightfall.

Bar San Rocco BAR
(Map p808; Piazzetta San Rocco; ⊙5pm-late) Head to San Rocco, the smoothest of several bars on Piazzetta San Rocco, for early evening *aperitivi* (complete with bountiful bar snacks) and late-night cocktails. Inside, it's a narrow, stone-vaulted affair, but the main action is outside on the vivacious piazzetta where summer crowds gather until the early hours. Occasional live music and DJ sets fuel the laid-back vibe.

Bar Zen BAR
(Map p806; ⊙9am-midnight mid-Jun–Sep) At this seaside bar affiliated with Jonico restaurant, you can plunge off the rocks and sunbathe all day, then retire to the outdoor deck for evening drinks and live music.

Il Blu WINE BAR
(Map p808; Via Nizza; ⊙6pm-late) A superb wine bar with a cosy front porch near the waterfront, this is a great place to take in the sun between dips in the sea.

Café Giufá MUSIC
(Map p808; ☑093 146 53 95; Via Cavour 25; ⊙closed Mon in winter) A fun bar that spreads onto the tiny square at the back, the Giufá has some good DJs who like reggae, jungle and dub beats.

 Entertainment

Piccolo Teatro dei Pupi PUPPET THEATRE
(Map p808; ☑093 146 55 40; www.pupari.com; Via della Giudecca 17) Syracuse's thriving puppet theatre hosts regular performances; see the website for a calendar. You can also buy puppets at its workshop next door.

 Shopping

Browsing Ortygia's quirky boutiques is great fun.

Untitled CLOTHING
(Map p808; ☑093 16 45 74; www.untitled-trend-wear.com; Via Serafino Privitera 39; ⊙10.30am-2.30pm & 4.30-8.30pm) With pieces by Italian and international designers, this boutique has clothes to die for and prices to give you a heart attack.

Massimo Izzo JEWELLERY
(Map p808; www.massimoizzo.com; Piazza Archimede 25; ⊙4.30-8.30pm Mon, 9am-1pm & 4.30-8.30pm Tue-Sat) The flamboyant jewellery of Messina-born Massimo Izzo features bold idiosyncratic designs made with Sciacca coral, gold and precious stones, inspired by the sea, theatre and classical antiquity.

Galleria Bellomo ARTISANAL
(Map p808; www.bellomogallery.com; Via Capodieci 15; ⊙10.30am-1.30pm & 4.30-8pm Mon-Sat) This gallery near Fontana Aretusa specialises in papyrus products, including greeting cards, bookmarks and writing paper and watercolour landscapes.

 Information

Ortygia tourist office (Map p808; ☑093 146 42 55; Via Maestranza 33; ⊙8am-2pm & 2.30-5.30pm Mon-Fri, 8am-2pm Sat) English-speaking staff and lots of good information.

Ospedale Umberto I (☑093 172 40 33; Via Testaferrata 1)

Police station (☑093 16 51 76; Piazza S Giuseppe)

Tourist office (Map p808; ☑0800 05 55 00; infoturismo@provsr.it; Via Roma 31; ⊙8am-8pm Mon-Sat, 9.15am-6.45pm Sun) English-speaking staff, city maps and other useful information.

 Getting There & Away

Syracuse's train and bus stations are a block apart from each other, halfway between Ortygia and the archaeological park.

BUS

Long-distance buses operate from the bus stop along Corso Umberto, just east of Syracuse's train station.

Interbus (☑093 16 67 10; www.interbus.it) runs buses to Catania (€6, 1½ hours, 15 daily Monday to Saturday, eight on Sunday) and its airport, Noto (€3.40, 55 minutes, two to four daily) and Palermo (€12, 3¼ hours, three daily).

AST (☑093 146 27 11; www.aziendasicilianatrasporti.it) offers services to Piazza Armerina (€8.80, four hours, one daily) and Ragusa (€6.90, 2¼ hours, four daily Monday to Saturday, two Sunday).

CAR & MOTORCYCLE

The modern A18 and SS114 highways connect Syracuse with Catania and points north, while the SS115 runs south to Noto and Modica. Arriving by car, exit onto the eastbound SS124 and follow signs to Syracuse and Ortygia.

Traffic on Ortygia is restricted; you're better off parking and walking once you arrive on the island. The large Talete parking garage on Ortygia's north side is a bargain – free between 5am and 9pm, and only €1 for overnight parking.

TRAIN

From Syracuse's **train station** (Via Francesco Crispi), several trains depart daily for Messina (InterCity/regional train €18.50/9.70, 2½ to 3¼ hours) via Catania (€9.50/6.35, 1¼ hours). Some go on to Rome, Turin and Milan as well as other long-distance destinations. For Palermo, the bus is a better option. There are also local trains from Syracuse to Noto (€3.45, 30 minutes) and Ragusa (€7.65, 2¼ hours).

ⓘ Getting Around

For travel between the bus and train stations and Ortygia, catch the free AST shuttle bus 20 (every 20 to 60 minutes). To reach Parco Archeologico della Neapolis from Ortygia, take AST city bus 1, 3 or 12 (two-hour ticket €1.10), departing from Ortygia's Piazza Pancali.

Noto

POP 23,800 / ELEV 160M

Flattened by the devastating earthquake of 1693, Noto was grandly rebuilt by its nobles into the finest baroque town in Sicily. Now a Unesco World Heritage Site, the town is especially impressive in the early evening, when its golden-hued sandstone buildings seem to glow with a soft inner light, and at night when illuminations accentuate the beauty of its intricately carved facades. The baroque masterpiece is the work of Rosario Gagliardi and his assistant, Vincenzo Sinatra, local architects who also worked in Ragusa and Modica.

◉ Sights

Two piazzas break up the long Corso Vittorio Emanuele: Piazza dell'Immacolata to the east and Piazza XVI Maggio to the west. The latter is overlooked by the beautiful Chiesa di San Domenico and the adjacent Dominican monastery, both designed by Rosario Gagliardi. On the same square, Noto's elegant 19th-century Teatro Comunale is worth a look. For sweeping views of Noto's baroque splendour, climb to the rooftop terrace at **Chiesa di Santa Chiara** (Corso Vittorio Emanuele; admission €2; ⓧ 9.30am-1pm & 3-7pm) or the *campanile* (bell tower) of **Chiesa di**

San Carlo al Corso (Corso Vittorio Emanuele; admission €2; ⓧ 9am-12.30pm & 4-7pm).

⭐**Cattedrale di San Nicolò**   CATHEDRAL
(www.cattedralenoto.it; Piazza Municipio; ⓧ 9am-1pm & 3-8pm) Pride of place in Noto goes to the renovated San Nicolò Cathedral. On 16 March 1996 the town was horrified when the roof and dome of the cathedral collapsed during a thunderstorm – luckily it was 10.30pm and the cathedral was empty. In 2007 the cathedral reopened, scrubbed of centuries of dust and dirt and once again gleaming in its peachy glow.

Piazza Municipio   SQUARE
In the centre of Noto's most graceful square is the Cattedrale di San Nicolò, surrounded by elegant town houses such as Palazzo Landolina, once home to Noto's oldest noble family, and Palazzo Ducezio (Town Hall), best known for its Sala degli Specchi (Hall of Mirrors).

Palazzo Nicolaci di Villadorata   PALACE
(☏ 320 556 80 38; www.palazzonicolaci.it; Via Nicolaci; adult/reduced €4/2; ⓧ 10am-1pm & 3-7.30pm) In the Palazzo Villadorata, the wrought-iron balconies are supported by a swirling pantomime of grotesque figures. Although empty of furnishings, the richly brocaded walls and frescoed ceilings of the *palazzo* give an idea of the sumptuous lifestyle of Sicilian nobles, as brought to life in the Giuseppe Tomasi di Lampedusa novel *Il Gattopardo* (The Leopard).

⚐ Festivals & Events

Noto's colourful two-week-long flower festival, **Infiorata**, is celebrated in mid- to late May with parades, historical re-enactments and a public art project in which artists decorate the length of Via Corrada Nicolaci with designs made entirely of flower petals.

⌂ Sleeping

B&Bs are plentiful in Noto; the tourist office keeps a detailed list.

Ostello Il Castello   HOSTEL €
(☏ 320 838 88 69; www.ostellodinoto.it; Via Fratelli Bandiera 1; dm €17, d without bathroom €45) Directly uphill from the centre, this old-school hostel with eight- to 16-bed dorms commands fabulous views over the *duomo* and offers great value for money, despite the paltry breakfast.

La Corte del Sole
RURAL INN €€

(☑320 82 02 10; www.lacortedelsole.it; Contrada Bucachemi; per person €55-126; P❄@🌐🏊) A few kilometres downhill from Noto, overlooking the Vendicari bird sanctuary, is this lovely rural retreat set around a central courtyard. The best of the 34 ceramic-clad, wood-beamed rooms overlook the pool. Other amenities include an in-house restaurant, a lovely breakfast area built around an ancient olive-oil press, bike hire, cooking courses and a shuttle bus to the nearby beach.

Hotel della Ferla
HOTEL €€

(☑093 157 60 07; www.hoteldellaferla.it; Via Gramsci; s €48-78, d €84-120; P❄🌐) This friendly family-run hotel in a residential area near the train station offers large, bright rooms with pine furnishings and small balconies, plus free parking.

 ## Eating

The people of Noto are serious about their food, so take time to enjoy a meal and follow it up with a visit to one of the town's excellent ice-cream shops.

★ Caffè Sicilia
GELATO €

(☑093 183 50 13; Corso Vittorio Emanuele 125; desserts from €2; ☺8am-10pm Tue-Sun) Dating from 1892 and especially renowned for its *granite*, this beloved place vies with its next-door neighbour, Dolceria Corrado Costanzo, for the honours of Noto's best dessert shop. Frozen desserts are made with the freshest seasonal ingredients (wild strawberries in springtime, for example) while the delicious torrone (nougat) bursts with the flavours of local honey and almonds.

★ Il Liberty
MODERN SICILIAN €€

(☑093 157 32 26; www.illiberty.com; Via Cavour 40; meals €27-35; ☺noon-2.30pm & 7.30-10pm Tue-Sun) Step into the atmospheric vaulted dining room and sample chef Giuseppe Angelino's contemporary spin on Sicilian cookery. An excellent local wine list supplements the inspired menu, which moves from superb appetisers like *millefoglie* – wafer-thin layers of crusty cheese and ground pistachios layered with minty sweet-and-sour vegetables – straight through to desserts like warm cinnamon-ricotta cake with homemade orange compote.

★ Trattoria Crocifisso
RISTORANTE €€

(☑093 157 11 51; www.ristorantecrocifisso.it; Via Principe Umberto 48; meals €30-35; ☺1-2.15pm & 8-11pm Thu-Tue) High up the many stairs of Noto Alta, this Slow Food–acclaimed trattoria with an extensive wine list is a Noto favourite. The rustic antipasto is rich in creamy aubergine, fried fennel, olives, cheeses and so on, and this is a great place to taste a Sicilian classic, in season - *macco di fave* (broadbean puree) with ricotta and toasted breadcrumbs.

Ristorante Il Cantuccio
MODERN SICILIAN €€

(☑093 183 74 64; www.ristoranteilcantuccio.it; Via Cavour 12; meals €30-35; ☺dinner Tue-Sun, lunch Sun) Chef Valentina presents a seasonally changing menu that combines familiar Sicilian ingredients in exciting new ways. Try her exquisite *gnocchi al pesto del Cantuccio* (ricotta-potato dumplings with basil, parsley, mint, capers, almonds and cherry tomatoes), then move on to memorable main courses such as lemon-stuffed bass with orange-fennel salad.

ℹ Information

Tourist office (☑093 157 37 79; www.comune. noto.sr.it; Piazza XVI Maggio; ☺9am-1pm & 3-8pm) An excellent and busy information office with multilingual staff and free maps.

ℹ Getting There & Around

BUS
From Largo Pantheon just east of Noto's historic centre, AST and Interbus serve Catania (€8.10, 1½ to 2¾ hours) and Syracuse (€3.40, 55 minutes).

TRAIN
There's frequent service to Syracuse (€3.45, 30 minutes, eight daily except Sunday), but Noto's station is inconveniently located 1km downhill from the centre.

Modica

POP 54,700 / ELEV 296M

A powerhouse in Grecian times, Modica may have lost its pre-eminent position to Ragusa, but it remains a superbly atmospheric town with its ancient medieval buildings climbing steeply up either side of a deep gorge.

The multilayered town is divided into Modica Alta (Upper Modica) and Modica Bassa (Lower Modica). A devastating flood in 1902 resulted in the wide avenues of Corso Umberto and Via Giarrantana (the river was dammed and diverted), which remain the main axes of the town, lined by *palazzi* and tiled stone houses.

◉ Sights

Aside from simply wandering the streets and absorbing the atmosphere, a visit to the extraordinary Chiesa di San Giorgio (⊙9am-noon & 4-7pm) is a highlight. This church, Gagliardi's masterpiece, is a vision of pure rococo splendour, a butter-coloured confection perched on a majestic 250-step staircase. Its counterpart in Modica Bassa is the Cattedrale di San Pietro (Corso Umberto I), another impressive church atop a rippling staircase lined with life-sized statues of the Apostles.

🛏 Sleeping

Modica's quality-to-price ratio tends to be excellent, making this a top destination for discerning travellers.

★ Villa Quartarella   AGRITURISMO €

(☑360 65 48 29; www.quartarella.com; Contrada Quartarella; s €40, d €75-80) Spacious rooms and welcoming hosts set the tone at this converted villa in the countryside south of Modica. Owners Francesco and Francesca are generous in sharing their love and encyclopaedic knowledge of local history, flora and fauna and can suggest multiple itineraries in the surrounding area. The delicious, ample breakfasts include everything from home-raised eggs to intriguing Modican sweets.

B&B Il Cavaliere   B&B €

(☑093 294 72 19; www.palazzoilcavaliere.it; Corso Umberto I 259; s €39-59, d €65-80, ste €95-130; ❄🕾) Stay in aristocratic style at this classy B&B in a 19th-century *palazzo*, just down from the bus station on Modica's main strip. Standard rooms have less character than the beautiful front suite and the large, high-ceilinged common rooms, which retain original tiled floors and frescoed ceilings. The elegant breakfast room has lovely views of San Giorgio church.

Hotel Relais Modica   HOTEL €

(☑093 275 44 51; www.hotelrelaismodica.it; Via Campailla; d €85-110; ❄@) Guests are assured of a warm welcome at this inviting old-school hotel. Housed in a converted *palazzo* just off Corso Umberto I, it's an attractive hostelry with 10 bright, cheery rooms, each slightly different but all spacious and quietly elegant. There's free internet in reception and satellite TV in the rooms.

✕ Eating

Dolceria Bonajuto   CHOCOLATE €

(☑093 294 12 25; www.bonajuto.it; Corso Umberto I 159; ⊙9am-1.30pm Mon-Sat, 4.30-8.30pm daily) Sicily's oldest chocolate factory is the perfect place to taste Modica's famous chocolate. Flavoured with cinnamon, vanilla, orange peel and even hot peppers, it's a legacy of the town's Spanish overlords who imported cocoa from their South American colonies.

Taverna Nicastro   SICILIAN €

(☑093 294 58 84; Via S Antonino 28; meals €14-20; ⊙dinner Tue-Sat) With over 60 years of history and a long-standing Slow Food recommendation, this is one of the upper town's most authentic and atmospheric restaurants, and a bargain to boot. The carnivore-friendly menu includes grilled meat, boiled veal, lamb stew and pasta specialities such as ricotta ravioli with pork *ragù* (meat sauce).

Fattoria delle Torri   SEAFOOD €€

(☑093 275 12 86; Vico Napolitano 14, Modica Alta; meals from €35; ⊙closed Sun evening & Mon) This is one of Modica's smartest restaurants. Housed in an elegant 18th-century *palazzo*, it has a beautiful dining area with tables set under stone arches, and bay windows looking onto a small internal garden. The seafood is particularly gorgeous, especially when combined with a crisp, dry white wine such as Cerasuolo di Vittoria.

La Locanda del Colonnello   SICILIAN €€

(☑093 275 24 23; Vico Biscari 6; meals €25-30; ⊙lunch & dinner Wed-Mon) This is a fantastic place to try Sicilian specialities with an original twist – like *macco di fave* (broad bean mash) with roasted octopus. For something more traditional, try the ravioli stuffed with ricotta and marjoram in a pork sauce, or the roast lamb with potatoes. Finish with a smooth *gelo di limone* (lemon jelly).

❶ Information

Tourist office (☑093 275 96 34; www.comune.modica.rg.it; Corso Umberto I 141; ⊙9am-1pm & 3.30-7.30pm Mon-Sat, 10am-1pm Sun) Can supply the odd map or list, but no English is spoken.

❶ Getting There & Away

BUS

Frequent buses run Monday to Saturday from Piazzale Falcone-Borsellino at the top of Corso Umberto I to Syracuse (€6), Noto (€3.90) and

SICILY MODICA

Ragusa (€2.40); on Sunday, service is limited to two buses in each direction.

TRAIN

From Modica's station, 600m southwest of the centre, there are three trains daily (one on Sunday) to Syracuse (€7, 1¾ hours) and six (one on Sunday) to Ragusa (€2.25, 25 minutes).

Ragusa

POP 72,800 / ELEV 502M

Like a grand old dame, Ragusa is a dignified and well-aged provincial town. Like every other town in the region, Ragusa collapsed after the 1693 earthquake; a new town called Ragusa Superiore was built on a high plateau above the original settlement. But the old aristocracy were loath to leave their tottering *palazzi* and rebuilt Ragusa Ibla on the original site. The two towns were only merged in 1927.

Ragusa Ibla remains the heart and soul of the town, and has all the best restaurants and the majority of sights. A sinuous bus ride or some very steep and scenic steps connect the lower town to its modern sister up the hill.

◉ Sights

Grand churches and *palazzi* line the twisting, narrow streets of Ragusa Ibla, interspersed with *gelaterie* and delightful piazzas where the local youth stroll and the elderly gather on benches. Palm-planted Piazza del Duomo, the centre of town, is dominated by the 18th-century **Cattedrale di San Giorgio** (Piazza Duomo; ⊙ 10am-12.30pm & 4-6.30pm), with its magnificent neoclassical dome and stained-glass windows.

At the eastern end of the old town is the **Giardino Ibleo** (⊙ 8am-8pm), a pleasant public garden laid out in the 19th century that is perfect for a picnic lunch.

🛏 Sleeping

L'Orto Sul Tetto   B&B €
(☑ 093 224 77 85; www.lortosultetto.it; Via Tenente Distefano 56; s €45-60, d €70-110; ❋ 🛜) This sweet little B&B behind Ragusa's *duomo* offers an intimate experience, with just three rooms and a lovely roof terrace where breakfast is served.

Locanda Don Serafino   INN €€
(☑ 093 222 00 65; www.locandadonserafino.it; Via XI Febbraio 15; s €80-138, d €90-168; ❋ @) This historic inn near the *duomo* has beautiful rooms, some with original vaulted stone ceilings, plus a well-regarded restaurant nearby. For €9 extra, guests get access to the Lido Azzurro beach at Marina di Ragusa, 25km away.

Caelum Hyblae   B&B €€
(☑ 093 222 04 02; www.bbcaelumhyblae.it; Salita Specula 11, Ragusa Ibla; d €100-120) With its book-lined reception and crisp white decor, this stylish, family-run B&B exudes quiet sophistication. Each of the seven rooms has views over the cathedral and while they're not the biggest, they're immaculately turned out with unadorned walls, pristine beds and functional modern furniture.

🍴 Eating

Quattro Gatti   SICILIAN €
(☑ 093 224 56 12; Via Valverde 95; meals €18; ⊙ dinner, closed Mon Oct-May & Sun Jun-Sep) This Sicilian-Slovak eatery near the Giardini Iblei serves an amazing four-course fixed-price menu bursting with fresh, local flavours. The antipasti spread is especially memorable, as are the seasonally changing specials scribbled on the blackboard up front. Slovak-inspired offerings such as goulash and apple strudel round out a menu of Sicilian classics.

Gelati DiVini   GELATO €
(☑ 093 222 89 89; www.gelatidivini.it; Piazza Duomo 20; ice cream from €2; ⊙ 10am-midnight) This exceptional *gelateria* makes wine-flavoured ice creams like marsala and muscat, plus unconventional offerings including rose, fennel, wild mint and the surprisingly tasty *gocce verdi*, made with local olive oil.

La Rusticana   TRATTORIA €€
(☑ 093 222 79 81; Corso XXV Aprile 68; meals €25; ⊙ Wed-Mon) Fans of the *Montalbano* TV series will want to eat here, as this is where scenes set in the fictional Trattoria San Calogero were filmed. In reality, it's a cheerful, boisterous trattoria whose generous portions and relaxed vine-covered terrace ensure a loyal clientele. The food is defiantly *casareccia* (home-style), so expect no-frills pastas and uncomplicated cuts of grilled meat. Slow Food recommended.

Ristorante Duomo   MODERN SICILIAN €€€
(☑ 093 265 12 65; Via Capitano Bocchieri 31; meals €90-100, tasting menus €135-140) This is generally regarded as one of Sicily's best restaurants. Behind the stained-glass door, small rooms are outfitted like private parlours, ensuring a suitably romantic ambience for Chef Ciccio Sultano's refined creations.

These combine ingredients in imaginative, unconventional ways while making constant use of classic Sicilian ingredients such as pistachios, fennel, almonds and Nero d'Avola wine. Book ahead.

ℹ Information

Tourist office (☎ 093 268 47 80; Piazza della Repubblica; ☉10am-1pm & 3.30-6.30pm) At the western edge of the lower town.

ℹ Getting There & Around

BUS

Long-distance and municipal buses share a terminal on Via Zama in the upper town. Buy tickets at the Interbus/Etna kiosk in the main lot or at cafes around the corner. **Interbus** (www.interbus.it) runs to Catania (€8.30, two hours, five to 12 daily). **AST** (☎ 093 268 18 18; www.aziendasicilianatrasporti.it) serves Syracuse (€6.90, three hours, eight daily Monday to Saturday, two on Sunday) via Modica (€2.40, 30 minutes) and Noto (€4.80, 2¼ hours).

City bus 33 (€1.10) runs hourly between the bus terminal and the lower town of Ragusa Ibla. From the train station, bus 11 (bus 1 on Sundays) makes a similar circuit.

TRAIN

From the station in the upper town, there are two trains to Syracuse (€7.65, 2¼ hours) via Noto (€5.75, 1½ hours) Monday to Saturday.

CENTRAL SICILY & THE MEDITERRANEAN COAST

Central Sicily is a land of vast panoramas, undulating fields, severe mountain ridges and hilltop towns not yet sanitised for tourists. Moving towards the Mediterranean, the perspective changes, as ancient temples jostle for position with modern high-rise apartments outside Agrigento, Sicily's most lauded classical site and also one of its busier modern cities.

Agrigento

POP 59,100 / ELEV 230M

Agrigento does not make a good first impression. Seen from a distance, the modern city's rows of unsightly apartment blocks loom incongruously on the hillside, distracting attention from the splendid Valley of the Temples below, where the ancient Greeks once built their great city of Akragas. Never

fear: once you get down among the ruins, their monumental grace becomes apparent, and it's easy to understand how this remarkable complex of temples became Sicily's preeminent travel destination, first put on the tourist map by Goethe in the 18th century.

Three kilometres uphill from the temples, Agrigento's medieval core is a pleasant place to pass the evening after a day exploring the ruins. The intercity bus and train stations are both in the upper town, within a few blocks of Via Atenea, the main street of the medieval city.

◎ Sights

◎ Valle dei Templi

★ **Valley of the Temples (Valle dei Templi)**   ARCHAEOLOGICAL SITE
(☎ 092 262 16 11; www.parcovalledeitempli.it; adult/EU under 18yr & over 65yr/EU 18-25yr incl Quartiere Ellenistico-Romano €10/free/5, incl Museo Archeologico €13.50/free/7) One of southern Europe's most compelling archaeological sites, the 1300-hectare Parco Valle dei Templi encompasses the ruins of the ancient city of Akragas. The highlight is the stunning Tempio della Concordia, one of the best-preserved Greek temples in existence and one of a series built on a ridge to act as beacons for homecoming sailors.

Three kilometres south of Agrigento, the park is divided into two distinct zones, separated by the main SS118 road. There are two ticket offices, one at the park's eastern edge and another at Piazza Alexander Hardcastle between the eastern and western zones. The car park is by the eastern entrance.

★ **Museo Archeologico**   MUSEUM
(☎ 092 24 01 11; Contrada San Nicola; admission incl Valley of the Temples adult/reduced €13.50/7; ☉9am-7pm Tue-Sat, 9am-1pm Sun & Mon) North of the temples, this wheelchair-accessible museum is one of Sicily's finest, with a huge collection of clearly labelled artefacts from the excavated site. Especially noteworthy are the dazzling displays of Greek painted ceramics and the aweinspiring reconstructed *telamone*, a colossal statue recovered from the nearby Tempio di Giove.

◎ Medieval Agrigento

Roaming the town's lively, winding streets is relaxing after a day among the temples.

Agrigento

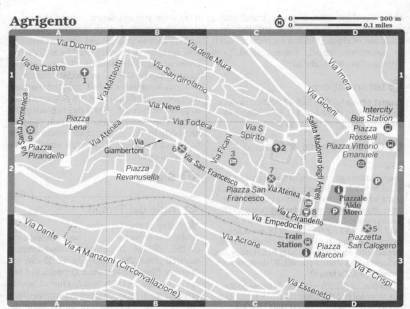

Agrigento

◎ Sights
1 Chiesa di Santa Maria dei Greci.......... A1
2 Monastero del Santo Spirito C2

◎ Sleeping
3 Camere a Sud...................................... C2
4 PortAtenea... D2

◎ Eating
5 Kalòs.. D3
6 L'Ambasciata di Sicilia....................... B2
7 Trattoria Concordia............................ C2

◎ Drinking & Nightlife
8 QOC.. D2

◎ Entertainment
9 Teatro Pirandello A2

Chiesa di Santa Maria dei Greci   CHURCH
(Salita Santa Maria dei Greci; ⊙ 9am-12.30pm &
4-6pm Mon-Sat) This 11th-century Norman
church is built on the site of a 5th-century
BC temple to Athena. Glass floor panels reveal the temple's foundations, while a narrow passageway left of the church allows
you to see the ancient Greek columns.

Monastero del Santo Spirito   CONVENT
This hillside convent was founded by Cistercian nuns at the end of the 13th century.
Ring the buzzer at the door marked No 8,
and their modern-day counterparts will sell
you a tray of delicious cakes and pastries
(€11), including *dolci di mandorla* (almond
pastries), *cuscusu* (almond and pistachio
'couscous') and – at Christmas time – *bucel-
lati* (rolled sweet dough with figs).

☞ Tours

The tourist office maintains a list of multilingual guides. The official rate is €140 for
a half-day tour, although discounts can be
negotiated.

🎎 Festivals & Events

Sagra del Mandorlo in Fiore   CULTURE
A huge folk festival held on the first Sunday
in February, when the Valley of the Temples
is cloaked in almond blossom.

🛏 Sleeping

Camere a Sud   B&B €
(📱 349 638 44 24; www.camereasud.it; Via Ficani 6;
r €60-70; ❄ @ 🛜) A lovely B&B in the centre
of Agrigento, Camere a Sud has three guest
rooms decorated with style and taste – traditional decor and contemporary textiles are

matched with bright colours and modern art. The sumptuous breakfast is served on the terrace in the warmer months.

PortAtenea B&B €

(📞349 093 74 92; www.portatenea.com; cnr Via Atenea & Via C Battisti; s €35-45, d €55-70; 🕸🛜) Five minutes from the train and bus stations at the entrance to Agrigento's main pedestrian thoroughfare, this B&B wins points for its large roof terrace overlooking the Valley of the Temples. The three double rooms and two triples are spacious and well appointed, with hairdryers and cheerful decor.

⭐ **Villa Athena** LUXURY HOTEL €€€

(📞092 259 62 88; www.hotelvillaathena.it; Via Passeggiata Archeologica 33; s €130-190, d €150-350, ste €240-890; 🅿🕸@🛜🏊) With the Tempio della Concordia lit up in the near distance and palm trees lending an exotic Arabian-nights feel, the views from this historic five-star are magnificent. Housed in an aristocratic 18th-century villa, the hotel's interior, gleaming after a recent makeover, is a picture of white, ceramic cool.

The Villa Suite, with two cavernous rooms floored in antique tiles, a freestanding jacuzzi tub and a vast terrace looking straight at the temples, vies for the title of coolest hotel room in Sicily.

🍴 Eating

Trattoria Concordia TRATTORIA €

(📞092 22 26 68; Via Porcello 8; meals €18-30; ⊙lunch & dinner) Tucked up a side alley, this rustic trattoria with exposed stone and stucco walls specialises in grilled fish along with traditional Sicilian *primi* like *casarecce con pesce spada, melanzane e menta* (pasta with swordfish, eggplant and mint).

⭐ **Kalòs** MODERN SICILIAN €€

(📞092 22 63 89; www.ristorantekalos.it; Piazzetta San Calogero; meals €30-40; ⊙lunch & dinner) Food is excellent at this smart restaurant with a couple of cute tables on the tiny balcony. Feast on *primi* such as fettucine with prawns and artichokes or pasta *all'agrigentina*, with fresh tomatoes, basil and pistachio; follow with *secondi* such as grilled lamb chops and citrus shrimp; and for dessert perhaps almond *semifreddo* or pear tart with chocolate and hazelnuts.

L'Ambasciata di Sicilia SICILIAN €€

(📞092 22 05 26; Via Giambertoni 2; meals €22-33; ⊙Mon-Sat) At the 'Sicilian Embassy', they do everything they can to improve foreign relations, plying tourists with tasty plates of traditional Sicilian fare and good seafood. Order an octopus and it arrives so fresh it feels as if it's staring you in the eyes. Try to get a table on the small outdoor terrace, which has splendid views.

🍷 Drinking & Nightlife

QOC BAR

(📞092 22 71 07; www.qoc.me; Via Cesare Battisti 8; ⊙Tue-Sun) A great place to hang out among young *agrigentini,* this trendy spot just off Via Atenea bills itself as an 'Outfit, Restaurant, Bar', but it does 'bar' best, with good, themed *aperitivi* and late-night cocktails. There's a nice-looking restaurant upstairs and a fixed-menu lunch (€10), although food is only average.

☆ Entertainment

Teatro Pirandello THEATRE

(📞092 22 50 19; www.teatroluigipirandello.it; Piazza Pirandello; tickets €18-23) This city-run theatre is Sicily's third largest, after Palermo's Teatro Massimo and Catania's Teatro Massimo Bellini. Works by local hero Luigi Pirandello figure prominently in the program, which runs from November to April.

ℹ Information

There are banks on Piazza Vittorio Emanuele I and Via Atenea.

Ospedale San Giovanni di Dio (📞092 244 21 11; Contrada da Consolida) North of the centre.

Police station (📞112; Piazzale Aldo Moro 2)

Tourist information point (Train Station; ⊙8am-8pm Mon-Fri, 8am-2pm Sat)

Tourist office (📞800 236 837; www.comune. agrigento.it; Piazzale Aldo Moro 1; ⊙8am-2pm Mon-Fri, 8am-1pm Sat) Inside the Provincia building, offers information on the city and province.

ℹ Getting There & Away

BUS

The intercity bus station and ticket booths are located on Piazza Rosselli. **Autoservizi Camilleri** (📞092 247 18 86; www.camilleriargentoelattuca. it) runs buses to Palermo (€8.70, two hours) five times Monday to Saturday and once on Sunday; **Cuffaro** (📞091 616 15 10; www.cuffaro.info) offers more frequent Palermo services – three to eight departures daily. **SAL** (Società Autolinee Licata; www.autolineesal.it) also offers direct service to Palermo's Falcone-Borsellino airport (€12.10, 2½ hours, four Monday to Saturday). **Lumia** (📞092 22 04 14; www.autolineelumia.it)

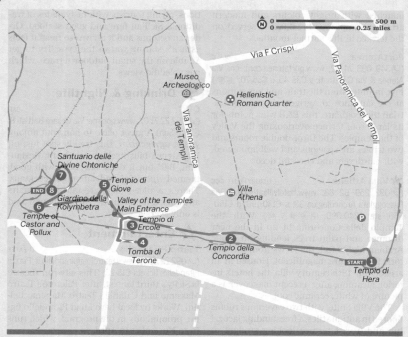

🏃 Archaeological Walking Tour
Valley of the Temples

LENGTH THREE HOURS

Begin your exploration in the so-called Eastern Zone, home to Agrigento's best-preserved temples. From the eastern ticket office, a short walk leads to the 5th-century BC **① Tempio di Hera** (Temple of Hera, aka Juno), perched on the ridgetop. Though partly destroyed by an earthquake, the colonnade remains largely intact as does a long sacrificial altar. Traces of red are the result of fire damage likely dating to the Carthaginian invasion of 406 BC.

Next descend past a gnarled 800-year-old olive tree and a series of Byzantine tombs to the **② Tempio della Concordia**. This remarkable edifice, the model for Unesco's logo, has survived almost entirely intact since its construction in 430 BC, partly thanks to its conversion into a Christian basilica in the 6th century, partly due to the shock-absorbing, earthquake-dampening qualities of the soft clay underlying its hard rock foundation.

Further downhill, the **③ Tempio di Ercole** (Temple of Hercules), is Agrigento's oldest, dat-ing from the end of the 6th century BC. Down from the main temples, the miniature **④ Tomba di Terone** (Tomb of Theron) dates to 75 BC.

Now cross the road to the Western Zone, stopping first at the **⑤ Tempio di Giove** (Temple of Olympian Zeus). This would have been the world's largest Doric temple had its construction not been interrupted by the Carthaginian sacking of Akragas. A later earthquake reduced it to the crumbled ruin you see today. Lying flat on his back amid the rubble is an 8m-tall *telamon* (a sculpted figure of a man with arms raised), originally intended to support the temple's weight. It's actually a copy; the original is in Agrigento's archeological museum.

Take a brief look at the ruined 5th-century BC **⑥ Temple of Castor and Pollux**, and the 6th-century BC complex of altars and small buildings known as the **⑦ Santuario delle Divine Chtoniche** (Sanctuary of the Chthonic Deities), before ending your visit in the **⑧ Giardino della Kolymbetra**, a lush garden in a natural cleft near the sanctuary, with more than 300 (labelled) species of plants and some welcome picnic tables.

has departures to Trapani and its Birgi Airport (€11.80, three to four hours, three daily Monday to Saturday, one on Sunday); and **SAIS** (☑ 092 22 93 24; www.saistrasporti.it) runs buses to Catania (€12.40, three hours, 10 to 15 daily).

CAR & MOTORCYCLE

The SS189 links Agrigento with Palermo, while the SS115 runs along the coast, northwest towards Trapani and southeast to Syracuse.

Driving in the medieval town is near impossible due to all the pedestrianised streets. There's metered parking at the train station and free parking along Via Esseneto just below.

TRAIN

From Agrigento Centrale station (Piazza Marconi), direct trains run regularly to Palermo (€8.30, 2¼ hours, seven to 10 daily). Service to Catania (€10.40 to €14.50, four hours) is less frequent and usually requires a change of trains. For other destinations, you're better off taking the bus.

ⓘ Getting Around

TUA (Trasporti Urbani Agrigento; ☑ 092 241 20 24) buses run down to the Valley of the Temples from the Piazza Rosselli bus station, stopping in front of the train station en route. Take bus 1, 2 or 3 (€1.10 with pre-purchased ticket, €1.65 on board) and get off at either the museum or the Piazzale dei Templi. Bus 1 continues to Porto Empedocle and bus 2 continues to San Leone. The Linea Verde (Green Line) bus runs hourly from the train station to the cathedral.

WESTERN SICILY

Directly across the water from North Africa and still retaining vestiges of the Arab, Phoenician and Greek cultures that once prevailed here, western Sicily has a bit of the Wild West about it. There's plenty to stir the senses, from Trapani's savoury fish couscous, to the dazzling views from hilltop Erice, to the wild coastal beauty of Riserva Naturale dello Zingaro.

Marsala

POP 82,300

Best known for its sweet dessert wines, Marsala is an elegant town of stately baroque buildings within a perfect square of walls.

The city was originally founded by Phoenician escapees from the Roman onslaught at nearby Mozia. Not wanting to risk a second attack, they fortified their new home with 7m-thick walls, ensuring that it was the last Punic settlement to fall to the Romans. In AD 830 it was conquered by the Arabs, who gave it its current name, Marsa Allah (Port of God).

It was here in 1860 that Giuseppe Garibaldi, leader of the movement for Italian unification, landed in his rickety old boats with his 1000-strong army – a claim to fame that finds its way into every tourist brochure.

◉ Sights & Activities

For a taste of local life, take a stroll at sunset around pretty **Piazza della Repubblica**, heart of the historic centre.

Cantine Florio   WINERY
(☑ 092 378 11 11; www.duca.it/cantineflorio; Via Vincenzo Florio 1; tours €10; ☹ wine shop 9am-1pm & 3.30-6pm Mon-Fri, 9.30am-1pm Sat, English-language tours 3.30pm Mon-Fri & 10.30am Sat year-round, plus 11am Mon-Fri Apr-Oct) These venerable wine cellars just east of town open their doors to visitors to explain the Marsala-making process and the fascinating history of local viticulture. Afterwards visitors can sample the goods in Florio's spiffy new tasting room. Take bus 16 from Piazza del Popolo.

Museo Archeologico Baglio Anselmi   MUSEUM
(☑ 092 395 25 35; Lungomare Boeo; adult €4, EU citizen 18-25yr or over 65yr €2; ☹ 9am-8pm Tue-Sun, 9am-1.30pm Mon) Marsala's finest treasure is the partially reconstructed remains of a Carthaginian *liburna* (warship) sunk off the Egadi Islands during the First Punic War. Displayed alongside objects from its cargo, the ship's bare bones provide the only remaining physical evidence of the Phoenicians' seafaring superiority in the 3rd century BC and offer a glimpse of a civilisation extinguished by the Romans.

Whitaker Museum   MUSEUM
(☑ 092 371 25 98; adult/child €9/5; ☹ 9.30am-1.30pm & 2.30-6.30pm Mar-Sep) On the island of Mozia, 10km north of Marsala, this museum displays archaeologist Joseph Whitaker's unique collection of Phoenician artefacts, assembled over decades. The museum's greatest treasure (on loan to the Getty Museum in Los Angeles at research time) is *Il Giovinetto di Mozia,* a marble statue of a young man in a pleated robe, suggesting Carthaginian influences.

FIONLINE / GETTY IMAGES ©

1. Teatro Greco, Taormina 2. Selinunte ruins 3. Doric Temple, Segesta 4. Mosaic, Villa Romana del Casale, Sicily

A Graeco-Roman Legacy

As the crossroads of the Mediterranean since the dawn of time, Sicily has seen countless civilisations come and go. The island's classical treasure trove includes Greek temples and amphitheatres, Roman mosaics and a host of fine archaeological museums.

Valle dei Templi

Crowning the craggy heights of Agrigento's Valle dei Templi (p817) are five Doric temples – including stunning Tempio della Concordia, one of the best preserved in all of Magna Graecia. Throw in the superb archaeological museum and you've got Sicily's most cohesive and impressive collection of Greek treasures.

Villa Romana del Casale

Bikini-clad gymnasts and wild African beasts prance side by side in remarkable floor decorations in this ancient Roman hunting lodge (p824). Buried under mud for centuries and now gleaming from restoration work completed in 2013, they're the most extensive mosaics in Sicily and a Unesco World Heritage Site.

Segesta

Segesta's perfect Doric temple (p830) perches on a windswept hilltop above a rugged river gorge.

Taormina

With spectacular views of snowcapped Mt Etna and the Ionian Sea, Taormina's Teatro Greco (p795) makes the perfect venue for the town's summer film and arts festivals.

Selinunte

Selinunte's vast ruins (p825) poke out of wildflower-strewn fields beside the sparkling Mediterranean.

Syracuse

Once the most powerful city in the Mediterranean, Syracuse (p805) brims with reminders of its ancient past, from the Greek columns supporting Ortygia's cathedral to the annual festival of classical Greek drama, staged in a 2500-year-old amphitheatre.

WORTH A TRIP

SICILY'S BEST-PRESERVED ROMAN MOSAICS

Near the town of Piazza Armerina in central Sicily is the stunning 3rd-century Roman **Villa Romana del Casale** (☑ 093 568 00 36; www.villaromanadelcasale.it; adult/reduced €10/5; ☺ 9am-6pm summer, 9am-4pm winter), a Unesco World Heritage Site and one of the few remaining sites of Roman Sicily. This sumptuous hunting lodge is thought to have belonged to Diocletian's co-emperor Marcus Aurelius Maximianus. Buried under mud in a 12th-century flood, it remained hidden for 700 years before its magnificent floor mosaics were discovered in the 1950s. Visit out of season or early in the day to avoid the hordes of tourists.

The mosaics cover almost the entire floor (3500 sq metres) of the villa and are considered unique for their narrative style, the range of subject matter and variety of colour – many are clearly influenced by African themes. Along the eastern end of the internal courtyard is the wonderful **Corridor of the Great Hunt**, vividly depicting chariots, rhinos, cheetahs, lions and the voluptuously beautiful Queen of Sheba. Across the corridor is a series of apartments, where floor illustrations reproduce scenes from Homer. But perhaps the most captivating of the mosaics is the so-called **Room of the Ten Girls in Bikinis**, with depictions of sporty girls in scanty bikinis throwing a discus, using weights and throwing a ball; they would blend in well on a Malibu beach. These most famous of Piazza Armerina's mosaics were fully reopened to the public in 2013 after years of painstaking restoration and are among Sicily's greatest classical treasures.

Travelling by car from Piazza Armerina, follow signs south of town to the SP15, then continue 5km to reach the villa.

Getting here without a car is more challenging. Buses operated by Interbus (p803) from Catania (€8.90, 1¾ hours) or **SAIS** (☑ 093 568 01 19; www.saisautolinee.it) from Enna (€3.40, 40 minutes) run to Piazza Armerina; from here catch a local bus (€0.70, 30 minutes, summer only) or a taxi (€20) the remaining 5km.

🛏 Sleeping & Eating

Marsala has few hotels within the historic centre.

⭐ Il Profumo del Sale   B&B €

(☑ 092 3189 0472; www.ilprofumodelsale.it; Via Vaccari 8; s €35, d €50-60; ☑) A dream B&B in every imaginable sense, Profumo del Sale has a perfect city centre location and three attractive rooms – including a palatial front unit with cathedral views from its small balcony – all enhanced by welcoming touches like almond cookies and fine soaps. Sophisticated owner Celsa is full of great tips about Marsala and the local area.

Hotel Carmine   HOTEL €€

(☑ 092 371 19 07; www.hotelcarmine.it; Piazza Carmine 16; s €70-105, d €100-130; ☑☀@☑) This lovely hotel in a 16th-century monastery has elegant rooms (especially rooms 7 and 30), with original blue-and-gold majolica tiles, stone walls, antique furniture and lofty beamed ceilings. Enjoy your cornflakes in the baronial-style breakfast room with its historic frescoes and over-the-top chandelier, or sip your drink by the roaring fireplace in winter. Modern perks include a rooftop solarium.

⭐ San Lorenzo Osteria   SICILIAN €€

(SLO; ☑ 092 371 25 93; Via Garraffa 60; meals €25-35; ☺ closed Tue; ☑) With roots as a wedding catering business, this stylish eatery opened to universal acclaim in 2012. It's a class act all around – from the ever-changing menu of market-fresh seafood scrawled daily on the blackboard to the interior's sleek modern lines to the gorgeous presentation of the food. The stellar wine list features some local choices you won't find elsewhere.

Il Gallo e l'Innamorata   SICILIAN €€

(☑ 092 3195 4446; www.osteriailgalloelinnamorata.com; Via Bilardello 18; meals €25-30; ☺ closed Tue) Warm orange walls and arched stone doorways lend an artsy, convivial atmosphere to this Slow Food–acclaimed eatery. The à la carte menu is short and sweet, featuring a few well-chosen dishes each day, including the classic *scaloppine al Marsala* (veal cooked with Marsala wine and lemon).

ℹ️ Information

Tourist office (☑092 399 33 38, 092 371 40 97; ufficioturistico.proloco@comune.marsala.tp.it; Via XI Maggio 100; ⊗8.30am-1.30pm & 3-8pm Mon-Sat) Spacious office with comfy couches right off the main square; provides a wide range of maps and brochures.

ℹ️ Getting There & Away

From Marsala, bus operators include **Lumia** (www.autolineelumia.it) to Agrigento (€9.90, 2½ hours, one to three daily); and **Salemi** (☑092 398 11 20; www.autoservizisalemi.it) to Palermo (€9.20, 2½ hours, at least nine daily).

The train is the best way to get to Trapani (€3.45, 30 minutes, 10 daily, five on Sunday).

Selinunte

The ruins of Selinunte are the most impressively sited in Sicily. The huge city was built in 628 BC on a promontory overlooking the sea, and over two and a half centuries became one of the richest and most powerful in the world. It was destroyed by the Carthaginians in 409 BC and finally fell to the Romans in about 350 BC, at which time it went into rapid decline and disappeared from historical accounts.

The city's past is so remote that the names of the various temples have been forgotten and they are now identified by the letters A to G, M and O. The most impressive, **Temple E**, has been partially rebuilt, its columns pieced together from their fragments with part of its tympanum. Many of the carvings, particularly from **Temple C**, are now in the archaeological museum in Palermo. Their quality is on a par with the Parthenon marbles and clearly demonstrates the high cultural levels reached by many Greek colonies in Sicily.

The ticket office and entrance to the **ruins** (☑092 44 62 51; www.selinunte.net; adult €6, EU citizen 18-25yr €3, under 18yr or over 65yr free; ⊗9am-6pm summer, 9am-4pm winter) is located near the eastern temples. Try to visit in spring when the surroundings are ablaze with wildflowers.

For overnight stays, **Sicilia Cuore Mio** (☑092 44 60 77; www.siciliacuoremio.it; Via della Cittadella 44; d €68-95; 🌐📶) is a lovely B&B with an upstairs terrace overlooking both the ruins and the sea. Guests enjoy breakfast (including homemade jams, *cannoli*, and more) on a shady patio bordered by olive trees. Escape the touristy and mediocre res-taurants near the ruins by heading for **Lido Zabbara** (☑092 44 61 94; Via Pigafetta; buffet per person €12), a beachfront place in nearby Marinella di Selinunte with good grilled fish and a varied buffet, or drive 15km east to **Da Vittorio** (☑092 57 83 81; www.ristorante vittorio. it; meals €28-45) in Porto Palo, another great place to enjoy seafood, sunset and the sound of lapping waves.

Selinunte is midway between Agrigento and Trapani, about 10km south of the junction of the A29 and SS115 near Castelvetrano. **Autoservizi Salemi** (☑092 48 18 26; www.autoservizisalemi.it) runs five to seven buses daily from Selinunte to Castelvetrano (€2, 25 to 35 minutes), where you can make onward bus connections to Agrigento (€8.30, two hours), or train connections to Marsala (€3.95, 35 to 55 minutes), Trapani (€5.75, 1¼ hours) and Palermo (€7.65, 2½ hours).

Trapani

POP 70,600

The lively port city of Trapani makes a convenient base for exploring Sicily's western tip. Its historic centre is filled with atmospheric pedestrian streets and some lovely churches and baroque buildings, although the heavily developed outskirts are rather bleak. The surrounding countryside is beautiful, ranging from the watery vastness of the coastal salt ponds to the rugged mountainous shoreline north of town.

Once situated at the heart of a powerful trading network that stretched from Carthage to Venice, Trapani's sickle-shaped spit of land hugs the precious harbour, nowadays busy with a steady stream of tourists and traffic to and from Tunisia, Pantelleria and the Egadi Islands.

⊙ Sights

The narrow network of streets in Trapani's historic centre remains a Moorish labyrinth, although it takes much of its character from the fabulous 18th-century baroque of the Spanish period – a catalogue of examples can be found down the pedestrianised **Via Garibaldi**. The best time to walk down here is in the early evening (around 7pm) when the *passeggiata* is in full swing.

Trapani's other main street is Corso Vittorio Emanuele, punctuated by the huge **Cattedrale di San Lorenzo** (Corso Vittorio Emanuele; ⊗8am-4pm), with its baroque facade and stuccoed interior. Facing off the

Trapani

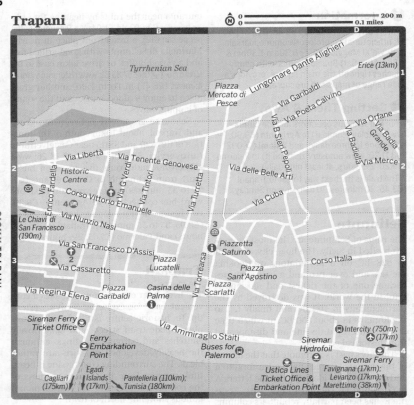

SICILY TRAPANI

east end of the corso is another baroque confection, the **Palazzo Senatorio** (cnr Corso Vittorio Emanuele & Via Torrearsa).

Chiesa del Purgatorio   CHURCH
(☎092 356 28 82; Via San Francesco d'Assisi; voluntary donation requested; ☺7.30am-noon & 4-7pm Mon-Sat, 10am-noon & 4-7pm Sun) Just off the corso in the heart of the city, this church houses the impressive 18th-century *Misteri*, 20 life-sized wooden effigies depicting the story of Christ's Passion, which take centre stage during the city's dramatic Easter Week processions. Explanatory panels in English, Italian, French and German help visitors to understand the story behind each figure.

Museo Nazionale Pepoli   MUSEUM
(☎092 355 32 69; Via Conte Pepoli 200; adult €6, EU citizen under 18yr or over 65yr free, EU citizen 18-25yr €3; ☺9am-1.30pm & 2.30-7.30pm Tue-Sat, 9am-12.30pm Sun; tours hourly 9am-noon & 2.30-6.30pm) In a former Carmelite monastery,

this museum houses the collection of Conte Pepoli, who devoted his life to salvaging Trapani's local arts and crafts, most notably the garish coral carvings – once all the rage in Europe before Trapani's offshore coral banks were decimated. The museum also has a good collection of Gagini sculptures, silverwork, archaeological artefacts and religious art. It's 12km east of town.

Egadi Islands   ISLANDS
The islands of Levanzo, Favignana and Marettimo make a pleasant day trip from Trapani. For centuries the lucrative tuna industry formed the basis of the islands' economy, but overfishing of the surrounding waters means that the Egadi survives primarily on income from tourists who come to cycle, dive or simply enjoy the relaxed pace of life.

The best range of meals and accommodation can be found on **Favignana**, while the islands' single greatest tourist attraction is **Grotta del Genovese** (☎339 741

Trapani

88 00, 092 392 40 32; www.grottadelgenovese.it; guided cave tour €10, incl transport one way/round trip €16/22.50; ⏲tours 10.30am daily, extra tour 2.30pm or 3pm Jul & Aug) on **Levanzo**, a cave decorated with Mesolithic and Neolithic art work, including a famous image of a prehistoric tuna. To really get away from it all, head to **Marettimo**, whose main attractions are the lovely whitewashed port and the surrounding network of walking trails. **Siremar** (✆092 354 54 55; www.siremar.it; Via Ammiraglio Staiti) and **Ustica Lines** (✆092 387 38 13; www.usticalines.it; Via Ammiraglio Staiti) run year-round hydrofoil services to the islands from Trapani and Marsala.

🎉 Festivals & Events

I Misteri   RELIGIOUS
(www.processionemisteritp.it) Sicily's most venerated Easter procession is a four-day festival of extraordinary religious fervour. Nightly processions, bearing life-sized wooden effigies, make their way through the old quarter to a specially erected chapel in Piazza Lucatelli. The high point is on Good Friday when the celebrations reach fever pitch.

Couscous Fest   FOOD
(www.couscousfest.it) In San Vito Lo Capo, 40km north of Trapani, this late-September festival celebrates Sicilian multiculturalism with world music concerts and international couscous cook offs.

🛏 Sleeping

The most convenient – and nicest – place to stay is in Trapani's pedestrianised historic centre, just north of the port.

Ai Lumi B&B   B&B €
(✆092 354 09 22; www.ailumi.it; Corso Vittorio Emanuele 71; s €40-70, d €70-100, tr €90-125, q €100-150; ❋🛜) Housed in an 18th-century *palazzo,* this centrally located B&B offers 13 rooms of varying size. Best are the spacious apartments (numbers 33, 34 and 35), with kitchenettes and balconies overlooking Trapani's most elegant pedestrian street. Upstairs apartment 23 is also lovely, with a private balcony reached by a spiral staircase. Guests get discounts at the hotel's atmospheric restaurant next door.

Le Chiavi di San Francesco   HOTEL €
(✆092 343 80 13; www.lechiavidisanfrancesco. com; Via Tartaglia 18; d €80-110, ste €140; ❋🛜) Opposite the Chiesa di San Francesco, this popular hotel has 16 rooms featuring cheerful colour schemes and small but clean bathrooms. Angle for one of the superior rooms up front, which offer more space, better light and optional kitchen facilities.

✖ Eating

Sicily's Arab heritage and Trapani's unique position on the sea route to Tunisia have made couscous ('*cuscus*' or '*kuscus*' as they sometimes spell it around here) a local speciality.

La Rinascente   PASTRIES & CAKES €
(✆092 32 37 67; Via Gatti 3; cannoli €1.80; ⏲9am-1pm & 3-7pm, closed Sun afternoon & Wed) When you enter this bakery through the side door, you'll feel like you've barged into someone's kitchen – and you have! Thankfully, owner Giovanni Costadura's broad smile will quickly put you at ease, coupled with some of the best *cannoli* on the planet, which you can watch being created on the spot.

★ Al Solito Posto   SICILIAN €€
(✆092 32 45 45; www.trattoria-alsolitoposto.com; Via Orlandini 30; meals €20-35; ⏲closed Sun & 15-31 Aug) A 15-minute walk east of the centre, this wildly popular trattoria is a well-deserved wearer of the Slow Food badge. From superb *primi* (try the trademark *busiate con pesto alla trapanese*) to super-fresh seafood *secondi* (don't miss the local tuna in May and June) to the creamy-crunchy homemade *cannoli*, everything is top-notch.

★ Osteria La Bettolaccia   SICILIAN €€
(✆092 32 16 95; www.labettolaccia.it; Via Enrico Fardella 25; meals €30-45; ⏲closed Sat & Sun lunch all year, plus Sun dinner Nov-Easter) An unwaveringly authentic, Slow Food favourite, this centrally located eatery just two blocks from the ferry terminal is the perfect place to try *cous cous con zuppa di mare* (couscous with mixed seafood in a spicy fish sauce, with tomatoes, garlic and parsley). In response to its great popularity, the dining

PANTELLERIA

Halfway between Trapani and Tunisia, this volcanic outcrop is Sicily's largest offshore island. Buffeted year-round by winds, Pantelleria is characterised by jagged lava stone, low-slung caper bushes, dwarf vines, steaming fumaroles and mudbaths. There are no true beaches, but Pantelleria's gorgeous, secluded coves – including **Cala Tramontana**, **Cala Levante** and **Balata dei Turchi** – are perfect for snorkelling, diving and boat excursions.

The island has excellent hiking trails, along the coast and in the high vineyard country of **Piana di Ghirlanda**. Near **Mursia** on the west coast, there are signposted but poorly maintained remnants of *sesi* (Bronze Age funerary monuments). Throughout the island you'll also find Pantelleria's famous *dammusi* (houses with thick, whitewashed walls and shallow cupolas). The island's exotic and remote atmosphere has long made it popular with celebrities, including Truman Capote, Sting, Madonna and Giorgio Armani.

Darwin (p828) offers regular flights to Pantelleria from Palermo and Trapani, and **Siremar** (www.siremar.it) runs one ferry daily to/from Trapani (€34, six hours).

For further information about Pantelleria see www.pantelleria.com.

room was expanded in 2013, but it's still wise to book ahead.

ℹ Information

The city centre has several banks with ATMs.

Ospedale Sant'Antonio Abate (☏ 092 380 91 11; Via Cosenza 82)

Police station (☏ 092 359 81 11; Piazza Vittoria Veneto)

Tourist office (☏ 092 354 45 33; point@ stradadelvinoericedoc.it; Piazzetta Saturno; ⊕ 9am-1pm & 4-7pm Mon-Sat) Trapani's tourist office offers city maps, bike sightseeing tours, bike rental (€8 per day), tour guides and information about wineries along the Strada del Vino Erice DOC. The subsidiary Casina delle Palme (Piazza Garibaldi; ⊕ 9am-1pm & 4-7pm Mon-Sat) branch is opposite the ferry terminal in Piazza Garibaldi.

ℹ Getting There & Around

For bus, plane and ferry tickets, try **Egatours** (☏ 092 32 17 54; www.egatourviaggi.it; Via Ammiraglio Staiti 13), a travel agency located opposite the port.

AIR

Trapani's small **Vincenzo Florio Airport** (TPS; Birgi Airport; www.airgest.it) is 17km south of town at Birgi. **Ryanair** (www.ryanair.com) offers direct flights to London Luton and a dozen other European cities; **Air One** (flyairone.com) serves cities on the Italian mainland, while **Darwin** (www.darwinairline.com) goes to the Mediterranean island of Pantelleria. AST buses connect the airport with downtown Trapani (€4.70, 45 minutes, hourly) and Marsala (€2.50, 45 minutes, four daily).

BOAT

Ferry ticket offices are inside Trapani's ferry terminal, opposite Piazza Garibaldi.

For Ustica Lines and Siremar hydrofoils, the ticket office and embarkation point is 150m further east along Via Ammiraglio Staiti.

Grimaldi Lines (www.grimaldi-ferries.com) runs weekly services to Tunisia (deck/cabin from €60/85, 8½ hours) and Civitavecchia (€120, 14½ hours).

Tirrenia (www.tirrenia.it) runs a weekly service to Cagliari (deck/cabin from €40/160, 12 hours).

Ustica Lines (p827) and Siremar (p827) both operate hydrofoils year-round to the Egadi Islands. Ustica Lines also offers summer-only Saturday morning services to Ustica (€28, 2½ hours) and Naples (€94, seven hours), while Siremar and **Traghetti delle Isole** (www. traghettidelleisole.it) offer nightly ferry service to Pantelleria (€34, six hours).

BUS

Intercity buses arrive and depart from the terminal 1km east of the centre (just southeast of the train station).

Segesta (☏ 092 32 84 04; www.segesta.it) runs express buses to Palermo (€9, two hours, hourly). Board at the bus stop across the street from Egatours or at the bus station.

Lumia (☏ 092 32 17 54; www.autolineelumia. it) buses serve Agrigento (€11.80, 2¾ to 3½ hours, one to three daily).

Two free city buses (No 1 and 2) operated by **ATM** (☏ 092 355 95 75; www.atmtrapani.it) do circular trips through Trapani, connecting the bus station, the train station and the port.

CAR & MOTORCYCLE

To bypass Trapani's vast suburbs and avoid the narrow streets of the city centre, follow signs from the A29 autostrada directly to the port, where you'll find abundant paid parking along the broad waterside avenue Via Ammiraglio Staiti, within walking distance of most attractions.

TRAIN

From Trapani's station on Piazza Umberto I, there are rail links to Palermo (€8, 2¼ to 3½ hours, three to four direct trains daily) and Marsala (€3.45, 30 minutes, 10 Monday to Saturday, four on Sunday).

Erice

POP 28,800 / ELEV 751M

One of Italy's most spectacular hill towns, Erice combines medieval charm with astounding 360-degree views. Erice sits on the legendary Mt Eryx (750m); on a clear day, you can see Cape Bon in Tunisia. Wander the medieval tangle of streets interspersed with churches, forts and tiny cobbled piazzas. The town has a seductive history as a centre for the cult of Venus. Settled by the mysterious Elymians, Erice was an obvious abode for the goddess of love, and the town followed the peculiar ritual of sacred prostitution, with the prostitutes themselves accommodated in the Temple of Venus. Despite countless invasions, the temple remained intact – no guesses why.

Erice's tourist infrastructure is excellent. Posted throughout town, you'll find bilingual (Italian–English) informational displays along with town maps displaying suggested walking routes.

◎ Sights

The best views can be had from **Giardino del Balio**, which overlooks the turrets and wooded hillsides south to Trapani's salt-pans, the Egadi Islands and the sea. Looking north, there are equally staggering views of San Vito Lo Capo's rugged headlands.

Castello di Venere   CASTLE
(www.comune.erice.tp.it/minisitocastello; Via Castello di Venere; adult €3, 8-14yr or over 65yr €1.50, child under 8yr free; ☉10am-6pm daily Apr-Oct, 10am-4pm Sat & holidays Nov-Mar) Erice's Norman castle was built in the 12th and 13th centuries over the Temple of Venus, which had long been a site of worship for the ancient Elymians. The views from up top, extending to San Vito Lo Capo on one side and the Saline di Trapani on the other, are spectacular.

SICILY ERICE

WORTH A TRIP

SICILY'S OLDEST NATURE RESERVE

Saved from development and road projects by local protests, the tranquil **Riserva Naturale dello Zingaro** (☎092 43 51 08; www.riservazingaro.it; adult €3, child 8-14yr €2, under 8yr or over 65yr free; ☉7am-7.30pm Apr-Sep, 8am-4pm Oct-Mar) is the star attraction on the Golfo di Castellammare, halfway between Palermo and Trapani. Founded in 1981, this was Sicily's first nature reserve. Zingaro's wild coastline is a haven for the rare Bonelli's eagle along with 40 other species of bird. Mediterranean flora dusts the hillsides with wild carob and bright yellow euphorbia, and hidden coves, such as Capreria and Marinella Bays, provide tranquil swimming spots. The main entrance to the park is 2km north of the village of Scopello. Several walking trails are detailed on maps available free at the entrance or downloadable from the park website. The main 7km trail along the coast passes by the visitor centre and five museums documenting everything from local flora and fauna to traditional fishing methods.

Once home to tuna fishers, Scopello now mainly hosts tourists, although outside of peak summer season it retains some of its sleepy village atmosphere. Its port, 1km below town, has a picturesque beach backed by a rust-red *tonnara* (tuna-processing plant) and dramatic *faraglioni* (rock towers) rising from the water.

★ **Pensione Tranchina** (☎092 454 10 99; www.pensionetranchina.com; Via Diaz 7; B&B per person €36-46, half-board per person €55-72; ❉☎) is the nicest of several places to stay and eat clustered around the cobblestoned courtyard at Scopello's village centre. Friendly hosts Marisin and Salvatore offer comfortable rooms, a roaring fire on chilly evenings and delicious home-cooked meals featuring local fish and home-grown fruit and olive oil.

Erice Monuments Circuit CHURCH
(admission €5; ⊙ 10am-6pm Apr-Jun & Oct, 10am-8pm Jul & Aug, 10am-7pm Sep, 10am-12.30pm Nov-Feb, 10am-4pm Mar) A single ticket grants admission to Erice's five major ecclesiastical attractions: the 14th-century cathedral's treasury and 28m-high campanile (climb to the top for great views), San Martino's wood sculptures, San Giuliano's Gruppa Misteri (Good Friday group sculptures) and San Giovanni's marble sculptures. Buy your ticket at any of the churches.

🛏 Sleeping & Eating

Hotels, many with their own restaurants, are scattered along Via Vittorio Emanuele, Erice's main street. After the tourists have left, the town assumes a beguiling medieval air.

Erice has a tradition of *dolci ericini* (Erice sweets) made by the local nuns. There are numerous pastry shops in town, the most famous being Maria Grammatico (☑ 092 386 93 90; www.mariagrammatico.it; Via Vittorio Emanuele 14; ⊙ 9am-10pm May, Jun & Sep, to 1am Jul & Aug, to 7pm Oct-Apr), revered for its *frutta martorana* (marzipan fruit) and almond pastries.

Hotel Elimo HOTEL €€
(☑ 092 386 93 77; www.hotelelimo.it; Via Vittorio Emanuele 23; s €80-110, d €90-130, ste €150-170; [P][@][🛜]) Communal spaces at this atmospheric historic house are filled with tiled beams, marble fireplaces, intriguing art, knick-knacks and antiques. The bedrooms are more mainstream, although many (along with the hotel terrace and restaurant) have breathtaking vistas south and west towards the Saline di Trapani, the Egadi Islands, and the shimmering sea.

❶ Information

The main **tourist office** (☑ 092 350 23 22; strerice@regione.sicilia.it; Porta Trapani; ⊙ 10.30am-1.30pm & 3.30-5.30pm Tue-Sat, 10.30am-1.30pm Sun, 2.30-5.30pm Mon) is adjacent to Porta Trapani (Erice's Old Town gate); there's a subsidiary branch in the **town centre** (☑ 092 386 93 88; strerice@regione.

sicilia.it; Via Tommaso Guarrasi 1; ⊙ 10.30am-1.30pm Tue-Sun).

❶ Getting There & Away

Regular AST buses run to and from Trapani (€2.80, 45 minutes). Connecting Erice and Trapani there is a **funicular** (Funivia; ☑ 092 356 93 06; www.funiviaerice.it; one way/return €5.50/9; ⊙ 1-8pm Mon, 8.10am-8pm Tue-Fri, 10am-10pm Sat, 10am-8pm Sun) situated opposite the car park at the foot of Erice's Via Vittorio Emanuele. This drops you in Trapani near the corner of Via Manzoni and Via Capua and you'll need to catch AST bus 21 or 23 (€1) westbound to get to the centre of Trapani.

Segesta

ELEV 304M
Set on the edge of a deep canyon in the midst of wild, desolate mountains, the 5th-century BC ruins of Segesta (☑ 092 495 23 56; adult €6, EU citizen 18-25yr €3, EU citizen under 18yr or over 65yr free; ⊙ 9am-4pm Oct-Mar, 9am-6pm Apr-Sep) are a magical site. On windy days the 36 giant columns of its magnificent temple are said to act like an organ, producing mysterious notes.

The city, founded by the ancient Elymians, was in constant conflict with Selinunte in the south, whose destruction it sought with dogged determination and singular success. Time, however, has done to Segesta what violence inflicted on Selinunte; little remains now, save the theatre and the never-completed Doric temple, the latter dating from around 430 BC and remarkably well preserved. A shuttle bus (€1.50) runs every 30 minutes from the temple entrance 1.5km uphill to the theatre.

Tarantola (☑ 092 43 10 20; www.tarantolabus.com) runs three buses daily from Trapani (one way/return €3.80/6.20, 35 to 50 minutes), plus two daily buses from Via Balsamo near Palermo's train station (one way/return €6.70/10.70, 1¼ hours). Alternatively, catch a train from Trapani (€3.45, 30 minutes, one or two daily) to Segesta Tempio station, turn left under the double underpass, then climb 1.5km (20 minutes) to the site.

Sardinia

Best Places to Eat

➡ St Remy (p839)

➡ La Botteghina (p855)

➡ Osteria del Mare (p861)

➡ Agriturismo Saltara (p864)

Best Places to Stay

➡ Agriturismo Guthiddai (p867)

➡ Casa Solotti (p866)

➡ Lemon House (p871)

➡ Il Cagliarese (p838)

➡ B&B Lu Pastruccialeddu (p863)

Why Go?

As DH Lawrence so succinctly put it: 'Sardinia is different.' Indeed, where else but on this 365-village, four-million-sheep island could you travel from shimmering bays to alpine forests, granite peaks to cathedral-like grottoes, rolling vineyards to one-time bandit towns – all in the space of a day? Sardinia baffles with prehistory at 7000 *nuraghic* sites, dazzles with its kaleidoscopic blue waters and whets appetites with island treats like spit-roasted suckling pig, sea urchins and crumbly pecorino.

Over millennia islanders have carved out a unique identity, cuisine, culture and language, leaving the forces of nature to work their magic on the landscape. And whether you're swooning over the megayachts in the Costa Smeralda's fjord-like bays or feasting on spit-roasted suckling pig at a rustic *agriturismo* (farm stay accommodation), you can't help but appreciate this island's love of the good life. Earthy and glamorous, adventurous and blissfully relaxed, Sardinia delights in being that little bit different.

When to Go
Cagliari

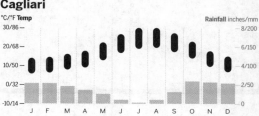

Feb Pre-Lenten shenanigans, from beastly *mamuthones* in Mamoiada to medieval jousting at Sa Sartiglia.

Mar–May Spring wildflowers, Easter parades, and hiking and climbing without the heat and crowds.

Jun–Aug Sunkissed beaches, open-air festivals and reckless horse races at the S'Ardia.

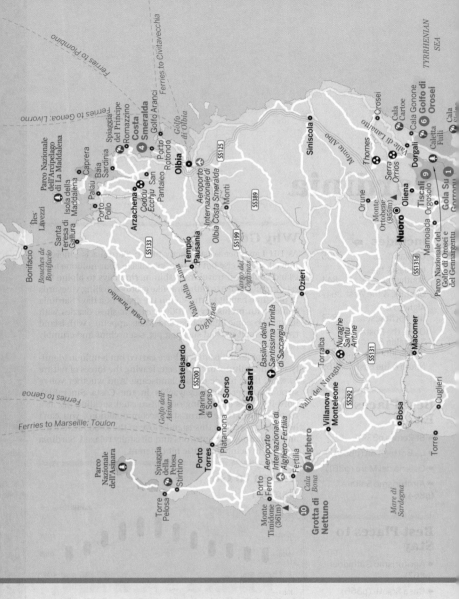

Sardinia Highlights

1 Walking on the wild side in the spectacular **Gola Su Gorropu** (p869).

2 Feeling the lure of the sea on the windswept beaches of the **Costa Verde** (p847).

3 Wandering the medieval backstreets of **Il Castello** (p835), Cagliari's rocky citadel.

4 Rubbing bronzed shoulders with the rich and super-famous on the **Costa Smeralda** (p862).

5 Boning up on prehistory at **Nuraghe Su Nuraxi** (p850), Sardinia's sole World Heritage Site.

6 Dropping anchor in the brilliant aquamarine waters of the **Golfo di Orosei** (p870).

MEDITERRANEAN SEA

OGLIASTRA

Ferries to Civitavecchia; Genoa

Cala Mariolu
Cala Goloritzè
Altoliano del Golgo
Santa Maria Navarrese
Aeroporto Nazionale di Tortoli
Tortoli
Arbatax
Ferries to Civitavecchia; Naples
Ferries to Palermo

Urzulei
Baunei
SS125
SS125
SS389
Monte del Gennargentu
Foresta di Montes
Santa Maria Navarrese

Tonara
Sorgono

Sadali
Isili
Serri
Santuario Santa Vittoria di Serri

Tertenia
SS125
Salto di Quirra
Flumendosa
Gerrei

Villaputzu
Capo Ferrato
Spiaggia Piscina Rei
Spiaggia Costa Rei

Monte dei Sette Fratelli (1023m)
Sarrabus
Cala Sinzias
Golfo di Carbonara
Villasimius
SS125

Stagno Notteri
Ferries to Trapani

MEDITERRANEAN SEA

Barumini
Nuraghe Su Nuraxi Mandas
La Marmilla
Tuili
La Giara di Gesturi
SS197
SS131
Monastir

Poetto
Golfo degli Angeli
Cagliari
Aeroporto Internazionale Cagliari-Elmas
Golfo di Cagliari
SS130
Mannu

Capoterra
Pula
Nora
Chia

Santa Caterina di Pittinuri
Monti Perru
Abbasanta
Lago Omodeo
Riola
S'Archittu
Sinis Peninsula
Santa Cristina
Santa
Sardo
Putzu Idu
Is Arenas
Isola di Mal di Ventre
Is Aruttas
San Salvatore
San Giovanni di Sinis
Tharros
Cabras
Oristano
Santa Giusta
Marina di Torre Grande
Golfo di Oristano
Terralba
Tirso

Montevecchio
Guspini
Arbus
Ingurtosu
Capo Pecora
Portixeddu
Buggerru
Grotta di Su Mannau
Fluminimaggiore
Tempio di Antas
Domusnovas
Iglesias
SS126
Carbonia

Torre dei Corsari
Spiaggia Piscinas
Spiaggia Scivu
Costa Verde

Cala Domestica
Masua
Nebida
Nebida
Funtanamare
Portoscuso
Portovesme
Carloforte
Isola di San Pietro
Calasetta
Sant'Antioco
Isola Sant'Antioco
Golfo di Gonnesa
Golfo di Palmas

Le Grotte Is Zuddas
Teulada
Porto Teulada
Capo Malfatano
Costa del Sud
Tuerredda
SS195

MEDITERRANEAN SEA

7 Soaking up the Spanish vibe of **Alghero** (p853), roaming its cobbled alleyways.

8 Taking a drive along the serpentine **SS125** for captivating views of the mountains and the Med (p869).

9 Marvelling at the mysterious *nuraghic* ruins of **Tiscali** (p870), high in the Supramonte.

10 Exploring stalactites and stalagmites at the fairy-tale **Grotta di Nettuno** (p856).

0   15 miles
0   30 km
N

History

Little is known about Sardinia's prehistory, but the first islanders probably arrived from mainland Italy around 350,000 BC. By the neolithic period (8000 BC to 3000 BC) tribal communities were thriving in north-central Sardinia. Their Bronze Age descendants, known as the *nuraghic* people, dominated the island until the Phoenicians arrived around 850 BC. The Carthaginians came next, followed by the Romans, who took over in the 3rd century BC.

In the Middle Ages, the island was divided into four independent *giudicati* (kingdoms) but by the 13th century the Pisans and Genoese were battling for control. They in turn were toppled by the Catalan-Aragonese from northern Spain, who also had to subdue bitter Sard resistance led by Eleonora d'Arborea (1340–1404), Sardinia's very own Joan of Arc.

Sardinia became Spanish territory after the unification of the Spanish kingdoms in 1479 and today there remains a tangible Hispanic feel to towns such as Alghero and Iglesias. In the ensuing centuries, Sardinia suffered as Spain's power crumbled; in 1720 the Italian Savoys took possession of the island. After Italian unity in 1861, Sardinia found itself under the boot of Rome.

In the aftermath of WWII, efforts were made to drag the island into the modern era. In 1946 a huge project was launched to rid the island of malaria and in 1948 Sardinia was granted its own autonomous regional parliament.

Coastal tourism arrived in the 1960s and has since become a mainstay of the Sardinian economy. Environmentalists breathed a sigh of relief in 2008 when NATO withdrew from the Maddalena islands after a 35-year sojourn.

ⓘ Getting There & Away

AIR

Flights from Italian and European cities serve **Elmas** (☑ 070 21 12 11; www.cagliariairport. it) airport in Cagliari; Alghero's **Fertilia** (☑ 079 93 52 82; www.aeroportodialghero.it); and the **Aeroporto Olbia Costa Smeralda** (☑ 0789 56 34 44; www.geasar.it) in Olbia. As well as major international carriers, several no-frills airlines operate direct flights, including **Ryanair** (www. ryanair.com), **easyJet** (www.easyjet.com) and **TUIfly** (www.tuifly.com). Some routes are restricted to between April and October. From Sardinia's Olbia airport, **Meridiana** (www.meridiana.it) now flies to London Gatwick and easyJet

flies to London Luton. **Thomsonfly** (www. thomsonfly.com) now also connects Alghero to London Gatwick.

BOAT

Sardinia is accessible by ferry from Genoa, Livorno, Piombino, Civitavecchia and Naples, and from Palermo and Trapani in Sicily. Ferries also run from Bonifacio and Porto Vecchio in Corsica, and from Marseilles via the Corsican ports of Ajaccio and Propriano. The arrival points in Sardinia are Olbia, Golfo Aranci, Santa Teresa di Gallura and Porto Torres in the north; Arbatax on the east coast; and Cagliari in the south. Services are most frequent from mid-June to mid-September, when it is advisable to book well ahead. Useful online resources include www.traghettiweb.it and www.traghettionline.com.

FERRY OPERATORS

CMN La Méridionale (☑ France 0810 20 13 20; www.cmn.fr) To Porto Torres from Marseille via Corsica.

Corsica Ferries, Sardinia Ferries (☑ 0825 09 50 95; www.corsica-ferries.co.uk) To Golfo Aranci from Civitavecchia and Livorno. Also Sardinia to Corsica (April to September).

Grandi Navi Veloci (☑ 010 209 45 91; www.gnv.it) To Olbia and Porto Torres from Genoa.

Moby Lines (☑ 199 303040; www.moby.it) To Olbia from Civitavecchia, Genoa, Livorno and Piombino; to Porto Torres from Genoa. Also has ferries between Sardinia and Corsica (April to September).

Saremar (☑ 199 118877; www.saremar.it) Runs seasonal ferry services between Santa Teresa Gallura (Sardinia) and Bonifacio.

SNCM (☑ 079 51 44 77; www.sncmitalia.it) To Porto Torres from Marseille via Corsica. In July and August some services depart from Toulon.

Tirrenia (☑ 892123; www.tirrenia.it) To Cagliari from Civitavecchia, Naples, Palermo and Trapani; to Olbia from Civitavecchia and Genoa; to Arbatax from Civitavecchia and Genoa; to Porto Torres from Genoa.

ⓘ Getting Around

BUS

Sardinia's main bus company, **ARST** (☑ 800 86 50 42; www.arst.sardegna.it), runs most local and long-distance services.

CAR & MOTORCYCLE

Sardinia is best explored by road. There are rental agencies in Cagliari as well as in airports and major towns.

TRAIN

Trenitalia (☑ 892 021; www.trenitalia.com) services link Cagliari with Oristano, Sassari, Porto

Torres, Olbia and Golfo Aranci. Services are slow but generally reliable. Slow **ARST** (☏ 070 34 31 12; http://arst.sardegna.it) trains serve Sassari, Alghero and Nuoro. Between mid-June and early September, ARST also operates a tourist train service known as the Trenino Verde (p843).

CAGLIARI

POP 149,343

Forget flying: the best way to arrive in Cagliari is by sea to witness the city rising in a jumble of golden-hued *palazzi* (mansions), domes and facades up to the rocky centrepiece, Il Castello. Cultured and cosmopolitan, Cagliari is Sardinia's most Italian-flavoured city. Vespas buzz down tree-fringed boulevards and locals relax at cafes tucked under the graceful arcades by the seafront. Swing east and you reach Poetto beach, the hub of summer life with its limpid waters and upbeat party scene.

At every turn, Cagliari's gripping history is spelled out, especially through archaeological sites, museums and churches. The city was founded by the Phoenicians in the 8th century BC, but came of age as a Roman port. Later, the Pisans arrived and treated it to a major medieval facelift, the results of which impress to this day.

⊙ Sights

Cagliari's trophy sights cluster in the Castello, Stampace, Marina and Villanova districts.

★ Il Castello   HISTORIC QUARTER

Precipitous stone walls enclose Cagliari's medieval citadel, known to locals as Su Casteddu, once the fortified home of the city's aristocracy and religious authorities. Inside the battlements, the old medieval city unfolds like origami. The university, cathedral, museums, honey-coloured Pisan palaces and towers are wedged into a jigsaw of narrow high-walled alleys.

Museo Archeologico Nazionale   MUSEUM

(www.archeocaor.beniculturali.it; Piazza dell' Arsenale; adult/reduced €3/1.50; ⊙9am-8pm Tue-Sun) The star of the Citadella dei Musei's four museums, this archaeological museum showcases artefacts spanning millennia of ancient history, including pint-sized *nuraghic bronzetti* (bronze figurines). In the absence of any written records, these are a vital source of information on Sardinia's mysterious *nuraghic* culture.

> ℹ️ **MUSEUM-FREE MONDAYS**
> The vast majority of Cagliari's museums close on Mondays – a point worth bearing in mind when you are devising your sightseeing itinerary.

Cattedrale di Santa Maria   CATHEDRAL

(www.duomodicagliari.it; Piazza Palazzo 4; ⊙7.30am-8pm Mon-Sat, 8am-1pm & 4.30-8.30pm Sun) **FREE** Cagliari's graceful cathedral stands proud on Piazza Palazzo. Apart from the square-based bell tower, little remains of the original 13th-century Gothic structure – the interior is 17th-century baroque and the Pisan-Romanesque facade is a 20th-century imitation. Inside are two intricate stone pulpits, sculpted by Guglielmo da Pisa and donated to the city in 1312.

Torre dell'Elefante   TOWER

(www.camuweb.it; Via Università; adult/reduced €4/2.50; ⊙10.30am-7pm Tue-Sun summer, 9am-5pm winter) One of only two Pisan towers still standing, the Torre dell'Elefante is named after the sculpted elephant by the vicious-looking portcullis. The 42m-high tower became something of a horror show, thanks to its foul decor: the Spaniards beheaded the Marchese di Cea here and left her severed head lying around for 17 years! Climb to the top for far-reaching city views.

Anfiteatro Romano   ROMAN SITE

(www.anfiteatroromano.it; Viale Sant'Ignazio; ⊙closed for restoration) This amphitheatre is Cagliari's must-see Roman monument. Although much of the original 2nd-century theatre was cannibalised for building material, enough has survived to pique the imagination. The amphitheatre was closed for restoration at the time of writing, but it's still worth taking a look from the outside.

Torre di San Pancrazio   TOWER

(Piazza Indipendenza; adult/reduced €4/2.50; ⊙10.30am-7pm Tue-Sun summer, 9am-5pm winter) Over by the citadel's northeastern gate, this 36m-high tower is the Torre dell'Elefante's twin. Completed in 1305, it is built on the city's highest point and has grandstand views of the Golfo di Cagliari.

Bastione San Remy   LOOKOUT

The monumental stairway that ascends from busy Piazza Costituzione to Bastione San Remy is the most impressive way to reach Il Castello; save your legs by

Cagliari

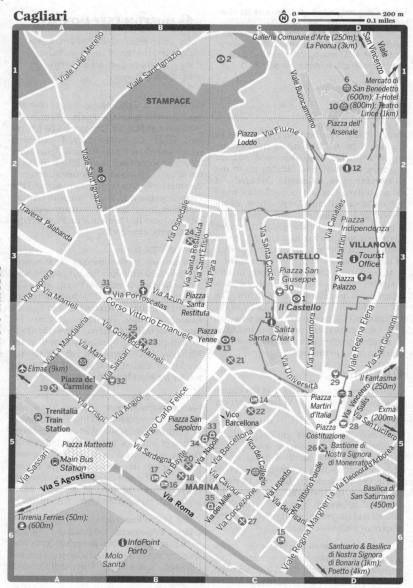

taking the panoramic elevator. A mix of neoclassical and Liberty styles, the lookout affords sweeping views over Cagliari's higgledy-piggledy rooftops to the glittering Mediterranean.

Pinacoteca Nazionale ART GALLERY (www.pinacoteca.cagliari.beniculturali.it; Piazza dell' Arsenale; adult/reduced €3/1.50; ⏰9am-8pm Tue-Sun) **FREE** Above and behind the archaeological museum, this gallery contains a prized collection of 15th- to 17th-century

Cagliari

art, including four outstanding works by Pietro Cavaro, father of the so-called Stampace school and arguably Sardinia's most important artist.

Orto Botanico GARDEN
(Viale Sant'Ignazio da Laconi 11; adult/reduced €4/2; ⊙8.30am-6pm Mon-Sat) Slightly downhill from the amphitheatre is one of Italy's most famous botanical gardens, bristling with palm trees, cacti, ficus trees and local carobs and oaks. Ancient ruins tastefully litter the gardens.

Galleria Comunale d'Arte ART GALLERY
(www.galleriacomunalecagliari.it; Viale San Vincenzo 2; adult/reduced €6/2.60; ⊙10am-8pm Wed-Mon, garden 6am-11pm summer, 7am-8pm winter) Housed in a neoclassical villa north of Il Castello, this gallery zooms in on modern Sardinian art, including works by island artists such as Tarquinio Sini (1891–1943). There are terrific views of Cagliari's skyline from the palm-dotted **garden** outside.

Chiesa di San Michele CHURCH
(Via Ospedale 2; ⊙8am-11am & 6-9pm Mon-Sat, 8am-noon & 7-9pm Sun) This 16th-century church is celebrated for its lavish 18th-century rococo decor. In the atrium note the four-columned pulpit from which the Spanish emperor Carlos V is said to have delivered a stirring speech before setting off on a fruitless campaign against Arab corsairs in Tunisia.

Basilica di San Saturnino CHURCH
(Piazza San Cosimo; ⊙9am-1pm Tue-Sat) A five-minute walk east of Piazza Contituzione, this 5th-century basilica is one of Sardinia's oldest churches and a striking example of palaeo-Christian architecture. It stands over a Roman necropolis where Saturninus, a much-revered local martyr, was buried in AD 304.

**Santuario & Basilica di
Nostra Signora di Bonaria** CHURCH, LOOKOUT
(www.bonaria.eu; Piazza Bonaria 2; donations welcome; ⊙6.30am-noon & 4.30pm-7.30pm) Around 1km southeast of Via Roma, and crowning the Bonaria hill, is this hugely popular pilgrim site. Devotees come from all over the world to pray to *Nostra Signora di Bonaria,* a statue of the Virgin Mary that is said to have saved a 14th-century Spanish ship during a storm. To the right of the sanctuary, the much larger basilica still acts as a landmark for returning sailors.

SAND IN THE CITY

An easy ride on buses PF or PQ from Piazza Matteotti, Cagliari's fabulous **Poetto** beach extends for 6km beyond the green Promontorio di Sant'Elia, nicknamed the **Sella del Diavola** (Devil's Saddle). In summer much of the city's youth decamps here to sunbathe and party in the restaurants, bars and discos that line the sand.

Water sports are big and you can hire canoes at the beach clubs. From its base at Marina Piccola, the **Windsurfing Club Cagliari** (☑ 070 37 26 94; www.windsurfingclub-cagliari.org; Viale Marina Piccola) offers a range of courses. A course of six one-hour windsurfing lessons costs €160, while three hours of surfing/stand-up paddling instruction will set you back €60.

Piazza Yenne
PIAZZA

Crowned with a statue of King Carlo Felice, this square is a favourite local hang-out, especially on summer nights when its bars, gelaterie and pavement cafes buzz with young Cagliaritani.

Museo d'Arte Siamese
ART GALLERY

(www.museicivicicagliari.it; Piazza dell'Arsenale; adult/reduced €2/1; ⊙ 10am-8pm Tue-Sun, to 6pm winter) Showcases an eclectic collection of Asian art, crafts and weaponry.

Museo del Tesoro e Area Archeologica di Sant'Eulalia
MUSEUM

(Vico del Collegio 2; adult/reduced €5/3.50; ⊙ 10am-1pm & 4-7pm Tue-Sun) Contains a rich collection of religious art, as well as an archaeological area, which extends for up to 200 sq metres beneath the adjacent **Chiesa di Sant'Eulalia**.

Exmà
ART GALLERY

(www.camuweb.it; Via San Lucifero 71; adult/reduced €3/2; ⊙ 9am-1pm & 4-8pm Tue-Sun) Occupying Cagliari's former abattoir, this cultural centre stages contemporary art exhibitions and summer concerts.

👉 Tours

City Tour Cagliari
BUS TOUR

(adult/reduced €10/8; ⊙ 9.30am-7.30pm) This open-topped bus does an hour's loop of the key landmarks and sights, with multilingual commentary available. Departures are hourly from Piazza Yenne.

✨ Festivals & Events

Cagliari puts on a good show for Carnevale in February and Easter Holy Week, when a procession of hooded participants climbs up to the cathedral in Il Castello.

Festa di Sant'Efisio
RELIGIOUS

Held between 1 and 4 May, on the opening day the saint's effigy is paraded around the city on a bullock-drawn carriage amid extravagantly costumed crowds.

🛏 Sleeping

★ Il Cagliarese
B&B €

(☑ 339 654 40 83; www.ilcagliarese.it; Via Vittorio Porcile 19; s €45-70, d €60-90; ❇ 🛜) This wonderfully snug and homey B&B sits in the heart of the Marina district, with nautical-inspired rooms dressed in cool blues and whites. Mauro runs the place with a passion, giving invaluable sightseeing tips and rustling up legendary breakfasts, with local *salumi* and cheeses, fresh fruit and homemade cakes.

La Peonia
B&B €

(☑ 070 51 31 64; www.lapeonia.com; Via Riva Villasanta 77; s €50-65, d €72-90; ❇ 🛜) Antonello and Vanna are your kindly hosts at this romantic neoclassical abode, 3km northeast of town. Turn-of-the-century interiors, decorated with polished wood furnishings, antiques and family heirlooms, contrast strikingly with the sleek monochrome bathrooms. Bus M stops in front of the B&B.

Hostel Marina
HOSTEL €

(☑ 070 67 08 18; www.hostelmarinacagliari.it; Scalette S Sepolcro; dm/s/d/q €22/40/60/100; ❇ 🛜) Housed in a beautifully converted 16th-century monastery, this hostel has oodles of historic charm. Many of the well-kept dorms have great city views and rates include a very basic breakfast.

Marina di Castello
B&B €

(☑ 070 28 90 477; www.bedandbreakfastcagliaricity.it; Via Roma 75a; d €80-110; ❇ 🛜) Sabrina makes you feel instantly at ease at this cheery B&B, housed in a *palazzo* (mansion) on Cagliari's main boulevard. The rooms are tastefully done out in silvers, bronzes and golds, with exposed brickwork, art and detailed fabrics lending a boutiquey touch. The roof terrace overlooking the marina is a relaxed spot for an afternoon coffee or sundowner.

La Ghirlanda
B&B €

(☏ 070 20 40 610; www.laghirlandacagliari.it; Via Baylle 7; s €48-60, d €75-95, tr €100-120; ❄ 🕸) Antiques, frescoes and high-ceilinged rooms whisk you back to the 18th century at this handsome town house in the Marina district.

T Hotel
HOTEL €€

(☏ 070 4 74 00; www.thotel.it; Via dei Giudicati 66; s €114-134, d €134-209, ste €249; P ❄ 🕸 🖳) This hard-to-miss steel and glass tower adds a dash of contemporary design to the cityscape. The rooms reveal a linear, modish look, and the spa invites relaxation with its hydrotherapy pool, jets and treatments. It's a 15-minute walk northeast of Il Castello. Or hop on bus M to Via Bacaredda, 200m from the hotel.

✖ Eating

Dining hot spots include the Marina area, Via Sassari and Corso Vittorio Emanuele. From November to March (mollusc season), *chioschi* (kiosks) serve sea-fresh sea urchins and mussels on Poetto beach.

Il Fantasma
PIZZERIA €

(☏ 070 65 67 49; Via San Domenico 94; pizzas €3-10; ⊙ Mon-Sat) A five-minute walk east of Piazza Martiri d'Italia, this boisterous pizzeria does the best pizza in Cagliari. Friendly waiters adroitly navigate the crowded barrel-vaulted interior to deliver bubbling pizzas straight from the wood-fired oven. Book or expect to queue.

Trattoria Gennargentu
SARDINIAN €

(☏ 070 65 82 47; Via Sardegna 60; meals €20-25; ⊙ closed Sun winter) Tables fill quickly at this no-frills trattoria that dishes up excellent seafood. Try spaghetti with clams and *bottarga* (mullet roe) or *tonno alla carlofortina* (tuna chunks served cold in a sweet tomato and onion sauce).

★ St Remy
SARDINIAN €€

(☏ 070 65 73 77; www.stremy.it; Via Torino 16; meals €25-35; ⊙ 1-3pm & 7-10.30pm Mon-Fri, 7-10.30pm Sat) Tucked away on a sidestreet, St Remy keeps the mood intimate in a vaulted, lime-washed space with stone arches. The menu puts a creative spin on Sardinian flavours, with homemade pasta preluding mains like John Dory in a white wine and black olive sauce – all cooked to a T and presented with panache.

Per Bacco
SARDINIAN €€

(☏ 070 65 16 67; www.enoperbacco.it; Via Santa Restituta 72; meals €25-35; ⊙ 8.30-11pm Mon-Sat) Hidden in the alleys of Stampace is this friendly, low-key find, with stone walls and cheek-by-jowl tables. The chef, Sabrina, allows ingredients to shine in simple, season-focused dishes. You might begin with antipasti such as Cabras *bottarga* with artichokes, followed by *primi* including *lorighittas ai ricci* (ring-shaped Sardinian pasta with sea urchins) and *secondi* such as saffron-infused sea bream.

SARDINIA CAGLIARI

DON'T MISS

FAVOURITE SNACK SPOTS

Le Patate & Co (Scalette Santo Sepulcro 1; fries €2.50; ⊙ 11.30am-3pm & 6pm-midnight, closed Thu evening) Antonio knocks up the freshest fries in town – cooked in olive oil until crisp, and not overly salty.

Isola del Gelato (Piazza Yenne 35; ice creams €1.50-4; ⊙ 7am-2am Wed-Mon) A hugely popular hang-out with ice-creamy treats including semifreddo and sorbet.

Gocce di Gelato e Cioccolato (Piazza del Carmine 21; ice creams & desserts €2-5; ⊙ noon-10pm winter, to 1am summer) Totally divine handmade gelati, desserts (try the mille feuille), spice-infused pralines and truffles.

Locanda Caddeo (Via Sassari 75; snacks €2.50-7; ⊙ daily) A cool, gallery-style haunt for focaccia, pizza and freshly prepared salads.

I Sapori dell'Isola (Via Sardegna 50; ⊙ 9.30am-9pm) Friendly deli with top-notch Sardinian bread, pastries, salami, cheese, *bottarga* (mullet roe), olive oil, wine and more.

Antica Cagliari   SARDINIAN €€
(☑ 070 73 40 198; www.anticacagliari.it; Via Sardegna 49; meals €25-40; ☻ Wed-Mon) A cut above most places in the Marina district, this beamed restaurant always has a good buzz. Go for Sardinian dishes like *fregola* (semolina pasta) with shellfish or whatever fish is fresh that day. Reserve ahead to snag one of the few tables on the pavement terrace.

Ristorante Ammentos   SARDINIAN €€
(☑ 070 65 10 75; Via Sassari 120; meals €20-30; ☻ Wed-Mon) Dine on authentic Sardinian fare in rustic surroundings at this popular trattoria. *Culurgiones* (ravioli) in herby tomato sauce are a delicious lead-in to succulent meat dishes such as wild boar or goat stew.

Drinking & Nightlife

On warm nights, Piazza Yenne becomes one huge beer garden. It's a lively gathering spot to kick-start an evening.

Antico Caffè   CAFE
(www.anticocaffe1855.it; Piazza Costituzione 10; ☻ 7am-2am) DH Lawrence and Grazia Deledda once frequented this grand old cafe, which opened in 1855. Join locals to chat over leisurely coffees and frilly crêpes.

Inu   WINE BAR
(Via Sassari 50; ☻ 7pm-1am Mon-Sat) Become versed in Sardinian wine at this contemporary, high-ceilinged *enoteca*, which pairs throaty Cannonau reds and tangy Vermentino whites with top-quality tasting plates of local *salumi* and cheese.

Caffè Librarium Nostrum   BAR
(Via Santa Croce 33; ☻ 7.30am-2am Tue-Sun) This modish Castello bar has panoramic seating on top of the city's medieval ramparts and occasional live music in the brick-lined interior.

Caffè degli Spiriti   BAR
(Bastione San Remy; ☻ 10am-3am) This slick lounge bar perched on the Bastione moves to a mellow groove and commands phenomenal views of the skyline, making it a prime spot for sunset imbibing.

Il Merlo Parlante   PUB
(Via Portoscalas 69; ☻ Tue-Sun) Shoehorned into a narrow alley off Corso Vittorio Emanuele, this popular student pub serves lager and rock to a young international crowd.

Emerson   CLUB
(www.emersoncafe.it; Viale Poetto 4) Near the fourth bus stop at Poetto beach, this swanky seafront place is part cocktail lounge, part restaurant and part beach club. It's a chilled spot for a sundowner and occasionally hosts live music.

☆ Entertainment

Cagliari's nightlife revolves around the city's bars and cafes, which in summer means the beach at Poetto. For the lowdown, ask at the tourist office or pick up a copy of the local newspaper *L'Unione Sarda*. Online, you'll find listings at www.sardegnaconcerti.com (in Italian).

Teatro Lirico   THEATRE
(☑ 070 408 22 30; www.teatroliricodicagliari.it; Via Sant'Alenixedda) This is Cagliari's premier venue for classical music, opera and ballet. It's a 15-minute stroll east of Il Castello.

🛍 Shopping

For boutiques and designer labels, head to Via Roma and boutique-studded Via Giuseppe Garibaldi. The Marina district harbours some enticing craft and speciality shops.

★ Durke   CONFECTIONERY
(Via Napoli 66; ☻ 10.30am-1.30pm & 4.30-8pm Mon-Sat) This is an Aladdin's cave of Sardinian sweets and pastries, all prepared according to traditional recipes. Some of the best are made with nothing more than sugar, egg whites and almonds.

Sapori di Sardegna   FOOD
(Vico dei Mille 1; ☻ 9.30am-9pm) Browse this breezy Marina emporium for fine *pecorino* (sheep's milk cheese), salami, *bottarga*, bread, wine and pretty-packed *dolci* (sweets).

Loredana Mandas   JEWELLERY
(Via Sicilia 31; ☻ 9.30am-1pm & 4.30pm-8pm Mon-Sat) A jewellery workshop selling the fine gold filigree for which Sardinia is famous.

Mercato di San Benedetto   MARKET
(Via San Francesco Cocco Ortu; ☻ 7am-2pm Mon-Sat) Seafood, salami, *pecorino* the size of wagon wheels, horse steaks, you name it – it's all at this morning food market in Villanova, a 10- to 15-minute walk east of Il Castello.

ℹ Information

Cagliari is dotted with free wi-fi zones, but annoyingly you can only log on if you have an Italian SIM card (the password is sent to your mobile phone).

Banks and ATMs are widely available, particularly around the port and station, and on Piazza del Carmine and Corso Vittorio Emanuele.

Guardia Medica (☑ 070 52 24 58; Via Talete) For an emergency call-out doctor.

Lamarù (Via Napoli 43; per hr €3; ☺ 8.30am-9pm Mon-Sat) Speedy internet and wi-fi.

Main Post Office (Piazza del Carmine 27; ⊙ 8am-6.50pm Mon-Fri, 8am-1.15pm Sat)

Tourist Office (☑ 070 409 23 06; Palazzo Viceregio, Piazza Palazzo; ⊙ 10am-7pm) This tourist office should be your first port of call for the lowdown on Cagliari and the surrounding province.

InfoPoint Porto (☑ 338 649 84 98; www.cagliariturismo.it; Molo Sanità, Stazione Marittima; ⊙ 8am-3pm Mon-Fri) At the port, this kiosk is handy for city info and maps.

ⓘ Getting There & Away

AIR

Cagliari's **Elmas airport** (☑ 070 21 12 11; www.cagliariairport.it) is 9km northwest of the centre. Flights connect with mainland Italy and European destinations including Barcelona, London, Paris and Stuttgart. In summer there are additional charter flights.

BOAT

Cagliari's ferry port is just off Via Roma. **Tirrenia** (☑ 892 123; www.tirrenia.it; Via dei Ponente 1) is the main operator, with year-round services to Civitavecchia, Naples, Palermo and Trapani. Book tickets at the port or at travel agencies.

BUS

From the main bus station on Piazza Matteotti, **Turmo Travel** (☑ 0789 2 14 87; www.gruppoturmotravel.com) runs a twice-daily service to Olbia (€19, 4¼ hours) and a daily bus to Santa Teresa di Gallura (€22.50, 5½ hours). ARST (p834) buses serve the following destinations.

TO	FARE (€)	DURATION (HR)	FREQUENCY
Chia	4	1¼	10 daily
Iglesias	4.50	1-1½	2 daily
Nuoro	15.50	2½-5	2 daily
Oristano	7	1½	2 daily
Pula	3	¾	hourly
Sassari	14.50	3¼	3 daily
Villasimius	3.50	1½	6-8 daily

CAR & MOTORCYCLE

The island's main dual-carriage road, the SS131 Carlo Felice Hwy, links the capital with Porto Torres via Oristano and Sassari, and Olbia via Nuoro. The SS130 leads west to Iglesias.

TRAIN

The main Trenitalia (p834) station is on Piazza Matteotti. Trains serve the following destinations.

TO	FARE (€)	DURATION (HR)	FREQUENCY
Carbonia	4.50	1	7 daily
Golfo Aranci	18	5-7	5 daily
Iglesias	3.85	1	16 daily
Olbia	17	4	5 daily
Oristano	6	1-2	15 daily
Porto Torres	17	4¼	1 daily
Sassari	15.75	3¾	5 daily

ⓘ Getting Around

TO/FROM THE AIRPORT

Buses run from Piazza Matteotti to Elmas airport (€4, 10 minutes, 32 daily) from 5.20am to 10.30pm. Between 9am and 10.30pm, departures are every hour and half past the hour. A taxi costs about €25.

BUS

CTM (☑ 070 209 12 10; www.ctmcagliari.it) bus routes cover the city and surrounding area. A standard ticket costs €1.20 and is valid for 90 minutes; a daily ticket is €3.

CAR & MOTORCYCLE

On-street parking within the blue lines costs €1 per hour. Alternatively, there's a useful car park next to the train station, which costs €10 for 24 hours. **CIA Rent a Car** (☑ 070 65 65 03; www.rentcagliari.com; Via S Agostino 13) hires out bikes, cars and scooters from €10/29/30 daily.

TAXI

There are taxi ranks at Piazza Matteotti, Piazza della Repubblica and on Largo Carlo Felice. Or call **Quattro Mori** (☑ 070 400 101) or **Rossoblù** (☑ 070 66 55).

AROUND CAGLIARI

Stretching east and north of Cagliari, the lonely Sarrabus is one of Sardinia's least developed areas. From its central wild hinterland rise the bushy green peaks of the Monte dei Sette Fratelli.

East of Poetto the SP17 hugs the coast prettily (if precariously) all the way round to Villasimius and then north along the Costa Rei.

A few kilometres short of Villasimius, a road veers south to **Capo Carbonara**, Sardinia's most southeasterly point. On the

SARDINIA CAGLIARI

western side of the peninsula is a marina and what remains of a Spanish tower, the **Fortezza Vecchia**. To the south is lovely **Spiaggia del Riso**. The eastern side is dominated by the **Stagno Notteri** lagoon, often host to flamingos in winter. On its seaward side is the stunning **Spiaggia del Simius** beach with its Polynesian-blue waters.

Villasimius

A cheerful summertime resort, Villasimius is a launch pad for exploring the gorgeous sandy bays that necklace the coast. At the Porto Turistico, about 3km outside of town, you can arrange boat tours (about €65 per person) and dives (from €36) to nearby reefs and wrecks.

From May to September, campers converge on **Spiaggia del Riso** (☑ 070 79 10 52; www.villaggiospiaggiadelriso.it; Via Degli Aranci 2; camping 2 people, car & tent €21-42, 4-bed bungalows €80-160; ☢) near the Porto Turistico. It has excellent facilities but gets hellishly crowded in summer.

Set in pristine gardens, the attractive, low-slung **Hotel Mariposas** (☑ 070 79 00 84; www.hotelmariposas.it; Viale Matteotti; s €72-136, d €92-186, f €112-206; ℙ✳🛜🔁☢) is just a five-minute stroll from the beach.

Dine alfresco on Sardinian classics like *burrida* (marinated dogfish) and spaghetti with *ricci* at **Ristorante Le Anforè** (☑ 070 79 20 32; www.hotelleanfore.com; Via Pallaresus 16; meals €30; ☺ dinner Tue-Sun).

ARST buses run to and from Cagliari (€3.50, 1½ hours, six to eight daily) throughout the year.

Costa Rei

From Villasimius, the SP17 skirts the coast north to the Costa Rei. About 25km out of Villasimius you hit **Cala Sinzias**, a pretty sandy strand with two campgrounds. Continue for a further 6km and you come to the Costa Rei resort, a holiday village full of villas, shops, bars, clubs and a few indifferent eateries. **Spiaggia Costa Rei** is a dazzling-white beach lapped by remarkably clear blue-green water.

By the resort's southern entrance and open from May to October, pine-shaded **Camping Capo Ferrato** (☑ 070 99 10 12; www.campingcapoferrato.it; Via Cilea 98 ; camping 2 peo-

FERRIES TO SARDINIA

Prices quoted here are approximate adult high-season single fares for a 2nd-class *poltrona* (reclinable seat) and small car, excluding supplements. Children aged four to 12 generally pay around half price; those under four go free. Most companies offer discounts for early booking and online deals – it's always worth checking.

FROM	DESTINATION	FARE (€)	CAR (€)	DURATION (HR)
Bonifacio	Santa Teresa di Gallura	22	32	1
Civitavecchia	Arbatax	49	104	10½
Civitavecchia	Cagliari	58	120	14½
Civitavecchia	Olbia	32	80	4½-10
Civitavecchia	Golfo Aranci	78	100	5½
Genoa	Arbatax	96	157	19
Genoa	Olbia	80	85	11
Genoa	Porto Torres*	68	116	10
Livorno	Golfo Aranci*	83-117	21-90	6
Livorno	Olbia	45	65	8
Marseille	Porto Torres	93	121	15-17
Naples	Cagliari	47	108	16¼
Palermo	Cagliari	70	82	14½
Piombino	Olbia	40	46	5
Trapani	Cagliari	75	87	11

* indicates a high-speed service

TRENINO VERDE

If you're not in a rush, take a slow, nostalgic ride through Sardinia's rugged interior on the narrow-gauge **Trenino Verde** (☑ 070 58 02 46; www.treninoverde.com). There are four routes: Mandas–Arbatax (5¼ hours, one-way/return €20/28), Mandas–Isili–Sorgono (3½ hours, one-way/return €15.50/21.50), Macomer–Bosa (two hours, one-way/return €11.50/16.50) and Sassari–Tempo–Palau (4¼ hours, one-way/return €20/28). Of these, the twisting Mandas–Arbatax line is particularly spectacular, crossing the remote highlands of the Parco Nazionale del Golfo di Orosei e del Gennargentu.

From the metro station on Piazza Repubblica in Cagliari, a metro runs to Monserrato where you can connect with trains for Mandas. The Trenino Verde runs between mid-June and early September.

ple, car & tent €16-37.50; ⊙ Apr-Oct) has direct access to the beach.

North of the resort, **Spiaggia Piscina Rei** continues the theme of blinding-white sand and turquoise water. A couple more beaches fill the remaining length of coast up to **Capo Ferrato**, beyond which drivable dirt trails lead north.

Nora & Around

About 30km southwest of Cagliari, the archaeological zone of **Nora** (adult/reduced €5.50/4; ⊙ 9am-8pm summer, to 5.30pm winter) is what's left of a once-powerful ancient city. Founded by Phoenicians in the 11th century BC, it passed into Carthaginian hands before being taken over by the Romans and becoming one of the most important cities on the island. Upon entry, you pass a single melancholy **column** from a former temple and then a small but beautifully preserved Roman **theatre**. To the west are the substantial remains of the **Terme al Mare** (Baths by the Sea). Four columns stand at the heart of what was a patrician villa; the surrounding rooms retain their mosaic floor decoration.

In nearby **Pula**, the one-room **Museo Archeologico** (Corso Vittorio Emanuele 67; adult/reduced €2.50/2, incl Nora €7.50/4.50; ⊙ 9am-8pm Tue-Sun summer, to 5.30pm winter) displays finds from Nora, including ceramics found in Punic and Roman tombs, some gold and bone jewellery, and Roman glassware. At the time of writing, the museum was closed for restoration.

Accommodation tends to be expensive in these parts, but you can still find some affordable, locally run places. Close to the river in the heart of town, the **Marin Hotel** (☑ 070 920 80 59; www.marinhotel.it; Viale Segni 58; s €65-90, d €80-150, tr €120-180, q €140-220;

P ❋ ❈ ☏) has light, generously sized rooms, with warm Mediterranean colour schemes and either balconies or patios.

Fiore is your sweet, helpful host at **B&B Fiore** (☑ 070 924 60 10; www.bedandbreakfast-fiore.it; SS195 km31; d €60-100; **P ❋ ❈**), which sits serenely amid fruit, palm and citrus trees, 2km south of town. The bright rooms open onto verandas and you can laze in the garden hammock or walk to the pale-sand beach of Porto d'Agumu, 800m away.

For further information about Pula and the surrounding area, ask the helpful staff at the **tourist office** (☑ 347 237 78 42; Piazza del Popolo; ⊙ 9.30am-12.30am & 4.30-7.30pm Mon-Sat) just off the town's main hub, Piazza del Popolo.

From Pula, the SS195 follows the coast round to **Chia** and the stunning Costa del Sud. But unless you're staying at one of the self-contained resort hotels that hog this stretch of coast, you're unlikely to glimpse much sea.

Regular buses connect Pula and Cagliari (€3, 45 minutes). From Pula there are frequent shuttle buses down to Nora (€1.20), 4km away.

Costa del Sud & Around

One of the most beautiful stretches of coast in southern Sardinia, the Costa del Sud runs 25km from **Chia** to **Porto Teulada**. Popular with windsurfers and kitesurfers, Chia's two ravishing beaches are golden strips of sand divided by a Pisan watchtower, while 3km away there's a magnificent strip of sand at **Tueredda**. As you wind your way towards the high point of **Capo Malfatano** there are wonderful views around every corner.

Budget accommodation is available in two campgrounds at either end of the

SARDINIA NORA & AROUND

coastal run – this is a fantastic area for camping. At Chia, there's **Campeggio Torre Chia** (☑070 923 00 54; www.campeggio-torrechia.it; camping 2 people, car & tent €36), a busy spot a few hundred metres back from the beach, while 25km to the west, **Portu Tramatzu Camping Comunale** (☑070 928 30 27; camping 2 people, car & tent €29) has modest facilities and an on-site diving centre near Porto Teulada.

Some 20km inland, **Le Grotte Is Zuddas** (www.grotteiszuddas.com; Loc Is Zuddas, Santadi; adult/reduced €10/7; ☉10am-noon & 3-5.30pm) is a spectacular cave system, with 500m of chambers taking you into a fantasy forest of stalagmites and stalactites.

From Cagliari, there are buses to and from Chia (€4, 1¼ hours, 10 daily). Between mid-June and mid-September, two daily buses ply the Costa del Sud.

IGLESIAS & THE SOUTHWEST

Iglesias

POP 27,552

Surrounded by the skeletons of Sardinia's once-thriving mining industry, Iglesias bubbles in the summer and slumbers in the colder months. Its historical centre, an appealing ensemble of lived-in piazzas, sun-bleached buildings and Aragonese-style wrought-iron balconies, creates an atmosphere that is as much Iberian as Sardinian – a vestige of its history as a Spanish colony. Visit at Easter to experience a quasi-Seville experience during the extraordinary drum-beating processions.

The Romans called the town Metalla after the precious metals mined here, especially lead and silver. Mining equipment dating back to the Carthaginian era was discovered in the 19th century.

◉ Sights

Centro Storico   HISTORIC QUARTER

Iglesias' central square, **Piazza Quintino Sella** was laid out in the 19th century in what was at the time a field outside the city walls. Just off the square, scruffy stairs lead up to a stout tower which is all that remains of **Castello Salvaterra**, a Pisan fortress built in the 13th century. A stretch of the

northwestern perimeter wall survives along Via Campidano.

Dominating the eastern flank of Piazza del Municipio in the heart of the *centro storico* (historic centre), the **Duomo** (Piazza del Municipio) is still closed for renovation, but retains a lovely Pisan-flavoured facade, as does the bell tower, with its chequer-board stonework.

Museo dell'Arte Mineraria   MUSEUM

(www.museoarteminineraria.it; Via Roma 47; adult/reduced €4/2; ☉6.30-8.30pm Sat-Sun summer, by appointment rest of year) Bone up on Iglesias' mining history at this former mining school. You can experience the harsh conditions in which miners worked in a series of recreated mine shafts.

🛏 Sleeping & Eating

B&B Mare Monti Miniere   B&B €

(☑078 14 17 65; www.maremontiminiere-bb.it; Via Trento 10; s €35, d €50-60, tr €80; ❄ 🛜 🐾) Outshining most budget picks in town, this home-style B&B is a cracking find. Rooms are cheery and immaculately kept, with above-par touches such as DVD players and bathrobes, and breakfast is a good spread of all-Sardinian produce. Whether you want to borrow a bike or use the kitchen, just ask the friendly family that runs the place.

La Babbajola B&B   B&B €

(☑347 614 46 21; www.lababbajola.it; Via Giordano 13; s €27-30, d €50-60; 🐾) This laid-back, homey B&B is in a gorgeous old mansion, inside the *centro storico,* run by the friendly Carla and her mother. Accommodation is in a mini-apartment or one of three big double rooms, each of which features patterned old floor tiles, bold colours and tasteful furniture. There's a kitchen and TV room for guest use. Two of the three double rooms share a bathroom.

Gazebo Medioevale   SARDINIAN €€

(☑078 13 08 71; Via Musio 21; meals €20-30; ☉Mon-Sat) Unassuming on the face of things, with its simple decor and long stone-and-brick arches, Gazebo Medievale rolls out fresh, authentic, attractively presented Sardinian fare. Dishes such as *trofie* pasta with tuna and pesto and couscous with seafood hit the mark every time.

ℹ Getting There & Away

Buses for Cagliari (€4.50, 1 to 1½ hours, two daily) arrive at and depart from Via XX Settembre. Get tickets from **Bar Giardini** (Via Oristano 8) across the park. From the train station on Via Garibaldi, a 15-minute walk from the town centre, there are up to 10 daily trains to Cagliari (€3.85, one hour, 16 daily).

Around Iglesias

A winding 15km drive north of Iglesias (follow signs for Fluminimaggiore) brings you to the sand-coloured **Tempio di Antas** (adult/reduced €3/2; ⊘ 9.30am-7.30pm summer, to 4.30pm Tue-Sun winter), an impressive Roman temple set in bucolic scenery. The 3rd-century temple was built by the Roman emperor Caracalla over a 6th-century-BC Punic sanctuary, which itself stood over an earlier *nuraghic* settlement. From near the ticket office a path marked *Antica Strada Romana, Antas Su Mannau* leads to what little remains of this settlement. Walk another 1½ hours along the path to the **Grotta de Su Mannau** (www.sumannau.it; adult/reduced €10/8; ⊘ 9.30am-6.30pm summer, to 5.30pm winter), an 8km-long cave complex with incredible rock formations.

About 10km east of Iglesias, the unremarkable town of **Domusnovas** sits at the centre of one of Sardinia's most exciting rock-climbing areas. The outlying countryside is peppered with limestone rocks, cliffs and caves, many of which are ideal for sports climbing. For technical information, check out www.climb-europe.com and www.sardiniaclimb.com.

Four kilometres north of town, the 850m-long **Grotta di San Giovanni** is an impressive sight. Eight daily buses connect Iglesias and Domusnovas (€1.50, 15 minutes).

Iglesiente Coast

Iglesias' local beach is at **Funtanamare** (also spelt Fontanamare), about 8km west of town. From Funtanamare, the SP83 coastal road affords spectacular views as it dips, bends and climbs its way northward. Dominating the seascape off **Nebida**, 5.5km to the north, is the 133m-high **Scoglio Pan di Zucchero** (Sugarloaf Rock), the largest of several *faraglioni* (sea stacks) that rise out of the glassy blue waters. A small and rather drab village, Nebida is a former mining settlement sprawled along the road high above the sea. Near its southern entrance, **Pan di Zucchero** (☑ 0781 4 71 14; www.hotelpandizucchero.it; Via Centrale 365; s/d/tr €50/70/94; half-board per person €70) is a family-run *pensione* with neat, modestly furnished rooms and a panoramic restaurant (meals €30 to €35).

A few kilometres north, **Masua** is another former mining centre. Seen from above, it looks pretty ugly, but it's not without interest. The main draw is the town's unique mining port, **Porto Flavia** (☑ 0781 491 300; adult/reduced €8/4.50; ⊘ by appointment). In 1924 two 600m tunnels were dug into the cliffs. In the lower of the two, a conveyor belt received zinc and lead ore from the underground deposits and transported it via an ingenious mobile loading arm directly to the ships moored below.

Local buses run between Iglesias and Masua, stopping off at Nebida (€2, 30 minutes, 10 daily).

Beyond Masua, and signposted off the SP83, **Cala Domestica** is a cool sandy beach wedged into a natural inlet. **Buggerru**, the biggest village on this stretch of coastline, is another former mining settlement.

The road out of Buggerru climbs high along the cliffs for a couple of kilometres before descending down to **Spiaggia Portixeddu**, one of the area's best beaches. At its southern tip, you can dine on pizza and fresh fish at **Ristorante San Nicolò** (☑ 0781 543 59; pizzas/meals €7/30; ⊘ 7.30-10pm).

Accommodation in the area is limited, but the **Hotel Golfo del Leone** (☑ 0781 5 49 52; www.golfodelleone.it; Loc Portixeddu; s/d/tr/q €58/90/120/142) boasts sunny, seafacing rooms about 1km back from the beach. Service is friendly and the helpful staff can organise horse-riding excursions. The adjacent restaurant serves up decent local food for about €25 to €30 per head.

Inland, there are several *agriturismi*, including **Biologico Fighezia** (☑ 348 069 83 03; www.agriturismofighezia.it; half-board per person €55-60, B&B in winter per person €35-40). Set in tranquil countryside, it offers lush views and cabin-style rooms decorated with terracotta tiles, solid wooden fixtures and private terraces. Dinner is served on a large communal table on the terrace of the main house.

Carbonia & Around

POP 28.676

You won't miss much if you bypass **Carbonia**, a drab town built by Mussolini to house workers from the nearby Sirai-Serbariu coalfield. However, in the vicinity there are a couple of sights worth a detour. The **Museo del Car-**

bone (www.museodelcarbone.it; adult/reduced €6/4; ⊙10am-7pm daily summer, 10am-5pm Tue-Sun winter) offers a chastening look into the life of Carbonia's miners, with an interesting collection of machines, photos and equipment, and guided tours into the claustrophobic mine shafts.

Sant'Antioco & San Pietro

POP 18,230

These islands off Sardinia's southwestern coast display very different characters. Both are popular summer destinations but Isola Sant'Antioco, the larger and more developed of the two, is less obviously picturesque, with a rocky Sardinian landscape and a gritty working port. Barely half an hour across the water, the pastel houses and bobbing fishing boats of Isola di San Pietro are much more what you'd expect of a holiday island.

⊙ Sights & Activities

The main sights are in Sant'Antioco. Up in the high part of town, the Basilica di Sant'Antioco Martire (Piazza Parrocchia 22; ⊙9am-12pm & 3-6pm Mon-Sat, 10.30-11.15am & 3-6pm Sun) is a sublimely simple 5th-century church set over an extensive system of creepy catacombs (guided tours €3; ⊙9am-noon & 3-6pm).

On the outskirts of town, the excellent Museo Archeologico (www.archeotur.it; admission €6/3.50; ⊙9am-7pm) contains a fascinating collection of local archaeological finds.

For beaches head to Maladroixa and Spiaggia Coa Quaddus on the eastern coast.

Over on Isola San Pietro the main activity is wandering the streets of laid-back Carloforte, the main town. On the seafront, several outfits offer boat tours for about €30 per person. From late May to early June, Carloforte's big annual event, the four-day Girotonno (www.girotonno.org) festival, is dedicated to the island's traditional tuna kill, known locally as the *mattanza*.

🛏 Sleeping

Hotel California HOTEL €
(☎0781 85 44 70; www.hotelcaliforniacarloforte. com; Via Cavallera 15, Carloforte; s €50-60, d €70-100; ❋) It ain't on a dark desert highway, but this Hotel California is still a lovely (if modest) place, where you can expect a super-friendly family welcome and spacious, sun-filled rooms. It's in a residential street a few blocks back from the *lungomare* (seafront promenade).

Hotel Moderno HOTEL €
(☎0781 8 31 05; www.hotel-moderno-sant-antioco. it; Via Nazionale 82; s €55-60, d €92-100, tr €122-132, q €132-142; ❋ 🛜 🛗) A bright, welcoming hotel on the main road into Sant'Antioco. Rooms are agreeable with a relaxing cream-and-salmon colour scheme and big, comfy beds. Downstairs, the airy restaurant (open

---

TOP FIVE OUTDOOR ACTIVITIES

➡ **Hiking** Head to the magnificent Parco Nazionale del Golfo di Orosei e del Gennargentu (p867) for exhilarating coastal and mountain trekking.

➡ **Climbing** The Supramonte (p867), Golfo di Orosei (p870), Ogliastra (p871) and Domusnovas are rock-climbing wonderlands. For the lowdown on routes, pick up *Arrampicare a Cala Gonone* (€18) by expert climber Corrado Conca in local bookshops, or visit http://klimbingkorns.de/climbing-in-sardinia-updates-2012 for details of guided climbing excursions. Maurizio Oviglia's *Pietra di Luna* guide is an excellent introduction to climbing in Sardinia, covering 3600 single-pitch sport routes.

➡ **Cycling** Ogliastra offers highly scenic road cycling and jaw-dropping downhill routes on old mule trails. At the Lemon House (p871) Peter gives invaluable tips or visit www. mountainbikeogliastra.it (in Italian).

➡ **Diving** Sardinia's gin-clear waters are a diver's dream. Check out the Med's largest underwater grotto, Nereo Cave near Alghero, or the depths of the Parco Nazionale dell'Arcipelago di La Maddalena (p864).

➡ **Windsurfing** Winds course through the Bonifacio Strait between Sardinia and Corsica, making Porto Pollo a top venue. Chia (p843) is another favourite spot.

April to October) serves a good line in local fish.

✕ Eating

Tuna is king of San Pietro cuisine and features on almost all island menus (May to August only).

Rubiu   MICROBREWERY, PIZZERIA €
(www.rubiubirra.it; Viale Trento 22, Sant'Antioco; pizza €6.50-11; ⊙7pm-1am Wed-Mon) This upbeat, contemporary microbrewery has an easy-going vibe and a terrific selection of home-brewed beers and ales. It also whips up tasty salads, antipasti and pizzas (choose from a basil or saffron base), such as Cabras with mozzarella, fresh tomatoes and *bottarga di muggine* (mullet roe).

Osteria della Tonnara   OSTERIA €€
(☑0781 85 57 34; Corso Battellieri 36; meals €35; ⊙Jun-Sep) Run by Isola San Pietro's tuna co-operative, this is the place to try *tonno alla carlofortina*. Bookings are recommended and credit cards are not accepted.

❶ Information

Proloco Carloforte (☑0781 85 40 09; www. prolococarloforte.it; Corso Tagliafico 2; ⊙10am-1pm & 5-8pm Mon-Sat)
A handy stop for information on Isola di San Pietro.

❶ Getting There & Around

Sant'Antioco is connected to the mainland by a bridge and is accessible by bus from Iglesias (€3.50, 1¾ hours) and Carbonia (€2, 50 minutes). To get to Isola San Pietro (Carloforte), you'll need to catch a **Saremar** (☑0781 84 01 60; www.saremar.it; Piazza Italia 3, Sant'Antioco) ferry from Portovesme (€2.60/12.50 per person/car, 40 minutes, 17 daily) or from Calasetta on Isola Sant'Antioco (€2.30/12 per person/car, 30 minutes, nine daily).

Local buses run around Sant'Antioco, and limited summertime services operate on San Pietro. Tickets cost €1.20.

Costa Verde

One of Sardinia's great undeveloped coastal stretches, the Costa Verde (Green Coast) extends northward from Capo Pecora to the small resort of Torre dei Corsari. This is an area of wild, exhilarating beauty and spectacular, unspoilt beaches.

To reach the area's two best beaches, head inland from Portixeddu along the SS126 and

TOP FIVE BEACHES IN SARDINIA

→ **Spiaggia Piscinas** (p847)
→ **Chia** (p843)
→ **Spiaggia del Principe** (p862)
→ **Is Aruttas** (p851)
→ **Cala Mariolu** (p870)

follow signs for Arbus. Signs off to the left direct you to Gennamari, Bau and **Spiaggia Scivu**, a golden beach backed by 70m-high sand dunes. A further 4km beyond this turn-off is another for the ghost town of **Ingurtosu** and beyond that, the magnificent and untamed **Spiaggia Piscinas**, a broad swath of virgin sand wedged between a desert of imposing dunes and the wild sea. Note that the route down to the beach involves at least 10km of dirt-track driving.

If you want to stay in the area, there's an excellent *agriturismo* off the SP65 between Montevecchio and Torre dei Corsari. **Agriturismo L'Oasi del Cervo** (☑347 301 13 18; www.oasidelcervo.com; half-board per person €43-60) is as authentic as it gets, a working farm at the end of a 2.5km dirt track in the middle of silent green hills. Rooms are extremely simple, but the location and the superb homemade food more than compensate.

You'll really need a car to explore the Costa Verde; however, during July and August, a bus runs daily from Oristano to Torre dei Corsari (€4.50, 1½ hours).

ORISTANO & THE WEST

Oristano

POP 32.156

With its elegant shopping streets, ornate piazzas and popular cafes, Oristano's animated centre makes a great base for exploring this part of the island. The city was founded in the 11th century and became capital of the Giudicato d'Arborea, one of Sardinia's four independent provinces.

Eleonora d'Arborea, a heroine in the Joan of Arc mould, became head of the *giudicato* in 1383 and led the fierce resistance against the island's Spanish invaders. But with her death, anti-Spanish opposition crumbled and Oristano was incorporated into the rest

Oristano

SARDINIA ORISTANO

of Aragon-controlled Sardinia. Eleonora is also remembered for her celebrated *Carta di Logu* (Code of Laws), an extraordinary law code that tackled land and property legislation as well as introducing a raft of women's rights.

⊚ Sights

Torre di Mariano II TOWER
(Piazza Roma) One of the few vestiges of Oristano's medieval past, the 13th-century tower was the town's northern gate and an important part of the city defences. From here, pedestrianised Corso Umberto I leads to Piazza Eleonora d'Arborea.

Queen Eleonora's Statue PIAZZA
(Piazza Eleonora d'Arborea) In the centre of Piazza Eleonora d'Arborea, Oristano's elegant outdoor salon, stands an ornate 19th-century statue of Eleonora, raising a

finger as if about to launch into a political discourse.

Chiesa di San Francesco
CHURCH

(Via Sant'Antonio) This neoclassical church harbours a 14th-century wooden sculpture, the *Crocifisso di Nicodemo*, considered one of Sardinia's most precious carvings.

Duomo
CATHEDRAL

(Piazza del Duomo) The duomo was built in the 13th century but remodelled 500 years later. Its free-standing *campanile* (bell tower), topped by a conspicuous majolica-tiled dome, adds an exotic Byzantine look to Oristano's skyline.

Museo Antiquarium Arborense
MUSEUM

(www.antiquariumarborense.it; Piazza Corrias; adult/reduced €5/2.50; ⊙9am-8pm) This museum contains one of the island's major archaeological collections, with prehistoric artefacts from the Sinis Peninsula and finds from Carthaginian and Roman Tharros. There's also a small collection of *retablos* (painted altarpieces), including the 16th-century Retablo del Santo Cristo, which depicts a decorative series of Franciscan saints.

🎇 Festivals & Events

Sa Sartiglia
RELIGIOUS

One of Sardinia's top festivals, Oristano's Sa Sartiglia is held over two days: Sunday and *martedì grasso* (Shrove Tuesday or Mardi Gras). It involves a costumed medieval joust and some amazing acrobatic horse riding.

🛏 Sleeping

Eleonora B&B
B&B €

(☑0783 7 04 35; www.eleonora-bed-and-breakfast. com; Piazza Eleonora d'Arborea 12; s €35-60, d €60-75, tr €75-95; ❉ 🕲) Surely the most charming B&B in town, the Eleonora is housed in a pretty medieval *palazzo* on Oristano's central piazza. The rooms are tastefully decorated with antique furniture and the floors are covered in gorgeous old tiles.

Duomo Albergo
HOTEL €€

(☑0783 77 80 61; www.hotelduomo.net; Via Vittorio Emanuele 34; s €65-80, d €108-135; ❉ @) Inside and out, Oristano's top hotel is refined and elegantly understated. Behind the discreet facade, spacious rooms reveal a low-key look with traditional fabrics and cooling white tones. Breakfast is served in the inner courtyard on fine days.

🍴 Eating & Drinking

La Torre
PIZZERIA €

(☑0783 30 14 94; Piazza Roma 52; pizzas €4.50-10, meals €20-25; ⊙Tue-Sun) This place doesn't look like much from outside; in fact, it's not so amazing inside either. No matter, it serves the best pizza in town. If you're off pizza but just want to enjoy the hectic atmosphere, there's a full menu of pastas and grilled mains.

Josto al Duomo
SARDINIAN €€

(☑0783 77 80 61; www.jostoalduomo.net; Via Vittorio Emanuele 34; meals €30-45; ⊙lunch & dinner Mon-Sat) Refined yet familiar, this restaurant is gathered around an inner courtyard perfect for alfresco dining. The menu is richly influenced by the seasons and market-fresh produce. Specialities such as lamb ravioli with wild fennel and candied lemon, and fillet of Montiferru beef are beautifully cooked and presented with an artistic eye for detail.

Lola Mundo
CAFE

(Piazzetta Corrias 14; ⊙Mon-Sat; 🛜) With its piazza seating and relaxing music, Lola Mundo is a good spot to hang out over a coffee or an aperitif. A favourite with the locals.

Pasticceria Eleonora
CAFE

(Piazza Eleonora d'Arborea 1; ⊙7.30am-9pm) The people-watching terrace of this *pasticceria* (pastry shop) overlooking the piazza is a prime spot for coffee and cake, ice cream or a pre-dinner drink.

ℹ Information

Tourist Office (☑0783 368 32 10; turismo@ provincia.or.it; Piazza Eleonora d'Arborea 19; ⊙8.30am-1pm & 3-6pm Mon-Thu, 8.30am-1pm Fri) Friendly, English-speaking staff are eager to offer information on Oristano and the region.

ℹ Getting There & Around

From the bus station on Via Cagliari buses leave for the following destinations.

TO	FARE (€)	DURATION (HR)	FREQUENCY
Cagliari	7	1½	2 daily
Nuoro	7	2½	6 daily
Santa Giusta	1.20	¼	half-hourly
Sassari	8-10	2	3 daily

The main train station is in Piazza Ungheria, east of the town centre. Up to 15 daily trains run

PREHISTORIC WONDERS

To the untrained eye, the strange stone circles that litter Sardinia's interior are mysterious and incomprehensible. But to archaeologists they provide one of the few windows into the dark world of the Bronze Age *nuraghe* people. There are said to be up to 7000 *nuraghi* (stone towers) across the island, most built between 1800 and 500 BC. No one is absolutely certain what they were used for, although most experts think they were defensive watchtowers.

Even before they started building *nuraghi*, the Sardinians were busy digging tombs into the rock, known as *domus de janas* (fairy houses). More elaborate were the common graves fronted by stele called **tombe dei giganti** (giants' tombs).

Evidence of pagan religious practices is provided by **pozzi sacri** (well temples). Built from around 1000 BC, these were often constructed to capture light at the yearly equinoxes, hinting at a naturalistic religion as well as sophisticated building techniques. The well temple at Santa Cristina is a prime example.

between Oristano and Cagliari (€6, one to two hours).

City buses on the *azzurra* (blue) line run from Via Cagliari to the beach at Marina di Torregrande (€1.20, 20 minutes).

Barumini & Around

In the heart of voluptuous green countryside near Barumini, the **Nuraghe Su Nuraxi** (www.nuraghi.org; adult/reduced €10/6.50; ⏱9am-7pm summer, to 4pm winter) is Sardinia's sole World Heritage Site and the island's most visited *nuraghi* (stone tower). The focal point is the tower dating from 1500 BC, which originally stood on its own but was later incorporated into a fortified compound. The first village buildings were erected in the Iron Age, and it's these that constitute the beehive of circular interlocking buildings that spread across the grass.

Five kilometres west of Barumini, the village of **Tuili** is a gateway to **La Giara di Gesturi**, a high basalt plateau famous for its population of wild *cavallini* (literally 'minihorses'). These are most likely to be seen beside shallow *pauli* (seasonal lakes) at daybreak or dusk.

To the east, it's a 25km drive to the village of Serri and the **Santuario Santa Vittoria di Serri** (Serri; adult/concession €4/3; ⏱9am-1pm & 3-7pm), the most extensive *nuraghic* settlement unearthed in Sardinia.

Three weekday buses run from Cagliari to Barumini (€5, 1½ hours); otherwise, you'll need your own transport.

Sinis Peninsula

West of Oristano, the Sinis Peninsula feels like a world apart with its glassy lagoons, low-lying countryside and snow-white beaches. The main sight is the ancient town of Tharros.

Tharros & Around

The blue choppy waters of the Golfo di Oristano form the ideal backdrop to the ruins of ancient **Tharros** (adult/reduced €7/4; ⏱9am-8pm summer, to 5pm winter). Founded by the Phoenicians in the 8th century BC, Tharros thrived as a Carthaginian naval base and was later taken over by the Romans. Much of what you see today dates from the 2nd and 3rd centuries AD, when the basalt streets were laid and the aqueduct, baths and other major monuments were built.

On the side of the road just before Tharros, you'll see the 6th-century **Chiesa di San Giovanni di Sinis** (⏱9am-7pm summer, to 5pm winter), one of oldest churches in Sardinia.

Some 4km north, the weird village of **San Salvatore** is worth a quick look. Used as a spaghetti-western film set during the 1960s, it is centred on a dusty town square surrounded by rows of tiny terraced houses, known as *cumbessias*. In the piazza, the 16th-century **Chiesa di San Salvatore** (⏱9.30am-1pm year-round, 3.30-6pm Mon-Sat summer) is built over a pagan sanctuary dating from the *nuraghic* period.

A fantastic place to eat nearby is **Peschiera Pontis** (☎0783 39 17 74; Strada Provinciale 6; menus €25-30) a restaurant fronting the Pontis fishing cooperative, on the road between

Cabras and Tharros. You'll get abundant antipasti, *primo* (first course), *secondo* (second course), desserts and wine in the fixed-price menus, and the freshest fish you're likely to taste on the island.

Just beyond the turn-off for the village, the excellent Agriturismo Su Pranu (☑0783 39 25 61; www.agriturismosupranu.com; half-board per person €55-65; ⊞) is a genuine working farm offering six bright guestrooms and superb home-grown food.

In July and August, there are five daily buses for San Giovanni in Sinis from Oristano (€2, 35 minutes).

Cabras

POP 9169

This straggling lagoon town is really only worth stopping at for the Museo Civico (www.penisoladelsinis.it; Via Tharros 121; adult/reduced €4/3, incl Tharros €7/4; ⊙9am-1pm & 4-8pm summer, 9am-1pm & 3-7pm winter) at the southern end of the town. It houses finds from the prehistoric site of Cuccuru Is Arrius, 3km to the southwest, and Tharros. Buses run every 20 minutes or so from Oristano (€1.50, 15 minutes).

Riola Sardo

POP 2146

The single main reason to stop off at this otherwise nondescript town is to stay at the wonderful Hotel Lucrezia. (☑0783 41 20 78; www.hotellucrezia.it; Via Roma 14a; s €104-114, d €129-169; ⊞ @ ⊞) Housed in an ancient family *cortile* (courtyard house), the luxuriously rustic rooms surround an inner courtyard complete with a wisteria-draped pergola and fig and citrus trees. Free bikes are provided, and the welcoming staff regularly organise cooking, painting and wine-tasting courses.

North Oristano Coast

North of the Sinis Peninsula, there are some superb beaches in and around the popular resort of Santa Caterina di Pittinuri. These include Spiaggia dell'Arco at S'Archittu, and further south, Is Arenas, one of the longest beaches in the area. Nearby, Camping Is Arenas (☑0783 5 21 03; www.camping-isarenas.co.uk; camping 2 people, car & tent €17-31, 2-person bungalows €50-90; ☎) is one of three camping grounds in the vicinity. Large and well-equipped, it has tent sites and bungalows surrounded by pine trees.

Inland, the Monti Ferru massif (105m) is a beautiful and largely pristine area of ancient forests, natural springs and small market towns. There's some great walking in the area and gourmets will enjoy the wonderful food.

From Oristano, five weekday buses run to Santa Caterina (€2.50, 40 minutes) and S'Archittu (€2.50, 40 minutes). Extra services are added in July and August.

SARDINIA NORTH ORISTANO COAST

WORTH A TRIP

THE BEACHES OF THE SINIS PENINSULA

The Sinis Peninsula's beaches are among the best on the island. One of the most famous is Is Aruttas, whose prized white quartz sand was for years carted off to be used in aquariums and on beaches on the Costa Smeralda. However, it's now illegal to take any. The beach is signposted and is 5km west off the main road north from San Salvatore.

Within walking distance of the beach, Camping Is Aruttas (☑0783 192 54 61; www.campingisaruttas.it; Loc Marina; camping 2 people, car & tent €27-36; ⊙May-Sep; ☎) has modest camping facilities set amid olive trees and Mediterranean shrubbery.

At the north of the peninsula, the popular surfing beach of Putzu Idu is backed by a motley set of holiday homes, beach bars and surfing outlets. One such, the Capo Mannu Kite School (☑347 007 70 35; www.capomannukiteschool.it), runs kitesurfing lessons for all levels. For underwater thrills, 9511 Diving (☑335 605 94 12; www.9511.it) runs dives and snorkelling trips, as well as excursions to the eloquently named Isola di Mal di Ventre (Stomach-ache Island), 10km off the coast. As a rough guide, reckon on €35 to €40+ for a standard dive and about €50 for an excursion over to Isola di Male di Ventre.

Two weekday buses run to Putzu Idu from Oristano (€2.50, 55 minutes). In July and August, there are four additional services.

Lago Omedeo Circuit

Follow the SS131 north out of Oristano for the **Nuraghe Santa Cristina** (adult/reduced incl Museo Archeologico-Etnografico Paulilatino €5/3.50; ☉8.30am-sunset), an important whose extraordinary Bronze Age *tempio a pozzo* (well-temple) is one of the best preserved in Sardinia. Finds from the site can be viewed a few kilometres up the road at Paulilatino's small **Museo Archeologico-Etnografico** (Via Nazionale 127; adult/reduced incl Nuraghe Santa Cristina €5/3.50; ☉9.30am-1pm & 3-6.30pm Tue-Sun summer, to 5.30pm winter).

Just north of Paulilatino is another major *nuraghe*, the impressive **Nuraghe Losa** (www.nuraghelosa.net; adult/reduced €5/3.50; ☉9am-1hr before sunset) dating from 1500 BC.

You will need your own transport to get to most of these sights, although buses do run from Oristano to Abbasanta (€3, 55 minutes), via Paulilatino. These will drop you within walking distance of Nuraghe Losa.

Bosa

POP 8026

Bosa is one of Sardinia's most attractive towns. Seen from a distance, its rainbow townscape resembles a vibrant Paul Klee canvas, with pastel houses stacked on a steep hillside, tapering up to a stark, grey castle. In front, moored fishing boats bob on the glassy Temo river and palm trees line an elegant riverfront. Three kilometres west, Bosa Marina, the town's satellite beach resort, is less obviously attractive, with modern low-rise hotels, restaurants and holiday homes.

◉ Sights & Activities

It's quite a climb up to Bosa's hilltop castle, **Castello Malaspina** (adult/reduced €4/3; ☉10am-7pm), built in 1112 by a noble Tuscan family. Note that these opening times often change, and it might well be open for longer during summer.

Down below, the **Museo Casa Deriu** (Corso Vittorio Emanuele 59; adult/reduced €4.50/3; ☉10am-1pm & 3-5pm Tue-Sun) illustrates the town's history, including a section on Bosa's old tanning industry. Also of interest is the Gothic-Romanesque **Cattedrale di San Pietro Extramuros**, 2km from the old bridge on the south bank of the Temo.

Bosa has much to offer outdoor enthusiasts. You can hire bikes and scooters at **Cuccu** (☏0785 37 32 98; Via Roma 5), a me-

chanics' on the southern side of the river, for €10/40 per day for a bike/scooter. At Bosa Marina, **Bosa Diving** (☏335 8189748; www.bosadiving.it; Via Colombo 2) runs dives (from €40) and snorkelling excursions (€20), and rents out canoes (double canoe €10 per hour) and dinghies (from €25 per hour).

🛏 Sleeping & Eating

La Torre di Alice   B&B €
(☏0785 85 04 04; www.latorredialice.it; Via del Carmine 7; s €30-40, d €50-70; @) Alice and Marco are your affable hosts at this charmingly restored townhouse in Bosa's medieval centre – you'll notice it by its bright colours and wacky signpost outside. The rooms are comfortable, with wrought-iron beds and relaxing decor. Alice prepares a delectable spread of homemade cakes and muffins at breakfast.

S'Ammentu   B&B €
(☏0785 37 61 80; www.sammentu.com; Via Del Carmine 55; d €60-80; 🛜) Squirreled away in the backstreets of Bosa's old town, S'Ammentu offers warm hospitality in a lovingly restored 17th-century townhouse. A rickety lift (keep your finger on the button!) rises to rooms big on original flair, with wrought-iron bedsteads, tiled floors, beams and stone arches. The vaulted breakfast room doubles as a shared kitchen.

Hotel Sa Pischedda   HOTEL €€
(☏0785 37 30 65; www.hotelsapischedda.com; Via Roma 8; s €60-85, d €90-140; ❋🛜) The apricot façade of this elegantly restored house greets you on the southern side of the Ponte Vecchio. Several rooms have original frescoed ceilings, some are split-level, and there are terraces overlooking the river. This place is a real gem, and the restaurant is exceptional.

Al Gambero Rosso   SARDINIAN €€
(☏0785 37 41 50; Via Nazionale 12; meals €20-30; ☉daily; ⓘ) Brimming with regulars, this restaurant has few airs and graces, but stands head and shoulders above most of Bosa's restaurants with its friendly service and winningly fresh pasta and seafood. Pizzas are delivered bubbling hot from a wood oven.

Sa Pischedda   SEAFOOD €€
(☏0785 37 30 65; Via Roma 8; meals €30-35, pizzas €7; ☉daily summer, Wed-Mon winter) At the hotel of the same name, this is one of Bosa's best restaurants. Speciality of the house is stylishly presented fish, both seawater and

freshwater, but it also does excellent pizza and pasta. Reservations in summer are a good idea.

ℹ️ Getting There & Away

All buses terminate at Piazza Zanetti. There are services to and from Alghero (€4.50, 1½ hours, two daily), Sassari (€6, 2¼ hours, three daily) and Oristano (€5.50, two hours, six daily Monday to Saturday). Get tickets from the bus depot on Via Nazionale (opposite Sa Pischedda restaurant) or ask the driver.

ALGHERO & THE NORTHWEST

Alghero

POP 40,641

Pretty and petite, Alghero is one of Sardinia's most beautiful towns, and even though it can be very touristy, the town hasn't given up its unique character. The town's charm is in the medieval centre, where cobbled caramel-coloured streets are shaded by Gothic *palazzi* and enlivened by busy squares bubbling with cafes and restaurants. The robust sea walls that enclose the old town are lined with restaurants and bars, and they overlook the harbour and the long sandy beaches to the north, and the rocky coves to the south.

Presiding over everything is a palpable Spanish atmosphere, a hangover from the 14th century when Sardinia's Aragonese invaders tried to replace the local populace with Catalan colonists.

◎ Sights

Centro Storico   HISTORIC QUARTER
A leisurely stroll round Alghero's animated *centro storico* is a good way of getting into the holiday atmosphere. Overlooking Piazza Duomo, the oversized **Cattedrale di Santa Maria** (☉ 7am-noon & 5-7.30pm) is an odd mishmash of Moorish, baroque, Renaissance and other influences. Of greater interest is the **campanile** (bell tower; ☎ 079 973 30 41; Via Principe Umberto; adult/child €2/free; ☉ 10.30am-12.30pm Mon-Fri & 7-9pm Mon & Fri Jun-Aug, 10.30am-12.30pm Mon, Tue, Thu, Fri & 4-6pm Mon & Fri Sep-Oct, on request Nov-May) round the back, which is a fine example of Catalan-Gothic architecture.

On the old town's main street, the **Chiesa di San Francesco** (Via Carlo Alberto) hides some beautiful 14th-century cloisters behind an austere stone facade.

Several 14th-century towers remain from the medieval city, including **Torre Porta a Terra** (Piazza Porta Terra; adult/child €3/2; ☉ 9am-midnight summer, 9am-1pm & 4-8pm winter), which was once one of the city's two main gates. It now houses a small museum dedicated to the city's past, and a terrace with sweeping, 360-degree views.

To the north, the **Bastione della Maddalena**, with its eponymous tower, is the only extant remnant of the city's former land battlements. To the south and west, respectively, the Mediterranean crashes against the seaward walls of the **Bastioni di San Marco** and **Bastioni Cristoforo Colombo**. Along these bulwarks are some inviting restaurants and bars where you can watch the sunset over a cocktail.

🏃 Activities

North of Alghero's yacht-jammed port, Via Garibaldi sweeps up to the town's beaches, **Spiaggia di San Giovanni** and the adjacent **Spiaggia di Maria Pia**. Nicer by far, though, are the beaches near Fertilia. From the port you can take boat trips along the impressive northern coast to **Capo Caccia**. Prices range from about €40 to €100 per person.

🛏️ Sleeping

Booking ahead is essential in July and August, and a good idea during the rest of the year.

B&B Benebenniu   B&B €
(☎ 380 174 67 26; www.benebenniu.com; Via Carlo Alberto 70; s €40-75, d €50-95, tr €70-130; ❄️ 🛜 👪) Wedged into a pretty corner of the old town, this B&B exudes warmth and familiarity. The generously sized, well-kept rooms are bathed in natural light, and the best of the lot (Tiricca) has a corner balcony overlooking the piazza.

Hotel San Francesco   HOTEL €
(☎ 079 98 03 30; www.sanfrancescohotel.com; Via Ambrogio Machin 2; s €58-63, d €90-101, tr €120-135; ❄️ @ 🛜) One of the few hotels in Alghero's *centro storico*. Housed in an ex-convent – monks still live on the 3rd floor – it has plain, comfortable rooms set around an attractive 14th-century cloister.

★ Angedras Hotel   HOTEL €€
(☎ 079 973 50 34; www.angedras.it; Via Frank 2; s/d €105/115; ❄️ 🛜) A model of whitewashed

Alghero

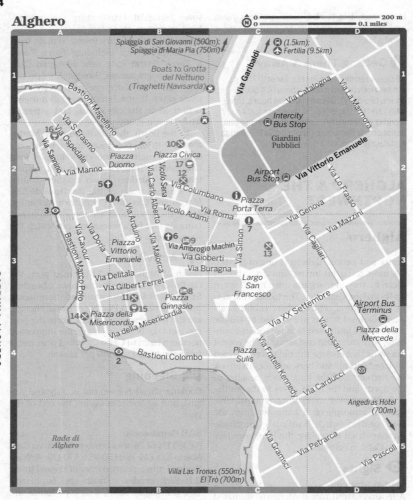

Spiaggia di San Giovanni (500m);
Spiaggia di Maria Pia (750m)

Boats to Grotta
del Nettuno
(Traghetti Navisarda)

(1.5km);
Fertilia (9.5km)

Via Garibaldi

Via Catalogna

Via La Marmora

Intercity
Bus Stop

Giardini
Pubblici

Bastioni Magellano

Via S. Erasmo

Via Ospedale

16

Via Sannino

Piazza
Duomo

Piazza Civica

10

Via Manno

5

4

17

12

Via Columbano

3

Via Carlo Alberto

Vicolo Sena

Airport
Bus Stop

Via Vittorio Emanuele

Via Lo Frasso

Via Roma

Piazza
Porta Terra

7

Via Genova

Via Mazzini

Via Cagliari

Via Arduino

Vicolo Adami

6

9

Via Ambrogio Machin

Via Gioberti

Via Simon

13

Piazza
Vittorio
Emanuele

Via Malorca

Via Buragna

Via Dora

Bastioni Marco Polo

Via Cavour

Via Delitala

Via Gilbert Ferret

11

15

8

Piazza
Ginnasio

Largo
San
Francesco

Airport Bus
Terminus

14

Piazza della
Misericordia

Via della Misericordia

Via XX Settembre

Via Sassari

Piazza della
Mercede

2

Bastioni Colombo

Piazza
Sulis

Via Fratelli Kennedy

Via Carducci

Angedras Hotel
(700m)

Rada di
Alghero

Via Gramsci

Via Petrarca

Via Pascoli

Villa Las Tronas (550m);
El Trò (700m)

SARDINIA ALGHERO

Mediterranean style, the Angedras has bright rooms with big French doors opening on to sunny patios. The airy terrace is good for iced drinks on hot summer evenings. Note that it's a good 15-minute walk south from the *centro storico*.

Villa Las Tronas LUXURY HOTEL **€€€**
(☑ 079 98 18 18; www.hotelvillalastronas.it; Via Lungomare Valencia 1; s €224-272, d €259-363) Splash out and stay at this palatial 19th-century hotel, situated on a promontory with balconies overlooking the waves. The rooms are pure *fin de siècle* plush with acres of brocade, ele-

gant antiques and moody oil paintings. A spa with a saltwater pool, sauna, hydromassage and hammam invites lingering. A minimum three-night stay applies in high season.

Eating

Self-caterers can stock up at Alghero's weekday **market** (Via Sassari 23; ⊙7am-1pm) between Via Sassari and Via Cagliari.

Lu Furat PIZZERIA **€**
(☑ 079 973 60 52; Via Columbano 8; snacks €2-6; ⊙Tue-Sun) Squeeze into this vaulted, hole-in-the-wall pizzeria and for a few euro you can

Alghero

snack on perfectly thin, crisp pizza or *fainè* made with chickpea dough (a cross between a pancake and pizza, often cooked with chopped onions and sausage). If you can't bag one of the few tables, get a take-away.

Il Ghiotto   FAST FOOD €
(☑ 079 97 48 20; Piazza Civica 23; mains €5-11; ⊙ 6am-midnight) Fill up for as little as €10 from the tantalising lunchtime spread of *panini*, pastas, salads and main courses. There's seating in a dining area behind the main hall or outside on a busy wooden terrace.

★ **La Botteghina**   SARDINIAN €€
(☑ 079 97 38 375; www.labotteghina.biz; Via Principe Umberto 63; meals €25-35; ⊙ closed Sat dinner) A crisp place in the *centro storico,* La Botteghina only deals in local food bought from small producers, which means the ingredients are simple and tastes are intense. Try the *fregola* (small pasta made from semolina) with seafood, or a gourmet pizza such as the one with swordfish, rocket and mozzarella.

The Kings   SARDINIAN €€
(☑ 079 97 96 50; www.thekingsrestaurant.it; Via Cavour 123; meals €30-40; ⊙ daily; ☑ ⊛) With a sea-facing terrace on Alghero's honey-coloured ramparts, this restaurant cranks up the romance as day softens into dusk.

Clean, bright Mediterranean flavours shine through in dishes like tagliatelle with clams and *bottarga* (mullet roe) and grilled swordfish cooked with aubergines and tomatoes. There are dedicated menus for kids and vegetarians.

⚱ Drinking & Entertainment

Blanc Bar   BAR
(Piazza Santa Croce) Fabulous cocktails, mellow music, golden views – what more could you want of a seafront bar? This slick lounge bar has pavement seating on a little piazza and three much-coveted tables on the western walls.

Baraonda   WINE BAR
(Piazza della Misericordia) Burgundy walls and black-and-white jazz photos set the tone at this moody wine bar. In summer, sit out on the piazza and watch the world parade by.

Caffè Costantino   CAFE
(Piazza Civica 31) Skip the mediocre, overpriced food, but by all means watch the world go by over a drink at one of this cafe's piazza-side tables.

El Trò   CLUB
(Via Lungomare Valencia 3) El Trò becomes a steamy mosh pit on hot summer weekends as hyped-up holidaymakers boogie until dawn on the seafront dance floor.

ℹ Information

Farmacia Bulla (☑ 079 95 21 15; Via Garibaldi 13; ⊙ 9am-1pm & 4.30-8.30pm)
Ospedale Civile (☑ 079 99 62 00; Via Don Minzoni) The main hospital.
Police Station (☑ 079 972 00 00; Piazza della Mercede 4)
Post Office (Via Carducci 35; ⊙ 8.20am-7.05pm Mon-Fri, 8.20am-12.35pm Sat)
Tourist Office (☑ 079 97 90 54; www.alghero-turismo.it; Piazza Porta Terra 9; ⊙ 8am-8pm, closed Sun winter) This should be your first port of call for info on Alghero.

ℹ Getting There & Away

AIR
Fertilia airport (☑ 079 93 52 82; www.aeroportodialghero.it), 10km north of town, serves domestic flights to and from Italy, and **Ryanair** (www.ryanair.com) flights to and from London and Frankfurt.

SARDINIA ALGHERO

BUS

InterCity buses stop at and leave from Via Catalogna, by the Giardini Pubblici. Buy tickets at the ticket office in the gardens. Up to 18 daily buses run to and from Sassari (€3, one hour). There are also services to Porto Torres (€3, one hour, six daily) and Bosa (€3.50, 1½ hours, two daily).

TRAIN

The train station is 1.5km north of the old town on Via Don Minzoni. Up to 12 trains run to and from Sassari (€2.20, 35 minutes).

❶ Getting Around

Buses travel between Via Cagliari and the airport hourly between 5am and 11pm (€1.20, 25 minutes). A taxi to/from the airport will cost between €20 and €25.

Bus line AO runs from Via Cagliari to the beaches. Tickets are available at newsagents and *tabaccai* (tobacconists) across town.

Cicloexpress (☑ 079 98 69 50; www.cicloexpress.com; Via Garibaldi) hires out cars (from €60 per day), scooters (from €30) and bikes (from €8).

Around Alghero

Riviera del Corallo

A few kilometres west of Alghero are two favourite beaches: **Spiaggia delle Bombarde** and **Spiaggia del Lazzaretto**. Both are signposted off the main road, but if you don't have a car the Capo Caccia bus from Alghero passes nearby. Divers should continue westward to the **Diving Centre Capo Galera** (☑ 079 94 21 10; www.capogalera.com; d €70-110, dives from €20), which offers superlative diving in the **Nereo Cave**, the biggest underwater grotto in the Mediterranean, and cheerful accommodation in a big, white villa.

Heading on to Porto Conte you'll pass the impressive **Nuraghe di Palmavera** (adult/reduced €3/2; ⊙9am-7pm summer, 10am-2pm winter), a 3500-year-old *nuraghic* village. You'll need your own transport to get there as the AF local bus from Alghero passes by but returns via an inland route, leaving you stranded.

Beyond the *nuraghe*, **Porto Conte** is on a lovely unspoilt bay, centred on **Spiaggia Mugoni**, a good spot for windsurfing, canoeing, kayaking and sailing. Regular buses run between Porto Conte and Alghero (€1.50, 30 minutes, six daily).

Just west of Porto Conte at the base of Monte Timidone, **Le Prigionette Nature Reserve** (☑ 079 94 90 60; admission free but ID required; ⊙8am-4pm Mon-Sat, to 5pm Sun) is home to deer, albino donkeys, Giara horses and wild boar. It has well-marked forest paths and tracks suitable for walkers and cyclists.

At the end of the road, **Capo Caccia** is a dramatic cape jutting out high above the sea. From the car park, a vertiginous 654-step staircase descends 110m of sheer cliff to the **Grotta di Nettuno** (☑ 079 94 65 40; adult/reduced €13/9; ⊙9am-7pm summer, to 3pm winter), an underground fairyland of stalactites and stalagmites. If you don't fancy the staircase, there are ferries from Alghero run by **Traghetti Navisarda** (☑ 079 95 06 03; www.navisarda.it; Via IV Novembre 6, Alghero; adult/child return €15/8), departing hourly between 9am and 5pm from June to September, and four times daily the rest of the year. Otherwise, there's a daily bus from Via Catalogna (€2.50, 50 minutes), which departs Alghero at 9.15am and returns at midday. From June to September, there are two extra runs at 3.10pm and 5.10pm, returning at 4.05pm and 6.05pm.

Those with transport should explore the flat, green land north of Capo Caccia. Hot spots include **Torre del Porticciolo**, a tiny natural harbour, backed by a small arc of beach, and 6km to the north, one of the island's longest stretches of wild sandy beach, **Porto Ferro**.

Inland

About 7km north of Alghero, just to the left (west) of the road to Porto Torres, lie the scattered ancient burial chambers of the **Necropoli di Anghelu Ruiu** (adult/reduced €3/2; ⊙9am-7pm summer, 10am-2pm winter). The 38 tombs carved into the sandstone rock date from the Ozieri era, between 3300 and 2700 BC. Known as *domus de janas* (fairy houses), some have ornately carved architraves, pillars and alcoves.

Further up the road is the 650-hectare estate of Sardinia's top wine producer, **Sella e Mosca** (☑ 079 99 77 00; www.sellaemosca.com). Here you can join a free guided tour of the estate's **museum** (⊙5.30pm Mon-Sat summer, by request rest of the year) and stock up at the **enoteca** (⊙8.30am-8pm Mon-Sat, to 6.30pm winter).

Porto Torres

POP 22.567

A busy working port surrounded by a fuming petrochemical plant, Porto Torres is no picture. But if you find yourself passing through – and you might, if heading to Corsica – take an hour or so to visit the impressive **Basilica di San Gavino** (crypt €1.50; ⊙ 9am-1pm & 3-7pm summer, 9am-1pm & 3-6pm winter), Sardinia's largest Romanesque church. Built between 1030 and 1080 to honour three Roman-era Christian martyrs, it is notable for the apses on either end (there is no facade) and its two-dozen marble columns, pilfered by the Pisan builders from the nearby Roman site. Underneath, a crypt is lined with religious statuary and stone tombs.

Buses leave from Via Mare for Sassari (€2, 35 minutes, hourly), Alghero (€3, one hour, six daily) and Stintino (€2.50, 30 minutes, five daily).

Stintino & Parco Nazionale dell'Asinara

Once a forgotten fishing village, Stintino is now a sunny little resort and a good base for exploring the surrounding area. There are some fine beaches in these parts, but the pick of the bunch is **Spiaggia della Pelosa**, a salt-white strip of sand fronted by shallow, turquoise waters and strange, low-lying licks of land. On the road to Pelosa beach, the **Asinara Diving Center** (☏ 079 52 70 00; www.asinaradivingcenter.it) offers a range of dives starting at about €40. On the beach itself, the **Windsurfing Center Stintino** (☏ 079 52 70 06; www.windsurfingcenter.it) rents out windsurfers (€18 per hour) and canoes (from €8 per hour).

Over the water from Pelosa lies Isola Asinara, home to native *asini bianchi* (albino donkeys), and until recently off limits due to its maximum-security prison. The prison is now closed and the island has been designated a national park, **Parco Nazionale dell'Asinara** (www.parcoasinara.org). From Stintino, **Linea del Parco** (☏ 079 52 31 18; www.lineadelparco.it) offers a number of packages, including bus/4WD tours (€36/55) and yacht/fishing boat excursions (€65/70 including lunch). If you want to visit on your own, you'll have to take a bike as there's no public transport on the island and access is limited to certain restricted areas. Reckon on €25 for transport with bike and park admission.

Accommodation in the area is mainly in large, resort-style hotels, but there are some pleasant lower-key choices. In Stintino, **Albergo Silvestrino** (☏ 079 52 30 07; www.hotelsilvestrino.it; Via Sassari 14 ; d €70-160, half-board per person €60-110; ❉ 🔊) is a summery three-star place with cool, tiled rooms and an excellent seafood restaurant (meals €35).

At laid-back **Lu Fanali** (☏ 079 52 30 54; www.lufanali.it; Lungomare C Columbo 89; pizzas €6-9, meals €30; ⊙ daily; 🔊) you can watch boats bob by as you dig into reliably good pizza and seafood classics such as *calamari e seppie grigliati* (grilled calamari and cuttlefish).

There are five weekday buses to Stintino from Porto Torres (€2.50, 30 minutes) and Sassari (€4, 70 minutes). Services increase between June and September.

Sassari

POP 130.658

Sardinia's second city is a proud and cultured university town with a medieval heart and a modern outlook. It's not an immediately appealing place, but once you've broken through the drab outskirts you'll discover a grand centre and an evocative, lived-in historical core.

The city's golden age came in the 14th century, firstly as capital of the medieval Giudicato di Logudoro and then as an autonomous city-state. But decline followed and for centuries the city was ruled by Spanish colonialists.

◉ Sights

Museo Nazionale Sanna　　　MUSEUM
(www.museosannasassari.it; Via Roma 64; adult/reduced €4/2; ⊙ 9am-8pm Tue-Sun) This is Sassari's main attraction and the archaeological collection is quite comprehensive. The highlight is the *nuraghic* bronzeware, including weapons, bracelets, votive boats and figurines depicting humans and animals. It also has an interesting picture gallery and a small collection of Sardinian folk art.

Centro Storico　　　HISTORIC QUARTER
In the heart of the *centro storico*, Sassari's **Duomo** (Piazza Duomo; ⊙ 8.30am-noon & 4-7.30pm) dazzles with its 18th-century baroque facade: a giddy free-for-all of statues,

PHILIP AND KAREN SMITH / GETTY IMAGES ©

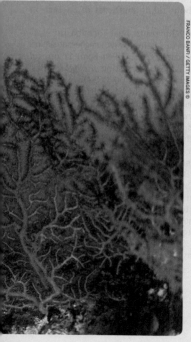

3

1. Climbing, Santa Teresa di Gallura (p863)
Sardinia's rock formations make for breathtaking climbing.

2. Windsurfing
Porto Pollo and Chia are top spots for windsurfing in Sardinia.

3. Hiking, Gola Su Gorropu (p869)
This spectacular gorge, flanked by vertical 400m rock walls, has been dubbed the 'Grand Canyon of Europe'.

4. Diving
The gin-clear waters in Sardinia are a dream for divers.

reliefs, friezes and busts. Inside, the cathedral reverts to its original Gothic character.

Nearby, imposing 19th-century buildings flank **Piazza Italia**, one of Sardinia's most impressive public spaces.

Sleeping

B&B Quattrogatti   B&B €
(☑ 349 4060481, 079 23 78 19; www.quattrogatti. eu; Via S Eligio 5; s/d/tr €40/75/105; ※ 🛜) You can expect a heartfelt *benvenuto* (welcome) at this cosy B&B, with quirky, colourful rooms and a wonderfully relaxed vibe. It's named after the four cats that can often be found slumbering in the inner courtyard. Breakfast is an appetising spread of local goodies and homemade jams.

Hotel Vittorio Emanuele   HOTEL €€
(☑ 079 23 55 38; www.hotelvesassari.it; Corso Vittorio Emanuele II 100-102; s €70-105, d €75-150; ※ @ 🛜) Housed in a medieval *palazzo*, this good-value, three-star place is awash with antiques and colourful paintings. Rooms are spacious if sterile with their corporate white-grey decor. Weekend discounts are available.

✕ Eating

Fainè alla Genovese Sassu   FAST FOOD €
(Via Usai 17; fainè €5; ⊙ 7-11pm Mon-Sat) This no-frills spot is the place to fill up on *fainè*, a cross between a pancake and pizza. There's nothing else on the menu, but with a wide range of toppings, you should find something to suit your tastes.

L'Antica Hostaria   SARDINIAN €€
(☑ 079 20 00 60; www.lanticahostaria.it; Via Cavour 55; meals €20-35; ⊙ Mon-Sat) L'Antica enjoys a reputation as one of Sassari's top addresses. In intimate surroundings you are treated to inventive cuisine rooted in local tradition. Meat lovers should try the *tagliata di manzo con rucola* (thinly sliced beef with rocket).

❶ Information

Nuovo Ospedale Civile (☑ 079 206 10 00; Via De Nicola) Hospital.

Post Office (Via Brigata di Sassari; ⊙ 8.20am-1.35pm Mon-Fri, 8.20am-12.35pm Sat)

Tourist Office (☑ 079 200 80 72; Via Sebastiano Satta 13; ⊙ 9am-1.30pm & 3-6pm Tue-Fri, 9am-1.30pm Sat)

❶ Getting There & Away

Sassari's main bus station is on Via XXV Aprile and services the following destinations.

TO	FARE (€)	DURATION (HR)	FREQUENCY
Alghero	3	1	11 daily
Cagliari	14.50	3¼	3 daily
Castelsardo	3	1	11 daily Mon-Sat
Nuoro	8-10	2	7 daily
Oristano	8-10	2	3 daily
Porto Torres	2.50	½	hourly

For Cagliari (€15.75, 3¾ hours, five daily) and Olbia (€7.35, two hours, six daily), you're better off taking the train. The train station is just beyond the western end of the old town on Piazza Stazione.

Around Sassari

The countryside south and east of Sassari is a patchwork of rugged slopes and golden wheat fields peppered by delightful Romanesque churches. The most impressive is the **Basilica della Santissima Trinità di Saccargia** (admission €2; ⊙ 9am-6pm) about 18km southeast of Sassari on the SS597.

Some 25km south, near Torralba, the **Nuraghe Santu Antine** (www.nuraghesantuantine. it; adult/reduced €9/6; ⊙ 9am-8pm) is one of Sardinia's most interesting *nuraghic* sites, dating from about 1600 BC. On weekdays, there are up to eight buses from Sassari to Torralba (€3, 1½ hours), although to get to the *nuraghe* from the village you'll have to walk about 4km.

On the coast north of Sassari, there are popular beaches at **Platamona** and **Marina di Sorso**, both accessible by the summer Buddi Buddi bus (line MP) from Via Eugenio Tavolara.

From here, the SS200 hugs the coast up to **Castelsardo**, a picturesque town with a dramatic medieval centre rising out of a rocky seafront peak. Regular buses run from Sassari (€3, one hour, 11 daily Monday to Saturday).

OLBIA, THE COSTA SMERALDA & THE GALLURA

Costa Smeralda evokes Sardinia's classic images: pearly-white beaches, wind-whipped licks of rock tapering into azure seas, and ageing oligarchs cavorting with bikini-clad beauties on zillion-dollar yachts. In inland Gallura, you could be on another island entirely, with vine-striped hills rolling to quaint villages, granite mountains and mysterious *nuraghi*. Gallura's northern coast is wild, the preserve of the dolphins, divers and windsurfers that splash around in the crystal waters of La Maddalena marine reserve.

Olbia

POP 54,833

Often ignored in the mad summer dash to the Costa Smeralda, Olbia has more to offer than at first meets the eye. Look beyond its industrial outskirts and you'll find a fetching city with a *centro storico* full of boutiques, wine bars and cafe-rimmed piazzas. Above all, Olbia is a refreshingly authentic and affordable alternative to the purpose-built resorts to the north and south.

◎ Sights

Museo Archeologico   MUSEUM
(Isolotto di Peddone; ◎ 10am-1pm Mon-Fri, 4-6pm Mon & Wed) FREE Architect Vanni Macciocco designed Olbia's striking new museum near the port. The museum spells out local history in artefacts, from Roman amulets to *nuraghic* finds. The highlight is the relic of a Roman vessel discovered in the old port.

Chiesa di San Simplicio   CHURCH
(Via San Simplicio; ◎ 7am-6pm Mon-Sat, 7am-9.30am & 11.30am-6pm Sun) Considered to be Gallura's most important medieval monument, this Romanesque granite church was built in the late 11th century and is a curious mix of Tuscan and Lombard styles.

⌴ Sleeping

★ **Hotel Panorama**   HOTEL €€
(☑ 0789 2 66 56; www.hotelpanoramaolbia.it; Via Giuseppe Mazzini 7; s €89-129, d €109-169, ste €179-249; P✳︎☎) The name says it all: the rooftop terrace has unbeatable views of the city, sea and Monte Limbara at this friendly, central hotel. Rooms are spacious and contemporary, with gleaming wood floors and

marble bathrooms. It costs an extra €22 to use the spa area, with a whirlpool, hammam and sauna.

La Locanda del Conte Mameli   BOUTIQUE HOTEL €€
(☑ 0789.2 30 08; www.lalocandadelcontemameli. com; Via delle Terme 8; s €59-149, d €74-149, tr €114-189; P✳︎☎) Housed in a 19th-century *locanda* (inn) built for Count Mameli, this boutique hotel oozes style, grace and original brickwork. An original Roman well is the centrepiece of the vaulted basement breakfast room.

✕ Eating & Drinking

Osteria del Mare   SEAFOOD €€
(☑ 0789 2 58 01; www.osteriadelmare.it; Via delle Terme 8; meals €25-35; ◎ daily) As the giant fish mural suggests, the big deal is seafood at this intimate, stone-walled osteria. The chef cooks with flair and precision, with dishes such as monkfish tortelli with shellfish sauce and courgette flowers and sea bass with scallops and basil revealing true depth and breadth of flavour.

La Lanterna   TRADITIONAL ITALIAN €€
(☑ 0789 2 30 82; Via Olbia 13; pizzas €6-16, meals €25-35; ◎ daily summer, closed Wed winter) The Lanterna distinguishes itself with its cosy subterranean setting, ever-friendly welcome and winningly fresh food. Starters such as homemade fettuccine with cherry tomatoes, chilli and ricotta are an appetising lead to whatever fish is on the menu that day.

KKult   BAR
(www.kkult.com; Corso Umberto 39) This contemporary lounge bar-cafe hybrid has a terrace on Olbia's main drag for watching the world go by over a coffee or cocktail. The pace picks up at the weekend with live music and DJ nights.

ℹ Information

Tourist Office (☑ 0789 5 22 06; www.olbiaturismo.it; Municipio, Corso Umberto; ◎ 9am-1pm Mon-Fri, plus 4-7pm Wed & Fri) This tourist office has stacks of info and brochures. Lucianda speaks English and is a mine of information on Olbia and the surrounding region.

ℹ Getting There & Around

AIR

Olbia's Aeroporto Internazionale di Olbia Costa Smeralda (p834) is about 5km southeast of the centre and handles flights from mainland Italian and major European cities. Low-cost operators include Air Berlin, easyJet, Jet2.com and Niki.

BOAT

Regular ferries arrive in Olbia from Genoa, Civitavecchia and Livorno. Book tickets at travel agents in town, or directly at the port.

BUS

Buses run from Olbia to the following destinations.

TO	FARE (€)	DURATION (HR)	FREQUENCY
Arzachena	2.50	¾	12 daily
Golfo Aranci	2	½	6 daily
Nuoro	9	2½	8 daily
Porto Cervo	3.50	1½	5 daily
Santa Teresa di Gallura	5	1½	7 daily
Sassari	7	1½	2 daily
Tempio Pausania	3.50	1½	2 daily

Get tickets from **Bar della Caccia** (Corso Vittorio Veneto 26, cnr Via Fiume D' Italia; ☺5.50am-9pm), just over the road from the main bus stops. Local bus 2 (€1, or €1.50 if bought on bus) runs half-hourly between 6.15am and 11.40pm from the airport to Via Goffredo Mameli in the centre.

TRAIN

The train station is just off Corso Umberto. There are trains to Cagliari (€17, four hours, five daily), Sassari (€7.35, two hours, six daily) and Golfo Aranci (€2.35, 25 minutes, four daily).

Golfo Aranci

POP 2288

Some 18km northeast of Olbia, Golfo Aranci is an important summer port, with services to Livorno and Civitavecchia. Most people pass through without a second glance, but it is worth a stop for its three white sandy beaches, particularly if activities like diving and speargun fishing rock your boat.

For a truly memorable experience, join the **Bottlenose Diving Research Institute** (☏0789 183 11 97; www.thebdri.com; Via Diaz 4) on one of its half-day cruises (€70/50 per adult/ child) to spot bottlenose dolphins. Sightings aren't guaranteed but the odds are excellent.

Costa Smeralda & Around

Stretching 55km from Porto Rotondo to the Golfo di Arzachena, the Costa Smeralda (Emerald Coast) is Sardinia's most fêted summer destination: a gilded enclave of luxury hotels, secluded beaches and exclusive marinas. Ever since the Aga Khan bought the coast for a pittance in the 1960s, it has attracted A-listers and paparazzi hoping to snap celebs in compromising clinches. But despite all the superficial fluff, it remains stunning, with granite mountains plunging into emerald waters in a series of dramatic fjord-like inlets.

The Costa's capital is **Porto Cervo**, a weird, artificial town whose pseudo-Moroccan architecture and perfectly manicured streets give it a strangely sterile atmosphere. It's dead out of season, but between June and September is party central, with tanned beauties posing on the **Piazzetta** and cashed-up shoppers perusing the designer boutiques.

To the west, **Baia Sardinia** faces onto a gorgeous strip of sand, while to the south, aficionados head for **Capriccioli** and **Spiaggia Liscia Ruia**, both near the exclusive Hotel Cala di Volpe. Near the signposted Hotel Romazzino, **Spiaggia del Principe** is a magnificent crescent of white sand bordered by Caribbean-blue waters – and the Aga Khan's favourite.

Inland, the rustic village of **San Pantaleo** merits a quick look, particularly on summer evenings when its picturesque piazza hosts a bustling market. Further on, the workaday town of **Arzachena** offers a number of interesting archaeological sites, including the **Nuraghe di Albucciu** (admission €3; ☺9am-7pm) on the main Olbia road, and **Coddu Ecchju** (admission €3; ☺9am-7pm), one of Sardinia's most important *tombe di giganti* (giants' tombs).

🛏 Sleeping & Eating

Villaggio Camping La Cugnana CAMPGROUND €
(☏0789 3 31 84; www.campingcugnana.it; Località Cugnana; camping 2 people, car & tent €20.50-40; 🛜🖵🚿) This slick, seaside camp ground is on the main road just north of Porto Rotondo. It has a supermarket, swimming pool and free beach shuttle bus.

★ B&B Lu Pastruccialeddu
B&B €€

(☑ 0789 8 17 77; www.pastruccialeddu.com; Località Lu Pastruccialeddu, Arzachena; s €70-100, d €90-120; P ⊠ ⊞) This is the real McCoy – a smashing B&B housed in a typical stone farmstead. It's run by the ultrahospitable Caterina Ruzittu, who prepares the sumptuous breakfasts and keeps the rooms pristine. Outside, a swimming pool shimmers in the lush green garden.

B&B Costa Smeralda
B&B €€

(☑ 0789 9 98 11; www.bbcostasmeralda.com; Lu Cumitoni, Poltu Quatu; d €80-130; ✳ @ ☞) Tucked in the hills above the Poltu Quatu harbour, this is an especially charming B&B. Piero and Luciana go out of their way to make you feel at home. Sunlight streams into rooms which are a blaze of blue and white. There are tantalising sea views from the verandah, where you can enjoy freshly made cakes and pastries at breakfast.

Agriturismo Rena
AGRITURISMO €€

(☑ 0789 8 25 32; www.agriturismorena.it; Località Rena, Arzachena; half-board per person €40-60; P ⊞) ✐ It's half-board only at this hilltop *agriturismo*, but that's no great sacrifice as the farmhouse food is a delight – cheese, honey, meat and wine are all home produced. Rooms have a rural look, with heavy wooden furniture and beamed ceilings.

La Vecchia Costa
SARDINIAN €

(☑ 0789 9 86 88; meals €15-25; ☺ daily) Great-value home cooking means this rustic restaurant is always booked solid. *Lorighittas* (ring-shaped pasta) in a porcini and lamb sauce is a delicious lead-in to sea bass with rocket, fresh tomatoes and basil. La Vecchia Costa is on the Arzachena–Porto Cervo road.

Spinnaker
MODERN ITALIAN €€

(☑ 0789 9 12 26; www.ristorantespinnaker.com; Liscia di Vacca; meals around €40; ☺ closed Wed low season) Fashionable Spinnaker attracts a buzzy crowd of yachties and socialites with its stylish ambience and fabulous seafood. Choose a crisp Vermentino white wine to go with sautéed calamari with fresh artichokes or rock lobster.

❶ Getting There & Away

Between June and September, **Sun Lines** (☑ 348 260 98 81) operates buses from Olbia airport to the Costa Smeralda, stopping at Porto Cervo and various other points along the coast. During the rest of the year, there's one daily bus between Porto Cervo and Olbia (€3.50, 1½ hours).

For Arzachena there are regular year-round services to and from Olbia (€2.50, 45 minutes, 12 daily).

Santa Teresa di Gallura
POP 5225

Bright, breezy and oh-so relaxed, Santa Teresa di Gallura bags a prime seafront position on Gallura's north coast. The resort gets extremely busy in high season yet somehow retains a distinct local character. Nearby, Capo Testa is famous for its surreal wind-sculpted rocks, while Corsica is a short ferry-hop away.

◉ Sights & Activities

When not on the beach, most people hang out at cafe-lined Piazza Vittorio Emanuele. Otherwise, you can wander up to the 16th-century **Torre di Longonsardo**, perched above the **Spiaggia Rena Bianca**, a glorious sweep of pale sand lapped by shallow aquamarine water (look out for the resident tortoise).

Four kilometres west of Santa Teresa, **Capo Testa** resembles a bizarre sculptural garden. Giant boulders lay strewn about the grassy slopes, their weird and wonderful forms the result of centuries of wind erosion.

Follow Via Capo Testa west of town and it's around an hour's hike to the cape. The

---

WORTH A TRIP

CANTINE SURRAU

Scenically surrounded by vineyards and mountains, the contemporary **Cantine Surrau** (☑ 0789 8 29 33; www.vignesurrau.it; Località Chilvagghja; ☺ 10am-9pm Mon-Fri, 10.30am-10pm Sat, 10.30am-9pm Sun) takes a holistic approach to winemaking. Take a look around the cellar and admire Sardinian art in the gallery before sniffing and swirling some of the region's crispest Vermentino white and beefiest Cannonau red wines (€3.50 to €4.50 per glass). There are free 30-minute guided tours of the cellar from 10am to noon and 3pm to 6pm. You'll find the winery on the Arzachena–Porto Cervo road.

walk itself is stunning, passing through boulder-strewn scrub and affording magnificent views of rock formations, rocky coves and the cobalt Mediterranean. You can stop en route for a swim and to admire the views of not-so-distant Corsica.

The **Consorzio delle Bocche** (☑0789 75 51 12; www.consorziobocche.com; Piazza Vittorio Emanuele; ☺9am-1pm & 5pm-12.30am May-Sep) runs trips to the Maddalena islands and down the Costa Smeralda, which cost between €40 and €45 per person. Go diving with **Centro Sub Marina di Longone** (☑338 627 00 54; www.marinadilongone.it; Viale Tibula 11), where prices start at about €40.

🛏 Sleeping & Eating

Most hotels only open from Easter to October. Head to Piazza Vittorio Emanuele for alfresco drinks and people-watching.

Camping La Liccia CAMPGROUND € (☑0789 75 51 90; www.campinglaliccia.com; SP for Castelsardo km59; camping 2 people, car & tent €20-31, 2-person bungalows €42-105; 🛜🖶) 🧭 This eco-friendly campground has fab facilities including a playground and sports area. It is 5km west of town on the road towards Castelsardo.

B&B Domus de Janas B&B €€ (☑338 499 02 21; www.bbdomusdejanas.it; Via Carlo Felice 20a; s €50-100, d €70-120, tr €80-140, q €100-160; 🖶🛜🖶) Daria and Simon are your affable hosts at this sweet B&B in the centre of town. There are cracking sea views from the terrace and the rooms are cheery, scattered with art and knick-knacks.

Hotel Moderno HOTEL €€ (☑0789 75 42 33, 0789 75 51 08; www.modernohotel.eu; Via Umberto 39; s €50-80, d €65-140, tr €90-180; 🖶🖶) This is a homey, family-run place near the piazza. Rooms are bright and airy with traditional blue-and-white Gallurese bedspreads and tiny balconies.

Agriturismo Saltara SARDINIAN €€ (☑0789 75 55 97; www.agriturismosaltara.it; Località Saltara; meals €40; ☺dinner daily; 🖶) Forget menus: just bring an open mind and a big appetite. Tables are positioned under the trees for course after delicious course of dishes such as ricotta-filled *culurgiones* and *porceddu* (suckling pig). Saltara is 10km south of town off the SP90 (follow the signs up a dirt track).

Il Grottino MEDITERRANEAN €€ (☑0789 75 42 32; Via del Mare 14; pizzas from €5, meals €30; ☺daily) Il Grottino sets a rustic scene with bare grey stone walls and warm, low lighting. The food is similarly wholesome with hearty, no-nonsense pastas, fresh seafood and juicy steaks.

ℹ️ Information

Bar Sport (Via Mazzini 7; per hr €5; ☺6am-midnight) Internet access.

Tourist Office (☑0789 75 41 27; www.comunesantateresagallura.it; Piazza Vittorio Emanuele 24; ☺10am-1pm & 4-8.30pm daily summer, 9am-1pm & 4-6pm Mon-Fri winter) Very helpful with loads of information.

ℹ️ Getting There & Around

From the bus terminus on Via Eleonora d'Arborea, buses run to and from Olbia (€5, 1½ hours, seven daily) and Sassari (€7, 2½ hours, three daily).

There are ferry services that run to Bonifacio in Corsica.

Palau & Arcipelago di La Maddalena

On Sardinia's northeastern tip, Palau is a well-to-do summer resort crowded with surf shops, boutiques, bars and restaurants. From here, year-round ferries make the short crossing over to **Isola della Maddalena**, the biggest of the more than 60 islands and islets that comprise the **Parco Nazionale dell'Arcipelago di La Maddalena** (www.lamaddalenapark.it). An area of spectacular, windswept seascapes, La Maddalena is best explored by boat, although the two main islands have plenty of charm with their sunbaked ochre buildings, cobbled piazzas and infectious holiday atmosphere.

🔍 Sights & Activities

The main activity in these parts is beach-bumming or boating around the islands. Down at the port in Palau, **Petag** (☑0789 70 86 81; www.petag.it) offers trips for about €35 per person from mid-May to mid-October, which include lunch and swimming time on well-known beaches. On La Maddalena, operators congregate around Cala Mangiavolpe.

Windsurfers converge on **Porto Pollo**, about 7km west of Palau, for some of the best wind conditions on the island. You can also try kitesurfing, canoeing, diving and sailing, with kit and lessons available along the beachfront.

There's also some excellent diving in the marine park. In Palau, **Nautilus** (☑0789 70 90 58; www.divesardegna.com; Piazza Fresi 8) runs dives from €50.

Linked to La Maddalena by a narrow causeway is **Isola Caprera**, a tiny island where Giuseppe Garibaldi once lived. His home, the **Compendio Garibaldino** (☑0789 72 71 62; www.compendiogaribaldino.it; adult/reduced €5/2.50; ⊙9am-7.15pm Tue-Sun), is visitable by guided tours (in Italian) only.

About 1.5km north of the Compendio, a walking trail drops down to the steep and secluded **Cala Coticcio** beach. Marginally easier to get to is **Cala Brigantina** (signposted), southeast of the complex.

Sleeping & Eating

It's strictly summer only in Palau and La Maddalena, where nearly everything closes from mid-October to Easter.

★**B&B Petite Maison**   B&B €
(☑0789 73 84 32; www.lapetitmaison.net; Via Livenza 7, La Maddalena; d €70-110) Liberally sprinkled with paintings and art deco furnishings, this B&B is a five-minute amble from the main square. Miriam's artistically presented breakfasts, with fresh, homemade goodies, are served in a bougainvillea-draped garden. Credit cards (and kids) are not accepted.

L'Orso e Il Mare   B&B €
(☑331 22 22 000; www.orsoeilmare.com; Vicolo Diaz 1, Palau; d €60-110, tr €70-130; ❋) Pietro gives a genuinely warm welcome at this B&B, just steps from Piazza Fresi. The spacious rooms sport breezy blue and white colour schemes. Breakfast is a fine spread of cakes, biscuits and fresh fruit salad.

Camping Baia Saraceno   CAMPGROUND €
(☑0789 70 94 03; www.baiasaraceno.com; Punta Nera, Palau; camping 2 people, car & tent €18-37, 2-person bungalows €90-174; ❋) Beautifully located on Palau's beach and shaded by pine trees, this campground has an on-site pizzeria, playground and dive centre.

San Giorgio   SARDINIAN €€
(☑0789 70 80 07; Via La Maddalena 4, Palau; pizzas €6-9, meals €30; ⊙Wed-Mon) The open-plan kitchen tells you all you need to know about this pizzeria-cum-restaurant. The spaghetti *allo scoglio* (with mixed seafood) is an excellent bet, as is the grilled fish.

❶ Information

Tourist offices Palau (☑0789 70 70 25; www.palauturismo.com; Palazzo Fresi; ⊙9am-1pm & 4-8pm summer, 9am-1pm Mon-Fri, plus 3-5pm Tue & Thu winter)
La Maddalena (☑0789 73 63 21; www.comune.lamaddalena.ot.it; Cala Gavetta; ⊙8.30am-1.30pm Mon-Fri, plus 3.30-5.30pm Mon & Wed)

❶ Getting There & Around

BOAT
Frequent car ferries to Isola Maddalena are operated by **Saremar** (☑199 118877; www.saremar.it) and **Delcomar** (☑0781 85 71 23; www.delcomar.it). The 15-minute crossing costs €6 per passenger and €13 for a small car (€1 less if you return the same day).

BUS
Services connect Palau with Olbia (€3.50, 1¼ hours, 10 daily), Santa Teresa di Gallura (€2, 40 minutes, five daily) and Arzachena (€1.50, 20 minutes, eight daily). In summer, **Nicos-Caramelli** (☑0789 67 06 13) runs buses to Porto Pollo (€2, 35 minutes), Baia Sardinia (€4.50, 35 minutes) and Porto Cervo (€4.50, 50 minutes). All buses leave from the port.

NUORO & THE EAST

If the Sardinians were to nominate one place as their geographical, cultural and spiritual heartland, this would surely be it. Nowhere is the force of nature more overpowering than here, where the Supramonte's limestone mountains give way to the Golfo di Orosei's plunging cliffs, grottoes and startling aquamarine waters.

Although larger towns are accessible by bus, you'll see more with your own set of wheels. A roller coaster of country roads leads to deep valleys concealing prehistoric *nuraghe*, the lonesome villages of the Barbagia steeped in bandit legends, and to holm oak forests where wild pigs roam.

Nuoro

POP 36,635

Once an isolated hilltop village and a byword for banditry, Nuoro had its cultural renaissance in the 19th and early 20th centuries when it became a hotbed of artistic talent. Today museums in the historic centre pay homage to local legends like Nobel Prize–winning author Grazia Deledda,

SARDINIA'S TOP FIVE CLIMBS & HIKES

➡ **Gola Su Gorropu** (p869) The trail to Gorropu from Genna 'e Silana pass is spectacular, taking in holm oak woods, boulder-strewn slopes and cave-riddled cliffs. It takes about two hours to go up, 1½ hours to come down.

➡ **Selvaggio Blu** This is the big one: an epic four- to seven-day, 45km trek along the Golfo di Orosei's dramatic coastline, traversing wooded ravines, cliffs and caves. A guide is recommended as the trail is not well signposted and there's no water en route. If you are going it alone, be aware that it involves scrambling, fixed-rope routes and abseiling, so some alpine mountaineering experience is necessary. Visit the website, www.selvaggioblu.it or get a copy of Enrico Spanu's *Book of Selvaggio Blu*.

➡ **Cala Luna** There's fabulous climbing above a beautiful bay, which is a scenic two-hour clifftop walk from Cala Fuili or a speedy boat ride from Cala Gonone. The 56 routes range from 5c to 8b+ and include some tricky single pitches in caves with overhangs.

➡ **La Poltrona** This massive limestone amphitheatre close to Cala Gonone has compact rock and 75 bolted routes from grades 4 to 8a. Mornings get too hot here in summer, so wait until late afternoon.

➡ **Golgo–Cala Goloritzè** It's an easy half-day hike along old mule trails from the plateau of Golgo to Cala Goloritzè, a perfect half-moon of white sand pummelled by astonishingly blue waters. Climbers can tackle its bizarre limestone pinnacles, including the Aguglia, a tough multipitch climb.

acclaimed poet Sebastiano Satta, novelist Salvatore Satta and sculptor Francesco Ciusa.

The city's spectacular backdrop is the granite peak of Monte Ortobene (955m), capped by a 7m-high bronze statue of the *Redentore* (Christ the Redeemer). The thickly wooded summit commands dress-circle views of the valley and the limestone mountains surrounding Oliena.

◉ Sights

Museo della Vita e delle Tradizioni Sarde   MUSEUM
(Via Antonio Mereu 56; adult/reduced €3/1; ⊙9am-7pm daily summer, 9am-1pm & 3-6pm Tue-Sun winter) This museum provides a fascinating insight into Sardinian traditions, folklore, superstitions and celebrations. Its pride and joy is the display of colourful traditional costumes.

Museo d'Arte   ART GALLERY
(MAN; www.museoman.it; Via S Satta 15; adult/reduced €3/2; ⊙10am-1pm & 3-7pm Tue-Sun) Set in a restored 19th-century town house, MAN is Sardinia's only serious modern art gallery. Its permanent collection boasts more than 400 works by the island's top 20th-century painters.

Museo Deleddiano   MUSEUM
(Via Grazia Deledda 53; adult/reduced €3/1; ⊙9am-7pm daily summer, 10am-1pm & 3-5pm Tue-Sun winter) Up in the oldest part of town, the birthplace of Grazia Deledda has been converted into this lovely little museum. The rooms, full of Deledda memorabilia, have been carefully restored to show what a well-to-do 19th-century Nuorese house actually looked like.

Festivals & Events

Sagra del Redentore   RELIGIOUS
In the last week of August, the 'Feast of Christ the Redeemer' is the main event in Nuoro, and one of Sardinia's most exuberant festivals, with parades, live music and a torchlit procession.

⌣ Sleeping & Eating

★ **Casa Solotti**   B&B €
(⌨328 602 89 75, 0784 3 39 54; www.casasolotti.it; Località Monte Ortobene; per person €26-35; P❄☎) This welcoming B&B sits in a rambling garden amid woods and walking trails near the top of Monte Ortobene, 5km from central Nuoro. Decorated with stone and beams, the elegantly rustic rooms have tremendous views of the surrounding valley and the Golfo di Orosei in the distance.

Nothing is too much trouble for your hosts, Mario and Frédérique, who can arrange everything from horse riding to packed lunches and guided hikes in the Supramonte.

Silvia e Paolo   B&B €
(☑ 0784 3 12 80; www.silviaepaolo.it; Corso Garibaldi 58; s €33-40, d €55-65; ❀ 🤝) Silvia and Paolo run this sweet B&B. Family treasures from dolls to old leather trunks make you feel right at home in the bright, spacious rooms. There's a roof terrace for observing the action on Corso Garibaldi by day and stargazing by night.

La Locanda Pili Monica   SARDINIAN €
(☑ 0784 3 10 32; Via Brofferio 31; meals around €15; ⊘ Mon-Sat) The €9.20 lunch is a bargain at this cheery, down-to-earth trattoria. Bag a table and you're in for a treat – think antipasti, fresh pasta and grilled steaks, washed down with highly quaffable house wine.

❶ Information

Tourist Office (☑ 0784 23 88 78; www.provincia.nuoro.it; Piazza Italia 7; ⊘ 8.30am-2pm Mon-Fri, plus 3.30-7pm Tue) Has plenty of useful information on Nuoro and environs.

❶ Getting There & Away

From the main bus station on Viale Sardegna there are services to the following destinations.

TO	FARE (€)	DURA-TION (HR)	FREQUENCY
Baunei	6	2	4 daily
Cagliari	15.50	2½-5	2 daily
Dorgali	3	¾	6 daily
Olbia	9	2½	8 daily
Oliena	1.50	½	frequent
Orgosolo	2.50	½	frequent
San Teodoro	7	1¾	8 daily
Santa Maria Navarrese	7	2½	5 daily
Tortolì	7	2¾	5 daily

Supramonte

Southeast of Nuoro rises the forbidding limestone massif of the Supramonte, its sheer walls like an iron curtain. This thrilling landscape forms the landward section of the **Parco Nazionale del Golfo di Orosei e del Gennargentu** (www.parcogennargentu.it), Sardinia's largest national park.

Oliena

POP 7355

From Nuoro you can see the multicoloured rooftops of Oliena cupped in the palm of Monte Corrasi (1463m). An atmospheric place with a grey-stone centre and a magnificent setting, it was founded in Roman times and is today famous for its blood-red Cannonau wine and traditional Easter celebrations.

◉ Sights & Activities

Piazza Santa Maria is the site of the Saturday market and the 13th-century **Chiesa di Santa Maria**. There are several other wonderful old churches here, including the blessedly simple 14th-century **Chiesa di San Lussorio** (Via Cavour).

The village's usual sleepy torpor is shattered on Easter Sunday for **S'Incontru** (The Meeting), a boisterous procession in which bearers carry a statue of Christ to meet a statue of the Virgin Mary in Piazza Santa Maria.

The countryside surrounding Oliena provides awesome trekking. **Sardegna Nascosta** (☑ 0784 28 85 50; www.sardegnanascosta. it), **Barbagia Insolita** (☑ 0784 28 60 05; www.barbagiainsolita.it; Corso Vittoria Emanuele 48) and **Cooperativa Enis** (☑ 0784 28 83 63; www.coopenis.it) all organise a range of excursions, including trekking, canoeing, abseiling, climbing and riding.

🛏 Sleeping & Eating

Hotel Monte Maccione   HOTEL, CAMPGROUND €
(☑ 0784 28 83 63; www.coopenis.it; Località Monte Maccione; s €39-49, d €66-80, tr €93-114, q €116-144, camping 2 people & tent €18; Ⓟ 🤝 ❀) Run by the Cooperativa Enis, this place offers breezy rooms done up in cool blues and greens, and grandstand views of the Supramonte from its hilltop location, 4km above Oliena. It also has a simple campground and a well-regarded restaurant (meals €22 to €35).

Hotel Cikappa   HOTEL €
(☑ 0784 28 80 24; www.cikappa.com; Corso Martin Luther King 2-4; s/d/tr €40/70/85; ❀ 🤝) Good modest digs above a popular restaurant (meals €25 to €35) in central Oliena. The best rooms have balconies overlooking the surrounding mountains.

★ **Agriturismo Guthiddai**   AGRITURISMO €€
(☑ 0784 28 60 17; www.agriturismoguthiddai. com; Nuoro-Dorgali bivio Su Gologone; half-board

per person €60-75; ❀ ☎ ⊞) On the road to Su Gologone, this whitewashed farmstead sits at the foot of rugged mountains, surrounded by fig, olive and fruit trees. Olive oil, Cannonau wine and fruit and veggies are all home produced. The rooms are exquisitely tiled in pale greens and cobalt blues.

Hotel Su Gologone　　　　　　HOTEL €€€
(☎ 0784 28 75 12; www.hotelsugologone.com; Località Su Gologone; s €105-170, d €160-250, ste €360-450; ⓟ ❀ ☎ ⊠) Treat yourself to a spot of rural luxury at Su Gologone, 7km east of Oliena. Rooms are decorated with original art works and handicrafts, and the facilities are top-notch – there's a pool, a wine cellar and a restaurant (meals around €50), where well-executed Sardinian specialities are served by an open fire or on the terrace.

Ristorante Masiloghi　　　　SARDINIAN €€
(☎ 0784 28 56 96; Via Galiani 68; meals €30-35; ☺ daily) A sunny Mediterranean villa on the main road into town. House specialities include homemade pasta, local lamb and boar stew.

ⓘ Information

Tourpass (☎ 0784 28 60 78; Corso Deledda 32; ☺ 9am-1pm & 4-6.30pm) The best source of information in Oliena is this private agency that can advise on activities in the area.

ⓘ Getting There & Away

ARST runs frequent buses from Via Roma to Nuoro (€1.50, 20 minutes, up to 12 Monday to Saturday, six Sunday).

Orgosolo & Mamoiada

For centuries Orgosolo was feared as a centre of banditry and kidnapping. Nowadays, it's better known for the vibrant graffiti-style murals that adorn its town centre. Like satirical caricatures, they depict all the big political events of the 20th century and are often very moving. An outstanding example is a series illustrating the death of 12-year-old Palestinian Mohammed el Dura as he hid behind his father during a Gaza shootout in 2000.

Ten kilometres to the west of Orgosolo, the undistinguished town of Mamoiada stages Sardinia's most sinister Carnevale celebrations. These kick off with the Festa di Sant'Antonio on 17 January, and climax on Shrove Tuesday and the preceding Sunday (February or early March). Stealing the limelight are the *mamuthones,* characters decked out in shaggy brown sheepskins and primitive wooden masks. Anthropologists believe that the *mamuthones* embodied all the untold horrors that primitive humans feared, and that the ritual parade is an attempt to exorcise these demons before the new spring.

Buses run to both Mamoiada (€2, 20 minutes) and Orgosolo (€2, 30 minutes) from Nuoro.

Dorgali

POP 8524

Dorgali is a down-to-earth town with a grandiose backdrop, nestled at the foot of Monte Bardia and framed by vineyards and olive groves. Limestone peaks rear above the centre's pastel-coloured houses and steep, narrow streets, luring hikers and climbers to their summits.

Other than perusing the local craftwork shops – Dorgali is famous for its leather goods, ceramics, carpets and filigree jewellery – the main attraction here is the great green wilderness, with the Golfo di Orosei and spectacularly rugged Supramonte within easy striking distance.

🛌 Sleeping & Eating

Sa Corte Antica B&B €
(📞 347 647 37 73; www.sacorteantica.it; Via Mannu 17; d €50-60, tr €65-75; 🌐) Gathered around an old stone courtyard, this B&B radiates old-world charm, with traditional reed ceilings and wrought-iron bedsteads. Homemade bread and *biscotti* (biscuits) are served at breakfast.

Ristorante Colibrì SARDINIAN €€
(📞 0784 9 60 54; Via Gramsci 14; meals €30; ⊙ Mon-Sat) Tucked away in an incongruous residential area (follow the signs), this is the bee's knees for meat eaters, with dishes like wild boar with rosemary and *porceddu*.

ℹ Information

Tourist Office (📞 0784 9 62 43; www.dorgali.it; Via Lamarmora 108b; ⊙ 10am-1pm & 4-8pm Mon-Fri) Provides information on Dorgali and Cala Gonone, including contact details for local trekking outfits and accommodation lists.

ℹ Getting There & Away

Buses serve Nuoro (€3, 45 minutes, six daily) and Olbia (€7.50, 2¾ hours, two daily). Up to six daily services shuttle back and forth between Dorgali and Cala Gonone (€1.20, 25 minutes).

Grotta di Ispinigoli

A short drive north of Dorgali, the fairy-tale-like **Grotta di Ispinigoli** (adult/reduced €7.50/3.50; ⊙ tours on the hour 9am-6pm summer, 10am-noon & 3-5pm winter) is a veritable forest of glittering stalagmites, including the world's second-tallest (the highest is in Mexico and stands at 40m). Unlike most caves of this type, which you enter from the side, here you descend 60m inside a giant 'well', at whose centre stands the magnificent 38m-high stalagmite. Photography is not permitted.

Serra Orrios & Thomes

The *nuraghic* village of **Serra Orrios** (adult/child €5/2.50; ⊙ hourly tours 9am-noon & 3-5pm) was inhabited between 1500 and 250 BC. Hidden among olive groves, the remains comprise a cluster of 70 or so horseshoe-shaped huts grouped around two basalt-hewn temples. The site lies 11km northwest of Dorgali (3km north off the Dorgali–Oliena road).

From Serra Orrios you could continue north to see the **Tomba dei Giganti S'Ena e Thomes** (⊙ dawn-dusk) `FREE`, a fine example of a *tomba dei giganti*, a Bronze Age megalithic tomb chamber. The stone monument is dominated by a central oval-shaped stele that once closed off an ancient burial chamber.

Gola Su Gorropu

The **Gola Su Gorropu** (📞 328 897 65 63; www.gorropu.info; adult/reduced €5/3.50; ⊙ tours 10.30am-3.30pm) is a spectacular gorge flanked by vertical 400m rock walls. From the Rio Flumineddu riverbed you can wander about 1km into the boulder-strewn gorge without climbing gear. After 500m you reach the narrowest point, just 4m wide.

There are two main approach routes. The more dramatic begins from the car park opposite Hotel Silana at the **Genna 'e Silana** pass on the SS125 at kilometre 183.

SARDINIA SUPRAMONTE

WORTH A TRIP

ROAD TRIPPING

It's well worth getting behind the wheel to drive the 60km stretch from Dorgali to Santa Maria Navarrese. Serpentine and at times hair-raising, the SS125 threads through the mountain tops where the scenery is distractingly lovely: to the right the ragged limestone peaks of the Supramonte rear above wooded valleys and deep gorges; to the left mountains tumble down to the bright-blue sea. The first 20km to the **Genna 'e Silana pass** (1017m) are the most breathtaking. Aside from the odd hell-for-leather Fiat, traffic is sparse, but you should take care at dusk, when wild pigs, goats, sheep and cows rule the road and bring down rocks.

The second and slightly easier route to Gorropu is via the Sa Barva bridge, about 15km from Dorgali. To get to the bridge, take the SS125 and look for the sign on the right for the Gola Su Gorropu and Tiscali between kilometres 200 and 201. Take this and continue until the asphalt finishes after about 20 minutes. Park here and cross the Sa Barva bridge, after which you'll see the trail for the Gola signposted off to the left. From here it's a scenic two-hour hike along the Rio Flumineddu to the mouth of the gorge.

Tiscali

Hidden in a mountain-top cave deep in the Valle Lanaittu, the *nuraghic* village of Tiscali (adult/reduced €5/2; ☺ 9am-7pm summer, to 5pm winter) is one of Sardinia's archaeological highlights. Dating from the 6th century BC and populated until Roman times, the village was discovered at the end of the 19th century. At the time it was relatively intact, but since then thieves have done a pretty good job of looting the place, stripping the conical stone-and-mud huts down to the skeletal remains that you see today.

Many local outfits offer guided tours (typically about €40), but if you want to go it alone the simplest route starts from the same point as for the Gola Su Gorropu. The trail is signposted and takes between 1½ and two hours; wear sturdy shoes and take ample water.

Golfo di Orosei

For sheer stop-dead-in-your-tracks beauty, there's no place like this gulf, forming the seaward section of the Parco Nazionale del Golfo di Orosei e del Gennargentu. Here high mountains abruptly meet the sea, forming a crescent of dramatic cliffs riven by false inlets, scattered with horseshoe-shaped bays and lapped by exquisitely aquamarine waters.

Cala Gonone

Climbers, divers, sea kayakers, hikers and beach bums all rave about Cala Gonone. Backed by imperious tree-specked cliffs, the resort has kept the low-key, family-friendly vibe of the small fishing village it once was. With an appealing line-up of hotels, bars and restaurants on its pine-fringed *lungomare*, Gonone makes a great base for outdoor adventures along this magnificent stretch of coast.

⊙ Sights & Activities

Kids love coming face to face with bubbling marine life at the new Acquario di Cala Gonone (www.acquariocalagonone.it; Via La Favorita; adult/reduced €10/7.50; ☺ 10am-6pm Apr-Oct). Or give them a lesson in prehistory at the romantic ruins of Nuraghe Mannu (adult/reduced €3/2; ☺ 9am-11am & 5-7pm, to 5pm low season, closed Nov-Mar), off the Cala Gonone–Dorgali road, with an eagle's-eye view over the whole coast.

DON'T MISS

THE BLUE CRESCENT

If you do nothing else in Sardinia, take a boat trip along Cala Gonone's southern coast. Some incredibly pretty cliff-flanked bays are accessible from town by car or on foot (eg, Cala Cartoe to the north, and Cala Fuili and Cala Luna to the south), but the best can only be reached by sea.

From the port, boats head south to the Grotta del Bue Marino (adult/reduced €8/4; ☺ guided tours hourly 10am-noon & 3-5pm Aug, 10am-noon & 3pm Jul, 10am, 11am & 3pm Sep, 11am & 3pm Oct-Nov & Mar-Jun), a haunting complex of stalactite- and stalagmite-filled caves where monk seals used to pup.

From there explore a string of coves and beaches, from the crescent-shaped Cala Luna and Cala Sisine, backed by a green valley, through to the dazzling-white pebbles and incredible cobalt-blue waters of Cala Mariolu.

The Nuovo Consorzio Trasporti Maritimi (☎ 0784 9 33 05; www.calagononecrociere.it; Porto Cala Gonone) whisks you along the beautiful coastline from March to late September. Its packages include return trips to Cala Luna (€15 to €23), Cala Sisine (€22 to €30) and Cala Mariolu (€30 to €40). A trip to the Grotta del Bue Marino costs between €19 and €22, which covers entry to the cave.

For the climbing lowdown and guided excursions, stop by **Prima Sardegna** (0784 9 33 67; www.primasardegna.com; Via Lungomare Palmasera 32). It also has bike/scooter/kayak rental for €24/48/30. **Argonauta** (349 473 86 52, 0784 9 30 46; www.argonauta.it; Via dei Lecci 10) offers a range of water-based activities, including snorkelling tours (€25), cavern and wreck dives (€45) and canyoning excursions (€40; minimum of five people).

🍴 Sleeping & Eating

The resort goes into hibernation from October until Easter; bookings are essential in summer. Besides the following options, the resort also has a campground. Snack bars, cafes and gelaterias line the *lungomare*.

★ Hotel L'Oasi
B&B €

(0784 9 31 11; www.loasihotel.it; Via Garcia Lorca 13; s €53-79, d €68-136; P ❋ 🛜) Perched on the cliffs above Cala Gonone and nestling in flowery gardens, this B&B offers enticing sea views from many of its breezy rooms. It's worth paying an extra €15 per person for half-board, as the three-course dinners are prepared with fresh local produce. L'Oasi is a 10-minute uphill walk from the harbour.

Agriturismo Nuraghe Mannu
AGRITURISMO, CAMPGROUND €

(0784 9 32 64; www.agriturismonuraghemannu. com; d €54-68, half-board per person €45-54, camping 2 people, car & tent €18-24; 🛍) 🌿 Off the SP26 Dorgali–Cala Gonone road, and immersed in greenery, this cracking *agriturismo* has four simple rooms, plus a tree-shaded camground with space for five tents. The farmhouse restaurant rustles up a feast of home-produced cheese, pork, lamb and wine.

Hotel Villa Gustui Maris
HOTEL €€

(0784 92 00 76; www.villagustuimaris.it; Via Marco Polo 57; s €136-200, d €148-200; ❋ @ 🛱 🛍) Wake up to sweeping views of the Golfo di Orosei at this Mediterranean villa-style hotel, a stiff 800m walk uphill from the resort centre. Quarters are bright and roomy, with tiled floors, lashings of cream and terracotta, and balconies or terraces (try for a sea-facing room). The pool is great for a scenic swim.

Il Pescatore
SEAFOOD €€

(0784 9 31 74; Via Acqua Dolce 7; meals €25-35; ⊙daily) Fresh seafood is what this place is about. Sit on the terrace for sea breezes and fishy delights like pasta with *ricci* and spaghetti with clams and *bottarga*.

THE LEMON HOUSE

A terrific base for outdoor escapades is the **Lemon House** (0782 66 95 07, 335 648 98 26; www.peteranne.it; Via Dante 10, Lotzorai; per person €30-43; 🛜), run by Peter and Anne. Peter has bolted some of the 800 climbing routes in the area and is a co-founder of Mountain **Bike Ogliastra** (visit www.mountain bikeogliastra.it). Their B&B is a relaxed base, with a roof terrace overlooking the mountains and sea, a bouldering wall, and homemade lemon marmalade served at breakfast. They can arrange bike hire and pick-ups, lend you a GPS and give you invaluable tips on hiking, climbing, mountain biking and kayaking.

Road House Blues
ITALIAN €€

(0784 9 31 87; Lungomare Palmasera 28; pizza €5-9.50, meals €20-30; ⊙daily) This laid-back haunt with a sea-facing terrace is great for a swift beer or a bite to eat. Dig into pizzas, Sardinian dishes like homemade pasta with sea anemones and *gnocchetti sardi* (shell-shaped pasta) with clams and mussels, grilled fish and steaks.

ℹ Information

Tourist Office (0784 9 36 96; www.dorgali.it; Viale Bue Marino 1a; ⊙9.30am-1.30pm & 3-7pm May-Sep, 9.30am-1.30pm Oct-Apr, 9.30am-8pm Jul & Aug) A very helpful office in the small park off to the right as you enter town.

ℹ Getting There & Away

Up to seven daily buses run to Cala Gonone from Dorgali (€1.20, 20 minutes, seven daily) and up to six to Nuoro (€3.50, 70 minutes).

Ogliastra

Wedged in-between the provinces of Nuoro and Cagliari, Ogliastra is a dramatic land of vast, unspoiled valleys, silent woods and windswept rock faces. The coastal stretches become increasingly dramatic the nearer you get to the Golfo di Orosei.

Baunei & the Altopiano del Golgo

Around 28km south of the Genna 'e Silana pass, you come to the uninspiring shepherd's town of Baunei. There's little reason to stop off here, but what is seriously worth your while is the 10km detour up to the **Altopiano del Golgo**, a strange, other-worldly plateau where goats and donkeys graze in dusty shrubland. From the town a signpost sends you up a 2km climb of impossibly steep switchbacks to the plateau. Head north and after 8km follow the **Su Sterru** (Il Golgo) sign for less than 1km, leave your vehicle and make for this remarkable feat of nature – a 270m abyss just 40m wide at its base. Its funnel-like opening is now fenced off but, knowing the size of the drop, just peering down is enough to bring on the vertigo.

In the heart of the plateau, the **Locanda Il Rifugio** (☑ 368 7028980, 0782 61 05 99; www.coopgoloritze.com; d €70, incl half board €110; ⊙ Apr-Oct) has six basic rooms in a converted farmstead and facilities for campers (€5 per tent). Managed by the **Cooperativa Goloritzè** (www.coopgoloritze.com), the refuge makes an excellent base for trekking and 4WD excursions. Many treks involve a descent from the plateau through dramatic *codula* (canyons) to the beautiful beaches of the Golfo di Orosei. Staff at the refuge also organise guides and logistical support for walkers attempting the once-in-a-lifetime Selvaggio Blu, Sardinia's toughest multiday trek.

Just beyond the refuge is the late-16th-century **Chiesa di San Pietro**, a humble construction flanked to one side by some even humbler *cumbessias* – rough, largely open stone affairs that are not at all comfortable for the passing pilgrims who traditionally sleep there on the saint's day.

Santa Maria Navarrese

At the southern end of the Golfo di Orosei sits the unpretentious and attractive beach resort of Santa Maria Navarrese. Shipwrecked Basque sailors built a small church here in 1052, dedicated to Santa Maria di Navarra on the orders of the Princess of Navarre, who happened to be one of the survivors. The church was set in the shade of a grand olive tree that is still standing – some say it's nearly 2000 years old.

Lofty pines and eucalyptus trees back the beach lapped by transparent water. Offshore are several islets, including the **Isolotto di Ogliastra**, a giant hunk of pink porphyritic

rock. The leafy northern end of the beach is topped by a watchtower built to look for raiding Saracens.

Down at the port, the **Consorzio Marittimo Ogliastra** (☑ 0782 61 51 73; www.mareogliastra.com) runs boat tours along the Golfo di Orosei for between €35 and €42 per person. Next door, **Nautica Centro Sub** (☑ 0782 61 55 22) organises dives (from €35) to some wonderful underwater spots.

The **Ostello Bellavista** (☑ 0782 61 40 39; www.ostelloinogliastra.com; Via Pedra Longa; s €35-65, d €50-100; ❄ 🖛) has light rooms with dreamy sea views. For drinks by the seafront, try the charismatic **Bar L'Olivastro** (☑ 0782 61 55 13; Via Lungomare Montesanto 1; ⊙ 8am-1am) below the branches of the town's famous olive tree.

A handful of buses link Santa Maria Navarrese with Tortolì (€1.50, 15 minutes, 11 daily), Dorgali (€5, 1½ hours, two daily) and Nuoro (€7, 2½ hours, five daily).

Tortolì & Arbatax
POP 10,826

Tortolì, Ogliastra's provincial capital, is unlikely to make a big impression with its large roadside hotels and uninspiring shops. About 4km away, **Arbatax** is little more than a port fronted by a few bars and restaurants. The only sight of any note is the *rocce rosse* (red rocks), a series of bizarre, weather-beaten rocks rising from the sea in Arbatax.

Near the port, you'll find the terminus for the **Trenino Verde**, the summer tourist train to Mandas.

There's no shortage of resort-style accommodation in these parts. Five minutes' stroll from the beach is **La Vecchia Marina** (☑ 0782 66 70 20; www.hotellavecchiamarina.com; Via Praga 1, Arbatax; d €70-140; 🅿❄🖛), a whitewashed hotel with an almost colonial feel, fringed by palm-dotted gardens. For Med-fresh seafood head to **Ittiturismo La Peschiera** (☑ 0782 66 44 15; Spiaggia della Cartiera, Arbatax; meals around €30; ⊙ daily), run by Tortolì's fishing cooperative.

Buses connect Tortolì with Santa Maria Navarrese (€1.50, 15 minutes, 11 daily), Dorgali (€5, one hour 50 minutes, one daily), and Nuoro (€7, 2¾ hours, five daily), as well as many inland villages.

Understand
Italy

Italy Today

Italy may be the beautiful country, but, regardless of their politics and circumstances, locals join in lamenting its state, concurring that the country is in an economic and political quagmire. Politics have long been a problem, with notoriously unstable governments – Berlusconi, with a record five-year stretch, was the longest serving prime minister since WWII. Unemployment rose from 6.2% in 2007 to 10.9% in 2012, while Italy's public debt had soared above 130% of GDP in 2013

Best Contemporary Songs

'Le Radici Ca Tieni' (Sud Sound System; 2003) Radical southern group sing about not forgetting your roots in a ragga-traditional music mash up.

'Nel blu dipinto di blu (Volare)' (Domenico Modugno; 1958) Infernally catchy, eternally sunny Eurovision hit.

'Ride on Time' (Black Box; 1989) Seminal Italo-house track stormed the dance floors in the late '80s.

'Albachiara' (Vasco Rossi; 1979) The poetic, rock Italian singer-songwriter's biggest hit.

Best Blogs

Beppe Grillo (www.beppegrillo.it/en/) Game-changing comedic and political musings of controversial comedian turned political leader.

Italian Politics with Watson (http://italpolblog.blogspot.se) Clear-cut and insightful discussions of political intrigues and intricacies.

La Tavola Marche (www.latavolamarche.blogspot.co.uk) American expat chef and food writer write on local cuisine and delicious recipes.

The Blonde Salad (www.theblondesalad.com) Influential fashion blogging by a Milanese student.

The Economy

The country is suffering economically and ordinary Italians are feeling the pain of austerity measures coupled with seemingly perpetual recession. In addition governments continue to be fragile and divided. As taxes and prices have risen, opportunities for employment have shrunk and wages flatlined; life in Italy is bleak for many. In 2013, one news story among many seemed to encapsulate the woes of the country: a couple in their 60s from Civitanova Marche committed suicide, unable to struggle on any longer on their small pension.

2013 Elections

The rise of former comedian Beppe Grillo's Five Star Movement, backed by 1 in 4 voters in the February 2013 elections, is an indication of how disillusioned Italians are, particularly the young, with traditional politics. Results from the election were inconclusive, resulting in a hung parliament.

Though ex–prime minister Silvio Berlusconi did not take office in 2013, he retained a hold on power, as Enrico Letta's new right-left coalition depends on the support of Berlusconi's People of Freedom (PdL) movement. It may seem incredible to outsiders, observing Berlusconi's scandal-mired life, but opinion polls continue to put the PdL movement out in front.

The Dreaded IMU

Besides Berlusconi's relative charisma and the country's fear of change, Berlusconi's enduring popularity may have been in part due to his promise to repay the unpopular Imposta Municipale Unica (IMU), a tax on properties. Never mind that Berlusconi's government originally introduced the tax (to apply to second homes and commence in 2014). The subsequent prime minister, Mario Monti, accelerated the introduction to 2012 and included people's primary residences, and therefore shouldered most of the blame.

Berlusconi's Trials & Tribulations

However, sensationally, in the summer of 2013, Berlusconi was successfully convicted of tax fraud, having exhausted the appeals process. The Supreme Court upheld his one-year sentence, but sent another part of the sentence – the five-year bar on holding public office – back to the Court of Appeal, so at the time of writing he was still able to continue in politics. Though it's worth considering that successful conviction may not be the end of Berlusconi as a leader: Beppe Grillo, who is unable to stand for government due to a manslaughter charge following a car accident, continues to lead the Five Star Movement from the sidelines.

Berlusconi has been facing trial over several cases, including tax evasion and bribery, but the most sensational trial is 'Rubygate'. In it, Berlusconi is accused of paying for sex with Karima El Mahroug, a nightclub dancer nicknamed Ruby Rubacuori (Ruby Heartstealer), while she was still 17 and therefore an underage prostitute. The encounters reputedly took place at so-called bunga bunga sessions; sex parties held at several of Berlusconi's villas. Berlusconi is further accused of providing false information to a Milan police chief in order to release El Mahroug from detention on unrelated theft charges (he allegedly claimed she was the granddaughter of President Mubarak of Egypt). In May 2013 a prosecutor in Milan told a court that Mr Berlusconi paid Ruby €4.5 million in late 2010.

Despite his prosecution and the numerous other ongoing cases, the former cruise-ship crooner insists that the claims are part of a plot orchestrated by the political left. But could it be that Italy's tumultuous relationship with Il Cavaliere ('the Knight') is finally in its death throes?

POPULATION: **61.5 MILLION**

AREA: **301,230 SQ KM**

NUMBER OF UNESCO WORLD HERITAGE SITES: **45**

AVERAGE CUPS OF COFFEE PER PERSON PER YEAR: **600**

if Italy were 100 people

93 would be Italian
4 would be Albanian & Eastern European
1 would be North African
2 would be others

belief systems
(% of population)

91
Roman Catholics

3.5
Other religions

1.5
Muslims

4
Other Christians

population per sq km

ROME   ITALY   USA

✝ ≈ 30 people

History

Few countries have been on such a roller-coaster ride as Italy. The Italian peninsula lay at the core of the Roman Empire; one of the world's great monotheistic religions, Catholicism, has its headquarters in Rome; and it was largely the dynamic city-states of Italy that set the modern era in motion with the Renaissance. But Italy has known chaos and deep suffering too. The rise of Europe's nation-states from the 16th century left the divided Italian peninsula behind. Italian unity was won in blood, but many Italians have since lived in abject poverty, sparking great waves of migration. The economic miracle of the 1960s propelled Italy to the top league of wealthy Western countries but, since the mid-1990s, the country has wallowed in a mire of frustration. A sluggish economy (hit hard by the global slump that began in 2008), unstable government, widespread corruption and the continuing open sore of the Mafia continue to overshadow the country's otherwise sunny disposition.

Etruscans, Greeks & Wolf-Raised Twins

A wide-ranging general site with potted Italian history is www. arcaini.com. It covers everything from prehistory to the post-war period, and includes a brief chronology.

Of the many tribes that emerged from the millennia of the Stone Age in ancient Italy, the Etruscans dominated the peninsula by the 7th century BC. Etruria was based on city-states mostly concentrated between the Arno and Tiber rivers. Among them were Caere (modern-day Cerveteri), Tarquinii (Tarquinia), Veii (Veio), Perusia (Perugia), Volaterrae (Volterra) and Arretium (Arezzo). The name of their homeland is preserved in the name Tuscany, where the bulk of their settlements were (and still are) located.

Most of what we know of the Etruscan people has been deduced from artefacts and paintings unearthed at their burial sights, especially at Tarquinia, near Rome. Argument persists over whether the Etruscans had migrated from Asia Minor. They spoke a language that today has barely been deciphered. An energetic people, the Etruscans were redoubtable warriors and seamen, but lacked cohesion and discipline.

At home, the Etruscans farmed, and mined metals. Their gods were numerous and they were forever trying to second-guess them and predict future events through such rituals as examining the livers of sacrificed animals. They were also quick to learn from others. Much of their

TIMELINE	c 700,000 BC	2000 BC	474 BC
	As long ago as 700,000 BC, primitive tribes lived in caves and hunted elephants, rhinoceros, hippopotamus and other hefty wild beasts on the Italian peninsula.	The Bronze Age reaches Italy. Hunter-gatherers have settled as farmers. The use of copper and bronze to fashion tools and arms marks a new sophistication.	The power of the Etruscans in Italy is eclipsed after Greek forces from Syracuse and Cumae join to crush an Etruscan armada off the southern Italian coast in the naval Battle of Cumae.

artistic tradition (which comes to us in the form of tomb frescoes, statuary and pottery) was influenced by the Greeks.

Indeed, while the Etruscans dominated the centre of the peninsula, Greek traders settled in the south in the 8th century BC, setting up a series of independent city-states along the coast and in Sicily that together were known as Magna Graecia. They flourished until the 3rd century BC and the ruins of magnificent Doric temples in Italy's south (at Paestum) and on Sicily (at Agrigento, Selinunte and Segesta) stand as testimony to the splendour of Greek civilisation in Italy.

Attempts by the Etruscans to conquer the Greek settlements failed and accelerated the Etruscan decline. The death knell, however, would come from an unexpected source – the grubby but growing Latin town of Rome.

The origins of the town are shrouded in myth, which says it was founded by Romulus (who descended from Aeneas, a refugee from Troy whose mother was the goddess Venus) on 21 April 753 BC on the site where he and his brother, Remus, had been suckled by a she-wolf as orphan infants. Romulus later killed Remus and the settlement was named Rome after him. At some point, legend merges with history. Seven kings are said to have followed Romulus and at least three were historical Etruscan rulers. In 509 BC, disgruntled Latin nobles turfed the last of the Etruscan kings, Tarquinius Superbus, out of Rome after his predecessor, Servius Tullius, had stacked the Senate with his allies and introduced citizenship reforms that undermined the power of the aristocracy. Sick of monarchy, the nobles set up the Roman Republic. Over the following centuries, this piffling Latin town would grow to become Italy's major power, gradually sweeping aside the Etruscans, whose language and culture disappeared by the 2nd century AD.

The Roman Republic

Under the Republic, *imperium,* or regal power, was placed in the hands of two consuls who acted as political and military leaders and were elected for non-renewable one-year terms by an assembly of the people. The Senate, whose members were appointed for life, advised the consuls.

Although from the beginning monuments were emblazoned with the initials SPQR (Senatus Populusque Romanus, or the Senate and People of Rome), the 'people' initially had precious little say in affairs. (The initials are still used and many Romans would argue that little has changed.) Known as plebeians (literally 'the many'), the disenfranchised majority slowly wrested concessions from the patrician class in the more than two centuries that followed the founding of the Republic. Some plebeians were even appointed as consuls and indeed by about 280 BC most of the distinctions between patricians and plebeians had disappeared.

Giuliano Procacci's *History of the Italian People* is one of the best general histories of the country in any language. It covers the period from the early Middle Ages until 1948.

The Romans devised a type of odometer that engaged with a vehicle's wheel to count every mile travelled.

264–241 BC	218-146 BC	133 BC	46 BC
War rages between Rome and the empire of Carthage, stretching across North Africa and into Spain, Sicily and Sardinia. By war's end Rome is the western Mediterranean's prime naval power.	Carthage sends Hannibal to invade Italy overland from the north in the Second Punic War. Rome invades Spain, Hannibal fails, and Carthage is destroyed in a third war in 149–146 BC.	Rome gains control of Sardinia, Sicily, Corsica, mainland Greece, Spain, most of North Africa and part of Asia Minor.	Julius Caesar assumes dictatorial powers.

That said, the apparently democratic system was largely oligarchic, with a fairly narrow political class (whether patrician or plebeian) vying for positions of power in government and the Senate.

The Romans were a rough-and-ready lot. Rome did not bother to mint coins until 269 BC, even though the neighbouring (and later conquered or allied) Etruscans and Greeks had long had their own currencies. The Etruscans and Greeks also brought writing to the attention of Romans, who found it useful for documents and technical affairs but hardly glowed in the literature department. Eventually the Greek pantheon of gods formed the bedrock of Roman worship. Society was patriarchal and its prime building block the household *(familia)*. The head of the family *(pater familias)* had direct control over his wife, children and extended family. He was responsible for his children's education. Devotion to household gods was as strong as to the increasingly Greek-influenced pantheon of state gods, led at first by the triad of Jupiter (the sky god and chief protector of the state), Juno (the female equivalent of Jupiter and patron goddess of women) and Minerva (patron goddess of craftsmen). Mars, the god of war, had been replaced by Juno in the triad.

Slowly at first, then with gathering pace, Roman armies conquered the Italian peninsula. Defeated city-states were not taken over directly; rather they were obliged to become allies. They retained their government and lands but had to provide troops on demand to serve in the Roman army. This relatively light-handed touch was a key to success. Increasingly, the protection offered by Roman hegemony induced many cities to become allies voluntarily. Wars with rivals like Carthage and in the East led Rome to take control of Sardinia, Sicily, Corsica, mainland Greece, Spain, most of North Africa and part of Asia Minor by 133 BC.

As the Empire grew, so did its ancient system of 'motorways'. With the roads came other bright concepts – postal services and wayside inns. Messages could be shot around the Empire in a matter of days or weeks by sending dispatch riders. At ancient 'truck stops', the riders would change mounts, have a bite and continue on their way (a more efficient system than many modern European postal systems).

By the second half of the 2nd century BC, Rome was the most important city in the Mediterranean, with a population of 300,000. Most were lower-class freedmen or slaves living in often precarious conditions. Tenement housing blocks (mostly of brick and wood) were raised alongside vast monuments. One of the latter was the Circus Flaminius, stage of some of the spectacular games held each year. These became increasingly important events for the people of Rome, who flocked to see gladiators and wild beasts in combat.

For Ancient Awe

Pantheon, Rome

Colosseum, Rome

Pompeii, Campania

Segesta, Sicily

Cerveteri, Lazio

30 BC	AD 79	100-138	476
Octavian (later Augustus) invades Egypt, Antony and Cleopatra commit suicide and Egypt becomes a province of Rome.	Mt Vesuvius showers molten rock and ash upon Pompeii and Herculaneum. Pliny the Younger later describes the eruption in letters and the towns are only rediscovered in the 18th century.	The Roman Empire reaches its most dominant extent, during the reign of Hadrian.	German tribal leader Odovacar proclaims himself king in Rome. The peninsula sinks into chaos and only the eastern half of the Empire survives intact.

Seizing the Day

Born in 100 BC, Gaius Julius Caesar would prove to be one of Rome's most masterful generals, lenient conquerors and capable administrators. He was also avid for power and this was probably his undoing.

He was a supporter of the consul Pompey (later known as Pompey the Great) who, since 78 BC, had become a leading figure in Rome after putting down rebellions in Spain and eliminating piracy. Caesar himself had been in Spain for several years, dealing with border revolts and, on his return to Rome in 60 BC, formed an alliance with Pompey and another important commander and former consul, Crassus. They backed Caesar's candidacy as consul.

To consolidate his position in the Roman power game, Caesar needed a major military command. This he received with a mandate to govern the province of Gallia Narbonensis, a southern swath of modern France stretching from Italy to the Pyrenees, from 59 BC. Caesar raised troops and in the following year entered Gaul proper (modern France) to head off an invasion of Helvetic tribes from Switzerland and subsequently to bring other tribes to heel. What started as an essentially defensive effort soon became a full-blown campaign of conquest. In the next five years, he subdued Gaul and made forays into Britain and across the Rhine. In 52–51 BC he stamped out the last great revolt in Gaul, led by Vercingetorix. Caesar was generous to his defeated enemies and so won the Gauls over to him. Indeed, they became his staunchest supporters in coming years.

By now, Caesar also had a devoted veteran army behind him. Jealous of the growing power of his one-time protégé, Pompey severed his political alliance with him and joined like-minded factions in the Senate to outlaw Caesar in 49 BC. On 7 January, Caesar crossed the Rubicon river into Italy and civil war began. His three-year campaign in Italy, Spain and the eastern Mediterranean proved a crushing victory. Upon his return to Rome in 46 BC, he assumed dictatorial powers.

He launched a series of reforms, overhauled the Senate and embarked on a building program (of which the Curia and Basilica Giulia remain).

By 44 BC it was clear Caesar had no plans to restore the Republic, and dissent grew in the Senate, even among former supporters like Marcus Junius Brutus, who thought he had gone too far. Unconcerned by rumours of a possible assassination attempt, Caesar had dismissed his bodyguard. A small band of conspirators led by Brutus finally stabbed him to death in a Senate meeting on the Ides of March (15 March) 44 BC, two years after he had been proclaimed dictator for life.

In the years following Caesar's death, his lieutenant, Mark Antony (Marcus Antonius), and nominated heir, great-nephew Octavian, plunged into civil war against Caesar's assassins. Things calmed down as

HISTORY SEIZING THE DAY

ROMAN SEX

Roman Sex by John Clarke is the result of decades of investigation into Roman eroticism, sexual mores and social attitudes. It is at once a serious anthropological retrospective and an amusing look at a society whose attitudes to sex were very different from our own.

568

Lombards invade and occupy northern Italy, leaving just Ravenna, Rome and southern Italy in the Empire's hands. Other tribes invade Balkan territories and cut the eastern Empire off from Italy.

754–56

Frankish king Pepin the Short enters Italy at the request of Pope Stephen II, defeats the Lombards and declares the creation of the Papal States.

902

Muslims from North Africa complete the occupation of Sicily, encouraging learning of the Greek classics, maths and other sciences. Agriculture flourishes and Sicily is relatively peaceful for two centuries.

FRENCH SCHOOL / GETTY IMAGES ©

➡ Tomb of Pepin the Short

The Roman Empire

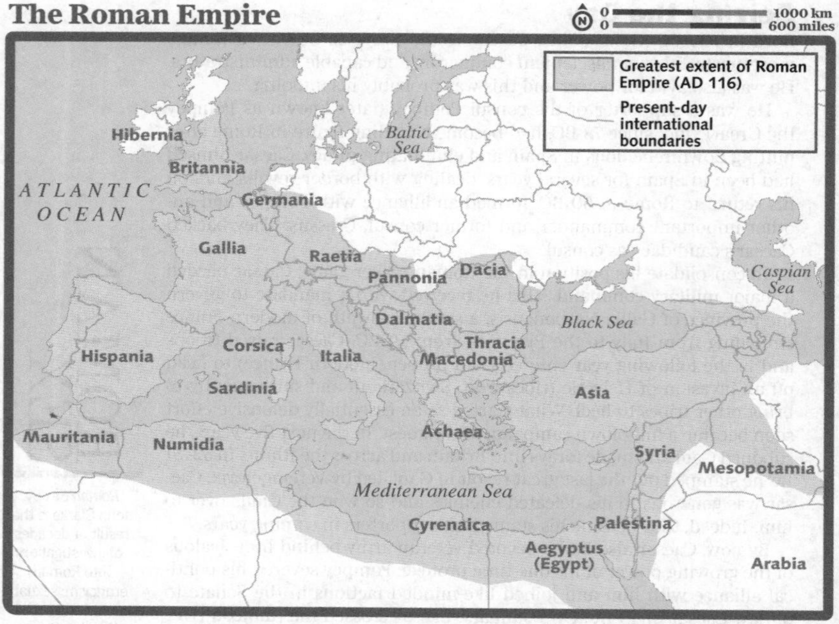

Greatest extent of Roman Empire (AD 116)

Present-day international boundaries

Map labels: Hibernia, Britannia, Baltic Sea, ATLANTIC OCEAN, Germania, Gallia, Raetia, Pannonia, Dacia, Caspian Sea, Dalmatia, Black Sea, Corsica, Italia, Thracia, Macedonia, Hispania, Sardinia, Asia, Mauritania, Numidia, Achaea, Syria, Mesopotamia, Mediterranean Sea, Cyrenaica, Palestina, Aegyptus (Egypt), Arabia

Octavian took control of the western half of the empire and Antony headed to the east, but when Antony fell head over heels for Cleopatra VII in 31 BC, Octavian went to war and finally claimed victory over Antony and Cleopatra at Actium, in Greece. The next year, Octavian invaded Egypt, Antony and Cleopatra committed suicide and Egypt became a province of Rome.

Augustus & the Glories of Empire

Octavian was left as sole ruler of the Roman world and by 27 BC had been acclaimed Augustus (Your Eminence) and conceded virtually unlimited power by the Senate. In effect, he had become emperor.

Under him, the arts flourished. Augustus was lucky in having as his contemporaries the poets Virgil, Horace and Ovid, as well as the historian Livy. He encouraged the visual arts, restored existing buildings and constructed many new ones. During his reign the Pantheon was raised

962	1130	1202–03	1271
Otto I is crowned Holy Roman Emperor in Rome, the first in a long line of Germanic rulers. His meddling in Italian affairs leads to clashes between papacy and empire.	Norman invader Roger II is crowned king of Sicily, a century after the Normans landed in southern Italy and so creating a united southern Italian kingdom.	Venice leads the Fourth Crusade to the Holy Land on a detour to Constantinople in revenge for attacks on Venetian interests there. The Crusaders topple the Byzantine emperor, installing a puppet ruler.	Venetian merchant Marco Polo embarks on a 24-year journey to Central Asia and China with his father and uncle. His written travel accounts help enlighten Europeans about Asia.

and he boasted that he had 'found Rome in brick and left it in marble'. The long period of comparatively enlightened rule that he initiated brought unprecedented prosperity and security to the Mediterranean.

By AD 100, the city of Rome is said to have had more than 1.5 million inhabitants and all the trappings of the imperial capital – its wealth and prosperity were obvious in the rich mosaics, marble temples, public baths, theatres, circuses and libraries. People of all races and conditions converged on the capital. Poverty was rife among an often disgruntled lower class. Augustus had created Rome's first police force under a city prefect *(praefectus urbi)* to curb mob violence, which had long gone largely unchecked. He had also instituted a 7000-man fire brigade and night watchman service.

Augustus carried out other far-reaching reforms. He streamlined the army, which was kept at a standing total of around 300,000 men. Military service ranged from 16 to 25 years, but Augustus kept conscription to a minimum, making it a largely volunteer force. He consolidated Rome's three-tier class society. The richest and most influential class remained the Senators. Below them, the so-called Equestrians filled posts in public administration and supplied officers to the army (control of which was essential to keeping Augustus' position unchallenged). The bulk of the populace filled the ranks of the lower class. The system was by no means rigid and upward mobility was possible.

A century after Augustus' death in AD 14 (at age 75), the Empire had reached its greatest extent. Under Hadrian (76–138), the Empire stretched from the Iberian peninsula, Gaul and Britain to a line that basically followed the Rhine and Danube rivers. All of the present-day Balkans and Greece, along with the areas known in those times as Dacia, Moesia and Thrace (considerable territories reaching to the Black Sea), were under Roman control. Most of modern-day Turkey, Syria, Lebanon, Palestine and Israel were occupied by Rome's legions and linked up with Egypt. From there a deep strip of Roman territory stretched along the length of North Africa to the Atlantic coast of what is today northern Morocco. The Mediterranean was a Roman lake.

This situation lasted until the 3rd century. By the time Diocletian (245–305) became emperor, attacks on the Empire from without and revolts within had become part and parcel of imperial existence. A new religious force, Christianity, was gaining popularity and under Diocletian persecution of Christians became common, a policy reversed in 313 under Constantine I (c 272–337) in his Edict of Milan.

Inspired by a vision of the cross, Constantine defeated his own rival, Maxentius, on Rome's Ponte Milvio (Milvian Bridge) in 312, becoming the Roman Empire's first Christian leader and commissioning Rome's first Christian basilica, San Giovanni in Laterano.

HISTORY AUGUSTUS & THE GLORIES OF EMPIRE

For Ancient Booty

Vatican Museums, Rome

Capitoline Museums, Rome

Museo Archeologico Nazionale, Naples

Museo Archeologico Paolo Orsi, Syracuse

Museo Nazionale Etrusco di Villa Giulia, Rome

1282	1309	1321	1348
Charles of Anjou creates enemies in Sicily with heavy taxes on landowners, who rise in the Sicilian Vespers revolt. They hand control of Sicily to Peter III, King of Aragón.	Pope Clement V shifts the papacy to Avignon, France, for almost 70 years. Clement had been elected pope four years earlier but refused to rule in a hostile Rome.	Dante Alighieri completes his epic poem *La divina commedia* (The Divine Comedy). The Florentine poet, considered Italy's greatest literary figure, dies the same year.	The Black Death (bubonic plague) wreaks havoc across Italy and much of the rest of western Europe. Florence is said to have lost three-quarters of its populace.

The Empire was later divided in two, with the second capital in Constantinople (founded by Constantine in 330; today known as Istanbul), on the Bosporus in Byzantium. It was this, the eastern Empire, which survived as Italy and Rome were overrun. This rump empire stretched from parts of present-day Serbia and Montenegro across to Asia Minor, a coastal strip of what is now Syria, Lebanon, Jordan and Israel down to Egypt and a sliver of North Africa as far west as modern Libya. Attempts by Justinian I (482–565) to recover Rome and the shattered western half of the Empire ultimately came to nothing.

Papal Power & Family Feuds

In an odd twist, the minority religion that Emperor Diocletian had tried so hard to stamp out saved the glory of the city of Rome. Through the chaos of invasion and counter-invasion that saw Italy succumb to Germanic tribes, the Byzantine reconquest and the Lombard occupation in the north, the papacy established itself in Rome as a spiritual and secular force.

The popes were, even at this early stage, a canny crowd. The papacy invented the Donation of Constantine, a document in which Emperor

---

IMPERIAL INSANITY

Bribes? Booty jokes? *Bunga bunga* parties? Spare a thought for the ancient Romans, who suffered their fair share of eccentric leaders. We salute some of the Empire's wackiest, weirdest and downright kinkiest rulers.

Tiberius (14–37) – A steady governing hand but prone to depression, Tiberius had a difficult relationship with the Senate and withdrew in his later years to Capri, where, they say, he devoted himself to drinking, orgies and fits of paranoia.

Gaius (Caligula) (37–41) – 'Little Shoes' made grand-uncle Tiberius look tame. Sex (including with his sisters) and gratuitous, cruel violence were high on his agenda. He emptied the state's coffers and suggested making a horse consul, before being assassinated.

Claudius (41–54) – Apparently timid as a child, he proved ruthless with his enemies (among them 35 senators), whose executions he greatly enjoyed watching. According to English historian Edward Gibbon, he was the only one of the first 15 emperors not to take male lovers (unusual at the time).

Nero (54–68) – Augustus' last descendant, Nero had his pushy stage mum murdered, his first wife's veins slashed, his second wife kicked to death and his third wife's ex-husband killed. The people accused him of playing the fiddle while Rome burned to the ground in 64. He blamed the disaster on the Christians, executed the evangelists Peter and Paul and had others thrown to wild beasts in a grisly public spectacle.

1506	1508–12	1534	1582
Work starts on St Peter's Basilica, to a design by Donato Bramante, over the site of an earlier basilica in Rome. Work would continue on Christendom's showpiece church until 1626.	Pope Julius II commissions Michelangelo to paint the ceiling frescoes in the Sistine Chapel. Michelangelo decides the context, and the central nine panels recount stories from Genesis.	The accession of Pope Paul III marks the beginning of the Counter-Reformation.	Pope Gregory XIII replaces the Julian calendar (introduced by Julius Caesar) with the modern-day Gregorian calendar. The new calendar adds the leap year to keep in line with the seasons.

Constantine I had supposedly granted the Church control of Rome and surrounding territory. What the popes needed was a guarantor with military clout. This they found in the Franks and a deal was done.

In return for formal recognition of the popes' control of Rome and surrounding Byzantine-held territories henceforth to be known as the Papal States, the popes granted the Carolingian Franks a leading (if ill-defined) role in Italy and their king, Charlemagne, the title of Holy Roman Emperor. He was crowned by Leo III on Christmas Day 800. The bond between the papacy and the Byzantine Empire was thus broken and political power in what had been the Western Roman Empire shifted north of the Alps, where it would remain for more than 1000 years.

The stage was set for a future of seemingly endless struggles. Similarly, Rome's aristocratic families engaged in battle for the papacy. For centuries, the imperial crown would be fought over ruthlessly and Italy would frequently be the prime battleground. Holy Roman Emperors would seek time and again to impose their control on increasingly independent-minded Italian cities, and even on Rome itself. In riposte, the popes continually sought to exploit their spiritual position to bring the emperors to heel and further their own secular ends.

The clash between Pope Gregory VII and Emperor Henry IV over who had the right to appoint bishops (who were powerful political players and hence important friends or dangerous foes) in the last quarter of the 11th century showed just how bitter these struggles could become. They became a focal point of Italian politics in the late Middle Ages and across the cities and regions of the peninsula two camps emerged: Guelphs (Guelfi, who backed the pope) and Ghibellines (Ghibellini, in support of the emperor).

The Wonder of the World

The Holy Roman Empire had barely touched southern Italy until Henry, son of the Holy Roman Emperor Frederick I (Barbarossa), married Constance de Hauteville, heir to the Norman throne in Sicily. The Normans had arrived in southern Italy in the 10th century, initially as pilgrims en route from Jerusalem, later as mercenaries attracted by the money to be made fighting for rival principalities and against the Arab Muslims in Sicily. Of Henry and Constance's match was born one of the most colourful figures of medieval Europe, Frederick II (1194–1250).

Crowned Holy Roman Emperor in 1220, Frederick was a German with a difference. Having grown up in southern Italy, he considered Sicily his natural base and left the German states largely to their own devices. A warrior and scholar, Frederick was an enlightened ruler with an absolutist vocation. A man who allowed freedom of worship to Muslims and

SPAGHETTI

The Arabs introduced spaghetti to Sicily, where 'strings of pasta' were documented by the Arab geographer Al-Idrissi in Palermo in 1150.

1600

Dominican monk and proud philosopher Giordano Bruno is burned alive at the stake in Rome for heresy after eight years of trial and torture at the hands of the Inquisition.

→ Statue of Giordano Bruno

1714

The War of the Spanish Succession ends forcing the Spanish to withdraw from Lombardy. The Spanish Bourbons establish an independent Kingdom of the Two Sicilies.

1805

Napoleon is proclaimed king of the newly constituted Kingdom of Italy, comprising most of the northern half of the country. A year later he takes the Kingdom of Naples.

A WHIFF OF HELLFIRE

Politics in Italy's mercurial city-states could take a radical turn. When Florence's Medici clan rulers fell into disgrace (not for the last time) in 1494, the city's fathers decided to restore an earlier republican model of government. This time there was a twist.

Since 1481, the Dominican friar Girolamo Savonarola had been in Florence preaching repentance. His blood-curdling warnings of horrors to come if Florentines did not renounce their evil ways somehow captured everyone's imagination and the city now submitted to a fiery theocracy. He called on the government to act on the basis of his divine inspiration. Drinking, whoring, partying, gambling, flashy fashion and other signs of wrongdoing were pushed well underground. Books, clothes, jewellery, fancy furnishings and art were burned on 'bonfires of the vanities'. Bands of children marched around the city ferreting out adults still attached to their old habits and possessions.

Pleasure-loving Florentines soon began to tire of this fundamentalism, as did Pope Alexander VI (possibly the least religiously inclined pope of all time) and the rival Franciscan religious order. The local economy was stagnant and Savonarola seemed increasingly out to lunch with his claims of being God's special emissary. Finally the city government, or *signoria*, had the fiery friar arrested. After weeks at the hands of the city rack-master, he was hanged and burned at the stake as a heretic, along with two supporters, on 22 May 1498.

Jews, he was not to everyone's liking, as his ambition was to finally bring all of Italy under the imperial yoke.

A poet, linguist, mathematician, philosopher and all-round fine fellow, Frederick founded a university in Naples and encouraged the spread of learning and translation of Arab treatises. From his early days at the imperial helm, he was known as Stupor Mundi (the Wonder of the World) for his extraordinary talents, energy and military prowess.

Having reluctantly carried out a crusade (marked more by negotiation than the clash of arms) in the Holy Land in 1228 and 1229 on pain of excommunication, Frederick returned to Italy to find Papal troops invading Neapolitan territory. Frederick soon had them on the run and turned his attention to gaining control of the complex web of city-states in central and northern Italy, where he found allies and many enemies, in particular the Lombard League. Years of inconclusive battles ensued, which even Frederick's death in 1250 did not end. Several times he had been on the verge of taking Rome and victory had seemed assured more than once. Campaigning continued until 1268 under Frederick's successors, Manfredi (who fell in the bloody Battle of Benevento in 1266) and Corradino (captured and executed two years later by French noble Charles of Anjou, who had by then taken over Sicily and southern Italy).

For Medieval Mystique

Gubbio, Umbria

Bologna, Emilia-Romagna

Perugia, Umbria

Assisi, Umbria

Scanno, Abruzzo

1814–15	1848	1860	1861
After Napoleon's fall, the Congress of Vienna is held to re-establish the balance of power in Europe. The result for Italy is largely a return of the old occupying powers.	European revolts spark rebellion in Italy, especially in Austrian-occupied Milan and Venice. Piedmont's King Carlo Alberto joins the fray against Austria, but within a year Austria recovers Lombardy and Veneto.	In the name of Italian unity, Giuseppe Garibaldi lands with 1000 men, the Red Shirts, in Sicily. He takes the island and lands in southern Italy.	By the end of the 1859–61 Franco-Austrian War, Vittorio Emanuele II controls Lombardy, Sardinia, Sicily, southern and parts of central Italy and is proclaimed king of a newly united Italy.

Rise of the City-States

While the south of Italy tended to centralised rule, the north was heading the opposite way. Port cities such as Genoa, Pisa and especially Venice, along with internal centres such as Florence, Milan, Parma, Bologna, Padua, Verona and Modena, became increasingly insolent towards attempts by the Holy Roman Emperors to meddle in their affairs.

The cities' growing prosperity and independence also brought them into conflict with Rome, which found itself increasingly incapable of exercising influence over them. Indeed, at times Rome's control over some of its own Papal States was challenged. Caught between the papacy and the emperors, it was not surprising that these city-states were forever switching allegiances in an attempt to best serve their own interests.

Between the 12th and 14th centuries, they developed new forms of government. Venice adopted an oligarchic, 'parliamentary' system in an attempt at limited democracy. More commonly, the city-state created a *comune* (town council), a form of republican government dominated at first by aristocrats but then increasingly by the wealthy middle classes. The well-heeled families soon turned their attentions from business rivalry to political struggles, in which each aimed to gain control of the *signoria* (government).

In some cities, great dynasties, such as the Medici in Florence and the Visconti and Sforza in Milan, came to dominate their respective stages.

War between the city-states was constant and eventually a few, notably Florence, Milan and Venice, emerged as regional powers and absorbed their neighbours. Their power was based on a mix of trade, industry and conquest. Constellations of power and alliances were in constant flux, making changes in the city-states' fortunes the rule rather than the exception. Easily the most stable and long the most successful of them was Venice.

In Florence, prosperity was based on the wool trade, finance and general commerce. Abroad, its coinage, the *firenze* (florin), was king.

In Milan, the noble Visconti family destroyed its rivals and extended Milanese control over Pavia and Cremona, and later Genoa. Giangaleazzo Visconti (1351–1402) turned Milan from a city-state into a strong European power. The policies of the Visconti (up to 1450), followed by those of the Sforza family, allowed Milan to spread its power to the Ticino area of Switzerland and east to the Lago di Garda.

The Milanese sphere of influence butted up against that of Venice. By 1450 the lagoon city had reached the height of its territorial greatness. In addition to its possessions in Greece, Dalmatia and beyond, Venice had

ORIGINS OF BANKING

Europe's first modern banks appeared in Genoa in the 12th century. The city claims the first recorded public bond (1150) and the earliest known exchange contract (1156). Italy's Banca Monte dei Paschi di Siena is the world's oldest surviving bank, counting coins since 1472.

1889	1908	1915	1919
Raffaele Esposito invents *pizza margherita* in honour of Queen Margherita, who takes her first bite of the Neapolitan staple on a royal visit to the city.	On the morning of 28 December, Messina and Reggio di Calabria are struck by a 7.5-magnitude earthquake and a 13-metre-high tsunami. More than 80,000 lives are lost.	Italy enters WWI on the side of the Allies to win Italian territories still in Austrian hands after Austria's offer to cede some of the territories is deemed insufficient.	Former socialist journalist Benito Mussolini forms a right-wing militant group, the Fasci Italiani di Combattimento (Italian Combat Fasces), precursor to his Fascist Party.

886

HISTORY A NATION IS BORN

expanded inland. The banner of the Lion of St Mark flew across northeast Italy, from Gorizia to Bergamo.

These dynamic, independent-minded cities proved fertile ground for the intellectual and artistic explosion that would take place across northern Italy in the 14th and 15th centuries – an explosion that would come to be known as the Renaissance and the birth of the modern world. Of them all, Florence was the cradle and launch pad for this fevered activity, in no small measure due to the generous patronage of the long-ruling Medici family.

A Nation is Born

The French Revolution at the end of the 18th century and the rise of Napoleon awakened hopes in Italy of independent nationhood. Since the glory days of the Renaissance, Italy's divided mini-states had gradually lost power and status on the European stage. By the late 18th century, the peninsula was little more than a tired, backward playground for the big powers and a Grand Tour hot spot for the romantically inclined.

Napoleon marched into Italy on several occasions, finishing off the Venetian republic in 1797 (ending 1000 years of Venetian independence) and creating the so-called Kingdom of Italy in 1805. That kingdom was in no way independent but the Napoleonic earthquake spurred many Italians to believe that a single Italian state could be created after the emperor's demise.

It was not to be so easy. The reactionary Congress of Vienna restored all the foreign rulers to their places in Italy.

Count Camillo Benso di Cavour (1810–61) of Turin, the prime minister of the Savoy monarchy, became the diplomatic brains behind the Italian unity movement. Through the pro-unity newspaper, *Il Risorgimento* (founded in 1847) and the publication of a parliamentary *Statuto* (Statute), Cavour and his colleagues laid the groundwork for unity.

Cavour conspired with the French and won British support for the creation of an independent Italian state. His 1858 treaty with France's Napoleon III foresaw French aid in the event of a war with Austria and the creation of a northern Italian kingdom, in exchange for parts of Savoy and Nice.

The bloody Franco-Austrian War (also known as the Second Italian War of Independence; 1859–61), unleashed in northern Italy, led to the occupation of Lombardy and the retreat of the Austrians to their eastern possessions in the Veneto. In the meantime, a wild card in the form of professional revolutionary Giuseppe Garibaldi had created the real chance of full Italian unity. Garibaldi took Sicily and southern Italy in a military blitz in the name of Savoy king Vittorio Emanuele II in 1860. Spotting the chance, Cavour and the king moved to take parts of central

America was named after Amerigo Vespucci, a Florentine navigator who, from 1497 to 1504, made several voyages of discovery in what would one day be known as South America.

For Renaissance Elegance

Duomo, Florence

Galleria degli Uffizi, Florence

Tempietto di Bramante, Rome

La Rotonda, Vicenza

The Last Supper, Milan

1922
Mussolini and his Fascists stage a march on Rome in October. Doubting the army's loyalty, a fearful King Vittorio Emanuele III entrusts Mussolini with the formation of a government.

1929
Mussolini and Pope Pius XI sign the Lateran Pact, which declares Catholicism as Italy's sole religion and the Vatican an independent state. Satisfied, the papacy acknowledges the Kingdom of Italy.

→ View of St Peter's Basilica, Vatican City

Italy (including Umbria and Le Marche) and so were able to proclaim the creation of a single Italian state in 1861.

In the following nine years, Tuscany, the Veneto and Rome were all incorporated into the fledgling kingdom. Unity was complete and parliament was established in Rome in 1871.

The turbulent new state saw violent swings between socialists and the right. Giovanni Giolitti, one of Italy's longest-serving prime ministers (heading five governments between 1892 and 1921), managed to bridge the political extremes and institute male suffrage. Women, however, were denied the right to vote until after WWII.

From the Trenches to Fascism

When war broke out in Europe in July 1914, Italy chose to remain neutral despite being a member of the Triple Alliance with Austria and Germany. Italy had territorial claims on Austrian-controlled Trento (Trentino), southern Tyrol, Trieste and even in Dalmatia (some of which it had tried and failed to take during the Austro-Prussian War of 1866). Under the terms of the Triple Alliance, Austria was due to hand over much of this territory in the event of occupying other land in the Balkans, but Austria refused to contemplate fulfilling this part of the bargain.

The Italian government was divided between a non-interventionist and war party. The latter, in view of Austria's intransigence, decided to deal with the Allies. In the London pact of April 1915, Italy was promised the territories it sought after victory. In May, Italy declared war on Austria and thus plunged into a 3½-year nightmare.

Italy and Austria engaged in a weary war of attrition. The Austro-Hungarian forces collapsed in November 1918, whereupon the Austrian Empire ceded the South Tyrol, Trieste, Trentino, and Istria to Italy in the Treaty of Saint-Germain-en-Laye. However, it was felt that the postwar Treaty of Versailles failed to award Italy the remaining territories it wanted, a perception that was exploited by the Italian fascists led by Mussolini.

These were slim pickings after such a bloody and exhausting conflict. Italy lost 600,000 men and the war economy had produced a small concentration of powerful industrial barons while leaving the bulk of the civilian populace in penury. This cocktail was made all the more explosive as hundreds of thousands of demobbed servicemen returned home or shifted around the country in search of work. The atmosphere was perfect for a demagogue, who was not long in coming forth.

Benito Mussolini (1883–1945) was a young war enthusiast who had once been a socialist newspaper editor and one-time draft dodger. This time he volunteered for the front and only returned, wounded, in 1917.

The experience of war and the frustration shared by many at the disappointing outcome in Versailles led him to form a right-wing militant

John Julius Norwich's *A History of Venice* is one of the all-time great works on the lagoon city in English and is highly readable. He has also published *Venice: Paradise of Cities*.

1935	1940	1943	1944
Italy seeks a new colonial conquest through the invasion of Abyssinia (Ethiopia) from Eritrea. The League of Nations condemns the invasion and imposes limited sanctions on Italy.	Italy enters WWII on Nazi Germany's side and invades Greece, which quickly proves to be a mistake. Greek forces counter-attack and enter southern Albania. Germany saves Italy in 1941.	King Vittorio Emanuele III sacks Mussolini. He is replaced by Marshall Badoglio, who surrenders after Allied landings in southern Italy. German forces free Mussolini.	Mount Vesuvius explodes back into action on 18 March. The eruption is captured on film by USAAF (United States Army Air Forces) personnel stationed nearby.

political group that by 1921 had become the Fascist Party, with its black-shirted street brawlers and Roman salute. These were to become symbols of violent oppression and aggressive nationalism for the next 23 years. After his march on Rome in 1922 and victory in the 1924 elections, Mussolini, who called himself Il Duce (the Leader), took full control of the country by 1926, banning other political parties, trade unions not affiliated to the party, and the free press.

By the 1930s, all aspects of Italian society were regulated by the party. The economy, banking, a massive public works program, the conversion of coastal malarial swamps into arable land and an ambitious modernisation of the armed forces were all part of Mussolini's grand plan.

On the international front, Mussolini at first showed a cautious hand, signing international cooperation pacts (including the 1928 Kellogg Pact solemnly renouncing war) and until 1935 moving close to France and the UK to contain the growing menace of Adolf Hitler's rapidly re-arming Germany.

That all changed when Mussolini decided to invade Abyssinia (Ethiopia) as the first big step to creating a 'new Roman empire'. This aggressive side of Mussolini's policy had already led to skirmishes with Greece over the island of Corfu and to military expeditions against nationalist forces in the Italian colony of Libya.

The League of Nations condemned the Abyssinian adventure (King Vittorio Emanuele III was declared Emperor of Abyssinia in 1936) and from then on Mussolini changed course, drawing closer to Nazi Germany. They backed the rebel General Franco in the three-year Spanish Civil War and in 1939 signed an alliance pact.

WWII broke out in September 1939 with Hitler's invasion of Poland. Italy remained aloof until June 1940, by which time Germany had overrun Norway, Denmark, the Low Countries and much of France. It seemed too easy and so Mussolini entered on Germany's side in 1940, a move Hitler must have regretted later. Germany found itself pulling Italy's chestnuts out of the fire in campaigns in the Balkans and North Africa and could not prevent Allied landings in Sicily in 1943.

By then, the Italians had had enough of Mussolini and his war and so the king had the dictator arrested. In September, Italy surrendered and the Germans, who had rescued Mussolini, occupied the northern two-thirds of the country and reinstalled the dictator.

The painfully slow Allied campaign up the peninsula and German repression led to the formation of the Resistance, which played a growing role in harassing German forces. Northern Italy was finally liberated in April 1945. Resistance fighters caught Mussolini as he fled north in the hope of reaching Switzerland. They shot him and his lover, Clara Petacci, before stringing up their corpses (along with others) in Milan's Piazzale

For more on the history of Fascist Italy, see www.thecorner.org/home.htm. Here you can trace Mussolini's rise to power and the tumultuous years of his rule.

Roberto Rossellini's *Roma, Città Aperta* (Rome, Open City), starring Anna Magnani, is a classic of Italian neorealist cinema and a masterful look at wartime Rome. The film is the first in his Trilogy of War, followed by *Paisà* and *Germania anno zero* (Germany: Year Zero).

1946	1957	1957	1960
Italians vote in a national referendum to abolish the monarchy and create a republic. King Umberto II leaves Italy and refuses to recognise the result.	Italy joins France, West Germany and the Benelux countries to sign the Treaty of Rome, which creates the European Economic Community (EEC). The treaty takes effect on 1 January 1958.	Turin-based car manufacturer Fiat launches the Fiat 500 in July. Designed by Dante Giacosa, the compact vehicle would become an icon of Italian industrial design.	Federico Fellini's iconic film *La Dolce Vita* is released. Capturing life in a newly affluent postwar Rome, the film is nominated for four Academy Awards.

Lotto. This was a far cry from Il Duce's hopes for a glorious burial alongside his ancient imperial idol, Augustus, in Rome.

The Grey and Red Years

In the aftermath of war, the left-wing Resistance was disarmed and Italy's political forces scrambled to regroup. The USA, through the economic largesse of the Marshall Plan, wielded considerable political influence and used this to keep the left in check.

Immediately after the war, three coalition governments succeeded one another. The third, which came to power in December 1945, was dominated by the newly formed right-wing Democrazia Cristiana (DC; Christian Democrats), led by Alcide De Gasperi, who remained prime minister until 1953. Italy became a republic in 1946 and De Gasperi's DC won the first elections under the new constitution in 1948.

Until the 1980s, the Partito Comunista Italiano (PCI; Communist Party), at first under Palmiro Togliatti and later the charismatic Enrico Berlinguer, played a crucial role in Italy's social and political development, in spite of being systematically kept out of government.

The very popularity of the party led to a grey period in the country's history, the *anni di piombo* (years of lead) in the 1970s. Just as the Italian economy was booming, Europe-wide paranoia about the power of the Communists in Italy fuelled a secretive reaction that, it is said, was largely directed by the CIA and NATO. Even today, little is known about Operation Gladio, an underground paramilitary organisation supposedly behind various unexplained terror attacks in the country, apparently designed to create an atmosphere or fear in which, should the Communists come close to power, a right-wing coup could be quickly carried out.

> Although much has happened since it was written, Paul Ginsborg's *A History of Contemporary Italy: Society and Politics, 1943–1988* remains one of the most readable and insightful books on postwar Italy.

GOING THE DISTANCE FOR THE RESISTANCE

In 1943–44, the Assisi Underground hid hundreds of Jewish Italians in Umbrian convents and monasteries, while the Tuscan Resistance forged travel documents for them – but the refugees needed those documents fast, before they were deported to concentration camps by Fascist officials. Enter the fastest man in Italy: Gino Bartali, world-famous Tuscan cyclist, Tour de France winner and three-time champion of the Giro d'Italia. After his death in 2003, documents revealed that during his 'training rides' throughout the war years, Bartali had carried Resistance intelligence and falsified documents to transport Jewish refugees to safe locations. Bartali was interrogated at the dreaded Villa Triste in Florence, where suspected anti-Fascists were routinely tortured – but he revealed nothing. Until his death, the long-distance hero downplayed, even to his children, his efforts to rescue Jewish refugees, saying, 'One does these things, and then that's that.'

1966	1970	1980	1980
A devastating flood inundates Florence in early November, leaving around 100 people dead, 5000 families homeless and 14,000 movable artworks damaged. The flood is the city's worst since 1557.	Parliament approves the country's first-ever divorce legislation. Unwilling to accept this 'defeat', the Christian Democrats call a referendum in 1974. Italians vote against the referendum.	A bomb in Bologna kills 85 and injures hundreds more. The Red Brigades and a Fascist cell both claim responsibility. Analysis later points to possible para-state terrorism in Operation Gladio.	At 7.34pm on 25 November, a 6.8–Richter scale earthquake strikes Campania. The quake kills almost 3000 people and causes widespread damage, including in the city of Naples.

The 1970s were thus dominated by the spectre of terrorism and considerable social unrest, especially in the universities. Neo-Fascist terrorists struck with a bomb blast in Milan in 1969. In 1978, the Brigate Rosse (Red Brigades, a group of young left-wing militants responsible for several bomb blasts and assassinations), claimed their most important victim – former DC prime minister Aldo Moro. His kidnap and murder some 54 days later (the subject of the 2003 film *Buongiorno, notte*) shook the country.

Despite the disquiet, the 1970s was also a time of positive change. In 1970, regional governments with limited powers were formed in 15 of the country's 20 regions (the other five, Sicily, Sardinia, Valle d'Aosta, Trentino-Alto Adige and Friuli Venezia Giulia, already had strong autonomy statutes). In the same year, divorce became legal and eight years later abortion was also legalised, following anti-sexist legislation that allowed women to keep their own names after marriage.

Claudia Cardinale starred in the 1984 Italian film *Claretta*, about the racy life and tragic end of Clara Petacci, Mussolini's lover. Given the chance to flee when they were captured, she instead tried in vain to shield Il Duce from the partisan execution squad's bullets.

Clean Hands, Berlusconi & Five Star

A growth spurt in the aftermath of WWII saw Italy become one of the world's leading economies, but by the 1970s the economy had begun to stagnate, and by the mid-1990s a new and prolonged period of crisis had set in. High unemployment and inflation, combined with a huge national debt and mercurial currency (the lira), led the government to introduce Draconian measures to cut public spending, allowing Italy to join the single currency (euro) in 2001.

As political parties splintered and economic crisis set in, the 1990s saw the Italian political scene rocked by the Tangentopoli ('kickback city') scandal, which broke in Milan in 1992. Led by a pool of Milanese magistrates, including the tough Antonio di Pietro, investigations known as *Mani Pulite* (Clean Hands) implicated thousands of politicians, public officials and businesspeople in scandals ranging from bribery and receiving kickbacks to blatant theft.

The old centre-right political parties collapsed in the wake of these trials and from the ashes rose what many Italians hoped might be a breath of fresh political air. Media magnate Silvio Berlusconi's Forza Italia (Go Italy) party swept to power in 2001 and (after an inconclusive two-year interlude of centre-left government under former European Commission head Romano Prodi from 2006) again in April 2008. Berlusconi's carefully choreographed blend of charisma, confidence, irreverence and promises of tax cuts appealed to many Italian voters. His transformation from cruise-ship crooner to populist media mogul (and football club owner) encapsulated the ultimate self-made success story, and his own corporate success was widely acknowledged as proof of an innate economic know-how.

1995	2001	2004–05	2005
Maurizio Gucci, heir to the Gucci fashion empire, is gunned down outside his Milan offices. Three years later, his estranged wife Patrizia Reggiani is jailed for ordering his murder.	Silvio Berlusconi's right-wing Casa delle Libertà (Liberties House) coalition wins an absolute majority in national polls. The following five years are marked by economic stagnation.	Tension between rival Camorra clans explodes on the streets of suburban Naples. In only four months, almost 50 people are gunned down in retribution attacks.	Pope John Paul II dies aged 84, prompting a wave of sorrow and chants of 'santo subito' ('sainthood now'). He is succeeded by Benedict XVI, the German Cardinal Ratzinger.

Berlusconi's tenure turned out to not be just more of the same, but if anything, even worse. A series of laws were passed that protected his extensive business interests, and the economy went from bad to worse.

However, in 2011, Berlusconi was forced to resign due to Italy's worsening economic situation in relation to the eurozone's sovereign debt crisis (see also p875 for more on Berlusconi's Trials and Tribulations). A government of technocrats, headed by economist Mario Monti took over until the inconclusive elections of February 2013. After lengthy post-electoral negotiations, Enrico Letta, a member of the Partito Democratico (PD), was named prime minister, heading a precarious right-left coalition.

It's difficult to see how any of contemporary Italy's problems, relating mainly to the black economy, mafia, corruption, nepotism, lack of growth, unemployment (particularly among the young) and the low birth rate coupled with an ageing population, may be addressed with any success, in such an uncertain political and economic climate.

Some Italians believe that the Five Star Movement, started by comedian-activist Beppe Grillo, offers a glimmer of hope. The movement won around 25% of the votes in the February 2013 election, despite not appearing on TV and campaigning only via the internet and huge rallies across Italy. This new, young movement (the average age of its politicians is 37, two decades younger than other parties) subsequently refused to make any post-electoral deals with the other parties, wanting to differentiate itself from the old political class. 'Five Star' refers to its principal policy issues of access to water, environmentalism, sustainable transport, internet connectivity and development. Only time will tell if the Five Star movement will cause the sea change that it desires.

POPE JOHN PAUL II

The death of Pope John Paul II in April 2005 saw a gob-smacking four million mourners pour into Rome in a single week amid chants of 'santo subito' ('sainthood now').

2006	2011	2011	2013
Juventus, AC Milan and three other top Serie A football teams receive hefty fines in a match-rigging scandal that also sees Juventus stripped of its 2005 and 2006 championship titles.	Berlusconi stands trial in Milan in April on charges of abuse of power and paying for sex with under-aged Moroccan prostitute Karima El Mahroug (aka Ruby Heartstealer).	Berlusconi is forced to quit, and economist Mario Monti is put in charge, heading a government of technocrats.	After an inconclusive February election, Enrico Letta is named prime minister of a shaky left-right coalition. Beppe Grillo's Five Star Movement, having won 25% of the votes, refuses to make any pacts with other parties.

Italian Art & Architecture

The history of Italian art and architecture is in may ways also the history of Western art and architecture. From the classical, Renaissance and baroque to the futurist and Metaphysical, the artistic world's seminal movements and periods have been forged by a pantheon of Italian greats including Giotto, Botticelli, da Vinci, Michelangelo, Bernini and more recently, Piano and Hadid.

Italy's dedicated art police, the Comando Carabinieri Tutela Patrimonio Culturale, tackles the looting of Italy's priceless heritage. It's estimated that over 100,000 ancient tombs have been ransacked by *tombaroli* (tomb raiders) alone; the contents often sold to private and public collectors around the world.

Art

The Ancient & the Classical

In art, as in so many other realms, the ancient Romans looked to the Greeks for examples of best practice. The Greeks had settled many parts of Sicily and southern Italy as early as the 8th century BC, naming it Magna Graecia and building great cities such as Syracuse and Taranto. These cities were famous for their magnificent temples, many of which were decorated with sculptures modelled on, or inspired by, masterpieces by Praxiteles, Lysippus and Phidias.

Sculpture flourished in southern Italy into the Hellenistic period. It also gained popularity in central Italy, where the primitive art of the Etruscans (the people of ancient central Italy) was influenced and greatly refined by the contribution of Greek artisans, who arrived through trade.

In Rome, sculpture, architecture and painting flourished under first the Republic and then the Empire. But the art that was produced here during this period was different in many ways from the Greek art that influenced it. Essentially secular, it focused less on harmony and form and more on accurate representation, mainly in the form of sculptural portraits. Innumerable versions of Pompey, Titus and Augustus all show a similar visage, proving that the artists were seeking verisimilitude in their representations and not just glorification.

And while the Greeks saw art as being solely about harmony, beauty and drama, Roman emperors like Augustus were happy to utilise art as a political tool, using it to celebrate status, power and image. This form of narrative art often took the form of relief decoration recounting the story of great military victories – the Colonna di Traiano (Trajan's Column) and the Ara Pacis Augustae (Altar of Peace) in Rome exemplify this tradition. Both are magnificent, monumental examples of art as propaganda, exalting the emperor and Rome in a form that no one could possibly ignore.

Wealthy Roman citizens also dabbled in the arts, building palatial villas and adorning them with statues looted from the Greek world or copied from Hellenic originals. Today, museums in Rome burst at the seams with such trophies, from the Capitoline Museums' copy of *Galata morente* (Dying Gaul, c 240–200 BC) to the Vatican Museums' original Greek *Laocoön and His Sons* (c 160–140 BC).

And while the Etruscans had used wall painting – most notably in their tombs at centres like Tarquinia and Cerveteri in modern-day Lazio, it was the Romans who refined the form, refocusing on landscape scenes to adorn the walls of the living. A visit to Rome's Museo Nazionale Romano: Palazzo Massimo alle Terme or to Naples' Museo Archeologico Nazionale offers sublime examples of the form.

The Glitter of Byzantine

In 330, Emperor Constantine, a convert to Christianity, made the ancient city of Byzantium his capital and renamed it Constantinople. The city became the great cultural and artistic centre of Christianity and it remained so up to the time of the Renaissance, though its influence on the art of that period was never as fundamental as the art of ancient Rome.

The Byzantine period was notable for its sublime ecclesiastical and palace architecture, its extraordinary mosaic work and – to a lesser extent – its painting. Its art was influenced by the decoration of the Roman catacombs and the early Christian churches, as well as by the Oriental Greek style, with its love of rich decoration and luminous colour. Byzantine art works de-emphasised the naturalistic aspects of the classical tradition and exalted the spirit over the body, so glorifying God rather than humanity or the state.

In Italy, the Byzantine virtuosity with mosaics was showcased in Ravenna, the capital of the Byzantine Empire's western regions in the 6th century. The city's Basilica di Sant'Apollinare in Classe, Basilica di San Vitale and Basilica di Sant'Apollinare Nuovo house some of the world's finest Byzantine art, their hand-cut glazed tiles *(tesserae)* balancing extraordinary naturalness with an epic sense of grandeur and mystery.

Yet, the Byzantine aesthetic was not limited to Ravenna. In Venice it would influence the exotic design of the Basilica di San Marco, while in

Masterpiece Mosaics
....
Basilica di Sant'Apollinare in Classe, Ravenna
....
Basilica di San Vitale, Ravenna
....
Basilica di San Marco, Venice
....
Cattedrale di Monreale, Monreale

CAPITAL SCANDALS: CONTROVERSIAL ART IN ROME

➜ **The Last Judgment (1537–41), Michelangelo** There were more than just arms and legs dangling from Michelangelo's Sistine Chapel fresco in Rome's Vatican Museums. The depiction of full-frontal nudity on the chapel's altar horrified Catholic Counter-Reformation critics. No doubt Michelangelo turned in his grave when the offending bits were covered up.

➜ **Madonna and Child with St Anne (1605–06), Caravaggio** St Anne looks more 'beggar-woman' than 'beatified grandmother', but it's Mary who made the faithful blush on Caravaggio's canvas, her propped-up cleavage a little too 'flesh-and-bone' for the mother of God. The sexed-up scene was too much for the artist's client, who offered a *'Grazie, but no grazie'*. The painting now hangs in Rome's Museo e Galleria Borghese.

➜ **St Matthew and the Angel (1602), Caravaggio** In the original version, personal space (or the sheer lack of it) was the main problem for Caravaggio's client Cardinal del Monte. Featuring a sensual, handsome angel snuggling up to St Matthew, exactly what kind of inspiration the winged visitor was offering the saint was anybody's guess. And so Caravaggio went back to his easel, producing the prime-time version now gracing the Chiesa di San Luigi dei Francesi in Rome.

➜ **Conquering Venus (1805–08), Antonio Canova** When asked whether she minded posing nude, Paolina Bonaparte Borghese provocatively replied 'Why should I?'. Given her well-known infidelities, this marble depiction of Napoleon's wayward sister as the Roman goddess of love merely confirmed her salacious reputation. This fact was not lost on her husband, Italian prince Camillo Borghese, who forbade the sculpture from leaving their home. You'll also find it the Museo e Galleria Borghese.

Rome it would leave its mark in the technicolour interior of the Chiesa di San Prassede.

In Sicily, Byzantine, Norman and Arab influences fused to create a distinct regional style showcased in the mosaic-encrusted splendour of Palermo's Cappella Palatina, as well as the cathedrals of Monreale and Cefalù.

The Not-so-Dark Ages

Italy has more World Heritage–listed sites than any other country in the world; many of its 47 listings are there in the guise of repositories of great art.

The Italian Middle Ages have often been dismissed as a 'dark' age between the Roman and Byzantine Empires and the Renaissance. However, to ignore this period would make it difficult to understand all subsequent Italian history. This is because Italy as we know it was born in the Middle Ages. The barbarian invasions of the 5th and 6th centuries began a process that turned a unified empire into a land of small independent city-states, and it was these states – or rather the merchants, princes, clergy, corporations and guilds who lived within them – that started the craze in artistic patronage that was to underpin the great innovations in art and architecture that would define the Renaissance.

Continuing the trend kick-started in the Byzantine period, ideas of clarity and simplicity of religious message began to outweigh ideals of faithful representation during the medieval period. This is why, at first glance, many pictures of the period look rather stiff.

Indeed, painting and sculpture of this period played second fiddle to its architecture, commonly known as 'Romanesque'. Complementing this architectural style was the work of the Cosmati, a Roman guild of

ART, ANGER & ARTEMESIA

Sex, fame and notoriety: the life of Artemesia Gentileschi (1593–1652) could spawn a top-rating soap opera. One of the early baroque's greatest artists (and one of the few females), Gentileschi was born in Rome to Tuscan painter Orazio Gentileschi. Orazio wasted little time introducing his young daughter to the city's working artists. Among her mentors was Michelangelo Merisi da Caravaggio, whose chiaroscuro technique would deeply influence her own style.

At the tender age of 17, Gentileschi produced her first masterpiece, *Susanna and the Elders* (1610), now in the Schönborn Collection in Pommersfelden, Germany. Her depiction of the sexually harassed Susanna proved eerily foreboding: two years later Artemesia would find herself at the centre of a seven-month trial, in which Florentine artist Agostino Tassi was charged with her rape.

Out of Gentileschi's fury came the gripping, technically brilliant *Judith Slaying Holofernes* (1612–13). While the original hangs in Naples' Museo di Capodimonte, you'll find a larger, later version in Florence's Uffizi. Vengeful Judith would make a further appearance in *Judith and her Maidservant* (c 1613–14), now in Florence's Palazzo Pitti. While living in Florence, Gentileschi completed a string of commissions for Cosimo II of the Medici dynasty, as well as becoming the first female member of the prestigious Accademia delle Arti del Disegno (Academy of the Arts of Drawing).

After separating from her husband, Tuscan painter Pietro Antonio di Vincenzo Stiattesi, Gentileschi headed south to Naples sometime between 1626 and 1630. Here her creations would include *The Annunciation* (1630), also in Naples' Museo di Capodimonte, and her *Self-Portrait as the Allegory of Painting* (1630), housed in London's Kensington Palace. The latter work received praise for its simultaneous depiction of art, artist and muse; an innovation at the time. Gentileschi's way with the brush was not lost on King Charles I of England, who honoured the Italian talent with a court residency from 1638 to 1641.

Despite her illustrious career, Gentileschi inhabited a man's world. Nothing would prove this more than the surviving epitaphs commemorating her death, focused not on her creative brilliance, but on the gossip depicting her as a cheating nymphomaniac.

mosaic and marble workers who specialised in assembling fragments of coloured stones and glass mosaics and combining them with large stone disks and strips of white marble to create stunning intricate pavements, columns and church furnishings as seen in Rome's Chiesa di Santa Maria in Cosmedin, Basilica di Santa Maria Maggiore and Chiesa di Santa Maria Sopra Minerva.

Gothic Refinement

The Gothic style was much slower to take off in Italy than it had been in the rest of Europe. But it did, marking the transition from medieval restraint to the Renaissance, and seeing artists once again drawing inspiration from life itself rather than solely religion. Occurring at the same time as the development of court society and the rise of civic culture in the city-states, its art was both sophisticated and elegant, highlighting attention to detail, a luminous palette and an increasingly refined technique. The first innovations were made in Pisa by sculptor Nicola Pisano (c 1220–84), who emulated the example of the French Gothic masters and studied classical sculpture in order to represent nature more convincingly, but the major strides forward occurred in Florence and Siena.

Giotto & the 'Rebirth' of Italian Art

The Byzantine painters in Italy knew how to make use of light and shade and had an understanding of the principles of foreshortening (how to convey an effect of perspective). It only required a genius to break the spell of their conservatism and to venture into a new world of naturalism. Enter Florentine painter Giotto di Bondone (c 1266–1337), whose brushstrokes focused on dramatic narrative and the accurate representation of figures and landscape. The Italian poet Giovanni Boccaccio wrote in his *Decameron* (1350–53) that Giotto was 'a genius so sublime that there was nothing produced by nature...that he could not depict to the life; his depiction looked not like a copy, but the real thing.'

Boccaccio wasn't the only prominent critic of the time to consider Giotto revolutionary – the first historian of Italian art, Giorgio Vasari, said in his *Lives of the Artists* (1550) that Giotto initiated the 'rebirth' (*rinascità* or *renaissance*) in art. Giotto's most famous works are all in the medium of the fresco (where paint is applied on a wall while the plaster is still damp), and his supreme achievement is the cycle gracing the walls of Padua's Cappella degli Scrovegni. It's impossible to overestimate Giotto's achievement with these frescoes, which illustrate the stories of the lives of the Virgin and Christ. Abandoning popular conventions such as the three-quarter view of head and body, he presented his figures from behind, from the side or turning around, just as the story demanded. Giotto had no need for lashings of gold paint and elaborate ornamentation either, opting to convey the scene's dramatic tension through a naturalistic rendition of figures and a radical composition that created the illusion of depth.

Giotto's oeuvre isn't limited to the frescoes in the Cappella degli Scrovegni. His Life of St Francis cycle in the Upper Church of the Basilica di San Francesco in Assisi is almost as extraordinary and was to greatly influence his peers, many of whom worked in Assisi during the decoration of the church. One of the most prominent of these was the Dominican friar Fra' Angelico (c 1395–1455), a Florentine painter who was famed for his mastery of colour and light. His *Annunciation* (c 1450) in the convent of the Museo di San Marco in Florence is arguably his most accomplished work.

Click onto www. exibart.com (mostly in Italian) for up-to-date listings of art exhibitions throughout Italy, as well as exhibition reviews, articles and interviews.

ITALIAN ART & ARCHITECTURE ART

GIOTTO

Many Renaissance painters included self-portraits in their major works. Giotto didn't, possibly due to the fact that friends such as Giovanni Boccaccio described him as the ugliest man in Florence. With friends like those...

CARAVAGGIO

In *M: The Man Who Became Caravaggio*, Peter Robb gives a passionate personal assessment of the artist's paintings and a colourful account of Caravaggio's life, arguing he was murdered for having sex with the pageboy of a high-ranking Maltese aristocrat.

The Sienese School

Giotto wasn't the only painter of his time to experiment with form, colour and composition and create a radical new style. The great Sienese master Duccio di Buoninsegna (c 1255–1319) successfully breathed new life into the old Byzantine forms using light and shade. His preferred medium was panel painting and his major work is probably his *Maestà* (Virgin Mary in Majesty; 1311) in Siena's Museo dell'Opera Metropolitana.

It was in Siena, too, that two new trends took off: the introduction of court painters and the advent of secular art.

The first of many painters to be given ongoing commissions by one major patron or court, Simone Martini (c 1284–1344) was almost as famous as Giotto in his day. His best-known painting is the stylised *Maestà* (1315–16) in Siena's Museo Civico, in which he pioneered his famous iridescent palette (one colour transformed into another within the same plane).

Also working in Siena at this time were the Lorenzetti brothers, Pietro (c 1280–1348) and Ambrogio (c 1290–1348), who are considered the greatest exponents of what, for a better term, can be referred to as secular painting. Ambrogio's magnificent *Allegories of Good and Bad Government* (1337–40) in the Museo Civico lauds the fruits of good government and the gruesome results of bad. In the frescoes, he applies the rules of perspective with an accuracy previously unseen, as well as significantly developing the Italian landscape tradition. In *Life in the Country,* one of the allegories, Ambrogio successfully depicts the time of day, the season, colour reflections and shadows – a naturalistic depiction of landscape that was quite unique at this time.

The Venetians

While Byzantine influence lingered longer in Venice than in many other parts of Italy, its grip on the city loosened by the early to mid-15th century. In *Polyptych of St James* (c 1450) by Michele Giambono (c 1400–62) in Venice's Galleria dell'Accademia, the luscious locks and fair complexion of the archangel Michael channel the style of early Renaissance master Pisanello (c 1395–1455). The winds of change blow even stronger in fellow Accademia resident *Madonna with Child* (c 1455) by Jacopo Bellini (c 1396–1470). Featuring a bright-eyed baby Jesus and a patient, seemingly sleep-deprived Mary, it's an image any parent might relate to. Relatable emotions are equally strong in the biblical scenes of Andrea Mantegna (1431–1506); one can almost hear the sobbing in his *Lamentation over the Dead Christ* (c 1480) in Milan's Pinacoteca di Brera.

Tuscan painter Gentile da Fabriano (c 1370–1427) was in Venice during the early stages of his transition to Renaissance realism, and his evolving style reputedly influenced Venetian Antonio Vivarini (c 1415–80), the latter's *Passion* polyptych in Venice's Ca' d'Oro radiating tremendous pathos. Antonio's brother, Bartolomeo Vivarini (c 1432–99) created a delightful altarpiece in Venice's I Frari, in which a baby Jesus wriggles out of the arms of his mother, squarely seated on her marble Renaissance throne.

In 1475, visiting Sicilian painter Antonello da Messina (c 1430–1479) introduced the Venetians to oil paints. It would prove a perfect match, the Venetians' knack for layering and blending colours creating a new luminosity that would ultimately redefine the city's art. Among the early ground-breakers was Giovanni Bellini (c 1430–1516). The son of Jacopo Bellini, his Accademia *Annunciation* (1500) deployed glowing reds and ambers to focus attention on the solitary figure of the kneeling Madonna, the angel Gabriel arriving in a rush of geometrically rumpled drapery.

Bellini's prowess with the palette was not lost on his students, among them Giorgione (1477–1510) and Titian (c 1488–1576). Giorgione preferred to paint from inspiration without sketching out his subject first, as in his enigmatic, *La Tempesta* (The Storm; 1500), also in the Accademia. The younger Titian set himself apart with brushstrokes that brought his subjects to life, from his early and measured *St Mark Enthroned* (1510) in Venice's Chiesa di Santa Maria della Salute to his thick, textured swansong *Pietà* (1576) in the Accademia.

Titian raised the bar for a new generation of northern Italian masters, including Jacopo Robusti, aka Tintoretto (1518–94). Occasionally enhancing his colours with finely crushed glass, Tintoretto's action-packed biblical scenes read like a modern graphic novel. His wall and ceiling paintings in Venice's Scuola Grande di San Rocco are nail-bitingly spectacular, laced with holy superheroes, swooping angels, and deep, ominous shadows. Paolo Caliari, aka Veronese (1528–88) was another 16th-century superstar, the remarkable radiance of his hues captured in the *Feast in the House of Levi* (1573), another Accademia must-see.

British art critic Andrew Graham-Dixon has written three authoritative books on Italian art: *Michelangelo and the Sistine Chapel*; *Caravaggio: A Life Sacred & Profane*; and *Renaissance*, the companion book to the BBC TV series.

ITALIAN ART & ARCHITECTURE ART

WHO'S WHO IN RENAISSANCE & BAROQUE ART

➡ **Giotto di Bondone (c 1266–1337)** Said to have ushered in the Renaissance; two masterworks: the Cappella degli Scrovegni (1304–06) in Padua and the upper church (1306–11) in Assisi.

➡ **Donatello (c 1382–1466)** Florentine born and bred; his *David* (c 1440–50) in the collection of the Museo del Bargello in Florence was the first free-standing nude sculpture produced since the classical era.

➡ **Fra' Angelico (1395–1455)** Made a saint in 1982; his best-loved work is the *Annunciation* (c 1450) in the convent of the Museo di San Marco in Florence.

➡ **Sandro Botticelli (c 1444–1510)** *Primavera* (c 1482) and *The Birth of Venus* (c 1485) are among the best-loved of all Italian paintings; both in the Uffizi.

➡ **Domenico Ghirlandaio (1449–94)** A top Tuscan master; his frescoes include those in the Tornabuoni Chapel in Florence's Basilica di Santa Maria Novella.

➡ **Michelangelo Buonarotti (1475–1564)** The big daddy of them all; everyone knows *David* (1504) in the Galleria dell'Accademia in Florence, and the Sistine Chapel ceiling (1508–12) in Rome's Vatican Museums.

➡ **Raphael Santi (1483–1520)** Originally from Urbino; painted luminous Madonnas and fell in love with a baker's daughter, immortalised in his painting *La Fornarina*, in Rome's Galleria Nazionale d'Arte Antica: Palazzo Barberini.

➡ **Titian (c 1490–1576)** Real name Tiziano Vecelli; seek out his *Assumption* (1516–18) in the Chiesa di Santa Maria Gloriosa dei Frari (I Frari), Venice.

➡ **Tintoretto (1518–1594)** The last great painter of the Italian Renaissance, known as 'Il Furioso' for the energy he put into his work; look for his *Last Supper* in Venice's Chiesa di Santo Stefano.

➡ **Annibale Caracci (1560–1609)** Bologna-born and best known for his baroque frescoes in Rome's Palazzo Farnese.

➡ **Michelangelo Merisi da Caravaggio (1573–1610)** Baroque's bad boy; his most powerful work is the *St Matthew Cycle* in Rome's Chiesa di San Luigi dei Francesi.

➡ **Gian Lorenzo Bernini (1598–1680)** The sculptor protégé of Cardinal Scipione Borghese; best known for his *Rape of Persephone* (1621–22) and *Apollo and Daphne* (1622–25) in Rome's Museo e Galleria Borghese.

The Renaissance

Of Italy's countless artistic highs, none surmount the Renaissance. The age of Botticelli, da Vinci and Michelangelo, this period of renewed interest in classical learning and humanist philosophy heralded the end of medieval obscurantism and the rise of the modern world.

Florence, Classicism & the Quattrocento

Giotto and the painters of the Sienese school introduced many innovations in art: the exploration of proportion, a new interest in realistic portraiture and the beginnings of a new tradition of landscape painting. At the start of the 15th century (Quattrocento), most of these were explored and refined in one city – Florence.

Sculptors Lorenzo Ghiberti (1378–1455) and Donatello (c 1382–1466) replaced the demure robe-clad statues of the Middle Ages with anatomically accurate figures evoking ancient Greece and Rome. Donatello's bronze *David* (c 1440–50) and *St George* (c 1416–17), both in Florence's Museo del Bargello, capture this spirit of antiquity.

Ghiberti's greatest legacy would be his bronze east doors (1424–52) for the baptistry in Florence's Piazza del Duomo. The original 10 relief panels heralded a giant leap from the late-Gothic art of the time, not only in their use of perspective, but also in the individuality bestowed upon the figures portrayed.

When the neighbouring Duomo's dome was completed in 1436, author, architect and philosopher Leon Battista Alberti called it the first great achievement of the 'new' architecture, one that equalled or even surpassed the great buildings of antiquity. Designed by Filippo Brunelleschi (1377–1446), the dome was as innovative in engineering terms as the Pantheon's dome had been 1300 years before.

A New Perspective

While Brunelleschi was heavily influenced by the classical masters, he was able to do something that they hadn't – discover the mathematical rules by which objects appear to diminish as they recede. In so doing, Brunelleschi gave artists a whole new visual perspective.

The result was a new style of masterpiece, including Masaccio's *Trinity* (c 1424–25) in Florence's Basilica di Santa Maria Novella and Leonardo da Vinci's fresco *The Last Supper* (1495–98) in the refectory of Milan's Chiesa di Santa Maria delle Grazie. Andrea Mantegna (1431–1506) was responsible for the painting that is the most virtuosic of all perspectival experiments that occurred during this period – his highly realistic *Dead Christ* (c 1480), now in Milan's Pinacoteca di Brera.

This innovation in perspective also created new problems. Painters found that the rigid new formulas often made harmonious arrangements of figures difficult. Artists such as Sandro Botticelli (c 1444–1510) led the way in pursuing a solution to this challenge, seeking to make a painting both perspectively

1. Basilica di Santa Croce (p488), Florence 2. Lorenzo Ghiberti's bronze panels, Battistero di San Giovanni (p476), Florence

accurate and harmonious in composition. His *The Birth of Venus* (c 1485), now in Florence's Uffizi, was one of the most successful attempts to solve this problem. It's not perfect – witness Venus' unnaturally elongated neck – but it was certainly an impressive attempt.

High Renaissance Masters

By the early 16th century (Cinquecento), the epicentre of artistic innovation shifted from Florence to Rome and Venice. This reflected the political and social realities of the period, namely the transfer of power in Florence from the Medicis to the moral-crusading, book-burning friar Girolamo Savonarola (1452–98), and the desire of the popes in Rome to counter the influence of Martin Luther's Reformation through turning the city into a humbling showpiece. While the age delivered a bounty of talent, some of its luminaries shone exceedingly bright.

Donato Bramante

Donato Bramante (1444–1514) knew the power of illusion. In Milan's Chiesa di Santa Maria presso San Satiro, he feigned a choir using the trompe l'œil technique. In Rome, his classical obsession would shine through in his perfectly proportioned Tempietto of the Chiesa di San Pietro in Montorio, arguably the pinnacle of High Renaissance architecture. The Urbino native would go on to design St Peter's Basilica, though his Greek-cross floor plan would never be realised.

Leonardo da Vinci

Polymath (aka Renaissance Man) Leonardo da Vinci (1452–1519) took what some critics have described as the decisive step in the history of Western art – abandoning the balance that had previously been maintained between colour and line in painting and choosing to modulate his contours using colour. This technique, called sfumato, is perfectly displayed in his *Mona Lisa* (now in the Louvre in Paris). In Milan's

1. Detail from Botticelli's *La Primavera*, Galleria degli Uffizi (p477), Florence 2. Michelangelo's *David*, Galleria dell'Accademia (p486), Florence

Chiesa di Santa Maria delle Grazie, his *The Last Supper* bestowed cutting-edge individuality to each depicted figure.

Raphael Santi

Raphael Santi (1483–1520) would rise to the aforementioned challenge faced by the Quattrocento painters – achieving harmonious and perspectively accurate arrangement of figures – in works like *Triumph of Galatea* (c 1514) in Rome's Villa Farnesina and *La Scuola d'Atene* (The School of Athens) in the Vatican Museums' Stanza della Segnatur. Other inspiring works include his enigmatic *La Fornarina* in Rome's Galleria Nazionale d'Arte Antica: Palazzo Barberini, and *Portrait of Alessandro Farnese* in Naples' Palazzo Reale di Capodimonte.

Michelangelo Buonarotti

Michelangelo Buonarotti (1475–1564) saw himself first and foremost as a sculptor, creating incomparable works like the *Pietà* in St Peter's Basilica and *David* (1504) in Florence's Galleria dell'Accademia. As a painter, he would adorn the ceiling of Rome's Sistine Chapel, creating figures that were not just realistic, but emotive visual representations of the human experience. A verified Renaissance Man, Michelangelo's talents extended to architecture – the dome atop St Peter's Basilica is another Michelangelo creation.

Andrea Palladio

Bramante's Tempietto would influence Andrea Palladio (1508–80) when designing La Rotonda in Vicenza. Like Bramante, northern Italy's greatest Renaissance architect was enamoured with classicism. His Palladian villas, such as the Brenta Riviera's Villa Foscari, radiate an elegant mathematical logic, perfectly proportioned and effectively accentuated with pediments and loggias. Classical influences also inform his Chiesa di San Giorgio Maggiore in Venice.

ITALIAN ARTISTS: THE EXCLUSIVE SCOOP

Painter, architect and writer Giorgio Vasari (1511–74) was one of those figures rightfully described as a 'Renaissance Man'. Born in Arezzo, he trained as a painter in Florence, working with artists including Andrea del Sarto and Michelangelo (he idolised the latter). As a painter, he is best remembered for his floor-to-ceiling frescoes in the Salone dei Cinquecento in Florence's Palazzo Vecchio. As an architect, his most accomplished work was the elegant loggia of the Uffizi (he also designed the enclosed, elevated corridor that connected the Palazzo Vecchio with the Uffizi and Palazzo Pitti, which was dubbed the 'Corridoio Vasariano' in his honour). But posterity remembers him predominantly for his work as an art historian. His *Lives of the Most Excellent Painters, Sculptors and Architects, from Cimabue to Our Time,* an encyclopedia of artistic biographies published in 1550 and dedicated to Cosimo I de' Medici, is still in print (as *The Lives of the Artists*) and is full of wonderful anecdotes and – dare we say it – gossip about his artistic contemporaries in 16th-century Florence. Memorable passages include his recollection of visiting Donatello's studio one day only to find the great sculptor staring at his extremely lifelike statue of the *Prophet Habakkuk* and imploring it to talk (we can only assume that Donatello had been working too hard). Vasari also writes about a young Giotto (the painter whom he credits with ushering in the Renaissance) painting a fly on the surface of a work by Cimabue that the older master then tried to brush away. The book makes wonderful pre-departure reading for anyone planning to visit Florence and its museums.

From Mannerism to Baroque

By 1520, artists such as Michelangelo and Raphael had pretty well achieved everything that former generations had tried to do and, alongside other artists, began distorting natural images in favour of heightened expression. This movement, skilfully illustrated in Titian's luminous *Assunta* (Assumption, 1516–18), in Venice's I Frari, and in Raphael's *La trasfigurazione* (Transfiguration, 1517–20), in the Vatican Museums' Pinacoteca, was derided by later critics, who labelled it mannerism.

By the end of the 16th century, two artists who had grown tired of mannerism took very different approaches to painting in an attempt to break the deadlock caused by their predecessors.

Milanese-born enfant terrible Michelangelo Merisi da Caravaggio (1573–1610) had no liking for classical models or respect for 'ideal beauty'. He was condemned by some contemporaries for seeking truth rather than ideal beauty in his art and shocked them with his radical practice of copying nature faithfully, regardless of its aesthetic appeal. But even they were forced to admire his skill with the technique of chiaroscuro (the bold contrast of light and dark) and his employment of tenebrism, where dramatic chiaroscuro becomes a dominant and highly effective stylistic device. One look at his *Conversion of St Paul* and the *Crucifixion of St Peter* (both 1600–01), both in Rome's Chiesa di Santa Maria del Popolo, or his *Le sette opere di Misericordia* (The Seven Acts of Mercy) in Naples' Pio Monte della Misericordia, and the raw emotional intensity of his work becomes clear.

This intensity reflected the artist's own notorious temperament. Described by the writer Stendhal as a 'great painter [and] a wicked man', Caravaggio fled to Naples in 1606 after killing a man in a street fight in Rome. Although his sojourn in Naples lasted only a year, it had an electrifying effect on the city's younger artists. Among these artists was Giuseppe (or Jusepe) de Ribera (1591–1652), an aggressive, bullying Spaniard whose *capo lavoro* (masterpiece), the *Pietà*, hangs in the Museo Nazionale di San Martino in Naples. Along with the Greek artist Belisiano Crenzio and Naples-born painter Giovanni Battista Caracciolo (known as Battistello), Ribera formed a cabal to stamp out any potential

Top Renaissance Sculptures

David, Michelangelo, Galleria dell'Accademia, Florence

David, Donatello, Museo del Bargello, Florence

Gates of Paradise, Ghilberti, Museo dell'Opera di Santa Maria del Fiore, Florence

Pietà, Michelangelo, St Peter's Basilica, Rome

Tomb of Pope Julius II, Michelangelo, Basilica di San Pietro in Vincoli, Rome

competition. Merciless in the extreme, they shied away from nothing to get their way. Ribera reputedly won a commission for the Cappella del Tesoro in the Duomo by poisoning his rival Domenichino (1581–1641) and wounding the assistant of a second competitor, Guido Reni (1575–1642). Much to the relief of other nerve-racked artists, the cabal eventually broke up when Caracciolo died in 1642.

North of Rome, Annibale Caracci (1560–1609) was the major artist of the baroque Emilian, or Bolognese, school. With his painter brother Agostino he worked in Bologna, Parma and Venice before moving to Rome to work for Cardinal Odoardo Farnese. In works such as his magnificent frescoes of mythological subjects in Rome's Palazzo Farnese, he employed innovative illusionistic elements that would prove inspirational to later baroque painters such as Cortona, Pozzo and Gaulli. However, Caracci never let the illusionism and energy of his works dominate the subject matter, as these later painters did. Inspired by Michelangelo and Raphael, he continued the Renaissance penchant for idealising and 'beautifying' nature.

The roots of baroque art lay in religious spirituality and stringent aestheticism. Its artists and patrons used it to combat the rapidly spreading Protestant Reformation while simultaneously exalting Catholicism. Considering this, it's somewhat ironic that its style displayed worldly joy, exuberant decoration and uninhibited sensuality. It seems that the baroque artists cottoned on to the modern mantra of advertising – sex sells.

Arguably the best known of all baroque artists was the sculptor Gian Lorenzo Bernini (1598–1680), who used works of religious art such as his *Ecstasy of St Theresa* in Rome's Chiesa di Santa Maria della Vittoria to arouse feelings of exaltation and mystic transport. In this and many other works he achieved an extraordinary intensity of facial expression and a totally radical handling of draperies. Instead of letting these fall in dignified folds in the approved classical manner, he made them writhe and whirl to intensify the effect of excitement and energy.

The New Italy

By the 18th century, Italy was beginning to rebel against years of foreign rule – first under the French in Napoleon's time and then under the Austrians. But although new ideas of political unity were forming, there was only one innovation in art – the painting and engraving of views, most notably in Venice, to meet the demand of European travellers wanting 'Grand Tour' souvenirs. The best-known painters of this school are Francesco Guardi (1712–93) and Giovanni Antonio Canaletto (1697–1768).

Despite the slow movement towards unity, the 19th-century Italian cities remained as they had been for centuries – highly individual centres of culture with sharply contrasting ways of life. Music was the supreme art of this period and the overwhelming theme in the visual arts was one of chaste refinement.

The major artistic movement of the day was neoclassicism and its greatest Italian exponent was the sculptor Antonio Canova (1757–1822). Canova renounced movement in favour of stillness, emotion in favour of restraint and illusion in favour of simplicity. His most famous work is a daring sculpture of Paolina Bonaparte Borghese as a reclining *Venere vincitrice* (Conquering Venus), in Rome's Museo e Galleria Borghese.

Canova was the last Italian artist to win overwhelming international fame. Italian architecture, sculpture and painting had played a dominant role in the cultural life of Europe for some 400 years, but with Canova's death in 1822, this supremacy came to an end.

ITALIAN ART & ARCHITECTURE ART

MACCHIAIOLI

The Italian equivalent of Impressionism was the Macchiaioli movement based in Florence. Its major artists were Telemaco Signorini (1835–1901) and Giovanni Fattori (1825–1908). See their work in the Palazzo Pitti's Galleria d'Arte Moderna in Florence.

Modern Movements

The two main developments in Italian art at the outbreak of WWI could not have been more different. Futurism, led by poet Filippo Tommaso Marinetti (1876–1944) and painter Umberto Boccioni (1882–1916), sought new ways to express the dynamism of the machine age. Metaphysical painting *(Pittura metafisica)*, in contrast, looked inwards and produced mysterious images from the subconscious world.

Futurism demanded a new art for a new world and denounced every attachment to art of the past. It started with the publication of Marinetti's *Manifesto del futurismo* (Futurist Manifesto, 1909) and was reinforced by the publication of a 1910 futurist painting manifesto by Boccioni, Giacomo Balla (1871–1958), Luigi Russolo (1885–1947) and Gino Severini (1883–1966). The manifesto declared that 'Everything is in movement, everything rushes forward, everything is in constant swift change.' An excellent example of this theory put into practice is Boccioni's *Rissa in galleria* (Brawl in the Arcade, 1910) in the collection of Milan's Pinacoteca di Brera. This was painted shortly after the manifesto was published and clearly demonstrates the movement's fascination with frantic movement and with modern technology and life. While the movement lost its own impetus with the outbreak of WWI, its legacy has been revived with Milan's Museo del Novecento. Dedicated to 20th-century art, the museum houses what is arguably Italy's finest collection of futurist works.

Like futurism, Metaphysical painting also had a short life. Its most famous exponent, Giorgio de Chirico (1888–1978), lost interest in the style after the war, but his work held a powerful attraction for the surrealist movement that developed in France in the 1920s. Stillness and a sense of foreboding are the haunting qualities of many of De Chirico's works of this period, which show disconnected images from the world of dreams in settings that usually embody memories of classical Italian architecture. A good example is *The Red Tower* (1913), now in Venice's Peggy Guggenheim Collection.

After the war, a number of the futurist painters began to flirt with Fascism, believing that the new state offered opportunities for patronage and public art and that Italy could once again lead the world in its arts practice. This period was known as 'second futurism' and its main exponents were Mario Sironi (1885–1961) and Carlo Carrà (1881–1966).

The local art scene became more interesting in the 1950s, when artists such as Alberto Burri (1915–95) and the Argentine-Italian Lucio Fontana (1899–1968) experimented with abstract art. Fontana's punctured canvases were characterised by *spazialismo* (spatialism) and he

Modern Art Musts

Galleria Nazionale d'Arte Moderna e Contemporanea, Rome
....
Peggy Guggenheim Collection, Venice
....
Museo del Novecento, Milan
....
Castello di Rivoli, Turin
....
MADRE, Naples

Italy's major contemporary art event is the world-famous Venice Biennale, held every odd-numbered year. It's the most important survey show on the international art circuit.

TOP FIVE ARCHITECTS

→ **Filippo Brunelleschi (1377–1446)** Brunelleschi blazed the neoclassical trail; his dome for Florence's Duomo announcing the Renaissance's arrival.

→ **Donato Bramante (1444–1514)** After a stint as court architect in Milan, Bramante went on to design the tiny Tempietto and huge St Peter's Basilica in Rome.

→ **Michelangelo (1475–1564)** Architecture was but one of the many strings in this great man's bow; his masterworks are the dome of St Peter's Basilica and the Piazza del Campidoglio in Rome.

→ **Andrea Palladio (1508–80)** Western architecture's single-most influential figure, Palladio turned classical Roman principles into elegant northern Italian villas.

→ **Gian Lorenzo Bernini (1598–1680)** The king of the Italian baroque is best known for his work in Rome, including the magnificent baldachin, piazza and colonnades at St Peter's.

also experimented with 'slash paintings', perforating his canvases with actual holes or slashes and dubbing them 'art for the space age'.

Burri's work was truly cutting edge. His assemblages were made of burlap, wood, iron and plastic and were avowedly anti-traditional. *Grande sacco* (Large Sack) of 1952, housed in Rome's Galleria Nazionale d'Arte Moderna e Contemporanea, caused a major controversy when it was first exhibited.

In the 1960s, a radical new movement called *Arte Povera* (Poor Art) took off. Its followers used simple materials to trigger memories and associations. Major names include Mario Merz (1925–2003), Giovanni Anselmo (b 1934), Luciano Fabro (b 1936–2007), Giulio Paolini (b 1940) and Greek-born Jannis Kounellis (b 1936). All experimented with sculpture and installation work.

The 1980s saw a return to painting and sculpture in a traditional (primarily figurative) sense. Dubbed 'Transavanguardia', this movement broke with the prevailing international focus on conceptual art and was thought by some critics to signal the death of avant-garde. The artists who were part of this movement include Sandro Chia (b 1946), Mimmo Paladino (b 1948), Enzo Cucchi (b 1949) and Francesco Clemente (b 1952).

Current Italian contemporary artists of note include Paolo Canevari (b 1963), Rä di Martino (b 1975), Paola Pivi (b 1971), Pietro Roccasalva (b 1970) and Francesco Vezzoli (b 1971).

Architecture

Architects working in Italy have always celebrated the classical. The Greeks, who established the style, employed it in the southern cities they colonised; the Romans refined and embellished it; Italian Renaissance architects rediscovered and tweaked it; and the Fascist architects of the 1930s referenced it in their powerful modernist buildings. Even today, architects such as Richard Meier are designing buildings in Italy that clearly reference classical prototypes. Why muck around with a formula that works, particularly when it can also please the eye and make the soul soar?

Classical

Only one word describes the buildings of ancient Italy: monumental. The Romans built an empire the size of which had never before been seen and went on to adorn it with buildings cut from the same pattern. From Verona's Roman Arena to Pozzuoli's Anfiteatro Flavio, giant stadiums rose above skylines. Spa centres like Rome's Terme di Caracalla were veritable cities of indulgence, boasting everything from giant marble-clad pools to gymnasiums and libraries. Aqueducts like those below Naples provided fresh water to thousands, while temples such as Pompeii's Tempio di Apollo provided the faithful with awe-inspiring centres of worship.

Having learned a few valuable lessons from the Greeks, the Romans refined architecture to such a

8th–3rd Century BC Magna Graecia

Greek colonisers grace southern Italy with stoic temples, sweeping amphitheatres and elegant sculptures that later influence their Roman successors.

6th Century BC– 4th Century AD Roman

Epic roads and aqueducts spread from Rome, alongside proud basilicas, colonnaded markets, sprawling thermal baths and frescoed villas.

4th–6th Century Byzantine

Newly Christian and based in Constantinople, the Empire turns its attention to the construction of churches with exotic, Eastern mosaics and domes.

8th–12th Century Romanesque

Attention turns from height to the horizontal lines of a building. Churches are designed with a stand-alone *campanile* (bell tower) and baptistry.

13th & 14th Century Gothic

Northern European Gothic gets an Italian makeover, from the Arabesque spice of Venice's Cá d'Oro to the Romanesque flavour of Siena's cathedral.

Late 14th–15th Century Early Renaissance

Filippo Brunelleschi's elegant dome graces the Duomo in Florence, heralding a return to classicism and a bold new era of humanist thinking and rational, elegant design.

Architectural Wonders

Italy is Europe's architectural overachiever, bursting at its elegant seams with triumphant temples, brooding castles and dazzling basilicas. If you can't see it all in one mere lifetime, why not start with five of the best?

Duomo, Milan

A forest of petrified pinnacles and fantastical beasts, Italy's Gothic golden child (p243) is pure Milan: a product of centuries of pillaging, fashion, one-upmanship and mercantile ambition. Head to the top for a peek at the Alps.

Duomo, Florence

Florence's most famous landmark (p476) is more than a monumental spiritual masterpiece. It's a living, breathing testament to the explosion of creativity, artistry, ambition and wealth that would define Renaissance Florence.

Piazza dei Miracoli, Pisa

Pisa (p508) promises a threesome you won't forget: the Duomo, the Battistero and the infamous Leaning Tower. Together they make up a perfect Romanesque trio, artfully arranged like objets d'art on a giant green coffee table.

Colosseum, Rome

Almost 2000 years on, Rome's mighty ancient stadium (p67) still has the X factor. Once the domain of gladiatorial battles and ravenous wild beasts, its 50,000-seat magnitude radiates all the vanity and ingenuity of a once-glorious, intercontinental empire.

Basilica di San Marco, Venice

It's a case of East–West fusion at this Byzantine beauty (p337), founded in AD 829 and rebuilt twice since. Awash with glittering mosaics and home to the remains of Venice's patron saint, its layering of eras reflects the city's own worldly pedigree.

1. Duomo, Milan 2. Duomo, Florence 3. Colosseum, Rome
4. Battistero and Leaning Tower, Pisa

degree that their building techniques, designs and mastery of harmonious proportion underpin most of the world's architecture and urban design to this day.

And though the Greeks invented the architectural orders (Doric, Ionic and Corinthian), it was the Romans who employed them in bravura performances. Consider Rome's Colosseum, with its ground tier of Doric, middle tier of Ionic and penultimate tier of Corinthian columns. The Romans were dab hands at temple architecture too. Just witness Rome's exquisitely proportioned Pantheon, a temple whose huge but seemingly unsupported dome showcases the Roman invention of concrete, an ingredient as essential to the modern construction industry as Ferrari is to the F1 circuit.

Byzantine

After Constantine became Christianity's star convert, the empire's architects and builders turned their talents to the design and construction of churches. The emperor commissioned a number of such buildings in Rome, but he also expanded his sphere of influence east, to Constantinople in Byzantium. His successors in Constantinople, most notably Justinian and his wife Theodora, went on to build churches in the style that became known as Byzantine. Brick buildings built on the Roman basilican plan but with domes, they had sober exteriors that formed a stark contrast to their magnificent, mosaic-encrusted interiors. Finding its way back to Italy in the mid-6th century, the style expressed itself on a grand scale in Venice's Basilica di San Marco, as well as more modestly in buildings like the Chiesa di San Pietro in Otranto, Puglia. The true stars of Italy's Byzantine scene, however, are Ravenna's Basilica di San Vitale and Basilica di Sant'Apollinare in Classe, both built on a cruciform plan.

Romanesque

The next development in ecclesiastical architecture in Italy came from Europe. The European Romanesque style became momentarily popular in four regional forms – the Lombard, Pisan, Florentine and Sicilian Norman. All displayed an emphasis on width and the horizontal lines of a building rather than height, and featured churches where the *campanile* (bell tower) and baptistry were separate to the church.

The use of white and green marble alternatively defined the facades of the Florentine and Pisan styles, as seen in iconic buildings like Florence's Basilica di Santa Maria Novella and Duomo baptistry, as well as in Pisa's cathedral and baptistry.

The Lombard style featured elaborately carved facades and exterior decoration featuring bands and arches. Among its finest examples are the Lombard cathedral in Modena, Pavia's Basilica di San Michele and Brescia's unusually shaped Duomo Vecchio.

Down south, the Sicilian Norman style blended Norman, Saracen and Byzantine influences, from marble columns to Islamic-inspired pointed arches to glass tesserae detailing. One of the greatest examples of the form is the Cattedrale di Monreale, located just outside Palermo.

Gothic

The Italians didn't embrace the Gothic as enthusiastically as the French, Germans and Spanish did. Its flying buttresses, grotesque gargoyles and over-the-top decoration were just too far from the classical ideal that was (and still is) bred into Italian genes. The local version was generally much more restrained, a style beautifully exemplified by Naples' simple, elegant Basilica di San Lorenzo Maggiore. There were, of course, exceptions. Never averse to a bit of frivolity, the Venetians used the style in grand *palazzi* (mansions) such as the Ca' d'Oro and on the facades of

For a Blast of Baroque

Lecce, Puglia

Noto, Sicily

Rome, Lazio

Naples, Campania

Catania, Sicily

Michelangelo's *David* is no stranger to close calls. In 1527, the lower part of his arm was broken off in a riot. In 1843, a hydrochloric 'spruce-up' stripped away some of the original surface, while in 1991 a disturbed, hammer-wielding Italian painter smashed the statue's second left toe.

Prize in 1990, and was known for both his writing (eg *The Architecture of the City* in 1966) and design work. Paolo Portoghesi is an architect, academic and writer with a deep interest in classical architecture. His best-known Italian building is the Central Mosque (1974) in Rome, famed for its luminously beautiful interior.

After a long period of decline, Italian architecture is back on the world stage, with architects and firms such as Massimiliano Fuksas; King, Roselli & Ricci; Cino Zucchi; Ian+; ABDR Architetti Associati; 5+1; Garofalo Miura; and Beniamino Servino designing innovative buildings.

The current king of the scene is Renzo Piano, whose international projects include London's scene-stealing Shard skyscraper and the Centre Culturel Tjibaou in Nouméa, New Caledonia. At home, recent projects include his bold Museo delle Scienze (MUSE) in Trento. Composed of a series of voids and volumes that seemingly float on water, its striking design echoes the area's dramatic mountain landscape. Further south in Rome, Piano's 2002 Auditorium Parco della Musica is considered one of his greatest achievements to date.

Piano's heir apparent is Massimiliano Fuksas, whose projects are as whimsical as they are visually arresting. Take, for instance, his brand new Nuovo Centro Congressi (New Congress Center) in Rome's EUR, dubbed the *'Nuvola'* (Cloud) for its 'floating', glass-encased auditorium. Other Fuksas highlights include the futuristic Milan Trade Fair Building and the San Paolo Parish Church in Foligno.

High-profile foreign architects have also shaken things up. In Florence, Arata Isozaki extended the Uffizi gallery. In Venice, David Chipperfield extended the Isola di San Michele's cemetery, while Tadao Ando oversaw the city's acclaimed Punta della Dogana and Palazzo Grassi renovation. In Rome, Richard Meier divided opinion with his 2006 Ara Pacis pavilion. The first major civic building in Rome's historic centre in more than half a century, the travertine, glass and steel structure was compared to a petrol station by popular art critic Vittorio Sgarbi, who described it as an 'indecent cesspit by a useless architect'. Less controversial is Meier's wave-like Chiesa di Dio Padre Misericordioso, a light-drenched church in suburban Rome commissioned by the Vatican to celebrate the 2000 Great Jubilee.

A little more love was given to Zaha Hadid's bold, sinuous MAXXI art gallery in northern Rome, which earned the Iraqi-British starchitect the prestigious RIBA (Royal Institute of British Architects) Sterling prize in 2010. Art and culture will also rule the roost at Rome's new arts centre for the Fondazione Alda Fendi. Set in a Fascist-era housing block and expected to open in 2014, its creator is French architect Jean Nouvel.

Not to be outdone, Milan is catapulting its skyline into the 21st century with the ambitious redevelopment of its Porta Nuova district. Home to Italy's tallest building (the 231m, César Pelli-designed UniCredit tower), the project also features Stefano Boeri's Bosco Verticale (Vertical Forest), a pair of eco-conscious apartment towers covered in luxuriant vegetation. Equally ambitious is Milan's CityLife project (under construction), a commercial, residential and parkland development dominated by three geometrically experimental skyscrapers by Zaha Hadid, Arata Isozaki and Daniel Liebeskind. City authorities have their fingers crossed that these head-turning additions will inject Italy's world metropolis with some much-needed edge.

Mid–Late 20th Century Modern

Industrialised and economically booming, mid-century Italy shows off its wealth in commercial projects like Giò Ponti's slim-lined Pirelli skyscraper.

21st Century Contemporary

Italian architecture gets its groove back with the international success of starchitects like Renzo Piano, Massimiliano Fuksis and Gae Aulenti.

ITALIAN ART & ARCHITECTURE ARCHITECTURE

The Italian Way of Life

Imagine you wake up tomorrow and discover you're Italian. How would life be different, and what could you discover about Italy in just one day as a local? Read on...

A Day in the Life of an Italian

Sveglia! You're woken not by an alarm but by the burble and clatter of the *caffettiera,* the ubiquitous stovetop espresso-maker. You're running late, so you bolt down your coffee scalding hot (an acquired Italian talent) and pause briefly to ensure your socks match before dashing out the door. Yet still you walk blocks out of your way to buy your morning paper from Bucharest-born Nicolae, your favourite news vendor and (as a Romanian) part of Italy's largest migrant community. You chat briefly about his new baby – you may be late, but at least you're not rude.

On your way to work you scan the headlines: more coalition-government infighting, another match-fixing scandal and an announcement of new EU regulations on cheese. Outrageous! The cheese regulations, that is; the rest is to be expected. At work, you're buried in paperwork until noon, when it's a relief to join friends for lunch and a glass of wine. Afterwards you toss back another scorching espresso at your favourite bar and find out how your barista's latest audition went – turns out you went to school with the sister of the director of the play, so you promise to put in a good word.

Back at work by 2pm, you multitask Italian-style, chatting with co-workers as you dash off work emails, text your schoolmate about the barista on your *telefonino* (mobile phone) and surreptitiously check *l'Internet* for employment listings – your work contract is due to expire soon. After a busy day like this, *aperitivi* are definitely in order, so at 6.30pm you head directly to the latest happy-hour hot spot. Your friends arrive, the decor is *molto design,* the vibe *molto cool* and the DJ *abbastanza hot,* until suddenly it's time for your English class – everyone's learning it these days, if only for the slang.

By the time you finally get home, it's already 9.30pm and dinner will have to be reheated. *Peccato!* (Shame!) You eat, absent-mindedly watching *X Factor Italia* while recounting your day and complaining about cheese regulations to whoever's home – no sense giving reheated pasta your undivided attention. While brushing your teeth, you discuss the future of Italian theatre and dream vacations in Anguilla, though without a raise, it'll probably be Abruzzo again this year. Finally you make your way to bed and pull reading material at random out of your current bedside stack: art books, *gialli* (mysteries), a hard-hitting Mafia exposé or two, the odd classic, possibly a few *fumetti* (comics). You drift off wondering what tomorrow might hold... Imagine if you woke up British or American. English would be easier, but how would you dress and what would you be expected to eat? *Terribile!* You shrug off that nightmare and settle into sleep. *Buona notte.*

Being Italian

The People

Who are the people you'd encounter every day as an Italian? Just over 22% of your fellow citizens are smokers and 75.5% drive to work, compared to only 3.2% who cycle. A growing proportion of Italians are already retired. Indeed, one out of five is over 65, which explains the septuagenarians you'll notice on parade with dogs and grandchildren in parks, affably arguing about politics in cafes, and ruthlessly dominating bocce tournaments.

You might also notice a striking absence of children. Italy's birth rate is one of the lowest in Europe, at around 1.41 per woman in 2013.

North versus South

In his film *Ricomincio da tre* (I'm Starting from Three; 1980), acting great Massimo Troisi comically tackles the problems faced by Neapolitans forced to head north for work. Laughter aside, the film reveals Italy's very real north–south divide; a divide still present more than 30 years on. While the north is celebrated for its fashion empires and moneyed metropolises, Italy's south (dubbed the 'Mezzogiorno') is a PR nightmare of high unemployment, crumbling infrastructure and Mafia arrests. At a deep semantic level, *settentrionale* (northern Italian) equals reservation, productivity and success, while *meridionale* (southern Italian) equates with conservatism, melodrama and laziness. From the Industrial Revolution to the 1960s, millions of southern Italians fled to the industrialised northern cities for factory jobs. Disparagingly nicknamed *terroni* (literally meaning 'of the soil'), these in-house 'immigrants' were often exposed to racist attitudes from their northern cousins. Decades on, the overt racism may have dissipated but the prejudices remain. Many northerners resent their taxes being used to 'subsidise' the south – a sentiment well exploited by the Milan-based Lega Nord (Northern League) party.

From Emigrants to Immigrants

From 1876 to 1976, Italy was a country of net emigration. With some 30 million Italian emigrants dispersed throughout Europe, the Americas and Australia, remittances from Italians abroad helped keep Italy's economy afloat during economic crises after Independence and WWII.

The tables have since turned. Political and economic upheavals in the 1980s brought new arrivals from Central Europe, Latin America and North Africa, including Italy's former colonies in Tunisia, Somalia and Ethiopia. More recently, waves of Chinese and Filipino immigrants have given Italian streetscapes a Far Eastern twist. While immigrants account for just 7.1% of Italy's own population today, the number is growing. Since the 2001 census, the country's foreign population (a number that excludes foreign-born people who take Italian citizenship) has tripled from 1.3 million to around 4 million.

From a purely economic angle, these new arrivals are vital for the country's economic health. While most Italians today choose to live and work within Italy, fewer are entering blue-collar agricultural and industrial fields. Without immigrant workers to fill the gaps, Italy would be sorely lacking in tomato sauce and shoes. From kitchen hands to hotel maids, it is often immigrants who take the low-paid service jobs that keep Italy's tourism economy afloat.

Despite this, not everyone is putting out the welcome mat. In 2010, the shooting of an immigrant worker in the town of Rosarno, Calabria, sparked Italy's worst race riots in years. Three years later in 2013, a top-level football match between AC Milan and Roma was suspended after

---

On average, Italians get six weeks of holidays a year, but spend the equivalent of two weeks annually on bureaucratic procedures required of working Italian citizens.

In 2013, Italy swore in its first black Cabinet minister, Congo-born Cecile Kyenge. Appointed Minister of Integration, the surgeon's appointment reflects the country's increasingly multicultural make up. Kyenge is one of two naturalised Italians in the government, the other being German-born former international canoeist, Josefa Idem.

LANGUAGES

fans chanted racist abuse at Mario Balotelli, AC Milan's black, Italian-born striker.

Yet not all Italians are comfortable with racist views. In May 2009, a radical law to punish undocumented immigrants – including potential refugees – with summary deportation and fines was denounced by Italian human rights groups, the Vatican, the UN and mass protests in Rome. As writer Claudio Magris observed in *The Times,* recalling Italy's recent past as a nation of emigrants, 'We, above all, should know what it is like to be strangers in a strange land.'

Religion, Loosely Speaking

While almost 80% of Italians identify as Catholics, only around 15% of Italy's population regularly attends Sunday Mass. Recent church scandals have Italians feeling increasingly cynical of the Vatican's moral authority, while shifting attitudes on issues such as gay marriage and abortion see many at odds with official church doctrine. That said, *La Famiglia Cristiana* (The Christian Family) remains Italy's most popular weekly magazine and crucifixes continue to adorn state buildings and classrooms, even if they're justified as 'cultural', not religious, artefacts.

Indeed, the Church continues to exert considerable influence on public policy and political parties, especially those of the center- and far-right. But in the land of the double park, even God's rules are up for interpretation. Sure, *mamma* still serves fish on Good Friday, but while she might consult *la Madonna* for guidance, chances are she'll get a second opinion from the *maga* (fortune-teller) on channel 32. The European Consumer Association estimates that Italians spend a whopping €5 billion annually on fortune-tellers and astrologers. While the current climate of economic uncertainty has seen a rise in the use of esoteric services, the trend is not surprising. Italians are a highly superstitious bunch. From not toasting with water to not opening umbrellas inside the home, the country offers a long list of tips to keep bad luck at bay.

Superstitious beliefs are especially strong in Italy's south. Here *corni* (horn-shaped charms) adorn everything from necklines to rear-view mirrors to ward off the *malocchio* (evil eye) and devotion to local saints takes on an almost cultish edge. Every year in Naples, thousands cram into the Duomo to witness the blood of San Gennaro miraculously liquefy in the phial that contains it. When the blood liquefies, the city breathes a sigh of relief – it symbolises another year safe from disaster. When it didn't in 1944, Mt Vesuvius erupted, and when it failed again in 1980 an earthquake struck the city that year. Coincidence? Perhaps. But even the most cynical Neapolitan would rather San Gennaro perform his magic trick...just in case.

It's Not What You Know...

From your day as an Italian, this much you know already: conversation is far too important to be cut short by tardiness or a mouthful of toothpaste. All that chatter isn't entirely idle, either: in Europe's most ancient, entrenched bureaucracy, social networks are essential to get things done. Putting in a good word for your barista isn't just a nice gesture, but an essential career boost. As a Ministry of Labour study recently revealed, most people in Italy still find employment through personal connections. For better or worse, *clientelismo* (nepotism) is as much a part of the Italian lexicon as *caffè* (coffee) and *tasse* (taxes). Just ask former Prime Minister Silvio Berlusconi who, in 2009 chose a *Grande Fratello* (Big Brother) contestant, a soap-opera starlet, a TV costume-drama actress and a Miss Italy contestant to represent Italy as members of the European Union parliament. In a case of art imitating life, Massimiliano Bruno's film *Viva*

There are 12 minority languages officially recognised in Italy, consisting of native languages Friulian, Ladin and Sardinian, and the languages of neighbouring countries, including French, Franco-Provençal, German, Catalan, Occitan, Slovene, Croatian, Albanian and Greek.

FASHION FAMILY SAGAS

Tight as they may be, Italian families are not always examples of heart-warming domesticity. Indeed, some of Italy's most fashionable *famiglie* (families) prove that every clan has its problems, some small, some extra, extra large.

Consider the Versace bunch, fashion's favourite catwalking Calabrians. One of Italy's greatest exports, the familial dynasty was founded by Gianni, celebrity BFF and the man who single-handedly made bling chic. But not even the fashion gods could save the bearded genius, inexplicably shot dead outside his Miami mansion by serial killer Andrew Cunanan in 1997. With Gianni gone, creative control was passed to Donatella, Gianni's larger-than-life little sister. The subject of Anna Wintour's most unusual fashion memory – full-body spandex on horseback – the former coke-addled party queen flew herself to rehab on daughter Allegra's 18th birthday.

Then there are the Florentine fashion rivals, the Gucci clan. Established by Guccio Gucci in 1904, the family firm reads like a bad Brazilian soap – power struggles between Rodolfo and Aldo (Guccio's sons) in the 1950s; assault charges by Paolo (Aldo's son) against siblings Roberto and Giorgio, and cousin Maurizio Gucci, in 1982; and a major fallout between Paolo and father Aldo over the offshore siphoning of profits.

The last Gucci to run the company was Maurizio, who finally sold his share to Bahrain investment bank Investcorp in 1993 for a healthy US$170 million. Two years later, Maurizio was dead, gunned down outside his Milan office on the order of ex-wife, Patrizia Reggiani. Not only had Reggiani failed to forgive her husband's infidelity, she was far from impressed with her US$500,000 annual allowance. After all, this was the woman who famously quipped that she'd rather cry in a Rolls Royce than be happy on a bicycle. Offered parole in 2011 on condition of finding employment, Reggiani stayed true to form, stating she'd rather water the plants in her cell than go out and find a job.

L'Italia (2012) features a crooked, well-connected senator who secures jobs for his three children, among them a talentless TV actress with a speech impediment. The Italian film industry itself came under attack in 2012 when newspaper *Il Fatto Quotidiano* accused several members of the Italian Academy (which votes for the prestigious David di Donatello film awards) of having conflicts of interest. As the satirist Beppe Severgnini wryly comments in his book *La Bella Figura: A Field Guide to the Italian Mind*, 'If you want to lose an Italian friend or kill off a conversation, all you have to say is "On the subject of conflicts of interest..." If your interlocutor hasn't disappeared, he or she will smile condescendingly.'

Hotel Mamma

If you're between the ages of 18 and 29, there's a 60.7% chance that's not a roommate in the kitchen making your morning coffee: it's mum or dad. Tick the 30-to-44 age box and your chance is 25.3%. This is not because Italy is a nation of pampered *bamboccioni* (big babies) – at least, not entirely. With a general unemployment rate of 11.5% and a youth unemployment rate of 38.4% in early 2013, it's no wonder that so many refuse to cut those apron strings.

While Italy's family-based social fabric provides a protective buffer for many during these challenging economic times, intergenerational solidarity has always been the basis of the Italian family. According to the time-honoured Italian social contract, you'd probably live with your parents until you start a career and a family of your own. Then after a suitable grace period for success and romance – a couple of years should do the trick – your parents might move in with you to look after your kids, and be looked after in turn.

As for those who don't live with family members, chances are they're still a quick stroll away, with 54% living within a 30-minute walk from

John Turturro's film *Passione* (2010) is a *Buena Vista Social Club*–style exploration of Naples' rich and eclectic musical traditions. Spanning folk songs to contemporary tunes, it offers a fascinating insight into the city's complex soul.

THE OLD PROVERBIAL

They might be old clichés, but proverbs can be quite the cultural revelation. Here are six of Italy's well-worn best:

'*Donne e motori, gioie e dolori.*' (Women and motors, joy and pain.)

'*Chi trova un'amico trova un tesoro.*' (He who finds a friend, finds a treasure.)

'*A ogni uccello il suo nido è bello.*' (To every bird, his own nest is beautiful.)

'*Fidarsi va bene, non fidarsi va meglio.*' (To trust is good, not to trust is better.)

'*Meglio essere invidiati che compatiti.*' (Better to be envied than pitied.)

'*Il diavolo fa le pentole ma non i coperchi.*' (The devil makes the pots but not the lids, ie the truth always comes out in the end.)

close relatives. All this considered, it's hardly surprising to hear that famous mobile phone chorus at evening rush hour: '*Mamma, butta la pasta!*' (Mum, put the pasta in the water!).

What it Feels Like for a Girl

It might string straight As in fashion, food and design, but Italy's prowess in gender equality leaves much room for improvement. Despite the cultural, economic and political gains made elsewhere in the 1960s and 1970s, sexism remains deeply entrenched in Italian society. On TV, women are often little more than scantily dressed props. On radio, female voiceovers range from quasi-hysterical to blushingly orgasmic. Despite his well-publicised sexist gaffes and alleged sexcapades, ex-Prime Minister Silvio Berlusconi remained a septuagenarian stud in the eyes of many Italian men, themselves influenced by the country's macho traditions. Indeed, male politicians rumoured to be dallying with mistresses have more often enjoyed a surge in public popularity than a slump.

Many Italian women must wish these men were half as passionate about pulling their weight at home. Statistics released by the Organisation for Economic Co-operation and Development (OECD) revealed that Italian men spend 103 minutes per day cooking, cleaning or caring, less than a third as long as Italian women, who spend an average of 326 minutes per day on domestic work. Kitchens seem to be especially overused by women; a 2013 report released by research firms Coldiretti and Censis claimed that Italian women spend 21 days of the year cooking, compared to eight days for Italian men.

Yet the winds of change are slowly picking up speed. On 13 February 2011, almost one million Italian women (and their male supporters) took to the streets demanding the dismissal of then-Prime Minister Berlusconi and an end to the Italian media's sexist representation of women. A few years on, one-third of Italy's Cabinet consists of respected female politicians. This sharp rise in esteemed women representatives is an explicit break from the Berlusconi administration, infamous for appointing a former topless model as the minister for equal opportunities.

According to a 2012 OECD report, entry rates into higher education for women in Italy were 57% in 2010, compared to 42% for men. Overall, women make up around 59% of all university-level first-degree graduates in Italy, as well as constituting 52% of advanced research qualifications (doctorates) awarded in the country – one of the highest percentages among OECD countries.

And the smuggest stat of all? While one in 10 Italian women still lives with her parents by age 35, twice as many men do.

The World Economic Forum's 2012 Global Gender Gap Report ranked Italy 80th worldwide in terms of overall gender equality, sliding from 74th position in 2011. It ranked 101st in female economic participation and opportunity, 65th in educational attainment and 71st in political empowerment.

While Rome is a Bermuda Triangle for rockers with drug habits – Kurt Cobain and Mark Sandman (the latter of Morphine fame) overdosed there – Milan is out to prove punk's not dead with the annual indie-fest Rock In Idrho (www.rockinidrho.com).

Italian Passions

Co-ordinated wardrobes, strong espresso and general admiration are not the only things that make Italian hearts sing. And while Italian passions are wide and varied, few define Italy like football and opera.

Better Living by Design

As an Italian, you actually did your co-workers a favour by being late to the office to give yourself a final once-over in the mirror. Unless you want your fellow employees to avert their gaze in dumbstruck horror, your socks had better match. The tram can wait as you make *la bella figura* (cut a fine figure).

Italians have strong opinions about aesthetics and aren't afraid to share them. A common refrain is *Che brutta!* (How hideous!), which may strike visitors as tactless. But consider it from an Italian point of view – everyone is rooting for you to look good, so who are you to disappoint? The shop assistant who tells you with brutal honesty that yellow is *not* your colour is doing a public service, and will consider it a personal triumph to see you outfitted in orange instead.

If it's a gift, though, you must allow 10 minutes for the sales clerk to *fa un bel pacchetto,* wrapping your purchase with string and an artfully placed sticker. This is the epitome of *la bella figura* – the sales clerk wants you to look good by giving a good gift. When you do, everyone basks in the glow of *la bella figura:* you as the gracious gift-giver and the sales clerk as savvy gift consultant, not to mention the flushed and duly honoured recipient.

As a national obsession, *la bella figura* gives Italy its undeniable edge in design, cuisine, art and architecture. Though the country could get by on its striking good looks, Italy is ever mindful of delightful details. They are everywhere you look and many places you don't: the intricately carved cathedral spire only the bell-ringer could fully appreciate, the toy duck inside your chocolate *uova di pasqua* (Easter egg), the absinthe-green silk lining inside a sober grey suit sleeve. Attention to such details earns you instant admiration in Italy – and an admission that, sometimes, non-Italians do have style.

Calcio (Football): Italy's Other Religion

Catholicism may be your official faith, but as an Italian your true religion is likely to be *calcio* (football). On any given weekend from September to May, chances are that you and your fellow *tifosi* (football fans) are at the *stadio* (stadium), glued to the TV, or checking the score on your mobile phone. Come Monday, you'll be dissecting the match by the office water cooler.

Like politics and fashion, football is in the very DNA of Italian culture. Indeed, they sometimes even converge. Silvio Berlusconi first found fame as the owner of AC Milan and cleverly named his political party after a well-worn football chant. Fashion royalty Dolce & Gabbana declared football players 'the new male icons', using five of Italy's hottest on-field stars to launch its 2010 underwear collection. Decades earlier, '60s singer Rita Pavone topped the charts with *La partita di pallone* (The Football Match), in which the frustrated pop princess sings *'Perchè, perchè la domenica mi lasci sempre sola per andare a vedere la partita di pallone?'* ('Why, why do you always leave me alone on Sunday so you can go and watch the football match?'). It's no coincidence that in Italian *tifoso* means both 'football fan' and 'typhus patient'. When the ball ricochets off the post and slips fatefully through the goalie's hands, when

THE ITALIAN WAY OF LIFE ITALIAN PASSIONS

Italian Style Icons

Bialetti *coffee-maker*

Cinzano *vermouth*

Acqua di Parma *cologne*

Piaggio *Vespa*

Olivetti 'Valentine' *typewriter*

Italy's culture of corruption and *calcio* (football) is captured in *The Dark Heart of Italy,* in which English expat author Tobias Jones wryly observes, 'Footballers or referees are forgiven nothing; politicians are forgiven everything.'

half the stadium is swearing while the other half is euphorically shouting *Goooooooooooooooool!,* 'fever pitch' is the term that comes to mind.

Nothing quite stirs Italian blood like a good (or a bad) game. Nine months after Italy's 2006 World Cup victory against France, hospitals in northern Italy reported a baby boom. In February the following year, rioting at a Palermo–Catania match in Catania left one policeman dead and around 100 injured. Blamed on the Ultras – a minority group of hard-core football fans – the violence shocked both Italy and the world, leading to a temporary ban of all matches in Italy and increased stadium security. A year earlier, the match-fixing 'Calciopoli' scandals resulted in revoked championship titles and temporary demotion of Serie A (top-tier national) teams, including the mighty Juventus.

Yet, the same game that divides also unites. You might be a Lazio-loathing, AS Roma supporter on any given day, but when the national *Azzurri* (The Blues) swag the World Cup, you are nothing but a heart-on-your-sleeve *italiano* (Italian). In his book *The 100 Things Everyone Needs to Know About Italy,* Australian journalist David Dale writes that Italy's 1982 World Cup win 'finally united twenty regions which, until then, had barely acknowledged that they were part of the one country.'

> Italy was introduced to modern *calcio* in the late 19th century when the English factory barons of Turin, Genoa and Milan established teams to keep their workers fit.

> According to figures released in 2011 by Istat, Italy's bureau of statistics, 58.8% of Italian households have a computer, while only 54.5% have internet access. The prevalence of mobile phones in Italian households is a much higher 91.6%.

Opera: Let the Fat Lady Sing

At the stadium, your beloved *squadra* (team) hits the field to the roar of Verdi. Okay, so you mightn't be first in line to see *Rigoletto* at La Fenice, but Italy's opera legacy remains a source of pride. After all, not only did you invent the art form, you gave the world some of its greatest composers and compositions. Gioachino Rossini (1792–1868) transformed Pierre Beaumarchais' *Le Barbier de Séville* (The Barber of Seville) into one of the greatest comedic operas, Giuseppe Verdi (1813–1901) produced the epic *Aida,* while Giacomo Puccini (1858–1924) delivered staples such as *Tosca, Madama Butterfly* and *Turandot.*

Lyrical, intense and dramatic – it's only natural that opera bears the 'Made in Italy' label. Track pants might be traded in for tuxedos, but Italy's opera crowds can be just as ruthless as their pitch-side counterparts.

MUSIC FOR THE MASSES

Most of the music you'll hear booming out of Italian cafes to inspire sidewalk singalongs is Italian *musica leggera* (popular music); a term covering home-grown rock, jazz, folk, hip hop and pop ballads. The scene's annual highlight is the San Remo Music Festival (televised on RAI1), a Eurovision-style song comp responsible for launching the careers of chart-topping contemporary acts like Eros Ramazzotti, Giorgia, Laura Pausini and, more recently, singer-songwriter Marco Mengoni. In 2013, Mengoni won San Remo for his ballad *L'essenziale,* using the same song later that year to represent Italy at Eurovision.

In the early 1960s, San Remo helped launch the career of living music legend, Mina Mazzini. Famed for her powerful, three-octave voice and a musical versatility spanning pop, soul, blues, R&B and swing, the songstress dominated the charts throughout the 1960s and 1970s, her emancipated image and frank tunes about love and sex ruffling a few bourgeois feathers. Equally controversial was the late Fabrizio de André, an Italian Bob Dylan celebrated for his poetic lyrics, musing monotone and cutting criticism of religious hypocrisy.

Still-active singer-songwriter Vinicio Capossela sounds like the long-lost Italian cousin of Tom Waits, while internationally renowned Pino Daniele is best known for fusing Neapolitan music with blues and world music influences. Naples' distinct culture shines through in the work of hip-hop outfit La Famiglia and ska band Bisca, known for mixing Italian sounds over heavy beats and Neapolitan dialect. Fusion is also the word further south in Puglia, where artists like Sud Sound System remix Jamaican dancehall and Italy's hyperactive tarantella folk music into an offspring genre: 'tarantamuffin'.

OPTIMAL OPERA VENUES

➡ **Milan's** Teatro alla Scala (p243) Standards for modern opera were set by La Scala's great iron-willed conductor Arturo Toscanini and are ruthlessly enforced by La Scala's feared *loggione*, opera's toughest and most vocal critics in the cheap seats upstairs.

➡ **Venice's** La Fenice (p343) Risen twice from the ashes of devastating fires, 'The Phoenix' features great talents on its small stage.

➡ **Verona's** Roman Arena (p390) Rising talents ring out here, thanks to forward-thinking organisers and the phenomenal acoustics of this Roman amphitheatre.

➡ **Rome's** Terme di Caracalla (p98) The dramatically decrepit summer venue for the Teatro dell'Opera di Roma was the site of the first concert by the Three Tenors (Luciano Pavarotti, Placido Domingo and Jose Carreras), with a recording that sold an unprecedented 15 million copies.

➡ **Naples'** Teatro San Carlo (p658) Europe's oldest opera house, a Unesco World Heritage site and the former home of Italy's most famous *castrati* – male sopranos traditionally with surgically altered upper ranges.

Centuries on, the dreaded *fischi* (mocking whistles) still possess a mysterious power to blast singers right off stage. In December 2006, a substitute in street clothes had to step in for Sicilian-French star tenor Roberto Alagna when his off-night aria met with vocal disapproval at Milan's legendary La Scala. Best not to get them started about musicals and 'rock opera', eh?

The word *diva* was invented for legendary sopranos such as Parma's Renata Tebaldi and Italy's adopted Greek icon Maria Callas, whose rivalry peaked when *Time* quoted Callas saying that comparing her voice to Tebaldi's was like comparing 'champagne and Coca-Cola'. Both were fixtures at La Scala, along with the wildly popular Italian tenor to whom others are still compared, Enrico Caruso. Tenor Luciano Pavarotti (1935–2007) remains beloved for attracting broader public attention to opera, while best-selling blind tenor Andrea Bocelli became a controversial crossover sensation with what critics claim are overproduced arias sung with a strained upper register. A new generation of stars include soprano Fiorenza Cedolins, who performed a requiem for the late Pope John Paul II, recorded *Tosca* arias with Andrea Bocelli, and scored encores in Puccini's iconic *La Bohème* at the Arena di Verona Festival. Another recent great was tenor Salvatore Licitra. Famed for stepping in for Pavarotti on his final show at New York's Metropolitan Opera, the 43-year-old died tragically after a motorcycle accident in 2011.

Born an Assisi heiress, introduced to the joys of poverty by St Francis himself, and co-founder of the first Franciscan abbey, St Clare gained another claim to fame in 1958 as the patron saint of TV.

Italy on Page & Screen

From ancient Virgil to modern-day Eco, Italy's literary canon is awash with world-renowned scribes. The nation's film stock is equally robust, lavished with visionary directors, iconic stars and that trademark Italian pathos.

Literature

Latin Classics

Roman epic poet Virgil (aka Vergilius) decided Homer's *Iliad* and *Odyssey* deserved a sequel, and spent 11 years and 12 books tracking the outbound adventures and inner turmoil of Aeneas, from the fall of Troy to the founding of Rome – and died in 19 BC with just 60 lines to go in his *Aeneid*. As Virgil himself observed: 'Time flies'.

Legend has it that fellow Roman Ovid (Ovidius) was a failed lawyer who married his daughter, but there's no question he told a ripping good tale. His *Metamorphose* chronicled civilisation from murky mythological beginnings to Julius Caesar, and his how-to seduction manual *Ars amatoria* (The Art of Love) inspired countless Casanovas.

Timeless Poets

Some literature scholars claim that Shakespeare stole his best lines and plot points from earlier Italian playwrights and poets. Debatable though this may be, the Bard certainly had stiff competition from 13th-century Dante Alighieri as the world's finest romancer. Dante broke with tradition in *La Divina commedia* (The Divine Comedy; c 1307–21) by using the familiar Italian, not the formal Latin, to describe travelling through the circles of hell in search of his beloved Beatrice. Petrarch (aka Francesco Petrarca) added wow to Italian woo with his eponymous sonnets, applying a strict structure of rhythm and rhyme to romance the idealised Laura.

If sonnets aren't your shtick, try 1975 Nobel laureate Eugenio Montale, who wrings poetry out of the creeping damp of everyday life, or Ungaretti, whose WWI poems hit home with a few searing syllables.

Cautionary Fables

The most universally beloved Italian fabulist is Italo Calvino, whose titular character in *Il barone rampante* (The Baron in the Trees; 1957) takes to the treetops in a seemingly capricious act of rebellion that makes others rethink their own earthbound conventions. In Dino Buzzati's *Il deserto dei Tartari* (The Tartar Steppe; 1940), an ambitious officer posted to a mythical Italian border is besieged by boredom, thwarted expectations and disappearing youth while waiting for enemy hordes to materialise – a parable drawn from Buzzati's own dead-end newspaper job.

Over the centuries, Niccolo Machiavelli's *Il principe* (The Prince; 1532) has been referenced as a handy manual for budding autocrats, but also as a cautionary tale against unchecked 'Machiavellian' authority.

Sidebar 1:

For Dante with a pop-culture twist, check out Sandow Birk and Marcus Sanders' satirical, slangy translation of *The Divine Comedy*, which sets *Inferno* in hellish Los Angeles traffic, *Purgatorio* in foggy San Francisco and *Paradiso* in New York.

Sidebar 2:

Italy's most coveted literary prize, the Premio Strega, is awarded annually to a work of Italian prose fiction. Its youngest recipient to date is physicist-cum-writer Paolo Giordano, who, at 26, won for his debut novel *La solitudine dei numeri primi* (The Solitude of Prime Numbers; 2008).

Crime Pays

Crime fiction and *gialli* (mysteries) dominate Italy's best-seller list, and one of its finest writers is Gianrico Carofiglio. The former head of Bari's anti-Mafia squad, Carofiglio's novels include the award-winning *Testimone inconsapevole* (Involuntary Witness; 2002), which introduces the shady underworld of Bari's hinterland.

Art also imitates life for judge-cum-novelist Giancarlo de Cataldo, whose best-selling novel *Romanzo criminale* (Criminal Romance; 2002) spawned both a TV series and film. Another crime writer with page-to-screen success is Andrea Camilleri, his savvy Sicilian inspector Montalbano starring in capers like *Il ladro di merendine* (The Snack Thief; 1996).

Umberto Eco gave the genre an intellectual edge with *Il nome della rosa* (The Name of the Rose; 1980) and *Il pendolo di Foucault* (Foucault's Pendulum; 1988). In Eco's *Il cimitero di Praga* (The Prague Cemetery; 2010), historical events merge with the tale of a master killer and forger.

Historical Epics

Set during the Black Death in Florence, Boccaccio's *Decameron* (c 1350–53) has a visceral gallows humour that foreshadows Chaucer and Shakespeare. Italy's 19th-century struggle for unification parallels the story of star-crossed lovers in Alessandro Manzoni's *I promessi sposi* (The Betrothed; 1827, definitive version released 1842), and causes an identity crisis among Sicilian nobility in Giuseppe Tomasi di Lampedusa's *Il gattopardo* (The Leopard; published posthumously in 1958).

Wartime survival strategies are chronicled in Elsa Morante's *La storia* (History; 1974) and in Primo Levi's autobiographical account of Auschwitz in *Se questo è un uomo* (If This Is a Man; 1947). WWII is the uninvited guest in *Il giardino dei Finzi-Contini* (The Garden of the Finzi-Continis; 1962), Giorgio Bassani's tale of a crush on a girl whose aristocratic Jewish family attempts to disregard the rising tide of anti-Semitism. In Margaret Mazzantini's *Venuto al mondo* (Twice Born; 2008) it's the Bosnian War that forms the backdrop to a powerful tale of motherhood and loss.

Social Realism

Italy has always been its own sharpest critic and several 20th-century Italian authors captured their own troubling circumstances with

---

Best in Print

The Italians (Luigi Barzini) A revealing look at Italian culture beyond the well-worn clichés.

Gomorrah (Roberto Saviano) Fascinating, disturbing exposé of the power of the Campanian Camorra.

The Pursuit of Italy (David Gilmour) Interesting insights into Italy's past and present.

La Bella Figura: A Field Guide to the Italian Mind (Beppe Severgnini) Satirist Severgnini offers a crash course in what makes modern Italians tick.

THE GREAT DIRECTORS

➡ **Vittorio De Sica** Actor-turned-neorealist director whose Honorary Oscar for *Sciuscià* (Shoeshine; 1946) spawned the Academy's 'Best Foreign Film' category. Must-see: *Two Women* (1960)

➡ **Roberto Rossellini** Film critic Francois Truffaut called the influential neorealist the 'father of the French New Wave'. Must-see: *Roma, Città Aperta* (Rome, Open City; 1945)

➡ **Luchino Visconti** Famed for the Oscar-nominated *The Damned* (1969) and the lavish aesthetics of his films. Must-see: *Death in Venice* (1971)

➡ **Federico Fellini** One of history's most influential and awarded filmmakers, best known for fusing dreams and reality. Must-see: *8½* (1963)

➡ **Pier Paolo Pasolini** Controversial neorealist who championed the damned of postwar Italy. Must-see: *Mamma Roma* (1962)

➡ **Sergio Leone** King of spaghetti westerns and inventor of the extreme close-up in Westerns. Must-see: *C'era una volta il West* (Once Upon a Time in the West; 1968)

➡ **Bernardo Bertolucci** His explicit *Last Tango in Paris* (1972) led to the film's ban in Italy, and to a suspended prison sentence for Bertolucci. Must-see: *The Last Emperor* (1987)

LOCATION! LOCATION!

Italy's cities, hills and coastlines set the scene for countless celluloid classics. Top billing goes to Rome, where Bernardo Bertolucci used the Terme di Caracalla in the oedipal *La luna* (1979), Gregory Peck gave Audrey Hepburn a fright at the Bocca della Verità in William Wyler's *Roman Holiday* (1953) and Anita Ekberg cooled off in the Trevi Fountain in Federico Fellini's *La Dolce Vita*. Fellini's love affair with the Eternal City culminated in his silver-screen tribute, *Roma* (1972), while American director Woody Allen showed his affection with the romantic comedy, *To Rome with Love* (2012).

Florence's Piazza della Signoria recalls James Ivory's *Room With a View* (1985). Further south, Siena's Piazza del Palio and Piazza della Paglietta stir fantasies of actor Daniel Craig – both featured in the 22nd James Bond instalment, *Quantum of Solace* (2008).

In Venice, Angelina Jolie and Johnny Depp sped down the Grand Canal in *The Tourist* (2010). The city enjoyed a cameo in *The Talented Mr Ripley* (1999), in which Matt Damon and Gwyneth Paltrow also tanned and toasted on the islands of Procida and Ischia. Fans of *Il Postino* will recognise Procida's pastel-hued Corricella, while deep down in Basilicata, Matera's cavernous landscape moonlit as Palestine in Mel Gibson's *Passion of the Christ* (2004).

unflinching accuracy. Grazia Deledda's *Cosima* (1937) is her fictionalised memoir of coming of age and into her own as a writer in rural Sardinia. Deledda became one of the first women to win the Nobel Prize for Literature (1926) and set the tone for such bittersweet recollections of rural life as Carlo Levi's *Cristo si è fermato a Eboli* (Christ Stopped at Eboli; 1945).

Jealousy, divorce and parental failings are grappled head-on by pseudonymous author Elena Ferrante in her brutally honest *I giorni dell'abbandono* (The Days of Abandonment; 2002). Confronting themes also underline Alessandro Pipero's *Persecuzione* (Persecution; 2010), which sees an esteemed oncologist accused of child molestation. Its sequel, *Inseparabili* (2012), won the 2012 Premio Strega literature prize.

Best on Screen

Ladri di bicicletta
(Bicycle Thieves)
Vittorio De Sica,
1948

La Dolce Vita
Federico Fellini,
1960

Cinema Paradiso
Giuseppe Tornatore, 1988

Il postino (The Postman) Michael Radford, 1994

La vita è bella
(Life is Beautiful)
Roberto Benigni,
1997

Cinema

Neorealist Grit

Out of the smouldering ruins of WWII emerged unflinching tales of woe, including Roberto Rossellini's *Roma, Città Aperta* (Rome, Open City; 1945), a story of love, betrayal and resistance in Nazi-occupied Rome. In Vittorio De Sica's Academy-awarded *Ladri di biciclette* (The Bicycle Thieves; 1948), a doomed father attempts to provide for his son without resorting to crime in war-ravaged Rome, while Pier Paolo Pasolini's *Mamma Roma* (1962) revolves around an ageing prostitute trying to make an honest living for herself and her deadbeat son.

Crime & Punishment

Italy's acclaimed new dramas combine the truthfulness of classic neorealism, the taut suspense of Italian thrillers and the psychological revelations of Fellini. Among the best is Matteo Garrone's brutal Camorra expose *Gomorra* (2008). Based on Roberto Saviano's award-winning novel, the film won the Grand Prix at the 2008 Cannes Film Festival. Another Cannes success story is Paolo Sorrentino's *Il divo* (2008), which explores the life of former prime minister Giulio Andreotti, from his migraines to his alleged Mafia ties. Mafiosi are among the cast in the deeply poignant *Cesare deve morire* (Caesar Must Die; 2012), a documentary about maximum-security prisoners preparing to stage Shakespeare's *Julius Caesar*. Directed by octogenarian brothers Paolo and Vittorio Taviani, the film scooped the Golden Bear at the 2012 Berlin Film Festival.

Romance all'italiana

It's only natural that a nation of hopeless romantics should provide some of the world's most tender celluloid moments. In Michael Radford's *Il postino* (The Postman; 1994), exiled poet Pablo Neruda brings poetry and passion to a drowsy Italian isle and a misfit postman, played with heart-breaking subtlety by the late Massimo Troisi. Another classic is Giuseppe Tornatore's Oscar-winning *Nuovo cinema paradiso* (Cinema Paradiso; 1988), a bittersweet tale about a director who returns to Sicily and redis-covers his true loves: the girl next door and the movies. In Silvio Sordini's *Pane e tulipani* (Bread and Tulips; 2000), a housewife left behind at a tour-bus pit stop runs away to Venice, where she befriends an anarchist florist, an eccentric masseuse and a suicidal Icelandic waiter – and gets pursued by an amateur detective. Equally contemporary is Ferzan Öz-petek's *Mine vaganti* (Loose Cannons; 2010), a situation comedy about two gay brothers and their conservative Pugliese family.

A one-man 'Abbott and Costello', Antonio de Curtis (1898–1967), aka Totò, famously depicted the Neapolitan *furbizia* (cunning). Appearing in over 100 films, including *Miseria e nobiltà* (Misery & Nobility; 1954), his roles as a hustler living on nothing but his quick wits have guaranteed him cult status in Naples.

Spaghetti Westerns

Emerging in the mid-1960s, Italian-style Westerns had no shortage of high-noon showdowns featuring flinty characters and Ennio Morricone's terminally catchy whistled tunes (*doodle-oodle-ooh, wah wah wah...*). Top of the directorial heap was Sergio Leone, whose Western debut *Per un pugno di dollari* (A Fistful of Dollars; 1964) helped launch a young Clint Eastwood's movie career. After Leone and Clintwood teamed up again in *Il buono, il brutto, il cattivo* (The Good, the Bad, and the Ugly; 1966), it was Henry Fonda's turn in Leone's *C'era una volta il West* (Once Upon a Time in the West; 1968), a story about a revenge-seeking widow.

Tragicomedies

Italy's best comedians skewer the exact spot where pathos intersects the funny bone. A group of ageing pranksters turn on one another in Mario Monicelli's *Amici miei* (My Friends; 1975), a satire reflecting Italy's own postwar midlife crisis. Italy's recent woes feed Massimiliano Bruno's biting *Viva L'Italia* (2012), its cast of corrupt politicians and nepotists cutting close to the core. Italy is slapped equally hard by Matteo Gar-rone's *Reality* (2012). Winner of the Grand Prix at the 2012 Cannes Film Festival, the darkly comic film revolves around a Neapolitan fishmonger desperately seeking fame through reality TV. Darker still is *La vita è bella* (Life is Beautiful; 1997), in which a father tries to protect his son from the brutalities of a Jewish concentration camp by pretending it's all a game – an Oscar-winning turn for actor-director Roberto Benigni.

Crueller and bloodier than their American counterparts, Ital-ian zombie films enjoy interna-tional cult status. One of the best is director Lucio Fulci's *Zombi 2* (aka Zombie Flesh Eaters; 1979). Fulci's other gore classics include *City of the Living Dead* (1980), *The Beyond* (1981) and *The House by the Cemetery* (1981).

Shock & Horror

Sunny Italy's darkest dramas deliver more style, suspense and fall-ing bodies than Prada platform heels on a slippery Milan runway. In Michelangelo Antonioni's *Blow-Up* (1966) a swinging-'60s fashion pho-tographer spies dark deeds unfolding in a photo of an elusive Vanessa Redgrave. Gruesome deeds unfold at a ballet school in Dario Argento's *Suspiria* (1977), while in Mario Monicelli's *Un borghese piccolo piccolo* (An Average Little Man; 1977), an ordinary man goes to extraordinary lengths for revenge. The latter stars Roman acting great Alberto Soldi in a standout example of a comedian nailing a serious role.

The Italian Table

Let's be honest: you came for the food, right? Wise choice. Just don't go expecting the stock-standard fare served at your local Italian restaurant back home. In reality, Italian cuisine is a handy umbrella term for the country's diverse regional cuisines. Despite the diversity, there is almost always one constant – whether you're tucking into a hearty *farro* soup in some Tuscan *osteria* or devouring a *pizza margherita* in its home town, Naples, you'll be struck with culinary amnesia. Has anything tasted this good, ever? Probably not.

Fifty years ago, Italy's *Domus* magazine dispatched journalists nationwide to collect Italy's best regional recipes. The result is Italy's food bible, *The Silver Spoon*, now available in English from Phaidon (2005).

The secret is in the ingredients. Each is chosen with careful consideration to scent, texture, ripeness and the ability to play well with others. This means getting to the market early and often, and remaining open to seasonal inspiration. To balance these ingredients in exactly the right proportions, Italian cooks apply an intuitive Pythagorean theorem of flavours you won't find spelled out in any recipe – but that is unmistakable with your first bite.

Tutti a Tavola

'Everyone to the table!' Traffic lights are merely suggestions and queues are fine ideas in theory, but this is one command every Italian heeds without question. To disobey would be unthinkable – what, you're going to eat your pasta cold? And insult the cook? Even anarchists wouldn't dream of it.

You never really know Italians until you've broken a crusty loaf of *pagnotta* with them – and once you've arrived in Italy, jump at any opportunity to do just that.

Morning Essentials

In Italy, *colazione* (breakfast) is a minimalist affair. Eggs, pancakes, ham, sausage, toast and orange juice are only likely to appear at weekend *brrrunch* (pronounced with the rolled Italian *r*), an American import now appearing at trendy urban eateries. Expect to pay upwards of €20 to graze a buffet of hot dishes, cold cuts, pastries and fresh fruit, usually including your choice of coffee, juice or cocktail.

Italy's breakfast staple is *caffè* (coffee). Scalding-hot espresso, cappuccino (espresso with a good dollop of foamed milk) or *caffè latte* – the hot, milky espresso beverage Starbucks mistakenly calls a *latte,* which will get you a glass of milk in Italy. An alternative beverage is *orzo,* a slightly nutty, noncaffeinated roasted-barley beverage that looks like cocoa.

With a *tazza* (cup) in one hand, use the other for that most Italian of breakfast foods – a pastry. Some especially promising options include the following:

➡ **Cornetto** The Italian take on the French croissant is usually smaller, lighter, less buttery and slightly sweet, with an orange-rind glaze brushed on top. Fillings might include *cioccolato* (chocolate), *cioccolato bianco* (white chocolate), *crema* (custard) or varying flavours of *marmelata* (jam).

➡ **Crostata** The Italian breakfast tart with a dense, buttery crust is filled with your choice of fruit jam, such as *amarena* (sour cherry), *albicocca* (apricot) or *frutti di bosco* (wild berry). You may have to buy an entire tart instead of a single slice, but you won't be sorry.

➡ **Doughnuts** Homer Simpson would approve of the *ciambella* (also called by its German name, *krapfen*), the classic fried-dough treat rolled in granulated sugar and sometimes filled with jam or custard. Join the line at kiosks and street fairs for *fritole*, fried dough studded with golden raisins and sprinkled with confectioners' sugar, and *zeppole* (also called *bigné di San Giuseppe*), chewy doughnuts filled with ricotta or *zucca* (pumpkin), rolled in confectioners' sugar, and handed over in a paper cone to be devoured dangerously hot.

➡ **Viennoiserie** Italy's colonisation by the Austro-Hungarian Empire in the 19th century had its upside: a vast selection of sweet buns and other rich baked goods. Standouts include cream-filled brioches and *strudel di mele,* an Italian adaptation of the traditional Viennese *apfelstrudel*.

Lunch & Dinner

Italian food culture directly contradicts what we think we know of Italy. A nation prone to perpetual motion with Vespas, Ferraris and Bianchis pauses for *pranzo* (lunch) – hence the term *la pausa* to describe the midday break. In the cities, power-lunchers settle in at their favourite *ristoranti* and trattorias, while in smaller towns and villages, workers often head home for a two- to three-hour midday break, devouring a hot lunch and resting up before returning to work fortified by espresso.

Where *la pausa* has been scaled back to a scandalous hour and a half – barely enough time to get through the lines at the bank to pay bills and bolt some *pizza al taglio* (pizza by the slice) – *rosticcerie* (rotisseries) or *tavole calde* (literally 'hot tables') keep the harried sated with steamy, on-the-go options like roast chicken and *supplì* (fried risotto balls with a molten mozzarella centre). Bakeries and bars are also on hand with focaccia, *panini* and *tramezzini* (triangular, stacked sandwiches made with squishy white bread) providing a satisfying bite.

THE ITALIAN TABLE TUTTI A TAVOLA

Less is more: most of the recipes in Ada Boni's classic *The Talisman Italian Cookbook* have fewer than 10 ingredients, yet the robust flavours of her osso bucco, polenta, and wild duck with lentils are anything but simple.

THE BIG FORK MANIFESTO

The year is 1987. McDonald's has just begun expansion into Italy and lunch outside the bun seems to be fading into fond memory. Enter Carlo Petrini and a handful of other journalists from small-town Bra, Piedmont. Determined to buck the trend, these *neo-forchettoni* ('big forks', or foodies) created a manifesto. Published in the like-minded culinary magazine *Gambero Rosso,* they declared that a meal should be judged not by its speed, but by its pure pleasure.

The organisation they founded would soon become known worldwide as **Slow Food** (www.slowfood.com), and its mission to reconnect artisanal producers with enthusiastic, educated consumers has taken root with more than 100,000 members in 150 countries – not to mention Slow Food *agriturismi* (farmstay accommodation), restaurants, farms, wineries, cheesemakers and revitalised farmers markets across Italy.

Held on even-numbered years in a former Fiat factory in Turin, Italy's top Slow Food event is the biennial **Salone del Gusto & Terre Madre** (www.salonedelgusto.it). Slow Food's global symposium, it features Slow Food producers, chefs, activists, restaurateurs, farmers, scholars, environmentalists and epicureans from around the world... not to mention the world's best finger food. Thankfully, odd years don't miss out on the epicurean enlightened either, with special events such as **Slow Fish** (p173) in Genoa, **Cheese** (www.cheese.slowfood.it) in Bra and the annual **Slow Food on Film** (www.slow-foodonfilm.it) in Bologna.

APERITIVI: BUDGET FEASTING

Aperitivi are often described as a 'before-meal drink and light snacks'. Don't be fooled. Italian 'happy hour' is a recession-friendly dinner disguised as a casual drink, accompanied by a buffet of antipasti, pasta salads, cold cuts and some hot dishes (this may include your fellow diners: *aperitivi* is prime time for hungry singles). You can methodically pillage buffets in Milan, Turin, Rome and Naples from about 5pm to 8pm for the price of a single drink – which crafty diners nurse for the duration – while Venetians enjoy *ombre* (wine by the glass) and bargain seafood *cicheti* (Venetian tapas). *Aperitivi* are wildly popular among the many young Italians who can't afford to eat dinner out, but still want a place to enjoy food with friends – leave it to Italy to find a way to put the glam into recession.

Traditionally, *cena* (dinner) is lunch's lighter sibling and cries of 'Oh, I can hardly eat anything tonight' are still common after a marathon weekend lunch. 'Maybe just a bowl of pasta, a salad, some cheese and fruit...' Don't be fooled: even if you've been invited to someone's house for a 'light dinner', wine and elastic-waisted pants are always advisable.

But while your Italian hosts may insist you devour one more cream-filled *cannolo* (surely you don't have them back home...and even if you did, surely they're not as good?!), your waiter will usually show more mercy. Despite the Italians' 'more is more' attitude to food consumption, restaurant diners are rarely obliged to order both a *primo* and *secondo,* and antipasti and dessert are strictly optional.

That said, a lavish dinner at one of Italy's fine-dining hot spots, such as Milan's Cracco-Peck or Rome's Open Colonna is a highlight few will want to skip.

Many top-ranked restaurants open only for dinner, with a set-price *degustazione* meal that leaves the major menu decisions to your chef and frees you up to concentrate on the noble quest to conquer four to six tasting courses. *Forza e coraggio!* (Strength and courage to you!)

Although some producers find these official Italian classifications unduly costly and creatively constraining, the DOCG (Denominazione di origine controllata e garantita) and DOC (Denominazione di origine controllata) designations are awarded to wines that meet regional quality-control standards.

Italian Menu 101

The *cameriere* (waiter) leads you to your table and hands you the menu. The scent of slow-cooked *ragù* (meat and tomato sauce) lingers in the air and your stomach rumbles in anticipation. Where might this culinary encounter lead you? Unfurl that *tovagliolo* (napkin), lick those lips, and read on...

Antipasti (Appetiser)

The culinary equivalent of foreplay, antipasti are a good way to sample a number of different dishes. Tantalising offerings on the antipasti menu may include the house bruschetta (grilled bread with a variety of toppings, from chopped tomato and garlic to black-truffle spread) or regional treats like *mozzarella di bufala* (buffalo mozzarella) or *salatini con burro d'acciughe* (pastry sticks with anchovy butter). Even if it's not on the menu, it's always worth requesting an *antipasto misto* (mixed antipasto), a platter of morsels including anything from *olive fritte* (fried olives) and *prosciutto e melone* (cured ham and cantaloupe) to *friarielli con peperoncino* (Neapolitan broccoli with chilli). At this stage, bread (and sometimes *grissini* – Turin-style breadsticks) are also deposited on the table as part of your €1 to €3 *pane e coperto* ('bread and cover' or table service).

Tomatoes were not introduced to Italy until the 16th century, brought from the Americas. The word 'pomodoro' literally means 'golden apple'.

Primo (First Course)

Starch is the star in Italian first courses, from pasta and gnocchi, to risotto and polenta. You may be surprised how generous the portions are – a *mezzo piatto* (half-portion) might do the trick for kids.

Primi menus usually include ostensibly vegetarian or vegan options, such as pasta *con pesto* – the classic Ligurian basil paste with *parmigiano reggiano* (Parmesan) and pine nuts – or *alla norma* (with basil, eggplant, ricotta and tomato), *risotto ai porcini* (risotto with pungent, earthy porcini mushrooms) or the extravagant *risotto al Barolo* (risotto with high-end Barolo wine, though actually any good dry red will do). But even if a dish sounds vegetarian in theory, before you order you may want to ask about the stock used in that risotto or polenta, or the ingredients in that suspiciously rich tomato sauce – there may be beef, ham or ground anchovies involved.

Meat eaters will rejoice in such legendary dishes as pasta *all'amatriciana* (Roman pasta with a spicy tomato sauce, *pecorino* cheese and *guanciale*, or bacon-like pigs' cheeks), osso bucco *con risotto alla milanese* (Milanese veal shank and marrow melting into saffron risotto), Tuscan speciality *pappardelle alle cinghiale* (ribbon pasta with wild boar sauce) and northern favourite *polenta col ragù* (polenta with meat sauce). Near the coasts, look for seafood variations like *risotto al nero* (risotto cooked with black squid ink), *spaghetti alle vongole* (spaghetti with clam sauce) or *pasta ai frutti di mare* (pasta with seafood).

Secondo (Second Course)

Light lunchers usually call it a day after the *primo,* but *buongustai* (foodies) pace themselves for meat, fish or *contorni* (side dishes, such as cooked vegetables) in the second course. These options may range from the outrageous *bistecca alla fiorentina,* a 3in-thick steak served on the bone in a puddle of juice, to more modest yet equally impressive *fritto misto di mare* (mixed fried seafood), *carciofi alla romana* (Roman artichokes stuffed with mint and garlic) or *pollo in tegame con barbe* (chicken casserole with salsify). A less inspiring option is *insalata mista* (mixed green salad), typically unadorned greens with vinegar and oil on the side – croutons, crumbled cheeses, nuts, dried fruit and other frou-frou ingredients have no business in a classic Italian salad.

Frutti e dolci

'Siamo arrivati alla frutta' ('We've arrived at the fruit') is an idiom roughly meaning 'we've hit rock bottom' – but hey, not until you've had one last tasty morsel. Your best bets on the fruit menu are local and seasonal. *Formaggi* (cheeses) are another option, but only diabetics or the French would go that route when there's room for *dolci* (sweets). *Biscotti* (twice-baked biscuits) made to dip in wine make for a delicious closure to the meal, but other great desserts include *zabaglione* (egg and marsala custard), *torta di ricotta e pera* (pear and ricotta cake), cream-stuffed profiteroles, or *cannoli Siciliani,* the ricotta-stuffed shell pastry immortalised thus in *The Godfather:* 'Leave the gun. Take the *cannoli.'*

Caffè (Coffee)

Most Italian mornings start with a creamy, frothy cappuccino (named for the Capuchin monks, with their brown hoods), which is rarely taken after about 11am and usually served not too hot. Otherwise it's espresso all the way, though you could ask for a tiny stain of milk in a *caffè macchiato*. On the hottest days of summer, a *granita di caffè* (coffee with

ESPRESSO

Don't believe the hype about espresso: one diminutive cup packs less of a caffeine wallop than a large cup of French-pressed or American-brewed coffee, and leaves drinkers less jittery.

WINE & COOKERY COURSES

You can hardly throw a stone in Italy without hitting a culinary course in progress, but there are better ways of finding a cookery school. You'll find some of the big hitters below.

➡ **Città del Gusto** (p118) Six floors of hot, nonstop gourmet-on-gourmet action in Rome, from live cooking demonstrations and TV-show tapings to wine courses in the 'Theatre of Wine'. All workshops and demos are run by *Gambero Rosso,* Italy's most esteemed food magazine. You'll find a second branch in **Naples** (☎081 1980 8900; Via Coroglio 57/104e).

➡ **Culinary Adventures** (www.peggymarkel.com) Indulge in and learn about cooking Italian dishes with local, sustainably sourced ingredients at decadent week-long courses in Sicily, Amalfi and Tuscany.

➡ **Eataly** This monument to artisanal food, with branches in Rome (p136) & Turin (p205), offers samples, wine tasting, workshops and courses, some of which go on for up to two days. Italian-speakers will have more options.

➡ **Italian Food Artisans** (www.foodartisans.com/workshops) Slip behind the scenes in restaurant kitchens and private homes and discover Italy's best-kept food secrets in Cinque Terre, Piedmont, Emilia-Romagna, Campania and Sicily on one-day workshops or week-long adventures with cookbook author Pamela Sheldon Johns.

➡ **Tasting Places** (www.tastingplaces.com) Recent offerings include excursions to regional Slow Food festivals, a 'White Truffle and Wine' weekend in Piedmont and gourmet getaways in the Veneto and Tuscany.

➡ **La Vecchia Scuola Bolognese** (p437) In food-heaven Bologna, this offers three-hour pasta-making courses (in English and Italian) plus lunch (€86).

shaved ice and whipped cream) is ideal. For more on the Italian Coffee Culture see p422.

The Vino Lowdown

A sit-down meal without *vino* (wine) in Italy is as unpalatable as pasta without sauce. Not ordering wine at a restaurant can cause consternation – are you pregnant or a recovering alcoholic? Was it something the waiter said? Italian wines are considered among the most versatile and 'food friendly' in the world, specifically cultivated over the centuries to elevate regional cuisine.

Here, wine is a consideration as essential as your choice of dinner date. Indeed, while the country's perfectly quaffable pilsner beers and occasional red ale pair well with roast meats, pizza and other quick eats, *vino* is considered appropriate for a proper meal – and since many wines cost less than a pint in Italy, this is not a question of price, but a matter of flavour.

Some Italian wines will be as familiar to you as old flames, including pizza-and-a-movie chianti or reliable summertime fling pinot grigio. But you'll also find some captivating Italian varietals and blends for which there is no translation (eg Brunello, Vermentino, Sciacchetrá), and intriguing Italian wines that have little in common with European and Australian cousins by the same name (eg merlot, pinot nero aka pinot noir, chardonnay).

Many visitors default to carafes of house reds or whites, which in Italy usually means young, fruit-forward reds to complement tomato sauces and chilled dry whites as seafood palate-cleansers. But with a little daring, you can pursue a wider range of options by the glass or half-bottle.

The average Italian adult consumes around 42L of wine per annum – a sobering figure compared with the 100L consumed on average back in the 1950s. Somewhat surprisingly, the world's top consumers of wine live in the Vatican City (54.78L per person).

➡ **Sparkling wines** Franciacorta (Lombardy), prosecco (Veneto), Asti (aka Asti Spumante; Piedmont), Lambrusco (Emilia-Romagna)

➡ **Light, citrusy whites with grassy or floral notes** Vermentino (Sardinia), Orvieto (Umbria), Soave (Veneto), Tocai (Friuli)

➡ **Dry whites with aromatic herbal or mineral aspect** Cinque Terre (Liguria), Gavi (Piedmont), Falanghina (Campania), Est! Est!! Est!!! (Lazio)

➡ **Versatile, food-friendly reds with pleasant acidity** Barbera d'Alba (Piedmont), Montepulciano d'Abruzzo (Abruzzo), Valpolicella (Veneto), Chianti Classico (Tuscany), Bardolino (Lombardy)

➡ **Well-rounded reds, balancing fruit with earthy notes** Brunello di Montalcino (Tuscany), Refosco dal Pedulunco Rosso (Friuli), Dolcetto (Piedmont), Morellino di Scansano (Tuscany)

➡ **Big, structured reds with velvety tannins** Amarone (Veneto), Barolo (Piedmont), Sagrantino di Montefalco secco (Umbria), Sassicaia and other 'super-Tuscan' blends (Tuscany)

➡ **Fortified and dessert wine** Sciacchetrá (Liguria), Colli Orientali del Friuli Picolit (Friuli), Vin Santo (Tuscany), Moscato d'Asti (Piedmont)

For a thirst-quenching adventure through Italy's most celebrated wine region, visit Tuscany's Il Chianti.

Liquori (Liqueurs)

Failure to order a postprandial espresso may shock your server but you may yet save face by ordering a *digestivo* (digestive), such as a grappa (a potent grape-derived alcohol), *amaro* (a dark liqueur prepared from herbs) or *limoncello* (lemon liqueur). Fair warning though: Italian digestives can be an acquired taste and they pack a punch that might leave you snoring before *il conto* (the bill) arrives.

Festive Favourites

Perhaps you've heard of ancient Roman orgies with trips to the vomitorium to make room for the next course, or Medici family feasts with sugar sculptures worth their weight in gold? In Italy, culinary indulgence is the epicentre of any celebration and major holidays are defined by their specialities. Lent is heralded by Carnevale (Carnival), a time for *migliaccio di polenta* (a casserole of polenta, sausage, *pecorino* and *parmigiano reggiano* cheeses), *sanguinaccio* ('blood pudding' made with dark chocolate and cinnamon), *chiacchiere* (fried biscuits sprinkled with icing sugar) and Sicily's *mpagnuccata* (deep-fried dough tossed in soft caramel).

If you're here around 19 March (St Joseph's Feast Day), expect to eat *bignè di San Giuseppe* (fried doughnuts filled with cream or chocolate) in Rome, *zeppole* (fritters topped with lemon-scented cream, sour cherry and dusting sugar) in Naples and Bari, and *crispelle di riso* (citrus-scented rice fritters dipped in honey) in Sicily.

Lent specialities like Sicilian *quaresimali* (hard, light almond biscuits) give way to Easter binging with the obligatory lamb, *colomba* (dove-shaped cake) and *uove di pasqua* (foil-wrapped chocolate eggs with toy surprises inside). The dominant ingredient at this time is egg, also used to make traditional regional specialities like Genoa's *torta pasqualina* (pastry tart filled with ricotta, *parmigiano*, artichokes and hard-boiled eggs), Florence's *brodetto* (egg, lemon and bread broth) and Naples' legendary *pastiera* (shortcrust pastry tart filled with ricotta, cream, candied fruits and cereals flavoured with orange water).

At the other end of the calendar, Christmas means stuffed pasta, seafood dishes and one of Milan's greatest inventions: *panettone* (a yeasty, golden cake studded with raisins and dried fruit). Equally famous are Verona's simpler, raisin-free *pandoro* (a yeasty, star-shaped cake dusted

CHIANTI CLASSICO

Italy's oldest known wine is Chianti Classico, with favourable reviews dating from the 14th century and a growing region clearly defined by 1716.

Top Food & Wine Regions

Emilia-Romagna

Tuscany

Piedmont

Campania

Sicily

with vanilla-flavoured icing sugar) and Siena's *panforte* (a chewy, flat cake made with candied fruits, nuts, chocolate, honey and spices). Further south, Neapolitans throw caution (and scales) to the wind with *raffioli* (sponge and marzipan biscuits), *struffoli* (tiny fried pastry balls dipped in honey and sprinkled with colourful candied sugar) and *pasta di mandorla* (marzipan), while their Sicilian cousins toast to the season with *cucciddatu* (ring-shaped cake made with dried figs, nuts, honey, vanilla, cloves, cinnamon and citrus fruits).

Of course, it's not all about religion. Some Italian holidays dispense with the spiritual premise and are all about the food. During spring, summer and early autumn, towns across Italy celebrate *sagre*, the festivals of local foods in season. You'll find a *sagra del tartufo* (truffles) in Umbria, *del pomodoro* (tomatoes) in Sicily and *del cipolle* (onions) in Puglia (wouldn't want to be downwind of that one). For a list of *sagre*, check out www.prodottitipici.com/sagre (in Italian).

To learn more about eating in Italy see Eat & Drink Like a Local, p39.

Survival Guide

Directory A–Z

Accommodation

Accommodation in Italy can range from the sublime to the ridiculous with prices to match. The options are incredibly varied, from family-run *pensioni* and designer hotels, to characterful B&Bs, serviced apartments, *agriturismi* (farm stays), and even *rifugi* (mountain huts) for weary mountain trekkers. Capturing the imagination even more are options spanning luxurious country villas and castles, tranquil convents and monasteries. When considering where to slumber, note the following tips:

➡ It pays to book ahead in high season, especially in popular coastal areas in the summer and popular ski resorts in the winter. In the urban centres you can usually find something if you leave it to luck, though reserving a room is essential during key events (such as the furniture and fashion fairs in Milan) when demand is extremely high.

➡ Accommodation rates can fluctuate enormously depending on the season,

with Easter, summer and the Christmas/New Year period being the typical peak tourist times. Seasonality also varies according to location. Expect to pay top prices in the mountains during the ski season (December to March) or along the coast in summer (July and August). Conversely, summer in the parched cities can equal low season; in August especially, many city hotels charge as little as half price.

➡ Price also depends greatly on location. A bottom-end budget choice in Venice or Milan will set you back the price of a decent midrange option in, say, rural Campania. Where possible, we present the high-season rates for each accommodation option. Half-board equals breakfast and either lunch or dinner; full board includes breakfast, lunch and dinner.

➡ Some hotels, in particular the lower-end places, barely alter their prices throughout the year. In low season there's no harm in bargaining for a discount, especially if you intend to stay for several

days. It's also always worth checking for last-minute online deals on websites like www.lastminute.com, www.booking.com and www.hotelsitalyonline.com.

➡ Hotels usually require that reservations be confirmed with a credit-card number. No-shows will be docked a night's accommodation.

B&Bs

B&Bs are a burgeoning sector of the Italian accommodation market and can be found throughout the country in both urban and rural settings. Options include everything from restored farmhouses, city *palazzi* (mansions) and seaside bungalows to rooms in family houses. Tariffs per person cover a wide range, from around €30 to €100. For more information, contact **Bed & Breakfast Italia** (www.bbitalia.it).

Camping

Most campgrounds in Italy are major complexes with swimming pools, restaurants and supermarkets. They are graded according to a star system. Charges usually vary according to the season, peaking in July and August. Note that some places offer an all-inclusive price, while others charge separately for each person, tent, vehicle and/or campsite. Typical high-season prices range from €10 to €20 per adult, up to €12 for children under 12, and from €5 to €25 for a site.

Italian campgrounds are generally set up for people travelling with their own vehicle, although some are accessible by public transport. In the major cities, grounds are often a long way from the historic centres. Most but not all have space for RVs. Tent campers are expected to bring their own equipment, although a few grounds offer tents for hire. Many also offer the alternative of bungalows or even simple, self-contained (self-catering) flats. In high season, some only offer deals for a week at a time.

Major bookshops also sell the annual *Campeggi e Villaggi turistici* (Camping and Holiday Villages, €14.90), a list of Italian, Corsican, French, Spanish and Croatian camp grounds published by Touring Club Italiano (TCI).

Lists of campgrounds are available from local tourist offices or online:

Campeggi.com (www.campeggi.com)

Camping.it (www.camping.it)

Italcamping.it (www.italcamping.it)

Canvas Holidays (www.canvasholidays.co.uk)

Eurocamp (www.eurocamp.co.uk)

Keycamp (www.keycamp.co.uk)

Select Sites (www.select-site.com)

Convents & Monasteries

Some Italian convents and monasteries let out cells or rooms as a modest revenue-making exercise and happily take in tourists, while others only take in pilgrims or people who are on a spiritual retreat. Many impose a fairly early curfew, but prices tend to be quite reasonable.

A useful if ageing publication is Eileen Barish's *The Guide to Lodging in Italy's Monasteries*. A more recent book on the same subject is Charles M Shelton's *Beds and Blessings in Italy: A Guide to Religious Hospitality*. Other resources can assist you in your search:

MonasteryStays.com (www.monasterystays.com) A well-organised online booking centre for monastery and convent stays.

In Italy Online (www.initaly.com/agri/convents.htm) Well worth a look for monastery and convent accommodations in Abruzzo, Emilia-Romagna, Lazio, Liguria, Lombardy, Puglia, Sardinia, Sicily, Tuscany, Umbria and the Veneto. You pay US$6 to access the online newsletter with addresses.

Chiesa di Santa Susana (www.santasusanna.org/comingToRome/convents.html) This American Catholic church in Rome has searched out convent and monastery accommodation options around the country and posted a list on its website. Note that some places are just residential accommodation run by religious orders and not necessarily big on monastic atmosphere. The church doesn't handle bookings; to request a spot, you'll need to contact each individual institution directly.

Hostels

Ostelli per la gioventù (youth hostels) are run by the **Associazione Italiana Alberghi per la Gioventù** (AIG; Map p94; ☑06 487 11 52; www.aighostels.com) affiliated with **Hostelling International** (HI; www.hihostels.com). A valid HI card is required in all associated youth hostels in Italy. You can get this in your home country or directly at many hostels.

THE SLUMBER TAX

Introduced in 2011, Italy's controversial *tassa di soggiorno* (accommodation tax) sees visitors charged an extra €1 to €5 per night 'room occupancy tax'.

Exactly how much you're charged may depend on several factors, including the type of accommodation (campground, guesthouse, hotel), a hotel's star rating and the number of people under your booking. Children are exempt from paying the tax in some cities and towns, though age limits can vary between destinations.

Most of our listings do not include the hotel tax, although it's always a good idea to confirm whether taxes are included when booking. At the time of research, the hotel tax was in force in more than 40 municipalities, including Ancona, Aosta, Assisi, Bologna, Cagliari, Capri, Catania, Florence, Friuli Venezia Giulia, Genoa, Ischia, Milan, Lago di Como, Lago di Garda, Lago Maggiore, Lecce, Lipari, Otranto, Padua, Pisa, Ravello, Rimini, Rome, Salerno, Sicily, Siena, Sorrento, Stresa, Trentino, Turin, Verbania and Venice.

SLEEPING PRICE RANGES

The following price ranges refer to a double room with bathroom (breakfast not included) in high season.

CATEGORY	REST OF ITALY	ROME	VENICE
€	less than €110	€120	€120
€€	€110-200	€120-250	€120-220
€€€	more than 200	€250	€220

OFFBEAT ACCOMMODATION

Looking for something out of the ordinary? Italy offers a plethora of sleeping options that you won't find anywhere else in the world.

➜ Down near Italy's heel, rent a *trullo*, one of the characteristic whitewashed conical houses of southern Puglia.

➜ On the island of Pantelleria, halfway between Sicily and Africa, sleep in a *dammuso* (traditional house with thick, whitewashed walls and a shallow cupola).

➜ Cruise northern Italy on the *Ave Maria,* a hotel barge that sails from Mantua to Venice over seven leisurely days, with cultural and foodie pit stops, and the chance to cycle between locations.

➜ In Friuli Venezia Giulia, experience village life in an *albergo diffuso*, an award-winning concept in which self-contained (self-catering) apartments in neighbouring houses are rented to guests through a centralised hotel-style reception.

A full list of Italian hostels, with details of prices and locations, is available online or from hostels throughout the country. Nightly rates in basic dorms vary from around €16 to €30, which usually includes a buffet breakfast. You can often get lunch or dinner for an extra €10 or so. Many hostels also offer singles and doubles (for around €30/50) and family rooms.

A few AIG hostels still have a midday lockout period as well as a curfew at 11pm or midnight, although these restrictions are less common than in years past.

A growing contingent of independent hostels offers alternatives to HI hostels. Many are barely distinguishable from budget hotels. One of many hostel websites is www.hostelworld.com.

Hotels & Pensioni

While the difference between an *albergo* (hotel) and a *pensione* is often minimal, a *pensione* will generally be of one- to three-star quality while an *albergo* can be awarded up to five stars. *Locande* (inns) long fell into much the same category

as *pensioni,* but the term has become a trendy one in some parts and reveals little about the quality of a place. *Affittacamere* are rooms for rent in private houses. They are generally simple affairs.

Quality can vary enormously and the official star system gives limited clues. One-star hotels/*pensioni* tend to be basic and usually do not offer private bathrooms. Two-star places are similar but rooms will generally have a private bathroom. Three-star options usually offer reasonable standards. Four- and five-star hotels offer facilities such as room service, laundry and dry-cleaning.

Prices are highest in major tourist destinations. They also tend to be higher in northern Italy. A *camera singola* (single room) costs from €30. A *camera doppia* (twin beds) or *camera matrimoniale* (double room with a double bed) will cost from around €50.

Tourist offices usually have booklets with local accommodation listings. Many hotels are also signing up with (steadily proliferating) online accommodation-

booking services. You could start your search here:

Alberghi in Italia (www.alberghi-in-italia.it)

All Hotels in Italy (www.hotelsitalyonline.com)

Hotels web.it (www.hotel-sweb.it)

In Italia (www.initalia.it)

Travel to Italy (www.travel-to-italy.com)

Mountain Huts

The network of *rifugi* in the Alps, Apennines and other mountains is usually only open from July to September. Accommodation is generally in dormitories but some of the larger refuges have doubles. The price per person (which typically includes breakfast) ranges from €20 to €30 depending on the quality of the *rifugio* (it's more for a double room). A hearty post-walk single-dish dinner will set you back another €10 to €15.

Rifugi are marked on good walking maps. Those close to chair lifts and cable-car stations are usually expensive and crowded. Others are at high altitude and involve hours of hard walking. It is important to book in advance. Additional information can be obtained from the local tourist offices.

The **Club Alpino Italiano** (CAI; www.cai.it) owns and runs many of the mountain huts. Members of organisations such as the New Zealand Alpine Club and British Mountaineering Council can enjoy discounted rates for accommodation and meals by obtaining a reciprocal rights card (for a fee).

Rental Accommodation

Finding rental accommodation in the major cities can be difficult and time-consuming; rental agencies (local and foreign) can assist, for a fee. Rental rates are higher for short-term leases. A small apartment or a studio anywhere near the centre of

Rome will cost around €1000 per month and it is usually necessary to pay a deposit (generally one month in advance). Expect to spend similar amounts in cities such as Florence, Milan, Naples and Venice.

Apartments and villas for rent are listed in local publications such as Rome's twice-weekly **Porta Portese** (www.portaportese. it) and the fortnightly **Wanted in Rome** (www.wantedin-rome.com). Another option is to share an apartment; check out university notice-boards for student flats with vacant rooms. Tourist offices in resort areas (coastal towns in summer, ski towns in winter) also maintain lists of apartments and villas for rent.

If you're looking for an apartment, studio or room to rent for a short stay (such as a week or two) check out the websites of agencies dealing in this kind of thing:

Guest in Italy (www.guestinitaly.com) An online agency focusing exclusively on Italy, with apartments (mostly for two to four people) ranging from about €120 to €450 a night.

Homelidays (www.homelidays.com) More than 16,000 rental accommodations of every description throughout Italy.

Holiday Lettings (www.holidaylettings.co.uk) Has more than 14,000 apartments and villas all over the country.

Interhome (www.interhome.co.uk) Book houses and apartments for weekly blocks, starting at around UK£600 for two or three people in central Rome.

Villas

Long the preserve of the Tuscan sun, the villa-rental scene in Italy has taken off in recent years, with agencies offering villa accommodation up and down the country – often in splendid rural spots not far from enchanting medieval towns or Mediterranean beaches. There are dozens of operators.

FARMHOUSE HOLIDAYS

Live out your bucolic fantasies at one of Italy's growing number of *agriturismi* (farm-stays). A long-booming industry in Tuscany and Umbria, farm-stays are spreading across the country like freshly churned butter. While all *agriturismi* are required to grow at least one of their own products, the farm-stays themselves range from rustic country houses with a handful of olive trees to elegant country estates with sparkling pools, to fully functioning farms where guests can pitch in.

To find lists of *agriturismi*, ask at any tourist office or check online at one of these sites:

➡ **Agritour** (www.agritour.net)

➡ **Agriturist** (www.agriturist.com)

➡ **Agriturismo.it** (www.agriturismo.it)

➡ **Agriturismo.net** (www.agriturismo.net)

➡ **Agriturismo.com** (www.agriturismo.com)

➡ **Agriturismo-Italia.net** (www.agriturismo-italia.net)

➡ **Agriturismo Vero** (www.agriturismovero.com)

Cuendet (www.cuendet.com) One of the old hands in this business; operates from Mestre, just outside Venice.

Ilios Travel (www.iliostravel.com) UK-based company with villas and apartments in Venice, Tuscany, Umbria, Lazio, Le Marche, Abruzzo and Campania.

Invitation to Tuscany (www.invitationtotuscany.com) Wide range of properties, with a strong focus on Tuscany.

Summer's Leases (www.summerleases.com) Properties in Tuscany and Umbria.

Long Travel (www.long-travel.co.uk) Specialises in Puglia, Sicily, Sardinia and other regions.

Think Sicily (www.thinksicily.com) Strictly Sicilian properties.

Cottages to Castles (www.cottagestocastles.com) UK-based operator specialising in villas.

Parker Villas (www.parkervillas.co.uk) Despite the UK web address, this is a US-based agency with an Italian office, offering exclusive listings of villas all over Italy.

Customs Regulations

Duty-free sales within the EU no longer exist (but goods are sold tax-free in European airports). Visitors coming into Italy from non-EU countries can import some items duty free.

DUTY-FREE ALLOWANCES

spirits	1L (or 2L wine)
perfume	50g
eau de toilette	250mL
cigarettes	200
other goods	up to a total value of €175

PRACTICALITIES

Weights and measurements Metric

Smoking Banned in all enclosed public spaces

Newspapers The major national dailies are centre-left; try Rome-based *La Republicca*, and the liberal-conservative, Milan-based *Corriere della Sera*.

Radio Tune into Vatican Radio (www.radiovaticana.org; 93.3 FM and 105 FM in the Rome area; in Italian, English and other languages) for a rundown of what the pope is up to; or state-owned Italian RAI-1, RAI-2 and RAI-3 (www.rai.it), which broadcast all over the country and abroad. Commercial stations such as Rome's Radio **Centro Suono** (www. centrosuono.com) and **Radio Città Futura** (www.radiocittafutura.it), Naples' Radio **Kiss Kiss** (www.kisskissnapoli.it) and Milan-based left-wing **Radio Popolare** (www.radiopopolare.it) are all good for contemporary music.

TV Channels include state-run RAI-1, RAI-2 and RAI-3 (www.rai.it) and the main commercial stations **Canale 5** (www.canale5.mediaset.it), **Italia 1** (www.italia1.mediaset.it) and **Rete 4** (www. rete4.mediaset.it) run by Silvio Berlusconi's Mediaset company, as well as **La 7** (www.la7.it).

Anything over the limits must be declared on arrival and the appropriate duty paid. On leaving the EU, non-EU citizens can reclaim any value-added tax on expensive purchases.

Discount Cards

Those under 18 and over 65 may get free admission to many galleries and cultural sites and visitors aged between 18 and 25 often qualify for a 50% discount (sometimes only for EU citizens).

Special discount cards are issued by cities or regions, such as **Roma Pass** (www. romapass.it; 3 days €34), which offers free use of public transport and free or reduced admission to Rome's museums.

In many places around Italy, you can also save money by purchasing a *biglietto cumulativo*, a ticket that allows admission to a number of associated sights for less than the combined cost of separate admission fees.

The European Youth Card offers thousands of discounts on Italian hotels, museums, restaurants, shops and clubs, while a student, teacher or youth travel card can save money on flights to Italy. Many cards are available from the **Centro Turistico Studentesco e Giovanile** (CTS; www.

cts.it), a youth travel agency with branches throughout Italy. The latter three cards are available worldwide from student unions, hostelling organisations and youth travel agencies such as **STA Travel** (www.statravel.com).

Electricity

Electricity goes by the European standard of 220-230V, with a frequency of 50Hz. Wall outlets typically accommodate plugs with two or three round pins (the latter grounded, the former not).

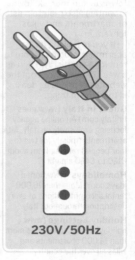

230V/50Hz

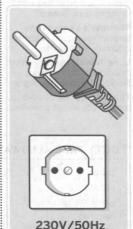

230V/50Hz

Embassies & Consulates

For foreign embassies and consulates in Italy not listed here, look up 'Ambasciate' or 'Consolati'. Some countries also run honorary consulates in other cities.

Australian Embassy/Consulate Rome (☑06 85 27 21; www. italy.embassy.gov.au; Via Antonio Bosio 5); **Milan** (☑02 7767 4200; www.austrade.it; Via Borgogna 2; Ⓜ San Babila)

YOUTH, STUDENT & TEACHER CARDS

CARD	WEBSITE	COST	ELIGIBILITY
European Youth Card (Carta Giovani)	europeanyouthcard.org; cartagiovani.it	€11	under 30yr
International Student Identity Card (ISIC)	www.isic.org	US$25, UK£9, €13	full-time student
International Teacher Identity Card (ITIC)		US$25, UK£9, €10–18	full-time teacher
International Youth Travel Card (IYTC)		US$25, UK£9, €13	under 26yr

Austrian Embassy/Consulate Rome (☑06 844 01 41; www.aussenministerium.at/rom; Via Pergolesi 3); **Milan** (☑02 78 37 43; www.aussenministerium.at/mailandgk; Piazza del Liberty 8/4)

Canadian Embassy (www.canadainternational.gc.ca/italy-italie)

French Embassy/Consulate Rome (☑06 68 60 11; www.ambafrance-it.org; Piazza Farnese 67); **Milan** (☑02 655 91 41; www.ambafrance-it.org/-Milan-; Via della Moscova 12; Ⓜ Turati); **Naples** (☑081 598 07 11; www.ambafrance-it.org; Via Francesco Crispi 86) **Turin** (☑011 573 23 11; www.ambafrance-it.org; Via Roma 366)

German Embassy/Consulate Rome (☑06 49 21 31; www.rom.diplo.de; Via San Martino della Battaglia 4); **Milan** (☑02 623 11 01; www.mailand.diplo.de; Via Solferino 40; Ⓜ Moscova); **Naples** (☑081 248 85 11; www.neapel.diplo.de; Via Francesco Crispi 69)

  Irish Embassy (☑06 585 23 81; www.ambasciata-irlanda.it; Villa Spada, Via Giacomo Medici 1, Rome)

Japanese Embassy/Consulate Rome (☑06 48 79 91; www.it.emb-japan.go.jp; Via Quintino Sella 60); **Milan** (☑02 624 11 41; www.milano.it.emb-japan.go.jp; Via Cesare Mangili 2/4; Ⓜ Turati)

Dutch Embassy/Consulate Rome (☑06 3228 6001; www.olanda.it; Via Michele Mercati 8); **Milan** (☑02 485 58 41; Via Gaetano Donizetti 20)

New Zealand Embassy/Consulate Rome (☑06 853 75 01; www.nzembassy.com; Via Clitunno 44); **Milan** (☑02 7217 0001; www.nzembassy.com/italy; Via Terraggio 17; Ⓜ Cadorna)

Slovenian Embassy/Consulate Rome (☑06 8091 4310; www.rim.veleposlanistvo.si; Via Leonardo Pisano 10, Rome); **Trieste** (☑040 30 78 55; Via San Giorgio 1)

Swiss Embassy/Consulate Rome (☑06 80 95 71; www.eda.admin.ch/roma; Via Barnaba Oriani 61, Rome); **Milan** (☑02 777 91 61; www.eda.admin.ch/milano; Via Palestro 2; Ⓜ Turati)

UK Embassy/Consulate Rome (☑06 4220 0001; ukinitaly.fco.gov.uk; Via XX Settembre 80a, Rome); **Milan** (☑06 4220 2431; Via San Paolo 7; Ⓜ San Babila); **Naples** (☑081 423 89 11; Via dei Mille 40)

US Embassy/Consulate Rome (☑06 4 67 41; italy.usembassy.gov; Via Vittorio Veneto 121, Rome); **Florence** (☑055 26 69 51; italy.usembassy.gov; Lungarno Vespucci 38, Florence); **Milan** (☑02 29 03 51; http://milan.usconsulate.gov; Via Principe Amedeo 2/10; Ⓜ Turati); **Naples** (☑081 583 81 11; italy.usembassy.gov; Piazza della Repubblica)

Food

For detailed information on eating in Italy see the chapters Eat & Drink Like a Local (p39) and The Italian Table (p924).

Gay & Lesbian Travellers

Homosexuality is legal in Italy and well tolerated in the major cities. Overt displays

---

EATING PRICE RANGES

The following price ranges used throughout this book refer to a meal of two courses, a glass of house wine, and *coperto* (cover charge) for one person.

€	under €25
€€	€25–45
€€€	over €45

These figures represent a halfway point between expensive cities such as Milan and Venice and the considerably cheaper towns across the south. Indeed, a restaurant rated as midrange in rural Sicily might be considered dirt cheap in Milan. Note that most eating establishments add *coperto* of around €2 to €3. Some also include a service charge (*servizio*) of 10% to 15%.

GOVERNMENT TRAVEL ADVICE

The following government websites offer up-to-date travel advisories.

➡ **Australian Department of Foreign Affairs** (www.smartraveller.gov.au)

➡ **British Foreign Office** (www.gov.uk/foreign-travel-advice)

➡ **Canadian Department of Foreign Affairs** (travel.gc.ca/travelling/health-safety)

➡ **US State Department** (http://travel.state.gov)

of affection by homosexual couples, however, could attract a negative response in the more conservative south and in smaller towns.

There are gay clubs in Rome, Milan and Bologna, and a handful in places such as Florence and Naples. Some coastal towns and resorts (such as the Tuscan town of Viareggio or Taormina in Sicily) have much more action in summer.

See the following resources for more information:

Arcigay (www.arcigay.it) Bologna-based national organisation for the LGBTI community.

AZ Gay (www.azgay.it) Rome-based organisation that publishes a free *Gay Rome* guide, available at tourist booths.

Circolo Mario Mieli (www.mariomieli.org) Rome-based cultural centre that publishes *Aut*, a free alternative monthly covering news, culture and politics.

Gay.it (www.gay.it) Website featuring LGBT news, feature articles and gossip.

GayFriendlyItaly.com (www.gayfriendlyitaly.com) English-language site produced by Gay.it, featuring information on everything from hotels and events, to LGBT politics and rights.

Pride (www.prideonline.it) National monthly magazine of art, music, politics and gay culture.

Health

Required Vaccinations

No jabs are required to travel to Italy, though the World Health Organization (WHO) recommends that all travellers should be covered for diphtheria, tetanus, the measles, mumps, rubella, polio and hepatitis B.

Health Insurance

If you're an EU citizen (or from Switzerland, Norway or Iceland), a European Health Insurance Card (EHIC) covers you for most medical care in public hospitals free of charge, but not for private medical healthcare or emergency repatriation home. The card is available from health centres and, depending on your country, online. For more information, see http://ec.europa.eu/social/main.jsp?langId=en&catId=509. Citizens from other countries should find out if there is a reciprocal arrangement for free medical care between their country and Italy (Australia, for instance, has such an agreement; carry your Medicare card).

If you do need health insurance, make sure you get a policy that covers you for the worst possible scenario, such as an accident requiring an emergency flight home. Find out in advance if your insurance plan will make payments directly to providers or reimburse you later for overseas health expenditures.

Availability of Health Care

Health care is readily available throughout Italy, but standards can vary significantly. Public hospitals tend to be less impressive the further south you travel. Pharmacists can give you valuable advice and sell over-the-counter medication for minor illnesses. They can also advise you when more-specialised help is required and point you in the right direction. In major cities you are likely to find English-speaking doctors or a translator service available.

Pharmacies generally keep the same hours as other shops, closing at night and on Sundays. However, a handful remain open on a rotation basis *(farmacie di turno)* for emergency purposes. These are usually listed in newspapers. Closed pharmacies display a list of the nearest ones open.

If you require an ambulance anywhere in Italy, call 118. For emergency treatment, head straight to the *pronto soccorso* (casualty) section of a public hospital, where you can also get emergency dental treatment.

Insurance

A travel-insurance policy to cover theft, loss and medical problems is a very good idea. It may also cover you for cancellation or delays to your travel arrangements. Paying for your ticket with a credit card can often provide limited travel accident insurance and you may be able to reclaim the payment if the operator doesn't deliver. Ask your credit-card company what it will cover.

Worldwide travel insurance is available at www.lonelyplanet.com/travel-insurance. You can buy, extend and claim online anytime – even if you're already on the road.

Internet Access

→ Internet access in Italy has improved markedly in the past couple of years, with Rome, Bologna, Venice and other municipalities instituting city-wide hot spots.

→ On the downside, public wi-fi and internet cafes (€2 to €6 per hour) remain thinner on the ground than elsewhere in Europe, signal strength is variable, and access is not yet as widespread in rural and southern Italy as in urban and northern areas.

→ An ever-increasing number of hotels, B&Bs, hostels and even *agriturismi* offer free wi-fi. Unfortunately, you will still have to pay at many top-end hotels (upwards of €10 per day).

→ Some internet cafes will request identification before allowing you to use their facilities.

Language Courses

Italian language courses are run by private schools and universities throughout Italy. Rome and Florence are teeming with schools, while most other cities and major towns have at least one. For a list of language schools around the country, see **Saena Iulia** (www.saenaiulia.it).

Università per Stranieri di Perugia (www.unistrapg.it) The well-established and reasonably priced programs make this Italy's most famous language school for foreigners. Language classes are supplemented with extracurricular or full-time courses in painting, art history, sculpture and architecture.

Università per Stranieri di Siena (www.unistrasi.it) A similarly well-regarded program in one of Italy's most beautiful medieval cities.

Italian Foreign Ministry (www.esteri.it) Publishes a list on its website of the 90 worldwide branches of the Istituto Italiano di Cultura (IIC), a government-sponsored organisation promoting Italian culture and language. An excellent resource for studying Italian before you leave or finding out more about language learning opportunities in Italy. Locations include Australia (Melbourne and Sydney), the UK (London and Edinburgh), Ireland (Dublin), Canada (Vancouver, Toronto and Montreal), and the USA (Los Angeles, San Francisco, Chicago, New York and Washington, DC). Click on 'Italian Cultural Institutes' under 'The Ministry' list.

Legal Matters

The average tourist will only have a brush with the law if robbed by a bag-snatcher or pickpocket.

Police

If you run into trouble in Italy, you're likely to end up dealing with the *polizia statale* or the *carabinieri*. The former wear powder-blue trousers with a fuchsia stripe and a navy blue jacket, the latter wear black uniforms with a red stripe and drive dark-blue cars with a red stripe.

To contact the police in an emergency, dial 113.

Drugs & Alcohol

→ Under Italy's tough drug laws, possession of any controlled substances, including cannabis or marijuana, can get you into hot water. Those caught in possession of 5g of cannabis can be prosecuted as traffickers. The same applies to tiny amounts of other drugs. Those caught with amounts below this threshold can be subject to minor penalties.

→ The legal limit for blood-alcohol when driving is 0.05% and random breath tests do occur.

Your Rights

→ You should be given verbal and written notice of the charges laid against you within 24 hours by arresting officers.

→ You have no right to a phone call upon arrest.

→ The prosecutor must apply to a magistrate for you to be held in preventive custody awaiting trial (depending on the seriousness of the offence) within 48 hours of arrest.

→ You have the right not to respond to questions without the presence of a lawyer.

→ If the magistrate orders preventive custody, you have the right to then contest this within the following 10 days.

Maps

The city maps provided in Lonely Planet guides, combined with the good, free local maps available at most Italian tourist offices, will be

---

ITALIAN POLICE ORGANISATIONS

Polizia statale (state police)	Thefts, visa extensions and permits
Carabinieri (military police)	General crime, public order and drug enforcement (often overlapping with the *polizia statale*)
Vigili urbani (local traffic police)	Parking tickets, towed cars
Guardia di finanza	Tax evasion, drug smuggling
Guardia forestale (aka *corpo forestale*)	Environmental protection

sufficient for many travellers. For more-specialised maps, browse the good selection at national bookshop chain Feltrinelli, or consult the websites listed here.

Touring Club Italiano (TCI; www.touringclub.com) Italy's largest map publisher operates shops around Italy and publishes decent 1:500,000 and 1:200,000 maps of Italy (€11.90 and €19.90 respectively), plus a series of 15 regional maps at 1:200,000 (€7.90 each) and an exhaustive series of walking guides with maps, co-published with the Club Alpino Italiano (CAI).

Tabacco (www.tabaccoeditrice.com) Publishes an excellent 1:25,000 scale series of walking maps, covering an area from Bormio in the west to the Slovenia border in the east.

Kompass (www.kompass-italia.it) Publishes 1:25,000 and 1:50,000 scale hiking maps of various parts of Italy, plus a nice series of 1:70,000 cycling maps.

Edizioni Multigraphic Florence (www.edizionimultigraphic.it) Produces a series of walking maps concentrating mainly on the Apennines.

Stanfords (www.stanfords.co.uk) Excellent UK-based shop that stocks many useful maps.

Omni Resources (www.omnimap.com) US-based online retailer with an impressive selection of Italian maps.

Money

The euro is Italy's currency. The seven euro notes come in denominations of €500, €200, €100, €50, €20, €10 and €5. The eight euro coins are in denominations of €2 and €1, and 50, 20, 10, five, two and one cents.

ATMs & Credit Cards

➜ ATMs (called 'Bancomats') are widely available throughout Italy and the best way to obtain local currency. International credit and debit cards can be used in any ATM displaying the appropriate sign.

➜ Visa and MasterCard are among the most widely recognised credit cards, but others like Cirrus and Maestro are also well covered. Only some banks give cash advances over the counter, so you're better off using ATMs.

➜ Cards are also good for payment in most hotels, restaurants, shops, supermarkets and tollbooths.

➜ Check any charges with your bank. Most banks now build a fee of around 2.75% into every foreign transaction. In addition, ATM withdrawals can attract a further fee, usually around 1.5%.

If your card is lost, stolen or swallowed by an ATM, you can telephone toll-free to have an immediate stop put on its use:

Amex (☏800 928391)

Diners Club (☏800 393939)

MasterCard (☏800 870866)

Visa (☏800 819014)

Moneychangers

You can change money in banks, at the post office or in a *cambio* (exchange office). Post offices and banks tend to offer the best rates; exchange offices keep longer hours, but watch for high commissions and inferior rates.

Taxes & Refunds

A value-added tax of around 22%, known as IVA (Imposta di Valore Aggiunto), is slapped onto just about everything in Italy. If you are a non-EU resident and spend more than €155 (€154.94 to be more precise!) on a purchase, you can claim a refund when you leave. The refund only applies to purchases from affiliated retail outlets that display a 'tax free for tourists' (or similar) sign. You have to complete a form at the point of sale, then have it stamped by Italian customs as you leave. At major airports you can get

an immediate cash refund; otherwise it will be refunded to your credit card. For information, visit **Tax Refund for Tourists** (www.taxrefund.it) or pick up a pamphlet on the scheme from participating stores.

Tipping

Tipping is not generally expected nor demanded in Italy as it is in some other countries. This said, a discretionary tip for good service is appreciated in some circumstances. Use the following as a guide.

Restaurant: 10–15%, if service charge not included.

Bar: €0.10–0.20 if drinking at bar, 10% for table service.

Top-end hotel: €2, for porter, maid, room service.

Taxi: Round up to the nearest euro.

Post

Le Poste (www.poste.it), Italy's postal system, is reasonably reliable.

Francobolli (stamps) are available at post offices and authorised tobacconists (look for the big white-on-black 'T' sign). Since letters often need to be weighed, what you get at the tobacconist for international airmail will occasionally be an approximation of the proper rate. Tobacconists keep regular shop hours.

The cost of sending a letter by *aerea* (airmail) depends on its weight, size and where it is being sent. Most people use *posta prioritaria* (priority mail), Italy's most efficient mail service, guaranteed to deliver letters sent to Europe within three days and to the rest of the world within four to nine days. Letters up to 20g cost €0.85 within Europe, €2 to Africa, Asia and North and South America, and €2.50 to Australia and New Zealand. Letters weighing 21g to 50g cost €2.60 within Europe, €3.50 to Africa,

Asia and the Americas, and €4.50 to Australia and New Zealand.

Public Holidays

Most Italians take their annual holiday in August, with the busiest period occurring around 15 August, known locally as Ferragosto. As a result, many businesses and shops close for at least part of that month. Settimana Santa (Easter Holy Week) is another busy holiday period for Italians.

National public holidays:

New Year's Day (Capodanno or Anno Nuovo) 1 January

Epiphany (Epifania) 6 January

Easter Monday (Pasquetta) March/April

Liberation Day (Giorno della Liberazione) 25 April

Labour Day (Festa del Lavoro) 1 May

Republic Day (Festa della Repubblica) 2 June

Feast of the Assumption (Assunzione or Ferragosto) 15 August

All Saints' Day (Ognissanti) 1 November

Feast of the Immaculate Conception (Immaculata Concezione) 8 December

Christmas Day (Natale) 25 December

Boxing Day (Festa di Santo Stefano) 26 December

Telephone
Directory Enquiries

National and international phone numbers can be requested at 1254 (or online at 1254.virgilio.it).

Domestic Calls

➡ Italian telephone area codes all begin with 0 and consist of up to four digits. The area code is followed by anything from four to eight digits. The area code is an integral part of the telephone number and must always be dialled, even when calling from next door.

➡ Mobile-phone numbers begin with a three-digit prefix such as 330.

➡ Toll-free (free-phone) numbers are known as *numeri verdi* and usually start with 800.

➡ Nongeographical numbers start with 840, 841, 848, 892, 899, 163, 166 or 199.

➡ Some six-digit national rate numbers are also in use (such as those for Alitalia, rail and postal information).

As elsewhere in Europe, Italians choose from a host of providers of phone plans and rates, making it difficult to make generalisations about costs.

International Calls

➡ The cheapest options for calling internationally are free or low-cost computer programs/smartphone apps such as Skype and Viber.

➡ Cut-rate call centres, found in all of the main cities, are also a cheaper option. You simply place your call from a private booth inside the centre and pay for it when you've finished.

➡ International calling cards, sold at newsstands and tobacconists, also offer cheaper call rates. They can be used at public telephones. Dial 00 to get out of Italy, then the relevant country and area codes, followed by the telephone number.

➡ To call Italy from abroad, call your international access number, then Italy's country code (39) and then the area code of the location you want, including the leading 0.

Mobile Phones

➡ Italy uses GSM 900/1800, compatible with the rest of Europe and Australia but not

OPENING HOURS

BUSINESS TYPE	GENERAL HOURS	NOTES
Banks	8.30am-1.30pm & 3.30-4.30pm Mon-Fri	Exchange offices usually keep longer hours.
Bars, pubs & clubs	10pm-4am	May open earlier if they have eateries on the premises; things don't get seriously shaking until after midnight
Cafes	7.30am-8pm	.
Central post offices	8am-7pm Mon-Fri, 8.30am-noon Sat	Smaller branch post offices often close at 2pm on weekdays
Restaurants	noon-2.30pm & 7.30-11pm or midnight	Sometimes even later in summer and in the south; kitchen often shuts an hour earlier than final closing time; most places close at least one day a week
Shops	9am-1pm & 3.30-7.30pm (or 4-8pm) Mon-Sat	In larger cities, department stores and supermarkets may stay open at lunchtime or on Sundays

with North American GSM 1900 or the totally different Japanese system.

➡ Most modern smart phones are multiband, meaning that they are compatible with a variety of international networks. Before bringing your own phone to Italy, check with your service provider to make sure it is compatible, and beware of calls being routed internationally (very expensive for a 'local' call).

➡ Unlocking your phone for use with an Italian SIM card is often the cheapest option, but always check with your home mobile-service provider to ascertain whether your handset allows use of another SIM card.

➡ You can get a temporary or prepaid account from most phone company stores in Italy if you already own a GSM, multiband cellular phone (take your passport). Activating a local prepaid SIM card can cost as little as €10 (sometimes with €10 worth of calls on the card). Pay-as-you-go SIM cards are also readily available at telephone and electronics stores throughout Italy.

➡ You can easily top up your Italian account with recharge cards (*ricariche*), available from most tobacconists, some bars, supermarkets and banks.

➡ Another option is to buy or lease an inexpensive Italian phone for the duration of your trip.

➡ Of the main mobile phone companies, TIM (Telecom Italia Mobile), Wind and Vodafone have the best networks of outlets across the country.

Payphones & Phonecards

➡ Telecom Italia is the largest communications organisation in Italy. Telecom payphones are commonly found on streets, in train stations and in Telecom offices.

➡ Most payphones accept only *carte/schede telefoniche* (phonecards), although some also accept credit cards.

➡ Telecom offers a wide range of prepaid cards for domestic and international use; for a full list, see www.telecomitalia.it/telefono/carte-telefoniche.

➡ You can buy phonecards (most commonly €3 or €5) at post offices, tobacconists and newsstands. Break off the top left-hand corner of the card before use. All phonecards have an expiry date, printed on the face of the card.

Time

➡ Italy is one hour ahead of GMT. When it is noon in London, it is 1pm in Italy.

➡ Daylight-saving time (when clocks are moved forward one hour) starts on the last Sunday in March and ends on the last Sunday in October.

➡ Italy operates on a 24-hour clock.

Tourist Information

Four tiers of tourist office exist: local, provincial, regional and national.

Local & Provincial Tourist Offices

Despite their different names, provincial and local offices offer similar services. All deal directly with the public and most will respond to written and telephone requests for information. Staff can usually provide a city map, lists of hotels and information on the major sights. In larger towns and major tourist areas, English is generally spoken, along with other languages depending on the region (for example, German in Alto Adige, French in Valle d'Aosta).

Main offices are generally open Monday to Friday; some also open on weekends, especially in urban areas or during peak summer season. Affiliated information booths (at train stations and airports, for example) may keep slightly different hours.

Regional Tourist Authorities

Regional offices are generally more concerned with planning, budgeting, marketing and promotion than with offering a public information service. However, they still maintain some useful websites. In some cases you'll need to look for the Tourism or Turismo link within the regional site.

TOURIST OFFICES

OFFICE NAME	DESCRIPTION	MAIN FOCUS
Azienda di Promozione Turistica (APT)	Main provincial tourist office	Information on the town and its surrounding province
Azienda Autonoma di Soggiorno e Turismo (AAST) or Informazione e Assistenza ai Turisti (IAT)	Local tourist office in larger towns and cities	Town-specific information only (bus routes, museum opening times etc)
Pro Loco	Local tourist office in smaller towns and villages	Similar to AAST and IAT

Abruzzo (www.abruzzoturismo.it)

Basilicata (www.aptbasilicata.it)

Calabria (www.turiscalabria.it)

Campania (www.incampania.com)

Emilia-Romagna (www.emiliaromagnaturismo.it)

Friuli Venezia Giulia (www.turismo.fvg.it)

Lazio (www.ilmiolazio.it)

Le Marche (www.le-marche.com)

Liguria (www.turismoinliguria.it)

Lombardy (www.turismo.regione.lombardia.it)

Molise (www.regione.molise.it/turismo)

Piedmont (www.piemonteitalia.eu)

Puglia (www.viaggiareinpuglia.it)

Sardinia (www.sardegnaturismo.it)

Sicily (www.regione.sicilia.it/turismo)

Trentino-Alto Adige (www.visittrentino.it)

Tuscany (www.turismo.intoscana.it)

Umbria (www.regioneumbria.eu)

Valle d'Aosta (www.regione.vda.it/turismo)

Veneto (www.veneto.to)

Tourist Offices Abroad

The Italian National Tourist Office (ENIT; www.enit.it) maintains offices in 23 cities on five continents. Contact information for all offices can be found on its website.

Travellers with Disabilities

Italy is not an easy country for travellers with disabilities and getting around can be a problem for wheelchair users. Even a short journey in a city or town can become a major expedition if cobblestone streets have to be negotiated. Although many buildings have lifts, they are not always wide enough for wheelchairs. Not an awful lot has been done to make life any easier for the hearing- or vision-impaired.

The Italian National Tourist Office in your country may be able to provide advice on Italian associations for travellers with disabilities and information on what help is available.

Italy's national rail company, Trenitalia (🖀199 303060; www.trenitalia.com), offers a national helpline for passengers with disabilities (6.45am to 9.30pm daily).

A handful of cities also publish general guides on accessibility, among them Bologna, Milan, Padua, Reggio Emilia, Turin, Venice and Verona. In Milan, Milano per Tutti (www.milanopertutti.it) is a helpful resource.

Some organisations that may help include the following:

Accessible Italy (🖀378 94 11 11; www.accessibleitaly.com) A San Marino–based company that specialises in holiday services for the disabled. This is the best first port of call.

Cooperative Integrate Onlus (COIN; 🖀06 712 90 11; www.coinsociale.it) Based in Rome, CO.IN provides information on the capital (including transport and access) and is happy to share its contacts throughout Italy.

Italia (www.italia.it) Italy's official tourism website offers a number of links for travellers with disabilities, covering destinations like Rome, Campania, Piedmont and the South Tyrol.

Visas

➧ European citizens whose country is part of the Schengen Treaty may enter Italy with nothing more than a valid identity card or passport.

➧ Residents of 28 non-EU countries, including Australia, Brazil, Canada, Israel, Japan, New Zealand and the USA, do not require visas for tourist visits of up to 90 days (this list varies for those wanting to travel to the UK and Ireland).

➧ All non-EU and non-Schengen nationals entering Italy for more than 90 days or for any reason other than tourism (such as study or work) may need a specific visa. See www.esteri.it/visti/home_eng.asp or contact an Italian consulate for details.

➧ EU citizens do not require any permits to live or work in Italy but, after three months' residence, are supposed to register at the municipal registry office where they live and offer proof of work or sufficient funds to support themselves.

➧ Non-EU foreign citizens with five years' continuous legal residence may apply for permanent residence.

Permesso di Soggiorno

Non-EU citizens planning to stay at the same address for more than one week are supposed to report to the police station to receive a permesso di soggiorno (a permit to remain in the country). Tourists staying in hotels are not required to do this.

A permesso di soggiorno only really becomes a necessity if you plan to study, work (legally) or live in Italy. Obtaining one is never a pleasant experience; it involves long queues and the frustration of arriving at the counter only to find you don't have the necessary documents.

The exact requirements, such as specific documents, are always subject to change. Updated requirements can be found online at www.poliziadistato.it (click on 'Foreign nationals').

EU citizens do not require a permesso di soggiorno.

Study Visas

Non-EU citizens who want to study at a university or language school in Italy must have a study visa. These can be obtained from your nearest Italian embassy or consulate. You will normally require confirmation of your enrolment, proof of payment of fees and adequate funds to support yourself. The visa covers only the period of the enrolment. This type of visa is renewable within Italy but, again, only with confirmation of ongoing enrolment and proof that you are able to support yourself (bank statements are preferred).

Volunteering

Concordia International Volunteer Projects

(☎01273 422218; www.concordiavolunteers.org.uk; 19 North St, Portslade, UK) Short-term community-based projects covering the environment, archaeology and the arts. You might find yourself working as a volunteer on a restoration project or in a nature reserve.

European Youth Portal

(europa.eu/youth) Has various links suggesting volunteering options across Europe. Navigate to the Volunteering/exchanges page and then narrow down the search to Italy.

World Wide Opportunities on Organic Farms

(www. wwoof.it) For a membership fee of €25 this organisation provides a list of farms looking for volunteer workers.

Women Travellers

Italy is not a dangerous country for women to travel in. Clearly, as with anywhere in the world, women travelling alone need to take certain precautions and, in some parts of the country, be prepared for more than their fair share of unwanted attention. Eye-to-eye contact is the norm in Italy's daily flirtatious interplay. Eye contact can become outright staring the further south you travel.

Lone women may find it difficult to remain alone. In many places, local Lotharios will try it on with exasperating insistence, which can be flattering or a pain. Foreign women are particular objects of male attention in tourist towns like Florence and more generally in the south. Usually the best response to undesired advances is to ignore them. If that doesn't work, politely tell your interlocutors you're waiting for your *marito* (husband) or *fidanzato* (boyfriend) and, if necessary, walk away. Avoid becoming aggressive as this may result in an unpleasant confrontation. If all else fails, approach the nearest member of the police.

Watch out for men with wandering hands on crowded buses. Either keep your back to the wall or make a loud fuss if someone starts fondling your behind. A loud *'Che schifo!'* (How disgusting!) will usually do the trick. If a more serious incident occurs, report it to the police, who are then required to press charges.

Transport

GETTING THERE & AWAY

A plethora of airlines link Italy with the rest of the world, and cut-rate carriers have significantly driven down the cost of flights from other European countries. Excellent rail and bus connections, especially with northern Italy, offer efficient overland transport, while car and passenger ferries operate to ports throughout the Mediterranean.

Flights, tours and rail tickets can be booked online at lonelyplanet.com/bookings.

Entering the Country

➡ European Union and Swiss citizens can travel to Italy with their national identity card alone. All other nationalities must have a valid passport and may be required to fill out a landing card (at airports).

➡ By law you are supposed to have your passport or ID card with you at all times. You'll need one of these documents for police registration every time you check into a hotel.

➡ In theory there are no passport checks at land crossings from neighbouring countries, but random customs controls do occasionally still take place between Italy and Switzerland.

Air

Airports & Airlines

Italy's main intercontinental gateways are Rome's **Leonardo da Vinci airport** (☎06 65 9 51; www.adr.it/fiumicino) and Milan's **Malpensa airport** (☎02 23 23 23; www.milanomalpensa1.eu/en). Both are served by non-stop flights from around the world. Venice's **Marco Polo airport** (☎041 260 92 60; www.veniceairport.it; Viale Galileo Galilei 30/1, Tessera) is also served by a handful of intercontinental flights.

Dozens of international airlines compete with the country's national carrier, Alitalia, rated a 3-star airline by UK aviation research company Skytrax. If you're flying from Africa or Oceania, you'll generally need to change planes at least once en route to Italy.

Intra-European flights serve plenty of other Italian cities; the leading mainstream carriers include Alitalia, Air France, British Airways, Lufthansa and KLM.

Cut-rate airlines, led by Ryanair and easyJet, fly from a growing number of European cities to more than two dozen Italian destinations, typically landing in smaller airports such as Rome's **Ciampino** (☎06 65 9 51; www.adr.it/ciampino).

CLIMATE CHANGE & TRAVEL

Every form of transport that relies on carbon-based fuel generates CO_2, the main cause of human-induced climate change. Modern travel is dependent on planes which might use less fuel per kilometre per person than most cars but travel much greater distances. The altitude at which aircraft emit gases (including CO_2) and particles also contributes to their climate change impact. Many websites offer 'carbon calculators' that allow people to estimate the carbon emissions generated by their journey and, for those who wish to do so, to offset the impact of the greenhouse gases emitted with contributions to portfolios of climate-friendly initiatives throughout the world. Lonely Planet offsets the carbon footprint of all staff and author travel.

Land

There are plenty of options for entering Italy by train, bus or private vehicle.

Border Crossings

Aside from the coast roads linking Italy with France and Slovenia, border crossings into Italy mostly involve tunnels through the Alps (open year-round) or mountain passes (seasonally closed or requiring snow chains). The list below outlines the major points of entry.

Austria From Innsbruck to Bolzano via A22/E45 (Brenner Pass); Villach to Tarvisio via A23/E55

France From Nice to Ventimiglia via A10/E80; Modane to Turin via A32/E70 (Fréjus Tunnel); Chamonix to Courmayeur via A5/E25 (Mont Blanc Tunnel)

Slovenia From Sežana to Trieste via SS58/E70

Switzerland From Martigny to Aosta via SS27/E27 (Grand St Bernard Tunnel); Lugano to Como via A9/E35

Bus

Buses are the cheapest overland option to Italy, but services are less frequent, less comfortable and significantly slower than the train.

Eurolines (www.eurolines. com) is a consortium of coach companies with offices throughout Europe. Italy-bound buses head to Milan, Rome, Florence, Venice and other Italian cities. It offers a low-season bus pass valid for 15/30 days that costs €215/320 (reduced €185/250). This pass allows unlimited travel between 51 European cities, including Milan, Venice, Florence and Rome. Fares increase to €355/465 (reduced €300/385) in midsummer.

Car & Motorcycle

FROM CONTINENTAL EUROPE

➡ Every vehicle travelling across an international border should display a nationality plate of its country of registration.

➡ Always carry proof of vehicle ownership and evidence of third-party insurance. If driving an EU-registered vehicle, your home country insurance is sufficient. Ask your insurer for a European Accident Statement (EAS) form, which can simplify matters in the event of an accident.

➡ A European breakdown assistance policy is a good investment and can

ibe obtained through the Automobile Club d'Italia.

➡ Italy's scenic roads are tailor-made for motorcycle touring, and motorcyclists swarm into the country every summer. With a motorcycle you rarely have to book ahead for ferries and can enter restricted-traffic areas in cities. Crash helmets and a motorcycle licence are compulsory.

➡ The US-based **Beach's Motorcycle Adventures** (www.bmca.com) offers a number of two-week tours from April to October, with destinations including the Alps, Tuscany and Umbria, Sicily and Sardinia. For longer-term auto leasing (14 days or more) or campervan and motorhome hire, check **IdeaMerge** (www.ideamerge. com).

FROM THE UK

You can take your car to Italy via France by ferry or via the **Channel Tunnel** (www. eurotunnel.com). The latter runs four crossings (35 minutes) an hour between Folkestone and Calais in the high season.

For breakdown assistance, both the **AA** (www.theaa.com) and the **RAC** (www.rac.co.uk) offer comprehensive cover in Europe.

Train

Regular trains on two western lines connect Italy with France (one along the coast and the other from Turin into the French Alps). Trains from Milan head north into Switzerland and on towards the Benelux countries. Further east, two main lines head for the main cities in Central and Eastern Europe. Those crossing the Brenner Pass go to Innsbruck, Stuttgart and Munich. Those crossing at Tarvisio proceed to Vienna, Salzburg and Prague. The main international train line to Slovenia crosses near Trieste.

Depending on distances covered, rail can be

DIRECT INTERCONTINENTAL FLIGHTS

AIRPORT	DIRECT INTERCONTINENTAL CONNECTIONS (YEAR-ROUND)
Rome (Leonardo da Vinci)	Atlanta, Boston, Chicago, Los Angeles, Miami, New York, Philadelphia, Washington DC, Montreal, Toronto, Buenos Aires, Rio de Janeiro, São Paulo, Caracas, Algiers, Amman, Beirut, Cairo, Casablanca, Doha, Dubai, Riyadh, Tehran, Tel Aviv, Tripoli, Tunis, Abu Dhabi, Dubai, Osaka, Tokyo, Seoul, Hong Kong, Shanghai, Bangkok, Singapore
Milan (Malpensa)	New York, São Paulo, Algiers, Cairo, Jeddah, Muscat, Tel Aviv, Tunis, Abu Dhabi, Dubai, Beijing, Hong Kong, Shanghai, Bangkok, Singapore
Venice (Marco Polo)	New York, Casablanca, Tunis, Doha, Dubai

DIRECT TRAINS TO ITALY FROM CONTINENTAL EUROPE

FROM	TO	FREQUENCY	DURATION (HR)	COST (€)
Geneva	Milan	four daily	4	78
Geneva	Venice	one daily	7	108
Munich	Florence	one nightly	9¼	111
Munich	Rome	one nightly	12¼	145
Munich	Venice	one nightly	9	116
Paris	Milan	three daily	7	98
Paris	Rome	one nightly	12½	120
Paris	Turin	three daily	5½	98
Paris	Venice	one nightly	13½	120
Vienna	Milan	one nightly	14	109
Vienna	Rome	one nightly	14	99
Zurich	Milan	six daily	3¾	69

highly competitive with air travel. Those travelling from neighbouring countries to northern Italy will find it is frequently more comfortable, less expensive and only marginally more time-consuming than flying.

Those travelling longer distances (say, from London, Spain, northern Germany or Eastern Europe) will doubtless find flying cheaper and quicker. Bear in mind, however, that the train is a much greener way to go – a trip by rail can contribute up to 10 times less carbon dioxide emissions per person than the same trip by air.

FROM CONTINENTAL EUROPE

➡ The comprehensive European Rail Timetable (UK£14.99), updated monthly, is available from **Thomas Cook Publishing** (www.thomascookpublishing. com).

➡ Reservations on international trains to/from Italy are always advisable, and sometimes compulsory.

➡ Some international services include transport for private cars.

➡ Consider taking long journeys overnight, as the

supplemental fare for a sleeper costs substantially less than Italian hotels.

FROM THE UK

➡ High-velocity passenger train **Eurostar** (www.eurostar. com) travels between London and Paris, or London and Brussels. Alternatively, you can get a train ticket that includes crossing the Channel by ferry.

➡ For the latest fare information on journeys to Italy, including the Eurostar, contact the **Rail Europe Travel Centre** (www.raileurope.co.uk) or **International Rail** (www. internationalrail.com).

Sea

Multiple ferry companies connect Italy with countries throughout the Mediterranean. Many routes only operate in summer, when ticket prices also rise. Prices for vehicles vary according to their size.

The helpful website www. traghettionline.com (in Italian) covers all the ferry companies in the Mediterranean. Another useful resource for ferries from Italy to Greece is www.ferries.gr.

International ferry companies that serve Italy:

Adria Ferries (www.adriaferries.com)

Agoudimos Lines (www. agoudimos-lines.com)

Anek Lines (www.anek.gr)

Blue Star Ferries (www. bluestarferries.com)

Commodore Cruises (www. commodore-cruises.hr)

GNV (Grandi Navi Veloci; www. gnv.it)

Grimaldi (www.grimaldi-lines. com)

Jadrolinija (www.jadrolinija.hr)

Minoan Lines (www.ferries. gr/minoan)

Moby Lines (☎199 30 30 40; www.moby.it)

Montenegro Lines (www. montenegrolines.net)

SNAV (www.snav.it)

Superfast (www.superfast. com)

Tirrenia (☎0923 03 19 11; www.tirrenia.it)

Venezia Lines (☎041 882 11 01; www.venezialines.com)

Ventouris (www.ventouris.gr)

Virtu Ferries (☎095 703 12 11; www.virtuferries.com)

GETTING AROUND

Italy's network of train, bus, ferry and domestic air transport allows you to reach most destinations efficiently and relatively affordably.

With your own vehicle, you'll enjoy greater freedom, but *benzina* (petrol) and autostrada (motorway) tolls are expensive and Italian drivers have a style all their own. For many, the stress of driving and parking in urban areas may outweigh the delights of puttering about the countryside. One solution is to take public transport between large cities and rent a car only to reach more-remote rural destinations.

Air

Italy enjoys an extensive network of internal flights. The privatised national airline, Alitalia, is the main domestic carrier. A useful search engine for comparing multiple carriers' fares and purchasing low-cost domestic flights is **AZfly** (www.azfly.it).

INTERNATIONAL FERRY ROUTES FROM ITALY

Destination Country	Destination Port(s)	Italian Port(s)	Company
Albania	Durrës	Bari	Ventouris
	Durrës	Bari, Ancona, Trieste	Adria Ferries
	Vlora	Brindisi	Agoudimos Lines
Croatia	Dubrovnik	Bari	Jadrolinija
	Hvar	Pescara	SNAV
	Split	Ancona, Pescara	SNAV
	Split, Zadar	Ancona	Jadrolinija
	Umag, Poreč, Rovinj, Pula, Rabac, Mali Lošinj,	Venice	Venezia Lines
Greece	Kefallonia, Corfu, Igoumenitsa, Patras, Zante	Brindisi	Agoudimos Lines
	Corfu, Igoumenitsa, Patras	Bari	Blue Star Ferries, Superfast
	Igoumenitsa, Patras	Ancona	Superfast, Anek Lines, Blue Star Ferries
	Igoumenitsa, Patras	Venice	Anek Lines
	Igoumenitsa, Patras	Trieste, Ancona	Minoan Lines
Malta	Valletta	Pozzallo, Catania	Virtu Ferries
Montenegro	Bar	Bari	Montenegro Lines
Morocco	Tangier	Genoa	GNV
	Tangier	Livorno	Grimaldi
Slovenia	Piran	Venice	Commodore Cruises
Spain	Barcelona	Genoa	GNV
	Barcelona	Civitavecchia, Livorno, Porto Torres	Grimaldi
Tunisia	Tunis	Genoa, Palermo	GNV
	Tunis	Genoa	Tirrenia
	Tunis	Civitavecchia, Palermo, Salerno, Trapani	Grimaldi
France (Corsica)	Bastia	Livorno, Genoa	Moby Lines
	Bonifacio	Santa Teresa di Gallura (Sardinia)	Moby Lines

ROAD DISTANCES (KM)

	Bari	Bologna	Florence	Genoa	Milan	Naples	Palermo	Perugia	Reggio di Calabria	Rome	Siena	Trento	Trieste	Turin	Venice
Bologna	681														
Florence	784	106													
Genoa	996	285	268												
Milan	899	218	324	156											
Naples	322	640	534	758	858										
Palermo	734	1415	1345	1569	1633	811									
Perugia	612	270	164	432	488	408	1219								
Reggio di Calabria	490	1171	1101	1325	1389	567	272	816							
Rome	482	408	302	526	626	232	1043	170	664						
Siena	714	176	70	296	394	464	1275	103	867	232					
Trento	892	233	339	341	218	874	1626	459	1222	641	375				
Trieste	995	308	414	336	420	948	1689	543	1445	715	484	279			
Turin	1019	338	442	174	139	932	1743	545	1307	702	460	349	551		
Venice	806	269	265	387	284	899	799	394	1296	567	335	167	165	415	
Verona	808	141	247	282	164	781	1534	377	1139	549	293	97	250	295	120

> **Note**
> Distances between Palermo and mainland towns do not take into account the ferry from Reggio di Calabria to Messina. Add an extra hour to your journey time to allow for this crossing

Airport taxes are factored into the price of your ticket.

The many cut-rate airlines within Italy include the following:

Air One (☏89 24 44; www.flyairone.com)

AirAlps (☏06 22 22; www.airalps.at)

Blu-express (☏06 9895 6666; www.blu-express.com)

Darwin Airline (☏06 8997 0422; www.darwinairline.com)

easyJet (☏199 201840; www.easyjet.com)

Meridiana (☏89 29 28; www.meridiana.it)

Ryanair (☏899 552589; www.ryanair.com)

Volotea (☏895 8954404; www.volotea.com)

Bicycle

Cycling is very popular in Italy. The following tips will help ensure a pedal-happy trip:

➜ If bringing your own bike, you'll need to disassemble and pack it for the journey, and may need to pay an airline surcharge.

➜ Make sure to bring tools, spare parts, a helmet, lights and a secure bike lock.

➜ Bikes are prohibited on Italian autostradas (motorways).

➜ Bikes can be wheeled onto any domestic train displaying the bicycle logo. Simply purchase a separate bicycle ticket, valid for 24 hours (€3.50). Certain international trains, listed on Trenitalia's 'In treno con la bici' page, also allow transport of assembled bicycles for €12, paid on board. Bikes dismantled and stored in a bag can be taken for free, even on night trains.

➜ Most ferries also allow free bicycle passage.

➜ In the UK, **Cyclists' Touring Club** (CTC; www.ctc.org.uk) can help you plan your tour or organise a guided tour. Membership costs £41 for adults, £25 for seniors and £16 for under-18s.

➜ Bikes are available for hire in most Italian towns. City bikes start at €10/50 per day/week; mountain bikes a bit more. Some municipalities, including Rimini and Ravenna, offer free bikes for visitors, as do a growing number of Italian hotels.

Boat

Craft *Navi* (large ferries) service Sicily and Sardinia, while *traghetti* (smaller ferries) and *aliscafi* (hydrofoils) service the smaller islands. Most ferries carry vehicles; hydrofoils do not.

Routes Main embarkation points for Sicily and Sardinia are Genoa, Livorno, Civitavecchia and Naples. Ferries for Sicily also leave from Villa San Giovanni and Reggio Calabria. Main arrival points in Sardinia are Cagliari, Arbatax, Olbia and Porto Torres; in Sicily they're Palermo, Catania, Trapani and Messina.

Timetables and tickets Comprehensive website **Traghetti-Online** (www.traghettionline.com) includes links to multiple Italian ferry companies, allowing you to compare prices and buy tickets.

Overnight ferries Travellers can book a two- to four-person cabin or a *poltrona*, which is an airline-type armchair. Deck class (which allows you to sit/ sleep in lounge areas or on deck) is available only on some ferries.

Bus

Routes Italy has everything from meandering local routes to fast, reliable InterCity connections provided by numerous bus companies.

Timetables and tickets Available on bus company websites and from local tourist offices. Tickets are generally competitively priced with the train and often the only way to get to smaller towns. In larger cities most of the InterCity bus companies have ticket offices or sell tickets through agencies. In villages and even some good-sized towns, tickets are sold in bars or on the bus.

Advance booking Generally not required, but advisable for overnight or long-haul trips in high season.

Car & Motorcycle

Italy's extensive network of roads span numerous categories. The main ones include:

➔ Autostradas – An extensive, privatised network of motorways, represented on road signs by a white 'A' followed by a number on a green background. The main north–south link is the Autostrada del Sole

(the 'Motorway of the Sun'), which extends from Milan to Reggio di Calabria (called the A1 from Milan to Rome, the A2 from Rome to Naples, and the A3 from Naples to Reggio di Calabria). There are tolls on most motorways, payable by cash or credit card as you exit.

➔ *Strade statali* (state highways) – Represented on maps by 'S' or 'SS'. Vary from toll-free, four-lane highways to two-lane main roads. The latter can be extremely slow, especially in mountainous regions.

➔ *Strade regionali* (regional highways connecting small villages) – Coded 'SR' or 'R'.

➔ *Strade provinciali* (provincial highways) – Coded 'SP' or 'P'.

➔ *Strade locali* – Often not even paved or mapped.

For information in English about distances, driving times and fuel costs, see en.mappy.com. Additional information, including traffic conditions and toll costs, is available at www.autostrade.it.

Automobile Associations

The **Automobile Club d'Italia** (ACI; ☑ from non-Italian phone account 800 116800, roadside assistance 803116; www.aci.it) is a driver's best resource in Italy. Foreigners do not have to join to get 24-hour roadside emergency service but instead pay a per-incident fee.

Driving Licences

All EU member states' driving licences are fully recognised throughout Europe. In practice, many non-EU licences (such as Australian, Canadian, New Zealand and US) are accepted by car-hire outfits in Italy. Travellers from other countries should obtain an International Driving Permit (IDP) through their national automobile association.

Fuel & Spare Parts

Italy's petrol prices are among the highest in Europe and vary from one service station (*benzinaio, stazione di servizio*) to another. At the time of writing, lead-free gasoline (*senza piombo;* 95 octane) was averaging €1.79 per litre, with diesel (*gasolio*) costing €1.69 per litre.

Spare parts are available at many garages or via the 24-hour ACI motorist assistance number, ☑ 803116 (or ☑ 800 116800 if calling with a non-Italian mobile phone account).

Hire

CAR

➔ Pre-booking via the internet often costs less than hiring a car in Italy. Online booking agency **Rentalcars.com** (www.rentalcars.com) compares the rates of numerous car-rental companies.

➔ Renters must generally be aged 25 or over, with a credit card and home-country driving licence or IDP.

➔ Consider hiring a small car, which will reduce your fuel expenses and help you negotiate narrow city lanes and tight parking spaces.

➔ Check with your credit-card company to see if it offers a Collision Damage Waiver, which covers you for additional damage if you use that card to pay for the car. Multinational car-rental agencies:

Auto Europe (www.autoeurope.com)

Avis (www.avis.com)

Budget (☑ 800 472 33 25; www.budget.com)

Europcar (www.europcar.com)

Hertz (www.hertz.it)

Holiday Cars (www.holiday-cars.com)

Italy by Car (☑ 334 6481920; www.italybycar.it)

Maggiore (☑ 199 151120; www.maggiore.it)

MOTORCYCLE

Agencies throughout Italy rent motorbikes, ranging from small Vespas to larger touring bikes. Prices start at around €35/150 per day/week for a 50cc scooter, or upwards of €80/400 per day/week for a 650cc motorcycle.

Road Rules

➡ Cars drive on the right side of the road and overtake on the left. Unless otherwise indicated, you must always give way to cars entering an intersection from your right.

➡ Seatbelt use (front and rear) is required by law; violators are subject to an on-the-spot fine. Helmets are required on all two-wheeled transport.

➡ Headlights are compulsory day and night for all vehicles on the autostradas, and advisable for motorcycles even on smaller roads.

➡ In the event of a breakdown, a warning triangle is compulsory, as is use of an approved yellow or orange safety vest if you leave your vehicle. Recommended accessories include a first-aid kit, spare-bulb kit and fire extinguisher.

➡ No licence is required to ride a scooter under 50cc but you should be aged 14 or over and you can't carry passengers or ride on an autostrada. To ride a motorcycle or scooter up to 125cc, you must be aged 16 or over and have a licence (a car licence will do). For motorcycles over 125cc you need a motorcycle licence. Do not venture onto the autostrada with a bike of less than 150cc.

➡ Motorbikes can enter most restricted traffic areas in Italian cities, and traffic police often turn a blind eye to motorcycles or scooters parked on footpaths.

➡ Italy's blood-alcohol limit is 0.05%, and random breath tests occur. If you're involved in an accident while under the influence, the penalties can be severe.

➡ Speeding fines follow EU standards and are proportionate with the number of kilometres that you are caught driving over the speed limit, reaching up to €3119 with a possible six-to 12-month suspension of your driving licence. Speed limits are as follows:

Autostradas 130-150km/h

Other main highways 110km/h

Minor, non-urban roads 90km/h

Built-up areas 50km/h

Mopeds The speed limit is always 40km/h

Local Transport

Major cities have good transport systems, including bus and underground-train networks. In Venice, the main public transport option is *vaporetti* (small ferries).

Bus & Metro

➡ Extensive *metropolitane* (metros) exist in Rome, Milan, Naples and Turin, with smaller metros in Genoa and Catania. The space-age *Minimetrò* in Perugia connects the train station with the city centre.

➡ Cities and towns of any size have an efficient *urbano* (urban) and *extraurbano* (suburban) bus system. Services are generally limited on Sundays and holidays.

➡ Purchase bus and metro tickets before boarding and validate them once on board. Passengers with unvalidated tickets are subject to a fine (between €50 and €75 in most cities). Buy tickets from *tabaccaio* (tobacconist's shops), newsstands, ticket booths or machines at bus stations and in metro stations. Tickets usually cost around €1.30 to €1.80. Most cities offer good-value 24-hour or daily tourist tickets.

Taxi

➡ You can catch a taxi at the ranks outside most train and bus stations, or simply telephone for a radio taxi. Radio taxi meters start running from when you've called rather than when you're picked up.

➡ Charges vary from one region to another. Most short city journeys cost between €10 and €15. Generally, no more than four people are allowed in one taxi.

Train

Trains in Italy are convenient and quite cheap compared with other European countries. The better train categories are fast and comfortable.

Trenitalia (☎199 303060; www.trenitalia.com) is the partially privatised state train system that runs most services. Its privately owned competitor **Italo** (☎06 07 08; www.italotreno.it) runs

TRAINS: HIGH-VELOCITY VS INTERCITY

FROM	TO	HIGH-VELOCITY DURATION (HR)	PRICE (€)	INTER-CITY DURATION (HR)	PRICE (€)
Turin	Naples	5½	105	9¾	70.50
Milan	Rome	3¼	86	6¾	55.50
Venice	Florence	2	45	3	27
Rome	Naples	1¼	43	2¼	24.50
Florence	Bologna	37min	24	1	11.50

EURAIL & INTERRAIL PASSES

Generally speaking, you'll need to cover a lot of ground to make a rail pass worthwhile. Before buying, consider where you intend to travel and compare the price of a rail pass to the cost of individual tickets on the **Trenitalia** (☏892021; www.trenitalia.com) website.

InterRail (www.interrailnet.com) passes, available online and at most major stations and student-travel outlets, are for people who have been a resident in Europe for more than six months. A Global Pass encompassing 30 countries comes in five versions, ranging from five days' travel within a 10-day period to a full month's unlimited travel. There are four age brackets: child (4 to 11), youth (12 to 25), adult (26 to 59) and senior (60+), with different prices for 1st and 2nd class. The InterRail one-country pass for Italy can be used for three, four, six or eight days in one month and does not offer senior discounts. See the website for full price details. Cardholders get discounts on travel in the country where they purchase the ticket.

Eurail (www.eurail.com) passes, available for non-European residents, are good for travel in 24 European countries (not including the UK). They can be purchased online or from travel agencies outside of Europe.

The original Eurail pass, now known as the **Global Pass**, is valid for a continuous period of 10 days, 15 days, 21 days, one, two or three months. Youth under 26 are eligible for a 2nd-class pass; all others must buy the more expensive 1st-class pass (offered at half-price for children aged between four and 11).

Eurail offers several alternatives to the traditional Global Pass:

➡ The **Select Pass** allows five to 15 days of travel within a two-month period in three to five bordering countries of your choice.

➡ The two-country **Regional Pass** (France/Italy, Spain/Italy or Greece/Italy) allows four to 10 days of travel within a two-month period.

➡ The **One Country Pass** allows three to 10 days of travel in Italy within a two-month period.

---

high-velocity trains on two lines, one between Turin and Salerno, and one between Venice and Naples.

Train tickets must be stamped in the yellow machines (usually found at the head of rail platforms) just before boarding. Failure to do so usually results in fines.

Italy operates several types of trains:

Regionale/interregionale Slow and cheap, stopping at all or most stations.

InterCity (IC) Faster services operating between major cities. Their international counterparts are called Eurocity (EC).

Alta Velocità (AV) State-of-the-art, high-velocity trains, including Frecciarossa, Frecciargento, Frecciabianca and Italo trains. with speeds of up to 300km/hr and connections to the major cities. More expensive than InterCity express trains, but journey times are cut by almost half.

Classes & Costs

Prices vary according to the class of service, time of travel and how far in advance you book. Most Italian trains have 1st- and 2nd-class seating; a 1st-class ticket typically costs from a third to half more than 2nd-class.

Travel on Trenitalia's InterCity and Alta Velocità (Frecciarossa, Frecciargento, Frecciabianca) trains means paying a supplement, included in the ticket price, determined by the distance travelled. If you have a standard ticket for a slower train and end up on an IC train, you'll have to pay the difference on board.

Reservations

➡ Reservations are obligatory on AV trains. On other services, outside of peak holiday periods, you should be fine without them.

➡ Reservations can be made on the Trenitalia and Italo websites, at railway station counters and self-service ticketing machines, or through travel agents.

➡ Both Trenitalia and Italo offer a variety of advance purchase discounts: the earlier you book, the greater the saving. Discounted tickets are limited, and refunds and changes are highly restricted. For tickets and prices, see the Trenitalia and Italo websites.

Train Passes

Trenitalia offers various discount passes, including the Carta Verde for youth and Carta d'Argento for seniors, but these are mainly useful for residents or long-term visitors, as they only pay for themselves with regular use over an extended period.

More interesting for short-term visitors are Eurail and InterRail passes.

Language

Standard Italian is taught and spoken throughout Italy. Regional dialects are an important part of identity in many parts of the country, but you'll have no trouble being understood anywhere if you stick to standard Italian, which we've also used in this chapter.

The sounds used in spoken Italian can all be found in English. If you read our col-oured pronunciation guides as if they were English, you'll be understood. The stressed syllables are indicated with italics. Note that ai is pronounced as in 'aisle', ay as in 'say', ow as in 'how', dz as the 'ds' in 'lids', and that r is a strong and rolled sound. Keep in mind that Italian consonants can have a stronger, emphatic pronunciation – if the consonant is written as a double letter, it should be pronounced a little stronger, eg *sonno son·*no (sleep) versus *sono so·*no (I am).

BASICS

Hello.	*Buongiorno.*	bwon·*jor*·no
Goodbye.	*Arrivederci.*	a·ree·ve·*der*·chee
Yes./No.	*Sì./No.*	see/no
Excuse me.	*Mi scusi.* (pol)	mee *skoo*·zee
	Scusami. (inf)	*skoo*·za·mee
Sorry.	*Mi dispiace.*	mee dees·*pya*·che
Please.	*Per favore.*	per fa·*vo*·re
Thank you.	*Grazie.*	*gra*·tsye
You're welcome.	*Prego.*	*pre*·go

WANT MORE?

For in-depth language information and handy phrases, check out Lonely Planet's *Italian Phrasebook*. You'll find it at **shop.lonelyplanet.com**, or you can buy Lonely Planet's iPhone phrase-books at the Apple App Store.

How are you?
| *Come sta/stai?* (pol/inf) | *ko*·me sta/stai |

Fine. And you?
| *Bene. E lei/tu?* (pol/inf) | *be*·ne e lay/too |

What's your name?
| *Come si chiama?* (pol) | *ko*·me see *kya*·ma |
| *Come ti chiami?* (inf) | *ko*·me tee *kya*·mee |

My name is ...
| *Mi chiamo ...* | mee *kya*·mo ... |

Do you speak English?
| *Parla/Parli* | *par*·la/*par*·lee |
| *inglese?* (pol/inf) | een·*gle*·ze |

I don't understand.
| *Non capisco.* | non ka·*pee*·sko |

ACCOMMODATION

campsite	*campeggio*	kam·*pe*·jo
guesthouse	*pensione*	pen·*syo*·ne
hotel	*albergo*	al·*ber*·go
youth hostel	*ostello della gioventù*	os·*te*·lo de·la jo·ven·*too*

Do you have a ... room?	*Avete una camera ...?*	a·*ve*·te oo·na *ka*·me·ra ...
double	*doppia con letto matri-moniale*	*do*·pya kon *le*·to ma·*tree*·mo·*nya*·le
single	*singola*	*seen*·go·la

How much is it per ...?	*Quanto costa per ...?*	*kwan*·to *kos*·ta per ...
night	*una notte*	oo·na *no*·te
person	*persona*	per·*so*·na

air-con	*aria condizionata*	*a*·rya kon·dee·tsyo·*na*·ta
bathroom	*bagno*	*ba*·nyo
window	*finestra*	fee·*nes*·tra

DIRECTIONS

Where's ...?
Dov'è ...?   do·ve ...

What's the address?
Qual'è l'indirizzo? kwa·le leen·dee·ree·tso

Could you please write it down?
Può scriverlo,   pwo skree·ver·lo
per favore?   per fa·vo·re

Can you show me (on the map)?
Può mostrarmi   pwo mos·trar·mee
(sulla pianta)?   (soo·la pyan·ta)

EATING & DRINKING

What would you recommend?
Cosa mi consiglia?   ko·za mee kon·see·lya

What's the local speciality?
Qual'è la specialità kwa·le la spe·cha·lee·ta
di questa regione?   dee kwe·sta re·jo·ne

Cheers!
Salute!   sa·loo·te

That was delicious!
Era squisito!   e·ra skwee·zee·to

Please bring the bill.
Mi porta il conto,   mee por·ta eel kon·to
per favore?   per fa·vo·re

I'd like to	*Vorrei*	vo·ray
reserve a	*prenotare un*	pre·no·ta·re oon
table for ...	*tavolo per ...*	ta·vo·lo per ...
(eight)	*le (otto)*	le (o·to)
o'clock		
(two)	*(due)*	(doo·e)
people	*persone*	per·so·ne
I don't eat ...	*Non mangio ...*	non man·jo ...
eggs	*uova*	wo·va
fish	*pesce*	pe·she
nuts	*noci*	no·chee

Key Words

bar	*locale*	lo·ka·le
bottle	*bottiglia*	bo·tee·lya
breakfast	*prima*	pree·ma
	colazione	ko·la·tsyo·ne
cafe	*bar*	bar
dinner	*cena*	che·na
drink list	*lista delle*	lee·sta de·le
	bevande	be·van·de
fork	*forchetta*	for·ke·ta
glass	*bicchiere*	bee·kye·re
knife	*coltello*	kol·te·lo

KEY PATTERNS

To get by in Italian, mix and match these simple patterns with words of your choice:

When's (the next flight)?
A che ora è   a ke o·ra e
(il prossimo volo)? (eel pro·see·mo vo·lo)

Where's (the station)?
Dov'è (la stazione)? do·ve (la sta·tsyo·ne)

I'm looking for (a hotel).
Sto cercando   sto cher·kan·do
(un albergo).   (oon al·ber·go)

Do you have (a map)?
Ha (una pianta)?   a (oo·na pyan·ta)

Is there (a toilet)?
C'è (un gabinetto)? che (oon ga·bee·ne·to)

I'd like (a coffee).
Vorrei (un caffè).   vo·ray (oon ka·fe)

I'd like to (hire a car).
Vorrei (noleggiare   vo·ray (no·le·ja·re
una macchina).   oo·na ma·kee·na)

Can I (enter)?
Posso (entrare)?   po·so (en·tra·re)

Could you please (help me)?
Può (aiutarmi),   pwo (a·yoo·tar·mee)
per favore?   per fa·vo·re

Do I have to (book a seat)?
Devo (prenotare   de·vo (pre·no·ta·re
un posto)?   oon po·sto)

lunch	*pranzo*	pran·dzo
market	*mercato*	mer·ka·to
menu	*menù*	me·noo
plate	*piatto*	pya·to
restaurant	*ristorante*	ree·sto·ran·te
spoon	*cucchiaio*	koo·kya·yo
vegetarian	*vegetariano*	ve·je·ta·rya·no

Meat & Fish

beef	*manzo*	man·dzo
chicken	*pollo*	po·lo
herring	*aringa*	a·reen·ga
lamb	*agnello*	a·nye·lo
lobster	*aragosta*	a·ra·gos·ta
mussels	*cozze*	ko·tse
oysters	*ostriche*	o·stree·ke
pork	*maiale*	ma·ya·le
prawn	*gambero*	gam·be·ro
salmon	*salmone*	sal·mo·ne
scallops	*capasante*	ka·pa·san·te

shrimp	gambero	gam·be·ro
squid	calamari	ka·la·ma·ree
trout	trota	tro·ta
tuna	tonno	to·no
turkey	tacchino	ta·kee·no
veal	vitello	vee·te·lo

Fruit & Vegetables

apple	mela	me·la
beans	fagioli	fa·jo·lee
cabbage	cavolo	ka·vo·lo
capsicum	peperone	pe·pe·ro·ne
carrot	carota	ka·ro·ta
cauliflower	cavolfiore	ka·vol·fyo·re
cucumber	cetriolo	che·tree·o·lo
grapes	uva	oo·va
lemon	limone	lee·mo·ne
lentils	lenticchie	len·tee·kye
mushroom	funghi	foon·gee
nuts	noci	no·chee
onions	cipolle	chee·po·le
orange	arancia	a·ran·cha
peach	pesca	pe·ska
peas	piselli	pee·ze·lee
pineapple	ananas	a·na·nas
plum	prugna	proo·nya
potatoes	patate	pa·ta·te
spinach	spinaci	spee·na·chee
tomatoes	pomodori	po·mo·do·ree

Other

bread	pane	pa·ne
butter	burro	boo·ro
cheese	formaggio	for·ma·jo
eggs	uova	wo·va
honey	miele	mye·le
jam	marmellata	mar·me·la·ta
noodles	pasta	pas·ta
oil	olio	o·lyo
pepper	pepe	pe·pe
rice	riso	ree·zo
salt	sale	sa·le
soup	minestra	mee·nes·tra
soy sauce	salsa di soia	sal·sa dee so·ya
sugar	zucchero	tsoo·ke·ro
vinegar	aceto	a·che·to

Drinks

beer	birra	bee·ra
coffee	caffè	ka·fe
juice	succo	soo·ko
milk	latte	la·te
red wine	vino rosso	vee·no ro·so
tea	tè	te
water	acqua	a·kwa
white wine	vino bianco	vee·no byan·ko

EMERGENCIES

Help!
Aiuto!   a·yoo·to

Leave me alone!
Lasciami in pace!   la·sha·mee een pa·che

I'm lost.
Mi sono perso/a. (m/f)   mee so·no per·so/a

Call the police!
Chiami la polizia!   kya·mee la po·lee·tsee·a

Call a doctor!
Chiami un medico!   kya·mee oon me·dee·ko

Where are the toilets?
Dove sono i gabinetti?   do·ve so·no ee ga·bee·ne·tee

I'm sick.
Mi sento male.   mee sen·to ma·le

SHOPPING & SERVICES

I'd like to buy ...
Vorrei comprare ...   vo·ray kom·pra·re ...

I'm just looking.
Sto solo guardando.   sto so·lo gwar·dan·do

Can I look at it?
Posso dare un'occhiata?   po·so da·re oo·no·kya·ta

How much is this?
Quanto costa questo?   kwan·to kos·ta kwe·sto

It's too expensive.
È troppo caro.   e tro·po ka·ro

There's a mistake in the bill.
C'è un errore nel conto.   che oo·ne·ro·re nel kon·to

Signs	
Closed	**Chiuso**
Entrance	**Entrata/Ingresso**
Exit	**Uscita**
Men	**Uomini**
Open	**Aperto**
Prohibited	**Proibito/Vietato**
Toilets	**Gabinetti/Servizi**
Women	**Donne**

ATM	Bancomat	ban·ko·mat
post office	ufficio postale	oo·fee·cho pos·ta·le
tourist office	ufficio del turismo	oo·fee·cho del too·reez·mo

TIME & DATES

What time is it?
Che ora è? ke o·ra e

It's (two) o'clock.
Sono le (due). so·no le (doo·e)

Half past (one).
(L'una) e mezza. (loo·na) e me·dza

in the morning	di mattina	dee ma·tee·na
in the afternoon	di pomeriggio	dee po·me·ree·jo
in the evening	di sera	dee se·ra
yesterday	ieri	ye·ree
today	oggi	o·jee
tomorrow	domani	do·ma·nee

Monday	lunedì	loo·ne·dee
Tuesday	martedì	mar·te·dee
Wednesday	mercoledì	mer·ko·le·dee
Thursday	giovedì	jo·ve·dee
Friday	venerdì	ve·ner·dee
Saturday	sabato	sa·ba·to
Sunday	domenica	do·me·nee·ka

TRANSPORT

boat	nave	na·ve
bus	autobus	ow·to·boos
ferry	traghetto	tra·ge·to
metro	metropolitana	me·tropo·lee·ta·na
plane	aereo	a·e·re·o
train	treno	tre·no

bus stop	fermata dell'autobus	fer·ma·ta del ow·to·boos
ticket office	biglietteria	bee·lye·te·ree·a
timetable	orario	o·ra·ryo
train station	stazione ferroviaria	sta·tsyo·ne fe·ro·vyar·ya

... ticket	un biglietto ...	oon bee·lye·to
one-way	di sola andata	dee so·la an·da·ta
return	di andata e ritorno	dee an·da·ta e ree·tor·no

Numbers		
1	uno	oo·no
2	due	doo·e
3	tre	tre
4	quattro	kwa·tro
5	cinque	cheen·kwe
6	sei	say
7	sette	se·te
8	otto	o·to
9	nove	no·ve
10	dieci	dye·chee
20	venti	ven·tee
30	trenta	tren·ta
40	quaranta	kwa·ran·ta
50	cinquanta	cheen·kwan·ta
60	sessanta	se·san·ta
70	settanta	se·tan·ta
80	ottanta	o·tan·ta
90	novanta	no·van·ta
100	cento	chen·to
1000	mille	mee·lel

Does it stop at ...?
Si ferma a ...? see fer·ma a ...

Please tell me when we get to ...
Mi dica per favore quando arriviamo a ... mee dee·ka per fa·vo·re kwan·do a·ree·vya·mo a ...

I want to get off here.
Voglio scendere qui. vo·lyo shen·de·re kwee

I'd like to hire a ...	Vorrei noleggiare una ...	vo·ray no·le·ja·re oo·na ...
bicycle	bicicletta	bee·chee·kle·ta
car	macchina	ma·kee·na
motorbike	moto	mo·to

bicycle pump	pompa della bicicletta	pom·pa de·la bee·chee·kle·ta
child seat	seggiolino	se·jo·lee·no
helmet	casco	kas·ko
mechanic	meccanico	me·ka·nee·ko
petrol	benzina	ben·dzee·na
service station	stazione di servizio	sta·tsyo·ne dee ser·vee·tsyo

Is this the road to ...?
Questa strada porta a ...? kwe·sta stra·da por·ta a ...

Can I park here?
Posso parcheggiare qui? po·so par·ke·ja·re kwee

GLOSSARY

abbazia – abbey

agriturismo – farm-stays

(pizza) al taglio – (pizza) by the slice

albergo – hotel

alimentari – grocery shop

anfiteatro – amphitheatre

aperitivo – pre-dinner drink and snack

APT – Azienda di Promozione Turistica; local town or city tourist office

autostrada – motorway; highway

battistero – baptistry

biblioteca – library

biglietto – ticket

borgo – archaic name for a small town, village or town sector

camera – room

campo – field; also a square in Venice

cappella – chapel

carabinieri – police with military and civil duties

Carnevale – carnival period between Epiphany and Lent

casa – house

castello – castle

cattedrale – cathedral

centro storico – historic centre

certosa – monastery belonging to or founded by Carthusian monks

chiesa – church

chiostro – cloister; covered walkway, usually enclosed by columns, around a quadrangle

cima – summit

città – town; city

città alta – upper town

città bassa – lower town

colonna – column

comune – equivalent to a municipality or county; a town or city council; historically, a self–governing town or city

contrada – district

corso – boulevard

duomo – cathedral

enoteca – wine bar

espresso – short black coffee

ferrovia – railway

festa – feast day; holiday

fontana – fountain

foro – forum

funivia – cable car

gelateria – ice-cream shop

giardino – garden

golfo – gulf

grotta – cave

isola – island

lago – lake

largo – small square

lido – beach

locanda – inn; small hotel

lungomare – seafront road/ promenade

mar, mare – sea

masseria – working farm

mausoleo – mausoleum; stately and magnificent tomb

mercato – market

monte – mountain

necropoli – ancient name for cemetery or burial site

nord – north

nuraghe – megalithic stone fortress in Sardinia

osteria – casual tavern or eatery

palazzo – mansion; palace; large building of any type, including an apartment block

palio – contest

parco – park

passeggiata – traditional evening stroll

pasticceria – cake/pastry shop

pensione – guesthouse

piazza – square

piazzale – large open square

pietà – literally 'pity' or 'compassion'; sculpture, drawing or painting of the dead Christ supported by the Madonna

pinacoteca – art gallery

ponte – bridge

porta – gate; door

porto – port

reale – royal

rifugio – mountain hut; accommodation in the Alps

ristorante – restaurant

rocca – fortress

sala – room; hall

salumeria – delicatessen

santuario – sanctuary; 1. the part of a church above the altar; 2. an especially holy place in a temple (antiquity)

sassi – literally 'stones'; stone houses built in two ravines in Matera, Basilicata

scalinata – staircase

scavi – excavations

sestiere – city district in Venice

spiaggia – beach

stazione – station

stazione marittima – ferry terminal

strada – street; road

sud – south

superstrada – expressway; highway with divided lanes

tartufo – truffle

tavola calda – literally 'hot table'; pre-prepared meals, often self-service

teatro – theatre

tempietto – small temple

tempio – temple

terme – thermal baths

tesoro – treasury

torre – tower

trattoria – simple restaurant

Trenitalia – Italian State Railways; also known as Ferrovie dello Stato (FS)

trullo – conical house in Perugia

vaporetto – small passenger ferry in Venice

via – street; road

viale – avenue

vico – alley; alleyway

villa – town house; country house; also the park surrounding the house

Behind the Scenes

SEND US YOUR FEEDBACK

We love to hear from travellers – your comments keep us on our toes and help make our books better. Our well-travelled team reads every word on what you loved or loathed about this book. Although we cannot reply individually to postal submissions, we always guarantee that your feedback goes straight to the appropriate authors, in time for the next edition. Each person who sends us information is thanked in the next edition – the most useful submissions are rewarded with a selection of digital PDF chapters.

Visit **lonelyplanet.com/contact** to submit your updates and suggestions or to ask for help. Our award-winning website also features inspirational travel stories, news and discussions.

Note: We may edit, reproduce and incorporate your comments in Lonely Planet products such as guidebooks, websites and digital products, so let us know if you don't want your comments reproduced or your name acknowledged. For a copy of our privacy policy visit lonelyplanet.com/privacy.

OUR READERS

Many thanks to the travellers who used the last edition and wrote to us with helpful hints, useful advice and interesting anecdotes:

Alex JK West, Andrea Graf, Andrea Mancini, Andrew Volin, Anna Mashman, Ben Grozier, Benjamin Stoll, Caitlin Gianniny, Chris Spencer, Christianna Kreiss, Cinzia Gloria Redaelli, Duncan Campbell, Ebby Cudlipp, Elizabeth Dobisz, Erika Gustavsson, Esteban Jaramillo, Frank Boyce, Garry Aslanyan, Gayle Galletta, Ilianna Anagnostakou, Jennifer Tomaiolo, Johan Reyneke, Judy Davies, Julia Swift, Ken Ohlsen, Leah Prescott, Linda Werner, Lynette Groszmann, Mark Langman, Martin Weiss, Merilyn Moos, Nick Radloff, Oliver Cohen, Patrycja Borowska, Paul Seaver, Piero Giadrossi, Ralph Bain, Richard Walker, Rob McDonald, Robert Kozlowski, Roman Petyk, Sabrina Lo Piano, Sheila Jacobs, Terry Millett, Torben Snarup Hansen, William R Long, Yoav Bloch

AUTHOR THANKS

Cristian Bonetto

First and foremost, an epic thank you to my hawk-eyed coauthors, who bring to this guide the absolute best Italy has to offer. On the ground, an equally epic *grazie* to my *Re e Regina di Napoli*, as well as to the incredibly generous Lorenzo Andrei, Vincenzo Mattiucci, Joe Brizzi, Andrea Maglio, Giancarlo Di Maio, Susy Galeone, Voza family, Luca Coda, Harriet Driver and Valentina Vellusi.

Abigail Blasi

A huge thank you to Joe Bindloss and Helena Smith for giving me the chance to write about my favourite country once again. Thanks to Cristian Bonetto for his excellent stewardship, and to all the other *Italy* authors for their contributions. *Molto grazie* to Luca, Gabriel, Jack and Valentina, to la *famiglia* Blasi for all their kindness and insight into Italian life, and to Georgina for help at home.

Kerry Christiani

Mille grazie to all the friends, hospitable locals and tourism pros I met in Sardinia, Umbria and Le Marche — I couldn't have written this without you. I'd also like to say a special thank you to Peter and Anne in Lotzorai and to climbing expert Corrado Conca for his *arrampicata* tips. At Lonely Planet I'd like to thank Joe Bindloss for giving me the gig, my fellow authors and the entire production team. Last but not least, big thanks to my husband and fellow Fiat 500 travel companion, Andy Christiani.

Gregor Clark

Grazie mille to all of the kind-hearted Italians who helped make this trip so memorable, especially Angela and Nicoletta in Palermo, the Tagliavia family in Polizzi Generosa, Francesca in Stromboli, Marisin and Salvatore in Scopello, Stefano in Milazzo and Diana in Lipari. Thanks to Gurty Spam for joining me on the Aeolians and helping me renew my Stromboli obsession. Finally, big hugs to Gaen, Meigan and Chloe, who always make returning home the happiest part of the trip.

Duncan Garwood

A big thanks to fellow scribe Abi Blasi for her suggestions and great work in Rome, and to Joe Bindloss, Annelies Mertens and the SPP gurus for their in-house help and support. *Grazie* to Barbara Lessona for her pointers, and, as always, a huge hug to Lidia, Ben and Nick for keeping me company in the Viterbo countryside and surviving such appalling seasickness en route to Ponza.

Paula Hardy

Firstly thanks to sterling Venetian and Lakes coauthors, Alison Bing and Anthony Ham for their ability to find the very best tips and recommendations. Also, *grazie mille*, Susan Steer, Cristina Toffolo, Toni Tombola, Paolo du Rossi, Tobia Morro, Mario Piccinin, Silvia Spera, Ivan Geronazzo, Graziano & Martina Spada, Roberto Frozza, Claudio Bonacina, Lorenzo Boiocchi, Marco Broglia, Jaana and Francesco (Villa Arcadio) and Chantal and Marsha. *Brava*, too, to ever-inspiring coordinator Cristian Bonetto, and thanks to Joe Bindloss for steering a steady course.

Virginia Maxwell

Love and thanks to my partner and travelling companion, Peter Handsaker. Thanks also to Ilaria Crescioli, Alberto Peruzzini, Susanna Scali, Roberta Vichi, Eva Zettelmayr, Sigrid Fuchs, Chiara Ponzuoli, Luigina Benci, Cecilia Rosa, Fulvia in San Gimignano, Arturo Comastri, Sean Lawson, Silvia Bucci, Italia Luchini, and my colleague Nicola Williams, who researched Florence, Northwestern Tuscany, the Central Coast and Elba for the Florence chapter.

Brendan Sainsbury

Many thanks to all the untold bus drivers, tourist info volunteers, wine pourers, opera singers and innocent bystanders who helped me during my research. Special thanks to my wife Liz and seven-year-old son Kieran for their company in countless bars, buses, interactive museums and hotel rooms.

Helena Smith

Thanks to everyone who helped with advice, good food and hospitality along the way.

Donna Wheeler

Hospitality often entirely exceeds expectation in my regions – *grazie/dankeschön* to Emanuela Grandi and Stefano Libardi, Raimonda Sabucco, Carmen Kruselburger and Klaus Alber, Martin Kirchlechner, and the restaurants of Bolzano who offered broth and half serves when I was poorly. Special mention to Wayne Young, for the warm welcome and great tips. Much gratitude to Joe Guario for somehow working out what the Ladin tractor driver said and subsequent avalanche avoidance. Finally, big thanks to Cristian Bonetto for unflagging support and boundless bonhomie.

ACKNOWLEDGMENTS

Climate Map Data Climate map data adapted from Peel MC, Finlayson BL & McMahon TA (2007) 'Updated World Map of the Köppen-Geiger Climate Classification', *Hydrology and Earth System Sciences*, 11, 1633¬44.

Illustrations pp76-7, pp346-7, pp482-3, pp678-9 by Javier Martinez Zarracina.

Cover photograph: Leaning Tower and tiled rooftops, Pisa, Tuscany; Travel Pix Collection/ AWL.

THIS BOOK

This 11th edition of Lonely Planet's *Italy* guidebook was researched and written by Cristian Bonetto, Alison Bing, Abigail Blasi, Kerry Christiani, Gregor Clark, Duncan Garwood, Anthony Ham, Paula Hardy, Vesna Maric, Virginia Maxwell, Brendan Sainsbury, Helena Smith and Donna Wheeler. This guidebook was commissioned in Lonely Planet's London office, and produced by the following:

Commissioning Editors Joe Bindloss, Helena Smith

Coordinating Editors Tracy Whitmey, Amanda Williamson

Senior Cartographers Valentina Kremenchutskaya, Anthony Phelan

Coordinating Layout Designer Wendy Wright

Managing Editors Brigitte Ellemor, Annelies Mertens

Managing Layout Designer Jane Hart

Assisting Editors Michelle Bennett, Penny Cordner, Adrienne Costanzo, Kate Daly, Sally O'Brien, Katie O'Connell, Charlotte Orr, Kirsten Rawlings, Sam Trafford

Assisting Cartographers Corey Hutchison, Jennifer Johnston, David Kemp, Genesys (India)

Assisting Layout Designers Carol Jackson, Wibowo Rusli

Cover Research Naomi Parker

Internal Image Research Rebecca Skinner, Aude Vauconsant

Language Content Branislava Vladisavljevic

Thanks to Anita Bahn, Sasha Baskett, Bruce Evans, Ryan Evans, Larissa Frost, Chris Girdler, Jouve India, Trent Paton, Martine Power, Gerard Walker

Index

NOTES

973

NOTES

Map Legend

Sights

Information

Routes

Geographic

Boundaries

Activities Courses & Tours

Population

Hydrography

Transport

Areas

Sleeping

Eating

Drinking & Nightlife

Entertainment

Shopping

Map Legend

Sights
- Beach
- Bird Sanctuary
- Buddhist
- Castle/Palace
- Christian
- Confucian
- Hindu
- Islamic
- Jain
- Jewish
- Monument
- Museum/Gallery/Historic Building
- Ruin
- Sento Hot Baths/Onsen
- Shinto
- Sikh
- Taoist
- Winery/Vineyard
- Zoo/Wildlife Sanctuary
- Other Sight

Activities, Courses & Tours
- Bodysurfing
- Diving
- Canoeing/Kayaking
- Course/Tour
- Skiing
- Snorkelling
- Surfing
- Swimming/Pool
- Walking
- Windsurfing
- Other Activity

Sleeping
- Sleeping
- Camping

Eating
- Eating

Drinking & Nightlife
- Drinking & Nightlife
- Cafe

Entertainment
- Entertainment

Shopping
- Shopping

Information
- Bank
- Embassy/Consulate
- Hospital/Medical
- Internet
- Police
- Post Office
- Telephone
- Toilet
- Tourist Information
- Other Information

Geographic
- Beach
- Hut/Shelter
- Lighthouse
- Lookout
- Mountain/Volcano
- Oasis
- Park
- Pass
- Picnic Area
- Waterfall

Population
- Capital (National)
- Capital (State/Province)
- City/Large Town
- Town/Village

Transport
- Airport
- Border crossing
- Bus
- Cable car/Funicular
- Cycling
- Ferry
- Metro station
- Monorail
- Parking
- Petrol station
- S-Bahn/Subway station
- Taxi
- T-bane/Tunnelbana station
- Train station/Railway
- Tram
- Tube station
- U-Bahn/Underground station
- Other Transport

Note: Not all symbols displayed above appear on the maps in this book

Routes
- Tollway
- Freeway
- Primary
- Secondary
- Tertiary
- Lane
- Unsealed road
- Road under construction
- Plaza/Mall
- Steps
- Tunnel
- Pedestrian overpass
- Walking Tour
- Walking Tour detour
- Path/Walking Trail

Boundaries
- International
- State/Province
- Disputed
- Regional/Suburb
- Marine Park
- Cliff
- Wall

Hydrography
- River, Creek
- Intermittent River
- Canal
- Water
- Dry/Salt/Intermittent Lake
- Reef

Areas
- Airport/Runway
- Beach/Desert
- Cemetery (Christian)
- Cemetery (Other)
- Glacier
- Mudflat
- Park/Forest
- Sight (Building)
- Sportsground
- Swamp/Mangrove

Duncan Garwood

Rome & Lazio Born in the UK, Duncan currently lives in the Castelli Romani hills just outside Rome. He first fell for the Italian capital in 1996 after arriving at the crack of dawn on an overnight train and walking the almost-deserted streets in beautiful morning sunlight. Since then he has worked on the past five *Rome* guides and a whole host of Lonely Planet Italy titles. He has also written on Italy for newspapers and magazines.

Paula Hardy

Milan & the Lakes; Venice & the Veneto From the slopes of Valpolicella to the shores of Lago di Garda and the spritz-fuelled bars of Padua, Venice and Milan, Paula has been contributing to Lonely Planet's Italian guides for over 10 years, including guides to Milan, the Italian Lakes, Venice & the Veneto, Puglia, Sicily and Sardinia. When she's not scooting around the *bel paese*, she writes for a variety of travel publications and websites. You can find her tweeting from lakes, islands and mountains @paula6hardy.

Virginia Maxwell

Florence & Tuscany Based in Australia, Virginia spends part of every year in Italy indulging her passions for history, art, architecture, food and wine. She is the coordinating author of Lonely Planet's *Florence & Tuscany* and the *Florence Encounter* guide, and has covered both Tuscany and other parts of the country for the *Western Europe* guide and for previous editions of this title. Though reticent to nominate her favourite Italian destinations (arguing that they're all wonderful), she usually nominates Florence and Rome if pressed.

Brendan Sainsbury

Liguria, Piedmont & the Italian Riviera; Emilia-Romagna & San Marino Born and bred in Hampshire, England, but now resident in Vancouver, Canada, Brendan first tackled Italy with a famed Inter-rail pass in the 1980s. He has been back innumerable times since as a travel guide, cyclist and – very occasionally – a tourist. This is his fourth Italy-related guidebook (he also wrote Lonely Planet's *Hiking in Italy*), though he has covered numerous other countries for Lonely Planet, including Angola, Cuba and the USA. His favourite Italian city is Bologna.

Helena Smith

Abruzzo & Molise; Puglia, Basilicata & Calabria Helena has been visiting Italy since she was five. At that time chocolate spread on toast was the main draw – now she goes back for the warmth, the art and the atmosphere. Researching this edition took her from mountain villages in Abruzzo to baroque Lecce and the ancient cave city of Matera.

Donna Wheeler

Trento & the Dolomites; Friuli Venezia Giulia Italy's northeastern border regions are Donna's dream assignment: complex histories, mountains, the sea, plus all that spectacular white wine and Viennese cake. Donna has travelled throughout Italy for two decades and lived in Turin's Quadrilatero Romano until 2011. She has also written for Lonely Planet on Milan, southern France, Tunisia and Algeria. An erstwhile editor and producer, she now writes about art, architecture and food for several publications and is a creative consultant specialising in the travel experience.

OUR STORY

A beat-up old car, a few dollars in the pocket and a sense of adventure. In 1972 that's all Tony and Maureen Wheeler needed for the trip of a lifetime – across Europe and Asia overland to Australia. It took several months, and at the end – broke but inspired – they sat at their kitchen table writing and stapling together their first travel guide, *Across Asia on the Cheap*. Within a week they'd sold 1500 copies. Lonely Planet was born.

Today, Lonely Planet has offices in Melbourne, London and Oakland, with more than 600 staff and writers. We share Tony's belief that 'a great guidebook should do three things: inform, educate and amuse'.

OUR WRITERS

Cristian Bonetto

Coordinating Author; Naples & Campania An ex-writer of farce and TV drama, it's not surprising that Cristian clicks with Italy. Born to a Venetian father and a Piedmontese mother, the Italo-Australian scribe was proudly bred the Italian way, and has both lived and holidayed in the *bel paese* (beautiful country). His musings on the motherland have appeared in newspapers, magazines and websites across the globe. When he's not in Italy hunting down perfect coffee or pastries, you'll find him scouring the rest of the globe for insight and delight. Cristian's Lonely Planet titles to date also include *New York City*, *Denmark*, *Scandinavia* and *Singapore*. You can follow his adventures on Twitter @CristianBonetto. Cristian also wrote the Plan Your Trip, Italian Art & Architecture, The Italian Way of Life, Italy on Page & Screen and Survival Guide chapters.

Abigail Blasi

Abigail moved to Rome in 2003 and lived there for three years, she married an Italian and her first son was born in Rome. Nowadays the *famiglia* divide their time between Rome, Puglia and London. She has worked on four editions of Lonely Planet's *Rome* and *Italy* guides, including the latest *Discover Italy* and *Discover Rome* guides, and cowrote the first edition of *Puglia & Basilicata*. She also regularly writes on Italy for various publications, including *Lonely Planet Magazine*, *Wanderlust* and i-escape.com. Abigail wrote the Italy Today, History, and The Italian Table chapters.

Kerry Christiani

Umbria & Le Marche; Sardinia Kerry's relationship with Italia began one hazy, post-graduation summer when she set off for a grand tour in a 1960s bubble caravan. Memorable moments researching this edition include spring coastal walks along Sardinia's cliff-flanked Golfo di Orosei, hill-town slow touring in Umbria and getting stuck in a rare snow storm in Urbino. An award-winning travel writer, Kerry has authored some 20 guidebooks, including Lonely Planet's *Sardinia*, and contributes to publications including bbc.com/travel and *Lonely Planet Traveller*. She tweets @kerrychristiani and lists her latest work at www.kerrychristiani.com.

Gregor Clark

Sicily Gregor caught the Italy bug at age 14 while living in Florence with his professor dad, who took him to see every fresco, mosaic and museum within a 1000km radius. He's lived in Le Marche, huffed and puffed across the Dolomites, and fallen head-over-heels for Sicily while researching Lonely Planet's *Cycling Italy* and the last three editions of the *Italy* guide. A lifelong polyglot with a romance languages degree, his peak experience this trip was celebrating his birthday atop an erupting Stromboli.

OVER PAGE | MORE WRITERS

Published by Lonely Planet Publications Pty Ltd
ABN 36 005 607 983
11th edition – Feb 2014
ISBN 978 1 74220 729 2
© Lonely Planet 2014   Photographs © as indicated 2014
10 9 8 7 6 5 4 3 2 1
Printed in China